COMBAT FLEETS OF THE WORLD 1980/81

Their Ships, Aircraft, and Armament

Edited by
JEAN LABAYLE COUHAT

English translation prepared by A. D. Baker III

This guide was first published in 1897 by Captain de Balincourt, French Navy. It was continued from 1928 to 1943 by Captain Vincent-Bréchignac, French Navy, and from 1943 to 1974 by Henri Le Masson.

Naval Institute Press

WORKS BY JEAN LABAYLE COUHAT

- *French Warships of World War I*
- *French Warships of World War II* — Published by Ian Allan, London. Sold in France by Editions Maritimes et d'Outre-Mer
- Articles for *"La Revue Maritime," "Marine," "Revue de Défense Nationale,"* and *"Armées d'aujourdhui"*
- Monographs on the French, American, British, and Soviet Navies, published by Éditions Ozanne. These works are all out of print.
- *Flottes de Combat 1974* in collaboration with H. LeMasson
- *Flottes de Combat 1976*
- *Flottes de Combat 1978*
- *Combat Fleets of the World 1976/77*
  Their Ships, Aircraft, and Armanent — published in the United States, Canada, and Great Britain under the auspices of the U.S. Naval Institute
- *Combat Fleets of the World 1978/79*
  Their Ships, Aircraft, and Armament

Library of Congress Catalog Card Number: 78-50192
ISBN 0-87021-123-4

All photographs are official, unless otherwise credited, and have
been issued by the national authorities concerned; new drawings
in this issue are by Henri Simoni, unless otherwise credited.

Printed in the United States of America

CONTENTS

PREFACE TO THE FRENCH EDITION

The 1980 edition of *Flottes de Combat* emphasizes descriptions of new and recent-construction warships, giving greater detail on their characteristics and capabilities than has hitherto been the practice. It contains a great many new photographs, some of which are of new ships, while others are replacements to bring coverage up to date. New, annotated drawings have been added and older drawings updated.

As with previous editions, I am indebted primarily to the French Navy, but the naval and military attachés and the ministries of the navy or of defense of other nations have given me invaluable assistance in the form of information and illustrations. I am also grateful to Captain John Moore, editor of *Jane's Fighting Ships*, Giorgio Giorgerini, editor of *Almanacco Navale*, and Gerhard Albrecht, editor of *Weyer's Flottentaschenbuch*.

Much credit is also due to long-time friends of *Flottes de Combat* who have kindly provided much data and photography: Commander Aldo Fraccaroli, Italian Navy; Carlo Martinelli; Norman Polmar, editor of *The Ships and Aircraft of the U.S. Fleet*; J. F. Pellegrini; J. Taibo; and Stefan Terzibaschitsch, author of many books and articles on the U.S. Navy, its ships, and its aircraft. A great many of the new illustrations come from the widely traveled Dr. Giorgio Arra, an expert on ships who is also well known as a superb naval photographer. Drawings not otherwise attributed are by Henri Simoni.

J. LC.

PREFACE TO THE ENGLISH LANGUAGE EDITION

The English-language edition of *Flottes de Combat* appears after its French parent and consequently benefits somewhat from later information. Additional photography has been provided from U.S. sources, and there are minor differences in format: for example, propulsion power is given in horsepower only, as the dual presentation in kilowatts proved too space-consuming. Besides the data on new ships provided in the French edition, information on older ships has been expanded and corrected; building data for all ships are now greatly expanded and, wherever possible, have been checked against official records.

In addition to those listed above, the following have been of particular assistance to the U.S. edition: Robert A. Carlisle and the staff of the Still Photos Branch, Office of Information, U.S. Navy; Peter Dakin, Boeing Marine Services; Charles Dragonette; Jerry Hoffpauir, president of Swiftships, Inc.; John Jedrlinic; Robert L. Lawson, editor of *The Hook;* Larry C. Manning and staff, Legislative and Public Affairs Office, Military Sealift Command; Paul Martineau, Ingalls Shipbuilding Division, Litton Industries; Samuel L. Morison, of *Jane's Fighting Ships;* A. J. Rizzo, Halter Marine, Inc.; John Roberts, editor of *Warship;* Robert L. Scheina, Historian of the U.S. Coast Guard; Albert T. Tappman; and Christopher C. Wright, editor of *Warship International.* Many others provided help as well. Particular thanks must go to Mary Veronica Amoss and the staff of the Book Department, U.S. Naval Institute, who performed the formidable task of assembling a book from many hundreds of pages of pen-and-ink changes and interpolated notes, and to Commander J. Bodin, French Navy, who was of assistance in translating the introduction.

Any work of this scope can only strive for perfection. Political events change shipbuilding programs, ships are altered during refits, are sold, scrapped, or lost, and new data become available constantly. The publisher will be only too glad to accept suggestions for changes or additions to the text and—above all—for reproducible photography, which is a major source of new information.

A.D.B. III

INTRODUCTION

UNITED STATES

Annual posture statements to the U.S. Congress over the last decade have constantly stated that the U.S. Navy, while remaining the world's most powerful, is being closely challenged for that position by the Soviet Navy. The relative—and highly subjective—rankings always push off into the future the date at which the might of Fleet Admiral Gorshkov's navy will surpass that of the U.S. Navy, but it cannot be denied that a fleet that has a definite plan for its future and a firm grasp of its strategic and political responsibilities will sooner or later achieve ascendancy over one that does not.

Since the close of the war in Vietnam, the U.S. Navy has been sorely troubled by the lack of a clear concept of its duties and by constant changes to its shipbuilding plans. The changes result not only from astronomical increases in the cost of shipbuilding and aircraft manufacturing, but also from a lack of understanding of the uses of sea power at the highest political levels. Political, social, and economic pressures have combined to produce a situation in which the congressionally mandated Five-Year Shipbuilding Programs change at least annually, often differing radically from their no-doubt carefully drawn predecessors. Until very recently, the general trend has been toward less procurement, but recent flagrant actions by the Soviet Union appear to give hope that the U.S. Navy, which has shrunk to its weakest position in more than forty years, will enter a period of expansion.

Unfortunately, any expansion in ship production will take a considerable time to bear fruit. Today's complex warships cannot be built in a hurry: an aircraft carrier now takes nine years from authorization to commissioning, while destroyers whose design was frozen before 1970 are still being delivered, more than a decade later. It takes four years to build even so simple a design as a fleet tug. When warships are produced in series over a long period, as is the case with the *Spruance*-class destroyers and the *Oliver Hazard Perry*-class frigates, what was a technologically current design at the outset stands a good chance of being obsolescent by the time the last units of a class are completed. Coordination of the various facets that make a naval ship a "weapon system" requires feats of scheduling that are not always attainable; the first *Oliver Hazard Perry*-class frigate was commissioned in 1977, yet the ASW helicopter for which she was intended to be the platform, and upon which she depends for any pretense of having a realistic ASW capability, will not be operational until at least 1984.

The cost of shipbuilding has inspired another unfortunate trend in naval ship design. In order to make them affordable, succeeding classes are to be less expensive, and hence, inevitably, less *capable*, than current designs. Thus, a new, cheaper, nuclear-powered attack submarine is programmed for introduction under the Fiscal Year 1984 budget, a new frigate that will cost but half as much as a *Perry*—one wonders if it will have even half as much combat capability—is in the planning stages, the new DDX to follow the *Spruance* design is intended to be smaller, and the Carter administration's unlamented conventionally propelled "CVV" aircraft carrier of 60,000-odd tons was a cut well below the capability of a *Nimitz*. The U.S. Navy simply cannot afford to buy large numbers of such ships as the CG–47-class Aegis cruisers, which were promoted from the status of "destroyer" in time for their cost to approach $1 billion *per ship*. And yet it has been stated that no ship of lesser capabilities than a CG–47 is safe against the *current* generation of Soviet air, surface, and undersea-launched anti-ship cruise missiles!

Despite the present lack of a clear definition of its roles, the U.S. Navy's responsibilities remain enormous. It is the one fleet in the world truly able to operate effectively anywhere on the world ocean for extended periods of time. That ability is the envy of the Soviet Navy, which still lacks an adequate logistics train. The U.S. Navy must still be able to send one—or more, as in the recent Iranian crisis—aircraft carrier to a remote location at a moment's notice and to operate it there for indefinite periods. That it can still do this is testimony to its outstanding leadership and long traditions of seamanship and service. But there are limitations. The ships are heavily worked, and many are getting old. A plan, drawn up in 1978, to create an Indian Ocean "Fifth Fleet" had to be dropped—there are not enough aircraft carriers to sustain such a capability. A year later, to deploy two aircraft carriers in the Indian Ocean the *Nimitz* had to be withdrawn from the Mediterranean theater. Nevertheless, in that sea, the superiority of the West remains the same, thanks to the two French aircraft carriers.

The aircraft carrier is still the centerpiece of what the chief of naval operations, Admiral Thomas B. Hayward, refers to as the U.S. "battle fleet." It is cause for rejoicing, then, that Congress has forced its will upon the administration and a fourth *Nimitz*-class carrier, CVN–71, will be built. Of course, the ship will not be fully operational until 1990. The third *Nimitz*-class carrier, *Carl Vinson* (CVN–70), should be commissioned in 1982. Still operational are the *Midway* (CV–41) and the *Coral Sea* (CV–43), both of which will have seen nearly forty years of hard service by the time they are retired. The future of carrier aviation is still in doubt, however; the Service Life Extension Program (SLEP) for updating the *Forrestal*-class carriers remains mired in politics, while Congress has appropriated $10 million in the Fiscal Year 1980 budget for the continuing study of a "Light Carrier Design."

The navy's strategic deterrence is embodied in its force of nuclear-powered ballistic-missile submarines. Yet no new unit has been commissioned since 1967, during which time the U.S.S.R. has built more than sixty such ships. The successor U.S. program, the *Ohio*-class SSBN, was to have gone to sea in 1978, but labor and technological problems have postponed its operational date into late 1981. In the meantime, a dozen of the existing *Lafayette*-class and *Benjamin Franklin*-class submarines are being altered to accept the Trident-I ballistic missile. The first operational Trident patrol was begun by the *Francis Scott Key* (SSBN–657) on 20 October 1979. Eight *Ohio*-class submarines have been authorized, and the program is to build three more before a new design is introduced, the first of which will probably not be ready before 1989. As with so many such programs, the new ship is to be smaller and less capable.

In 1979 the world's first nuclear-powered ship, Admiral Hyman G. Rickover's epoch-making *Nautilus*, was decommissioned. The same year saw the commissioning of three *Los Angeles*-class nuclear-powered attack submarines, the ninth, tenth, and eleventh of what is now a thirty-five-ship program, whose first unit was authorized under the Fiscal 1970 budget. The 1980 five-year construction program called for four more to be built before the switch to a smaller design is made. Although SSNs will continue to be built, the rate of construction is such that the present fleet of seventy-four will inevitably shrink with the disposal of the *Permit* and *Sturgeon* classes in the 1990s. Only five conventionally powered submarines are now active fleet units, and their days are numbered. Attack submarines are rapidly being equipped with the Harpoon submerged-launch anti-ship missile, and will carry the longer-ranged Tomahawk when it becomes available in the mid-1980s.

It seemed that the cruiser as a type in the U.S. Navy had come to an end when the construction of the nuclear-powered, Aegis-equipped CGN–42 was rejected and no nuclear-powered cruisers were listed in any building program. But a stroke of the administrative pen has created a new cruiser class, the CG–47, out of the DDG–47 program. Certainly, a ship so formidable and sizeable deserves to be called a cruiser and requires a commanding officer of the rank and experience of a captain. Two CG–47-class ships have now been authorized, and it would appear that—despite their incredible cost—at least a dozen more will be requested. The delay in getting Aegis to the fleet, however, has taken its toll: CG–47 will not be commissioned until 1983, and there will not be enough of them to provide each carrier with one such escort until the 1990s. Old cruisers continue to be discarded, but the *Albany* (CG–10) has been given a short reprieve because her services as a flagship are still required. Since the last edition nine cruisers and command ships have been stricken, two of them, the *Oklahoma City* (CG–5) and the *Chicago* (CG–11), from the active fleet. There are now but two big-gun cruisers remaining on the Navy List, neither of which has seen active service in almost twenty years. The 203-mm Mk. 71 gun program was canceled in 1978 and the largest gun now on any active U.S. ship is of 127-mm bore. The twenty-five commissioned cruisers in service are to be joined in 1980 by the newly built *Arkansas* (CGN–41) and the *Belknap* (CG–26), rebuilt after damage sustained in a collision in 1975. Many of these ships have not so much as a 20-mm AA gun in their ordnance suits, depending primarily on missiles for battle—an optimism shared by no other navy.

One of the few benefits of the revolution in Iran, from the U.S. Navy's point of view, was that the new government canceled an order for four "DD–993"-class destroyers. Because of the advanced state of their construction, these magnificant ships were incorporated into the U.S. Navy as the *Kidd* class and retyped as DDG—Guided-Missile Destroyer; the hull numbers, however, were not changed, leaving a very odd discontinuity in the numbering of such ships. The first will be completed in 1980 and the others in 1981. Twenty-five of the thirty-one *Spruance*-class large destroyers, upon which the designs of the *Kidd* and CG–47 classes were based, had been commissioned by the end of 1979, and of the remainder, all but one were to be operational by mid-1980; the thirty-first unit, an orphan that the navy did not ask for, was only ordered in September 1979 and will not be completed until 1983 at the earliest. It had been planned to dispose of all but nine of the remaining destroyers of the World War II era during Fiscal 1980, but Congress, apparently working on that theory that "a destroyer is a destroyer is a destroyer," required that twelve of the twenty ships scheduled for decommissioning be retained and overhauled; none is worth the trouble, all being obsolete for modern warfare.

The second of thirty-eight *Oliver Hazard Perry*-class guided-missile frigates authorized to date for the U.S. Navy was commissioned at the end of 1979, with future requests evidently to be restricted to three or four per year through perhaps 1984. The ships will be delivered at such a rapid rate during the early 1980s that most will be completed well ahead of schedule—an almost unheard-of occurrence in the U.S. shipbuilding industry. These ships have been criticized for their very high cost and low combat effectiveness. A new class of even more austere ships is being planned, to be manned in part by the Naval Reserve Force, which will operate them when the World War II destroyers have been phased out. The relatively new forty-six ships of the *Knox* class are being given new sensors and having their hulls modified to make them more seaworthy, but eighteen *Brooke*-, *Garcia*-, and *Bronstein*-class ships, which are very little older, are being allowed to become obsolescent before their time. One frigate was "gained" in 1979 when the experimental ship *Glover* (AGFF–1) was redesignated FF–1098.

Mine warfare continues to suffer from almost total neglect, the newest of the U.S. Navy's disproportionately small force of minesweepers having been delivered in 1958. Plans for building a new class have been continually delayed; planners have not been able to agree on the size or capabilities required. Most of the amphibious-warfare force is of fairly recent construction, but only *one* new ship is now planned for delivery during the 1980s, the last *Tarawa*-class LHA. A follow-on dock landing ship class, LSD–41, long in the planning stages, has been continually deferred, and the eight *Thomaston* class LSDs will be leaving service as they reach thirty years of service, which will be during this period. One amphibious cargo ship and two amphibious personnel transports were discarded between 1979 and 1980, and the five *Charleston*-class amphibious cargo ships seem destined to be turned over to the Naval Reserve Force. Plans for series construction of an air-cushion landing craft appear to have been abandoned, as does a program for a new 20-knot LCM. The Fiscal 1981 budget request will include the first of a type that, to dust off an old stillborn concept from the late 1960s, might be called "Forward Deployment Logistic Ships," fourteen of which are planned. Capable of unloading their cargoes of combat stores over the beach, if necessary, these ships are intended for positioning around the globe to support rapidly deployed troops, who would be flown in. The concept appears to be extraordinarily expensive and open to charges of imperialist intent; a similar scheme from the Johnson administration was rejected by Congress for those reasons, and it remains to be seen how the new version will fare.

The U.S. Navy operates virtually no minor combatants, the new *Pegasus*-class guided-missile patrol boats being the only ones entering service; they were not desired by the navy and their role has not been defined, but they might operate from Key West as a counter to the growing power of the Cuban Navy in the Caribbean. After the expenditure of more than a decade of effort and perhaps $1 billion, the program for surface-effect ships seems to be dead, no funds having been appropriated for 1980. No useful role for a 3,000-ton SES has been perceived, and its operating expenses would have been astronomical. The few remaining conventional patrol craft are involved in experimental and training duties.

The auxiliary force of the U.S. Navy is a bright area; a number of large and extremely capable repair types are entering service to replace those built during World War II. Most underway replenishment and other service duties are being transferred to the civilian-manned Military Sealift Command, although the navy plans to operate the new *Cimarron*-class oilers. Nevertheless, in general, the ability to transfer fuel, stores, provisions, and munitions at sea will decline over the next decade because old ships are not being replaced on a one-for-one basis, new ships are less versatile than those built in the 1960s and 1970s, and, in the name of economy, some replenishment equipment is being removed from existing ships.

The U.S. Coast Guard, faced with the responsibility for patrolling the new 200-nautical-mile economic zone, is being rejuvenated, with new medium-endurance patrol ships, patrol aircraft, and helicopters on order. But no replacements are foreseen for the one-third of its high-endurance cutters that were completed well over forty years ago. Similarly, although a modernization program is in effect, no new patrol craft are programmed.

SOVIET UNION

The Soviet Navy keeps improving in quality and expanding in the area of major surface combatants and submarines. Its main strength continues to rest in the power of its missile-equipped, land-based bomber force and in its large force of submarines—the latter including more than seventy nuclear-powered, ballistic-missile boats, twenty-eight of which are of the recent Delta-I, Delta-II, and Delta-III series. The Delta-III, whose submerged displacement is more than 13,000 tons, is currently the largest submarine ever built, although it will be surpassed when the U.S. Navy's *Ohio* class is commissioned in the 1980s. Delta-class submarines carry either SS–N–8 or SS–N–18 missiles, both of which can reach targets more than 4,000 nautical miles away—a range much longer than that achievable by Western submarine-launched ballistic missiles until the advent of the U.S. Trident-I. It is thought possible that Soviet missiles are technically less sophisticated and less accurate than their U.S. counterparts, but their individual payloads are larger—indeed, payloads that are very large when compared with Western weapons are characteristic of virtually all Soviet offensive missile systems. Delta-class submarines in the Northern and Pacific fleets have enough missile range to hit any target in the United States, Europe, or Asia without having to leave the sanctuary of their home waters, where they have the protection of "pro-submarine" antisubmarine forces. An even larger submarine class "Tayfun" (Typhoon) is said to be in development in response to the U.S. Trident program, which shows that the Soviets are firmly committed to maintaining a formidable strategic-missile submarine force.

The size of the Soviet attack submarine force—more than 260 units, nearly 90 of them nuclear-powered—is highly impressive. Nonetheless—and despite the ability of a number of submarines to launch tactical cruise missiles while submerged— the majority of the submarines must be judged as less than the technical equals of many Western submarines. Reportedly, the principal Soviet weaknesses still lie in the noisiness of their nuclear-powered submarines and the lesser effectiveness of their sensor suits. But the Soviet Navy continues to strive for quality; the new Alfa-class submarines have caused anxiety in the West because of their very high speed of over 40 knots, greater diving depths than Western submarines or weapons can achieve, and probable reduction in radiated noise. Alfa is reportedly constructed of titanium, a technological tour de force that the West cannot hope to emulate. The highly capable Victor series of attack submarines and Charlie series of tactical cruise-missile submarines—both nuclear-powered—continue in production, as does the conventionally propelled Tango class, at least the equal of similar units in the West. But the remaining units of the huge number of boats built or designed in the 1950s still constitute a large proportion of the Soviet submarine fleet, and even the earliest nuclear-powered November, Hotel, and Echo classes are approaching a quarter-century of service. Therefore, it is hardly likely that the Soviet Union will slacken its submarine-building program, which calls for about a dozen new units of all types each year.

The late 1970s saw the end of the surface-combatant construction programs introduced at the beginning of the decade, but this seems to be only a pause to allow the series construction of new and even more impressive designs to begin. Perhaps the most startling development is the construction of the Soviet Union's first nuclear-powered surface combatants, the *Kirov*-class "cruisers" of more than 25,000 tons' full-load displacement. The purpose of these large vessels is not clear. They are derived from the strike cruiser type, a project the U.S. Navy gave up, and their tonnage is reminiscent of the battle cruisers of a past era. Better knowledge of their specifications will probably shed some light on why the Soviets are building such ships. But other cruiser programs are also under way: a new conventionally powered design of around 7,500 tons' displacement is being built in quantity at Leningrad, and a class of nearly twice that size is said to be under construction at Nikolayev as a follow-on to the Kara class. When this edition was going to press, news arrived via the U.S. press of yet a fourth class of cruisers, 8,400-ton ships, tailored for ASW (*see* Addenda). As they are completed during the course of the 1980s, all these designs, and perhaps others, will be adding to the power of the Soviet blue-water fleet. The 1970s saw the completion of ten Kresta-II-class and seven or more Kara-class guided-missile cruisers. At the same time, the old *Sverdlov*-class cruisers, with their powerful gun batteries and extensive command-and-control facilities, continue to be modernized.

More surprising than the growth of the cruiser force has been the growing commitment of the Soviet Navy to carrier aviation. Two *Kiev*-class hybrid missile cruiser/aircraft carriers are now in service, and two more are expected in the early 1980s. Some naval specialists believe, as has always been the case with hybrid-type ships, that these aircraft carriers are "capable of everything and good for nothing." Of more importance, however, are the persistent reports of a program to build a 60,000-ton, nuclear-powered carrier equivalent in concept to such ships in the West. The ships would presumably operate conventional catapult-launched fighter and attack aircraft, rather than the less capable (if technically ingenious) Forger-type V/TOL attack aircraft carried on the *Kiev*s. After decades of decrying such ships as tools of Western

imperialism, the Soviets have apparently decided to acquire a few such useful tools of their own. The first of these ships cannot be expected immediately, perhaps not until the second half of the 1980s, but its introduction will mark a new dimension in Soviet sea power. But it is almost certain that this carrier—if built—will present problems to the Soviet Navy, which lacks experience in this field. Building true aircraft carriers with modern planes on board may interfere with the building of other categories of ships that the Soviet Navy needs badly. Soviet land-based naval aviation continues to receive emphasis. Approximately one half of all Backfire missile-carrying supersonic bombers are built for the navy, while the very-long-ranged Bear series of turboprop-powered patrol and ASW bombers continue to be built. Helicopters for coastal ASW and, very likely, for minesweeping, are in production, while land-based attack fighters have been seen in use by naval aviation in the Baltic.

Less clear is the direction being taken by the Soviet Navy in the production of small surface combatants. In contrast with extensive new frigate and destroyer programs in other major navies, the Soviets seem to have no such ships programmed, other than continued construction of the 1970-vintage Krivak series, recently demoted in Soviet terminology from "large ASW ship" to "patrol ship." No ships describable as "destroyers" seem to be under construction for home use, although three improved versions of the Kashin class are being built for India. Surprising to Western observers is the fact that none of these ASW ships have permanently assigned helicopters, whereas other navies would not think of modern ASW ships without helicopters. If for no other purpose than to provide escort for the new, large combatants, some new class of large frigate or destroyer will probably begin to appear in the early 1980s.

Continuing in construction are large numbers of the small combatants required by Soviet doctrine to protect the coasts of the motherland. Koni-class frigates, Grisha corvettes, Nanuchka missile corvettes (and a new design, the Tarantul), Matka missile patrol boats, Turya hydrofoil torpedo boats all continue to appear, while trials continue with more technologically sophisticated craft, such as the Sarancha large missile hydrofoil and the Babochka ASW hydrofoil, which may provide the basis for new designs for the 1980s. The Soviet Union continues to build small combatants for export, a growing stream of such craft being sent to Soviet clients each year.

A variety of mine-warfare ships and craft are being built, largely as replacements for units completed in the 1950s. The Soviet Navy maintains by far the largest mine-countermeasures force of any navy, perhaps reflecting its longtime interest in mine warfare. Other than the new probably magnetic minesweepers of the Andryusha class, Soviet designs show no significant technological innovations, but there are a great many of them. In production are Natya-class metal-hulled fleet minesweepers (some for export), Sonya-class wood-and-fiberglass coastal minesweepers, Yevgenya-class inshore minesweepers, Olya-class river minesweepers, Ilyusha-class minesweeping drones, and the aforementioned Andryusha class. Some older mine-warfare units are being converted to other purposes: the T–58-class fleet minesweepers are all now believed to have been reconfigured either as patrol ships or as radar pickets.

Amphibious warfare remains primarily a support element for the Red Army's land forces, and the capabilities of the Naval Infantry, which consists of perhaps no more than 15,000 men, can hardly be said to compare with those of the U.S. Marines, particularly as it is divided among four widely separated fleets. Nevertheless, great strides have been made in the ability of the Soviet Navy to transport and support seaborne troops and their equipment. The Polnocny-class small landing ships built in Poland for the U.S.S.R. and Poland, and still in production for export, have been followed by the far larger and longer-ranged Ropucha class. In 1978, the first really large amphibious landing ship, *Ivan Rogov*, appeared. At nearly 14,000 tons full-load displacement (the size of a U.S. Navy LPD), the *Rogov*, whose design is somewhat unusual, carries several helicopters, has a bow ramp, incorporates a stern well to accommodate two or more air-cushion landing craft, carries a battalion landing team of more than 500 men and all its vehicles, provides its own fire support by means of guns and an automatic barrage rocket launcher, and has the sensor suit and defensive gun and missile systems of a frigate. Such a ship, and her successors, cannot alone stage an invasion, but her presence on a deployed station in the Indian Ocean or off the West Coast of Africa provides potent assurance of Soviet power. Added to the *naval* component of Soviet amphibious warfare capability must be the potential of the merchant fleet, which now has around three dozen roll-on/roll-off cargo ships (some with bow ramps) that would provide immediate assistance in preparation for an amphibious landing.

The Soviet logistic support fleet has grown in size and capability, thanks to the completion of a sixth *Boris Chilikin*-class replenishment oiler, two more Finnish-built *Dubna*-class small replenishment oilers, and the first of the *Berezina* class, a ship of 40,000 tons full-load displacement with a stores load roughly equivalent to that of a U.S. *Wichita*-class AOR and the armament and sensor suit of a frigate. Like the U.S. Navy, with its Military Sealift Command, and the British Navy, with its Royal Fleet Auxiliary, the Soviet Navy depends heavily on its civilian-manned Naval Auxiliary Service for afloat logistics support; indeed, the *Berezina* appears to be the *only* armed and naval-manned replenishment auxiliary. Increasing use is being made of underway, alongside replenishment, but delivery rates are still slow and little use is made of the capabilities provided for transferring solid stores. Nonetheless, despite their smaller size and lack of sophistication, the Soviet Navy now has at its disposal roughly the same number of oilers capable of under-way replenishment as does the U.S. Navy— thanks to a program of backfitting older units with alongside replenishment rigs.

In other support functions, the Soviet Navy continues to acquire new ships. Among the navy's duties are many of the oceanographic-research, hydrographic-survey, and navigational-aid support functions performed in the United States by the Coast Guard and the National Oceanic and Atmospheric Administration (NOAA) fleets. Indeed, the Soviet Union operates easily half the world's research ships, and roughly half of those are navy-subordinated. Many of these scientific ships are built in East German and Polish shipyards; the latter have also delivered more than thirty small repair ships to the Soviet Navy in recent years. Also of importance is the large number of specialized training ships being built.

Major worldwide naval exercises, such as Okean, conducted by the Soviet Navy, as well as operations in home waters, indicate that training has greatly improved and has departed from the stereotyped scenarios used for so many years. Although Soviet ships in general spend far less time deployed beyond home waters than do U.S. Navy ships, important forces remain deployed at great distances from the U.S.S.R. for many months, often half a year. This requires a commendable endurance on the part of their crews, in spite of the fact that for much of the deployed time they are inactive, with the ships at anchor.

Most of the enlisted personnel of the Soviet Navy are draftees, who serve a three-year term. This permits only rudimentary training in the repair of their equipment, and most are trained in no more than one narrow field of specialization. As a result, the Soviet Navy depends heavily on its officer corps for hands-on repair and maintenance, and its ships, particularly the more sophisticated ones, have a higher percentage of officers and a much lower number of experienced petty officers than do their foreign counterparts. Soviet officers, most of whom are graduates of one of the eleven Higher Naval Training Schools, are at least on a par in quality with other naval officers in knowledge and experience. They remain in their posts for far longer periods than is common elsewhere, especially in the U.S. Navy. Furthermore, the communist regime, with its dual political and military hierarchy at all levels, accentuates tendencies that existed in the days of the Tsars: extreme centralization of decision-making at a very high, indeed the highest level; lack of initiative and imagination in action;

a typically slavic fatalistic, even passive, attitude on lower levels; and a college-type management.

In analyzing overall capabilities, it must be borne in mind that geography plays a greater role in the strategies of the Soviet Navy than it does in those of other navies. Two of the four major fleets, the Baltic and the Black Sea, have only narrow outlets— controlled by foreign powers—to the high seas, while the Northern Fleet and Pacific Ocean Fleet must travel great distances to reach their deployed operational areas. The Soviet Navy has no major overseas bases, although its claim that it has *none* is not valid; Cuba and the People's Democratic Republic of Yemen (Aden) provide more-or-less permanent berthing facilities, while for years repairs to naval ships have been routinely carried out in Yugoslav, Singaporean, and Tunisian shipyards, among others. All of its overseas facilities, including frequently used open anchorages, however, would be vulnerable the instant a war began.

Geography and its own composition have given the Soviet Navy two major missions:

Military: To be always prepared to make a surprise strategic strike against enemy naval forces and their bases, using nuclear munitions. This mission would be entrusted to submarines, naval aviation's land-based bombers, and cruise missiles launched by major surface combatants. This threat naturally obsesses Western planners.

Political: To support the policies and interests of the Soviet Union in "peacetime." Thus the mere presence of Soviet naval elements implies support for friends and hindrance of the freedom of action of other navies. In this mode, the Soviet Navy can be said to have been remarkably successful in recent years, particularly as its efforts are in part aided by foreign naval commentators who are inclined to overstate its capabilities. This twofold mission can be described by the Western term *sea-denial* and requires neither a fleet as sophisticated nor sailors as well trained as those of, for instance, the U.S. Navy.

Many commentators, particularly in the United States, tend to view Soviet naval-construction programs in a one-on-one context. But if an attempt is made to view the naval threat through Soviet eyes, it can be seen that the West as a whole continues to outbuild the U.S.S.R. Assuming Western alliances remained in effect in wartime, the Soviet Navy, particularly on the open sea, would still be outnumbered.

Through the machinery of the Warsaw Pact, the Soviet Navy is itself assisted by the small navies of its satellites. East Germany is particularly important as the first line of defense against any attack through the Baltic, and it has recently received the first two of an expected four Koni-class frigates to replace old Riga-class patrol ships. Both East Germany and Poland maintain considerable amphibious-landing capabilities, the former with its new Frosch-class landing ships, and the latter with a larger number of older, smaller, and less capacious Polnocnys. Neither Bulgaria nor Romania poses much threat, or much potential for assistance, in the Black Sea, although their navies do from time to time receive new small combatants. Poland operates four aged Soviet Whiskey-class submarines, while Bulgaria has two somewhat more modern Romeos.

GREAT BRITAIN

While greatly diminished in size in recent years, the Royal Navy can still lay claim to being a major naval power—and certainly its ships and men are second to none in quality. Its warships are, on average, admirably youthful, thanks to the fact that the economic pressures of overcapacity in the shipbuilding industry have helped to inspire continued programs of warship construction, and they, in turn, have caused the retirement of a number of still-useful warships in order to provide crews for the new ships. The decommissioning of the last conventional aircraft carrier, the *Ark Royal*, in December 1978 has ended an era of naval aviation that began during World War

I. Even the introduction into active service of the first of three *Invincible*-class helicopter and V/STOL fighter carriers in the early 1980s cannot fill the gap, because the capabilities of the Harrier can by no means be said to approach those of the Phantoms, Buccaneers, and Gannets flown from the *Ark Royal*. Retention of the *Hermes*, whose capability is similar to that of the *Invincibles*, and the recommissioning of the aged and less-capable *Bulwark* as interim measures, will give the Royal Navy at least a minimal aviation capability at sea from 1981 on.

The last active British cruiser, the *Blake*, will have been decommissioned by the time this book appears in print, while decommissionings have reduced the number of "County"-class guided-missile destroyers to six. As compensation, however, a vigorous program of building *Sheffield*-class Sea Dart-equipped guided-missile destroyers is being pursued, with the eleventh and later units to be enlarged by some 16.1 meters in length, .6 meters in beam, and 400 tons in displacement—all it would seem without an increase in their weapon or sensor capabilities. Of similar size, but typed as frigates, are the *Broadsword* class, six of which have been ordered to date; armed with the remarkable Sea Wolf missile for defense, these ships probably have the best capability against anti-ship missiles of any ships now in service. Programs have been announced for a new Type 24 frigate for export sales (*see* Addenda), while Type 23 will apparently be an enlarged version of the *Broadsword* class.

Besides building new ships, the Royal Navy has been modernizing many of its old frigates, in particular the very seaworthy *Leander* class. A program to update the first sixteen (half with Ikara ASW missiles and half with Exocet anti-ship missiles) is nearly complete, while the *Andromeda*, the first of the ten "broad-beam" *Leanders*, has begun extensive modernization with Sea Wolf and Exocet.

Heavy emphasis is being placed on the construction of nuclear-powered submarines. In January 1980 it was announced that Great Britain would be procuring U.S. Trident-I missiles, to be equipped with British warheads and, evidently, carried by a new class of ballistic-missile submarines. In the meantime, the Polaris for these SSBN will be modernized (6 MRV heads hardened for better penetration). The *Trafalgar* and two sisters of a new nuclear-powered attack submarine class are on order, and all British submarines of that type, eleven of which have been completed, are to carry the U.S. submerged-launch Harpoon anti-ship missile, beginning in the 1980s. To replace the existing conventionally powered *Oberon*-class submarines, planning is underway for a new class, the first of which would be completed in the late 1980s; one candidate design is described in the Addenda.

New, glass-reinforced plastic minehunters of great size, the Hunt class, are in series production, while a dozen Extra-Deep Armed Team Sweeps, based on commercial stern-haul trawler designs, are to be completed by 1985 for operation by the rejuvenated Royal Navy Volunteer Reserve. A new class of Offshore Patrol Vessels for duties in the North Sea oilfields will follow on the heels of the just-completed Island class; these too are described in the Addenda. Also for North Sea duties is the *Speedy*, a Boeing-built hydrofoil that may presage construction of up to a dozen sisters. A great many small combatant designs ranging in size from a few tons to more than 400 tons full-load are being built by British shipyards for export. Amphibious warfare ships are few in number and no new ones are planned; it can be said that Great Britain has just about abandoned that form of naval warfare.

Also worthy of note is the Royal Navy's superb logistics fleet, which affords considerable strategic flexibility. Most recently, it has been enriched by the completion of the two Fort-class fleet replenishment ships, and the acquisition of two commercial tankers to replace two that have been returned to their owner. A sea-bed operations vessel was ordered recently to replace the *Reclaim*, which is to be decommissioned. But the situation of the the Royal Navy is not as idyllic as it seems. There is too little support from industry because of the irresponsible behavior of unions. For example,

the *Swiftsure* has been waiting in Chatham for a general refit for more than a year while arguments about working schedules and so forth go on.

FRANCE

For the French Navy, the most important developments since the last edition are the decision to build a sixth ballistic-missile submarine, the *Inflexible*, to be fitted with M–4 missiles (2,300 nautical miles, 6 MRV of 150 kt each), and the launching in July 1979 of *La Provence*, France's first nuclear-powered attack submarine. All four conventional submarines of the *Agosta* class are now in service, as are the *Georges Leygues* destroyers, and nine of the *d'Estienne d'Orves*-class corvettes. The new Tripartite minehunter program is well under way, with simultaneous production by the Netherlands and Belgium of the same glass-reinforced, plastic-hulled design. New patrol craft and auxiliaries are also being built. One major ship program, announced more than five years ago, has not yet begun; the PA 75 nuclear-powered helicopter carrier has not been laid down and, for budgetary reasons, seems destined to remain in the future for some time to come. Such a ship—or class of ships—will be badly needed by the 1990s when the aircraft carriers *Clemenceau* and *Foch* will have to be retired.

JAPAN

The size and capability of the Japanese Maritime Self-Defense Force and its vigorous new construction programs make it a major naval power, although one capable of little more than home defense because of its near-total lack of a logistics force—a second small fleet oiler was only just completed in 1979. Current programs include new ASW helicopter-carrying destroyers, two new guided-missile destroyer classes, a new frigate, a superb new conventional-submarine design, and continued construction of minesweepers, auxiliaries, and service craft. Of equal importance is the massive expansion of Japan's coast guard, the Maritime Safety Agency which, since the last edition, has ordered more than two dozen major patrol ships, most of which will be in service before the end of 1980. This edition of *Combat Fleets* has taken special pains to provide a full description of the MSA, which is now the largest and most diversified coast guard of any nation. Both the Maritime Self-Defense Force and the Maritime Safety Agency are also acquiring numbers of new aircraft and helicopters, with the U.S. P–3C coming into service and providing a major new capability for long-range reconnaissance and ASW.

WEST GERMANY

Thanks to its numerous guided-missile patrol boats and small, silent submarines, the navy of the Federal German Republic is well equipped for its NATO role in the Baltic. For North Sea operations and duties elsewhere on the open ocean, the four *Hamburg*-class destroyers have been modernized, and the *Bremen*, the first of an eventual dozen Type-122 frigates, has been launched; the design of the latter is based on that of the Dutch *Kortenaer* class. Mine-countermeasures capabilities are being modernized by the conversion of existing minesweepers into minehunters and of others into control ships for the unique Troika-type remote-controlled minesweepers. Altogether, however, West Germany is not building enough ships to maintain current capabilities, and new programs in several areas—particularly submarines—will have to be pursued in the near future.

THE NETHERLANDS

Proportionate to size, few navies have undergone so thorough a rejuvenation as is taking place within the Royal Netherlands Navy. Not only are a dozen of the highly capable *Kortenaer*-class frigates being rapidly brought into service (with a thirteenth, modified to a command/surface-to-air missile configuration, programmed), but the existing six *Van Speijk*-class frigates are being extensively modernized. The *Friesland*-class destroyers, completed in the late 1950s, have begun phasing out, and a new frigate class to replace them and the aging Roofdier-class corvettes for North Sea patrol duties has been announced; these 2,300-ton ships will be scarcely less capable than the 3,000-ton *Kortenaer*s. Also on order are two new *Walrus*-type conventional submarines and fifteen Tripartite-design minehunters.

SPAIN

The Royal Spanish Navy is also undergoing a remarkable renewal, although funding constraints may delay some of the programs that have been announced. A new U.S.-designed V/STOL fighter- and helicopter-carrier is to be laid down in 1980 to replace the *Dedalo* (the West's first such ship, although little noted as such), while four new French *Agosta*-class submarines should begin entering service shortly. The eight-ship *Descubierta*-class light-frigate program is to be followed by four slightly larger ships with combined gas-turbine and diesel propulsion, while plans to construct three U.S. *Oliver Hazard Perry*-class guided-missile frigates appear to have encountered delays. Considerable numbers of new patrol boats and craft are being built, and export sales of units ranging from the *Descubierta* class down to tiny patrol craft have been expanding. At the same time as Spain has been building new warships, most of its collection of obsolescent destroyers, frigates, corvettes, and minesweepers has been discarded, relieving an expensive maintenance burden.

ITALY

The Italian Navy is building a small aircraft carrier, the *Garibaldi*, but political pressures will keep it from reaching its full potential by denying it V/STOL aircraft, which are felt in some influential circles to be "too offensive" in nature. Six *Maestrale*-class frigates will shortly join four new *Lupo*-class units in service; the smaller *Lupo* has been ordered by Venezuela and Peru, and other Italian-built warship designs are seeing increasing sales in the export market. Two more fast submarines are to join the pair of *Nazario Sauro*-class craft already completed, while six guided-missile-equipped hydrofoils are to be completed by 1981 and four mine-countermeasures ships are on order. On the other hand, the rapid rise of shipbuilding costs in Italy has forced cancellation of the construction of two more *Audace*-class guided-missile destroyers and two *Maestrale*-class frigates and has postponed the ordering of six mine-counter-measures ships. To fill the latter gap, some ten old U.S.-designed minesweepers dating from the 1950s are being converted to minehunters.

CHINA

It may seem strange that the world's second largest navy—in terms of numbers of ships—is given so brief a mention, but it is quite evident that little of technical interest is occurring in Chinese shipyards and little major new construction is being undertaken. Recent visits to China by observers from the West have revealed ships that are very well built by any standard but whose design and capabilities are a quarter-century behind the times. No new combatant classes of any consequence have been introduced since the early 1970s, and expected purchases of Western ships—or at least equipment

for ships—have failed to materialize. The Chinese Navy is extremely well maintained and its huge number of ships and craft would provide formidable resistance to any invader, but poses no threat on the high seas.

OTHER NAVIES

Readers of this edition of *Combat Fleets* who are interested in the smaller navies will note that virtually all of them are striving to modernize and augment their resources, either by purchases abroad or by construction in their own shipyards. There are now very few navies of any size that do not have at least a few ships or craft armed with anti-ship guided missiles. The development of industries for the building of naval combatants in countries such as Argentina, Brazil, Peru, South Korea, Israel, and Singapore deserves attention. Unless the Brazilian Navy does more, the Argentine Navy may soon rank number one in South America. It has ordered from West Germany four very fine frigates, type Meko 360H2, and, with the help of German yards, is going to build six 1,400-ton corvettes, type Meko 140, four 1,700-ton and two 1,400-ton submarines. Many of the small navies are funded by oil revenues and headed by governments whose intentions are not always peaceful. Of particular importance in that category is Libya, which is receiving numbers of ships and submarines from France, Italy, and the U.S.S.R. far beyond what might be needed for its own defense. Libya's naval ambitions and mercurial leadership could easily upset the balance of forces in the Mediterranean, and it is to be hoped that the sale of offensive systems to Libya by France and Italy does not turn out to have been irresponsible.

SUMMARY

This introduction was intended to be as brief as possible a *tour d'horizon* of the current naval scene, for it is felt that such matters are best handled in other forums. The function of a naval manual such as *Combat Fleets* is the presentation of as much and as accurate data as possible on the composition of the fleets of the world, and editorial analyses are of distinctly less importance. For that reason, readers are invited to study the pages that follow and to form for themselves a view of the directions in which naval fleet developments are leading.

J. LC.

TERMS AND ABBREVIATIONS

Most ships' characteristics are given in the following form:

	Bldr	Laid down	L	In serv.
D 602 SUFFREN	Lorient	12-62	15-5-65	1967

D: 5,090 tons (6,090 fl)   **Dim:** 157.6 (148.0 pp) × 15.54 × 7.25 (max.)
S: 34 kts   **Range:** 2,000/30, 2,400/29, 5,100/18
Man: 23 officers, 164 petty officers, 168 men
A: 1/Masurca system (II × 1)—4/MM 38 Exocet—2/100-mm, Model 1953 (I × 2)—4/20-mm AA (I × 4)—1/Malafon system (13 missiles)—2/catapults for L-5 torpedoes (10 torpedoes)
Electron Equipt: Radars: 1/DRBI 23, 1/DRBV 50, 2/DRBR 51, 1/DRBC 32A, 1/DRBN 32
       Sonars: 1/DUBV 23, 1/DUBV 43—SENIT 1, 2 Syllex systems
Boilers: 4 multitube, automatic-control, 45 kg/cm² pressure—superheat 450° C
Electric: 3,440 kw (2 × 1,000-kw turbogenerators, 3 × 480-kw diesel alternators)
M: 2 Rateau double-reduction GT; 2 props; 72,500 hp

Ships' hull numbers and names are in capitals and small capitals. Hull dimensions are in meters, calibers in millimeters, speeds in knots, ranges in nautical miles; speeds and ranges of aircraft are in kilometers/hour and kilometers, unless otherwise indicated.

D: Displacement. In most cases, standard displacement, as defined by the Treaty of Washington (1922), is given. Where possible, full load (fl) is given; otherwise, normal (avg) displacement or trial displacement is given. In the case of most submarines, two displacements are given: the first figure is surfaced displacement; the second is submerged displacement. When available, the figure for standard displacement precedes the surfaced and submerged figures.

Dim: Hull dimensions are given as follows: length overall × beam × draft (full load, unless otherwise stated). Length between perpendiculars is given as "pp"; length at the waterline as "wl." In cases where two figures are given for one of the dimensions, e.g., the beam of the flight deck and of the hull of an aircraft carrier, the hull measurement is given as "h."

S: Speed. This is given in knots and generally refers to maximum speed; in some cases trial speed is given. Where two speeds are given for a surface ship, the top speed is given first, followed by the cruising speed. For submarines, surfaced speed is given first and is followed by submerged speed.

Man: Ship's company.

Range: Cited in nautical miles at a given speed.

A: Armament. Number of guns/caliber; or number of torpedo tubes or launchers with caliber. Figures in parentheses show the number of mounts and whether they are single, double, triple, etc., e.g., (III × 2) indicates two triple mounts.

Armor: Armor protection, thickness given in millimeters.

M: Machinery. Geared turbine is shown as GT; in some cases, the type of turbine is given, e.g., Parsons, etc. COSAG, CODAG/CODOG, COGAG/COGOG are used when such combinations of machinery have to be shown. "Props" indicates propellers.

Electric: Electric generating power.

Boilers: In most cases, number and type are shown. Steam pressure is expressed in kilograms/square centimeter and steam superheat in degrees Centigrade.

Dates: Dates are given in the following sequence: day-month-year.

A	Armament
AA	Antiaircraft
A & C, At & Ch	Shipbuilding yard
AAW	Anti-air warfare
AEW	Airborne early warning
ARM	Anti-radiation missile
ASCAC	Airborne ASW control center
Ast Nav	Naval shipyard
ASW	Antisubmarine warfare
Author.	Authorized
avg	Average, normal
BB	Boatbuilding
Bldr	Builder
BPDMS	Base Point Defense Missile System
BW	Boat Works
BY	Boat Yard
Ch, Ch Nav	Builder, naval shipyard
C N, Cant Nav	Naval shipyard
COD	Carrier Onboard Delivery
COGAG/CODAG/COSAG/ COGOG/CODOG	Combined propulsive machinery systems, gas turbine, diesel, steam. *CO* means *combined, a* means *and, o* means *on.* For example, CODOG means *combined diesel on gas.*
CSGN	Nuclear-powered, guided-missile strike cruiser
D	Displacement
DD, DDM	Dry dock, dry dock company
Dim	Dimensions
DP	Dual-purpose
DSRV	Deep Submergence Rescue Vessel
ECM	Electronic countermeasures
ECCM	Electronic counter-countermeasures
Electron Equipt	Electronic equipment
ELINT	Electronic intelligence
EMD	Electronique Marcel Dassault
Eng	Engineering
ESM	Electronic support measures
FF, FFG	Frigate, guided-missile frigate
fl	Full load
FR, FRAM	Fleet Rehabilitation and Modernization
fwd	Forward
GE	General Electric Co.
GFCS	Gunfire-control system
GM	General Motors Corp.

grt	Gross register tons
GT	Geared turbine
H	Helicopter
h	Hull
HF	High frequency
HMDY	Her Majesty's dockyard
HSA	Hollandse Signaal Apparaaten
hp	Horsepower
IFF	Identification Friend or Foe
kg	Kilogram
Kon. Mij.	Royal company
kt	Kiloton
kts	Knots
kva	Kilovolt-ampere
kw	Kilowatt
L	Launched
l	Light
LF	Low frequency
loa	Length overall
M	Machinery
m	Mean
MAD	Magnetic (or Anomaly) Detection
Man	Manpower on board ship, crew, ship's company
MAP	Military Assistance Program (U.S. and allies)
MF	Medium frequency
ML	Missile launcher
mm	Millimeters
MSC	Military Sealift Command
N.B.	New Brunswick
NBC	Nuclear, biological, and chemical
NDY	Naval dockyard
nrt	Net register tons
N.S.	Nova Scotia
NSY	Naval shipyard
NTDS	Naval Tactical Data System
NY	Navy Yard
oa	Overall
PADLOC	Passive/Active Detection and Location
PLAT	Pilot Landing Air Television
pp	Between perpendiculars
PUFFS	Passive Underwater Fire-Control System
RDY	Royal dockyard
RL	Rocket launcher
rpm	Revolutions per minute
S	Speed
SAM	Surface-to-air missile
SAR	Search and Rescue
SB	Shipbuilding
S.F.C.N.	Société Française de Construction Navale
SINS	Ship's Inertial Navigation System
SLEP	Service Life Extension Program
SSBN	Nuclear-powered fleet ballistic-missile submarine
SSM	Surface-to-surface missile

STIR	Surveillance Target Indicator Radar
	Separate Track and Illumination Radar
SURTASS	Surface Towed Array Surveillance System
SY	Shipyard
TACTASS	Tactical Towed Acoustic Sensor System
TASS	Towed Array Surveillance System
TT	Torpedo tubes/launchers
VDS	Variable-depth sonar
Wks	Works
wl	Waterline

CONVERSION TABLES

♦ METERS (m.) to FEET (ft.)
based on 1 inch = 25.4 millimeters

m	0	1	2	3	4	5	6	7	8	9
	ft.	ft.	ft.	ft.	ft.	ft.	ft.	ft.	ft.	ft.
—	—	3.28084	6.5617	9.8425	13.1234	16.4042	19.6850	22.9659	26.2467	29.5276
10	32.8084	36.0892	39.3701	42.6509	45.9317	49.2126	52.493	55.774	59.005	62.336
20	65.617	68.898	72.178	75.459	78.740	82.021	85.302	88.583	91.863	95.144
30	98.425	101.706	104.987	108.268	111.549	114.829	118.110	121.391	124.672	127.953
40	131.234	134.514	137.795	141.076	144.357	147.638	150.919	154.199	157.480	160.761
50	164.042	167.323	170.604	173.884	177.165	180.446	183.727	187.008	190.289	193.570
60	196.850	200.131	203.412	206.693	209.974	213.255	216.535	219.816	223.097	226.378
70	229.659	232.940	236.220	239.501	242.782	246.063	249.344	252.625	255.905	259.186
80	262.467	265.748	269.029	272.310	275.590	278.871	282.152	285.433	288.714	291.995
90	295.276	298.556	301.837	305.118	308.399	311.680	314.961	318.241	321.522	324.803
100	328.084	331.365	334.646	337.926	341.207	344.488	347.769	351.050	354.331	357.611
10	360.892	364.173	367.454	370.735	374.016	377.296	380.577	383.858	387.139	390.420
20	393.701	396.982	400.262	403.543	406.824	410.105	413.386	416.667	419.947	423.228
30	426.509	429.790	433.071	436.352	439.632	442.913	446.194	449.475	452.756	456.037
40	459.317	462.598	465.879	469.160	472.441	475.722	479.002	482.283	485.564	488.845
50	492.126	495.407	498.688	501.97	505.25	508.53	511.81	515.09	518.37	521.65
60	524.93	528.22	531.50	534.78	538.06	541.34	544.62	547.90	551.18	554.46
70	557.74	561.02	564.30	567.59	570.87	574.15	577.43	580.71	583.99	587.27
80	590.55	593.83	597.11	600.39	603.67	606.96	610.24	613.52	616.80	620.08
90	623.36	626.64	629.92	633.20	636.48	639.76	643.04	646.33	649.61	652.89
200	656.17	659.45	662.73	666.01	669.29	672.57	675.85	679.13	682.41	685.70
10	688.98	692.26	695.54	698.82	702.10	705.38	708.66	711.94	715.22	718.50
20	721.78	725.07	728.35	731.63	734.91	738.19	741.47	744.75	748.03	751.31
30	754.59	757.87	761.15	764.44	767.72	771.00	774.28	777.56	780.84	784.12
40	747.40	790.68	793.96	797.24	800.52	803.81	807.09	810.37	813.65	816.93
50	820.21	823.49	826.77	830.05	833.33	836.61	839.89	843.18	846.46	849.74
60	853.02	856.30	859.58	862.86	866.14	869.42	872.70	875.98	879.26	882.55
70	885.83	889.11	892.39	895.67	898.95	902.23	905.51	908.79	912.07	915.35
80	918.63	921.92	925.20	928.48	931.76	935.04	938.32	941.60	944.88	948.16
90	951.44	954.72	958.00	961.29	964.57	967.85	971.13	974.41	977.69	980.97
300	984.25	987.53	990.81	994.09	997.38	1000.66	1003.94	1007.22	1010.50	1013.78
10	1017.06	1020.34	1023.62	1026.90	1030.18	1033.46	1036.75	1040.03	1043.31	1046.59
20	1049.87	1053.15	1056.43	1059.71	1062.99	1066.27	1069.55	1072.83	1076.12	1079.40
30	1082.68	1085.96	1089.24	1092.52	1095.80	1099.08	1102.36	1105.64	1108.92	1112.20
40	1115.49	1118.77	1122.05	1125.33	1128.61	1131.89	1135.17	1138.45	1141.73	1145.01
50	1118.29	1151.57	1154.86	1158.14	1161.42	1164.70	1167.98	1171.26	1174.54	1177.82

♦ MILLIMETERS (mm.) to INCHES (in.)
based on 1 inch = 25.4 millimeters

mm	0	1	2	3	4	5	6	7	8	9
	in.	in.	in.	in.	in.	in.	in.	in.	in.	in.
—	—	0.03937	0.07874	0.11811	0.15748	0.19685	0.23622	0.27559	0.31496	0.35433
10	0.39370	0.43307	0.47244	0.51181	0.55118	0.59055	0.62992	0.66929	0.70866	0.74803
20	0.78740	0.82677	0.86614	0.90551	0.94488	0.98425	1.02362	1.06299	1.10236	1.14173
30	1.18110	1.22047	1.25984	1.29921	1.33858	1.37795	1.41732	1.45669	1.49606	1.53543
40	1.57480	1.61417	1.65354	1.69291	1.73228	1.77165	1.81102	1.85039	1.88976	1.92913

mm	0	1	2	3	4	5	6	7	8	9
	in.	in.	in.	in.	in.	in.	in.	in.	in.	in.
50	1.96850	2.00787	2.04724	2.08661	2.12598	2.16535	2.20472	2.24409	2.28346	2.32283
60	2.36220	2.40157	2.44094	2.48031	2.51969	2.55906	2.59843	2.63780	2.67717	2.71654
70	2.75591	2.79528	2.83465	2.87402	2.91339	2.95276	2.99213	3.03150	3.07087	3.11024
80	3.14961	3.18898	3.22835	3.26772	3.30709	3.34646	3.38583	3.42520	3.46457	3.50394
90	3.54331	3.58268	3.62205	3.66142	3.70079	3.74016	3.77953	3.81890	3.85827	3.89764
100	3.93701									

CONVERSION FACTORS

Meter	Yard	Foot	Inch	Centimeter	Millimeter
1	1.093 61	3.280 84	39.370 1	100	1 000
0.914 4	1	3	36	91.44	914.4
0.304 8	0.333 333	1	12	30.48	304.8
0.254	0.027 777 8	0.083 333	1	2.54	25.4 j
0.01	0.010 936 1	0.032 808 4	0.393 701	1	10
0.001	0.001 093 61	0.003 280 84	0.039 370 4	0.1	1

Nautical mile	Statute mile	Meters
1	= 1.151 52	= 1 853.18

♦ Boiler working pressure

Kilogram per square centimeter (*atmosphere*) — *Pounds per square inch*

1	equivalent →	14.223 3
0.070 307	← equivalent	1

♦ Conversion for Fahrenheit and Centigrade scales

1 degree Centigrade = 1.8 degrees Fahrenheit
1 degree Fahrenheit = 5/9 degree Centigrade
$t\,°F = 5/9(t - 32)\,°C.$
$t\,°C = (1.8\,t + 32)\,°F.$

♦ Weights

1 kilogram = 2.204 62 *pounds* (av)
1 *pound* = 0.453 592
1 ton (metric) = 0.984 21 *ton*
1 ton = 1.016 05 *metric ton*

♦ Power

1 (CV) = 0.986 32 *horsepower* (HP) 0.735 88 kilowatt (Greenwich) (75 kgm/s)
1 *horsepower* (HP) = 1.013 87 (CV) 0.746 08 kilowatt (Greenwich)

ALBANIA

PERSONNEL: 3,000 men

MERCHANT MARINE (1978): 16 ships—43,623 grt

Neither the U.S.S.R. nor China is now supporting Albania, and the material condition of the ships listed below must be suffering.

The following are of either Soviet or Chinese origin:

◆ **3 W-class submarines** (1,050 tons surfaced, 1,350 submerged, 17/16 kts), two operational

◆ **4 Kronstadt-class patrol boats** (310 tons, 18 kts)

◆ **6 Shanghai-II-class patrol boats**

    D: 155 tons (fl)   **S:** 28 kts
    A: 4/37-mm AA (II × 2)—4/25-mm AA (II × 2)

REMARK: Four transferred in 1974, two in 1975.

◆ **2 T-43-class ocean minesweepers** (500 tons, 14 kts)

◆ **6 T-301-class coastal minesweepers** (145.8 tons, 12.5 kts)

◆ **4 P-4-class torpedo boats** (19.3 tons, 55 kts)

◆ **35 Huchwan-class hydrofoil torpedo boats**

◆ **1 Toplevo-class fuel barge**

◆ **1 Khobi-class small tanker**

◆ **2 small transports**

◆ **1 Nyryat-class diving tender**

◆ **1 Sekstan-class degaussing ship**

◆ **4 tugs**

◆ **2 Poluchat-class torpedo-recovery ships**

◆ **1 barracks ship**

Huchwan-class hydrofoil torpedo boat   1976

ALGERIA

PERSONNEL (1975): 3,000 men with about 300 to 350 officers, not necessarily on full-time active duty with the navy.

MERCHANT MARINE (1978): 121 ships—1,152,086 grt (tankers 20—642,675 grt)

NAVAL AVIATION: The Algerian Air Force uses 11 twin-engine Fokker F-27 (Maritime) patrol aircraft for maritime surveillance.

The Algerian Navy is made up of ships from the U.S.S.R. See that section for characteristics.

MISSILE- AND TORPEDO-LAUNCHING SMALL CRAFT

◆ **4 guided-missile patrol boats** Bldr: ONCN/CNE, Mers-el-Kebir

    D: **S:**   **Dim:** 40.0 × 7.0 × 1.75
    A: 2 SSM (Otomat?)—2/76-mm DP OTO Melara Compact (I × 2)
    M: 2 diesels; 2 props; 11,000 hp   **Man:** 18 men

REMARKS: Program announced and boats ordered 1979, for delivery by 1983. Armament uncertain; most equipment probably Italian.

◆ **8 Osa-II-class guided-missile boats**

Algerian Osa-II   1977

REMARK: Transferred 1976-79.

◆ **3 Osa-I-class guided-missile boats:** R 167, R 267, R 367

REMARK: Transferred 1967.

◆ **6 Komar-class guided-missile boats:** 671 to 676

REMARK: Transferred 1966.

◆ **4 P-6-class torpedo boats**

REMARK: Transferred 1963-68. Two without torpedo tubes were transferred to the Coast Guard, two are hulks, two are unarmed training craft.

MINE WARFARE SHIPS

◆ **2 T-43 class:** M 221, M 222

REMARKS: Transferred in 1968. M-221 in reserve since 1974.

ALGERIA (continued)

LANDING SHIPS

◆ **1 Polnocny-class medium landing ship**

REMARK: Transferred 8-76.

PATROL BOATS

◆ **6 S.O.-1 class: P 651 to P 656**

REMARKS: Transferred 10-65 to 10-67. Three carry 2 torpedo tubes removed from P-6-class torpedo boats.

VARIOUS SHIPS

A 640 VASISA, *Sekstan*-class degaussing tender
A 641, *Poluchat*-class torpedo-recovery ship
VP 650 YAVDEZAN, harbor tug

REMARKS: A-640 procured in 1964; VP-650, also used as a diving tender, procured in 1965.

COAST GUARD

◆ **4 Mangusta-class patrol boats** Bldr: Baglietto, Italy.

331 REQUIN   332 ESPADON   333 MARSOUIN   334 MURÈRIE

Requin (now renumbered)   C. Martinelli, 1977

D:	91 tons (fl)	**S:**	32 kts	**Dim:**	30.0 × 5.84 × 2.1
A:	1/20-mm AA	**Man:**	3 officers, 11 men	**Range:**	800/24, 1,400/12.5
M:	3 diesels; 3 props; 4,050 hp			**Electron Equipt:**	Radars: 3RM 20 SMA

REMARK: In service 1977-78.

◆ **10 24-GC-class patrol craft** Bldr: Baglietto, Italy
235, 236, 325, 335, ...

D:	52 tons (fl)	**S:**	32 kts	**Dim:**	24.26 × 5.2 × 1.8
A:	1/20-mm AA	**Man:**	13 men	**Range:**	660/22, 1,200/12
Fuel:	8 tons	**M:**	2 CRM 18DS diesels; 2 props; 2,700 hp		
M:	2 CRM 18DS diesels; 2 props; 2,700 hp				

Baglietto coast guard patrol craft   C. Martinelli, 1977

REMARKS: The first two entered service in 8-76, the others were delivered at two-month intervals.

◆ **2 Soviet P-6-class torpedo boats** without tubes, transferred from the Navy.

◆ **several smaller patrol craft.**

ANGOLA

MERCHANT MARINE: (1978): 29 ships — 21,820 grt (tankers: 2 — 1,875 grt)

A small navy was established in 1976 by employing units left by the Portuguese. Subsequently, the U.S.S.R. has provided assistance. Believed operational are:

◆ **5 Soviet Shershen-class torpedo boats** Transferred 12-77 to 2-79

◆ **5 Argos-class patrol boats** (ex-*Centauro*, ex-*Escorpiao*, ex-*Lira*, ex-*Orion*, ex-*Pegaso*): 180 tons, 18 kts, 2/40-mm AA (I × 2). Blt. 1961-64

◆ **1 Soviet Zhuk-class patrol craft**

D:	50 tons (60fl)	**S:**	30 kts	**Dim:**	26.0 × 4.9 × 1.5
A:	4/14.5-mm machine guns (II × 2)	**M:**	2 M50 diesels; 2 props; 2,400 hp		

REMARK: Transferred 1977.

ANGOLA (continued)

◆ **1 Jupiter-class patrol craft** (ex-*Venus*): 32 tons, 20 kts, 1/20-mm AA. Blt. 1964

◆ **5 Bellatrix-class patrol craft** (ex-*Altair*, ex-*Espiga*, ex-*Fomalhaut*, ex-*Pollux*, ex-*Rigel*): 23 tons, 15 kts, 1/20-mm AA. Blt. 1961-63

◆ **2 Soviet Polnocny-B medium landing ships**

REMARK: Transferred 1977-78.

◆ **1 Alfange-class landing craft:** 500 tons, 11 kts, 57 × 11.8 × 1.3, 2/20-mm AA

◆ **9 smaller landing craft** (LCM, LCVP types)

ARGENTINA

PERSONNEL: 21,000 men, including 2,300 officers and 3,000 Marines

MERCHANT MARINE (1978): 432 ships — 2,000,879 grt (tankers: 70 — 652,047 grt)

NAVAL AVIATION: The air squadron in the *25 de Mayo* consists of 12 A-4Q Skyhawks, 4 SH-3D helicopters, and 6 S-2A Trackers. In addition, 3 A-4Q are held in reserve. Land-based aircraft include 4 P2-H Neptunes, 3 HU-16 Albatros patrol planes, 30 T-28 trainers, 8 C-47, 3 C-54, 3 L-188 Electra, 5 short Skyvan, 1 twin Otter, 6 C-45, 1 H.S. 125A, 3 Beaver, 2 Beech Super King Air, and 3 Fairchild-Porter transports. Helicopters also include 2 Sea Lynx (for the *Sheffield*-class DDGs), 4 Alouette III, 6 Bell 47, 6 Hughes Cayuse, 2 Sikorsky S-61, and 5 Sikorsky S-55.

WARSHIPS IN SERVICE OR UNDER CONSTRUCTION AS OF 1 JANUARY 1980

	L	Tons	Main Armament
◆ **10 submarines**			
2 GERMAN TR-1400	1980-82	1,450	6/533-mm TT
4 GERMAN TR-1700	1980-82	1,750	6/533-mm TT
2 GERMAN 209	1972-73	980	8/533-mm TT
2 GUPPY IA, II	1944-45	1,517	10/533-mm TT
◆ **1 aircraft carrier**			
25 DE MAYO	1943	15,892	9/40-mm AA
			22 aircraft

	L	Tons	Main Armament
◆ **2 crusiers**			
2 BROOKLYN	1936-38	10,800	15/152-mm
◆ **9 destroyers**			
2 SHEFFIELD	1972-74	3,150	1 Sea Dart SAM, 1/114-mm DP, 1 ASW helicopter
1 GEARING, FRAM II	1944	2,400	4 Exocet SSM, 6/127-mm DP
4 ALLEN M. SUMNER, FRAM II	1944	2,200	4 Exocet SSM, 6/127-mm DP
2 FLETCHER	1942-43	2,050	4/127-mm DP, 4/533-mm TT
◆ **11 frigates**			
6 MEKO 360	198 . .	2,900	4 Exocet, Albatros, 1/127-mm DP
3 A-69	1977	1,170	2 Exocet, 1/100-mm DP
2 MURATURE	1943-45	1,000	3/105-mm DP
◆ **8 corvettes**			
2 CHEROKEE	1944-45	1,235	4/40-mm AA
6 SOTOYOMO	1944-45	689	1/40-mm AA
◆ **10 patrol boats**			
◆ **6 minesweeper/minehunters**			
◆ **2 landing ships**			

AIRCRAFT CARRIER

◆ **1 British Colossus-class**

	Bldr	Laid down	L	In serv.	Modernized
25 DE MAYO (ex-*Venerable*, ex-*Karel Doorman*)	Cammell Laird	12-42	30-12-43	5-45	8-1969

D: 15,892 tons (19,896 fl)   **S:** 24.5 kts
Dim: 212.67 (192.04 pp) × 24.49 (40.66) × 7.5
Man: 1,509 men   **Range:** 6,200/23, 12,000/14
A: 9/40-mm AA — 22 aircraft: 18 planes, 4 helicopters
Electron Equipt: Radars: Dutch: 2/LW 02, 1/SGR 109 (height-finding), 1/SGR 105, 1/SGR 103
M: Parsons GT; 2 props   **Electric:** 2,500 kw
Boilers: 4 Admiralty 3-drum type; steam pressure 30.23 kg/cm² since refit; 40,000 hp
Fuel: 3,200 tons

REMARKS: Purchased by The Netherlands from the British Navy in 1948. Rebuilt from 1955 to 1958 by Wilton-Fijenoord, angled flight deck of 165.80 meters, steam catapult, mirror optical landing equipment, new anti-aircraft guns, and new radar equipment of Dutch conception and construction. Modified for service in the tropics. Partially air-conditioned. In 1967 new boilers were installed from the British aircraft carrier *Leviathan* which was never completed. Purchased in 1968 by Argentina. She is equipped with the British C.A.A.I.S. data display system. The British Sea Harrier V/STOL attack aircraft is to be acquired to augment the A-4Q Skyhawks carried.

AIRCRAFT CARRIER (continued)

25 de Mayo

SUBMARINES

◆ **2 TR-1400 class** Bldr: AFNE, Rio Santiago

	L		L
N . . .	. . .	N . . .	. . .

    D: 1,450 tons   **Dim:** 58.1 × 7.3 × 6.5
    S: 21 kts (submerged) – 13 with snorkel, 15 kts (surfaced)
    A: 6/533-mm TT forward, 22 torpedoes   **Man:** . . .
    M: Diesel-electric: 4/1,000-kw generators; 1 motor; . . .hp

REMARKS: Ordered at same time as the TR-1700 class below. Intended for coastal operations with less endurance required. Same bow and stern components as TR-1700 class.

◆ **4 TR-1700 class** Bldr: Thyssen Nordseewerke, Germany, and AFNE, Rio Santiago

	L		L
N . . .	. . .	N . . .	. . .
N . . .	. . .	N . . .	. . .

    D: 1,750 tons (2,050 surfaced fl)   **Dim:** 64.1 × 7.3 × 6.5
    S: 25 kts (submerged) – 13 with snorkel, 15 kts (surfaced)

    A: 6/533-mm TT, 22 torpedoes   **Man:** 26 men
    M: Diesel-electric: 4/1,000-kw generators; 1 motor; 1 prop, 6,000 hp
    Range: 15,000/5

REMARKS: First unit laid down in Germany 7-78 for delivery 1-82; last three to be built in Argentina. Battery has eight groups of 120 cells, 5,858 amp/hr. capacity.

◆ **2 Salta** (German 209 class)

	Bldr	L	In serv.
S 31 SALTA	Howaldtswerke, Kiel	22-11-72	5-74
S 32 SAN LUIS	Howaldtswerke, Kiel	7-73	5-74

    D: 980 tons standard, 1,230 submerged   **Dim:** 55.0 × 6.6 × 5.9
    S: 21 kts submerged – 12 with snorkel   **Man:** 5 officers, 26 men
    A: 8/533-mm TT – 6 reserve torpedoes
    M: 4 MTU type 12V-493-TY60 diesels, Siemens electric motor; 3,600 hp; 1 prop
    Fuel: 50 tons diesel

REMARKS: Built in four sections in Kiel and assembled at the navy yard in Rio Santiago. Part of the electronic equipment is French. An extension of the German 205/206 class (IKL plans of Professor Ulrich Gabler); submarine is of single-hull construction.

SUBMARINES (continued)

Salta   1972

◆ 2 ex-U.S. Guppy class

	Bldr	L
S 21 SANTA FE (ex-*Catfish*, SS-339)	Electric Boat Co.	19-11-44
S 22 SANTIAGO DEL ESTERO (ex-*Chivo*, SS-341)	Electric Boat Co.	14-1-45

For photograph, see *Murat Reis* in the section on Turkey.

D: 1,517 tons surfaced; 1,870 normal; 2,340 submerged
S: 18/14 kts   **Range:** 10,000/10   **Dim:** 93.6 × 8.4 × 5.25
A: 10/533-mm TT (6 forward, 4 aft)   **Man:** 9 officers, 76 men
M: 3 (S-22; 4) GM 16-278A diesels, each of 1,625 hp, with 2 electric motors of 2,700 hp each; 2 props   **Fuel:** 300 tons diesel

REMARKS: Transferred 7-71. S-21 is a Guppy II; S-22 is a Guppy IA.

CRUISERS

◆ 2 ex-U.S. Brooklyn class

	Bldr	Laid down	L	In serv.
C 4 GENERAL BELGRANO (ex-*Diecisiete de Octubre*, ex-*Phoenix*, CL-46)	New York SB Co.	15-4-35	12-3-38	3-10-38
C 5 NUEVE DE JULIO (ex-*Boise*, CL-47)	Newport News	1-4-35	3-12-36	12-8-38

D: 10,800 tons (13,479 fl)   **S:** 25/24 kts   **Dim:** 185.32 × 18.77 × 7.62
Man: 980 men   **Range:** 2,500/30, 9,850/12
A: *General Belgrano:* 15/152-mm (III × 5)−8 Sea Cat SAM (IV × 2)−
     8/127-mm DP (I × 8)−20/40-mm AA (IV × 2,
     II × 6)−2/20-mm AA

Nueve de Julio: 15/152-mm (III × 5)−6/127-mm DP (I × 6)−28/40-mm
     AA (IV × 4, II × 6)−12/20-mm AA (II × 6)
Electron Equipt: Radars: C-4−1/SGR-110, 1/SGR-105, 1/SGR-114, 1/NA-10, 2/Mk 8,
     1/Mk 28
     C-5−1/SGR-116, 2/SG-6, 2/Mk 8, 2/Mk 28
Armor: Belt, 102; Decks, 76; Turret, 102; Conning tower, 203
M: Parsons GT; 4 props; 100,000 hp
Boilers: 8 Babcock Express, 31 kg pressure

REMARKS: Purchased in the U.S.A., 12-1-51. Ships have two helicopters. Chilean Navy has two sisters. *General Belgrano*'s Sea Cat systems are controlled by 2 Selenia RTN-10. *Nueve de Julio* has only a skeleton crew. Neither ship has bulges.

DESTROYERS

◆ 2 Sheffield-class guided-missile

	Bldr	Laid down	L	In serv.
D 1 HERCULES	Vickers, Barrow	1971	24-10-72	10-5-76
D 2 SANTISIMA TRINIDAD	Ast. Nav. Rio Santiago	2-72	9-11-74	. . .

Hercules   G. Arra, 1977

D: 3,150 tons (3,600 fl)   **Dim:** 125 (119.5 pp) × 14.6 × 5.2
S: 28/18 kts   **Range:** 4,000/18   **Man:** 270 men
A: 1/114-mm DP Mk 8−2/20-mm AA−1 Sea Dart (II × 1)−1 WG 13 Lynx ASW and anti-ship helicopter−6/324-mm Mk 32 ASW TT (III × 2)−2 Knebworth Corvus chaff launchers
Electron Equipt: Radars: 1/965M, 1/992, 2/909, 1/1006, ADAWS-4 control
     Sonars: 1/177, 1/174, 1/170B, 1/162
M: COGOG propulsion: 2 Olympus TM 3B gas turbines, 27,200 hp each for boost; 2 Tyne RM 1A gas turbines, 4,100 hp each for cruising; 2 controllable-pitch, 5-bladed props
Electric: 4,000 kw

DESTROYERS (continued)

REMARKS: Ordered 18-5-70. D-1 has "Loxton Bends" angled exhausts like HMS *Sheffield*. D-2 was sabotaged on 22-8-75 and will be delayed. Formerly numbered D-28 and D-29. The Sea Dart system is Mk 30 mod. 2 and has 20 missiles.

◆ 1 ex-U.S. Gearing class

	Bldr	L	In serv.
D 27 COMODORO PY (ex-*Perkins*, DD-877)	Consolidated Steel	7-12-44	4-45

Comodoro Py 1973

D: 2,400 tons (3,600 fl) **S:** 36 kts **Dim:** 119.17 × 12.45 × 5.8
Man: 15 officers, 260 men **Range:** 2,400/25, 4,800/15
A: 4/MM 38 Exocet—4/127-mm AA 38-cal. (II × 2)—2 Hedgehogs—6/324-mm ASW TT (III × 2) Mk 32 for Mk 44 torpedoes—1/Alouette-III helicopter
Electron Equipt: Radars: 1/SPS 40, 1/SPS 10—Sonar: 1/SQS 23
M: Westinghouse GT; 2 props; 60,000 hp **Fuel:** 650 tons
Boilers: 4 Babcock & Wilcox

REMARKS: Transferred 1-73. Had undergone Fram II modernization. Exocet added 1977-78 in place of 127-mm just before bridge. Mk 37 fire-control system with Mk 25 radar.

◆ 4 ex-U.S. Allen M. Sumner class

	Bldr	L	In serv.
D 25 SEGUI (ex-*Hank*, DD-702)	Federal SB & DD	21-5-44	8-44
D 26 HIPOLITO BOUCHARD (ex-*Borie*, DD-704)	Federal SB & DD	4-7-44	9-44
D 30 PIEDRABUENA (ex-*Collett*, DD-730)	Bath Iron Works	5-3-44	5-44
D 31 ESPORA (ex-*Mansfield*, DD-728)	Bath Iron Works	29-1-44	4-44

D: 2,200 tons (3,300 fl) **Dim:** 114.75 × 12.45 × 5.8
S: 30 kts **Man:** 14 officers, 260 men **Range:** 1,260/30, 4,600/15
A: 4/MM 38 Exocet—4/127-mm DP (II × 2)—D-25: 4/76-mm AA (II × 2) also—6/324-mm ASW TT Mk 32—2 Hedgehogs—1/Alouette-III helicopter
Electron Equipt: Radars: 1/SPS 40, 1/SPS 10 Mk 25
Sonars: 1/SQS 29 or 30, VDS (not on D-25)
M: GT; 2 props, 60,000 hp
Boilers: 4 Babcock **Fuel:** 650 tons

REMARKS: Two transferred 7-72, and two 4-76. Exocet anti-ship missiles added to D-26 and D-30 in 1977-78, just before bridge. D-25 was not modernized. She still has 6/127-mm (II × 3) and has SPS-6 radar. D-31, which was transferred 4-76 for cannibalization, has SPS-29 radar. She was placed in commission in 1978.

Segui—Mk 56 fire-control system aft with Mk 35 radar 1975

Hipolito Bouchard—D-30 and D-31 similar 1975

◆ 2 ex-U.S. Fletcher class

	Bldr	L	In serv.
D 23 ALMIRANTE DOMECQ GARCIA (ex-*Braine*, DD-630)	Bath Iron Works	7-3-43	5-43
D 24 ALMIRANTE STORNI (ex-*Cowell*, DD-547)	Bethlehem, San Pedro	18-4-43	8-43

D: 2,050 tons (2,850 fl) **S:** 30 kts **Dim:** 114.85 × 12.03 × 5.5
Man: 15 officers, 247 men **Range:** 1,260/30, 4,400/15
A: 4/127-mm DP (I × 4)—6/76-mm AA (II × 3)—4/533-mm TT (IV × 1)—D-23 and D-24: 6/324-mm ASW TT Mk 32 (III × 2)—2 Hedgehogs—1 depth-charge rack
Electron Equipt: Radars: 1/SPS 6, 1/SPS 10 Sonar: 1/SQS 4
M: GE GT; 2 props; 60,000 hp
Boilers: 4 Babcock & Wilcox **Fuel:** 650 tons

REMARKS: Transferred 1962-63 and 1971-72. Fire-control radars: 1/Mk 25, 2/Mk 34, 1/Mk 35. The *Knapp* (DD-653) of this class was purchased for spare parts. The *Brown* (ex-*Heerman*, DD-532) was stricken 12-77.

FRIGATES

◆ **6 Meko-360 class** Ordered 1978 Bldr: Thyssen/Rheinstahl (2) and AFNE, Rio Santiago (4)

	L		L		L
N . . .	. . .	N . . .	. . .	N . . .	. . .
N . . .	. . .	N . . .	. . .	N . . .	. . .

D: 2,900 tons (fl) **S:** 30 kts **Dim:** 125.4 × 15.0 × 4.3

A: 4/MM 38 Exocet−8/Albatros-Aspide (VIII × 1)−1/127-mm DP OTO Melara−4/40-mm Breda AA (II × 2)−6/324-mm ASW TT Mk 32−1/Sea Lynx ASW helicopter−2/SCLAR chaff launchers

Electron Equipt: Radar: AWS 5 **Man:** 200 men

M: CODOG: 2 Olympus TM 3 GT; 2 MTU 331 TC 81 diesels; 2 controllable-pitch props; 56,000/10,680 hp

REMARKS: Replace six planned U.K. *Amazon* class. First to be completed 6-81.

◆ **3 A-69 class**

	Bldr	L	In serv.
F 701 DRUMMOND (ex-*Good Hope*, F-432)	Lorient DY	5-3-77	10-78
F 702 GUERRICO (ex-*Transvaal*, F-102)	Lorient DY	. . .	10-78
F . . . GRANVILLE (ex-. . .)	• • •	. . .	. . .

D: 1,170 tons **S:** 24 kts **Dim:** 80.0 (76.0 pp) × 10.3 × 3.0

A: 2/MM 38 Exocet−1/100-mm DP mod. 1968−1/40-mm AA−2/20-mm AA (I × 2)−6/324-mm ASW TT (III × 2)

Man: 5 officers, 70 men **Range:** 3,000/18, 4,500/15

Electron Equipt: Radars: 1/DRBV 51A, 1/DRBC 32C, 1/Decca 1228

Sonar: Diodon

M: 2 SEMT-Pielstick 12 PC 2 diesels; 2 controllable-pitch props; 11,000 hp

Electric: 840 kw

REMARKS: The first two were originally ordered by South Africa, but delivery was embargoed. Purchased by Argentina, 25-9-78, to augment fleet in case of war with Chile. Armament and some electronic gear differs from French Navy version. A third unit was ordered in 1979.

◆ **2 Murature class**

	Bldr	Laid down	L	In serv.
P 20 MURATURE	Ast. Nav. Rio Santiago	6-38	7-45	11-46
P 21 KING	Ast. Nav. Rio Santiago	1939	43	7-46

King

D: 913 tons, 1,000 normal, 1,032 fl **S:** 16 kts **Dim:** 76.8 × 8.85 × 2.5

Range: 6,000/12 **Man:** 140 men

A: 3/105-mm DP−4/40-mm AA−4 depth-charge mortars

M: Werkspoor 4-stroke diesels; 2 props; 2,500 hp **Fuel:** 90 tons diesel

REMARK: Both used for training.

CORVETTES

◆ **2 U.S. Cherokee Class**

	Bldr	L
A 1 COMANDANTE GENERAL IRIGOYEN (ex-ATF-152)	Charleston SB & DD	2-11-44
A 3 FRANCISCO DE CHURRUCA (ex-*Luiseno*, ATF-156)	Charleston SB & DD	17-3-45

D: 1,235 tons (1,675 fl) **S:** 16 kts **Dim:** 62.5 (59.45 pp) × 11.65 × 4.7

A: 4/40-mm AA (II × 1, I × 2)−2/20-mm AA

M: Diesel-electric propulsion; 1 prop; 3,000 hp

REMARKS: Former U.S. tugs, transferred 1961-75, used on patrol duties.

◆ **6 U.S. Sotoyomo Class**

A 5 DIAGUITA (ex-ATA-124)	A 8 SANAVIRON (ex-ATA-228)
A 6 YAMANA (ex-ATA-126)	A 9 ALFEREZ SOBRAL (ex-ATA-210)
A 7 CHIRIGUANO (ex-ATA-227)	A 10 COMODORO SOMELLERA (ex-ATA-187)

Bldr: Levingston Shbldg., Texas, 1944-45

D: 689 tons (800 fl) **S:** 12 kts **Dim:** 43.6 (40.75 pp) × 10.37 × 3.65

Man: 49 men **Range:** 16,500

A: 2/20-mm AA (none in A-7, A-8)

M: Diesel-electric propulsion; 1 prop; 1,850 hp **Fuel:** 154 tons diesel

REMARK: A-7 and A-8 used primarily as tugs.

GUIDED-MISSILE AND PATROL BOATS

◆ **2 West German Type 148**

N . . . N . . .

D: 234 tons (265 fl) **S:** 38 kts **Dim:** 44.9 (42.3 pp) × 7.1 × 2.5

A: 5/Gabriel SSM−1/76-mm DP OTO Melara−1/40-mm AA

M: 4 MTU diesels; 4 props; 14,000 hp **Range:** 1,450/20

REMARK: Ordered from Lürssen, 1976.

◆ **2 Intrepida class**

	Bldr	L	In serv.
ELPR 1 INTREPIDA	Lürssen (Bremen-Vegesack)	12-12-74	20-7-74
ELPR 2 INDOMITA	Lürssen (Bremen-Vegesack)	5-74	Spring 1975

D: 240 tons **Dim:** 44.9 × (42.3 pp) × 7.1 × 2.5 (prop.)

S: 40 kts **Range:** 1,450/20 **Man:** 34 men

A: 1/76-mm DP OTO Melara−2/40-mm AA (I × 2)−2/81-mm Oerlikon rocket launchers (II × 1)−2/533-mm wire-guided TT

M: 4 MTU diesels; 4 props; 12,000 hp **Electric:** 330 kw

REMARK: Anti-rolling stabilizers.

GUIDED-MISSILE AND PATROL BOATS (continued)

Intrepida   S. Terzibaschitsch, 1974

◆ **4 Israeli Dabur class**   Bldr: Israeli Aircraft Industries, Israel

BARADERO   BARRANQUERAS   CLORINDA   CONCEPCION DEL URUGUAY

   D: 25 tons (35 fl)   **S:** 25 kts   **Dim:** 19.8 × 5.8 × 0.8
   A: 2/20-mm AA (I × 2) – 4/12.7-mm machine guns (II × 2)
   M: 2 GM diesels; 2 props; 960 hp   **Range:** 1,200/17

REMARK: In service 1978.

◆ **2 former 24-meter torpedo boats**   Bldr: Higgins, New Orleans, in serv., 1948

ALAKASH   TOWARA   **A:** 2/40-mm AA

MINE WARFARE SHIPS

◆ **6 British "-ton" class**   Bought 1967

	L		L
M 1 NEUQUEN (ex-*Hickleton*)	26-1-55	M 4 TIERRA DEL FUEGO	17-3-53
		(ex-*Bevington*)	
M 2 RIO NEGRO (ex-*Tarlton*)	1954	M 5 CHACO	27-11-58
		(ex-*Rennington*)	
M 3 CHUBUT (ex-*Santon*)	18-8-55	M 6 FORMOSA	1954
Transferred in 1968.		(ex-*Ilmington*)	

   D: 370 tons (425 fl)   **S:** 15 kts   **Dim:** 46.33 (42.68 pp) × 8.76 × 2.50
   A: 1/40-mm   **M:** Diesels; 2 props; 2,500/3,000 hp   **Fuel:** 45 tons diesel

REMARK: M-5 and M-6 are fitted out as minehunters, with Plessey Type 193M sonar.

HYDROGRAPHIC SHIPS

◆ **2 Puerto Deseado class**

	Bldr	L	In serv.
Q 8 PUERTO DESEADO	Astarza, San Fernando	12-77	26-2-79
Q . . . ALVARO ALBERTO	Alianza, Avellaneda	. . .	. . .

   D: 2,133 tons   **S:** 15 kts   **Dim:** 76.81 (67.0 pp) × 13.2 × 4.5
   M: 2 Fiat diesels; 2 props; 2,700 hp   **Man:** 83 men   **Range:** 12,000/12

REMARK: Used for hydrometeorological reporting.

Q 11 COMODORO RIVADAVIA   Bldr: Mestrina, Argentina
   L: 29-11-73   In serv. 6-12-76

   D: 655 tons (830 fl)   **S:** 12 kts   **Dim:** 52.2 × 8.8 × 2.6
   M: 2 Werkspoor diesels; 1,160 hp   **Man:** 27 men   **Range:** 6,000/12

Q 15 CORMORAN Coastal survey craft, 82 tons, 13 kts In serv. 1964
Q . . . PETREL Coastal survey craft,   52 tons   In serv. 1965

◆ **2 ex-U.S. Maritime Commission V4-M-A1-class tugs**

Q 17 GOYENA (ex-*Dry Tortugas*)
A 4 THOMPSON (ex-*Sombrero Key*)
   Bldr: Pendleton SY, New Orleans, 1943
   D: 1,630 tons (1,863 fl)   **S:** 11 kts   **Dim:** 59.23 × 11.43 × 5.72
   A: 2/40-mm AA (II × 1)   **Man:** 90 men   **Range:** 19,000/14
   M: 2 Enterprise diesels; 2 props; 2,340 hp   **Fuel:** 566 tons

REMARKS: Transferred 1965. Q-17 for Antarctic research. A-4 for oceanographic research and patrol.

Q 4 GENERAL SAN MARTIN   Bldr: A. G. Weser, Bremen
   D: 4,850 tons (5,300 fl)   **S:** 16 kts   **Dim:** 84.7 × 18.6 × 6.4
   A: 2/40-mm AA   **Man:** 160 men   **Range:** 35,000/10   **Cargo:** 1,600 tons
   M: Diesel-electric propulsion; 2 props; 6,500 hp   **Fuel:** 1,100 tons diesel

REMARKS: Launched 24-6-54. Oceanographic research vessel with icebreaker configuration. Has a helicopter.

Q 7 EL AUSTRAL (ex-*Atlantis*)
   D: 571 tons (fl)   **S:** 9 kts   **Dim:** 43.0 (33.5 pp) × 8.2 × 6.1
   M: 1 diesel; 400 hp   **Man:** 19 men

REMARKS: Schooner, purchased from U.S.A. 4-66. In service since 1931.

AMPHIBIOUS WARFARE SHIPS

◆ **1 ex-U.S. LSD**

PY 3 CANDIDO DE LASALA (ex-*Gunston Hall*, LSD-5) Bldr: Moore DD
L: 1-5-43.
   D: 4,032 tons (8,700 fl)   **S:** 15 kts   **Dim:** 139 × 21.9 × 4.9
   Man: 17 officers, 309 men   **Range:** 8,000/15
   A: 12/40-mm AA   **M:** 2 triple expansion, 7,000 hp

REMARKS: Transferred 24-4-70. Docking well: 103 × 13.30. 2 cranes: 35 tons. Now used as a patrol craft tender.

◆ **1 De Soto County-class LST**

Q 42 CABO SAN ANTONIO   Bldr: AFNE, Rio Santiago, 1968
   D: 4,300 tons (8,000 fl)   **S:** 17 kts   **Dim:** 135.0 × 18.8 × 5.5
   A: 12/40-mm AA (IV × 3)   **Man:** 124 men   **M:** Diesels; 14,000 hp

REMARKS: Completion greatly delayed. In service 1978. Has Stülcken heavy-lift crane, Plessey AWS-1 radar.

◆ **LCM and LCVP landing craft**

EDVP 1, 2, 3, 7, 8, 10, 12, 13, 17, 19, 21, 24, 28, 29, 30 (ex-U.S. LCVPs)
LCM-1 to LCM-4   Bldr: Argentina, 1971

ICEBREAKER

Q 5 ALMIRANTE IRIZAR   Bldr: Wärtsila, Helsinki, Finland

D: 13,878 (fl)   **S:** 16.5 kts   **Dim:** 119.3 × 24.6 × 9.4
Electron Equipt: Radar: Plessey AWS-2   **Electric:** 2,640 kw
A: 2/40-mm AA (I × 2)   **Man:** 123 crew plus 100 scientists
M: Diesel-electric: 4 SEMT-Pielstick 8 PC 2.5 L/400 diesels; 2 Stromberg motors; 2 props; 16,200 hp

REMARKS: Ordered 17-12-75. In service 15-12-78.

AUXILIARY SHIPS

◆ **3 Canal-Beagle-class transports**   Bldr: Principe SY

	L	In serv.
B 3 CANAL BEAGLE	14-10-77	28-4-78
B 4 CABO DE HORNOS	. . .	. . .
B 5 BAHIA SAN BLAS	28-4-78	. . .

D: 7,640 tons (fl)   **S:** 15 kts   **Dim:** 119.9 × 17.5 × 6.4
A: None   **M:** 2 AFNE-Sulzer diesels; 2 props; 6,400 hp

REMARKS: To supply remote stations. 4,600 grt/5,800 dwt. 9,700 cubic meters cargo. Also carry passengers.

◆ **3 Bahia Aguirre-class transports**

	Bldr	L	In serv.
B 2 BAHIA AGUIRRE	Halifax, Canada	15-5-49	1951
B 6 BAHIA BUEN SUCESO	Halifax, Canada	15-6-49	1951

D: 3,100 tons (5,255 fl)   **S:** 15 kts   **Dim:** 95.1 × 14.33 × 7.9
M: 2 Nordberg diesels; 3,750 hp   **Fuel:** 400 tons diesel

B 7 SAN JULIAN (ex-FS-281) (1-45)   Bldr: Wheeler SB Co.

D: 930 tons   **S:** 10 kts   **Dim:** 55.0 × 9.95 × 3.4
M: Diesels; 2 props; 1,000 hp

Bahia Aguirre

REMARK: Former U.S. Army cargo ship.

◆ **2 oilers**

	Bldr	L	In serv.
B 18 PUNTA MEDANOS	Swan Hunter	20-2-50	10-50

D: 16,300 tons (fl)   **S:** 18 kts   **Dim:** 153.0 (143.2 pp) × 18.9 × 8.7
Cargo: 8,250 tons   **Range:** 13,700/12   **Man:** 99 men

M: Parsons GT; 2 props; 9,500 hp   **Fuel:** 1,500 tons
Boilers: 2 Babcock and Wilcox, 28 kg/cm² pressure

B 16 PUNTA DELGADA (ex-U.S. AOG-66)   In serv. 4-45

D: 6,000 tons   **M:** 1,400 hp

◆ **2 tugs**   Bldr: V. Forte

R . . . QUERANDI   R . . . TEHUELCHE
D: 370 tons (fl)   **S:** 12 kts   **Dim:** 33.6 × 8.4 × 3.0
M: 2 M.A.N. diesels; 1,200 hp   **Range:** 1,200/12   **Man:** 30 men

REMARK: In service 1979.

◆ **3 tugs**

R 30 TONOCOTE In serv. 1954   **D:** 330 tons   **M:** 600 hp
R 32 QUILMES and R 33 GUYAYCURU In serv. 1960   **D:** 368 tons   **M:** 650 hp

◆ **6 former U.S. Navy tugs—Transferred 1965-69**

R 6   CALCHAQUI (ex-YTL-445)
R 16   CAPAYAN (ex-YTL-443)
R 18   CHIQUILLAN (ex-YTL-444)
R 10   CHULUPI (ex-YTL-426
R 5   MOCOVI (ex-YTL-441)
R 19   MORLOYAN (ex-YTL-448)

D: 70 tons   **S:** 10 kts   **Dim:** 20.4 × 4.3 × 4.0
M: 1 diesel; 310 hp   **Man:** 5 men

◆ **1 sailing training vessel**

Q 2 LIBERTAD   Bldr: Ast. Nav. Rio Santiago. L: 30-5-56. In serv.: 1962.

Libertad

D: 3,025 tons (3,625 fl)   **Dim:** 94.25 × 13.75 × 6.75
S: 12 kts   **Man:** 222 men and 140 cadets   **Range:** 12,000

ARGENTINA (*continued*)
AUXILIARY SHIPS (*continued*)

> **A:** 1/76-mm – 4/40-mm – 4/47-mm saluting
> **M:** Diesels; 2 props; 2,400 hp

◆ **2 small sail training yachts**

ITATI II   **Bldr:** Cadenazzi SY, 1979   **D:** 80 tons (fl)   **S:** 15 kts
FORTUNA II   Yawl for ocean racing

COAST GUARD

PATROL SHIPS AND CRAFT

◆ **9 ocean patrol ships**   **Bldr:** Bazan, El Ferrol, Spain
N . . .   N . . .   N . . .   N . . .   N . . .

> **D:** 900 tons (fl)   **S:** Over 20 kts   **Dim:** 67.0 (65.0 pp) × . . . × . . .
> **A:** 1/76-mm DP OTO Melara – 1/40-mm AA – 1 helicopter
> **M:** 2 MTU diesels; 2 props; . . . hp

REMARK: Ordered 3-79.

GC 13 DELPHIN

> **D:** 1,000 tons   **S:** 15 kts   **Dim:** 60.0 × 9.0 × 4.7
> **A:** 1/40-mm AA   **Man:** 32 men   **M:** Diesel; 2,300 hp

REMARK: Former whaler, built 1958, acquired 1975 to replace *Bouchard*-class mine-sweeper *Spiro*.

GC 21 LYNCH   GC 22 TOLL   GC 23 EREZCANO
   Bldr: Navy Yard, Rio Santiago, 1964-65

> **D:** 100 tons (117 fl)   **S:** 22 kts   **Dim:** 27.44 × 5.8 × 1.85
> **A:** 1/20-mm AA   **Man:** 16 men   **M:** 2 Maybach diesels; 2,700 hp

◆ **8 patrol craft**   **Bldr:** Cadenazzi SY, Tigre, 1978-79

> **D:** 13 tons   **S:** 25 kts   **Dim:** 12.54 × 3.57 × 1.1
> **A:** 1 machine gun   **M:** 2 GM diesels; 2 props; 560 hp

◆ **20 LLE-class patrol boats**   **Bldr:** Bazan, El Ferrol, Spain

> **D:** 80 tons (fl)   **S:** . . .kts   **Dim:** 28.0 × . . . × . . .
> **A:** . . .   **M:** 2 diesels; 2 props; 800 hp

REMARK: Ordered 1979.

AUSTRALIA

PERSONNEL: approx. 17,000, 2,000 officers

MERCHANT MARINE (1977): 424 ships – 1,374,197 grt
(tankers: 16 – 284,272 grt)

WARSHIPS IN SERVICE OR UNDER CONSTRUCTION
AS OF 1 JANUARY 1980

	L	Tons	Main armament
◆ **1 aircraft carrier**			
MELBOURNE	1945	16,000	17 aircraft
◆ **6 submarines**			
6 OBERON	1965-75	1,610	8/533-mm TT
◆ **5 destroyers**			
3 CHARLES F. ADAMS	1963-66	3,370	1 Tartar system, 2/127-mm, 2 Ikara
2 VENDETTA	1951-56	2,800	6/114-mm
◆ **9 frigates**			
3 OLIVER HAZARD PERRY	1978-80	3,000	1 Tartar system, 1/76-mm, 6 ASW TT
6 RIVER	1958-68	2,100	2/114-mm, 1 Ikara
◆ **5 minesweepers**			
◆ **1 amphibious warfare ship**			

NAVAL AVIATION: Only ship-based aircraft belong to the Navy. On 5-12-76 a fire destroyed 12 of the total of 13 S-2E Tracker ASW aircraft. These were replaced by 6 ex-U.S. Navy aircraft and 6 other former USN aircraft already on order. Other than these, the Australian Fleet Air Arm operates: 8 A-4G Skyhawk fighter-bombers and 8 Sea King helicopters for shipboard use, and retains 4 Wessex 31-B helicopters formerly used aboard *Melbourne*.

Shore-based aviation is under the direction of the RAAF; it includes a squadron of 12 SP2H Neptunes and another of 25 P3 Orions. Eight or more P3C are on order to replace the Neptunes. Other land-based aircraft include 7 TA-4G Skyhawk and 7 MB-326H for training, 2 HS-748 transports, and 4 Bell UH-1H and 2 Bell 206B helicopters.

WEAPONS AND SYSTEMS: The Australian Navy uses U.S. equipment and systems on its U.S.-built warships and British weapons and systems on its other ships, but some of its air-search and fire-control radars have been purchased in The Netherlands (LWO-2, M-20, etc.). Some 71 U.S. Mk 48 torpedoes have been purchased for use by submarines.

Except for the U.S.-built ships, the sonars are all of British or Australian (Mulloka) origin. The Australian Navy has perfected an unusual ASW weapon, the Ikara. Similar in basic concept to the French Malafon, it is a Mk 44 or Mk 46 torpedo coupled with a guided missile and guidance equipment, and has a maximum range of about 20,000 yards.

AIRCRAFT CARRIER

	Bldr	Laid down	L	In serv.
R 21 MELBOURNE	Vickers-Armstrong	15-4-43	28-2-45	28-10-55
(ex-*Majestic*)				

D: 16,000 tons (20,320 fl)   **Dim:** 217.7 (198 wl) × 24.5 (39 max.) × 7.15
S: 23 kts   **Man:** 1,335 men, including 347 air group
A: 12/40-mm AA (II × 4, I × 4)—about 17 aircraft
Electron Equipt: Radars: 1/LWO 2, 1/293, 1/978, 1/SPN 35 CCA
M: Parsons GT; 2 props; 42,000 hp   **Range:** 6,200/23, 12,000/14
Boilers: 4 Admiralty, 28 kg pressure   **Fuel:** 3,200 tons

Melbourne   G. Arra, 1977

REMARKS: Will require replacement by 1985. Steam catapults, 5½° angled flight deck, mirror landing equipment. Modernized in 1969 to operate ASW aircraft, and again refitted in 1971, 1972-73, and 1978-79, when a flight-deck extension to starboard abaft the island was added to park aircraft.

SUBMARINES

◆ **6 British Oberon-class torpedo attack submarines**

	Bldr	Laid down	L	In serv.
S 57 OXLEY	Scott's	2-7-64	24-9-65	27-3-67
S 59 OTWAY	Scott's	29-6-65	29-11-66	22-4-68
S 60 ONSLOW	Scott's	26-5-67	29-8-68	22-12-69
S 61 ORION	Scott's	6-10-72	16-9-74	15-6-77
S 62 OTAMA	Scott's	28-5-73	3-12-75	27-4-78
S 70 OVENS	Scott's	17-6-66	5-12-67	18-4-69

Oxley

D: 1,610 tons, 2,070 surfaced, 2,410 submerged   **S:** 17.5/15 kts
Dim: 89.9 (87.45 pp) × 8.07 × 5.48   **Man:** 6 officers, 57 men
A: 8/533-mm TT (6 fwd, 2 aft) all contained within pressure hull—14 torpedoes in reserve (U.S. Mk 37 and Mk 48)
Electron Equipt: Radar: 1/1006
           Sonars: 1/187 C, 1/197, 1/2007, "Micro-puffs"
M: Two 3,680-hp Admiralty Standard Range 16 VVS-AS 21 diesel engines; diesel-electric propulsion; 6,000 hp

REMARKS: Completion of S-61 and S-62 delayed by deficiencies in the electrical equipment. The four earlier units are being given new U.S. and West German sonars and U.S. Singer Librascope fire-control equipment. Sub-Harpoon missiles may be purchased from the United States. Seventy-one U.S. Mk 48 wire-guided torpedoes have been acquired for use by these submarines.

DESTROYERS

◆ **3 U.S. Charles F. Adams-class guided-missile destroyers**

	Bldr	Laid down	L	In serv.
D 38 PERTH	Defoe S.B. Co. (U.S.)	21-9-62	26-9-63	17-7-65
(ex-U.S. DDG-25)				
D 39 HOBART	Defoe S.B. Co. (U.S.)	26-10-62	9-1-64	18-12-65
(ex-U.S. DDG-26)				
D 41 BRISBANE	Defoe S.B. Co. (U.S.)	15-2-65	5-5-66	16-12-67
(ex-U.S. DDG-27)				

Brisbane   G. Arra, 1977

D: 3,370 tons (4,618 fl)   **Dim:** 134.18 (128 pp) × 14.32 × 6.0
S: 35 kts   **Man:** 21 officers, 312 men   **Range:** 1,600/30—6,000/14
A: 1/Mk 13 Standard SM-1A (40 missiles)—2/127-mm DP (I × 2) Mk 42—6 ASW Mk 32 torpedo tubes (III × 2)—2 ASW Ikara launching systems, one to each side

DESTROYERS *(continued)*

Electron Equipt: Radars: 1/978, 1/SPS 40, 1/SPS 10, 1/SPS 52, 2/SPG 51 C,1/SPG-53A —NTDS
Sonar: 1/SQS 23F   TACAN: 1/URN-20
M: GT: 2 props; 70,000 hp   **Fuel:** 900 tons
Boilers: 4 Babcock & Wilcox, 84 kg/cm² – superheat 520°
Electric: 2,000 kw

REMARKS: D-38 modernized in the U.S. 3-9-74 to 2-1-75 with SM-1A Standard missiles, NTDS, and Mk 42, mod. 10, guns. The other two were refitted to the same standard in Australia. All are scheduled eventually to receive Harpoon anti-ship missiles. Missile-fire control is Mk 74, mod. 8, with two radar directors; guns are controlled by one Mk 63 radar director (optical range-finder removed).

◆ 2 Vendetta-class destroyers

		Bldr	Laid down	L	In serv.
D 08	VENDETTA	Williamstown Naval DY	4-7-49	3-5-54	26-11-58
D 11	VAMPIRE	Cockatoo D. & Eng. Co.	1-7-52	27-10-56	23-6-59

Vendetta   G. Arra, 1978

D: 2,800 tons (3,670 fl)   **Dim:** 118.87 (111.55 pp) × 13.1 × 5.1
S: 30 kts   **Man:** 321 men   **Range:** 3,700/20
A: 6/114-mm DP Mk 6 (II × 3)–6/40-mm AA (II × 2, I × 2)–1 Limbo Mk 10 ASW mortar
M: Parsons GT; 2 props; 54,000 hp
Boilers: 2 Foster Wheeler   **Fuel:** 584 tons
Electron Equipt: Radars: 1/LW0 2, 1/8GR 301, 2/HSA M22
Sonars: 1/162, 1/170, 1/174

REMARKS: D-08 and D-11 completed modernization in 1971 and 1973 with Dutch fire-control and air-search radars. D-08 placed in reserve 1979. Both will be discarded on delivery of new FFGs. The *Duchess*, D-154, converted to training ship, was discarded 1977.

FRIGATES

◆ 3 Oliver Hazard Perry-class guided-missile frigates

		Bldr	Laid down	L	In serv.
F . . .	ADELAIDE	Todd, Seattle	29-7-77	21-6-78	30-8-80
(ex-U.S. FFG-17)					
F . . .	CANBERRA	Todd, Seattle	1-3-78	1-12-78	31-12-80
(ex-U.S. FFG-18)					
F . . .	SYDNEY	Todd, Seattle	1980	26-9-80	31-12-82
(ex-U.S. FFG-35)					

D: 3,678 tons (fl)   **S:** 28.5 kts   **Dim:** 135.6 (126 pp) × 13.7 × 7.5
Man: 226 men total   **Range:** 5,000/18
A: 1/Mk 13, mod. 4, launcher for Standard SM-1A SAM and Harpoon–1/76-mm DP OTO Melara Compact (U.S. Mk 75)–6/Mk 32 ASW TT for Mk 46 torpedoes– 2 helicopters
Electron Equipt: Radars: 1/SPS 55, 1/SPS 49, 1/SPG 60, 1/Mk 92 fire-control
Sonar: 1/SQS 56   ESM: 1/SLQ 32
M: 2 GE LM 2500; 1 controllable-pitch prop; 40,000 hp
Electric: 4,000 kw   **Fuel:** 651 tons

REMARKS: First two ordered 27-2-76 in lieu of Australian DDL design. The third was ordered 23-1-79. Two drop-down, diesel-electric-driven propellers are located forward beneath the hull for emergency propulsion and maneuvering. No fin stabilizers fitted. Will not have U.S. Vulcan/Phalanx close-defense gun. The type of helicopter to be carried has not been decided between the U.S. Lamps III and the British/French Lynx. Crew larger than in U.S. sisters.

◆ 6 River-class frigates

		Bldr	Laid down	L	In serv.
F 45	YARRA	Williamstown Nav. DY	9-4-57	30-9-58	27-7-61
F 46	PARRAMATTA	Cockatoo D. & Eng. Co.	3-1-57	31-1-59	4-7-61
F 48	STUART	Cockatoo D. & Eng. Co.	20-3-59	8-4-61	28-6-63
F 49	DERWENT	Williamstown Nav. DY	16-6-59	17-4-61	30-4-64
F 50	SWAN	Williamstown Nav. DY	18-8-65	16-12-67	20-1-70
F 53	TORRENS	Cockatoo D. & Eng. Co.	18-8-65	28-9-68	19-1-71

Stuart—before modernization   G. Arra, 1976

FRIGATES (continued)

D: 2,100 tons (2,750 fl)   **S:** 27 kts   **Dim:** 112.75 (109.75 pp) × 12.5 × 3.9
Man: 13 officers, 238 men   **Range:** 4,500/12
A: 2/114-mm DP Mk 6 (II × 1 fwd) − 1/Sea Cat missile launcher − 1/Limbo Mk 10
    mortar (not in F-45) − 1/Ikara ASW missile launcher − 6/324-mm Mk 32 ASW TT
    (III × 2; F-49 only)
Electron Equipt: Radars: 1/978, 1/LWO 2, HSA M 22, (1/275 on F-45)
    Sonars: 1/162, 1/177, 1/170 (F-50 and F-53 only), 1/199 VDS,
    Mulloka on F-45
M: GT; 2 props; 34,000 hp   **Fuel:** 400 tons   **Electric:** 1,140 kw
Boilers: 2 Babcock & Wilcox, 38.7 kg/cm² pressure − superheat 450°C

Swan − Compare profile with that of the **Stuart**   1972

REMARKS: Improved versions of the British *Rothesay* class. Profiles of the F-50 and
F-53 differ from those of other four, resembling more the British *Leander* class. F-45
completed a half-life refit in 12-77. F-46, F-48, and F-49 are currently being given a
more extensive overhaul, to be completed by 1981; they are receiving two triple Mk 32
ASW torpedo tubes in place of the Limbo mortar, Mulloka sonar in place of their
original suits, HSA M 22 gunfire-control systems, having their boilers converted to
use diesel fuel, and have had their accommodations improved. Their LWO-2 radar is to
replace type 978. The Ikara missile carries a U.S. Mk 44 ASW torpedo as its payload.
Variable-depth sonars are being removed, where fitted. F-50 has been used in Mulloka
experiments since 1975.

Ikara ASW missile and launcher

PATROL BOATS

◆ **15 Fremantle class** Bldr: First ship: Brooke Marine, U.K.; others: North Queensland
Eng. Cairns, Australia.

P . . . FREMANTLE	P . . . GEELONG	P . . . TOWNSVILLE
P . . . GAWLER	P . . . LAUNCETON	P . . . CESSNOCK
P . . . IPSWICH	P . . . WOLLONGONG	P . . . DUBBO
P . . . WHYLLA	P . . . BUNBURY	P . . . GLADSTONE
P . . . BENDIGO	P . . . GERALDTON	P . . . WARRNAMBOOL

PATROL BOATS (continued)

PCF-420 design   1978

> **D:** 190 tons (220 fl)   **S:** 30 kts   **Dim:** 42.0 × 7.15 × 1.8
> **A:** 1/40-mm AA−1/81-mm mortar−2/12.7-mm machine guns
> **Man:** 22 men   **Range:** 1,450/28, 4,800/8
> **M:** 2 MTU MD 16V538 TB 91 diesels; 2 props; 72,000 hp−1 Dorman 12JTM diesel; 1 prop; . . . hp for cruising.

REMARKS: Brooke Marine PCF-420 design. Ordered 9-77. In service 6-79 through 1985. The *Fremantle* was laid down 3-11-77 and launched 15-2-79 as pattern craft. The 40-mm AA will be replaced with newer weapons. To replace the *Attack* class.

◆ **12 Attack-class coastal-patrol boats**

P 81 ACUTE	P 87 ARDENT	P 91 AWARE	P 99 BOMBARD
P 82 ADROIT	P 89 ASSAIL	P 97 BARBETTE	P 100 BUCCANEER
P 83 ADVANCE	P 90 ATTACK	P 98 BARRICADE	P 101 BAYONET

Buccaneer   1972

Bldr: Evans Deakin, Ltd. (except P-83, P-97, P-99, P-101: Walkers, Ltd.). Ordered in 1965, delivered 1967-69.

> **D:** 146 tons (fl)   **S:** 24/21 kts   **Dim:** 32.76 (30.48 pp) × 6.2 × 1.9
> **Range:** 1,220/13   **Man:** 3 officers, 19 men   **Fuel:** 20 tons diesel
> **A:** 1/40-mm AA−2 machine guns   **Radar:** 1/Decca RM 916
> **M:** 2 Davey-Paxman Ventura, 16 YJCM diesels; 2 props; 3,500 hp

REMARKS: Steel hull; light-alloy superstructure; air-conditioned. P-91 is unarmed. Sisters P-84 *Aitape*, P-92 *Lavada*, P-93 *Lae*, P-94 *Madang*, P-85 *Samarai* transferred to Papua New Guinea, in 1974. P-86 *Archer* and P-95 *Bandolier* sold in 1973 to Indonesia and transferred in 1973 and 1974, respectively. P-88 *Arrow* sunk 25-12-74 in Typhoon Tracey.

MINE WARFARE SHIPS

◆ **2 MHCAT-class catamaran minehunters**

N . . .   N . . .
> **D:** 100 tons (160 fl)   **S:** 10 kts   **Dim:** 31.0 × 9.0 × 1.8
> **A:** 2 machine guns   **M:** 2 diesels; 2 props; 530 hp

REMARKS: In service 1982. Fiberglass hulls, each 3 meters in beam. For coastal service, will have modularized payloads. If successful, more units will be built.

◆ **3 British "-ton"-class coastal minesweepers**

	Bldr	Laid down	L	In serv.
M 1102 SNIPE (ex-*Alcaston*)	Thornycroft, U.K.	7-51	5-1-53	1953
M 1121 CURLEW (ex-*Chediston*)	Montrose, U.K.	4-53	6-10-53	1954
M 1183 IBIS (ex-*Singleton*)	Montrose, U.K.	10-53	18-11-55	1956

> **D:** 370 tons (489 fl)   **S:** 15 kts   **Dim:** 46.6 (42.68 pp) × 8.76 × 2.5
> **Man:** 34 to 38 men   **Range:** 2,300/13, 3,500/8
> **A:** 2/40-mm AA (I × 2)   **Electron Equipt:** Radar: 1/978
> **M:** Napier Deltic 18A-7A diesels; 2 props; 3,000 hp   **Fuel:** 45 tons diesel

Ibis   1973

MINE WARFARE SHIPS (*continued*)

REMARKS: Bought in 1962 after refitting. Air-conditioned and stabilized. M-1102 and M-1121 are equipped as minehunters, with type 193 sonar and four divers. M-1183 has only one gun. It is proposed to replace these three survivors of a group of six ex-RN minesweepers with a new class of oceangoing minehunters in the mid-1980s.

AMPHIBIOUS WARFARE SHIPS

◆ **1 modified British Sir Bedivere class**

	Bldr	Laid down	L	In serv.
L 50 TOBRUK	Carrington Slipways, Tomago	7-2-79	. . .	. . .

Tobruk   1978

D: 5,800 tons (fl)   **S:** 17 kts   **Dim:** 129.5 × 19.6 × 4.3
A: 2/40-mm Bofors AA   **Man:** approx. 18 officers, 50 men
M: 2 Mirrlees-Blackstone KDM8 diesels; 2 props; 9,600 hp

REMARKS: Construction announced 8-76 as a replacement for the *Sydney*. Will carry Wessex Mk 31B troop helicopters operating from platforms amidships and aft, and will be able to carry 300-500 troops, Leopard tanks, and other military vehicles. Bow and stern ramps will be fitted. Two LCVP carried. Can carry two LCM-8 on deck.

◆ **6 Balikpapan-class LCU**   Bldr: Walkers Ltd.

L 126 BALIKPAPAN	L 128 LABUAN	L 130 WEWAK
L 127 BRUNEI	L 129 TARAKAN	L 133 BETANO

D: 316 tons (503 fl)   **S:** 10 kts   **Dim:** 44.5 × 10.1 × 1.9
A: 2 machine guns   **Man:** 2 officers, 11 men   **Range:** 3,000/10
M: 2 GM diesels; 2 props; 675 hp

REMARKS: In service 1971-74. The *Salamaua* (L-131) and *Buna* (L-132) were transferred to Papua New Guinea in 1974. Can carry three Leopard tanks. Originally Army-subordinated.

◆ The Australian Army operates a number of landing craft, including 11 U.S. LCM-8-class LCMs (**AB 1050** to **1053, 1055** to **1061**), 6 LCVPs, 2 small tugs for support, and a cargo tender.

HYDROGRAPHIC SHIPS

◆ **1 improved Moresby class**

	Bldr	Laid down	L	In serv.
A 291 COOK	Williamstown Nav. DY	30-9-74	27-8-77	12-79

Cook

D: 1,910 tons (2,550 fl)   **Dim:** 96.6 (91.2 pp) × 13.41 × 4.6
S: 17 kts   **Range:** 11,000/14   **Man:** 150 crew, 13 scientists
Electron Equipt: Radar: 1/TM 829   Sonar: 1/Simrad SU 2
M: 4 Caterpillar D398TA diesels; 2 props; 3,400 hp   **Fuel:** 640 tons

REMARK: Intended for oceanographic research, to replace *Diamantina*.

◆ **1 Moresby class**

	Bldr	Laid down	L	In serv.
A 573 MORESBY	State DY, Newcastle, NSW	5-62	7-9-63	3-64

Moresby

HYDROGRAPHIC SHIPS (*continued*)

D: 1,714 tons (2,340 fl)   **Dim:** 95.7 (86.7 pp) × 12.8 × 4.6
S: 19 kts   **Man:** 13 officers, 133 men
Electron Equipt: Radar: 1/TM 829   Sonar: 1/Simrad SU 2
M: Diesel-electric propulsion; 3 CSVM generators, each 1,330 kw/800 rpm; 2 electric motors, each 2,500 hp/250 rpm; 2 props

REMARKS: A Bell 206B helicopter can be carried on board. Ship is air-conditioned. 2/40-mm AA removed, stack heightened 1973-74.

◆ **1 Flinders class**

	Bldr	Laid down	L	In serv.
A 312 FLINDERS	Williamstown Nav. DY	12-70	29-7-72	27-4-73

Flinders   1975

D: 765 tons (fl)   **Dim:** 49.1 × 10.05 × 3.7
S: 13.5 kts   **Range:** 5,000/9   **Man:** 4 officers, 34 men
Electron Equipt: TM 829 radar; Simrad SU 2 sonar
M: 2 Paxman Ventura diesels; 2 props; 1,680 hp

REMARKS: Similar to the Philippine ship *Atyimba*. Replaces the *Paluma* stricken in 1974. Operates along Barrier Reef. A sister may be built to replace the *Kimbla*.

◆ **1 former netlayer**

GOR 314 KIMBLA   Bldr: Walkers, Australia   L: 23-3-55

D: 762 tons (1,021 fl)   **Dim:** 54.55 × 9.75 × 3.7
S: 9.5 kts   **Man:** 4 officers, 36 men
Electron Equipt: Radar: 1/975   Sonar: 1/Simrad SU 2
M: Triple-expansion; 1 prop; 350 hp

REMARK: Converted for oceanographic research in 1959.

AUXILIARIES

◆ **1 proposed oiler**

D: 17,800 tons (fl)   **S:** 19 kts   **Dim:** 157.3 (149 pp) × 21.2 × 10.8
A: . . .   **Range:** 9,000/15   **Fuel:** 750 tons
M: 2 SEMT-Pielstick 16PC2-5 diesels; 1 controllable-pitch prop; 20,000 hp

REMARKS: Contract let to DTCN, France, in 1977 to design a version of the French Navy's *Durance*-class fleet oiler to be built in Australia to replace the *Supply*. Construction planned to start in 1980 but has been delayed.

◆ **1 British oiler**

AO 195 SUPPLY (ex-*Tide Austral*)   Bldr: Harland & Wolff

Supply

D: 15,000 tons (26,500fl)   **Dim:** 177.8 (167.8 pp) × 21.7 × 9.8
S: 17 kts   **Range:** 8,500/13   **Man:** 205 men
A: 6/40-mm AA (II × 2, I × 2)   **M:** GT; 2 props; 15,000 hp

REMARKS: Launched 1-9-54. In service 3-55. Operated in Royal Navy 1955-62 and in Royal Australian Navy since 8-62. 17,600 deadweight tons.

◆ **1 destroyer tender**

	Bldr	Laid down	L	In serv.
A 215 STALWART	Cockatoo D & E, Sydney	6-64	7-10-66	4-2-68

Stalwart

AUXILIARES (*continued*)

D: 15,500 tons (fl)   **S:** 20 kts   **Dim:** 157.12 (143.25 pp) × 20.57 × 9.0
A: 4/40-mm AA (II × 2)   **Man:** 396 men
Electric: 3,200 kw   **Range:** 12,000/12
M: Scott-Sulzer diesels, (6 cyl) Mk RD 68; 2 props; 14,400 hp

REMARKS: Helicopter platform and hangar for two Wessex or Sea King. Workshops and foundry (400 m²); boiler shop (100 m²); electric shop; electronic shop (300 m²); mechanical workshop (500 m²); and shops for precision equipment and plastic-boat repairs. Four 3-ton and two 6-ton cranes. Carries spare missiles for destroyers and frigates.

◆ 1 training ship

	Bldr	Laid down	L	In serv.
GT 203 JERVIS BAY	State DY, Newcastle	18-8-67	17-2-69	25-8-77 (in RAN)
(ex-*Australian*				
Trader)				

Jervis Bay

D: 8,915 tons (fl)   **S:** 17 kts   **Dim:** 135.7 (123.5 pp) × 21.5 × 6.1
A: None   **Fuel:** 820 tons   **Man:** 111 crew plus 40 trainees
M: 2 Crossley-Pielstick 16 PC 2V 400 diesels; 2 props; 13,000 hp
Electric: 2,000 kw

REMARKS: A former roll-on/roll-off cargo ferry converted to a training ship to replace the *Duchess*. Name commemorates an armed merchant cruiser of World War II. Can also serve as a transport and cargo ship.

◆ 2 general-purpose tankers

G 247 BASS, G 244 BANKS Bldr: Walkers, Ltd., Maryborough, 1960

D: 260 tons (fl)   **S:** 10 kts   **Dim:** 30.8 × 6.7 × 2.5
Man: 14 men   **M:** Diesels

REMARK: G-247 was originally equipped as a hydrographic ship and G-244 for fisheries protection, but both are used primarily for reserve training.

◆ 2 diving tenders

DTV 1001 SEAL (ex-*Wintringham*, 24-5-55)
DTV 1002 PORPOISE (ex-*Neasham*, 1955)
  Bldr: White, Cowes

D: 120 tons (159 fl)   **S:** 14 kts   **Dim:** 32.43 (30.48 pp) × 6.45 × 1.7
Man: 7 men   **Range:** 1,500/12   **Fuel:** 15 tons diesel
M: Davey-Paxman diesels; 2 props; 1,000 hp

REMARKS: Former British "-ham"-type inshore minesweepers, transferred in 1966. Assigned to the school of diving and underwater demolition in Sydney. Can support fourteen divers. Sister *Otter* (Y-299) sold 1974.

◆ 3 501-class tugs

501, 502, 504 (1969, 1972)

D: 47.5 tons   **Dim:** 15.4 × 4.6 × . . .
S: 9 kts   **Man:** 3 men
M: 2 GM diesels; 2 props; 340 hp

REMARK: Sister 503 to Papua New Guinea 1974.

◆ 2 ex-U.S. Army wooden-hull tugs

TB 9 SARDIUS   TB 1536 . . .

D: 60 tons (fl)   **Dim:** 13.7 × . . . × . . .
S: 10 kts   **Man:** 4 men
M: 1 Hercules diesel; 240 hp

REMARK: Built 1944.

◆ 3 torpedo-recovery craft

TRV 801   TRV 802   TRV 803

D: 91.6 tons   **Dim:** 27.0 × 6.4 × 1.4
S: 13 kts   **Man:** 9 men
M: 3 GM diesels; 3 props; 890 hp

REMARKS: Built 1970-71. TRV-802 normally used as a diving tender.

◆ 4 water tenders

MRL 253 GAYUNDAH   MWL 254   MWL 256   MWL 257

D: 300 tons (600 fl)   **Dim:** 36.5 × 7.3 × . . .
S: 9.5 kts
M: 2 Ruston & Hornsby diesels; 2 props; 440 hp

REMARKS: Built in 1940s. MRL-253 used as dry-stores carrier. Sisters to hydrographic ship *Paluma*, scrapped in 1974.

◆ 3 stores lighters

CSL 01   CSL 02   CSL 03

D: . . .   **Dim:** 23.7 × 9.8 × 2.0
M: 2 GM diesels

REMARKS: Built 1972. Catamarans. One 3-ton electric crane. Based on AWL-304 design but with pilothouse aft.

AUSTRALIA (*continued*)

AUXILIARIES (*continued*)

◆ **1 aircraft lighter**

AWL-304

REMARKS: Built 1967 to service the MELBOURNE, can carry 2 Skyhawk or 1 Tracker. Similar to CSL-01 class but with A-frame crane aft and low pilothouse forward.

◆ **1 aircraft-rescue launch**

Y 256 AIR SPRITE

   D: 23.5 tons   **Dim:** 19.2 × 4.7 × 1.0
   S: 25 kts
   M: 2 Hall-Scott gasoline engines

REMARKS: Built 1960. Based on U.S. Navy 63-foot AVR design; sisters are in RAAF service. Two 11.6-m Bertram yachts, 38101 and 38102, purchased as rescue launches, are used as yachts.

NOTE: There are a number of other yard and service craft, including non-self-propelled oil barges, stores lighters, etc., as well as approximately 20 12.2-m motor workboats.

AUSTRIA

MERCHANT MARINE (1978): 15 ships—3,670 grt

◆ **2 patrol craft for the Danube**

A 604 NIEDERÖSTERREICH Bldr: Korneuberg, In serv. 4-70

Niederösterreich

   D: 71 tons (fl)   **Dim:** 29.0 × 5.4 × 1.1
   S: 22 kts   **Man:** 9 men
   A: 1/20-mm AA—2 machine guns   **M:** 2 diesels; 1,600 hp

A 602 OBERST BRECHT
  Bldr: Korneuberg

   D: 10 tons   **Dim:** 12.3 × 2.5 × 0.7
   S: 10 kts   **Man:** 5 men
   A: 1 machine gun   **M:** 2 diesels; 214 hp

◆ **10 U.S.-built M-3-class launches** (4 in serv. 1965, 6 in serv. 1976)

   D: 2.9 tons   **Dim:** 8.3 × 2.5 × . . .
   S: 18 kts   **M:** 2 gasoline/diesels; 204/184 hp

BAHAMAS

MERCHANT MARINE (1978): 93 ships—84,269 grt (tankers: 4—14,506 grt)

POLICE MARINE DIVISION

◆ **2 Vosper-Thornycroft 103-foot patrol craft**

P 01 MARLIN   P 02 FLAMINGO

Marlin   Vosper, 1978

BAHAMAS (*continued*)

D: 100 tons (125 fl)   **S:** 24 kts   **Dim:** 31.5 × 5.9 × 1.6
Man: 3 officers, 16 men   **Range:** 2,000/13
A: 1/20-mm AA   **M:** 2 Paxman-Ventura diesels; 2 props; 2,900 hp

REMARKS: In service 22-5-78. Fin stabilizers, steel hulls. Two 50-mm flare launchers.

◆ **7 patrol craft** Bldr: Keith Nelson, G. B.

P 21 ACKLINS   P 23 ELEUTHERA   P 25 EXUMA   P 27 INAGUA
P 22 ANDROS   P 24 SAN SALVADOR   P 26 ABACO
First four in serv. 3-71, last three in 12-77

Andros   1972

D: 30 tons   **S:** 19.5 kts   **Dim:** 18.68 × 4.77 × 1.4
A: Machine guns   **Man:** 11 men   **Range:** 650/16
Electron Equipt: Radar: 1/Decca 110
M: 2 Caterpillar 3408 TA diesels; 2 props; 950 hp

REMARKS: Fiberglass construction, air-conditioned. Keith Nelson is a division of Vosper Thornycroft.

BAHRAIN

MERCHANT MARINE (1978): 32 ships—7,161 grt (tankers: 2—913 grt)

During 1979, four fast patrol boats were ordered from Lürssen, Vegesack, West Germany: two TNC-45 class identical to those ordered by the United Arab Emirates and two of a new FPB-38, 38-meter design.

◆ **1 Tracker-class patrol craft** Bldr: Fairey Marine, G. B.

1 BAHRAIN

D: 26 tons (fl)   **S:** 28 kts   **Dim:** 19.6 × 4.9 × 1.5
A: 1/20-mm AA   **Range:** 500   **M:** 2 GM diesels; 2 props; 1,120 hp

REMARK: In service 1975.

◆ **2 Spear-class patrol craft** Bldr: Fairey Marine, G. B.

4 SAHEM   5 KHATAF

D: 4.5 tons (10 fl)   **S:** 26 kts   **Dim:** 9.1 × 2.75 × 0.84
A: 2 machine guns   **Man:** 3 men   **Range:** 220
M: 2 Perkins diesels; 2 props; 290 hp

REMARK: In service 1975.

◆ **3 27-foot patrol craft** Bldr: Cheverton, Cowes, G. B.

15 NOON   16 ASKAR   17 SUWAD

D: 3.3 tons   **S:** 15 kts   **Dim:** 8.23 × 2.44 × 0.81
M: 2 diesels; 1 prop; 150 hp

REMARK: In service 1977.

◆ **2 50-foot patrol craft** Bldr: Cheverton, Cowes, G. B.

6 MASHTAN   N . . .

D: 9 tons   **S:** 12 kts   **Dim:** 15.2 × 4.3 × 1.4
M: 2 Perkins diesels; 2 props; 150 hp

◆ **2 patrol craft** Bldr: Vosper, Singapore

2 JIDA   3 HOWAR

D: 15 tons   **S:** 23 kts   **Dim:** 13.9 × 6.1 × 1.1
M: 2 diesels; 2 props; 1,080 hp

REMARK: In service 1974.

◆ **1 Loadmaster-class landing craft** Bldr: Cheverton, Cowes, G. B.

7 SAFRA

D: 90 tons (fl)   **S:** 10 kts   **Dim:** 18.23 × 6.1 × 1.0
M: 2 diesels; 2 props; 240 hp

REMARK: In service 1976. Can carry 40 tons of vehicles or dry cargo, or 60 tons of liquid cargo.

◆ **10 dhows for logistics and patrol duties**

BANGLADESH

PERSONNEL: 3,500 men

MERCHANT MARINE (1978): 141 ships—284,496 grt
(tankers: 26—41,863 grt)

◆ 1 British Leopard-class frigate

	Bldr	Laid down	L	In serv.
F . . . ALI HAIDER	Wm. Denny, Dumbarton	11-53	30-7-57	12-59
(ex-*Jaguar*, F-37)				

Ali Haider—as the **Jaguar**   G. Arra, 1972

D: 2,300 tons (2,520 fl)   **S:** 23 kts
Dim: 103.63 (100.58 pp) × 12.19 × 4.8 (fl)
A: 4/114-mm Mk 6 DP (II × 2)—1/40-mm Mk 9 AA   **Man:** 10 officers, 200 men
Electron Equipt: Radars: 1/965, 1/978, 1/993, 1/275 fire-control
Range: 2,300/23, 7,500/16   **Electric:** 1,200 kw   **Fuel:** 230 tons
M: 8 Admiralty Standard Range-1 diesels; 2 props; 12,400 hp

REMARKS: Sold 6-7-78; arrived Bangladesh 11-78 after overhaul. Squid ASW mortar and sonars removed while in Royal Navy.

◆ 1 British Salisbury-class frigate

	Bldr	Laid down	L	In serv.
F 16 UMAR FAROOQ	Hawthorn Leslie, G. B.	8-53	30-11-55	4-58
(ex-*Llandaff*, F-61)				

D: 2,170 tons (2,408 fl)   **Dim:** 103.6 (100.58 pp) × 12.19 × 4.8
S: 24 kts   **Range:** 2,300/24, 7,500/16   **Man:** 14 officers, 223 men
A: 2/114-mm Mk 6 DP (II × 1)—2/40-mm AA (II × 1)—1/Mk 4 Squid ASW mortar (III × 1)

Umar Farooq   1979

Electron Equipt: Radars: 1/985, 1/993, 1/277Q, 1/982, 1/975, 1CT/275
Sonars: 1/174, 1/170B
M: 8 Admiralty Standard Range-1 diesels; 2 props; 12,400 hp

REMARKS: Former aircraft-direction frigate, transferred 10-12-76.

◆ 4 Kraljevica-class patrol boats

P 301 KARNAPHULI (ex-Yugoslav PBR-502)   P . . . N . . . (ex-Yugoslav PBR-. . .)
P 302 TISTA (ex-Yugoslav PBR-505)   P . . . N . . . (ex-Yugoslav PBR-. . .)

Karnaphuli   1976

BANGLADESH (*continued*)

D: 190 tons (202 fl)   **S:** 18 kts   **Dim:** 41.0 × 6.3 × 2.2
Man: 4 officers, 40 men   **Range:** 1,000/12
A: 2/40-mm AA (I × 2) − 4/20-mm AA (I × 4) − 2 Mk 6 depth-charge throwers − 2 depth-charge racks
Electron Equipt: Radar: Decca 45   Sonar: QCU 2
M: 2 M.A.N. W8V 30/38 diesels; 2 props; 3,300 hp

REMARK: Transferred 6-6-75, . . . 79.

◆ **2 Chinese Shanghai-II-class patrol boats**

N . . .   N . . .

D: 155 tons (fl)   **S:** 28 kts   **Dim:** 38.8 × 5.4 × 1.6
A: 4/37-mm AA (II × 2) − 4/25-mm AA (II × 2)
M: 4 diesels; 4 props; 4,800 hp

REMARK: Transferred 1974.

◆ **2 Ajay-class surveillance patrol boats**
Given by India Bldr: Hooghly D & E, Calcutta, 1-62

P 201 PADMA (ex-*Akshay*, P-3136)   P 202 SURMA (ex-*Ajay*, P-3135)

D: 120 tons (160 fl)   **S:** 12.5 kts   **Dim:** 35.75 (33.52 pp) × 6.1 × 1.9
A: 1/40-mm AA   **Man:** 3 officers, 32 men   **Range:** 5,000/10
M: 2 Paxman diesels; 2 props; 1,000 hp

◆ **5 river patrol boats** Bldr: DEW Narayengonj, Dacca

P 101 PABNA (6-72)   P 103 PATUAKHALI (11-74)   P 105 RANGAMATI (6-77)
P 102 NOAKHALI (7-72)   P 104 BOGRA (6-77)

D: 69.5 tons (fl)   **S:** 10 kts   **Dim:** 22.9 × 6.1 × 1.9
A: 1/40-mm AA   **Man:** 3 officers, 30 men   **Range:** 700/8
M: 2 Cummins diesels; 2 props

REMARK: Last two differ in configuration, gun forward.

◆ **1 training ship**

SHAHEED RUHUL AMIN (ex-*Anticosti*, Canadian merchant)
Bldr: Canada, 1969

D: 710 tons (fl)   **S:** 11.5 kts   **Dim:** 47.5 × 11.1 × 3.1
A: 1/40-mm AA   **Man:** 8 officers, 72 men   **Range:** 4,000/10
M: 1 Caterpillar diesel

REMARK: In service 12-74.

BARBADOS

PERSONNEL: 61 (4 officers, 57 men)

MERCHANT MARINE (1978): 33 ships − 4,448 grt

◆ **1 Halmatic, 20-meter, Guardian-class police patrol craft**
Bldr: Aquarius Boat, G. B.

GC 601 GEORGE FERGUSON

D: 30 tons   **S:** 24 kts   **Dim:** 20.0 × 5.25 × 1.5
A: 1/20-mm AA   **Man:** 11 men   **Range:** 650/12
M: 2 GM 12V71 diesels; 1,300 hp

REMARK: In service 12-74.

◆ **3 Halmatic, 12-meter, Guardian-class police patrol craft**
Bldr: Aquarius Boat, G. B.

GC 402 COMMANDER MARSHALL   GC 403 T. T. LEWIS   GC 404 J. T. C. RAMSAY

D: 11.5 tons   **S:** 21 kts   **Dim:** 12.0 × 3.7 × 1.0
M: 2 Caterpillar Mk 334 TA diesels; 2 props; 580 hp   **Man:** 4 men

BELGIUM

PERSONNEL: 4,350, including 300 officers

MERCHANT MARINE (1978): 268 ships − 1,634,692 grt (tankers: 15 − 303,767 grt)

NAVAL AVIATION: Five helicopters (2 Sikorsky S-58 and 8 Alouette IIIB) used for mine-hunting. One Alouette may be taken on board the *Zinnia* or the *Godetia*.

FRIGATES

◆ **4 Wielingen class, Type E 71**

	Bldr	Laid down	L	In serv.
F 910 WIELINGEN	Boëlwerf, Temse	5-3-74	30-3-76	3-76
F 911 WESTDIEP	Cockerill, Hoboken	2-9-74	8-12-75	6-77
F 912 WANDELAAR	Boëlwerf, Temse	5-3-75	21-6-77	27-10-78
F 913 WESTHINDER	Cockerill, Hoboken	8-12-75	31-1-77	27-10-78

D: 1,880 tons (2,283 fl)   **Dim:** 106.38 (103 pp) × 12.3 × 5.3 (over sonar)
S: 28 kts on gas turbine   **Man:** 15 officers, 145 men
A: 4 Exocet MM 38 − 1/100-mm DP − 1 NATO Sea Sparrow (8 missiles) − 2/20-mm AA (I × 2) − 1/375-mm Bofors sextuple ASW rocket launcher − 2 launching racks for L-5 torpedoes

FRIGATES (*continued*)

Wielingen   1978

Wandelaar   1978

Electron Equipt: Radars: 1 DA 05, 1 Raytheon TM 1645/9X navigation, 1 HSA
WM-25, 2 Knebworth Corvus 8-tube chaff launchers,
SEWACO
Sonar: 1 SQS-505A   ESM: Elcos-1
Fuel: 190 tons diesel   **Electric:** 2,000 kw   **Range:** 4,500/18, 5,000/14

Westhinder   1978

M: CODOG propulsion, 2 shafts with variable-pitch props, 2 Cockerill CO-240V-12
diesels, each 3,000 hp (1,000 rpm); 1 Rolls-Royce Olympus TM 3B gas turbine of
28,000 hp (5,600 rpm)

REMARKS: Welded hull, two self-activating Vosper Thornycroft stabilizers; 15 knots
on one diesel, 20 knots on two; for more than 20 knots the gas turbine is brought on
the line. Canadian hull sonar. French 100-mm, Model 1968. Belgian-Dutch automatic
surface and air-search radar system, including fire control and an automatic tactical
data system with two DMAB optical sights. The ASW rocket launcher also carries
six rocket-flare rails. Two chaff launchers are fitted and Nixie torpedo decoy is carried.

MINE WARFARE SHIPS

◆ **10 Tripartite class**   Bldr: Polyship Consortium

		L			L
M . . .	N . . .	. . .	M . . .	N . . .	. . .
M . . .	N . . .	. . .	M . . .	N . . .	. . .
M . . .	N . . .	. . .	M . . .	N . . .	. . .
M . . .	N . . .	. . .	M . . .	N . . .	. . .
M . . .	N . . .	. . .	M . . .	N . . .	. . .

D: 511 tons (544 fl)   **S:** 15 kts   **Dim:** 51.6 (47.1 pp) × 8.96 × 2.45
A: 1/20-mm AA   **Man:** 34 men   **Range:** 3,000/12
Electron Equipt: Radar: Decca 1229   Sonar: DUBM-21A
M: 1 Brons/Werkspoor A-RUB 215X 12 diesel; 1 controllable-pitch prop; 1,900 hp
(1,200 rpm); 2 maneuvering props (active rudder); bow-thruster
Electric: 750 kw

MINE WARFARE SHIPS (*continued*)

REMARKS: Same as French *Eridan* and Dutch *Alkmaar* classes. First unit to be laid down in 1981. Three Astazov geared-turbine generators. Two PAP-104 remote-controlled mine locators; automatic pilot; automatic track-plotter; TORAN and Sydelis navigation systems; conventional wire sweep also. Will be of glass-reinforced-plastic construction. To replace MSO and MSC classes.

◆ 7 AM/MSO oceangoing minesweepers

	L	In serv.
M 902 VAN HAVERBEKE (ex-MSO-522)	29-10-59	7-11-60
M 903 A. F. DUFOUR (ex-*Lagen*, ex-MSO-498)	13-8-54	27-9-55
M 904 DE BROUWER (ex-*Nansen*, ex-MSO-499)	15-10-54	1-11-55
M 906 BREYDEL (ex-AM-504)	25-3-55	24-1-56
M 907 ARTEVELDE (ex-AM-503)	19-6-54	12-12-55
M 908 GEORGES TRUFFAUT (ex-AM-515)	1-11-55	21-9-56
M 909 FRANÇOIS BOVESSE (ex-AM-516)	28-2-56	21-12-56

Artevelde   J.-C. Bellonne, 1973

D: 720 tons (780 fl)   **Dim:** 52.67 (50.3 pp) × 10.67 × 3.2
S: 15/14 kts   **Man:** 5 officers, 67 men
A: 1/40-mm AA Mk 3 (M-907 only)   **Range:** 3,000/10, 2,400/12
Fuel: 53 tons diesel   **Electron Equipt:** Sonar: SQQ-14 (not in M-907)
M: GM diesels; 2 variable-pitch props; 1,600 hp

REMARKS: Transferred 1955-60, except M-903 and M-904 transferred from Norway in 1966. M-907 has no sonar and serves as divers' clearance ship, rest as minehunters. Wooden hulls.

◆ 6 U.S. AMS/MSC coastal minesweepers

2 U.S. construction

M 934 VERVIERS (ex-AMS-259)   M 935 VEURNE (ex-AMS-260)

Bldr: Hodgdon Bros., Maine   In serv. 1956

Veurne—Note the differences in bridge structure between her and **Rochefort**

REMARK: Converted to minehunters, with Voith-Schneider vertical cycloidal props and Plessey 193M sonar.

◆ 4 Belgian construction

	L		L
M 928 STAVELOT	26-3-55	M 932 NIEUWPOORT	12-3-55
M 930 ROCHEFORT	5-6-54	M 933 KOKSIJDE	4-6-55

Bldr: M-928: Boëlwerf; M-930, M-932, M-933: Béliard, Ostend

D: 330 tons (390 fl)   **S:** 13.5/12 kts   **Dim:** 44.0 (42.1 pp) × 8.3 × 2.6
A: 1/40-mm AA   **Man:** 4 officers, 17 petty officers, 19 men
Range: 2,700/10.5   **Fuel:** 30 m³ diesel
Electron Equipt: Sonar: AN/UQS-1
M: GM diesels; 2 props; 880 hp

Rochefort

MINE WARFARE SHIPS (*continued*)

REMARKS: Minehunters have enclosed bridge, deckhouse aft. Three sisters serve as auxiliaries.

◆ 13 Herstal-class inshore minesweepers

	L		L
M 471 HASSELT	5-68	M 479 HUY (ex-MSI-91)	17-11-56
M 473 LOKEREN	18-5-57	M 480 SERAING (ex-MSI-92)	16-3-57
M 474 TURNHOUT	7-9-57	M 482 VISE (ex-MSI-94)	7-9-57
M 475 TONGEREN	16-11-57	M 483 OUGRÉE (ex-MSI-95)	16-11-57
M 476 MERKSEM	5-4-58	M 484 DINANT (ex-MSI-96)	5-4-58
M 477 OUDENAERDE	3-5-58	M 485 ANDENNE (ex-MSI-97)	3-5-58
M 478 HERSTAL	6-8-56		

Bldr: Mercantile Marine Yard, Kruibeke

Dinant

D: 160 tons (190 fl)   **Dim:** 34.5 (32.5 pp) × 6.7 × 2.1
A: 2/12.7-mm machine guns (II × 1)
Man: 1 officer, 7 petty officers, 9 men   **Fuel:** 18 m³ diesel
M: 2 diesels; 2 props; 1,260 hp   **S:** 15 kts   **Range:** 2,300/10

REMARKS: Wooden hulls. Designed to sweep the Schelde River. Fitted for magnetic, acoustic, and mechanical sweeping to a depth of 4.50 to 10 m. Modified version of British "-ham" class. M-479 to M-485 built with U.S. funds.

AUXILIARY SHIPS

◆ 2 mine countermeasures support ships

	Bldr	Laid down	L	In serv.
A 961 ZINNIA	Cockerill (Hoboken)	8-11-66	6-5-67	5-9-67

D: 1,705 tons (2,685 fl)   **Dim:** 99.5 (94.2 wl) × 14.0 × 3.6
S: 18 kts (20 on trials)   **Range:** 14,000/12.5

Zinnia   G. Arra, 1976

Man: 13 officers, 46 petty officers, 64 men
A: 3/40-mm AA (I × 3)−1 Alouette IIIB helicopter with telescoping hangar
Fuel: 150 m³ diesel, 300 m³ for supply to minesweepers
M: Cockerill-Ougrée V 12 TR 240 CO diesels; 1 controllable-pitch prop; 5,000 hp

REMARK: Anti-rolling devices.

	Bldr	Laid down	L	In serv.
A 960 GODETIA	Boëlwerf, Temse	1-64	7-12-65	23-5-66

Godetia   J.-C. Bellonne, 1973

D: 1,700 tons (2,500 fl)   **Dim:** 91.83 (87.85 pp) × 14.0 × 3.5
S: 18 kts   **Man:** 10 officers, 37 petty officers, 48 men
A: 2/40-mm AA (II × 1)   **Range:** 2,250/15, 8,700/12
M: 4 ACEC-M.A.N. diesels; 2 controllable-pitch props; 5,400 hp

BELGIUM (*continued*)
AUXILIARY SHIPS (*continued*)

REMARKS: Used as fishery protection ship. 15 knots on one diesel engine. Stabilized by liquid anti-rolling devices. Ship can be protected against radioactive fallout by closed-circuit ventilation. Can accommodate oceanographic research personnel on board and has space for laboratory. Cargo hold with crane to unload supplies or small boats. Minesweeping cables are stowed on reels on the helicopter deck, which has been extended aft to continue to permit one Aloutte-III to land.

PATROL CRAFT

◆ **6 river gunboats**

P 901 LEIE   P 903 MEUSE   P 905 SCHELDE
P 902 LIBERATION   P 904 SAMBRE   P 906 SEMOIS

Bldr: Hitzler, Regensburg

Libération   1970

D:	30 tons (fl)	**S:** 19 kts	**Dim:** 23.25 × 3.8 × 0.9
A:	2/12.7-mm machine guns		**Man:** 1 officer, 6 men
M:	2 MWM Diesels; 440 hp		

REMARKS: Built 1953-54. P-902 is 26 meters in length, 4 meters in beam. P-906 is employed as a diving tender. Sister *Tresignes* (ex-*Rupel*) is a cadet-training boat.

AUXILIARIES

◆ **1 oceanographic research craft and sail training ship**

A 958 ZENOBE GRAMME

D: 149 tons   **S:** 10 kts   **Dim:** 28.15 × 6.85 × 2.1
M: 1 MWM diesel; 220 hp   **Man:** 14 men

REMARK: Fitted out as Bermudian ketch (240m³ sail area).

◆ **6 tugs**

A 950 SUB-LIEUTENANT VALCKE: 110 tons, 600 hp. A 951 HOMMEL, A 952 WESP: 22 tons, 300 hp. A 953 BIJ, A 956 KREKEL: 71 tons, 400 hp. A 959 MIER: 17.5 tons, 90 hp.

◆ **3 ex-MSC-class minesweepers**

A 962 MECHELEN (ex-M-926) Used as an oceanographic research ship
A 963 SPA (ex-M-927) Used as a degaussing tender
A 964 HEIST (ex-M-929) Used as a missile transport in support of the *Wielingen*-class frigates

Mechelen   1974

◆ **3 fuel barges:** FN 4, FN 5, FN 6 – 300 tons, 32 m. (1957)

◆ **1 ammunition transport:** EKSTER – 140 tons, 36 m. (1953)

◆ **1 diving tender:** ZM 4 – 8 tons, 10 m. (1954)

◆ **1 personnel launch:** SPIN – 32 tons, 14.6 m., 250 hp (1958)

◆ **1 training boat:** B 30 TRESIGNES (ex-*Rupel*), former patrol craft. Used for seamanship training for cadets. For data, *see* river gunboats under Patrol Craft.

BELIZE

PERSONNEL: approx. 50 men

MERCHANT MARINE (1978): 3 ships – 620 grt

◆ **2 Brooke Marine patrol craft**

PBM 01 BELIZE   PBM 02 BELMOPAN

D: 15 tons (fl)   **S:** 22 kts   **Dim:** 12.2 × 3.6 × 0.6
A: 3 machine guns   **M:** 2 Caterpillar diesels; 2 props; 370 hp

REMARK: Built 1972.

BENIN

(formerly Dahomey)

MERCHANT MARINE (1978): 8 ships — 1,074 grt

◆ **2 Soviet P-6-class torpedo boats** Transferred from Algeria, 1977

BOLIVIA

PERSONNEL (1978): 1,500

◆ **1 seagoing cargo ship**

LIBERATADOR BOLIVAR (ex-*Simon Bolivar*, ex-*Ciudad de Barquisimeto*)
  Bldr: Fairfield, G. B., 1951

D: 9,000 tons	**S:** 14.5 kts	**Dim:** 128.3 (120.4 pp) × 16.76 × 6.7
M: 1 Doxford diesel; 4,350 hp	**Range:** 7,000/14	

REMARKS: Donated by Venezuela, 1977. Homeported in Argentina. Used to generate revenue and for training in preparation for possible ceding to Bolivia of a "corridor to the sea" between Peru and Chile. 4,214 grt/6,390 dwt/2,352 nrt.

◆ **7 river patrol craft/transports**

MO 1 ALMIRANTE GRAU, 52 tons   MO 5 COMANDANTE ARANDIA, 82 tons

Almirante Grau

MO 2 NICOLAS SUAREZ, 26 tons   MO 6 TOPATER
MO 3 MARISCAL SANTA CRUZ, 52 tons   MO 8 CORONEL EDUARDO AVAROA, 82 tons
MO 4 PRESIDENTE BUSCH, 52 tons

REMARK: Iron-or wooden-hulled, raftlike craft with high superstructures and speeds of 8-10 knots.

◆ **1 or more Brown-class patrol launches**

ALMIRANTE GUILLERMO BROWN

D: 4 tons	**S:** 12 kts	**Dim:** 7.0 × 2.3 × 1.0
M: 1 Ford Penta diesel; 116 hp	**Man:** 12 men	

REMARK: Built 1978-. . . .

◆ **2 ex-U.S. PBR Mk-II patrol boats**

REMARK: Transferred 1974.

◆ **24 miscellaneous Lake Titicaca and river service launches** (several oar-propelled)

◆ **2 hospital launches**
  JULIAN APAZA   BRUNO RACUA

REMARK: Launched 1977-78; 17 tons.

BRAZIL

PERSONNEL: 3,800 officers, 21,200 men, plus 650 officers and 10,850 men in the Fuzileiros Navais (Marine Corps equivalent)

MERCHANT MARINE (1978): 565 ships — 3,701,731 grt
  (tankers: 48 — 1,259,776 grt)

NAVAL AVIATION: Established in 1963. Uses Westland Whirlwind, 4 U.S. SH3-D Sea King, 6 Westland Wasp, 18 Bell 206B Jetranger II helicopters, and 9 Westland WG 13 Lynx. Six SA 350 Ecureuil are on order from France, and Gazelles may be purchased. The Air Force makes available to the Navy: 7-S-2A/E Trackers, 6 RC-130E Hercules, 6 Grumman Albatros amphibians, and 12 EMBM Baudeirante in a sea-surveillance version.

MAIN WARSHIPS IN SERVICE OR UNDER CONSTRUCTION AS OF 1 JANUARY 1980

	L	Tons	Main armament
◆ **1 light aircraft carrier (ASW)**			
MINAS GERAIS	1944	15,890	10/40-mm AA, 20 aircraft
◆ **10 submarines**			
3 OBERON	1972-75	1,610	8 TT
2 GUPPY III	1945	1,650	10 TT
5 GUPPY II	1942	1,525	10 TT

◆ 10 destroyers

2 GEARING, FRAM I	1944-45	2,400	2/127-mm DP, 6 ASW TT Asroc
4 ALLEN M. SUMNER, FRAM II	1944	2,200	6/127-mm DP, 6 ASW TT
3 FLETCHER	1942-44	2,050	4-5/127-mm DP, 5/533-mm TT
1 ALLEN M. SUMNER	1944	2,200	6/127-mm DP, 1 Sea Cat SAM, 6 ASW TT

◆ 6 frigates

4 NITEROI	1974-77	3,200	1/114-mm DP, 2/40-mm AA, 1 Branik missile launcher, 2 Sea Cat missile launchers, 1 Bofors rocket launcher, 6 ASW TT, 1 helicopter
2 CONSTITUCÃO	1974-75	3,200	2/114-mm DP, 2/40-mm AA, 4 Exocet missile launchers, 2 Sea Cat missile launchers, 1 Bofors rocket launcher, 6 ASW TT, 1 helicopter

◆ 10 patrol vessels

10 IMPERIAL MARINHEIRO	1954	911	1/76-mm DP

◆ 6 patrol craft

◆ 6 river patrol craft

◆ 6 mine warfare ships

◆ 2 amphibious warfare ships

LIGHT AIRCRAFT CARRIER (ASW)

◆ 1 British Colossus class

	Bldr	Laid down	L	In serv.
A 11 MINAS GERAIS (ex-*Vengeance*)	Swan Hunter	11-42	23-3-44	1-45

D: 15,890 tons (19,890 fl) **Dim:** 211.25 × 36.44 (24.50 hull) × 7.15
S: 24 kts **Man:** 1,000 ship's company plus 300 aviation personnel
A: 10/40-mm AA (IV × 2, II × 1) − 7 S-2A or E aircraft − 13 helicopters
Range: 12,000/14, 6,200/23
Electron Equipt: Radars: 1/SPS-12, 1/SPS-8B, 1/SPS-4, 1/1402, 2/SPG34 fire-control.
M: Parsons GT; 2 props; 42,000 hp **Electric:** 2,500 kw
Boilers: 4, 28 kg/cm² pressure **Fuel:** 2,200 tons

REMARKS: Purchased from Great Britain in 12-56; refitted in Rotterdam, completing in 1960 with new weapons, steam catapult, angled flight deck (8.5°), mirror optical landing equipment, new radars, and new elevators. In refit 1976-79. A data link system for cooperation with the *Niteroi* class has been installed.

Minas Gerais

SUBMARINES

◆ 3 British Oberon-class torpedo attack submarines

	Bldr	Laid down	L	In serv.
S 20 HUMAITÁ	Vickers-Barrow	3-11-70	5-10-71	18-6-73
S 21 TONELERO	Vickers-Barrow	18-21-70	22-11-72	8-9-78
S 22 RIACHUELO	Vickers-Barrow	26-5-73	6-9-75	12-3-77

D: 1,610 tons standard, 2,030 surfaced, 2,400 submerged
Dim: 89.9 × 8.07 × 5.48 **S:** 17.5/12 kts **Man:** 5 officers, 57 men
A: 8/533-mm TT, 6 forward, 2 aft
Electron Equipt: Sonars: 1/187, 1/2007
M: 2 Admiralty Standard Range 16VVS-ASR1 diesels; 2 electric generators, each 1,280 kw; 2 electric motors; 2 props; 6,000 hp

Humaitá

1975

SUBMARINES (*continued*)

REMARKS: S-21 several years late entering active service due to a fire on board during construction. Batteries made up of 224 elements in two sections, with a 7,240-ampere capacity for five hours. Underway cruising with snorkel may be maintained for six weeks at a maximum speed of 11 knots. "One-man control" system for emersion and diving. Digital tactical data system. Eighteen torpedoes, B.G. Mk 8 and U.S. Mk 37. Satellite navigation receiver installed.

◆ 2 ex-U.S. Guppy III class

	Bldr	L
S 15 GOIÁS (ex-*Trumpetfish*, SS-425)	Cramp S.B.	13-5-45
S 16 AMAZONAS (ex-*Greenfish*, SS-351)	Electric Boat Co.	21-12-45

Goiás   1975

D: 1,650 tons standard, 1,975 surfaced, 2,540 submerged
Dim: 99.4 × 8.2 × 5.2   **S:** 20/13-15 kts
Man: 86 men   **Range:** 10,000/10
A: 10/533-mm torpedo boats, 6 fwd, 4 aft
Electron Equipt: sonar: BQG 4, BQR-2
M: Diesel-electric propulsion; 4 groups of generators (6,400 hp); 2 electric motors (5,400 hp)

REMARKS: S-15 transferred 17-10-73, S-16 on 19-12-73. Both have Puffs passive-ranging fire-control sonar.

◆ 5 ex-U.S. Guppy II class

	Bldr	L
S 10 GUANABARA (ex-*Dogfish*, SS-350)	Electric Boat Co.	27-10-45
S 11 RIO GRANDE DO SUL (ex-*Grampus*, SS-523)	Boston NSY	15-12-44
S 12 BAHIA (ex-*Sea Leopard*, SS-483)	Portsmouth NSY	2-3-45
S 13 RIO DE JANEIRO (ex-*Odax*, SS-484)	Portsmouth NSY	10-4-45
S 14 CEARA (ex-*Amberjack*, SS-522)	Boston NSY	15-12-44

D: 1,517 tons standard, 1,950 surfaced, 2,540 submerged
Dim: 93.8 × 8.2 × 5.2   **S:** 18/13-15 kts   **Range:** 10,000/10
A: 10/533-mm TT, 6 fwd and 4 aft   **Man:** 86 men
M: Diesel-electric propulsion; 3 generator groups; 2 electric motors; 2 props; 4,800/5,400 hp   **Fuel:** 300 tons diesel

REMARKS: Purchased in 5-72, 7-72, and 1973. A fourth group of diesel generators has been removed. Two batteries of 126 elements. Converted in 1952-54. S-11 originally Guppy I.

Rio de Janeiro   1972

DESTROYERS

◆ 2 ex-U.S. Gearing class, FRAM I

	Bldr	L	In serv.
D 25 MARCILIO DIAZ (ex-*Henry W. Tucker*, DDR-875)	Consolidated Steel Corp.	8-11-44	3-45
D 26 MARIZ E BARROS (ex-*Brinkley Bass*, DD-887)	Consolidated Steel Corp.	26-5-45	10-45

D: 2,400 tons (3,600 fl)   **Dim:** 119.17 × 12.45 × 5.8
S: 30 kts   **Range:** 2,400/25, 4,800/15   **Man:** 14 officers, 260 men
A: 4/127-mm (II × 2)−1 Asroc ASW system−6/324-mm ASW TT (III × 2) Mk 32 for Mk 44 torpedoes

Marcilio Diaz   1974

DESTROYERS (continued)

Electron Equipt: Radars: 1/SPS 10, 1/SPS 40, 1 MK 25 fire-control
Sonar: 1/SQS 23
M: GT; 2 props; 60,000 hp   **Boilers:** 4 Babcock & Wilcox   **Fuel:** 650 tons

REMARKS: Transferred in 12-73 and reached Brazil in 6-74. Four additional units will not be transferred as planned. D-25 badly damaged in collision, 1978.

◆ 5 ex-U.S. Allen M. Sumner class

	Bldr	L
D 34 MATO GROSSO (ex-*Compton*, DD-705)	Federal SB, Kearney	17-9-44
D 35 SERGIPE (ex-*Buck*, DD-761)	Bethlehem, San Fran.	11-2-44
D 36 ALAGOAS (ex-*James C. Owens*, DD-776)	Bethlehem, San Pedro	1-10-44
D 37 RIO GRANDE DO NORTE (ex-*Strong*, DD-758)	Bethlehem, San Fran.	23-4-44
D 38 ESPIRITO SANTO (ex-*Lowry*, DD-770)	Bethlehem, San Pedro	6-2-44

Mato Grosso 1975

Sergipe—Note the variable-depth sonar 1975

Rio Grande do Norte 1978

D: 2,200 tons (3,320 fl)   **S:** 30 kts   **Dim:** 114.75 × 12.45 × 5.8
Man: 15 officers, 260 men   **Range:** 1,260/30, 4,600/15
A: 6/127-mm (II × 3)—(D-34 only: 1/quadruple Sea Cat SAM)—2 Hedgehogs—6/324-mm ASW TT Mk 32 (III × 2)
Electron Equipt: Radars: 1/SPS 10, 1/SPS 40 (D-34: 1/SPS 6, D-38: 1/SPS 37), 1 Mk 25 fire-control
Sonars: 1/SQS 29-32, D-35 and D-38: VDS also
M: GT; 2 props; 60,000 hp   **Boilers:** 4 Babcock & Wilcox   **Fuel:** 460 tons

REMARKS: All except D-34 are FRAM II. D-34 transferred 27-9-72, the others in 1973. Sea Cat system in D-34 uses M 20 optical director.

◆ 3 ex-U.S. Fletcher class

	Bldr	L
D 29 PARANA (ex-*Cushing*, DD-797)	Bethlehem Steel	30-9-43
D 30 PERNAMBUCO (ex-*Hailey*, DD-556)	Todd SY, Seattle	9-3-43
D 33 MARANHÃO (ex-*Shields*, DD-596)	Puget Sound B&DD	25-9-44

D: 2,050 tons (2,850 fl)   **Dim:** 114.85 × 12.03 × 5.5
S: 30 kts   **Man:** 15 officers, 247 men   **Range:** 1,260/30, 4,400/15
A: D-29, D-33: 5/127-mm DP (I × 5)—10/40-mm AA (D-33: none)—D-30: 4/127-mm DP; on D-29, D-30: 5/533-mm ASW TT (V × 1)—6/324-mm ASW TT Mk 32 (III × 2)—2 Hedgehogs—1/depth-charge rack
Electron Equipt: Radars: 1/SPS 10, 1/SPS 6, 1/MK 25 fire-control
Sonar: 1/SQS 4, 29, or 32
M: GE GT; 2 props; 60,000 hp; 4 Babcock & Wilcox boilers
Fuel: 450 tons

REMARKS: Transferred under Mutual Aid Agreement: D-29 and D-30 in 1961, D-33 in 1972. *Piaui* (D-31) and *Santa Catarina* (D-32) stricken 1977, *Para* (D-27) and *Paraiba* (D-28), 10/78.

DESTROYERS (*continued*)

Maranhão   1975

FRIGATES

◆ **6 Vosper Thornycroft Mk-10 class**

ASW types:

	Bldr	Laid down	L	In serv.
F 40 NITEROI	Thornycroft, Woolston	5-72	8-2-74	11-76
F 41 DEFENSORA	Thornycroft, Woolston	12-72	11-3-75	3-77
F 44 INDEPENDENCIA	Ast. Ilha das Cobras, Rio	6-72	2-9-74	11-79
F 45 UNIÃO	Ast. Ilha das Cobras, Rio	6-72	14-3-75	1980
General-purpose types:				
F 42 CONSTITUCÃO	Thornycroft, Woolston	3-72	4-76	2-78
F 43 LIBERAL	Thornycroft, Woolston	5-75	7-2-77	19-11-78

D: 3,200 tons (3,800 fl)
S: 30.5 kts (28 cruising on gas turbines, 22 on diesels)

Niteroi—ASW version   Vosper, 1976

Constitucão—General-purpose version   Vosper, 1978

FRIGATES (continued)

Dim: 129.24 (121.92 pp) × 13.49 × 5.94 (includes sonar)

Range: 1,300/28, 4,200/19 (4 diesels), 5,300/17.5 (2 diesels)

A: ASW type: 1/114-mm Mk 8 Vickers automatic DP—2/40-mm Bofors AA (I × 2)—
    Branik ASW system—1/Bofors 375-mm, twin-barrel ASW system—
    2/Sea Cat SAM systems (III × 2)—6/324-mm Mk 32 ASW TT (III × 2)
    —1/Lynx WG 13 helicopter—1/depth-charge rack (5 charges)
General-purpose type: similar but without the Branik system and with a sec-
    ond 114-mm Mk 8 aft and 4 launchers (II × 2) for the MM 38 Exocet
    SSM system

Electron Equipt: Radars: 1/Plessey AWS 2 with Mk 10 IFF (air search),
    1/Hollandse Signaalapparaten ZWO-6 with RRA,
    2/Selenia RTN-10 X fire-control
    Sonars: all ships have 1/EDO 610 E; ASW ships also have 1/EDO
    700 E VDS

Fuel: 450 tons diesel, 50 tons fresh water, 26 tons helicopter fuel

Endurance: 45 days **Electric:** 4,500 kw **Man:** 21 officers, 180 men

M: CODAG propulsion: 2 Rolls-Royce Olympus TM3B gas turbines, each 28,000 hp;
    4 M.A.N. V8V 23/23 diesels, 3,940 hp each, coupled to one drive shaft in pairs;
    2 controllable-pitch Escher-Wyss props

Niteroi   Vosper, 1976

Defensora   Vosper, 1977

REMARKS: Ordered 20-9-70. Fitted with retractable stabilizers. Branik is the name of
the system devised for handling the Australian Ikara ASW missile in these ships. All
have CAAIS action data system (Ferranti 1600B computers) and are equipped with
Decca ECM gear. Construction of a seventh unit, at Rio de Janeiro, has been dis-
cussed; the ship would be equipped for cadet training to replace the *Custódio de Mello*
and would differ greatly in equipment from the other six. The Brazilian units experienced considerable delays in fitting out.

PATROL BOATS AND CRAFT

◆ **10 Imperial Marinheiro class**

V 15 IMPERIAL MARINHEIRO (24-11-54)   V 20 ANGOSTURA (55)
V 16 IGUATEMI (54)   V 21 BAHIANA (11-54)
V 17 IPIRANGA (29-6-54)   V 22 MEARIM (8-54)
V 18 FORTE DE COIMBRA (11-6-54)   V 23 PURUS (6-11-54)
V 19 CABOCLO (28-8-54)   V 24 SOLIMÕES (24-11-54)

Imperial Marinheiro   1971

D: 911 tons   **S:** 15 kts   **Dim:** 55.72 × 9.55 × 4.6

A: 1/76-mm—4/20-mm AA (I × 4)   **Man:** 60 men

M: Sulzer diesels; 2 props; 2,160 hp   **Fuel:** 135 tons diesel

PATROL BOATS AND CRAFT (*continued*)

REMARKS: Heavy tugs built in Holland. Were intended to be convertible for mine-sweeping or minelaying. The V-15 is used as a submarine tender. Officially designated "corvettes" and used in District patrols and in support of the 200-mile economic boundary.

◆ 6 Piratini-class patrol craft

		In serv.			In serv.
P 10	PIRATINI (ex-PGM-109)	30-11-70	P 13	PARATI (ex-PGM-119)	7-71
P 11	PIRAJÁ (ex-PGM-110)	1-71	P 14	PENEDO (ex-PGM-120)	9-71
P 12	PAMPEIRO (ex-PGM-118)	3-71	P 15	POTI (ex-PGM-121)	10-71

Parati   1972

    D: 105 tons (fl)   **S:** 15.5 kts
    Dim: 30.5 (29 pp) × 6.05 × 1.9   **Man:** 2 officers, 14 men
    A: 1/81-mm mortar with 12.7-mm machine gun—2/12.7-mm machine guns
    Range: 1,000/15, 1,700/12
    M: 4 Cummins diesels; 2 props; 1,100 hp

REMARK: These patrol craft are based on the 95-foot WPBs of the U.S. Coast Guard.

MINE WARFARE SHIPS

◆ 6 German Schütze-class (R55) minesweepers

    Bldr: Abeking and Rasmussen, German Federal Republic

		L			L
M 15	ARATU	27-5-70	M 18	ARACATUBA	1971
M 16	ANHATOMIRIM	4-11-70	M 19	ABROLHOS	7-5-74
M 17	ATALAIA	14-4-71	M 20	ALBARDÃO	9-74

Anhatomirim   1972

Aratu   1971

    D: 230 tons (280 fl)   **S:** 24 kts   **Dim:** 47.2 × 7.16 × 2.1
    A: 1/40-mm AA   **Range:** 710/20
    Fuel: 22 tons diesel   **Man:** 39 men
    M: 4 Maybach diesels; 2 Escher-Wyss variable-pitch props; 4,500 hp

REMARKS: Four ordered 4-69, two 11-73. Fitted for magnetic, mechanical, and acoustic minesweeping. Wooden hulls.

AMPHIBIOUS WARFARE SHIPS

◆ 2 ex-U.S. LSTs

G 26 DUQUE DE CAXIAS (ex-*Grant County*, LST-1174)

    Bldr: Avondale. In serv. 11-57

Duque de Caxias

    D: 4,164 tons (7,800 fl)   **Dim:** 135.7 × 18.9 × 5.3
    S: 16 kts   **A:** 6/76-mm AA (II × 3)
    M: 4 Nordberg diesels; 2 controllable-pitch props; 14,000 hp

REMARKS: Transferred 11-72. Can carry 700 men. Air-conditioned. Four LCVP in davits; and four causeways (pontoon sections) which can be dropped where needed. Platform for helicopters.

G 28 GARCIA DAVILA (ex-*Outagamie County*, LST-1073) 1944

    D: 1,490 tons (4,100 fl)   **Dim:** 100.0 × 15.25 × 3.36
    M: 2 GM diesels; 2 props; 1,700 hp   **A:** 8/40-mm AA (II × 2, I × 4)

REMARK: Transferred 25-5-71.

AMPHIBIOUS WARFARE SHIPS (*continued*)

Garcia Davila   1972

◆ **4 U.S. LCU-1610 type landing craft**   Bldr: Navy Yard, Rio, 1974-77

L 10 GUARAPARI	L 22 TIMBAU
L . . CAMBORIU	L . . TRAMANDAI

   D: 200 tons (396 fl)   **S:** 11 kts   **Dim:** 41.0 × 9.0 × 2.0
   M: 2 GM 12V71 diesels; 2 props; 1,000 hp   **Range:** 1,200/8

◆ **28 LCVP** Built in Japan, 1959-60

◆ **7 EDVP** Built in Brazil, 1971

   Dim: 11.0 × 3.2 × 0.6 (fwd), 1 (aft)   **M:** Brazilian Scania diesel

REMARKS: Hulls built of synthetic materials. Can carry 36 men with full pack or one jeep with trailer and 17 men or 1/105-mm howitzer or an anti-tank gun and 18 men.

RIVER PATROL CRAFT

◆ **3 Roraima-class river patrol craft**

	Bldr	L	In serv.
P 30 RORAIMA	MacLaren, Niteroi	9-11-72	21-2-75
P 31 RONDÔNIA	MacLaren, Niteroi	10-1-73	3-12-75
P 32 AMAPÁ	MacLaren, Niteroi	9-3-73	1-76

Rondônia   1975

D: 340 tons (365 fl)   **Dim:** 45.0 × 8.45 × 1.37
S: 14.5 kts   **Man:** 9 officers, 54 men   **Range:** 6,000/11
A: 1/40 mm AA – 6/machine guns – 2/81-mm mortars
M: 2 M.A.N. diesels: 912 hp; 2 props

REMARKS: In Amazon Flotilla. Carry one LCVP.

◆ **2 river patrol craft**

P 20 PEDRO TEIXEIRA   L: 11-6-72   P 21 RAPOSO TAVARES   L: 11-6-72

Raposo Tavares   1975

D: 700 tons   **Dim:** 62.0 × 9.35 × 1.65
S: 16 kts   **Range:** 5,500/10
A: 1/40-mm AA – 6/machine guns – 2/81-mm mortars
M: 4 MEP-M.A.N. diesels, V6V type; 2 props; 3,840 hp

REMARKS: Ordered in 1970 from Ilha das Cobras Naval Dockyard. Platform and hangar for one helicopter. In service 17-12-73.

◆ **1 old river monitor**   Bldr: Arsenal de Marinha, Rio

U 17 PARNAIBA

Parnaiba   1976

RIVER PATROL CRAFT (*continued*)

D: 620 tons (720 fl) **S:** 12 kts **Dim:** 55.0 × 10.1 × 1.6
A: 1/76.2-mm DP − 2/47-mm − 2/40-mm AA (I × 2) − 6/20-mm AA (I × 6)
Man: 90 men **Range:** 1,350/10 **Fuel:** 90 tons
M: 2 sets triple-expansion reciprocating steam; 2 props; 1,300 hp
Boilers: 2/3-drum

REMARK: In service since 11-37. In Mato Grosso Flotilla.

HYDROGRAPHIC AND OCEANOGRAPHIC SHIPS

◆ **1 new construction research ship**

ALVARO ALBERTO

D: . . . **S:** 13 kts **Dim:** 60.0 × 12.0 × 4.3
Man: 26 crew, 17 scientists

REMARK: Ordered 1973, but construction does not seem to have yet begun.

◆ **1 ex-U.S. oceanographic ship**

H 41 ALMIRANTE CAMARA (ex-*Sands*, T-AGOR-6)

Almirante Camara   1974

D: 1,020 tons (1,370 fl) **Dim:** 70.0 (63.7 pp) × 11.28 × 6.3 (fl)
S: 13.5 kts **Range:** 12,000/12
Man: 8 officers, 18 men, 15 oceanographers
M: Diesel-electric; 1 prop; 1,000 hp

REMARKS: Transferred 1974. An auxiliary motor powers a small maneuvering propeller for stationkeeping purposes at extremely low rpm. Has echo-sounders capable of measuring 11,000-meter depths.

◆ **2 Sirius class**

	Bldr	Laid down	L	In serv.
H 21 SIRIUS	Ishikawajima	12-56	30-7-57	12-57
H 22 CANOPUS	Ishikawajima	12-56	20-11-57	3-58

Canopus

D: 1,463 tons (1,800 fl) **S:** 15 kts **Dim:** 77.9 × 12.03 × 3.7
Range: 12,000/11
Man: 102 men **M:** Sulzer diesels; 2 controllable-pitch props; 2,700 hp

REMARKS: 1 helicopter, 1 LCVP, 3 small survey craft. Fully equipped. Armament removed.

◆ **6 wooden-hulled hydrographic boats**

	In serv.		In serv.
H 11 PARAIBANO	10-68	H 15 ITACURUSSÁ	3-71
H 12 RIO BRANCO	10-68	H 16 CAMOCIM	1971
H 14 NOGUEIRA DA GAMA	3-71	H 17 CARAVELAS	1971
(ex-*Jaceguai*)			

Bldr: Bormann (Rio de Janeiro)

Nogueira da Gama   1971

HYDROGRAPHIC AND OCEANOGRAPHIC SHIPS (*continued*)

D: 32 tons (50 fl)   **S:** 11 kts   **Dim:** 16.0 × 4.6 × 1.3
Man: 2 officers, 9 men   **Range:** 600/11
M: 1 GM 6-71 diesel; 165 hp

REMARK: In Amazon Flotilla.

	Bldr	L	In serv.
U 10 ALMIRANTE SALDANHA	Vickers	19-12-33	6-34

Almirante Saldanha

D: 3,225 tons (3,825 fl)   **Dim:** 92.0 × 15.7 × 5.5
S: 11 kts   **Man:** 218 men   **Range:** 12,000/10

REMARKS: Former 4-masted schooner, refit completed in 7-61 as an oceanographic research ship. Employed in training.

H 31 ARGUS (6-12-57)   H 32 ORION (5-2-28)   H 33 TAURUS (7-1-58)

Bldr: Arsenal de Marinha, Rio

D: 250 tons (300 fl)   **Dim:** 44.8 (42.06 pp) × 6.1 × 2.45
S: 17 kts (15 cruising)   **Range:** 1,200/15
M: Caterpillar diesels; 2 props; 1,200 hp   **Fuel:** 35 tons diesel

Orion

REMARKS: Based on the Portuguese *Azevia*-class gunboat. H-32 modernized in 1973/74, with new propulsion machinery, auxiliaries, and electronic equipment.

AUXILIARY SHIPS

◆ **4 transports**

	Bldr	Laid down	L	In serv.
U 26 CUSTÓDIO DE MELLO	Ishikawajima, Tokyo	12-53	10-6-54	9-54
G 16 BARROSO PEREIRA	Ishikawajima, Tokyo	12-53	7-8-54	12-54
G 21 ARI PARREIRAS	Ishikawajima, Tokyo	12-55	24-8-56	12-56
G 22 SOARES DUTRA	Ishikawajima, Tokyo	12-55	13-12-56	3-57

Custódio de Mello   1976

D: 4,800 tons (8,600 fl)   **Dim:** 119.2 × 16.0 × 6.1
S: 16 kts   **Man:** 118 men. Can carry 1,972 troops (497 average)
A: 4/76-mm (U-26)—2/76-mm and 2/20-mm on the others
Cargo capacity: 4,200 tons   **M:** GT; 2 props; 4,800 hp   **Boilers:** 2

REMARKS: Refrigerated storeroom. Living spaces mechanically ventilated and partially air-conditioned. *Custódio de Mello* is used as an underway training ship.

◆ **1 ex-U.S. LST repair ship**

G 24 BELMONTE (ex-*Helios*, ARB-12, ex-LST-1127)

Bldr: Maryland Dry Dock, Baltimore. In serv. 2-45

Belmonte

AUXILIARY SHIPS (continued)

D: 2,030 tons (4,100 fl)   **Dim:** 100.0 × 15.25 × 3.36
S: 9 kts   **A:** 8/40-mm AA (IV × 2)
M: GM 5-267 diesels; 2 props; 1,800 hp   **Range:** 6,000/9

REMARKS: Transferred 1963. 1/60-ton winch crane, 2/10-ton booms. Used mainly as a transport.

◆ 2 oilers

G 27 MARAJO (31-1-68) Bldr: Ishikawajima do Brasil, Rio

Marajo   1977

D: 10,500 tons   **Dim:** 137.1 (127.69 pp) × 19.22 × 7.35
S: 13.6 kts   **Range:** 9,200/14.5   **Man:** 80 men
M: 1 Sulzer diesel; 8,000 hp   **Cargo capacity:** 7,200 tons

G 17 POTENGI (16-3-38) Bldr: Papendrecht (Holland)

D: 600 tons   **S:** 10 kts   **Dim:** 54.0 × 7.2 × 1.8
M: Diesel; 550 hp   **Cargo capacity:** 450 tons

REMARK: In Mato Grosso Flotilla.

◆ 1 submarine-rescue ship Bldr: Charleston SB & DD Co.

K 10 GASTÃO MOUTINHO (ex-U.S. *Skylark*, ASR-20; ex-*Yustaga*, ATF-165)

D: 1,780 tons (2,140 fl)   **Dim:** 62.48 × 11.73 × 4.7
S: 14.5 kts   **A:** 2/20-mm AA (I × 2)
M: 2 GM 12-278A diesels, electric drive; 1 prop; 3,000 hp

REMARKS: Launched 19-3-46. Purchased in 6-1973. Employed in hydrographic survey duties.

◆ 3 ex-U.S. ATA-class tugs

R 21 TRITÃO (ex-ATA-234) R 22 TRIDENTE (ex-ATA-235), R 23 TRIUNFO (ex-ATA-236).
   Bldr: Gulfport, Texas

D: 534 tons (835 fl)   **Dim:** 43.61 × 10.34 × 4.03
S: 13 kts   **A:** 2/20-mm AA
M: Diesel-electric; 1,500 hp

REMARK: Launched in U.S.A. in 1944; purchased in 1947.

◆ 1 tug

R 14 LAURINDO PITTA Bldr: Vickers, 1910, rebuilt 1969

D: 514 tons: **Dim:** 39.04 × 7.77 × 3.35 (aft)

◆ 6 tugs Bldr: Holland Nautic Yard. In serv. 1953

R 31 AUDAZ   R 33 GUARANI   R 35 PASSO DE PATRIA
R 32 CENTAURO   R 34 LAMEGO   R 36 VOLUNTARIO

D: 130 tons   **S:** 11 kts   **Dim:** 27.6 × 7.2 × 3.1
M: 1 Womag diesel; 765 hp   **Man:** 12 men

◆ 3 Isaias de Noronha-class tugs

R . . . ISAIAS DE NORONHA   R . . . D.N.O.G.
R . . . TENIENTE LAHMEYER

D: 1,000 tons (fl)   **Dim:** 47 × . . . × . . .

REMARK: In service 1972-74.

◆ 1 personnel and stores transport Bldr: Ebraso, Santa Catarina

R 47 SARGENTO BORGES

D: 108.5 tons   **Dim:** 28.0 × 6.5 × 1.5
S: 10 kts   **Range:** 400/10
M: 2 diesels; 2 props; 480 hp

REMARK: Launched 29-8-74. Can carry 106 passengers.

◆ 4 passenger ferries Bldr: Inconav Niteroi Shipbuilders

U 40 RIO PARDO   U 42 RIO CHUI
U 41 RIO NEGRO   U 43 RIO OIAPOQUE

D: 150 tons   **Dim:** 35.38 × 6.5 × 1.9
M: 2 diesels; 548 hp   **S:** 14 kts

REMARKS: Delivered 1975-76. Can carry 600 passengers. Used in and around naval bases.

◆ 6 river transports Bldr: The Netherlands, 1956

U 20 RIO DOCE   U 23 RIO REAL
U 21 RIO DAS CONTAS   U 24 RIO TURVO
U 22 RIO FORMOSO   U 25 RIO VERDE

D: 150 tons   **Dim:** 35.0 × 6.0 × 2.1
M: 2 Sulzer diesels; 2 props; 450 hp   **S:** 14 kts

REMARK: Can carry 600 passengers.

◆ 7 personnel launches Bldr: Brazil

ACARÁ, AGULHA, ANCHOVA, ARENQUE, ARGENTINA, ARUANA, ATUM

D: 13 tons (fl)   **S:** 25 kts   **Dim:** 13.0 × 3.8 × 1.2
M: 2 diesels; 280 hp   **Man:** 3 men
Cargo: 12 passengers   **Range:** 400/20

REMARK: In service 1965-67.

BRAZIL (*continued*)

AUXILIARY SHIPS (*continued*)

◆ **1 command transport ship**

G 15 PARAGUASSU

    D: 285 tons   **S:** 12 kts   **Dim:** 40.0 × 7.0 × 1.2
    M: Diesel; 1 prop   **Range:** 2,500/10

REMARKS: Former river transport ship *Guarapuava*, bought in 1971, refitted for the Mato Grosso Flotilla, and used as a river buoy tender.

◆ **2 small service transports**

TENENTE FABIO   TENENTE RAUL

    D: 55 tons   **S:** 10 kts
    Dim: 20.28 × 5.1 × 1.2   **Range:** 350
    M: Diesel; 135 hp; 1/10-ton derrick   **Cargo capacity:** 22 tons

◆ **5 munitions lighters**

SÃO FRANCISCO DOS SANTOS (1964), UBIRAJARA DOS SANTOS (1968), OPERATÏO LUIS LEAL (1968), MIGUEL DOS SANTOS (1968), APRENDIZ LÉDIO CONCEIÇÃO (1968)

REMARK: Last two for torpedoes.

◆ **2 water tankers**

R 43 PAULO AFONSO   R 42 ITAPURA

    D: 485.3 tons   **Dim:** 42.8 × 7.0 × 2.5
    M: 1 diesel   **Cargo:** 389 tons

REMARK: Launched 1957.

◆ **3 floating docks**

G 25 AFONSO PENA (ex-U.S. ARD-14)   **D:** 5,200 tons (fl)   **Dim:** 150.0 × 24.7
G 26 ALMIRANTE J. GONCALVES (ex-U.S. AFDL-4) can lift 1,000 tons.
    Dim: 60 × . . .
G 27 CIDADE DE NATAL (ex-U.S. AFDL-39) can lift 2,800 tons.
    Dim: 119.0 × . . .

◆ **8 130-ton buoy-maintenance ships**

H 13 MESTRO JOÃO DOS SANTOS	H 30 FAROLEIRO NASCIMENTO
H 24 CASTELHANOS	H . . CABO BRANCO
H 27 FAROLEIRO AREAS	H . . CABO CALLANHAR
H 28 FAROLEIRO SANTANA	H . . CABO FRIO

◆ **1 lighthouse and buoy tender**

	Bldr	Laid down	L	In serv.
H 34 GRAÇA ARANHA	Elbin, Niteroi	end 1970	23-6-74	10-76

    D: 1,253 tons   **S:** 13 kts   **Dim:** 75.57 × 13.0 × 3.71
    M: Diesel; 1 controllable-pitch prop; 2,000 hp; 1 bow thruster   **Man:** 101 men

REMARKS: Telescoping helicopter hangar. Two LCVPs carried as transports.

Graça Aranha   1976

BRUNEI

PERSONNEL: 350 men

MERCHANT MARINE (1978): 18 ships—4,158 grt

◆ **2 guided-missile patrol boats projected**

REMARK: To be ordered from France.

◆ **3 guided-missile patrol boats**   Bldr: Vosper-Thornycroft, Singapore

	L	In serv.
P 02 WASPADA	3-8-77	7-78
P 03 PEJUANG	3-78	1979
P 04 SETERIA	22-6-78	1979

    D: 150 tons (fl)   **S:** 32 kts   **Dim:** 36.88 (33.53 pp) × 7.16 × 1.8
    A: 2/MM 38 Exocet SSM—2/30-mm AA (II × 1)—2 machine guns
    Electron Equipt: Radar: Decca AC 1229   **Man:** 24 men
    Range: 1,200/14   **Fuel:** 16 tons
    M: 2 MTU 20V538 TB91 diesels; 2 props; 9,000 hp (7,500 sust.)

REMARKS: P-02 has enclosed upper bridge (open on other two) and facilities for training. All have Sperry Sea Archer fire control and two 50-mm rocket-flare launchers. The 30-mm mount is BMARC/Oerlikon GCM-BOI.

◆ **3 patrol craft**

P 14 PERWIRA (5-74)   P 15 PEMBURU (30-1-75)   P 16 PENYARANG (20-3-75)

Perwira   1974

Bldr: Vosper-Thornycroft, Singapore

D: 38.5 tons (fl)   **S:** 32 kts   **Dim:** 21.7 × 6.1 × 1.2
Range: 600/20
A: 2/20-mm (I × 2)−2 machine guns
M: 2 MTU 12V331 TC 81 diesels; 2,700 hp
Electron Equipt: Radar: Decca RM 616

◆ **3 Masna-class patrol craft**   Bldr: Vosper-Thornycroft, Singapore

P 11 MASNA (19-9-70)   P 12 SALEHA (18-9-70)
P 13 NORAIN (11-71)

Bldr: Vosper-Thornycroft Private Ltd., Singapore. In serv: 1971-73

D: 23.5 tons   **S:** 25/23 kts   **Dim:** 18.9 × 4.8 × 1.4
A: 2/20-mm Hispano−2 machine guns   **Range:** 600/23
M: 2 GM diesels 16-cyl. Mk V 71 N; 1,240 hp
Electron Equipt: Radar: Decca RM 616

REMARK: Wooden hull, light-metal superstructure.

◆ **3 small patrol craft**

P 21 BENDAHARA   P 23 KEMAINDERA   P 22 MAHARAJALELA
D: 10 tons   **Dim:** 14.1 × 3.6 × 0.9
S: 20 kts   **Man:** 6 men
A: 2 machine guns   **Electron Equipt:** Radar: Decca RM 616
M: 2 GM diesels; 334 hp

REMARK: Built 1974-75.

◆ **2 Loadmaster-class landing craft**   Bldr: Cheverton, G. B.

L 31 DAMUAN (5-76)   L 32 PUNI (2-77)
D: 64.3 tons (light)   **S:** 8.5 kts   **Dim:** 22.86 × 6.1 × 1.07
Electron Equipt: Radar: Decca RM 1216   **Range:** 300/8.5, 1,000/6
M: 2 GM 6-71 diesels; 2 props; 348 hp   **Cargo:** 30 tons

MARINE POLICE

◆ **4 patrol craft**   Bldr: Vosper-Thornycroft, Singapore, 1978

TENANG   ABADI   N . . .   N . . .
D: 14 tons (fl)   **S:** 28 kts   **Dim:** 18.0 × 4.88 × 0.79
A: Machine guns   **M:** 2 MTU diesels; 2 water jets

REMARKS: Glass-reinforced plastic hulls. The second pair was ordered early in 1979.

◆ **3 patrol craft**   Bldr: Vosper-Thornycroft, Singapore

MAKMOR   TENTERAM−17 meters   AMAN DAMAI−11 meters

Makmor

◆ **25 small armed river craft**   **M:** 100 hp   **A:** 1/7.62-mm machine gun

BULGARIA

PERSONNEL: approx. 4,000 men

MERCHANT MARINE (1978): 189 ships—1,082,477 grt
(tankers: 22—352,617 grt)

NAVAL AVIATION: 6 Soviet Hound and 2 Mi-2 helicopters

NOTE: For additional ships' data, see U.S.S.R. section

SUBMARINES

◆ **2 Soviet Romeo class**

SLAVA   POBIEDA

D: 1,330 tons, surfaced, 1,700 submerged   **Dim:** 77.0 × 6.7 × 5.0
S: 15 kts surfaced, 13 submerged   **Range:** 14,000/9
A: 8/533-mm TT (6 fwd, 2 aft)—14 torpedoes or 24 mines
Electron Equipt: Radar: Snoop Plate   **Endurance:** 60 days
M: 2 diesels; electric drive; 4,000 hp

REMARKS: Transferred 1971-72. Replaced two Whiskey class with same names. Can
dive to 300 meters.

FRIGATES

◆ **2 Soviet Riga class**

DERSKY   SMELY

D: 1,450 tons (fl)   **S:** 28 kts   **Dim:** 91.0 × 11.0 × 3.4
A: 3/100-mm DP—3/533-mm TT—2 ASW MBU 2500 rocket launchers
Electron Equipt: Radars: 1/Slim Net, 1/Neptune, 1/Sun Visor B
        IFF: 2/Square Head, 1/High Pole
M: 2 sets GT; 2 props; 20,000 hp; 2 boilers

REMARK: Transferred 1957-58.

CORVETTES

◆ **3 Soviet Poti class**

D: 500 tons (fl)   **S:** 34 kts   **Dim:** 60.3 × 8.0 × 3.0
A: 2/57-mm AA (II × 1)—2 MBU 2500A ASW rocket launchers—2/533-mm ASW TT
Electron Equipt: Radars: 1/Spin Trough, 1/Strut Curve, 1/Muff Cob
        IFF: 2/Square Head, 1/High Pole B
        Sonar: 1 high-frequency
M: CODAG: 2 M-503A diesels of 4,000 hp each plus 2 gas turbines of 20,000 hp each;
        2 props

REMARK: Transferred 1975.

PATROL BOATS

◆ **3 Soviet Stenka class**

D: 150 tons (fl)   **S:** 38 kts   **Dim:** 37.5 × 8.5 × 1.8
A: 4/30-mm AA (II × 2)—4/400-mm ASW TT (I × 4)—2 depth-charge racks

Electron Equipt: Radars: 1/Pot Drum, 1/Drum Tilt
        IFF: 2/Square Head, 1/High Pole B
M: 3 M-503A diesels; 3 props; 12,000 hp

◆ **6 Soviet S.O.-1 class**

D: 190 tons (215 fl)   **S:** 25 kts   **Dim:** 42.0 × 6.1 × 1.9
A: 4/25-mm AA—4 ASW MBU 1800 rocket launchers—depth charges
Electron Equipt: Radar: 1/Pot Head
        IFF: 1/Dead Duck, 1/High Pole

REMARK: Transferred 1963.

GUIDED-MISSILE PATROL AND TORPEDO BOATS

◆ **1 Soviet Osa-II-class patrol boat**

D: 240 tons (fl)   **S:** 36 kts   **Dim:** 39.0 × 7.7 × 1.8
A: 4/SS-N-2 Styx—4/30-mm AA (II × 2)   **Range:** 800/25
Electron Equipt: Radars: 1/Square Tie, 1/Drum Tilt
        IFF: 2/Square Head, 1/High Pole B
M: 3 M-504 diesels; 3 props; 15,000 hp

REMARK: Transferred 1977.

◆ **3 Soviet Osa-I-class patrol boats**

D: 175 tons (210 fl)   **S:** 36 kts   **Dim:** 39.0 × 7.7 × 1.8
A: 4/SS-N-2 Styx—4/30-mm (II × 2)
Electron Equipt: Radars: 1/Square Tie, 1/Drum Tilt
        IFF: 2/Square Head, 1/High Pole B
M: 2 M-503A diesels; 3 props; 12,000 hp

REMARK: Transferred 1970-71.

◆ **6 Soviet Shershen-class torpedo boats**

D: 150 tons (180 fl)   **S:** 45 kts   **Dim:** 34.0 × 7.2 × 1.5
A: 4/533-mm TT—4/30-mm AA (II × 2)
Electron Equipt: Radars: 1/Pot Drum, 1/Drum Tilt
M: 3 M-503A diesels; 3 props; 12,000 hp

REMARK: Transferred 1970.

◆ **4 Soviet P-4-class torpedo boats**

D: 19.3 tons (22.4 fl)   **S:** 55 kts
A: 2/450-mm TT—2/14.5-mm AA (II × 1)
Electron Equipt: Radar: 1/Skin Head

REMARK: Transferred 1956.

MINE WARFARE SHIPS

◆ **4 Soviet Vanya-class minesweepers**

D: 220 tons (245 fl)   **S:** 18 kts   **Dim:** 40.0 × 7.6 × 1.8
A: 2/30-mm AA (II × 1)—mines
Electron Equipt: Radar: 1/Don-2
        IFF: 1/Square Head, 1 High Pole B
M: 2 diesels; 2 props; 2,200 hp

REMARK: Transferred 1971-72.

BULGARIA (*continued*)

MINE WARFARE SHIPS (*continued*)

◆ **2 Soviet T-43-class minesweepers**

VUKOV KLANAC   N . . .

    D: 500 tons (580 fl)   **S:** 14 kts   **Dim:** 58.0 × 8.4 × 2.3
    A: 4/37-mm AA (II × 2) – 8/14.5-mm AA (II × 4) – mines
    Electron Equipt: Radars: 1/Ball End, 1/Neptune
                  IFF: 1/Square Head, 1/High Pole A

REMARKS: Transferred 1953. The two Bulgarian T-43s are early versions of the class with flush bridge faces. They are the only known units of that configuration with tripod, rather than pole, masts.

◆ **4 T-301-class minesweepers**

    D: 145.8 tons (160 fl)   **S:** 12.5 kts   **Dim:** 38.0 × 5.1 × 1.6
    A: 2/37-mm AA (I × 2)

◆ **1 Soviet Yevgenya-class inshore minesweeper**

    D: 80 tons (90 fl)   **S:** 12 kts   **Dim:** 26.0 × 6.0 × 1.5
    A: 2/14.5-mm AA (II × 1)   **Man:** 12 men
    Electron Equipt: Radar: 1/Spin Trough   IFF: 1/High Pole B
    M: 2 diesels; 2 props; 600 hp

REMARKS: Plastic hull. Equipped with towed television minehunting and marking system effective to 30-meter depths.

◆ **12 PO-2-class inshore minesweepers**

    D: 50 tons (fl)   **S:** 9 kts   **Dim:** 21.0 × . . . × 1.0
    A: 1 machine gun

REMARK: Transferred in early 1960s.

AMPHIBIOUS WARFARE SHIPS

◆ **10 Soviet Vydra-class LCU**

    D: 600 tons (fl)   **S:** 10.5 kts   **Dim:** 54.8 × 8.1 × 2.0
    M: Diesels; 600 hp

◆ **10 German MFP-class LCU**   Bldr: Bulgaria, 1950s

VARIOUS SHIPS Most built in Bulgaria

◆ **1 Soviet Moma-class survey ship** Transferred 1977

◆ **3 coastal oilers**

◆ **7 tugs**

◆ **2 salvage ships**

◆ **2 diving vessels**

◆ **6 barracks ships**

BURMA

PERSONNEL: approx. 7,000, including reserves and naval infantry

MERCHANT MARINE (1978): 73 ships – 70,848 grt (tankers: ? – 6,258 grt)

CORVETTES

◆ **1 British Algerine class**

YAN MYO AUNG (ex-*Mariner*) Bldr: Port Arthur SY, Canada (9-5-44)

    D: 1,040 tons (1,355 fl)   **S:** 16 kts   **Dim:** 68.58 × 10.82 × 3.5
    A: 1/102-mm – 4/40-mm AA – fitted to plant 16 mines   **Man:** 140 men
    M: Triple-expansion; 2 props; 2,400 hp; 2 boilers   **Range:** 5,200/10

REMARK: Purchased 1958.

◆ **2 ex-U.S. escort vessels** Purchased 1965-66

YAN GYI AUNG (ex-U.S. *Creddock*, MSF-356) Bldr: Willamette

REMARK: Launched 22-7-44.

YAN TAING AUNG (ex-U.S. *Farmington*, PCE-894) Bldr: Willamette, 1943

    D: 600 tons (903 fl)   **S:** 17 kts   **Dim:** 56.24 × 10.06 × 2.8
    A: 1/76-mm – 6/40-mm AA (II × 3) – 8/20-mm AA (II × 4) – 1 Hedgehog – 2 depth-charge throwers – 2 depth-charge racks   **Man:** 80/95 men
    M: GM diesels; 2 props; 2,400 hp

PATROL BOATS

PGM 401 to PGM 406 (ex-U.S. PGM-43 to PGM-46, PGM-51, and PGM-52)
Bldr: U.S.A. 1959

    D: 100 tons (141 fl)   **S:** 16 kts   **Dim:** 30.8 × 6.4 × 2.3
    A: 1/40-mm AA – 4/20-mm AA (II × 2) – 2 machine guns   **Man:** 17 men
    M: 8 GM diesels; 2 props; 2,040 hp

MGB 101, 102, 103, 105, 106, 108, 110

25-meter patrol boat

PATROL BOATS (continued)

D: 49 tons (66 fl)   **S:** 11 kts   **Dim:** 25.0 × 4.85 × 1.6
A: 2/40-mm AA   **Man:** 16 men   **M:** 4 GM diesels; 2 props; 800 hp

REMARKS: U.S.C.G.-type boats with new hulls, built in Burma, 1960-61. Three or more may have been lost or discarded.

RIVERINE PATROL VESSELS

Y 311, Y 312   Bldr: Similak, Burma, 1967

D: 250 tons   **S:** 14 kts   **Dim:** 37.0 × 7.3 × 1.1
A: 2/40-mm AA (I × 2) − 2/20-mm AA (I × 2)
M: 2 Mercedes-Benz diesels; 2 props; 1,000 hp

NAWARAT   NAGAKYAY   Bldr: Dawbon DY, Rangoon, 1961

Nawarat

D: 400 tons (450 fl)   **S:** 12 kts   **Dim:** 49.7 × 8.23 × . . .
A: 2/25-pound guns (Army ordnance) − 2/40-mm AA   **Man:** 43 men
M: 2 Paxman-Ricardo diesels; 2 props; 1,160 hp

Y 301 to Y 310   Bldr: Uljanik, Pula, 1957-60

Y-301 class

D: 120 tons   **S:** 13 kts   **Dim:** 32.0 × 7.25 × 0.8
A: 2/40-mm AA − 2/20-mm AA   **Man:** 29 men
M: 2 Mercedes-Benz diesels; 4 cylinders; 1,100 hp

VARIOUS SHIPS

◆ 8 river transports

SABAN	SEINDA	SETYAHAT	SHWEPAZUN
SAGU	SETKAYA	SHWETHIDA	SINMIN

Armed river transports

D: 98 tons   **S:** 12 kts   **Dim:** 28.8 × 6.7 × 1.4
A: 1/40-mm AA − 3/20-mm AA (I × 3)   **M:** 2 Crossley ERL-6 diesels; 160 hp

◆ 10 30-to-40-ton river boats   Bldr: Burma, 1951-52

◆ 25 30-to-40-ton river boats   Bldr: Yugoslavia, 1965

◆ 2 hydrographic ships

THU TAY THI   Bldr: Yugoslavia, 1965   **D:** 1,100 tons

YAY BO   Bldr: The Netherlands, 1957   **D:** 108 tons

REMARK: The first has a helicopter platform.

Thu Tay Thi

BURMA (*continued*)

VARIOUS SHIPS (*continued*)

◆ **4 landing craft**   Bldr: Yokohama Yacht

AIYAR MAUNG   AIYAR MAI
AIYAR MIN THAR   AIYAR MIN THA MEE

D: 250 tons (fl)   **S:** 10 kts   **Dim:** 38.25 × 9.14 × 1.4
M: 2 diesels; 2 props; 560 hp   **Cargo:** 100 tons

REMARK: Launched 3-69.

◆ **2 landing craft**   Bldr: Yokohama Yacht

D: . . .   **S:** 10 kts   **Dim:** 29.5 × 6.72 × 1.4
M: 2 diesels; 2 props; 300 hp   **Cargo:** 50 tons, 30 passengers

◆ **8 ex-U.S. LCM (3) class**

LCM 701 to LCM 708   **D:** 52 tons   **S:** 9 kts

◆ **1 landing craft**

AIYAR LULIN (ex-U.S. LCU-1620)

D: 190 tons (390 fl)   **S:** 11 kts   **Dim:** 41.0 × 9.0 × 2.0
A: 2/20-mm AA   **M:** 4 GM 6-71 diesels; 2 props; 1,200 hp

REMARK: Used as a transport.

◆ **1 torpedo transport**   Bldr: Japan, 1967

YAN LONG AUNG   **D:** 520 tons

REMARK: Now used as a diving and repair tender.

CAMEROON

PERSONNEL: 300 men

MERCHANT MARINE (1978): 29 ships — 83,777 grt (tanker: 1 — 47,527 grt)

PATROL BOATS

◆ **1 French PR-48 class**   Bldr: Soc. Française Constructions Navales

L'AUDACIEUX

D: 240 tons (fl)   **S:** 18.5 kts   **Dim:** 47.5 (45.5 pp) × 7.1 × 2.5
A: 2/40-mm AA (I × 2)   **Man:** 3 officers, 22 men   **Range:** 2,000/15
M: 2 MGO diesels; 2 props; 2,400 hp   **Electric:** 100 kw

REMARK: In service 11-5-76.

◆ **2 Chinese Shanghai-II class**

101   102

D: 155 tons (fl)   **S:** 28 kts   **Dim:** 38.8 × 5.4 × 1.6
A: 4/37-mm AA (II × 2) — 4/25-mm AA (II × 2)   **Man:** 25 men
Electron Equipt: Radar: 1/Pot Head   **M:** 4 diesels; 4 props; 4,800 hp

REMARK: Transferred 7-76.

PATROL CRAFT

◆ **3 small coastal surveillance craft**

LE VALEUREUX   Bldr: Estérel Naval SY, 1970

Le Valeureux   Estérel, 1970

D: 45 tons   **S:** 25 kts   **Dim:** 26.8 × 4.97 × 1.55
A: 2/20-mm AA   **Man:** 1 officer, 8 men   **M:** 2 diesels; 2 props; 960 hp

BRIGADIER M'BONGA TOUNDA   Bldr: Estérel Naval SY, 1967

D: 20 tons (fl)   **S:** 22.5 kts   **Dim:** 18.15 (17.03 pp) × 4.03 × 1.1
A: 1/12.7-mm machine gun   **Man:** 8 men
M: Caterpillar diesels D 333 TA; 2 props; 540 hp

REMARKS: Customs ship, manned by the Navy. Same characteristics as the Mauritanian *Imrag'Ni* class.

QUARTIER MAÎTRE ALFRED MOTTO   Bldr: A.C.R.E., Libreville, Gabon

D: 96 tons (fl)   **S:** 15.5 kts   **Dim:** 29.1 × 6.2 × 1.85 (aft)
Man: 2 officers, 15 men
A: 2/20-mm AA — 2 machine guns   **M:** 2 Baudoin diesels; 1,290 hp

AMPHIBIOUS WARFARE CRAFT

◆ **1 LCM**

BAKASI   Bldr: Carena, Abidjan, Ivory Coast, 1973

D: 57 tons (fl)   **S:** 9 kts   **Dim:** 17.5 × 4.28 × 1.3
M: 2 Baudoin diesels; 490 hp

CAMEROON (*continued*)

AMPHIBIOUS WARFARE CRAFT (*continued*)

◆ **5 LCVP-type landing craft**

Souellaba, Indépendance, Reunification, Manoka, Machtigal

D: 11 tons   S: 10 kts

REMARK: The *Souellaba* built at the A.C.R.E., Libreville, Gabon.

SERVICE CRAFT

◆ **2 10-ton harbor launches**

Sanaga, Bimbia

CANADA

The Canadian Armed Forces have been completely unified. Six operational commands have been set up: Mobile Command, Maritime Command, Air Transport Command, Air Defense Command Training Command, and Material Command. The Maritime Command is in charge of the naval ships, the ship-based aircraft, and all of the units of the former Maritime Air Command (RCAF). Its principal role is ASW, but it can also be called upon to transport men and equipment for the Mobile Command.

PERSONNEL (1979): about 14,200 men.

MERCHANT MARINE (1978): 1,289 ships − 2,954,499 grt
(tankers: 62 − 276,665 grt)

NAVAL AVIATION: Made up of ship-based helicopters on ASW helicopter destroyers (DDH), maritime patrol aircraft, and ASW aircraft, formerly carrier-based but now maintained at land bases.

Identifying letters are as follows: HS (ASW helicopter), HU (supply helicopter), VS (ASW plane), MP (maritime patrol plane), VU (supply plane), VS (experimental plane).

Primary strength as follows:

−32 ASW CHSS 2 (CH-124) Sea King helicopters (*see* U.S.A. section). These helicopters are armed with Mk 44 or Mk 46 torpedoes and sensors (AQS 13 sonar, for example) and are used to search for hostile submarines. Upon landing, they are automatically secured and parked in the hangar, thanks to the ingenious Bear Trap recovery system. Several are used in logistics service aboard the three replenishment oilers.

−26 CS-2F (CP-107) ASW 2-engine Tracker aircraft (*see* U.S.A. section).
−16 4-engine CL-28 (CP-121) Argus aircraft.

The CL-28 Argus is an ASW plane with an extended flight radius. **Wingspan:** 43.50. **Length:** 39.20. **Weight:** 67 tons. **Engines:** 4 Wright, each of 3,700 hp. **Speed:** 250 knots. **Search speed:** 163 knots. **Endurance:** 20 hours. **Range:** 3,900 miles. **Ceiling:** 25,000 feet. Radar dome. Can carry mines, torpedoes, depth charges, including an atomic depth charge, and air-to-surface rockets.

As a follow-on for this plane, Canada signed a contract on 25-7-76 with Lockheed for the manufacture of 18 CP-140 Aurora maritime patrol aircraft based on the U.S. Navy's P-3 C Orion. The first plane flew on 22-3-79 but was to undergo tests and be delivered during 5-80 with the second and third; all were to arrive by 3-81. The Canadian version of the plane will differ considerably from the American P-3. It will be fitted not only for reconnaissance, ASW, and electronic warfare, but for detecting atmospheric and maritime pollution and for analyzing oil spills at sea. It will have a crew of twelve.

The Aurora will, of course, be given the Orion's A-NEW system based on the miniaturized computer Univac ASQ 114, which can store 65,000 words of 30 bits and has a retrieval time of 4 microseconds. This equipment integrates all the ASW information put into it. It has 36 launching chutes for dropping active and passive sonobuoys and can carry racks for 120 reserve sonobuoys in the rear of the fuselage. It will carry ASW torpedoes or depth charges or a combination of these weapons. Its other principal systems will be:

2 ASN-84 inertial navigation computers
1 Doppler radar
1 tactical recorder flight-control director
1 tactical data link system
1 FLIR (Forward-Looking Infrared)
SLAR (Side-Looking Airborne Radar) antennas
Detectors for lasers
A low-light television pod

WARSHIPS IN SERVICE OR UNDER CONSTRUCTION AS OF 1 JANUARY 1980

	L	Tons (Surfaced)	Main armament
◆ **3 submarines**			
3 Ojibwa	1962-65	2,070	8/533-mm TT
◆ **4 destroyers**		Tons	
4 Iroquois	1970-71	3,551	1/127-mm DP, 2 Can. Sea Sparrow, ASW weapons, 2 Sea King helicopters
◆ **16 frigates**			
2 Annapolis	1961-63	2,400	4/76-mm DP, ASW weapons, 1 Sea King helicopter
4 Mackenzie	1961-62	2,380	4/76-mm DP, ASW weapons
4 Restigouche	1954-57	2,390	2/76-mm DP, Asroc, other ASW weapons
6 St. Laurent	1952-56	2,260	2/76-mm DP, ASW weapons, 1 Sea King helicopter

WEAPONS AND SYSTEMS

A. MISSILES

◆ **Surface-to-air missiles.** The Canadian Navy has adopted the short-range surface-to-air NATO Sea Sparrow for its four *Iroquois*-class destroyers. The missile is designed to attack aircraft or missiles flying at a low altitude or at a transonic speed. Its characteristics are:

Length: 3.660 m. **Diameter:** 0.200 m. **Wingspan:** 1.020 m. **Weight:** 204 kg. **Speed:** Mach 3.5. **Practical antiaircraft range:** 8,000 to 10,000 m.

Its GMLS launching system, designed by Raytheon Canada, is made up of two loaders and two launchers. The launchers are fixed one to port and one to starboard, perpendicular to the axis of the ship. They are retractable, can be trained and elevated, and are housed in the structure forward of the bridge. Each launcher has four missiles ready to be fired.

B. GUNS

The following guns are currently in use:

76-mm Mk 22. Twin DP (U.S. Mk 34 mount) mounted behind a plastic spray shield.
Length: 50 calibers. **Muzzle velocity:** 822 m/s.
Maximum firing rate: 50 rounds per minute per barrel. **Arc of elevation:** 15° to +85°.
Maximum effective antiaircraft range: 4,000 to 5,000 m.
Fitted on the *St. Laurent, Restigouche, Mackenzie,* and *Annapolis* classes of frigates.

76-mm Mk. 6. Twin barrel, automatic (British model).
Length: 70 calibers. **Muzzle velocity:** . . . m/s. **Maximum firing rate:** 60 pounds per minute per barrel.
Maximum effective antiaircraft range: 5,000 m.
Installed forward on the *Restigouche* and *Mackenzie* classes of frigates.

127-mm OTO-Melara (*see* Italy section)
Installed on the *Iroquois*-class destroyers.

C. ASW WEAPONS

◆ **Depth-charge and torpedo launchers**

— British Mk 10 Limbo triple-barreled mortar on all destroyers and frigates
— U.S. Asroc on 4 *Restigouche*-class frigates
— U.S. Mk 32 ASW torpedo tubes on all destroyers and 12 frigates
— ASW torpedo side-throwers on 4 training frigates

◆ **Torpedoes**

— U.S. Mk 43, 44, and 46 ASW torpedoes aboard ships, and the latter two aboard Sea King helicopters and maritime patrol aircraft
— U.S. Mk 37 and British Mk 8 aboard submarines

D. ELECTRONICS

◆ **Radars:**
— SPS 12 long-range air search.
— SPS 501 long-range air search (version of Dutch LWO-2) installed in *Iroquois*-class destroyers.
— SPS 10 and Sperry Mk 2 navigation/surface search.
— SPQ 2 D combination search (Italian radar) installed in the *Iroquois* class.

◆ **Sonars:**
— SQS 501 for detection of submarines lying on the sea bottom.
— SQS 503 hull MF.
— SQS 504 towed MF, Type 503 transducer.
— SQS 505 hull LF installed in the *Iroquois* class.
— SQS 505 towed LF installed in the *Iroquois* class (SQA-502 hoist).

SUBMARINES

◆ **3 Ojibwa class**

	Bldr	Laid down	L	In serv.
SS 72 OJIBWA	H.M. DY, Chatham	9-62	29-2-64	23-9-65
SS 73 ONANDAGA	H.M. DY, Chatham	6-64	25-9-65	22-6-67
SS 74 OKANAGAN	H.M. DY, Chatham	3-65	17-9-66	22-6-68

Okanagan—pendant number no longer displayed   1970

Ojibwa

D: 1,610 tons standard, 2,070 surfaced, 2,410 submerged
Dim: 89.9 (87.45 pp) × 8.07 × 5.48   **S:** 17.5/15 kts
A: 8/533-mm TT (6 fwd, 2 aft)—22 torpedoes   **Man:** 6 officers, 59 men
Electron Equipt: Radar: 1/1006
            Sonars: 1/2007, 1/187, 1/197, 1/719
M: 2 Admiralty Standard Range 16VVS-AS21 diesels; diesel-electric drive; 2 props; 6,000 hp

REMARKS: Same basic characteristics as the British *Oberon* class. The *Ojibwa* was begun under the name of "Onyx" for the Royal Navy and transferred while still under construction. The living spaces have been modified for Canadian weather conditions.

DESTROYERS

◆ **4 Iroquois class**

	Bldr	Laid down	L	In serv.
280 IROQUOIS	Marine Industries, Sorel	1-69	28-11-70	7-72
281 HURON	Marine Industries, Sorel	1-69	3-4-71	12-72
282 ATHABASCAN	Davie S.B., Lauzon	6-69	27-11-70	11-72
283 ALGONQUIN	Davie S.B., Lauzon	9-69	23-4-71	9-73

DESTROYERS (continued)

Huron G. Arra, 1977

Huron G. Arra, 1977

D: 3,551 tons (4,200 fl) **S:** 30/29 kts
Dim: 128.92 (121.31 pp) × 15.24 × 4.42
Man: 27 officers, 258 men **Range:** 4,500/20
A: 2 Canadian Sea Sparrow systems – 1/127-mm DP – 1 Mk 10 Limbo mortar – 6 Mk 32 TT (III × 2) – 2 Sea King ASW helicopters – 1 multiple flare and chaff launcher
Electron Equipt: Radars: 1/SPS 502, 1/SPQ 2D, 2/WM 22 directors, TACAN
   Sonars: 1/SQS 505 (hull), 1/SQS 505 (towed), 1/SQS 501 (bottomed target)
M: COGOG propulsion: 2 Mk FT 4A2 Pratt & Whitney gas turbines, 25,000 hp each, and, for a cruising speed of 18 kts, 2 Mk FT 12H solar gas-turbine generators, 33,700 hp each; 2 five-bladed, reversible-pitch props **Electric:** 2,750 kw

Huron G. Arra, 1977

DESTROYERS (*continued*)

REMARKS: Two paired stacks, angled to avoid corrosion of the antennas by stack gases. Bear Trap positive-control helicopter landing system. Passive-tank anti-rolling system fitted to improve stability at low speeds.

FRIGATES

◆ 6 new construction

A first increment of six gas-turbine frigates is to be ordered in 1980 to begin replacement of the sixteen old frigates still in service. Characteristics are as yet by no means firm, but the ships should displace between 3,500 and 4,200 tons (fl) and will carry a Sea King helicopter, one OTO Melara 76-mm gun, Sea Sparrow and Harpoon missiles, and two triple Mk 32 ASW TT. The first should be completed in 1985 and the sixth in 1989.

◆ 2 Annapolis class

	Bldr	Laid down	L	In serv.
265 ANNAPOLIS	Halifax Shipyards Ltd	7-60	27-4-63	19-12-64
266 NIPIGON	Marine Industries, Sorel	4-60	10-12-61	30-5-64

Annapolis 1970

D: 2,400 tons (3,000 fl)   **S:** 28 kts   **Dim:** 113.1 × 12.8 × 4.4
Man: 18 officers, 210 men   **Range:** 4,750/14
A: 2/76-mm DP Mk 22 (II × 1)−1 Mk 10 Limbo mortar−6/324-mm ASW TT (III × 2) −1 Sea King helicopter
Electron Equipt: Radars: 1/SPS 12, 1/SPS 10, 1/Sperry Mk 2, Mk 48 fire-control, TACAN
Sonars: 1/SQS 503, 1/SQS 504, 1/SQS 501
M: English-Electric GT; 2 props; 30,000 hp   **Boilers:** 2 Babcock & Wilcox
Electric: 1,400 kw

◆ 4 Mackenzie-class training frigates

	Bldr	Laid down	L	In serv.
261 MACKENZIE	Canadian-Vickers	10-58	25-5-61	10-62
262 SASKATCHEWAN	Victoria Machinery	8-59	1-2-61	2-63
263 YUKON	Burrard, Vancouver	10-59	27-7-61	5-63
264 QU'APPELLE	Davie S.B., Lauzon	1-60	2-5-62	9-63

Saskatchewan G. Arra, 1977

Yukon G. Arra, 1977

D: 2,380 tons (2,890 fl)   **S:** 28 kts   **Dim:** 111.5 × 12.8 × 4.1
Man: 11 officers, 199 men   **Range:** 4,750/14
A: 4/76-mm DP (II × 1 Mk 22, II × 1 Mk 6)−2 Mk 10 Limbo mortars−2 ASW TT
Electron Equipt: Radars: 1/SPS 12, 1/SPS 10, 1/Sperry Mk 2, 1/SPG 48, 1/SPG 34
Sonars: 1/SQS 503, 1/SQS 501
M: English-Electric GT; 2 props; 30,000 hp   **Boilers:** 2 Babcock & Wilcox
Electric: 1,400 kw

REMARKS: All employed in the Pacific. U.S. Mk 69 gunfire-control forward, Mk 63 aft.

◆ 4 modified Restigouche-class ASW frigates

	Bldr	Laid down	L	In serv.
236 GATINEAU	Davie SB, Lauzon	4-53	3-6-57	2-59
257 RESTIGOUCHE	Canadian-Vickers	7-53	22-11-54	6-58
258 KOOTENAY	Burrard, Vancouver	8-52	15-6-54	3-59
259 TERRA NOVA	Victoria Machinery	6-53	21-6-55	6-59

FRIGATES (continued)

D: 2,390 tons (2,900 fl)   **S:** 28 kts   **Dim:** 113.1 × 12.8 × 4.3
Man: 13 officers, 201 men   **Range:** 4,750/14
A: 2/76-mm DP Mk 6 (II × 1) fwd — 1 Asroc system — 1 Mk 10 Limbo mortar — multiple flare and chaff launcher
Electron Equipt: Radars: 1/SPS 12, 1/SPS 10, 1/Sperry Mk 2, 1/SPG 48 fire-control
               Sonars: 1/SQS 501, 1/SQS 503, 1/SQS-505 (VDS)
M: English-Electric GT; 2 props; 30,000 hp   **Boilers:** 2 Babcock & Wilcox
Electric: 1,400 kw

Restigouche   1973

Gatineau   1972

REMARKS: Reconstruction with lengthened hull for VDS and Asroc in place of aft 76-mm mount and one Limbo completed 1968-73. U.S. Mk 69 fire-control system. Unmodified sisters *Chaudière*, *Columbia*, and *St. Croix* were reduced to disposal reserve in 1974.

◆ **6 St. Laurent-class helicopter frigates**

		Bldr	Laid down	L	In serv.
206	SAGUENAY	Halifax Shipyards	4-51	30-7-53	12-56
207	SKEENA	Burrard, Vancouver	6-51	19-8-52	3-57
229	OTTAWA	Canadian-Vickers	6-51	29-4-53	11-56
230	MARGAREE	Halifax Shipyards	9-51	29-3-56	10-57
233	FRASER	Burrard, Vancouver	12-51	19-2-53	6-57
234	ASSINIBOINE	Marine Industries, Sorel	5-52	12-2-54	8-56

Margaree — now has TACAN   J. Jedrlinic, 1974

D: 2,260 tons (2,860 fl)   **S:** 28 kts   **Dim:** 111.5 × 12.8 × 4.2
Man: 18 officers, 210 men   **Range:** 4,750/14
A: 2/76-mm DP Mk 22 — Mk 10 Limbo mortar — 6/324-mm Mk 32 ASW TT (III × 2) — 1 Sea King helicopter
Electron Equipt: Radars: 1/SPS 12, 1/SPS 10, 1/Sperry Mk 2, 1/SPG 48
               Sonars: 1/SQS 503, 1/SQS 501, 1/SQS 504
M: English-Electric GT; 2 props; 30,000 hp   **Boilers:** 2 Babcock & Wilcox
Electric: 1,400 kw

Assiniboine   1977

FRIGATES (continued)

Skeena

REMARKS: The *St. Laurent*, 205, was taken out of service in 1974. The *Fraser*, which was completed by Yarrow, Ltd., has a lattice mast between her funnels to support a TACAN dome; the others carry their TACAN atop a pole mast. Nos. 207, 229, and 233 given major overhauls 1977-78.

SUBMARINE CHASER

◆ **1 experimental hydrofoil ship**

	Bldr	L	Trials
FHE 400 BRAS D'OR	Marine Industries, Sorel	7-68	1969

(FHE—fast hydrofoil escort)

D: 237.5 tons (fl) **Dim:** (hull) 46.0 × 6.55 × 5.08 (cruising)
S: 50/60 kts in calm seas **Man:** 17 men
A: 12 ASW TT (III × 4) two groups each side, not mounted
M: Pratt and Whitney Mk FT 4 A gas turbine; 22,000 hp

REMARKS: Outboard length of lifting foils: 27.43 m. Draft: hullborne, 7.21, foilborne: 1.32. At 15 knots cruising speed, a Davey-Paxman diesel (2,000 hp) drives 2 controllable-pitch props. After experiments, this ship was placed in reserve in 1971; she remains stored on land.

OCEANOGRAPHIC AND HYDROGRAPHIC SHIPS

	Bldr	Laid down	L	In serv.
AGOR 172 QUEST	Burrard DD, Vancouver	1967	9-7-68	8-69

D: 2,130 tons **S:** 15 kts **Dim:** 77.2 (71.62 pp) × 12.8 × 4.6
Man: 37 men **Range:** 10,000/12

REMARKS: A modification of the *Endeavour* (AGOR-171) with the same machinery. Can carry a Bell UH-1B helicopter. *See* remarks on the *Endeavour*.

	Bldr	L	In serv.
AGOR 171 ENDEAVOUR	Yarrow, Ltd., Victoria	17-8-61	2-65

D: 1,560 tons **S:** 16 kts **Dim:** 71.85 (65.53 wl) × 11.73 × 4.0
Man: 37 crew plus 14 scientists **Range:** 10,000/12
M: Fairbanks-Morse 38D8 1/8 9-cylinder diesels/GE electric drive; 2 props; 2,960 hp

Quest 1970

Endeavour 1970

REMARKS (for both ships): Reinforced hulls for navigation in icefields. Excellent loading equipment, 5- and 9-ton cranes. Bulb-shaped stems. Anti-rolling and anti-pitching devices. Civilian crews.

AGOR 114 BLUETHROAT

Bluethroat 1969

OCEANOGRAPHIC AND HYDROGRAPHIC SHIPS *(continued)*

D: 785 tons (870 fl) **S:** 13 kts **Dim:** 47.0 × 9.9 × 3.0
M: Diesel; 2 props; 1,200 hp **Man:** 27 men

REMARK: Former cable ship and minelayer, launched in 1955.

AGOR 140 FORT STEELE

D: 85 tons **S:** 18 kts **Dim:** 36.0 × 6.4 × 2.1
M: 2 Paxman Ventura diesels; 2 props; 2,800 hp

REMARKS: Built by Canadian Shipbuilding Co. and launched in 1955. Primarily used as a naval reserve training craft.

DEEP SUBMERGENCE EXPERIMENTAL SHIP

ASXL 20 CORMORANT (ex-*Aspa Quarto*)

Reconstructed by Davie SB, Lauzon In serv. 10-11-78

D: 2,350 tons (fl) **S:** 14 kts **Dim:** 74.6 (72.0 pp) × 11.9 × 5.0
Man: 9 officers, 53 men
M: 3 Deutz diesels, electric drive; 1 controllable-pitch prop, 2,100 hp

REMARKS: Ex-Italian stern-haul trawler bought in 1975 and adapted to handle and service the SDL-1 submersible, which can dive to 600 m. A large hangar for SDL-2 and a gallows crane have been built on the stern. The ship can also support conventional and saturation divers and has extensive compressor facilities, decompression chambers, etc.

REPLENISHMENT OILERS

◆ **2 Protecteur-class multi-purpose supply ships**

	Bldr	Laid down	L	In serv.
AOR 509 PROTECTEUR	St. John SB & DD (NB)	10-67	18-7-68	6-69
AOR 510 PRESERVER	St. John SB & DD (NB)	8-67	20-5-69	9-70

D: 9,000 tons (24,000 fl) **S:** 20 kts **Dim:** 172.0 (166.42 pp) × 23.16 × 9.15
Man: 15 officers, 212 men, 57 passengers **Range:** 7,500/11.5
A: 2/76-mm DP Mk 33 (II × 1)
Electron Equipt: Radars: 1/Sperry Mk 2, 1/Decca TM 969, TACAN
M: Canadian GE GT; 1 prop; 21,000 hp **Boilers:** 2 **Electric:** 3,500 kw
Cargo capacity: 13,250 tons, with 12,000 tons of distillate fuel, 600 tons of diesel oil, 400 tons of jet fuel, frozen and dry foods, spare parts, munitions, etc.

Preserver 1973

REMARKS: Flight deck, hangar space, and repair facilities for three Sea King helicopters. Four replenishment-at-sea stations, one elevator aft of the navigation bridge, two 15-ton cranes on the afterdeck. One bow-thruster. Daily fresh-water distillation capacity is 80 tons. Sea Sparrow SAM was to replace the 76-mm, but never fitted. The gun mount is precariously situated in the eyes of the ship and has been washed away several times; fire control is local. Can be used to carry military vehicles and troops for commando purposes. Carry four LCVPs.

◆ **1 Provider-class multi-purpose supply ship**

	Bldr	Laid down	L	In serv.
AOR 508 PROVIDER	Davie SB, Lauzon	6-61	5-7-62	9-63

Provider

D: 7,300 tons (22,000 fl) **S:** 20 kts **Dim:** 168.0 (159.4 pp) × 23.17 × 9.15
Man: 15 officers, 151 men **Range:** 5,000/20
M: GT; 1 prop; 21,000 hp **Boilers:** 2 Electric: 2,140 kw **Fuel:** 1,200 tons

REMARKS: Platform and hangar for two Sea King helicopters. Can carry 12,000 tons of distillate fuel, 1,200 tons of diesel, 1,000 tons of aviation gas, 250 tons of provisions, munitions, and various spare parts.

SMALL OILERS

AOTL 501 DUNDALK AOTL 502 DUNDURN

D: 950 tons **S:** 10 kts **Dim:** 54.5 × 9.8 × 3.9
M: 1 diesel; 700 hp

Dundalk 1969

REPAIR SHIP

ARE 101 CAPE SCOTT (ex-*Beachy Head*) Bldr: Burrard DD, Vancouver

Cape Scott

D: 8,450 tons (11,270 fl)   **S:** 11 kts   **Dim:** 133.8 × 18.88 × 8.84
M: GT; 2,500 hp   **Boilers:** 2 Foster-Wheeler

REMARKS: Launched in 1944 and purchased from the Royal Navy in 1951. Refitted 1958-59. Equipped for pierside service at Esquimault and not expected ever to steam again. Sister *Cape Breton* (ARE-100) discarded in 1977.

RESERVE TRAINING SHIPS AND CRAFT

NOTE: In addition to the ships and craft listed below, the four obsolescent *Mackenzie*-class frigates are used exclusively for training. The units below retain hull numbers associated with their former function.

◆ **6 Bay class**

	Bldr	Laid down	L	In serv.
PFL 159 FUNDY	Davie S.B., Lauzon	3-55	14-6-56	11-56
PFL 160 CHIGNECTO	Davie S.B., Lauzon	10-55	26-2-57	8-57
PFL 161 THUNDER	Port Arthur S.B., Ont.	9-55	27-10-56	10-57
PFL 162 COWICHAN	Yarrows Ltd., Victoria	7-56	26-2-57	12-57
PFL 163 MIRAMICHI	Victoria Machinery	2-56	22-2-57	10-57
PFL 164 CHALEUR	Marine Industries, Sorel	2-56	17-11-56	9-57

Cowichan   1969

D: 370 tons (415 fl)   **S:** 15 kts   **Dim:** 50.0 (46.05 pp) × 9.21 × 2.8
Man: 3 officers, 35 men   **Range:** 4,500/11   **Fuel:** 52 tons diesel
M: GM diesels; 2 props; 2,500 hp

REMARKS: Former minesweepers, reclassified as patrol escorts in 1972 and used for training reserve personnel. They took the names of minesweepers transferred to France in 1954. The *Gaspé* (143), *Comox* (146), *Ungava* (148), and *Trinity* (157) were transferred to Turkey in 1958. Hull of composite construction. One 40-mm AA removed.

◆ **5 Porte class**

YMG 180 PORTE ST. JEAN	YMG 185 PORTE QUEBEC
YMG 183 PORTE ST. LOUIS	YMG 186 PORTE DAUPHINE
YMG 184 PORTE DE LA REINE	

D: 300 tons (429 fl)   **S:** 11 kts   **Dim:** 38.0 × 8.5 × 3.9
M: Diesel-electric; 1 prop; 600 hp   **Man:** 3 officers, 20 men

REMARKS: Launched 1950-52. Trawlerlike profile. Built as auxiliary minesweepers and net tenders.

◆ **5 former Mounted Police patrol craft**

PB 191 ADVERSUS	PB 193 CAPTOR	PB 195 SIDNEY
PB 192 DETECTOR	PB 194 ACADIAN	

D: 48 tons   **S:** 12 kts   **Dim:** 19.8 × 4.6 × 1.2
M: 1 Cummins diesel; 200 hp

◆ **1 former Mounted Police patrol craft**

PB 196 NICHOLSON Blt: 1967

D: 85 tons   **S:** 18 kts   **Dim:** 36.0 × 6.4 × 2.1   **Man:** 18 men
M: 2 Paxman YJCM diesels; 2 controllable-pitch props; 2,800 hp

◆ **5 Ville-class former tugs** Bldr: Russell Bros., 1944

YTL 582 BURRARD	YTL 587 PLAINSVILLE	YTL 589 LOGANVILLE
YTL 586 QUEENSVILLE	YTL 588 YOUVILLE	

D: 25 tons   **S:** . . .   **Dim:** 12.2 × 3.2 × 1.5
M: 1 diesel; 150 hp

◆ **3 miscellaneous reserve training craft**

YAG 116 (18 tons)	YFL 104 (12 tons)	YDT 2 (70 tons)

TUGS

◆ **2 Saint class** Bldr: St. John DD In serv. 1957

ATA 531 SAINT ANTHONY	ATA 532 SAINT CHARLES

D: 600 tons (840 fl)   **S:** 14 kts   **Dim:** 46.2 × 10.0 × 5.2
M: 1 diesel; 1 prop; 1,920 hp

◆ **5 Glen class** Blt: 1975-77

YTB 640 GLENDYNE	YTB 642 GLENEVIS	YTB 644 GLENSIDE
YTB 641 GLENDALE	YTB 643 GLENBROOK	

D: 255 tons (3,997 fl)   **S:** 11.5 kts   **Dim:** 28.2 × 8.5 × 4.4
M: 2 Ruston AP-3 diesels; 2 vertical cycloidal props; 900 hp   **Man:** 6 men

TUGS *(continued)*

◆ **5 new Ville class** Blt: 1974

YTL 590 LAWRENCEVILLE YTL 592 LISTERVILLE YTL 594 MARYSVILLE
YTL 591 PARKSVILLE YTL 593 MERRICKVILLE

> **D:** 70 tons (fl) **S:** 9.8 kts **Dim:** 19.5 × 4.7 × 2.7
> **M:** 1 diesel; 365 hp **Man:** 3 men

◆ **2 Wood class** Blt: 1944

YTL 550 EASTWOOD YTL 553 WILDWOOD

> **D:** 65 tons (fl) **S:** 10 kts **Dim:** 18.3 × 4.9 × 1.5
> **M:** 1 diesel; 250 hp **Man:** 3 men

DIVING TENDERS

◆ **3 steel-hulled** Bldr: Ferguson, Pictou, N.S., 1962-63

YDT 10 YDT 11 YDT 12

> **D:** 70 tons (132 fl) **S:** 11 kts **Dim:** 38.3 × 8.0 × . . .
> **M:** 1 GM 6-71 diesel; 228 hp

◆ **3 miscellaneous 70-ton**

YDT 6, YDT 8 YDT 9

FIREBOATS

◆ **2 130-ton**

YTR 561 FIREBIRD YTR 562 FIREBRAND

◆ **2 48-ton**

YTR 556 FIRE TUG 1 YTR 557 FIRE TUG 2

TORPEDO RETRIEVERS

◆ **4 miscellaneous**

YPT SONGHEE YPT 4 YPT 120 NIMPKISH YPT 532

MISCELLANEOUS SERVICE CRAFT

◆ approximately 12 self-propelled units in the categories of fuel-oil lighter, water tanker, degaussing tender, water tender, floating crane, etc., plus a number of non-self-propelled cargo and fuel barges, power barges, sludge-removal craft, etc.

COAST GUARD

The Canadian Coast Guard is a civilian organization in the Federal Transportation Ministry. It mans some 150 ships, including two weather-station cutters, 20 icebreakers, and about 30 helicopters.

◆ **weather ships for Pacific Ocean service** Bldr: Burrard DD, Vancouver

QUADRA (4-7-66) VANCOUVER (29-6-65)

> **D:** 5,600 tons (fl) **S:** 18 kts **Dim:** 121.0 × 15.5 × 5.3
> **Man:** 96 men **Range:** 8,400/14
> **M:** Turbo-electric propulsion; 2 props; 7,500 hp **Boilers:** 2 Babcock

REMARKS: Have a telescoping hangar and are equipped with fin-stabilizers.

Quadra 1969

ICEBREAKERS

◆ **1 new construction** (proposed)

> **D:** 33,000 tons (fl) **S:** 20 kts **Dim:** 192.0 × 32.3 × 12.2
> **Man:** 118 men plus 56 cadets
> **M:** CODAG; electric drive; 90,000 hp **Range:** 20,000/15

REMARKS: This project remains under discussion, as does an even more powerful design with nuclear propulsion.

◆ **2 R-class new construction** Bldr: Burrards, Vancouver

	L	In serv.
PIERRE RADISSON	3-6-77	1978
FRANKLIN	10-3-78	1980

Pierre Radisson 1977

> **D:** 8,180 tons (fl) **S:** 13.5 kts **Dim:** 98.15 (87.9 pp) × 19.5 × 9.91
> **Man:** 75 men **Range:** 15,000/13.5 **Fuel:** 2,240 tons
> **M:** Diesel-electric: 6 Montreal Loco MLW 251V-16F diesels (17,580 hp total); 6 G.E.C. alternators (11,100 kw); 2 G.E.C. motors; 2 props; 13,600 hp

ICEBREAKERS (*continued*)

REMARKS: Telescopic hangar and flight deck for one Bell-212 helicopter. Passive-tank stabilization. Will be used on St. Lawrence River and Great Lakes in winter, in Arctic in summer.

NORMAN MCLEOD ROGERS   Bldr: Vickers, Montreal, 1969

Norman McLeod Rogers   1970

D: 6,320 tons (fl)   S: 15 kts   **Dim:** 90.0 × 19.5 × 6.1
M: CODAG: 4 diesels, 2 GT; electric drive; 2 props; 12,000 hp

REMARKS: Also navigation tender. One helicopter.

LOUIS S. ST. LAURENT   Bldr: Vickers, Montreal, 1966

Louis S. St. Laurent   1970

D: 13,000 tons (fl)   S; 17.5 kts   **Dim:** 111.8 × 24.39 × 9.45
M: Turbo-electric propulsion; 3 props; 24,000 hp   **Range:** 16,000/13

REMARKS: Quarters for 216 men. Two helicopters.

JOHN CABOT   Bldr: Vickers, Montreal, 1965

John Cabot   1969

D: 6,375 tons (fl)   S: 15 kts   **Dim:** 94.0 × 18.0 × 6.45
Range: 10,000/12   **Man:** 85 men
M: Diesel-electric propulsion: 9,000 hp

REMARKS: Equipped as a cable-layer and repair ship also. Occasionally chartered by the U.S. Navy.

JOHN A. MACDONALD   Bldr: Davie SB, Lauzon, 1959

D: 9.160 tons (fl)   S: 15.5 kts   **Dim:** 96.0 × 21.3 × 8.55
M: Diesel-electric propulsion; 15,000 hp

REMARK: One helicopter.

MONTCALM (1957)   WOLFE (1959)

D: 3,005 tons (fl)   S: 13 kts   **Dim:** 72.7 × 14.6 × 4.9
M: Reciprocating steam; 2 boilers; 2 props; 4,000 hp

REMARK: One helicopter.

LABRADOR

D: 6,490 tons (fl)   S: 16 kts   **Dim:** 88.5 × 19.4 × 8.8
M: 6 diesels, electric drive; 2 props; 10,000 hp

REMARKS: Built 1954 and transferred from Royal Canadian Navy 1958. Patterned after U.S. Coast Guard *Wind* class. Two helicopters.

D'IBERVILLE (1953)

D: 9,930 tons (fl)   S: 15 kts   **Dim:** 94.6 × 20.3 × 9.2
M: Reciprocating steam; 2 props; 10,800 hp

REMARK: One helicopter.

VARIOUS SHIPS

◆ **27 navigation tenders**   Most also icebreakers

	In serv.	D	hp
NAMAO	1975	370 tons (fl)	1,350
GRIFFON	1970	3,096 tons (fl)	4,000
BARTLETT	1970	1,620 tons (fl)	1,760
PROVO WALLIS	1970	1,620 tons (fl)	1,760
ROBERT FOULIS	1969	260 tons (fl)	960
TRACY	1968	1,300 tons (fl)	2,000
J. E. BERNIER	1967	3,096 tons (fl)	4,250
NARWHAL	1963	2,064 grt	2,000
MONTMAGNY	1963	565 tons (fl)	1,000
SIMCOE	1962	1,300 tons (fl)	2,000
THOMAS CARLETON	1960	1,532 tons (fl)	2,000
SIMON FRASER	1960	1,876 tons (fl)	2,900
TUPPER	1959	1,876 tons (fl)	2,900
SIR WM. ALEXANDER	1959	3,565 tons (fl)	4,250
CAMSELL	1959	3,072 tons (fl)	4,250
SIR H. GILBERT	1959	3,000 tons (fl)	4,250
ALEXANDER HENRY	1959	2,497 tons (fl)	3,550
VERENDRYE	1959	400 tons (fl)	760
MONTMORENCY	1957	1,006 tons (fl)	1,200
SIR JAS. DOUGLAS	1956	720 tons (fl)	1,000
WALTER E. FOSTER	1954	2,715 tons (fl)	2,000
ALEX. MACKENZIE	1950	720 tons (fl)	1,000
EDWARD CORNWALLIS	1949	3,700 tons (fl)	2,800
ERNEST LAPOINTE	1941	1,675 tons (fl)	2,000
N. B. MCLEAN	1930	5,034 tons (fl)	6,500
NOKOMIS	—	64 tons (fl)	120
KENOKI	—	270 tons (fl)	940

◆ **1 fisheries-protection cutter**

CAPE RODGERS   Bldr: Ferguson, Pictou, N.S., 1976

   D: 1,400 tons   **S:** 16.5 kts   **Dim:** 62.5 × 12.2 × 4.1
   M: 2 diesels; 1 prop; 2,200 hp   **Range:** 7,000/13   **Man:** 42 men

◆ **1 offshore-patrol cutter**

ALBERT   Bldr: Davie SB, Lauzon, 1969

   D: 2,025 tons (fl)   **S:** 18.8 kts   **Dim:** 71.5 × 12.2 × 4.6
   M: Diesel-electric; 2 props; 7,716 hp   **Range:** 6,000/15

REMARKS: One helicopter. Was to have been prototype for a class. Icebreaking bow.

◆ **1 offshore-patrol cutter**

DARING (ex-*Wood*) (1958)

   D: 600 tons (780 fl)   **S:** 16 kts   **Dim:** 54.3 × 8.8 × 3.0
   M: 2 Fairbanks-Morse diesels; 2 props; 2,660 hp

REMARK: Transferred to Coast Guard 1971.

◆ **3 Cape-class patrol boats**   Bldr: Breton Industrial & Marine, Part Hawkesbury

CAPE HARRISON (1977)

CAPE LOUISBURG (1978)

N . . . (1979)

   D: 120 tons   **S:** 20 kts   **Dim:** 38.1 (36.6 pp) × . . . × 2.5
   M: 2 MTU 12V538 TB91 diesels; 2 props; 4,500 hp

◆ **6 Racer-class patrol boats**   Bldrs: Various, all 1963

RACER	RAPID	RELAY
RALLY	READY	RIDER

Rapid   1969

   D: 153 grt   **S:** 20 kts   **Dim:** 29.0 × 6.1 × 2.0
   M: 4 Cummins diesels; 2 props; 2,400 hp

REMARK: Patterned after U.S. Coast Guard Cape class.

SPINDRIFT   SPRAY   SPUME (1963-64)

   D: 57 grt   **S:** 19 kts   **Dim:** 21.4 × 5.1 × 1.4
   M: 2 Paxman diesels; 2 props; 1,050 hp

◆ **14 motor rescue lifeboats**

CG 101-109   CG 114-118

REMARK: Patterned after U.S.C.G. craft. 18 tons.

◆ **4 hydrographic survey and sounding vessels**

BEAUPORT (1960)

   D: 767 tons (fl)   **S:** 16 kts   **Dim:** 51.1 × 7.3 × 2.7
   M: Diesels; 1,300 hp

DETECTOR

   D: 584 tons (fl)   **S:** 14 kts   **Dim:** 42.7 × 10.7 × 3.1
   M: Reciprocating steam

CANADA (*continued*)

VARIOUS SHIPS (*continued*)

NICOLET

    D: 935 tons (fl)   **S:** 16 kts   **Dim:** 58.0 × 10.7 × 2.9
    M: Diesels; 1,350 hp

VILLE MARIE

    D: 493 tons (fl)   **S:** 18 kts   **Dim:** 48.9 × 8.5 × 2.9
    M: Diesel-electric; 1,000 hp

◆ **2 cargo ships for northern supply**

EIDER   SKUA (1946)

    D: 1,100 grt   **S:** 9 kts   **Dim:** 70.5 × 11.6 × 2.1
    M: 2 diesels; 2 props; 1,000 hp

REMARK: Former British LCT-8s, bought 1957, 1961.

◆ **5 river tenders**

DUMIT   ECKALOO   MISKANAW   TEMBAH   NAHIDIK

◆ **2 training ships**

MIKULA **D:** 617 tons (fl)—former lightship
SKIDEGATE **D:** 200 tons (fl)—former navigation tender

ROYAL CANADIAN MOUNTED POLICE

About 30 small patrol craft. Most larger units transferred to the Ministry of Defense, 1975-76.

CAPE VERDE ISLANDS

PERSONNEL: . . .

PATROL BOATS

◆ **2 Soviet Shershen class**

    D: 180 tons (fl)   **S:** 45 kts   **Dim:** 34.0 × 7.2 × 1.5
    A: 4/30-mm AA (II × 2)   **Range:** 450/34, 700/20
    M: 3 M503A diesels; 3 props; 12,000 hp

REMARK: Transferred 1979.

CHILE

PERSONNEL: 23,000 men, including 3,680 Marines and 1,320 officers. Civil Service personnel with a more or less military status number about 6,600.

MERCHANT MARINE (1978): 146 ships—466,319 grt (tankers: 5—60,540 grt)

NAVAL AVIATION: Established in 1923, merged in 1930 with the aviation arm of the military, Fuerza Aera de Chile, and reestablished in 1953. However, its growth has been restrained by the Air Force, which retains responsibility for the airspace over the ocean. The naval air arm has 16 aircraft (8 Bandeirante maritime surveillance aircraft, 5 T-34B Mentor trainers, 3 C-47 transports) and 26 helicopters (10 Alouette III, 4 Bell Jetranger, 7 Bell 47-G, 3 Bell 47, 2 Bell 47-J). Six Casa-212 light transports were ordered from Spain in 1979. The principal air base is at El Belloto, near Valparaiso.

WARSHIPS IN SERVICE OR UNDER CONSTRUCTION AS OF 1 JANUARY 1980

	L	Tons (Surfaced)	Main armament
◆ **3 submarines**			
1 OBERON	1973	2,030	8/533-mm TT
1 BALAO	1944	1,810	10/533-mm TT
◆ **3 cruisers**		Tons	
1 TRE KRONOR	1944	8,200	7/152-mm AA, 4/57-mm AA, 6/533-mm TT
2 BROOKLYN	1936	9,700	15/152-mm, 8/127-mm
◆ **6 destroyers**			
2 ALMIRANTE WILLIAMS	1958	2,730	4/102-mm DP, 4 Exocet
2 ALLEN M. SUMNER	1944	2,200	6/127-mm DP
2 FLETCHER	1943	2,050	4/127-mm DP, 5/533-mm TT
◆ **3 frigates**			
2 LEANDER	1972-73	2,450	2/114-mm DP, 4 Exocet
1 CHARLES LAWRENCE	1943	1,400	1/127-mm DP
◆ **4 torpedo boats**	1965-66	134	2/40-mm AA, 4/533-mm TT

WEAPONS AND SYSTEMS

Most of the Chilean Navy's equipment is of U.S. or British origin. Among the most modern weapons are the guns of the cruiser *Almirante Latorre* and the *Almirante Williams*-class destroyers.

152-mm Bofors

This gun, which dates from 1942 and is mounted in twin- and triple-barreled turrets, is on the *Almirante Latorre*. Its characteristics are:

Muzzle velocity: 900m/sec
Arc: +70°
Maximum firing rate: 10 rounds/minute/barrel
Projectile: 46 kg
Maximum range, surface target: 26,000 m

WEAPONS AND SYSTEMS (*continued*)

Maximum range, surface target (effective): 15,000 m
Maximum range, air target (effective): 10,000 m

102-mm Vickers AA

This single-barreled automatic mount dates from 1955 and is not used by any other navy. It is on the *Almirante Riveros* and the *Almirante Williams*. Its characteristics are:

Turret weight: about 26 tons
Muzzle velocity: 900m/sec
Arc: +75°
Maximum firing rate: 40 rounds/minute
Projectile: 16 kg
Maximum range, surface target: 18,500 m
Maximum range, surface target (effective): 12,000 m
Maximum range, air target: 12,000 m
Maximum range, air target (effective): 8,000 m

Missiles

The Chilean Navy has adopted the French MM38 Exocet anti-ship system and the British Sea Cat short-range SAM.

SUBMARINES

◆ 2 British Oberon class

	Bldr	Laid down	L	In serv.
S 22 O'BRIEN	Scott Lithgow	1970	22-12-72	1976
S 23 HYATT	Scott Lithgow	1971	26-9-73	1977

O'Brien   G. Arra, 1977

D: 1,610 tons standard, 2,030 surfaced, 2,400 submerged   **S:** 17.5/15 kts
Dim: 89.92 (87.45 pp) × 8.07 × 5.48   **Man:** 65 men
A: 8/533-mm TT (6 fwd, 2 aft) — 22 torpedoes
M: 2 Admiralty Standard Range 16 VVS-AS21 diesels, diesel-electric drive; 2 props; 6,000 hp

REMARK: Delivery of these submarines was a year late because of a number of malfunctions in the electrical equipment.

◆ 1 U.S. Balao class

S 21 SIMPSON (ex-*Spot*, SS-413)   Bldr: Mare Island NSY, 1944

D: 1,526 tons light, 1,810 surfaced, 2,425 submerged
Dim: 95.02 × 8.34 × 5.18   **S:** 18.5 kts surfaced/10 submerged
A: 10/533-mm TT (6 fwd, 4 aft) — 22 torpedoes   **Man:** 80 men
M: 4 Fairbanks-Morse 38D81/8 diesels, 5,400 hp, electric drive; 2 props; 4,600 hp
Range: 12,000/13.5, 9,700/6.5 (snorkeling)

REMARKS: Transferred in 1961, the *Simpson* was decommissioned in 1975 but reactivated in 1977. She had a 127-mm deck gun as late as 1972. Streamlined, high, Guppytype sail. Sister *Thompson*, S-20, (ex-*Springer* SS-414) still exists as a training hulk.

CRUISERS

◆ 1 Swedish Tre Kronor class

	Bldr	Laid down	L	In serv.
04 ALMIRANTE LATORRE	Eriksberg	9-43	17-11-45	15-12-47
(ex-*Göta Lejon*)				

Almirante Latorre   1972

D: 8,200 tons (10,000 fl)   **S:** 33 kts   **Dim:** 182.0 (174.0 wl) × 16.5 × 6.5
Man: 26 officers, 429 men (peacetime), 30 officers, 618 men (wartime)
A: 7/152-mm AA (III × 1, II × 2) — 4/57-mm AA — 11/40-mm AA — 6/533-mm TT (III × 2) — 2 depth-charge racks — 120 mines
Electron Equipt: Radars: 1/LWO-3 (Dutch), 1/277 and 1/293 (British), Band I fire-control
Armor: Belt: 80-100   **Main deck:** 40-60
Turrets: 135 fwd, 30 sides, 50 top
M: De Laval GT; 2 props; 100,000 hp
Boilers: 4 Penhoët, 32 kg pressure, superheat to 375°C

REMARK: Purchased 7-71.

◆ 2 U.S. Brooklyn class

	Bldr	Laid down	L	In serv.
02 O'HIGGINS	New York NYD	12-3-35	30-11-36	18-7-38
(ex-*Brooklyn*, CL-40)				
03 PRAT	New York SB Corp	24-1-35	2-10-37	25-11-38
(ex-*Nashville*, CL-43)				

D: 02: 10,000 tons (13,500 fl) 03: 9,700 tons (13,000 fl)   **S:** 30/25 kts
Dim: 185,42 × 21.03 (03: 18.77) × 7.62   **Man:** 890/970 men
A: 15/152-mm (III × 5) — 8/127-mm (I × 8) — 28/40-mm AA (VI × 4, II × 2) — 12/20-mm AA (II × 6) — 1 SH-57A Jetranger helicopter
Electron Equipt: Radars: 1/SPS 6, 2/SPS 4, 2/Mk 8, 4/Mk 28
Armor: Belt: 76-127   Main deck: 76   Upper deck: 52   Turrets: 127
Range: 2,500/30, 9,850/12   **Fuel:** 2,377 tons

CRUISERS (continued)

Prat   1971

    M: Westinghouse GT; 4 props; 100,000 hp
    Boilers: 8 Babcock & Wilcox, 31 kg pressure

REMARKS: Bought 1951, refitted in U.S.A. 1957-58. *O'Higgins*, damaged in collision in 1974 and laid up as an accommodation hulk, was repaired and recommissioned in 1978. Both have two Mk 34 directors for 152-mm guns, two Mk 33 for 127-mm guns, and two Mk 57 and Mk 51 fire-control systems for 40-mm guns. *Prat* has bulges, *O'Higgins* does not.

DESTROYERS

◆ **2 Almirante Williams class**

	Bldr	Laid down	L	In serv.
D 18 ALMIRANTE RIVEROS	Vickers-Armstrong	12-4-57	12-12-58	31-12-60
D 19 ALMIRANTE WILLIAMS	Vickers-Armstrong	20-6-56	5-5-58	26-3-60

    D: 2,730 tons (3,300 fl)   **S:**   34.5 kts   **Dim:**   122.5 (113.99 pp) × 13.1 × 3.9
    Man: 17 officers, 249 men   **Range:**   7,800
    A: 4/MM 38 Exocet – 2 Sea Cat SAM systems – 4/102-mm DP (I × 4) – 4/40-mm AA (I × 4) – 6 Mk 32 ASW TT (III × 2) – 2 ASW Squid mortars

Almirante Williams   1977

Electron Equipt: Radars: Plessey AWS-1, 1 Marconi Type IV, Type III, 2/SGR 102, 2/SNG 20
         Sonar: 164B
    M: Parsons-Pamatreda GT; 2 props; 50,000 hp   **Boilers:**   2 Babcock & Wilcox

REMARKS: Refitted in Great Britain, D-18 in 1973-75 and D-19 in 1971-74. Dutch M-4 radar directors for Sea Cat. Exocet replaced by four 533-mm TT (IV × 1).

◆ **2 U.S. Allen M. Sumner class**

	Bldr	L	In serv.
D 16 MINISTRO ZENTENO (ex-*Charles S. Sperry*, DD-697)	Todd-Pacific	30-9-44	26-12-44
D 17 MINISTRO PORTALES (ex-*Douglas H. Fox*, DD-779)	Federal SB	13-3-44	17-5-44

Ministro Zenteno   1977

Ministro Portales   1975

    D: 2,200 tons (3,300 fl)   **S:**   30 kts   **Dim:**   114.75 × 12.45 × 3.8 (light)
    Range: 1,260/30, 4,600/15   **Man:**   14 officers, 260 men
    A: 6/127-mm DP 38-cal. (II × 3) – 6/324-mm Mk 32 ASW TT (III × 2) – 2 hedgehogs – 1 helicopter
    Electron Equipt: Radars: 1/SPS 40 (D-17) or SPS 37 (D-16), 1/SPS 10
                  Sonar: 1/SQS 40 (with VDS)
    M: GT; 2 props; 60,000 hp   **Boilers:**   4 Babcock & Wilcox   **Fuel:**   650 tons

REMARK: FRAM-II conversions, delivered 1-74.

DESTROYERS *(continued)*

◆ **2 U.S. Fletcher class**

	Bldr	L	In serv.
D 14 BLANCO ENCALADA	Bath Iron Works	7-8-43	19-10-43
(ex-*Wadleigh*, DD-689)			
D 15 COCHRANE	Todd-Pacific	6-6-44	2-9-44
(ex-*Rooks*, DD-804)			

Blanco Encalada   1977

D: 2,050 tons (2,850 fl)   **S:** 32 kts   **Dim:** 114.85 × 12.03 × 5.5
Man: 15 officers, 247 men   **Range:** 1,385/32, 3,800/12
A: 4/127-mm DP 38-cal. (I × 4) — 6/76-mm AA (II × 3) — 5/533-mm TT (V × 1) — 2 ASW
     torpedo racks — 2 hedgehogs — 1 depth-charge rack
Electron Equipt: Radars: 1/SPS 6C, 1/SPS 10, 1/Mk 25, 2/Mk 34, 1/Mk 35
                Sonar: 1/SQS 29

Electric: 660 kw   **Fuel:** 512 tons
M: GE GT; 2 props; 60,000 hp   **Boilers:** 4 Babcock & Wilcox
REMARKS: Transferred in 1962. The *Cochrane* refitted and recommissioned 1977-78.

FRIGATES

◆ **2 British Leander class**

	Bldr	Laid down	L	In serv.
PF 06 CONDELL	Yarrow & Co	6-71	6-12-72	21-12-73
PF 07 LYNCH	Yarrow & Co	12-72	12-6-73	25-5-74

D: 2,450 tons (2,900 fl)   **Dim:** 113.38 (109.73 pp) × 12.5 × 5.49 (fl)
S: 27 kts   **Range:** 4,500/12   **Man:** 263 men
A: 4 MM 38 Exocet 2/114-mm Mk VI DP (II × 1) — 1 Sea Cat SAM system (IV × 1) —
     2/20-mm AA — 6/324-mm ASW TT Mk 32 (III × 2) — 1 helicopter
Electron Equipt: Radars: 1/965, 1/992 Q, 1/978, 1/GWS 22, 1 MRS 3
                Sonars: 1/177, 1/170 B, 1/162
M: General Electric GT; 2 props
Boilers: 2 Babcock & Wilcox   **Fuel:** 460 tons

Condell   1977

Lynch   1977

REMARK: Ordered 14-1-70.

◆ **1 U.S. Charles Lawrence class**

	Bldr	L	In serv.
29 VIRGILIO URIBE	Bethlehem, Hingham	25-2-43	9-6-43
(ex-*Daniel Griffin*, APD-38)			

D: 1,691 tons (2,130 fl)   **S:** 23 kts   **Dim:** 93.27 × 11.25 × 4.8
Range: 1,747/23, 4,800/12   **Electric:** 340 kw
A: 1/127-mm DP — 6/40-mm AA (II × 3) — 2 hedgehogs — 2 depth-charge racks
Electron Equipt: Radar: SPS 6   **Boilers:** 2 Foster-Wheeler, 32.3 kg/cm²
M: Turbo-electric: 2 GE turbines, 2/4,600 kw gen.; 2 props; 12,000 hp

REMARKS: Transferred 12-66. Sisters *Serrano* (ex-*Odum*, APD-71) and *Orella* (ex-*Jack C. Robinson*, APD-72) remain as hulks. *Uribe* refitted 1977-78 with SPS-6 atop lattice mast aft. Carries two LCVP.

CORVETTES

◆ **1 U.S. Cherokee class**

63 SERGENTE ALDEA (ex-*Arikara*, ATF-98)

CORVETTES (*continued*)

Sergente Aldea 1975

    D: 1,235 tons (1,675 fl)   **S:** 15 kts   **Dim:** 62.5 × 11.6 × 4.7

    A: 1/76-mm DP − 2/20-mm AA   **Man:** 85 men

    Electron Equipt: Radar: 1/SPS 5

    M: Diesel-electric: 4 Busch-Sulzer 539 diesels; 1 prop; 3,000 hp

REMARK: Transferred 7-71.

◆ **2 U.S. Sotoyomo class**

60 LIENTUR (ex-ATA-177)   62 LAUTARO (ex-ATA-122)

    Bldr: Levingston SB, Orange, Texas, 1943-44

Lautaro 1970

    D: 534 tons (835 fl)   **S:** 12.5 kts   **Dim:** 43.9 × 10.15 × 5.2

    A: 1/76-mm DP − 2/20-mm AA   **Man:** 46 men   **Fuel:** 187 tons diesel

    M: GM diesels; 2 props; 1,500 hp

REMARK: Transferred 9-47.

TORPEDO BOATS

◆ **4 German Lürssen class**

81 FRESIA   83 QUIDORA

82 GUACOLDA   84 TEHUALDA

    Bldr: Bazan, Cadiz, 1965-66

Fresia 1970

    D: 134 tons (fl)   **S:** 30 kts   **Dim:** 36.2 × 5.6 × 1.64

    A: 2/40-mm AA − 4/533-mm TT   **Man:** 20 men   **Range:** 1,500/15

    M: 2 Mercedes-Benz MB839Bb diesels; 2 props; 4,800 hp

PATROL BOATS AND CRAFT

◆ **4 Spanish Barcelo class**

        L   L

N . . .   . . .   N . . .   . . .

N . . .   . . .   N . . .   . . .

    Bldr: Bazan, La Carraca, Ordered 1978

    D: 135 tons   **S:** 36.5 kts   **Dim:** 36.2 × 5.3 × 1.9

    A: 1/40-mm AA − 1/20-mm AA   **M:** 2 MTU-Bazan diesels; 2 props; 6,000 hp

◆ **1 U.S. PC-1638 class**

P 37 PAPUDO (ex U.S. PC-1646)   Bldr: ASMAR, Talcahuano, 1971

Papudo 1977

PATROL BOATS AND CRAFT *(continued)*

D: 313 tons (417 fl)   **S:** 20 kts   **Dim:** 52.9 × 7.0 × 3.1
A: 1/40-mm AA—4/20-mm AA (II × 2)—1 trainable Mk 15 hedgehog—4 depth-
charge throwers—1 depth-charge rack
M: 2 GM diesels; 2 props; 2,800 hp

◆ **2 small trawlers**

PC 75 MARINERO FUENTALBAS   PC 76 CABO ODGER

Bldr: ASMAR, Talcahuano, 1966-67

D: 215 tons   **S:** 9 kts   **Dim:** 24.4 × 6.4 × 2.75
A: 1/20-mm   **M:** 1 Cummins diesel; 340 hp   **Range:** 2,600/9

REMARKS: Purchased 1966. Profile of U.S.-type trawler.

HYDROGRAPHIC SURVEY AND RESEARCH SHIPS

AGS 64 YELCHO (ex-U.S. *Tekesta*, ATF-93, 1943). Transferred 1960

Yelcho   1970

D: 1,235 tons (1,675 fl)   **S:** 16.5 kts   **Dim:** 62.5 × 11.65 × 4.7
A: 2/20-mm AA   **Man:** 5 officers, 59 men
M: Diesel-electric propulsion; 3,000 hp

REMARKS: Used for oceanographic research.

◆ **1 Antarctic patrol, transport, and research ship**

	Bldr	Laid down	L	In serv.
AP 45 PILOTO PARDO	Haarlemsche Scheepsbouw	1957	1958	8-58

D: 1,250 tons (2,545 fl)   **S:** 14 kts   **Dim:** 83.0 × 11.9 × 7.4 (fl)
Man: 44 crew, 24 passengers   **Range:** 6,000
M: Diesel-electric propulsion; 1 prop; 2,000 hp

REMARKS: Armament removed; can carry 2 Bell 47-G helicopters.

Piloto Pardo   1977

AUXILIARY SHIPS

◆ **3 tankers**

AO 55   N . . .

D: approx. 30,000 tons (fl)   **S:** . . .   **Dim:** 176.1 × 25.5 × . . .
M: Diesels; 18,300 hp

REMARKS: 19,500 tons deadweight. Ordered 1976 from ASMAR, Talcahuano.

AO 53 ARAUCANO   Bldr: Burmeister & Wain (21-6-66)

D: 23,000 tons (fl)   **S:** 17 kts   **Dim:** 160.93 × 21.95 × 8.8
A: Removed   **Range:** 12,000/14.5
M: Burmeister & Wain diesel, type 62 VT 2 BF 140, 9-cyl.; 1 prop; 10,800 hp

Araucano   1977

AUXILIARY SHIPS (continued)

REMARKS: Can replenish two ships at sea simultaneously. Carries 21,126 cu. meters liquid and 1,444 cu. meters dry cargo. Can carry 8/40-mm AA (II × 4).

AOG 54 BEAGLE (ex-U.S. *Genesee*, AOG-8) Transferred 7-72

Beagle   1977

    D: 1,850 tons (4,570 fl)   S: 14 kts   Dim: 93.5 × 13.6 × 4.75
    Range: 6670/10
    A: 1/76-mm DP—2/20-mm AA   M: Diesel electric; 3,100 hp

◆ 8 transports

AP 47 AQUILES (ex-Danish *Tjaldur*) Bldr: Aalborg Vaerft, 1953

Aquiles   1977

    D: 2,660 tons (fl)   S: 16 kts   Dim: 87.8 (82.0 pp) × 13.42 × 5.2
    A: 1/40-mm AA   Man: 32 crew, 406 passengers
    M: B and W diesel; 1 prop; 3,600 hp   Range: 5,500/16

REMARK: Former mixed-cargo ship purchased in 1967.

AP 88 COMANDANTE HEMMERDINGER (ex-U.S. *New London County*, T-LST-1066)
AP 89 COMANDANTE ARAYA (ex-U.S. *Nye County*, T-LST-1067)
AP 97 COMANDANTE TORO (ex-U.S. T-LST-277)

    Bldr: U.S.A., 1943-44

Comandante Hemmerdinger   1977

    D: 4,080 tons (fl)   S: 11 kts   Dim: 100.04 × 15.24 × 4.35
    M: GM diesels; 2 props; 1,700 hp   Range: 6,000/11

Comandante Toro   1977

REMARKS: Former U.S. Military Sealift Command ships; one transferred in February and two in August 1973. No armament.

AP 94 OROMPELLO   Bldr: U.S.A., 15-9-64
AP 95 ELICURA   Bldr: ASMAR, Talcahuano, 10-12-68

    D: 290 tons (750 fl)   S: 10.5 kts   Dim: 43.9 (42.05 pp) × 10.3 × 6.9
    A: 3/20-mm AA   Man: 20 men   Range: 2,900/9
    M: 2 Cummins VT-17-700M diesels; 2 props; 900 hp   Fuel: 71 tons diesel

CHILE (*continued*)

AUXILIARY SHIPS (*continued*)

AP 110 METEORO Bldr: ASMAR, Talcahuano, 1967
AP . . . HUEMEL 1975

    D: 205 tons (fl)   **S:** 8 kts   **Dim:** 24.4 × 6.7 × . . .
    M: Diesel   **Man:** 220 passengers (ferries)

◆ **1 submarine tender**

70 ANGAMOS (ex-*Puerto Montt*, ex-Danish *Kobenhavn*)

  Bldr: Orenst & Koppel, Germany, 1966

    D: 3,560 tons   **S:** 16 kts   **Dim:** 93.92 × 16.2 × 4.5
    M: 2 Pielstick diesels; 2 props; 6,500 hp

REMARKS: Former car and passenger ferry, purchased 4-77. Now fitted with workshops, spare parts stores, ammunition and torpedo magazines.

◆ **1 training ship**

	Bldr	L	In serv.
BE 43 ESMERALDA (ex-*Don Juan de Austria*)	Bazan, Cadiz	12-5-53	9-54

Esmeralda   1973

    D: 3,673 tons   **S:** 11 kts   **Dim:** 94.1 × 13.1 × 8.7
    A: 4/47-mm   **Man:** 271 crew, 80 midshipmen   **Range:** 8,000/8
    M: Fiat diesel; 1,400 hp

REMARKS: Four-masted schooner, ordered by Spain, sold to Chile in 1953. Similar to the Spanish *Juan Sebastian de Elcano*.

◆ **1 hospital ship**

111 CIRUJANO VIDELA Bldr: ASMAR, Talcahuano, 1964

    D: 140 tons (fl)   **S:** 14 kts   **Dim:** 31.0 × 6.5 × 2.0
    M: 2 Cummins diesels; 2 props; 700 hp

REMARK: Modified U.S. PGM-59 design.

◆ **1 buoy tender and lighthouse-servicing ship**

ATA 73 COLO COLO Bldr: England, 1929

    D: 790 tons   **S:** 11 kts   **Dim:** 41.38 × 8.72 × 4.07
    M: Reciprocating; 1 prop; 1,050 hp

◆ **6 tugs**

YT . . . GALVEZ Bldr: Southern Shipbuilders, G.B., 1975

    D: 112 grt   **S:** . . .   **Dim:** 25.5 × 7.3 × 2.8

YT 104 ANCUD   YT 120 REYES   YT 128 CORTEZ
YT 105 MONREAL   YT 127 CAUPOLICAN

◆ **2 3,000-ton-capacity floating docks**

132 MUTILLA (ex-U.S. ARD-32), leased 15-12-60
131 INGENIERO MERY (ex-U.S. ARD-25), bought 20-8-73

    D: 5,200 tons   **Dim:** 150.1 × 25.6 × 1.7

CHINA

People's Republic of

Today, the Chinese Navy is the size of a little finger. I hope that in a few years it will be a bit larger than a thumb.

               MAO TSE-TUNG

PERSONNEL: 116,000 men in the following categories:
  Seagoing personnel: 36,000
  Naval air arm: 20,000
  Shore establishment: 60,000 (including 20,000 naval infantry)

MERCHANT MARINE (1977): . . . ships—3,904,677 grt (tankers: 75—996,412 grt)

NAVAL AVIATION: The naval air arm, which is under the control of the navy, consists of about 400 aircraft, including 200 MIG-17, MIG-19, and MIG-21 interceptors, 150 light bombers, such as IL-28 and TU-2, and about 100 transports, seaplanes, and helicopters. Its principal mission is defense of the coast and of naval surface forces near the coast. A few of the aircraft are believed to be equipped for minelaying. Control of naval aircraft is integrated with the continental air-defense system. Some of the recently purchased French Super-Frélon helicopters may belong to the navy.

WARSHIPS IN SERVICE OR UNDER CONSTRUCTION
AS OF 1 JANUARY 1980

	L	Tons (Surfaced)	Main armament
◆ **79-81 submarines**			
2 HAN	1971?	. . .	TT
1 SOVIET GOLF	. . .	2,300	3 ballistic missiles, 10/533-mm TT
2 MING	1975	1,500	6/533-mm TT
56-58 SOVIET ROMEO	1964 on	1,330	8/533-mm TT
18 SOVIET WHISKEY	1960-64	1,050	6/533-mm TT
◆ **11 destroyers**		Tons	
7 LUTA	1970 on	3,500	4/130-mm, 6 Styx
4 SOVIET GORDY	1938-40	1,660	4/130-mm, 4 Styx
◆ **16 frigates**			
5 KIANG HU	1974 on	1,800	2/100-mm, 4 Styx
2 KIANG TUNG	1972 on	1,800	4/100-mm, 2 SAM
5 KIANGNAN	1966-68	1,500	3/100-mm
4 SOVIET RIGA	1953-56	1,450	3/100-mm, 2 Styx

◆ **168-189 guided-missile patrol boats**

◆ **200-225 torpedo boats**

◆ **650+ patrol boats and craft**

◆ **15-20 minesweepers**

SUBMARINES

◆ **2 Han-class, nuclear**

	Bldr	In serv.
N . . .	Luta	1974
N . . .	Luta	?

REMARKS: Experimental units. The existence of a second ship is doubtful. Construction and trials on the first took a very long time. Modern hull form, single propeller, one nuclear reactor.

◆ **1 Soviet Golf-class, ballistic missile**

D: 2,300 tons surfaced, 2,750 submerged   **S:** 14 kts submerged
Dim: 98.8 × 8.5 × 6.5   **A:** 3 ballistic missiles—10/533-mm TT (6 fwd, 4 aft)

REMARKS: Plans furnished by the Soviet Union at a time when relations between the two countries were good. Medium-range missiles, if any, would be of Chinese origin.

◆ **2 Ming class**

D: 1,500 tons, 1,900 submerged   **S:** 17/15 kts   **Dim:** 76.0 × . . . × . . .
A: 6/533-mm TT   **M:** Diesel-electric; 2 props

REMARKS: Launched 1975. Evidently a Chinese design derived from the Romeo.

◆ **40-45 Soviet Romeo class**

D: 1,330 tons surfaced, 1,700 submerged   **S:** 15 kts surfaced, 13 submerged

Chinese Romeo-class submarine   1978

Dim: 77.0 × 6.7 × 4.95   **Range:** 14,000/9   **Man:** 56 men
M: Diesel-electric: 2 diesels, 2,000 hp each; 2 props; 3,000 hp

REMARKS: Endurance: 45 days. Diving depth: 200 meters.

◆ **18 Soviet Whiskey class**

D: 1,050 tons surfaced, 1,350 submerged   **S:** 17/16 kts
Dim: 76.0 × 6.3 × 4.8   **A:** 6/533-mm TT (4 fwd, 2 aft)—14 torpedoes

REMARKS: A few were delivered by the U.S.S.R., the others were built in China (1960-), probably at the Chiang Nan shipyard at Kao Chang Miao, near Shanghai. These are several more that are nonoperational and used for instruction, and one Soviet 1939-vintage S-1-class unit.

DESTROYERS

◆ **7 Luta class, guided-missile**   In serv., 1972-77

D: 3,960 tons (fl)   **S:** 32 kts   **Dim:** 127.5 × 12.9 × 5.2
A: 6 SSM similar to Styx (III × 2)—4/130-mm (II × 2)—8/57-mm or 37-mm AA (II × 4)—4/25-mm AA (II × 2)—2 ASW rocket launchers—4 depth-charge launchers—2 depth-charge racks
M: GT; 2 props; 60,000 hp   **Range:** 4,000/15   **Man:** 300 men

Luta-class destroyer   1974

DESTROYERS (continued)

REMARKS: Superficially resembles Kotlin but is larger and has a flat transom stern, larger superstructure, etc. Some systems of Soviet design; the ASW rocket launchers are derived from Soviet designs, but have more tubes.

◆ **4 Gordy class, guided-missile**

ANSHAN   CHI LIN
CHANG CHUN   FU CHUN

D: 1,657 tons (2,039 fl)   **S:** 38 kts when built, certainly much less today
Dim: 112.86 × 10.2 × 3.8   **Man:** 197 men   **Range:** 800/38, 2,600/20
A: 4 Styx missiles (II × 2)—4/130-mm (I × 4)—8/37-mm AA (II × 4)
M: GT; 2 props; 48,000 hp   **Boilers:** 3   **Fuel:** 540 tons

REMARK: Ex-Soviet *Razyashchy*, *Reshitelny*, *Retivy*, and *Resky*, all built in the Far East, launched 1936-41, and transferred by the U.S.S.R. in 1955.

FRIGATES

◆ **3 Kiang Hu class, guided-missile**

Kiang-Hu-class frigate   1978

D: 1,800 tons (2,200 fl)   **S:** 28 kts   **Dim:** 100.0 × 11.0 × 4.0
A: 4 SSM similar to Styx (II × 2)—2/100-mm DP—8/37-mm AA (II × 4)—2/MBU-1800—2 depth-charge projectors
M: Diesel; 2 props; 24,000 hp

REMARKS: Launched 1975. A variation of the Kiang Tung class with SSM vice SAM.

◆ **2 Kiang Tung class, guided-missile**

D: 1,800 tons (2,200 fl)   **S:** 28 kts   **Dim:** 100.0 × 11.0 × 4.0
A: 2 SAM systems—4/100-mm DP (II × 2)—8/37-mm AA (II × 4)—2/MBU-1800—2 depth-charge projectors
M: Diesels; 2 props; 24,000 hp

REMARKS: Launched 1974. SAM system, of Chinese design, not yet operational.

◆ **5 Kiangnan class**   Bldr: Chiang Nan SY, Shanghai, 1967-69

D: 1,500 tons   **S:** 28 kts   **Dim:** 92.0 × 10.0 × 3.9
A: 3/100-mm (I × 3, 1 fwd, 2 aft)—8/37-mm AA (II × 4)—4/14.5-mm AA (II × 2)—2/MBU-1800—4 depth-charge projectors—2 depth-charge racks
M: 4 diesels; 2 props; 24,000 hp

Kiangnan-class frigate

REMARK: Chinese version of the Soviet Riga class.

◆ **4 Soviet Riga class**   Bldr: Chiang Nan SY, Shanghai, 1954-57

CHIENG TU   KUEI YANG
KUEI LIN   K'UN MING

D: 1,450 tons (fl)   **S:** 28 kts   **Dim:** 91.0 × 11.0 × 3.4
A: 2 Styx systems (II × 1)—3/100-mm (I × 3)—4/37-mm AA (II × 2)—4 depth-charge projectors—2 depth-charge racks
M: GT; 2 props; 20,000 hp   **Range:** 2,000/10

GUIDED-MISSILE PATROL BOATS

◆ **1 Hola class**

An enlarged version of Osa-I, armed with four surface-to-surface missiles, and equipped with a large radome.

◆ **85-100 Soviet Osa-I class**   Bldr: Chiang Nan SY, Shanghai, 1960-

Chinese-built, Osa-I-class, guided-missile patrol boats   1978

D: 175 tons (210 fl)   **S:** 40 kts (36 cruising)   **Dim:** 39.0 × 7.7 × 1.8
A: 4 SSM similar to Styx—4/25-mm AA (II × 2)   **Man:** 25 men
M: 3 M503A diesels; 3 props; 12,000 hp

GUIDED-MISSILE PATROL BOATS *(continued)*

REMARKS: The electronic equipment of these ships is slightly different from that of the Soviet version and different guns are fitted. No fire-control radar.

◆ **75-80 Hoku class**

D: 80 tons (fl)	**S:** 39 kts	**Dim:** 28.0 × 6.3 × 1.8
A: 2 Styx SSM — 2/25-mm AA (II × 1)		**Man:** 18 men
M: 4 M50 diesels; 4 props; 4,800 hp		**Range:** 200/25

Hoku-class, guided-missile patrol boat with Homa hydrofoil variant inboard   1978

REMARKS: Steel-hulled improvement on Komar. A slightly longer variant, with hydrofoils and a second 25-mm AA mount aft, is nicknamed Homa.

◆ **7-8 Soviet Komar class**

D: 71 tons (82 fl)	**S:** 40 kts	**Dim:** 25.3 × 7.0 × 2.0
A: 2 Styx SSM — 2/25-mm AA (II × 1)		
M: 4 M50 diesels; 4 props; 4,000 hp		

REMARK: Transferred about 1960.

TORPEDO BOATS

◆ **70-80 Huchwan-class hydrofoils**

D: 39 tons (fl)	**S:** 54 kts	**Dim:** 21.8 × 4.9 × 1.0; foilborne: 7.5 × .31
A: 2/450-mm TT — 2/14.5-mm machine guns (II × 1)		
M: 3 diesels; 3 props; 3,600 hp		

REMARKS: In service since about 1966. Identical to the hydrofoils delivered to Albania, Pakistan, and Tanzania. Also built in Romania.

◆ **80-90 Soviet P-6 class**   Bldr: China, 1960s

D: 56 tons (66.5 fl)	**S:** 43 kts	**Dim:** 25.3 × 6.1 × 1.7

A: 2/533-mm TT — 4/25-mm AA (II × 2)		
M: 4 M50 diesels; 4 props; 4,800 hp		

◆ **50-55 Soviet P-4 class**

D: 19.3 tons (22.4 fl)	**S:** 55 kts	**Dim:** 19.3 × 3.7 × 1.0
A: 2/14.5-mm machine guns (II × 1) — 2/450-mm TT		
Electron Equipt: Radar: Skin head		**M:** 2 M50 diesels; 2 props; 2,400 hp

REMARK: Since 1952.

PATROL BOATS AND CRAFT

◆ **15-20 Hainan class**

D: 400 tons	**S:** 24 kts	**Dim:** 59.0 × 7.3 × 2.4
A: 4/57-mm AA (II × 2) — 4/25-mm AA (II × 2) — 4/MBU-1800 — 2 depth-charge projectors — 2 depth-charge racks		
Electron Equipt: Radar: Pot Head		**M:** 4 diesels; 4 props; 8,000 hp

Three Hainan-class patrol boats   1977

REMARKS: From 1964 onward. Early units had 2/76-mm DP vice 4/57-mm AA. Two were transferred to Pakistan, 1976.

◆ **20 Soviet Kronstadt class**

D: 300 tons (330 fl)	**S:** 18 kts	**Dim:** 52.1 × 6.5 × 2.2
A: 1/85-mm — 2/37-mm AA — 6/14.5-mm machine guns (II × 3) — 2 depth-charge projectors — mines — 2 depth-charge racks. Some: 2/MBU-1800		
M: 3 diesels; 3 props; 3,300 hp		

REMARKS: 1956-57. Six could have been delivered by the U.S.S.R., the others built in Shanghai and Canton. Other information indicates that only two were built in China, the balance in the Soviet Union.

◆ **300-350 Shanghai-II class**

D: 155 tons (fl)	**S:** 28 kts	**Dim:** 38.8 × 5.4 × 1.6
A: 4/37-mm AA (II × 2) — 4/25-mm AA (II × 2) — depth charges — mines. Some: 2 recoilless rifles (II × 1)		
Electron Equipt: Radar: Pot Head or Skin Head		**Man:** 25 men
M: diesels; 4 props; 4,800 hp		

PATROL BOATS AND CRAFT *(continued)*

Shanghai-class patrol boat 1978

REMARKS: A large number have been transferred to foreign navies. Very unsophisticated and sparsely equipped. Shanghai-I class was smaller and had 2/57-mm (II × 1) forward.

◆ **Shantung class**

Similar to Swatow class, but with hydrofoils. Very few built. Probably not successful.

◆ **50-60 Swatow class**

D: 80 tons (fl) S: 28 kts Dim: 25.1 × 6.0 × 1.8
A: 4/37-mm AA (II × 2)—2 heavy-machine-gun mounts—8 depth charges
M: 4 diesels; 3,000 hp

REMARKS: 1955-60. Similar to P-6, but broader and with a steel hull.

◆ **30-35 Whampoa class** Bldr: China, 1954-58

D: 45 tons S: 12 kts Dim: 27.0 × 4.0 × 1.5
A: 2/37-mm AA (II × 1)—2 machine guns M: 2 diesels; 2 props; 600 hp

◆ **Several hundred craft of the following classes:** Yu Lin, Ying Kou, Wu Hsi, Pei Hai, Tai Shan, Fukien, etc.

Most 10 to 50 tons with 14.5-mm machine guns or twin 25-mm AA.

MINE WARFARE SHIPS

◆ **15-20 Soviet T-43-class fleet minesweepers**

D: 610 tons (fl) S: 14 kts Dim: 60.0 × 8.6 × 2.15
A: 4/37-mm AA (II × 2)—4/25-mm AA (II × 2)—4/14.5-mm machine guns—2 depth-charge projectors
M: 2 diesels; 2 props; 2,200 hp

REMARKS: A few were transferred from the U.S.S.R., the majority were built in China. A few older units are only 58 meters overall and 580 tons (fl). Several were built or converted as surveying ships and civilian research ships.

◆ **100 auxiliary minesweepers convertible from fishing boats or motor junks**

AMPHIBIOUS WARFARE SHIPS

◆ **20-ex-U.S. LST**

Possible names:
CHANG PAI SHAN CHUNG MENG SHAN
TA PIEH SHAN CHING KANG SHAN

D: 4,100 tons (fl) S: 11 kts

REMARKS: Transferred before the civil war to Nationalist China and captured by the communist forces. Used as transports or station vessels.

◆ **10-12 Yu Ling class**

REMARKS: 1971-. Design reportedly derived from U.S. LSM class.

◆ **14 ex-U.S. LSM**

Three ex-U.S. LSM-1 class in the Chinese Navy 1978

REMARKS: Date from 1944-45. Some used as minelayers.

◆ **5-6 LCU (ex-LCT)**

REMARK: Of U.S. and British origin.

◆ **440-500 LCM**

REMARKS: Built in China or of U.S. Navy origin. 300-350 are Yunnan class.

AUXILIARY SHIPS

There is no comprehensive information on the Chinese fleet's logistic support, but China has designed and built large numbers of auxiliary vessels, reportedly running the spectrum of logistics support, repair, hydrographic survey, and research types, including a great many tugs and small oilers.

Some old U.S. (for example, LST) and Japanese ships that have no military value today have probably been converted to depot ships, repair ships, etc.

COLOMBIA

PERSONNEL: 8,000 men, including 1,500 marines

MERCHANT MARINE (1978): 59 ships — 265,483 grt (tankers: 5 ships — 29,585 grt)

OVERSEAS PURCHASE PROGRAM: Colombia is seeking to expand and replenish her aging fleet by the purchase of used naval ships from other nations. Arrangements for the transfer of five other U.S. Navy ships in 1977-78 and four ex-Portuguese frigates in 1978 fell through, however, and no substitutes have been found.

SUBMARINES

◆ 2 German Type 209

	Bldr:	L	In serv.
SS 28 PIJAO	Howaldtswerke, Kiel	19-6-74	17-4-75
SS 29 TAYRONA	Howaldtswerke, Kiel	. . .	18-7-75

D: 980 tons standard, 1,050 surfaced, 1,230 submerged
S: 22 kts for a few minutes **Endurance:** 30 days
Dim: 56.0 × 6.2 × 5.9 **Man:** 5 officers, 26 men
A: 8/533-mm TT fwd — 6 reserve torpedoes **Fuel:** 50 tons diesel
M: 4 MTU 12V-493-TY60 diesels, Siemens electric motor, 3,600 hp; 1 prop

◆ 2 Italian S.X. 506 midget Bldr: Cosmos, Livorno, Italy (1972-74)

SS 20 INTREPIDO   SS 21 INDOMABLE

D: 58 tons surfaced, 70 tons submerged **S:** 8.5 kts **Dim:** 23.0 × 2.0 × 4.0
Man: 5 men **Range:** 1,200/7
Cargo capacity: 2,050 kg of explosives; 8 frogmen fully equipped; 2 submarine vehicles (for the frogmen) supported by a fixed system on lower part of the hull, one on each side.

REMARKS: Similar submarines have been bought by the Pakistani and Taiwanese navies. The *Roncador* (SS-23) and *Quita Sueno* (SS-24) are no longer in service.

DESTROYERS

◆ 1 Swedish Hälland class

	Bldr	Laid down	L	In serv.
06 SIETE DE AGOSTO	Götaverken	11-55	19-6-56	31-10-58
(ex-*13 de Junio*)				

D: 2,650 tons (3,300 fl) **S:** 25 kts **Dim:** 121.05 × 12.4 × 4.7 (fl)
Range: 450/25 **Man:** 21 officers, 227 men
A: 6/120-mm AA automatic (II × 3) — 4/40-mm AA (I × 4) — 4/533-mm TT (IV × 1) — 4/375-mm Bofors ASW rocket launcher (IV × 1)
Electron Equipt: Radars: 1/LWP-3, 1 DAO-2, HSA fire-control (6 sets)
M: De Laval double-reduction GT; 2 props; 55,000 hp
Boilers: 2 Penhoët-Motala-Verkstad **Fuel:** 524 tons

Siete de Agosto

◆ 1 Allen M. Sumner class

	Bldr	Laid down	L	In serv.
03 SANTANDER	Federal SB & DD	16-11-43	26-3-44	8-6-44
(ex-*Waldron*, DD-699)				

D: 2,200 tons (3,300 fl) **S:** 30 kts **Dim:** 114.75 × 12.45 × 5.8
A: 6/127-mm 38-cal. DP (II × 3) — 6/324-mm Mk 32 ASW TT (III × 2)
Electron Equipt: Radars: 1/SPS 40, 1/SPS 10, 1/Mk 25 fire-control
Sonar: SQS 30 **Range:** 4,800/15
M: GT; 2 props; 60,000 hp **Boilers:** 4 Babcock & Wilcox **Fuel:** 650 tons

REMARKS: Transferred 16-12-73. Has had FRAM II modernization and can handle a small helicopter. VDS and hedgehogs removed before transfer. Mk 37 gunfire-control director. Sister *Caldas* (02) was decommissioned in 1976.

FRIGATES

◆ 1 Courtney class

	Bldr	Laid down	L	In serv.
07 BOYACA	New York SB	10-55	24-11-56	6-57
(ex-*Hartley*, DE-1029)				

D: 1,450 tons (1,914 fl) **S:** 25 kts **Dim:** 95.7 × 11.26 × 4.3
Man: 11 officers, 150 men **Range:** 4,500/15 **Fuel:** 400 tons
A: 2/76-mm DP (II × 1) — 6/Mk 32 ASW TT (III × 2) — 1 depth-charge rack
Electron Equipt: Radars: 1/SPS 6, 1/SPS 10, 1/Mk 34
Sonar: SQS 23
M: De Laval GT; 1 prop; 20,000 hp **Boilers:** 2 Foster-Wheeler

REMARKS: Transferred by U.S. 8-7-72. Twin rudders. Superstructure built of light-metal alloy. Flight deck and hangar for small helicopter.

◆ 1 ex-U.S. LPR

	Bldr	Laid down	L	In serv.
DT 15 CORDOBA	Phila. Navy Yd	2-44	15-6-44	6-45
(ex-*Ruchamkin*, LPR-89)				

D: 1,450 tons (2,050 fl) **S:** 23 kts **Dim:** 93.26 × 11.28 × 4.7
Man: 204 men **Range:** 2,000/23, 5,000/15 **Fuel:** 350 tons

FRIGATES (continued)

Cordoba   1973

   A: 1/127-mm DP−4/40-mm AA (II × 2)−6/324-mm Mk 32 ASW TT (III × 2)−1
      depth-charge rack
   Electron Equipt: Radar: 1/SPS 10
   M: Turbo-electric propulsion; 2 props; 12,000 hp   **Boilers:** 2

REMARKS: Transferred 1969. Can be used as fast transport for 100 men. Had FRAM-II
modernization. Sister *Almirante Tono* decommissioned 11-76; two others discarded
1972-73.

CORVETTES

◆ 3 Cherokee-class fleet tugs

	Bldr	L	In serv.
N . . . (ex-*Carib*, ATF-82)	Charleston SB & DD	7-2-43	7-43
N . . . (ex-*Hidatsa*, ATF-102)	Charleston SB & DD	29-12-43	4-44
N . . . (ex-*Jicarilla*, ATF-104)	Charleston SB & DD	25-2-44	6-44

   D: 1,235 tons (1,675 fl)   **S:** 16.5 kts   **Dim:** 62.48 × 11.73 × 4.67
   A: 1/76.2-mm DP−2/40-mm AA (I × 2)−4/20-mm AA (II × 2)
   M: Diesel-electric, 4 GM 12-278 diesels (ex-ATF-102, ex-ATF-104: 4 Busch-Sulzer
      B5-539 diesels); 1 prop; 3,000 hp   **Electric:** 300 kw

REMARK: Reactivated from U.S. Maritime Commission reserve fleet and transferred
3-79 for use as patrol and rescue ships.

RIVER PATROL BOATS AND CRAFT

CF 35 RIO HACHA   CF 37 ARAUCA

   Bldr: Unial Barranquilla, 1955

   D: 170 tons (184 fl)   **S:** 13 kts   **Dim:** 47.25 × 8.23 × 1.0
   A: 2/76-mm AA (I × 2)−4/20-mm AA (I × 4)   **Man:** 27-43 men
   M: 2 Caterpillar diesels; 2 props; 800 hp   **Range:** 1,000/12

REMARK: Sister *Leticia* disarmed and equipped as a hospital boat.

Arauca

CF 33 CARTAGENA Bldr: Yarrow & Co., Glasgow, 1930

   D: 142 tons   **S:** 15.5 kts   **Dim:** 41.9 × 7.16 × 0.8
   Man: 39 men   **Range:** 2,100/15   **Fuel:** 24 tons diesel
   A: 2/76-mm−1/20-mm AA−4/7.7-mm machine guns
   M: 2 Gardner diesels; 2 props (in tunnels); 600 hp

REMARK: Principal parts of the ship protected against small arms.

Cartagena

OCEANOGRAPHIC RESEARCH SHIPS

BO 151 SAN ANDRES (ex-*Rockville*, PCER-851)
   Bldr: Pullman Standard Car Co., Chicago, 1944

OCEANOGRAPHIC RESEARCH SHIPS *(continued)*

D: 674 tons (858 fl)   **S:** 15 kts   **Dim:** 56.23 × 10.05 × 3.0
Man: 60 men   **Electric:** 180 kw
M: 2 GM 12-567A diesels; 2 props; 1,800 hp

San Andres   1976

REMARK: Bought 5-6-69.

BO 153 QUINDIO (ex-U.S. YFR-443)

D: 380 tons (600 fl)   **Dim:** 40.4 × 9.10 × 2.5
Man: 17 men   **M:** 1 Union diesel; 600 hp

REMARK: Built in 1942 as a refrigerated cargo lighter by Niagara SB, Buffalo, N.Y. Transferred 7-64.

HYDROGRAPHIC SURVEY SHIP

FB 161 GORGONA Bldr: Lindigoverken

D: 560 tons   **S:** 13 kts   **Dim:** 41.15 × 9.0 × 2.83
M: 2 Nohab diesels; 2 props; 900 hp

REMARK: Launched 28-5-54 and originally intended as a lighthouse tender.

AUXILIARY SHIPS

◆ **1 oiler**

BT 67 TUMACO (ex-U.S. *Chewaucan,* AOG-50) Bldr: Cargill, Inc., Savage, Minn.

D: 4,570 tons (fl)   **S:** 14 kts   **Dim:** 94.7 (89.0 pp) × 14.78 × 4.9
A: 2/76-mm DP (I × 2)   **Man:** 45 men   **Range:** 8,350/11.5
M: 2 General Motors 16-278A diesels; 2 props; 3,300 hp
Cargo capacity: 2,575 tons fuel

REMARK: Launched 22-7-44 and transferred 7-71.

Tumaco   1976

◆ **1 small transport /cargo ship**

TM 43 CIUDAD DE QUIBO Bldr: Sander, Delfzijl, Netherlands.

D: 633 tons   **S:** 11 kts   **Dim:** 50.3 × 7.2 × 2.8
M: Diesel; 1 prop; 390 hp   **Man:** 11 men   **Fuel:** 32 tons

REMARK: Purchased 1953.

◆ **2 hospital boats**

BD 36 LETICIA Former river patrol boat, see under *Arauca* class. Has 6 beds, surgery facilities, etc.

BD 33 SOCORRO Bldr: Cartagena Naval DY, 1956

D: 70 tons   **S:** 9 kts   **Dim:** 25.0 × 5.5 × 0.75
M: 2 GM diesels; 270 hp   **Man:** 10 men

REMARKS: Originally fitted to carry 56 troops on the rivers, now used for surgery.

◆ **10 tugs**

RM 72 PEDRO DE HEREDIA (ex-*Choctaw,* ATF-70) Bldr: Charleston SB

Pedro de Heredia   1975

COLOMBIA *(continued)*

AUXILIARY SHIPS *(continued)*

> **D:** 1,235 tons (1,675 fl)   **S:** 16.5 kts   **Dim:** 62.48 × 11.73 × 4.67
> **M:** Diesel-electric propulsion, 4 GM 12-278 diesels; 1 prop; 3,000 hp
> **Electric:** 160 kw

REMARK: 18-10-42, transferred 1961.

RM 75 BAHIA UTRIA (ex-*Koka*, ATA-185) Bldr: Levingston SB, Texas

> **D:** 534 tons (835 fl)   **S:** 13 kts   **Dim:** 43.6 × 10.3 × 4.0
> **M:** Diesel-electric propulsion, 2 GM 12-278A diesels; 1 prop; 1,500 hp

REMARKS: Launched 11-9-44 and transferred 1-7-71. Sister *Bahia Honda* lost 2-75.

RM 73 RICARDO SORZANO (ex-U.S. YTL-231)

> **D:** 80 tons (fl)   **S:** 9 kts   **Dim:** 20.2 × 5.2 × 1.5
> **M:** 1 diesel; 240 hp

REMARK: Transferred 1963.

RM 71 ANDAGOYA

> **D:** 117 grt   **S:** 12 kts   **Dim:** 28.0 × 6.1 × 3.0   **M:** Diesel; 400 hp

REMARK: Dates from 1928.

RR 81 CAPITAN CASTRO   RR 86 CAPITAN RIGOBERTO GIRALDO
RR 82 CANDIDO LEGUIZAMO   RR 87 CAPITAN VLADIMIR VALEK
RR 84 CAPITAN ALVARO RUIS   RR 88 TENIENTE LUIS BERNAL

> **D:** 50 tons   **S:** 10 kts   **Dim:** 20.0 × 4.25 × 0.75   **M:** 2 diesels; 260 hp

REMARK: All for river use.

◆ **1 school sailing ship**

Gloria   1976

GLORIA Bldr: Celaya, Bilbao

> **D:** 1,300 tons (fl)   **S:** 10.5 kts (on diesel)   **Dim:** 64.7 × 10.6 × 6.6
> **M:** 1 diesel; 500 hp   **Sail area:** 1,400 m²

REMARKS: Bark-rigged. Delivered 7-9-68.

◆ **1 floating dry dock**

JAIME ARIAS

COMORO ISLANDS

MERCHANT MARINE (1978): 3 ships — 765 grt

◆ **1 landing ship**

N . . .

L-9061   C. Limonier, 1975

> **D:** 657 tons (1,000 fl)   **S:** 9 kts   **Dim:** 70.48 × 11.9 × 1.8
> **A:** 2/20-mm AA (I × 2) — 1/120-mm mortar, Army model
> **M:** 4 Paxman diesels; 2 props; 1,840 hp   **Man:** 29 men

REMARK: Ex-British *Buttress* (LCT(8) 4099) bought 7-65 by France (LCT-9061), transferred by France, 1976.

CONGO
People's Republic of

PERSONNEL: 180 men

MERCHANT MARINE (1978): 16 ships—6,942 grt

The naval forces are divided into coastal navy and the river navy.
Coastal navy:

◆ **3 ex-Chinese Shanghai-II-class patrol boats**

P 401   P 402   P 403

    D: 155 tons (fl)   **S:** 28 kts   **Dim:** 38.8 × 5.4 × 1.6
    A: 4/37-mm AA (II × 2)—4/25-mm AA (II × 2)—depth charges
    M: 4 diesels; 4 props; 4,800 hp   **Man:** 25 men

REMARKS: Very unsophisticated boats. Delivered in 3-75.

River navy:

◆ **4 ex-Chinese Yu Lin-class 10-ton river patrol boats**

◆ **2 locally built small craft**

◆ **10 small craft**

    M: 40-to-75 hp Johnson outboards

REMARK: Probably in poor condition.

COSTA RICA

PERSONNEL: 100 men

MERCHANT MARINE (1978): 19 ships—10,462 grt

◆ **1 105-foot U.S. Swift ship**

FP . . .

    D: 118 tons (fl)   **S:** 36 kts   **Dim:** 31.73 × 7.1 × 2.16
    A: Machine guns   **Range:** 1,200/18
    M: 3 MTU 12V331 diesels; 3 props; . . . hp

REMARK: Acquired 1978.

◆ **5 65-foot U.S. Swift ships**

FP 407   FP 408   FP 409   FP 410   FP 411

    D: 33 tons (fl)   **S:** 32 kts   **Dim:** 19.77 × 5.56 × 1.98
    A: Machine guns   **Range:** 1,200/18
    M: 2 MTU 8V331 diesels; 2 props; . . . hp

REMARK: Acquired 1978.

CUBA

PERSONNEL: Approx. 9,000 men

MERCHANT MARINE (1978):   331 ships—779,187 grt
                (tankers: 15—71,022 grt)

SUBMARINES

◆ **1 Soviet Foxtrot class**

    D: 1,950 tons surfaced, 2,400 submerged   **S:** 18 kts surfaced, 16 submerged
    Dim: 96.0 × 7.5 × 6.0   **Man:** 78 men   **Endurance:** 70 days
    A: 10/533-mm TT (6 fwd, 4 aft)—22 torpedoes or 44 mines
    M: Diesels and electric motors; 3 props

REMARKS: Transferred 1-79. A nonoperational Whiskey-class submarine was transferred 4-79, possibly as a training hulk.

PATROL BOATS

◆ **4 Soviet Kronstadt class**

Cuban Kronstadt   1972

    D: 300 tons (330 fl)   **S:** 18 kts   **Dim:** 52.1 × 6.5 × 2.2
    A: 1/85-mm DP—2/37-mm AA (I × 2)—6/14.5-mm machine guns—2/MBU-1800—2
        depth-charge projectors—2 depth-charge racks
    Electron Equipt: Radar: Ball End   **Man:** 50 men   **Range:** 1,500/12
    M: 3 diesels; 3 props; 3,300 hp   **Fuel:** 20 tons diesel

REMARKS: Transferred 2-62. Two additional believed discarded.

◆ **10 Soviet S.O.-1 class**

    D: 190 tons (215 fl)   **S:** 28 kts   **Dim:** 42.0 × 6.1 × 1.9
    A: 4/25-mm AA (II × 2)—4/MBU-1800 ASW rocket launchers—2 depth-charge racks

PATROL BOATS (*continued*)

Cuban S.O.-1   1975

Electron Equipt: Radar: Pot Head   **Man:**   30 men
M: 3 diesels; 3 props; 6,000 hp

REMARKS: Six were transferred in 1964 and six in 1967. Two additional believed discarded.

GUIDED-MISSILE BOATS

◆ **6 Soviet Osa-II class**

    D: 240 tons (fl)   **S:**   36 kts   **Dim:**   39.0 × 7.7 × 1.8
    A: 4 Styx SSM (I × 4)–4/30-mm AA (II × 2)   **Range:**   800/25
    Electron Equipt: Radars: 1/Square Tie, 1/Drum Tilt
    M: 3 M504 diesels; 3 props; 15,000 hp   **Man:**   25 men

REMARK: Transferred 1976-79.

◆ **6 Soviet Osa-I class**

    D: 175 tons (210 fl)   **S:**   36 kts   **Dim:**   39.0 × 7.7 × 1.8
    A: 4 Styx SSM–4/30-mm AA (II × 2)   **Man:**   25 men
    Electron Equipt: Radars: 1/Square Tie, 1/Drum Tilt
    M: 3 M503A diesels; 3 props; 12,000 hp

REMARK: Two were delivered in 1972, two in 1973, and two in 1974.

◆ **18 Soviet Komar class**

    D: 71 tons (82 fl)   **S:**   40 kts   **Dim:**   25.3 × 7.0 × 2.0
    A: 2 Styx systems–2/25-mm AA (II × 1)   **Man:**   19 men
    Electron Equipt: Radar: 1/Square Tie
    M: 4 M50 diesels; 4 props; 4,800 hp   **Range:**   650/30

REMARKS: Date from 1961-63. Twelve were delivered in 1962 and six in 1966.

TORPEDO BOATS

◆ **2 Soviet Turya-class hydrofoils**

    D: 240 tons (fl)   **S:**   40 kts   **Dim:**   39.0 × 7.7 × 1.8 (without foils)
    A: 2/57-mm AA aft (II × 1)–2/25-mm AA (II × 1)–4/533-mm TT (I × 4)

Two Turya-class hydrofoils en route to Cuba   1979

    Electron Equipt: Radars: 1/Pot Drum, 1/Muff Cob
                         Sonar: None
    M: 3 M504 diesels; 3 props; 15,000 hp   **Man:**   16 men

REMARKS: Delivered 2-79, the first foreign transfer of this class. ASW capability deleted. Fixed forward hydrofoils; stern planes on surface. Uses Osa-II hull and propulsion.

◆ **6 Soviet P-6 class**

    D: 56 tons (66.5 fl)   **S:**   43 kts   **Dim:**   25.3 × 6.1 × 1.7
    A: 4/25-mm AA (II × 2)–2/533-mm TT–depth charges
    Electron Equipt: Radar: Skin Head   **Range:**   450/30
    M: 4 M50 diesels; 4 props; 4,800 hp

REMARKS: Post-1955. Delivered in 1962.

◆ **12 Soviet P-4 class**

    D: 19.3 tons (22.4 fl)   **S:**   55 kts   **Dim:**   19.3 × 3.7 × 1.0
    A: 2/14.5-mm machine guns (aft)–2/450-mm TT
    Electron Equipt: Radar: Skin Head   **M:**   2 M50 diesels; 2 props; 2,400 hp

REMARKS: Pre-1955. Delivered 1962-64.

PATROL CRAFT

◆ **10 Soviet Zhuk class**

    D: 50 tons (60 fl)   **S:**   30 kts   **Dim:**   26.0 × 4.9 × 1.5
    A: 4/14.5-mm machine guns (II × 2)   **M:**   2 M50 diesels; 2 props; 2,400 hp

REMARK: Transferred 1975-78.

CUBA (*continued*)

MINE WARFARE SHIPS

◆ **2 Soviet Yevgenya-class inshore minesweepers**

> **D:** 80 tons (90 fl)   **S:** 12 kts   **Dim:** 26.0 × 6.0 × 1.5
> **A:** 2/25-mm AA (II × 1)   **Man:** 12 men   **M:** 2 diesels; 600 hp

REMARK: Transferred 1978.

AUXILIARY SHIPS

◆ **7 hydrographic survey vessels**

H 101   **D:** 600 tons

REMARKS: Former trawler, built in Spain, 1972. Also used for training.

H 91   H 92   H 93   H 94   H 95   H 96

> **D:** 120 tons (fl)   **S:** 12 kts   **Dim:** 29.0 × 5.0 × 1.7
> **M:** 1 diesel   **Man:** 15 men   **Range:** 1,600/10

REMARKS: Date of transfer not known. Soviet Nyryat-1 class, known in U.S.S.R. as
GPB-480 class. Same class, with different equipment, also used as diving tenders.

◆ **2 lighthouse and buoy tenders**

ENRIQUE COLLAZO   Bldr: Great Britain, 1906

> **D:** 815 tons   **Dim:** 64.0 × 10.5 × 2.8
> **M:** Triple expansion; 2 props; 680 hp

SF 10 BERTHA

> **D:** 100 tons   **S:** 10 kts   **Dim:** 31.5 × 5.75 × 3.4
> **M:** 2 Gray diesels; 2 props; 450 hp

REMARK: Dates from 1944.

◆ **7 Soviet T-4-class landing craft (LCM)**

> **D:** 94 tons (fl)   **S:** 9 kts   **Dim:** 19.0 × 5.3 × 1.3
> **M:** 2 diesels; 2 props; 400 hp

REMARKS: Transferred 1967-74. Used as harbor craft.

◆ **1 yacht**

GRANMA   Small cabin cruiser in which Fidel Castro returned to Cuba in 1956. Maintained by the navy as a museum.

◆ **3 small service launches**   Bldr: U.S.A., 1949

A 1   A 2   A 3

> **D:** 58 tons   **Dim:** 22.50 × 4.6 × 1.6
> **M:** 2 Gray Marine diesels; 2 props; 225 hp

◆ **1 Soviet Okhtensky-class tug**

CARIBE

> **D:** 1,000 tons (fl)   **S:** 12 kts   **Dim:** 46.5 × 9.5 × 3.9
> **M:** 2 diesels; 2 props; 2,000 hp   **Man:** 34 men

REMARK: Transferred 1976.

COAST GUARD

◆ **7 craft**

GF 528   GF 725   GF 825   GF 720   similar to 40-foot U.S. Coast Guard small craft

GF 101   GF 102   GF 701   similar to 70-foot U.S. Coast Guard small craft

REMARKS: Assigned to the Department of the Interior. Hull numbers painted in red to
distinguish these boats from naval ships.

◆ **1 patrol craft**

GUANABACOA   Bldr: Cadiz

> **S:** 22 kts   **L:** . . .

◆ **6 fast launches**

CAMILO CIENFUEGOS   MACEO   MARTI
ESCAMBRAY CUARTEL MONCADA   FINLAY

Bldr: Spain, 1971-72

REMARK: No other information.

CYPRUS

PERSONNEL: 330 men

MERCHANT MARINE (1978):   774 ships—2,494,039 grt
(tankers: 23—204,993 grt)

◆ **2 ex-German R-class minesweepers**

R-class minesweeper in Cypriot service   G. Arra, 1971

> **D:** 130 tons (fl)   **S:** 18 kts   **Dim:** 37.8 × 5.8 × 1.4
> **A:** 1/40-mm AA—2/20-mm (I × 2)   **M:** 2 M.A.N. diesels; 2 props; 1,800 hp

REMARK: Date from 1943.

◆ **6 Soviet P-4-class torpedo boats**

> **D:** 19.3 tons (22.4 fl)   **S:** 55 kts   **Dim:** 19.3 × 3.7 × 1.0
> **A:** 2/14.5-mm machine guns (II × 1)—2/450-mm TT   **Man:** 12 men
> **Electron Equipt:** Radar: 1/Skin Head   **M:** 2 M50 diesels; 2 props; 2,400 hp

CYPRUS (*continued*)

REMARK: Four transferred in 10-64 and two in 2-65.

◆ **10 small former fishing boats**

   D: 50 tons   A: 1 or 2 machine guns

REMARK: Several were probably lost during the crisis in July 1974.

DENMARK

PERSONNEL: 6,100 men

MERCHANT MARINE (1978):   1,397 ships − 5,530,408 grt
                                        (tankers: 74 ships − 2,902,383 grt)

NAVAL AVIATION: About 15 helicopters, including 8 Alouette-III. Five WG-13 Sea Lynx were ordered during 1979 for service aboard the five fisheries-protection corvettes; they will replace Alouette-III helicopters.

WARSHIPS IN SERVICE OR UNDER CONSTRUCTION AS OF 1 JANUARY 1980

	L	Tons (Surfaced)	Main armament
◆ **6 submarines**			
2 TYPE 205	1968-69	370	8/533-mm TT
4 DELFINEN	1956-63	595	4/533-mm TT
		Tons	
◆ **2 frigates**			
2 PEDER SKRAM	1965	2,030	8 Harpoon, 1 Sea Sparrow, 2/127-mm DP, 4/40-mm AA
◆ **8 corvettes**			
3 NILS JUEL	1978-79	1,320	8 Harpoons, 1 Sea Sparrow, 1/76-mm DP
1 HVIDBJØRNEN, mod.	1975	1,970	1/76-mm DP, 1 helicopter
4 HVIDBJØRNEN	1961-62	1,345	1/76-mm DP, 1 helicopter
◆ **16 guided-missile and torpedo boats**			
10 WILLIMOES	1974-	250	1/76-mm, 4/533-mm TT
6 SØLØVEN	1963-66	95	2/40-mm AA, 4/533-mm TT
◆ **21 (+1) patrol boats**			
2 (+1) AGDLEK	1974	330	2/20-mm AA
9 BARSØ	1969-73	155	2/20-mm AA
2 MAAGEN	1960	175	1/40-mm AA
8 DAPHNE	1960-63	150	1/40-mm AA

◆ **6 minelayers**

2 LINDORMEN	1977	575	2/20-mm AA, 60 mines
4 FALSTER	1962-63	1,880	4/76-mm AA, 400 mines

◆ **8 coastal minesweepers**

SUBMARINES

NOTE: Denmark is considering the construction of six units of the German/Norwegian Type 210 replacement design to supplant, first, her *Delfinen*s and, then, her Type-205s.

◆ **2 type 205**

	Bldr	Laid down	L	In serv.
S 320 NARHVALEN	RDY Copenhagen	2-65	10-9-68	2-70
S 321 NORDKAPEREN	RDY Copenhagen	1-66	18-12-69	12-70

Narhvalen   1970

   D: 370 tons surfaced, 480 submerged   **Dim:** 45.41 × 4.6 × 4.58
   S: 17/12 kts   A: 8/533-mm TT, fwd   **Man:** 22 men
   M: 2 Mercedes-Benz diesels, diesel-electric drive; 1 prop; 1,200/1,700 hp

REMARK: Modeled on the German Type 205 and Norwegian Type Type 207 (*Kobben* class)

◆ **4 Delfinen class**

	Bldr	Laid down	L	In serv.
S 326 DELFINEN	RDY Copenhagen	7-54	5-5-56	9-58
S 327 SPÆKHUGGEREN	RDY Copenhagen	12-54	20-2-57	6-59
S 328 TUMLEREN	RDY Copenhagen	5-56	22-5-58	1-60
S 329 SPRINGEREN	RDY Copenhagen	1-61	26-4-63	10-64

Springeren   1970

SUBMARINES (*continued*)

D: 595 tons surfaced, 643 submerged   **Dim:** 54.0 × 4.7 × 3.8
S: 13/12 kts   **Man:** 33 men
A: 4/533-mm TT, fwd   **Range:** 4,000/8.5
M: Burmeister & Wain diesels and motors; 2 props; 1,200 hp

REMARKS: S-329 built with U.S. "offshore" funds, as U.S. SS-554. S-327 damaged in dry-dock accident 20-9-79; will probably be stricken.

FRIGATES

◆ **2 Peder Skram**

	Bldr	Laid down	L	In serv.
F 352 PEDER SKRAM	Helsingør Vaerft	9-64	20-5-65	6-66
F 353 HERLUF TROLLE	Helsingør Vaerft	12-64	8-9-65	4-67

Herluf Trolle   1977

Herluf Trolle   1977

D: 2,030 tons (2,720 fl)   **S:** 28 kts   **Dim:** 112.5 (108.0 pp) × 12.0 × 3.6
A: 8 Harpoon SSM—1 NATO Sea Sparrow system (VIII × 1)—2/127-mm DP (II × 1)
   —4/40-mm AA (I × 4)—4/533-mm TT (IV × 1)
Electron Equipt: Radars: 1/CWS 3, 1/CWS 2, 1/NWS 1, 1/NWS 2, 3/M 46 fire-control, 2/Mk 91 fire-control
              Sonar: 1/Plessey MS 26
M: CODOG propulsion: 2 diesels (4,800 hp); 2 gas turbines (37,000 hp); 2 Ka-Me-Wa props   **Man:** 200 men

REMARKS: Danish design, built with U.S. "offshore" funds. The gas turbines are GG4A-3 Pratt & Whitney Stal-Laval models and the diesels are General Motors 567D, V-16 V (800 rpm). Speed with diesels: 16 knots. The 127-mm guns are U.S. 38-caliber model. There are two radar directors for the Sea Sparrow system, which, along with Harpoon, was added 1977-79.

CORVETTES

◆ **3 Nils Juel (Type KV 72) class**

	Laid down	L	In serv.
F 354 NILS JUEL	1977	27-9-78	1979
F 355 OLFERT FISCHER	1977	. . .	1980
F 356 PETER TORDENSKJOLD	1977	. . .	1981

Bldr: Aalborg Vaerft

Nils Juel—*on trials*   1979

D: 1,320 tons (fl)   **S:** 30 kts (20 on diesel)
Dim: 84.0 (80.0 pp) × 10.3 × 3.1   **Man:** 18 officers, 9 CPO, 63 men
A: 8 Harpoon SSM (IV × 2)—NATO Sea Sparrow SAM (VIII × 1)—1/76-mm OTO Melara Compact DP—ASW torpedoes—1 depth-charge rack
Electron Equipt: Radars: 1/AWS 5, 2/M 46, 2 SCLAR chaff launchers
M: CODOG: 1 GE LM-2500 GT (25,000 hp), 1 MTU 20V-956 diesel (4,800 hp); 2 props

REMARK: Ordered 5-12-75.

◆ **1 modified Hvidbjørnen class**   Bldr: Aalborg Vaerft

	Laid down	L	In serv.
F 340 BESKYTTEREN	15-12-74	27-5-75	27-2-76

CORVETTES (continued)

Beskyterren 1976

D: 1970 tons (fl)   **S:** 18 kts   **Dim:** 74.4 × 11.8 × 4.5
Man: 60 men   **Range:** 6,000/13 (one engine)
A: 1/76-mm DP – 1 helicopter
Electron Equipt: Radars: 1/CWS 2, 1/NWS 1, 1/NWS 2
         Sonar: Plessey MS 26
M: 4 B & W Alpha diesels; 1 controllable-pitch prop; 7,440 hp

REMARKS: Serves as a fisheries-protection ship. The helicopter is an Alouette-III. An OTO Melara Compact 76-mm gun was to have been fitted.

◆ 4 Hvidbjørnen class

	Bldr	Laid down	L	In serv.
F 348 HVIDBJØRNEN	Aarhus Flydedok	6-61	23-11-61	12-62
F 349 VAEDDEREN	Aalborg SY	10-61	6-4-62	3-63
F 350 INGOLF	Svendborg Skibsvaerft	12-61	27-7-62	6-63
F 351 FYLLA	Aalborg SY	6-62	18-12-62	7-63

Ingolf 1970

D: 1,345 tons (1,650 fl)   **S:** 18 kts   **Dim:** 72.6 × 11.6 × 4.9
A: 1/76-mm DP – 1 Alouette-III helicopter   **Range:** 6,000/13

Electron Equipt: Radars: 1/CWS 1, 1/NWS 1
         Sonar: Plessey MS 46
M: 4 GM 16-567C diesels; 1 controllable-pitch prop; 6,400 hp
Man: 10 officers, 60 men

REMARKS: Used for fisheries-protection. Reinforced bow. F-350, used for hydrographic surveying, has no gun or helicopter but carries four 13-meter survey launches on her flight deck.

◆ 1 Italian Airone class

	Bldr	L	In serv.
F 347 TRITON	CN di Taranto, Italy	19-9-54	8-55

D: 760 tons (870 fl)   **S:** 20 kts (16 cruising)
Dim: 75.0 (69.49 pp) × 9.5 × 3.0   **Man:** 109 men
A: 2/76-mm DP – 1/40-mm – ASW weapons, including 2 Hedgehogs
Electron Equipt: Radars: 1/CWS 1, 1/NSW 1
         Sonar: QCU 2

REMARKS: The *Diana* (F-345) was discarded in 1974, the *Flora* (F-346) in 1979. The others will be scrapped on completion of the *Nils Juel* class. Built with U.S. "offshore" funds.

GUIDED-MISSILE BOATS

◆ 10 Willemoes class

	L	In serv.		L	In serv.
P 540 BILLE	26-3-76	10-76	P 545 NORBY	11-77	16-2-78
P 541 BREDAL	. . .	1-77	P 546 RODSTEEN	. . .	1-78
P 542 HAMMER	. . .	1-4-77	P 547 SEHESTED	5-5-77	3-78
P 543 HUITFELDT	. . .	15-6-77	P 548 SUENSON	26-8-77	6-78
P 544 KRIEGER	. . .	22-9-77	P 549 WILLEMOES	5-10-74	7-10-76

Bldr: Frederikshavn SY.

Willemoes 1977

GUIDED-MISSILE BOATS (*continued*)

Willemoes — with 20 mines in lieu of torpedo tubes   1976

Willemoes — with four Harpoon launchers   1979

D: 232 tons (265 fl)   **S:** 40 kts (36 normal)
Dim: 46.1 (42.4 pp) × 7.4 × 2.1 (2.7 over props)   **Man:** 5 officers, 21 men
A: 1/76-mm OTO Melara Compact — 4/533-mm TT (or 4 Harpoon — 2/533-mm TT) —
6 flare launchers
Electron Equipt: Radars: 1/NWS 3, 1/9LV 200 fire-control
Range: 400/36   **Electric:** 420 kw
M: CODOG: 3 Rolls-Royce Proteus 52M/544 gas turbines; 2 GM 8V-71 diesels; 3
Ka-Me-Wa props; 12,750/800 hp

REMARKS: Based on the Swedish Lürssen-designed Spica class and ordered in 1972.
The torpedoes are Swedish Type 61, wire-guided, with a range of 20,000 meters. Endurance is normally 36 hours. P-545 carried two Harpoon early in 1979.

TORPEDO BOATS

◆ **6 Søløven class**

	Bldr	Laid down	L	In serv.
P 510 SØLØVEN	Vosper, Portsmouth	8-62	19-4-63	2-65
P 511 SØRIDDEREN	Vosper, Portsmouth	10-62	22-8-63	2-65
P 512 SØBJORNEN	RDY Copenhagen	7-63	19-8-64	9-65
P 513 SØHESTEN	RDY Copenhagen	8-63	31-3-65	1966
P 514 SØHUNDEN	RDY Copenhagen	2-64	12-1-66	1-67
P 515 SØULVEN	RDY Copenhagen	6-64	27-4-66	3-67

Søridderen   1970

D: 95 tons (114 fl)   **S:** 50 kts (10 on diesel)
Dim: 30.26 (27.44 pp) × 7.3 × 2.15
A: 2/40-mm AA (I × 2) — 2/533-mm TT   **Man:** 4 officers, 22 men
M: Rolls-Royce Marine Proteus gas turbines; 3 props; 10,500 hp (12,750 max);
cruising, 2 GM 6V-71 diesels

REMARKS: A modification of the British Brave class. Two 533-mm TT were removed
when the after gun was enclosed. P-510 was built as PT-821 with U.S. funds. The
Falken-class torpedo boats were discarded 1977-78.

PATROL BOATS AND CRAFT

◆ **3 Agdlek class**

	In serv.
Y 386 AGDLEK	12-3-74
Y 387 AGPA	14-5-74
Y . . . N . . .	. . .

Agdlek   1976

PATROL BOATS AND CRAFT (*continued*)

Bldr: Svendborg

D: 330 tons (fl) **S:** 12 kts **Dim:** 31.4 × 7.7 × 3.3
A: 2/20-mm AA (I × 2) **Electron Equipt:** Radars: 2/Terma 20T48
M: 1 Burmeister & Wain Alpha diesel; 800 hp **Man:** 15 men

REMARKS: For service in Greenland waters. Can carry two survey launches. A third unit was ordered during 1978.

◆ **9 Barsø class** Bldr: Svendborg

Y 300 BARSØ	Y 303 SAMSØ	Y 305 VEJRØ	Y 307 LAESØ
Y 301 DREJØ	Y 304 THURØ	Y 306 FARØ	Y 308 ROMØ
Y 302 ROMSØ			

Barsø 1970

D: 155 tons (fl) **S:** 11 kts **Dim:** 25.5 × 6.0 × 2.8
A: 2/20-mm AA (I × 2) **M:** 1 diesel; 1 prop; 385 hp

REMARK: The first six were built in 1969, and the last three 1972-73.

◆ **2 Maagen class**

	Bldr	In serv.
Y 384 MAAGEN	Helsingør Vaerft	5-60
Y 385 MALLEMUKKEN	Helsingør Vaerft	5-60

D: 175 tons (190 fl) **S:** 10 kts **Dim:** 27.0 × 7.2 × 2.75
A: 1/40-mm AA **M:** Diesel; 1 prop; 350 hp

REMARKS: Steel hull. Profile of a whale-hunter ship. Based in Greenland. Gun normally not carried.

Maagen 1970

◆ **8 Daphne class**

	Laid down	L	In serv.
P 530 DAPHNE	4-60	10-11-60	12-61
P 531 DRYADEN	7-60	1-3-61	4-62
P 533 HAVFRUEN	3-61	4-10-61	12-62
P 534 NAJADEN	9-61	20-6-62	4-63
P 535 NYMFEN	4-62	1-11-62	10-63
P 536 NEPTUN	9-62	29-5-63	12-63
P 537 RAN	12-62	10-7-63	5-64
P 538 ROTA	6-63	26-11-63	1-65

Bldr: RDY, Copenhagen

Ran 1970

D: 150 tons (170 fl) **S:** 20 kts **Dim:** 38.0 × 6.75 × 2.0
A: 1/40-mm AA − 2 depth-charge projectors − 2 depth-charge racks
Electron Equipt: Radar: 1/NWS 3 Sonar: Plessey MS 26

PATROL BOATS AND CRAFT (*continued*)

M: 2 Maybach diesels, 1,300 hp, and 1 Foden FD-6 diesel, 100 hp; 3 props
Man: 23 men

REMARKS: The 100-hp engine is used for cruising. P-530, P-534, and P-536, which were paid for with U.S. "offshore" funds as PGM-47, PGM-49, and PGM-50, are completely disarmed. The *Havmanden* (P-532) was struck in 1978; others may follow soon.

◆ 3 Botved 9.8-meter class

Y 377   Y 378   Y 379

D: 9 tons (fl)   **S:** 27 kts   **Dim:** 9.8 × 3.3 × 0.9
Electron Equipt: Radar 1/NWS 3
M: 2 Volvo Penta inboard/outboard diesels; 2 props; 600 hp

REMARK: Date from 1975.

◆ 2 Botved 13.3-meter class

Y 375   Y 376

D: 12 tons (fl)   **S:** 26 kts   **Dim:** 13.3 × 4.5 × 1.1
M: 2 diesels; 2 props; 680 hp   **Electron Equipt:** Radar: 1/NWS 3

REMARK: Date from 1974.

PATROL CRAFT MANNED BY THE HOME GUARD

◆ 2 (+24) MHV class   Bldr: Ejvinds, Svendborg

D: . . .   **S:** 15 kts   **Dim:** . . . × . . . × . . .
A: 1/20-mm AA   **M:** 1 MTU diesel; . . . hp

REMARKS: These craft are intended to replace the older MHV units over the next few years. Glass-reinforced plastic hulls.

◆ 7 MHV-90 class

MHV 90   MHV 91   MHV 92   MHV 93   MHV 94   MHV 95   MHV 96

D: 85 tons (130 fl)   **S:** 10.7 kts   **Dim:** 19.8 × 5.7 × 1.6
A: 1/20-mm AA   **M:** 1 Burmeister & Wain diesel; 400 hp

REMARK: In service 1974-75.

◆ 3 MHV-70 class   Bldr: Navy Yard, Copenhagen

MHV 70   MHV 71   MHV 72

D: 78 tons (130 fl)   **S:** 10 kts   **Dim:** 20.1 × 5.1 × 2.5
A: 1/20-mm AA   **M:** 1 diesel; 200 hp

REMARK: In service 1958.

◆ 6 MHV-80 class

MHV 81 ASKØ   MHV 83 MANØ   MHV 85 HJORTØ
MHV 82 ENØ   MHV 84 BAAGØ   MHV 86 LYØ

D: 74 tons   **S:** 11 kts   **Dim:** 24.4 × 4.9 × 1.6
A: 1/20-mm AA   **M:** 1 diesel; 350 hp

REMARK: In service 1958. Former inshore minesweepers.

◆ 32 smaller craft, including:

MHV 1 through MHV 15; MHV 51, MHV 52, MHV 54, MHV 56 through MHV 68, MHV 74. No data known.

MINE WARFARE SHIPS

◆ 4 Falster-class minelayers

	Bldr	Laid down	L	In serv.
N 80 FALSTER	Nakskov Skibsvaerft	4-62	19-9-62	11-63
N 81 FYEN	Frederikshavn Vaerft	4-62	3-10-62	9-63
N 82 MØEN	Frederikshavn Vaerft	10-62	6-6-63	4-64
N 83 SJAELLAND	Nakskov Skibsvaerft	1-63	14-6-63	7-64

Møen   G. Arra, 1977

D: 1,880 tons (fl)   **S:** 16.5 kts   **Dim:** 77 (72.5 pp) × 12.5 × 3.0
Man: 10 officers, 108 men
A: 4/76-mm AA (II × 2) – 400 mines – 4 minelaying tracks
Electron Equipt: Radars: 1/CSW 2, 1/NWS 3, 1/M 46
M: GM 16-567D diesels; 2 variable-pitch props; 4,800 hp

Møen   1977

MINE WARFARE SHIPS (continued)

REMARKS: NATO design. The Turkish ship *Nusret* was identical. N-82 is a training ship for naval cadets. N-83 converted to submarine tender in 1976, to replace *Henrik Gerner* (can still lay mines). N-80 and N-82 built with U.S. "offshore" funds as MMC-14 and MMC-15. Now have ESM domes on the foremast yards.

◆ **2 Lindormen-class minelayers** Bldr: Svendborg

	Laid down	L	In serv.
N 43 LINDORMEN	20-1-77	7-6-77	1978
N 44 LOUSSEN	2-77	9-9-77	1978

D: 575 tons (fl)   S: 14 kts   Dim: 43.3 (40.0 pp) × 9.0 × 2.65
A: 2/20-mm AA (I × 2) – 50 to 60 mines   Man: 27 men
M: 2 Wichmann 7AX diesels; 2 props; 4,200 hp   Electric: 192 kw

REMARKS: Built to replace the *Lougen* class.

◆ **8 ex-U.S. coastal minesweepers**

M 571 AARØSUND	M 574 GRØNSUND	M 577 ULVSUND
M 572 ALSSUND	M 575 GULDBORGSUND	M 578 VILSUND
M 573 EGERNSUND	M 576 OMØSUND	

Bldr: U.S.A., 1953-56

Aarøsund   1970

D: 350 tons (376 fl)   Dim: 43.89 (41.50 pp) × 7.95 × 2.55
S: 13 kts (8 sweeping)   Range: 2,500/10
A: 2/20-mm AA (II × 1)   Man: 38 men
Electron Equipt: Radar: 1/NWS 3 Sonar: 1/UQS-1   Fuel: 40 tons diesel
M: 2 GM 8-268A diesels; 2 props; 1,000 hp

REMARKS: Transferred, 1955-56. Hull entirely of wood. The first three are ex-MSC-127 to MSC-129 and are 405 tons (fl); the others are ex-MSC-256, ex-MSC-257, ex-MSC-221, ex-MSC-263, and ex-MSC-264. M-575 has a charthouse between the stack and bridge so that she can act as a survey ship; she still has minesweeping equipment and carries 1/40-mm AA forward.

AUXILIARY SHIPS

◆ **2 coastal oilers**

A 568 RIMFAXE (ex-U.S. YO-226)   A 569 SKINFAXE (ex-U.S. YO-229)

Rimfaxe   1970

D: 1,390 tons (fl)   Dim: 53.0 × 9.75 × 4.0
S: 10 kts   Man: 23 men   Range: 2,000/8
M: 1 GM 8-278A diesel; 1 prop; 640 hp   Cargo: 900 tons

REMARKS: Launched 1945, transferred 8-62.

◆ **1 torpedo transport/retriever**

A 558 SLEIPNER

D: 150 tons (fl)   S: 9 kts   Dim: 30.0 × . . . × . . .
M: 1 diesel; . . . hp

◆ **1 royal yacht**

A 540 DANNEBROG

D: 1,130 tons   S: 14 kts   Dim: 74.9 × 10.4 × 3.7
M: 4 Burmeister & Wain diesels; 2 props; 1,800 hp

REMARK: Dates from 1931.

◆ **3 icebreakers**

DANBJØRN   ISBJØRN

D: 3,685 tons   S: 14 kts   Dim: 75.6 × 16.8 × 6.0
M: Diesel-electric; 11,880 hp   Man: 34 men

ELBJØRN

D: 898 tons (1,400 fl)   S: 12 kts   Dim: 47.0 × 12.1 × 4.35
M: Diesel-electric; 3,600 hp

REMARKS: These icebreakers are owned and manned by the Ministry of Commerce. The *Danbjørn* and the *Isbjørn* date from 1965, and the *Elbjørn* from 1953. A new, 6,300-hp icebreaker was ordered during 1979.

DENMARK (*continued*)

MINISTRY OF FISHERIES

FISHERIES-PATROL SHIP

◆ **1 FV 710 class**   Bldr: Frederikshavn SY

HAVØRNEN

   D: 660 tons (fl)   **S:** 20 kts   **Dim:** 49.98 (45.8 pp) × 10.5 × 2.75
   A: . . .   **Man:** 15 men   **Range:** 5,000/15   **Electric:** 359 kva
   M: 2 Burmeister & Wain Alpha 16V23L-VO diesels; 2 controllable-pitch props;
   4,640 hp

REMARKS: In service 1979. Has a hangar and flight deck for one Sea Lynx or Alouette-III helicopter and a recessed stern ramp for a 6.5-meter rubber inspection dinghy. Built to mercantile specifications, a modified British "Osprey" design.

DJIBOUTI REPUBLIC

On independence, in 1977, a small naval/police force was established and took over one patrol craft formerly operated by the French colonial police at Djibouti.

◆ **1 ex-French patrol craft**   Bldr: Tecimar

P-472 and P-474

Tecimar, 1974

   D: 30 tons   **S:** 25 kts   **Dim:** 13.3 × 4.1 × 1.1
   A: 1/12.7-mm and 1/7/5-mm machine gun
   M: 2 GM diesels; Model V-71; 6 cylinders; 240 hp

REMARK: Molded hull of stratified polyester. In service since 1974.

DOMINICAN REPUBLIC

PERSONNEL: 370 officers and 3,630 men

MERCHANT MARINE (1978): 21 ships—18,313
              (tanker: 1 ship—674 grt)

FRIGATE

◆ **1 Canadian river class**

	Bldr	L
451 MELLA (ex-*Presidente Trujillo*, ex-*Carlplace*)	Davie S.B. (Lauzon)	6-7-44

Mella—wearing old number and with second tripod mast just forward of original

   D: 1,445 tons (2,300 fl)   **S:** 19 kts   **Dim:** 92.35 × 11.45 × 4.3
   A: 1/102-mm—1/40-mm AA—4/20-mm AA—2/47-mm saluting guns
   Man: 15 officers, 135 men   **Range:** 7,700/12   **Fuel:** 645 tons
   M: Triple-expansion; 2 props; 5,500 hp   **Boilers:** 2 (3-drum)

REMARKS: Bought in 1947. Serves as a training ship; can carry 50 cadets.

CORVETTES

◆ **3 ex-U.S. Cohoes-class netlayers**

	Bldr	L
P 207 CAMBIASO (ex-*Etlah*, AN-79)	Marietta Mfg., W.Va.	16-12-44
P 208 SEPARACIÓN (ex-*Passaconaway*, AN-86)	Marine Iron & Ry, Duluth	30-6-44
P 209 CALDERAS (ex-*Passaic*, AN-87)	Leatham B. Smith, Wisc.	29-6-44

   D: 650 tons (785 fl)   **S:** 12.3 kts   **Dim:** 51.36 (44.5 pp) × 10.31 × 3.3
   A: 1/76-mm DP—3/20-mm AA (I × 3)   **Man:** 48 men
   Electron Equipt: Radar: 1/SPS 5D   **Electric:** 120 kw   **Fuel:** 88 tons
   M: Diesel-electric: 2 Busch-Sulzer B5-539 diesels, 1 motor; 1 prop; 1,200 hp

REMARKS: Recommissioned from the U.S. Maritime Commission's reserve fleet, where

CORVETTES (continued)

they had been laid up since 1963, and transferred 9-76. Despite low speed and general unsuitability, they are employed as patrol ships and tugs. Also used in general support, navigational tender, and hydrographic survey duties.

◆ **2 ex-U.S. Admirable-class minesweeper-escorts**

	Bldr	L
BM 454 PRESTOL BOTELLO (ex-*Separación*, ex-*Skirmish*, MSF-303)	Assoc. Shbldg.	16-8-43
BM 455 TORTUGERO (ex-*Signet*, MSF-302)	Assoc. Shbldg.	16-8-43

Prestol Botello   1976

D: 600 tons (903 fl)   **Dim:** 56.24 × 10.06 × 4.4
S: 15 kts   **Man:** 100 men
A: 1/76-mm DP—2/40-mm AA (I × 2)—6/20-mm AA (I × 6)
M: General Motors diesels; 2 props; 1,710 hp
Fuel: 260 tons diesel   **Range:** 5,600/9

REMARKS: Transferred in 1-66. BM-454 renamed 1976. All minesweeping equipment and ASW armament removed from both.

PATROL BOATS AND CRAFT

◆ **1 ex-U.S. PGM-71 class**   Bldr: Peterson, U.S.A., 1965

GC 102 BETELGEUSE (ex-PGM-77)

D: 130 tons (145.5 fl)   **S:** 17 kts   **Dim:** 30.8 (30.2 pp) × 6.4 × 1.85
Man: 20 men   **Range:** 1,000/12
A: 1/40-mm AA—4/20-mm AA (II × 2)—2/12.7-mm machine guns (I × 2)
M: 8 GM 6-71 diesels; 2 props; 2,200 hp

REMARK: Transferred 1-66. One of many gunboats of this class transferred to smaller navies by the United States.

◆ **3 ex-U.S. Coast Guard boats**

		In serv.
P 204 (ex-P-105) INDEPENDENCIA (ex-*Icarus*, PC-110)		1931
P 205 (ex-P-106) LIBERTAD (ex-*Rafael Atoa*, ex-*Thetis*, PC-115)		1931
P 206 (ex-P-104, P 203) RESTAURACIÓN (ex-*Galathea*, PC-108)		1932

D: 235 tons (335 fl)   **S:** 14 kts   **Dim:** 50.3 × 7.6 × 2.5
Man: 40 men   **Fuel:** 25 tons diesel
A: 1/76-mm DP—1/40-mm AA—1/20-mm AA
M: 2 Winton diesels; 2 props; 1,280 hp   **Range:** 1,300/15

REMARK: All in reserve.

◆ **1 former U.S. Army aircraft-rescue launch**

GC 105 CAPITAN ALSINA   L: 1944

D: 100 tons   **S:** 17 kts   **Dim:** 31.5 × 5.8 × 1.75
A: 2/20-mm AA (I × 2)   **Man:** 20 men
M: 2 GM diesels; 2 props; 1,000 hp

REMARK: Wooden hull. Used as Naval Acadamy training craft, refitted 1977.

◆ **4 patrol craft**

	In serv.		In serv.
GC 104 ALDEBARÁN	1972	GC 106 BELLATRIX	1967
GC 103 PROCION	1967	GC 107 CAPELLA	1968

Bldr: Sewart Seacraft, Berwick, La.

D: 60 tons   **S:** 21.7 kts   **Dim:** 25.9 × 5.7 × 2.1   **Range:** 800/20
A: 3/12.7-mm machine guns   **Man:** 9 men
M: 2 GM 16V71N diesels; 2 props; 1,400 hp

◆ **1 former U.S. 63-ft aircraft-rescue launch**

GC 101 RIGEL

D: 27 tons   **S:** 18.5 kts   **Dim:** 19.3 × 4.7 × 1.2
A: 2/12.7-mm machine guns   **Range:** 450/15
M: 2 GM diesels; 2 props; 800 hp   **Man:** 9 men

REMARK: In service since 1953.

◆ **4 small patrol craft**   Bldr: Navy Yard

ATUN   CARITE   MERO   PICUA

D: 30 tons   **S:** 12 kts   **Dim:** 12.7 × 4.0 × 1.8
A: 1/7.6-mm machine gun   **M:** 2 GM diesels; 200 hp

REMARK: In service since 1975. Have auxiliary sail power. Sisters *Albacora* and *Bonito* discarded.

AUXILIARY SHIPS

◆ **1 converted LSM cargo-carrier**   Bldr: Brown Bros., Houston

301 SIRIO (ex-LSM-483)

D: 734 tons (1,100 fl)   **S:** 12 kts   **Dim:** 62.8 × 10.4 × 2.1
Man: 30 men   **Fuel:** 164 tons diesel
M: 2 GM diesels; 1,800 hp

REMARKS: Launched 10-3-45, transferred in 1960. Decked over, bow doors plated up, bridge on centerline.

DOMINICAN REPUBLIC (*continued*)

AUXILIARY SHIPS (*continued*)

◆ **1 LCU** Bldr: Dominican Naval SY, 1958

LDM 302 (ex-LA-2) SAMANA

    D: 128 tons (310 fl)   **S:** 8/7 kts   **Dim:** 36.4 × 11.0 × 1.15
    A: 1/12.7-mm machine gun   **Man:** 17 men   **Fuel:** 80 tons diesel
    M: 3 GM diesels; 3 props; 450 hp

REMARKS: U.S. LCT(5) design, used for logistics duties. Sister *Enriquillo* discarded 1979.

◆ **2 buoy tenders**

BA 10 NEPTUNO (ex-*Toro*) Bldr: J. H. Mathis, U.S.A., 1954
    D: 72.2 tons (fl)   **S:** 10 kts   **Dim:** 19.5 × 5.7 × 2.4
    M: 1 GM diesel; 225 hp   **Man:** 7 men

FB 1 CAPOTILLO (ex-FB-101, ex-*Camillia*, WAGL-206) Bldr: U.S.A., 1911

    D: 327 tons   **S:** 10 kts

REMARK: *Capotillo* transferred 1949.

◆ **2 small oilers** Bldr: Ira S. Bushey, N.Y.

BT 4 CAPITAN W. ARVELO (ex-U.S. YO-213)
BT 5 CAPITAN BEOTEGUI (ex-U.S. YO-215)

    D: 1,076 tons (fl)   **S:** 8 kts   **Dim:** 47.6 × 9.3 × 4.0
    A: 1/20-mm AA   **Man:** 25 men   **Cargo:** 6,071 barrels fuel
    M: 2 Union diesels; 1 prop; 525 hp

REMARKS: BT-4 was launched in 1945, BT-5 in 1944. Both were loaned 4-64.

◆ **1 small survey ship**

BA 8 ATLANTIDA

◆ **7 tugs**

RM 21 MACORIX (ex-U.S. *Kiowa*, ATF-72)

    Bldr: Charleston SB & DD

    D: 1,280 tons (1,700 fl)   **S:** 15 kts   **Dim:** 62.5 × 11.7 × 4.7
    M: Diesel-electric, 4 GM 5-267 diesels; 1 prop; 3,000 hp

REMARK: Launched 5-11-42, transferred 10-72.

RM 18 CAONABO (ex-U.S. *Sagamore*, ATA-208)

    Bldr: Gulfport Boiler & Welding, Texas

    D: 534 tons (835 fl)   **S:** 13 kts   **Dim:** 43.6 × 10.3 × 4.0
    M: Diesel-electric, 2 GM 5-267 diesels; 1 prop; 1,500 hp

REMARKS: Launched 19-1-45, transferred 2-72.

RDM 303 OCOA Bldr: U.S.A.

    D: 50 tons (fl)   **S:** 9 kts   **Dim:** 17.1 × 4.3 × 1.2
    M: 2 diesels; 2 props; 450 hp   **Range:** 130/9

REMARK: Former U.S. LCM, modified as a tug about 1976.

RP 20 ISABELA   **M:** 300 hp
RP 14 MAGUANA   RP CALDERAS—small coastal tugs
RP 16 BOHECHIO (ex-U.S. YTL)   **M:** 240 hp   Transferred 1-71

ECUADOR

PERSONNEL: 3,800 total

MERCHANT MARINE (1978): 59 ships—201,244 grt
    (tankers: 17 ships—98,081)

NAVAL AVIATION: A small detachment with three French Alouette-III helicopters, three Israeli Arava light transports, two Cessna T-37, two T-41, one Cessna 320, and one Cessna 177.

NOTE: Ecuadorian pendant numbers change frequently; those listed below are the latest available.

SUBMARINES

◆ **2 German Type 209 (IK-79)**

	Bldr	L
S 11 SHYRI	Howaldtswerke, Kiel	8-10-76
S 12 HUANCAVILCA	Howaldtswerke, Kiel	18-3-77

    D: 1,100 tons standard, 1,260 surfaced, 1,390 submerged
    S: 21.5 kts (max. submerged for 5 minutes), 12 kts with snorkel
    Dim: 59.5 × 6.6 × 5.9   **Man:** 5 officers, 26 men   **Endurance:** 16 days
    A: 8/533-mm TT, fwd (plus 6 reserve torpedoes)
    M: 4 MTU type 12V-493-TY60 diesels; Siemens electric motor; 3,600 hp

REMARKS: Ordered in 1974. The latest version of a class previously sold to Argentina, Greece, and Peru. Two additional units not built.

◆ **1 U.S. Gearing class, FRAM-I**

	Bldr	L	In serv.
. . . PRESIDENTE ELOY ALFARO (ex-*Holder*, DD-819)	Consolidated, U.S.A.	25-8-45	5-46

    D: 2,425 tons (3,500 fl)   **S:** 30 kts   **Dim:** 119.1 × 12.4 × 5.8
    A: 4/127-mm DP (II × 2)—6/324-mm Mk 32 ASW TT (III × 2)
    Electron Equipt: Radars: 1/SPS 10, 1/SPS 40, 1/Mk 25 fire-control
        Sonar: SQS 23
    Man: 270 men   **Range:** 2,400/25, 4,800/15   **Fuel:** 650 tons
    M: GT; 2 props; 60,000 hp   **Boilers:** 4 Babcock & Wilcox

REMARKS: The *Alfaro* began overhaul in the U.S. 8-78, to arrive in Ecuador 7-79. Asroc deleted. Sale of the U.S.S. *Southerland* (DD-743) to Ecuador has been canceled.

FRIGATE

◆ **1 U.S. fast transport (LPR)**

	Bldr	L	In serv.
D 01 MORAN VALVERDE (ex-*26 de Julio*, ex-*Enright*, APD-66)	Phila. Navy Yd.	29-5-43	21-9-43

    D: 1,400 tons (2,130 fl)   **S:** 23 kts   **Dim:** 93.27 × 11.27 × 4.7
    A: 1/127-mm DP—6/40-mm AA (II × 3)—2 depth-charge racks
    Electron Equipt: Radars: 1/SPS 6, 1/SPS 10

FRIGATE (*continued*)

Moran Valverde   1974

Man: 212 men   **Range:** 2,000/23, 5,000/15   **Fuel:** 350 tons
M: GE turbo-electric drive; 2 props; 12,000 hp   **Boilers:** 2 Foster-Wheeler "D"

REMARKS: Transferred 7-67. Could carry 162 troops when in U.S. Navy. Davits can handle four LCPR/LCVP. Now has a raised helicopter deck over the stern area.

CORVETTES

◆ 6 Italian missile ships

		L			L	
. . .	N . . .	. . .	. . .	N . . .	. . .	
. . .	N . . .	. . .	. . .	N . . .	. . .	
. . .	N . . .	. . .	. . .	N . . .	. . .	

Bldr: CNR del Tirreno

D: 600 tons (fl)   **S:** 32.5 kts   **Dim:** 61.7 (57.8 pp) × 9.3 × . . .
A: 4/Otomat SSM – 1/76-mm OTO Melara Compact – 2/40-mm AA Breda – 1/Bofors 375-mm ASW rocket launcher (II × 1)
Electron Equipt: Radars: 1/RAN 11-LX, 1/NA 10 fire-control
        Sonar: Plessey MS 26
Man: 54 men   **Range:** 1,200/31, 3,900/16, 4,400/14   **Fuel:** 126 tons
M: 4 MTU 16V956 TB 91 diesels; 4 props; 18,000 hp   **Electric:** 480 kw

REMARKS: Ordered 1978. Three of these ships may receive 20-cylinder diesels for higher speeds; that version may have a helicopter platform and will not carry the Bofors rocket launcher. Similar in design to the Wadi Mragh class for Libya.

◆ 2 ex-U.S. PCE-821 class

BE 01 ESMERALDAS (ex-*Eunice*, PCE-846)
BE 02 MANABI (ex-*Pascagoula*, PCE-874)

Bldrs: Pullman Standard Car, Chicago/Albina Eng. & Mach., Portland

Esmeraldas   1973

D: 640 tons (903 fl)   **S:** 15 kts   **Dim:** 56.24 × 10.08 × 2.9
A: 1/76-mm DP – 6/40-mm AA (II × 3) – 2/20-mm AA (I × 2) – Hedgehog – 2 depth-charge projectors – 2 depth-charge racks
Man: 100 men   **Range:** 4,300/10   **Electron Equipt:** Radar: 1/SPS 5D
M: 2 GM 12-567A diesels; 1,800 hp

REMARKS: BE-01 launched 20-12-43 and BE-02 11-5-43. Both transferred in 1960. *Esmeraldas* is to be used as an oceanographic research ship.

GUIDED-MISSILE PATROL BOATS

◆ 3 Quito class

LM 31 QUITO   LM 32 GUAYAQUIL   LM 33 CUENCA

Bldr: Lürssen, Vegasack, West Germany

D: 250 tons (265 fl)   **S:** 35 kts   **Dim:** 47.0 × 7.0 × 2.4
A: 4/MM 38 Exocet systems – 1/76-mm OTO Melara Compact – 2/35-mm AA (II × 1)
Electron Equipt: Radar: Thomson-CSF fire-control   **Range:** 600/30
Man: 34 men   **Fuel:** 39 tons   **Electric:** 330 kw
M: 4 MTU 16V538 diesels; 4 props; 14,000 hp

REMARKS: LM-32 launched 5-4-76; the other two in 11-76. Another version of the Lürssen Type 148/*La Combattante* basic design. Carry 250 rounds of 76-mm and 1,100 rounds of 35-mm ammunition.

TORPEDO BOATS

◆ 3 Manta class

LT 41 MANTA   LT 42 TULCAN   LT 43 NUEVA ROCAFUERTE (ex-*Tena*)

Manta   1971

TORPEDO BOATS (*continued*)

Bldr: Lürssen, Vegasack, West Germany

  D: 119 tons (134 fl)   **S:** 35 kts   **Dim:** 36.2 × 5.8 × 1.7
  Man: 19 men   **Range:** 700/30, 1,500/15   **Fuel:** 21 tons
  A: 2/30-mm AA Emerlec (II × 1)—2/533-mm TT—2/81-mm Oerlikon rocket launchers (II × 1)
  M: 2 Mercedes-Benz diesels; 3 props; 9,000 hp

REMARKS: Similar to Chilean *Guacolda*, but faster. LT-41 launched in 1-71 and LT-42 in 12-70. New guns added 1979.

PATROL BOATS

◆ 2 ex-U.S. PGM

LC 71 VEINTECINCO DE JULIO (ex-*Quito*, ex-*PGM-75*)
LC 72 DIEZ DE AGOSTO (ex-*Guayaquil*, ex-*PGM-76*)

  Bldr: Petersen, U.S.A., 1965

Veintecinco de Julio—now LC-71   1967

  D: 130 tons (147 fl)   **S:** 20 kts   **Dim:** 30.81 (30.2 pp) × 6.45 × 2.3
  Man: 15 men   **Range:** 1,000/12
  A: 1/40-mm—4/20-mm (II × 2)—2/12.7-mm machine guns
  M: 4 Mercedes-Benz 820Bb diesels; 2 props; 2,200 hp

REMARK: Transferred in 1965.

PATROL CRAFT

◆ 3 port director class

COMANDANCIA DE BALAO   COMANDANCIA DE SALINAS
COMANDANCIA DE GUYAYQUIL

  Bldr: Halter, New Orleans, 1976

  D: 34 tons (fl)   **S:** 25 kts   **Dim:** 19.66 × 5.18 × 1.24
  A: . . .   **M:** 2 GM 12V71 TI diesels; 2 props; 960 hp

◆ 3 LPI class

LC 81 BABA HOYO (ex-*10 de Agosto*)
LC 82 PICHINCHA (ex-*9 de Octubre*)
LC 83 PORTOVIEJO (ex-*3 de Noviembre*)

Bldr: Schurenstedt, West Germany, 1954-55

  D: 45 tons (64 fl)   **S:** 20 kts   **Dim:** 23.4 × 4.6 × 1.8
  Man: 9 men   **Range:** 556/16
  A: Machine guns   **M:** 2 Böhn & Kahler diesels; 2 props; 1,200 hp

◆ 2 ex-U.S. Coast Guard utility boats

UT 111 RIO NAPO   UT 112 ISLA PUNA

  D: 10.6 tons   **S:** 19 kts   **Dim:** 12.27 × 3.45 × 1.0
  A: . . .   **Man:** 4-5 men   **Range:** 280/18
  M: 2 GM diesels; 2 props; 380 hp

REMARK: Transferred 1971.

AMPHIBIOUS WARFARE SHIPS

◆ 1 ex-U.S. LST

T 55 HUALCOPO (ex-*Summit County*, LST-1148)

  Bldr: Chicago Bridge

  D: 1,650 tons (4,080 fl)   **S:** 11.6 kts   **Dim:** 100.04 × 15.24 × 4.3
  A: 8/40-mm (II × 2, I × 4)   **Man:** 119 men   **Range:** 7,200/10

REMARKS: Launched 23-5-45, bought 2-77. Used as transport; has ice-reinforced waterline.

◆ 2 ex-U.S. LSM

T 51 JAMBELLI (ex-*LSM-539*)   T 52 TARQUI (ex-*LSM-555*)

  D: 513 tons (1,095 fl)   **S:** 12.5 kts   **Dim:** 62.0 × 10.5 × 2.2
  A: 2/40-mm AA   **Man:** 60 men   **Range:** 2,500/12
  M: 2 GM 16-278A diesels; 2 props; 2,800 hp

REMARKS: Built 1945, transferred 1958. Used as transports.

◆ 6 British Rotork 12-meter "Sea Trucks"

LF 91   LF 92   LF 93   LF 94   LF 95   LF 96

REMARKS: Used for logistic support. Mercury outboard motor.

AUXILIARY SHIPS

◆ 2 hydrographic survey ships

O 112 RIGEL   Bldr: Halter Marine, New Orleans
  D: 50 tons   **Man:** 10 men

HI 101 ORLON (ex-*Mulberry*, ex-*AN-27*)   Bldr: American SB, Cleveland, Ohio
  D: 560 tons (805 fl)   **S:** 12.5 kts   **Dim:** 49.7 (44.5 pp) × 9.3 × 3.6
  M: 1 Busch-Sulzer BS-539 diesel; electric drive; 800 hp   **Man:** 20 men

REMARKS: Armament removed, replaced by charthouse. 0-112 launched in 1975. HI-101, a former netlayer, launched 26-3-41 and transferred 1965.

◆ 1 ex-U.S. Army small cargo ship

T 12 CALICUCHIMA (ex-*FS-525*)

  D: 650 tons (950 fl)   **S:** 11.5 kts   **Dim:** 53.7 × 9.8 × 4.3
  M: 2 GM diesels; 2 props; 500 hp

REMARKS: In service since 1944, transferred 1963. Used to supply the Galápagos Islands.

ECUADOR (*continued*)

AUXILIARY SHIPS (*continued*)

◆ **1 ex-U.S. small water tanker**

T 41 ATALHUAPA (ex-YW-131) Bldr: Leatham D. Smith, Wisc., 1945

    D: 415 tons (1,235 fl)   **S:** 11.5 kts   **Dim:** 53.1 × 9.8 × 4.6
    M: 1 GM diesel; 1 prop; 640 hp   **Cargo:** 200,000 gallons fresh water

REMARK: Transferred 1963.

◆ **5 tugs**

R 51 CAYAMBE (ex-*Los Rios*, ex-*Cusabo*, ex-ATF-155)
R 52 CHIMBORAZO (ex-*Chowanoc*, ATF-100)

  Bldr: Charleston SB & DD

Cayambe—now R-51   1966

    D: 1,235 tons (1,675 fl)   **S:** 16.5 kts   **Dim:** 62.5 × 11.7 × 4.7
    A: 1/76-mm DP−2/40-mm AA (I × 2)−2/20-mm AA   **Man:** 85 men
    M: 4 GM 12-278A diesels, electric drive; 1 prop, 3,000 hp

REMARKS: Launched 26-2-45 and 20-8-43, respectively, and transferred 1960 and 1978. R-52 no armament, 4 Busch-Sulzer B5-539 diesels, pipe vice stack.

R 53 SANGAY (ex-*Losa*)

    D: 295 tons (390 fl)   **S:** 12 kts   **Dim:** 32.6 × 7.9 × 4.25
    M: 1 Fairbanks-Morse diesel.

REMARK: Launched 1952, bought 1964.

R 54 COTOPAXI (ex-*R. T. Ellis*)

    D: 150 tons   **S:** 9 kts   **Dim:** 25.0 × 6.62 × 2.9
    M: Diesel; 1 prop; 650 hp

REMARK: Launched 1945 and bought from U.S.A. 1947.

R 104 ANTIZANA—Small tug; no other information.

VARIOUS SHIPS

◆ **1 sail training ship**

BE 01 GUAYAS Bldr: Celaya SY, Bilbao, Spain

    D: 934 grt   **S:** 10.5 kts   **Dim:** 76.2 × 10.6 × 4.2
    M: GM 12V-149 diesel; 700 hp

REMARK: Three-masted bark, launched 22-10-76.

◆ **1 repair barge**

BT 62 PUTAMAYO (ex-YR-34) Bldr: New York Navy Yard, 1944

    D: . . .   **S:** . . .   **Dim:** 45.7 × 10.4 × . . .

REMARK: Transferred 7-62.

◆ **1 floating dry dock**

DF 61 AMAZONAS (ex-ARD-17)

    Dim: 149.9 × 24.7 × 10.0   **Capacity:** 3,500 tons

REMARK: Built in U.S.A. in 1944, transferred in 1961.

EGYPT

PERSONNEL: Approx. 17,500 men with more than 1,500 officers

MERCHANT MARINE (1978): 205 ships−456,291 grt
                             (tankers: 29 ships−130,940 grt)

WARSHIPS IN SERVICE OR UNDER CONSTRUCTION AS OF 1 JANUARY 1980

	L	Tons (Surfaced)	Main armament
◆ **12 submarines**			
6 ROMEO	1957	1,330	8/533-mm TT
6 WHISKEY	1955	1,050	6/533-mm TT
		Tons	
◆ **7 (+2) destroyers**			
4 SKORY	1950-54	2,400	4/130-mm, 2/85-mm or 4/57-mm AA, 10/533-mm TT
2 (+2) GEARING, FRAM-I	1944-45	2,245	4/127-mm DP
1 Z	1944	1,730	4/102-mm DP, 6/40-mm AA, 8/533-mm TT
◆ **3 frigates**			

WARSHIPS IN SERVICE OR UNDER CONSTRUCTION (*continued*)

◆ **14 (+6) guided-missile boats**

(6) RAMADAN	1981-82	. . .	8/Otomat, 1/76-mm DP
6 6 OCTOBER	1969-75	71	2/Otomat, 2/30-mm AA
6 OSA-I	. . .	175	4/Styx, 4/30-mm AA
2 KOMAR	1961-63	71	2/Styx, 2/25-mm

◆ **12 patrol boats**

◆ **30 torpedo boats**

◆ **12 minesweepers**

◆ **17 amphibious ships**

CANCELED PROGRAMS: Plans to purchase the former British guided-missile destroyers *Devonshire* and *Hampshire*, the frigates *Salisbury* and *Lincoln*, and the submarine *Cachelot* were all canceled for lack of funds to refit and modernize the ships. Long-rumored plans to acquire two new Italian-built *Lupo*-class frigates have apparently met the same fate.

SUBMARINES

◆ **6 Soviet Romeo class**

Egyptian Romeo   1977

D: 1,330 tons surfaced, 1,700 submerged   **S:** 15 kts surfaced, 13 submerged
Dim: 77.0 × 6.7 × 4.95
A: 8/533-mm TT (6 fwd, 2 aft) — 14 torpedoes or 28 mines
Man: 60 men   **Endurance:** 45 days   **Range:** 14,000/9
M: Diesel-electric, 2 diesels, 2,000 hp each; 2 props; 3,000 hp

REMARK: Transferred 1966-69.

◆ **6 Soviet Whiskey class**

D: 1,050 tons surfaced, 1,350 submerged   **Dim:** 74 × 6.6 × 4.8
S: 17/16 kts   **Man:** 60 men   **Range:** 6,000/5
A: 6/533-mm TT (4 fwd, 2 aft) — 14 torpedoes or 28 mines
M: Diesels and electric motors; 2 props; 4,000/2,500 hp
Endurance: 40-45 days

REMARK: Transferred from 6-57 to 8-62. Reported in poor condition. In refit 1978-79; to get British electronic intercept equipment.

DESTROYERS

◆ **4 Soviet Skory class**

	Bldr	Transferred
6 OCTOBER (ex-*El Nasser*)	U.S.S.R.	1956
EL ZAFFER	U.S.S.R.	1967
DAMIET	U.S.S.R.	1967
SUEZ	U.S.S.R.	1956

Egyptian Skory class

D: 2,400 tons (3,200 fl)   **Dim:** 120.0 × 12.0 × 4.3
S: 34 kts   **Man:** 250 men   **Range:** 900/32, 3,500/14
A: *Suez:*   4/130-mm DP (II × 2) — 2/85-mm AA (II × 1) — 8/37-mm AA (II × 4) — 4/25-mm AA (II × 2) — 10/533-mm TT (V × 2) — 2 depth-charge projectors — 2 depth-charge racks — 50 mines
    El Zaffer: 4/130-mm DP (II × 2) — 2 Styx — 6/37-mm AA (II × 3) — 4/25-mm AA (II × 2) — 10/533-mm TT (V × 2) — etc.
    6 October, Damiet: 4/130-mm DP (II × 2) — 4/57-mm AA (IV × 1) — 4/37-mm AA (II × 2) — 4/25-mm AA (II × 2) — 10/533-mm TT (V × 2) — 2 MBU-2500 — 2 depth-charge racks — 50 mines
M: GT; 2 props; 58,000 hp   **Boilers:** 4

REMARKS: The *El Zaffer* and the *Damiet* were replaced in 1968 by two ships of the same class and with the same names. The *Suez* has had two aft-firing Styx launchers from a discarded Komar added atop her after deckhouse in place of the twin 85-mm mount and one twin 37-mm AA; *El Zaffer* may have received similar treatment. All four carry SA-N-5 Grail shoulder-launched AA missiles.

◆ **4 U.S. Gearing FRAM-I**

	Bldr:	L	In serv.
. . . N . . . . (ex-*Harold J. Ellison*, DD-864)	Bethlehem, Staten Is.	14-3-45	23-5-45
. . . N . . . . (ex-*Damato*, DD-871)	Bethlehem, Staten Is.	10-5-45	18-8-45
. . . N . . . (ex-. . .)	. . .	. . .	. . .
. . . N . . . (ex-. . .)	. . .	. . .	. . .

D: 2,425 tons (3,480-3,520 fl)   **S:** 30 kts   **Dim:** 119.1 × 12.4 × 5.8
Man: 19 officers, 289 men   **Range:** 2,400/25, 4,800/15
A: 4/127-mm 38-cal. DP (II × 2) — 16/Mk 32 ASW TT (III × 2) — Asroc ASW system
Electron Equipt: Radars: 1/SPS 10, 1/SPS 40, 1/Mk 25
         Sonar: 1/SQS 23
M: GT; 2 props; 60,000 hp   **Boilers:** 4 Babcock & Wilcox   **Fuel:** 650 tons

REMARKS: Two transferred 6-10-79, two in 1980. Although older than Egypt's Skorys, they are in better condition and are superior for ASW.

DESTROYERS (*continued*)

Harold J. Ellison, before transfer   1976

◆ **1 British Z class**

	Bldr	Laid down	L	In serv.
EL FATEH (ex-*Zenith*)	Wm. Denny	19-5-42	5-6-44	22-12-44

El Fateh   1975

D: 1,730 tons (2,575 fl)   **S:** 31 kts   **Dim:** 110.6 × 10.9 × 5.2
Range: 2,800/20   **Man:** 250 men
A: 4/102-mm DP (I × 4) — 6/40-mm AA (II × 1, I × 4) — 8/533-mm TT — 4 depth-charge
projectors
M: GT; 2 props; 2 boilers; 40,000 hp   **Fuel:** 580 tons

FRIGATES

◆ **1 British Black Swan class**

	Bldr	Laid down	L	In serv.
555 EL TARIK (ex-*El Malek Farouk*, ex-HMS *Whimbrel*)	Yarrow & Co.	10-41	25-8-42	1-43

D: 1,470 tons (1,925 fl)   **S:** 14 kts   **Dim:** 91.3 × 11.73 × 3.45
Man: 180 men   **Range:** 4,500/12

A: 6/102-mm DP (II × 3) — 4/40-mm AA — 4 depth-charge projectors — 2 racks
M: Parsons GT; 2 props; 2 boilers; 4,300 hp   **Fuel:** 370 tons

REMARKS: Bought in 12-49. Used as a submarine tender.

◆ **1 British River class**

	Bldr	Laid down	L	In serv.
511 RACHID (ex-HMS *Spey*)	Smith's Dock Co., Ltd.	7-41	18-21-41	3-42

Rachid   1978

D: 1,460 tons (2,175 fl)   **S:** 19 kts   **Dim:** 91.85 × 11.17 × 4.34 (fl)
Range: 7,700/12, 5,000/16
A: 1/102-mm — 4/40-mm AA (II × 2) — 1/SA-N-5 Grail SAM system
M: Triple-expansion; 2 props; 5,500 hp   **Boilers:** 2   **Fuel:** 640 tons

REMARKS: Bought in 12-49. Used as a training ship.

◆ **1 British Hunt class**

	Bldr	L
PORT SAID (ex-*Mohamed Ali El Kebit*, ex-*Cottesmore*)	Yarrow & Co.	5-9-40

D: 1,000 tons (1,490 fl)   **S:** 25 kts   **Dim:** 85.3 × 8.8 × 4.3
Man: 146 men   **Range:** 2,000/12, 800/25
A: 4/102-mm DP (II × 2) — 2/25-mm AA — 2/12.7-mm machine guns
M: Parsons GT; 2 props; 19,000 hp   **Boilers:** 2   **Fuel:** 280 tons

REMARKS: Transferred 7-50.

GUIDED-MISSILE BOATS

◆ **6 Ramadan class**   Bldr: Vosper-Thornycroft

	L		L
N . . .	. . .	N . . .	. . .
N . . .	. . .	N . . .	. . .
N . . .	. . .	N . . .	. . .

D: 260 tons (fl)   **S:** 40 kts   **Dim:** 46.0 (42.0 wl) × 7.8 × 2.3
A: 4/Otomat SSM (II × 2) — 1/76-mm DP OTO Melara Compact — 2/40-mm AA Breda
(II × 1)
Man: 31 men   **Range:** 2,000/15   **Fuel:** 39 tons
M: 4 MTU MD 20V538 TB 91 diesels; 4 props; 16,000 hp

REMARKS: Little data released, based on *Tenacity* but with all-diesel propulsion. Ordered 4-9-77. To deliver 4-81 to 4-82.

GUIDED-MISSILE BOATS (*continued*)

◆ **6 6 October class**   Bldr: Egypt/Vosper-Thornycroft

D: 80 tons (fl)   **S:** 40 kts   **Dim:** 25.3 × 6.0 × 1.8
A: 2/Otomat SSM − 2/30-mm AA Type A32
M: 4 CRM 12D/55 YE diesels; 4 props; 5,000 hp   **Range:** 400/30

6 October class   Vosper, 1978

REMARKS: Wooden hulls, built at Alexandria DY, Egypt, 1969 onward. Being completed by Vosper-Thornycroft at Portchester, Portsmouth, with French missiles and British guns; diesels are Italian. Basic design is that the Soviet Komar class. Expected to deliver 1979-80.

◆ **6 ex-Soviet Osa-I class**

Soviet Osa-I

D: 175 tons   **S:** 36 kts   **Dim:** 39.0 × 7.7 × 1.8
A: 4/Styx systems (I × 4) − 4/30-mm AA (II × 2) − SA-N-5 Grail
Electron Equipt: Radars: 1/Square Tie, 1/Drum Tilt, 1/Kelvin-Hughes 1006
M: 3 M503A diesels; 3 props; 12,000 hp   **Range:** 450/34, 700/20

REMARKS: Transferred 1966. Reported being refitted with 3 MTU diesels.

◆ **2 ex-Soviet Komar class**

Soviet-built Egyptian Komar   1976

D: 71 tons (82 fl)   **S:** 40 kts   **Dim:** 25.3 × 7.0 × 2.0
A: 2 Styx systems (I × 2) − 2/25-mm AA   **Range:** 450/30
Electron Equipt: Radar: 1/Square Tie
M: 4 M50 diesels; 4 props; 4,800 hp

REMARK: Transferred since 1966.

PATROL BOATS

◆ **12 Soviet SO-I class**

D: 190 tons (215 fl)   **S:** 28 kts   **Dim:** 42.0 × 6.1 × 1.9
A: 4/25-mm AA (II × 2) − 4 MBU-1800 rocket launchers − 2 depth-charge racks − mines. Some are armed with 2/533-mm TT as well.
Electron Equipt: Radar: Pot Head   **Man:** 30 men
M: 3 diesels; 3 props; 6,000 hp

REMARK: Transferred since 1962-63. Also carry SA-N-5 Grail, shoulder-launched SAMs.

TORPEDO BOATS

◆ **6 Soviet Shershen class**

D: 150 tons (180 fl)   **S:** 45 kts   **Dim:** 34.0 × 7.2 × 1.5
A: 4/30-mm AA (II × 2) − 4/533-mm TT (I × 4)
Electron Equipt: 1/Square Tie, 1/Drum Tilt
M: 3 diesels; 3 props; 12,000 hp

REMARKS: Transferred from 1967 on. Three are armed with two 40-tubed 122-mm rocket launchers instead of torpedoes. Most carry SA-N-5 Grail missiles as well.

◆ **20 ex-Soviet P-6 class**

D: 56 tons (66.5 fl)   **S:** 43 kts (cruising)   **Dim:** 25.3 × 6.1 × 1.7
A: 4/25-mm AA (II × 2) − 2/533-mm TT
M: 4 M50 diesels; 4 props; 4,800 hp

TORPEDO BOATS (*continued*)

Egyptian P-6 equipped with multiple rocket launcher   1975

REMARKS: Transferred since 1960. A few are armed with one 40-tubed BM-21 122-mm rocket launcher, have no TT, and the after 25-mm mount removed; these carry 2/20-mm AA guns aft. Some of these boats were built in Egypt. At least two have 4/533-mm TT.

◆ **4 ex-Soviet P-4 class**

P-4 with octuple rocket launcher mounted on bow   1974

D: 19.3 tons (22.4 fl)   **S:** 55 kts   **Dim:** 19.3 × 3.7 × 1.0
A: 2/450-mm TT – 2/14.5-mm AA (II × 1) – 8/122-mm rockets (VIII × 1)
M: 2 M50 diesels; 2 props; 2,400 hp

PATROL CRAFT

◆ **30 fiberglass-hulled DC-35 class**   Bldr: Dawncraft, Wroxham, G. B.

D: 4 tons   **S:** 25 kts   **Dim:** 10.7 × 3.5 × 0.8
M: 2 Perkins T-6-354 diesels; 2 props; 290 hp   **Man:** 4 men

REMARKS: Delivered 1977. For police service.

◆ **3 or more Nisr class**   Bldr: De Castro, Port Said, 1963

D: 110 tons (fl)   **A:** 1/20-mm   **M:** 2 Maybach diesels

REMARK: Far Coast Guard work.

◆ **20 launches**   Bldr: Bertram, Miami, U.S.A., 1963

D: 8 tons (fl)   **S:** 24 kts   **Dim:** 8.5 × . . . × . . .
A: 2/12.7-mm machine guns – 4/122-mm rockets (I × 4)
M: Diesels; 2 props

MINE WARFARE SHIPS

◆ **4 ex-Soviet Yurka-class minesweepers**

ASSUAN   GUIZEN   QENA   SUHAG

D: 460 tons (fl)   **S:** 18 kts   **Dim:** 52.0 × 8.8 × 2.0
A: 4/30-mm AA (II × 2) – 20 mines
M: Diesels; 2 props; 4,000 hp   **Electron Equipt:** Radar: 1/Don

REMARK: Delivered 1969.

◆ **6 ex-Soviet T-43-class minesweepers**

BAHAIRA   CHARKIEH   GHARBIA
ASSIUT   DAQHALA   SINAI

Bldr: U.S.S.R., 1953

D: 500 tons (580 fl)   **S:** 14 kts   **Dim:** 58.0 × 8.4 × 2.3
A: 4/37-mm AA (II × 2) – 8/12.7-mm machine guns – depth charges
M: 2 diesels; 2 props; 2,200 hp

REMARK: Transferred since 1956; one in 1970.

◆ **2 Soviet T-301-class minesweepers**

EL FAYOUD   EL MANUFIEH

D: 145.8 tons (160 fl)   **S:** 12.5 kts   **Dim:** 38.0 × 5.1 × 1.6
A: 2/45-mm – 2 machine guns   **M:** 3 diesels; 3 props; 1,440 hp

REMARK: Delivered 1962-63.

AMPHIBIOUS WARFARE SHIPS

◆ **3 Soviet Polnocny-class, Type I LSM**

D: 900 tons (fl)   **S:** 18 kts   **Dim:** 72.5 × 8.5 × 2.0
A: 2/30-mm AA (II × 1) – 2/140-mm multiple rocket launchers (XVIII × 2)
M: 2 diesels; 2 props; 4,000 hp   **Cargo:** 3 tanks/200 tons

REMARK: Transferred 1974.

◆ **9 ex-Soviet Vydra-class LCUs**

D: 750 tons (fl)   **S:** 10 kts   **Dim:** 54.8 × 8.1 × 2.0

EGYPT (*continued*)

AMPHIBIOUS WARFARE SHIPS (*continued*)

Egyptian Vydra with rocket launchers   1976

  A: 4/40-mm AA (II × 2) – 8 15-tube rocket launchers
  M: 2 diesels; 2 props; 800 hp

REMARKS: Transferred 1967-69. Armament now landed. Some had 37-mm AA vice 40-mm.

◆ **5 ex-Soviet SMB-I-class LCUs**

  D: 335 tons (fl)   **S:** 10 kts   **Dim:** 48.5 × 6.5 × 2.0
  A: . . .
  M: 2 diesels; 2 props; 600 hp   **Cargo:** 200 tons   **Man:** 16 men

REMARK: Transferred 1965.

◆ **10 to 12 LCMs of various origins**

AUXILIARY SHIPS

◆ **4 Soviet Okhtenshiy-class tugs**

AL ISKANDARAN   EL MEY
EL AGAMI   N . . .

REMARK: Two transferred in 1966, two built in Egypt.

◆ **2 Soviet Nyryat-I-class diving tenders**

REMARK: Transferred in 1964.

◆ **2 Soviet Poluchat-I-class torpedo-recovery boats**

◆ **2 70-ton PO-2-class tenders**

◆ **1 Soviet Sekstan-class degaussing ship**

TRAINING SHIP

EL HORRIA (ex-*Mahroussa*)   Bldr: Samuda, Scotland, 1865

El Horria   G. Garier, 1976

  D: 4,561 tons (fl)   **S:** 16 kts   **Dim:** 145.6 (121.9 pp) × 13.0 × 5.3
  A: Several machine guns   **M:** GT; 3 props; 5,500 hp

REMARKS: Visited U.S.A. in July 1976. World's oldest active naval ship.

EL SALVADOR

PERSONNEL: 130 officers and men

MERCHANT MARINE (1978): 2 ships – 1,987 grt

PATROL CRAFT

◆ **3 aluminum-hulled**   Bldr: Camcraft, Crown Pt., Louisiana

GC 6 (10-75)   GC 7 (12-75)   GC 8 (11-75)

  D: . . .   **S:** 25 kts   **Dim:** 30.5 × 6.4 × 1.5
  A: 3/12.7-mm machine guns   **Man:** 10 men   **Range:** 780/24
  M: 3 GM 12 V TI diesels; 3 props; 1,200 hp

REMARK: Ordered 1974.

◆ **1 aluminum-hulled**   Bldr: Sewart Seacraft, Berwick, Louisiana

GC 5

  D: 33 tons (fl)   **S:** 25 kts   **Dim:** 19.8 × 4.9 × 1.5
  A: 3/12.7-mm machine guns   **M:** 3 GM 8V71 diesels; 3 props; 1,590 hp

REMARK: Transferred 9-67.

◆ **2 ex-U.S. Coast Guard utility boats**

GC 3   GC 4

  D: 10.6 tons   **S:** 18 kts   **Dim:** 12.3 × 3.4 × 1.0

EL SALVADOR (*continued*)

PATROL CRAFT (*continued*)

    A: 1/12.7-mm machine gun   **Range:** 160/18   **M:** 2 diesels; 2 props; 400 hp

REMARK: Launched in 1950.

◆ **1 ex-British HMDL**

GC 2 FLO-JA-LIS (ex-*Nohaba*)

    D: 46 tons (54 fl)   **S:** 11.5 kts   **Dim:** 21.9 × 4.8 × 1.7
    A: 1/12.7-mm machine gun   **M:** 2 diesels; 2 props; 300 hp

REMARK: In service since 1942, bought 1959.

◆ **25 small launches with outboard motors**

EQUATORIAL GUINEA

PERSONNEL: 100 men

MERCHANT MARINE (1978): 2 ships—370 grt

◆ **1 P-6-class torpedo boat**

    D: 56 tons (66.5 fl)   **S:** 43 kts   **Dim:** 25.3 × 6.1 × 1.7
    A: 4/25-mm AA (II × 2)−2/533-mm TT (I × 2)   **Man:** 12 men
    Electron Equipt: Radar: Skin Head
    M: 4 M50 diesels; 4 props; 4,800 hp   **Range:** 400/32, 700/15

REMARK: Delivered 1974.

◆ **1 Poluchat-class patrol boat**

    D: 80 tons (90 fl)   **S:** 18 kts   **Dim:** 29.6 × 5.8 × 1.5
    A: 2/14.5-mm machine guns   **Man:** 20 men
    M: 2 M50 diesels; 2 props; 2,400 hp

REMARK: Delivered 1974.

◆ **2 small patrol craft**

ETHIOPIA

PERSONNEL: 1,200 men including 230 officers

MERCHANT MARINE (1978): 17 ships—23,490 grt
             (tankers: 1 ship—2,051 grt)

GUIDED-MISSILE BOATS

◆ **1 Soviet Osa-II class**

    D: 175 tons (240 fl)   **S:** 36 kts   **Dim:** 39.0 × 7.7 × 1.8
    A: 4/Styx SSM−4/30-mm AA (II × 2)
    Electron Equipt: Radars: 1/Square Tie, 1/Drum Tilt
    M: 3 M504 diesels; 3 props; 15,000 hp   **Range:** 450/34, 700/20

Remarks: Transferred 1978. As many as six to eight ships may ultimately be transferred.

TORPEDO BOATS

◆ **3 Soviet MOL class**

    D: 175 tons (220 fl)   **S:** 36 kts   **Dim:** 39.0 × 7.6 × 1.8
    A: 4/533-mm TT (I × 4)−4/30-mm AA (II × 2)
    Electron Equipt: Radars: 1/Pot Head, 1/Drum Tilt
    M: 3 M503A diesels; 3 props; 12,000 hp

REMARKS: Transferred 1978. May not carry the torpedo tubes.

PATROL BOATS

◆ **4 aluminum-hulled boats** Bldr: Swiftships, Morgan City, Louisiana

P 201   P 202   P 203   P 204

Aluminum-hulled patrol boat with Emerlec 30-mm AA   Swiftships, 1977

PATROL BOATS (continued)

Aluminum-hulled patrol boat with 23-mm AA   1978

   D: 118 tons (fl)   **S:** 32 kts   **Dim:** 31.73 × 7.1 × 2.16
   A: 4/30-mm Emerlec AA (II × 2)   **Man:** 21 men   **Range:** 1,200/18
   Electron Equipt: Radar: Decca RM 916
   M: 2 MTU MB 16V538 TB90 diesels; 2 props; 7,000 hp

REMARKS: Ordered 1976, delivered 4-77; two additional units were cancelled by the U.S. arms embargo. P-203 and P-204 have four 23-mm AA (II × 2) and two 12.7-mm machine guns (II × 1)

◆ 4 ex-U.S. Coast Guard Cape design

PC 12 (ex-CG-WPB-95310)   PC 14 (ex-U.S. PGM-54)
PC 13 (ex-U.S. PGM-53)   PC 15 (ex-U.S. PGM-58)

   Bldr: Petersen, U.S.A., 1955-62

PC-14

   D: 80 tons (101 fl)   **S:** 20 kts   **Dim:** 28.8 × 5.8 × 1.55
   A: 1/40-mm AA – 1/20-mm AA   **Man:** 15 men
   M: 4 diesels; 2 props; 2,200 hp   **Range:** 1,500/10

REMARKS: Three transferred in 1958, one in 1961, and one in 1962. PC-11 lost in action, 4-77. All ASW weapons removed. Reportedly, only three are in service.

◆ 1 ex-Dutch minesweeper

41 (ex-M-829 *Elst*)   Bldr: Netherlands

   D: 373 tons (417 fl)   **S:** 14 kts   **Dim:** 46.62 × 8.78 × 2.3
   A: 2/40-mm AA (I × 2)   **Man:** 40 men
   M: 2 Werkspoor diesels; 2 props; 2,500 hp   **Range:** 2,500/10

REMARKS: Launched 21-3-56, bought in 1970. For profile, see *Wildervank* class, Netherlands section. All minesweeping gear removed.

◆ 1 ex-Yugoslav Kraljevica-class subchaser

51 (ex-509)

   D: 190 tons (202 fl)   **S:** 18 kts   **Dim:** 41.0 × 6.3 × 2.2
   A: 2/40-mm AA (I × 2) – 4/20-mm AA (I × 4)
   M: 2 M.A.N. diesels, 2 props; 3,300 hp

REMARKS: In service since 1953. Donated in 1975.

PATROL CRAFT

◆ 4 aluminum-hulled craft

GB 21 GB 22 GB 23 GB24 (ex-*John, Caroline, Patrick, Jacqueline*)

   Bldr: Sewart Seacraft, Berwick, La., 1966-67

GB-23   1976

   D: 15 tons   **S:** 20 kts   **Dim:** 13.1 × 3.9 × 0.9
   A: 2/12.7-mm machine guns   **Man:** 7 men
   M: 2 GM diesels; 2 props; 500 hp

AMPHIBIOUS SHIPS

◆ 2 French EDIC-class LCU   Bldr: SFCN, Villeneuve la Garonne

L 35 N . . .   L 36 N . . .

   D: 250 tons (670 fl)   **S:** 8 kts   **Dim:** 59.0 × 11.95 × 1.3
   A: 2/20-mm AA (I × 2)   **Man:** 1 officer, 15 men   **Range:** 1,800/8
   M: 2 MGO diesels; 2 props; 1,000 hp

REMARK: Launched 5-77.

◆ 2 ex-U.S. LCM

ETHIOPIA (*continued*)

AMPHIBIOUS SHIPS (*continued*)

◆ **2 ex-U.S. LCVP**

REMARK: Two transferred in 1962 and two in 1971.

◆ **4 Soviet T-4-class LCM**

REMARK: Transferred 1977-78.

TRAINING SHIP

	Bldr	L
A 01 ETHIOPIA (ex-*Orca*, AVP-49)	Lake Washington SY	4-10-42

Ethiopia

    D: 1,766 tons (2,800 fl)   **Dim:** 94.7 (91.5 pp) × 12.52 × 3.65
    S: 18 kts   **Man:** 215 men   **Range:** 15,000/12
    A: 1/127-mm DP−5/40-mm AA   **Electron Equipt:** Radar: 1/SPS-12
    M: 4 Fairbanks-Morse 38D8⅛ diesels; 2 props; 6,000 hp

REMARK: Transferred in 1-62. Probably inoperable due to age, poor condition, and lack of spares.

FIJI

A small naval force was established in 6-74 for coastal patrol, to prevent smuggling, and for local hydrographic surveying.

PERSONNEL: 159 men (19 officers)

MERCHANT MARINE (1978): 37 ships−10,023 grt (1 tanker−2,541 grt)

PATROL BOATS

◆ **3 ex-U.S. Bird-class minesweepers** Bldr: Bellingham SY, Washington

	In serv.
205 KULA (ex-*Vireo*, MSC-205)	6-55
206 KIRO (ex-*Warbler*, MSC-206)	7-55
204 KIKAU (ex-*Woodpecker*, MSC-209)	2-56

    D: 370 tons (fl)   **S:** 13 kts   **Dim:** 43.9 × 8.5 × 2.6
    A: 1/20-mm AA−2/12.7-mm machine guns   **Man:** 39 men
    Range: 2,500/10
    M: 2 GM 8-268A diesels; 2 props; 880 hp

REMARKS: The first two were transferred 10-75, the third 6-76. Most minesweeping gear removed.

AUXILIARY SHIPS

◆ **2 logistics support craft**

VASUA Bldr: . . . , 1978

    D: . . .   **S:** 8 kts   **Dim:** 40.0 × . . . × . . .
    M: 2 GM diesels; 2 props; 348 hp   **Cargo:** 220 tons

REMARK: Bow-ramped landing craft.

YAUBULA Bldr: Government SY, Suva, Fiji, 1978

    D: 500 tons (fl)   **S:** 8 kts   **Dim:** 42.5 × 9.1 × 1.7
    Man: 17 men   **Electric:** 100 kva   **Fuel:** 85 tons
    M: 2 GM 12V71 diesels; 2 props; 680 hp   **Cargo:** 200 tons plus 31 passengers

REMARKS: Subordinate to the Fiji Marine Department. Landing craft with bow ramp. 343.16 grt/230.99 nrt

◆ **1 survey ship**

RUVE (ex-*Volasiga*, ex-*Marinetta*)

    D: 100 tons   **S:** . . .   **Dim:** 28.7 × 5.3 × 2.3
    M: Diesels   **Man:** 14 men

REMARKS: Dates from 1929, transferred 6-76 from the Marine Department. A 30-meter replacement for this ship was expected to complete 4-79 at Government Shipyard, Suva.

FINLAND

The naval force, limited by the Treaty of Paris to 10,000 tons and 4,500 men, is a separate establishment under the orders of the chief of the armed forces. Submarines and torpedo boats are excluded from the fleet and there is no naval aviation.

PERSONNEL (1977): about 2,500, including 200 officers.

MERCHANT MARINE (1978): 341 ships−2,358,623 grt
                        (tankers: 46 ships−1,139,785 grt)

NAVAL PROGRAM: Present plans are to bring the Finnish navy up to at least 8,000 tons by 1983, reaching 8,600 by 1988, the warships being divided as follows:

- ◆ **6 frigates/corvettes (3 currently)**
- ◆ **24 fast small boats (12 currently)**
- ◆ **14 minesweepers (6 currently)**
- ◆ **8 patrol boats (5 currently) with minesweeping capability.**

This goal will require considerable effort because many of the Finnish Navy's ships are, at best, obsolescent.

WEAPONS

The *Turunmaa*-class corvettes and the new minelayer have a single-barrel automatic Bofors 120-mm gun with the following characteristics:

weight without munitions: 28.5 tons	arc of elevation: −10° to +80
length: 46 calibers	maximum rate of fire: 80 rounds/min
muzzle velocity: 800 m/sec	projectile weight: 35 kg
training speed: 40°/sec	maximum effective range, surface
elevation speed: 30°/sec	fire: 12,000 m

FRIGATES

◆ **1 Soviet Riga class**

HÄMEENMAA, Bldr: U.S.S.R.

Hämeenmaa before rearmament

D: 1,600 (fl)   **S:** 28/27 kts   **Dim:** 91.0 × 11.0 × 3.4
A: 3/100-mm AA—2/40-mm AA (I × 2)—2/30-mm AA (II × 1)—2/20-mm AA (I × 2) —3/533-mm TT (III × 1)—1 Hedgehog—4 depth-charge projectors—2 depth-charge racks
Man: 175 men   **Range:** 2,000/10
Electron Equipt: Radars: 1/Neptune, 1/Slim Net, 1/Sun Visor B
M: GT, 2 props; 20,000 hp   **Boilers:** 2

REMARKS: Transferred in 1964. The twin 30-mm mount is carried at the extreme bow. Sister *Uusimaa* was discarded early in 1979. The *Hämeenmaa* will operate until the end of the 1980s.

CORVETTES

◆ **2 Turunmaa class**

	Bldr	Laid down	L	In serv.
TURUNMAA	Wärtsilä, Helsinki	3-67	11-7-67	29-8-68
KARJALA	Wärtsilä, Helsinki	3-67	16-8-67	21-10-68

Karjala

D: 750 tons (890 fl)   **S:** 35 kts   **Dim:** 74.1 × 7.8 × 2.83
A: 1/120-mm Bofors automatic—2/40-mm AA (I × 2)—2/30-mm (II × 1)—2/MBU-1800—2 depth-charge racks
Man: 70 men   **Range:** 2,500/14   **Electric:** 880 kva   **Fuel:** 120 tons
Electron Equipt: Radars: 1/HSA M22, 1/navigational
M: CODOG propulsion: 1 Bristol-Siddeley Olympus gas turbine; 3 Mercedes-Benz diesels; 3 props; 22,000 hp

REMARKS: Flush-deck hull, closed bridge, sharp profile. Cruises on the diesels (3 × 1,100 hp) at 17 knots. Ka-Me-Wa controllable-pitch propellers. Have Vosper fin stabilizers. Soviet ASW rocket launchers are behind doors in main-deck superstructure, abreast the mast.

GUIDED-MISSILE PATROL BOATS

◆ **8 PB-80 class**

D: 250 tons (fl)   **S:** 40 kts   **Dim:** 45.0 × 7.1 × 1.8
A: . . .   **Man:** 40 men
M: 3 Rolls-Royce Proteus gas turbines; 3 props; 11,580 hp

REMARKS: Ordered 5-10-78. Design based on Swedish *Spica*-II class. To carry missiles, guns, and torpedoes.

◆ **4 Soviet Osa-II class**

D: 210 tons (240 fl)   **S:** 36 kts   **Dim:** 39.0 × 7.7 × 1.8
A: 4/SS-N-2 Styx—4/30-mm AA (II × 2)   **Range:** 450/34, 700/20
Electron Equipt: Radars: 1/Square Tie, 1/Drum Tilt, 1/navigational
M: 3 M504 diesels; 3 props; 15,000 hp

REMARKS: Transferred in 1975. Some Western electronic equipment has been added.

GUIDED-MISSILE PATROL BOATS (*continued*)

◆ **Isku**   Bldr: Reposaaren Konepaja, Pori, 1969

>   **D:**   115 tons (140 fl)   **S:**   15 kts   **Dim:**   26.35 × 8.7 × 2.0
>   **A:**   4/SS-N-2 Styx − 2/30-mm AA   **M:**   Soviet M50 diesels; 4 props; 3,600 hp

REMARKS: Bargelike hull, designed for a far more powerful propulsion plant. Used primarily for training.

PATROL BOATS

◆ **13 Nuoli class**

>   **D:**   64 tons (fl)   **S:**   40 kts   **Dim:**   22.0 × 6.65 × 1.5
>   **A:**   1/40-mm − 1/20-mm   **Electron Equipt:**   Radar: Decca 707
>   **M:**   3 Soviet M50 diesels; 3,600 hp

REMARKS: Date from 1961-63. Six are to be modernized, the other seven discarded.

◆ **5 Rihtniemi and Ruissalo class**

R 1 RIHTNIEMI	R 3 RUISSALO	R 5 RÖYTTA
R 2 RYMÄTTYLÄ	R 4 RAISIO	

Bldr: Rauma SY, 1956-59

Ruissalo before modernization   1972

>   **D:**   110 tons (130 fl)   **S:**   18 kts   **Dim:**   34.0 × 6.0 × 1.8
>   **A:**   4/30-mm AA (II × 2) − 2/MBU-1800 − mines   **Man:**   20 men
>   **M:**   Mercedes-Benz diesels; 2 controllable-pitch props; 2,500 hp

REMARKS: Former convertible minesweeper/gunboats, modernized 1977-80. R-1 and R-2 originally only 31 meters overall and 5.7 meters in beam. Now have bow bulwarks.

MINE WARFARE SHIPS

◆ **2 minelayers**

01 POHJANMAA   Bldr: Wärtsilä, Helsinki

>   **D:**   1,100 tons (fl)   **S:**   20 kts   **Dim:**   78.2 × 11.6 × 3.0
>   **A:**   1/120-mm Bofors DP − 2/40-mm AA (I × 2) − 8/23-mm AA (II × 4) − 2/MBU-1800
>   − mines

Pohjanmaa   Wärtsilä, 1979

>   **Man:**   80 men plus 70 cadets   **Range:**   3,500/17   **Electric:**   1,040 kva
>   **M:**   2 Wärtsilä-Vasa 16V22 diesels; 2 controllable-pitch props; 5,800 hp

REMARKS: Launched 28-8-78, in service 8-6-79. Training facilities are to be fitted in portable containers mounted on the two internal mine rails, easily removable if the ship is required for combat. There is a helicopter pad aft.

KEIHÄSSALMI   Bldr: Valmet Oy, Helsinki

>   **D:**   290 tons (360 fl)   **S:**   15 kts   **Dim:**   56.0 × 7.7 × 2.0
>   **A:**   4/30-mm AA (II × 2) − 2/20-mm AA − 100 mines
>   **Electron Equipt:**   Radar: Drum Tilt added in 1976   **Man:**   60 men
>   **M:**   2 Wärtsilä diesels; 2 props; 2,000 hp

REMARK: Launched 16-3-57.

◆ **6 Kuha-class inshore minesweepers**   Bldr: Laivateollisuus, Turku

	In serv.		In serv.
KUHA 21	28-6-74	KUHA 24	7-3-75
KUHA 22	-74	KUHA 25	17-6-75
KUHA 23	-75	KUHA 26	13-11-75

Kuha   1974

MINE WAREFARE SHIPS (*continued*)

D: 90 tons (fl) **S:** 12 kts **Dim:** 26.6 × 6.9 × . . .
A: 2/23-mm AA (II × 1) − 1/20-mm AA **Man:** 15 men
M: 2 Cummins NT-380M diesels; 2 outboard-drive props; 600 hp

REMARKS: Plastic hulls. Funds for eight additional were to be provided.

AMPHIBIOUS WARFARE SHIPS

◆ **3 Kampela-class LCU** Bldr: Enso-Gutzeit, Savonlinna

KAMPELA 1   KAMPELA 2   KAMPELA 3

D: 90 tons (260 fl) **S:** 9 kts **Dim:** 32.5 × 8.0 × 1.5
A: 2/20-mm AA (I × 2) − mines **Man:** 10 men
M: 2 Scania diesels; 2 props; 460 hp

REMARK: In service 1977-78.

◆ **6 Kala-class LCU** Bldr: Rauma-Repola

KALA 1 − KALA 6

D: 60 tons (200 fl) **S:** 9 kts **Dim:** 27.0 × 8.0 × 1.8
A: 1/20-mm AA − 34 mines **Man:** 10 men
M: 2 Valmet diesels; 2 props; 360 hp

REMARK: In service since 1956-59.

◆ **5 Kave-class LCM**

KAVE 1   KAVE 2   KAVE 3   KAVE 4   KAVE 6

D: 27 tons (60 fl) **S:** 9 kts **Dim:** 18.0 × 5.0 × 1.3
A: 1/20-mm AA **Man:** 3 men
M: 2 Valmet diesels; 2 props; 360 hp

REMARK: In service since 1956-60.

AUXILIARY SHIPS

◆ **2 headquarters tenders**

LOUHI (ex-*Sisu*) Bldr: Wärtsilä, Helsinki

D: 2,075 tons **S:** 16 kts **Dim:** 64.1 × 14.2 × 5.1
A: 2/40-mm AA (I × 2) **Man:** 100 men
M: 2 Atlas diesels, electric drive; 2 props; 4,000 hp

REMARK: Launched 24-9-38. Former icebreaker, converted 1975 as tender to missile boats.

KORSHOLM (ex-*Korsholm III*, ex-*Öland*)

D: 650 tons **S:** 11 kts **Dim:** 48.0 × 8.5 × 2.9
A: 2/20-mm AA **M:** Reciprocating steam; 1 prop; 865 hp

REMARK: In service since 1931. Former car ferry, bought 1967 for use as staff headquarters and small-craft tender.

◆ **1 cable ship**

PUTSAARI Bldr: Rauma-Repola

D: 430 tons **S:** 10 kts **Dim:** 45.5 × 8.9 × 2.3
M: 1 Wärtsilä diesel; 1 prop; 450 hp **Man:** 20 men

REMARK: Launched 15-12-65.

◆ **1 salvage tender**

PELLINKI

D: 700 tons **S:** 12 kts **Dim:** . . . × . . . × . . .
M: Diesels

REMARKS: Purchased 1978. Former rescue tug, has diving and fire-fighting facilities.

◆ **6 general-service tenders** Bldr: U.S.A., 1943-44

PIRTTISAARI   PYHTÄÄ   PURHA

D: 150 tons **S:** 8 kts **Dim:** 21.3 × 6.2 × 2.6
A: 1/20-mm AA **Man:** 10 men
M: 1 Wärtsilä or Atlas diesel; 1 prop; 400 hp

REMARKS: Used as miscellaneous transports. Pyhtää belongs to the Coast Artillery.

PUKKIO   PORKKALA   PANSIO Bldr: Valmet, Helsinki

D: 162 tons **S:** 10 kts **Dim:** 28.5 × 6.0 × 2.7
A: 1/40-mm − 1/20-mm − 20 mines **Man:** 10 men
M: 1 Wärtsilä diesel; 1 prop; 300 hp

REMARKS: In service 1939, 1940, and 1947. Used as tugs, transports, and minelayers.

◆ **4 Valas-class utility craft** Bldr: Hollming Oy, Roma

D: 275 tons (fl) **S:** 12 kts **Dim:** 30.0 × 7.5 × . . .
M: 1 Wärtsilä diesel; 1,300 hp **Man:** 15 men

REMARKS: Ordered 1978. One to be a diving tender. All can break four-meter ice. Can carry 30 tons cargo and 150 passengers.

◆ **4 Hauki-class personnel transports**

HAUKI   HAKUNI   HAVOURI   N . . .

D: 46 tons **S:** 10 kts **Dim:** 14.5 × 4.6 × . . .
M: 2 Valmet 611-CS diesels; 2 props; 280 hp

REMARKS: Ordered 1978. Can carry 45 troops or 6 tons supplies.

◆ **57 service launches, K, Y, L, YM, and H classes**

D: 2 to 34 tons **S:** 7 to 10 kts

REMARK: For local transport.

COAST GUARD

Operated by the Ministry of the Interior

PATROL BOATS

TURVA . . . Bldr: Laivateollisuus, Turku

D: 550 tons

REMARK: Ordered 1976. An improved *Valpas*, similar in appearance.

VALPAS Bldr: Laivateollisuus, Turku

COAST GUARD – PATROL BOATS (*continued*)

D: 545 tons **S:** 15 kts **Dim:** 48.3 × 8.7 × 4.0
A: 1/20-mm AA **Man:** 22 men
M: 1 Werkspoor TMABS-398 diesel; 1 controllable-pitch prop; 2,000 hp

REMARK: Launched 22-12-70. Ice-strengthened, equipped with sonar.

VIIMA Bldr: Laivateollisuus, Turku

D: 135 tons **S:** 23 kts **Dim:** 35.7 × 6.6 × 2.0
A: 1/40-mm AA **Man:** 12 men
M: 3 Mercedes-Benz diesels; 3 props; 4,050 hp

REMARK: Launched 20-7-64.

SILMA Bldr: Laivateollisuus, Turku

D: 530 tons **S:** 15 kts **Dim:** 48.3 × 8.3 × 4.3
A: 1/20-mm AA **Man:** 22 men
M: 1 Werkspoor diesel; 1 prop; 1,800 hp

REMARK: Launched 25-3-63.

UISKO Bldr: Valmet, Helsinki

Uisko

D: 370 tons **S:** 15 kts **Dim:** 43.4 × 7.3 × 3.83
A: 1/20-mm AA **Man:** 20 men
M: 1 Werkspoor diesel; 1 prop; 1,800 hp

REMARK: In service 1959.

| KAAKKURI | KOSKELO | KUOVI | TAVI |
| KIISLA | KUIKKA | KURKI | TELKKÄ |

Bldr: Valmet, Helsinki, 1956-59

D: 75 tons (97 fl) **S:** 23 kts **Dim:** 29.42 × 5.02 × 1.5
A: 1/20-mm AA **Man:** 11 men
M: Mercedes-Benz diesels; 2 props; 2,700 hp

REMARKS: Steel hull, ice-strengthened. *Kuikka, Kaakkuri:*

D: 90 tons (fl) **S:** 16 kts **M:** 1,000 hp.

PATROL CRAFT

◆ **98 small craft, Series RV, NV, and PV**

D: 1.1 to 20 tons **S:** Most, 9 to 13 kts **Dim:** 8 to 14 overall

REMARKS: The newest are RU-37 to RU-41, delivered 1978-79 by Hollming:

D: 20 tons **Dim:** 14.3 × 3.5 × . . . **M:** 1 diesel; 320 hp

◆ **1 training ship**

ECKERO Bldr: Kone & Silta, Helsinki

D: 55 tons **S:** 10 kts **Dim:** 40.7 × 7.2 × 4.4
M: 1 Mercedes-Benz diesel; 1 prop; 225 hp

REMARK: Built 1903, rebuilt 1954.

◆ **1 small cargo ship**

TURJA Bldr: Wärtsilä, Helsinki, 1928

D: 65 tons **S:** 11 kts **Dim:** 22.6 × 4.5 × 2.5
M: 1 Mercedes-Benz diesel; 1 prop; 225 hp

ICEBREAKERS (Under Board of Navigation)

◆ **2 Urho class** Bldr: Wärtsilä, Helsinki

URHO SISU

D: 7,500 tons (9,500 fl) **S:** 18 kts **Dim:** 104.6 × 23.8 × 8.3
M: 5 SEMT-Pielstick diesels, electric drive; 4 props; 22,000 hp

REMARKS: In service 1975-76. Sisters to Swedish *Atle.* One helicopter. Two props forward, two aft.

◆ **3 Tarmo class** Bldr: Wärtsilä, Helsinki

TARMO VARMA APU

D: 4,890 tons **S:** 17 kts **Dim:** 85.7 × 21.7 × 6.8
M: 4 Sulzer diesels, electric drive; 4 props; 10,000 hp

REMARK: In service 1963, 1968, and 1970, respectively. Two props forward, two aft.

◆ **3 Karhu class** Bldr: Wärtsilä, Helsinki

KARHU MURTJALA SAMPO

D: 3,540 tons **S:** 16 kts **Dim:** 74.2 × 17.4 × 6.4
M: Diesel-electric; 4 props (2 fwd), 7,500 hp

REMARK: In service 1958, 1959, and 1960, respectively.

◆ **1 Voima class** Bldr: Wärtsilä, Helsinki

D: 4,415 tons **S:** 16.5 kts **Dim:** 83.6 × 19.4 × 6.8
M: Diesel-electric; 4 props (2 fwd); 10,500 hp

FRANCE

For the first time in its history, the Navy is among the most important components in the military might of France and its contribution will become more significant every day.

GENERAL CHARLES DE GAULLE (1965)

For some time there have been increasing signs of the advent of a new, predominantly maritime phase in civilization.

VALÉRY GISCARD D'ESTAING

PERSONNEL (1979): 68,246 on active duty, including 4,322 officers, 29,616 chief petty officers and petty officers, and 34,308 other enlisted personnel.

MERCHANT MARINE (1-7-78): 1,317 ships — 12,197,354 grt
(tankers: 106 ships — 7,714,800 grt)

WARSHIPS IN SERVICE OR UNDER CONSTRUCTION
AS OF 1 JANUARY 1980

	L	Tons	Main armament
◆ 3 aircraft carriers			
2 CLEMENCEAU (fixed-wing)	1957-60	22,000	8/100-mm DP, 40 aircraft
1 JEANNE D'ARC (helicopter)	1961	10,000	4/100-mm DP, 6/MM38 Exocet, 8 heavy helicopters
◆ 26 (+7) submarines			
0(+1) L'INFLEXIBLE (nuclear)	. . .	7,500	16 missiles, 4 TT
4(+1) LE REDOUTABLE (nuclear)	1967-77	7,500	16 missiles, 4 TT
1 GYMNOTE	1964	3,000	2 missiles
0(+5) PROVENCE (nuclear)	1979-. . .	2,265	4 TT
4 AGOSTA	1974-76	1,200	4 TT
9 DAPHNÉ	1959-67	700	12 TT
2 ARÉTHUSE	1957-58	400	4 TT
6 NARVAL	1954-58	1,320	6 TT
◆ 1 guided-missile cruiser			
1 COLBERT	1956	8,500	1 Masurca, 2/100-mm DP, 12/57-mm AA
◆ 19 (+8) destroyers			
0(+3) C 70 AA	. . .	3,900	1/SM-1MR, 4/MM38, 2/100-mm DP, 2 TT
1(+5) GEORGES LEYGUES	1975-	3,800	1/100-mm DP, 4/MM38, 2 TT 2 WG 13 Lynx helicopters
3 TOURVILLE	1972-74	4,580	1 Malafon, 6/MM38, 1 Crotale, 2/100-mm DP, 2 TT, 2 WG 13 Lynx helicopters
2 SUFFREN	1965-66	5,090	1 Masurca, 2/100-mm DP, 1 Malafon
1 ACONIT	1970	3,500	2/100-mm DP, 1 Malafon, ASW mortar, 2 TT
1 LA GALISSONIÈRE	1960	2,750	2/100-mm DP, 1 Malafon, 1 helicopter
1 DUPERRÉ	1956	3,900	1/100-mm DP, 4/MM38
5 D'ESTRÉES	1954	3,900	2/100-mm DP, 1 Malafon, ASW weapons
4 KERSAINT	1953-54	2,750	1 SM-1MR, 6/57-mm AA, 1 ASW rocket launcher, 6 TT
1 LA BOURDONNAIS	1955	2,750	4/127-mm DP, 4/57-mm AA, 6 TT, 1 ASW rocket launcher
◆ 23 (+6) frigates and corvettes			
1 BALNY	1962	1,750	2/100-mm DP, 1 ASW mortar, 6 TT
8 COMMANDANT RIVIÈRE	1958-63	1,750	4/MM38, 2/100-mm DP, 1 ASW mortar, 6 TT
3 L'ALSACIEN	1957	1,250	4/57-mm AA, 12 TT, 1 ASW mortar
2 LE NORMAND	1954-56	1,250	4 or 6/57-mm AA, 12 TT, 1 rocket launcher
9 (+6) D'ESTIENNE D'ORVES	1973-80	1,170	1/100-mm DP, 2/MM38, 1 ASW rocket launcher, 2 TT
◆ 21 (+7) patrol boats			
1 LE FOUGUEUX	1957-59	325	1/40-mm AA
0(+6) NEW CONSTRUCTION	. . .	290	1/40-mm AA
4 TRIDENT	1976-77	115	1/40-mm, 6/SS 12 SSM
1 LA COMBATTANTE	1963	180	2/40-mm AA, 4/SS 12 SSM
4 LA LORIENTAISE	1952-54	370	1/40-mm AA
0(+1) MERCURE	1957	365	2/20-mm AA
5 SIRIUS	1953-57	400	1/40-mm AA, 1 or 2/20-mm
6 "-HAM"	1954-55	140	1/20-mm AA
◆ 35 (+15) minehunters and minesweepers			
0(+15) ERIDAN (minehunters)	1979-. . .		1/20-mm AA
5 CIRCÉ (minehunters)	1970-72	465	1/20-mm AA
10 U.S. MSO (5 minehunters)	1953-54	700	1/40-mm AA
5 SIRIUS	1955-56	400	1/40-mm AA
15 U.S. MSC	1953-54	300	2/20-mm AA
◆ 21 (+2) amphibious warfare ships			
2 OURAGAN	1963-67	5,800	4/40-mm AA
5 ARGENS	1958-60	1,750	3/40-mm AA
2 (+2) CHAMPLAIN	1973-. . .	770	. . .
12 EDIC	1958-69	250	2/20-mm AA

SHIPS ENTERING ACTIVE SERVICE DURING 1979
1 guided-missile destroyer: *Georges Leygues*
2 corvettes: *SM Le Behau, LV Le Henaff*

WARSHIPS IN SERVICE OR UNDER CONSTRUCTION *(continued)*

SHIPS RETIRED FROM SERVICE DURING 1979
    2 submarines: *Aréthuse, Ariane*
    1 destroyer: *Tartu*
    3 frigates: *Le Picard, Le Béarnais, Le Basque*
    3 coastal escorts: *L'Alerte, L'Ardent, L'Adroit*
    2 patrol boats: *Sagittaire, Aldebaran*

SHIPS SCHEDULED TO ENTER SERVICE BETWEEN 1980 AND 1982
    1 ballistic-missile submarine: *Le Tonnant*
    1 nuclear-powered attack submarine: *Provence*
    2 guided-missile destroyers: *Dupleix, Montcalm*
    4 A-69-class corvettes
    1 replenishment oiler: *Meuse*

SHIPS SCHEDULED TO BE RETIRED BETWEEN 1980 AND 1982
    1 frigate: *Le Savoyard*
    1 replenishment oiler: *La Saône* (on completion of the *Meuse*)

NEW CONSTRUCTION UNDER THE 4TH PLAN (1977-82)
    1 aircraft carrier (deferred?)
    4 nuclear-powered attack submarines
    3 guided-missile destroyers, AA version
    3 guided-missile destroyers, ASW version
    6 patrol boats
    14 minehunters

During the same period naval aviation will receive 40 Super Étendard fighter-bombers and 13 WG 13 Lynx helicopters (the remainder of an original order for 71 and 40 machines, respectively).

WEAPONS AND SYSTEMS

A. MISSILES

◆ Strategic ballistic

M 2

Two-stage engine, not aerodynamically stabilized, solid propulsion. Characteristics:
    Total height: 10.40 m
    First-stage height: 5.20 m
    Second-stage height: 2.60 m
    Diameter: 1.50 m
    Total weight: 20,000 kg
    Warhead: 500 kilotons
    Range: 3,000 km, approx.
The M 2 is being replaced by the M 20.

M 20

Externally identical to the M 2, the M 20 carries a thermonuclear warhead and its new equipment is more refined than that in the M 2. The chief elements controlling reentry and terminal flight are in the upper part of the missile. These may include a thermonuclear warhead in the megaton range, new systems to protect against antimissile efforts, and a greater ability to penetrate. It has about the same range as the M 2.

M 4

Beginning in 1985, this missile will replace the M 20. It will be an MRV (Multiple Reentry Vehicle) consisting of three stages and having a range of more than 4,000 km. Each of its six warheads will be on the order of 150 kilotons, will have a high degree of accuracy, and a greater ability to penetrate than the M 20. The launching system will have a rapid rate of fire, be relatively quiet, and capable of operation from a submarine's greatest depth. The missile will be put in service in the *Inflexible* and will gradually replace the M 20 in all ballistic-missile submarines, with the exception of *Le Redoutable*. Its installation will require that the submarines' launching tubes be enlarged.

◆ Surface-to-air

Masurca

A medium-range missile (30 nautical miles, can intercept between 100 ft and 75,000 ft) launched by a solid-propellant booster which, in a few seconds, brings it to a speed close to Mach 3; a slower-burning solid propellant maintains this speed throughout the

Masurca launcher

WEAPONS AND SYSTEMS (*continued*)

flight. The missile and booster together are 8.6 m long and weight 2,098 kg. Other characteristics are:

	Missile	Booster
Length	5.38 m	3.32 m
Diameter	0.406 m	0.57 m
Span of fins	—	1.5 m
Weight	950.0 kg	1,148.0 kg
Warhead	100.0 kg	—

The Mod 2 beam-riding missile is no longer used. Mod 3, a semi-active homing missile, is the only one now in service. It follows a trajectory determined by proportional navigation, keeping its antenna pointed at the target, which is illuminated by the launching ship's radar transmitter.

Masurca, which is installed in the *Suffren*-class guided-missile destroyers and in the *Colbert* guided-missile cruiser, consists of (1) a target-designator and weapon-assignment console, including a computer, which uses the shipboard search radar and the Senit automatic tactical data system, and (2) two guidance systems, each with:

DRBR 51 tracking radar

A director carrying the rear-reference beam and illumination beam for the control
    system

An illumination beam

A twin launcher

Storage and maintenance facilities, including two horizontal ready-service drums
    containing eighteen missiles in addition to reserve missiles in the magazines

IFF and control equipment.

Masurca is scheduled to be modernized between 1981 and 1985. This updating is intended to keep the system up to date to the end of its expected service life (1995).

Standard SM-1 MR

A one-stage engine with solid propulsion. Characteristics:

Length: 4.6 m

Diameter: .41 m

Weight: 590 kg

Guidance: semi-active homing, proximity fuse

Range: 50,000 m, max.

Interception altitude: 60 ft to 80,000 ft

The complete system consists of, in addition to the missile:

1 single Mk 13 launcher

1 vertical stowage-loader containing forty missiles

Various computers

SPS 39B height-finding radar

2 SPG 51C tracking radars

SM-1MR is mounted on T-47-type destroyers modified for Tartar and will be installed in the planned C-70 AAW-type destroyers, which will have DRBJ 11 height-finding radar. It has replaced the earlier Tartar ITR and SM-1A in the French naval service.

Crotale

An Air Force missile adapted for naval use. Electronics are by Thomson-CSF and the missile by Matra. Characteristics:

Length: 2.93 m

Diameter: 0.156 m

Span: cruciform (0.54 m with wings extended), antipitching ailerons mounted for-
    ward

Weight: 85.1 kg

Mk 13 launcher—with Standard missile

Crotale launcher—on board the **Georges Leygues**   Thomson-CSF, 1979

WEAPONS AND SYSTEMS (*continued*)

Range: 8,000 m
Interception ranges: 150 ft to 12,000 ft
Warhead: 14 kg
Guidance: beam-riding, then detonation by infrared fuse incorporated in the missile
Launcher: octuple

Crotale is to be installed on the F-67 and C-70 types of destroyers. It will be used with DRBV 51C radar and will have a special extractor and a Thomson tracking radar in the KU band. Eighteen missiles will be carried in the magazine. The prototype was installed in the test ship *Ile d'Oléron* in May 1977, while the first operational installation was aboard the *Georges Leygues* in 1978.

◆ **Surface-to-surface**

MM 38 Exocet

A homing missile with solid-fuel propellant. Characteristics:
Weight: 700 kg, approx (explosive charge: more than 150 kg)
Speed: Mach 1
Range: 37 km, min
Length: 5.2 m
Diameter: .35 m
Wingspan: 1 m

Built by SNIAS. Usual missile silhouette, cylindrical body with a pointed nose, cruciform wings with arrow shape.

The fire-control solution requires a fix on the target provided by the surface radar of the firing ship and uses the necessary equipment for launching the missile and determining the correct range and height bearing of the target.

The missile is launched at a slight elevation (about 15°). After the boost phase, it reaches its flight altitude and is stabilized between 3 and 15 meters. Stabilization is maintained by a radar altimeter.

MM-38 launchers—on board the **Tourville**　　　　1975

During the first part of the flight, the missile is automatically guided by an inertial device which has received the azimuth of the target. When within a certain distance from the target, an automatic homing radar begins to seek the target, picks it up and directs the missile. Great effort has been made to protect the missile from enemy countermeasures during this phase.

Detonation takes place upon impact or by proximity fuse, according to interception conditions, size of the target ship, and the condition of the sea.

As of 10-79, the MM 38 was mounted on board the *Jeanne d'Arc*, the three *Tourville* class, the *Duperré*, eight *Commandant Rivière* class, the *Suffren* and *Duquesne*, five A-69-type corvettes, and planned for installation in the C-70 AA and ASW frigates.

MM 40 Exocet

An offshoot of the MM 38 and the AM 39 and also built by SNIAS, the MM 40 will be an over-the-horizon missile whose range will be adapted to radar performance, but it will be able to use fire-control data relayed by a third means. The range will be at least 65 km. Instead of the usual metal launcher, it will have a fiberglass, cylindrical one which, because it is lighter and has less fittings, will increase fire power by allowing more missiles to be carried on board.

It has been proposed to equip the future C-70 AA-type guided-missile destroyers with eight launchers each (four per side) for MM 40 if the system is acquired for the French Navy.

SS 11

A wire-guided system with line-of-sight alignment on the target. Characteristics:
Length:　1.215 m
Diameter: 0.164 m
Wingspan: 0.500
Weight:　30.4 kg
Range:　3,000 m

Not currently installed in any ships or craft; obsolescent.

SS 12 M

Similar system to SS 11. Characteristics:
Length:　1.870 m
Diameter: 0.210 m
Wingspan: 0.650
Weight:　75 kg (upon firing)
Warhead: 30 kg (about)
Range:　5,500 m

Mounted only on the missile patrol boat *La Combattante*.

B. AVIATION MISSILES

◆ **Air-to-ground**

AM 39

This is the air-to-sea version of the MM 38. After being detached by gravity and a retro-firing booster motor, it acquires a trajectory similar to that of the MM 38, whereafter it has the same flight characteristics as the MM 38.
Builder:　SNIAS
Length:　4.633 m
Diameter:　0.348 m
Wingspan:　1.004 m
Weight:　65 kg (before launching)
Range:　50-70 km, according to altitude and speed at launch
Radar:　Active home-seeking head (EMD)

WEAPONS AND SYSTEMS (*continued*)

AM 39 is known as a "fire and forget" missile because it permits an aircraft that has fired to renew its attack or to seek a new target. It may be used with the Atlantic (and the Atlantic's proposed successor) and the Super Étendard aircraft. It is equally suitable for use by such medium-weight helicopters as the Super Frélon.

AS 11

A wire-guided system with optical alignment on the target. Used for training for the CM 175 and the HSS 1.

Builder:	SNIAS
Length:	1.210 m
Diameter:	0.164 m
Wingspan:	0.50 m
Weight:	29.900 kg

AS 12

A wire-guided system with optical alignment on the target. Used by the BR 1150 Atlantic and the BR 1050 Alizé.

Builder:	SNIAS
Length:	1.870 m
Diameter:	0.210 m
Wingspan:	0.650 m
Weight:	75 kg
Range:	Maximum 7,500 to 8,000 m; minimum 1,500 m

AS 20

Builder:	SNIAS
Length:	2.60 m
Diameter:	0.25 m
Wingspan:	0.80 m
Weight:	140 kg
Guidance:	radio command
Range:	4,000 m to 8,000 m

Used in firing training of the AS 30 on the Étendard IV M.

AS 30

System developed for firing from a maneuvering aircraft at middle, low, or very low altitude. Used by the Étendard IV M and the Super Étendard.

Builder:	SNIAS
Length:	3.785 m
Diameter:	0.342 m
Wingspan:	1.000 m
Total weight:	528 kg
Range:	maximum 9 to 12,000 m; minimum 1,500 m
Guidance:	radio command

AS 37 Martel

Two types, television and anti-radar. Only the latter is used in the French Navy.

Builders:	Matra and Hawker Siddeley Dynamics
Length:	4.122 m
Diameter:	0.40 m
Wingspan:	1.192 m
Total weight:	531 kg
Range:	over 20,000 m

Passive homing head (EMD); the missile homes on the radar emissions of the enemy vessel. Immediately after being fired, the missile is on its own, permitting the aircraft to depart or evade. To be used with BR 1150 Atlantic aircraft.

◆ Air-to-air

R 530

There are two versions of this missile: infrared (IR) and radar-homing (EMD).

Builder:	Matra
Length:	IR type: 3.198 m; EMD type: 3.284 m
Diameter:	0.263 m
Wingspan:	1.103 m
Weight:	IR type: 193.5 kg, EMD type: 192 kg
Range:	maximum 10,000 m: minimum 5,000 m
Guidance:	Semi-passive-homing (MD) or infrared-homing

Sidewinder

The French Navy uses this air-to-air American missile (*see* U.S.A. section).

Magic

Builder:	Matra
Length:	2.900 m
Diameter:	0.157 m
Wingspan:	0.660 m
Weight:	89 kg
Range:	300/8,000 m
Guidance:	Infrared-homing

C. GUNS

127-mm Model 1948

Twin-barrel semi-automatic for use against aircraft, surface vessels, or land targets. Now only aboard the destroyer *Forbin*. Can use American ammunition, as used in the now-discarded U.S. Mk 39 version.

Length of barrel: 54 calibers
Muzzle velocity: 810 m/sec
Maximum anti-aircraft range: 14,000 m
Effective anti-aircraft range: 9,000 m
Maximum surface range: 22,400 m
Effective surface range: 18,000 m
Weight: 48 tons
Weight of mount: 14 tons
Maximum rate of fire: 18 rounds per minute

100-mm, Models 1953 and 1968

Singe-barrel automatic, for use against aircraft, surface vessels, or land targets. Model 1968 is a lighter version of Model 1953. The ammunition is the same. Characteristics of Model 1968:

Weight of mount: 22 tons
Length of barrel: 55 calibers
Range at 40° elevation: 17,000 m
Maximum effective range for surface fire: 15,000 m
Maximum effective range for anti-aircraft fire: 8,000 m
Maximum rate of fire: 60 rounds/minute

WEAPONS AND SYSTEMS (*continued*)

Arc of elevation: −15° to +80°
Maximum speed: training, 40°/sec, elevation, 25°/sec

Model 1953 uses an analog fire-control system with electro-mechanical and electronic equipment for the fire-control solution. The director can be operated in optical and radar modes.

Model 1968 uses a digital fire-control system, with central units, and memory disks, or magnetic tape for data storage. Light radar gun director. Optical direction equipment can be added.

57-mm Model 1951

Twin-barrel automatic:
Length of barrel: 60 calibers
Muzzle velocity: 865 m/sec
Maximum range: 13,000 m
Effective anti-aircraft range: 5,000 m
Maximum rate of fire: 60 rounds/min per barrel
Arc of elevation: −8° to 90°
Maximum rate of fire: 60 rounds per minute, per barrel.

30-mm

Single-barrel automatic:
Length: 2.440 m
Weight: 4 tons
Muzzle velocity: 1,000 m/sec
Maximum effective range: 2,800 m
Maximum rate of fire: 650 rounds per minute

Also in service are typical **40-mm** guns based on Bofors designs and **20-mm** guns of Oerlikon design.

D. ANTISUBMARINE WEAPONS

Malafon

A glider that carries L-4 torpedoes and is launched with the assistance of a double booster. It is stabilized by automatic pilot and guided by radio command.
Glider: speed, 230 m/sec; range, 12,000 m
Missile: length, 6.15 m; diameter, 0.65 m; span, 3.30 m; weight, including torpedo, 1,500 kg

The Malafon, built by Latécoère in partnership with St. Trôpez, is installed in the two *Suffren*-class destroyers, *La Galissonnière*, the Type T 47 ASW conversions, the *Aconit*, and the *Tourville*-class destroyers.

375-mm Rocket Launchers, Models 1964 or 1972

Sextuple mount. Automatic loading in vertical position. Firing rate, 1 rocket/second. Range: 1,600 m. Time or proximity fuse. Based on Bofors quadruple mounting. Normally has six illumination-flare rocket rails mounted also.

305-mm Mortar

Quadruple mount; automatic loading. ASW projectile weight: 230 kg; range: 400 to 3,000 m. Can also fire a 100-kg projectile against land targets; range: 6,000 m. Normally has four illumination-flare rocket rails mounted on the face of the rotating housing.

Automatic-loading 305-mm ASW and bombardment mortar — with flare rails

Automatic-loading, six barreled, 325-mm ASW rocket launcher — with six flare rails

E. TORPEDOES

◆ For surface ships

	Weight in kg	Diameter in mm	Speed in kts
K 2	1,100	550	50
L 3	900	550	25

WEAPONS AND SYSTEMS (*continued*)

L 4	500	533	30
L 5, Mod 1 and Mod 4	1,000	533	35

◆ **For submarines**

Z 13	1,700	550	30
E 12	1,600	550	25
E 14	900	550	25
L 5, Mod 3	1,300	533	35
F 17	1,300	533	35

◆ **For aircraft**

In addition to the U.S. torpedoes, **Mk 44** and **Mk 46**, French naval aircraft use the **L 4** torpedo.

F. SONARS

◆ **For surface ships**

	Type	Frequency	Average range
DUBA 1	Hull	HF	2,500 m
DUBA 3	Hull	HF	3,000 m
DUBV 24	Hull	LF	6,000 m
DUBV 23	Bow	LF	*see* Remarks
DUBV 43	Towed	LF	*see* Remarks
DUBA 25	Hull	MF	*see* Remarks
DUBA 26	Hull	MF	*see* Remarks
DUBM 20	Hull—on *Circé*-class minehunters		
DUBM 21	Hull—on new Tripartite and modernized MSO minehunters		
DUBM 41	Towed—on modernized MSO		

REMARKS: **DUBV 23** and **DUBV 43** are used simultaneously and, under normal sound-propagation conditions, achieve ranges of 8,000 to 10,000 meters. In certain bathy-metric conditions, the range is 20,000 meters.

DUBA 25 is a new sonar designed for the A-60 corvettes.

DUBA 26 is under development.

◆ **For submarines**

Listening devices, active-passive sonars, and telemetric equipment.

◆ **For helicopters**

	Frequency	Remark
AQS 13	MF	U.S. sonar
DUAV 1	HF	
DUAV 4	HF	In the WG 13 Lynx

G. COMBAT INFORMATION SYSTEMS

SENIT

This system serves four principal purposes:

It establishes the combat situation from the manual collection of information derived from detection equipment on board and from the automatic or manual collection of information from external sources.

It disseminates the above data to the ship and to other vessels by automatic means (Links 11 and 14).

It assists in decision-making.

It transmits to the target-designation console all the information it requires.

The several versions of the Senit are similar in general concept but differ in construction and programming in order to ensure fulfillment of the various missions assigned to each type of ship.

Senit 1: A system with one or two computers. Installed in the *Suffren*, the *Duquesne*, and the *Colbert*.

Senit 2: A single-computer system. Installed in the T-47-type *Kersaint*-class destroyers, as well as in the *Duperré*, which uses two computers.

Senit 3: A central system consisting of two computers and two memory banks, the entire group designed for the control of various weapons (guns, Malafon ASW system, torpedoes). Installed in the *Aconit*, and the three *Tourville*-class ships.

The above three systems are based on equipment of U.S. origin, some built in France under license.

Senit 4: A system conceived by the French Navy's programming center and designed around the French Iris N 55 computer. Fitted in the *Georges Leygues* class.

Senit 5: Also designed by the French Navy's programming center, this system will be fitted on small ships. It uses the French M 15 minicomputer.

Senit 6: Another system designed by the French Navy's programming center. It will equip the future C-70 AAW version of the *Georges Leygues* class. It combines a number of M 15 computers and a new generation of display devices particularly adapted for command purposes.

H. RADARS

◆ **Air search**

DRBV 20 A: Metric

DRBV 20 C: Metric, long-range. Mounted on aircraft carriers

DRBV 22 A: Mounted in T 47 ASW version destroyers, frigates, and corvettes

DRBV 22 C: *Ile d'Oléron*

DRBV 22 D: *Jeanne d'Arc, Henri Poincaré*

DRBV 23 C: Mounted in the *Colbert* and the aircraft carriers

DRBV 26: Mounted in the *Tourville* are the *Georges Leygues*

DRBV 13: Doppler pulse radar. Has several uses, installed in the *Aconit*

◆ **Height-finding/three-dimensional**

DRBI 10: Mounted in aircraft carriers, T-53 destroyers, the *Colbert*, the *Jeanne d'Arc*, the *Ile d'Oléron*

DRBI 23: Mounted in the *Duquesne* and *Suffren*

SPS-39B: American radar. Mounted on Standard-equipped T-47-class destroyers

DRBJ 11: Pulse-coded radar for the C-70 AAW class guided-missile destroyers

◆ **Surface and low-altitude air search**

DRBV 50: Mounted on aircraft carriers, *Jeanne d'Arc*, T-47 ASW-class destroyers, the *Rhin*, the *Ile d'Oléron*, the *Colbert*, and the *La Galissonnière*

DRBV 51: Mounted on A-69 corvettes and the *Duperré*

DRBV 51B: Mounted on the *Tourville* class

DRBV 51C: Mounted on the *Georges Leygues* class

◆ **Navigational**

Decca RM 416

DRBN 31: Mounted on some minesweepers and coastal patrol craft

DRBV 31: Mounted on the Standard-equipped T-47-class destroyers, on the T-53 class, and on some frigates

WEAPONS AND SYSTEMS (*continued*)

◆ Fire-control

DRBC 31: For the 100-mm of the *Duperré*. The *Foch* has DRBC 31C and the *Clemenceau* DRBC 31D

DRBC 32A: For 100-mm guns on ASW-modified T-47-class destroyers, some frigates, the *Jeanne d'Arc*, and the *Clemenceau*

DRBC 32B: For 100-mm guns on the *Aconit*

DRBC 32C: Mounted on the *Colbert*, the *Duperré*, and the *Foch*

DRBC 32D: Mounted on the *Tourville* class and the *Georges Leygues* class

DRBC 32E: Mounted on the A-69-class corvettes

SPG 51C: U.S. tracking radar used with the Standard system on the T-47-type AAW destroyers

DRBR 51: Tracking radar for the Masurca on the *Colbert*, *Suffren*, and *Duquesne*

I. COUNTERMEASURES

The French Navy uses the eight-barreled Syllex chaff launcher (a version of the British Knebworth/Corvus), which will eventually be replaced by the Sagaie, a better system. Smaller ships will receive the Dagaie system. Both Sagaie and Dagaie are fired automatically by the electronic intercept system.

AIRCRAFT CARRIERS

	Budget	Bldr	Laid down	L	In serv.
R 98 CLEMENCEAU	1953	Brest	11-55	21-12-57	22-11-61
R 99 FOCH	1955	Ch. Atlantique	2-57	28-7-60	15-7-63

D: 22,000 tons (27,307 mean) R-98: 32,780(fl) R-99: 32,185 (fl)

Dim: 265.0 (238.0 pp) × 31.72 beam × 51.2 flight deck × 7.5 light draft × 8.5 fl

S: 32 kts (33 on trials) **Range:** 4,800/24, 7,500/18

A: 8/100-mm DP Model 1953 (I × 8)–40 aircraft (*see* Remarks)

Electron Equipt: Radars: 1/DRBV 20C, 1/DRBV 23B, 2/DRBI 10, 1/DRBV 50, 1/DRBC 31, 1/Decca, 1/NRBA, 2/DRBC 31C (R-99) or D (R-98), 2/DRBC 32A (R-98) or C (R-99)

  Sonar: 1/SQS 505 – TACAN: 1/URN 6

Armor: Reinforced flight deck, armored bulkheads in engine room and magazines, reinforced-steel bridge superstructure

Man: Peacetime: As aircraft carriers: 64 officers, 476 petty officers, 798 other enlisted. Total: 1,338 men

  As helicopter carriers: 45 officers, 392 petty officers, 547 other enlisted. Total: 984 men

Boilers: 6, 45 kg/cm² – superheat 450° **Fuel:** 3,720 tons

M: 2 Parsons GT; 2 props; 126,000 hp

REMARKS: Flight deck 257 m in length; deck angled at 8°, 165.5 × 29.5; deck forward of the angled deck: 93 × 28; width of the deck abeam the island: 35. Hangar dimensions, 180 × 22 to 24 × 7 (height). Two elevators 16 m long, 11 m in width, one forward on the main flight deck, one slightly abaft the island, able to raise a 15-ton aircraft 8.50 m in 9 seconds. Two 50-meter Mitchell-Brown type BS5 steam catapults, able to launch 15/20-ton aircraft at 110 knots, one forward, another on the angled deck. Optical-mirror landing equipment of French manufacture.

The propulsion machinery was built by the Chantiers de l'Atlantique. Living spaces are air-conditioned. Medium-sized island with three bridges: flag, navigation, aviation. Communication systems, especially with fighter aircraft, are a significant aspect of the ships' capabilities.

Clemenceau   1979

Foch   1978

The *Foch*, built in a special dry dock at St. Nazaire, was towed to Brest for the installation of her armament.

Aviation fuel: 1,800 m³ of jet fuel and 109 m³ of aviation gasoline carried by the *Foch*; 1,200 m³ of jet fuel and 400 m³ of aviation gasoline by the *Clemenceau*.

Between September 1977 and November 1978, the *Clemenceau* underwent a significant refit in the Toulon dockyard. The work consisted of a general overhaul of her installations and her living spaces, taking into account the new system of naval ranks, modernization of her flight deck, reinforcement of her arresting gear, strengthening of her catapults, an engine overhaul, and the addition of two supplementary boilers. Her

AIRCRAFT CARRIERS (continued)

electronic systems were modernized and she was given the Senit 2 that was removed from the inactivated destroyer *Jaurreguibery*. On the *Clemenceau*, this system has three main functions: establishment of a situation based on information from external sources (land-based radars, aircraft, ships); dissemination of those data to the ship and to other ships; and assistance in decision-making. The ship has been equipped with a closed-circuit television system that displays needed information in interested parts of the ship: flight-deck control, the combat operations center, the ready rooms, the air operations office. To operate the Super Étendard, the *Clemenceau* has been fitted with a central inertial guidance system that transfers information to the inertial guidance system in each plane. Her magazines have been modified to carry tactical nuclear weapons. The *Foch* is scheduled to undergo the same refit in 1980: she will receive the Senit 2 from the inactivated destroyer *Tartu*. As an aircraft carrier, the *Clemenceau* has an air group that consists of 16 Super Étendard, 3 Étendard IV P, 10 F-8E Corsair, 7 Alizé, and 2 Alouette III; as a helicopter carrier, she carries 30 to 40 helicopters, depending on their size.

◆ **1 nuclear propulsion, Type PA 75 (ASW and amphibious assault)**

	Bldr	Laid down	In serv.
N . . .	Brest Navy Yard	1981	. . .

D: 16,400 tons (18,400 fl) **S:** 28 kts
Dim: 208 × 202 flight deck × 26.4 (wl) × 46 flight deck × 6.5
Man: 840 men, 50 staff—plus up to 1,500 troops
Range: Under nuclear power, unlimited—3,000/18 (diesel engines)
A: 2 Crotale systems (VIII × 2)—2/100-mm DP Model 1968 (I × 2)—helicopters (*see* Remarks)
Electron Equipt: Radars: 1/DRBV 26, 1/DRBV 51 C, 2/Decca, 2/DRBC 32
  Sonars: 1/DUBA 25—2 Sagaie systems—SENIT

Foch 1978

Clemenceau Guiglini, 1979

Foch 1978

AIRCRAFT CARRIERS (*continued*)

M: 1 CAS 230 (230 megawatt) reactor furnishing steam to 2 turbo-reduction-con-
denser groups; 65,000 hp; 2 props; 2 AGO standby diesels

Electric: 9,400 kw

REMARKS: Due to budgetary restrictions, the laying down of the ship has been postponed from 1976 until at least 1981. It is entirely possible that, by that date, the design may have been considerably modified. In any case, the ship could not now be
operational before the late 1980s. The installations for aircraft operation will include
the following: 1 hangar 84 × 21 × 6.50, 2 deck-edge elevators (15 tons in 11 seconds),
1 fixed crane, 1 mobile crane, munition-handling rooms, magazines, workshops, fuel
tanks for 1,000 m³ of TR jet fuel. 1,250 tons of fuel are to be carried to replenish escorting ships.

Originally, the ship was to be able to launch about 25 WG 13 Lynx, about 10 Super
Frélon, or 15 Army-type Puma helicopters, or a combination of these, space being
available for all of them on the hangar deck. It was later planned to carry fixed-wing
aircraft of the V/STOL or V/TOL type as well—hence the change in designation from
PH (Porte-Hélicoptères) to PA (Porte Aéronefs).

◆ **1 helicopter-carrier**

	Budget	Bldr	Laid down	L	In serv.
R 97 JEANNE D'ARC	1957	Brest	7-60	30-9-61	30-6-64
(ex-*La Résolue*)					

Jeanne d'Arc—with three Sikorsky HSS-1 helicopters on deck   1975

D: 10,000 tons (12,365 fl)   **S:** 26.5 kts (cruising)

Dim: 182.0 (172.0 wl) × 24.0 × 22.0 (wl) × 6.6 (7.3 aft)

A: 6/MM 38 Exocet—4/100-mm DP Model 1953 (I × 4)—8 helicopters (*See* Remarks)

Electron Equipt: Radars: 1/DRBV 22D, 1/DRBV 50, 1/DRBN 32, 1/DRBI 10,
3/DRBC 32A

Sonar: SQS 503—2 Syllex countermeasures installations—
TACAN

Man: Ship's company: 31 officers, 182 petty officers, 414 other enlisted

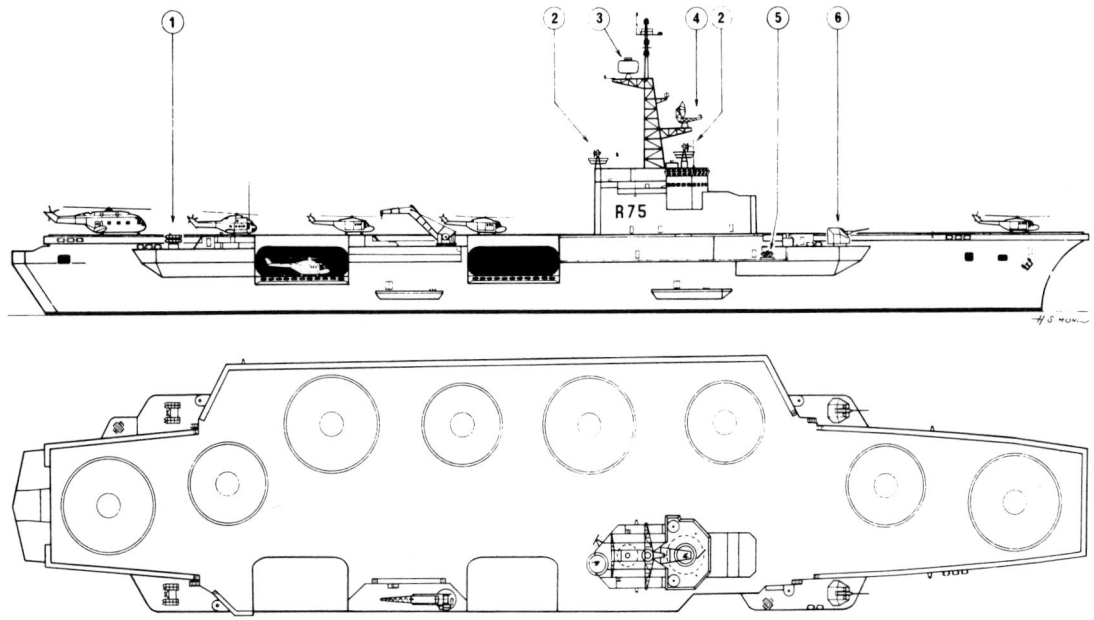

1. Crotale launcher 2. DRBC-32 radar 3. DRBV-51C radar 4. DRBV-26 radar 5. Sagaie system 6. 100-mm mount, Model 1968

AIRCRAFT CARRIERS (*continued*)

Range: 3,000/26.5, 3,750/25, 5,500/20, 6,800/16   Fuel: 1,360 tons
Boilers: 4 asymmetric, multitube, 45 kg/cm² — superheat 450°C
M: 2 Rateau-Bretagne GT; 2 props; 40,000 hp   Electric: 4,400 kw

REMARKS: Replaced the former cruiser *Jeanne d'Arc* as a training ship for officer cadets. When on this mission, she carries only four heavy helicopters. In wartime, she would be used for ASW missions, amphibious assault, or as a troop transport. The number of heavy helicopters embarked can be quickly augmented by simple structural changes.

The landing platform is 62 × 21 m. The hull is welded throughout.

Aviation facilities include:

Aft of the island structure, a flight deck that permits the simultaneous takeoff of two Super Frélon helicopters, while two machines can be stationed forward of the takeoff area and two others astern, one on each side of the elevator.

An elevator (12-ton capacity) at the after end of the flight deck.

A hangar deck that, if some of the living quarters used by midshipmen are used, can accommodate eight helicopters.

At the after end of the hangar deck there are all the machine shops necessary for maintenance and repair, including helicopter electronic equipment, and an area for inspection. There, also, are the compartments for handling weapons and ammunition (torpedoes, rockets, etc.).

There are three fire-control directors for the 100-mm guns, each served by three automatically controlled radar directors.

In addition to the navigation bridge, the superstructure contains a helicopter-control bridge, a modular-type information and operations center, and a combined control center for amphibious operations.

The engineering spaces are divided into two compartments, each with two boilers and a turbine, separated by a bulkhead.

The *Jeanne d'Arc* is scheduled for a refit from 1982-83; at that time, the Senit 2 computerized tactical data handling system is expected to be installed.

NAVAL AVIATION

The Naval Air establishment is made up of combatant flotillas, maintenance squadrons or sections, bases, schools, and the special services necessary to ensure the efficient operation of the flight components. It is manned by naval personnel.

Administrative problems are handled by the Aeronautical Division of the Naval General Staff and the Central Service Branch of Naval Air, both headed by flag officers. Operational and training matters are directed by the Navy Staff, whose various bureaus include aviation officers.

Primary training in fixed-wing planes is provided by the Air Force; helicopter pilots are given initial training by the Army as well as the Air Force. Specialization of these pilots in multi-engine aircraft or in carrier-based fixed-wing and rotary aircraft is provided by Naval Air. The latter also trains navigators and maintenance crews at the Naval Air School, Rochefort.

The combat flotillas are:

(a) those embarked which, flying from aircraft carriers or helicopter carriers, carry out intercept, attack, reconnaissance, or CAP missions and engage in antisubmarine warfare.

(b) maritime patrol flotillas and antisubmarine warfare flotillas that are land-based.

Jeanne d'Arc   1975

Super Étendard

NAVAL AVIATION (*continued*)

The service support squadrons and sections have various missions: schools, training exercises, transportation, logistical support for seagoing forces, experimental and salvage operations.

Authority over embarked flotillas and squadrons is assigned to a rear admiral, Commander, Aircraft Carriers and seagoing aviation (ALPA).

Maritime patrol squadrons are commanded by a rear admiral (ALPATMAR).

Shore-based flotillas, squadrons, and sections are commanded by the Préfets Maritimes (Naval District Commandants) through the regional aviation commanders.

Bases: Nîmes-Garon, Saint-Mandrier (helicopters), Saint-Raphaël (experimental station), Hyères, Cuers (maintenance), Ajaccio-Aspretto (training), Lorient-Lann Bihoué, Lanvéoc-Poulmic (helicopters), Landivisiau.

For training, the French Navy uses the Nord-262, Douglas C-47, CM-175, the Alouette II helicopter, and the Rallye-880 light plane. Aircraft of the MS-760, Nord-262, Rallye-880, C-47, C-54, CM-175, and Falcon-10 types, as well as Alouette II and III, HSS-1, and Super Frélon helicopters are used by support organizations. The Pacific Experimental Center uses P-2H Neptune aircraft and Alouette III helicopters for support duties.

Naval aircraft carry on the fuselage sides the French tricolor insignia with a yellow surround and a superimposed black anchor; the word *Marine* is also displayed near the insignia.

Super Étendard

COMBAT ORGANIZATION

Flotilla	Subordination	Bases	Equipment	Missions
4 F	ALPA	Lann-Bihoué	12 Alizé	ASW/AEW
6 F	ALPA	Nîmes-Garons	12 Alizé	ASW/AEW
11 F	ALPA	Landivisiau	12 Super-Étendard	Attack
12 F	ALPA	Landivisiau	15 Crusader (F-8E)	Interception
14 F	ALPA	Landivisiau	12 Super-Étendard	Attack
16 F	ALPA	Landivisiau	6 Étendard IV P 2 Étendard IV M	Reconnaissance
17 F	ALPA	Hyères	12 Étendard IV M/ Super-Étendard	Attack
21 F	ALPATMAR	Nîmes-Garons	7 Atlantic	Maritime patrol
22 F	ALPATMAR	Nîmes-Garons	7 Atlantic	Maritime patrol
23 F	ALPATMAR	Lann-Bihoué	7 Atlantic	Maritime patrol
24 F	ALPATMAR	Lann-Bihoué	7 Atlantic	Maritime patrol
25 F	ALPATMAR	Lann-Bihoué	12 Neptune (P-2H)	Maritime patrol
31 F	ALPA	St-Mandier	8 WG 13 Lynx	ASW
32 F	ALPA	Lanvéoc-Poulmic	10 Super-Frélon	ASW & troop transport
33 F	ALPA	St-Mandrier	12 Super-Frélon	Troop transport
34 F	ALPA	Lanvéoc-Poulmic	10 Alouette III/ WG 13 Lynx	ASW

Super Étendard—with AM-39 missile

Étendard-IVM

F-8E Crusader

Alizé

WG-13 Lynx

Super Frélon

Alouette-III

WG-13 Lynx

WG-13 Lynx

Atlantic

Atlantic

P-2H Neptune

Alouette-III

WG-13 Lynx

Alizé – landing on the Clemenceau

COMBAT AIRCRAFT

Type	Mission	Wingspan	Length	Height	Weight (max.) kilos	Engine	Maximum speed in mach or in knots	Maximum ceiling	Range	Weapons	Remarks
◆ SHIP-BASED PLANES											
Crusader F8-E (FN) (Ling-Temco-Vought)	All-weather interceptor	10.72	16.61	4.80	13,000	1 J57 P20 *A* Pratt & Whitney turbojet with after-burner	Mach 1.8	50,000 ft	1,500 miles 2 hr 30 min	4/20-mm guns, Air-to-air missiles	(1) Alize aircraft will be modernized 1980-83 with Iguane radar, Omega radio-navigation equipment, and ARAR 12A intercept gear.
Super-Étendard (Dassault)	Fleet air defense, attack, reconnaissance photo	9.60	14.35	3.85	11,900	1 8 K 50 SNECMA turbojet developing 5 tons of thrust	Mach 1 at 11,000 m; Mach 0.97 at low altitude			2/30-mm guns, bombs, rockets, combination or AM 39	(2) May be outfitted with a small photo pod for reconnaissance missions. The ANG Atlantic which will enter service in 1985 will have the same airframe, engines, and characteristics as the Mk I but its weapon system will be entirely new, built around a Type 15 M digital tactical computer. It will be able to transport 3 tons of weapons, e.g., 4 Martel under the wings or 2 AM 39 inboard. 42 aircraft will be procured.
Étendard-IVM (Dassault)	Attack aircraft	9.60	14.35	3.85	10,200	1 SNECMA Atar 8 turbojet	Mach 1.3	35,000 ft	750 miles 1 hr 45 min or 2 hr 15 min with supplemental reserve tank	2/30-mm guns, air surface missiles (or air-to-air) 68-mm and 100-mm rockets, various bombs of 50 to 400 kg	
Étendard-IVP (Dassault)	Reconnaissance photo	9.60	14.50	3.85	10,200	1 SNECMA Atar 8 turbojet	Mach 1.3	35,000 ft	750 miles 1 hr 45 or 2 hr 15 with supplemental reserve tank	100-mm rockets, 68-mm rockets, photo-flash bombs	
Alizé (BR 1050) (1) (Bréguet)	AEW, ASW	15.60	13.66	5	8,200	1 Rolls-Royce Dart 21 turbo-prop (1,925 hp + 230 kt of thrust)	240 kts	11,000 ft	685 miles 3 hr 45	Air-to-surface missiles, Mk 44 torpedoes, 100-mm rockets, ASW depth charges, 50 to 250 kg bombs, acoustic buoys, mortar type projectiles	(3) Localization, classification and attack of contacts picked up by an anti-submarine ship.
◆ LAND-BASED PLANES											
P2-H Neptune (Lockheed)	Patrol, ASW	31.50	31.70	10.80	34,280	2 R 3350 32 *Wa* Wright engines × 3,250 hp + 2 Westing-house turbojets type J34 × 1,540 kg	240 kts	25,000 ft	3,200 miles 16 hr	L 4 or Mk 44 or 46 torpedoes, ASW depth charges, sono-buoys, mortar type projectiles (ASW), photo-flash bombs	(4) Detection, identification and neutralization of small surface vessels with weak anti-aircraft defense.
Atlantic Mk 1 (BR 1150) (Bréguet)	Patrol, ASW (2)	36.30	31.75	11.33	43,500	2 Rolls-Royce Tyne 20 turbo-props, 6,000 hp each	300 kts	30,000 ft	4,300 miles 17 hr	Air-to-surface missiles, L 4 or Mk 44 or 46 torpedoes, ASW depth charges, sono-buoys, mortar type projectiles (ASW), photo flash bombs	(5) Equipped with retractable MAD gear.
◆ HELICOPTERS											
HSS-1 (Sikorsky)	ASW, troop carrier	17.07 (rotor diameter)	20.06	4.73	6,000	1 R 1820.84 Wright, 1,525 hp	110 kts	9,000 ft	380 miles 4 hr 30 min	Mk 44 and Mk 46 torpedoes, air-to-surface missiles, ASW depth charges	

COMBAT AIRCRAFT (*continued*)

Type	Mission	Wingspan	Length	Height	Weight (max.) kilos	Engine	Maximum speed in mach or in knots	Maximum ceiling	Range	Weapons	Remarks
Super-Frélon (SNIAS)	ASW	18.90 (rotor diameter)	23	6.35	13,000	3 C3 Turboméca III turbo-shafts, each with 1,500 hp	145 kts	10,000 ft	420 miles 3 hr 30 min	Mk 44 and Mk 46 torpedoes, ASW torpedoes	
Lynx (WG 13) (Westland-SNIAS)	ASW (3)	12.80 (rotor diameter)	15.2	3.20	4,150	2 BS 360 Rolls-Royce turbo-shafts, of 900 hp each	150 kts	12,000 ft	1 hr 30, half hovering, half in flight 2 hr 30 min with 3 men and 4 missiles	Mk 44 and Mk 46 torpedoes, air-to-surface missiles	
	Surface attack aircraft (4)										
Alouette-III (SNIAS)	ASW (5)	11.02 (rotor diameter)	12.8	3.0	2,200	1 Turbomeca Astazou turboshaft, 870 hp	110 kts	10,000 ft	325 miles 2 hr 30 min	Mk 44 torpedoes	

BALLISTIC-MISSILE SUBMARINES

NOTE: The French Navy is studying a new generation of strategic-missile submarines to be evolved from the designs of *L'Inflexible* and *Le Redoutable* class.

	Bldr	Laid down	L	In serv.
S . . . (Q . . .) L'INFLEXIBLE	Cherbourg	1980	. . .	1985

D: 7,500-7,900 tons surfaced   **S:** over 20 kts
Dim: 128.0 × 10.6 × 10.0
A: 16 M 4 ballistic missiles — 4/533-mm TT fwd (18 torpedoes)
Man: 2 crews in rotation, each of 15 officers, 120 men
M: 1 nuclear reactor producing pressurized steam for propulsion; 1 prop

REMARKS: *L'Inflexible* will have most characteristics in common with the five preceding SSBNs of *Le Redoutable* class but will take advantage of many technological advances in propulsion, sonar systems, navigation systems, etc., and will be able to dive 100 m deeper. The ship will be equipped from the outset with the M 4 missile, which will have seven Multiple Independent Re-entry Vehicle (MIRV) warheads.

◆ **5 nuclear-powered Le Redoutable class**

	Laid down	L	Trials	In serv.
S 611 (Q 252) LE REDOUTABLE	11-64	29-3-67	1969	1-12-71
S 612 (Q 253) LE TERRIBLE	22-6-67	12-12-69	1971	1-1-73
S 610 (Q 257) LE FOUDROYANT	12-69	4-12-71	5-73	6-6-74
S 613 (Q 258) L'INDOMPTABLE	12-71	17-9-74	12-75	23-12-76
S 614 (Q 259) LE TONNANT	1973	17-9-77	. . .	5-80

Bldr: Cherbourg

Le Redoutable   E.C.P.A., 1970

Le Redoutable   E.C.P.A., 1971

BALLISTIC-MISSILE SUBMARINES (*continued*)

Le Terrible E.C.P.A., 1971

D: 7,500 tons surfaced, 9,000 submerged   **S:** 20 kts, max
Dim: 128.0 × 10.6 × 10.0
A: 16 M20 ballistic missiles—4/350-mm TT fwd (18 torpedoes)
Man: Twin crews of 15 officers and 120 men for each ship, manning in rotation
M: 1 nuclear reactor producing pressurized steam for propulsion; 1 prop

REMARKS: The *Redoutable* (authorized in March 1963) and other submarines of this class are the principal elements of the French naval deterrent. They can dive more than 200 meters.

The propulsion system consists of a reactor with enriched uranium and distilled water under pressure giving the required heat energy for the production of steam to produce the power of two turbine installations and two turbo-alternators. An auxiliary main engine with electrical energy can substitute for the main engines in an emergency. The range on the diesel-electric auxiliary propulsion engine is about 5,000 nautical miles.

◆ 1 experimental submarine

	Bldr	Laid down	L	In serv.
S 655 GYMNOTE	Cherbourg	17-3-63	17-3-64	17-10-66

Gymnote J.-C. Bellonne, 1977

D: 3,000 tons surfaced, 3,250 submerged
S: 11 kts surfaced, 10 kts submerged
Dim: 84.0 × 10.6 × 7.6   **Man:** 8 officers, 38 petty officers, 45 other enlisted
M: 4 sets 620-kw diesel generators; 2 electric motors; 2 props; 2,600 hp

REMARKS: Used for testing missiles designed for the SSBNs. Has two vertical missile-launching tubes to port. Bow diving planes do not retract. Noncombatant. Currently involved in M-4 developmental trials. The pressure hull was laid down in 1958 for a nuclear-powered attack submarine that was canceled in 1959.

ATTACK SUBMARINES

◆ **5 nuclear-powered Provence class, Type SNA 72**

	Bldr	Laid down	L	In serv.
S 616 PROVENCE	Cherbourg	11-12-76	7-7-79	1982
S . . . BRETAGNE	Cherbourg	. . .	. . .	1985
S . . . BOURGOGNE	Cherbourg	. . .	. . .	. . .
S . . . N (Q 268)	Cherbourg	. . .	. . .	. . .
S . . . N (Q 269)	Cherbourg	. . .	. . .	. . .

Provence—at her launching DCAN, 1979

D: 2,265 tons, 2,385 surfaced, 2,670 submerged (fl)   **S:** 25 kts
Dim: 72.1 × 7.6 × 6.9
A: 4/550-mm TT fwd (14 torpedoes, or SM 39 missiles, or mines)
Man: 8 officers, 36 chief petty officers, 22 other enlisted
M: A nuclear power system made up of an integrated reactor-exchanger able to deliver constant power of 48 MW for the necessary steam to two turbo-alternators. A single electric motor drives a single shaft, and an emergency diesel generator group can be cut into the propulsion line in case of a nuclear breakdown.

ATTACK SUBMARINES (*continued*)

REMARKS: New class of nuclear attack submarines. Fire-control, torpedo-launching, and submarine-detection systems are the same as the *Agosta* class. The *Provence* was financed under the Third Military Equipment Plan. The second through the fifth come under the Fourth Plan (1977-82). *Bretagne* was ordered under the 1977 Budget, *Bourgogne* under the 1979 Budget.

◆ 4 Agosta class

	Bldr	Laid down	L	In serv.
S 620 AGOSTA	Cherbourg	10-11-72	19-10-74	11-2-78
S 621 BÉVÉZIERS	Cherbourg	17-5-73	14-6-75	10-77
S 622 LA PRAYA	Cherbourg	1974	15-5-76	9-3-78
S 623 OUESSANT	Cherbourg	1974	23-10-76	27-7-78

Bévéziers   1977

Agosta   S. Cioglia, 1979

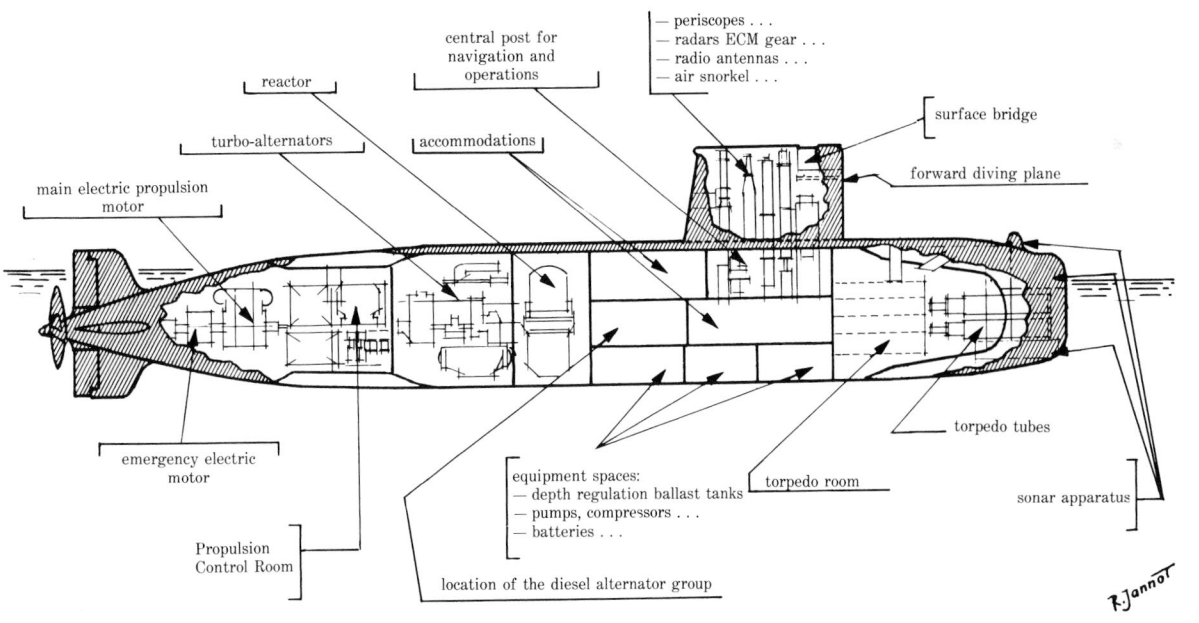

SNA 72 — Longitudinal Cutaway

ATTACK SUBMARINES (continued)

Ouessant   1978

D: 1,230 tons, 1,490 surfaced, 1,740 submerged (fl)
S: 20 kts (submerged)   **Dim:** 67.57 × 6.8 × 5.4
A: 4/550-mm TT fwd — 20 torpedoes (rapid-loading)

La Praya — sail   1978

Electron Equipt: Radar: 1/Calypso
                      Sonars: DUUA 2, DSUV, DUBM
Man: 7 officers, 46 men   **Endurance:** 45 days   **Fuel:** 200 tons
Range: 8,500/9 (snorkel), 178/3.5 (creep motor)
M: 2 SEMT-Pielstick 16 PA 4 185 diesel generator sets (850 kw each); 1 × 3,500-kw
       propulsion motor; 4,600 hp (1 × 23-hp creep motor)

REMARKS: Oceangoing submarines, authorized in the 1970-75 program. Weapons and
equipment similar to the refitted *Daphné* class. Fire control centralized in one computer bank. Air-conditioned. Retractable deck fittings on hull exterior. Advanced
techniques for quiet operations both inboard and outboard. The torpedo tubes will
accept torpedoes of either 550 mm or 533 mm in diameter. Spain has ordered four of
this class of submarine and Pakistan, two — from the embargoed South African order.

◆ **9 Daphné class**

		Budget	Bldr	Laid down	L	In serv.
S 641	DAPHNÉ	1955	Dubigeon	3-58	20-6-59	1-6-64
S 642	DIANE	1955	Dubigeon	7-58	4-10-60	20-6-64
S 643	DORIS	1955	Cherbourg	19-58	14-5-60	26-8-64
S 645	FLORE	1956	Cherbourg	19-58	21-12-60	21-5-64
S 646	GALATÉE	1956	Cherbourg	19-58	22-9-61	25-7-64
S 648	JUNON	1960	Cherbourg	7-61	11-5-64	25-2-66
S 649	VÉNUS	1960	Cherbourg	8-61	24-9-64	1-1-66
S 650	PSYCHÉ	1964	Brest	5-65	28-6-67	1-7-69
S 651	SIRÈNE	1964	Brest	5-65	28-6-67	1-3-70

D: 700 tons, 869 surfaced, 1,043 submerged (fl)   **S:** 13.5/16 kts
Dim: 57.75 × 6.76 × 4.62   **Man:** 6 officers, 39 men
A: 12/550-mm TT, 8 fwd, 4 aft   **Range:** 4,500/5 (snorkel)
Electron Equipt: Radar: 1/Calypso II
                      Sonars: DUUA 2, passive sets
M: 2 SEMT-Pielstick 450-kw diesel generator sets; 2 × 1,000 hp (1,300 for a brief
       period) electric motors; 2 props

ATTACK SUBMARINES (*continued*)

Vénus   J.-C. Bellonne, 1972

Doris   1976

Flore   J.-C. Bellonne, 1975

REMARKS: Development of the *Aréthuse* class. Very quiet when submerged. Modernized, beginning in 1971, with special attention given to detection equipment and weapons. Can submerge to more than 300 meters. No spare torpedoes are carried. This class of submarine has been purchased by the following countries: Portugal, four in 1964; Pakistan, four in 1966; South Africa, three in 1967. Spain has built four with French technical assistance. One Portuguese unit was sold to Pakistan in 1976. Sister *Sirène* lost in 1972, salvaged and scrapped. The *Flore* began a second modernization in 1978.

◆ **2 Aréthuse class**

	Budget	Bldr	Laid down	L	In serv.
S 636 ARGONAUTE	1953	Cherbourg	3-55	29-6-57	11-2-59
S 639 AMAZONE	1954	Cherbourg	End 1955	3-4-58	1-7-59

Argonaute   J.-C. Bellonne, 1977

D: 400 tons, 543 surfaced, 669 submerged (fl)
A: 4/550-mm TT fwd (8 torpedoes)
Man: 6 officers, 34 men   S: 12.5 kts (surfaced), 16 kts (submerged)
M: Diesel-electric propulsion; 12-cylinder SEMT-Pielstick motors; 1 prop; 1,060/1,300 hp

REMARKS: Ballast tanks reduced to a minimum, can submerge to more than 200 meters. Quiet, maneuverable submarines. The *Aréthuse* (S-635) and *Ariane* (S-640) were in 1979.

◆ **6 Narval class**

	Author	Bldr	Laid down	L	In serv.
S 631 NARVAL	1949	Cherbourg	6-51	11-12-54	1-12-57
S 632 MARSOUIN	1949	Cherbourg	9-51	21-5-55	1-10-57
S 633 DAUPHIN	1950	Cherbourg	5-62	17-9-55	1-8-58
S 634 REQUIN	1950	Cherbourg	6-52	3-12-55	1-8-58
S 637 ESPADON	1954	A. Normand	12-55	15-9-58	2-4-60
S 638 MORSE	1954	Seine Maritime	2-56	10-12-58	2-5-60

D: 1,320 tons, 1,635 surfaced, 1,910 submerged
S: 15 kts (surfaced), 18 (submerged)   Dim: 77.63 × 7.82 × 5.4
A: 6/550-mm TT fwd — 14 torpedoes in reserve — mines
Man: 7 officers, 57 men   Range: 15,000/8 (snorkel)   Endurance: 45 days
M: 3 SEMT-Pielstick 12 PA 4 motor generator sets; 2 electric motors; 2 props; 3,000 hp (2 × 40-hp creep motors)

REMARKS: Exceptionally strong hull, welded throughout, streamlined sail. Rebuilt from 1966 to 1970 with special attention to the machinery spaces, complete modernization of detection devices and weapons. The *Marsouin* (S-632) had a serious fire 4-8-78 but was repaired.

Marsouin   1976

GUIDED-MISSILE CRUISER

	Budget	Bldr	Laid down	L	In serv.
C 611 COLBERT	1953	Brest	12-53	24-3-56	5-5-59

D: 8,500 tons (11,300 fl)   **S:** 31.5 kts

Dim: 180.0 (175.0 pp) × 19.7 (20.2 max.) × 7.66

A: 1 Masurca system (48 missiles) — 2/100-mm DP, Model 1968 (I × 2) — 12/57-mm AA (II × 6)

Electron Equipt: Radars: 1/Decca RM 416, 1/DRBV 50, 1/DRBV 23C, 1/DRBV 20, 2/DRBR 51, 1/DRBR 32C, 1/DRBC 31, 1/DRBI 10D

SENIT 1 — 2 Syllex countermeasures systems — TACAN — URN: 22

Armor: Deck: 50, Belt: 50 to 80   **Range:** 4,000/25

Man: 25 officers, 208 petty officers, 329 men

Boilers: 4 asymmetric, multitube, 45 kg/cm², superheat 450°C

M: C.E.M. Parsons GT; 2 props; 86,000 hp   **Electric:** 4,920 kw

REMARKS: Converted into a surface-to-air guided-missile cruiser between 4-70 and 10-72. Together with the guided-missile destroyers *Duquesne* and *Suffren*, this ship, thanks to the Masurca system, provides a high degree of anti-aircraft protection to ships at sea at a medium range. The capability of the SENIT 1 tactical data system enables real-time control of the surface and air situation at the center of a widely dispersed formation to be maintained, which makes this an excellent command ship, able as well to coordinate the air defense of the formation. If necessary the ship can be used as a command post for an inter-service operation overseas. During the refit the bridge superstructure was rebuilt, the electronic equipment for command and control was modernized, the electric power increased, and living spaces were improved, including air-conditioning. Four MM 38 Exocet anti-ship missiles have not been installed as was planned; racks to support the missile containers are mounted on the deck immediately abaft the upper 100-mm gun mount. In addition to the two DRBR 51 radar directors for the 57-mm AA guns, there are also four lead-computing visual directors. Machinery and boilers are installed in two separate compartments, each with two boilers and a turbine, separated by an 18-meter-long watertight bulkhead.

Colbert   J.-C. Bellonne, 1976

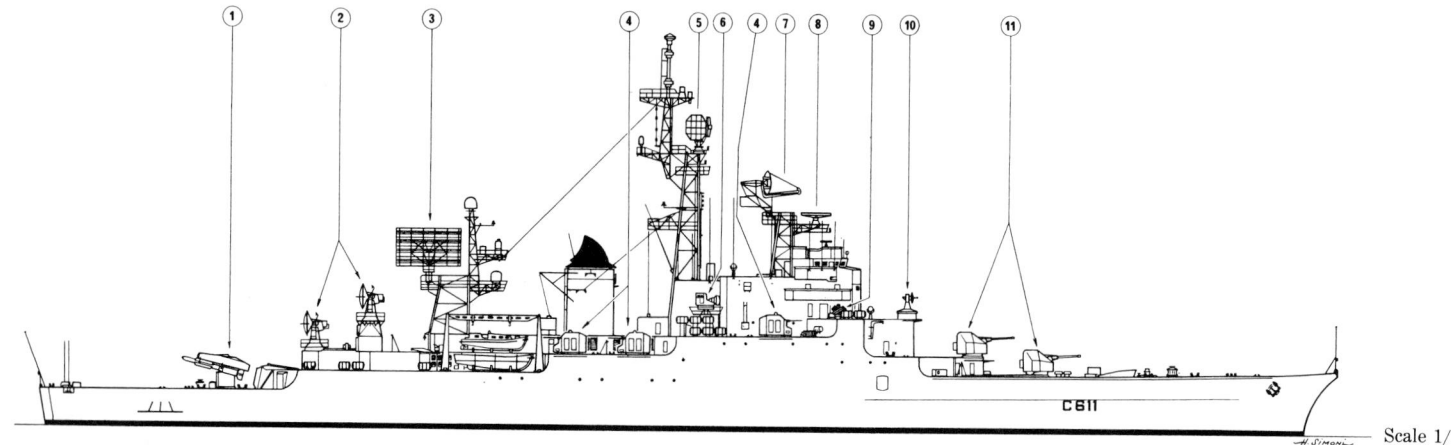

Scale 1/1000

1. Masurca launcher 2. DRBR-51 radars 3. DRBV-20 radar 4. 57-mm mounts 5. DRBI-10D radar 6. 57-mm director (DRBC-31) 7. DRBV-23C radar 8. DRBV-50 radar 9. Syllex systems 10. DRBC-32C radar 11. 100-mm mounts, Model 1968

GUIDED-MISSILE CRUISER (*continued*)

Colbert

1978

Colbert

GUIDED-MISSILE DESTROYERS

◆ **3 C-70 class, AA**

	Bldr	Laid down	L	In serv.
D...N...	...	1979	...	1986
D...N...	...	1980	...	1987
D...N...	...	1982	...	1989

D: 3,900 tons (approx.)   **S:** 30 kts   **Dim:** 139.0 × 14.0 × 5.5
Man: 200 men   **Range:** 5,000/24, 8,200/17
A: 4/MM 38 (or 8/MM 39) SSM – 1 Mk 13 launcher (40 Standard SM1-MR missiles)
  – 2/100-mm DP, Model 1968 (I × 2) – 2/20-mm AA (I × 2) – 2/fixed catapults for
  Type L-5 ASW torpedoes (10 torpedoes)
Electron Equipt: Radars: 1/DRBJ 11, 1/DRBV 26, 2/SPG 51C, 1/DRBC 32D
       Sonar: 1/DUBV 25 – SENIT-6 data system, 2 Dagaie and 2
          Sagaie countermeasures systems
Electric: 3,400 kw   **Fuel:** 600 tons
M: 4 SEMT-Pielstick 18 PA 6 BTC diesels; 2 props; 42,300 hp (31,760 kw)

REMARKS: 1977-82 program; the first was authorized under the 1978 budget, the second
  under the 1979 budget. The launchers for MM-38 Exocet (or MM-39), two or four per
  beam, are to be mounted perpendicular to the ship's centerline in a form of "duck
  blind" superstructure box (*see* drawing). There will be a helicopter platform but no
  facilities for permanent embarkation.

The problem of equipment-positioning caused by the amount of space taken up by
the fresh-air intakes and gas exhausts of a CODOG system, such as that installed in
the *George Leygues*, has been overcome in these ships by the adoption of diesels which,
because of double supercharging, have a high power-to-weight ratio.

◆ **6 Georges Leygues C-70 class, ASW**

	Bldr	Laid down	L	Trials	In serv.
D 640 GEORGES LEYGUES	Brest	6-74	6-9-75	1977	10-79
D 641 DUPLEIX	Brest	9-75	2-12-78	end-79	3-81
D 642 MONTCALM	Brest	9-75	...	early-81	7-82
D 643 JEAN DE VIENNE	Brest	9-79	26-10-79	...	...
D...N...	Brest	...	...	...	...
D...N...	Brest	...	...	...	...

D: 3,830 tons (4,170 fl)
Dim: 139.0 (129.0 pp) × 14.0 × 5.5 (hull) 5.73 (props)
S: 30 kts (GT), 21 kts (diesels)   **Range:** 1,000/30, 9,500/17 diesels
Man: Peacetime: 15 officers, 90 petty officers, 111 men (accommodations for 250
  total)
A: 4/MM 38 Exocet – 1/100-mm DP, Model 1968, with Vega fire-control system –
  – 1/Crotale BPDMS – 2/20-mm AA (I × 2) – 2 catapults for L-5 ASW torpedoes
  (10 torpedoes) – 2 WG 13 Lynx helicopters with sonar and torpedoes; by replac-

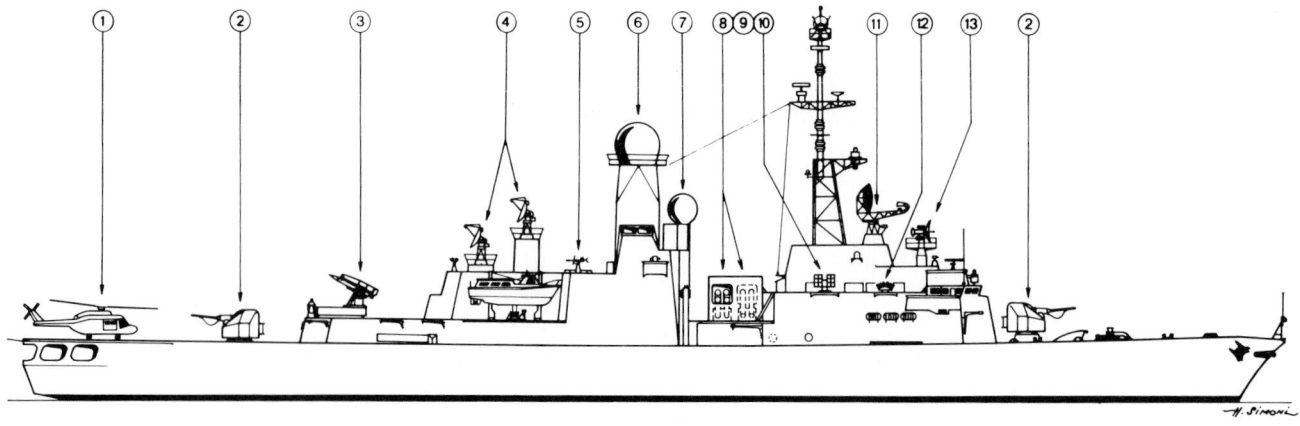

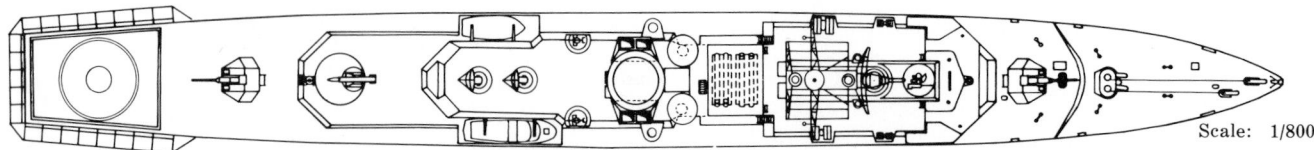

Scale: 1/800

1. WG-13 Lynx helicopter 2. 100-mm gun mounts 3. MK-12 launcher for Standard missile 4. SPG-51C missile-control radars 5. 20-mm AA
6. DRBJ-11 radar 7. Satellite communications antenna radomes 8. and 9. MM-38 or MM-39 missile installations 10. Sagaie decoy
rocket-launching system 11. DRBV-26 radar 12. Dagaie decoy rocket-launching system 13. DRBC-32D gunfire-control radar

GUIDED-MISSILE DESTROYERS (*continued*)

ing these with 4/AS-12 missiles, the helicopters can be used in an anti-surface role

Electron Equipt: Radars: 1/DRBV 26, 1/DRBV 51C, 1/DRBC 32D, 2/Decca 1226
Sonars: 1/DUBV 23, 1/DUBV 43 — SENIT 4, 2 Syllex systems

Electric: 3,400 kw (4 × 850-kw diesel alternator sets)

Fuel: 600 tons distillate

M: CODOG propulsion, 2 Rolls-Royce Olympus TM3B gas turbines; 2 SEMT-Pielstick 16 PA 6 CV 280 diesels; 2 controllable-pitch props; 52,000 hp (gas turbine), 10,400 hp (diesel)

REMARKS: Three are under the 1970-75 plan and three under the 1977-82 plan. The principal mission of these ships is antisubmarine warfare, their secondary mission being anti-ship warfare. Main propulsion and auxiliary equipment is divided among four compartments from forward to aft as follows: a forward auxiliary room, the turbine room, the diesel room with the reduction gears, and an after auxiliary room. On diesel power and with the DUBV-43 sonar in the water, maximum speed is 19 knots. Centralized control of the propulsion machinery from the bridge greatly reduces the engineering staff required (3 officers, 23 petty officers, 24 men).

As in the *De Grasse*, much attention has been given to habitability, which measures have caused the addition of 5 meters of length and 150 tons of weight to the original plans. The ships of the *Georges Leygues* class have Denny Brown automatic stabilizers.

Georges Leygues   DCAN, Brest, 1978

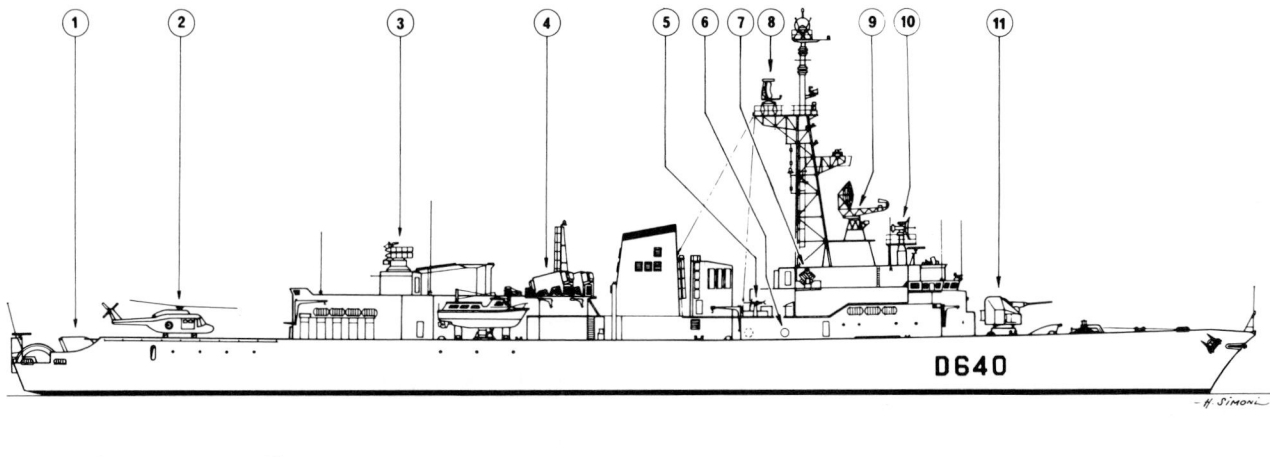

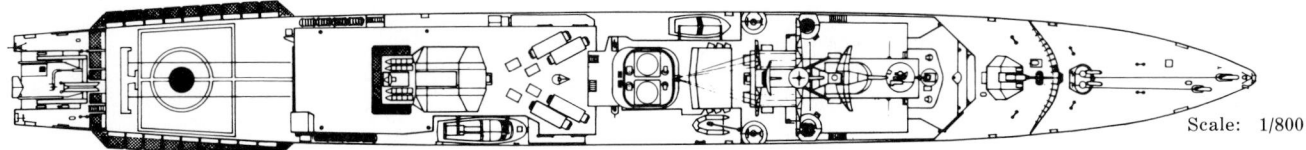

Scale: 1/800

1. DUBV-43 sonar 2. WG-13 Lynx helicopter 3. Crotale launcher 4. Exocet launchers 5. 20-mm AA 6. ASW torpedo catapults 7. Syllex system 8. DRBV-51C radar 9. DRBV-26 radar 10. DRBC-32D radar 11. 100-mm gun mount, Model 1968

GUIDED-MILLILE DESTROYERS (*continued*)

Georges Leygues   DCAN, Brest, 1978

Georges Leygues   DCAN, Brest, 1978

◆ 3 Tourville class, Type F-67, ex-C-67A

	Budget	Bldr	Laid down	L	In serv.
D 610 TOURVILLE	1967	Lorient	3-70	13-5-72	21-6-74
D 611 DUGUAY TROUIN	1967	Lorient	1-71	1-6-73	17-9-75
D 612 DE GRASSE	1970	Lorient	1972	30-11-74	1-10-77

De Grasse   1979

De Grasse — with WG-13 Lynx   1979

GUIDED-MISSILE DESTROYERS (*continued*)

1. DUBV-43 sonar 2. WG-13 Lynx helicopter 3. Crotale launcher 4. Torpedo catapults 5. Syllex system 6. DRBV-51B radar 7. DRBV-26 radar 8. Malafon launcher 9. Exocet launchers 10. Decca-1226 navigation radar 11. DRBC-32D radar 12. 100-mm gun mounts, Model 1968

Scale: 1/800

De Grasse

1979

GUIDED-MISSILE DESTROYERS (continued)

Tourville   1979

D: 4,800 tons (5,800 fl)   **Dim:** 152.75 (142.0 pp) × 15.3 × 5.7 (hull) 6.48 (props)
S: 32 kts   **Man:** 17 officers, 122 petty officers, 143 men
A: 6/MM 38 Exocet−1 Crotale BPDMS−2/100-mm DP, Model 1968 (I × 2)−2/20-mm AA (I × 2)−1 Malafon missile launcher (13 missiles)−2 catapults for L-5 antisubmarine torpedoes (10 torpedoes)−2 WG 13 Lynx helicopters
Electron Equipt: Radars: 1/DRBV 26, 1/DRBV 51B, 1/DRBC 32D, 2/Decca 1226
                  Sonars: 1/DUBV 23, 1/DUBV 43−SENIT 3, 2 Syllex systems
Range: D-610, burning fuel oil: 1,900/30, 3,600/24, 4,550/20, 5,000/18
        D-611 and D-612, burning distillate fuel: 1,900/30, 4,500/18
Boilers: 4 asymmetric, multitube, automatic-control, 45 kg/cm² pressure−superheat 450°C

Electric: 4,440 kw (2 × 1,500-kw turbogenerators, 3 × 480-kw diesel alternators)
M: 2 Rateau double-reduction GT; 2 props; 54,400 hp

REMARKS: Built under the 1965-70 plan, these ships were designed for antisubmarine warfare and can operate in a high-air-threat environment. The *Duguay-Trouin* was equipped with the Crotale antiaircraft missile system during 1979; the *Tourville* will receive it in 1980 and the *De Grasse* in 1981. In preparation for Crotale, the third 100-mm gun mount atop the helicopter hangar on the *Tourville* and the *Duguay-Trouin* was removed; it was never carried by the *De Grasse*. During her Crotale installation refit, the *Tourville* will have her boilers converted to burn distillate fuel, which has been burned by the *De Grasse* from the outset. Denny Brown automatic stabilizers are fitted. These ships, particularly the *De Grasse*, have a very high standard of habitability and seakeeping qualities on a par with those of the *Suffren* class.

◆ 2 Suffren class

	Bldr	Budget	Laid down	L	Trials	In serv.
D 602 SUFFREN	Lorient	1960	12-62	15-5-65	12-65	7-67
D 603 DUQUESNE	Brest	1960	11-64	11-2-66	7-68	4-70

D: 5,090 tons (6,090 fl)   **Dim:** 157.6 (148.0 pp) × 15.54 × 7.25 (max.)
S: 34 kts   **Range:** 2,000/30, 2,400/29, 5,100/18
Man: 23 officers, 164 petty officers, 168 men
A: 1/Masurca system (II × 1)−4/MM 38 Exocet−2/100-mm, Model 1953 (I × 2)−4/20-mm AA (I × 4)−1/Malafon system (13 missiles)−2 catapults for L-5 torpedoes (10 torpedoes)
Electron Equipt: Radars: 1/DRBI 23, 1/DRBV 50, 2/DRBR 51, 1/DRBC 32A, 1/DRBN 32
                  Sonars: 1/DUBV 23, 1/DUBV 43−SENIT 1, 2 Syllex systems

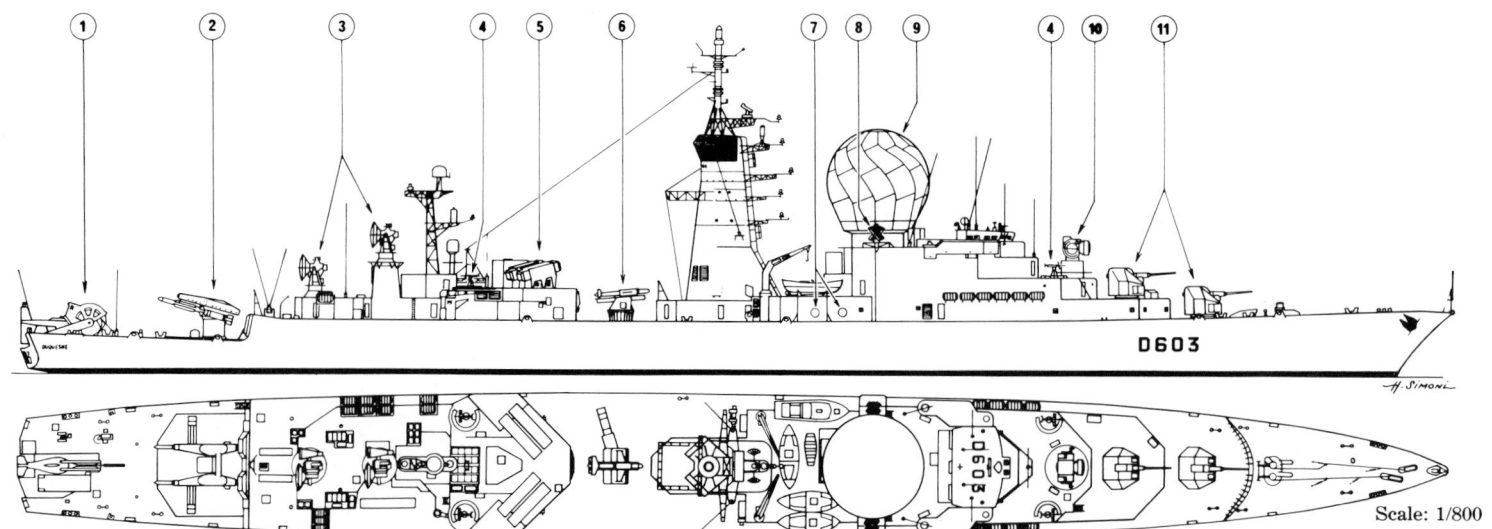

Scale: 1/800

1. DUBV-43 sonar   2. Masurca launcher   3. DRBR-51 radars   4. 20-mm AA gun mounts   5. Exocet launchers   6. Malafon launcher   7. Catapults for L-5 torpedoes 8. Syllex system   9. DRBI-23 radar   10. 100-mm gun director with DRBC-32A radar 11. 100-mm gun mounts, Model 1953

GUIDED-MISSILE DESTROYERS (*continued*)

Boilers: 4 multitube, automatic-control, 45 kg/cm² pressure—superheat 450°C
Electric: 3,440 kw (2 × 1,000-kw turbogenerators, 3 × 480-kw diesel alternators)
M: 2 Rateau double-reduction GT; 2 props; 72,500 hp

REMARKS: Built under the 1960-65 plan, these ships are extremely seaworthy; they roll and pitch only slightly and vibrate very little. Three pairs of nonretractable, anti-rolling stabilizers are energized by two central gyroscopes, only one of which is normally in use. Living and operating spaces are air-conditioned. The *Suffren* will receive MM 38 Exocet missile launchers during her 1980 refit. She used to carry 2/30-mm AA (I × 2) on her after superstructure and no 20-mm AA.

Suffren—before installation of Exocet

1976

Duquesne

1977

GUIDED-MISSILE DESTROYERS (*continued*)

◆ **1 C-65 class**

	Bldr	Laid down	L	In serv.
D 609 ACONIT	Lorient	1967	7-3-70	30-3-73

D: 3,500 tons (3,840 fl)   **S:** 27 kts   **Dim:** 127.0 × 13.4 × 4.05, 5.8 (props)
Man: 15 officers, 103 petty officers, 114 men
Range: 1,600/27, 5,000/18   **Electric:** 2,960 kw
A: 2/100-mm DP, Model 1968 (I × 2) — 1/Malafon system (13 missiles) — 1/305-mm
ASW mortar — 2 catapults for L-5 ASW torpedoes (10 torpedoes)

Electron Equipt: Radars: 1/DRBV 13, 1/DRBN 32, 1/DRBV 22A, 1/DRBC 32B
                      Sonars: 1/DUBV 23, 1/DUBV 43 — SENIT 3, 2 Syllex systems
Boilers: 2 asymmetric, multitube, automatic-control, 45 kg/cm² pressure — super-
              heat 450°C
M: Rateau double-reduction GT; 1 prop; 28,650 hp (31,500 hp for short periods)

REMARKS: Built under the 1965-70 plan, the *Aconit* is the predecessor of the Type-F-67
destroyer but does not carry a helicopter. One computer controls the SENIT functions and the weapons. Propulsion machinery is very compact. Ship is equipped with
fin stabilizers. A major refit is scheduled for 1983.

Aconit   C. Martinelli, 1974

Aconit   C. Martinelli, 1974

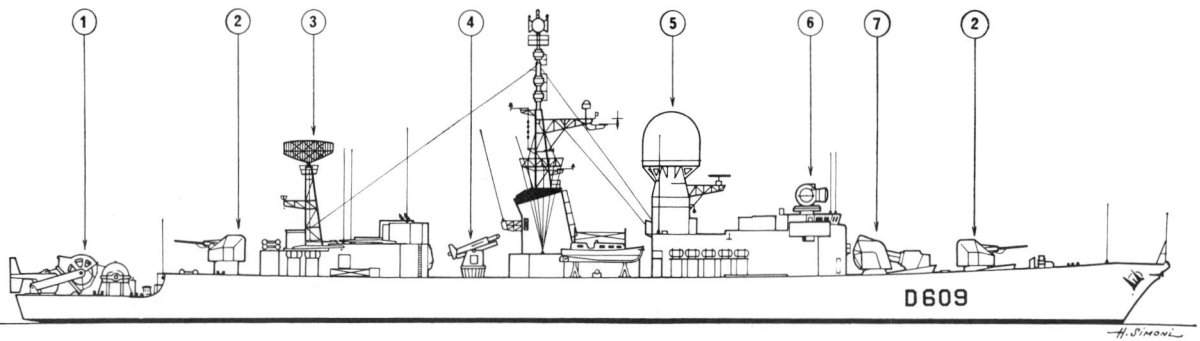

1. DUBV-43 sonar 2. 100-mm gun mounts, Model 1968 3. DRBV-22A radar 4. Malafon launcher 5. DRBV-13 radar 6. 100-mm gun director with DRBC-32B radar
7. 305-mm mortar

GUIDED-MISSILE DESTROYERS (*continued*)

◆ 1 T-56 class

	Bldr	Laid down	L	In serv.
D 638 LA GALISSONNIÈRE	Lorient	11-58	12-3-60	7-62

La Galissonière — with hangar closed   J.-C. Bellonne, 1977

D: 2,750 tons (3,740 fl) **S:** 34 kts (32 fl)
Dim: 132.8 × 12.7 × 5.4 (fwd) 5.9 (props) **Range:** 1,500/30, 5,000/18
A: 2/100-mm DP, Model 1954 (I × 2) – 1/Malafon ASW missile system (13 missiles) –
 6/550-mm TT (III × 2) for K-2 and L-3 torpedoes – 1/Alouette III ASW helicopter
 (the hangar's overhead folds down to become the landing platform)
Electron Equipt: Radars: 1/DRBV 22A, 1/DRBV 50, 1/DRBN 32, 1/DRBC 32A
       Sonars: 1/DUBV 23, 1/DUBV 43 – TACAN:URN 22
Man: Peacetime: 15 officers, 92 petty officers, 165 men
Boilers: 4 ACB-Indret, 35 kg/cm² pressure – superheat 385°C
M: 2 sets Rateau GT; 2 props; 63,000 hp **Fuel:** 800 tons oil

REMARKS: Formerly an experimental vessel for ASW sonar with two bow-mounted
sonars. A quadruple 305-mm ASW mortar and six torpedo tubes (III × 2) have been
removed.

La Galissonnière — with hangar open

◆ 1 modified T-53 class, ASW

	Bldr	Laid down	L	In serv.
D 633 DUPERRÉ	Lorient	11-54	23-6-56	8-10-57

Duperré — with Alouette-III   G. Arra, 1977

D: 2,750 tons (3,740 fl) **S:** 34 kts (32 fl)
Dim: 132.8 × 12.7 × 5.9 (props) **Range:** 1,500/30, 5,000/18
Man: Peacetime: 15 officers, 102 petty officers, 142 men
A: 4/MM 38 Exocet – 1/100-mm DP, Model 1968 – 2 catapults for L-5 torpedoes
 (8 torpedoes) – 1 WG 13 Lynx helicopter
Electron Equipt: Radars: 1/DRBV 22A, 1/DRBV 51, 1/DRBC 32C, 1/DRBC 31,
       2/Decca
       Sonars: 1/DUBV 23, 1/DUBV 43 – SENIT 2, 2 Syllex systems
Boilers: 4 ACB-Indret, 35 kg/cm² pressure – superheat 385°C
M: 2 sets Rateau GT; 2 props; 63,000 hp **Electric:** 1,640 kw

REMARKS: From 1967 to 1971, the *Duperré* was unarmed and was used for towed-sonar
research, using the huge array now mounted in the auxiliary *Aunis*. Reconverted at
Brest from 1972 to 21-5-74, as the final step in the long evolution of the T-47, *Surcouf*-
class destroyer design. The hangar is fixed and has maintenance facilities and the
flight deck has a helicopter-recovery system similar to that on the *Tourville* and
Georges Leygues classes. Although the *Duperré* is credited with a DRBC-32C radar
fire-control director for the 100-mm gun, it had not been installed in 1977. The ship
ran aground in 1978 and was badly damaged, but was repaired using components
cannibalized from the inactivated *La Bourdonnais*.

◆ 5 D'Estrées class, converted Type T-47, ASW

	Bldr	Laid down	L	In serv.
D 627 MAILLE BRÉZÉ	Lorient	10-53	26-9-54	4-5-57
D 628 VAUQUELIN	Lorient	3-54	26-9-54	3-11-56
D 629 D'ESTRÉES	Brest	5-53	27-11-54	19-3-57
D 631 CASABIANCA	F.C. de la Gironde	10-53	13-11-54	4-5-57
D 632 GUÉPRATTE	A.C. de Bretagne	8-53	8-11-54	6-6-57

GUIDED-MISSILE DESTROYERS (*continued*)

Guépratte   J.-C. Bellonne, 1976

Maille Brézé   J.-C. Bellonne, 1975

D: 2,750 tons (3,740 fl)   **S:** 32 kts   **Dim:** 132.5 × 12.72 × 5.9 (props)
Man: Peacetime: 15 officers, 103 petty officers, 151 men
Range: 1,500/30, 5,000/18   **Electric:** 1,440 kw   **Fuel:** 800 tons
A: 2/100-mm DP, Model 1953 (I × 2) − 2/20-mm AA (I × 2) − 1/Malafon ASW missile
system (13 missiles) − 1/375-mm Bofors ASW rocket launcher − 6 TT (III × 2)
for K-2 or L-3 ASW torpedoes
Electron Equipt: Radars: 1/DRBV 22A, 1/DRBV 50, 1/DRBN 32, 2/DRBC 32A,
2/SPG 51 C
Sonars: 1/DUBV 23, 1/DUBV 43 − TACAN: URN 22
Boilers: 4 ACB-Indret, 35 kg/cm² pressure − superheat 385°C
M: 2 sets Rateau GT; 2 props; 63,000 hp

REMARKS: ASW conversions completed between 1-68 and 1-71: weapon system renewed,
living spaces air-conditioned, electrical system and safety installations completely
redesigned. These ships do not have the SENIT system. The D'Estrées has carried the
British SCOT satellite-communications system as an experiment. A new, smaller
TACAN is fitted in the D-628, D-629, and D-632.

D'Estrées   H. Kowark, 1976

Casabianca   H. Kowark, 1978

Vauquelin   1979

GUIDED-MISSILE DESTROYERS (*continued*)

◆ **4 Kersaint class, converted Type T-47, with Standard**

	Bldr	Laid down	L	In serv.
D 622 KERSAINT	Lorient	6-51	3-10-53	20-3-56
D 624 BOUVET	Lorient	11-51	3-10-53	13-5-56
D 625 DUPETIT THOUARS	Brest	3-51	4-3-54	15-9-56
D 630 DU CHAYLA	Brest	7-53	27-11-54	4-6-57

D: 2,750 tons (3,850 fl) **Dim:** 128.5 × 12.96 × 6.3 (fwd) 5.0 (aft)

S: 32 kts (at 3,800 tons) **Range:** 1,200/32, 3,500/20, 4,100/14

A: 1/Mk 13 Standard launcher (40 missiles)—6/57-mm AA (II × 3)—1/375-mm ASW rocket launcher (VI × 1) Model 1954—6/550-mm TT (III × 2) for K-2 or L-3 ASW torpedoes

Electron Equipt: Radars: 1/DRBV 20 (DRBV 22 on D-625 and D-630), 1/SPS 39 A or B, 1/DRBV 31, 2/SPG 51B, 1/DRBC 31
  Sonars: 1/DUBA 1, 1/DUBV 24—SENIT 2, TACAN: URN 22

Man: Peacetime: 15 officers, 87 petty officers, 173 men

Boilers: 4 ACB-Indret, 35 kg/cm² pressure—superheat 385°C

Electric: 1,600 kw

M: 2 sets Rateau GT; 2 props; 63,000 hp

REMARKS: Converted to carry U.S. Tartar missile system, 1961-65. Obsolescent DRBV 20 air-search radar being replaced by later DRBV 22.

Bouvet   J.-C. Bellonne, 1977

Dupetit Thouars—before substitution of DRBV-22   1976

Du Chayla—before substitution of DRBV-22   1979

Kersaint   G. Arra, 1972

DESTROYERS

◆ **1 La Bourdonnais-class, Type T-53 training ship**

	Bldr	Laid down	L	In serv.
D 635 FORBIN	Brest	8-54	15-10-55	1-2-58

D: 2,750 tons (3,740 fl) **S:** 34 kts (32 fl) **Dim:** 128.6 × 12.7 × 5.4 (fwd)

Man: ... **Range:** 1,500/30, 5,000/18 **Fuel:** 800 tons

DESTROYERS (continued)

Forbin

A: 4/127-mm DP (II × 2) − 4/57-mm AA (II × 2) − 6/550-mm TT for ASW K-2 and L-3 torpedoes (III × 2) − 1/375-mm ASW rocket launcher, Model 1954 (VI × 1)
Electron Equipt: Radars: 1/DRBV 22A, 1/DRBI 10A, 1/DRBV 31
Sonars: 1/DUBA, 1/DUBV 24
Boilers: 4 ACB-Indret, 35 kg/cm² pressure − superheat 385°C
Electric: 1,160 kw
M: 2 sets Rateau GT; 2 props; 63,000 hp

REMARKS: Originally fitted for aircraft direction and detection. Attached as school ship in 1973, forward 57-mm and aftermost 127-mm mounts removed and helicopter platform substituted. The *Forbin* has the last 127-mm guns in the French Navy. Serves with the *Jeanne d'Arc* as a training ship for the École d'Application des Enseignes de Vaisseau. Sisters *La Bourdonnais* (D-634), *Jauréguiberry* (D-637), and *Tartu* (D-636) stricken in 1976, 1977, and 1979, respectively.

FRIGATES

◆ 1 Balny class

	Budget	Bldr	Laid down	L	In serv.
F 729 BALNY	1956	Lorient	3-60	17-3-62	2-70

Balny — now with 30-mm AA   1975

D: 1,750 tons (2,230 fl)   **S:** 26 kts
Dim: 102.7 (98.0 pp) × 11.8 × 5.0 (prop)
Man: 9 officers, 67 petty officers, 93 men   **Range:** 13,000/10
A: 2/100-mm DP, Model 1953 (I × 2) − 2/30-mm AA (I × 2) − 6/TT for L-3 ASW torpedoes (III × 2)
Electron Equipt: Radars: 1/DRBV 22, 1/Decca 1226, 1/DRBC 32C
Sonars: 1/DUBA 3, 1/SQS 17
M: CODAG: 1 Turbomeca M 38 gas turbine (11,500 hp), 2 AGO V-16 diesels (3,600 hp each); 1 controllable-pitch prop; 18,700 hp
Electric: 1,280 kw

REMARKS: In 1964 the *Balny* was allocated for trials with the French Navy's first combined gas-turbine *and* diesel plant (CODAG). The gas turbine is a naval version of the Atar-8 turbojet used in the Étendard fighter, reduced in rate from 15,000 shp to 11,500 hp. Both diesels and the gas turbine can be clutched together to drive the single propeller, which is 3.6 meters in diameter and extends 1 meter beneath the keel. The compactness of the *Balny's* propulsion plant compared with that of the all-diesel plants in her half sisters of the *Commandant Rivière* class permits her to carry approximately 100 more tons of fuel, which accounts for her great endurance on diesels alone. Because one of her 100-mm guns is mounted atop her lengthened after superstructure, it has not been possible to install Exocet anti-ship missiles.

◆ 8 Commandant Rivière class

	Budget	Laid down	L	In serv.
F 733 COMMANDANT RIVIÈRE	1955	4-57	11-10-58	12-62
F 725 VICTOR SCHOELCHER	1956	10-57	11-10-58	10-62
F 726 COMMANDANT BORY	1956	3-58	11-10-58	3-64
F 727 AMIRAL CHARNER	1956	11-58	12-3-60	12-62
F 728 DOUDART DE LAGRÉE	1956	3-60	15-4-61	3-63
F 740 COMMANDANT BOURDAIS	1956	4-59	15-4-61	3-63
F 748 PROTET	1957	9-61	7-12-62	5-64
F 749 ENSEIGNE DE VAISSEAU HENRY	1957	1962	14-12-63	1-65

Bldr: Lorient

Commandant Rivière   1978

FRIGATES (*continued*)

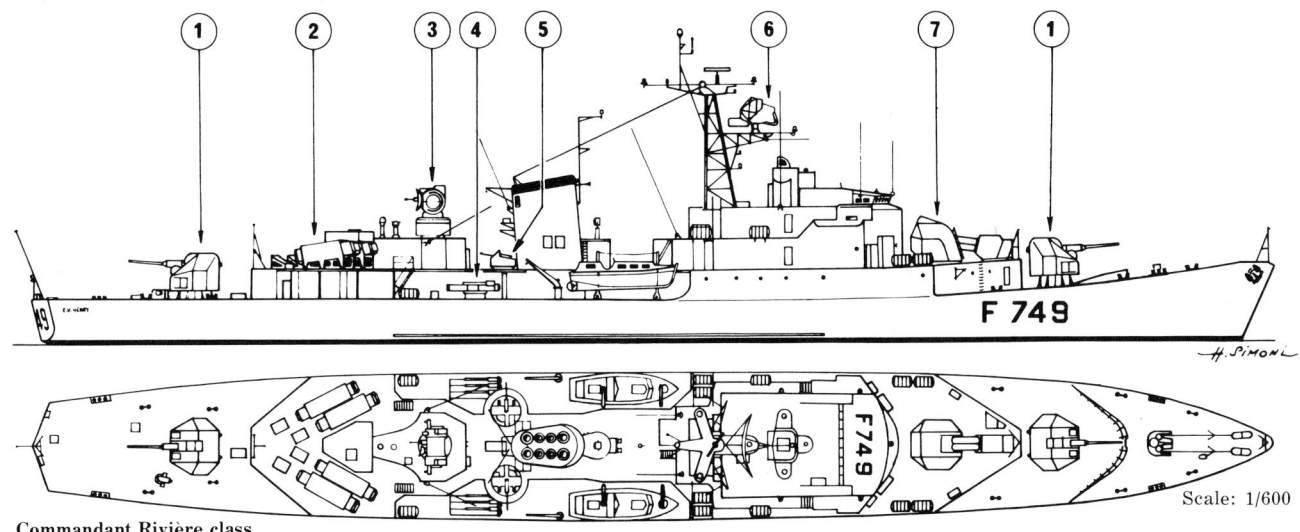

Commandant Rivière class

Scale: 1/600

1. 100-mm DP gun mounts, Model 1953   2. Exocet launchers   3. Gun-director radar
4. ASW torpedo tubes   5. 30-mm or 40-mm AA gun mounts   6. DRBV-22 radar
7. 305-mm quadruple mortar

D: 1,750 tons (2,070 normal, 2,230 fl)   **S:** 26 kts (26.6 on trials)
Dim: 102.7 (98.0 pp) × 11.8 × 4.35 (max.)
Man: 9 officers, 66 petty officers, 91 men   **Fuel:** 210 tons
A: 4/MM 38 Exocet−2/100-mm DP, Model 1963 (I × 2)−2/30- or 40-mm AA−1/305-
     mm mortar (IV × 1)−6 TT for K-2 and L-3 ASW torpedoes (III × 2)
Electron Equipt: Radars: 1/DRBV 22, 1/Decca 1226, 1/DRBC 32C
                 Sonars: 1/DUBA 3, 1/SQS 17
Range: 2,300/26, 7,500/16.5   **Electric:** 1,280 kw
M: 4 SEMT-Pielstick PC diesels, V-12 cylinders; 2 props; 16,000 hp

Victor Schoelcher   J.-C. Bellonne, 1976

Commandant Bourdais   C. Martinelli, 1977

FRIGATES (continued)

Enseigne de Vaisseau Henry   G. Arra, 1977

REMARKS: Designed for escort duty in various climates; air-conditioned; storage space for 45 days' fresh food. Can embark a flag officer and staff or an 80-man commando unit. These maneuverable ships are very successful. The *Commandant Bory* originally had free-piston generators driving turbines, but these were replaced with a standard diesel plant in 1974-75. Four Exocet missiles replaced a 100-mm gun atop the after superstructure, beginning in the mid-1970s. Few, if any, have the 30-mm AA gun.

◆ **3 L'Alsacien class, Type E-52B**

	Bldr	Laid down	L	In serv.
F 776 L'ALSACIEN	Lorient	7-56	26-1-57	27-8-60
F 777 LE PROVENÇAL	Lorient	2-57	5-10-57	6-11-59
F 778 LE VENDÉEN	F.C. de la Mediterranée	3-57	27-7-57	1-10-60

Le Vendéen   C. Martinelli, 1977

Le Provençal   J.-C. Bellonne, 1976

D: 1,250 tons (1,528 trials, 1,700 fl)   **S:** 27 kts
Dim: 99.8 (95.0 pp) × 10.3 × 4.1 (hull)   **Range:** 4,500/15
A: 4/57-mm AA (II × 2) — 2/20-mm AA (I × 2) — 12/TT (III × 4) for K-2 and L-3 ASW torpedoes — 1/305-mm mortar (IV × 1)
Electron Equipt: Radars: 1/DRBV 22A, 1/DRBV 31, 1/DRBC 32
                 Sonars: 1/DUBV 24, 1/DUBV 1
Man: 10 officers, 51 petty officers, 110 men   **Electric:** 790 kw
Boilers: 2 ACB-Indret, 35 kg/cm² pressure — superheat 385°C
M: 2 sets Parsons or Rateau GT; 2 props; 20,000 hp

◆ **2 Le Normand class, Type E-52A**

	Bldr	Laid down	L	In serv.
F 765 LE NORMAND	F.C. de la Mediterranée	7-53	13-2-54	3-11-56
F 771 LE SAVOYARD	F.C. de la Mediterranée	11-53	7-5-55	14-6-56

Le Savoyard   J.-C. Bellonne, 1974

FRIGATES (continued)

D: 1,250 tons (1,528 trials, 1,700 fl)   **S:** 27 kts (29 kts on trials)
Dim: 99.8 (95.0 pp) × 10.3 × 5.8 (max.)   **Range:** 4,500/15
A: 6/57-mm AA (II × 3)—F-771: 4/57-mm AA—2/20-mm AA—12/TT (III × 4) for K-2
and L-3 ASW torpedoes—1/375-mm rocket launcher, Model 1954 (VI × 1)
Electron Equipt: Radars: 1/DRBV 22A, 1/DRBV 31, 1/DRBC 31 or 32
Sonars: 1/DUBV 24, 1/DUBA 1
Man: 9 officers, 52 petty officers, 109 men   **Electric:** 720 kw
Boilers: 2 ACB-Indret, 35 kg/cm² pressure—superheat 385°C
M: 2 sets Parsons or Rateau GT; 2 props; 20,000 hp

REMARKS: *Le Lorain* (F-768) and *Le Champenois* (F-770) were stricken in 1975, *Le Gascon* (F-767) in 1976, *Le Picard* (F-766), *L'Agenais* (F-774), and *Le Basque* (F-733) in 1979; *Le Béarnais* (F-775) was to be stricken during the first quarter of 1980. *Le Savoyard* operates with Group M (the Atlantic Missile Range) as a missile-tracking ship and has a tracking radar in place of the fantail 57-mm gun mount.

CORVETTES

◆ **15 D'Estienne D'Orves class, Type A-69**

	Laid down	L	In serv.
F 781 D'ESTIENNE D'ORVES	8-72	1-6-73	10-9-76
F 782 AMYOT D'INVILLE	9-73	30-11-74	30-7-76
F 783 DROGOU	10-73	30-11-74	30-9-76
F 784 DÉTROYAT	12-74	31-1-76	24-3-77
F 785 JEAN MOULIN	12-74	31-1-76	29-5-77
F 786 QUARTIER-MAÎTRE ANQUETIL	8-75	7-8-76	2-1-78
F 787 COMMANDANT DE PIMODAN	9-75	7-8-76	20-5-78
F 788 SECOND MAÎTRE LE BIHAN	11-76	13-8-77	6-79
F 789 LIEUTENANT DE VAISSEAU LE HENAFF	3-77	18-9-78	12-79
F 790 LIEUTENANT DE VAISSEAU LAVALLÉE	10-77	. . .	10-80
F 791 COMMANDANT L'HERMINIER	12-77	. . .	8-81
F 792 PREMIER MAÎTRE L'HER	7-78	. . .	1-82
F 793 COMMANDANT BLAISON	9-78	. . .	6-82
F 794 ENSEIGNE DE VAISSEAU JACOUBET	4-79	. . .	10-82
F . . . N . . .	. . .	. . .	. . .

Bldr: Lorient

D: 1,100 tons (1,250 fl)   **S:** 24 kts   **Dim:** 80.0 (76.0 pp) × 10.3 × 3.0
Man: 7 officers, 42 petty officers, 56 men   **Endurance:** 15 days
A: 2/MM 38 Exocet on 5 units—1/100-mm DP, Model 1968—2/20-mm AA (I × 2)—
1/375-mm ASW rocket launcher (VI × 1)—4/TT for L-3 and L-5 ASW torpedoes
Electron Equipt: Radars: 1/DRBV 51, 1/DRBC 32E, 1/DRBN 32 (Decca 1226)
Sonar: 1/DUBA 25—2 Dagaie countermeasures systems
Range: 4,500/15   **Electric:** 840 kw
M: 2 SEMT-Pielstick 12 PC 2 diesels; 2 controllable-pitch props; 11,000 hp

REMARKS: Very economical and seaworthy ships designed for coastal antisubmarine warfare but available for scouting missions, instruction, and showing the flag. Can carry a troop detachment of one officer and seventeen men. The control system for

Drogou   M. Bar, 1978

Amyot d'Inville   J.-C. Bellonne, 1976

the 100-mm gun consists of a DRBC-32E monopulse, X band radar and a semi-analog, semi-digital computer; it also has an optical sight. Only ships destined for the Mediterranean Squadron will carry 2 MM 38 missiles, but foundations for their containers will be installed on all units. All have a stabilization system. The fifteenth ship was ordered in 1979. Stacks and masts have been modified from the *Jean Moulin* (F-785) onward. The heightened stack is being backfitted in earlier units. Plans to add a helicopter facility to the *Commandant Blaison* (F-793) and *Enseigne de Vaisseau Jacoubet* (F-794) have evidently been abandoned. The *Commandant L'Herminier* (F-791) is to receive 2 SEMT-Pielstick 12 PA 6 BTC diesels totaling 14,400 hp; later units may get the same plant. As many as seven more may be ordered. The original *Lieutenant de Vaisseau Le Henaff* and *Commandant L'Herminier* were completed to a slightly modified design for South Africa and then sold to Argentina, which has ordered an additional unit.

CORVETTES (*continued*)

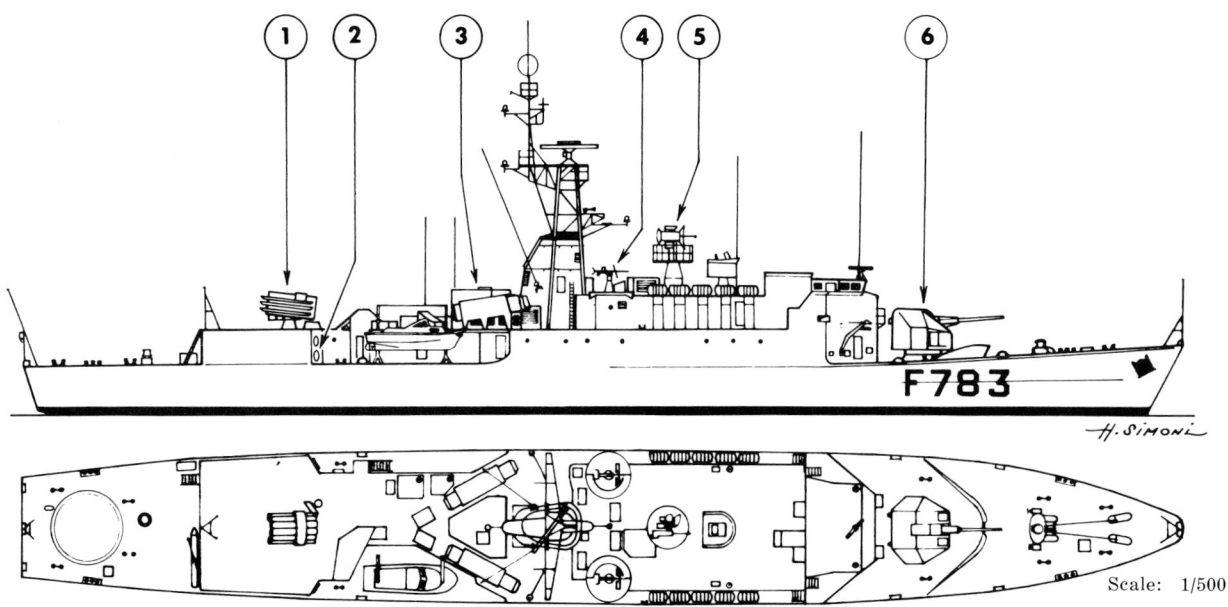

1. Sextuple Bofors ASW rocket-launcher, Model 1954   2. ASW torpedo tubes   3. Exocet launchers   4. 20-mm AA gun mounts   5. DRBC-32E fire-control radar   6. 100-mm DP gun mount, Model 1968

Commandant de Pimodan   DCAN, Lorient, 1978

D'Estienne d'Orves   M. Bar, 1977

CORVETTES (continued)

Quartier-maître Anquetil 1978

Jean Moulin 1977

SUBMARINE CHASER

◆ 1 Le Fougueux class

	Bldr	L
P 640 LE FRINGANT	F.C. Méditerranée	6-2-59

L'Ardent – now stricken. **Le Fringant** has a deckhouse aft 1975

D: 325 tons (400 fl)   **S:** 18.7 kts (22 kts on trials)
Dim: 53.03 × 7.26 × 3.1 (fl)
Man: 4 officers, 9 petty officers, 33 men   **Range:** 2,000/15, 3,000/12
A: 1/40-mm AA – 1/20-mm mortar fwd – 2 depth-charge projectors – 2 depth-charge racks
Electron Equipt: Radar: Decca . . . – Sonar: QCU 2
M: 4 SEMT-Pielstick diesels; 2 props; 3,240 hp

REMARKS: *Le Fringant* is employed on fisheries-protection duties and has a large deckhouse over the former after 40-mm AA position. She will probably be replaced by the *Mercure* (ex-M-765) during 1980. Sisters *L'Ardent* (P-635), *L'Adroit* (P-644), and *L'Alerte* (P-645) were stricken in 1979. Survivor of a class of fourteen in the French Navy; others were built for foreign navies.

PATROL BOATS

◆ 6 boats

	Bldr	L	In serv.		Bldr	L	In serv.
P . . . N . . .	. . .	. . .	. . .	P . . . N . . .	. . .	. . .	. . .
P . . . N . . .	. . .	. . .	. . .	P . . . N . . .	. . .	. . .	. . .
P . . . N . . .	. . .	. . .	. . .	P . . . N . . .	. . .	. . .	. . .

D: 320 tons   **S:** 28.5 kts   **Dim:** 50.0 (pp) × 7.0 × 1.9
A: 2/MM 38 Exocet (eventually) – 1/40-mm AA – 2/20-mm AA (I × 2)
Electron Equipt: Radars: 1/Decca . . . , 1/fire-control (eventually)
Electric: 200 kw   **Range:** 2,500/15
M: 2 SEMT-Pielstick 18 PA 4 200 diesels; 2 controllable-pitch props; 9,000 hp

REMARK: Projected under the 1977-82 plan, to be ordered in 1980.

◆ 4 Trident class

	Bldr	L	In serv.
P 670 TRIDENT	Auroux, Arcachon	31-5-76	17-12-76
P 671 GLAIVE	Auroux, Arcachon	25-8-76	3-77
P 672 ÉPÉE	C.N.M. Cherbourg	31-3-76	9-10-76
P 673 PERTUISANE	C.N.M. Cherbourg	2-6-76	20-1-77

Épée 1976

D: 115/130 tons   **S:** 26 kts   **Dim:** 37.0 × 5.5 × 1.6
A: 1/40-mm AA – 6/SS-12 missiles – 1/12.7-mm machine gun
Man: 2 officers, 5 petty officers, 12 men   **Range:** 750/20, 1,750/10
M: 2 AGO V 12 CZSHR diesels; 2 controllable-pitch props; 4,000 hp

PATROL BOATS (*continued*)

Trident   1976

REMARKS: Thirty were planned, then fourteen, but only these four are to be built. Two sisters have been built for the Ivory Coast. The *Epée* and *Trident* are stationed overseas.

◆ 1 La Combattante-I class

	Bldr	Laid down	L	In serv.
P 730 LA COMBATTANTE	Const. Méc. de Normandie	4-62	20-6-63	3-64

La Combattante   1974

D: 180 tons (202 fl)   **S:** 23 kts   **Dim:** 45.0 × 7.35 × 2.45 (fl)
Man: 3 officers, 22 men   **Range:** 2,000/12   **Electric:** 120 kw
A: 4/SS-12 missiles (IV × 1)–2/40-mm AA (I × 2)
M: 2 SEMT-Pielstick diesels; 2 controllable-pitch props; 3,200 hp

REMARKS: Anti-magnetic, laminated-wood-and-plastic hull. For a short passage can carry eighty men and their equipment.

◆ 1 Type DB-1 former minesweeper

	Bldr	Laid down	L	In serv.
P . . . MERCURE	Const. Méc. de Normandie	1-55	21-2-57	12-58

Mercure—as a minesweeper

D: 365 tons (400 fl)   **S:** 15 kts   **Dim:** 44.35 (42.0 pp) × 8.27 × 4.04
A: 2/20-mm AA (II × 1)   **Man:** 5 officers, 14 petty officers, 18 men
M: 2 Mercedes-Benz MB 820 EB diesels; 2 Ka-Me-Wa controllable-pitch props; 4,000 hp

REMARKS: Six sisters built for West Germany have since been transferred to Turkey. The *Mercure* is being converted to a fisheries-protection ship, to enter service late 1980. Minesweeping equipment removed. Insulated against cold climate. Habitability modernized. Carries two 6-man rubber inspection boats with 20-hp motors. Former pendant number M-765. Construction financed by U.S. as MSC-254. Six sisters built for West Germany have since been transferred to Turkey.

◆ 4 former Canadian Bay-class coastal minesweepers

	Bldr	L	In serv.
P 652 LA LORIENTAISE (ex-*Miramichi*)	St. John DD	1953	1953
P 653 LA DUNKERQUOISE (ex-*Fundy*)	St. John DD	17-7-53	1954
P 655 LA DIEPPOISE (ex-*Chaleur*)	Port Arthur SY	21-6-52	1952
P 657 LA PAIMPOLAISE (ex-*Thunder*)	Can. Vickers	7-7-53	1953

D: 370 tons (470 fl)   **S:** 15 kts   **Dim:** 50.0 (46.05 pp) × 9.21 × 2.8
Man: 3 officers, 11 petty officers, 19 men   **Range:** 4,500/11
A: 1/40-mm AA   **Fuel:** 52 tons
M: GM diesels; 2 props; 2,500 hp

PATROL BOATS (continued)

La Dieppoise   C. Limonier, 1975

REMARKS: Wooden hulls with aluminum-alloy frames. All minesweeping gear deleted. Air-conditioned. All stationed overseas. Transferred to France in 1954 under the Military Assistance program.

◆ 5 Sirius-class ex-coastal minesweepers

	Bldr	L
P 650 ARCTURUS	C.N. Caen	12-3-54
P 656 ALTAIR	C.M.N., Cherbourg	27-3-56
P 659 CANOPUS	Augustin Normand	31-12-55
P 660 ÉTOILE POLAIRE	Seine Maritime	5-3-57
P 759 LYRE	Penhoët	3-5-56

Altair

D: 400 tons (440 fl)   **S:** 15 kts   **Dim:** 46.4 (42.7 pp) × 8.55 × 2.5
Man: 3 officers, 13 petty officers, 22 men   **Range:** 3,000/10
A: 1/40-mm AA – 1 or 2/20-mm AA   **Fuel:** 48 tons
M: 2 SEMT-Pielstick 16-cylinder diesels; 2 props; 2,000 hp

REMARKS: French-built version of the British "-ton" class. Engines built by S.G.C.M. Minesweeping equipment removed. All except the *Lyre* (P-759) stationed overseas. The *Vega* (P-707), *Aldebaran* (ex-*Eridan*, P-741), and *Sagittaire* (P-743) stricken. The *Croix du Sud* (P-658) transferred to the Seychelles in 1979. The *Canopus* (P-659) was financed by the U.S. under the Offshore Procurement Program as USN MSC-228.

◆ 6 ex-minesweepers, British "-ham" class

	Bldr	In serv.
P 661 JASMIN (ex-*Stedham*)	Blackmore, Bideford	1955
P 662 PETUNIA (ex-*Pineham*)	McLean, Renfrew	1956
P 742 PAQUERETTE (ex-*Kingham*)	J. S. White	1955
P 784 GÉRANIUM (ex-*Tibenham*)	McGruer	1955
P 787 JONQUILLE (ex-*Sulham*)	Fairlie Yacht Co.	1955
P 788 VIOLETTE (ex-*Mersham*)	J. S. White	1955

Petunia   1975

D: 140 tons (170 fl)   **S:** 14 kts   **Dim:** 33.43 × 6.45 × 1.7
Man: 1 officer, 10 petty officers, 2 men   **Endurance:** 4 days
A: 1/20-mm AA   **Fuel:** 15 tons
M: 2 Paxman YHAXM diesels; 2 props; 550 hp

REMARKS: Except for the *Petunia* (P-662), which is used by the Navy as a buoy tender and patrol boat, all are manned by the Gendarmerie. Built with U.S. Offshore Procurement funds as USN MSI-86, MSI-87, MSI-82, MSI-84, MSI-83, and MSI-77, respectively.

PATROL CRAFT

◆ 4 P 778 class

P 778   P 779   P 780 (*Karukera*)   P 781 (*Gugane*)

D: 20 tons (30 fl)   **S:** 25 kts   **Dim:** . . . × . . . × . . .
A: . . .   **M:** . . .

◆ 3 Tecimar type

P 770   P 772   P 774

D: 30 tons   **S:** 25 kts   **Dim:** 13.3 × 4.1 × 1.1
A: 1/12.7-mm machine gun – 1/7.5-mm machine gun
M: 2 GM 6-71 diesels; 2 props; 670 hp

PATROL CRAFT (continued)

P-772 and P-774   Tecimar, 1974

REMARKS: In service since 1974. Hull molded of stratified polyester. Manned by the Gendarmerie. P-771 transferred to Djibouti.

MINE WARFARE SHIPS

NOTE: The tender *Loire* (A-615) is, in effect, a mine-countermeasures support ship. However, because she has an auxiliary "A" pendant and for convenience, she is listed with her *Rhin*-class sisters under Support Tenders.

◆ 5 (+10) Eridan-class minehunters

	Budget	Laid down	L	In serv.
M 641 ERIDAN	1976	20-12-77	5-2-79	1st quarter-81
M . . . N . . .	1977	. . .	. . .	4th quarter-81
M . . . N . . .	1977	. . .	. . .	3rd quarter-82
M . . . N . . .	1979	. . .	. . .	. . .
M . . . N . . .	1979	. . .	. . .	. . .

Bldr: Lorient

D: 500 tons (544 fl)   **S:** 15 kts on main engine, 7 kts while hunting
Dim: 51.6 (47.1 pp) × 8.96 × 2.45 (hull) 2.6 (max.)
Man: 49 men   **Range:** 3,000/12   **Electric** 750 kw

A: 1/20-mm AA – 2/PAP 105 remote-control mine-locators
Electron Equipt: Radars: 1/Decca 1229, 1/automatic track-plotter with numerical calculator, automatic pilot, Toran and Syledis radio navigation systems, Decca HiFix
         Sonar: DUBM 21 – EVEC 20 automatic plotting table
M: 1 Brons-Werkspoor A-RUB 215 × 12 diesel; 1 controllable-pitch prop; 1,900 hp; 2 electric maneuvering props, 120 hp each; bow-thruster

REMARKS: Hull built of glass and polyester resin. Will have one mechanical drag sweep. France, Belgium, and The Netherlands will cooperate in building these ships for the requirements of the three countries. A total of 15 are programmed to be built for France under the 1977-82 plan. Starting with the fifth, they are to enter service at nine-month intervals.

◆ 5 Circé-class minehunters

	Laid down	L	In serv.
M 712 CYBELE	15-9-70	2-3-72	28-9-72
M 713 CALLIOPE	4-4-70	20-10-71	28-9-72
M 714 CLIO	4-9-69	10-6-71	18-5-72
M 715 CIRCÉ	30-1-69	15-12-70	18-5-72
M 716 CÉRÈS	2-2-71	10-8-72	8-3-73

Bldr: Const. Méc. de Normandie, Cherbourg

Cybele   G. Arra, 1976

D: 460 tons (495 fl)   **Dim:**   50.9 (46.5 pp) × 8.9 × 3.6 (max.)
S: 15 kts   **Man:**   Peacetime: 4 officers, 19 petty officers, 24 men
A: 1/20-mm AA – 2 PAP-104 remote control mine-locators
Electron Equipt: Radar: Decca 1229 – Sonar: DUBM 20 (minehunting)
M: 1 MTU diesel; 1 prop; 1,800 hp   **Range:**   3,000/12

REMARKS: Designed for the detection and destruction of mines laid as deep as 60 meters. Hull made of laminated wood. Stress is on anti-magnetism and silence. Two independent propulsion systems, one for navigation, the other for minesweeping, both with remote control. Special rudders with small, screw propellers mounted at the base of the rudder's after end and powered by a 260-hp electric motor, giving a speed of 7 knots and permitting exceptional maneuverability. Mines are destroyed

MINE WARFARE SHIPS (continued)

Clio   1972

either by divers (six in each crew) or by the PAP-104 (*poisson auto-propulsé*) wire-guided sled device, which is 2.7 meters long, 1.1 meters in diameter, weighs 700 kg, is moved by two electric motors that drive it at 6 knots for a distance up to 500 meters, and has a television camera that displays an image of the mine. It can deposit its explosive charge of 100 kg near the mine. When the sled has been recovered, the charge is detonated by ultra-sonic waves. These ships to not have minesweeping gear.

◆ 5 ex-U.S. Agile class, converted to minehunters

	In serv.	Converted
M 615 CANTHO (ex-MSO-476)	11-54	1-79
M 616 DOMPAIRE (ex-MSO-454)	6-54	21-1-78
M 617 GARIGLIANO (ex-MSO-452)	4-54	5-79
M 618 MYTHO (ex-MSO-475)	9-54	...
M 619 VINH-LONG (ex-MSO-477)	1-55	...

Bldr: Bellingham Shipyard, Bellingham, Washington

Dompaire   1979

D: 700 tons (780 fl)   **S:** 13.5 kts (14 kts on trials)
Dim: 50.29 × 10.67 × 3.15   **Range:** 3,000/10
A: 1/40-mm AA — 2/PAP 104 remote-control mine-locators
Man: Peacetime: 4 officers, 22 petty officers, 28 men
Electron Equipt: Radar: ...
                  Sonar: DUBM 21 — EVEC 11 automatic plotting table
M: 2 GM 8-278A diesels; 2 controllable-pitch props; 1,600 hp; bow-thruster

REMARKS: Conversion to minehunters to be completed in 1980. Mechanical minesweeping capability retained. All have new bridge superstructure.

◆ 5 ex-U.S. Agile-class ocean minesweepers

	Bldr	In serv.
M 610 OUISTREHAM (ex-MSO-513)	Peterson Bldrs., Sturgeon Bay, Wisc.	8-56
M 612 ALENÇON (ex-MSO-453)	Bellingham SY, Wash.	6-54
M 613 BERNEVAL (ex-MSO-450)	Bellingham SY, Wash.	12-53
M 620 BERLAIMONT (ex-MSO-500)	Bellingham SY, Wash.	1-56
M 623 BACCARAT (ex-MSO-505)	Tacoma Boat, Wash.	3-56

Alençon   J.-C. Bellonne, 1975

D: 700 tons (780 fl)   **S:** 13.5 kts (14 kts on trials)
Dim: 50.29 × 10.67 × 3.15   **Man:** 5 officers, 53 men
A: 1/40-mm AA   **Range:** 3,000/10   **Fuel:** 47 tons
M: 2 GM 8-268A diesels; 2 controllable-pitch props; 1,600 hp

REMARKS: Budget restrictions have caused the conversion of these five ships to minehunters to be abandoned. However, they began receiving the new DUBM-41 sonar
in 1978. The *Narvik* (M-609) was reclassified 1-1-76 as a trials ship for the AP-4 drag
sweep and a new lens-type sonar — *see* Experimental Ships.

◆ 5 coastal Sirius-class minesweepers

	L		L
M 737 CAPRICORNE	8-8-56	M 756 CÉPHÉE	3-1-56
M 749 PHÉNIX	23-5-55	M 757 VERSEAU	26-4-56
M 755 CAPELLA	6-10-55		

Bldr: Constructions Mécaniques de Normandie, Cherbourg

MINE WARFARE SHIPS (*continued*)

D: 400 tons (440 fl)   **S:** 15 kts (11.5 kts when sweeping)
Dim: 46.4 (42.7 pp) × 8.55 × 2.5
Man: 3 officers, 35 men   **Electric:** 1,471 kw
A: 1/40-mm AA, 1 or 2/20-mm AA   **Range:** 3,000/10   **Fuel:** 48 tons
M: 2 SEMT-Pielstick 16-cylinder diesels; 2 props; 1,600 hp

Capricorne   1973

REMARKS: French-built versions of the British "-ton" class. Engines built by S.G.C.M. Hull is laminated wood and light aluminum, which produce a strong, rigid, light body. Keel and stem in heavy wood. Have gear for sweeping mechanical, magnetic, and acoustic mines. The *Capricorne* (M-737) has greater degaussing capability than the others. All have one diesel sweep-generator (500 hp). The *Aries* (M-758) was loaned to Morocco in 1975. The *Bételgeuse* (A-747) was reclassified 1-5-77 as an experimental ship and used for trials with the DUBM 41 sonar and its computer. Of the other survivors, five were converted to patrol boats. M-749 through M-757 were financed under the U.S. Offshore Procurement program as MSC-232 to MSC-235.

◆ 9 ex-U.S. Adjutant class

		Bldr	In serv.
M 632	PERVENCHE (ex-MSC-141)	Southcoast Co., Cal.	6-54
M 633	PIVOINE (ex-MSC-125)	Stephen Bros.	8-54
M 639	ACANTHE (ex-MSC-70)	F.L. Sample, Maine	5-53
M 671	CAMÉLIA (ex-MSC-68)	Harbor Boat, Terminal Isl., Cal.	8-53
M 681	LAURIER (ex-MSC-86)	Stephen Bros.	3-54
M 682	LILAS (ex-MSC-93)	National Steel, San Diego	2-54
M 687	MIMOSA (ex-MSC-99)	Tacoma Boat, Wash.	8-54
M 688	MUGUET (ex-MSC-97)	Tacoma Boat, Wash.	6-54

◆ 6 ex-U.S. Adjutant class for which degaussing/deperming standards are no longer maintained

M 635	RÉSÉDA (ex-MSC-126)	Stephen Bros.	11-54
M 638	ACACIA (ex-MSC-69)	F.L. Sample, Maine	3-53
M 668	AZALÉE (ex-MSC-67)	Harbor Boat, Terminal Isl., Cal.	6-53
M 674	CYCLAMEN (ex-MSC-119)	National Steel, San Diego	10-53
M 675	EGLANTINE (ex-MSC-117)	Tacoma Boat, Wash.	2-54
M 684	LOBELIA (ex-MSC-96)	Tacoma Boat, Wash.	6-54

Muguet   C. Martinelli, 1976

Lilas   C. Martinelli, 1974

D: 300 tons (372 fl)   **S:** 13 kts (8 kts when sweeping)
Dim: 43.0 (41.5 pp) × 7.95 × 2.55   **Man:** 3 officers, 9 petty officers, 20 men
A: 2/20-mm AA (II × 1)   **Range:** 2,500/10   **Fuel:** 40 tons
M: 2 GM 8-268A diesels; 2 props; 1,200 hp (cruising)

REMARKS: These minesweepers are the survivors of a series of twenty-seven transferred 1953-54 under the Military Assistance Program. The hulls are constructed entirely of wood. Five have been converted to auxiliaries: the *Ajonc* as a tender to the diving school, the *Liseron*, *Gardenia*, and *Magnolia* as base ships for mine-demolition divers, and the *Jacinthe* as an experimental ship and minelayer. The others have been stricken or transferred abroad: the *Coquelicot* and *Marjolaine* to Tunisia, the

MINE WARFARE SHIPS (continued)

Marguerite to Uruguay, and the *Pavot* and *Renoncule* to Turkey. The six for which anti-magnetic standards are no longer maintained are used as training tenders: M-635 and M-638 at the school of navigation and the others at the French Naval Academy; they are not likely to be used as minesweepers in the future.

AMPHIBIOUS WARFARE SHIPS

◆ **2 Ouragan-class dock landing ships**

	Budget	Bldr	Laid down	L	In serv.
L 9021 OURAGAN	1960	Brest	6-62	9-11-63	6-65
L 9022 ORAGE	(22-7-65)	Brest	6-66	22-4-67	3-68

Ouragan   J.-C. Bellonne, 1975

Orage – now armed   J.-C. Bellonne, 1973

D: 5,800 tons (8,500 fl)   **S:** 17.3 kts   **Range:** 4,000/15
Dim: 149.0 (144.5 pp) × 21.5 × 5.4 (8.7, max.)   **Electric:** 2,650 kw
Man: 10 officers, 66 petty officers, 135 men (L-9021: 138 men)
A: 4/40-mm AA (I × 4) – 2/20-mm mortars (on L-9021 only)
Electron Equipt: Radar: 1/DRBN 32 – Sonar: 1/SQS 17 on L-9021
M: 2 SEMT-Pielstick diesels; 2 controllable-pitch props; 8,640 hp

REMARKS: Transports whose mission is to carry for long distances and place in operation (a) helicopters that can land a full commando, sustain troops ashore, and provide fire support and communications; (b) landing craft for personnel or material (tanks, vehicles, supplies, etc.). Can carry 349 troops, including 14 officers, or 470 troops for a short distance.

A 20-meter-long well with a 14-by-5.5-meter stern gate can be sunk under 3 meters of water. When ships are ballasted down, displacement reaches 14,400 tons. Movement of the sluices and valves is automatic, using pumps (3,000 m³/h) controlled from a central position. A removable deck in six sections covers 36 meters of the after part of the well and allows the landing and takeoff of heavy helicopters. A 90-meter-long temporary deck in fifteen sections can be used to stow cargo or vehicles, but its use reduces the number of landing craft that can be carried, because the well is then diminished by half.

Ouragan   J.-C. Bellonne, 1975

If used as transports, they can embark either two EDIC landing craft for infantry and tanks, carrying 11 light tanks or trucks, or 18 LCM Mk 6 with tanks, or vehicles and, in addition, heavy helicopters on a landing platform. If used as cargo-carriers, they can embark 1,500 tons of material. Lifting equipment includes two 35-ton cranes. A combined command center permits the simultaneous direction of helicopter and amphibious operations.

AMPHIBIOUS WARFARE SHIPS (continued)

◆ 5 Argens-class tank landing ships

	Bldr	Laid down	L	In serv.
L 9003 ARGENS (BDC-2)	A.C. de Bretagne	10-58	7-4-59	6-60
L 9004 BIDASSOA (BDC-5)	Seine Maritime	1-60	30-12-60	7-61
L 9007 TRIEUX (BDC-1)	A.C. de Bretagne	12-58	6-12-58	3-60
L 9008 DIVES (BDC-4)	Seine Maritime	5-59	29-6-60	4-61
L 9009 BLAVET (BDC-3)	A.C. de Bretagne	4-59	15-1-60	1-61

Argens   G. Arra, 1972

Trieux and Blavet – both with hangars   1970

D: 1,400 tons, 1,750 (av), 4,225 (fl)   **S:** 11 kts
Dim: 102.12 (96.6 pp) × 15.54 × 3.2
A: 3/40-mm AA (I × 3) – 1/120-mm mortar mounted fwd
Man: 6 officers, 69 men   **Range:** 18,500/10
M: 2 SEMT-Pielstick 16PA1 diesels; 2 props; 2,000 hp

REMARKS: Design derived from U.S. LST-1 class. Can carry 1,800 tons of cargo, 4 LCVP landing craft, and a maximum of 807 passengers (normally 170 troops). MacGregor-type loading hatches. *Trieux* and *Blavet* have been modified with a hangar for two Alouette III helicopters.

◆ 4 Champlain-class medium landing ships

	Bldr	Laid down	L	In serv.
L 9030 CHAMPLAIN	Brest	1973	17-11-73	5-10-74
L 9031 FRANCIS GARNIER	Brest	1973	17-11-73	21-6-74
L . . . N . . .	. . .	. . .	. . .	. . .
L . . . N . . .	. . .	. . .	. . .	. . .

Champlain   J.-C. Bellonne, 1977

D: 750 tons (1,330 fl)   **Dim:** 80.0 (68.0 pp) × 13.0 × 3.0 (max.)
S: 16 kts (13 cruising)   **Man:** 4 officers, 35 men
M: 2 diesels; 2 props; 1,800 hp   **Range:** 4,500/13

REMARKS: Bow-door design, embarkation ramp and helicopter platform aft. Living quarters for a landing team (5 officers, 15 non-commissioned officers, 118 men) and its 12 vehicles, including Leopard armored personnel carriers. Can carry 2/40-mm AA, 2/81-mm mortars as defensive armament. Two additional units are to be built under the 1979 budget.

◆ 12 EDIC-class tank landing craft

L 9091 (7-1-58)	L 9094 (24-7-58)	L 9072 (1968)	L 9082 (1964)
L 9092 (2-12-58)	L 9096 (11-10-58)	L 9073 (1968)	L 9083 (1964)
L 9093 (17-4-58)	L 9070 (30-3-67)	L 9074 (22-7-69)	L 9084 (. .)

Bldrs: 7 Ch. Franco-Belges; 2 Toulon Naval DY; 2 Ch. de La Perrière; 1 Lorient

D: 250 tons (670 fl)   **S:** 8 kts   **Dim:** 59.0 × 11.95 × 1.3 (1.62 fl)
A: 2/20-mm AA (I × 2)   **Man:** 5 petty officers, 12 men
M: 2 MGO diesels; 2 props; 1,000 hp   **Range:** 1,800/8

AMPHIBIOUS WARFARE SHIPS (*continued*)

L-9096 DCAN, 1974

REMARKS: L-9082, L-9083, and L-9084: 310 tons (685 fl). Can carry 11 trucks or 5 LVTs. Two each can be carried aboard the *Ouragan* and the *Orage*. L-9095 transferred to Senegal, 1-7-74. L-9071 stricken 19-4-77.

◆ **16 U.S. LCM (8) class** Bldr: France, 1966-67

CTM 1 to CTM 16

D: 56 tons (150 fl) **S:** 9.5 kts **Dim:** 23.8 × 6.35 × 1.17
Man: 6 men **Fuel:** 3.4 tons diesel **Cargo:** 90 tons
M: 2 Hispano-HS 103 S diesels; 2 props; 450 hp

REMARK: Bow doors.

◆ **11 U.S. LCM (3) class**

LCM-1031	LCM-1035	LCM-1041	LCM-1045	LCM-1052	LCM-1056
LCM-1074	LCM-1076	LCM 1084	LCM 1087	VETERAN-2	

D: 26 to 52 tons **S:** 8 kts **Dim:** 15.25 × 4.3 × 1.2
Load: 1 30-ton tank **M:** 2 diesels

EXPERIMENTAL SHIPS

◆ **1 missile-range tracking ship**

	Bldr	L	In serv.
A 603 HENRI POINCARÉ (ex-*Maina Morasso*)	Adriatico	10-60	3-68

Henri Poincaré DCAN, 1974

D: 24,000 tons (fl) **S:** 15 kts **Dim:** 180.0 (160.0 pp) × 22.2 × 9.4
Man: 11 officers, 75 petty officers, 133 men, and several civilian technicians
A: 2/20-mm AA **Range:** 11,800/13.5 **Electric:** 7,355 kw
Electron Equipt: Radars: 1/DRBV 22D, 1/Savoie, 2/Bearn
Boilers: 2 Foster Wheeler, 48 kg/cm² pressure—superheat 445°C
M: Parsons GT; 1 prop; 10,000 hp; bow thruster

REMARKS: Flagship of Group M (the Naval Test and Measurement Group), which makes at-sea tests, takes measurements, and conducts experiments, as requested by the Navy or any other organization, civilian or military. The chief mission of the *Henri Poincaré* is to measure the trajectory of ballistic missiles (MSBS and SSBS) fired from the experimental station at Landes or from missile-carrying nuclear submarines and to compute their flight characteristics, especially from re-entry to impact. Her secondary mission is to assist the flag officer in controlling the naval and air elements in the test area, particularly recovery and security.

A former Italian tanker, the ship was entirely rebuilt by DCAN at Brest between 1964 and 1967, during which time she was given three radars for tracking and trajectory-measuring in ballistic tests and a sonar dome. She also has: an automatic tracking station; celestial position-fixing equipment: a camera-equipped theodolite; infrared equipment; a Transit navigational system; aerological, meteorological, and oceanographic equipment; excellent communications equipment; a programming and transcribing center for all experiments and installations; and a platform and hangar for two heavy and five light helicopters.

◆ **1 guided-missile trials ship**

A 610 ILE D'OLÉRON (ex-*München*) Bldr: Germany, 1939

Ile d'Oléron C. Martinelli, 1974

D: 5,500 tons (6,500 fl) **S:** 14.5 kts **Dim:** 115.05 × 15.24 × 6.5
Man: 9 officers, 46 petty officers, 113 men **Fuel:** 340 tons
Electron Equipt: Radars: 1/DRBV 22C, 1/DRBV 50, 1/DRBI 10
Range: 5,900/14, 7,200/12 **Electric:** 1,240 kw
M: 2 M.A.N. 6-cylinder diesels; 1 prop; 3,500 hp

REMARKS: Taken from the Germans as a prize of war and converted, 1957-58, to an ex-

EXPERIMENTAL SHIPS (*continued*)

perimental ship for missiles. Besides the radars listed, she carries guidance radars for the systems under test. She was used for Exocet trials and, since 1977, has been used for Crotale.

◆ 1 Sirius-class mine-countermeasures trials ship

A 474 BÉTELGEUSE

Bételgeuse   Skyfotos, Ltd., 1979

REMARKS: For trials with the DUBM-41 minehunting sonar. Retains most minesweeping gear and 1/40-mm AA. Enlarged forward superstructure. For other data, see Sirius-class minesweepers.

◆ 1 electronics experimental ship

A 644 BERRY (ex-*Medoc*)   Bldr: Roland Werft, Bremen

Berry   J.-C. Bellonne, 1977

D: 2,700 tons (fl)   **S:** 15 kts   **Dim:** 86.7 (78.5 pp) × 11.6 × 4.6
A: 2/20-mm AA (I × 2)   **Range:** 7,000/15
M: 2 MWM diesels; 2 props; 2,400 hp

REMARKS: An ex-stores ship, launched 10-9-58, converted, 1976-77, at Toulon, and recommissioned 2-77. Used for trials with electronic-warfare equipment. Former sister *Aunis* is a sonar-trials ship.

◆ 1 ex-U.S. Agile-class ocean minesweeper

A 769 NARVIK (ex-M-609, ex-MSO-512)   Bldr: Peterson Builders, Sturgeon Bay, Wisc.

REMARKS: In service since 6-56. Conducts experiments with the AP-4 drag sweep and a new lens-type sonar. For data, *see* ex-U.S. *Agile*-class under Mine Warfare Ships.

◆ 1 ex-U.S. Adjutant-class coastal minesweeper

A 680 JACINTHE (ex-M-680, ex-MSC-115)   Bldr: Tacoma Boat, Wash.

REMARKS: In service since 3-54. Equipped as a trials ship and minelayer. For data, *see* ex-U.S. *Adjutant*-class under Mine Warfare Ships.

◆ 1 deep-diving submarine

A 648 ARCHIMÈDE   Bldr: Toulon Dockyard

Archimède   J.-C. Bellonne, 1972

D: 200 tons (submerged)   **Dim:** 21.0 × 5.0 × 5.2   **Weight:** 60 tons (light)

REMARKS: Painted bright yellow. Can go 11,000 meters deep.

◆ 1 underwater-research ship

	Budget	Bldr	Laid down	L	In serv.
A 646 TRITON	1967	Lorient	1967	7-3-70	1972

D: 1,410 tons (1,510 fl)   **S:** 13 kts   **Electric:** 640 kw
Dim: 74.0 (68.0 pp) × 11.85 × 3.65 (aver.)   **Range:** 4,000/13
Man: Ship's company: 4 officers, 44 men. Divers: 5 officers, 12 men
M: Aft: 2 MGO V 12 ASHR diesels; 1 Voith-Schneider 30 G cycloidal propeller; 880 hp. Forward: 2 electric motors, 1 Voith-Schneider 26 G cycloidal propeller; 530 hp

EXPERIMENTAL SHIPS (*continued*)

Triton   J.-C. Bellonne, 1971

REMARKS: Assigned to GISMER (Groupe d'Intervention sous la Mer) for deep-sea diving and observation. Has a decompression chamber, laboratories, television, navigational radar, sonar for deep-water area search, etc. Helicopter platform. Good maneuverability at very slow speeds; capable of remaining positioned above a point 300 meters deep. Can be used in submarine-rescue operations. Her 15-ton crane can lower and raise: (a) a 13.5-ton chamber that can be sunk to 250 meters and can carry two four-man diving teams—this bell does not float, it is wire-tethered; (b) the two-man submarine *Griffon*, which is capable of diving to 600 meters for underwater exploration; (c) diving devices, sleds (troika, automatically guided). The *Griffon* has a manipulator arm, and her other characteristics are:

D: 14.2 to 16.7 tons   **Dim:** 7.8 × 2.3 × 3.1 (height)
Range: 24 hours/4 kts   **M:** 1 electric motor
The *Triton* is painted white.

NOTE: The *Chamois*-class local support tender *Isard* is also subordinated to GISMER and supports the ERIC (Engin de Recherche et d'Intervention par Cable) wire-guided submersible. For data, *see* the *Chamois* class under Miscellaneous Auxiliary Ships.

◆ 1 submersible support ship

	Bldr	In serv.
A 759 GUSTAVE ZEDÉ	Stetinner Orderwerke, AG	1-8-37
(ex-*Marcel Le Bihan*, ex-*Grief*)		

Gustave Zedé   J.-C. Bellonne, 1973

D: 800 tons (1,250 fl)   **S:** 13 kts   **Dim:** 72.0 (69.4 pp) × 10.6 × 3.2
A: 4/20-mm AA (II × 2)   **Range:** 2,500/13
Man: 3 officers, 47 men, plus accommodations for 22
M: 2 GM 16-278A diesels; 2 Voith-Schneider vertical cycloidal props; 2,800 hp

REMARKS: An ex-net-tender and ex-seaplane-tender. Transferred from the U.S. Navy 2-48. Has a 13-ton traveling crane. Tender to the submersible *Archimède;* subordinated to GISMER (Group d'Intervention sous la Mer). Renamed in 1977.

◆ 1 sonar-trials ship

A 643 AUNIS (ex-*Regina Pacis*) Bldr: Roland Werft, 1956

Aunis   1978

D: 2,900 tons   **S:** 12 kts   **Dim:** 94.43 × 11.6 × . . .
Man: 3 officers, 47 men   **Range:** 4,500/12
M: 2 M.A.N. diesels; 1 prop; 2,400 hp

REMARKS: Former Italian cargo ship purchased as a transport in 1966. Modified at Toulon, 1972-74. Used in the Cormoran deep-submerged towed-sonar project in the deep sound channel, using equipment formerly carried by the *Duperré* (D-633).

OCEANOGRAPHIC RESEARCH SHIPS

◆ 1 expeditionary ship

	Bldr	Laid down	L	In serv.
A 757 D'ENTRECASTEAUX	Brest	7-69	30-5-70	1971

D: 2,400 tons (fl)   **S:** 15 kts   **Dim:** 89.0 × 13.0 × 3.9
Man: 6 officers, 73 men, up to 38 scientists and technicians
Electron Equipt: Radars: 1/DRBV 50, 1/DRBN-32   **Range:** 10,000/12
M: 2 diesel-electric main engines × 1,000 kw; 2 controllable-pitch props. For extremely slow maneuvering, 2 retractable Schöttel propellers, one fwd, one aft.

D'Entrecasteaux   J.-C. Bellonne, 1974

OCEANOGRAPHIC RESEARCH SHIPS (continued)

REMARKS: For oceanographic research and hydrographic duties. Can take soundings and surveys to a depth of 6,000 meters. Two radars, one sonar; helicopter platform and hangar (Alouette III helicopter). Booms, one landing craft, three hydrographic launches. Painted white.

◆ 1 ex-U.S. Agile-class ocean minesweeper

A 640 ORIGNY (ex-M 621, ex-MSO-501) Bldr: Bellingham SY, Wash.

Origny   1974

D: 700 tons (780 fl)   **S:** 13.5 kts   **Dim:** 50.29 × 10.67 × 3.15
M: 2 GM 8-278A diesels; 2 controllable-pitch props; 1,600 hp

REMARKS: In service since 1-56. Converted, 1961-62. Wooden hull. Painted white.

◆ 1 underwater archeological research ship

A 789 ARCHÉONAUTE Bldr: Auroux, Arcachon

Archéonaute   J.-C. Bellonne, 1972

D: 120 tons (fl)   **S:** 12 kts   **Dim:** 29.3 × 6.0 × 1.7
Man: 2 officers, 4 men, 3 scientific research personnel, 6 divers
M: Baudoin diesels; 2 controllable-pitch props; 600 hp

REMARKS: Ordered by the Office of Cultural Affairs, manned by Navy personnel. Launched 25-8-67. Laboratory and workshops, decompression chamber, underwater television.

HYDROGRAPHIC SURVEY SHIPS

◆ 2 converted ex-trawlers

	L	In serv. with French Navy
A 756 L'ESPERANCE (ex-*Jacques Coeur*)	1962	1969
A 766 L'ESTAFETTE (ex-*Jacques Cartier*)	1962	1972

Bldr: Gdynia, Poland

L'Estafette   1973

D: 956 tons (1,360 fl)   **Dim:** 63.45 (59.75 pp) × 9.82 × 5.85 (fl)
S: 13.5 kts   **Man:** 3 officers, 29 men; 14 hydrographic service personnel
M: M.A.N. diesels; 1 prop; 1,870 hp   **Range:** 7,500/13

REMARKS: Former oceangoing fishing trawlers, purchased, 1968-69. Large oceanographic winch on stern, articulated crane amidships. Painted white.

	Bldr	L	In serv.
A 758 LA RECHERCHE (ex-*Guyane*)	Ziegler, Dunkerque	4-51	3-62

La Recherche   J.-C. Bellonne, 1972

HYDROGRAPHIC SURVEY SHIPS (continued)

D: 810 tons (910 fl) **S:** 13.5 kts **Dim:** 67.5 (62 pp) × 10.4 × 4.5
Man: 2 officers, 10 petty officers, 26 men **Range:** 3,100/10
M: 1 Werkspoor MABS 398 diesel, 8 cylinders 4 t.; 1,535 hp

REMARKS: Operated for the French Overseas Ministry. Bought in 1960. Hull bulged for stability. Painted white.

◆ 2 Astrolabe-class coastal survey ships

	Bldr	Laid down	L	In serv.
A 780 ASTROLABE	Seine Maritime	1962	27-5-63	7-64
A 781 BOUSSOLE	Seine Maritime	6-62	11-4-63	7-64

Astrolabe   1968

D: 330 tons (440 fl) **S:** 12.5 kts **Dim:** 42.7 (36.65 pp) × 8.45 × 2.9
Man: 1 officer, 32 men **Range:** 4,000/12
A: A-780: 1/40-mm − 2/12.7-mm machine guns (not normally mounted)
M: 2 Baudoin DV 8 diesels; 1 controllable-pitch prop; 800 hp

REMARKS: Authorized in 1961. Air-conditioned. Carries two radio-equipped, 4.5-ton survey launches. Painted white.

◆ 2 coastal survey ships

A 683 OCTANT (ex-*Michel Marie*)

Octant   J.-C. Bellonne, 1976

D: 128 tons (133 fl) **S:** 9 kts **Dim:** 24.0 × 6.1 × 3.23
Man: 1 officer, 12 men **Range:** 2,000 **Endurance:** 12 days
M: 2 diesels; 1 controllable-pitch prop; 200 hp

A 794 CORAIL (ex-*Marc Joly*)

Corail   1975

D: 54.78 tons (light) **S:** 10.3 kts **Dim:** 17.8 × 4.92 × 1.83
M: 1 Caterpillar diesel; 250 hp

REMARKS: Ex-fishing boats, modified, 1962-63. The *Octant*, built in 1955, operates in the Mediterranean. Her sister *Alidade* (A-682) was stricken 4-77. The *Corail*, built in Belgium in 1967 by Thuin, operates from New Caledonia. Both are painted white.

SUPPORT TENDERS

◆ 1 Jules Verne-class multi-purpose repair ship

	Budget	Bldr	Laid down	L	In serv.
A 620 JULES VERNE (ex-*Achéron*)	1961	Brest	1969	30-5-76	3-76

D: 6,485 tons (10,250 fl) **S:** 18 kts **Dim:** 147.0 × 21.56 × 6.5
Man: 16 officers, 150 petty officers, 116 men
A: 2/40-mm AA (I × 2) **Range:** 9,500/18 **Electric:** 3,800 kw
M: 2 SEMT-Pielstick T2PC diesels; 1 prop; 11,200 hp

REMARKS: Six years after being launched as an ammunition ship, the *Jules Verne* was converted to a floating workshop for providing support to a force of from three to six surface warships. Has significant capabilities for both regular maintenance and battle-damage repair: mechanical, engine, electrical, sheet-metal, electronic workshops, etc. She carries a stock of torpedoes and other munitions. Has a platform and hangar for two Alouette-III helicopters.

SUPPORT TENDERS (*continued*)

Jules Verne   ECPA, 1976

Jules Verne   J.-C. Bellonne, 1976

◆ **5 Rhin class**

	Budget	Purpose	Bldr	Laid down	L	In serv.
A 621 RHIN	1959	Electronics	Lorient	5-61	17-3-62	3-64
A 622 RHÔNE	1960	Submarines	Lorient	2-62	8-12-62	10-64
A 615 LOIRE	1962	Minesweepers	Lorient	7-65	10-66	6-67

Rhin   J.-C. Bellonne, 1977

D: 2,075 tons (2,445 fl)   **Dim:** 101.05 (92.05 pp) × 13.1 × 3.65
S: 16.5 kts   **Man:** A-621: 6 officers, 42 petty officers, 76 men
A: 3/40-mm AA (I × 3)   **Range:** 13,000/13
Electron Equipt: Radar: 1/DRBV 50   **Electric:** 920 kw
M: 2 SEMT-Pielstick 16 PA 2V diesels; 1 prop; 3,200 hp

Rhône   J.-C. Bellonne, 1972

	Budget	Purpose	Bldr	Laid down	L	In serv.
A 618 RANCE	1964	Experimental	Lorient	8-64	5-5-65	2-66

Rance   J.-C. Bellonne, 1976

Man: 10 officers, 39 petty officers, 69 men   **A:** None
Electron Equipt: Radars: 1/DRBV 24, 1/DRBV 50
M: SEMT-Pielstick 12 PA 4 diesels; 3,600 hp

	Budget	Purpose	Bldr	Laid down	L	In serv.
A 617 GARONNE	1964	Repair	Lorient	11-63	8-8-64	9-65

SUPPORT TENDERS (*continued*)

Garonne J.-C. Bellonne, 1977

D: 2,320 tons **S:** 15 kts **Dim:** 101.5 (92.05 pp) × 13.8 × 3.7
Man: 6 officers, 39 petty officers, 69 men **Range:** 13,000/13
A: 1/40-mm AA – 2/20-mm AA
M: 2 SEMT-Pielstick 12 PA 4 diesels; 1 prop; 3,600 hp

REMARKS: The *Rhin* has 1,700 m³ of store rooms and 700 m³ of workshops, many air-conditioned. She has a hangar and flight deck for one helicopter, which is equipped to serve minesweepers with spare sweep gear, cable, and repairs. The *Rhône* is fitted to service submarines. She has a helicopter deck but no hangar. The *Loire* has a helicopter deck but no hangar. All have one 5-ton crane with a 12-meter reach. The profile of the *Rance* is different from that of the other ships of this group. An additional deck has been fitted between her navigating bridge and her stack. She has a laboratory, radioactive decontamination stations, and carries up to three Alouette helicopters. The *Garonne* was designed for overseas service. She has metalworking and carpentry shops, an extra deck with lower overhead, and a 30-ton crane mounted in the center of her fantail. She has no helicopter facilities.

FLEET REPLENISHMENT SHIPS

◆ 3 Durance-class fleet oilers

	Bldr	Laid down	L	In serv.
A 629 DURANCE	Brest	10-12-73	6-9-75	1-12-76
A 607 MEUSE	Brest	2-6-77	2-12-78	8-80
A . . . N . . .	Brest	12-78	. . .	1983

Durance 1977

D: 7,600 tons (17,800 fl) **Dim:** 157.3 (149.0 pp) × 21.2 × 8.65 (10.8 fl)
S: 19 kts (fl) **Man:** 8 officers, 62 petty officers, 89 men
A: 2/40-mm AA (I × 2) **Range:** 9,000/15 **Electric:** 5,400 kw
M: 2 SEMT-Pielstick 16 PC 2.5 diesels; 2 controllable-pitch props; 20,000 hp
Fuel: 750 tons

Durance 1977

REMARKS: Two dual solids/liquids underway-replenishment stations per side. Can supply two ships alongside and one astern. *Durance:* 7,500 tons fuel oil, 1,500 tons diesel fuel, 500 tons JP-5, 130 tons distilled water, 170 tons fresh provisions, 150 tons munitions, 50 tons spare parts; *Meuse:* 5,000 tons fuel oil, 3,200 tons diesel, 1,800 tons JP-5—the remainder the same as the *Durance.* Hangar for one Alouette-III and flight deck for larger helicopters. A near-sister will be built in Australia for the RAN.

◆ 1 Isère class

A 675 ISÈRE (ex-*Caltex Strasbourg*) Bldr: A.C. Seine Maritime

Isère J.-C. Bellonne, 1977

FLEET REPLENISHMENT SHIPS (*continued*)

D: 7,440 tons (26,700 fl)   **Dim:** 170.38 (167.0 pp) × 21.72 × 10.27 (max.)
S: 16 kts   **Man:** 6 officers, 41 petty officers, 59 men
Boilers: 2   **Cargo capacity:** 18,200 tons
M: Parsons GT; 1 prop; 8,260 hp

REMARK: French tanker launched 22-6-59 and purchased in 1965. She can refuel two ships alongside and one astern.

◆ 1 La Seine class

A 628 LA SAÔNE (ex-*Stormarn*) Bldr: A.C. de France

La Saône   1976

D: 8,600 tons (23,410 fl)   **S:** 18 kts (14 cruising)
Dim: 160.0 × 22.0 × 10.75 (aft, fl) 8.75 (fwd, fl)
A: 3/40-mm AA   **Man:** 9 officers, 53 petty officers, 117 men
Boilers: 3 Penhöet, 27 kg/cm² pressure — superheat 350°C
M: Parsons GT; 2 props; 15,800 hp   **Range:** 6,400/17.5, 11,000/10

REMARKS: Laid down in 1940 and taken over for Germany. Launched 27-2-48. Modernized 1962-63. Carries 9,100 tons black oil, 1,800 tons jet fuel, 730 tons diesel fuel, 200 tons fresh provisions, including 83,165 liters wine. Five transfer positions, one with automatic, constant-tension rig, two for light transfers and two for heavy loads. *La Seine* (A-627) stricken 13-10-76. *La Saône* will be stricken on completion of the *Meuse*.

TRANSPORT OILERS

◆ 1 La Charente class, converted for command-ship duties

A 626 LA CHARENTE (ex-*Beaufort*) Bldr: Haldnes, Tönsberg, 1957

La Charente   1974

La Charente   1974

D: 7,440 tons (26,000 fl)   **Dim:** 179.0 × 21.9 × 9.25 (10.4 fl)
S: 17.5 kts   **Man:** 6 officers, 94 men
A: 4/40-mm AA (I × 4).   **Cargo capacity:** 19,000 tons
M: GE GT; 1 prop; 2 boilers; 12,000 hp

REMARKS: Norwegian tanker purchased in 5-64. Modified to serve as admiral's flagship in the Indian Ocean (staff: 5 officers, 13 petty officers, 5 men). Helicopter platform and hangar on stern. Capability for astern refueling only.

◆ 2 Punaruu class

A 625 PAPENOO (ex-*Bow Queen*)   A 632 PUNARUU (ex-*Bow Cecil*)

Bldr: Norway, 1969

Punaruu   1975

D: 1,195 tons (2,927 fl)   **S:** 12 kts   **Dim:** 83.0 × 13.85 × 5.8
M: 2 diesels; 1 controllable-pitch prop; 2,050 hp; bow thruster

REMARKS: Former Norwegian tankers purchased at the end of 1969. Highly automated ships. Capacity: 2,500 m³. Ten washable "inox" cargo tanks that can accept any liquid. Astern fueling capability.

◆ 1 fuel carrier

A 638 SAHEL Bldr: C.N. de Caen, 1951

D: 630 tons (1,450 fl)   **S:** 12 kts   **Dim:** 53.7 × 9.0 × 4.4
A: 2/20-mm AA   **Cargo capacity:** 646 tons
M: 2 Sulzer diesels; 2 props; 1,400 hp

TRANSPORT OILERS (*continued*)

Sahel   Guiglini, 1974

REMARKS: One of eleven units of a class begun for Germany during World War II. Three sisters are in the East German Navy. Carries fuel and water.

◆ **1 ex-U.S. YO-55 class**

A 630 LAC TONLÉ SAP (ex-*Pumper*, YO-56) Bldr: R.T.C. Shipbuilding, Camden, N.J.

Lac Tonlé Sap   J.-C. Bellonne, 1972

> **D:** 800 tons (2,700 fl) **S:** 11 kts **Dim:** 71.65 × 11.3 × 4.8
> **A:** 3/20-mm AA **Range:** 6,300/11 **Man:** 2 officers, 35 men
> **M:** 25-cyl. Fairbanks-Morse 37E14-5 diesels; 2 props; 1,150 hp

REMARKS: Launched 9-42, transferred 1945, and will be retained until 1981. Cargo capacity: 1,700 tons. Capable of replenishing at sea.

LIGHT-FUELS TANKER

	Bldr	Laid down	L	In serv.
A 619 ABER WRACH	C.N.M., Cherbourg	11-62	11-63	1966

Aber Wrach   1972

> **D:** 1,220 tons (3,500 fl) **S:** 12 kts **Dim:** 86.55 (80.0 pp) × 12.2 × 4.8
> **A:** 1/40-mm AA **Man:** 3 officers, 45 men **Range:** 5,000/12
> **M:** 1 SEMT-Pielstick 6 PL diesel; 1 controllable-pitch prop; 2,000 hp

REMARKS: Cargo capacity: 2,200 tons. Carries diesel oil, jet fuel, and gasoline in point-to-point service. Capable of underway fueling, astern or anchored alongside.

PROVISIONS SHIP

A 733 SAINTONGE (ex-*Santa Maria*, ex-*Sven Germa*)

    Bldr: Duchèsne et Bossière, 1956

Saintonge

> **D:** 300 tons (990 fl) **S:** 10 kts **Dim:** 54.0 × 8.5 × 3.22
> **Man:** 2 officers, 6 petty officers, 13 men **Fuel:** 51 tons
> **M:** 1 MAK diesel; 760 hp

REMARK: Cargo capacity: 500 tons.

MISCELLANEOUS AUXILIARY SHIPS

◆ **5 Chamois-class local support tenders**

	In serv.		In serv.
A 767 CHAMOIS	1976	A 775 GAZELLE	13-1-78
A 768 ELAN	1977	A 776 ISARD	28-9-78
A 774 CHEVREUIL	7-10-77		

Bldr: Ch. de la Perrière, Lorient

Chamois   1976

D: 400 tons   **S:** 14.5 kts   **Dim:** 41.5 (36.96 pp) × 7.5 × 3.18
Man: 2 officers, 16 petty officers, 2 men
M: 2 SACM MGO V-16 AFHR diesels; 2 controllable-pitch props; 2,200 hp

REMARKS: Except for a 5.6-ton crane, the first four are identical to the fourteen civilian-manned FISH class designed for the supply of petroleum platforms. Hydraulic 50-ton stern crane mounted. Can be used for coastal towing and cleaning up oil spills. Two rudders and an 80-hp bow thruster. After winch with 28-ton bollard pull. Can be used as transports for twenty-eight passengers, as minelayers, or as torpedo-retrievers. The *Isard* is equipped as a divers' support ship and tender for the ERIC wire-guided submersible (2 tons, 4 meters overall, 600-meter diving depth). She has a ULISM decompression chamber capable of simulating pressures to a water depth of 150 meters. She also has a longer aft structure, supporting rubber divers' dinghys and a small helicopter deck. The ship is subordinated to GISMER.

◆ **7 "-ham"-class ex-inshore minesweepers for base support**

A 710 MYOSOTIS (ex-*Riplingham*)	A 738 CAPUCINE (ex-*Petersham*)
A 735 HIBISCUS (ex-*Sparham*)	A 739 ŒILLET (ex-*Isham*)
A 736 DAHLIA (ex-*Whippingham*)	A 740 HORTENSIA (ex-*Mileham*)
A 737 TULIPE (ex-*Frettenham*)	

D: 140 tons (170 fl)   **S:** 14 kts (9, sweeping)
Dim: 32.43 × 6.45 × 1.7   **Man:** 2 officers, 10 men
A: 1/20-mm AA or none   **Endurance:** 4 days   **Fuel:** 15 tons
M: 2 Paxman YHAXM diesels; 2 props; 550 hp

REMARKS: Wooden hulls. The *Myosotis* (A-710) is a diving tender; the others carry personnel and supplies. Built with U.S. Offshore Procurement funds as U.S. MSI-89,

Œillet   J.-C. Bellonne, 1975

MSI-85, MSI-88, MSI-75, MSI-78, MSI-79, and MSI-76, respectively. Six sisters serve the Navy and the Gendarmerie as patrol boats.

NET TENDERS

◆ **1 seagoing net tender**

	Bldr	Laid down	L	In serv.
A 731 TIANÉE	Brest	1-4-73	1-11-73	1975

Tianée   1974

D: 842 tons (905 fl)   **S:** 12 kts   **Dim:** 54.3 × 10.6 × . . .
Man: 1 officer, 12 petty officers, 24 men   **Range:** 5,200/12
M: 2 diesels; diesel-electric drive; 1 prop; 1,200 hp

REMARK: Living quarters air-conditioned, transverse bow thruster. Used primarily as a mooring-buoy tender.

NET TENDERS (*continued*)

◆ **5 Cigale-class tenders, ex-U.S. AN-93 class**

	Bldr	L
A 760 CIGALE (ex-AN-98)	A.C. de la Rochelle-Pallice	23-9-54
A 761 CRIQUET (ex-AN-96)	A.C. Seine Maritime	3-6-54
A 762 FOURMI (ex-AN-97)	A.C. Seine Maritime	6-7-54
A 763 GRILLON (ex-AN-95)	Penhoët	18-2-54
A 764 SCARABÉE (ex-AN-94)	Penhoët	21-11-53

Criquet   G. Arra, 1972

D: 770 tons (850 fl)   **Dim:** 46.28 (44.5 pp) × 10.2 × 3.2
A: 1/40-mm AA − 4/20-mm AA   **Range:** 5,200/12
Man: 1 officer, 36 men   **Fuel:** 125 m³ diesel oil
M: 2 SEMT PA-1 diesels; diesel-electric drive; 1 prop; 1,600 hp

REMARKS: U.S. "Offshore" mutual assistance. One sister built for Spain, two others
built in Italy. Used as mooring-buoy and salvage tenders.

◆ **3 La Prudente-class port netlayers**

	Bldr	L
Y 749 LA PRUDENTE	A.C. de la Manche	13-5-68
Y 750 LA PERSÉVÉRANTE	A.D. de la Rochelle-Pallice	14-5-68
Y 751 LA FIDÈLE	A.C. de la Manche	26-8-68

D: 446 tons (626 fl)   **S:** 10 kts   **Dim:** 43.5 (42.0 pp) × 10.0 × 2.8
Man: 1 officer, 8 petty officers, 21 men   **Electric:** 440 kw
Range: 4,000/10
M: 2 Baudoin diesels, diesel-electric drive; 1 prop; 620 hp

REMARKS: Used as mooring-buoy tenders. Lifting power, via pivoting crane forward:
25 tons.

◆ **1 Tupa class**

Y 667 TUPA

D: 292 tons   **S:** 6 kts   **Dim:** 28.5 × 8.3 × 0.85
M: 1 diesel; 1 prop; 210 hp

La Prudente   1976

DIVING TENDERS

◆ **1 base tender**

A 722 POSEIDON   Bldr: SIGNAV, St. Malo

Poseidon   J.-C. Bellonne, 1977

D: 200 tons (220 fl)   **S:** 13 kts   **Dim:** 40.5 (38.5 pp) × 7.2 × . . .
Man: 42 men   **Endurance:** 8 days   **M:** 1 diesel; 600 hp

REMARKS: Launched 5-12-74, in service 14-1-77. Used for training combat frogmen.

DIVING TENDERS (*continued*)

◆ 4 ex-U.S. Adjutant-class coastal minesweepers

		Bldr	In serv.
A 701	AJONC (ex-M-667, ex-MSC-71)	F.L.Sample, Maine	8-53
A 711	GARDENIA (ex-M-676, ex-MSC-114)	Tacoma Boat, Wash.	2-54
A 723	LISERON (ex-M-683, ex-MSC-98)	Tacoma Boat, Wash.	6-54
A 770	MAGNOLIA (ex-M-685, ex-MSC-87)	Stephen Bros.	3-54

Gardenia   J.-C. Bellonne, 1976

REMARKS: The *Ajonc* (A-701) is a tender to the French Navy's diving school; the others support mine-demolition divers. A deckhouse has replaced the minesweeping winch and the forward superstructure has been enlarged. For data, see *Adjutant*-class minesweepers.

TORPEDO-RECOVERY SHIPS

A 698 PÉTREL (ex-*Cap Lopez*, ex-*Yvon Loic II*) Bldr: Dubigeon, 1960

Pétrel   Y. Grangeon

D: 277 tons (318 fl)   **S:** 10 kts   **Dim:** 30.0 × 7.8 × 3.5
Man: 5 petty officers, 14 men
M: 2 Baudoin DV 6 diesels; 1 controllable-pitch prop; 600 hp

A 699 PÉLICAN (ex-*Kerfany*) Bldr: Avondale, U.S.A., 1951

Pélican   J.-C. Bellonne, 1976

D: 362 tons (425 fl)   **S:** 11 kts   **Dim:** 37.0 × 8.55 × 4.0
Man: 5 petty officers, 14 men
M: Burmeister & Wain diesel; 1 prop; 650 hp

REMARKS: Purchased 1965. Former tuna-fishing boat. Torpedo tube at stern.

COASTAL TRANSPORTS

◆ 8 Ariel class

Y 604 ARIEL (27-4-63)	Y 696 ALPHÉE (10-6-69)	Y 613 FAUNE (8-9-71)
Y 661 KORRIGAN (6-3-64)	Y 741 ELFE (14-4-70)	Y 622 DRYADE (1973)
	Y 700 NEREIDE (17-2-77)	Y 701 ONDINE (1977)

Alphée   1976

COASTAL TRANSPORTS (*continued*)

Bldr: Soc. Française de Constr. Navale (formerly Franco-Belges), except D.C.A.N., Brest, for *Nereide* and *Ondine*. All based at Brest, except *Ariel*, at Toulon.

D: 195 tons (225 fl) **S:** 15 kts **Dim:** 40.5 × 7.45 × 3.3
Man: 9 men, 400 passengers (250 seated)
M: 2 MGO (1,640 hp) or Poyaud (1,730 hp) diesels; 2 props

◆ 3 Merlin class

Y 735 MERLIN   Y 736 MÉLUSINE   Y 671 MORGANE

Bldrs: Y-735 and Y-736: C.N. Franco-Belges, 1967-68; Y-671: A. du Mourillon

Mélusine   1968

D: 170 tons **S:** 11 kts **Dim:** 31.5 × 7.06 × 2.4
M: MGO diesels; 2 props; 960 hp **Man:** 400 passengers

Y 664 LUTIN

D: 68 tons **S:** 10 kts **M:** 400 hp

REMARKS: Ex-small craft *Georges Clemenceau*, purchased in 1965. Assigned to the Sonar School, Toulon.

Y 710 SYLPHE Bldr: C.N. Franco-Belges, 1959-60

Sylphe   1976

D: 142 tons (189 fl) **Dim:** 38.5 (36.75 pp) × 6.9 × 2.5
S: 12 kts **Man:** 9 men **M:** 1 MGO diesel; 1 prop; 425 hp

REMARK: Operates from Toulon.

SEAGOING TUGS

NOTE: After the affair of the *Amoco Cadiz*, the French government leased for three years the commercial salvage tug *Abeille Normandie*, built by Beliard & Murdoch, Ostend. Characteristics include:

D: 3,500 tons **S:** 16 kts **Dim:** 67.0 × 14.0 × 6.5
M: 2 diesels; 2 controllable-pitch props; 9,000 hp; 2 550-hp bow thrusters

REMARKS: Bollard-pull capacity: 120 tons. The civilian-manned tug is based at Brest under the control of the Maritime Prefect of the Second Region.

◆ 3 Tenace class

A 664 MALABAR—Bldr: Oelkers, Hamburg L: 16-4-75; in serv: 3-2-76
A 669 TENACE—Bldr: Oelkers, Hamburg, 1971-73
A 674 CENTAURE—Bldr: de la Rochelle-Pallice, 1972-74

Tenace   ECPA, 1975

Malabar   J.-C. Bellonne, 1976

SEAGOING TUGS (*continued*)

Centaure   J.-C. Bellonne, 1975

D: 970 tons (1,440 fl)   **S:** 13.5 kts   **Dim:** 51.0 × 11.5 × 5.7
Man: 4 officers, 30 petty officers, 24 men   **Range:** 9,500/13
M: 2 diesels; 1 prop; 4,600 hp   **Fuel:** 500 tons

REMARKS: Bollard-pull capacity: 60 tons. Living quarters air-conditioned. All based at Brest.

A 666 ÉLEPHANT (ex-*Bar*)

D: 880 tons (1,150 fl)   **S:** 11 kts   **Dim:** 51.0 × 9.4 × 5.32
M: . . .; 1 prop; 2,000 hp   **Man:** 1 officer, 13 petty officers, 27 men

◆ 2 ex-U.S. Sotoyomo class

A 660 HIPPOPOTAME (ex-*Utrecht*)   A 668 RHINOCÉROS (ex-ATA-226)

Rhinocéros   J.-C. Bellonne, 1976

Man: 1 officer, 12 petty officers, 26 men
M: 2 GM 12-278A diesels, electric drive: 1 prop; 1,850 hp

REMARKS: Both built by Levingston Brothers, Texas, but they differ slightly. Bollard-pull capacity: 20 tons. A-668 was launched 5-45 and sold to France 7-47. A-660 was sold commercially after the war and bought by France in 1964. A-668 is based at Toulon, A-660 in Tahiti.

COASTAL TUGS

◆ 12 Actif class

A 693 ACHARNE	A 667 HERCULE	A 685 ROBUSTE
A 686 ACTIF	A 687 LABORIEUX	A 692 TRAVAILLEUR
A 706 COURAGEUX	A 671 LE FORT	A 672 UTILE
A 694 EFFICACE	A 673 LUTTEUR	A 688 VALEUREUX

Lutteur   DCAN, 1974

D: 230 tons (300 fl)   **S:** 11.8 kts   **Dim:** 28.3 (25.3 pp) × 7.9 × 4.3
M: 1 MGO ASHR diesel; 1,100 to 1,450 hp   **Range:** 2,400/11

REMARKS: Bollard-pull capacity: 17 tons. Four completed in 1960, four 1962-63, two in late 1960s, and A-693 and A-694 in 1974.

◆ 2 of 200 tons (fl) and 11 kts

Y 608 BAMBOU   Y 652 HAUR BARR

HARBOR TUGS

NOTE: Two-letter contractions of names used on bows instead of official pendant numbers.

◆ 2 Bonite class

Y 634 ROUGET   Y 630 BONITE

D: 93 tons (fl)   **S:** 11 kts   **M:** 380 hp

REMARK: Bollard-pull capacity: 7 tons. Y-634 built in 1974, Y-630 in 1975.

HARBOR TUGS (continued)

Bonite

J.-C. Bellonne, 1975

◆ 29 Acajou class

Y 601 Acajou	Y 618 Érable	Y 668 Mélèze	Y 689 Pin
Y 607 Balsa	Y 635 Equeurdreville	Y 669 Merisier	Y 695 Platane
Y 612 Bouleau	Y 644 Frêne	Y 739 Noyer	Y 720 Santal
Y 623 Charme	Y 654 Hêtre	Y 682 Okoumé	Y 708 Saule
Y 620 Chataigner	Y 655 Hevea	Y 719 Olivier	Y 704 Sycomore
Y 624 Chêne	Y 663 Latanier	Y 686 Palétuvier	
Y 629 Cormier	Y 666 Manguier	Y 740 Papayer	
Y 717 Ébène	Y 638 Marronier	Y 688 Peuplier	

Mélèze

1975

D: 105 tons (fl)   **S:** 11 kts   **Dim:** 21.0 × 6.9 × 3.2
M: 1 diesel; 700 hp

REMARK: Bollard-pull capacity: 10 tons.

◆ 29 Oiseau class

Y 602 Aigrette	Y 723 Engoulevent	Y 725 Marabout	Y 691 Pinson
Y 720 Alouette	Y 687 Fauvette	Y 675 Martin Pêcheur	Y 694 Pivert
Y 730 Ara	Y 748 Gelinotte	Y 636 Martinet	Y 724 Sarcelle
Y 611 Bengali	Y 648 Goeland	Y 670 Merle	Y 726 Toucan
Y 625 Cigogne	Y 728 Grand Duc	Y 621 Mésange	Y 722 Vanneau
Y 628 Colibri	Y 653 Héron	Y 673 Moineau	
Y 632 Cygne	Y 747 Loriot	Y 617 Mouette	
Y 729 Eider	Y 727 Macreuse	Y 687 Passereau	

Bengali

DCAN, 1975

D: 200 tons (fl)   **S:** 9 kts   **Dim:** 18.4 × 5.7 × 2.5
M: 1 Poyaud diesel; 250 hp   **Range:** 1,700/9

REMARKS: Bollard-pull capacity: 3.5 tons. *Ibis* (Y-658) on loan to Senegal. *Pingoun* (Y-690) and *Tourterelle* (X-643) stricken.

Y 680 Murene

D: 33 tons   **S:** 7 kts   **M:** 1 diesel; 120 hp

TRAINING CRAFT

◆ 2 ex-trawlers

A 772 Engageante (ex-*Cayolle*)   A 774 Vigilante (ex-*Iseran*)

D: 286 tons fl (156 grt)   **S:** 11 kts   **Dim:** 30.0 (25.0 pp) × 6.7 × 3.8 (aft)
M: 1 Deutz diesel; 1 prop; 560 hp

REMARKS: Built 1964; purchased 1975. Used by petty officers' navigation school. Decca radar.

◆ 2 tenders   Bldr: Bayonne, 1971

Y 706 Chimère   Y 711 Farfadet

D: 100 tons   **S:** 11 kts   **M:** 1 diesel 200 hp

REMARK: Used by the Naval Academy for training in maneuvering. Sail-equipped.

◆ 2 auxiliary barkentines

A 649 L'Étoile
A 650 La Belle Poule

TRAINING CRAFT (*continued*)

La Belle Poule   1974

D: 227 tons (275 fl)   **Dim:** 32.25 × 7.0 × 3.2
M: Sulzer diesel; 125 hp   **S:** 6 kts

REMARKS: Assigned to the Naval Academy. Both built in 1932.

A 653 LA GRANDE HERMINE (ex-*La Route Est Belle*, ex-*Menestrel*)

REMARK: Fourteen-meter yawl built in 1932 and purchased in 1964 for the reserve officers' school.

A 652 MUTIN

  Bldr: Chauffeteau, les Sables, 1927

D: 57 tons   **Dim:** 22.0 × 6.3 × 3.4 (1.5 fwd)
M: 1 Deutz diesel; 120 hp   **Sails:** 240 m²

REMARK: Assigned to the Dundee annex of the Seamanship School.

MISCELLANEOUS SERVICE CRAFT

◆ **2 launches**

A 702 GIRELLE

  D: . . .   **S:** . . .   **M:** . . .

Girelle   ECPA, 1976

A 714 TOURMALINE   Bldr: C.M.N. Cherbourg

  D: 37 tons (45 fl)   **S:** 15 kts   **Dim:** 26.8 × 4.97 × 1.53
  M: 2 diesels; 2 props; 480 hp

Tourmaline   1974

◆ **6 fireboats**

Y 745 AIGUIÈRE   Y 618 CASCADE   Y 746 EMBRUN
Y 645 GAVE   Y 646 GEYSER   Y 684 OUED

  D: 70 tons (85 fl)   **S:** 11.3 kts   **Dim:** 23.8 × 5.3 × 1.7
  M: 2 Poyaud 6 PZM diesels; 2 props; 405 hp

◆ **1 degaussing (deperming) tender**

Y 732

Y-732   DCAN, 1970

FRANCE (*continued*)

MISCELLANEOUS SERVICE CRAFT (*continued*)

D: 260 tons   **S:** 10 kts   **Dim:** 38.2 × 4.3 × 2.4
M: 1 diesel; 1 prop; 375 hp

◆ **1 radiological surveillance ship**

Y 743 PALANGRIN

    D: 44 tons   **M:** 1/220-hp diesel

REMARK: Commissioned in 1969.

Palangrin   1969

◆ **1 self-propelled mooring lighter**

Y 698 CALMAR

    D: 129 tons   **S:** 6 kts   **Dim:** . . . × . . . × . . .
    M: 1 diesel; 1 prop; 175 hp

◆ **16 motor lighters, converted from landing craft**

CHA 1, 6, 7, 8, 9, 13, 14, 15, 16, 17, 18, 19, 22, 23, 24, 25

CHA-13   G. Arra, 1972

    D: 20 tons   **S:** 7 kts   **M:** 1 diesel; 100 hp (CHA-1, CHA-6: 115 hp)

◆ **12 water lighters**

NOS. 1 to 12

    D: . . .   **S:** 9 kts   **Dim:** . . . × . . . × . . .   **M:** 1 diesel; 420 hp

REMARKS: Nos. 5 and 6 in Tahiti, No. 2 at Brest, Nos. 1 and 11 at Toulon, No. 12 at Lorient, the others at the CEP (Centre d'Experimentation Pacifique).

◆ **4 water lighters for SSBNs**

    D: Over 44 tons   **S:** 6 kts   **Dim:** . . . × . . . × . . .
    M: 1 diesel; 480 hp

GABON

Republic of

MERCHANT MARINE (1978):   15 ships — 77,520 grt
                                 (tankers: 2 ships — 74,471 grt)

PATROL BOATS

◆ **1 wooden-hulled**   Bldr: de l'Esterel, Cannes

PRESIDENT EL HADJ OMAR BONGO

President El Hadj Omar Bongo   de l'Esterel, 1977

PATROL BOATS (*continued*)

D: 155 tons (fl)   **S:** 40 kts   **Dim:** 42.0 × 7.8 × 1.9
A: 4/SS-12 missiles – 1/40-mm Bofors AA – 1/20-mm AA
Man: 25 men   **Electron Equipt:** Radar: Decca RM 1226
Range: 1,000/18
M: 3 MTU 16V538TB91 diesels; 2 props, 10,500 hp

REMARK: In service 1977.

◆ **4 N'Golo class** Bldr: Intermarine, Sarzana, Italy

GC 04	N'GOLO	In serv. 1976	GC . . .	N . . .	In serv. 1977
GC . . .	N . . .	In serv. 1977	GC . . .	N . . .	In serv. 1977

N'Golo   1976

D: 65 tons (88 fl)   **S:** 43 kts   **Dim:** 27.3 × 6.8 × 2.1
A: 1/40-mm AA – 2/20-mm AA   **Man:** 13 men
M: 2 MTU diesels; 2 props, 7,000 hp

◆ **1 U.S. design** Bldr: Swiftships, Morgan City

GC 03 N'GUENE

D: 118 tons (fl)   **S:** 35 kts   **Dim:** 32.17 (29.18 pp) × 2.3 (props)
A: 2/40-mm AA (I × 2) – 2/20-mm AA (I × 2) – 2/12.7-mm machine guns
Electron Equipt: Radar: Decca RM 916   **Man:** 21 men   **Range:** 825/25
M: 3 GM 16V 149TE diesels; 3 props; 4,800 hp   **Electric:** 80 kw

REMARKS: In service 2-76. Aluminum.

GC 02 COLONEL DJOUÉ DABANY (ex-*President Albert Bernard Bongo*)

Bldr: de l'Esterel

D: 80 tons   **S:** 30 kts   **Dim:** 32.0 × 5.8 × 1.5
A: 2/20-mm   **Man:** 17 men   **M:** 2 MTU diesels; 2,700 hp

REMARKS: In service 3-72. Wooden hull treated with résorcine (an anti-boring-worm product).

Colonel Djoué Dabany   de l'Esterel, 1972

PATROL CRAFT

MANGA Bldr: Dakar Dockyard, 1978

D: 152 tons (fl)   **S:** 9 kts   **Dim:** 24.0 × 6.4 × 1.3
Man: 6 men   **Range:** 600/5   **M:** 2 diesels; 2 props; . . . hp

		Bldr	Laid down	L	In serv.
GC 01	PRESIDENT LÉON M'BA	Gabon	1967	6-1-68	1968

President Léon M'Ba   1968

D: 85 tons   **S:** 12.5 kts   **Dim:** 28.0 × 6.2 × 1.54
A: 1/75-mm recoilless rifle – 1/12.7-mm machine gun   **Range:** 1,000/12
Man: 1 officer, 3 petty officers, 12 men   **M:** Diesel; 1 prop

◆ **2 harbor patrol craft** Bldr: La Manche, Dieppe

D: . . .   **S:** 10 kts   **Dim:** 12.4 × 3.7 × .9
M: 1 Baudouin DNP-5 diesel; 171 hp

REMARK: Launched 9-77.

GABON (*continued*)

PATROL CRAFT (*continued*)

◆ **7 small Arcoa patrol craft**   **S:** 15 to 25 kts

◆ **2 SRN-6 hovercraft**   Delivered 1977

◆ **1 buoy tender**

N'GOMBE   Bldr: La Manche, Dieppe

   D: . . .   **S:** 10 kts   **Dim:** 17.0 × 4.5 × 1.3
   M: 1 Baudouin DNP-6 diesel; 215 hp

REMARK: Launched 9-77.

◆ **1 transport**

GC . . .   MANGA   Bldr: Dakar SY, 1976

   D: 152 tons   **S:** 9 kts   **Dim:** 24.0 × 6.4 × 1.3
   A: 2/12.7-mm machine guns   **Electron Equipt:** Radar: Decca 101
   M: 2 Poyaud V8-520 diesels; 2 props; 480 hp

THE GAMBIA

MERCHANT MARINE (1978): 8 ships – 4,224 grt

PATROL CRAFT

◆ **3 Tracker class**   Bldr: Fairey Marine, G. B.

P 2 JATO   P 3 CHALLENGE   P 4 CHAMPION

   D: 31.5 tons (fl)   **S:** 29 kts   **Dim:** 19.25 × 4.98 × 1.45
   A: 1/20-mm AA – 2/7.62-mm machine guns   **Man:** 11 men
   Range: 650/20
   M: 2 GM 12V-71 TI diesels; 2 props; 990 hp

REMARK: In service 1977-78.

◆ **1 Lance class**   Bldr: Fairey Marine, G. B., 1976

P 1 SEA DOG

   D: 17 tons (fl)   **S:** 24 kts   **Dim:** 14.81 × 4.76 × 1.3
   A: 1/20-mm AA – 3/7.62-mm machine guns (I × 3)
   Man: 6 men plus 10-man boarding party   **Range:** 500/15
   M: 2 GM 8V-71 TI diesels; 2 props; 850 hp

◆ **1 Keith Nelson 75-foot class**   Bldr: Camper & Nicholson, G.B., 1974

MANSA KILA IV

   D: 70 tons (fl)   **S:** 24.5 kts   **Dim:** 22.9 × 6.0 × 1.6
   A: 2/20-mm AA (I × 2)   **Man:** 11 men   **Range:** 800/20
   M: 2 diesels; 2 props; 1,840 hp

GERMANY

Democratic Republic of

PERSONNEL: 15,500 men

MERCHANT MARINE (1977): 452 ships – 1,539,994 grt
(tankers: 17 ships – 275,651 grt)

NAVAL AVIATION: About 15 Soviet MI-4 Hound helicopters used for ASW and assault operations.

WEAPONS AND SYSTEMS: Nearly all of Soviet design. *See* U.S.S.R. section for details.

WARSHIPS IN SERVICE OR UNDER CONSTRUCTION AS OF 1 OCTOBER 1979

	L	Tons	Main armament
◆ **2 frigates**	1977-78	1,800	1/SA-N-4, 4/76-mm,
2 KONI			4/30-mm, 2 ASW RL
◆ **12 corvettes**			
12 HAI-III	1962-70	350	4/30-mm AA, 4 ASW RL
◆ **60 missile and torpedo boats**			
15 OSA-I	1964-	175	4 Styx systems, 4/30- mm AA
15 SHERSHEN	1966-	150	4/30-mm AA, 4/533-mm TT
30 LIBELLE	1975-	30	2/533-mm TT
◆ **50 minesweepers**			
50 KONDOR I, II	1968-71	225/310	2 or 6/25-mm AA

FRIGATES

◆ **2 Soviet Koni class**   Bldr: U.S.S.R.

141 ROSTOCK   142 BERLIN

   D: 1,800 tons (2,000 fl)   **S:** 30 kts   **Dim:** 95.0 × 11.3 × 3.8
   A: SA-N-4 SAM (II × 1) – 4/76-mm DP (II × 2) – 4/30-mm AA (II × 2) – 2/MBU-2500A – mines – 2 depth-charge racks

FRIGATES (*continued*)

Rostock – on delivery voyage, wearing old number   1978

    Electron Equipt: Radars: 1/Strut Curve, 1/Don 2, 1/Pop Group,
                                1/Hawk Screech, 1/Drum Tilt
    M: CODAG: 1 gas turbine; 2 diesels; 2 props; 30,000 hp
REMARK: Transferred 1978-79.

CORVETTES

◆ 12 Hai III class

Possible names: BAD DOBERAN, BÜTZOW, DIRNA, GADEBUSCH, GREVESMÜHLEN, LUD-WIGSLUST, LÜBZ, PERLEBERG, RIBNITZ-DAMGARTEN, STERNBERG, TETEROW, WISMAR

    Bldr: Peenewerft, Wolgast, 1962-70

Hai-III class   1976

    D: 350 tons (400 fl)   **S:**   32 kts   **Dim:**   51.0 × 6.2 × 2.4
    A: 4/30-mm (II × 2) – 4/MBU-1800 ASW rocket launchers – depth-charge racks –
         mines   **Man:**   28 men   **Range:**   1,000/18
    Electron Equipt: Radars: 1/Pot Head, 1/Drum Tilt
                         Sonar: 1/Tamir 11

    M: CODAG propulsion system; 1 gas turbine × 10,000 hp; 2 diesels, 4,800 hp each;
         3 props; 19,600 hp
REMARK: Hull numbers, 400 series.

GUIDED-MISSILE AND TORPEDO PATROL BOATS

◆ 15 Soviet Osa-I-class missile boats

Possible names: ALBERT GAST, ALAIN KÖBIS, A. SAEFKOW, FRIEDRICH SCHULZE, FRITZ GAST, KARL MESEBERG, MAX REICHPIETSCH, PAUL WIEKZOREK, RICHARD SORGE, RUDOLF AUGUST LÜTTGENS, PAUL EISENSCHNEIDE, PAUL ENGLEHOFER SCHULZ, WALTER KRÄMER, N . . .   N . . .

    Bldr: U.S.S.R., 1964

East German Osa-I class   1970

    D: 175 tons (205 fl)   **S:**   35 kts   **Dim:**   39.0 × 7.6 × 1.8
    A: 4/Styx (SS-N-2) systems – 4/30-mm AA (II × 2)
    Electron Equipt: Radars: 1/Square Tie, 1/Drum Tilt
    M: 3 M503A diesels; 3 props; 12,000 hp

REMARK: Hull numbers, 700 series.

◆ 15 Soviet Shershen-class torpedo boats

    Bldr: U.S.S.R., since 1966

East German Shershen class   1976

GUIDED-MISSILE AND TORPEDO PATROL BOATS (*continued*)

EDGAR ANDRÉ, WILLI BÄNSCH, BERNHARD BÄSTLEIN, ARTHUR BECKER, FRITZ BEHN, RUDOLF BREITSCHEID, ERNST GRUBE, ARVID HARNACK, HEINZ KAPELLE, FRITZ HECKERT, ADAM KUCKHOFF, BRUNO KÜHN, ERNST SCHNELLER, N . . . N . . .

D: 150 tons (fl) **S:** 45 kts **Dim:** 34 × 7.2 × 1.5
A: 4/533-mm torpedoes (2 on each side) — 4/30-mm AA (II × 2)
Electron Equipt: Radars: 1/Pot Drum, 1/Drum Tilt
M: 3 M503A diesels; 3 props; 12,000 hp

REMARK: Hull numbers, 800 series.

◆ **26 Libelle-class light torpedo boats**

Libelle class   1976

D: 30 tons (fl) **S:** 50 kts **Dim:** 19.6 × 4.5 × 2.0
A: 2/533-mm TT — 2/33-mm AA (II × 1)
M: 3 diesels; 3 props; 3,600 hp

REMARKS: Hull numbers, 900 series. Completed since 1975. Can quickly convert to commando/frogman carriers. Torpedoes discharged over stern; short tubes on deck may be for wire-guidance system.

Libelle class   1975

PATROL CRAFT

◆ **19 Bremse class**

Bremse class

D: 25 tons **S:** 14 kts **Dim:** 23.0 × 5.0 × 1.1
A: Small arms **M:** 2 diesels; 2 props; 600 hp

REMARKS: Date from 1971. Also known as KB-123 class. Operated by the Border Guard on rivers and inland waterways. The Border Guard also has a number of smaller craft.

◆ **7 "fishing cutter" class**

G 91 to G 97

REMARK: Wooden-hulled former fishing boats operated by the Border Guard.

"Fishing cutter" class

MINE WARFARE SHIPS

◆ **28 Kondor-II-class inshore minesweepers**

Bldr: Peenewerft, Wolgast

ALTENBURG, BERNAU, BITTERFELD, BOLTENHAGEN, DESSAU, EILENBURG, FREIBERG, GENTHIN, GREIZ, GUBEN, KAMENZ, KLÜTZ, KYRITZ, MEININGEN, NEURUPPIN, POESSNICK, RATHENOW, RIESA, ROBEL, ROSSLAU, SCHOENEBECK, STRALSUND, STRASBURG, TANGERHÜTTE, TIMMENDORF, TORGAU, WITTSTOCK, ZERBST

Kondor-II class   1976

Kondor-II class — training squadron hull number   1976

   D: 310 tons (fl)   **S:**   17 kts   **Dim:**   55.0 × 7.0 × 2.4
   A: 6/25-mm AA (II × 3) — mines
   M: 2 M-40 diesels; 2 controllable-pitch props; 5,000 hp

REMARKS: Date from 1971; hull numbers, 300 series. One additional unit, V-32, is a trials craft.

◆ **22 Kondor-I-class inshore minesweepers**

Bldr: Peenewerft, Wolgast, 1968-70

AHRENSHOOP, ANKLAM, BERGEN, DEMMIN, EISLEBEN, GRAAL-MÜRITZ, GREIFSWALD, HETTSTED, KUHLUNGSBORN, MEISSEN, NEUSTRELITZ, PRITZWALK, PRENZLAU, PREROW, RERIK, STENDAL, UECKERMÜNDE, VITTE, WEISSWASSER, WOLGAST, ZINGST, ZWICKAU

Kondor-I class   1976

   D: 225 tons (275 fl)   **S:**   17 kts   **Dim:**   52.0 × 7.0 × 2.4
   A: 2/25-mm AA (II × 1) — mines
   M: 2 M-40 diesels; 2 controllable-pitch props; 5,000 hp

REMARKS: Eighteen units, G-11 to G-16, G-21 to G-26, and G-41 to G-46, attached to Border Guard as patrol boats. Two have been converted as torpedo-recovery craft; two others, the *Komet* and *Meteor*, altered as intelligence-collectors; another is the state yacht *Ostseeland;* V-31 is a trials craft; the *Ernst Thaelmann* was converted to a youth-training ship in 1977.

AMPHIBIOUS SHIPS AND CRAFT

◆ **10 Frosch-class tank landing ships**   Bldr: Peenewerft, Wolgast, 1976-79

Possible names: COTTBUS, HOYERSWERDA, LÜBBEN, NEUBRANDENBERG, SCHWERIN, N . . .   N . . .   N . . .   N . . .   N . . .

Frosch class   1978

AMPHIBIOUS SHIPS AND CRAFT (*continued*)

Frosch class   1978

   D: 2,000 tons (fl)   **S:** 18 kts   **Dim:** 98.0 × 12.5 × . . .
   A: 4/57-mm AA (II × 2) – 4/30-mm AA (II × 2) – 2/barrage rocket launchers – mines
   Electron Equipt: Radars: 1/Strut Curve, 1/Muff Cob, 1/German TSR 333
                               (navigational)
   M: 2 diesels; 2 props; . . . hp

REMARKS: Cargo capacity 400 to 600 tons. Similar in general form to new Soviet Ropucha class, but smaller and with a blunter bow, heavier armament, etc. Have a large number of communications antennas, possibly indicating an ability to act as command ships in amphibious operations. Two rocket launchers of the type carried by the Soviet ship *Ivan Rogov* are being added forward of the bridge.

◆ **2 Robbe class**   **Bldr:** Peenewerft, Wolgast

N . . .   N . . .

Robbe class

   D: 500 tons (1,100 fl)   **S:** 13/12 kts   **Dim:** 64.0 × 12.0 × 1.5 (2.2 aft)
   A: 2/57-mm AA (II × 1) – 4/25-mm AA (II × 2) – mines   **Range:** 2,000 (econ.)
   M: 2 diesels; 2 props; 5,000 hp

REMARKS: Utility load, 500 tons. Being rapidly replaced by the Frosch class; originally six were in service. The Labo-100-class landing craft have been discarded.

INTELLIGENCE-GATHERING VESSELS

◆ **2 modified Kondor-I class**

KOMET   METEOR

Komet   1974

REMARKS: No armament. Collection antennas added, otherwise as for Kondor-I-class minesweepers.

◆ **1 Soviet Okean-class trawler**

HYDROGRAPH

Hydrograph   1976

   D: 700 tons (fl)   **S:** 10 kts   **Dim:** 50.8 × 8.8 × 3.4
   Man: 32 men   **Range:** 7,900/11   **M:** 1 diesel; 540 hp

REMARKS: Dates from 1958. Equipped with Sigint collection devices.

HYDROGRAPHIC SURVEY SHIPS

NOTE: All survey ships, buoy tenders, and the cable tender *Dornbusch* are operated under SHD, the Naval Hydrographic Service, and are civilian-manned.

◆ **1 modified Kondor-II class**

KARL FRIEDRICH GAUSS

REMARKS: Since 1978. No armament. Data as for Kondor-II-class minesweepers. Has more extensive superstructure, twin kingposts aft for handling boats, buoys, etc.

◆ **1 Soviet Kamenka class**   Bldr: Szczecin SY, Poland, 1972

BUK

    D: 703 tons (fl)   **S:** 13.7 kts   **Dim:** 53.5 × 9.1 × 2.6
    M: 2 Zgoda diesels; 2 props; 1,765 hp   **Range:** 4,000/10

◆ **3 Arkona class, also buoy tenders**

ARKONA   DARSSER ORT   STUBBENKAMMER

    D: 55 tons   **S:** 10 kts   **M:** Diesel

REMARK: Built 1965-70.

◆ **1 cable and buoy tender**

DORNBUSCH

    D: 700 tons (fl)

REMARK: Bow cable sheaves, large crane, superstructure aft.

◆ **8 buoy tenders (1971-72)**

BREITLING, ESPER ORT, GOLWITZ, GRASS ORT, LANDTIEFF, PALMER ORT, RAMZOW, ROSEN ORT

    D: 158 tons (fl)   **S:** 11.5 kts   **Dim:** 29.6 × 6.2 × 1.9
    M: 1 diesel; 1 prop; 580 hp

REMARK: Built 1971-72.

EXPERIMENTAL SHIPS   V = *Versuch* (Research)

◆ **1 ex-civilian research ship**

V 71   1976

V 71 (ex-*Meteor*)

REMARK: Built as a fishing boat.

◆ **1 ex-corvette, Hai-II class (1964)**

V 81 PARCHIM

Parchim   1976

REMARK: Used in minesweeping research.

◆ **1 Kondor-II-class minesweeper**

V 32

◆ **1 Kondor-I-class minesweeper**

V 31

OILERS

◆ **1 Soviet Baskunchak class**

C 27 USEDOM

Usedom

OILERS (*continued*)

D: 2,500 tons **S:** 13 kts **Dim:** 70.0 × 8.9 × 3.8
M: 1 diesel; . . . hp

◆ 3 Hiddensee class

C 37 (ex-*Hiddensee*), C 76 (ex-*Riems*), C . . . (ex-*Poel*)

Bldr: Peenewerft, Wolgast, 1960-61

Hiddensee class — before being armed

D: 1,450 tons (fl) **S:** 12 kts **Dim:** 53.7 × 9.0 × 4.5
A: 4/25-mm (II × 2) **Man:** 26 men
M: 2 diesels; 1,400 hp **Cargo:** 650 tons

REMARKS: Laid down during World War II. *Sahel* in French Navy is a sister.

GENERAL SUPPORT SHIPS

◆ 3 Kuemo class

RUDEN VILM RÜGEN

Bldr: Matthias Thiesen Werft, Wismar, 1955-57

Ruden 1976

D: 585 tons (fl) **S:** 9 kts **Dim:** 36.0 × 7.3 × 2.7
M: 1 diesel; 1 prop; 300 hp

REMARK: *Ruden* is a cargo ship, *Vilm* is an oiler, and *Rügen* is a torpedo trials ship.

TRAINING SHIP S = *Schulschiff* (Schoolship)

◆ 1 Polish Wodnik class Bldr: Gdansk SY

S 61 WILHELM PIECK

Wilhelm Pieck 1976

D: 2,000 tons (fl) **S:** 17 kts **Dim:** 73.0 × 12.0 × 4.0
A: 4/30-mm AA (II × 2) − 4/25-mm AA (II × 2)
Electron Equipt: Radars: 2/TSR 333, 1/Drum Tilt
M: 2 Zgoda diesels; 2 props; 3,600 hp **Electric:** 530 kw

REMARKS: In service 6-7-76. Sister to *Wodnik* and *Gryf* in Polish Navy and *Oka* and *Luga* in Soviet Navy. Design developed from Soviet Moma-class surveying ships.

NOTE: In addition to the *Wilhelm Pieck*, the following are used for training (data earlier): 3 Osa-I-class missile boats, 3 Shershen-class torpedo boats, 3 Kondor-II-class minesweepers, and 3 Kondor-I-class minesweepers. All have S-series hull numbers.

SALVAGE SHIP

◆ 1 Polish Piast class Bldr: Gdansk SY, 1977

A 46 OTTO VON GUERICKE

D: 1,560 tons (1,732 fl) **S:** 16.5 kts **Dim:** 73.2 × 10.0 × 4.0
M: 2 Zgoda GTD 48 diesels; 2 props; 3,800 hp **Range:** 3,000/12

REMARKS: Sister to Polish *Piast* and *Lech*. Can mount 8/25-mm AA (II × 4). Has diving bell. Build on Soviet Moma-class survey ship hull and propulsion plant.

DIVING TENDER

◆ 1 converted Havel-class fishing trawler

U 33 HUGO ECKENER

GERMANY – DEMOCRATIC REPUBLIC (*continued*)

DIVING TENDER (*continued*)

Hugo Eckener   1977

D:	450 tons (fl)	**S:** 10.5 kts	**Dim:** 37.7 (33.0 pp) × 8.2 × 3.0	
M:	1 type 8 NVD36A diesel; 578 hp	**Electric:** 280 kw		

REMARKS: Built 1971. Stern-haul trawler with equipment for mine-clearance divers.

VARIOUS SHIPS

◆ **2 torpedo retriever/target ships**

B 73   B 74

B 74   1976

REMARKS: Converted Kondor-I-class minesweepers, which they basically resemble. No armament. Ramp at stern for torpedo-recovery. Radar reflector array on mast, below TSR-333 radar.

◆ **1 yacht**

OSTSEELAND

REMARKS: Kondor-I minesweeper hull; large, rakish superstructure. Used for head of state.

◆ **several small diving tenders**

◆ **up to 11 Jugend-class barracks barges**

◆ **1 small cable tender**

FREESENDORF   Built 1963

◆ **1 seagoing tug (also salvage tug)**

A 14

    D: 800 tons   **S:** 12 kts

◆ **11 harbor tugs**

◆ **5 Gustav Koenigs-class harbor fuel lighters**   Bldr: VEB, Rosslau/Elbe

SOCIETY FOR SPORTS AND MECHANICS

The Naval College of this paramilitary youth organization maintains a number of craft for training, the largest of which is the *Ernst Thaelmann*.

◆ **1 converted Kondor-I-class minesweeper**

ERNST THAELMANN

REMARKS: In service 19-8-77. Superstructure enlarged; carries 10 crew and 28 trainees.

GERMANY

Federal Republic of

PERSONNEL: approx. 35,000 men

MERCHANT MARINE (1978):   1,999 ships – 9,776,667 grt
                                  (tankers: 121 ships – 3,418,607 grt)

SHIPS IN SERVICE, UNDER CONSTRUCTION, OR ORDERED AS OF 1 JANUARY 1980

	L	Tons	Main armament
◆ **24 submarines**			
18 TYPE 206	1972-74	450	8/533-mm TT
6 TYPE 205	1961-68	370	8/533-mm TT

SHIPS IN SERVICE, UNDER CONSTRUCTION, OR ORDERED (*continued*)

◆ 11 destroyers

3 LÜTJENS	1967-69	3,370	1/Tartar system, 2/127-mm DP, 1/Asroc
4 HAMBURG	1960-63	3,400	4/MM38, 3/100-mm, 8/40-mm AA, 4/ASW TT
4 Z	1942-43	2,050	4/127-mm DP, 6/76-mm AA, 5/533-mm TT

◆ 14 frigates

8 TYPE 122	1980-83	2,900	8/Harpoon, 1/Sea Sparrow, 2/ ASMD, 1/76-mm, 4/ASW TT, 2/helicopters
6 KÖLN	1958-62	1,750	2/100-mm DP, 6/40-mm AA, 2/ASW RL, 4/ASW TT

◆ 5 corvettes

5 THETIS	1960-62	604	2/40-mm AA, 1/ASW RL, 4/ASW TT

◆ 40 guided-missile boats

10 TYPE 143A	1981-83	300	4/MM 38, 1/76-mm AA, 1/RAM system, mines
10 TYPE 143	1973-76	295	4/MM38, 2/76-mm AA, 2/533-mm TT
20 TYPE 148	1972-75	234	4/MM38, 1/76-mm DP, 1/40-mm AA

◆ 10 torpedo boats

10 TYPE 142	1961-63	160	2/40-mm AA, 2/533-mm TT

◆ 79 minesweepers/minehunters

Bréguet Atlantic 1973

NAVAL AVIATION:

2 groups of Starfighter (F-104G) all-weather interceptor attack and reconnaissance airplanes (110-120 planes). Characteristics are:

Length: 16.61 meters
Wingspan: 6.68 meters
Takeoff weight: 9.900 kg
Motor: 1 GE S79 SE 11A turbojet, 7,170 kg thrust
Max. speed: Mach 2
Altitude: 50,000 feet
Range: 250 to 600 nautical miles, depending on equipment
Weapons: 4,000 kg maximum (bombs, rockets, Bullpup, etc.)

1 squadron of 20 Bréguet Atlantic-1150 aircraft, 5 of which have been modified for electronic warfare.

1 squadron of 22 Mk 41 Sea King helicopters for search and rescue operations.

On 7-4-76 the German government decided to begin construction of 112 MRCA Tornado variable-geometry fighter-bombers for the Navy. The first entered service in late 1979. Characteristics are:

Length: 16.70 meters
Wingspan: 13.90 meters max./8.60 meters min.
Maximum takeoff weight: 24,500 kg.
Maximum speed: Mach 2.2

Westland/Brequet Sea Lynx WG-13 helicopters have been ordered for the new Type 122 frigates.

WEAPONS AND SYSTEMS

With few exceptions, West German ships have weapons and systems of foreign navies.

(A) MISSILES

◆ Surface-to-air

Standard Tartar SM-1MR on board the 3 *Lütjens*-class destroyers.

◆ Surface-to-surface

MM38 Exocet on board *Hamburg*-class destroyers and Types 143 and 148 guided-missile patrol boats.

(B) GUNS

Automatic 127-mm U.S. Mk 42 mod. 10 on Lütjens-class destroyers *Köln*-class frigates, and 9 *Rhein*-class tenders
OTO Melara compact 76-mm guns on board Types 143 and 148 guided-missile patrol boats
40-mm (70-caliber) Bofors, in single or twin mounts
40-mm/70 Breda
20-mm Oerlikon

(C) ANTISUBMARINE WARFARE

◆ Rocket launchers

Quadruple 375-mm Bofors, similar to French models automatically loaded in a vertical position

◆ Torpedoes

U.S. Mk 37 on submarines
U.S. Mk 44 and Mk 46 on *Lütjens* guided-missile destroyers and Bréguet Atlantic-1150 ASW patrol aircraft

WEAPONS AND SYSTEMS (*continued*)

Wire-guided Seal type (20,000 m range) on Type 143 missile boats, Type 142 torpedo boats, and submarines.

(D) ELECTRONICS

In addition to the U.S. radars mounted in the *Lütjens* DDGs, the West German Navy uses the following Dutch radars (Hollandse Signaal-apparaaten):

LW 02 long-range air search (Band D)
SGR 105 multi-purpose search (Band E-F)
SGR 103 surface search (Band I)
Band X for 100-mm and 40-mm fire control

Type 148 missile patrol boats have a Thomson-CSF Triton target-designation radar and Vega fire-control system with Pollux radar.

Type 143 missile patrol boats carry the AGIS fire-control system combined with Dutch HSA WM 27 M radar. AGIS has two UNIVAC computers, one for fire control and the other for real-time threat-processing. WM 27 has two antennas within its dome, one for search and one for tracking. An automatic data link permits AGIS to relay information with other units of the Type 143, *Lütjens* DDGs, and with future combatants destined for service with the fleet operating from Glücksberg-Meierwik. The *Lütjens*-class destroyers are receiving the Lockheed-built Mk 86 gunfire-control system, with SPQ-9 radar.

SUBMARINES

◆ . . . Type 210

A 750-ton (submerged) submarine to replace the Norwegian *Kobben* (Type 207) and German 205 classes in the 1980s is under study by IKL Lübeck in conjunction with the Norwegian Navy.

◆ 18 Type 206

	L		L		L
S 192 U 13	28-9-71(A)	S 198 U 19	15-12-72(A)	S 174 U 25	23-5-73(A)
S 193 U 14	1-2-72(B)	S 199 U 20	16-1-73(B)	S 175 U 26	20-11-73(B)
S 194 U 15	15-6-72(A)	S 170 U 21	9-3-73(A)	S 176 U 27	21-8-73(A)
S 195 U 16	29-8-72(B)	S 171 U 22	27-3-73 (B)	S 177 U 28	22-1-74(B)
S 196 U 17	10-10-72(A)	S 172 U 23	22-5-73(B)	S 178 U 29	5-11-73(A)
S 197 U 18	31-10-72(B)	S 173 U 24	26-6-73(B)	S 179 U 30	26-3-74(B)

Bldrs: (A) Howaldtswerke-Deutsche Werft, Kiel; (B) Rheinstahl Nordseewerke, Bremen

U-29   1975

D: 450 tons surfaced, 600 submerged   **S:** 17 kts (5 cruising)
Man: 22 men   **Range:** 4,500/5   **Dim:** 48.6 × 4.5 × 4.3
A: 8/533-mm TT—16 wire-guided Seal or Mk 37 torpedoes, or 12 to 18 mines
M: 2 MTU diesels; 750 hp each, 2 500-kw generators; 1 1,500-hp electric motor

U-13   1974

REMARKS: *U-13* to *U-24* authorized in 1969, *U-25* to *U-30* in 2-70. An external "mine-belt" container is being developed for these submarines to permit them to carry a full complement of torpedoes plus 24 mines. Range submerged is 200/5. Three batteries, 92 cells each.

◆ 6 Type 205

	L		L		L
S 180 U 1	17-2-67(A)	S 188 U 9	20-10-66 (A)	S 190 U 11	2-9-68(A)
S 181 U 2	15-7-66(B)	S 189 U 10	20-7-67(A)	S 191 U 12	10-9-68(A)

Bldrs: (A) Howaldtswerke-Deutsche Werft, Kiel; (B) Rheinstahl Nordseewerke, Bremen

U-2   1975

SUBMARINES (*continued*)

D: 370 tons surfaced, 450 submerged   **S:** 17/10 kts
Dim: 43.5 × 4.6 × 3.8   **Man:** 21 men   **A:** 8/533-mm TT
M: 2 MTU 820Db diesels; 2 electric motors; 1 prop; 1,200-1,500 hp

REMARKS: The poor quality of the antimagnetic steel used in the first six of this class caused serious pitting, which made it necessary to rebuild the *U-1* and *U-2* (originally launched 21-10-61 and 25-1-62) with regular steel. Beginning with the *U-9*, laid down in 1964, these submarines were built with a new antimagnetic steel. The *U-1* and *U-2* are now training ships; the *U-3* was stricken in 1968, the *U-4* and *U-8* in 1974, the *U-5* in 1975, and the *U-6* in 1976.

◆ 1 Type XXI

Y 880 WILHELM BAUER (ex-*U-2540*)   Bldr: Blohm & Voss

D: 1,620 tons surfaced, 1,820 submerged   **S:** 12/14 kts
Dim: 76.7 × 6.6 × 6.86   **Man:** 57 men   **Range:** 11,000/12, 490/3 (sub)
A: 4/533-mm TT, forward
M: 2 MTU diesels, electric motors; 2 props; 1,200-1,500 hp

REMARKS: Launched 13-1-45, sank in shallow water that same year. Raised and returned to service as an experimental submarine in 9-60. Officially removed from service for scrapping 26-4-68, but rebuilt and put back in service 15-5-70 as an experimental submarine. Not considered a combatant unit. New propulsion plant, much less powerful than the original, duplicates that of a Type 206.

GUIDED-MISSILE DESTROYERS

◆ 3 Lütjens (Charles F. Adams) class

	Laid down	L	In serv.
D 185 LÜTJENS (ex-DDG-28)	1-3-66	11-8-67	22-3-69
D 186 MÖLDERS (ex-DDG-29)	12-4-66	13-4-68	20-9-69
D 187 ROMMEL (ex-DDG-30)	22-8-67	1-2-69	2-5-70

Bldr: Bath Iron Works

Mölders   G. Arra, 1976

D: 3,370 tons (4,544 fl)   **S:** 35 kts   **Dim:** 134.4 (128.1 pp) × 14.32 × 6.1 (fl)
A: 1/Tartar Mk 13 missile launcher (40 SM-1MR missiles)—2/127-mm Mk 42 DP (I × 2)—6/Mk 32 ASW TT (III × 2)—1/Asroc ASW missile launcher

Electron Equipt: Radars: 1/SPS 40, 1/SPS 10, 1/SPS 52, 1/Kelvin-Hughes 149, 2/SPG 51, 1/SPQ 9
         Sonar: 1/SQS 23   ECM: Satir-1 system—URN/22 TACAN
Man: 21 officers, 319 men   **Range:** 1,600/30, 6,000/14   **Fuel:** 900 tons
M: GT; 2 props; 70,000 hp   **Electric:** 3,000 kw
Boilers: 4 Combustion Engineering, 84 kg/cm² pressure, superheat 500°C

Mölders   J.-C. Bellonne, 1977

REMARKS: Authorized 1964. They differ in several ways, especially in profile, from the *Charles F. Adams* design, on which they are based. Installation of the SM-1MR system and digitalization of some computer equipment has been completed on D-187; the others will complete modernization 1981-82. All being fitted with new Mk 86 gunfire-control system (with SPG 60 and SPQ 9 radar) in place of Mk 68.

◆ 4 Hamburg class (modified Type 101)

	Laid down	L	In serv.
D 181 HAMBURG	29-1-59	26-3-60	23-3-64
D 182 SCHLESWIG-HOLSTEIN	20-8-59	20-8-60	12-10-64
D 183 BAYERN	14-9-60	14-8-62	6-7-65
D 184 HESSEN	15-2-61	4-5-63	8-10-68

Bldr: H. C. Stülcken, Hamburg

Hessen   1976

GUIDED-MISSILE DESTROYERS (continued)

Hessen—with new bridge   1978

Hamburg   J.-C. Bellonne, 1978

D: 3,400 tons (4,400 fl)　**S:** 35 kts　**Man:** 280 men
Dim: 133.7 (128.0 pp) × 13.4 × 5.2 (fl)
A: 4/MM38 Exocet SSM—3/100-mm automatic DP (III × 1)—8/40-mm Breda AA
　　(II × 4)—4/533-mm ASW TT—2/4-barreled 375-mm Bofors ASW rocket launch-
　　ers—can carry 60 to 80 mines
Electron Equipt: Radars: 1/DA-08, 1/SGR 105, 1/SGR 103—3 M45 FC
　　　　　Sonar (German Atlas): 1 medium-frequency, hull—2 Breda
　　　　　SCLAR 20-cell chaff launchers
M: GT; 2 props; 68,000 hp　　**Electric:** 5,400 kw
Boilers: 4, 64 kg/cm² pressure, superheat 465°C

REMARKS: Between the beginning of 1975 and the end of 1977, refitted with 4/MM38 to
　replace mount C, in the following order: D-184, D-181, D-182, and D-183. Five fixed
　anti-ship torpedo tubes (3 in bows, 2 aft) removed, 40-mm replaced by later model,
　new air search radar.

DESTROYERS

◆ **4 Z (ex-U.S. Fletcher) class**

	Bldr	L	In serv.
D 171 Z 2 (ex-*Ringgold* DD-500)	Federal SB&DD	11-11-42	30-12-42
D 172 Z 3 (ex-*Wadsworth* DD-516)	Bath Iron Works	10-1-43	16-3-43
D 178 Z 4 (ex-*Claxton* DD-571)	Consolidated Steel	1-4-42	8-12-42
D 179 Z 5 (ex-*Dyson* DD-572)	Consolidated Steel	15-4-42	23-2-60

Z-4   1977

D: 2,050 tons (2,750 fl)　**S:** 30/32 kts　**Dim:** 114.85 × 12.03 × 5.5
A: 4/127-mm 38-cal DP (I × 4)—6/76-mm DP (II × 3) *Z-2:* 4/76-mm—2/533-mm ASW
　　TT (I × 2)—2 Hedgehogs—1 depth-charge rack—mines
Electron Equipt: Radars: 1/SPS 6, 1/SPS 10, 1/Mk 25, 2/Mk 34, 1/Mk 35
　　　　　Sonar: SQS 29
Man: 350 men　**Range:** 1,260/35, 4,400/15　**Fuel:** 650 tons
M: GE GT; 2 props; 60,000 hp　**Boilers:** 4 Babcock & Wilcox
Electric: 800 kw

REMARKS: *Z-2* to *Z-4* transferred 1959; *Z-5* in 1960. *Z-6* removed from service in 1968,
　Z-1 in 1972. *Z-4* does not have after twin 76-mm mount, the position having been used
　for trials with the 76-mm OTO Melara Compact gun, since removed. Fire-control sys-
　tems include Mk 37 forward, two Mk 63 amidships, and Mk 56 aft.

GUIDED-MISSILE FRIGATES

◆ **8 Type 122**

	Bldr	Laid down	L	In serv.
F . . . BREMEN	Bremer-Vulkan	. . .	. . .	7-81
F . . . N . . .	AG Weser, Bremen	. . .	. . .	5-82
F . . . N . . .	Howaldtswerke, Kiel	. . .	. . .	11-82
F . . . N . . .	Nordseewerke, Emden	. . .	. . .	5-83
F . . . N . . .	Blohm & Voss, Hamburg	. . .	. . .	11-83
F . . . N . . .	Blohm & Voss, Hamburg	. . .	. . .	5-84
F . . . N . . .	. . .	. . .	. . .	. . .
F . . . N . . .	. . .	. . .	. . .	. . .

D: 2,900 tons (3,800 fl)　**S:** 30 kts　**Dim:** 128.0 × 14.4 × 6.0
A: 8/Harpoon SSM (IV × 2)—1/NATO Sea Sparrow SAM (8-cell)—2/ASMD SAM (8-
　　cell)—1/76-mm OTO Melara DP—4/324-mm Mk 32 ASW TT (I × 4)—2/Sea Lynx
　　ASW helicopters

GUIDED-MISSILE FRIGATES (continued)

Model of Type 122   Bremer-Vulkan, 1978

Electron Equipt: Radars: 1/DA 08, 1/WM 25, 1/STIR, 1/3RM20
   Sonar: DSQS 21BZ (bow-mounted)—SRBOC chaff launchers—
   FL 1800S intercept array
Man: 203 men   **Range:** 4,000/20   **Electric:** 3,000 kw
M: CODOG: 2 GM LM 2500 GT (50,000 hp); 2 MTU 20V956 TB92 diesels (10,400 hp);
   2 controllable-pitch props

REMARKS: Germanized version of Dutch *Kortenaer* class. To complete 1981-86. First six ordered 7-77; two additional authorized 1979. Four more of a modernized version, Type 122A, are planned to enter service beginning 1990. The helicopters will be equipped with DAQS-13D dipping sonar.

FRIGATES

◆ 6 Köln class (Type 120)

Bldr: H. C. Stülcken, Hamburg

	Laid down	L	In serv.
F 220 KÖLN	21-12-57	6-12-58	15-4-61
F 221 EMDEN	15-4-58	21-3-59	24-10-61
F 222 AUGSBURG	29-10-58	15-8-59	7-4-62
F 223 KARLSRUHE	15-12-58	24-10-59	15-12-62
F 224 LÜBECK	28-10-59	23-7-60	6-7-63
F 225 BRAUNSCHWEIG	28-7-60	3-2-62	16-6-64

D: 1,750 tons (2,090 normal, 2,996 fl)   **S:** 30 kts (20 on diesels)
Dim: 109.83 (105.0 pp) × 10.5 × 4.61 (fl)   **Man:** 212 men
A: 2/100-mm French model 1953 DP (I × 2)—6/40-mm AA (II × 2, I × 2)—2/4-barreled 375-mm Bofors ASW rocket launchers—4/533-mm ASW TT (I × 4)—82 mines

Lübeck

Electron Equipt: Radars: 1/DA 02, 1/SGR 103, 1/Kelvin-Hughes 149, 2/Mk 44 fire-control, 1/Mk 45 fire-control
   Sonar: 1 PAE/CWE hull-mounted M/F
Range: 900/30, 2,700/22   **Fuel:** 333 tons   **Electric:** 2,700 kw
M: CODAG: 4 M.A.N. V-16-cylinder diesels (each 3,000 hp); 2 Brown-Boveri GT (each 13,000 hp); 2 controllable-pitch props

REMARKS: The rocket-launcher magazines carry 72 projectiles. Two diesels and one gas turbine on each of the two shafts. Made 33 knots on trials.

CORVETTES

◆ 5 Thetis class (Type 420)

P 6052 THETIS (21-3-60)   P 6055 TRITON (5-8-61)
P 6053 HERMES (9-8-60)   P 6056 THESEUS (20-3-62)
P 6054 NAJADE (6-12-60)

Bldr: Roland Werft, Bremen-Hemelingen

Triton   S. Terzibaschitsch, 1978

D: 575 tons (658 fl)   **S:** 23.5 kts   **Dim:** 69.8 × 8.2 × 2.65
A: 2/40-mm AA (II × 1, aft)—1/4-barreled Bofors 375-mm rocket launcher (fwd)—4/533-mm ASW TT (I × 4)—mines

CORVETTES (*continued*)

Electron Equipt: Radars: Kelvin-Hughes 149, TRS-N
            Sonar: ELAC 1BV
Man: 5 officers, 43 men   **Range:** 2,760/15   **Electric:** 540 kw
M: 2 M.A.N. diesels; 2 props; 6,800 hp

REMARKS: Former torpedo-recovery boats, well designed for operations in the Belts and the Baltic. May receive OTO Melara 76-mm in place of 40-mm. P-6054 has larger forward superstructure. P-6052 is 68.21 meters, overall.

NOTE: Former corvette *Hans Bürkner* is now listed under experimental auxiliaries.

GUIDED-MISSILE PATROL BOATS

◆ **10 Type 143A**

	L	In serv.		L	In serv.
P . . . S . . .	. . .	1982	P . . . S . . .	. . .	. . .
P . . . S . . .	. . .	. . .	P . . . S . . .	. . .	. . .
P . . . S . . .	. . .	. . .	P . . . S . . .	. . .	. . .
P . . . S . . .	. . .	. . .	P . . . S . . .	· . . .	. . .
P . . . S . . .	. . .	. . .	P . . . S . . .	. . .	. . .

Bldrs: 7 by Lürssen, Vegasack, 3 by Kröger, Rendsburg

D: 300 tons (390.6 fl)   **S:** 36 kts (32 fl)   **Dim:** 57.6 (54.4 pp) × 7.76 × 2.99
A: 4/MM 38 Exocet – 1/RAM ASMD (XXIV × 1) – 1/76-mm OTO Melara DP – mines
Electron Equipt: Radars: HSA WM-27 with AGIS data system, 1/3RM 20
Man: 34 men   **Range:** 600/30, 2,600/16   **Electric:** 540 kw
M: 4 MTU 16V956 TB91 diesels; 4 props; 16,000 hp   **Fuel:** 116 tons

REMARKS: Ordered 1978. A repeat Type 143 with a point-defense SAM system in place of the 76-mm gun, and mine rails in place of the wire-guided torpedoes. Wood-planked hull on steel frame. To complete 1982-84, will replace the Type-142 class.

◆ **10 Type 143, composite-hulled**

	L	In serv.		L	In serv.
P 6111 S 61	22-10-73	1-11-76	P 6116 S 66	5-9-75	25-11-76
P 6112 S 62	21-3-74	13-4-76	P 6117 S 67	6-3-75	1-77
P 6113 S 63	18-9-74	2-6-76	P 6118 S 68	17-11-75	28-3-77
P 6114 S 64	14-4-75	14-8-76	P 6119 S 69	5-6-75	23-12-77
P 6115 S 65	15-1-74	27-9-76	P 6120 S 70	14-4-76	29-7-77

Bldrs: S-65, S-67, S-69: Kröger, Rendsburg; remainder: Lürssen, Vegasack

S-63   1976

S-62 – on trials   1976

D: 295 tons (398 fl)   **S:** 36 kts (32 fl)   **Dim:** 57.6 (54.4 pp) × 7.76 × 2.82
A: 4/MM 38 Exocet – 2/76-mm OTO Melara AA (I × 2) – 2/533-mm TT (aft-launching, for Seal wire-guided torpedoes)
Electron Equipt: Radars: HSA WM-27 with AGIS data system, 1/3RM 20
Man: 40-42 men   **Range:** 600/30, 2,600/16   **Fuel:** 116 tons
M: 4 MTU 16V956 diesels; 4 props; 16,000 hp   **Electric:** 540 kw

◆ **20 Type 148, steel-hulled**

	L		L
P 6141 S 41	27-9-72	P 6143 S 43	7-3-73
P 6142 S 42	12-12-72	P 6144 S 44	5-5-73
P 6145 S 45	3-7-73	P 6153 S 53	4-7-74
P 6146 S 46	21-5-73	P 6154 S 54	8-7-74
P 6147 S 47	20-9-72	P 6155 S 55	15-11-74
P 6148 S 48	10-9-73	P 6156 S 56	30-10-74
P 6149 S 49	11-1-74	P 6157 S 57	13-2-75
P 6150 S 50	10-12-73	P 6158 S 58	26-2-75
P 6151 S 51	26-4-74	P 6159 S 59	15-5-75
P 6152 S 52	25-3-74	P 6160 S 60	26-5-75

Bldr: Constructions Mécaniques de Normandie, Cherbourg, with Lürssen, Vegasack, who built the boats carrying even number designations from number P-6146. All were fitted out at Lorient.

S-52   1975

GUIDED-MISSILE PATROL BOATS (*continued*)

S-41   1973

D: 234 tons (265 fl)   S: 35.8 kts   Dim: 47.0 (45.9 pp) × 7.1 × 2.66 (fl)
Man: 4 officers, 17 petty officers, 9 men   Range: 570/30, 1,600/15
A: 4/MM38 Exocet—1/76-mm DP OTO Melara (fwd)—1/40-mm Bofors AA (aft)—
8 mines in place of the 40-mm AA
Electron Equipt: Radars: 1/3 RM 20 navigation, 1/Triton target designation, 1/
Vega FC system with Pollux
Fuel: 39 tons   Electric: 270 kw
M: 4 MTU MD 872-type diesels; 4 props; 14,400 hp (12,000 sust.)

TORPEDO BOATS

♦ **10 Type 142 Zobel-class**

P 6092 Zobel (21-8-61)   P 6097 Puma (26-10-61)
P 6093 Wiesel (16-3-61)   P 6098 Gepard (14-4-62)
P 6094 Dachs (10-6-61)   P 6099 Hyäne (31-3-62)
P 6095 Hermelin (5-8-61)   P 6100 Frettchen (20-11-62)
P 6096 Nerz (5-9-61)   P 6101 Ozelot (4-2-63)

Wiesel   1975

D: 210 tons (230 fl)   S: 38 kts   Dim: 42.62 × 7.14 × 2.2
A: 2/40-mm AA (I × 2)—2/533-mm TT (aft-launching for Seal wire-guided tor-
pedoes)   Man: 42 men
Electron Equipt: Radars: HSA M 20 fc, Kelvin Hughes 14/9 navigational
M: 4 MTU 20V 538 diesels; 4 props; 12,000 hp

REMARKS: Modernized 1971-72. Wooden hull, light-alloy superstructure. To be stricken
1982-84 on completion of Type 142A class.

NOTE: All the Type 141 (*Jaguar*) torpedo boats have been retired; seven were transferred to Greece and seven to Turkey.

MINE WARFARE SHIPS

♦ **. . . Type 355 pressure-mine sweepers**

REMARKS: A project to design a ship capable of detecting and disposing of the "un-
sweepable" pressure mine. To be built during the mid-1980s.

♦ **10 Type 343 minelayer-minehunters**

REMARKS: A design project to begin replacement of the existing Type 331A minehunters. To receive DSQS-11 minehunting sonar. The Type 331/332 minesweeper-
minehunter program has been delayed.

♦ **6 Type 351 drone minesweeper-control ships**   Bldr: Burmester, Bremen

M 1073 Schleswig (2-10-57)   M 1081 Konstanz (30-9-58)
M 1076 Paderborn (5-12-57)   M 1082 Wolfsburg (10-12-58)
M 1079 Düren (12-6-58)   M 1083 Ulm (10-2-59)

D: 465 tons (fl)   S: 16.5 kts   Dim: 47.1 × 8.5 × 2.75
A: 1/40-mm AA   Man: 44 men   Range: 2,200/16
Electron Equipt: Radar: TRS-N   Sonar: DSQS-11A
M: 2 KM 8771 UM/1D diesels; 2 controllable-pitch props; 3,300 hp

REMARKS: Type 320 minesweepers to be converted in the early 1980s. Each ship will
control three F-1 "Troika" drone magnetic mechanical minesweepers.

♦ **18 Type F-1 "Troika" drones**   Bldr: MAK, Kiel

F-1 "Troika" trials craft   1977

D: 99.4 tons (fl)   S: 9.4 kts   Dim: 27.0 × 3.53 × 2.1
A: None   Man: 3 men   Range: 520/8.8   Electric: 208 kw
M: 1 TRHS 518A diesel; Schöttel prop; 445 hp

MINE WARFARE SHIPS (continued)

REMARKS: Ordered 1977. Remote-controlled, self-propelled, magnetic minesweeping solenoids with all machinery highly shock-protected. Will also tow Oropesa Type SDG-21 mechanical minesweeping gear. Crew debarked while in operation. Type 351 minesweeper conversions will control and service three drones each. Three prototypes, *Seekuh 1* to *Seekuh 3*, are still in service as well.

◆ 10 Type 331A minehunters

M 1070 GÖTTINGEN (1-4-57)	M 1077 WEILHEIM (4-2-58)
M 1071 KOBLENZ (6-5-57)	M 1078 CUXHAVEN (11-3-58)
M 1072 LINDAU (16-2-57)	M 1080 MARBURG (4-8-58)
M 1074 TÜBINGEN (12-8-57)	M 1085 MINDEN (9-6-59)
M 1075 WETZLAR (24-6-57)	M 1087 VÖLKLINGEN (20-10-59)

Tübingen—with two PAP-104 on deck　　　　　　　　　　　1978

◆ 2 Type 331B minehunters

M 1084 FLENSBURG (7-4-59)	M 1086 FULDA (19-8-59)

Bldr: Burmester, Bremen

D: 419.4 tons (fl)　　**S:** 17 kts　　**Dim:** 47.45 × 8.3 × 3.68 (sonar down)
A: 1/40-mm AA　　**Man:** 46 men　　**Range:** 2,200/16, 3,450/9
Electron Equipt: Radar: TRS-N
　　　　　　　　　Sonars: DSQS 11 (Type 331B: Plessey 193M Mk 20G)
M: 2 Maybach diesels; 2 controllable-pitch props; 4,000 hp　　**Electric:** 220 kw

REMARKS: All are conversions from the Type 320, *Lindau*-class, wooden-hulled minesweepers. The first ten above were converted 1975-80 and the other two 1968-71. The earlier Type 331B conversions have British sonar and do not carry the two French PAP-104 minehunting devices fitted to the later Type 331As. None has mechanical sweep gear.

◆ 22 Type 340(a) and Type 341(b) patrol minesweepers

M 1051 CASTOR (12-7-62)(a)	M 1064 DENEB (11-9-61)(b)
M 1054 POLLUX (15-9-60)(a)	M 1065 JUPITER (15-2-61)(b)
M 1055 SIRIUS (15-3-61)(a)	M 1067 ALTAIR (20-4-61)(b)
M 1056 RIGEL (2-4-62)(a)	M 1069 WEGA (10-10-62)(b)
M 1057 REGULUS (18-12-61)(a)	M 1090 PERSEUS (22-9-60)(b)
M 1063 WAAGE (9-4-59)(b)	M 1092 PLUTO (9-8-60)(b)
M 1058 MARS (1-12-60)(a)	M 1093 NEPTUN (9-6-60)(b)
M 1059 SPICA (25-5-60)(a)	M 1094 WIDDER (13-3-59)(b)
M 1060 SKORPION (29-5-63)(b)	M 1095 HERKULES (25-8-60)(b)
Y 849 STIER (30-10-58)(b)	M 1096 FISCHE (14-7-59)(b)
M 1062 SCHÜTZE (20-5-58)(b)	M 1097 GEMMA (6-10-59)(b)

Bldr: Schlichting, Travemünde; Schürenstedt, Bardenfleth; Abeking and Rasmussen, Lemwerde, 1958-63

Herkules　　　　　　　　　　　　　　　　　　　　　　　1974

Waage—in patrol-boat configuration　　　　　　　S. Terzibaschitsch

D: 241 tons (266.5 fl)　　**S:** 24.6 kts　　**Dim:** 47.44 × 7.2 × 2.2
A: 1/40-mm AA (*see* Remarks)　　**Man:** 39 men
Fuel: 22 tons　　**Electric:** 120 kw plus 340-kw sweep generator
Range: 640/22, 1,000/18
M: Maybach or Mercedes-Benz diesels; 2 Escher-Wyss cycloidal props; 4,000/4,200 hp

MINE WARFARE SHIPS (*continued*)

REMARKS: Multi-purpose ships that can be employed as minesweepers, coastal patrol craft (2/40-mm AA), and minelayers (2 mine rails), the minesweeping gear having been removed in the latter two instances. *Stier* (former M-1061), used as a submarine-rescue ship, has been given a new hull number and disarmed; decompression chamber on new stern deckhouse. Ten with Mercedes-Benz diesels are Type 340; the remainder, with Maybach diesels, are Type 341. Several have been discarded.

◆ 1 Type 390 inshore minesweeper

	Bldr	Laid down	L	In serv.
Y 836 HOLNIS	Abeking	1964	20-5-65	31-3-66

D: 180 tons (fl)　**S:** 14.5 kts　**Dim:** 36.87 × 7.4 × 1.8
A: None　**Man:** 21 men　**Fuel:** 13 tons
M: 2 MB diesels; 2 props; 2,000 hp

REMARKS: Converted 1968 as trials ship for "Troika" magnetic minesweeping system, which uses three radio-controlled, 27-meter *Seekuh* launches. *Holnis* now has a deck-house aft and bulwarks around her stern. Nineteen projected sisters were canceled.

◆ 18 Types 393 (a) and 394 (b) inshore minesweepers

(*a*)	(*b*)
M 2650 ARIADNE (23-4-60)	M 2658 FRAUENLOB (26-2-65)
M 2651 FREYA (25-6-60)	M 2659 NAUTILUS (19-5-65)
M 2652 VINETA (17-9-60)	M 2660 GEFION (19-6-65)
M 2653 HERTHA (18-2-61)	M 2661 MEDUSA (25-1-66)
M 2654 NYMPHE (20-9-62)	M 2662 UNDINE (16-5-66)
M 2655 NIXE (13-12-62)	M 2663 MINERVA (25-8-66)
M 2656 AMAZONE (27-2-63)	M 2664 DIANA (13-12-66)
M 2657 GAZELLE (14-8-63)	M 2665 LORELEY (14-3-67)
	M 2666 ATLANTIS (20-6-67)
	M 2667 ACHERON (11-10-67)

Bldr: Kröger, Rendsburg.

Ariadne (Type 393)　　　　　　　　　　1975

Loreley (Type 394)　　　　　　　　　　1975

D: (*a*): 185 tons (210 fl) (*b*) 204 tons (249 fl)　**S:** 14 kts
Dim: (*a*): 38.01 × 7.85 × 1.88 (*b*) 38.01 × 8.29 × 2.1
A: 1/40-mm AA　**Man:** 4 officers, 20 men
Range: (*a*): 830/12 (*b*): 648/14, 1,770/7
M: 2 MB diesels; 2 props; 2,000 hp　**Electric:** 440 kw　**Fuel:** 30 tons

REMARKS: Wooden hulls. Formerly had Y-series hull numbers and, earlier, W-series. M-2654 to M-2657 are 8.29 meters in beam. Type 393 have 260-kw gas-turbine, sweep-current generator; Type 394 diesel.

◆ 2 Hansa-class converted inshore minesweepers

Y 806 HANSA (18-11-57)

Bldr: Kröger, Rendsburg

D: 150 tons (175 fl)　**S:** Y-806: 14 kts　Y-1653: 16 kts
Dim: 35.18 × 6.84 × 1.7 (Y-806: 1.95)
A: None　**Man:** 19/22 men　**Range:** 800/12 (Y-806: 1,500/12)
M: Y-806: 1 MTU diesel; 1 prop; 1,000 hp　Y-1653: 2 MTU diesels; 2 props; 2,000 hp

REMARKS: *Hansa* (Type 392) now tender for training mine-clearance divers. *Niobe* (Type 391) has been used for minesweeping experiments with the "Troika" drone system; she was stricken in 1979. Wooden hulls.

AMPHIBIOUS WARFARE CRAFT

◆ 22 Type 520 utility landing craft

L 760 FLUNDER (6-1-66)	L 767 TÜMMLER (14-6-66)	L 792 DORSCH (17-3-66)
L 761 KARPFEN (5-1-66)	L 768 WELS (15-6-66)	L 793 FELCHEN (19-4-66)
L 762 LACHS (17-2-66)	L 769 ZANDER (13-7-66)	L 794 FORELLE (20-4-66)
L 763 PLÖTZE (16-2-66)	L 788 BUTT (28-3-65)	L 795 INGER (14-7-66)
L 764 ROCHEN (18-3-66)	L 789 BRASSE (28-3-65)	L 796 MAKRELE (22-8-66)
L 765 SCHLEI (17-5-66)	L 790 BARBE (26-11-65)	L 797 MÜRÄNE (23-8-66)
L 766 STÖR (18-5-66)	L 791 DELPHIN (25-11-65)	L 798 RENKE (22-9-66)
		L 799 SALM (23-9-66)

Bldr: Howaldtswerke, Hamburg, 1965-66

AMPHIBIOUS WARFARE CRAFT (*continued*)

Lachs   1975

D: 166 tons (403 fl)   **S:** 11 kts   **Dim:** 40.04 (36.7 pp) × 8.8 × 1.6
A: 2/20-mm AA (II × 1)   **Man:** 17 men   **Range:** 1,200/11
M: 2 MWM diesels; 1,200 hp   **Electric:** 130 kw   **Cargo:** 237 tons

REMARKS: Design based on the American LCU-1646 class. Receiving two 20-mm Rhein-metall AA. *Renke* (L-798) and *Salm* (L-799) in reserve; *Inger* (L-795) used for reserve training.

◆ **28 Type 521 landing craft**   Bldr: Blohm & Voss, 1964-74

LCM 1 to LCM 28

D: 116 tons (168 fl)   **S:** 10.6 kts   **Dim:** 23.56 × 6.4 × 1.46
M: 4 GM diesels; 1,368 hp   **Electric:** 28 kw   **Cargo:** 60 tons

REMARKS: Design based on U.S. LCM (8). LCM-11 to LCM-20 have a two-ton boom and can carry eighteen torpedoes. LCM-1 to LCM-8 and LCM-21 to LCM-28 are in reserve.

AUXILIARY SHIPS

◆ **11 Rhein-class tenders, Types 401, 402, and 403**

(*a*) Type 401, for fast combatants

		Bldr	L	In serv.
A 58	RHEIN	Schlieker, Hamburg	10-12-59	6-11-61
A 61	ELBE	Schlieker, Hamburg	5-5-60	17-4-62
A 63	MAIN	Lindenauwerft, Kiel	23-7-60	29-6-63
A 66	NECKAR	Lürssen, Vegasack	26-6-61	7-12-63
A 68	WERRA	Lindenauwerft, Kiel	26-3-63	2-9-64
A 69	DONAU	Schlichting, Travemünde	26-11-60	23-5-64

(*b*) Type 402, for mine-countermeasures ships

		Bldr	L	In serv.
A 54	ISAR	Blohm & Voss, Hamburg	14-7-62	25-1-64
A 65	SAAR	Norderwerft, Hamburg	11-3-61	11-5-63
A 67	MOSEL	Schlieker, Hamburg	15-12-60	8-6-63

(*c*) Type 403, for submarines

		Bldr	L	In serv.
A 55	LAHN	Flenderwerke, Lübeck	21-11-61	24-3-64
A 56	LECH	Flenderwerke, Lübeck	8-5-62	8-12-64

Mosel (Type 402)   1975

D: (*a*): 2,370 tons (2,740 fl)   (*b*): 2,330 tons (2,930 fl)
     (*c*): 2,400 tons (2,956 fl)   **S:** 20 kts (trials, 22)
Dim: 98.6 × 11.8 × 3.96   **Range:** 2,500/16
Man: 98 men (space for 40 officers, 40 petty officers, 130 nonrated men)
A: 2/100-mm AA (I × 2) (not in A-55, A-56)—4/40-mm AA (I × 4, except II × 2 in
     A-55 and A-56)—mines
Electron Equipt: Radars: 1/SGR 105, 1/SGR 103, 2/Mk 45 fire-control
                          A-55 and A-56: SGR 103 only
M: 6 Maybach diesels (Mercedes-Benz in A-55 and A-56); 2 controllable-pitch props;
     11,400 hp   **Electric:** 2,250 kw   **Fuel:** 334 tons

Lech (Type 403)   1975

REMARKS: A-54, A-55, A-56, A-65, A-67 have electric drive. Tenders carry 200 tons of fuel oil, 40 reserve torpedoes; A-55, A-56, and A-58 have an additional 200 tons of stores; A-66, A-68, and A-69 can be used as training ships. *Weser* (A-62) and *Ruhr* (A-64) transferred to the Greek and Turkish navies in 1975 and 1976, respectively. Two of the combatant-tender version are to be re-equipped to support the new Type-143A missile boats as Type-401D tenders.

AUXILIARY SHIPS (continued)

Neckar (Type 401) H. Kowark, 1976

UNDERWAY REPLENISHMENT SHIPS

NOTE: These ships are grouped together here because, despite their dissimilar functions, they are variations on the same basic design.

◆ 8 Type 701 and Type 701C multi-purpose supply ships

a) Type 701

	Bldr	L	In serv.
A 1411 LÜNEBURG	Flensburger SY	3-5-65	31-1-66
A 1413 FREIBURG	Blohm & Voss, Hamburg	15-4-66	27-5-68
A 1416 NIENBURG	Flensburger SY	28-7-66	1-8-68
A 1417 OFFENBURG	Blohm & Voss, Hamburg	10-9-66	21-5-68

b) Type 701C

	Bldr	L	In serv.
A 1412 COBURG	Flensburger SY	15-12-65	9-7-68
A 1414 GLÜCKSBURG	Flensburger SY	3-5-66	9-7-68
A 1415 SAARBURG	Blohm & Voss, Hamburg	15-7-66	30-7-68
A 1428 MEERSBURG	Flensburger SY	22-3-66	25-6-68

Freiburg (Type 701)—unmodified 1977

Saarburg (Type 701C)—lengthened 1976

D: 3,483 tons (fl)   Type 701C: 3,679 tons (fl)   **S:** 17 kts
Dim: 104.18 × 13.2 × 4.2 Type 701C: 114.9 overall
A: 4/40-mm AA (II × 2) in preservation   **Man:** 103 men
Range: 3,000/17, 3,200/14   **Electric:** 1,935 kw
M: 2 Maybach MD 874 diesels; 2 controllable-pitch props; 5,600 hp

REMARKS: Originally configured to carry more than 1,100 tons of cargo, including 640 tons fuel oil, 200 tons ammunition, 100 tons spare parts (10,000 separate items), and 130 tons fresh water. A-1415 lengthened 11.5 meters in 1974-75 to carry spare Exocet missiles and other supplies for the new Type-143 and Type-148 classes; stowage for spare parts increased to 30,000 items, with inventory management by the Nixdorf computer system. A-1411, A-1412, and A-1418 also converted to Type 702C standard, 1975-77. A-1414 (in 1982) and A-1412 (in 1984) will complete conversion to support the new Type-122 frigates; they will be equipped with helicopter facilities to permit vertical replenishment.

◆ 2 Type 760 ammunition ships

A 1435 WESTERWALD (25-2-66)   A 1436 ODENWALD (5-5-66)

Bldr: Orenstein & Koppel, Lübeck

Westerwald 1974

D: 3,460 tons (4,032 fl)   **S:** 17 kts   **Dim:** 105.3 × 14.0 × 3.7
A: 4/40-mm AA (II × 2) in preservation   **Man:** 58 men

UNDERWAY REPLENISHMENT SHIPS (*continued*)

Range: 3,500/17   **Electric:** 1,285 kw   **Cargo:** 1,080 tons
M: 2 Maybach MD 874 diesels; 2 controllable-pitch props; 5,600 hp

REMARK: Similar to Type 701 but carry only ammunition.

◆ **2 Type 762 mine-supply ships**   Bldr: Blohm & Voss, Hamburg

A 1437 SACHSENWALD (10-12-66)   A 1438 STEIGERWALD (10-3-67)

Steigerwald   1974

D: 2,962 tons (3,850 fl)   **S:** 17 kts   **Dim:** 110.9 × 13.9 × 4.2
A: 4/40-mm AA (II × 2)   **Man:** 65 men   **Range:** 3,500/17
M: 2 Maybach MD 864 diesels; controllable-pitch props; 5,600 hp
Electric: 1,300 kw

REMARKS: The designation "supply ships" is something of a euphemism, since these ships have four mine ports at the stern and are actually minelayers. Construction of a torpedo-transport version was canceled.

REPAIR SHIPS

◆ **2 former U.S. Aristaeus class**

	Bldr	L	In serv.
A 512 ODIN (ex-*Ulysses*, ARB-9)	Bethlehem, Hingham	2-12-44	27-12-44
A 513 WOTAN (ex-*Diomedes*, ARB-11)	Chicago Bridge & Iron	11-11-44	23-1-45

Odin

D: 3,435 tons (4,100 fl)   **S:** 11 kts   **Dim:** 100.0 × 15.28 × 3.96
Man: 143 men (civilian personnel)   **Range:** 13,200/11   **Fuel:** 438 tons
M: 2 GM 12-278A (A-513: 12-567A) diesels; 2 props; 1,800 hp

REMARKS: Modified former LST-967 and LST-1119, respectively, transferred in 6-61. A 10-ton traveling crane moves on rails between the bridge and the forward sheer.

OILERS

◆ **2 Type 704 former merchant tankers**

	Bldr	L	In serv.
A 1443 RHÖN (ex-*Okapi*)	Kröger, Rendsburg	23-8-74	5-9-77
A 1442 SPESSART (ex-*Okene*)	Kröger, Rendsburg	13-2-75	23-9-77

Rhön   1977

D: 17,590 tons (fl); 6,209 grt/10,950 dwt   **S:** 16 kts
Dim: 130.2 × 19.6 × 8.2   **Man:** 42 men   **Electric:** 2,000 kw
M: 1 MAK 12-cyl. diesel; controllable-pitch prop; 8,000 hp   **Cargo:** 11,763 m³

REMARKS: Converted while building. Purchased from Bulk Acid Carriers, Monrovia, in 1976 to replace *Emsland* (A-1440) and *Münsterland* (A-1441), which were stricken in 1977-78. Fitted with one underway-replenishment station per side.

◆ **4 Type 703**   Bldr: Lindenau, Kiel

A 1424 WALCHENSEE (10-7-66)	A 1426 TEGERNSEE (27-10-66)
A 1425 AMMERSEE (22-9-66)	A 1427 WESTENSEE (8-4-67)

Ammersee   1975

OILERS (continued)

D: 2,174 tons (fl) **S:** 12.5 kts **Dim:** 71.2 × 11.2 × 4.28
Man: 21 men **Range:** 3,250/12 **Cargo capacity:** 1,130 m³
M: 2 MWM diesels; 2 props; 1,200 hp

◆ **1 Type 763 former merchant tanker**

A 1407 WITTENSEE (ex-*Sioux*) Bldr: Lindenau, Kiel

Wittensee   1975

D: 1,237 tons (1,970 fl) **S:** 12 kts **Dim:** 67.45 × 9.84 × 4.25
Man: 21 men (civilian crew) **Range:** 6,240/12 **Cargo:** 1,238 tons
M: 1 MAK diesel; 1,250 hp **Electric:** 216 kw

REMARKS: Launched 23-9-58, purchased 29-3-59. Sister *Bodensee* transferred to Turkey 8-77.

◆ **1 Type 766 former merchant tanker**

A 1429 EIFEL (ex-*Friedrich Jung*) Bldr: Norderwerft, Hamburg

D: 6,640 tons (fl) **S:** 13 kts **Dim:** 101.76 × 14.43 × 7.1
Man: 40 men **Range:** 7,300/12 **Cargo:** 4,720 tons
M: 2 M.A.N. diesels; 1 prop; 3,360 hp

REMARKS: Launched 2-4-58, purchased 1963. Equipped for underway replenishment.

◆ **1 Type 766 former merchant tanker**

A 1428 HARZ (ex-*Clare Jung*) Bldr: Norderwerft, Hamburg

Harz

D: 5,380 tons (fl) **S:** 12 kts **Dim:** 92.4 × 13.6 × 6.7
Man: 28 men **Range:** 7,200/11 **Cargo:** 3,525 tons
M: 2 OEW 8-cyl. diesels; 1 prop; 2,520 hp

REMARKS: Launched 2-9-53, purchased 1963. Equipped for underway replenishment, one station per side.

SEAGOING TUGS

◆ **3 Type 722 Baltrum class**

A 1451 WANGEROOGE   A 1452 SPIEKEROOG   A 1455 NORDERNEY

Bldr: Schichau, Bremerhaven, 1966-68

Langeoog (now Y-1665)—as a diving tender   1969

D: 854 tons (1,025 fl) **S:** 13.6 kts **Dim:** 51.78 × 12.1 × 4.2
A: 1/40-mm AA **Man:** 31 men **Range:** 5,000/10 **Electric:** 540 kw
M: 2 MWM diesels; electric motors; 1 prop; 2,400 hp

REMARKS: Also employed as salvage tugs and port icebreakers. The *Baltrum* has been used as a diving-training tender since 1974. The *Juist* and *Langeoog* were reconfigured for training duties during 1977-78.

◆ **2 Type 720 Helgoland-class salvage tugs**

A 1457 HELGOLAND (8-4-65)   A 1458 FEHMARN (25-11-65)

Bldr: Schichau, Bremerhaven

Fehmarn—gun mount now removed   1974

SEAGOING TUGS (*continued*)

D: 1,620 tons (fl)   **S:** 16.6 kts   **Dim:** 67.9 × 12.74 × 5.0
A: None   **Man:** 34 men   **Range:** 6,400/16   **Electric:** 1,065 kw
M: 4 MWM diesels, electric drive; 2 props; 3,300 hp

REMARKS: Two 40-mm AA (II × 1) removed. *Fehmarn* serves as a tender to the submarine training establishment.

◆ **2 Eisvogel-class icebreaking tugs**   Bldr: Hitzler, Laurenburg

A 1401 EISVOGEL (28-4-60)   A 1402 EISBÄR (9-6-60)

D: 496 tons (576 fl)   **S:** 13 kts   **Dim:** 37.8 × 9.5 × 4.2
M: 2 Maybach diesels; 2 props; 2,400 hp   **Man:** 16 men   **Range:** 2,000/12

HARBOR TUGS

◆ **3 Type 724 Neuende-class tugs**   Bldr: Schichau, Bremerhaven

Y 1680 NEUENDE   Y 1681 HEPPENS   Y 1682 ELLERBEK

Ellerbek   S. Terzibaschitsch

D: 122 tons (232 fl)   **S:** 12 kts   **Dim:** 26.6 × 7.4 × 2.6
Man: 6 men   **M:** 1 MWM diesel; 800 hp

REMARK: In service since 1971.

◆ **4 Type 724 Sylt-class tugs**   Bldr: Schichau, Bremerhaven

Y 820 SYLT   Y 821 FÖHR   Y 822 AMRUM   Y 823 NEUWERK

D: 266 tons (fl)   **S:** 12 kts   **Dim:** 30.6 × 7.45 × 4.0
Man: 10 men   **Range:** 1,775/12   **M:** 1 MAK diesel; 800-1,000 hp

REMARK: In service 1962-63.

◆ **8 Type 723 tugs**

Y 812 LÜTJE HÖRN   Y 814 KNECHTSAND   Y 816 VOGELSAND   Y 818 TRISCHEN
Y 813 MELLUM   Y 815 SCHARNHORN   Y 817 NORDSTRAND   Y 819 LANGENESS

D: 52.2 tons (fl)   **S:** 10 kts   **Dim:** 15.7 × 5.1 × 2.2
Man: 4 men   **Range:** 550/9
M: 2 Deutz diesels; 2 Voith-Schneider cycloidal props; 300 hp

REMARK: In service 1958-59.

WATER TANKERS

◆ **5 Type 705 FW-1 class**

Y 864 FW 1   Y 865 FW 2   Y 866 FW 3   Y 867 FW 4   Y 868 FW 5

FW-5   S. Terzibaschitsch

D: 626 tons (fl)   **S:** 9.5 kts   **Dim:** 44.1 × 7.8 × 2.6
Man: 12 men   **Range:** 2,150/9   **Cargo capacity:** 350 m³
M: 1 MWM diesel; 230 hp

REMARKS: Date from 1963-64. Sister FW-6 sold to Turkey in 1975.

TORPEDO-RECOVERY BOATS

◆ **13 boats**

Y 851	Y 853	Y 855	Y 872	Y 874	Y 883	Y 886
Y 852	Y 854	Y 856	Y 873	Y 882	Y 884	

D: 43 tons (fl)   **S:** 17 kts   **Dim:** 22.1 × 3.7 × 1.5
M: 1 Deutz diesel; 250 hp (Y-851 to Y-856 and Y-872 to Y-874: 950 hp)

TORPEDO-RECOVERY BOATS (continued)

Y-855   1975

REMARKS: Y-883 to Y-886 are much older than the others. Stern ramps to recover torpedoes on Y-851 to Y-874.

INTELLIGENCE COLLECTORS

◆ **2 Type 753B converted trawlers** Bldr: Unterweser, Bremerhaven, 1960-61

A 50 ALSTER (ex-*Mellum*)   A 53 OKER (ex-*Hoheweg*)

   D: 1,187 tons (1,497 fl)   **S:** 15 kts   **Dim:** 84.0 × 10.5 × 5.6
   Man: 90 men   **M:** Diesel-electric; 1 prop; 1,800 hp

REMARKS: Also have one small "cruise" diesel. Converted 1971-72.

◆ **1 Type 753 converted tug** Bldr: Akers, Oslo, 1943

A 52 OSTE (ex-U.S. 101, ex-*Puddefjord*)

   D: 1,083 tons (fl)   **S:** 11 kts   **Dim:** 49.65 × 9.1 × 5.8
   M: 1 Akers diesel; 1,600 hp   **Man:** 30 men

AIR-SEA RESCUE CRAFT

◆ **6 KW series**

Y 827 KW 15   Y 832 KW 18   Y 845 KW 17
Y 830 KW 16   Y 833 KW 19   Y 846 KW 20

   D: 60 tons (70 fl)   **S:** 25 kts   **Dim:** 28.9 × 4.7 × 1.42
   M: 2 MTU diesels; 2 props; 2,000 hp   **Man:** 17 men

REMARK: Date from 1951-53.

TRAINING SHIPS

◆ **1 Type 440 cruiser type**

	Bldr	Laid down	L	In serv.
A 59 DEUTSCHLAND	Nobiskrug, Rendsburg	17-9-59	5-11-60	25-5-63

   D: 4,880 tons (5,450 fl)   **S:** 22 kts (18 cruising)
   Dim: 138.2 (130.0 pp) × 16.0 × 4.8   **Man:** 33 officers, 521 men (250 cadets)

Deutschland   1974

   A: 4/100-mm AA (I × 4) – 8/40-mm AA (II × 2, I × 4) – 4/533-mm ASW TT – 8/375-mm
      Bofors ASW rocket launchers (IV × 2)
   Electron Equipt: Radars: 1/LWO 8, 1/SGR 114, 1/SGR 105, 1/SGR 103, 4/M 45 fire-
                                       control
                        Sonar: 1 ELAC 1BV (M/F)
   Range: 6,000/17   **Fuel:** 640 tons   **Boilers:** 2 Wahodag, 450°C
   M: 4 diesels (2 Maybach and 2 Mercedes-Benz), each of 2,000 hp; 1 Wahodag GT
      8,000 hp; 3 props, 2 controllable-pitch   **Electric:** 1,500 kw

REMARKS: Quarters for 7 instructors and 250 cadets. Can be used as a minelayer.

◆ **1 Type 441 sail training ship**

A 60 GORCH FOCK Bldr: Blohm & Voss, Hamburg

   D: 1,760 tons (1,880 fl)   **S:** 10 kts   **Dim:** 81.44 × 12.02 × 5.0
   M: 1 M.A.N. diesel; 890 hp

REMARKS: Launched 23-8-58. 1,964 m² of sail. Living spaces for 200 cadets. Length over bowsprit is 89.3 m.

◆ **1 ketch**

Y 834 NORDWIND

   D: 110 tons   **S:** 11 kts   **Dim:** 24.0 × 6.4 × 2.5   **Range:** 1,200/7
   M: 1 Demag diesel; 137 hp

REMARKS: Launched in the United States 1945, purchased 1951.

◆ **68 smaller sail training craft**

EXPERIMENTAL AND TRIALS SHIPS

◆ **1 Type 742 magnetic research ship**

Y 841 WALTHER VON LEDEBUR Bldr: Burmester, Bremen

   D: 775 tons (825 fl)   **S:** 19 kts   **Dim:** 63.2 × 10.6 × 3.0
   Man: 19 men plus technicians   **M:** 2 MTU diesels; 2 props; 5,200 hp

REMARKS: Launched 30-6-66. One of the largest wooden ships built in modern times. Used in mine-warfare research.

EXPERIMENTAL AND TRIALS SHIPS (continued)

◆ **1 Type 421 former corvette**

A 1449 HANS BÜRKNER Bldr: Atlaswerke, Bremen

Hans Bürkner   1975

D: 983 tons (1,203 fl)   **S:** 24 kts   **Dim:** 80.6 × 9.27 × 2.87
A: 1/375-mm Bofors 4-barreled ASW rocket launcher (*see* Remarks)
Man: 50 men   **Range:** 2,180/15
M: 4 M.A.N. diesels; 2 controllable-pitch props; 13,600 hp

REMARKS: Launched 16-7-61, in service 5-63. Employed as an ASW trials ship. Has recently carried a small variable-depth sonar. Position for two 40-mm AA (II × 1) retained, and has previously carried two 533-mm ASW torpedo tubes. Fitted with mine rails.

◆ **2 Type 741 net tenders**

Y 837 SP 1 (21-6-66)   Y 838 WILHELM PULLWER (16-8-66)

Bldr: Schürenstedt K. G., Bardenfleth

SP-1   S. Terzibaschitsch

D: 132 tons (160 fl)   **S:** 12.5 kts   **Dim:** 31.54 × 7.5 × 2.2
M: 2 Mercedes-Benz diesels; 2 Voith-Schneider cycloidal props; 700 hp

REMARK: Used in experimental trials.

◆ **1 Type 740 torpedo-trials ship**

Y 871 HEINZ ROGGENKAMP (ex-*Grief*) Bldr: AG Weser, Bremerhaven

D: 996 tons (fl)   **S:** 12 kts   **Dim:** 57.2 × 9.0 × 3.1
A: 3/533-mm TT (I × 3)   **Man:** 19 men   **M:** 1 KHD diesel; 800 hp

REMARKS: Launched 8-11-52, purchased 1963. One underwater torpedo tube. Civilian-manned ex-trawler.

◆ **1 weapons-trials barge**

BARBARA Bldr: Howaldtswerke, Kiel

D: 3,500 tons (fl)   **Dim:** 52.1 × 24.0 × 3.0

REMARKS: In service 6-64. Non-self-propelled. Extensive superstructure. Used to test guns.

◆ **1 former fishing cutter**

Y 882 OTTO MEYCKE (ex-*Meteor II*) Bldr: Lürssen, Vegasack

D: 50 tons   **S:** 9 kts   **Dim:** 15.0 × 5.0 × 1.9
Man: 6 men   **M:** 1 diesel

REMARKS: Wooden craft, launched 6-47, purchased 1960. Primarily a diving tender. Civilian crew.

◆ **1 trials tender**

Y 888 FRIEDRICH VOGE (ex-*Kurefjord*) Bldr: Nyslands, Oslo

Friedrich Voge   1975

D: 260 tons (298 fl)   **S:** 12 kts   **Dim:** 33.2 × 6.7 × 3.3
Man: 14 men   **M:** 1 M.A.N. diesel; 550 hp

REMARK: Launched 16-3-43. Acquired 12-59.

EXPERIMENTAL AND TRIALS SHIPS (*continued*)

◆ **3 ex-U.S. YMS-class minesweepers**

Y 847 OT 2   Y 881 ADOLF BESTELMEYER   Y 889 RUDOLF DIESEL

> **D:** 270 tons (350 fl)   **S:** 15 kts   **Dim:** 41.2 × 7.63 × 2.4
> **M:** 2 MTU diesels; 2 props; 930 hp

REMARKS: Sister *H. C. Oersted* used as degaussing tender. Full-load displacements vary. Y-881 and Y-889 have 2 GM diesels.

DEGAUSSING TENDERS

◆ **1 ex-U.S. YMS-class minesweeper**

Y 877 H. C. OERSTED (ex-YMS-247)   Bldr: Weaver, Orange, Texas

H. C. Oersted   S. Terzibaschitsch

> **D:** 302 tons (fl)   **M:** 2 GM diesels.

REMARKS: Launched 14-10-42. *See* data under Experimental and Trials Ships above.

DIVING TENDERS

◆ **3 Baltrum-class former seagoing tugs**

Y 1661 BALTRUM   Y 1664 JUIST   Y 1665 LANGEOOG

REMARKS: Converted 1974-78. For details, *see* under Seagoing Tugs.

◆ **Y 1678 TB 1**

> **D:** 70 tons   **S:** 14 kts   **Dim:** 27.8 × 5.8 × 1.9   **M:** 950 hp

REMARK: Dates from 1972.

VARIOUS SHIPS

◆ **1 torpedo workshop**

Y 805 MEMMERT (ex-U.S. 106, ex-*India*)

> **D:** 164 tons (210 fl)   **S:** 8 kts   **Dim:** 32.5 × 9.5 × 1.8
> **Man:** 8 men   **Range:** 440/8   **M:** 2 MWM diesels; 2 props; 300 hp

Memmert   1975

REMARK: Dates from 1940.

◆ **2 floating barracks**

Y 811 KNURRHAN

> **D:** 1,250 tons   **Dim:** 58.9 × 11.0 × 2.6

Y 809 ARCONA (ex-*Royal Prince*)

> **D:** 380 tons   **Dim:** 66.4 × 10.0 × 1.6

REMARKS: Non-self-propelled. Y-811 dates from 1916. Y-809, a former river liner, dates from 1943.

◆ **2 tank-cleaning craft**   Bldr: Deutsche Werft, Hamburg

Y 1641 FÖRDE   Y 1642 JADE

> **D:** 1,830 tons (fl)   **S:** 8 kts   **Dim:** 58.5 × 10.4 × 4.1
> **Man:** 16 men   **Range:** 750/8   **M:** 1 WMW diesel; 390 hp

REMARKS: Date from 1967. For steam-cleaning fuel tanks and for sludge-removal. Resemble small tankers.

◆ **2 self-propelled floating cranes**   Bldr: Rheinwerft, Walsum, 1962

Y 875 HIEV   Y 876 GRIEP

> **D:** 1,857 tons (fl)   **S:** 6 kts   **Dim:** 52.9 × 22.0 × 2.1
> **M:** 3 MWM 600-hp diesels, electric drive; 3 vertical cycloidal props; 1,425 hp

REMARKS: Electric-crane capacity: 100 tons. Civilian crews.

◆ **3 battery-charging craft**

LP 1 (1964)   LP 2 (1964)   LP 3 (1974)

> Bldrs: Jadewerft, Wilhelmshaven (LP-2: Oelkers, Hamburg)
>
> **D:** 234 tons (fl)   LP-3: 267 tons   **S:** 8 kts   **Dim:** 27.6 × 7.0 × 1.6
> **Man:** 6 men   **M:** 1 MTU diesel; 250 hp

REMARKS: Each has two 405-kw generators and one (LP-3: two) 150-kw generator for charging submarine batteries. LP-3 is 7.5 m. in beam, 1.8 m draft.

VARIOUS SHIPS (*continued*)

◆ numerous small service craft, personnel launches, fuel barges, etc.

◆ 6 floating dry docks

HYDROGRAPHIC SHIP

A 1450 PLANET   Bldr: Norderwerft, Hamburg

Planet   A. and J. Pavia

D: 1,513 tons (1,943 fl)   **S:** 13.5 kts   **Dim:** 80.4 (74.0 pp) × 12.6 × 3.97
Man: 40 men plus 22 technicians   **Range:** 9,400/13.4
M: 4 MWM 850-hp diesels, electric drive; 1 prop; 1,200 hp; active rudder and bow thruster

REMARKS: Launched 23-9-65. Operated for the Ministry of Communications by a civilian crew. Hangar for one helicopter.

COAST GUARD

NOTE: A separate paramilitary force of 1,000 men (Bundesgrenzschutz-See).

PATROL BOATS

◆ 8 Neustadt Class

BG 11 NEUSTADT	BG 14 DUDERSTADT	BG 17 BAYREUTH
BG 12 BAD BRAMSTEDT	BG 15 ESCHWEGE	BG 18 ROSENHEIM
BG 13 UELTZEN	BG 16 ALSFELD	

Bldrs: Lürssen, Vegasack, except B-13: Schlichting, Travemünde

D: 140 tons (203 fl)   **S:** 30 kts   **Dim:** 38.3 × 7.0 × 2.15
A: 2/40-mm AA (I × 2)   **Man:** 23 men   **Range:** 450/27
M: 3 MTU diesels; 3 props; 7,885 hp

REMARKS: In service 1969-70. Centerline engine of 685 hp for cruise. Two additional planned were canceled.

◆ a number of smaller craft plus helicopters

◆ 1 tug

BG 5 RETTIN   Bldr: Mützelbeldt-Werft, Cuxhaven

D: 99.9 grt   **S:** 9 kts   **Dim:** 22.5 (20.0 pp) × 6.6 × 2.9
M: 2 MWM diesels; 1 prop; 590 hp

REMARK: Launched 29-1-76.

FISHERIES PROTECTION

NOTE: Operated by the Ministry of Agriculture and Fisheries.

◆ 7 patrol ships

N . . .   Bldr . . .

D: . . .   **S:** 20.5 kts   **Dim:** 82.0 × 12.8 × 4.3   **M:** Diesels

REMARK: Authorized 1979.

MEERKATZE   Bldr: Lürssen, Vegasack, 1976

D: 2,386 tons   **S:** 15 kts   **Dim:** 76.5 × 11.8 × 5.5   **Man:** 30 men
M: 3 MWM diesels, electric drive; 2 props; 2,300 hp

SOLEA   Bldr: Sieghold, Bremerhaven, 1974

D: 337 grt   **S:** 12 kts   **Dim:** 33.5 × 9.0 × 3.6
M: 1 Deutz diesel; 640 hp   **Man:** 11 men

WALTHER HERWIG   Bldr: Schlichting, Travemünde, 1972

D: 2,500 tons   **S:** 15.5 kts   **Dim:** 77.0 × 14.9 × 5.2   **Man:** 35 men
M: 2 M.A.N. diesels; 2 props; 3,380 hp

FRITHJOF   Bldr: Schlichting, Travemünde, 1967

D: 2,140 tons   **S:** 15 kts   **Dim:** 76.0 × 11.8 × 5.2
M: 3 Maybach diesels, electric drive; 2 props; 2,650 hp   **Man:** 35 men

ANTON DOHRN (ex-*Walther Herwig*)   Bldr: Seebeck, Bremerhaven, 1963

D: 1,986 grt   **S:** 15 kts   **Dim:** 83.0 × 12.5 × 5.2
M: Maybach diesels; 2,210 hp   **Man:** 38 men

POSEIDON   Bldr: Mützelfeldt, Cuxhaven, 1957

D: 934 grt   **S:** 12 kts   **Dim:** 58.8 × 10.2 × . . .
M: 1 Verschure diesel; 800 hp   **Man:** 20 men

GOVERNMENT CIVIL RESEARCH SHIPS

NOTE: Operated by the German Hydrographic Institute, which is subordinate to the Ministry of Transport.

◆ 6 oceanographic research and survey ships

N . . .   Bldr: Schlichting Werft, Travemünde, 1979

D: 1,372 tons (light)   **S:** 13.5 kts   **Dim:** 68.7 (61.0 pp) × 13.0 × 4.0
M: Diesel-electric

POSEIDON   Bldr: Schichau, Unterweser, 1976

D: 1,050 grt   **S:** 15 kts   **Dim:** 58.0 × 11.4 × . . .
M: MWM diesels; 1,800 hp

KOMET   Bldr: Jadewerft, Wilhelmshaven, 1969

D: 1,253 grt   **S:** 15 kts   **Dim:** 68.0 × 11.5 × 4.0
M: 2 Maybach diesels; 1 prop; 2,650 hp   **Man:** 42 men

METEOR   Bldr: Seebeck, Bremerhaven, 1963

GERMANY — FEDERAL REPUBLIC (continued)

GOVERNMENT CIVIL RESEARCH SHIPS (continued)

D: 2,800 tons   **S:** 15 kts   **Dim:** 81.0 × 13.5 × . . .
M: Diesel-electric; 765 hp   **Man:** 57 men

ATAIR   WEGA   Bldr: Schlichting, Travemünde, 1962

D: 157 grt   **S:** 10.5 kts   **Dim:** 31.7 × 6.5 × 2.3
M: 1 Deutz diesel; 205 hp   **Man:** 13 men

GHANA

PERSONNEL: 2,000 men

MERCHANT MARINE 1978: 85 ships — 186,079 grt

CORVETTES

◆ 2 Vosper Mk 1

	Bldr	L	In serv.
F 17 KROMANTSE	Vosper Ltd	5-9-63	9-64
F 18 KETA	Vickers-Armstrong	18-1-65	8-65

Keta   G. Arra, 1975

D: 435 tons (500 fl)   **S:** 18 kts   **Dim:** 53.95 (49.38 pp) × 8.7 × 3.05
Man: 5 officers, 49 men   **A:** 1/102-mm — 1/40-mm AA — 1 Squid ASW mortar
Electron Equipt: Radars: 1/Type 978 navigational, 1/Plessey ASW-1

Fuel: 60 tons   **Range:** 1,100/18, 2,900/14   **Electric:** 360 kw
M: 2/16-cyl. Bristol Siddeley-Maybach diesels; 2 props; 5,720 hp

REMARKS: Stabilizers. Quarters are air-conditioned. Both refitted 1974-75.

PATROL BOATS

◆ 2 Jaguar-III (FPB-57) class   Bldr: Lürssen, Vegasack

P 28 ACHIMOTO   P 29 YOGAGA

D: 380 tons (410 fl)   **S:** 30 kts   **Dim:** 58.1 × 7.6 × 2.8
A: 2/40-mm AA (I × 2)   **M:** 3 MTU diesels; 3 props; . . . hp

REMARKS: Ordered at the end of 1976; launched 11-5-79. No missiles to be carried.

◆ 2 Jaguar-II (TNC-45) class   Bldr: Lürssen, Vegasack

P 26 DZATA   P 27 SEBO

D: 255 tons (fl)   **S:** 38.5 kts   **Dim:** 44.9 × 7.0 × 2.3
A: 2/40-mm AA (I × 2)

REMARKS: Ordered at the end of 1976. P-26 in service 12-78; P-27, 5-79.

◆ 2 Sahene class Bldr: Ruthoff, Mainz, Germany, 1976

P 24 SAHENE   P 25 DELA

Dela   1976

D: 160 tons (fl)   **S:** 30 kts   **Dim:** 35.2 × 6.5 × 1.8
A: 1/40-mm AA (with flare launchers attached)   **Man:** 32 men
Range: 1,000/30   **M:** 2 MTU MD16V538 TB90 diesels; 2 props; 3,000 hp

REMARKS: Ordered 1973; builder went bankrupt and four others were not delivered. Designed for rescue and fisheries protection. Rescue equipment aft.

◆ 2 British Ford class Bldr: Yarrow

P 13 ELMINA (18-10-62)   P 14 KOMENDA (17-5-62)

D: 120 tons (160 fl)   **S:** 15 kts   **Dim:** 35.7 × 6.2 × 2.1
A: 1/40-mm — depth charges   **Man:** 19 men
Fuel: 23 tons   **M:** 2 Paxman YHAXM diesels; 2 props; 1,100 hp

REMARK: Seaward defense boats.

GHANA (continued)

MINE WARFARE SHIPS

♦ **1 British "-ton"-class coastal minesweeper**

M 16 EJURA (ex-*Aldington*) Bldr: Camper & Nicholson, 1955

> **D:** 370 tons (425 fl) **S:** 15 kts **Dim:** 46.33 × 8.76 × 2.5
> **A:** 1/40-mm AA — 2/20-mm AA (II × 1)
> **Electron Equipt:** Radar: Type 978 **Range:** 2,300/13, 3,000/8
> **Fuel:** 45 tons **Man:** 27 men **M:** 2 Deltic 18A-7A diesels; 2 props; 3,000 hp

REMARKS: Loaned 1964, bought 1974. Two former British "-ham"-class minesweepers, *Yogada* and *Afadzato*, were discarded in 1977.

REPAIR SHIP

ASUANTSI (ex-MRC-1122)

> **D:** 657 tons (fl) **S:** 9 kts **Dim:** 70.5 × 11.9 × 1.5
> **M:** 4 Paxman diesels; 2 props; 1,840 hp

REMARKS: British LCT(4)-class landing craft converted to floating workshop. Purchased 1965.

GREAT BRITAIN

Now, we are third . . .
> DAILY MAIL

We can no longer afford to patrol the World's sea lanes.
> ROY MASON
> Ministry of Defense (1975)

The nation that would rule upon the sea must always attack . . .
> MONCK

PERSONNEL (1979):

	Officers	Nonofficers	Total
Royal Navy and Royal Marines	9,583	59,662	69,245
Women's Royal Naval Service	447	3,389	3,836
Total	10,030	63,051	73,081

MERCHANT MARINE (1978): 3,559 ships — 30,896,606 grt
(tankers: 441 – 14,731,430 grt)

NAVAL PROGRAM: There is no publicly announced long-range construction program. However, as of 1 January 1980 there were on order or under construction 4 nuclear-powered attack submarines, 2 small aircraft carriers, 7 guided-missile destroyers, 3 guided-missile frigates, 4 minehunters, and a number of auxiliaries.

WARSHIPS IN SERVICE, UNDER CONSTRUCTION, OR PROJECTED
AS OF 1 JANUARY 1980

	L	Tons	Main armament
♦ **2 (+3) aircraft carriers**			
(3) INVINCIBLE	1977-	16,000	1/Sea Dart, 5/Sea Harrier, 9/Sea King
1 HERMES	1953	23,900	5/Sea Harrier, 9/Sea King
1 BULWARK	1948	23,300	9/Sea King, 6/Wessex
♦ **30 (+5) submarines**		Tons (surfaced)	
4 RESOLUTION (nuclear ballistic missile)	1966-68	7,500	16/Polaris A3, 6/533-mm TT
(3) TRAFALGAR (nuclear attack)	. . .	. . .	. . .
4 (+2) SWIFTSURE (nuclear attack)	1971-80	4,200	5/533-mm TT
5 VALIANT (nuclear attack)	1963-70	4,000	6/533-mm TT
1 DREADNOUGHT	1960	3,500	6/533-mm TT
16 PORPOISE/OBERON	1956-66	2,030	6/533-mm TT
♦ **2 cruisers**		Tons	
2 TIGER	1945	9,550	2/152-mm DP, 2/76-mm DP, 2/Sea Cat, 4/Sea King
♦ **13 (+8) guided-missile destroyers**			
(4) TYPE 42C	1984	. . .	1/Sea Dart, 1/114-mm DP, 1/helicopter
6 (+4) SHEFFIELD	1971-82	3,150	1/Sea Dart, 1/114-mm DP, 1/Sea Lynx
1 BRISTOL	1969	6,100	1/Sea Dart, 1/Limbo, 1/Ikara, 1/114-mm DP
6 COUNTY	1961-67	5,440	1/Sea Slug, 2/Sea Cat, 4/114-mm DP, 1/Wessex
♦ **53 (+5) frigates**			
1 (+5) BROADSWORD	1976-80	3,500	2/Sea Wolf, 2/40-mm AA, 2/Sea Lynx
8 AMAZON	1971-75	2,750	4/MM38 Exocet, 1/Sea Cat, 1/114-mm DP, 1/Sea Lynx or Wasp
26 LEANDER	1961-71	2,450-650	1, 2, or 3/Sea Cat, 2/114-mm and/or 40-mm, 1/Wasp, 1/MM38 Exocet or Ikara in 16, ASW weapons
7 TRIBAL	1959-62	2,300	2/114-mm DP, 1/Limbo, 1/Wasp
9 ROTHESAY	1957-60	2,380	2/114-mm DP 1/Sea Cat, 1/Wasp, 1/Limbo
1 WHITBY	1954	2,150	2/114-mm DP, 1/Limbo
1 LEOPARD	1955	2,300	4/114-mm DP, 1/40-mm AA

WARSHIPS IN SERVICE, UNDER CONSTRUCTION, OR PROJECTED (*continued*)

◆ **21 (+4) patrol ships, boats, and craft**

◆ **37 (+16) mine warfare ships**

◆ **12 amphibious warfare ships**

WEAPONS AND SYSTEMS

A. MISSILES

◆ **strategic ballistic missiles**

The Royal Navy uses the U.S. Polaris A3, but the three nonmaneuverable re-entry warheads, 200 kilotons each, are of British design and construction.

◆ **surface-to-air missiles**

Sea Dart (GWS 30)   Bldr: Hawker Siddeley Dynamics
Medium-range system (25 miles, interception altitudes from 100 to 60,000 ft)
  Length: 4,400 m   Wingspan: 0.91 m
  Diameter: 0.42 m   Weight: 550 kg
  Propulsion: solid propellant then ramjet
  Guidance: semi-active homing
  Fire control: Type 909 radar
Fitted on the *Bristol*, the *Sheffield*, and the *Invincible*
Mk 30 Mod 0 launcher on the *Bristol*; the lighter Mk 30 Mod 2 on the *Sheffield* class
A lightweight version of the entire system is in development

Sea Slug Mk 1 and Mk 2   Bldr: Hawker Siddeley Dynamics
Short-range system (15 miles slant range, 500 to 50,000 ft)
  Length: 5.94 m   Wingspan: 1.420 m (1.600 with fins)
  Diameter: 0.41 m   Weight: 900 kg (2,000 kg with boosters)
  Speed: Mach 1.8
  Propulsion: solid propulsion system with four solid boosters
  Fire control: Type 901, a beam-riding radar
  Fitted on the County-class DDG

Sea Wolf (GWS 25)   Bldr: BAC
Short-range missile system (5,000 m)
  Length: 1.9 m   Wingspan: 0.45 m
  Diameter: 0.3 m   Weight: 82 kg
  Guidance: radar
  Fire control: Marconi Type 910 pulse-doppler radar, which permits control of 2-missile salvoes
Fitted on *Broadsword*-class frigates; to be installed on some *Leander* class
Launcher contains six missiles (total weight with missiles: 3,500 kg)
Target designation is via the combined Type 967-968 radar

Sea Wolf (GWS 40)   Bldr: BAC
Intended to replace the Sea Cat systems on the Type 21 frigates as well as smaller warships, GWS 40 is a lightweight system now under development. It will use a quadruple reloadable launcher and will have a new combined warning pulse-doppler control radar system being developed by BAC and HSA of the Netherlands.

Sea Cat (GWS 20, 21, 22, and 24)   Bldr: Short and Harland
  Length: 1.47 m   Wingspan: 0.65 m

  Diameter: 0.2 m   Weight: 68 kg
  Propulsion: 2-stage solid propellant
  Guidance: GWS 21, GWS 22, or GWS 24, radar or GWS 20 optical system
  Launcher contains 4 missiles

◆ **surface-to-surface missiles**

The Royal Navy has purchased the MM38 Exocet (*see* section on France) and builds it under license.
In August 1977, it was announced that the U.S. Harpoon system would be bought for use from submarines.

◆ **air-to-surface missiles**

AS 11 (*see* section on France) is used from Wasp helicopters on frigates

Sea Skua   Bldr: BAC

Solid propellant
  Length: 2.83 m   Wingspan: 0.6 m
  Diameter: 0.2 m   Weight: 210 kg (20 kg of explosive)
  Speed: . . .   Range: 9,000 m
  Guidance: semi-active
  Being developed for use by Lynx helicopters

B. GUNS

114-mm Mk 5

Single barrel, semi-automatic, deck-installed, hand-loaded
  Maximum effective range in surface fire: 11,000 m
  Maximum effective range in anti-aircraft fire: 5,000 m
  Rate of fire: 8/10 rounds/min
Fitted on the Tribal-class frigates

114-mm Mk 6

Double-barreled, semi-automatic, triple-purpose (air, surface, and land targets)
  Muzzle velocity: 850 m/sec
  Maximum effective range in surface fire: 13,000 m
  Maximum effective range in anti-aircraft fire: 6,000 m
  Rate of fire: 10/12 rounds/min/barrel
Installed on some *Leander*, all *Rothesay*, *Whitby*, and *Leopard*-class frigates, and on County-class destroyers

114-mm Mk 8

Singe-barreled, automatic, triple-purpose (air, surface, and land targets); muzzle brake
  Length of barrel: 55 calibers
  Maximum effective range in surface fire: 13,000 m
  Maximum effective range in anti-aircraft fire: 6,000 m
  Rate of fire: 25 rounds/min
  Arc of elevation: −10° +53°
Light gun mount in synthetic resin reinforced with fiberglass
Installed on the *Bristol*, *Sheffield*-class destroyers, and *Amazon*-class frigates

152-mm Mk 26

Twin-barreled automatic, triple-purpose (air, surface, and land targets)
  Length of tube: 50 calibers
  Muzzle velocity: 800 m/sec

WEAPONS AND SYSTEMS (continued)

Maximum effective range in surface fire: 15,000 m
Maximum effective range in anti-aircraft fire: 8,000 m
Rate of fire: 25 rounds/min
Turret weight: 156 tons
Fire control: MRS 3
Fitted in the cruisers *Blake* and *Tiger*

76-mm Mk 6

Twin-barreled automatic anti-aircraft
Length of tube: 70 calibers
Muzzle velocity: 1,400 m/sec
Maximum effective range in surface fire: 5,000 m
Rate of fire: 120 rounds/min/barrel
Fitted in the cruisers *Blake* and *Tiger*

Bofors 40-mm

60-caliber guns are used on single Mk 7 and Mk 9 mounts; all Mk 5 twin mounts have now been discarded except on the *Bulwark*

Oerlikon 20-mm

Standard 80-caliber single mountings are used in many classes

C. ANTISUBMARINE WEAPONS

Mk 10 Mortar (Limbo)

Triple-barreled mortar based on the Squid of World War II. Range: 700 to 1,000 m

Ikara

Mk 44 or Mk 46 torpedo below a guided missile launched by a solid-fuel rocket motor
Maximum range: 18,000 m
Fitted on the *Bristol* and eight *Leander*-class frigates

D. TORPEDOES

U.S. Mk 44 and Mk 46 ASW torpedoes

The principal torpedoes of British origin are:
the wire-guided, submarine-launched ASW Mk 23
the wire-guided Mk 24 Tigerfish (ex-Ongar). This torpedo is designed for use by nuclear attack submarines
a new torpedo designated NST 75 11 Stingray is scheduled to enter service in 1980. It is intended for launch by helicopters and by the RAFs *Nimrod* ASW aircraft

E. SONARS

◆ On surface ship

No.	Type	Frequency band	Average range (above layer)
170B	Hull	High	2,500 m
174	Hull	High	2,500 m
177	Hull, 360° scan	Medium	6,000 m
184	Hull, 360° scan	Medium	7,000 m
199	Towed	Medium	7,000 m
2016	Hull, 360° scan	Multiple	. . .

199 is the British version of the Canadian SQS 504. Most VDS have been removed from *Leander*- and Tribal-class frigates (Ikara *Leander*s retain them); the reason given is that the equipment is not needed in the normal Eastern Atlantic operating area for RN ships. But the real reason is insufficient mastery of VDS employment techniques and a lack of spare parts.

◆ On submarines

186	Passive	Low
187	Active-Passive	Low-Medium
2001	Active-Passive	Low
2007	Passive	Low-Medium

◆ On helicopters

195		Medium	3,000 m

F. DATA SYSTEMS

The data systems outlined below are either in service or will soon enter service:
ADA (Action Data Automation)
ADAWS 1 Aerial defense system. Fitted on County-class destroyers
ADAWS 2 Integrated AAW and ASW defense system. Fitted on the *Bristol*
ADAWS 4 Integrated AAW and ASW defense system. Fitted on the *Sheffield*-class destroyers
ADAWS 5 Aerial and ASW defense. Fitted on the *Invincible*-class aircraft carriers
CAAIS (Computer Assisted Action Information System)
In *Amazon*-class frigates for tactical data-handling; linked to WSA 4 fire control system

G. RADARS

◆ Navigation

978 (3 cm, I band)
1002 (9,650 MHz) for *Porpoise*-class submarines
1006 (9,445 MHz) in newest surface ships and submarines, navalized Kelvin-Hughes 19/9A.

◆ Air-search

965   Metric radar (long range)
965M The M is composed of two 965 antennas, one placed on top of the other with the Mk 10 IFF interrogator built in

966   STIR (Surveillance Target Indicator Radar) is new radar designed for the *Invincible* and can operate in a strong electronic countermeasures environment
1022 Dutch LW-08 air search with a Marconi antenna, on *Invincible* class

◆ Surface-to-air, low-altitude search (combination)

992, 992 Q, and 993 (E-F bands)

967   Pulse doppler: combination of radar bands H, G, and I, found in the Sea Wolf
968   system (GWS 25)

◆ Height-finding

277 and 982 (E-F bands)
278 and 983 (E-F bands)

WEAPONS AND SYSTEMS (*continued*)

◆ Gun-direction

275 (F band) is used in the older FC system for Mk 6 twin 114-mm gun mounts in the *Whitby* and *Leopard* frigates

903 (I band) is used in all other Mk 6 and Mk 5 114-mm directors (MRS 3), as well as with the 152-mm and 76.2-mm guns on the *Tiger*-class cruisers

◆ Missile-guidance

262	Sea Cat GWS 21 system on MRS 8 directors, Tribal class only
901	Sea Slug system (I band)
903	MRS 3 and GWS 22 fire control for the Sea Cat
909	Sea Dart system (also 114-mm Mk 8 gun in the *Sheffield*-class destroyers)
910	Tracking radar used with the Sea Wolf (GWS 25) system
RTN-10X	Used for Sea Cat and 114-mm control in *Amazon*-class frigates

◆ For aircraft

Sea Spray (. . . band) for helicopters
Blue Fox (. . . band) for Sea Harrier

H. COUNTERMEASURES

A launched decoy system (chaff) called Knebworth Corvus is used on major combat units. All ships so equipped have two eight-tubed launchers. A new chaff rocket is in development for the launcher, with much greater "bloom."

Invincible   R. Hodgson, 1979

AIRCRAFT CARRIERS

◆ 3 Invincible class

		Bldr	Laid down	L	In serv.
C 01	INVINCIBLE	Vickers, Barrow	20-7-73	3-5-77	1980
C 02	ILLUSTRIOUS	Swan Hunter	7-10-76	14-12-78	. . .
C 03	ARK ROYAL	Swan Hunter	14-12-78	. . .	. . .

D: 16,000 tons (19,500 fl)   **S:** 28 kts
Dim: 206.6 (192.87 wl) × 31.89 (27.5 wl) × 6.4 (mean)
A: 1/Sea Dart system (22 missiles) — Aircraft: 5/Sea Harrier — 9/Sea King Mk 4
Electron Equipt: Radars: 1/1006, 1/992R, 1/1022, 2/909 — ADAWS 5 — 2/Knebworth
       Corvus   Sonar: 1/184
Electric: 12,000 kw   **Range:** 5,000/18
Man: 129 officers, 869 men (plus aircrew)
M: 4 Rolls-Royce Olympus TM3B gas turbines; 2 controllable-pitch props; 112,000 hp

REMARKS: *Invincible*, ordered 17-4-73 and intended for V/STOL aircraft and helicopters only, has a flight deck 180 meters long with a 7-degree "ski jump" at the forward end to assist Sea Harrier aircraft in making rolling takeoffs at full combat load. The flight deck on the later pair will be at 9 degrees and 10 to 12 meters longer. The flight deck is slightly angled to port to clear the Sea Dart launcher, which is awkwardly located on the ship's centerline and has been given an elaborate blast shield to protect the aircraft aboard. The single-level hangar has three separate bays, with the amidships bay narrower to permit passage of the gas-turbine exhausts. There are two elevators. The Type 1022 long-range air-search radar uses a Marconi antenna but has the same electronics as the HSA LW-08. Four MM38 Exocet launchers were deleted from the design, but the emplacements intended for them (to starboard of the Sea Dart launcher) remain, taking up valuable flight-deck space.

NOTE: The previous *Ark Royal* was decommissioned 12-78.

	Bldr	Laid down	L	In serv.
R 12 HERMES	Vickers, Barrow	6-44	16-2-53	11-59

D: 23,900 tons (28,700 fl)   **S:** 28 kts
Dim: 226.85 (198.12 pp) × 27.43 (wl) × 8.8
A: 2/Sea Cat systems (IV × 2) — Aircraft: 5/Sea Harrier — 9/Sea King Mk 2
Electron Equipt: Radars: 1/965, 1/978, 1/993, GWS 22 FC — TACAN
       Sonar: 1/184
Boilers: 4 Admiralty   **Fuel:** 4,200 tons   **Electric:** 9,000 kw
Man: 143 officers, 1,027 men   **M:** Parsons GT; 2 props; 83,000 hp

REMARKS: Converted 1971-73 by the Devonport Naval Dockyard into a helicopter-carrying commando carrier (LPH). Converted again 1976/1-77 as an ASW carrier for Sea King and Wessex helicopters and, by 1980, will be converted for operational employment of the first of 24 Sea Harrier V/STOL strike aircraft now on order. She will continue in service until 1985 as an interim version of the *Invincible* class. *Hermes* retains the ability to embark a commando group (750 men) and continues to carry four LCVPs in davits. Catapults and arresting gear removed 1971. Flight deck angled 6.5 degrees and strengthened for Harriers. A 12-degree "ski jump" takeoff ramp was intended to be fit to her bow during 1979, in anticipation of the Sea Harriers she will receive in 1981. In 1978 a Ferranti 1600E computer was added to aid in tactical data handling.

AIRCRAFT CARRIERS (*continued*)

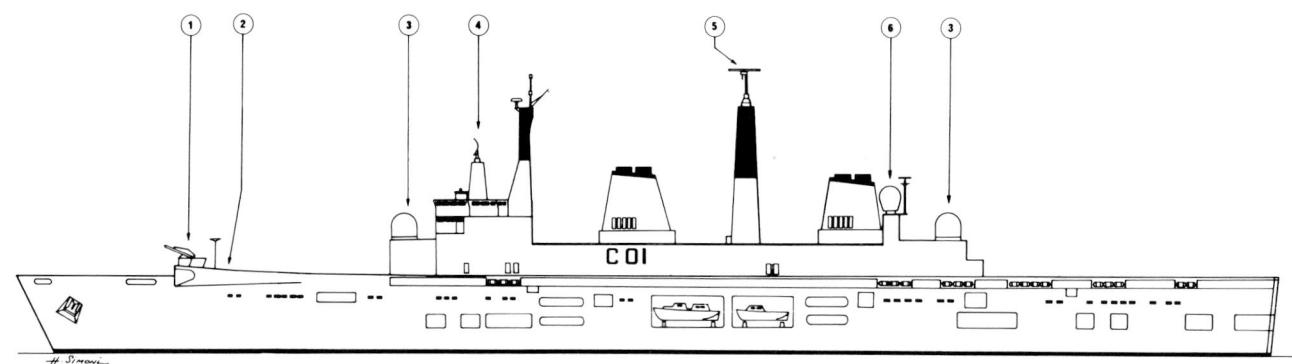

1. Sea Dart   2. "Ski jump" takeoff ramp   3. Type 909 fire-control radar   4. Type 1022 radar   5. Type 992R radar   6. SCOT satellite communications system

Invincible—official model

1978

AIRCRAFT CARRIERS (continued)

Hermes   S. Terzibaschitsch, 1977

Hermes   1977

Hermes   J.-C. Bellonne, 1977

	Bldr	Laid down	L	In serv.
R 08 BULWARK	Harland & Wolff	5-45	22-6-48	10-54

D: 23,300 tons (27,705 fl)   **S:** 28 kts
Dim: 224.9 (198.12 pp) × 37.49 (27.0 wl) × 8.5
A: 8/40-mm AA (II × 4) — Aircraft: 9/Sea King Mk 2, 61 Wessex Mk 5
Electron Equipt: Radars: 1/983, 1/993, 1/978
Man: 900 men (2,000 with air group)
Armor: Flight deck: 50 mm — Watertight bulkheads on each side below the waterline: 25 mm
Boilers: 4 Admiralty
Electric: 3,200 kw   **Fuel:** 3,880 tons   **M:** Parsons GT; 2 props; 83,000 hp

Bulwark   J.-C. Bellonne, 1972

REMARKS: Converted in 1959-60 to commando carrier. She was reduced to reserve in 4-76 but was recommissioned 23-2-79 to serve as ASW support and/or commando carrier until the *Illustrious* is completed in the early 1980s. There are two centerline elevators. The commando (750 men) can be put ashore by helicopter or by four LCVP landing craft, which are hung in davits aft, two on each side. For short distances, two commandos can be carried. Living quarters are air-conditioned. Sisters *Albion* and *Centaur* were stricken in 1972. Although *Bulwark* has handled Harriers, no Sea Harriers will be included in her air complement. Sea King Mk 4 will replace Wessex Mk 5 for troop carrying.

NAVAL AVIATION

Ship-based aviation, the Fleet Air Arm, is the only air component in the Royal Navy. All 12 Phantom and 14 Buccaneer aircraft were handed over to the RAF when the *Ark Royal* was decommissioned in 1978; the remaining eight Gannet early-warning aircraft were discarded.

Except at the level of formation commanders, there is no naval air command. Land-based ASW aircraft belong to the RAF and, since the reorganization of the latter, have constituted the Eighteenth, or Maritime, Group of Strike Command. While the group is part of the RAF as regards personnel and equipment, its employment is determined by the Royal Navy.

The Fleet Air Arm consists of:

First-line squadrons (designation characterized by a group of three figures beginning with an 8) whose missions are: attack, ASW, and helicopter assault.

NAVAL AVIATION (continued)

Sea Harrier   1978

Nimrod   1970

Westland Wasp

Second-line squadrons (designation characterized by a group of three figures beginning with a 7) that are used in schools, tests, and maintenance.

The total of operational aircraft available to the Royal Navy includes 30 Sea King, 7 Wessex Mk 3, and 40 Wasp ASW helicopters, and about 20 Wessex Mk 5 troop-carrying helicopters. For short-based training and other duties, Sea King, Wessex Mk 3, Wasp, and Gazelle helicopters are available, as well as 16 Jetstream T-2 and a few Canberra and Hunter fixed-wing aircraft. As of 1-1-79, 15 Sea King Mk 4, 30 Sea Lynx, 6 Gazelle, and 24 Sea Harrier were on order. In early 1979 it was announced that the WG 34, a replacement for Sea King Mk 2, would be developed by Westland.

BASES

Fleet Air Arm bases are given ships' names. They are:
RNAS, Yeovilton (HMS Heron)
RNAS, Culdrose (HMS Sea Hawk)
RNAS, Prestwick (HMS Gannet)
RNAS, Lee-on-Solent (HMS Daedalus)
RNAS, Portland (HMS Osprey)

Westland WG 13 Lynx   1974

NAVAL AVIATION (continued)

COMBAT AIRCRAFT

Type and builder	Mission	Wingspan	Length	Height	Weight	Engine	Max. speed in Mach or in knots	Practical maximum ceiling in feet	Range	Weapons	Remarks
◆ **FIXED-WING**											
Sea Harrier (Hawker Siddeley)	Attack	7.6	14.1	3.35	10,500	1 Rolls-Royce Pegasus turbojet with 9,750 kg thrust	Mach 0.96 Mach 1.2 (diving)	50,000	VTOL: 50 miles STOL: 250 miles	2,270 kg, including P3T Martel ASM	For the *Invincible* class, *Hermes*, and *Bulwark*. The Sea Harrier plane will have a more corrosion-resistant Pegasus 104 engine in place of the 103, which is used by RAF aircraft. In defense missions the Sea Harrier will have AIM-9L Sidewinder air-to-air missiles and 2/30-mm Aden guns
Nimrod (Hawker Siddeley) (RAF-operated)	ASW detection and engagement	35.1	38.03	9	79,000	4 Rolls-Royce Spey (RB 168-20) Mk 250 jet engines, 5,200 hp thrust each	450 kts	40,000	11 hrs	Bomb bay for 15-m weapons (6 torpedoes + 10 buoys) 2/Martel or 4/AS 12	Can carry nuclear depth charges
◆ **HELICOPTERS** **Wasp** (Westland)	ASW, anti-surface	Rotor diam. 9.82	12.23	3.27	1,370	1 Blackburn Nimbus 102 turboshaft, 1,050 hp	109 kts 96 kts (cruising)	12,000		1/Mk 44 torpedo or 2/AS 11 ASM	On board the Tribal, *Whitby*, *Rothesay*, and *Leander* frigate classes
WG 13 Lynx (Westland)	ASW, anti-surface	12.8	15.2	3.2	4,150	2 Rolls-Royce BS 360 turboshafts, 900 hp each	150 kts	12,000	1 hr 30 min. (half hovering, half cruising)	2/Mk 44 or Mk 46 torpedoes Seal Skua air-surface missiles	Franco-British helicopter. On board the *Sheffield*, *Amazon*, and *Broadsword* classes. Some to carry AN/ANS-18 dipping sonar
Wessex Mk3 Mk5 (Westland)	ASW transport assault	17.06	20.05	4.82	Mk 3: 5,700 Mk 5: 5,800	Mk 3: 1 Napier Gazelle 161 NGA 13 turboshaft with 1,650 hp Mk 5: 2 linked Bristol-Siddeley Gnome H 1400 turbo-shafts with 1,400 hp each	Mk 3: 120 kts Mk 5: 130 kts	6,000 hovering 14,000 cruising	3 hrs	Mk 3: 2/Mk 44 or 46 torpedoes or 4/ depth charges Sonar	Mk 3: on board the County class; has APN-97 radar, Type 194 sonar. Mk 5: for troop carrying; on *Bulwark*, *Fearless* class, etc.
Sea King Mk 1 Mk 2 Mk 4 (Westland)	ASW	19	22		9,300	2 Rolls-Royce Gnome H turboshafts, 1,500 hp each driving a 5-bladed rotor and a tail rotor	124 kts	10,000	3 hr 15 min	4/Mk 44 or 46 torpedoes or 4/ Mk 11 depth charges. Sonar, radar (Mk 4: 4 tons stores or 27 troops)	58/Sea King Mk 1 are in service and 21/Mk 2 are in service or on order with Type 195 sonar, AW 392 radar, and Marconi-Elliot doppler navigation systems. On board *Bulwark*, *Hermes*, and to be on the *Invincible* class. MK 4 for troop carrying, no ASW gear

NAVAL AVIATION (*continued*)

Westland Wessex Mk 3

Westland Sea King HAS Mk 1   1978

Westland Wessex Mk 5 – delivering supplies to the **Fearless**

NOTE: Royal Navy submarines no longer wear hull numbers. The assigned numbers are included here for reference only.

BALLISTIC-MISSILE SUBMARINES

◆ **4 Resolution class**

		Bldr	Laid down	L	In serv.
S 22	RESOLUTION	Vickers-Armstrong	26-2-64	15-9-66	2-10-67
S 23	REPULSE	Vickers-Armstrong	12-3-65	4-11-67	28-9-68
S 26	RENOWN	Cammell Laird	25-6-64	25-2-67	15-11-68
S 27	REVENGE	Cammell Laird	19-5-65	15-3-68	4-12-69

Resolution—bow planes hinge at half-span　　　　　Vickers

Resolution　　　　　1978

D: 7,500 tons surfaced, 8,400 submerged　　　**S:** 25/20 kts
Dim: 129.54 × 10.05 × 9.15　　**Man:** 13 officers, 130 men
A: 16/Polaris A3 – 6/533-mm TT
Electron Equipt: Radar: 1/1003　　　Sonars: 1/2001, 1/2007
M: 1 Rolls-Royce pressurized-water reactor; 1 English-Electric turbine; 1 prop

Revenge　　　　　1976

BALLISTIC-MISSILE SUBMARINES (*continued*)

REMARKS: Characteristics are very similar to those of the U.S. *Lafayette* class, including the propulsion machinery, the launching and guidance systems, and the inertial navigation system. The A3 missiles with 3 MRV warheads of 200 kilotons each were furnished by the U.S., but the re-entry vehicles are of British conception and construction. Substitution of the Polaris A3 by the Poseidon or the Trident I is no longer being considered.

NUCLEAR-PROPELLED ATTACK SUBMARINES

◆ **3 Trafalgar class**   Bldr: Vickers, Barrow

	Laid down	L	In serv.
S 113 TRAFALGAR	4-79	. . .	. . .
S 114 . . .	. . .	. . .	. . .
S 115 . . .	. . .	. . .	. . .

REMARKS: Few details available; will be enlarged and improved *Swiftsure*-class submarines. S-113 was ordered 7-4-77, S-114 on 28-7-78, and S-115 5-79. Will carry Sub-Harpoon SSMs.

◆ **4 (+2) Swiftsure class**   Bldr: Vickers, Barrow

	Laid down	L	In serv.
S 104 SCEPTRE	25-10-73	20-11-76	1979
S 108 SOVEREIGN	18-9-70	22-2-73	22-7-74
S 109 SUPERB	16-3-72	30-11-74	13-11-76
S 111 SPARTAN	26-3-76	7-4-78	1980
S 112 SPLENDID (ex-*Severn*)	23-11-77	1979	. . .
S 126 SWIFTSURE	6-6-69	7-9-71	17-4-73

D: 4,000 tons light, 4,200 surfaced, 4,500 submerged
Dim: 82.9 × 10.12 × 8.2   **S:**   28/30 kts
A: 5/533-mm bow TT (20 torpedoes)
Electron Equipt: Radar: 1/1003   Sonars: 1/2001, 1/2007, 1/197, 1/183
Man: 12 officers, 85 men
M: 1 reactor; 1 turbine; 1 prop; 20,000 hp (1 Paxman auxiliary propulsion diesel, electric drive; 400 hp)

REMARKS: High-performance, very quiet submarines with excellent passive sonars. Carry the wire-guided Mk 24 Tigerfish torpedo. Will carry the U.S. Sub-Harpoon missile. Intended for ASW defense of surface forces.

Sovereign   1975

Superb   G. Arra, 1977

Superb   G. Arra, 1977

NUCLEAR-PROPELLED ATTACK SUBMARINES (*continued*)

Sceptre

1978

◆ 5 Valiant class

	Bldr	Laid down	L	In serv.
S 46 CHURCHILL	Vickers, Barrow	6-67	20-12-68	15-7-70
S 48 CONQUEROR	Cammell Laird	12-67	29-8-69	9-11-71
S 50 COURAGEOUS	Vickers, Barrow	10-68	7-3-70	16-10-71
S 102 VALIANT	Vickers, Barrow	22-1-62	3-12-63	18-7-66
S 103 WARSPITE	Vickers, Barrow	12-63	25-9-65	18-4-67

D: 3,500 tons standard, 4,000 surfaced, 4,900 submerged
Dim: 86.87 × 10.12 × 8.25   **S:** 25/20 kts   **Man:** 13 officers, 90 men
A: 6/533-mm TT fwd (26 torpedoes)
Electron Equipt: Radar: 1/1003   Sonars: 1/2001, 1/2007, 1/197, 1/183
M: 1 pressurized-water reactor; 2 English-Electric GT; 1 prop; 20,000 hp

REMARKS: The propulsion plant of the *Valiant* and the *Warspite* (20,000 hp) is of entirely British design and construction (Admiralty, Vickers, Rolls-Royce, and English-Electric). The hull form of this class is a development of the *Dreadnought*. In 1967 the *Valiant* made a nonstop, submerged cruise from Singapore to Great Britain in 28 days (12,000 miles). To receive Sub-Harpoon Missiles. S-106 completed long refit and refuelling 7-78.

Courageous

1972

Churchill

G. Arra, 1977

NUCLEAR-PROPELLED ATTACK SUBMARINES (*continued*)

◆ 1 Dreadnought class

	Bldr	Laid down	L	In serv.
S 101 DREADNOUGHT	Vickers, Barrow	12-6-59	21-10-60	17-4-63

Dreadnought   Pradignac & Leo, 1971

D: 3,000 tons standard, 3,500 surfaced, 4,000 submerged
Dim: 81.08 × 9.75 × 7.80
S: 25/15 kts   **A:** 6/533-mm TT fwd   **Man:** 11 officers, 77 men
Electron Equipt: Radar: 1003   Sonars: 2001/2007, 197, 183
M: 1 U.S./S5W reactor; GT; 1 prop; 15,000 hp

REMARKS: Authorized in 1956. The first Admiralty studies for the ship were entrusted to the nuclear branch of the Vickers Company, including Rolls-Royce for the reactor, Foster-Wheeler for the heat exchanger, and Vickers for the turbines. Finally, however, a Westinghouse S5W engine, furnished by the U.S. (1958), was adopted. The hull shape is similar to the U.S. nuclear submarine *Skipjack* except for the forward one-third. Endurance: 70 days. During major overhaul from 5-68 to 9-70, the core was renewed. Later in 1970 the ship made a cruise under the North Pole.

TORPEDO ATTACK SUBMARINES

◆ 3 Porpoise class

	Bldr	Laid down	L	In serv.
S 01 PORPOISE	Vickers-Armstrong	6-54	25-4-56	4-58
S 07 SEALION	Cammel Laird	6-58	31-12-59	7-61
S 08 WALRUS	Scott's SB, Greenock	2-53	22-9-59	2-61

◆ 13 Oberon class

	Bldr	Laid down	L	In serv.
S 09 OBERON	HM Dockyard, Chatham	11-57	18-7-59	2-61
S 10 ODIN	Cammell Laird	3-59	4-11-60	5-62
S 11 ORPHEUS	Vickers-Armstrong	4-59	17-11-59	11-60
S 12 OLYMPUS	Vickers-Armstrong	3-60	14-6-61	7-62
S 13 OSIRIS	Vickers-Armstrong	1-62	20-11-62	1-64
S 14 ONSLAUGHT	HM Dockyard, Chatham	4-59	24-9-60	8-62
S 15 OTTER	Scott's SB, Greenock	1-60	15-5-61	8-62
S 16 ORACLE	Cammell Laird	4-60	26-9-61	2-63
S 17 OCELOT	HM Dockyard, Chatham	11-60	5-5-62	8-63
S 18 OTUS	Scott's SB, Greenock	5-61	17-10-62	10-63
S 19 OPOSSUM	Cammell Laird	12-61	23-5-63	6-64
S 20 OPPORTUNE	Scott's SB, Greenock	10-62	14-2-64	12-64
S 21 ONYX	Cammell Laird	11-64	16-8-66	11-67

Onslaught   G. Arra, 1976

Osiris   S. Terzibaschitsch, 1977

D: 1,610 tons, 2,030 surfaced, 2,400 submerged   **S:** 17.5/15 kts
Dim: 89.92 (87.45 pp) × 8.07 × 5.48
Man: 6 officers, 62 men (S-01, S-08: 65 men)
A: 6/533-mm TT fwd, 2 aft (22 torpedoes)
Electron Equipt: Radars: 1/1002 (p) 1/1006 (o)
                   Sonars: 1/186, 1/187
M: 2/3,680-hp Admiralty Standard Range 16 VVS-AS21 diesels; diesel-electric drive; 2 props; 6,000 hp

TORPEDO ATTACK SUBMARINES *(continued)*

REMARKS: Conventional propulsion and hull form. Streamlined sail. Maximum depth: 200 meters. Snorkel. Air-conditioned. Excellent living spaces. Long endurance. Plastics used throughout in the design of the superstructure of the second series (*Oberon, Odin, Onslaught,* for example) as well as light alloys (*Orpheus*). The first *Onyx* transferred to Canada (1-64) and renamed the *Ojibwa;* another *Onyx* was built. Canada ordered three ships of this class, Australia six, Chile two, and Brazil three. The *Porpoise* is used as a submarine target. The *Grampus* (S-04) of the same class was stricken in 1976, the *Rorqual* (S-02) in 1976, the *Narwhal* (S-03) and *Cachelot* (S-06) in 1977, and the *Finwhale* (S-05) in 1978. Sale of the *Cachelot* to Egypt was canceled.

Sea Lion   G. Arra

NOTE: In 1974 it was announced that the Royal Navy would resume building conventional diesel-engine submarines. The first units of this new class, however, will not be ordered until the early 1980s.

CRUISERS

◆ **2 Tiger class**

	Bldr	Laid down	L	In serv.
C 99 BLAKE (ex-*Tiger*)	J. Brown, Clydebank	17-8-42	20-12-45	8-3-61
C 20 TIGER (ex-*Bellerophon*)	Fairfield SB, Govan	1-10-41	25-10-45	18-3-59

D: 9,550 tons (12,000 fl)   **S:** 31.5 kts (29.5 cruising)
Dim: 172.8 (164 pp) × 19.5 × 7.0   **Man:** 85 officers, 800 men
A: 2/152-mm DP (II × 1)—2/76-mm DP (II × 1)—2/Sea Cat systems (IV × 2)—4/Sea King Mk 1 ASW helicopters
Electron Equipt: Radars: 1/965, 1/992Q, 1/978, 1/278, 4/903
Armor: Belt: 90   Conning tower: 100   Deck: 52   Turrets: 26/52
Electric: 4,000 kw   **Boilers:** 4 Admiralty, 28.5 kg/cm² pressure—superheat to 355°C
Range: 6,500/13, 4,000/20, 2,100/29   **Fuel:** 1,850 tons
M: Parsons GT; 4 props; 72,500 hp

REMARKS: These ships are survivors of a series of eight cruisers of the *Swiftsure* class laid down during World War II. Converted into helicopter cruisers, the *Blake* from 1965 to 1968, and the *Tiger* from 1969 to 1972. The after 152-mm and 76-mm gun

Tiger   G. Arra, 1976

mounts were replaced by a hangar and a flight deck. The port and starboard 76-mm gun mounts were replaced by two Sea Cat launchers. The conversion of sister *Lion* was canceled and the ship was stricken. *Tiger* was reduced to reserve in late 1978 to provide crew for *Bulwark*. Both will probably be stricken in the early 1980s as the *Invincible* class is commissioned. Both ships have SCOT satellite communications domes beside their upper bridges.

Blake   S. Terzibaschitsch, 1977

CRUISERS (continued)

Blake   G. Arra, 1977

GUIDED-MISSILE DESTROYERS

NOTE: The prototype, *Sheffield* (shown in the drawing), had an experimental funnel design with the uptakes bent sideways in a form referred to as "Loxton Bends." *Hercules*, the first Argentine unit, has a similar stack. This feature was intended to keep the exhaust gases away from the after part of the ship, but it was found to be unnecessary, and the remainder of the class have reverted to a normal configuration. In D-86 and later units, the Mk 32 torpedo tubes are on the deckhouse at the base of the after mast.

◆ **4 . . . class (Type 42C)**

	Bldr	Laid down	L	In serv.
D . . . MANCHESTER	Vickers, Barrow	19-5-79	. . .	1984
D . . . GLOUCESTER	Vosper Thornycroft	1979	. . .	. . .
D . . . EDINBURGH	Cammell Laird	1979	. . .	. . .
D . . . YORK	Swan Hunter	1979	. . .	. . .

REMARKS: Unit 11 and later of the *Sheffield* class (Type 42C) are to be 12 meters longer and 0.6 meters greater in beam, leading to a full-load displacement on the order of 4,400 tons. Armament and other equipment are to remain as on the first 11 units, which may be a good indication that the original design is cramped and possibly a poor sea boat. The *Manchester* was ordered 10-11-78, the other three in 4-79. There is a possibility that two more will be ordered later.

◆ **6 (+4) Sheffield class (Type 42)**

	Bldr	Laid down	L	In serv.
D 80 SHEFFIELD	Vickers, Barrow	15-1-70	10-6-71	16-2-75
D 86 BIRMINGHAM	Cammell Laird	28-3-72	30-7-73	3-12-76
D 87 NEWCASTLE	Swan Hunter	21-2-73	24-4-75	23-3-78
D 88 GLASGOW	Swan Hunter	7-3-74	14-4-76	24-5-79
D 89 EXETER	Swan Hunter	22-7-76	25-4-78	. . .
D 90 SOUTHAMPTON	Vosper Thornycroft	21-10-76	29-1-79	. . .
D 91 NOTTINGHAM	Vosper Thornycroft	6-2-78	4-79	. . .
D 92 LIVERPOOL	Cammell Laird	5-7-78	. . .	. . .
D 108 CARDIFF	Vickers, Barrow	3-11-72	22-2-74	19-10-79
D 118 COVENTRY	Cammell Laird	22-3-73	21-6-74	10-11-78

D: 3,150 tons (4,100 fl) **Dim:** 125.0 (119.5 pp) × 14.34 × 5.0
S: 30 kts (18 cruising) **Man:** 26 officers, 273 enlisted
A: 1/Sea Dart GWS 30 (II × 1) (20 missiles) – 1/114-mm Mk 8 DP – 2/20-mm AA (I × 2) – 1/WG 13 Lynx ASW and anti-surface helicopter – 6/Mk 32 ASW TT (III × 2)
Electron Equipt: Radars: 1/965M, 1/992Q, 2/909, 1/1006 – ADAWS 4 – 2/Knebworth Corvus
 Sonars: 1/184, 1/174, 1/170B, 1/162

Birmingham   G. Arra, 1977

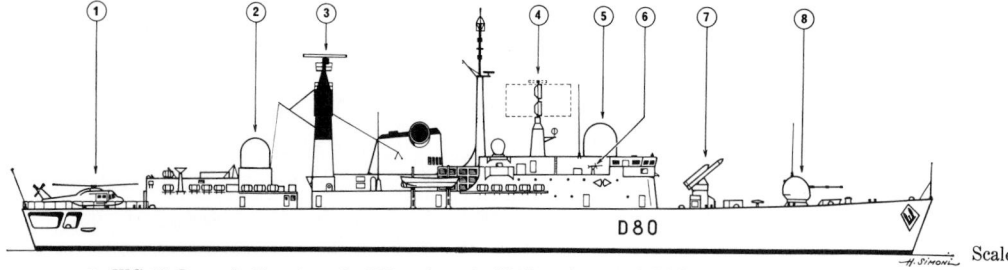

D 80   Scale 1/1000

1. WG 13 Lynx helicopter 2. 909 radar 3. 992Q radar 4. 965M radar 5. 909 radar
6. 20-mm AA 7. Sea Dart launcher 8. 114-mm DP mount Mk 8

GUIDED-MISSILE DESTROYERS (*continued*)

Sheffield   1975

Coventry   1978

GUIDED-MISSILE DESTROYERS (continued)

Birmingham—with radomes removed from Type 909 radar   1976

Range: 650/30, 4,500/18   **Electric:** 4,000 kw
M: COGOG propulsion; 2 Olympus TM3B gas turbines × 27,200 hp for high speed;
2 Tyne RM1A gas turbines × 4,100 hp for cruising; 2 five-bladed controllable-pitch props

REMARKS: First ordered 11-68. The cruising and high-speed turbines are not linked to
each other; each shaft must be driven by one or the other. Mk 30 Mod 2 launcher for
the Sea Dart system. The *Sheffield* initially did not have any ASW torpedo tubes; later
units do. The *Cardiff*, delayed by labor problems, was completed by Swan Hunter.
Completion of the *Glasgow* delayed by fire 9-76. All will receive two SCOT radomes for
Skynet satellite communications system. Very cramped ships. Helicopter is for surveillance and attack (Sea Skua missiles) rather than ASW.

◆ 1 Type 82

		Bldr	Laid down	L	In serv.
D 23	BRISTOL	Swan Hunter	15-11-67	30-6-69	31-3-73

D: 6,100 tons (7,100 fl)   **Dim:** 154.6 (149.9 wl) × 16.77 × 5.2 (7.0 over sonar)
S: 28 kts   **Man:** 29 officers, 378 men
A: 1/Sea Dart system (II × 1)(40 missiles) — 1/114-mm Mk 8 DP — 2/20-mm AA (I × 2)
— 1/Mk 10 Limbo ASW mortar — 1/Ikara ASW system (32 missiles) — 2/Knebworth
Corvus
Electron Equipt: Radars: 1/965M, 1/992Q, 1/978, 2/909, 1/1006 — ADAWS 2
                Sonars: 1/162, 1/170, 1/182, 1/184, 1/185, 1/189
M: COSAG propulsion; 2 props. On each shaft, 1 A.E.I. GT (15,000 hp) and 1 Rolls-
Royce Olympus TMIA gas turbine (22,300 hp): 74,600 hp total
Boilers: 2 Babcock & Wilcox, 49.2 kg/cm² pressure — 510°C superheat
Electric: 7,000 kw   **Range:** 5,000/18

Bristol   J.-C. Bellonne, 1974

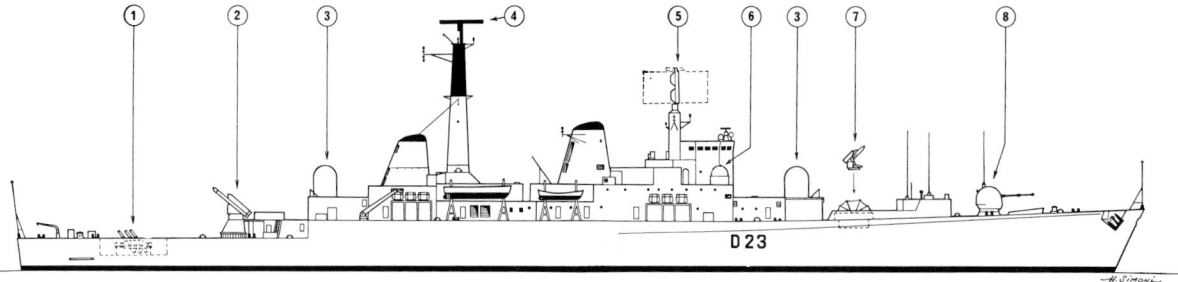

1. Limbo mortar 2. Sea Dart launcher 3. 909 radar 4. 992Q radar 5. 965M radar
6. Ikara fire-control radar 7. Ikara ASW system 8. 114-mm DP Mk 8

GUIDED-MISSILE DESTROYERS (*continued*)

Bristol—before full operational appearance   1975

REMARKS: Designed as an escort for the 50,000-ton aircraft carrier *Furious* when construction of the latter was being considered. There were to be eight in the class, but this ship, ordered in 10-66, was the only one built. Fin stabilizers and air-conditioning. The Sea Dart launcher is Mk 3 Mod 0. Missiles are stowed in a vertical position. Although nominally commissioned in 1973, she had not been accepted for active service by the time of her first refit in 1976-78. At that time full military equipment, including two 20-mm AA and chaff rocket launchers, were fitted; still to be added were electronic intercept gear (ECM) and SCOT antennae for the Skynet satellite communications system. Generally considered an expensive failure.

Antrim   S. Terzibaschitsch, 1977

◆ 6 County class

			Bldr	Laid down	L	In serv.
(a)	D 12	KENT	Harland & Wolff	1-3-60	27-9-61	8-63
	D 16	LONDON	Swan Hunter	26-2-60	7-12-61	11-63
(b)	D 19	GLAMORGAN	Fairfield SB&E	13-9-62	9-7-64	10-66
	D 18	ANTRIM	Fairfield SB&E	20-1-66	19-10-67	3-71
	D 20	FIFE	Vickers-Armstrong	1-6-62	9-7-64	6-66
	D 21	NORFOLK	Swan Hunter	15-3-66	16-11-67	3-70

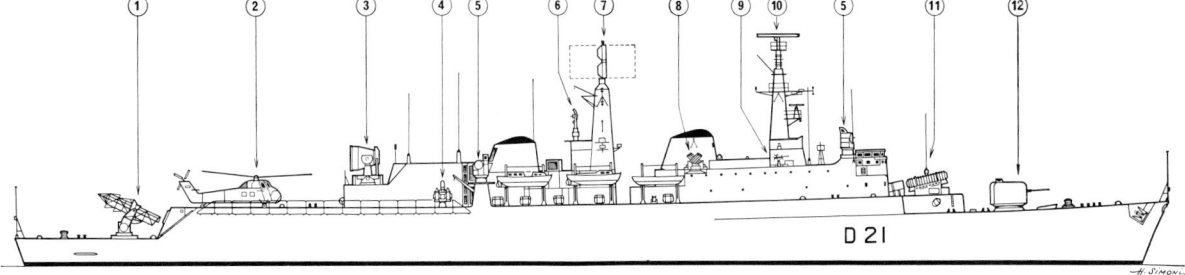

1. Sea Slug launcher 2. Wessex Mk 3 helicopter 3. 901 radar 4. Sea Cat system
5. MRS 3 fire-control radar 6. 278 radar 7. 965M radar 8. Corvus chaff launcher
9. 20-mm AA 10. 992Q radar 11. Exocet launchers 12. 114-mm DP Mk 6 mount

GUIDED-MISSILE DESTROYERS (continued)

London—showing electronics arrays, including port SCOT radome and single-row AKE-1 antenna for Type 965 radar   G. Arra, 1976

Fife—showing AKE-2 antenna for 965M radar   1978

D: 5,440 tons (6,200 fl)   **Dim:** 158.55 (153.9 pp) × 16.46 × 6.1 (fl)
S: 32.5 kts (30 cruising)   **Range:** 3,500/28
A: (a) 1/Sea Slug Mk 1 surface-to-air (30 missiles)−2/Sea Cat systems (one on each side) (IV × 2)−4/114-mm Mk 6 DP (II × 2) fwd−2/20-mm AA (I × 2)−1/ Wessex Mk 3 ASW helicopter. *See* Remarks
　　(b) 4/MM38 Exocet−1/Sea Slug Mk 2 system (30 missiles)−2/Sea Cat systems (IV × 2)−2/114-mm Mk 6 DP (II × 1)−2/20-mm AA (I × 2)−1/Wessex Mk 3 ASW helicopter
Electron Equipt: Radars: 1/965 (965M on the (b) group), 1/992Q, 1/901, 1/278, 3/903 fire control−2/Knebworth Corvus−ADAWS 1
　　　　　　　　Sonars: 1/184 or 177, 1/170B, 1/174, 1/162
Man: 33 officers, 438 men
M: COSAG propulsion; 2 props. On each shaft, 1 A.E.I. GT (15,000 hp) and 2 linked G 6 gas turbines (7,500 hp each): 60,000 hp total
Boilers: 2 Babcock & Wilcox, 49.21 kg/cm² pressure−superheat to 510°C
Fuel: 600 tons   **Electric:** (a) 3,750 kw   (b) 4,750 kw

REMARKS: Two County class authorized in each of the following years: 1955-56, 1956-57, 1961-62, 1964-65, and 1965-66. Fin Stabilizers. Twin rudders. Air-conditioned. Remote control of the boilers and engines from a command post that is completely protected from radioactive contamination. The Sea Slug launcher is on the stern and its fire-control radar is aft of the helicopter hangar. Missile stowage extends to the midships area and is more than 100 meters long; it is inboard, along the axis of the ship, and contains two parallel rows of 15 missiles, which can also be used against surface targets. The Sea Cat system is now GWS 22 in all units. The (b) group has its mast slightly farther aft than the (a) group. All (b) group units were fitted with four Exocet

Kent   S. Terzibaschitsch, 1977

anti-ship missiles in 1974-76. The *Hampshire* (D-08) was stricken 4-76, *Devonshire* (D-02) 28-7-78. *Norfolk* (D-21), long overhaul completed 4-78, has SCOT satellite communications antennae, as does *London* (D-16). These ships have virtually no ASW capability in poor weather, as the helicopter can only be flown in calm seas (because of the poor hangar arrangement) and there are no on-board ASW weapons.

GUIDED-MISSILE DESTROYERS (continued)

Fife

1977

1. WG 13 Lynx Helicopter 2. Sea Wolf system 3. 9.0 radar 4. Mk 32 TT 5. 40-mm
AA 6. 967-968 radar 7. Knebworth Corvus 8. Exocet launchers

Scale 1/1000

FRIGATES

◆ 1 (+5) **Broadsword (Type 22)** Bldr: Yarrow, Scotstoun

	Laid down	L	In serv.
F 88 BROADSWORD	7-2-75	12-5-76	3-5-79
F 89 BATTLEAXE	4-2-76	18-5-77	1980
F 90 BRILLIANT	24-3-77	15-12-78	. . .
F 91 BRAZEN (ex-*Boxer*)	19-8-78	. . .	. . .
F . . . N . . .	. . .	. . .	. . .
F . . . N . . .	. . .	. . .	. . .

D: 3,500 tons (4,400 fl)   **S:** 29 kts   **Dim:** 131.2 × 14.8 × 4.3 (avg)
A: 4/MM38 Exocet−2/Sea Wolf GWS 25 systems (VI × 2)−2/40-mm AA (I × 2)−
6/Mk 32 ASW TT (III × 2)−2/WG 13 Lynx helicopters
Electron Equipt: Radars: 1/967-968, 2/910 (GWS 25), 1/1006−2 Knebworth Corvus
  Sonars: 1/2008, 1/2016−CAAIS
Electric: 4,000 kw   **Range:** 4,500/18 (on Tyne GT), 1,200/24
Man: 249 men
M: COGOG propulsion; 2 Olympus TM3B gas turbines × 27,300 hp for high speed;
2 Tyne RM1A × 4,100 hp for cruising; 2 controllable-pitch props

FRIGATES (*continued*)

Broadsword   1979

REMARKS: The class is expected to number at least 14 ships. The first four were ordered 2-74, 4-75, 8-76, 10-77, and 1979. The fifth was to be ordered during 1979. The 2016 is a new multiple-frequency sonar. All will receive SCOT radomes for the Skynet communications satellite system. The WG 13 Lynx can carry both ASW and anti-ship weapons. The 967-968 radar is a back-to-back array with track-white-scan features.

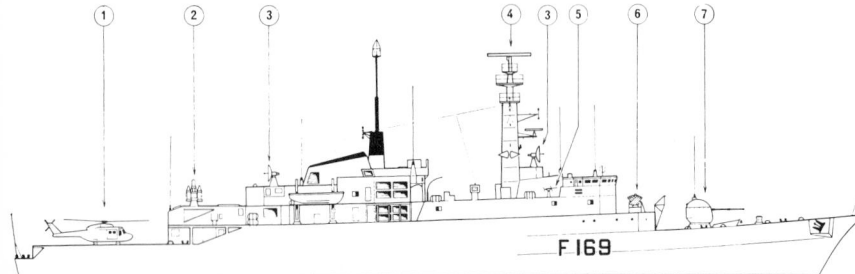

Amazon—as completed
1. WG 13 Lynx helicopter   2. Sea Cat system   3. RTN-10X Sea Cat guidance radar (GWS 22)   4. 992Q radar   5. 20-mm AA   6. Knebworth Corvus   7. 114-mm Mk 8 mount

Broadsword—on trials   1978

◆ 8 Amazon class (Type 21)

		Bldr	Laid down	L	In serv.
F 169	AMAZON	Vosper Thornycroft	6-11-69	26-4-71	11-5-74
F 170	ANTELOPE	Vosper Thornycroft	23-3-71	16-3-72	19-7-75
F 171	ACTIVE	Vosper Thornycroft	23-7-71	23-11-72	17-6-77
F 172	AMBUSCADE	Yarrow, Scotstoun	1-9-71	18-1-73	5-9-75
F 173	ARROW	Yarrow, Scotstoun	28-9-72	5-2-74	29-7-76
F 174	ALACRITY	Yarrow, Scotstoun	5-3-73	18-9-74	2-4-77
F 184	ARDENT	Yarrow, Scotstoun	26-2-74	9-5-75	13-10-77
F 185	AVENGER	Yarrow, Scotstoun	30-10-74	20-11-75	15-4-78

D: 2,750 tons (3,250 fl)   **S:** 32 kts

Dim: 117.04 × 12.8 × 4.4 (5.8 over sonar)

Man: 13 officers, 164 men

A: 4/MM38 Exocet—1 Sea Cat system GWS 24 (IV × 1)—1/114-mm Mk 8 DP—2/20-mm AA (I × 2)—1 Wasp or WG 13 Lynx helicopter—6 Mk 32 ASW TT

Electron Equipt: Radars: 1/992Q 1/978, 2/CT RTN-10X Orion—WSA 4 CAAIS—2/Knebworth Corvus

                Sonars: 1/184, 1/170B, 1/174, 1/162M

Range: 4,500/18, 1,200/30   **Electric:**   3,000 kw

FRIGATES (*continued*)

Alacrity　　　　　　　　　　　　　　　　　　G. Arra, 1977

Amazon　　　　　　　　　　　　　　　　　　G. Arra, 1977

Arrow—with Wasp helicopter　　　　　　　　　G. Arra, 1977

M: COGOG propulsion; 2 Olympus TM3 gas turbines × 25,000 hp each; 2 Tyne RB209 gas turbines × 4,250 hp each; 2 controllable-pitch props

REMARKS: Designed jointly by Vosper Thornycroft and Yarrow. Remote control of engine room from the bridge. Supplies on board for 60 days. Ferranti WSA 4 digital system used in fire-control, employing two Selenia RTN-10X radar directors for both

Sea Cat and the 114-mm gun. The CAAIS is a separate entity, whose data are automatically transmitted to WSA 4; both use a single FM-1600B computer. The Exocet launchers are paired, toed-in, and forward of the bridge. F-169, F-170, F-172 were completed without Exocet but were to have it retrofitted. Their Knebworth/Corvus chaff launchers are before the bridge, while on the others they are abaft the bridge, one deck higher. All are to receive two SCOT radomes for the Skynet communications satellite system. The torpedo tubes began to be installed during 1977. Sea Cat may be replaced by the Sea Wolf GWS 40 system now in development. Four 750-kw diesel generator sets supply the 450-volt, 3-phase, 60-Hz electrical current.

Arrow　　　　　　　　　　　　　　　　　　G. Arra, 1976

FRIGATES (*continued*)

Ardent—on trials   I. Furguson, 1977

Antelope   1978

Antelope—Group A   G. Arra, 1976

FRIGATES (continued)

◆ 26 Leander class

	Bldr	Laid down	L	In serv.
(a) F 109 LEANDER (ex-*Weymouth*)	Harland & Wolff	10-4-59	28-6-61	27-3-63
F 114 AJAX (ex-*Fowey*)	Cammell Laird	12-10-59	16-8-62	10-12-63
F 10 AURORA	John Brown	1-6-61	28-11-62	9-4-64
F 15 EURYALUS	Scotts SB&E	2-11-61	6-6-63	16-9-64
F 18 GALATEA	Swan Hunter	29-12-61	23-5-63	25-4-64
F 38 ARETHUSA	J. Samuel White	7-9-62	5-11-63	24-11-65
F 39 NAIAD	Yarrow, Scotstoun	30-10-62	4-11-63	15-3-65
(b) F 28 CLEOPATRA	HMDY, Devonport	19-6-63	25-3-64	4-1-66
F 104 DIDO (ex-*Hastings*)	Yarrow, Scotstoun	2-12-59	22-12-61	18-9-63
F 45 MINERVA	Vickers-Armstrong	25-7-63	19-12-64	14-5-66
F 42 PHOEBE	Alex. Stephen & Sons	3-6-63	8-7-64	15-4-66
F 40 SIRIUS	HMDY, Portsmouth	9-8-63	22-9-64	15-6-66
F 56 ARGONAUT	Hawthorn Leslie	27-11-64	8-2-66	17-8-67
F 52 JUNO	Thornycroft	16-7-64	24-11-65	18-7-67
F 47 DANAE	HMDY, Devonport	16-12-64	31-10-65	7-9-67
F 127 PENELOPE (ex-*Coventry*)	Vickers-Armstrong	14-3-61	17-8-62	31-10-63
(c) F 58 HERMIONE	Stephen/Yarrow	6-12-65	26-4-67	11-7-69
F 60 JUPITER	Yarrow, Scotstoun	3-10-66	4-9-67	9-8-69
F 57 ANDROMEDA	HMDY, Portsmouth	25-5-66	24-5-67	2-12-68
F 69 BACCHANTE	Vickers-Armstrong	27-10-66	29-2-68	17-10-69
F 71 SCYLLA	HMDY, Devonport	17-5-67	8-8-68	12-2-70
F 75 CHARYBDIS	Harland & Wolff	27-1-67	28-2-68	2-6-69
F 12 ACHILLES	Yarrow, Scotstoun	1-12-67	21-11-68	9-7-70
F 16 DIOMEDE	Yarrow, Scotstoun	30-1-68	15-4-69	2-4-71
F 70 APOLLO	Yarrow, Scotstoun	1-5-69	15-10-70	28-5-72
F 72 ARIADNE	Yarrow, Scotstoun	1-11-69	10-9-71	10-2-73

Aurora—Ikara **Leander** 1977

Achilles—broad-beam **Leander** (note Limbo well and Wasp aft) 1975

D: (a): 2,450 tons (2,860 fl); (b): 2,650 tons (3,200 fl) (c): 2,500 tons (2,962 fl)

Dim: (a) and (b): 113.38 (109.73 pp) × 12.5 × 5.49
(c): 113.38 (109.73 pp) × 13.12 × 5.49

S: 27 kts (30 on trials)   **Man:** (avg) 17 officers, 245 enlisted

A: (a): 2/40-mm AA (I × 2)—2/Sea Cat systems (IV × 2)—1/Ikara ASW system—1/Limbo Mk 10 ASW mortar (III × 1)—1/Wasp ASW helicopter
(b): 4/MM38 Exocet—2/40-mm AA—3/Sea Cat systems—6/324-mm Mk 32 ASW TT (III × 2)—1/Wasp ASW helicopter
(c): 2/114-mm DP Mk 6 (II × 1)—2/20-mm AA (I × 2)—1/Sea Cat system—1/Limbo Mk 10 ASW mortar—1/Wasp ASW helicoper (see Remarks)

Electron Equipt: Radars: 1/965 (not on (a) group), 1/993, 1/978 or 975, 1 or 2/903 (on MRS 3 and GWS 22 FC)—CAAIS on (a) group—2/Knebworth Corvus
Sonars: 1/177 or 184, 1/170B, 1/162 (1/199 on (a) group and some (c) group only)

Boilers: 2 Babcock & Wilcox 3-drum, 38.7 kg/cm² − superheat 450°C

Electric: (a) group plus F-28, F-104; 1,600 kw; other (b) group: 1,900 kw; (c) group: 2,500 kw

Range: approx. 4,500/12   **Fuel:** 460 tons; (c) group: 500 tons

M: White-English Electric GT; 2 5-bladed props; 30,000 hp

REMARKS: Improvement on the *Rothesay* class. Hull entirely welded; quarters air-conditioned; twin rudders; excellent sea-keeping qualities. Successive improvements to the propulsion and auxiliary machinery. All are gradually being fitted with two SCOT radomes for the Skynet satellite communications system. Many have received the Abbeyhill ECM/ESM system.

The (a) group, or "Ikara *Leander*" class, have been modernized, completions ranging from 12-72 to 11-76. The Ikara system replaced the 114-mm twin mount, while the number of Sea Cat launchers was doubled and two 40-mm AA were mounted abreast the bridge. These ships have the Ikara guidance radar in a radome atop the bridge and only one GWS 22 director, aft for the Sea Cat. All have VDS, and the 965 radar has been removed.

The (b) group, or "Exocet *Leander*" class, have had the 114-mm mount replaced by four MM38 Exocet and a Sea Cat launcher. The Limbo mortar was removed and two triple ASW TT were mounted abreast the hangar, which now has two Sea Cat launch-

FRIGATES (*continued*)

Naiad—Ikara **Leander** with SCOT domes   G. Arra, 1977

Cleopatra—Exocet **Leander** (SCOT aft)   G. Arra, 1977

ers atop it; two GWS 22 directors are carried, and single 40-mm mounts were placed abreast the bridge. The VDS well was plated up. F-28 completed conversion 11-75; the others (except F-127) were scheduled for completion 1977-79. F-127, otherwise disarmed, served as Sea Wolf system-trials ship, with a six-celled launcher on the stern, the 910 radar director atop the deckhouse on the former helicopter deck, and a 967-968 tracking radar atop her after mast; originally scheduled to be an Ikara conversion on completion of the Sea Wolf trials, she will now be given the Exocet conversion, to be completed during 1980. F-42 has carried a WG 13 Lynx helicopter.

The (*c*) group, or "broad-beam *Leander*" class, are 0.61 meters greater in beam to improve seaworthiness, provide larger fuel tanks, and permit installation of a more powerful electrical generator plant. All carried one Sea Cat GWS 22 system—unlike many of the earlier (*a*) and (*b*) groups, which did not get Sea Cat prior to modernization. *Hermione* (F-58) and some others have Type 199 VDS in a well at the stern; in others, the well is plated up, as it will be in all after modernization. The (*c*) group are

also scheduled for modernization during the early 1980s; *Andromeda*, the first, commenced reconstruction 1-78. As refitted, each ship will have a Sea Wolf launcher and four MM38 Exocet forward, two 40-mm AA, an enlarged hangar and flight deck for WG 13 Lynx, two triple-Mk 32 ASW TT, and new electronics (including Type 2016 sonar); Limbo, the twin 114-mm gun, and Sea Cat will be removed. Programs (starting with F-10): three in 1960-61, three in 1961-62, three in 1962-63, three in 1963-64, three in 1964-65, three in 1965-66, two in 1966-67, and two in 1967-68.

Naiad—Ikara under canvas to left, control radomes atop bridge; SCOT, 978 and 993 on mast   G. Arra, 1976

Cleopatra—with Sea Cat and four Exocet on forecastle, 40-mm AA beside foremast
                                                      G. Arra, 1977

FRIGATES (*continued*)

Andromeda – broad-beam **Leander** (before modernization)   1977

◆ 7 Tribal class (Type 81)

	Bldr	Laid down	L	In serv.
F 117 ASHANTI	Yarrow, Scotstoun	15-1-58	9-3-59	23-11-61
F 119 ESKIMO	J. Samuel White	22-10-58	20-3-60	21-2-63
F 122 GURKHA	Thornycroft, Woolston	3-11-58	11-7-60	13-2-63
F 125 MOHAWK	Vickers-Armstrong	22-12-60	5-4-62	29-11-63
F 131 NUBIAN	HMDY, Portsmouth	7-9-59	6-9-60	9-10-62
F 133 TARTAR	HMDY, Devonport	22-10-60	19-9-60	26-2-62
F 124 ZULU	Alex. Stephen & Sons	13-12-60	3-7-62	17-4-64

Gurkha – with Type 199 VDS   S. Terzibaschitsch, 1977

Mohawk – with a Wasp on the helicopter deck   1968

FRIGATES (continued)

Tartar   G. Arra, 1975

Eskimo   1976

D: 2,300 tons (2,700 fl)   **S:** 24/23 kts (actual)
Dim: 109.73 (106.68 pp) × 12.95 × 5.3 (fl)
A: 2/114-mm Mk 5 DP (I × 2), 1 fwd, 1 aft—2/20-mm AA (I × 2)—2/Sea Cat GWS 21 systems (IV × 2)—1/Mk 10 Limbo ASW mortar—1/Wasp ASW helicopter
Electron Equipt: Radars: 1/965, 1/978, 1/993, 1/903, 2/262—2/Knebworth Corvus
Sonars: 1/177, 1/170B, 1/162 (1/199 also on F-117 and F-122)
Man: 13 officers, 237-40 men   **Range:** 4,500/12
Fuel: 400 tons
Boiler: 1 Babcock & Wilcox, 38 kg/cm²—450°C   **Electric:** 1,500 kw
M: COSAG propulsion: 1 Metrovik GT (15,000 hp) and 1 A.E.I. G6 (7,500 hp) gas turbine geared to a single prop

REMARKS: Three Tribal class authorized in 1955-56, four in 1956-57. Living quarters air-conditioned. Remote control of propulsion machinery. The gas turbine permits almost instantaneous cold starts but is used only when high speeds are required. Denny-Brown stabilizers and twin rudders. Flush deck and welded hull, which had to be reinforced after the trials of the F-117. GWS 21 Sea Cat system uses modified MRS 8 directors abreast the after stack. The hangar is below the helo deck and is served by a small athwartships elevator; the Limbo triple mortar is just forward of the helo area. All seven frigates are now scheduled for early decommissioning, then modernization and sale to foreign customers.

◆ **9 Rothesay class (Type 12)**

	Bldr	Laid down	L	In serv
F 101 YARMOUTH	John Brown (Clyde)	29-11-57	23-3-59	26-3-60
F 103 LOWESTOFT	Alex Stephen & Sons	9-6-58	23-6-60	18-10-61
F 107 ROTHESAY	Yarrow, Scotstoun	6-11-56	9-12-57	23-4-60
F 108 LONDONDERRY	Thornycroft	15-11-56	20-5-58	22-7-60
F 115 BERWICK	Harland & Wolff	16-6-58	15-12-59	1-6-61
F 106 BRIGHTON	Yarrow, Scotstoun	23-7-57	30-10-59	28-9-61
F 113 FALMOUTH	Swan Hunter	23-11-57	15-12-59	26-7-61
F 126 PLYMOUTH	HMDY, Devonport	1-7-58	20-7-59	11-5-61
F 129 RHYL	HMDY, Portsmouth	29-1-58	23-4-59	31-10-60

D: 2,380 tons (2,800 fl)   **Dim:** 112.77 (109.73 pp) × 12.5 × 5.3
S: 30 kts (26/25 actual)   **Man:** 15 officers, 220 men
A: 2/114-mm Mk 6 DP (II × 1)—2/20-mm AA (I × 2)—1/Sea Cat GWS 20 system (IV × 1)—1/Mk 10 Limbo ASW mortar—1/Wasp ASW helicopter (see Remarks)
Electron Equipt: Radars: 1/978, 1/993, 1/903
Sonars: 1/174, 1/170, 1/162
Range: 4,500/12   **Electric:** 1,460 kw   **Fuel:** 400 tons
M: Same as *Whitby* class

REMARKS: Improved version of the *Whitby* class. Two in trials service. All modernized 1966-72 with Sea Cat GSW 20 system (no radar) and helicopter facility in place of one Limbo ASW mortar. MRS 3 fire-control system replaced the original Mk 6 director, and new electronics and air-conditioning were installed. F-108 began conversion 11-75 to serve as trials ship for the Admiralty Surface Weapons Establishment; completed 12-78. She now has pump-jet propellers and no longer has Limbo. F-103 conducted trials during 1978 with the DA-5 towed passive sonar array and had a deckhouse on her helicopter deck; her Limbo was removed.

Plymouth   1977

FRIGATES (*continued*)

Rhyl   G. Arra, 1976

◆ **1 Whitby class (Type 12)**

	Bldr	Laid down	L	In serv.
F 43 TORQUAY	Harland & Wolff	11-3-53	1-7-54	10-5-56

Torquay   1975

D: 2,150 tons (2,560 fl)   **S:** 30 kts (26/25 usual)
Dim: 112.77 (109.73 pp) × 12.5 × 5.26
A: 2/114-mm Mk 6 DP (II × 1) – 1/Mk 10 Limbo ASW mortar
Electron Equipt: Radars: 1/1006, 1/993, 1/275 (on Mk 6 dir.)
              Sonars: 1/174, 1/170, 1/162 – CAAIS
Boilers: 2 Babcock, 38.7 kg/cm² pressure – superheat 450°C
Fuel: 370 tons   **Range:** 4,500/12   **Electric:** 1,140 kw
M: English-Electric GT; 2 props; 30,000 hp

REMARKS: Training frigate assigned to Navigation and Aircraft Direction Training at Portsmouth. Welded hull, air-conditioned, twin rudders. Cruising turbines for normal underway passage, with automatic shift to high-speed turbines. In trials, 30 knots

were attained with 75 per cent of anticipated power. The *Eastbourne* (F-73), formerly assigned to the Machinists' School (weapons removed), was relegated to status of harbor training hulk in 1976. *Blackpool* (F-77), discarded in 1974, was used as a target ship and was scrapped in 1978. The *Scarborough* (F-63) and *Tenby* (F-65) of the same class, purchased in 1974 by Pakistan, were sold for scrap. The *Whitby* (F-36) was discarded in 1975.

◆ **1 Salisbury class (Type 61)**

	Bldr	Laid down	L	In serv.
F 99 LINCOLN	Fairfield SB & E	20-5-55	6-4-59	7-7-60

D: 2,170 tons (2,400 fl)   **S:** 23 kts   **Dim:** 103.63 (97.5 pp) × 12.19 × 4.8 (fl)
Man: 14 officers, 223 men
A: 2/114-mm Mk 6 DP (II × 1) – 2/20-mm AA (I × 2) – 1/Sea Cat GWS 20 (IV × 1)
Electron Equipt: Radars: 1/965 M, 1/982, 1/278, 1/993, 1/275, 1/978
              Sonars: removed
Fuel: 230 tons   **Range:** 7,500/16, 2,300/23   **Electric:** 1,200 kw
M: 8 Admiralty Standard Range I diesels; 2 props; 12,400 hp

REMARKS: Aircraft direction. In reserve since 1976; was to have been sold to Egypt 7-78 but transfer canceled. *Llandaff* (F-61) sold to Bangladesh 1-12-76. *Chichester* (F-59) stricken 7-77, *Salisbury* (F-32) 6-78; transfer of the latter to Egypt also canceled, and she remains on the sales list.

◆ **1 Leopard class (Type 41)**

	Bldr	Laid down	L	In serv.
F 27 LYNX	J. Brown (Clydebank)	13-8-53	12-1-55	14-3-57

Lynx   S. Terzibaschitsch, 1977

D: 2,300 tons (2,520 fl)   **Dim:** 103.63 (97.5 pp) × 12.19 × 4.8 (fl)
S: 23 kts   **Man:** 15 officers, 220 men
A: 4/114-mm Mk 6 DP (II × 2) – 1/40-mm AA
Electron Equipt: Radars: 1/965, 1/978, 1/993, 1/262
              Sonars: 1/174, 1/170B
Fuel: 230 tons diesel   **Electric:** 1,200 kw   **Range:** 7,500/16, 2,300/23
M: 8 Admiralty Standard I diesels

REMARKS: Anti-aircraft. The survivor of a class of four, *Lynx* is in ready-reserve. Squid ASW mortar removed. Anti-rolling fin stabilizers. Four 300-kw diesel generators as auxiliary machinery. The original lattice main mast was replaced by a mast-stack, or "mack" (contraction of "mast" and "stack"). In trials, these ships reached 25 knots.

FRIGATES (continued)

Panther of this series was sold to India in 1956 and renamed *Brahmaputra*. *Puma* (F-34) was stricken in 1973, *Leopard* (F-14) in 1976. *Jaguar* (F-37) was sold to Bangladesh in 1978. The two remaining Type 61 radar picket frigates, built to a very similar design, were both stricken 6-78. The two remaining Type 14-class utility frigates were stricken 1978-79.

CORVETTES

◆ (4) improved Isles-class offshore patrol vessels

Bldr: Hall Russel, Aberdeen

P . . . N . . .　　　P . . . N . . .　　　P . . . N . . .　　　P . . . N . . .

　D: 1,250 tons　　S: 22 kts　　Dim: 80.0 × . . . × . . .
　A: 1/40-mm AA – 2/7.6-mm machine guns　　Range: 5,000/. . .
　Man: 37 men
　M: 2 Ruston 12 RK 320 CM diesels; 2 controllable-pitch props; 4,380 hp

REMARKS: Final design in preparation 1979, to be delivered 1982-83. Clear deck aft to land WG 13 Lynx helicopter. Three-week endurance.

◆ 7 Isles-class offshore patrol vessels　Bldr: Hall Russell, Aberdeen

	L	In serv.
P 277 ANGLESEY	18-10-78	5-79
P 278 ALDERNEY	27-2-79	11-79
P 295 JERSEY	18-3-76	15-10-76
P 297 GUERNSEY	17-2-77	28-10-77
P 298 SHETLAND	22-11-76	14-7-77
P 299 ORKNEY	29-6-76	25-2-77
P 300 LINDISFARNE	1-6-77	26-1-78

Guernsey　　　　　　　　　　　　　　　　　　　　1977

　D: 1,000 tons (1,280 fl)　　S: 16 kts　　Dim: 59.51 (51.97 pp) × 10.9 × 4.26
　A: 1/40-mm AA Mk 3 – 2/7.6-mm machine guns　　Range: 7,000/12
　Electric: 536 kw　　Man: 7 officers, 32 men (plus marine detachment)
　Fuel: 310 tons
　M: 2 Ruston 12-RK 3 CM diesels (750 rpm); 1 controllable-pitch prop; 4,380 hp

REMARKS: Near duplicates of the Scottish Department of Fisheries ships *Jura* and *Westra*. The *Jura* (as P-296) was loaned to the the Royal Navy from 1975 to 1-77 for use in patrolling offshore oil rigs and the 200-nautical-mile economic zone, the purpose for which the Isles class was built. First five ordered 11-2-75, other pair 21-10-77. P-277 and P-278 have fin stabilizers. All are excellent sea boats, able to maintain speed in heavy weather.

PATROL BOATS

◆ 5 ex-"-ton"-class minesweepers

P 1007 BEACHAMPTON	P 1055 MONKTON	P 1089 WASPERTON
P 1093 WOLVERTON	P 1096 YARNTON	

　D: 360 tons (425 fl)　　S: 15 kts　　Dim: 46.3 (42.7 pp) × 8.8 × 2.5
　A: 2/40-mm AA (I × 2) – 2/7.6-mm machine guns
　Electron Equipt: Radar: 978　　Range: 2,300/13
　Fuel: 45 tons　　Man: 5 officers, 25 men
　M: 2 Deltic 18A-7A diesels; 2 props; 3,000 hp

Beachampton　　　　　　　　　　　　　　　　G. Arra, 1976

REMARKS: All employed at Hong Kong. Originally completed 1953-57. Modified, 1971-72. All sweep gear removed, light armor added around bridge. Scheduled to be replaced 1982-83 by patrol boats built in Hong Kong. An additional "-ton," *Laleston* (M-1158), has acted as a patrol ship in Ulster, and eight others act as fisheries-patrol craft (see under Minesweepers).

PATROL CRAFT

◆ 4 Kingfisher class　Bldr: Richard Dunston, Hessle

	Laid down	L	In serv.
P 260 KINGFISHER	7-73	20-9-74	8-10-75
P 261 CYGNET	10-73	26-10-75	8-7-76
P 262 PETEREL	11-73	14-5-76	7-7-77
P 263 SANDPIPER	12-73	20-1-77	16-9-77

PATROL CRAFT (continued)

Kingfisher   1975

Peterel—note lack of hull portholes   S. Terzibaschitsch, 1977

D: 187 tons   **S:** 25 kts   **Dim:** 36.6 (33.8 pp) × 7.0 × 2.0
A: 1/40-mm AA − 2/7.6-mm machine guns   **Man:** 4 officers, 10 men
Range: 2,000/14   **M:** 2 Paxman 16 YCJM diesels (1,500 rpm); 2 props; 4,000 hp

REMARKS: Unsuccessful design based on RAF *Seal*-class air-sea rescue craft. A large number of additional sisters were canceled. P-262 and P-263 are used for Naval Reserve training; the other two were employed in patrol work in the North Sea but have been reassigned to the mine countermeasures squadron at Rosyth. Have fin stabilizers, but evidently still have stability problems. All will be disarmed and converted for use as inshore survey craft. Note: *Peterel* (P-262) has no hull portholes.

◆ **1 (+1) Jetfoil class**   Bldr: Boeing, Seattle

	L	In serv.
P . . . SPEEDY	9-7-79	12-79

Speedy—on trials   Boeing Marine Systems, 1979

PATROL CRAFT (continued)

D: 117 tons (fl)   **S:** 43 kts   **Dim:** 27.43 (30.78 with foils up; 23.77 wl) × 9.14 × 1.83 (5.18 with foils down, at rest; 2.4 foiling)

A: 2/7.6-mm machine guns   **Man:** 18 men   **Range:** 3,500/5, 560/43
Fuel: 23 tons
M: 2 Allison 501-K20 A gas turbines, driving waterjets; 6,600 hp; 2 GM 8V-92 TI diesels; . . . hp (for hull-borne cruise)

REMARKS: Ordered 29-6-78 for use in patrolling North Sea fisheries and oil rigs. If successful, up to 11 additional ships may be acquired. Aluminum structure. Design evolved from U.S. Navy's *Tucumcari* (PGH-2) through a very successful commercial passenger hydrofoil.

◆ 2 "Loyal"-class ex-fleet tenders

A 510 ALERT (ex-*Loyal Governor*)   A 382 VIGILANT (ex-*Loyal Factor*)

REMARKS: Built 1974-75. For details, *see* under General-purpose Tenders. Used in local patrol duties in Ulster, with naval crews.

◆ 1 prototype

P 276 TENACITY Bldr: Vosper Thornycroft, 18-2-69

D: 165 tons (220 fl)   **S:** 39 kts   **Dim:** 44.1 × 8.1 × 2.4

A: 2/7.6-mm machine guns   **Range:** 2,500/15   **Man:** 4 officers, 28 men
M: CODOG propulsion: 3 Rolls-Royce Proteus gas turbines, 12,750 hp; 2 Paxman diesels, 1,200 hp; 3 props

REMARKS: Built as a private-venture experimental missile boat with dummy weapons. Employed for fisheries protection in the Irish Sea, for anti-smuggling patrol, and as a target craft. Purchased 21-1-72.

◆ 3 Scimitar class

P 271 SCIMITAR   P 274 CUTLASS   P 275 SABRE

Bldr: Vosper Thornycroft, Portsmouth

Scimitar

D: 102 tons (fl)   **S:** 40 kts   **Dim:** 30.5 × 8.1 × 1.95
Man: 2 officers, 10 men   **Range:** 1,500/21.5, 425/35
M: CODOG propulsion: 2 Rolls-Royce Proteus gas turbines (9,000 hp); 2 Fodens diesels (180 hp) for cruising; 2 props

REMARKS: Designed for anti-missile-boat training. Hull of laminated and glued wood. A third gas turbine allowed for in design. Can carry two 7.6-mm machine guns if required for patrol duties. *Scimitar* launched 4-12-69, *Cutlass* 19-2-70, and *Sabre* 21-4-70.

MINE WARFARE SHIPS

◆ 12 "Extra Deep Armed Team Sweeps (MSM/EDATS)"

REMARKS: The first of these adaptations of a commercial stern-haul trawler design to be ordered during 1979 for delivery in 1980, with the remainder entering service by 1985. They are evidently intended to sweep deep ocean mines by operating in pairs, with a wire sweep between them. In time of war, additional commercial fishing craft would be acquired for the same duties. The concept is being investigated with *Venturer* and *St. Davids* (see below), and the new ships will have similar characteristics. These ships will be linear (if not functional) replacements for "-ton"-class minesweepers.

◆ 1 (+4) Hunt-class minehunters

	Bldr	Laid down	L	In serv.
M 29 BRECON	Vosper Thornycroft	21-10-75	21-6-78	1979
M . . . LEDBURY	Vosper Thornycroft	5-10-77	1979	. . .
M . . . COTTESMORE	Yarrow, Scotstoun	. . .	. . .	. . .
M . . . MIDDLETON	Yarrow, Scotstoun	. . .	. . .	. . .
M . . . CATTISTOCK	Vosper Thornycroft	. . .	. . .	. . .

Brecon—lying alongside the fitting-out quay   1974

MINE WARFARE SHIPS (continued)

D: 615 tons (725 fl) **S:** 17 kts **Dim:** 60.0 (56.6 pp) × 9.85 × 2.2
A: 1/40-mm AA Mk 9 **Electron Equipt:** Radar: 1/1006 Sonar: 1/193M
Man: 45 men
Electric: 1,080 kw (3 diesel alternators of 200 kw each for ship's service plus one 480-kw diesel alternator for magnetic minesweeping)
M: 2 Ruston-Paxman Deltic 59K diesels (1,600 rpm); 2 props; 3,540 hp

REMARKS: Equipped for both hunting and sweeping mines. Hull constructed of glass-reinforced plastic. Up to 12 may be built, with Yarrow cooperating in the program. Will carry divers and 2 French PAP 104 wire-guided, remote-controlled mine locators.

◆ **2 ex-commercial stern trawlers**

Bldr: Cubow Ltd., Woolwich

M 07 ST. DAVIDS (ex-*Suffolk Monarch*)
M 08 VENTURER (ex-*Suffolk Harvester*)

D: 392 grt **S:** . . . kts **Dim:** 36.64 (34.14 pp) × 8.95 × . . .
A: none **Man:** . . . men **Electric:** 240 kw
M: 2 Mirrlees Blackstone 8-cyl. diesels; 1 controllable-pitch prop; 2,000 hp

REMARKS: Chartered 11-78. Manned by Royal Naval Reserve, M-07 (launched 9-73) at Cardiff and M-08 (launched 12-72) at Bristol. To test concept for "extra deep armed team sweeps." Chartered through 11-80.

◆ **1 prototype glass-reinforced plastic minehunter** Bldr: Vosper Thornycroft

	Ordered	L	In serv.
M 1116 WILTON	11-2-70	18-2-72	25-4-73

D: 450 tons (fl) **S:** 15 kts **Dim:** 46.33 × 8.76 × 2.6
A: 1/40-mm AA Mk 7 **Man:** 5 officers, 32 men
M: As for "-ton" class

REMARKS: First large warship with an all-glass-reinforced plastic hull. Machinery and fittings are from the *Derriton*, scrapped in 1970.

Wilton S. Terzibaschitsch, 1977

◆ **15 "-ton"-class minehunters** Bldrs: Various

M 1110 BILDESTON	M 1140 GAVINTON	M 1157 KIRKLISTON
M 1133 BOSSINGTON	M 1147 HUBBERSTON	M 1165 MAXTON
M 1113 BRERETON*	M 1151 IVESTON	M 1166 NURTON
M 1114 BRINTON*	M 1153 KEDLESTON**	M 1181 SHERATON*
M 1115 BRONINGTON	M 1154 KELLINGTON**	M 1182 SHOULTON

Nurton—minehunter G. Arra, 1976

◆ **18 "-ton"-class minesweepers** Bldr: Various

M 1103 ALFRISTON**	M 1158 LALESTON**	M 1187 UPTON**
M 1109 BICKINGTON*	M 1208 LEWISTON	M 1188 WALKERTON
M 1124 CRICHTON*	M 1173 POLLINGTON*	M 1175 WISTON**
M 1216 CROFTON**	M 1167 REPTON**	M 1195 WOTTON
M 1125 CUXTON*	M 1180 SHAVINGTON*	
M 1141 GLASSERTON*	M 1200 SOBERTON*	
M 1146 HODGESTON*	M 1204 STUBBINGTON*	

*Fisheries protection. **Naval Reserve training. M-1158 mine-clearance diving tender (*see* Remarks); M-1188 navigational training ship at Royal Naval College, Dartmouth (to be relieved by M-1103).

Walkerton—no guns or sweep gear G. Arra, 1975

MINE WARFARE SHIPS (*continued*)

Cuxton—fisheries-protection minesweeper   S. Terzibaschitsch, 1977

Crofton—Naval Reserve training minesweeper   S. Terzibaschitsch, 1977

  D: 370 tons (425 fl)   **Dim:** 46.33 (42.68 pp) × 8.76 × 2.5′
  S: 15 kts (cruising)   **Man:** 29 men sweepers/38 hunters
  A: 1/40-mm AA Mk 7 – plus 2/20-mm AA (II × 1) in some sweepers (M-1103, M-1141,
      M-1182, M-1188 disarmed)
  M: 2 Paxman Deltic 18A-7A diesels; 2 props; 3,000 hp – except M-1141, M-1158,
      M-1167: 2 Mirrlees JVSS 12 diesels; 2 props, 2,500 hp
Range: 3,000/8, 2,300/13   **Fuel:** 45 tons
Electron Equipt: Radar: 1/978   Sonar: 1/193 (hunters only)

REMARKS: Survivors of a class of 118 completed 1952-58; five others are equipped as
patrol boats. All minehunters are equipped with active rudders for low-speed operations, have a Type 193 sonar, and can carry mine-clearance divers (divers not in Fisheries Patrol units). All hunters and M-1216, M-1208, M-1173, M-1167, M-1204, M-1188,
and M-1175 have enclosed bridges. M-1182, as the prototype minehunter, was given

pump-jet propulsion and a bow thruster. M-1141 carries the Osbourne multiple sweep
array. M-1188 is to be replaced by M-1103 shortly. M-1158, used recently as a patrol
boat in Ulster, has an enlarged deckhouse aft and no sweep cable reel or winch. The
three units still having Mirrlees diesels will likely soon be stricken. M-1125 was first
commissioned 10-75, having gone into reserve on completion in 1953.

    All have wooden hulls, most sheathed with nylon below the waterline. Fin stabiliz-
ers are fitted. Fisheries Patrol units have a searchlight abaft the stack.

MINE COUNTERMEASURES SUPPORT SHIP

◆ **1 exercise minelayer and tender**

	Bldr	Laid down	L	In serv.
N 21 ABDIEL	Thornycroft, Woolston	23-5-66	22-1-67	17-10-67

Abdiel   1967

Abdiel   G. Arra, 1976

MINE COUNTERMEASURES SUPPORT SHIP (continued)

D: 1,375 tons (1,460 fl)   **Dim:** 80.42 (74.67 pp) × 11.74 × 2.85
S: 16 kts   **A:** 44 mines   **Electron Equipt:** Radar: 1/978
Man: 77 men   **Electric;** 1,225 kw
M: 2 Paxman Ventura 16-YSCM diesels; 2 props; 2,690 hp

REMARKS: Carries and repairs spare sweeping equipment and cable.

AMPHIBIOUS WARFARE SHIPS

ASSAULT SHIPS

◆ **1 Lyness class**

	Bldr	Laid down	L	In serv.
A 345 TARBATNESS	Swan Hunter	4-66	22-2-67	10-8-67

REMARKS: Landing platform assault ship (RFA). Under conversion 1979 to mid-1980 from a stores carrier. Will retain Royal Fleet Auxilliary status with civil crew. To be able to carry 1,300 marines. Former lifeboat and stores launch positions to be used for stowing six landing craft. Most hold space will be converted to accommodations. For data *see* under Fleet-replenishment Ships, *Lyness* class. No armament.

◆ **2 Fearless class**

	Author.	Bldr	Laid down	L	In serv.
L 10 FEARLESS	1961-62	Harland & Wolff	25-7-62	19-12-63	25-11-65
L 11 INTREPID	1962-63	J. Brown (Clyde)	11-12-62	5-6-64	11-3-67

Fearless   1978

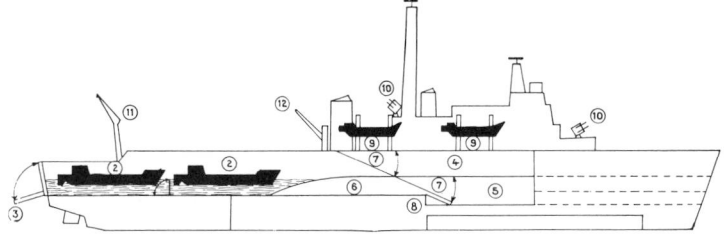

1. Well deck 2. LCM 9 3. Stern well gate 4. Tank deck 5. Lower deck (light vehicles) 6. Half-deck 7. Mobile ramps. 8. Fixed ramp 9. LCA 10. Sea Cat system 11, 12. Cranes

D:. 11,060 tons (12,120 fl) (16,950 tons, draft 9.15, with well deck flooded)
S: 21 kts   **Dim:** 158.5 (152.4 pp) × 24.38 × 6.2
A: 4/Sea Cat GWS 20 systems (IV × 4) – 2/40-mm AA (I × 2)
Electron Equipt: Radars: 1/978, 1/993 – CAAIS – 2/Knebworth Corvus
Man: 36 officers, 520 men, 380-700 troops   **Range:** 5,000/20
Boilers: 2 Babcock & Wilcox, 38.66 kg/cm² pressure – superheat 454°C
Electric: 4,000 kw
M: English-Electric GT; 2 props; 22,000 hp

REMARKS: These ships are equivalent to U.S. LPD and French TCD types, and have excellent command and communication facilities for amphibious operations. They can launch four to six Wessex Mk 5 assault helicopters (landing platform but no hangar), and have quarters for troop contingents of various sizes, depending on the duration and distance of operations, but usually a single light infantry battalion and an artillery battery. On board are four LCA landing craft, which can transport 35 men or a half-ton vehicle and four LCM(9) landing craft carrying two Chieftain or Centurion tanks, or four vehicles, or 100 tons of supplies; four additional tanks can be carried on the tank deck. The vehicles are divided between the tank deck, a lower deck, and a half-deck reserved for jeeps. *Intrepid* was placed in reserve in 1976, refitted during 1978, and replaced the *Fearless* in 1979. The active unit is normally assigned as officer cadet training ship at the Royal Naval College, Dartmouth, but is immediately available for amphibious operations as required.

LANDING SHIPS, TANK

◆ **6 Sir Bedivere class**

	Bldr	Laid down	L	In serv.
L 3004 SIR BEDIVERE	Hawthorn Leslie	10-65	20-7-66	18-5-67
L 3005 SIR GALAHAD	Alexander Stephen	2-65	19-4-66	17-12-66
L 3027 SIR GERAINT	Alexander Stephen	6-65	26-1-67	12-7-67
L 3029 SIR LANCELOT	Fairfield	3-62	25-6-63	16-1-64
L 3036 SIR PERCIVALE	Hawthorn Leslie	4-66	4-10-67	23-3-68
L 3505 SIR TRISTRAM	Hawthorn Leslie	2-66	12-12-66	14-9-67

Sir Percivale   G. Arra, 1978

LANDING SHIPS, TANK (*continued*)

Sir Geraint   S. Terzibaschitsch, 1977

D: 3,270 tons (5,674 fl)   **S:** 17 kts   **Dim:** 126.45 × 17.7 × 3.8
Man: 18 officers, 51 men   **Range:** 8,000/15
Fuel: 811 tons   **A:** 2/40-mm (not installed)
M: 2 Mirrlees diesels; 2 props; 9,400 hp (L-3029: 2 Denny-Sulzer diesels; 9,520 hp)

REMARKS: In 1963 the Ministry of Transportation ordered the first of six specially designed LST-class ships for the Army, chartered in peacetime to various private maritime firms. In 1970 these ships came under the control of the Royal Fleet Auxiliary Service, which mans them today. Beaching cargo capacity is 340 tons (military lift). Built into the bow and the stern are ramps and doors for the handling of vehicles (roll-on/roll-off system); interior ramps connect the two decks. Quarters are provided in the after superstructure for 402 men. The ships have a helicopter platform, and three cranes (two 4.5, one 8.5 tons); landing craft may be carried in cradles normally used for lifeboats. L-3029 has four cranes, and is 5,550 tons full load.

NOTE: *Empire Gull* (L-3513), the last active LST(3), was stricken 9-78. Five others serve as nonoperational stores/workshop/accommodations hulks: *Dieppe* (L-3016), *Lofoten* (K-07), *Messina* (L-3043), *Narvik* (L-3044), and *Stalker* (L-3515). **D:** 4,960 tons (fl); **Dim:** 105.9 × 16.8 × 3.7.

MEDIUM LANDING SHIPS

◆ **2 Ardennes-class logistic landing craft**   Bldr: Brooke Marine

	Laid down	L	In serv.
L 4001 ARDENNES	27-8-75	29-7-76	1977
L 4003 ARAKAN	16-2-76	23-5-77	9-6-78

D: 870 tons (1,413 fl)   **S:** 10.3 kts   **Dim:** 73.1 (71.7 pp) × 15.03 × 1.8
Range: 4,000/10   **Man:** 4 officers, 31 men
M: 2 Mirrlees-Blackstone GWSL 8-MGR 2 diesels; 2 props; 2,000 hp

REMARKS: Replacements for the LCT(8) class, operated by the Royal Corps of Transport. Can carry 5 70-ton tanks or 24 standard 20-foot containers (340 dwt) as well as 6 officers and 28 troops.

Ardennes   1977

◆ **2 LCT (8) class**

L 4041 ABBEVILLE   L 4061 AUDEMER

D: 657 tons (895 to 1,075 fl)   **Dim:** 70.18 × 11.9 × 1.8
S: 12 kts (9 cruising)   **Man:** 33 men
M: 4 Paxman diesels; 2 props; 1,840 hp

Audemer   S. Terzibaschitsch, 1977

REMARKS: Operated by the Army's Royal Corps of Transport. The following have been scrapped since 1974: *Aachen* (L-4062), *Andalnes* (L-4097), *Akyab* (L-4037), *Antwerp* (L-4071), *Arezzo* (L-4128), *Arakan* (L-4164) and *Agheila* (L-4002).

LANDING CRAFT

◆ **2 25-meter class**

REMARKS: Ordered 5-79. To be operated by the Army Royal Corps of Transport.

◆ **14 LCM (9) class**

LCM (9) 700 to 711, LCM (9) 3507 and LCM (9) 3508

REMARKS: The prototype of this new series, L-3507, was delivered in 1963. The *Fearless*

LANDING CRAFT (continued)

L-702   G. Arra, 1977

Lodden   G. Arra, 1977

(L-10) and the *Intrepid* (L-10) can each carry four of these. Bldrs: two by Vosper, six by Richard Dunston, four by Brooke Marine Ltd., and two by Bolson & Sons, 1964-66.

D: 75 tons (176 fl)   **Dim:** 25.7 × 6.5 × 1.7   **Man:** 6 men
M: 2 Paxman YHXAM diesels; Kort-nozzle props; 624 hp

REMARKS: Can carry two Centurion tanks or 100 tons of cargo. All naval-manned.

◆ 11 Avon class

RPL 01 AVON   RPL 07 GLEN
RPL 02 BUDE   RPL 08 HAMBLE
RPL 03 CLYDE   RPL 10 KENNET
RPL 04 DART   RPL 11 LODDEN
RPL 05 EDEN   RPL 12 MEDWAY
RPL 06 FORTH

D: 61 tons   **S:** 8 kts   **Dim:** 22.0 × 6.1
M: 2 diesels; 2 props; 870 hp

REMARKS: Two-deck superstructure aft. Used in U.K. coastal service. Operated by the Army's Royal Corps of Transport.

◆ 2 LCM (7) class

L 7037   L 7100

D: 28 tons (63 fl)   **S:** 9.8 kts   **Dim:** 18.4 × 4.9 × 1.2
M: 2 Gray Marine diesels; 2 props; 290 hp

REMARKS: Wartime construction, used as stores tenders; survivors of a once-numerous class. Naval-operated.

◆ 26 LCVP

LCVP (1): 102, 112, 118, 120, 123, 127, 128, 134, 136
LCVP (2): 142-149
LCVP (3): 150-158

     D: 8.5 tons (13.5 fl)   **S:** 8-10 kts   **Dim:** 12.7 or 13.1 × 3.1 × 0.8
     M: 2 diesels; 2 props; 130 or 200 hp

REMARKS: Eight of the LCVP (2) are carried in *Fearless* and *Intrepid*; *Tarbatness* will carry six.

◆ 3 LCP(L) (3)

501, 503, 556

     D: 6.5 tons (10 fl)   **S:** 12 kts   **Dim:** 11.3 × 3.4 × 1.0
     M: 225 hp

◆ 3 smaller craft: LCR 5507, LCR 5508, LCN 604

HOVERCRAFT

All Royal Navy hovercraft are operated by the Hovercraft Trials Unit, Lee-on-Solent. The craft remain in experimental status, and no quantity acquisition has been announced. In addition to assault landings, they have been used in mine countermeasures and logistics support trials.

◆ 1 VT-2 class

P 234   Bldr: Vosper

     D: 62.5 tons (105 max.)   **S:** 60+ kts   **Dim:** 30.17 × 13.3 × 0.86 (at rest)
     Fuel: 10.5 tons
     M: 2 Rolls-Royce Proteus gas turbines; 2/4.1-m dia. props; 9,000 hp

REMARKS: Intended for further experiments in mine countermeasures as precursor of a class to be built during the late 1980s. Has a 32-ton payload. Built 1975. Purchased 3-4-79.

HOVERCRAFT (*continued*)

◆ 1 BH-N7 Wellington Mk 4 class

XW 255   Bldr: British Hovercraft (1970)

BH-N7 Wellington class   G. Arra, 1977

   D: 33 tons (50 max.)   **S:** 60 kts   **Dim:** 23.9 × 13.0 × 1.7 (at rest)
   Man: 14 men   **M:** 1 Rolls-Royce Proteus gas turbine; 4,250 hp

◆ 3 SR N6 Winchester class

XV 615   XV 617   XV 852   Bldr: British Hovercraft, 1975

   D: 10 tons   **S:** 50 kts   **Dim:** 14.8 × 7.0 × 1.3 (at rest)
   M: 1 Rolls-Royce Gnome gas turbine; 900 hp

AUXILIARY SHIPS

Most auxiliary and supply vessels are responsible to the Royal Fleet Auxiliary (RFA), an organization peculiar to the Royal Navy. Built to the specifications of Lloyds of London (compartmentation, security, habitability), they also meet the standards of the Shipping Naval Acts of 1911 and of the Ministry of Transportation. Manned by the Civil Service, they fly the blue flag of the reserve, rather than the white ensign. In addition, about 40 tugs, salvage vessels, cable-layers, research vessels, etc. are assigned to the Royal Maritime Auxiliary Service (RMAS), whose personnel are also civil servants. The former Port Auxiliary Service (PAS) was absorbed by the RMAS on 1-10-76. Ships not listed below as either RFA or RMAS are manned by the Royal Navy. RMAS ships have black hulls and gray upperworks. They do not normally display hull numbers; most former PAS ships never had any. Former numbers, listed hereafter in parentheses for these ships, are for reference only.

HYDROGRAPHIC SHIPS

NOTE: All British survey ships, except the *Waterwitch*, are painted white, with buff-colored stacks and masts.

◆ 1 improved Hecla class

(A 138) HERALD   Bldr: Robb, Caledon

Herald   1976

   D: 2,125 tons (2,945 fl)   **S:** 14 kts   **Dim:** 79.3 × 14.9 × 4.7
   Man: 128 men   **Range:** 20,000/9, 12,000/11
   M: Diesel-electric propulsion (identical to the *Hecla* class); 1 prop

REMARKS: Improved version of the *Hecla* class. Carries one Wasp helicopter. Replaces the *Vidal*, stricken in 1972. Launched 4-10-73; in service since 31-10-74.

◆ 3 Hecla class   Bldr: Yarrow

(A 133) HECLA   (A 137) HECATE   (A 144) HYDRA

   D: 1,915 tons (2,733 fl)   **Dim:** 79.25 (71.63 pp) × 14.94 × 4.0
   S: 14 kts   **Range:** 20,000/9, 12,000/11
   Man: 14 officers, 104 men   **Fuel:** 450 tons
   M: Diesel-electric propulsion: 3 Paxman Ventura diesels (12 cyl.), each 1,280 hp; 2 electric motors for propulsion (2,000 hp, 190 rpm) linked to a single prop

REMARKS: Based on the oceanographic research vessel *Discovery*. Air-conditioned hull, reinforced against ice; bow propeller for navigation in narrow waters. Hangar and platform for one Wasp helicopter. Excellent scientific laboratories; usually carries seven civilian scientists in addition to crew. Carries two survey launches. *Hecla* launched 21-12-64; *Hecate* launched 31-3-65; *Hydra* launched 14-7-65.

Hecate   G. Arra, 1977

HYDROGRAPHIC SHIPS (*continued*)

◆ **4 Bulldog-class coastal survey ships** Bldr: Brooke Marine, Lowestoft

(A 317) BULLDOG	(A 320) FOX
(A 319) BEAGLE (ex-*Barracuda*)	(A 335) FAWN

D: 800 tons (1,088 fl)   **S:** 15 kts   **Dim:** 60.95 × 11.43 × 3.6
Man: 5 officers, 36 men   **Range:** 4,000/12   **Electric:** 720 kw
M: 4 Lister-Blackstone ERS-8-M diesels; 2 Ka-Me-Wa controllable-pitch props; 2,000 hp

REMARKS: Hulls built to commercial specifications and reinforced against ice damage. Carry one 8.7-meter survey launch. Passive tank stabilization. Decca "Hi-Fix" precision plot. One other built for Nigeria. *Bulldog* launched 12-7-67, *Beagle* 7-9-67, *Fox* 6-11-67, and *Fawn* 29-2-68.

Bulldog   G. Arra, 1977

◆ **3 Echo-class inshore survey craft**

	Bldr	L	In serv.
(A 70) ECHO	J. Samuel White, Cowes	1-5-57	12-9-58
(A 71) ENTERPRISE	M. W. Blackmore, Bideford	20-9-58	1959
(A 72) EGERIA	W. Weatherhead, Cockenzie	13-9-58	1959

D: 120 tons (160 fl)   **S:** 13/12 kts   **Dim:** 32.55 × 6.98 × 2.1
Man: 2 officers, 16 men   **Range:** 1,600/10   **Fuel:** 15 tons
M: 2 Paxman diesels; 2 controllable-pitch props; 700 hp

REMARKS: Built of laminated wood. Quarters for 22. Mount for 1/40-mm. Two echosounders; sonar for detecting shipwrecks. Modified version of "-ham" class

Echo   S. Terzibaschitsch, 1977

◆ **2 "-ham"-class minesweepers, modified as inshore survey craft**

(M 2720) WATERWITCH (ex-*Powderham*)	(M 2780) WOODLARK (ex-*Yaxham*)

Bldr: J. Samuel White, Cowes

D: 120 tons (160 fl)   **Dim:** 32.43 (30.48 pp) × 6.45 × 1.7
S: 13/12 kts   **Man:** 2 officers, 16 men
Fuel: 15 tons   **Range:** 1,500/12
M: 2 Paxman YHAXM diesels; 2 props; 1,100 hp

REMARKS: *Waterwitch*, built 11-57, has a black hull. *Woodlark* was built 1-58. RMAS-operated.

Woodlark   G. Arra, 1977

EXPERIMENTAL SHIPS

◆ 1 sonar-trials ship

	Bldr	Laid down	L	In serv.
A 285 AURICULA	Ferguson Bros.	16-2-79	8-79	1980

D: 1,100 grt **S:** . . . kts **Dim:** 52.0 × . . . × . . .
M: 2 Mirrlees-Blackstone ESL-6-MGR diesels; 2 props; 1,300 hp

REMARKS: Ship operated by RMAS. Ordered 5-1-78.

◆ 1 sonar-research ship

	Bldr	Laid down	L	In serv.
A 367 NEWTON	Scott Lithgow, Greenock	19-12-73	26-6-75	17-6-76

Newton G. Arra, 1977

D: 3,940 tons (fl) **S:** 15 kts **Dim:** 98.6 (88.7 pp) × 16.15 × 4.7
Range: 5,000/13 **Man:** 61 men (including 12 technicians)
Electron Equipt: Radar: 1/1006 Sonar: 1/182, 1/185, 1/2010, 1/2013
Electric: 2,150 kw **Fuel:** 300 tons
M: 3 Mirrlees-Blackstone EWSL-12 MA diesels, electric drive; 1 Kort-nozzle prop; 2,680 hp

REMARKS: Intended for sonar-propagation trials and also fitted to lay cable over the bows. Equipped with bow thruster and passive tank stabilization system. Propulsion plant extremely quiet, with a 300-hp electric motor for low speeds. Has four laboratories and seven special winches. Can carry and lay 400 tons of undersea cable. Navigation equipment includes SINS, satellite receivers, two optical range-finders, Decca Mk 21, and considerable other equipment. RMAS-operated.

◆ 1 torpedo-research vessel

A 364 WHITEHEAD Bldr: Scotts SB, Greenock

D: 3,040 tons (fl) **S:** 15.5 kts **Dim:** 97.23 (88.7 pp) × 14.63 × 5.2
A: 1/533-mm TT (bow, submerged)—3/324-mm Mk 32 ASW TT (III × 1)
Man: 10 officers, 47 men and scientists **Range:** 4,000/12
M: 2 Paxman 12 YLCM diesels; 1 prop; 3,400 hp

REMARKS: Designed not only to launch and recover exercise torpedoes but also to perform precision tracking in three dimensions, using passive hydrophone arrays, and post-firing checkout and maintenance on torpedoes. Launched 5-5-70. RMAS-operated.

Whitehead 1971

◆ 1 sonar-research barge

(RDV 01) CRYSTAL Bldr: HMDY, Devonport

D: 3,040 tons (fl) **Dim:** 126.0 × 17.0 × 1.7 **Man:** 60 men

REMARKS: No propulsion plant. Assigned to test new sonars at Portland. Launched 5-5-70. RMAS-operated.

Crystal G. Arra, 1977

EXPERIMENTAL SHIPS *(continued)*

◆ **1 weapons-research ship**

A 179 WHIMBREL (ex-MRC-1012) (1944)

D: 600 tons (fl) **S:** 10.5 **Dim:** 58.5 × 9.5 × 1.4
Man: . . . **Range:** 1,900/9 **Fuel:** 25 tons
M: 2 Paxman diesels; 2 props; 920 hp

REMARKS: Former repair-configured landing craft employed since 1964 by the Admiralty Underwater Weapons Establishment, Portland. Has a 3-dimensional underwater tracking system. RMAS-operated.

◆ **2 Miner-class stabilization-systems trials ships** Bldr: Philip, Dartmouth

. . . BRITANNIC (ex-*Miner V*)
. . . STEADY (ex-*Miner VII*)

D: 300 tons (355 fl) **S:** 10 kts **Dim:** 33.6 × 8.1 × 2.4
M: 2 Ruston & Hornsby diesels; 2 props; 360 hp

REMARKS: The *Steady*, built 1944, is a former minelayer employed in testing gyro systems at Portsmouth. Sister *Britannic*, built 1940 and equipped as a harbor cable layer, is in reserve as a standby for *Steady*. RMAS-operated.

REPAIR SHIPS

◆ **1 converted Colossus-class aircraft carrier**

	Bldr	Laid down	L	In serv.
A 108 TRIUMPH	Hawthorn Leslie	1-43	2-10-44	4-46

Triumph 1970

D: 13,500 tons (17,500 fl) **Dim:** 213.11 (198.17 wl) × 24.39 × 7.15
S: 24 kts **Man:** 27 officers, 472 men
A: 4/40-mm AA (removed) **Range:** 5,500/23, 10,000/14
Fuel: 3,000 tons **Boilers:** 4 Admiralty; 28 kg/cm² − 371°C
M: Parsons GT; 2 props; 40,000 hp

REMARKS: Conversion to repair ship 1958 to 1965. Landing and takeoff platform, three Wessex helicopters in one deck hangar, four cranes on the flight deck. In reserve at Chatham since 1970. In addition to the crew, carried 285-man repair force.

◆ **1 Head class**

	Bldr	Laid down	L	In serv.
A 134 RAME HEAD	Burrard, Vancouver	7-44	22-11-44	8-45

D: 9,000 tons (11,270 fl) **S:** 10 kts **Dim:** 134.6 (126.8 pp) × 17.5 × 6.9
A: 11/40-mm AA (I × 11) **Man:** 425 men
Boilers: 2 Foster-Wheeler, 17 kg/cm² − 330°C **Fuel:** 700 tons
M: Triple-expansion steam; 1 prop; 2,500 hp

REMARKS: Former escort maintenance ship employed as an accommodations ship at Portsmouth since 6-76. Repair equipment and armament maintained on board in preservation since 1972. Has one 12-ton and two 5-ton cranes.

Rame Head S. Terzibaschitsch, 1977

FLEET-REPLENISHMENT SHIPS

◆ **2 Fort-class ammunition, explosives, food, stores ships (AEFS)**

	Bldr	Laid down	L	In serv.
A 385 FORT GRANGE	Scotts	9-11-73	9-12-76	1978
A 386 FORT AUSTIN	Scotts	9-12-75	9-3-78	5-79

D: 22,749 tons (fl) **S:** 20 kts **Dim:** 183.8 (170.0 pp) × 24.1 × 8.6
Electron Equipt: Radar: Kelvin-Hughes 21/16 P
Electric: 4,120 kw **Man:** 201 men
M: 1 Sulzer 8 RND 90 diesel; 1 prop; 23,200 hp

Fort Grange 1978

FLEET-REPLENISHMENT SHIPS (continued)

REMARKS: Ordered 11-71 and 4-72; 16,009 grt/8,300 dwt/6,729 nrt. In addition to the flight deck on the stern, the roof of the hangar can land helicopters. Two Sea King will be carried, and the ships will have ASW torpedoes and other ASW stores for their use if needed. The design is a combination of features of the *Resource* and *Lyness* classes. Three sliding-stay, constant-tension, alongside-replenishment stations on each beam. RFA-operated.

◆ **2 Resource-class ammunition, explosives, food, stores ships (AEFS)**

	Bldr	Laid down	L	In serv.
A 480 RESOURCE	Scott's SB, Greenock	6-64	11-2-66	18-5-67
A 486 REGENT	Harland & Wolff, Belfast	9-64	9-3-66	6-6-67

Regent   J.-C. Bellonne, 1977

D: 23,000 tons (fl) (18,029 grt)   **S:** 17 kts
Dim: 195.07 (182.88 pp) × 23.47 × 7.95
Man: 182 men, including 11 RN   **Boilers:** 2 Foster-Wheeler
M: A.E.I. GT; 1 prop; 20,000 hp

REMARKS: Three sliding-stay, constant-tension, alongside-replenishment stations per side. One Wessex 5 helicopter. RFA-operated.

◆ **2 Lyness-class stores support ships**

	Bldr	Laid down	L	In serv.
A 339 LYNESS	Swan Hunter	4-65	7-4-66	22-12-66
A 344 STROMNESS	Swan Hunter	10-65	16-9-66	21-3-67

D: 9,010 tons, light (16,792 fl)   **S:** 17 kts
Dim: 159.76 (149.39 pp) × 21.95 × 6.7   **Man:** 25 officers, 126 men
Range: 12,000/16   **M:** Sulzer 8 RD 76 diesel; 1 prop; 11,520 hp

REMARKS: RFA-operated; 12,359 grt/7,782 dwt/4,744 nrt. Platform for two helicopters. Closed-circuit TV provided to monitor handling of stores. A-339, formerly especially configured to act as air-stores support ship, was reassigned to carry food and stores,

Lyness   1977

but not ammunition, in 1978 when *Ark Royal* was stricken. Sister *Tarbatness* (A-345) modified to "landing platform assault" 1979-80.

◆ **1 Retainer-class armament support ship**

A 280 RESURGENT (ex-*Changchow*)   Bldr: Scott's SB, Greenock

    D: 14,400 tons (fl)   **S:** 14 kts   **Dim:** 145.8 × 18.92 × 8.83 (fl)
    Man: 107 men   **Fuel:** 925 tons
    M: 1 Doxford diesel; 1 prop; 6,500 hp

REMARKS: Launched 31-7-50; purchased 1952; 9,357 grt. Former mixed-cargo ship of the China Line. Carries mainly ammunition, but also some combat stores. *Retainer* (A 329) stricken 4-78 on completion of *Fort Grange; Resurgent* will probably be discarded shortly. RFA-operated.

◆ **1 Bacchus-class cargo ship**

A 404 BACCHUS   Bldr: Henry Robb, Ltd.

    D: 2,740 tons light (8,173 fl)   **S:** 15 kts
    Dim: 115.52 (106.7 pp) × 16.76 × 6.4   **Man:** 11 officers, 25 men
    Fuel: 720 tons   **Range:** 14,000/15
    M: 2 Sulzer SRD 68 diesels; 1 prop; 5,500 hp

REMARKS: Built 1962; 4,823 grt, 5,318 dwt. Chartered for 19 years upon completion. Living spaces and machinery area aft. Transportation of cargo and provisions. Three holds. Refrigerated compartments. Can carry 800 tons fuel oil, 200 tons lube oil, 240 tons of fresh water. Not intended for underway replenishment. RFA-operated. Sister *Hebe* stricken 1-79.

FLEET OILERS

◆ **3 Olwen class**

	Bldr	L	In serv.
A 122 OLWEN (ex-*Olynthus*)	Hawthorn Leslie	10-7-64	21-6-65
A 123 OLNA	Hawthorn Leslie	28-7-75	1-4-66
A 124 OLMEDA (ex-*Oleander*)	Swan Hunter	19-11-64	18-10-65

    D: 10,890 tons light (36,000 fl)
    S: 20 kts
    Dim: 197.51 (185.92 pp) × 25.6 × 10.5

FLEET OILERS (continued)

Olwen   S. Terzibaschitsch, 1977

Man: 87 men
Boilers: 2 Babcock & Wilcox, 60 kg/cm² – superheat 510°C
M: Pamatreda GT; 1 prop; 26,500 hp

REMARKS: Hull reinforced against ice, living spaces air-conditioned. advanced automation, excellent facilities for replenishment at sea; 25,000 dwt, 18,600 grt. Helicopter platform; hangar to port recently enlarged to hold two Wessex 5 helicopters,
but normally only one is carried. Can carry 18,400 tons fuel oil, 1,720 tons diesel,
3,730 tons aircraft fuel, and 130 tons lube oil. RFA-operated.

◆ **2 later Tide class**   Bldr: Hawthorn Leslie, Hebburn-on-Tyne

	Laid down	L	In serv.
A 75 TIDESPRING	24-7-61	3-5-62	18-1-63
A 76 TIDEPOOL	4-12-61	11-12-62	28-6-63

Tidespring   G. Arra, 1977

D: 8,531 tons light (27,400 fl)   **Dim:** 177.6 (167.65 pp) × 21.64 × 9.75
S: 18.3 kts   **Man:** 110 men
Boilers: 2 Babcock & Wilcox, 60 kg/cm² – 510°C
M: 1 Pamatreda GT; 1 prop; 15,000 hp

REMARKS: RFA-operated; 18,900 dwt, 14,130 grt. As built, carried 17,400 tons fuel oil
and 700 tons diesel, but with RN dependence on gas-turbine propulsion, proportions
may have changed. Hangar and flight deck for 1 Wessex 5 helicopter.

SMALL FLEET OILERS

◆ **5 Rover class**   Bldr: Swan Hunter, Hebburn-on-Tyne

		L	In serv.
A 268 GREEN ROVER		19-12-68	15-8-69
A 269 GREY ROVER		17-4-69	10-4-70
A 270 BLUE ROVER		11-11-69	15-7-70
A 271 GOLD ROVER		7-3-73	22-3-74
A 273 BLACK ROVER		30-10-73	23-8-74

Grey Rover   G. Arra, 1978

Black Rover   G. Arra, 1976

SMALL FLEET OILERS (*continued*)

Blue Rover   G. Arra, 1975

D: 4,700 tons light (11,522 fl)   **S:** 19.25 kts
Dim: 140.5 × 19.2 × 7.3   **Man:** 47 men   **Range:** 15,000/15
Electric: 2,720 kw   **Fuel:** 965 tons
M: 2 SEMT-Pielstick 16PA 4 diesels (V-16); 1 controllable-pitch prop; 15,300 hp

REMARKS: RFA-operated; 6,822 dwt (A-271, A-273: 6,692 dwt), 7,510 grt. Carry 6,600 tons of fuel plus water, dry stores, and provisions. Helicopter deck but no hangar. A-271 is used for training.

SUPPORT OILERS

◆ **2 C13A class**   Bldr: Cammell Laird, Birkenhead

A . . . APPLELEAF (ex-*Hudson Cavalier*)
A . . . BRAMBLELEAF (ex-*Hudson Deep*)

D: . . . tons   **S:** 16.2 kts   **Dim:** 170.69 (163.51 pp) × 25.94 × 11.33
Fuel: 2,498 tons   **Man:** . . . men
M: 2 Crossley-Pielstick diesels; 1 controllable-pitch prop; 14,000 hp

REMARKS: RFA-operated; 19,975 grt/33,750 dwt. Launched 24-9-75. Laid up on completion in 1975; chartered 1979. *Appleleaf* in service 1981; *Brambleleaf* 1982. One sister, either *Hudson Deep* or *Hudson Progress*, may also be chartered.

◆ **2 Leaf-group support oilers**

A 78 PLUMLEAF   Bldr: Blythwood, Glasgow

Plumleaf   1978

D: 26,480 tons (fl)   **S:** 15.5 kts   **Dim:** 170.8 × 22.0 × 9.2
M: 1 6-cyl. Doxford diesel; 1 prop; 9,500 hp

REMARKS: Launched 29-3-60; 19,430 dwt, 12,459 grt. Chartered 7-60 to RFA. Can refuel at sea alongside (two stations) or astern.

A 77 PEARLEAF   Bldr: Blythwood, Glasgow

Pearleaf   S. Terzibaschitsch, 1977

D: 25,790 tons (fl)   **S:** 16 kts   **Dim:** 173.2 (162.7 pp) × 21.9 × 9.2
M: 1 Rowan-Doxford 6-cyl. diesel; 1 prop; 8,800 hp

REMARKS: Launched 15-10-59; 18,711 dwt, 12,353 grt. Can refuel at sea alongside (two stations) or astern. On charter to RFA.

NOTE: Mobile Reserve Tanker *Dewdale* (A-219) was returned to owners in 1978. Support Oiler *Orangeleaf* (A-80) was discarded 1978 and the charter of *Cherryleaf* (A-82) was due to expire 4-79.

◆ **1 Eddy-class coastal tanker**

A 261 EDDYFIRTH   Bldr: Lobnitz, Renfrew

D: 1,960 tons light (4,160 fl)   **Dim:** 87.65 (82.3 pp) × 13.44 × 5.26
S: 12.5 kts   **Man:** 26 men
Boilers: 2 Scotch-type, 17 kg/cm²

Eddyfirth

SUPPORT OILERS (continued)

Range: 7,550/11 **Fuel:** 515 tons
M: Triple-expansion; 1 prop; 1,750 hp

REMARKS: Last of a class of eight. In service 2-54; 2,200 dwt, 2,222 grt. Carries 1,500 tons light petroleum products, 246 tons dry cargo, 50 tons lube oil. No underway replenishment capability. RFA-operated.

MISCELLANEOUS AUXILIARY SHIPS

♦ **1 helicopter training ship**

	Bldr	Laid down	L	In serv.
K 08 ENGADINE	Henry Robb Ltd.	8-65	16-9-66	12-67

D: 3,640 tons light (8,960 fl) **S:** 16 kts
Dim: 129.31 × 17.86 × 6.73
Man: 61 RFA plus 14 RN (and 113 air group with 29 officers)
Electric: 1,200 kw **Fuel:** 450 tons
M: 1 Sulzer 5RD68, 5-cyl. diesel; 1 prop; 5,500 hp

REMARKS: Intended to train flight crews in ASW helicopter procedures at sea. The hangar can hold either four Wessex or two Sea King and two Wasp. A smaller hangar atop the superstructure serves a target drone launch facility. Equipped with Denny-Brown fin stabilizers and has remote bridge control for all engineering plant. Many internal compartments are voids. RFA-operated.

Engadine G. Arra, 1976

♦ **1 antarctic patrol ship**

A 171 ENDURANCE (ex-*Anita Dan*)
Bldr: Kröger-Werft, Rendsburg

Endurance Skyfotos Ltd., 1978

D: 3,600 tons (fl) **Dim:** 93.58 (82.9 pp) × 14.03 × 5.03
S: 14.5 kts **Man:** 13 officers, 106 men, up to 12 scientists
A: 2/20-mm AA (I × 2) **Range:** 12,000/14
M: 1 Burmeister & Wain 550VTBF, 5-cyl. diesel; 1 prop; 3,220 hp; (plus a bow thruster)

REMARKS: Built 25-5-56; purchased 20-2-67. Hull painted red, superstructure white. Carries two Wasp helicopters and two survey launches. Converted 1967-68 by Harland & Wolff, Belfast, to support the British Antarctic Survey and act as guard ship in the Falkland Islands; 2,641 grt. Large radome added atop hangar 1978 for antenna for MARISAT satellite communications system.

♦ **1 royal yacht**

	Bldr	Laid down	L	In serv.
(A 00) BRITANNIA	J. Brown (Clydebank)	7-52	16-4-53	14-1-54

Britannia G. Arra, 1977

MISCELLANEOUS AUXILIARY SHIPS (continued)

D: 3,990 tons (4,715 fl)   **Dim:** 125.9 (115.82 pp) × 16.76 × 4.86
S: 21 kts   **Man:** 270 men
Fuel: 490 tons   **Range:** 3,100/20
M: GT; 2 props; 12,000 hp   **Boilers:** 2

REMARKS: In wartime, would become a hospital ship (200 beds and 60 medical personnel) and have a helicopter platform. Gyrofin stabilizers.

◆ 1 submarine-support ship

A 236 WAKEFUL (ex-*Dan*, ex-*Herakles*)   Bldr: Cochrane, Selkirk

D: 1,100 tons (fl)   **S:** . . .   **Dim:** 44.43 (38.86 pp) × 10.7 × 4.74
Man: 14 men   **Fuel:** 247 tons   **Electric:** 380 kw
M: Ruston & Hornsby 9-cyl. diesels; 1 prop; . . . hp

REMARKS: Built 1965. Purchased 1974 from Sweden to act as submarine target ship and safety vessel at Faslane; subsequently, also used occasionally on fisheries patrol duties. Former commercial tug, 492 grt.

◆ 1 seabed operations tender   Bldr: Scotts, Govan

REMARKS: Ordered 5-79. Intended to replace *Reclaim;* no data available.

◆ 1 offshore support and salvage ship

. . . SEAFORTH HIGHLANDER   Bldr: Cochrane, Selby

D: 3,320 tons (fl)   **S:** 14 kts   **Dim:** 78.6 (68.7 pp) × 13.7 × 5.01
Man: 46 men (plus 20-man naval salvage group)   **Fuel:** 404 tons
Electric: 1,748 kw
M: 4 Mirrlees-Blackstone EZSL-12 diesels; 2 controllable-pitch, Kort-nozzle props; 7,320 hp

REMARKS: In service 1977; chartered 1978, extended through 1979. The ship was originally intended for oilfield support duties and for maintaining single-point deep moorings. Has a submersible diver's decompression chamber and a "moonpool" opening through the keel of the ship to ensure smooth waters for diving operations. Both bow and stern thrusters are fitted. Has a four-point mooring system and a 30-ton capacity electrohydraulic crane to port, aft. Four fire monitors atop the forward king post can each deliver 18,500 liters/min.

◆ 1 submarine-rescue and salvage ship

A 231 RECLAIM (ex-*Salverdant*)   Bldr: Simons, Renfrew

Reclaim   S. Terzibaschitsch, 1977

D: 1,200 tons (1,800 fl)   **S:** 12 kts   **Dim:** 66.4 × 11.6 × 4.7
Boilers: 2 Scotch, 17 kg/cm²
Range: 3,000/10   **Fuel:** 310 tons   **Man:** 100 men
M: Triple-expansion; 1 prop; 1,500 hp

REMARKS: Launched 12-3-48. Equipped for general-purpose salvage, wreck-location, tending divers, and submarine rescue. Carries sonar. Overdue for replacement.

◆ 1 cable-layer and repair ship

A 259 ST. MARGARETS   Bldr: Swan Hunter

D: 1,300 tons (2,500 fl)   **Dim:** 76.8 (69.7 pp) × 10.9 × 4.8
S: 12 kts   **Boilers:** 2 Scotch, 17 kg/cm²
M: Triple-expansion; 2 props; 1,250 hp

Remarks: Built 1944; 1,200 dwt, 1,524 grt. Lays and recovers cables over the bow. Sister *Bullfinch* stricken 1975. RMAS-operated.

MOORING, SALVAGE, AND NET TENDERS

◆ 2 Pochard class   Bldr: Robb Caledon

(P 197) POCHARD   (P 196) GOOSANDER

Goosander   Robb Caledon, 1974

D: 750 tons (1,200 fl)   **Dim:** 55.4 (48.8 pp) × 12.2 × 5.5
S: 10 kts   **Man:** 26 men
Range: 3,250/9.5
M: 2 Paxman RPHXM 16-cyl. diesels; 550 hp

REMARKS: RMAS-operated. *Pochard* launched 21-6-73; *Goosander* 12-4-73. All mooring, salvage, and boom vessels are multi-purpose and are capable of transporting and servicing moorings, performing salvage duties, and, in wartime, handling harbor-defense nets. Can dead-lift 200 tons over bow horns.

◆ 4 Wild Duck class

	Bldr	L	In serv.
(P 192) MANDARIN	Cammell Laird	17-9-63	2-64
(P 193) PINTAIL	Cammell Laird	3-12-63	3-64
(P 194) GARGANEY	Brooke Marine Ltd.	13-12-65	9-66
(P 195) GOLDENEYE	Brooke Marine Ltd.	31-3-66	12-66

MOORING, SALVAGE, AND NET TENDERS (*continued*)

Goldeneye　　　　　　　　　　　　　　　　　G. Arra, 1975

D:　850 tons (1,300 fl) (P-192, P-193: 041/1,622 tons)
Dim:　57.86 (47.24 pp) × 13.0 × 3.2 (P-192, P-193: 60.23 × 12.22 × 4.21)
S:　10.8 kts　　**Range:**　3,000/10
Man:　7 officers, 18 men
Electric:　P-194, P-195: 640 kw; P-192, P-193: 405 kw
M:　2 Davey-Paxman diesels, 16 cyl.; controllable-pitch prop; 550 hp (P-192, P-193: 750 hp)

REMARK: RMAS-operated.

◆ **1 Lay class**　Bldr: Wm. Simons & Co.

(P 190) LAYMOOR

D:　800 tons (1,050 fl)　　**Dim:**　58.83 (48.77 pp) × 10.36 × 3.5
S:　14 kts　　**Man:**　4 officers, 26 men
Boilers:　2 Foster-Wheeler, 17 kg/cm²
M:　Triple-expansion; 1 prop; 1,300 hp

REMARKS: Sister *Layburn* (P-191) sold commercially, 1978; P-190 (launched 6-8-59) may be stricken in early 1980. Can dead-lift 200 tons over bow horns. RMAS-operated.

◆ **4 Kin class**　Bldr: Hall (A-507: Smith's DY)

(A 281) KINBRACE	(A 482) KINLOSS
(A 232) KINGARTH	(A 507) UPLIFTER

D:　950 tons (1,050 fl)　　**S:**　9 kts
Dim:　54.0 × 10.6 × 3.6
Man:　34 men
M:　1 Atlas Polar M44M diesel; 630 hp

REMARKS: RMAS-operated; built 1944-45; 200-tons lift. Originally had reciprocating steam engines; diesels fitted 1964-67. Sister *Dispenser* sold commercially.

NOTE: The Insect-class fleet tender *Scarab* is also equipped as a moorings tender (10-ton lift).

SEAGOING TUGS

◆ **3 Roysterer class**　Bldr: C. D. Holmes, Hull

		L	In serv.
A 361	ROYSTERER	20-5-70	25-4-72
A 502	ROLLICKER	29-1-71	2-73
. . .	ROBUST	7-10-71	6-4-74

Roysterer　　　　　　　　　　　　　　　　　G. Arra, 1977

D:　1,630 tons (fl)　　**S:**　15 kts　　**Dim:**　54.8 (49.4 pp) × 11.6 × 5.5
Range:　13,000/12
Man:　31 men (plus 10-man RN salvage party if needed)
M:　2 Mirrlees KMR6 diesels; 2 props; 4,500 hp

REMARKS: RMAS-operated; 50-ton bollard pull. Although designed for long-distance towing, have been used primarily in port service.

◆ **1 Typhoon class**

A 95 TYPHOON　Bldr: H. Robb, Leith

Typhoon　　　　　　　　　　　　　　　　　G. Arra, 1975

SEAGOING TUGS (*continued*)

D: 800 tons (1,380 fl)   **S:** 17 kts   **Dim:** 60.5 × 12.3 × 4.0
M: 2 12-cyl. diesels; 1 controllable-pitch prop; 2,750 hp

REMARKS: RMAS-operated; launched 14-10-58; 32-ton bollard pull.

◆ 5 Confiance class

(A 88) AGILE, (A 89) ADVICE, (A 90) ACCORD, (A 289) CONFIANCE, (A 290) CONFIDENT

Bldr: Inglis, Glasgow, except A-88: Goole

Agile   G. Arra, 1976

D: 760 tons (fl)   **Dim:** 47.2 (42.7 pp) × 10.7 × 3.4
S: 13 kts   **Man:** 29 men (plus 13 salvage)
M: 4 Paxman HAXM diesels; 2 controllable-pitch props; 1,800 hp

REMARKS: In service 1956-59. RMAS-operated.

◆ 2 Samson class

(A 288) SEA GIANT   SUPERMAN   Bldr: A. Hall, Aberdeen

D: 1,200 tons (fl)   **S:** 15 kts   **Dim:** 54.9 × 11.3 × 4.3
M: 2 sets triple-expansion; 2 props; 3,000 hp   **Boilers:** 2

REMARKS: Built 1954-55. RMAS-operated. *Superman* in reserve. Sister *Samson* stricken 1974.

◆ 1 Bustler class

(A 111) CYCLONE (ex-*Growler*) Bldr: H. Robb, Leith

D: 1,118 tons (1,630 fl)   **S:** 16 kts   **Dim:** 62.5 (58.0 pp) × 12.3 × 5.1
Man: 42 men   **Fuel:** 405 tons   **Range:** 17,000/14
M: 2 Polar 8-cyl. diesels; 1 prop; 4,000 hp

REMARKS: RMAS-operated. Launched 10-9-42. Last of a class of four, in reserve. Sister *Reward* rammed and sunk 1976 while serving as North Sea patrol ship; salvaged and scrapped.

SERVICE CRAFT

AMMUNITION LIGHTERS

◆ 1 (+1) new construction   Bldr: Cleland, Wallsend

A 379 THROSK   A . . . KINTERBURY

D: 2,193 tons (fl)   **S:** 14 kts   **Dim:** 70.57 (64.31 pp) × 11.9 × 4.57
Man: 10 officers, 22 men   **Range:** 5,000/10
M: 2 Mirrlees-Blackstone diesels; 1 prop; 3,000 hp

REMARKS: Two holds, two 5-ton cranes; 1,150 dwt. A-379 ordered 12-75, launched 31-3-77; second unit ordered 1978, to be launched 1980. A third will be built for the Army Royal Corps of Transport. The original *Kinterbury* (A-378) was stricken 1979. RMAS-operated.

◆ 1 Gun class

(A 377) MAXIM Bldr: Lobnitz

D: 383 tons (707 fl)   **S:** 10.5 kts   **Dim:** 44.0 (40.8 pp) × 7.9 × 2.4
Man: 13 men   **Fuel:** 60 tons   **Range:** 1,200/10
M: Triple-expansion; 1 prop; 490 hp

REMARKS: RMAS-operated; built 1944; 340 dwt. In reserve.

DEGAUSSING TENDERS

◆ 2 new construction   Bldr: Clelands, Wallsend-on-Tyne

		Laid down	L	In serv.
A . . .	MAGNET	3-11-78	6-79	12-79
A . . .	LODESTONE	22-12-78	10-79	1980

D: 950 grt   **S:** 12 kts   **Dim:** 54.8 (50.0 pp) × 11.4 × 3.0
Man: 15 men   **Range:** 1,750/12
M: 2 diesels, electric drive; 2 props; . . . hp

REMARKS: Built to commercial standards. RMAS-operated.

◆ 3 converted "-ham" class

(M 2717) FORDHAM   (M 2790) THATCHAM   (M 2737) WARMINGHAM

REMARKS: RMAS-operated. Details as for "-ham"-class training craft. Deckhouse greatly enlarged, cable reel at stern.

TORPEDO RETRIEVERS

◆ 4 Tornado class   Bldr: Hall Russell, Aberdeen

		Laid down	L	In serv.
(A . . .)	TORNADO	11-78	6-79	1980
(A . . .)	TORCH	12-78	. . .	1980
(A . . .)	TORMENTOR	3-79	. . .	. . .
(A . . .)	TOREADOR	5-79	. . .	. . .

D: 660 tons (fl)   **S:** 14 kts   **Dim:** 47.47 (40.0 pp) × 8.53 × 3.0
Man: 17 men   **Range:** 3,000/. . .   **Fuel:** 110 tons

TORPEDO RETRIEVERS (*continued*)

M: 2 Lister-Blackstone ESL-8-MGR diesels; 2 props; 2,200 hp

REMARK: RMAS-operated.

◆ **2 Torrent class, seagoing** Bldr: Cleland, Wallsend

(A 127) TORRENT   (A 128) TORRID

D: 468 tons (685 fl)   **S:** 11.5 kts   **Dim:** 49.55 (44.2 pp) × 9.72 × 3.05
Man: 19 men   **Range:** 1,500/11   **Electric:** 300 kw   **Fuel:** 49 tons
M: Paxman 16 RPHM diesel; 1 prop; 700 hp

Torrent   1972

REMARKS: Can stow 32 torpedoes on deck and perform post-firing maintenance. Stern
ramp for recovery. RMAS-operated. *Torrent* in service 9-71; *Torrid* 1-72.

◆ **1 converted customs craft**

ENDEAVOR Bldr: R. Dunston

D: 88 tons (fl)   **S:** 10.5 kts   **Dim:** 23.2 × 4.4 × 2.0
M: 1 Lister-Blackstone diesel; 337 hp

REMARKS: Launched 1966. RMAS-operated. Resembles a small tug; cannot bring recovered torpedoes aboard. Also used as range safety craft at Portland.

◆ **6 converted "-ham" class**

(M 2614) BUCKLESHAM   (M 2622) DOWNHAM   (M 2626) EVERINGHAM
(M 2630) FRITHAM   (M 2635) HAVERSHAM   (M 2636) LASHAM

REMARKS: RMAS-operated. Details as for "-ham"-class training craft. Ramp in stern
for torpedo recovery.

NOTE: The torpedo retriever *Thomas Grant* was stricken 1979.

DIVING TENDERS

◆ **4 modified Cartmel class** Bldr: Gregson, Blyth

(A 305) ILCHESTER
(A 309) INSTOW
(A 311) IRONBRIDGE (ex-*Invergorden*)
(A 318) IXWORTH

REMARKS: RMAS-operated. All in service 1974. Details and appearance as for *Cartmel*-
class tenders, except for a decompression chamber on deck forward, beneath a stowage platform for a Gemini dinghey. Can be used for harbor mine clearance. Displacement is 150 tons (fl).

◆ **1 Datchet class**

DATCHET Bldr: Vosper, Singapore

Datchet   G. Arra, 1975

D: 70 tons (fl)   **S:** 12 kts   **Dim:** 22.86 × 5.79 × 1.22
Range: 500/12
M: 2 Gray Marine diesels; 2 props; 500 hp

REMARKS: RMAS-operated. In service 1968.

TRAINING CRAFT

◆ **3 "-ham"-class former inshore minesweepers**

M 2621 DITTISHAM   M 2628 FLINTHAM   M 2793 THORNHAM

D: 120 tons (157 fl)   **Dim:** 32.47 (30.48 pp) × 6.61 × 1.75
S: 14 kts   **Man:** 15 men
A: 1/20-mm AA   **Electron Equipt:** Radar: 978   **Range:** 2,350/9
M: 2 Paxman YHAXM 12-cyl. diesels; 2 props; 1,100 hp   **Fuel:** 15 tons

REMARKS: In service 1954-57. M-2621 and M-2628 employed for enlisted basic training
at Plymouth; M-2793 attached to Aberdeen University naval training unit. All minesweeping gear removed.

◆ **2 Ley-class former inshore minehunters**

M 2002 AVELEY   M 2010 ISIS (ex-*Cradley*)

TRAINING CRAFT (*continued*)

Aveley   G. Arra, 1976

  D: 123 tons (140 fl)   **Dim:** 32.44 (30.48 pp) × 6.1 × 1.68
  S: 14 kts   **Man:** 15 men
  A: M-2010 only: 1/40-mm AA   **Electric:** 108 kw
  M: 2 Paxman YHAXM 12-cyl. diesels; 2 props; 1,100 hp

REMARKS: Survivors of 10 built. *Aveley* launched 1953. Had sonars vice magnetic sweep gear; otherwise similar to "-ham" class but with larger superstructure. M-2010 attached to Southampton University; M-2002 is tender at Plymouth.

◆ 2 Ford-class former submarine chasers

P 3104 DEE (ex-*Beckford*)   P 3113 DROXFORD

  D: 115 tons (138 fl)   **Dim:** 35.76 (33.53 fl) × 6.1 × 1.68
  S: 18 kts   **Man:** 19 men
  A: Removed   **Range:** 500/12; 1,000/8 (cruise diesel)   **Fuel:** 23 tons
  M: 2 Paxman YHAXM diesels (500 hp each), 1 Foden FD 6 diesel (100 hp); 3 props

REMARKS: Survivors of a class of 20, some transferred abroad. *Dee* launched 1953; *Droxford* 1954. P-3104 attached to Liverpool University, P-3113 to Glasgow University for naval cadet training.

NOTE: General-purpose tenders *Cromarty*, *Clovelly*, and *Froxfield* of the *Cartmel* class and *Alnmouth* and *Bembridge* of the *Aberdovey* class are also employed in training; *see* under General-purpose Tenders for data.

FUEL LIGHTERS

◆ 6 Oil class   Bldr: Appledore

(Y 21) OILPRESS   (Y 23) OILWELL   (Y 25) OILBIRD
(Y 22) OILSTONE   (Y 24) OILFIELD   (Y 26) OILMAN

  D: 250 tons (535 fl)   **Dim:** 42.26 (39.62 pp) × 7.47 × 2.51
  S: 10 kts   **Man:** 4 officers, 7 men

Oilwell   G. Arra, 1976

  Range: 1,500/10   **Fuel:** 15 tons   **Electric:** 225 kw
  M: 1 Lister-Blackstone ES-6-MGR diesel; 405 hp

REMARK: First three carry diesel fuel and are 247 tons (527 fl); other three carry fuel oil. Built 1969. RMAS-operated.

WATER LIGHTERS

◆ 6 Water class   Bldr: Drypool, Hull

(Y 15) WATERCOURSE   (Y 17) WATERFALL   (Y 19) WATERSPOUT
(Y 16) WATERFOWL   (Y 18) WATERSHED   (Y 20) WATERSIDE

  D: 344 tons (478 fl)   **S:** 11 kts   **Dim:** 40.02 (37.5 pp) × 7.5 × 2.44
  Man: 11 men   **Range:** 1,500/11   **Electron Equipt:** Radar: 975 or 978
  Electric: 155 kw
  M: 1 lister-Blackstone ERS-8-MGR diesel; 600 hp

REMARKS: RMAS-operated. Built 1966-73. Carry 150 tons water cargo. Resemble Oil class. Y-15 and Y-16 (launched 1973) have deckhouse over after cargo tanks.

Waterside   G. Arra, 1977

WATER LIGHTERS (continued)

◆ 1 Spa class

(A 222) SPAPOOL   Bldr: Chas. Hill, Bristol

D: 1,219 tons (fl)   **S:** 9 kts   **Dim:** 52.43 × 9.14 × 3.66
Fuels: 90 tons coal   **Cargo:** 500 tons water   **Boilers:** 1
M: Triple-expansion; 1 prop; 675 hp

REMARKS: RMAS-operated. In service 1947. Survivor of a class of six; *Spabrook* (A-224) discarded 1977.

◆ 2 Fresh class

FRESHLAKE   FRESHSPRING

D: 594 tons (fl)   **S:** 9 kts   **Dim:** 38.47 × 7.77 × 3.28
Fuel: 42 tons coal (*Freshspring:* oil)   **Cargo:** 236 tons water   **Boilers:** 1
M: Triple-expansion; 1 prop; 450 hp

REMARKS: RMAS-operated. In service 1941-42. Both in reserve.

TANK-CLEANING CRAFT

◆ 3 Isles-class converted escorts

(A 332) CALDY   (A 336) LUNDY   (A 346) SWITHA

D: 560 tons (770 fl)   **S:** 12 kts   **Dim:** 49.99 (45.72 pp) × 8.43 × 4.19
Range: 4,200/8   **Fuel:** 183 tons coal   **Boilers:** 1
M: Triple-expansion; 1 prop; 850 hp

REMARKS: All in service 1942-43. Survivors of 155 built as ASW trawlers or minesweepers. Converted 1951-57 for cleaning fuel tanks of other ships. *Coll* stricken 1977; *Bern*, *Graemsay*, and *Skomer* stricken 1978. Sister *Mull* serves Army as a cargo ship.

GENERAL-PURPOSE TENDERS

◆ 7 100-foot Insect class   Bldr: C. D. Holmes

BEE	COCKCHAFER	GNAT	SCARAB
CICALA	CRICKET	LADYBIRD	

Bee   G. Arra, 1977

D: 213 tons (450 fl)   **Dim:** 34.06 (30.48 pp) × 8.53 × 3.2
S: 10.5 kts   **Man:** 10 men
M: 1 Lister-Blackstone ERS-8-HGR diesel; 660 hp

REMARKS: RMAS-operated; built 1970-73; 200 tons cargo, one 3-ton crane. *Scarab*, with 5-ton winch and bow horn, is used as a moorings tender.

◆ 8 Loyal class   Bldr: R. Dunston, Thorne

LOYAL CHANCELLOR	LOYAL MODERATOR	LOYAL VOLUNTEER
LOYAL HELPER	LOYAL PROCTOR	LOYAL WATCHER
LOYAL MEDIATOR	LOYAL SUPPORTER	

Loyal Proctor   G. Arra, 1977

REMARKS: RMAS-operated. Built 1974-78. Details as for *Cartmel* class but equipped to carry up to 200 personnel in cargo hold for short distances (except *Loyal Moderator*, RMAS training craft, 12 extra berths instead). Two sisters, *Vigilant* (A-382, ex-*Loyal Factor*) and *Alert* (A-510, ex-*Loyal Governor*) serve as patrol craft in Ulster waters, RN-manned.

◆ 30 (+4) 23-meter Cartmel class   Bldrs: Various

CARTMEL	ELKSTONE	GLENCOVE	LAMLASH
CAWSAND	ELSING	GRASMERE	LECHLADE
CLOVELLY	EPWORTH	HAMBLEDON	LLANDOVERY
CRICCIETH	ETTRICK	HARLECH	N . . .
CRICKLADE	FELSTED	HEADCORN	N . . .
CROMARTY	FINTRY	HEVER	N . . .
DENMEAD	FOTHERBY	HOLMWOOD	N . . .
DORNOCH	FROXFIELD	HORNING	
DUNSTER	FULBECK	IXWORTH	

GENERAL-PURPOSE TENDERS (continued)

Horning   G. Arra, 1976

D: 143 tons (fl)   **S:** 10.5 kts   **Dim:** 24.38 (22.86 pp) × 6.4 × 1.98
Man: 6 men   **Range:** 700/10   **Electric:** 106 kw
M: 1 Lister-Blackstone ERS-4-MGR diesel; 330 hp

REMARKS: RMAS-operated except *Ettrick* and *Elsing*, which are RN-manned. Built 1971-74. Improved version of *Aberdovey* class; 25 tons cargo. First two, 5.49-meter beam. Carry stores, personnel, food. Can tow. *Clovelly*, *Cromarty*, and *Froxfield* are also used for training. Four more were ordered during 1979.

◆ **12 23-meter Aberdovey class**

(a) ABERDOVEY	ALNMOUTH	(b) BEAULIEU	BIBURY
ABINGER	APPLEBY	BEDDGELERT	BLAKENEY
ALNESS	ASHCOTT	BEMBRIDGE	BRODICK

Bldrs: (a) I. Pimblott, Norwich; (b) I. S. Doig, Grimsby

Beaulieu   G. Arra, 1976

D: 117.5 tons (fl)   **S:** 10.5 kts   **Dim:** 24.16 (22.86 pp) × 5.79 × 1.68
Range: 700/10   **M:** 1 Lister-Blackstone ER-4-MGR diesel; 225 hp

REMARKS: RMAS-operated. (a) built 1963-68; (b) built 1966-71. Carry 25 tons cargo. *Alnmouth* used for Sea Cadet Corps training; *Bembridge* also used for training.

◆ **1 converted ex-stern trawler** Bldr: P. K. Harris, Appledore

DOLWEN (ex-*Hector Gull*)

D: 602 tons (fl)   **S:** . . . kts   **Dim:** 41.1 × 9.0 × 4.4
M: 1 National FSSM-6 diesel; 1 controllable-pitch prop; . . . hp

REMARKS: RMAS-operated. Built 1962. Gallows at stern for laying buoys; used as air bombardment safety range craft.

◆ **5 "-ham"-class former inshore minesweepers**

(M 2716) PAGHAM	(M 2784) PUTTENHAM	(M 2735) TONGHAM
(M 2781) PORTISHAM	(M 2726) SHIPHAM	

Pagham   S. Terzibaschitsch, 1977

REMARKS: RMAS-operated. Built 1953-57. Details as for "-ham"-class training craft; no armament, all sweep gear removed. Carry passengers and stores. M-2726 temporarily used as an inshore survey ship, 1978-79. *Thakeham* (M-2735) stricken 1978.

LARGE HARBOR TUGS

◆ **19 Dog class**   Bldrs: Various

(A 102) AIREDALE	(A 155) DEERHOUND	(A 188) POINTER
(A 106) ALSATIAN	(A 162) ELKHOUND	(A 182) SALUKI
(A 327) BASSET	(A 394) FOXHOUND	(A 187) SEALYHAM
(A 126) CAIRN	(ex-*Boxer*)	(A 189) SETTER
(A 328) COLLIE	(A 169) HUSKY	(A 250) SHEEPDOG
(A 330) CORGI	(A 168) LABRADOR	(A 201) SPANIEL
(A 129) DALMATIAN	(A 180) MASTIFF	

D: 206 tons (248 fl)   **S:** 12 kts   **Dim:** 28.65 (25.91 pp) × 7.72 × 3.51
Man: 8 men   **Electric:** 80 kw
M: 2 Lister-Blackstone ERS-86-MGR diesels; 1 prop; 1,320 hp

LARGE HARBOR TUGS (*continued*)

Setter   G. Arra, 1975

REMARKS: RMAS-operated; built 1962-72; 18.7-ton bollard pull. *Foxhound* renamed 1977.

◆ **2 Dexterous-class paddle tugs**   Bldrs: A-86: Yarrow; A-87: Ferguson

(A 86) FORCEFUL   (A 87) FAVOURITE

   D: 710 tons (fl)   **S:** 13 kts   **Dim:** 47.91 (44.2 pp) × 18.24 × 3.04
   Man: 21 men
   M: 4 Paxman diesels (500 hp each), 2 electric motors; 2 paddles; 1,600 hp

REMARKS: RMAS-operated. Built 1957-59 to handle aircraft carriers; world's only naval paddle tugs. Hull beam 9.14 meters. *Dexterous* (A-93), *Director* (A-94), *Faithful* (A-85), *Griper* (A-91), and *Grinder* (A-92) stricken 1978-79.

Favourite   G. Arra, 1977

◆ **4 new construction**   Bldr: R. Dunston

REMARKS: Ordered 8-3-79. A new class of "twin-unit tractors" with dual vertical cycloidal propeller systems.

MEDIUM HARBOR TUGS

◆ **8 Felicity-class water tractors**   Bldr: Hancock, Pembroke except *Felicity:* R. Dunston

FELICITY	GEORGINA	HELEN	FLORENCE
FIONA	GWENDOLINE	FRANCES	GENEVIEVE

Fiona   G. Arra, 1977

   D: 220 tons (fl)   **S:** 8 kts   **Dim:** 21.95 (20.73 pp) × 6.4 × 2.97
   Man: 6 men   **M:** 1 Lister-Blackstone ERS-8-MGR diesel; cycloidal prop; 6.5 hp

REMARKS: RMAS-operated. In service 1968-80. Three more were ordered from Dunston 13-12-78 for delivery in 1980.

◆ **8 modified Girl class**   Bldrs: (*a*) I. Pimblott; (*b*) R. Dunston

(*a*) CHARLOTTE	(*b*) DAISY	DOROTHY
CHRISTINE	DAPHNE	EDITH
CLARE	DORIS	

   D: 100 tons (fl)   **S:** 10.5 kts   **Dim:** 20.57 × 6.25 × 2.9
   Man: 4 men   **Range:** 900/10
   M: 1 Lister-Blackstone ERS-6-MGR diesel; 495 hp

REMARKS: RMAS-operated; in service 1966-74; 50 grt; 6.5-ton bollard pull. *Clare* is used as a patrol craft at Hong Kong. *Celia* (A-206) sold commercially, 1971.

GREAT BRITAIN (continued)

MEDIUM HARBOR TUGS (continued)

◆ **8 Girl class** Bldrs: (a) P. Harris; (b) R. Dunston

(a)	(A 116) AGATHA	(b)	(A 324) BARBARA
	(A 121) AGNES		(A 232) BETTY
	(A 113) ALICE		(A 335) BRENDA
	(A 117) AUDREY		(A 322) BRIDGET

Bridget G. Arra

D: 66.5 tons (81 fl) **S:** 10 kts **Dim:** 18.75 (17.3 pp) × 5.11 × 2.36
Man: 4 men **Range:** 980/9.8
M: 1 Lister-Blackstone ERS-6-MGR diesel; 495 hp

REMARKS: RMAS-operated; built 1961-63; 40 grt; 6.5-ton bollard pull.

SMALL HARBOR TUGS

◆ **12 (+4) Triton-class water tractors** Bldr: R. Dunston

IRENE	KATHLEEN	MARY	ADEPT
ISABEL	KITTY	MYRTLE	BUSTLER
JOAN	LESLEY	NANCY	CAPABLE
JOYCE	LILAH	NORAH	CAREFUL

D: 107.5 tons (fl) **S:** 7.75 kts **Dim:** 17.65 (16.76 pp) × 5.26 × 2.8
Man: 6 men **M:** 1 Lister-Blackstone ERS-4-M diesel; cycloidal prop; 330 hp

REMARKS: RMAS-operated; built 1972-73; 50 grt; 3-ton bollard pull. Voith vertical cycloidal prop to provide instant mobility and full power in any direction. Four additional ordered during 1979 from the same builder.

Isabel G. Arra

GREECE

PERSONNEL: About 16,500 men, including 1,900 officers

MERCHANT MARINE (1978): 3,666 ships—33,956,093 grt (tankers: 443 ships—10,653,499 grt)

NAVAL AVIATION: Greek naval aviation began in April 1975, when four Alouette-III ASW helicopters fitted with AS-12 anti-ship, wire-guided missiles went into service. Six Agusta-Bell AB-212 ASW helicopters were ordered from Italy in 5-77. The Air Force has eight Hu-16B Grumman Albatross amphibian planes for antisubmarine warfare.

Warships In Service or Under Construction As Of 1 January 1980

	L	Tons	Main armament
◆ **8 (+2) submarines**			
6 (+2) TYPE 209	1970-79	980	8/533-mm TT
1 GUPPY III	1945	1,660	10/533-mm TT
1 GUPPY II	1944	1,500	10/533-mm TT
◆ **14 destroyers**			
7 GEARING	1944-45	2,425	4-6/127-mm DP, 1/76-mm (in 4), Asroc (in 4), 6/ASW TT
1 ALLEN M. SUMNER	1944	2,200	6/127-mm DP, 6/ASW TT
6 FLETCHER	1942-43	2,050	4-5/127-mm DP, 6/76-mm AA or 10/40-mm AA, ASW weapons
◆ **5 frigates**			
1 RHEIN	1960	2,370	2/100-mm DP, 4/40-mm AA, mines
4 CANNON	1942-43	1,300	3/76-mm DP, ASW weapons
◆ **2 corvettes**			
2 EX-U.S. PGM	1943-44	325	1/76-mm, ASW weapons
◆ **23 (+6) guided-missile patrol boats and torpedo boats**			
4 LA COMBATTANTE III	1976-77	400	4/MM-38, 2/76-mm, 4/30-mm AA
4 (+6) LA COMBATTANTE II	1971-79	234	4/MM-38 or 6/Penguin, 4/35-mm AA
2 KELEFSTIS STAMOU	1975	80	2/20-mm AA, 4/SS-12 SSM
5 TJELD	1966-67	69	4/533-mm TT, 2/40-mm AA
1 BRAVE	1962	95	2/40-mm AA, 2/533-mm TT
7 JAGUAR	1958	195	2/40-mm AA, 4/533-mm TT

◆ **17 patrol craft**

◆ **15 minesweepers**

◆ **2 minelayers**

◆ **26 amphibious-warfare ships**

SUBMARINES

◆ **6 (+2) German Type 209** Bldr: Howaldtswerke, Kiel

	Laid down	L	In serv.
110 GLAVKOS	1969	9-70	5-11-71
111 NEREUS	1969	9-71	10-2-72
112 TRITON	1969	1971	23-11-72
113 PROTEUS	1970	12-71	8-8-72
. . . POSEIDON	15-4-76	3-78	6-79
. . . AMFRITITI	1976	14-6-78	9-79
. . . OKEANOS	1976	24-11-78	1980
118 PONTOS	. . .	22-3-79	1980

D: 980 tons, 1,105 surfaced, 1,230 submerged **Dim:** 55.0 × 6.6 × 5.9
S: 21 kts (max. submerged for 5 min), 12 kts with snorkel
A: 8/533-mm TT fwd (+6 reserve torpedoes) **Man:** 5 officers, 26 men
M: Diesel-electric propulsion; 4 Maybach diesels, each linked to an AEG generator of 420 kw; a single Siemens electric motor of 3,600 hp; 1 prop

REMARKS: Similar to the submarines ordered by Argentina, Peru, and other countries. Submersion depth better than 200 m. The second group of four are 58 m overall, 1,180 tons surfaced/1,300 tons submerged.

Glavkos   1977

SUBMARINES (continued)

Proteus   1972

◆ 1 ex-U.S. Guppy III class

	Bldr	L	In serv.
115 L. KATSONIS (ex-*Remora*, SS-487)	Portsmouth NSY	12-7-45	3-1-46

D: 1,660 tons, 1,975 surfaced, 2,540 submerged   **Dim:** 99.4 × 8.2 × 5.2
S: 20/13-15 kts
A: 10/533-mm TT (6 fwd, 4 aft)   **Electron Equipt:** Sonar: BQG-4 (PUFFS), BQR-2
M: Diesel-electric propulsion; 4 groups of generators (6,000 hp); 2 electric motors (5,400 hp)

REMARK: Transferred in 10-73.

Katsonis

◆ 1 ex-U.S. Guppy II class

	Bldr	L
114 PAPANIKOLIS (ex-*Hardhead*, SS-365)	Manitowoc SB	12-12-44

D: 1,500 tons, 1,840 surfaced, 2,245 submerged   **Dim:** 93.2 × 8.2 × 5.2
S: 18/15 kts   **Man:** 86 men   **Fuel:** 300 tons diesel
A: 10/533-mm TT (6 fwd, 4 aft)   **Range:** 10,000/10

M: Diesel-electric propulsion; 3 groups of generators; 2 electric motors; 2 props; 4,800/5,200 hp

REMARKS: Transferred 26-7-72. Originally the *Balao* type; the fourth group of generators was removed to permit enlargement of the sonar compartment. Two 126-cell batteries. *Triana* (S-86), ex-*Scabbardfish* (SS-397), is now used for pierside training.

DESTROYERS

◆ 5 ex-U.S. Gearing class

Transferred: 210 in 1971, 212 in 1972, 213 and 214 in 1973, 215 in 1977, 2 more in 1980.

	Bldr	Laid down	L	In serv.
210 THEMISTOCLES (ex-*Frank Knox*, DD-742)	Bath Iron Works	8-5-44	17-9-44	11-12-44
212 KANARIS (ex-*Stickell*, DD-888)	Consolidated Steel	5-1-45	16-6-45	26-9-45
213 KONTOURIOTIS (ex-*Rupertus*, DD-851)	Bethlehem, Quincy	2-5-45	21-9-45	8-3-46
214 SACHTOURIS (ex-*Arnold J. Isbell*, DD-869)	Bethlehem, Quincy	14-3-45	6-8-45	5-1-46
215 TOUMBAZIS (ex-*Gurke*, DD-783)	Todd SY, Seattle	1-7-44	15-4-45	5-12-45

D: 2,425 tons (3,500 fl)   **S:** 30 kts   **Dim:** 119.72 × 12.55 × 5.5
Man: 14 officers, 260 men   **Range:** 2,400/25, 4,800/15   **Fuel:** 650 tons
A: 210: 6/127-mm, 38-cal. (II × 3)−2/40-mm AA (I × 2)−6/20-mm AA (I × 6)−2 Hedgehogs−6/Mk 32 ASW TT (III × 2) Others: 4/127-mm, 38-cal. (II × 2)−1/76-mm OTO Melara−1/Asroc system−1/40-mm AA−2/12.7-mm machine guns−6/Mk 32 ASW TT (III × 2)−1 depth-charge rack
Electron Equipt: Radars: 1/SPS 10, 1/SPS 40 (SPS 37 on 210, 212, 215), 1/Mk 25, 1/NA 10 (not in 210)
  Sonars: SQS 23 (210: also SQA 10 VDS)−210: TACAN
M: GT; 2 props; 60,000 hp   **Boilers:** 4 Babcock & Wilcox

Sachtouris   1977

DESTROYERS (continued)

Kontouriotis   1977

Velos   G. Arra

REMARKS: 212, 213, 214, and 215 modernized under FRAM-I program, 210 under FRAM-II. 210 given modest modernization, including hangar and flight deck for one Alouette-III, 1976-77. Others have received an Elsag NA-10 fire-control system aft, 1/76-mm OTO Melara Compact on the helicopter deck and a 40-mm AA before the bridge. All also have a small navigational radar.

◆ 1 ex-U.S. Allen M. Sumner class

	Laid down	L	In serv.
211 MIAOULIS (ex-*Ingraham*, DD-694)	4-4-43	16-1-44	10-3-44

Bldr: Federal SB & DD

D: 2,200 tons (3,320 fl)   **S:** 30 kts   **Dim:** 114.75 × 12.45 × 5.8
Man: 14 officers, 260 men   **Range:** 2,400/25, 4,800/15   **Fuel:** 650 tons
A: 6/127-mm, 38-cal. (II × 3) – 2/40-mm AA (I × 2) – 6/20-mm AA (I × 6) – 2 Hedge-hogs – 6/Mk 32 ASW TT (III × 2)
Electron Equipt: Radars: 1/SPS 10, 1/SPS 40, 1/Mk 25
            Sonars: SQS 29, SQA 10 VDS
M: GT; 2 props; 60,000 hp   **Boilers:** 4 Babcock & Wilcox

REMARKS: Modernized in U.S. under FRAM-II program. Transferred 16-7-71. Mk-37 gunfire-control system.

◆ 6 ex-U.S. Fletcher class

	Bldr	L	In serv.
06 ASPIS (ex-*Conner*, DD-582)	Boston NSY	18-7-42	6-43
16 VELOS (ex-*Charette*, DD-581)	Boston NSY	3-6-42	5-43
28 THYELLA (ex-*Bradford*, DD-545)	Bethlehem, San Pedro	12-12-42	6-43
58 LONCHI (ex-*Hall*, DD-583)	Boston NSY	18-7-42	7-43
85 SPHENDONI (ex-*Aulick*, DD-569)	Consolidated SB	2-3-42	10-42
63 NAVARINON (ex-*Brown*, DD-546)	Bethlehem, San Pedro	22-4-43	7-43

D: 2,050 tons (2,850 fl)   **S:** 32/30 kts   **Dim:** 114.85 × 12.03 × 5.5
Man: 350 men   **Range:** 1,260/30, 4,400/15   **Fuel:** 650 tons
A: 06, 16, 58, 85: 4/127-mm, 38-cal. (I × 4) – 6/76-mm AA, 50-cal. (II × 3) – 5/533-mm TT (V × 1)
     28, 63: 5/127-mm AA (I × 5) – 10/40-mm AA (IV × 2, II × 1)
     All: 6/324-mm Mk 32 ASW TT (III × 2) – 2 Hedgehogs – 1 depth-charge rack
Electron Equipt: Radars: 1/SPS 10, 1/SPS 6, 1/Mk 25, 2/Mk 34
                06, 16, 58, 85: 1/Mk 35 also
M: GE GT; 2 props; 60,000 hp   **Boilers:** 4 Babcock & Wilcox
Electric: 580 kw

REMARKS: Transferred under the Military Assistance Program, three in 1959, 58 in 1960, 28 and 63 in 9-62. Loan renewed in 3-70. All have Mk-37 gunfire-control system; ships with 76-mm guns also have Mk-56 and two Mk-63 systems.

FRIGATES

◆ 1 German Rhein-class former tender

215 AEGEON (ex-*Weser*, A-62)   Bldr: Elsflether Werft

D: 2,370 tons (2,740 fl)   **S:** 20.5 kts
Dim: 98.18 (92.8 pp) × 11.8 × 3.9
A: 2/100-mm DP (I × 2) – 4/40-mm AA (I × 4) – 70 mines   **Man:** 110 men
Electron Equipt: Radars: 1/SGR 105, 1/SGR 103, 2/M 45
M: 6 Maybach 16-cyl. diesels; 2 controllable-pitch props; 12,600 hp
Range: 2,500/16

REMARKS: Launched 11-6-60, transferred 6-7-76. A small combatant tender used by Greece as a frigate. Still can act as tender.

◆ 4 ex-U.S. Cannon class

	Bldr	L
01 AETOS (ex-*Ebert*, DE-768)	Tampa Shipbldg	23-5-44
31 HIERAX (ex-*Slater*, DE-766)	Tampa Shipbldg	13-2-44
54 LEON (ex-*Garfield Thomas*, DE-193)	Federal, Port Newark	12-12-43
67 PANTHIR (ex-*Eldridge*, DE-173)	Federal, Port Newark	25-6-43

FRIGATES (*continued*)

Leon   1977

D: 1,300 tons (1,750 fl)   **Dim:** 93.0 (91.5 pp) × 11.17 × 3.25
S: 19 kts   **Range:** 5,500/19, 11,500/11   **Fuel:** 300 tons
Man: Peacetime: 150 men Wartime: 185 men   **Electric:** 680 kw
A: 3/76-mm AA − 6/40-mm AA (II × 3) − 14/20-mm AA (II × 7) − 6/324-mm Mk 32
  ASW TT (III × 2) − 2 Hedgehogs − 8 depth-charge projectors − 2 depth-charge
  racks
Electron Equipt: Radars: 1/SA, 1/Decca, 1/Mk 26
        Sonar: QCU 2
M: Diesel-electric propulsion; 4 GM 16-278A diesels and 2 electric motors; 2 props;
  6,000 hp

REMARK: Transferred in 1951.

CORVETTES

◆ **2 ex-U.S. 173-ft coastal patrol vessels** Bldr: Consolidated SB, New York

P 14 PLOTARCHIS ARSANOGLOU (ex-PGM-25, ex-PC-1556)
P 70 ANTIPLOIARCHOS PEZOPOULOS (ex-PGM-21, ex-PC-1552)

Plotarchis Arsanoglou − Hedgehog now removed

D: 280 tons (400 fl)   **S:** 18 kts   **Dim:** 52.95 × 7.05 × 3.25
Man: 65 men   **Range:** 2,300/18, 6,000/10
A: 1/76-mm − 6/20-mm AA (I × 6)
M: 2 GM 16-278A diesels; 2 props; 2,880 hp   **Electric:** 120 kw

REMARKS: P-14 launched 6-9-44; P-70, 25-5-44.

GUIDED-MISSILE PATROL BOATS

◆ **4 La Combattante III class** Bldr: Constr. Méc. de Normandie, Cherbourg

	L	In serv.
P 50 ANTIPLIARCHOS LASCOS	6-7-76	2-4-77
P 51 ANTIPLIARCHOS BLESSAS	10-11-76	19-7-77
P 52 ANTIPLIARCHOS TROUPAKIS	6-1-77	8-11-77
P 53 ANTIPLIARCHOS MYKONIOS	5-5-77	. . .-77

Antipliarchos Troupakis   G. Arra, 1977

Antipliarchos Lascos   1976

GUIDED-MISSILE PATROL BOATS (*continued*)

D: 400 tons (fl)   **S:** 32.6 kts   **Dim:** 56.0 × 7.9 × 2.5
A: 4 MM 38 Exocet—2/76-mm DP OTO Melara (I × 2)—4/30-mm Emerlec AA (II × 2)
—2/533-mm wire-guided TT
Electron Equipt: Radar: Thomson: 1 Castor, 1 Pollux, 1 Triton
Range: 700/32.5, 2,000/15   **Man:** 6 officers, 36 men
M: MTU 20V 538TB91 diesels; 4 props; 18,000 hp   **Electric:** 520 kw

◆ **10 La Combattante II class**

	L	In Serv.
P 53 IPOPLIARCHOS KONIDIS (ex-*Kimothoi*)	26-1-71	7-72
P 54 IPOPLIARCHOS BATSIS (ex-*Kalypso*)	27-4-71	12-71
P 55 IPOPLIARCHOS ANNINOS (ex-*Evniki*)	8-9-71	4-72
P 56 IPOPLIARCHOS ARLIOTIS (ex-*Navsithoi*)	12-71	6-72
P . . . N . . .	. . .	. . .
P . . . N . . .	. . .	. . .
P . . . N . . :	. . .	. . .
P . . . N . . .	. . .	. . .
P . . . N . . .	. . .	. . .
P . . . N . . .	. . .	. . .

Bldrs: P-53 to P-56 plus one: Constr. Méc. de Normandie, Cherbourg; others: Hellenic SY, Greece

Ipopliarchos Konidis   1976

D: 234 tons (255 fl)   **S:** 36.5 kts   **Dim:** 47.0 (44.0 pp) × 7.1 × 2.5 (fl)
A: 4/MM 38 Exocet missiles—(new units: 6 Penguin II, *see* Remarks)—4/35-mm AA
(II × 2)—2/ASW wire-guided TT aft
Electron Equipt: Radars: Thomson CSF: 1/Castor, 1/Pollux, 1/Triton
Range: 850/25, 2,000/15   **Man:** 4 officers, 36 men
M: 4 MTU 872 high-speed diesels; 4 props; 12,000 hp   **Fuel:** 39 tons

REMARKS: Steel hull, light-steel superstructure. Contract for six more with 6 Penguin SSM, 1/76-mm OTO Melara, 4/30-mm Emerlec AA (II × 2) signed 22-12-76; will have Decca TM 626 and Thomson D-1280 radars.

Ipopliarchos Batsis   1976

NOTE: Transfer of the *Beacon* (PG-99) and *Green Bay* (PG-101) has been under discussion with the U.S. Navy since 1976, but the transfer had not been made as of 1 January 1980, nor had any date been set. They were to have been named *Arsonoglou* and *Pegopoulos*.

◆ **2 Kelefstis Stamou class**   Bldr: de l'Esterel, Cannes

P 28 KELEFSTIS STAMOU (1975)   P 29 DIOPOS ANTONIOU (1975)

D: 80 tons (115 fl)   **S:** 30 kts   **Dim:** 32.0 × 5.8 × 1.5
A: 4/SS-12 SSM—2/20-mm AA
Man: 17 men   **Range:** 1,500/15
M: 2 MTU 12V331 TC81 diesels; 2 props; 2,700 hp

REMARK: These wooden-hulled ships were ordered by Cyprus but acquired by Greece.

Kelefstis Stamou   l'Esterel, 1975

TORPEDO BOATS

◆ 7 Jaguar class, ex-German S-141 class

P 196 ESPEROS (ex-*Seeadler*)(1-2-58)
P 197 KATAIGIS (ex-*Falke*)(30-8-58)
P 198 KENTAUROS (ex-*Habicht*)(21-2-59)
P 199 KYKLON (ex-*Greif*)(28-6-58)

P 228 LAIAPS (ex-*Kondor*)(17-5-58)
P 229 SCORPIOS (ex-*Kormoran*)(16-7-59)
P 230 TYFON (ex-*Geier*)(1-10-58)

   Bldrs: P-196, P-197, P-199, P-228, and P-230: Lürssen; P-198 and P-229: Kröger
   D: 195 tons (221 fl)   **S:** 42.5 kts   **Dim:** 42.6 × 7.1 × 2.4
   A: 2/40-mm AA (I × 2)—4/533-mm TT (I × 4)   **Range:** 500/39, 1,000/32
   M: 4 Maybach diesels; 4 props; 14,400 hp   **Electric:** 192 kw

REMARKS: Transferred 1976-77. The others, the ex-*Albatros*, ex-*Bussard*, and ex-*Sperber*, were transferred to be cannibalized for spares. Wooden-planked hull skin on metal frame.

◆ 5 Norwegian Tjeld class

P 21 ANDROMEDA
P 23 KASTOR

P 24 KYKONOS
P 25 PIGASSOS

P 26 TOXOTIS

Bldr: Mek. Verks. Mandal, Norway, 1967

Kykonos

   D: 69 tons (76 fl)   **Dim:** 24.5 (22.86 pp) × 7.5 × 1.95
   S: 43 kts (40 cruising)   **Man:** 22 men   **Range:** 450/40, 600/25
   A: 2/40-mm AA (I × 2)—4/533-mm TT (I × 4)   **Fuel:** 10 tons
   M: 2 Napier-Deltic Mk T 1827K diesels; 2 props; 6,280 hp

◆ 1 Brave class

P 20 ASTRAPI (ex-*Strahl*) Bldr: Vosper

Astrapi   1969

   D: 97 tons (102 fl)   **S:** 50 kts   **Dim:** 30.26 (29.26 wl) × 7.29 × 2.13
   Man: 3 officers, 19 men   **Range:** 400/45
   A: 2/40-mm AA—2/533-mm TT or 1/40-mm AA and 4/533-mm TT—or mines
   M: 3 Bristol-Siddeley Proteus gas turbines; 10,500 hp

REMARKS: Launched 10-1-62, in service 2-11-62. Bought in Germany in January 1967. Wood and light-metal hull. Welded superstructure in light alloys.

◆ 1 Ferocity class

P 19 AIOLOS (ex-*Pfeil*) Bldr: Vosper

   D: 75 tons (85 fl)   **S:** 54/50 kts   **Dim:** 28.96 (28.03 wl) × 7.28 × 2.16
   A: Same as the *Astrapi* (P-20)   **Man:** 14 men
   M: CODOG: 2 Bristol-Siddeley Proteus gas turbines; 8,500 hp; 2 Mathway-Daimler diesels; 300 hp

REMARKS: Launched 26-10-61, in service 27-6-62. Bought in Germany in January 1967. Same construction as the *Astrapi* (P-20).

NOTE: The five ex-German *Silbermöwe*-class torpedo boats were stricken 1977-78.

Aiolos   1971

PATROL CRAFT

◆ **15 Goulandris class** — Bldr: Neozioh, Syros (5) and Skaramanga (10)

		In serv.
P 14	Arsanoglou	. . .
P 22	N.I. Goulandris I	25-6-75
P 24	N.I. Goulandris II	1977
P 61	E. Panagopoulos	23-6-76
P 70	Pezopoulos	. . .

   D: 75 tons (86 fl)   **S:** 27 kts   **Dim:** 29.0 × 6.2 × 1.1   **Man:** 15 men
   A: 2/20-mm AA (I × 2)   **Range:** 1,600/25
   M: 2 MTU 12V331 TC81 diesels; 2 props; 2,700 hp

REMARKS: Designed by Abeking & Rasmussen, West Germany. Other names not known.

◆ **2 ex-German KFK class**

P 290 Archikelefstis Mallioupoulos (ex-W-8)
P 288 Archikelefstis Stasis (ex-W-2)

   A: 1/20-mm AA

REMARKS: Built in World War II, and in service since 1944. Transferred 30-8-75. For data, *see* sister *Anemos* (A-469), now a survey ship.

MINE WARFARE SHIPS

◆ **15 U.S. Adjutant-class and Falcon-class minesweepers**

M 202	Atalanti (ex-MSC-169)*	M 245	Doris (ex-MSC-298)
M 205	Antiopi (ex-MSC-153)*	M 246	Aigli (ex-MSC-299)
M 206	Phedra (ex-MSC-154)	M 247	Daphni (ex-MSC-307)
M 210	Thalia (ex-MSC-170)*	M 248	Aidon (ex-MSC-310)
M 211	Alkyon (ex-MSC-319)	M 213	Argo (ex-MSC-317)
M 240	Pleias (ex-MSC-314)	M 214	Avra (ex-MSC-318)
M 241	Kichli (ex-MSC-308)	M 254	Niovi (ex-MSC-171)*
M 242	Kissa (ex-MSC-309)		

   Bldr: U.S.A., *1954-55; others 1964-69

Antiopi — Falcon class   G. Arra, 1973

Pleias — Falcon class   1967

   D: 300 tons (372 fl)   **Dim:** 43.0 (41.50 pp) × 7.95 × 2.55
   S: 13 kts (8 sweeping)   **Man:** 4 officers, 27 men
   A: 2/20-mm (II × 1)   **Range:** 2,500/10
   M: GM diesels; 2 props; 880/1,000 hp   **Fuel:** 40 tons

REMARKS: Transferred, beginning in 1964, under MAP. The M-202, M-205, M-206, M-210, and M-254 of the *Adjutant* class (**D:** 330/402 fl) are the former Belgian ships *St. Truiden, Herne, Malmédy, Blankenbergue,* and *Laroche,* returned to the U.S.A. on 7-9-69 and then transferred to Greece. M-202 is fitted as a hydrographic survey ship.

◆ **2 minelayers**

N 04 Aktion (ex-LSM-301)   N 05 Amvrakia (ex-LSM-303)

   Bldr: Charleston NSY, 1943

Amvrakia

MINE WARFARE SHIPS (*continued*)

D: 720 tons (1,100 fl)   **S:** 13 kts   **Dim:** 62.0 × 10.5 × 2.4
Man: 65 men   **Range:** 3,500/12
A: 8/40-mm AA (II × 4) – 6/20-mm AA (I × 6) – 100 to 300 mines, depending upon type
M: 2 GM 16-278A diesels; 2 props; 2,800 hp

REMARKS: Transferred in 1953. Four derricks, two forward and two aft, for handling mines. Two minelaying rails. Four 30-cm searchlights, 1 of 60 cm. Twin rudders. Three of the same class ships were transferred to Turkey, and two to Norway, who passed them on to Turkey in 1961.

AMPHIBIOUS WARFARE SHIPS

◆ **1 ex-U.S. LSD**

L 153 NAFKRATOUSSA (ex-*Fort Mandan*, LSD-21)   Bldr: Boston NSY

Nafkratoussa   1975

D: 4,790 tons (9,375 fl)   **S:** 15 kts   **Dim:** 139.5 × 22.0 × 5.49
Man: 254 men   **Range:** 8,000/15
A: 8/40-mm AA (IV × 2)   **Electron Equipt:** Radars: SPS 10, SPS 6
M: GT; 2 props; 9,000 hp   **Boilers:** 2 water-tube, 3 drums

REMARKS: Launched 2-6-45. Modernized under the FRAM program (*see* U.S.A. section) and transferred 1-71. Flagship of the amphibious forces. Helicopter deck. Well deck: 103.0 × 13.3. Two 35-ton cranes. Can carry eighteen LCMs each with an LCVP nested in it. SPS-6 air-search radar recently added.

◆ **2 ex-U.S. Terrebonne Parish-class LSTs**

	Bldr	In serv.
L 104 OINOUSSAI	Bath Iron Works	19-3-53
(ex-*Terrell County*, LST-1157)		
L 116 KOS	Christy Corp.	14-9-54
(ex-*Whitfield County*, LST-1169)		

D: 2,590 tons (5,800 fl)   **S:** 15 kts   **Dim:** 117.1 × 16.7 × 5.2
A: 6/76-mm AA (II × 3)   **Man:** 115 men plus 395 troops
M: 4 GM diesels; 2 controllable-pitch props; 6,000 hp

REMARKS: Transferred 1976.

◆ **8 ex-U.S. LST-1 and LST-511 classes**   Bldr: U.S.A., 1943-45

L 144 SYROS (ex-LST-325)	L 171 KRITI (ex-LST-1076)
L 179 SAMOS (ex-LST-331)	L 154 IKARIA (ex-LST-1086)
L 195 CHIOS (ex-LST-35)	L 157 RODOS (ex-LST-391)
L 158 LEMNOS (ex-LST-36)	L 172 LESBOS (ex-LST-389)

Rodos   1975

D: 4,080 tons (fl)   **S:** 11 kts   **Dim:** 100.04 × 15.24 × 4.3
A: 10/40-mm AA or 8/40-mm – 6/20-mm (I × 6)
M: 2 GM 16-278A diesels; 1,700 hp   **Cargo:** 2,100 tons

REMARKS: Transferred in 1944, 1947, 1960, 1964, and 1971. L-144 (with reinforced waterline belt for ice operations!) was transferred 29-5-64 after a complete refit and modernization; L-171 in 3-71. All carry 4 LCVPS.

◆ **5 ex-U.S. LSMs**

L 161 IPOPLIARCHOS GRIGOROPOULOS	L 164 IPOPLIARCHOS ROUSEN
L 162 IPOPLIARCHOS TOURNAS	L 165 IPOPLIARCHOS KRYSTALLIDIS
L 163 IPOPLIARCHOS DANIOLOS	

D: 1,095 tons (fl)   **S:** 12.5 kts   **Dim:** 62.0 × 10.5 × 2.4
A: 2/40-mm AA (II × 1) – 4/20-mm AA (I × 4)   **Range:** 3,500/12
M: 2 diesels; 2 props; 2,800 hp

REMARKS: In service since 1944-45 and transferred in 1958, these ships were LSM-227, LSM-45, LSM-399, LSM-102, and LSM-541.

◆ **6 ex-LCU-501 class**   Bldr: U.S.A., 1944

L 145 KASSOS (ex-LCU-1382)	L 149 KYTHNOS (ex-LCU-763)
L 146 KARPATHOS (ex-LCU-1379)	L 150 SIFNOS (ex-LCU-677)
L 147 KIMONOS (ex-LCU-971)	L 152 SKYATOS (ex-LCU-827)

D: 143 tons (309 fl)   **S:** 8 kts   **Dim:** 36.3 × 10.05 × 1.5
A: 2/20-mm   **Man:** 13 men   **M:** 3 diesels; 440 hp

REMARK: Transferred 1960-72.

◆ **13 LCM**

◆ **34 LCVP**

REMARK: All carried aboard the 10 LSTs.

◆ **14 LCP**

REMARKS: Ordered 1977. No data available.

HYDROGRAPHIC SHIPS

◆ **A 478 NAFTILOS**   Bldr: Anastadiades Tsortanides Perama
D: 1,480 tons   **S:** 15 kts   **Dim:** 63.1 (56.5 pp) × 11.6 × 4.0
M: 2 Burmeister & Wain SS28LH diesels; 2 props; 2,640 hp   **Man:** 57 men

HYDROGRAPHIC SHIPS (continued)

Naftilos

REMARKS: In service 3-4-76. Near sisters *St. Lykoudis* (A-481) and *I. Theophilopoulos Karavoyiannos* (A-485) are lighthouse tenders. Helicopter-landing platform.

◆ 1 ex-U.S. Barnegat-class oceanographic research ship

A 413 HEPHAISTOS (ex-*Josiah Willard Gibbs*, AGOR-1, ex-*San Carlos*, AVP-51)

Bldr: Lake Washington SB, Seattle

D: 2,800 tons (fl)   **S:** 17 kts   **Dim:** 94.7 × 12.52 × 3.65
M: 2 Fairbanks-Morse 38D81/8 diesels; 6,080 hp   **Man:** 150 men

REMARKS: Launched 20-12-42, in service 21-3-44, transferred 12-71. Purchased outright 1977. Now in reserve.

◆ 1 ex-German KFK class

A 469 ANEMOS (ex-. . .)

D: 112 tons (fl)   **S:** 11 kts   **Dim:** 22.3 × 6.4 × 2.7
M: 1 Demag diesel; 150 hp   **Man:** 16 men   **Range:** 1,200/7

REMARKS: Wooden construction. Launched in 1944, acquired by Greece in 1969. Two sisters serve as patrol boats.

Anemos   1971

◆ 1 modified U.S. Adjutant-class minesweeper

M 202 ATALANTI

For data, *see* same class under Mine Warfare Ships.

AUXILIARY SHIPS

◆ 1 training ship   Bldr: Anastiadis Tsortanides, Perama

	Laid down	L	In serv.
A . . . ARIS	10-78	. . .	. . .

D: 3,100 tons (fl)   **S:** . . . kts   **Dim:** . . . × . . . × . . .
A: 1/76-mm DP OTO Melara—2/40-mm AA (I × 2)—helicopter
M: MAK diesels

REMARKS: Largest naval ship built in Greece. Remsembles a small passenger ship. Hangar and flight deck aft for one helicopter.

◆ 1 yacht/training ship

A . . . CHRISTINA (ex-*Matane*, ex-*Stormont*) Bldr: Canadian Vickers
D: 1,526 grt   **S:** 20 kts   **Dim:** 99.15 (86.59 pp) × 11.13 × 5.33
A: . . .   **Man:** . . .   **Range:** 7,400/15, 12,000/10   **Electric:** 400 kw
M: 2 sets 4-cyl., triple-expansion steam; 2 props; 5,500 hp
Boilers: 2 water-tube

REMARKS: Launched 29-5-53. Donated 12-7-78. Former yacht of Shipowner Aristotle Onassis, converted from a Canadian River-class frigate 1951-54 by Howaldtswerke, Kiel. Receipt of this expensive gift by the Greek Navy may prove something of an embarrassment, as a new training ship is already under construction.

◆ 2 ex-British Algerine-class transports and training ships

	Bldr	L
A 74 POLEMISTIS (ex-*Gozo*)	Redfern Const. Co.	27-1-43
A 76 PYRPOLITIS (ex-*Arcturus*)	Redfern Const. Co.	31-8-43

D: 990 tons (1,237 fl)   **S:** 16 kts   **Dim:** 68.58 × 10.82 × 3.5
Man: 85-90 men   **Range:** 2,270/14, 5,000/10   **Fuel:** 270 tons
A: A-76: 1/76-mm—4/20-mm—2 machine guns—A-74: No weapons
M: Triple-expansion; 2 props; 2,700 hp   **Boilers:** 2 Yarrow, 17.6 kg/cm² pressure

REMARKS: Acquired in 1947. Former fleet minesweepers, now generally used as administrative transports or for training. Three sisters, the *Armatolos*, *Mahitis*, and *Navmachos*, stricken 1976-77.

◆ 2 personnel ferries   Bldr: Perama

A 419 PANDORA   A 420 PANDROSOS

D: 350 tons   **S:** 11 kts   **Cargo:** 500 personnel.

REMARK: Launched 1972-73.

◆ 1 netlayer

D: 680 tons
Ordered 1977, Krögerwerft, Rendsburg. No other data.

◆ 1 netlayer   Bldr: Krögerwerft, Rendsburg

A 307 THETIS (ex-U.S. AN-103)

D: 560 tons (805 fl)   **S:** 13 kts   **Dim:** 51.7 (44.5 wl) × 10.3 × 3.6

GREECE (*continued*)

AUXILIARY SHIPS (*continued*)

    A: 1/40-mm AA – 4/20-mm AA (II × 2)   **Man:** 48 men
    M: 2 M.A.N. diesels; 1 prop; 1,400 hp

REMARKS: Launched 1959. Transferred 4-60.

◆ **2 ex-U.S. Patapsco-class oilers** Bldr: Cargill, Savage, Minn.

A 377 ARETHOUSA (ex-*Natchaug*, AOG-54)
A 414 ARIADNI (ex-*Tombigbee*, AOG-11)

Arethousa—wearing old number   1968

    D: 1,850 tons (4,335 fl)   **S:** 13 kts   **Dim:** 94.0 × 14.6 × 4.7
    Man: 46 men   **Cargo capacity:** 2,040 tons
    A: A-377: 4/76-mm AA (I × 4) – A-414: 2/76-mm (I × 2)
    M: 2 GM 16-278A diesels; 2 props; 3,300 hp

REMARKS: Former gasoline tankers. A-377 launched 6-12-44, transferred 7-59. A-414 launched 18-11-45, transferred 7-72.

◆ **2 coastal tankers** Bldr: Kynossqura, Piraeus

A 416 OURANOS   A . . . HYPERION

    D: 1,200 tons (fl)   **S:** 13 kts   **Dim:** 67.7 × . . . × . . .
    M: 1 MWM TPD-484BU diesel; 1,750 hp

REMARK: A-416 in service 29-1-77; *Hyperion*, 27-2-77.

◆ **4 small harbor oilers**

A 372 ZEUS (ex-U.S. YOG-98)

    D: 1,390 tons   **S:** 9 kts   **Dim:** 53.0 × 9.8 × 3.1   **Cargo:** 900 tons

A 345 SIRIOS (ex-*Poseidon*, ex-*Empire Faun*)

    D: 846 grt, 850 dwt   **S:** 9.5 kts   **Dim:** 59.8 × 9.5 × . . .

A 471 VIVIES   **Cargo:** 687 tons
A 373 KRONOS (ex-*Islay*, ex-*Dresden*)   **Cargo:** 110 tons

REMARKS: A-372 was built in 1944. A-345 was built in 1943 and bought in 1958.

◆ **1 ammunition ship** Bldr: Dubigeon, Nantes

A 415 EVROS (ex-German *Schwarzwald*, ex-French *Amalthée*)

    D: 2,395 tons   **S:** 15 kts   **Dim:** 80.18 × 11.99 × 4.65

    A: 4/40-mm AA (II × 2)   **Man:** 32 men   **Range:** 4,500/15
    M: 1 Sulzer 6-SD-60 diesel; 3,000 hp

REMARKS: Launched 31-1-56. Purchased 2-60 by the German Navy, transferred to Greece 2-6-76.

◆ **8 motorized water vessels**

A 474 ILIKI   A 470 KASTORIA   A 484 KERKINI (ex-German FW-3)   A 468 KALLIROI
A 467 VOLVI   A 473 TRICHONIS   A 434 PRESPA   A . . . DOIRANI

REMARKS: A-484 transferred 1976. A-434 and A-468 were built in 1976, **D:** 600 tons. The *Doirani* was built 1976, bought 1978, **D:** 450 tons

◆ **3 coastal tugs** Bldr: Perama Ordered 1977

A . . . N . . .   A . . . N . . .   A . . . N . . .

    D: 345 tons (fl)   **S:** . . . kts   **Dim:** 30.0 × 3.4 × . . .
    M: 1 MWM diesel; 1,200 hp

REMARK: Ordered in 1977.

◆ **12 harbor tugs**

A 406 AIAS	A 410 ATROMITIS	A 429 PERSEUS
A 406 ANTAIOS	A 418 ROMALEOS	A 430 SAMSON
A 408 ATLAS	A 421 MINOTAUROS	A 431 TITAN
A 409 ACHILLEUS	A 427 PATRAIKOS	A 432 CIGAS

REMARKS: From a variety of sources, including the U.S. and Great Britain. Three more harbor tugs were ordered in 1977.

◆ **1 salvage ship**

A 384 SOTIR (ex-HMS *Salventure*)   **D:** 700 tons (fl)

REMARK: Launched 24-11-42.

◆ **2 lighthouse tenders** Bldr: Perama, 1976-77

A 481 ST. LYKOUDIS
A 485 I. THEOPHILOPOULOS KARAVOYIANNOS

    D: 1,350 tons (1,450 fl)   **S:** 15 kts   **Dim:** 63.24 × 11.6 × 4.0
    M: 1 MWM TBD-500-8UD diesel; 2,400 hp   **Man:** 40 men

REMARK: Near sisters to hydrographic survey ship *Naftilos*.

GRENADA

◆ **1 patrol craft** Bldr: Brooke Marine, G.B., 1972

    D: 15 tons (fl)   **S:** 22 kts   **Dim:** 12.2 × 3.7 × 0.6
    A: 3/7.62-mm machine guns   **M:** 2 Caterpillar diesels; 2 props; 740 hp

REMARK: An old ex-RAF, Vosper-built air-sea rescue craft may also be in service as a patrol craft.

GUATEMALA

PERSONNEL: approx. 600 men

MERCHANT MARINE (1976): 6 ships — 8,197 grt

◆ **1 U.S. Broadsword class**   Bldr: Halter Marine, New Orleans, La.

P 1051 KUKULKAN

Kukulkan — on trials with the **Bitol** (P-655), **Picuda** (P-361), and **Barracuda** (P-362)
Halter, 1976

    D: 90.5 tons (fl)   **S:** 32 kts   **Dim:** 32.0 × 6.3 × 1.9
    Man: 5 officers, 15 men   **Range:** 1,150/20   **Electric:** 60 kw
    A: 1/75-mm recoilless rifle — 1/81-mm mortar with a 12.7-mm machine gun atop it —
    2/12.7-mm machine guns (I × 2)
    M: 2 GM 16V-149TI diesels; 3,200 hp

REMARK: In service 4-8-76.

◆ **2 U.S. 85-foot class**   Bldr: Sewart Seacraft, Berwick, La.

P 851 UTATLAN   P 852 SUBTENIENTE OSORIO SARAVIA

    D: 50 tons   **S:** 23 kts   **Dim:** 25.9 × 5.8 × 1.0
    A: 2/12.7-mm machine guns — 1/81-mm recoilless rifle
    M: 2 GM diesels; 2,200 hp   **Man:** 7 officers, 10 men   **Range:** 780/15

REMARK: Transferred 5-67 and 1972.

◆ **5 U.S. Cutlass class**   Bldr: Halter Marine, New Orleans, La., 1972, 1976

P 651 TECUNUMAN   P 653 AZUMANCHE   P 655 BITOL
P 652 KAIBILBALAN   P 654 TZACOL

    D: 34 tons (fl)   **S:** 25 kts   **Dim:** 19.7 × 5.2 × 0.9
    Man: 10 men   **Range:** 400/15   **Electric:** 20 kw

    A: 1/12.7-mm machine gun — 3/7.6-mm machine guns (I × 3)
    M: 2 GM 12V-71 diesels; 2 props; 960 hp

REMARK: P-654 in service 3-76, P-655 in 8-76.

◆ **1 ex-U.S. aircraft-rescue boat(AVR)**

P 632 HUNAPHU

    D: 328 tons   **S:** 25 kts   **Dim:** 19.0 × 4.7 × 0.9
    A: 2/12.7-mm machine guns   **M:** 2 GM diesels; 2 props

REMARK: Built in 1945.

◆ **2 U.S. Machete class**   Bldr: Halter Marine, New Orleans, La.

P 361 PICUDA   P 362 BARRACUDA

    D: 6 tons   **S:** 36 kts   **Dim:** 11.0 × 4.0 × 0.76
    M: 2 GM 6V 53PI diesels; 2 water jets

REMARKS: In service 4-8-76. Troop carriers. Square bows, aluminum construction.

◆ **1 ex-U.S. LCM (6) class**

561 CHINALTENANGO

REMARK: Transferred in 12-65.

GUINEA

PERSONNEL: 350 men

MERCHANT MARINE (1978): 11 ships — 15,280 grt

NOTE: For details on characteristics, *see* country of origin.

◆ **2 Soviet Shershen-class patrol boats**

REMARK: Ex-torpedo boats, transferred in 1978.

◆ **6 Shanghai-II class patrol boats**

P 733   P 734   P 736   P . . .   P . . .

REMARK: P-733 to P-736 were transferred by the People's Republic of China in 1974,
the other two in 1976.

◆ **1 Soviet T-58-class ocean minesweeper**

LAMINE SADJI KABA

REMARK: Transferred in 1979.

◆ **2 Soviet Poluchat-I-class patrol boats**

◆ **4 Soviet P-6-class torpedo boats**

REMARK: Have no torpedo tubes.

GUINEA-BISSAU

PERSONNEL: 180 men

MERCHANT MARINE (1978): 1 ship—219 grt

NOTE: For details on characteristics, *see* country of origin.

◆ **1 Soviet Shershen-class patrol boat**

REMARK: Ex-torpedo boat, transferred in 1978.

◆ **2 Soviet Poluchat-I-class patrol boats**

A: 2/25-mm AA (II × 1)—2/14.5-mm AA (II × 1)

REMARKS: Transferred in 1978. Other than armament, same as in U.S.S.R. section.

◆ **2 French Plascoa-1900-class patrol craft**

CABO ROXO   ILHEU POILAD

D: 30 tons (fl)   S: 25 kts   Dim: 19.0 × 5.35 × 1.2
A: 2/12.7-mm machine guns   Range: 650/25, 1,500/9
M: 2 GM diesels; 2 props; 1,050 hp

◆ **3 Spanish LVC-I-class patrol craft**   Bldr: Bazan, El Ferrol

REMARK: Ordered in 1978.

◆ **1 Soviet Biya-class survey ship**

REMARK: Transferred in 1978.

◆ **2 Soviet T-4-class landing craft**

REMARK: Transferred in 1978.

GUYANA

MERCHANT MARINE (1978): 69 ships—19,105 grt (tankers: 3 ships—818 grt)

◆ **1 103-foot British patrol boat**   Bldr: Vosper Thornycroft, Portsmouth

DF 1010 PECCARI

D: 96 tons (109 fl)   S: 27 kts   Dim: 31.4 × 6.0 × 1.6
A: 2/20-mm AA (I × 2)   Man: 22 men   Range: 1,400/14
M: 2 Paxman Ventura diesels; 2 props; 3,500 hp

REMARKS: Launched 3-77. A second unit was ordered in 1977 but has been canceled because of lack of funds.

◆ **3 patrol boats**   Bldr: Vosper Thornycroft

JAGUAR   MARGAY   OCELOT

D: 10 tons   S: 20 kts   Dim: 14.0 × 3.4 × 2.0
A: 1/7.62-mm machine gun   Man: 6 men   Range: 150/12
M: 2 Cummins D366A diesels; 2 props; 270 hp

REMARKS: Fiberglass hull; light-alloy superstructure. Delivered 1971.

◆ **3 45-foot boats, supplied by the U.S.**

CAMOUDIE   LABANA   RATTLER

◆ **2 ex-fishing boats**

EKEREKU   NUMBER 2

NOTE: Under AID, Guyana has also received the ex-U.S. Navy tug YTM-190 and the converted lighter YFN-960, both operated by the Guyana Harbor Board.

HAITI

PERSONNEL: 250 men

MERCHANT MARINE (1978): 1 ship—394 grt

COAST GUARD

◆ **3 U.S. 65-foot Commercial Cruiser class**   Bldr: Sewart, La., 1976

MH 21   MH 22   MH 23

D: 33 tons (fl)   S: 25 kts   Dim: 21.3 × 5.2 × 1.0
A: 2/12.7-mm machine guns   M: 3 GM 8V71 diesels; 3 props; 1,590 hp

◆ **1 U.S. Enforcer class**   Bldr: Bertram, Miami

MH 6   Dim: 9.5 × . . . × . . .   M: Inboard/outboard motor

◆ **1 U.S. Sotoyomo-class oceangoing tug**

HENRI CHRISTOPHE (ex-*Samoset*, ATA-190)   Bldr: Levingston SB, Orange, Texas

D: 689 tons (835 fl)   S: 13 kts   Dim: 43.6 (40.75 pp) × 10.37 × 3.65
Man: 40 men   Range: 16,500/9   Fuel: 154 tons
A: None   Electric: 120 kw
M: 2 GM 12-278A diesels, electric drive; 1 prop; 1,500 hp

REMARK: Launched 26-10-44, transferred 18-9-78. Sister *Accokeek* (ATA-181) was also offered for sale to Haiti in late 1979.

HONDURAS

MERCHANT MARINE (1978): 70 ships—130,831 grt (tankers: 3 ships—2,853 grt)

◆ **2 U.S. 105-foot class**   Bldr: Swiftships

N . . . (4-77)   N . . . . (1979)

   D: 103 tons (fl)   **S:** 32 kts   **Dim:** 31.5 × 6.6 × 2.1
   A: . . .   **Man:** 16 men   **Range:** 1,200/18
   M: 2 MTU diesels; 2 props; 7,000 hp

◆ **2 U.S. 65-foot Commercial Cruiser class**   Bldr: Swiftships

GC 6501 GRAL
GC 6502 J. T. CABANAS

   D: 32 tons (fl)   **S:** 27 kts   **Dim:** 21.3 × 5.2 × 1.0
   A: . . .   **Man:** 5 men   **Range:** 2,000/22
   M: 3 GM diesels; 3 props; 1,590 hp

HONG KONG

British Crown Colony

PERSONNEL: 71 officers, 1,221 men
MERCHANT MARINE (1978) 150 ships—874,850 grt
                (tankers: 22 ships—29,976 grt)

NOTE: In addition to the craft listed below, the Royal Navy maintains five converted "-ton"-class minesweepers as gunboats at Hong Kong.

PATROL CRAFT

◆ **2 command boats**   Bldr: Hong King United DY, 1965

No. 1   No. 2

   D: 222 tons (fl)   **S:** 11.8 kts   **Dim:** 33.9 × 7.3 × 3.2
   A: Small arms   **Man:** 29 men   **Range:** 5,200/11.8
   M: 2 Cummins diesels; 2 props; 674 hp

◆ **7 78-foot craft**   Bldr: Vosper Thornycroft, Singapore, 1972-73

Nos. 50 to 56

   D: 82 tons (fl)   **S:** 20.7 kts   **Dim:** 23.7 × 5.2 × 1.7
   A: 1/12.7-mm machine gun   **Man:** 16 men   **Range:** 4,000/20
   M: 2 Cummins diesels; 2 props; 1,500 hp

◆ **1 78-foot craft**   Bldr: Thornycroft, Singapore, 1958

No. 4

   D: 72 tons (fl)   **S:** 15.5 kts   **Dim:** 23.7 × 4.6 × 1.4
   A: Small arms   **Man:** 21 men   **Range:** 600/15.5
   M: 3 diesels; 3 props; 2,070 hp

◆ **9 70-foot craft**   Bldrs: 26-28: Hong Kong SY; 29-34: Cheoy Lee SY, 1954-55

Nos. 26 to 34

No. 27   G. Arra, 1977

   D: 52 tons (fl)   **S:** 10 kts   **Dim:** 21.3 × 5.2 × 1.6
   A: Small arms   **Man:** 12 men   **Range:** 1,600/10
   M: 2 diesels; 2 props; 430 hp

◆ **1 65-foot craft**

No. 6

   D: 48 tons (fl)   **S:** 10.5 kts   **Dim:** 19.8 × 4.4 × 1.6
   A: Small arms   **Man:** 11 men   **Range:** 1,400/9   **M:** 1 diesel; 152 hp

◆ **8 45-foot converted wooden tugs**   Bldr: Australia, 1944-45

Nos. 9 to 16

   D: 27.7 tons   **S:** 9 kts   **Dim:** 13.7 × 4.6 × 2.1
   A: Small arms   **Man:** 5 men   **Range:** 1,700/8
   M: 1 Gray Marine diesel; 144 hp

◆ **3 40-foot patrol launches**   Bldr: Cheoy Lee SY, 1971

No. 20   No. 21   No. 22

   D: 17 tons   **S:** 24 kts   **Dim:** 12.3 × 3.5 × 0.6
   A: Small arms   **Man:** 5 men   **Range:** 380/24
   M: 2 diesels; 2 props; 740 hp

HONG KONG (*continued*)

MISCELLANEOUS CRAFT

◆ **1 support craft** Bldr: Thornycroft, Singapore, 1958

No. 3

    D: 37 tons   **S:** 15 kts   **Dim:** 17.7 × . . . × . . .
    A: Small arms   **Man:** 8 men   **Range:** 240/15
    M: 2 diesels; 2 props; . . . hp

◆ **1 personnel launch** Bldr: Hip Hing Ching SY, 1975

No. 7

    D: 18.5 tons   **S:** 23.5 kts   **Dim:** 16.0 × . . . × . . .
    A: Small arms   **Man:** 6 men   **Range:** 300/20
    M: 2 diesels; 2 props; 700 hp

◆ **11 22-foot personnel launches** Bldr: Cheoy Lee SY, 1970

    D: 4.8 tons   **S:** 20 kts   **Dim:** 6.7 × . . . × . . .
    A: Small arms   **Man:** 2 men   **Range:** 160/20   **M:** 1 diesel; . . . hp

HUNGARY

Merchant Marine (1978): 23 ships — 77,378 grt

◆ **10 river patrol craft**

    D: 100 tons   **S:** . . .   **Dim:** . . . × . . . × . . .
    A: 1/14.5-mm AA   **M:** 2 diesels

◆ **5 LCM**

◆ **several small tugs**

ICELAND

Personnel: 170 men

Merchant Marine (1978): 383 ships — 175,097 grt (tankers — 4 ships — 2,491 grt)

Aviation: 2 Fokker F-27 Friendship patrol aircraft, 1 Hughes helicopter, 2 Bell 47-G helicopters

COAST GUARD

FISHERIES-PROTECTION SHIPS

◆ **2 Aegir class**

	Bldr	In serv.
Aegir	Aalborg SY, Denmark	1968
Tyr	Aarhus, Denmark	15-3-78

Aegir   J. Meister, 1971

Tyr   1975

    D: 1,150 tons (1,500 fl)   **S:** 20 kts   **Dim:** 69.65 (62.18 pp) × 10.0 × 4.7
    A: 1/57-mm (6-pdr.)   **Man:** 22 men   **Electric:** 630 kva
    M: 2 M.A.N. R8V 40/54 diesels; 2 Ka Me Wa controllable-pitch props; 8,600 hp

Remarks: Although built ten years apart, these two ships are nearly identical. Helicopter hangar between twin stacks. Three radar sets, fish-finding sonar. 20-ton bollard-pull towing winch.

ICELAND (*continued*)

FISHERIES-PROTECTION SHIPS (*continued*)

	Bldr	Laid down	L	In serv.
ODINN	Aalborg SY, Denmark	1-59	9-59	1-60

Odinn—now has hangar like the **Aegir**　　　　J. Meister, 1971

D: 1,000 tons (fl)　　**S:** 18 kts　　**Dim:** 63.63 (56.61 pp) × 10.0 × 4.8
A: 1/57-mm (6-pdr.) low-angle　　**Man:** 22 men
M: 2 Burmeister & Wain diesels; 2 props; 5,050 hp

REMARK: Rebuilt in 1975 with hangar and helicopter deck.

THOR　Bldr: Aalborg SY, Denmark, 1951

Thor　　　　　　　　　　　　　　　　　　　1973

D: 920 tons (fl)　　**S:** 17 kts　　**Dim:** 62.8 (55.9 pp) × 9.5 × 4.0
A: 1/57-mm (6-pdr.)—1/47-mm (3-pdr.)　　**Man:** 22 men
M: 2 MWM diesels; 2 props; 3,200 hp

REMARK: Fixed hangar and flight deck added in 1971.

ARVAKUR　Bldr: Bodewes, Netherlands

D: 716 tons (fl)　　**S:** 12 kts　　**Dim:** 32.3 × 10.0 × 4.0
A: 1/12.7-mm machine gun　　**Man:** 12 men　　**M:** 1 diesel; 1,000 hp

REMARKS: Built as a lightouse tender. Transferred to the Coast Guard in 1969.

NOTE: The 200-ton *Albert* was stricken in 1978. The 740-ton fishing trawler *Balder* was returned to commercial service in 1977.

◆ **1 Nelson 45-foot customs launch**　Bldr: W. S. Souter, Cowes, G.B., 1978
　S: 17 kts　　**M:** 2 Cummins V555M diesels

◆ **. . . 21-SS smuggler-patrol launches**　Bldr: Norway, 1975
　S: 36 kts　　**M:** Castold; water jets

INDIA

PERSONNEL: 46,000 men approx.

MERCHANT MARINE (1978): 591 ships—5,759,324 grt (tankers: 41 ships—1,131,891 grt)

NAVAL AVIATION: The Navy has 16 Sea Hawk and 11 Bréguet Alizé fixed-wing planes for the carrier *Vikrant* and 12 Sea King and 19 Alouette-III helicopters. Some Soviet Ka-25 Hormone-A helicopters are to be delivered for the newly transferred Kashin-class guided-missile destroyers. The Indian Air Force has turned over to the Navy 5 Lockheed Constellations for long-range reconnaissance, while the U.S.S.R. has delivered at least 3 IL-38 May aircraft. Eight Sea Harrier planes, two of which will be two-seaters, have been ordered from Great Britain to replace the *Vikrant*'s Sea Hawk fighters and 3 more Sea King helicopters have also been ordered.

WARSHIPS IN SERVICE, UNDER CONSTRUCTION, OR PROJECTED AS OF 1 JANUARY 1980

	L	Tons	Main armament
◆ **1 aircraft carrier**			
1 GLORY	1945	15,700	15 aircraft
◆ **8 submarines**		Tons (submerged)	
8 FOXTROT	1965	2,400	10/533-mm TT
◆ **1 cruiser**		Tons	
1 FIJI	1939	8,700	9/152-mm, 8/102-mm
◆ **0 (+2) destroyers**			
(2) KASHIN	1963-72	3,500	2 Goa SAM, 4/76-mm, ASW weapons, 1 helicopter

WARSHIPS IN SERVICE, UNDER CONSTRUCTION, OR PROJECTED (continued)

◆ 21 (+3) frigates

0 (+3) . . .	1980-. . .	3,000	4/SS-N-2C, 1/SA-N-4, 4/57-mm
6 LEANDER	1968-78	2,250	4/114-mm, 1 helicopter
10 PETYA II	1963	950	4/76-mm DP, 3/533-mm TT
3 LEOPARD	1957-59	2,250	4/114-mm DP, 1 Squid
2 WHITBY	1958	2,144	3/SS-N-2, 2 Limbo

◆ 3 corvettes

3 NANUCHKA	1977-78	780	4/SS-N-2C, 1/SA-N-4, 2/57-mm

◆ 16 guided-missile patrol boats

8 OSA II	1960-70	240 (fl)	4/SS-N-2, 4/30-mm
8 OSA I	1960-70	175	4/SS-N-2, 4/30-mm

◆ 12 minesweepers

4 NATYA	1977-78	650	4/30-mm, 4/25-mm
4 "-TON"	1955-56	370	1/40-mm
4 "-HAM"	1954-69	120	1/20-mm

◆ 6 amphibious ships

AIRCRAFT CARRIER

◆ 1 Glory class   Bldr: Vickers-Armstrong

	Laid down	L	In serv.
R 11 VIKRANT (ex-Hercules)	14-10-43	22-9-45	4-3-61

Vikrant

D: 15,700 tons (19,500 fl)   **Dim:** 211.25 (198.0 wl) × 24.29 × 7.15
S: 24 kts (fl) 17 kts (cruising)   **Range:** 6,200/23, 12,000/14
Man: Peacetime: 1,075 men Wartime: 1,340 men   **Fuel:** 3,200 tons
A: 15/40-mm (II × 4, I × 7) — 15 aircraft (max. capacity)
Electron Equipt: Radars: 1/960, 1/278, 1/293, 1/963 TACAN
M: Parsons GT; 2 props; 40,000 hp   **Boilers:** 4 Admiralty, 28 kg/cm² pressure

REMARKS: Bought in Great Britain in 1-57. Air-conditioned. One hangar, two elevators, angled flight deck, steam catapult. Flight deck: 210 × 34. Being modernized 1974-81 and will receive eight Sea Harrier (two 2-seat) to replace obsolete Sea Hawk fighters. The Alizé ASW aircraft are to be refurbished and the ship will also carry Alouette-III ASW helicopters and possibly Sea King helicopters.

SUBMARINES

◆ 8 Soviet Foxtrot class

S 20 KURURA	S 22 KANDHERI	S 40 VELA	S 42 VAGLI
S 21 KARANJ	S 23 KALVARI	S 41 VAGIR	S 43 VAGSHEER

Karanj   G. Arra, 1978

D: 2,000 tons surfaced, 2,500 submerged   **S:** 18/16 kts
Dim: 96.5 × 7.5 × 6.0   **Man:** 8 officers, 70 men   **Range:** 20,000
A: 10/533-mm TT (6 fwd, 4 aft) — 22 torpedoes or mines
M: 3 diesels and electric motors; 3 props; 6,000 hp

REMARKS: S-20 and S-21 were transferred in 4-68 and 1-69; S-22 and S-23 at the end of 1970; S-40 and S-41 in 9-73; S-42 in 12-73; and S-43 in 2-75.

CRUISER

◆ 1 British Fiji class   Bldr: Vickers-Armstrong

	Laid down	L	In serv.
C 60 MYSORE (ex-Nigeria)	8-2-38	18-7-39	23-9-40

D: 8,700 tons (11,000 fl)   **S:** 31 kts   **Dim:** 169.32 × 18.88 × 6.49 (fl)
A: 9/152-mm (III × 3) — 8/102-mm AA (II × 4) — 12/40-mm AA (II × 5, I × 2)
Electron Equipt: Radars: 1/960, 1/277, 1/293   **Man:** 800 men
M: Parsons GT; 4 props; 72,000 hp   **Boilers:** 4 Admiralty

CRUISER (continued)

Mysore 1973

REMARK: Bought in 1954, refitted from 1954-57. The old cruiser *Delhi* was stricken 30-6-78.

GUIDED-MISSILE DESTROYERS

◆ **2 Soviet Kashin class**

D...N...   D...N...

  D: 4,750 tons (fl)   **S:** 35/36 kts   **Dim:** 144.0 × 15.8 × 5.8 (mean)
  A: 4/SA-N-1 systems (II × 2) with 44 Goa missiles – 4/76-mm DP (II × 2) – 2/MBU-2500A ASW rocket launchers – 2/MBU-4500A ASW rocket launchers – 5/533-mm TT (V × 1) – 1 Ka-25 Hormone helicopter – mines
Electron Equipt: Radars: 2/Don 2, 2/Head Net A or 1/Head Net C and 1/Big Net, 2/Peel Group, 2/Owl Screech
            Sonar: 1 high-frequency, hull-mounted
  M: 4 gas turbines; 2 props; 94,000 hp   **Range:** 900/35, 4,500/18

REMARKS: Reportedly, the first was to be delivered in 1979. Whether these will be ex-Soviet Navy ships or new-construction units is not yet known.

FRIGATES

◆ **3 or more new-construction, guided-missile** Bldr: Mazagon Docks, Bombay

	Laid down	L	In serv.
F...N...	6-78	. . .	. . .
F...N...	. . .	. . .	. . .
F...N...	. . .	. . .	. . .

  D: 3,000 tons (3,500 fl)   **S:** 31 kts   **Dim:** 121.0 × 14.1 × 4.3
  A: 4/SS-N-2C Styx SSM – 1/SA-N-4 SAM system – 4/57-mm AA (II × 2) – 8/30-mm AA (II × 4) – 2/Sea King ASW helicopters
  Boilers: 2 Babcock & Wilcox, 3-drum, 38.7 kg/cm² pressure – superheat 450°C
  M: GT; 2 five-bladed props; 30,000 hp

REMARKS: Design derived from the *Leander* class, with the same propulsion plant but larger hull. Most weapon systems will be Soviet, but may use LWO-8 radar.

◆ **6 British Leander class** Bldr: Mazagon Docks, Bombay

	Laid down	L	In serv.
F 33 NILGIRI	10-66	23-10-68	6-72
F 34 HIMGIRI	1967	6-5-70	23-11-74
F 35 UDAYGIRI	9-70	24-10-72	1975

Udaygiri 1977

F 36 DUNAGIRI	1-73	9-3-74	1976
F 37 TARAGIRI	1974	25-10-76	1979
F 38 UINDHYAGIRI	1976	12-11-77	1980

  D: 2,250 tons (2,800 fl)   **S:** 30 kts   **Dim:** 113.38 × 13.1 × 4.27 (avg.)
  A: 2/114-mm DP (II × 1) – F-33, F-34: 1/Sea Cat GWS 22; Others; 2/Sea Cat with M-4 directors – 1/Limbo Mk-10 ASW mortar (not on F-37 and F-38) – 1 Alouette III ASW helicopter (Sea King on F-37 and F-38)
Electron Equipt: Radars: F-33 and F-34: 1/965, 1/993, 1/978, 2/903 From F-35 on: 1/SGR 103, 1/DA 08, 3/M 45
            Sonars: 1/177 – 1/199 VDS on F-33 and F-34
  Range: approx. 4,500/12   **Fuel:** 500 tons   **Electric:** 2,500 kw
  Boilers: 2 Babcock & Wilcox, 3-drum; 38.7 kg/cm² pressure – superheat 450°C
  M: 2 sets GT; 2 five-bladed props; 30,000 hp

REMARKS: The first two are very similar to British versions of the *Leander* class, but later units have been progressively improved, using HSA radars and an ever-greater proportion of Indian-built components. F-37 and F-38 have very large telescoping hangars situated much nearer the stern and requiring removal of the three-barreled Limbo, ASW mortar; the new hangar will hold a Westland Sea King ASW helicopter. F-37 and F-38 also have openings in the hull sides beneath the helicopter deck at the

Udaygiri 1977

FRIGATES (continued)

stern. F-33 and F-34 received Type 199 variable-depth sonar; later units did not. The single Sea Cat quadruple SAM launcher in the F-33 and F-34 has one MRS-3 director; later ships have two Dutch M-4 directors (with M-45 radar).

◆ **10 Soviet Petya-II class**

P 68 ARNALA	P 75 AMINI	P 79 KILTAN
P 69 ANDROTH	P 77 KAMORTA	P 80 KAVARATTI
P 73 ANJADIP	P 78 KADMATH	P 81 KATCHAL
P 74 ANDAMAN		

D: 950 tons (1,150 fl)   **S:** 28 kts   **Dim:** 80.0 (76.2 pp) × 9.8 × 3.0
A: 4/76-mm DP (II × 2) – 4 MBU-2500 rocket-launchers – 3/533-mm ASW TT (III × 1) – 2 depth-charge racks – mine rails
Man: 130 men
Electron Equipt: Radars: 1 Slim Net, 1 Hawk Screech
                Sonar: 1 Hercules

Andaman

Kavaratti   1970

M: CODOG propulsion: 1 diesel × 6,000 hp + 2 gas turbines × 15,000 hp; 3 props; 36,000 hp

REMARK: Transferred in 1969, 1972, and 1975.

◆ **3 British Leopard class**

	Bldr	Laid down	L	In serv.
F 31 BRAHMAPUTRA	J. Brown, Clydebank	1956	15-3-57	28-3-58
(ex-*Panther*)				
F 37 BEAS	Vickers-Armstrong	1957	9-10-58	24-5-60
F 38 BETWA	Vickers-Armstrong	1957	15-9-59	8-12-60

Brahmaputra   A. and J. Pavia

D: 2,250 tons (2,515 fl)   **S:** 25 kts   **Dim:** 103.0 × 12.2 × 4.9
Man: 240 men   **Range:** 7,500/15   **Electric:** 1,200 kw
A: 4/114-mm DP Mk 6 (II × 2) – 2/40-mm AA (II × 1) – 1/Squid triple ASW mortar
Electron Equipt: Radars: 1/960, 1/293, 1/978, 1/262
                Sonars: 1/177, 1/162, 1/174B
M: 8 Admiralty Standard Range-I diesels; 2 props; 12,380 hp

◆ **2 British Whitby class**

	Bldr	Laid down	L	In serv.
F 40 TALWAR	Cammell Laird	1957	18-7-58	4-60
F 43 TRISHUL	Harland & Wolff	1957	18-6-58	1-60

FRIGATES (continued)

Talwar 1977

D: 2,144 tons (2,560 fl)　**S:** 30 kts　**Dim:** 112.7 × 12.5 × 5.4 (over sonar)
Range: 4,500/12　**Fuel:** 370 tons　**Electric:** 1,140 kw
A: 3/SS-N-2 Styx – 4/40-mm AA (II × 1, I × 2) – 2/Limbo triple ASW mortars
Electron Equipt: Radars: 1/293, 1/277, 1/978, 1/Square Tie
　　　　　　　　　　 Sonars: 1/177, 1/174B, 1/162
Boilers: 2 Babcock & Wilcox, 38.7 kg/cm² pressure – superheat 450°C
M: 2 sets GT; 2 props; 30,000 hp

REMARKS: Three SS-N-2 Styx launchers removed from Osa-I-class, guided-missile patrol boats have replaced the twin 114-mm Mk-6 gun mount in these two ships. Soviet Square Tie radar associated with Styx replaced the gun director, atop the pilothouse.

GUIDED-MISSILE CORVETTES

◆ 3 Soviet Nanuchka class, modified

K 71 VISAYDURG	K 72 SINDHURDURG	K 73 HOSDURG

Sindhurdurg 1977

Sindhurdurg 1977

D: 780 tons (930 fl)　**S:** 30 kts　**Dim:** 60.0 × 13.2 × 2.7
Man: 60 men　**Range:** 3,600/15
A: 4/SS-N-2C (II × 2) – 1/SA-N-4 system – 2/57-mm AA (II × 1)
Electron Equipt: Radars: 1/Band Stand, 1/Pop Group, 1/Muff Cob, 1/Don 2
M: 3 M-507 twin diesels; 3 props; 24,000 hp

REMARK: Delivered 1977-78.

GUIDED-MISSILE PATROL BOATS

◆ 8 Soviet Osa-II class

K 90 PRACHAND	K 92 PRABAL	K 94 CHAMAK	K 96 CHAPAK
K 91 PRALAYA	K 93 PRATAP	K 95 CHAPAL	K 97 CHARAG

D: 240 tons (fl)　**S:** 36 kts　**Dim:** 39.0 × 7.7 × 1.8
A: 4/SS-N-2 Styx (I × 4) – 4/30-mm AA (II × 2)
Electron Equipt: Radars: 1 Square Tie, 1 Drum Tilt
　　　　　　　　　　 IFF: 2/Square Head, 1/High Pole B
M: 3 M-504 diesels; 3 props; 15,000 hp

REMARK: Transferred 1976-77.

◆ 8 Soviet Osa-I class

K 82 VEER	K 84 VIJETA	K 86 NIPAT	K 88 NIRBHIK
K 83 VIDYUT	K 85 VINASH	K 87 NASHAT	K 89 NIRGHAT

D: 175 tons (210 fl)　**S:** 36 kts　**Dim:** 39.0 × 7.7 × 1.8
A: 4/SS-N-2-Styx (I × 4) – 4/30-mm AA (II × 2)
Electron Equipt: Radars: 1 Square Tie, 1 Drum Tilt
　　　　　　　　　　 IFF: 2/Square Head, 1/High Pole B
M: 3 M 503A diesels; 3 props; 12,000 hp

REMARKS: Transferred 1971. Three of the K-84's missile launchers have been mounted on the frigate *Talwar* (F-40); she may therefore be considered out of service, along with one other whose missile launchers are now on the *Trishul* (F-43).

MINE WARFARE SHIPS

◆ 6 Soviet Natya class

M 61 PONDICHERY	M 63 BEDI	M 65 N . . .
M 62 PORBANDAR	M 64 BHAVNAGAR	M 66 N . . .

Pondichery   1978

     D: 650 tons (750 fl)   **S:** 20 kts   **Dim:** 61.0 × 10.0 × 2.7
     A: 4/30-mm AA (II × 2) − 4/25-mm AA (II × 2) − 2/MBU-1800 ASW rocket launchers
        (V × 2) − mines
     Electron Equipt: Radars: 1/Don 2, 1/Drum Tilt
                          IFF: 2/Square Head, 1/High Pole B
     M: 2 diesels; 2 props; 8,000 hp   **Man:** 80 men

REMARKS: Two transferred in 1978, two in 1979, and two in 1980. Differ from the units
in the Soviet Navy in that they do not have a ramp at the stern. Can be used as ASW
escorts.

◆ 4 British "-ton"-class minesweepers

M 90 CUDDALORE (ex-*Wennington*)	M 97 KARWAR (ex-*Overton*)
M 91 CANNAMORE (ex-*Whitton*)	M 1201 KAKINADA (ex-*Durweston*)

     D: 370 tons (425 fl)   **S:** 15 kts   **Dim:** 46.33 (42.68 pp) × 8.76 × 2.5
     Man: 27 men   **Range:** 2,300/13, 3,000/8   **Fuel:** 45 tons
     A: 1/40-mm − 2/20-mm AA
     M: 2 Napier Deltic 18A-7A diesels; 2 props; 2,500 hp

REMARKS: Launched 1955-56. M-91 has been used as the presidential yacht.

◆ 4 British "-ham"-class minesweepers

	Bldr	L
M 89 BHATKAL	Mazagon Docks, Bombay	5-67
M 90 BULSAR	Mazagon Docks, Bombay	17-5-69
2705 BIMLIPATHAM (ex-*Hildersham*)	Vosper, Portsmouth	5-2-54
2707 BASSEIN (ex-*Littleham*)	Brooke Marine, Lowestoft	4-5-54

     D: 120 tons (159 fl)   **S:** 14 kts (9, sweeping)
     Dim: 32.43 (30.48 pp) × 6.45 × 1.7   **Fuel:** 25 tons
     A: 1/20-mm AA   **Man:** 2 officers, 13 men
     M: Davey Paxman YHAXM diesels; 2 props; 1,000 hp

Bhatkal   1968

REMARKS: Nos. 2705 and 2707 were transferred in 1955. The Indian-built units have
teakwood hulls but are otherwise almost identical.

AMPHIBIOUS WARFARE SHIPS

◆ 4 Soviet Polnocny-III class

L 14 GHORPAD	L 15 KESARI	L 16 SHARDUL	L 17 SHARABH

     D: 1,150 (fl)   **S:** 18 kts   **Dim:** 82.0 × 10.0 × 2.0
     A: 4/30-mm AA (II × 2) − 2/140-mm rocket launchers (XVIII × 2)
     Electron Equipt: Radar: 1/Don-2
     M: 2 diesels; 2 props; 5,000 hp   **Cargo:** 350 tons

REMARK: Three transferred in 1975, one in 1976.

Shardul   1976

AMPHIBIOUS WARFARE SHIPS (*continued*)

◆ **2 Soviet Polnocny-I class**

L 13 GULDAR   L 14 GHARIAL

    D: 900 tons (fl)   **S:** 18 kts   **Dim:** 72.5 × 8.5 × 2.0
    A: 2/25-mm AA (II × 1) − 2/140-mm rocket-launchers (XVIII × 2)
    Electron Equipt: Radar: 1/DON-2
    M: 2 diesels; 2 props; 4,000 hp   **Cargo:** 200 tons

REMARK: Transferred 1966.

◆ **2 utility landing craft**   Bldr: Hooghly Dockyard, 1978

L . . .   N . . .   L . . .   N . . .

    D: 600 tons (fl)   **S:** 9 kts   **Dim:** 55.96 × 7.94 × 1.71
    A: . . .   **Electric:** 180 kva
    M: 3 Kirlasker-M.A.N. W8V 17.5/22 AMAL diesels; 3 Kort-nozzle props; 1,245 hp

AUXILIARY SHIPS

◆ **3 Sandhayak-class hydrographic-survey ships**   Bldr: Garden Reach DY, Calcutta

		L	In serv.
J . . .	SANDHAYAK	6-4-77	1979
J . . .	NIRDESHAK	16-11-78	. . .
J . . .	N . . .	. . .	. . .

    D: 2,050 grt   **S:** 15 kts   **Dim:** 78.3 × . . . × 3.7
    A: . . .   **M:** 1 M.A.N. G3V 30/45 ATL diesel; 1 controllable-pitch prop; 3,400 hp

REMARKS: To replace old *Sutlej*-class ships. Will carry four inshore-survey launches. Hangar for one Alouette-III helicopter.

◆ **1 hydrographic-survey ship**   Bldr: Hindustan SY, India.

J 14 DARSHAK

    D: 2,790 tons   **S:** 16 kts   **Dim:** 97.3 × 14.94 × 5.8
    A: 1/40-mm AA   **Man:** 150 men
    M: 2 diesels, electric drive; 2 props; 3,000 hp

REMARKS: Launched 2-11-59, in service 12-64. Carries one helicopter.

Darshak   1974

◆ **2 Gaveshani-class small inshore-survey craft**

J . . .   GAVESHANI   J . . .   N . . .

REMARK: Launched 2-76.

◆ **1 Soviet Ugra-class submarine tender**   Bldr: U.S.S.R., 1968

A 54 AMBA

Amba   1968

    D: 6,750 tons (9,500 fl)   **Dim:** 141.4 × 17.7 × 6.5
    S: 20 kts   **A:** 4/76-mm AA (II × 2)
    Electron Equipt: Radars: 1/Slim Net, 2/Hawk Screech
    M: Diesels; 2 props; 14,000 hp

REMARKS: Helicopter platform. Quarters for 750 men. Two 6-ton cranes, one 10-ton crane.

◆ **1 Soviet T-58-class submarine-rescue ship**

A 55 NISTAR

    D: 850 tons   **S:** 18 kts   **Dim:** 71.7 × 9.1 × 2.5
    Electron Equipt: Radar: 1/Don   **M:** 2 diesels; 2 props; 4,000 hp

REMARKS: Built during late 1950s, transferred 1971. Two rescue chambers, port and starboard sides of the stern. Decompression chamber, diving bells.

◆ **1 repair ship**

A 52 DHARINI (ex-*La Petite Hermine*, ex-*Ketowna Park*)

    D: 4,625 dwt   **S:** 9 kts   **Dim:** 99.0 × 13.9 × 4.0
    M: Triple-expansion; 1 prop; 800 hp   **Fuel:** 620 tons

REMARKS: Built in Canada, launched 25-7-44. In service in Indian Navy 5-60.

◆ **1 training ship**

F 256 TIR (ex-*Bann*)   Bldr: Charles Hill, Bristol

    D: 1,450 tons (2,100 fl)   **S:** 19/18 kts   **Dim:** 91.9 × 11.07 × 4.1
    Man: 100-120 men   **Range:** 9,500/12   **Fuel:** 540 tons
    A: 1/102-mm − 1/40-mm AA − 2/20-mm AA (I × 2)
    M: Triple-expansion; 2 props; 5,500 hp   **Boilers:** 2

REMARK: Former British frigate, launched 29-12-42.

OILERS

◆ **2 Deepak class**   Bldr: Bremer Vulkan Schiffbau, Bremen-Vegesack

A 50 DEEPAK   A 57 SHAKTI

OILERS (continued)

Shakti   G. Arra, 1978

D: 6,785 tons (22,000 fl)   **S:** 20 kts   **Dim:** 168.43 (157.5 pp) × 23.0 × 9.14
Man: 169 men   **Range:** 5,500/18.5   **Boilers:** 2 Babcock & Wilcox
A: 3/40-mm AA (I × 3) − 2/20-mm AA (I × 2)
M: GT; 1 prop; 16,500 hp

REMARKS: A-50 has been in service since 1972, A-57 since 31-12-75. 12,690 grt/15,800 dwt.
Two liquid-replenishment stations per side, with British-style rigs. Telescoping
hangar and flight deck for one helicopter. Carry 12,624 tons fuel oil, 1,280 tons diesel
fuel, 1,495 tons aviation fuel, 812 tons fresh water, and some dry cargo.

LOK ADHAR (ex-*Hooghly*)

REMARK: A 9,231-dwt tanker, taken over in 1972.

DESH DEEP

REMARK: An 11,000-dwt tanker, taken over in 1972.

YARD CRAFT

NOTE: Most of the Indian Navy's service craft are of local design and construction.
Oilers of up to 1,000 dwt have been built in Bombay, while a new class of 1,200-hp
tug is in series production—names include MATAN and BALSHIL, the former
launched in 10-77.

COAST GUARD

The Coast Guard was established 1-2-77 to ensure surveillance of India's 200-nautical-
mile economic zone. Commanded by an admiral, it consisted initially of ships and craft
transferred from the Indian Navy. The name "Coast Guard" is written in large black
letters on the sides of ship hulls, which are painted white.

The Coast Guard has announced that, in addition to the units listed below, it plans
to acquire three 700-ton patrol cutters, six 250-ton patrol boats, a salvage tug of 1,570
grt, a pollution-control ship, twelve patrol aircraft, and one search-and-rescue aircraft.

FRIGATES

◆ **2 British Blackwood class**

		Bldr	Laid down	L	In serv.
31	KIRPAN	Alex. Stephen, Glasgow	1957	19-8-58	7-59
32	KUTHAR	Samuel White, Cowes	1957	14-10-58	1960

D: 1,180 tons (1,456 fl)   **S:** 23 kts   **Dim:** 94.5 (91.44 pp) × 10.05 × 4.7
Range: 4,500/12   **Electric:** 1,108 kw
A: 3/40-mm AA (I × 3) − 2/Mk-10 Limbo triple ASW mortars

Kirpan—in naval service   1969

Electron Equipt: Radar: 1/978
                         Sonars: 1/174, 1/170B, 1/162
Boilers: 2 Babcock & Wilcox, 38.7 kg/cm² pressure − superheat 450°C
M: 1 set GT; 1 prop; 15,000 hp

REMARKS: Transferred to the Coast Guard 1-7-77. The *Khukri* was sunk 9-12-71 by a
Pakistani submarine.

◆ **8 SDB Mk-2 class** Bldr: Garden Reach DY, Calcutta

	L		L
N . . .	31-12-75	N . . .	. . .
N . . .	. . .	N . . .	. . .
N . . .	. . .	N . . .	. . .
N . . .	. . .	N . . .	. . .

D: 160 tons (fl)   **S:** 32 kts   **Dim:** 37.5 × 7.5 × 1.75
A: 1/40-mm AA   **Electric:** 220 kva
M: 2 Deltic 18-42K diesels; 2 props; 7,000 hp; 1 Cummins NH-220 cruise diesel;
165 hp

◆ **5 Soviet Poluchat class**

PANAJI	PANVEL	PAMBAN	PULI	PULICAT

D: 80 tons (90 fl)   **S:** 18 kts   **Dim:** 29.57 × 6.1 × 1.9
A: 2/14.5-mm AA (II × 1)   **Range:** 460/17
M: 2 M-50 diesels; 2 props; 2,400 hp

REMARK: Transferred 1967-69.

◆ **1 British "Ford" class** Bldr: Hooghly Dock, Calcutta

ABHAY

Indian "Ford" class   1968

INDIA (*continued*)

FRIGATES – COAST GUARD (*continued*)

D: 120 tons (151 fl)   **S:** 18 kts   **Dim:** 35.76 × 6.1 × 1.7
A: 1/40-mm AA   **Range:** 500/12, 1,000/8 (cruise engine)
M: 2 Paxman YHAXM diesels; 2 props; 1,000 hp; 1 Foden FD-6 cruise diesel; 100 hp
Fuel: 23 tons

REMARKS: In service since 13-11-61. Originally a class of six: two stricken, two to Bangladesh, one to Mauritius.

◆ **4 British HDML class**

SPC 3110 (ex-HDML-1110)   SPC 3117 (ex-HDML-1117)
SPC 3112 (ex-HDML-1112)   SPC 3118 (ex-HDML-1118)

D: 48 tons (54 fl)   **S:** 12 kts   **Dim:** 21.6 × 4.8 × 1.3
A: 2/20-mm AA (I × 2)   **M:** 2 diesels; 2 props; 320 hp

REMARKS: Built in 1943 and may have been stricken. Wooden construction, for harbor service.

INDONESIA

PERSONNEL: 40,000 men, including 5,000 Marines

MERCHANT MARINE (1978): 1,093 ships – 1,272,387 grt (tankers: 75 ships – 105,240 grt)

NAVAL AVIATION: Indonesia has a small coastal-surveillance and logistic-support force consisting of 12 Australian Nomad-22 STOL transport, 6 C-47, and 3 Aero Commander aircraft. Also in naval service are 4 BO-105 and 1 Alouette-II helicopters.

WARSHIPS IN SERVICE OR UNDER CONSTRUCTION
AS OF 1 JANUARY 1980

	L	Tons (Surfaced)	Main armament
◆ **2 (+2) submarines**			
0 (+2) TYPE 209	. . .	980	8/533-mm TT
2 WHISKEY	1958	1,050	6/533-mm TT
		Tons	
◆ **9 (+3) frigates**			
0 (+1) . . .	1981	1,850	4/Exocet, 1/57-mm DP
1 (+2) FATAHILAH	1977-79	1,160	4/Exocet, 1/120-mm DP, 1/40-mm
4 CLAUD JONES	1958-59	1,450	1 or 2/76-mm, 6/Mk-32 TT
3 RIGA	1954-57	1,200	3/100-mm DP, 3/533-mm TT
1 PATTIMURA	1956	950	2/85-mm DP

◆ **8 (+2) guided-missile patrol boats**			
2 (+2) PSSM MK-5	1978-79	250	4/Exocet, 1/57-mm,1/40-mm
6 KOMAR	1960	71	2/SS-N-2

◆ **4 torpedo patrol boats**

◆ **16 patrol boats**

◆ **7 minesweepers**

◆ **6 amphibious-warfare ships**

NOTE: The names of Indonesian ships are preceded by the designation KRI (Kapal perang Republik Indonesia, or Warship of the Republic of Indonesia).

SUBMARINES

◆ **2 West German Type 209**   Bldr: Howaldtswerke, Kiel

401 CAKRA   402 CANDRASA

D: 980 tons surfaced, 1,356 submerged   **Dim:** 60.0 × 6.2 × 5.2
S: 10/22 kts   **Man:** 32 men
A: 8/533-mm TT fwd – 14 total torpedoes
M: 4 MTU diesels, electric drive; 5,000 hp

REMARK: Ordered 2-4-77.

◆ **2 Soviet Whiskey class**

410 PASOPATI   412 BRAMASTRA

Pasopati   1976

D: 1,050 tons surfaced, 1,350 submerged   **S:** 17/16 kts
Dim: 76.0 × 6.3 × 5.0
A: 6/533-mm TT (4 fwd, 2 aft) – 14 torpedoes or 28 mines
Man: 60 men   **Endurance:** 40 to 45 days   **Range:** 6,000/5
M: 2 diesels (4,000 hp), electric drive; 2 props; 2,500 hp

REMARKS: Sister *Nagabanda* (403) serves as an alongside training ship. The *Bramastra*, which was thought to have been removed from the active list, has been refitted and returned to service.

FRIGATES

◆ **1 training frigate**   Bldr: Uljanic SY, Yugoslavia

	Laid down	L	In serv.
N . . .	5-79	. . .	. . .

D: 1,850 tons (fl)   **S:** 27 kts   **Dim:** 96.7 × 11.2 × 3.55
Man: 93 men + 100 students   **Range:** 4,000/20 (diesels)
A: 4/MM 38 Exocet SSM (II × 2) – 1/57-mm Bofors – 2/20-mm AA (I × 2) – 2/ASW TT
– mines – 1 helicopter
M: CODOG: 1 Rolls-Royce Olympus TM-3B gas turbine, 22,360 hp; 2 MTU 16V956
TB61 diesels, 7,500 hp; 2 controllable-pitch props

REMARKS: Same basic design as ship laid down in 1977 for Iraq. Ordered 14-3-78.

◆ **3 Fatahilah class**   Bldr: Wilton-Fijenoord, Schiedam, The Netherlands

	Laid down	L	In serv.
361 FATAHILAH	31-1-77	22-12-77	1979
362 MALAHAYATI	28-7-77	19-6-78	1980
363 NALA	27-1-78	1-79	1980

Fatahilah   1978

D: 1,160 tons (1,450 fl)   **S:** 30 kts   **Dim:** 83.38 × 11.1 × 3.35
Man: 82 men   **Range:** 4,250/16 (diesels)
A: 4/MM 38 Exocet SSM (II × 2) – 1/120-mm Bofors L-46 DP – 1/40-mm Bofors L-70
– 2/20-mm AA (I × 2) – 2/375-mm Bofors SR-375A ASW rocket launcher (II × 1)
– 6/324-mm Mk-32 ASW TT (III × 2)
Electron Equipt: Radars: 1/DA 05, 1/WM 28, 1/navigational
Sonar: Plessey PHS 32
DAISY data system – Decca RDL 1 ESM – 2 Knebworth Corvus
chaff launchers
M: CODOG: 1 Rolls-Royce Olympus TM-3B gas turbine, 22,360 hp; 2 MTU 16V956
TB61 diesels, 7,500 hp; 2 controllable-pitch props

REMARKS: Ordered 8-75. Three more may be ordered in 1980. Maximum speed on diesels is 21 knots. The *Nala* will have a new type of helicopter deck that folds around
the helicopter to form a hangar, and two single 40-mm AA instead of one.

◆ **4 ex-U.S. Claud Jones class**

	L	In serv.
341 SAMADIKUN (ex-*John R. Perry*, DE-1034)	29-7-58	5-5-59
342 MARTADINATA (ex-*Charles Berry*, DE-1035)	17-3-59	25-11-60
343 MONGINDISI (ex-*Claud Jones*, DE-1033)	27-5-58	10-2-59
344 NGURAH RAI (ex-*McMorris*, DE-1036)	26-5-59	4-3-60

Bldrs: 341, 343: Avondale Marine, Westwego, La., 342, 344: American SB, Toledo, Ohio

Martadinata   1974

D: 1,450 tons (1,750 fl)   **S:** 22 kts   **Dim:** 95.0 × 11.3 × 5.5
Man: 15 officers, 160 men
A: 1 or 2/76-mm AA (I × 1 or 2) – 0 or 2/37-mm AA (II × 1) – 2/25-mm AA (II × 1) –
6/ASW Mk 32 TT (III × 2)
Electron Equipt: Radars: 1/SPS-10, 1/SPS-6, 1/SPG-53
Sonar: SQS-29
M: 4 Fairbanks-Morse 38D81/8 diesels; 1 prop; 9,200 hp

REMARKS: No. 341 was transferred on 20-2-73, No. 342 on 31-1-74, Nos. 343 and 344 on
16-12-74. Nos. 341 and 342 have a twin Soviet 37-mm AA in place of one 76-mm on
fantail and a twin 25-mm at the forecastle break. ESM domes removed from No. 341,
retained in others.

◆ **3 ex-Soviet Riga class**   Bldr: U.S.S.R., 1954-57

351 JOS SUDARSO   357 LAMBUNG MANEGURAT   360 NUKU

FRIGATES (*continued*)

D: 1,200 tons (1,450 fl)   **S:** 28 kts   **Dim:** 91.0 × 10.0 × 3.4
A: 3/100-mm DP–4/37-mm AA (II × 2)–3/533-mm TT (III × 1)–1/MBU 600 Hedge-
hog– 4 depth-charge projectors–2 depth-charge racks–50 mines
Electron Equipt: Radars: 1/Don, 1/Slim Net, 1/Sun Visor A fire-control
M: GT; 2 props; 20,000 hp   **Man:** 150 men

REMARK: Transferred in 1964.

◆ **1 Pattimura class**

	Bldr	Laid down	L	In serv.
371 PATTIMURA	Ansaldo, Livorno	1-56	1-7-56	28-1-58

Pattimura   1975

D: 950 tons (1,200 fl)   **S:** 21.5 kts   **Dim:** 82.37 × 10.3 × 2.8
Man: 119 men   **Range:** 2,400/18   **Fuel:** 100 tons diesel
A: 2/85-mm DP–4/25-mm AA (II × 2)–4/14.5-mm AA (II × 2)–2 Hedgehogs–4
depth-charge launchers
M: Diesels; 2 props; 7,000 hp

REMARKS: Rearmed 1976-77 with Soviet guns removed from stricken units of the Kronstadt, P-6, and Komar classes. Sister *Sultan Hasanudin* (802) stripped and decommissioned in 1978.

NOTE: The two *Almirante Clemente*-class frigates, *Iman Bondjol* and *Surapati*, were
decommissioned in 1978.

GUIDED-MISSILE PATROL BOATS

◆ **4 PSSM Mk-5 class**   Bldr: Korea-Tacoma SY

621 MANDAU   622 RENCONG   623 BADEK   624 KERIS

D: 250 tons (280 fl)   **S:** 40 kts   **Dim:** 50.3 × 7.3 × 2.0
Man: 32 men   **Range:** 2,600/14
A: 4/MM 38 Exocet (II × 2)–1/57-mm AA Bofors–1/40-mm AA Bofors–2/20-mm
AA (I × 2)
M: CODOG: 1 GE-Fiat LM-2500 gas turbine, 25,000 hp; 2 MTU 12V331 TC81 diesels,
1,120 hp each; 2 controllable-pitch props

REMARKS: Building in South Korea to a U.S. design based on the *Asheville*-class hull.
First units scheduled for 1979-80 delivery.

Guawidjaya   1967

◆ **6 Soviet Komar class**

602 KALAMISANI	606 KALANADA	611 NAGA PASA
603 SARPAWISESA	608 SARUTAMA	612 GUAWIDJAYA

D: 71 tons (82 fl)   **S:** 40 kts   **Dim:** 25.5 × 5.0 × 2.0
A: 2/SS-N-2 Styx–2/25-mm AA (II × 1)   **Range:** 400/30
M: 4 M-50-F4 diesels; 4,800 hp

REMARKS: Transferred 1961-63. Nos. 603 and 606, and possibly others, are in reserve.
All now of very little value.

TORPEDO PATROL BOATS

◆ **4 German TNC-45 class**   Bldr: Lürssen, Vegesack, 1959-60

652 BERUANG	653 MADJAN KUMBANG
654 ANOA	655 HARIMAU

D: 140 tons (180 fl)   **S:** 40 kts   **Dim:** 42.0 × 7.6 × 1.8
A: 2/40-mm AA–4/533-mm TT   **Man:** 42 men
M: 4 Mercedes-Benz diesels; 4 props; 12,000 hp

REMARKS: Similar to German Jaguar class. Survivors of a class of eight, four of which
had steel, rather than standard, wooden hulls.

Harimau   1976

SUBMARINE CHASERS

◆ **4 Soviet Kronstadt class** Bldr: U.S.S.R., 1951-52

814 PANDRONG   815 SURA   816 KAKAP   817 BARAKUDA

Sura   1978

D: 300 tons (330 fl)   **S:** 18 kts   **Dim:** 52.1 × 6.5 × 2.2
A: 1/85-mm − 2/37-mm AA (I × 2) − 6/14.5-mm − 2/MBU 1200 ASW rocket launchers − 2 depth-charge projectors − 2 depth-charge racks − mines
M: 3 diesels; 3 props; 3,300 hp   **Fuel:** 20 tons   **Man:** 50 men

REMARKS: Transferred 1958-59. A number of others have been stricken.

◆ **7 ex-Yugoslav PBR-500 class**

819 KAYANG	821 KRAPU	823 TODAK	830 SEMBILANG
820 LEMADANG	822 DORANG	829 TOHOK	

Kayang   1976

D: 190 tons (235 fl)   **S:** 20 kts   **Dim:** 41.0 × 6.3 × 2.1
A: 1/76-mm − 1/40-mm AA − 6/20-mm AA (II × 3) − 2 Mousetraps − 2 depth-charge projectors − 2 depth-charge racks
Man: 54 men   **Range:** 1,500/12   **Fuel:** 15 tons
M: 2 M.A.N. diesels; 2 props; 3,300 hp

REMARK: Transferred in 1959.

PATROL BOATS

◆ **5 Samadar class** Bldr: De Havilland Marine

	In serv.		In serv.
851 SAMADAR	8-76	854 SAWANGI	11-76
852 SASILA	9-76	855 SADARIN	12-76
853 SABOLA	10-76		

D: 27 tons (fl)   **S:** 30 kts   **Dim:** 16.0 × 5.0 × 1.2
A: 2/12.7-mm machine guns   **Man:** 10 men   **Range:** 950/18
M: 2 MTU diesels; 2 props; 1,400 hp   **Fuel:** 18.5 tons

REMARKS: Grant-aid from Australia. Aluminum construction.

◆ **2 Australian Attack class**

847 SIBARU (ex-*Bandolier*)   848 SULIMAN (ex-*Archer*)

D: 146 tons (fl)   **S:** 24/21 kts   **Dim:** 32.76 × 6.2 × 1.9
A: 1/40-mm − 2 machine guns   **Man:** 3 officers, 19 men
M: 2 Davey-Paxman diesels; 3,460 hp   **Fuel:** 20 tons

REMARKS: Transferred in 1973. Light-alloys superstructure. Air-conditioned.

◆ **3 Kelabang class** Bldr: Surabaya DY, 1966-70

844 KELABANG   845 KALAHITAM   846 KOMPAS

Kelabang − wearing old number   1966

D: 147 tons (fl)   **S:** 21 kts   **Dim:** 36.0 × 5.0 × 2.0
A: 1/40-mm AA − 4/12.7-mm machine guns (II × 2)
M: 2 M.A.N. diesels; 2 props; . . . hp

REMARK: No. 846 is in reserve.

◆ **3 U.S. PGM-53 class**

841 BENTANG WAITATIRE (ex-PGM-55)   843 BENTANG KALAKUANG (ex-PGM-57)
842 BENTANG SILUNGKANG

PATROL BOATS (continued)

D: 122 tons (fl)   **S:** 17 kts   **Dim:** 30.5 × 6.4 × 2.6
A: 2/20-mm AA (I × 2) − 2/12.7-mm machine guns
M: 2 MTU MB820dB diesels; 2 props; 1,600 hp

REMARKS: Transferred 1-62. No. 842 is in reserve.

◆ 3 ex-U.S. 173-foot PC class

805 HIU (ex-*Malvern*, PC 580)   807 TJAKALANG (ex-*Pierre*, PC-1141)
806 TORANI (ex-*PC-581*)

D: 335 tons (400 fl)   **S:** 19 kts   **Dim:** 52.95 × 7.25 × 3.25
A: 1/37-mm − 4/25-mm (II × 2)   **Man:** 55 men   **Range:** 4,800/9
M: 2 GM diesels; 2 props; 2,880 hp   **Fuel:** 60 tons

REMARKS: Launched 1942-43, transferred 1959-60. Only No. 805 is active.

MINE WARFARE SHIPS

◆ 5 ex-Soviet T-43-class minesweepers

701 PULAU RANI   703 PULAU ROON   705 PULAU RADJA
702 PULAU RATEWO   704 PULAU RORBAS

D: 500 tons (580 fl)   **S:** 14 kts   **Dim:** 58.0 × 8.4 × 2.3
A: 4/37-mm AA (II × 2) − 8/12.7-mm machine guns (II × 4) − 2 depth-charge pro-
      jectors − 2 mine rails
M: 2 diesels; 2 props; 2,200 hp   **Range:** 3,200/10

REMARK: Transferred 1962-64. Used on patrol duties.

NOTE: Six ex-U.S. *Bluebird*-class coastal minesweepers (MSC) transferred in 1971
quickly disintegrated under constant usage as patrol boats and were stricken in 1976,
at the expiration of a five-year period.

◆ 2 German Raum Boote-class inshore minesweepers
Bldr: Abeking & Rasmussen, 1954-56

708 PULAU RUPAT   712 PULAU RENGAT

D: 130 tons   **S:** 24 kts   **Dim:** 39.0 × 5.7 × 1.58
A: 1/40-mm AA − 2/12.7-mm machine guns   **Man:** 26 men
M: 2 M.A.N. diesels; 2 props; 2,800 hp

REMARKS: Frame and inner hull of metal alloy. Planked in wood. No. 708 is in reserve.

Pulau Rupat

AMPHIBIOUS WARFARE SHIPS

◆ 6 ex-U.S. LSTs   Bldr: U.S.A., 1943

501 TELUK LANGSA (ex-LST-1128)   509 TELUK RATAI (ex-*Polk County*, LST-1084)
504 TELUK KAU (ex-LST-652)   510 TELUK SALEH (ex-LST-601)
505 TELUK MENADO (ex-LST-657)   511 TELUK BONE (ex-LST-639)

Teluk Menado   1967

D: 1,650 tons (4,080 fl)   **S:** 11 kts   **Dim:** 100.04 × 15.24 × 4.3
Man: 119 + 264 passengers   **Range:** 7,200/10   **Fuel:** 600 tons
A: 6 or 7/40-mm or 37-mm AA   **M:** GM diesels; 2 props; 1,800 hp

REMARKS: Transferred in 3-60, 1961, and Nos. 510 and 511 in 7-70 under the Military
Assistance Program. Bought since 1961. Can carry 2,100 tons of cargo. Sisters *Teluk
Bayer* and *Teluk Tomani* are in the Military Sealift Command, as is the Japanese-
built near-sister *Teluk Amboina*.

HYDROGRAPHIC SHIPS

931 BURUDJULASAD   Bldr: Schlichtingwerft, Travemünde

Burudjulasad   1979

HYDROGRAPHIC SHIPS (*continued*)

D: 1,800 tons (2,150 fl)   **S:** 19 kts   **Dim:** 82.0 × 11.4 × 3.5
Man: 129 men   **Range:** 14,500/15.7   **Fuel:** 600 tons
M: 4 M.A.N. V6V 22/30 diesels; 2 props; 6,400 hp   **Electric:** 1,008 kw

REMARKS: Launched in 8-65. Can accommodate 28 scientists and can carry one helicopter.

1005 JALANIDHI Bldr: Sasebo Heavy Industries, Japan

Jalanidhi   1972

D: 740 tons (985 fl)   **S:** 12.7 kts   **Dim:** 53.9 (48.5 pp) × 9.5 × 4.3
Range: 12,000/11.5   **Fuel:** 165 tons   **Electric:** 261 kw
M: 1 M.A.N. G6V 30/42 diesel; 1,000 hp

REMARKS: In service 12-1-63. Primarily for hydrometeorological and oceanographic research. Weather-balloon facility aft.

◆ **1 ex-Soviet PO-2 class**

1008 ARIES

D: 56 tons (fl)   **S:** 12 kts   **Dim:** 21.3 × 3.8 × 2.0
Man: 13 men   **M:** 1 3D12 diesel; 300 hp

REMARK: Transferred in 1964.

1002 BURDJAMHAL Bldr: De Waal Scheepswerf, Nijmegen

D: 1,200 tons (1,500 fl)   **S:** 10 kts   **Dim:** 64.5 (58.5 pp) × 10.1 × 3.3
Man: 90 men   **Fuel:** 150 tons
M: 2 Werkspoor TMA8-278 diesels; 2 props; 1,160 hp

REMARK: Launched 6-9-52 and manned in 7-53.

AUXILIARY SHIPS

◆ **1 ex-Soviet Don-class submarine tender** Bldr: U.S.S.R., 1960

301 RATULANGI (ex-441)

D: 6,700 tons (fl)   **S:** 21 kts   **Dim:** 137.2 × 16.8 × 5.2
A: 4/100-mm DP (I × 4) — 8/57-mm AA (II × 4) — 8/25-mm AA (II × 4)
M: 4 diesels; 2 props; 8,000 hp   **Man:** 300 men

REMARK: Transferred in 1962.

◆ **1 command ship** Bldr: Ishikawajima, Japan

561 MULTATULI

Multatuli   1979

D: 4,500 tons (fl)   **S:** 18.5 kts   **Dim:** 111.35 (103.0 pp) × 16.0 × 6.98
Man: 134 men   **Range:** 6,000/16   **Fuel:** 1,400 tons
A: 8/37-mm AA (II × 2, I × 4) — 4/14.5-mm AA (II × 2) — 1 Alouette-II helicopter
M: 1 Burmeister & Wain diesel; 5,500 hp

REMARKS: Launched 13-6-61. Built as a submarine-support ship, converted as a fleet command ship in the late 1960s. Has a helicopter platform aft.

◆ **1 ex-U.S. Achelous-class repair ship** Bldr: Chicago Bridge & Iron

921 JAJA WIDJAJA (ex-*Askari*, ARL-30)

D: 1,625 tons (4,100 fl)   **S:** 11 kts   **Dim:** 100.0 × 15.3 × 13.4
A: 8/40-mm AA (IV × 2)   **Man:** 280 men
M: 2 GM 12-267A diesels; 2 props; 1,800 hp

REMARK: Launched 2-3-45. Transferred 31-8-71.

◆ **1 replenishment oiler** Bldr: Yugoslavia, 1965

911 SORONG

D: 5,100 (dwt)   **S:** 15 kts   **Dim:** 112.0 × 15.4 × 6.6
A: 8/12.7-mm machine guns (II × 4)   **M:** 1 diesel

REMARK: Cargo: 3,000 tons fuel/300 tons water. Can conduct underway replenishments.

◆ **1 ex-Soviet Khobi-class oiler**

909 PAKAN BARU

D: 1,525 tons (fl)   **S:** 12.7 kts   **Dim:** 67.4 × 10.0 × 4.4
M: 2 diesels; 2 props; 1,600 hp

◆ **1 buoy and cable tender** Bldr: J. & K. Smit, Kinderijk, The Netherlands

1003 BIDUK

AUXILIARY SHIPS (*continued*)

D: 1,250 tons   **S:** 12 kts   **Dim:** 65.0 × 12.0 × 4.5
M: Triple-expansion; 1 prop; 1,600 hp   **Man:** 66 men

REMARK: Launched 30-10-51 and put in service 7-52.

◆ **4 tugs**

922 RAKATA (ex-U.S. *Menominee*, ATF-73)   Bldr: United Eng., Alameda, California

     D: 1,640 tons (fl)   **S:** 15 kts   **Dim:** 62.5 × 11.7 × 4.7
     A: 1/76.2-mm DP − 2/40-mm AA (I × 2) − 4/25-mm AA (II × 2)
     M: 4 GM 12-278A diesels, electric drive; 1 prop; 3,000 hp

934 LAMPO BATANG   Bldr: Japan

     D: 250 tons   **S:** 11 kts   **Dim:** 26.4 × 7.1 × 3.4
     Man: 23 men   **Range:** 1,000/11   **Fuel:** 18 tons
     M: 2 diesels; 2 props; 1,200 hp

935 TAMBORA   936 BROMO   Bldr: Japan

     D: 150 tons (fl)   **S:** 10.5 kts   **Dim:** 24.1 × 6.6 × 3.0
     Man: 15 men   **Range:** 690/10.5   **Fuel:** 15 tons
     M: 2 M.A.N. diesels; 2 props; 600 hp

REMARKS: The *Rakata* was launched 14-2-42 and transferred in 1961. The *Lampo Batang* was launched 4-61, the *Tambora* and *Bromo*, 6-61.

◆ **1 sail training ship**

DEWARUTJI   Bldr: Stülcken, Hamburg

Dewarutji   1977

D: 810 tons (1,500 fl)   **S:** 9 kts   **Dim:** 58.3 (41.5 pp) × 9.5 × 4.23
M: 1 M.A.N. diesel; 575 hp   **Man:** 110 men, 78 cadets

REMARKS: Launched 21-1-52. Sail area: 1,091 m². Will be replaced by the new training frigate.

MILITARY SEALIFT COMMAND (KOLINLAMIL)

Formed in 1978 to coordinate the Indonesian Navy's logistic support for its far-flung bases and outposts in the Indonesian archipelago. Some of the units have been taken over from the Indonesian Army and others from the Navy.

◆ **1 tank landing ship**

9 . . TELUK AMBOINA   Bldr: Sasebo Heavy Industries

     D: 4,145 tons (fl)   **S:** 13 kts   **Dim:** 99.9 × 15.2 × 4.6
     A: 4/40-mm AA − 1/37-mm AA   **Man:** 88 men + 212 passengers
     Range: 4,000/13   **Fuel:** 1,200 tons
     M: 2 M.A.N. diesels; 2 props; 2,850 hp

REMARKS: Built as reparations. Launched 17-3-61. Near duplicate of U.S. LST design. Guns may have been removed.

◆ **3 U.S. LSTs**

9 . . TELUK BAYER (ex-LST-616)   959 TELUK MENTAWAI (ex-LST . . .)
9 . . TELUK TOMANI (ex-LST-983)

     D: 1,650 tons (4,080 fl)   **S:** 11 kts   **Dim:** 100.0 × 15.24 × 4.3
     A: None   **Man:** 119 men + 264 passengers   **Range:** 7,200/10
     M: 2 GM diesels; 2 props; 1,800 hp   **Fuel:** 600 tons

REMARKS: Bought since 1961. *Teluk Tomani* is used as a cattle-carrier and does not carry passengers. *Teluk Mentawai* came from the Army and was in commercial service before that.

◆ **2 utility landing craft**   Bldr: Surabaya DY

9 . . KRUPANG   9 . . DILI

     D: 400 tons (fl)   **S:** 11 kts   **Dim:** 42.9 (36.27 pp) × 9.14 × . . .
     M: 2 diesels; 2 props; . . . hp   **Range:** 700/11   **Man:** 17 men

REMARKS: The *Krupang* went into service 3-11-78, the *Dili*, 27-2-79. Based on U.S. LCU-1610 class. Cargo: 200 tons.

◆ **2 Amurang class**   Bldr: Austria, 1968

9 . . AMURANG   9 . . DORE

     D: 182 tons (275 fl)   **S:** 8 kts   **Dim:** 38.3 × 10.0 × 1.8
     M: 2 diesels; 2 props; 420 hp   **Man:** 17 men

REMARK: Sister *Banten* and one other in merchant service.

◆ **1 oiler**   Bldr: Japan, 1965

901 BALIKPAPAN (ex-*Komado* V)

     D: 1,780 dwt   **S:** 11 kts   **Dim:** 69.6 × 9.6 × 4.9
     M: 1 diesel; 1,300 hp   **Man:** 26 men

REMARK: Purchased in 1977.

◆ **1 oiler**   SAMBU   No data available

INDONESIA (*continued*)

MILITARY SEALIFT COMMAND (*continued*)

◆ **5 Soviet Keyla-class cargo ships**

951 TELAUD	953 NATUNA	960 KARAMAJA
952 NUSATELU	957 KARIMUNDSA	

D: 2,000 tons (fl)   S: 12 kts   Dim: 78.5 × 10.5 × 4.6
M: 1 diesel; 1,000 hp   Man: 26 men   Range: 4,200/10.7

REMARKS: Transferred 1963-64. Taken over from the Army in 1978. Had originally been naval. 1,296 grt/1,280 dwt. Cargo: 1,100 tons.

◆ **2 transports**

931 TANSUNG PANDAN (ex-*Cut Nya Dhien*)   932 TANSUNG OISINA (ex-*Gununjati*)

REMARKS: Purchased in 1978. Large (approx. 6,000-8,000 grt) but elderly passenger-cargo ships.

MARITIME SECURITY AGENCY

Established in 1978 to patrol Indonesia's 200-nautical-mile economic zone and to maintain navigational aids. To date, very few assets have been acquired. Craft include:

◆ **6 PAT-class patrol craft** Bldr: Tanjung Priok SY, 1978-79

PAT 01 to PAT 06

D: 12 tons (fl)   S: 14 kts   Dim: 12.15 × 4.25 × 1.0
A: Machine guns   M: 1 Renault diesel; 260 hp

◆ **2 buoy tenders** Ordered from Japan in 1978

CUSTOMS SERVICE

◆ **18 patrol boats** Bldrs: CMN, Cherbourg, 11, Chantiers Navals de l'Esterel, Cannes, 7

BC 1001 to BC 1018

BC-1002   l'Esterel, 1975

D: 90 tons (fl)   S: 35 kts   Dim: 28.0 × 5.2 × 1.6
A: 1 machine gun   Man: 15 men   Range: 600/26
M: 2 MTU 12V331 TC81 diesels; 2 props; 2,700 hp   Fuel: 10 tons

REMARKS: In service 1975-80. Wooden hull. Similar in design to Moroccan *El Wacil* class.

◆ **5 patrol boats** Bldrs: Lürssen, Vegesack, and Abeking & Rasmussen, Lemwerder

DKN 901 to DKN 905

D: 140 tons (fl)   S: 24.5 kts   Dim: 39.0 × 5.8 × 1.6
A: 4/20-mm AA (II × 2)   M: 2 MTU diesels; 2 props; 3,000 hp

REMARKS: In service 1958-59. Probably no longer operational. DKN-907 to DKN-916, built in Italy and delivered in 1960, are out of service.

INDONESIAN ARMY (ADRI)

At one time the Indonesian Army operated a great variety of ships, including up to 29 units in the ADRI-I series, most of which were old passenger-cargo ships acquired for use as troop transports. Most of its serviceable ships were turned over to the new Military Sealift Command in 1977 and 1978, but a new series of logistics landing craft is under construction.

◆ **20 utility craft** Bldr: Tanjung Priok DY

ADRI XXXI to ADRI L

D: 300 tons   S: 9 kts   Dim: 42.0 × 10.7 × 1.8
M: 2 GM 6-71 diesels; 2 props; 300 hp

REMARK: Began entering servide 1978.

INDONESIAN AIR FORCE (AURI)

The Indonesian Air Force operates six passenger-cargo logistics ships that were completed in the mid-1960s. Of about 600 dwt, they are intended to beach and are equipped with bow doors.

IRAN

PERSONNEL: 12,500 men, including 1,100 officers (before the revolution)

MERCHANT MARINE (1978): 208 ships — 1,194,675 grt (tankers: 25 ships — 597,675 grt)

MARITIME AVIATION: On hand before the revolution were: 7 SH-3D Sea King, 7 AB-212, 5 AB-205A, 14 AB-206A, and 2 Sikorsky RH-53D helicopters, 6 P-3F Orion long-range patrol aircraft, 4 Fokker Friendship transports, and 6 Aero Commander -utility transports.

NOTE: Since the revolution in Iran, the sale to Iran of a number of new or newly renovated U.S. and European ships has been canceled. The ships involved include: six

West German Type-209 submarines ordered 11-3-78 from Howaldtswerke; two ex-U.S. *Tang*-class submarines that were to have been turned over in 1980 and 1982 — a third was transferred, but has been handed back; four U.S. DD-943-class (Modified *Spruance*) guided-missile "destroyers" ordered in 1974; and two LSTs on order in Great Britain. Negotiations in Western Europe for twelve guided-missile frigates, which were to have U.S.-supplied weapons and electronics, have been terminated, as have been plans to build a number of minesweepers. Other ongoing programs are in doubt at the time of writing, including the delivery of the last three *La Combattante*-II-class guided-missile boats from France and the replenishment oiler *Kharg* from Great Britain; for details, *see* entries below.

SUBMARINE

◆ 1 U.S. Tang class   Bldr: Gen. Dynamics, Groton

	Laid down	L	In serv.
101 KUSSEH (ex-*Trout*, SS-566)	1-12-49	21-8-51	27-6-52

D: 2,100 tons surfaced, 2,700 submerged   **S:** 16/16 kts
Dim: 87.4 × 8.3 × 6.2   **A:** 8/533-mm TT (6 fwd, 2 aft)
Man: 8 officers, 79 men
M: 3 Fairbanks-Morse diesels, electric drive; 2 props; 5,600 hp

REMARKS: After extensive renovation, transferred 17-12-77, but handed back to the U.S. Navy 5-79. Sale of the *Wahoo* (SS-565) and *Gudgeon* (SS-567) has been canceled. The *Kusseh* is considered by the United States to be Iranian property.

GUIDED-MISSILE DESTROYERS

◆ 1 ex-British Battle class   Bldr: Cammell Laird, Birkenhead

	Laid down	L	In serv.
51 ARTEMIZ (ex-*Sluys*, D-60)	24-11-43	28-2-45	30-9-46

Artemiz — wearing old number   Thornycroft, 1969

D: 2,325 tons (3,360 fl)   **S:** 31 kts   **Dim:** 115.32 (108.2 pp) × 12.95 × 5.2 (fl)
Man: 260 men   **Range:** 3,200/20   **Fuel:** 680 tons
A: 4/Standard SSM launchers (8 missiles) — 4/114-mm (II × 2, fwd) — 4/40-mm AA
   (I × 4) — 1/Sea Cat (IV × 1) — 1/Squid ASW mortar (III × 1)
Electron Equipt: Radars: 1/Plessey AWS-1 air-search, 1/Plessey surface-search,
                  Contraves Sea Hunter fire-control
           Sonar: Plessey MS-26 — Decca RDL-1 ESM
M: Parsons GT; 2 props; 50,000 hp   **Boilers:** 2 Admiralty

REMARKS: Modernized before transfer on 20-1-67. Anti-ship missiles added after refit in South Africa, 1975-76.

◆ 2 ex-U.S. Allen M. Sumner, FRAM II, class

	Bldr	Laid down	L	In serv.
61 BABR (ex-*Zellars*, DD-777)	Todd, Pacific	24-12-43	19-7-44	25-10-44
62 PALANG (ex-*Stormes*, DD-780)	Federal SB, Kearny	25-2-44	4-11-44	27-1-45

Babr   1976

D: 2,200 tons (3,320 fl)   **S:** 30 kts   **Dim:** 114.75 × 12.45 × 5.6
Man: 14 officers, 260 men   **Range:** 1,260/30, 4,600/14   **Fuel:** 650 tons
A: 4/Standard SSM systems (8 missiles) — 4/127-mm DP (II × 2) — 6/324-mm Mk-32
   ASW TT — 2 Hedgehogs — AB-204 ASW helicopter
Electron Equipt: Radars: 1/SPS 10, 1/SPS 37, 1/Mk 25
           Sonar: 1/SQS 29 — ULQ 6 ECM
M: GT; 2 props; 60,000 hp   **Boilers:** 4 Babcock & Wilcox

REMARKS: Assigned in 3-71 and delivered in 10-73 and 1974. The *Bordelon* (DD-881) and the *Kenneth D. Bailey* (DD-713) were transferred for cannibalization. The Standard missiles are on a platform between the stacks and on the 01 level forward of the bridge. Mk 37 fire-control for the 127-mm guns. VDS now removed from the *Babr*.

FRIGATES

◆ 4 Saam Mk-5 class

	Bldr	Laid down	L	In serv.
71 SAAM	Vosper Thornycroft	22-5-67	25-7-68	20-5-71
72 ZAAL	Vickers, Newcastle	3-3-68	25-7-68	1-3-71
73 ROSTAM	Vickers, Barrow	10-12-67	4-3-69	28-2-72
74 FARAMARZ	Vosper Thornycroft	25-7-68	30-7-69	28-2-72

D: 1,100 tons (2,350 fl)   **S:** 40/30 kts (17.5 with diesel)
Dim: 94.5 (88.4 pp) × 11.07 × 3.25   **Man:** 135 men
Range: 5,000/15   **Fuel:** 150 tons (250 with overload)
A: 1/114-mm DP Mk 8 — 2/35-mm AA (II × 1) — 1/Sea Killer SSM system (V × 1) —
   1/Sea Cat system (III × 1) — 1/Limbo Mk 10 ASW mortar (III × 1)

FRIGATES (*continued*)

Faramarz   1978

Zaal   1977

Electron Equipt: Radars: 1/Plessey AWS-1 air-search, 2/Contraves Sea Hunter
fire-control

M: CODOG: 2 Rolls-Royce Olympus TM3A gas turbines; 2 Paxman 16-cyl. Ventura
diesels for cruising; 2 controllable-pitch props; 46,000 hp (turbines), 3,800 hp
(diesels)

REMARKS: Air-conditioned. Retractable fin stabilizers. All now carry Mk 8 guns in
place of original Mk 6.

◆ **4 U.S. PF-103 class**   Bldr: Levingston SB, Orange, Texas

	Laid down	L	In serv.
81 BAYANDOR (ex-PF-103)	20-8-62	7-7-63	18-5-64
82 NAGHDI (ex-PF-104)	12-9-62	10-10-63	22-7-64
83 MILANIAN (ex-PF-105)	1-5-67	4-1-68	13-2-69
84 KAHNAMUIE (ex-PF-106)	12-6-67	4-4-68	13-2-69

D: 900 tons (1,135 fl)   **S:** 20 kts   **Dim:** 83.82 × 10.05 × 3.05

Man: 133 men   **Range:** 3,000/15

A: 2/76-mm DP (I × 2)−2/40-mm AA (II × 1)−2/23-mm AA (II × 1)−4 depth-charge
projectors−2 depth-charge racks

Electron Equipt: Radars: 1/SPS 6, 1/Raytheon navigational, 1/Mk 34
Sonar: SQS 17

M: 4 Fairbanks-Morse 38D81/8 diesels; 2 props; 6,000 hp

Kahnamuie   1978

REMARKS: Transferred under MAP. Twin Soviet 23-mm AA have been added forward
of the bridge in place of the single Hedgehog ASW mortar.

GUIDED-MISSILE PATROL BOATS

◆ **12 La Combattante-II class**   Bldr: Constr. Méc. de Normandie, Cherbourg

	L	In serv.		L	In serv.
P 221 KAMAN	8-1-76	6-77	P 227 SHAMSHIR	12-9-77	31-3-78
P 222 ZOUBIN	14-4-76	6-77	P 228 GORZ	28-12-77	15-9-78
P 223 KHADANG	15-7-76	15-3-78	P 229 GARDOUNEH	23-2-78	23-10-78
P 224 PEYKAN	12-10-76	15-3-78	P 230 KHANJAR	27-4-78	. . .
P 225 JOSHAN	21-2-77	31-3-78	P 231 NEYZEH	5-7-78	. . .
P 226 FALAKHON	2-6-77	31-3-78	P 232 TABARZIN	15-9-78	. . .

Zoubin   G. Arra, 1977

GUIDED-MISSILE PATROL BOATS (*continued*)

Kaman　　　　　　　　　　　　　　　　　　G. Arra, 1977

D: 249 tons (275 fl)　　**S:** 36 kts　　**Dim:** 47.0 × 7.1 × 1.9
Man: 31 men　　**Range:** 700/33.7　　**Fuel:** 41 tons
A: 4/Harpoon SSM (II × 2)–1/76-mm DP OTO Melara–1/40-mm AA
Electron Equipt: Radar: 1/WM 28 fire-control
M: 4 MTU 16V538 TB91 diesels; 4 props; 14,400 hp　　**Electric:** 350 kw

REMARKS: Contracted 19-2-74 and 14-10-74. The last three were embargoed at Cherbourg 4-79 pending payment. Only twelve Harpoon missiles were delivered.

PATROL BOATS

◆ **3 U.S. PGM-71 class**
　Bldrs: P-211: Peterson, Sturgeon Bay; P-212, P-213: Tacoma Boat

P 211 PARVIN　　　P 212 BAHRAM　　　P 213 NAHID

　　D: 105 tons (146 fl)　　**S:** 17 kts　　**Dim:** 30.5 × 6.7 × 3.1
　　A: 1/40-mm AA–4/20-mm AA (II × 2)–4/12.7-mm machine guns (II × 2)–2/Mk 22
　　Mousetrap–2 depth-charge racks
　　M: 8 GM 6-71 diesels; 2 controllable-pitch props; 2,000 hp

REMARK: In service 1967-70.

◆ **4 U.S. Cape class**　Bldr: U.S. Coast Guard, Curtis Bay, Md.

P 201 KEYVAN　　　P 202 TIRAN　　　P 203 MEHRAN　　　P 204 MAHVAN

　　D: 85 tons (107 fl)　　**S:** 20 kts　　**Dim:** 29.0 × 6.2 × 2.0
　　A: 1/40-mm AA–2/Mk 22 Mousetrap–2 depth-charge racks
　　M: 4 Cummins diesels; 2 props; 2,200 hp　　**Range:** 1,500/15

REMARK: In service 1956-59.

MINE WARFARE SHIPS

◆ **3 ex-U.S. Falcon-class minesweepers**

	Bldr	L
301 SHAHROKH (ex-MSC-276)	Peterson	1958
302 SIMORGH (ex-MSC-291)	Bellingham SY	3-3-61
303 KARKAS (ex-MSC-292)	Tacoma Boat	1962

Simorgh　　　　　　　　　　　　　　　　　　1961

D: 320 tons (378 fl)　　**Dim:** 43.0 (41.5 pp) × 7.95 × 2.55
S: 12.5 kts (8, sweeping)　　**Man:** 3 officers, 35 men　　**Fuel:** 27 tons
A: 2/20-mm AA (II × 1)　　**Range:** 2,500/10
Electron Equipt: Radar: Decca 707　　Sonar: UQS 1
M: 2 GM diesels; 2 props; 890 hp

REMARKS: Sister *Shabaz* lost through fire in 1975. The *Shahrokh* is the Iranian Navy's largest unit in the Caspian Sea.

◆ **2 ex-U.S. Cape-class inshore minesweepers**　Bldr: Tacoma Boatbuilding, 1964

311 HARISCHI (ex-*Kahnamuie*, ex-MSI-13)　　　312 RIAZI (ex-MSI-14)

Harischi　　　　　　　　　　　　　　　　　　1964

MINE WARFARE SHIPS (*continued*)

D: 180 tons (235 fl)　　**S:** 13 kts　　**Dim:** 34.0 × 7.0 × 1.8
A: 1/12.7-mm machine gun　　**Man:** 5 officers, 18 men
M: 2 diesels; 650 hp　　**Fuel:** 20 tons　　**Range:** 1,000/9

AMPHIBIOUS WARFARE SHIPS

◆ **4 Hengam-class LSTs**　Bldr: Yarrow & Co., Glasgow

	L	In serv.		L	In serv.
511 HENGAM	27-9-73	12-8-74	513 LAVAN	27-2-79	. . .
512 LARAK	7-5-74	12-11-74	514 TONB	. . .	. . .

Larak—wearing old number　　　　　　　　　　　1976

D: 2,540 tons (fl)　　**S:** 14.5 kts　　**Dim:** 93.0 (86.8 wl) × 14.95 × 2.21
A: 4/40-mm AA (I × 4)　　**Man:** 80 men + 227 troops
Electron Equipt: Radar: Decca 1229　　**Electric:** 1,100 kw
M: 4 Paxman Ventura Mk-2 12 YJCM diesels; 2 controllable-pitch props;, 5,600 hp

REMARKS: Two others, ordered in 7-77, were canceled in 3-79. Delivery of 513 and 514 is uncertain. Flight deck for one helicopter aft. Cargo capacity of 700 tons includes 300 tons of vehicle fuel. Vehicle deck is 42.7 × 9.4 meters and can accommodate 12 Soviet T-55 or 6 British Chieftain tanks. Bow doors and ramp for beaching. Upper deck forward has a 10-ton crane to handle two Uniflote cargo lighters (LCVP) and twelve Z-boat rubber personnel landing craft. Intended for logistics support (when ten 20-ton or thirty 10-ton containers would be carried) or for amphibious assult.

NOTE: The old LCU, *Gheshne*, was sunk as a Harpoon target during 1978.

HOVERCRAFT

◆ **6 BH.7 Wellington class**　Bldr: British Hovercraft, 1973-75

101 to 106

D: 50 to 55 tons (fl)　　**S:** 65 kts　　**Dim:** 23.9 × 13.8 × 10.36 (high)
A: Machine guns　　**Electron Equipt:** Radar: Decca 914
Range: 400/56　　**Fuel:** 9 tons　　**Electric:** 110 kva
M: 1 Rolls-Royce Gnome 15M549 gas turbine; 1 6.4-m diameter prop; 4,250 hp

REMARKS: Four are of the logistics-support version, with a 14-ton payload. Two are of the Mk-4 version with recess for two SSM, which have not been mounted. The Mk-4 uses the Gnome 15M541 engine of 4,750 hp and can carry sixty troops in side compartments as well as assault vehicles on its 56-m² cargo deck. Speed in both versions is reduced to 35 kts in a 1.4-meter sea.

◆ **8 SR-N6 Winchester class**

01 to 08

D: 10 tons　　**S:** 52 kts　　**Dim:** 14.8 × 7.7 × 3.8 (high)
A: 1/7.6-mm machine gun　　**Range:** 110/30
M: 1 Gnome Mk 1050 gas turbine

AUXILIARY SHIPS

◆ **1 large replenishment oiler**

	Bldr	Laid down	L	In serv.
91 KHARG	Swan Hunter, G.B.	1-76	3-2-77	. . .

D: 33,014 tons (fl)　　**S:** 21.5 kts　　**Dim:** 207.1 (195.0 pp) × 25.5 × 9.1
Man: 248 men　　**Electric:** 7,000 kw
A: 1/76-mm OTO Melara AA—4/40-mm Breda AA (II × 2)—3 helicopters
M: Westinghouse GT; 1 prop; 26,870 hp　　**Boilers:** 2 Babcock & Wilcox

REMARKS: Ordered 10-74. 21,100 grt/20,000 dwt. Design is a greatly modified version of the Royal Navy's *Olwen* class. Ran initial trials 11-78 but delays in fitting-out made delivery before the revolution impossible. Delivery status uncertain.

◆ **2 Bandar Abbas-class small replenishment oilers**

422 BANDAR ABBAS　　　　441 BOOSHEHR

Bldr: C. Lühring, Brake, West Germany

Bandar Abbas　　　　　　　　　　　　　1976

D: 5,000 tons (fl)　　**S:** 15 kts　　**Dim:** 108.0 × 16.6 × 4.5
A: 2/40-mm AA (I × 2)—1 helicopter　　**Man:** 60 men
M: 2 M.A.N. diesels; 2 props; 6,000 hp

REMARKS: No. 422 launched 14-8-73 and No. 441, 22-3-74. 3,250 dwt. Telescoping hangar. Carry fuel, food, ammunition, and spare parts.

AUXILIARY SHIPS (*continued*)

Bandar Abbas   1975

◆ **1 modified U.S. 174-foot-class yard oiler** Bldr: Nav. Mec. Castellammare, 1956

43 HORMUZ

    D: 1,200 tons (fl)   **S:** 9 kts   **Dim:** 54.4 × 9.8 × 4.3
    A: 2/20-mm AA (I × 2)   **Electron Equipt:** Radar: Decca 707
    M: 1 Ansaldo Q370 diesel; 600 hp   **Fuel:** 25 tons

Hormuz   1974

◆ **2 water tankers** Bldr: Mazagon Dock, India

411 KANGAN   412 TAHERI

    D: 12,000 tons (fl)   **S:** 12 kts   **Dim:** 147.95 (140.0 pp) × 21.5 × 5.0
    M: 1 M.A.N. 7L52/55A diesel; 7,385 hp

REMARKS: No. 411 launched in 4-78 and No. 412 on 17-9-78. 9,430 dwt. Resemble engines-aft oil tankers. Intended to supply Arabian Gulf islands. Liquid cargo: 9,000 m³.

◆ **1 U.S. 174-foot-class water tanker** Bldr: Zenith Dredge, Duluth, Minn., 1944

    D: 1,282 tons (fl)   **S:** 10 kts   **Dim:** 54.3 × 9.8 × 4.3
    M: 1 diesel; 580 hp

REMARK: Purchased in 1964.

◆ **1 ex-U.S. Amphion-class repair ship** Bldr: Tampa SB, Florida

CHAH BAHAR (ex-*Amphion*, AR-13)

    D: 14,450 tons (fl)   **S:** 16 kts   **Dim:** 150.0 × 21.4 × 8.4
    A: 2/76-mm (I × 2)   **Man:** Quarters for 921 men   **M:** 1 GT; 8,500 hp

REMARKS: Launched 15-5-45. Transferred in 10-71. Primarily stationary, but can steam.

◆ **2 imperial yachts**

CHAH SEVAR Bldr: Boele's SW, Bolnes, The Netherlands, 1936

    D: 530 tons   **S:** 15 kts   **Dim:** 53.0 × 7.65 × 3.2
    M: Stork diesels; 2 props; 1,300 hp

REMARK: In the Caspian Sea.

KISH Bldr: West Germany, 1970

    D: 175 tons   **Dim:** 37.0 × 7.6 × 2.2   **M:** 2 MTU diesels; 2,920 hp

REMARK: In the Persian Gulf.

◆ **2 barracks ships**

	Bldr	L	In serv.
MICHELANGELO	Ansaldo	9-62	. . .
RAFFAELLO	CRDA, Monfalcone	. . .	7-7-65

    D: 42,000 tons (fl)   **S:** 29 kts   **Dim:** 275.8 (244.0 pp) × 31.0 × 9.3
    M: GT; 4 props; 65,000 hp   **Boilers:** 4 Foster-Wheeler

REMARKS: Former cruise liners, purchased 12-12-76. Arrived July/August 1977 at Bandar Abbas for use as floating barracks for Iranian naval personnel and their families. Apparently will retain original names.

◆ **1 ex-U.S. Army tug**

45 BAHMAN SHIR (ex-ST-1002)
D: 150 tons

REMARK: Transferred in 1962.

◆ **2 ex-German tugs**

1 (ex-*Karl*)   2 (ex-*Ise*)
D: 134 tons

REMARK: Built 1962-63, and transferred in 6-74.

◆ **2 ammunition lighters** Bldr: Karachi DY, 1978

N . . .   N . . .

    D: 840 grt   **S:** 7.5 kts   **Dim:** 64.0 × 10.5 × 3.2
    M: 2 M.A.N. G6V-23.5/33ATL diesels; 2 props; 1,560 hp

◆ **2 water barges** Bldr: Karachi DY, 1977-78

    D: 1,410 grt   **Dim:** 65.0 × 13.0 × 2.6

NOTE: Upwards of 20 other non-self-propelled service barges were built for the Iranian Navy at the Karachi Dockyard, Pakistan, between 1976 and 1978.

◆ **1 floating dry dock**

400 (ex-ARD-28)

    D: 3,500 tons lift   **Dim:** 149.8 × 25.6 × 1.7 (light)

REMARKS: In service in 1944. Transferred 1-3-77.

IRAN (*continued*)

COAST GUARD

PATROL CRAFT

◆ **20 + 50 (?) U.S. 64-foot Mk III class** Bldr: Peterson, U.S.A.

> **D:** 28.6 tons (34.7 fl)   **S:** 30 kts   **Dim:** 19.8 × 5.6 × 2.0
> **A:** 3/20-mm AA (I × 3)—1/12.7-mm machine gun   **Man:** 5 men
> **M:** 3 GM 8V71-TI diesels; 3 props; 2,050 hp   **Range:** 500/30

REMARKS: Twenty were ordered in 1973 and up to fifty more in 1976. Some were to be built under license in Iran. Totals are uncertain.

◆ **20 U.S. 50-foot Mk II class** Bldr: Peterson, U.S.A., 1976-77

1201 to 1220

> **D:** 22 tons (fl)   **S:** 26 kts   **Dim:** 15.3 × 4.8 × 1.9
> **A:** 4/12.7-mm machine guns (II × 2)   **Man:** 6 men
> **M:** 2 GM 12V71 diesels; 2 props; 900 hp

◆ **6 U.S. 40-foot class** Bldr: Sewart, La., 1963, 197. .

| MAHMAVI-HAMRAZ | MAHMAVI-VANEDI | MORDARID |
| MAHMAVI-TAHERI | MARDJAN | SADAF |

> **D:** 10 tons   **S:** 30 kts   **Dim:** 12.2 × 3.4 × 1.1
> **A:** 2/7.6-mm machine guns   **M:** 2 GM diesels; 2 props; 600 hp

REMARKS: Four given to Sudan in 1978, two stricken.

◆ **40+ U.S. Bertram Enforcer harbor patrol craft** Dim: 9.5 and 6.1 oa

◆ **10 British Fairey Marine Medina-class motor lifeboats**

IRAQ

PERSONNEL: 5,000 men, including 400 officers

MERCHANT MARINE (1978): 115 ships—2,305,907 grt (tankers: 29 ships—1,141,120 grt)

FRIGATE

◆ **1 training frigate** Bldr: Uljanic SY, Yugoslavia

	Laid down	L	In serv.
N . . .	1977	1978	. . .

> **D:** 1,850 tons (fl)   **S:** 26 kts   **Dim:** 96.7 × 11.2 × 3.55
> **Man:** 93 men + 100 students   **Range:** 4,000/20 (diesels)

> **A:** 1/57-mm AA Bofors SAK 57—1/40-mm AA—8/20-mm AA (II × 4)—1 helicopter
> **M:** CODOG: 1 Rolls-Royce Olympus TM-3B gas turbine, 22,360 hp; 2 MTU 16V956 TB61 diesels, 7,500 hp; 2 controllable-pitch props

REMARKS: Same basic design as the ship laid down in 1979 for Indonesia. Will serve to provide experience in operating larger ships for future expansion of the Iraq fleet.

PATROL BOATS

◆ **3 ex-Soviet S.O.-1 class**

| 210 | 211 | 212 |

> **D:** 190 tons (215 fl)   **S:** 28 kts   **Dim:** 42.0 × 6.1 × 1.9
> **Man:** 3 officers, 27 men   **Range:** 1,500/12
> **A:** 4/25-mm AA (II × 2)—4 MBU-1800 ASW rocket launchers—2 depth-charge racks—mines
> **Electron Equipt:** Radar: 1/Pot Head   Sonar: High-frequency
> **M:** 3 diesels; 3 props; 7,500 hp

REMARK: Delivered in 1962.

GUIDED-MISSILE PATROL BOATS

◆ **8 Soviet Osa-II class**

> **D:** 240 tons (fl)   **S:** 36 kts   **Dim:** 39.0 × 7.7 × 1.8
> **A:** 4/SS-N-2B Styx (I × 4)—4/30-mm AA (II × 2)
> **Electron Equipt:** Radars: 1/Square Tie, 1/Drum Tilt
>   IFF: 2/Square Head, 1 High Pole A
> **M:** 3 M-504 diesels; 3 props; 15,000 hp

REMARK: Two transferred in 1974 and two in each year through 1977.

◆ **6 Soviet Osa-I class**

> **D:** 175 tons (210 fl)   **S:** 36 kts   **Dim:** 39.0 × 7.7 × 1.8
> **A:** 4/SS-N-2 Styx—4/30-mm AA (II × 2)   **Man:** 25 men
> **Electron Equipt:** Radars: 1/Square Tie, 1/Drum Tilt
>   IFF: 2/Square Head, 1/High Pole A
> **M:** 3 M-503A diesels; 3 props; 12,000 hp

REMARK: Two transferred 1971-72, two in 1973, and two in 1974.

◆ **4 Yugoslav Kraljevica class**

> **D:** 190 tons (202 fl)   **S:** 18 kts   **Dim:** 41.0 × 6.3 × 2.2
> **A:** 2/40-mm AA (I × 2)—4/MBU-1800 ASW rocket launchers—depth charges
> **M:** 4 M.A.N. W8V 30/38 diesels; 2 props; 3,300 hp   **Range:** 1,000/12

REMARKS: Transferred between end 1976 and early 1977. Information uncertain, may not have occurred.

TORPEDO BOATS

◆ **10 ex-Soviet P-6 class**

14 RAMADAN	TAMOUR	AL BAHI	SHULAS
AL TAMI	ALEF	AL SHAAB	
LAMAKI BIN ZIHYAD	AL ADRISI	TAREQ BEN ZOID	

> **D:** 65 tons (66.5 fl)   **S:** 43 kts   **Dim:** 25.3 × 6.1 × 1.7
> **Man:** 2 officers, 12 men   **Range:** 650/26
> **A:** 4/25-mm AA (II × 2)—2/533-mm TT (I × 2)

IRAQ (*continued*)
TORPEDO BOATS (*continued*)

Electron Equipt: Radar: Pot Head or Skin Head
M: 4 M50 diesels; 4 props; 4,800 hp

PATROL CRAFT

◆ **4 Soviet Zhuk class**

D: 50 tons (60 fl)   S: 30 kts   Dim: 26.0 × 4.9 × 1.5
A: 4/14.5-mm AA (II × 2)   M: 2 M50 diesels; 2 props; 2,400 hp

REMARK: Transferred in 1975.

◆ **2 Soviet Poluchat-I class** — Transferred in 1966

D: 80 tons (90 fl)   S: 18 kts   Dim: 29.6 × 5.8 × 1.5
A: 2/14.5-mm AA   M: 2 diesels; 2 props; 2,400 hp

REMARKS: Transferred in 1966. May in fact be torpedo-recovery versions of the Poluchat class.

◆ **4 river patrol craft**   Bldr: Thornycroft, 1937

D: 67 tons   S: 12 kts   Dim: 30.5 × 5.2 × 0.9
A: 1/90-mm howitzer — 4/12.7-mm machine guns
M: 2 diesels; 2 props; 280 hp

MINE WARFARE SHIPS

◆ **2 Soviet T-43-class fleet minesweepers**

465 AL YARMOUK   . . . AL KADISIA

D: 500 tons (580 fl)   S: 14 kts   Dim: 58.0 × 8.4 × 2.3
A: 4/37-mm AA (II × 2) — 8/12.7-mm machine guns (II × 4) — 2 depth-charge projectors — mines   Electron Equipt: Radar: Ball End
M: 2 diesels; 2 props; 2,200 hp   Range: 3,200/10

REMARK: Transferred in 1969.

◆ **3 Yevgenya-class inshore minesweepers**

D: 80 tons (90 fl)   S: 12 kts   Dim: 26.0 × 6.0 × 1.5
A: 2/25-mm AA   M: 2 diesels; 2 props; 600 hp

REMARKS: Transferred in 1975 as "oceanographic research craft." Have heavier guns than their Soviet Navy sisters.

AMPHIBIOUS WARFARE SHIPS

◆ **3 Soviet Polnocny-C class**   Bldr: Poland

ATIKA   GANDA   NOUH

D: 1,150 tons (fl)   S: 18 kts   Dim: 82.0 × 10.0 × 2.0
A: 4/30-mm AA (II × 2) — 2/122-mm rocket launchers (XL × 2)
M: 2 diesels; 2 props; 5,000 hp

REMARKS: Have a helicopter platform forward of the superstructure. Two transferred in 1977 and one in 1978.

VARIOUS SHIPS

◆ **4 Soviet Nyryat-2-class diving tenders**

D: 56 tons (fl)   S: 12 kts   Dim: 21.3 × 3.8 × 2.0
M: 1 3D12 diesel; 300 hp

REMARK: May also be used as tugs.

◆ **1 Soviet Pozharney-I-class fireboat**

D: 180 tons (fl)   S: 17 kts   Dim: 35.0 × 6.2 × 2.0
M: 2 diesels; 2 props; 1,800 hp

◆ **1 tug**   Bldr: Denmark, 1978

AKA

REMARKS: Design basically that of an oilfield-supply ship. A: 4/14.5-mm AA (II × 2)

CUSTOMS SERVICE

◆ **1 yacht used as a patrol boat**

AL THAWRA (1929)

D: 746 tons   S: 14 kts   M: Diesels; 2 props; 1,800 hp

◆ **8 pilot launches**   Bldr: Thornycroft, 1961-62

D: 10 tons   S: . . .   Dim: 11.0 × . . . × . . .
M: 1 diesel; 125 hp

◆ **4 pilot launches**   Bldr: Thornycroft

Dim: 6.4 × . . . × . . .   M: 40 hp

IRELAND
Eire

PERSONNEL: 866 officers and men

MERCHANT MARINE (1978): 110 ships — 212,143 grt (tankers: 3 ships — 3,989 grt)

FISHERIES-PROTECTION SHIPS

◆ **3 Emer class**   Bldr: Verolme, Cork

	L	In serv.
FP 21 EMER	-77	9-1-78
FP 22 AOIFE	12-78	6-79
FP 23 AISLING	3-10-79	. . .

FISHERIES-PROTECTION SHIPS (*continued*)

Emer—now has new number   1978

D: 1,020 tons (fl)   **S:** 18 kts   **Dim:** 65.2 (58.5 pp) × 10.4 × 4.36
Man: 5 officers, 41 men   **Range:** 4,500/18, 6,750/12
A: 1/40-mm AA−2/20-mm AA (I × 2)   **Fuel:** 170 tons
Electron Equipt: Radars: 2/Decca . . .   **Sonar:** Simrad side-scan
M: 2 SEMT-Pielstick 6 PA6L-280 diesels; 1 controllable-pitch prop; 4,800 hp

REMARKS: Developed version of the *Deirdre* with raised forecastle instead of bow bulwarks, to improve sea-keeping. Have advanced navigational aids, fin stabilizers. FP-
22 and FP-23 have satellite navigation receivers, a bow thruster, a computerized
plotting table, and a new-pattern Ka-Me-Wa propeller. Five larger units, with helicopter facilities, are planned.

◆ **1 Dierdre class**   Bldr: Verolme, Cork

	L	In serv.
FP 20 DEIRDRE	29-12-71	5-72

Deirdre   Batenian, 1972

D: 972 tons   **Dim:** 62.5 (56.2 pp) × 10.4 × 4.35
S: 18 kts (15.5 cruising)   **Man:** 5 officers, 41 men
Range: 3,000/15.5, 5,000/12
A: 1/40-mm AA−2/52-mm flare launchers   **Fuel:** 150 tons
M: 2 British Polar SF 112 VS-F diesels; 1 controllable-pitch prop; 4,200 hp

REMARK: Vosper fin stabilizers.

◆ **3 ex-British "-ton"-class minesweepers**

		Bldr	In ser.
CM 10	GRAINNE (ex-*Oulston*)	Thornycroft	1955
CM 11	BANBA (ex-*Alverton*)	Camper & Nicholson	1953
CM 12	FOLA (ex-*Blaxton*)	Thornycroft	1956

Grainne   1972

D: 370 tons (425 fl)   **S:** 15 kts   **Dim:** 46.33 (42.68 pp) × 8.76 × 2.5
Man: 33 men   **Range:** 2,300/13, 3,000/8
A: 1/40-mm AA−2/20-mm AA (II × 1)   **Fuel:** 45 tons
M: 2 Mirrlees or Napier Deltic diesels; 2 props; 2,500-3,000 hp

REMARK: Transferred in 1971. The portable sweep gear has been landed, but winches,
cable reels, and davits remain aboard.

MISCELLANEOUS SHIPS

◆ **1 training ship**   Bldr: Liffey, Dublin, 1953

A 15 SETANTA (ex-*Isolde*)

D: 1,173 tons (fl)   **S:** 11.5 kts   **Dim:** 63.5 × 11.6 × 4.0
A: 2/20-mm AA (I × 2)   **Man:** 44 men   **Range:** 3,500/10
M: Reciprocating steam; 2 props; 1,500 hp   **Fuel:** 276 tons

REMARK: Taken over in 1976 from the Irish Lighthouse Commission.

◆ **1 stores tender**   Bldr: R. Dunston, G.B., 1934

JOHN ADAMS

D: 94 grt   **S:** 10 kts   **Dim:** 25.9 × 5.6 × 2.1
M: 1 diesel; 216 hp

REMARK: The *Ferdia* (A-16), a former Danish trawler leased for Irish naval service,
was returned to her owners in 1978.

◆ **1 utility launch:** COLLEEN   **Dim:** 10.7 oa   **M:** 35 hp

◆ **1 stores lighter:** CHOWL   **D:** 100 tons   **M:** 50 hp

ISRAEL

PERSONNEL: Active: 3,500, of whom 250 officers and 500 men are especially trained as commandos and frogmen. In reserve: 500 men.

MERCHANT MARINE (1978): 55 ships—420,933 grt
(tankers: 2 ships—368 grt)

NAVAL AVIATION: During 1978 the Israeli Navy put into service three IAI Westwind 1124 Sea Scan maritime-reconnaissance aircraft, whose mission is to cooperate with surface forces.

SHIPS IN SERVICE OR UNDER CONSTRUCTION
AS OF 1 JANUARY 1980

	L	Tons (Surfaced)	Main armament
◆ **3 submarines**			
3 GERMAN TYPE 206	1975-76	420 Tons	8/533-mm TT
◆ **22 (+4) guided-missile patrol boats**			
0 (+2) SUPER FLAGSTAFF 1980		71	Gabriel and Harpoon missile systems, 2/30-mm
10 (+2) RESHEV	1973-79	415	Gabriel and Harpoon missile systems, 2/76-mm
12 SA'AR II and III	1967-69	220	Gabriel and Harpoon missile systems, 1/40-mm or 1/76-mm
◆ **53 or more patrol craft**			

WEAPONS AND SYSTEMS

Triple trainable Gabriel missile launcher

The Israeli Navy uses foreign equipment such as 76-mm OTO Melara Compact, Breda 40-mm, and Oerlikon guns, and it has perfected the Gabriel anti-ship missile system.

Gabriel is a 400-kg, solid-propellant, surface-to-surface missile. After being fired, it climbs about 100 meters, then, at 7,500 meters from the launcher, descends slowly to an altitude of 20 meters. Optical or radar guidance is provided in azimuth, and a radio altimeter determines altitude. At a distance of 1,200 meters from the target, the missile descends to 3 meters, under either radio command or semi-active homing. The explosive charge is a 75-kg conventional warhead. In the Yom Kippur War of 1973, 85 per cent of the Gabriel missiles fired reached their targets.

Chaff launchers on a Reshev-class guided-missile patrol boat   1975

WEAPONS AND SYSTEMS (*continued*)

In order to have an even more effective surface-to-surface missile on the international market, the Israeli Navy has introduced the Gabriel II. This missile carries a television camera and a transceiver for azimuth and altitude commands. The television is energized when the missile has attained a certain height and sends to the firing ship a picture of the areas that cannot be picked up by shipboard radar. The operator then can send any necessary corrections during the middle and final phases of the missile's flight, and thus find a target that cannot be seen either by the naked eye or on radar. The range of the Gabriel II is about 40,000 meters. The need to increase the range of the Gabriel is one of the lessons the Israeli learned from the Yom Kippur War.

The U.S. Harpoon was acquired beginning in 1978 and is used on guided-missile patrol boats in a mix with Gabriel.

SUBMARINES

◆ **3 German Type 206**   Bldr: Vickers, Barrow, G.B.

GAL   TANNIN   RAHAV

D: 420 tons surfaced, 600 submerged   **S:** 17/11 kts
Dim: 45.0 × 4.7 × 3.8   **Man:** 22 men   **A:** 8/533-mm TT, fwd
M: 2 MTU 12V-493-TY60 diesels (600 hp each); AEG generators; 1 prop; 1,800 hp

REMARKS: Ordered in 4-72. The *Gal* in service 12-76, the *Tannin* in 6-77, and the *Rahav* in 1978. Carry two spare torpedoes. The first unit ran aground on delivery voyage, but has been repaired.

Israeli Type-206 unit   1977

GUIDED-MISSILE CORVETTES

◆ **Sa'ar class**   Bldr: Israeli SY, Haifa

D: 850 tons (fl)   **S:** 40 kts   **Dim:** 77.1 × 9.1 × 3.04
A: 8/Harpoon SSM (IV × 2)—2/76-mm DP OTO Melara (I × 2)—4/30-mm AA Emerlec (II × 2)—1/short-range SAM system—1 helicopter   **Man:** 45 men

M: CODAG: 1 GE LM-2500 gas turbine, 20,000-25,000 hp; 2 MTU diesels, 8,000 hp; 2 props

REMARKS: This design is a project offered by the shipyard but not yet ordered by the Israeli Navy. The helicopter would provide over-the-horizon target data for the Harpoon.

GUIDED-MISSILE PATROL BOATS

◆ **2 Super Flagstaff-class hydrofoils**

		In serv.
N . . .	Grumman, Bethpage, L.I.	7-80
N . . .	Israeli SY, Haifa	1980

D: 71 tons (94 fl)   **S:** 50 kts   **Dim:** 25.74 × 7.3 × . . .
Range: 900/48   **Fuel:** 16 tons
A: 4/Harpoon SSM (II × 2)—2/Gabriel SSM (I × 2)—2/30-mm Emerlec (II × 1)
M: 1 Allison 501KE diesel; 5,400 hp—2 auxiliary propulsion diesels; 260 hp

REMARKS: Ordered in 1978. The hull for the Grumman unit was subcontracted to Lautana Boatyard, Jacksonville, Florida. If successful, as many as ten more may be built at the Israeli Shipyard, Haifa.

◆ **12 Reshev (Sa'ar-IV) class**   Bldr: Israeli SY, Haifa

	L	In serv.		L	In serv.
RESHEV	19-2-73	4-73	NITZAHON	10-7-78	9-78
KESHET	23-8-73	10-73	HATZMAAT	3-12-78	2-79
ROMACH	1-74	3-74	MOLEDET	22-3-79	5-79
KIDON	7-74	9-74	KOMEMIYUT	19-7-79	. . .
TARSHISH	1-75	3-75	N . . .	6-80	. . .
YAFO	2-75	4-75	N . . .	10-80	. . .

Yafo—with four Harpoon, four Gabriel   1978

D: 415 tons (450 fl)   **S:** 32 kts   **Dim:** 58.1 × 7.6 × 2.4
Man: 45 men   **Range:** 1,500/30, 4,000/17
A: 4/Harpoon SSM (II × 2)—4/Gabriel SSM (I × 4)—2/76-mm OTO Melara Compact (I × 2)—2/20-mm AA (I × 2)—2/12.7-mm machine guns—4 large and 72 small chaff launchers

GUIDED-MISSILE PATROL BOATS (*continued*)

Yafo 1975

Keshet—with seven Gabriel 1974

Electron Equipt: Radars: 1/Thomson CSF Neptune, 1/Selenia Orion
VHFD/F and intercept gear
M: 4 MTU MD871 diesels; 4 props; 14,000 hp

REMARKS: Quarters are air-conditioned. Can launch chaff for long-distance cluttering of radar screens. The *Tarshish* has carried a temporary helicopter deck in place of the after 76-mm gun for experiment with over-the-horizon targeting for Harpoon. Original missile armament was seven Gabriel. The Gabriel launchers are fixed. The 76-mm guns have been specially adapted for shore bombardment. Three have been built for the Republic of South Africa and three more are building at Durban.

◆ 6 Sa'ar III class

	L		L
SA'AR	25-11-69	HEREV	20-6-69
SOUFA	4-2-69	HANIT	1969
GAASCH	24-6-69	HETZ	14-12-69

◆ 6 Sa'ar II class

Bldr: Constr. Méc. de Normandie, Cherbourg

	L		L
MIVTACH	11-4-67	EILATH	14-6-68
MIZNAG	1967	HAIFA	14-6-68
MIFGAV	1967	AKKO	1968

Sa'ar-II type—now 40-mm aft in place of triple Gabriel 1970

Miznag 1978

GUIDED-MISSILE PATROL BOATS (*continued*)

Sa'ar-III type

D: 220 tons (250 fl)   S: 40 kts   Dim: 45.0 × 7.0 × 1.8 (2.5 fl)
Man: 5 officers, 30-35 men   Range: 1,000/30, 1,600/20, 2,500/15
A: Sa'ar II: 5/Gabriel SSM (III × 1, I × 2) – 2/40-mm AA Breda (I × 2) – 2/12.7-mm machine guns
     Sa'ar III: 2/Harpoon SSM (I × 2) – 3/Gabriel SSM (III × 1) – 1/76-mm DP OTO Melara – 2/12.7-mm machine guns
Electron Equipt: Radars: 1/Thomson CSF Neptune, 1/Selenia Orion VHFD/F and intercept gear
M: 4 MTU MD871 diesels; 4 props; 14,000 hp   Fuel: 30 tons

REMARKS: Excellent sea qualities and endurance. *Sa'ar I* is the name that was used for these ships in an all-gun configuration. The after 40-mm gun on the *Sa'ar II* version can be removed and two single U.S. 324-mm Mk-32 ASW TT substituted at the stern. An ELAC searchlight sonar is carried. *Sa'ar III* has no ASW capability. Armaments now fairly standardized, but triple Gabriel launchers can be interchanged with the after 40-mm mountings.

PATROL CRAFT

◆ **1 Dvora class** Bldr: Israeli Aircraft Industries, 1978

D: 47 tons (fl)   S: 36 kts   Dim: 21.62 × 5.49 × 0.94 (1.82 props)
Man: 8-10 men   Range: 700/32   Electric: 30 kw
A: 2/20-mm AA (I × 2) – 2/12.7-mm machine guns
Electron Equipt: Radar: Decca 926
M: 2 MTU 12V331 TC81 diesels; 2 props; 2,720 hp

REMARKS: Privately funded prototype, acquired in 1979 to begin replacing the Coast Guard's four "Wind"-class patrol boats. The design has been offered with two Gabriel SSM, and has been exported to Nicaragua.

◆ **25 Dabur class** Bldrs: 12 by Sewart Seacraft, U.S.A.; others by Israeli Air Industries, 1973-77

D: 25 tons (35 fl)   S: 25 kts   Dim: 19.8 × 5.8 × 0.8
Man: 1 officer, 5 men   Range: 1,200/17
A: 2/20-mm (I × 2) – 2/12.7-mm machine guns (I × 2)

Dabur class   1978

Electron Equipt: Radar: Decca 926   M: 2 GM diesels; 2 props; 960 hp

REMARKS: Quarters air-conditioned and spacious. Five given to Lebanon in 1976. Examples exported to Argentina and Nicaragua.

◆ **up to 28 Yatush class (U.S. PBR type)**

D: 6.5 tons   S: 25 kts   Dim: 9.8 × 3.4 × 0.8
A: 2 machine guns   Man: 5 men   M: 2 diesels; water jets

REMARKS: Early units bought in the United States in 1968, later ones built in Israel. Several may be stationed in the Red Sea. Two given to Lebanon, 1975-76.

AMPHIBIOUS WARFARE SHIPS

◆ Bat Sheva

Bat Sheva   1969

D: 900 tons (1,150 fl)   S: 10 kts   Dim: 95.1 × 11.2 × . . .
A: 4/20-mm – 4/12.7-mm machine guns   Man: 26 men
M: Diesels; 2 props

REMARK: Built in Germany in 1967 and bought in South Africa in 1968.

◆ **3 LCT type**

61 Ashdod   63 Ashkelon   65 Ahziv Bldr: Israeli SY, Haifa, 1966-67

ISRAEL (continued)
AMPHIBIOUS WARFARE SHIPS (continued)

Ashdod   1971

D: 400 tons (730 fl)   **S:** 10.5 kts   **Dim:** 62.7 × 10.0 × 1.8
A: 2/20-mm AA (I × 2)   **Man:** 20 men   **Fuel:** 37 tons
M: 3 MWM diesels; 3 props; 1,900 hp

51 ETZION GUEBER   53 SHIKMONA   55 . . .
     Bldr: Israeli SY, Haifa, 1965

Etzion Gueber

D: 182 tons (230 fl)   **S:** 10 kts   **Dim:** 30.5 × 5.9 × 1.3
A: 2/20-mm AA (I × 2)   **Man:** 10 men   **M:** Diesels; 2 props; 1,280 hp

◆ **3 ex-U.S. LSM-1 class**
N . . .   N . . .   N . . .
D: 1,095 tons (fl)   **S:** 12.5 kts   **Dim:** 62.1 × 10.5 × 2.2
A: 1/20-mm AA—several machine guns   **M:** 2 GM diesels; 2 props; 2,800 hp

REMARK: Built 1944-45 and bought in 1972.

VARIOUS SHIPS

BAT YAM

REMARKS: Small cargo ship fitted out as a transport and based at Eilath. Former Dutch
     motorized barge, refitted in Israel in 1967.

NOGAH

REMARK: Former small cargo vessel equipped as a training ship for the merchant
     marine.

NAHARYA

REMARK: Base craft for the missile craft stationed at Eilath.

MA'OZ

REMARKS: 4,000-ton oilfield-supply type used as a missile-boat tender in the Mediterra-
     ranean. Built by Todd, Seattle, 1976. Acquisition of U.S. 65D-13, *Casa Grande*, was
     superseded by the purchase of this ship.

ITALY

PERSONNEL (1978): 42,000, including 5,200 officers

MERCHANT MARINE (1978): 1,684 ships; 11,491,873 grt
                   (tankers: 289 ships; 4,874,279 grt)

NAVAL AVIATION: Fixed-wing ASW aircraft belong to the Air Force, which puts them
at the disposal of the Navy. For some time, American two-engined S-2 Trackers were
the primary planes in use but, following a contract entered into in October 1968, the
BR-1150 Atlantic became the principal type, the last 18 units being delivered in 1973.
One squadron of eight S-2F Trackers remains in service.
     Helicopters, of which there are 82, are under the control of the Navy. They are used
mainly for ASW, but can also be used in an anti-ship role; they can carry such missiles
as the AS-12. For antisubmarine warfare, the Italian Navy originally favored a light,
weapon-carrying helicopter working in combination with another helicopter of the
same size equipped with ASW sensors. Because this limits the ships that can partici-
pate in ASW operations to those that are fitted to carry both types of helicopter,
future orientation in ASW operations appears to be towards the use of a heavier helicopter (SH-3D) that carries both weapons and sensors. These helicopters, 24 of which
have been acquired, may be based ashore or on such ships as can handle them (*Giu-
seppe Garibaldi*, *Vittorio Veneto*, the two *Andrea Doria*-class cruisers, and the two
Audace-class destroyers). There are 30 AB-204B and 28 AB-212 light ASW helicopters
in service.

     The Bell AB-204B and AB-212 are built under American license by Agusta in Italy.
Principal characteristics are:

AB-204B
   Ceiling: 10,800 ft
   Range: 2 hr 5 min without torpedoes
          1 hr 15 min with torpedoes
   Armament: 2 Mk 44 or Mk 46 torpedoes or 4 AS-12
   Electronics: ASQ-13 sonar
   Crew: 3

Length: 17.4 m
Rotor: 14.6 m
Max. weight: 4,310 kg
Motor: 1 turboshaft, 1,200 hp
Max. speed: 104 kts
Cruising speed: 90 kts

AB-212

Ceiling: 5,000 ft
Range: 4 hr 15 min (360 n.m.)
Armament: 2 Mk 44 or Mk 46 torpedoes, depth
charges, or 4 AS-12 ASM
Electronics: ASQ-13B sonar
Crew: 3

Length: 17.2 m
Rotor: 17.4 m
Max. weight: 5,081 kg
Motor: 1 turboshaft, 1,290
hp
Max. speed: 106 kts
Cruising speed: 90 kts

WARSHIPS IN SERVICE, UNDER CONSTRUCTION, OR AUTHORIZED AS OF 1 JANUARY 1980

	L	Tons	Main armament
◆ 0 (+1) VTOL carrier			
GIUSEPPE GARIBALDI	. . .	10,043	4/Otomat, 2/Albatros, 12/helicopters and VTOL aircraft
		Tons (surfaced)	
◆ 10 (+2) submarines			
2 (+2) NAZARIO SAURO	1976-. . .	1,456	6/533-mm TT
4 ENRICO TOTI	1967-68	535	4/533-mm TT
2 TANG	1951	2,100	8/533-mm TT
2 GUPPY III	1944-46	1,975	10/533-mm TT
◆ 3 cruisers		**Tons**	
1 VITTORIO VENETO	1967	7,500	1/missile launcher, 8/76-mm, 9/helicopters
2 ANDREA DORIA	1962-63	6,500	1/missile launcher, 8/76-mm, 4/helicopters
◆ 6 destroyers			
2 AUDACE	1971	3,950	1/missile launcher, 2/127-mm, ASW weapons
2 IMPAVIDO	1962	3,201	1/missile launcher, 2/127-mm, ASW weapons
2 IMPETUOSO	1955-56	2,775	4/127-mm, ASW weapons
◆ 22 (+6) frigates and corvettes			
0 (+6) MAESTRALE	1979-. . .	3,040	4/Otomat, 1/Sea Sparrow, 1/127-mm, ASW weapons
4 LUPO	1976-79	2,208	8/Otomat, 1/Sea Sparrow, 1/127-mm, ASW weapons
2 ALPINO	1967	2,000	6/76-mm, ASW weapons
4 CARLO BERGAMINI	1960	1,410	2/76-mm, ASW weapons
4 CANOPO	1954-56	1,807	3/76-mm, ASW weapons
4 PIETRO DE CRISTOFARO	1964-65	850	2/76-mm, ASW weapons
4 ALBATROS	1954	800	2/40-mm, ASW weapons

WEAPONS AND SYSTEMS

A. MISSILES

◆ Surface-to-air

American Terrier, Tartar, SM1, and SM1-MR (*see* under U.S.A.)

Albatros Aspide (Italian version of the Sea Sparrow) Bldr: Selenia

Ceiling: 15 m (min.); 5,000 m (max.)
Length: 3.7 m   Diameter: 0.2 m
Wingspan: 1.02 m   Weight: 204 kg
Range: 10,000 m   Guidance: semi-active homing
This equipment employs an octuple launcher built by OTO Melara and weighing 7 tons; elevation: 5 to +65 degrees. Controlled by NA-22 system.

◆ Surface-to-surface

Otomat Mk 1 Bldr: OTO Melara/Matra

Length: 4,820 m   Diameter: 1,060 m (with boosters); 460 m (without boosters)
Wingspan: 1.19 m   Weight: 750 kg
Range: 60-80 km   Guidance: Thomson/CSF active homing
This missile flies almost at sea level after firing, climbs at a steep angle to a predetermined height, and strikes its target during descent.

Otomat Mk 2 (also known as Teseo)

This model differs from the Mk 1 in having an Italian (SMA) active radar homing head, instead of a French one. It is also a "sea-skimmer": that is, it flies close to the water after firing. Its explosive charge is about 200 kg, and its ramjet propulsion system allows it to be used at ranges limited only by its guidance system and its target designation.

◆ Air-to-surface

The French SNIAS AS-12 wire-guided anti-shipping missile has been adopted for use by helicopters.

B. GUNS

With the exception of some old American guns, such as the 127-mm twin-barreled 38-caliber semi-automatic, the following Italian systems are used.

40-mm Breda/Betors Compact

Length: 70 calibers
Muzzle velocity: . . .
Max. effective range, anti-aircraft fire: 3,500-4,00 m
Rate of fire: 300 rounds/min/barrel
Projectile weight: 0.96 kg
Number of ready-service rounds: 444 or 736 (depending on installation)
Fire control: Dardo system
Impact or proximity fusing

76-mm

Single- or twin-barreled, automatic, air, surface, and land targets

Length: 62 calibers
Muzzle velocity: 850 m/sec
Max. effective range, surface fire: 8,000 m
Max. effective range, anti-aircraft fire: 4,000-5,000 m
Rate of fire: 60 rounds/min/barrel

WEAPONS AND SYSTEMS (*continued*)

76-mm OTO Melara Compact

Single-barreled light anti-aircraft automatic fire; entirely remote control with muzzle brake and cooling system

Length: 62 calibers
Muzzle velocity: 925 m/sec
Max. effective range, surface fire: 8,000 m
Max. effective range, anti-aircraft fire: 4,000-5,000 m
Rate of fire: 85 rounds/min
Weight of mount: 7.35 tons, because of the use of light alloys and fiberglass; 80 ready-service rounds in the drum, which permits at least 1 minute of fire before reloading. There are no personnel in the mount; the ammunition-handlers in the magazine have only to feed the drum.
The gun has been purchased by many navies.

127-mm OTO Melara Compact

Single-barreled automatic, triple-purpose, remote control

Length: 54 calibers
Muzzle velocity: 808 m/sec
Max. effective range, surface fire: 15,000 m
Max. effective range, anti-aircraft fire: 7,000 m
Rate of fire: 45 rounds/min, automatic setting
Weight of the mount: 32 tons because of the use of light alloys and a fiberglass shield. The gun has a muzzle brake; it can automatically fire 66 rounds, thanks to 3 loading drums, each with 22 rounds. Two hoists serve two loading trays with rounds coming from the magazine, and a drum may be loaded even while the gun is firing. An automatic selection system allows a choice of ammunition (anti-aircraft, surface target, pyrotechnics, chaff for cluttering radar).
This equipment has also been purchased by the Canadian Navy for its *Iroquois*-class destroyers.

C. ANTISUBMARINE WEAPONS

Menon triple-barreled mortar

The system has a launcher carrying three 4.6-mm barrels. These tubes fire a 160-kg projectile at a fixed elevation of 45 degrees. The range (400 to 900 m) is reached by varying the quantity of gas admitted into the tubes from three powder chambers. The tubes are reloaded at a 90-degree elevation from a drum containing the depth charge projectiles.

Menon single-barreled mortar

The system has a single barrel with automatic loading. Fire control is usually directed in the underwater battery plot. The mortar is fired at a 45-degree angle with the range fixed by a system similar to that of the triple-barreled Menon; firing 160-kg depth-charges round by round; the gas relief valves have adjustable vents. The weapon is automatically reloaded from the magazine by hoist and a loading drum.

Torpedoes

American Mk 44 and Mk 46 torpedoes are used on ships (using the triple Mk 32 tube mount) and helicopters.
The Whitehead Moto Fides A-184 wire-guided torpedo is now in use, with a 533-mm carrier torpedo that ejects a Mk 46 passive homing torpedo; range is over 15,000 m. A replacement for Mk 46, A-244, is in development.

D. RADARS

The Italian Navy uses a number of American radars (SPS-6, SPS-39, SPS-52, etc.) but also uses a number of systems developed in Italy, including:

Type	Band	Remarks
Orion RTN-10X	I/J	Gun and missile fire control (Argo system)
RTN-20	I/J	With Dardo system (40-mm gun)
SPQ-2D	I/J	Combined surveillance
RAN-3L	D	Air search
RAN-10S	E/J	Combined surveillance
RAN-205	E/F	Three-dimensional
RTN-30X	I/J	Target acquisition (albatros system)
3 RM series	I/J	Navigation and surface search for small combatants

E. SONARS

Most of the newest equipment is American or Dutch.

	Type	Frequency		Type	Frequency
SQS 23	Hull	MF	SQS 4	Hull	MF
SQS 29	Hull	MF	SQA 10	Towed	MF
SQS 11A	Hull	MF	SQS 36	Towed	HF
SQS 10	Hull	MF	CWE 610	Hull	LF (Dutch)

F. TACTICAL INFORMATION SYSTEM

The Italian Navy has perfected the SADOC system, which is compatible with the American NTDS and the French SENIT. The Breda SCLAR chaff-rocket-launching system is widely used; it employs 20 105-mm rockets in a trainable/elevatable launcher controlled by the computer system.

HELICOPTER CARRIER

♦ 1 Garibaldi class

		Laid down	L	In serv.
		Bldr		
C 551 GARIBALDI	Italcantieri, Monfalcone	11-80	. . .	1984

D: 10,043 tons (13,250 fl)   **S:** 29 kts
Dim: 180.2 (162.8 pp) × 30.4 (23.8 wl) × 6.7
A: 4/Otomat Mk 2 Teseo SSM (I × 4)−2/Albatros SAM (VIII × 2)−6/40-mm AA Breda Compact (II × 3) with Dardo control system−6/324-mm Mk 32 ASW TT (III × 2)−12/SH-3D Sea King helicopters
Electron Equipt: Radars: 1/RAN-3L air search, 1/RAN-205 3D, 1/RAN-105 combined search, 1/SPS-702 surface search, 1/SPS-703 navigational−TACAN
Sonars: SQS-23−2/SCLAR chaff launchers (XX × 2)
Electric: 6,240 kw (4 GMT A230-12M diesel alternator sets)
Range: 7,000/20   **Man:**   560 men (accommodations for 825 men)
M: 4 GE/Fiat LM 2500 gas turbines; 2 controllable-pitch props; 80,000 hp

REMARKS: The *Garibaldi* is essentially an ASW ship for helicopters, although the design permits the handling of V/STOL aircraft as well. The flight deck is 173.8 meters long. There are to be two elevators, one forward of and one abaft the island. There are six flight deck spaces for flight operations. The hangar (110 × 15 × 6 meters) can accommodate 12 Sea King, or 10 Sea Harrier and 1 Sea King, although political considerations have precluded acquisition of the "offensive" Sea Harrier for the present. Steel superstructure and hull. To permit helicopter operations in heavy weather, much

HELICOPTER CARRIER (*continued*)

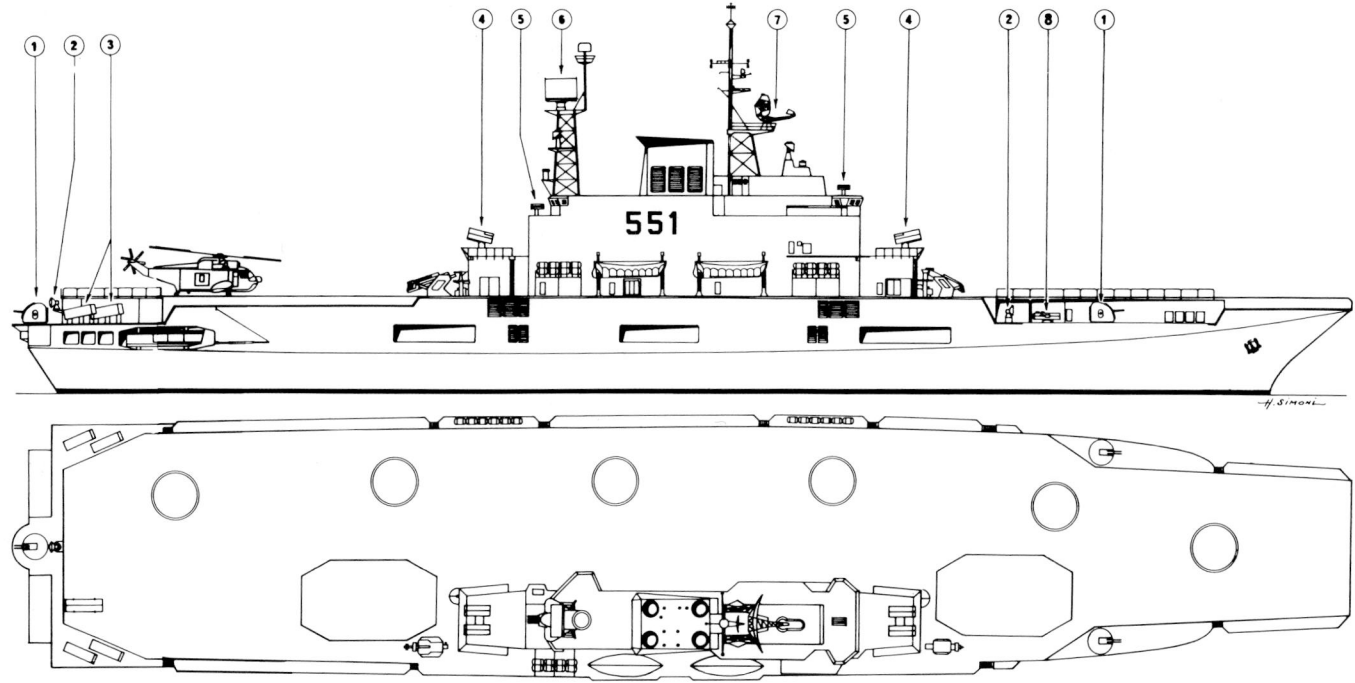

551

1. Twin 40-mm AA 2. RTN-20X Dardo fire-control system 3. Teseo SSM launchers
4. Albatros launchers for Aspide SAM 5. SCLAR chaff rocket launchers 6. RAN-205
3-D radar antenna 7. RAN-3L air-search radar antenna 8. Triple Mk 32 ASW TT
Scale: 1/1,000

attention was given to stability, and the ship has two pairs of fin stabilizers. There are five decks: the flight deck; the hangar deck, which is also the main deck; and two decks and a platform deck below the hangar deck. Thirteen watertight bulkheads divide the ship into fourteen sections. The island has four levels. The design of the ship, her armament, and her equipment might be modified during construction. The *Garibaldi* appears, on paper at least, to be better designed than the British *Invincible* class.

SUBMARINES

◆ **4 Nazario Sauro class** Bldr: C.R.D.A., Monfalcone

	Laid down	L	In serv.
S 518 NAZARIO SAURO	15-7-74	9-10-76	1979
S 519 CARLO FECIA DI COSSATO	15-11-75	16-11-77	1980
S 520 GUGLIELMO MARCONI	1978	. . .	. . .
S 521 LEONARDO DA VINCI	1978	12-10-79	. . .

D: 1,456 tons (surfaced), 1,641 tons (submerged)   **S:** 12/20 kts
Dim: 63.85 × 6.83 × 5.7   **Man:** 45 men   **Fuel:** 144 tons

Nazario Sauro—on trials   1978

SUBMARINES (continued)

A: 6/533-mm TT (6 reloads)
Electron Equipt: Radars: RM-20/SMG
Sonars: USEA/Selenia IPD-70 system, Velox M5
Range: 12,500/4 (snorkel), 7,000/12 **Endurance:** 45 days
M: 3 GMT A210 16M diesels (2,160 kw), electric drive; 1 prop; 4,000 hp

REMARKS: Can travel 20 knots submerged for 1 hour, or 100 hours at 4 knots. Maximum diving depth is 250 meters. All 12 torpedoes are of the A-184 type. Seven-bladed propeller. Second pair approved 1977.

◆ **4 Enrico Toti class** Bldr: C.R.D.A., Monfalcone

	Laid down	L	In serv.
S 505 ATTILIO BAGNOLINI	15-4-65	26-8-67	16-6-68
S 506 ENRICO TOTI	15-4-65	12-3-67	22-1-68
S 513 ENRICO DANDOLO	10-3-67	16-12-67	25-9-68
S 514 LAZZARO MOCENIGO	12-6-67	20-4-68	11-1-69

Enrico Dandolo   C. Martinelli, 1976

Enrico Toti   1978

D: 535 tons (surfaced) 591 (submerged)   **Dim:** 46.2 × 4.7 × 3.99
S: 14/20 kts   **Man:** 4 officers, 22 men
A: 4/533-mm TT (6 torpedoes)   **Range:** 7,500/4.5 (surfaced), 180/4 (submerged)
Electron Equipt: Radar: 1/3 RM 20/SMG   Sonar: Passive and active
M: Diesel-electric propulsion; 2 Fiat/MB 820 diesels; 1 electric motor; 1 prop; 2,200 hp

◆ **2 U.S. Tang class** Bldr: Electric Boat

	Laid down	L	In serv.
S 515 LIVIO PIOMARTA (ex-*Trigger*, SS-564)	24-2-49	14-6-51	31-3-52
S 516 ROMEO ROMEI (ex-*Harder*, SS-568)	30-6-50	3-12-51	19-8-52

Romeo Romei   G. Arra, 1976

D: 2,100 tons (surfaced), 2,700 (submerged)   **S:** 20/17 kts
Dim: 87.5 × 8.3 × 6.2   **A:** 8/533-mm TT (6 fwd, 2 aft)
Electron Equipt: Sonars: BQR-3, BQR-4   **Man:** 8 officers, 73 men
M: Diesel-electric propulsion: 3 Fairbanks-Morse 38ND8⅛ diesels; 2 props; 5,600 hp

REMARKS: The S-515 was transferred to Italy on 10-7-73; S-516 on 20-2-74. Both ships have BQR-2 "PUFFS" passive ranging sonar.

◆ **2 U.S. Guppy-III class**

	Bldr	Laid down	L	In serv.
S 502 GIANFRANCO GAZZANA PRIAROGGIA (ex-*Volador*, SS-490)	Portsmouth NSY	15-6-45	17-1-46	10-1-48
S 501 PRIMO LONGOBARDO (ex-*Pickerel*, SS-524)	Boston NSY	8-2-44	15-12-44	4-9-49

Gianfranco Gazzana Priaroggia   G. Arra, 1978

SUBMARINES (*continued*)

D: 1,650 tons, 1,975 (surfaced), 2,540 (submerged)   **S:** 20/13-15 kts
Dim: 99.4 × 8.2 × 5.2   **Man:** 86 men   **Range:** 10,000/10
A: 10/533-mm TT (6 fwd, 4 aft)   **Electron Equipt:** Sonar: BQR-2 PUFFS
M: 4 Fairbanks-Morse 38ND8⅛ diesels, 2 electric motors; 6,400/5,200 hp

REMARKS: Originally *Balao*-class submarines. Underwent FRAM II modernization in 1961-63: a 1.5-meter compartment was added to the sail to make room for an "attack center" operations area, and a 3.5-meter battery compartment was added. Two 126-cell batteries. Both transferred to Italy on 18-8-72.

CRUISERS

◆ **1 Vittorio Veneto class**

	Bldr	Laid down	L	In serv.
C 550 VITTORIO VENETO	Nav. Mec. Castellammare	10-6-65	5-2-67	12-7-69

D: 7,500 tons (9,500 fl)   **Dim:** 179.6 (170.61 pp) × 19.4 × 6.0
S: 30.5 kts   **Range:** 3,000/28, 6,000/20   **Man:** 72 officers, 493 men
A: 1/Mk 20 Mod 7 Aster launch system (Asroc and Standard) − 8/76-mm OTO Melara AA − 6/324-mm Mk 32 TT (III × 2) − 9/AB-204B or AB-212 or 4 SH-3D ASW helicopters
Electron Equipt: Radars: 1/SPS-40, 1/SPS-52, 1/SPQ-2B, 1/3RM-7, 2/SPG-55B, 4/RTN-10X (Argo systems) − URN-20A TACAN
     Sonars: SQS-23 − ECM: 2/SCLAR chaff launchers (XX × 2)
Fuel: 1,200 tons   **Electric:** . . .
Boilers: 4 Foster-Wheeler, 43 kg/cm² pressure − superheat 450°C
M: 2 sets Tosi GT; 2 props; 73,000 hp

REMARKS: The flight deck (40 × 18.5) is on the stern and is served from a hangar immediately below by two elevators (18 × 5.3). The hangar (27.5 × 15.3) is two decks in depth. When carrying SH-3 helicopters, none will fit into the hangar. Very extensive, stabilized intercept arrays. Eight Teseo SSMs are to be installed on this ship. Anti-rolling stabilizers. The Aster system can launch either Asroc ASW or Standard SAM and has a total capacity of 60 missiles on three magazine drums.

Vittorio Veneto   1977

Vittorio Veneto   1977

◆ **2 Andrea Doria class**

	Bldr	Laid down	L	In serv.
C 553 ANDREA DORIA	C. Nav. Tirreno, Riva Trigoso	5-58	27-2-63	2-64
C 554 CAIO DUILIO	Nav. Mec. Castellammare	5-58	22-12-62	4-64

D: 6,500 tons (7,300 fl)   **S:** 30 kts
Dim: 149.3 (144 pp) × 17.25 × 4.96 (7.5 fl)
A: 1/Mk 10 launcher (40 standard SM1-ER) − 8/76-mm AA (I × 8) − 6/324-mm Mk 32 ASW TT (III × 2) − 4/AB-204B helicopters
Electron Equipt: Radars: 1/SPS-40 (1/RAN-3L on 553), 1/SPQ-2, 1/SPS-52, 2/SPG-55C, 4/RTN-10X (Argo systems) − 1/URN-20A TACAN
     Sonars: SQS-23 − ECM: 2/SCLAR chaff launchers (XX × 2)
Range: 6,000/15   **Man:** 54 officers, 460 men

Andrea Doria   G. Arra, 1978

CRUISERS (*continued*)

Andrea Doria   G. Arra, 1976

Andrea Doria   G. Arra, 1976

Fuel: 1,100 tons   **Electric:** 4,700 kw
Boilers: 4 Foster-Wheeler, 43 kg/cm² pressure – superheat 450°C
M: GT; 2 props; 60,000 hp

REMARKS: The flight deck is 30 × 16 meters. Hangar on main deck. Anti-rolling stabilizers. The engineering spaces are divided into two groups, forward and aft: each has
a boiler room with two boilers and a turbine compartment separated by living spaces.
In each turbine space are two 1,000-kw turbo-alternators; there are also two 350-kw
emergency diesel alternators. The engineering groups are automatic and remote-
controlled.

C-554 was refitted in the mid-1970s with SPS-40 and SPS-52 radars, and Standard
SM1-ER SAM missiles. C-553 is currently being refitted with 8 Teseo SSM (I × 8),
an Albatros SAM system (VIII × 1, Aspide missiles), SADOC computerized tactical
data system, and Standard SM1 and SM1-MR missiles. Both will be brought to the
same standard but are expected to be stricken when *Garibaldi* is completed in the
mid-1980s.

CRUISERS (continued)

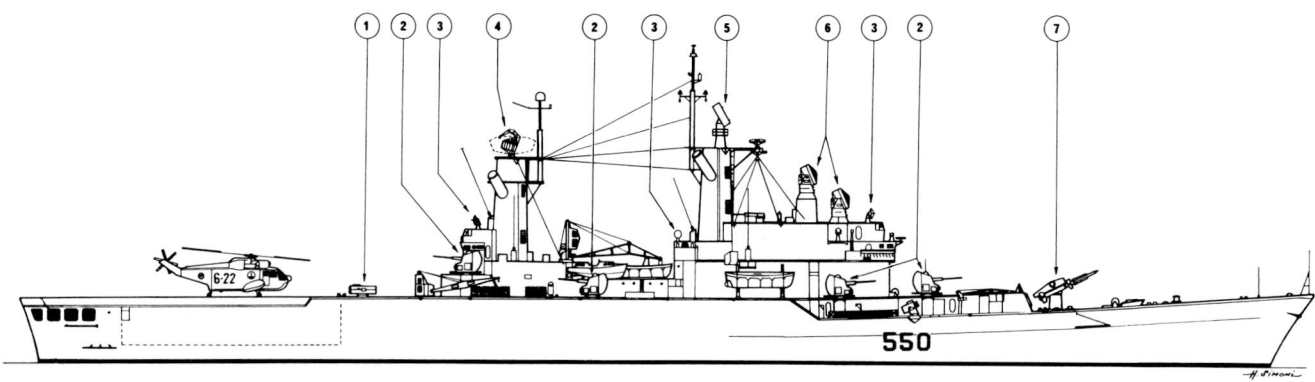

Vittorio Veneto 1. Mk 32 ASW TT 2. 76-mm DP 3. Argo fire-control radar 4. SPS-40 radar 5. SPG-52 radar 6. SPG-55 radar 7. Mk 10 mod 7 missile launcher Note: The radar above the after stack is an SPS-40

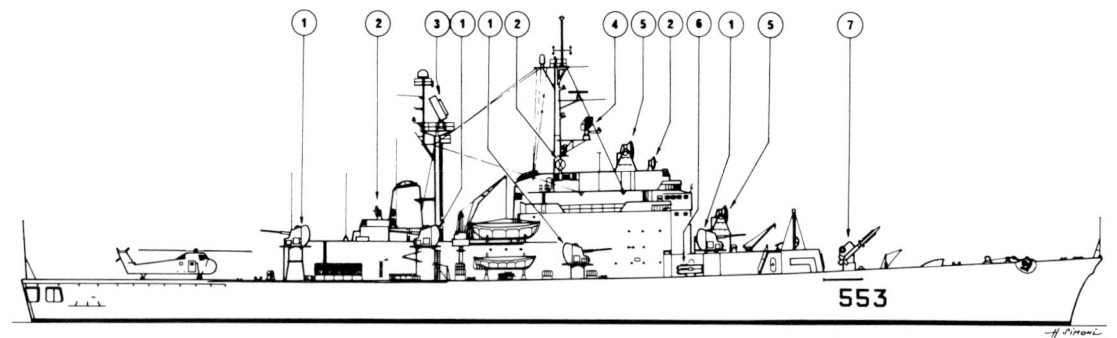

Andrea Doria 1. 76-mm DP 2. Argo fire-control radar 3. SPS-52 radar 4. RAN-3L radar 6. Mk 32 ASW TT 7. Mk 10 missile launcher

GUIDED-MISSILE DESTROYERS

◆ **2 Audace class**

	Bldr	Laid down	L	In serv.
D 550 ARDITO	Nav. Mec. Castellammare	19-7-68	27-11-71	5-12-73
D 551 AUDACE	C. Nav. del Tirreno	27-4-68	2-10-71	16-11-72

D: 3,950 tons (4,559 fl) **S:** 33/34 kts **Dim:** 136.6 × 14.23 × 4.6 (avg)

A: 1/Mk 13 missile launcher aft (40 Standard SM-1)−2/127-mm OTO Melara Compact (I × 2)−4/76-mm AA OTO Melara Compact (I × 4)−6/324-mm Mk 32 ASW TT (III × 2)−4/single TT for AS-184 wire-guided torpedoes−2/AB-204B or AB-212 or 1/SH-3D Sea King ASW helicopter

Electron Equipt: Radars: 1/SPS-12, 1/SPQ-2, 1/SPS-52, 2/SPG-51B, 3/RTN-10X (Argo systems)

Sonars: CWE 610−ECM: 2/SCLAR chaff launchers (XX × 2)

Audace J. C. Bellonne, 1975

GUIDED-MISSILE DESTROYERS (*continued*)

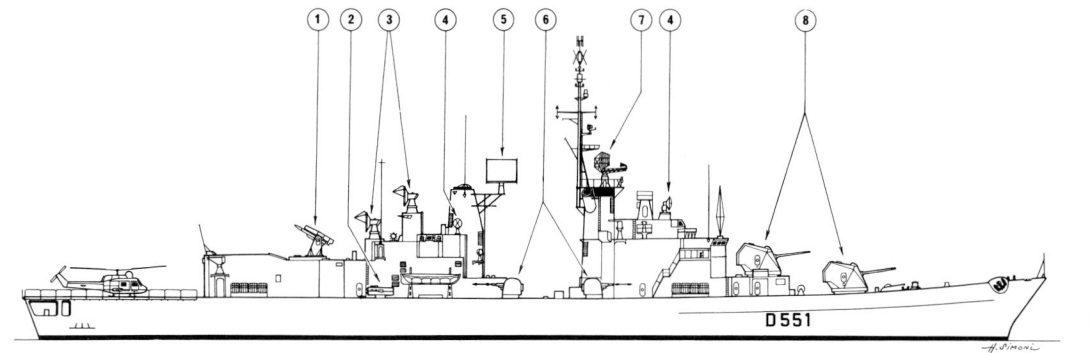

Audace 1. Mk 13 launcher 2. Mk 32 ASW TT 3. SPG-51B radars 4. Argo fire-control radar 5. SPS-52 radar 6. 76-mm DP 7. SPS-12 radar 8. 127-mm AA

Scale: 1/1,000

D 551

Audace

1978

GUIDED-MISSILE DESTROYERS (*continued*)

Ardito   A. Fraccaroli, 1978

Boilers: 4 Foster-Wheeler, 43 kg/cm² pressure—superheat 450°C
Range: 4,000/25   **Man:** . . . officers, . . . men
M: 2 sets GT; 2 props; 73,000 hp

REMARKS: Habitability has been given much attention in the design of these very fine ships. The four single 533-mm torpedo tubes are mounted at the extreme stern, below the fantail, and launch aftward. Plans for two more have been postponed.

Audace   J.-C. Bellonne, 1975

◆ **2 Impavido class**

	Bldr	Laid down	L	In serv.
D 570 IMPAVIDO	C. N. del Tirreno, Riva Trigoso	10-6-57	25-5-62	16-11-63
D 571 INTREPIDO	Ansaldo, Livorno	16-5-59	21-10-62	28-7-64

D: 3,201 tons (3,990 fl)   **S:** 33.5 kts   **Dim:** 131.3 × 13.65 × 4.43
A: 1/Mk 13 missile launcher aft (40 Standard SM-1 missiles)—2/127-mm 38-cal. DP (II × 1) fwd—4/76-mm DP (I × 4)—6/324-mm Mk 32 ASW TT (III × 2)

Impavido   1978

GUIDED-MISSILE DESTROYERS (*continued*)

Intrepido   G. Arra, 1976

Electron Equipt: Radars: 1/SPS-12, 1/SPQ-2, 1/SPS-52, 2/SPG-51, 3/RTN-10X
                        (Argo systems)
                   Sonars: 1/SQS-23 — ECM: 2/SCLAR chaff launchers (XX × 2)
Boilers: 4 Foster-Wheeler, 43 kg/cm² pressure — superheat 450°C
Range: 3/300/20, 2,900/25, 1,500/30   **Man:** 22 officers, 312 men
Fuel: 650 tons   **M:** 2 sets Tosi GT; 2 props; 70,000 hp

REMARKS: Refitted (D-571 in 1974-75, D-570 in 1976-77) with new fire control for guns
and new missiles. Extensive intercept arrays (ESM). Have fin stabilizers.

DESTROYERS

◆ **2 Impetuoso class**

	Bldr	Laid down	L	In serv.
D 558 IMPETUOSO	C. Nav. del Tirreno, Riva Trigoso	7-5-52	16-9-56	25-1-58
D 559 INDOMITO	Ansaldo, Livorno	24-4-52	9-8-55	23-2-58

Indomito   G. Arra, 1976

Impetuoso   1978

D: 2,775 tons (3,811 fl)   **S:** 34 kts   **Dim:** 127.6 (123.4 pp) × 13.15 × 4.5
A: 4/127-mm 38-cal. DP (II × 2) — 16/40-mm AA (IV × 2, II × 4) — 1/Menon triple
ASW mortar — 6/324-mm Mk 32 ASW TT (III × 2)
Electron Equipt: Radars: 1/SPS-6, 1/SPQ-2, 1/Mk-25, 3/SPG-34
                   Sonar: 1/SQS-11
Range: 3,400/20   **Man:** 24 officers, 330 men
Fuel: 650 tons   **Electric:** 1,300 kw
Boilers: 4 Foster-Wheeler, 43 kg/cm² pressure — superheat 450°C

REMARKS: Both given modest updating during the mid-1970s, but retain obsolescent
U.S. gear. Mk 25 f.r. radar is on the Mk 37 director for the 127-mm guns. The four
SPG-34 are carried two on the quadruple 40-mm AA mounts and on two of the four
twin 40-mm mounts; the radars support four Mk 63 control systems. D-558 has had
the forward superstructure enlarged around the stack.

GUIDED-MISSILE FRIGATES

◆ **6 Maestrale class** Bldr: CNR, Muggiano

	Laid down	L	In serv.
F 570 MAESTRALE	8-3-78	. . .	. . .
F 571 GRECALE	. . .	. . .	. . .
F 572 LIBECCIO	. . .	. . .	. . .
F 573 SCIROCCO	. . .	. . .	. . .
F 574 ALISEO	. . .	. . .	. . .
F 575 EURO	. . .	. . .	. . .

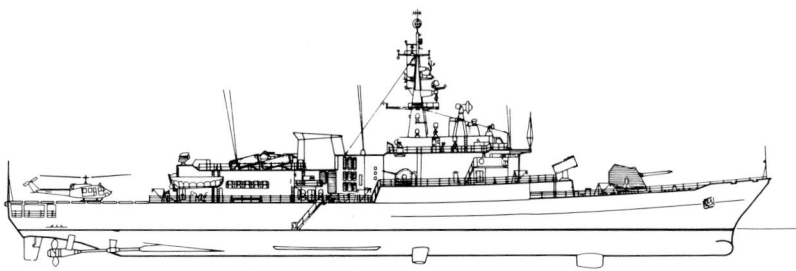

D: 3,040 tons (fl)   **S:** 30 kts   **Dim:** 122.73 (116.4 pp) × 12.88 × 4.1

A: 4/Otomat Mk 2 Teseo SSM (I × 4) – 1/Albatros SAM system (VIII × 1, Aspide missiles) – 1/127-mm DP OTO Melara – 4/40-mm AA Breda (II × 2) – 2/533-mm TT (A-184 torpedoes) – 6/324-mm Mk 32 ASW TT (III × 2) – 2/AB-212 helicopters

Electron Equipt: Radars: 1/RAN-105, 1/SMA-702, 1/SPQ-2D, 1/RTN-30X (NA-30 system), 2/RTN-20 (Dardo system), 1/RTN-10 (Argo system)

Sonars: 1/Raytheon 1160B, 1/Raytheon 1164 VDS – Selenia IPN-10 data system – ECM: 2/SCLAR chaff launchers (XX × 2)

Electric: 3,120 kw   **Range:** 5,000/12 (1 diesel) – 90-day autonomy

Man: 23 officers, 190 men

M: CODOG: 2GE/Fiat LM-2500 gas turbines, 50,000 hp; 2 GMT B 230-20 DV diesels, 10,146 hp; 2 controllable-pitch props

REMARKS: An enlarged version of *Lupo* with better seaworthiness and two helicopters at the expense of four anti-ship missiles and about 2.5 knots maximum speed. Two more units, *Espero* (F-576) and *Zeffiro* (F-577) were canceled in 1977. Completion of the remaining six is scheduled for 1980-83 but may change. The hull sonar is a commercial version of the U.S. Navy SQS-56 as used on the *Oliver Hazard Perry* (FFG-7) class.

◆ **4 Lupo class** Bldr: C. N. del Tirreno, Riva Trigoso

	Laid down	L	In serv.
F 564 LUPO	8-10-74	29-7-76	20-9-77
F 565 SAGITTARIO	4-2-76	22-6-77	18-11-78
F 566 PERSEO	18-1-76	8-7-78	26-2-79
F 567 ORSA	1-8-77	2-3-79	1979

D: 2,208 tons (2,340 trials; 2,525 fl)

S: 35.23 kts (trials, *Lupo*); 32 kts at 80% power; 20.3 kts on 2 diesels

Lupo　　　　　　　　　　　　　　　　C. Martinelli, 1978

Lupo　　　　　　　　　　　　　　　　C. Martinelli, 1978

GUIDED-MISSILE FRIGATES (continued)

Lupo—with new mast

C. Martinelli, 1978

Dim: 112.8 (106.0 pp) × 11.98 × 3.66
A: 8/Otomat Mk 2 Teseo SSM (I × 8)−1/Nato Sea Sparrow system (VIII × 1)−
1/127-mm OTO Melara DP−4/40-mm Breda AA (II × 2)−6/324-mm Mk 32 ASW
TT (III × 2)−1/AB-212 helicopter
Electron Equipt: Radar: 1/RAN-10S combined search, 1/SPQ-2F, 1/RAN-11/LX
combined search, 1/RTN-10X (NA-10 mod 2 Argo f.c.
system), 1/Mk 91 mod 1, 2/RTN-20 (Dardo system)
Sonars: Raytheon 1160B−ECM: active and passive systems,
2/SCLAR chaff launchers (XX × 2)−IPN-10 data system
Man: 16 officers, 95 senior enlisted, 75 men
Electric: 3,120 kw (4 Fiat 236 SS diesel alternator sets)
Range: 5,000/1 diesel−90-day autonomy
M: CODOG: 2 GE/Fiat LM-2500 gas turbines, 50,000 hp; 2 GMT A230-20M diesels,
8,490 hp; 2 controllable-pitch props

REMARKS: Fin stabilizers. Telescopic hangar. The Teseo launchers are mounted two
per side abreast the hangar and two per side on the forward superstructure; normally
only four missiles seem to be aboard. The *Lupo* had her radar antennae redistributed
1978-79 and a new mast added at the after end of the stack. The SAM system uses
the U.S. Mk 29 launcher and a U.S. director, rather than the later Albatros system
with the similar Aspide missiles of the *Maestrale* class. Machinery is mounted in
four compartments: auxiliaries, gas turbines, reduction gearing, and diesel alternator sets. Much automation is used. Conditions on board are cramped and Spartan.
Six ships of the same class were ordered for Venezuela and four for Peru.

FRIGATES

◆ **2 Alpino class** Bldr: C. N. del Tirreno, Riva Trigoso

	Laid down	L	In serv.
F 580 ALPINO (ex-*Circe*)	27-2-63	14-6-67	14-1-68
F 581 CARABINIERE (ex-*Climene*)	9-1-65	30-9-67	28-4-68

D: 2,000 tons (2,700 fl) **S:** 27 kts **Dim:** 113.3 (106.4 pp) × 13.1 × 3.76
A: 6/76-mm 62-cal. DP (I × 6)−1/single-barreled Menon ASW mortar−6/324-mm
MK 32 ASW TT (III × 2)−2/AB-204B or AB-212 helicopters
Electron Equipt: Radars: 1/SPS-12, 1/SPQ-2, 1/RTN-30X (NA-30 system), 3/RTN-
10X (Argo systems)

Sonars: 1/SQS-43, 1/SQA-10 VDS−ECM: MM/SPR-A intercept,
2/SCLAR chaff launchers (XX × 2)
Range: 4,200/17 **Man:** 20 officers, 244 men
Fuel: 275 tons **Electric:** 2,400 kw
M: CODAG propulsion: 4 Tosi OTV-320 diesels, 4,200 hp each; 2 Tosi-Metrovik G6
gas turbines, 7,700 hp each; 2 props; 31,800 hp

REMARKS: Stablizers. Cruising, 22 knots on diesels.

Carabiniere 1978

Carabiniere 1978

FRIGATES (continued)

◆ **4 Carlo Bergamini class**

	Bldr	Laid down	L	In serv.
F 593 CARLO BERGAMINI	C.R.D.A., Trieste	19-7-59	16-6-60	23-6-62
F 594 VIRGILIO FASAN	Castellammare	6-3-60	9-10-60	10-10-62
F 595 CARLO MARGOTTINI	Castellammare	26-5-57	12-6-60	5-5-62
F 596 LUIGI RIZZO	Castellammare	26-5-57	6-3-60	15-12-61

D: 1,410 tons (1,650 fl) **S:** 25 kts **Dim:** 93.95 (86.51 pp) × 11.35 × 3.1
A: 2/76-mm 62-cal. DP (I × 2)–1/single-barreled Menon ASW mortar–6/324-mm
Mk 32 ASW TT (III × 2)–1 AB-204B or AB-212 helicopter
Electron Equipt: Radars: 1/SPS-12, 1/SPQ-2, 1/Orion (OG-3 system)
Sonars: SQS-30–Intercept: MM/SPR-A

Virgilio Fasan

Virgilio Fasan   A. Molinari, 1972

Range: 4,500/16, 3,600/18   **Man:** 155 men   **Electric:** 1,200 kw
M: 4 high-speed Fiat 3012 RSS or Tosi diesels; 2 props; 16,000 hp

REMARKS: Equipped with Denny-Brown anti-rolling stabilizers to reduce rolling from
20 degrees to 3 degrees. Enlargement of the helicopter platform between 1968 and
1971 required the removal of the after 76-mm gun. Telescopic hangar.

	Bldr	Laid down	L	In serv.
F 552 CANOPO	C. Nav. di Taranto	15-5-52	20-2-55	1-4-58
F 553 CASTORE	C. Nav. di Taranto	14-3-55	8-7-56	14-7-57
F 554 CENTAURO	Ansaldo, Livorno	31-5-52	4-4-54	5-5-57
F 555 CIGNO	C. Nav. di Taranto	10-2-54	14-3-55	7-3-57

Cigno   1978

FRIGATES (*continued*)

Cigno 1978

Licio Visintini G. Arra, 1976

D: 1,807 tons (2,250 fl) **S:** 26 kts **Dim:** 103.1 (93.3 pp) × 12.0 × 3.8
A: 3/76-mm DP (1 fwd, 2 aft) − 1/triple-barreled Menon ASW mortar − 6/324-mm Mk 32 TT (III × 2)
Electron Equipt: Radars: 1/SPS-6, 1/SPQ-2, 1/RTN-10 Orion (OG-3 system)
Sonars: SQS-11 − Intercept: MM/SPR-A
Range: 2,600/20 **Man:** 160 men **Fuel:** 400 tons
Boilers: 2 Foster-Wheeler, 43 kg/cm² pressure − superheat 450°C.
M: 2 sets Tosi GT; 2 props; 22,000 hp

REMARKS: Originally had four 76-mm (II × 2) guns; reconfigured 1966-73. Refitted mid-1970s. OG-3 radar director is atop bridge; a U.S. Mk 51 visual-only director is located aft (on F-552 the OG-3 is aft).

CORVETTES

◆ **4 Pietro de Cristofaro class**

	Bldr	Laid down	L	In serv.
F 540 PIETRO DE CRISTOFARO	C. N. del Tirreno	30-4-63	29-5-65	19-12-65
F 541 UMBERTO GROSSO	Ansaldo, Livorno	21-10-62	12-12-64	25-4-66
F 546 LICIO VISINTINI	C.R.D.A., Monfalcone	30-9-63	30-5-65	25-8-66
F 550 SALVATORE TODARO	Ansaldo, Livorno	21-10-62	24-10-64	25-4-66

D: 850 tons (1,020 fl) **S:** 22-23 kts **Dim:** 80.2 (75.0 pp) × 10.0 × 2.5
A: 2/76-mm DP (I × 2) − 1/single-barreled Menon ASW mortar − 6/324-mm Mk 32 ASW TT (III × 2)
Electron Equipt: Radars: 1/SPQ-2 1/Orion (OG-3 system)
Sonars: 2/SQS-36 (1 hull, 1 VDS) − Intercept: MM/SPR-A
Range: 4,600/18 **Man:** 8 officers, 123 men **Fuel:** 100 tons
M: 2 diesels (*see* Remarks); 2 props; 8,400 hp

REMARKS: High-speed diesels: Fiat 3012 RSS on F-540, F-541, and F-550; Tosi on F-546, with reduction gears and Tosi-Vulcan hydraulic linkage. OG-3 gun director forward, U.S. Mk 51 director aft. The VDS uses an SQA-13 hoist.

◆ **4 Albatros class**

		Laid		
	Bldr	down	L	In serv.
F 542 AQUILA (ex-*Dutch Lynx*)	Breda Marghera, Venice	7-53	31-7-54	2-10-56
F 543 ALBATROS	Nav. Mec. Castellammare	1953	18-7-54	1-6-55
F 544 ALCIONE	Nav. Mec. Castellammare	1953	19-9-54	23-10-55
F 545 AIRONE	Nav. Mec. Castellammare	1953	21-11-54	2-10-55

D: 800 tons (950 fl) **S:** 19 kts **Dim:** 76.3 (69.49 pp) × 9.65 × 2.8
A: 2/40-mm 70-cal. AA (I × 2) − 6/324-mm Mk ASW TT (II × 2) − 2/Mk 11 Hedgehogs
Electron Equipt: Radar: 1/SPQ-2 Sonar: QCU-2
Range: 2,988/18 **Man:** 7 officers, 111 men

Alcione G. Arra, 1972

CORVETTES (continued)

Fuel: 100 tons   **Electric:** 1,200 kw
M: 2 Fiat M 409 diesels; 2 props; 5,200 hp

REMARKS: Ships built with U.S. "offshore" funds (ex-U.S. PC-1626, PC-1919, PC-1920, and PC-1921). One similar ship was delivered to The Netherlands (returned to Italy in 10-61) and four to Denmark. Originally had two 76-mm DP, two 40-mm AA (II × 1); rearmed 1963. F-544 had a third 40-mm AA aft in 1974. All are equipped for minesweeping (wire sweep only).

NOTE: The remaining *Ape*-class corvettes, *Bombarda* (F-549), *Chimera* (F-569), and *Sfinge* (F-579), were stricken 1976-77.

GUIDED-MISSILE PATROL BOATS

◆ **7 Sparviero class**   Bldr: CNR, La Spezia

	Laid down	L	In serv.
P 420 SPARVIERO	4-71	3-73	15-7-74
P . . . NIBBIO	. . .	. . .	1979
P . . . FALCONE	5-77	. . .	1979
P . . . CONDORE	. . . .	. . .	1980
P . . . ASTORE	. . .	. . .	1980
P . . . GRIFFONE	. . .	. . .	1981
P . . . GREPPIO	. . .	. . .	1981

D: 64.5 tons (fl)   **S:** 43 kts (heavy sea), 50 kts (calm sea)
Dim: 22.95 (24.56, foils retracted) × 7.01 (12.06 max. over foils) × 1.87 (1.45 over foils at speed, 4.37 over foils at rest)
A: 1/76-mm OTO Melara Compact—2/Otomat SSM (I × 2)

Sparviero   1978

Sparviero   G. Arra, 1976

Electron Equipt: Radars: 1/3RM7-250, 1/RTN-10X (NA-10 system)
Range: 1,050/8 (diesel), 400/45   **Man:** 2 officers, 8 men   **Fuel:** 11 tons
M: CODOG: 1 Rolls-Royce Proteus 15 M-560 gas turbine; 1 waterjet; 4,500 hp;
    1 GM 6V-53N diesel; 1 prop; 180 hp

REMARKS: Prototype studied by the Alinavi Society, which was formed in 1964 by Boeing, U.S.A., the Italian government's I.R.I., and Carlo Rodriguez of Messina, builder of commercial hydrofoils. Six more (of eight planned) were ordered 1977. The three hydrofoils are raised when cruising, and the diesel engine is engaged. All-aluminum construction. Project based on U.S. *Tucumcari.*

PATROL BOATS

◆ **2 Freccia class**

	Bldr	Laid down	L	In serv.
P 493 FRECCIA (ex-MC-590)	C. Nav. di Taranto	30-4-63	9-1-65	6-7-65
P 494 SAETTA (ex-MC-591)	C.R.D.A., Monfalcone	11-6-63	11-4-65	25-7-66

D: 175 tons (205 fl)   **S:** 40 kts   **Dim:** 46.1 × 7.2 × 1.54
A: As patrol boat: 3/40-mm 70-cal. AA (I × 3)—1 missile
    As torpedo boat: 2/40-mm AA (I × 2)—2/533-mm TT
    As minelayer: 1/40-mm AA—8 mines
Electron Equipt: Radar: 1/3ST7-250   **Man:** 4 officers, 33 men
M: CODAG: 2 Fiat diesels, 3,800 hp each; 1 Rolls-Royce Proteus
    1 gas turbine, 4,250 hp; 3 props; 11,860 hp

REMARKS: The plan to build two more has not materialized. P-494 served trials with the Sea Killer Mk 1 SSM (V × 1), later removed; she retains a Contraves gun director, with RTN-150 radar, while P-494 has only a Mk 51 lead-computing director.

PATROL BOATS (*continued*)

Freccia—in torpedo boat rig (now new director)   G. Arra, 1972

◆ **2 Lampo class** Bldr: C. Nav. di Taranto

	Laid down	L	In serv.
P 491 LAMPO	4-1-58	22-11-60	7-63
P 492 BALENO	22-11-60	10-5-64	16-7-65

Lampo—in torpedo boat rig   G. Arra, 1972

D: 197 tons (210 fl)   **S:** 39 kts   **Dim:** 43.0 × 6.3 × 1.5
A: As patrol boat: 3/40-mm 70-cal. AA
　　As torpedo boat: 2/40-mm 70-cal. AA—2/533-mm TT
Electron Equipt: Radar: 1/3ST7-250   **Man:** 5 officers, 28 men
M: CODAG: 2 MTU 518D diesels, 3,600 hp each; 1 Metrovik-Nuove
　　Reggiane gas turbine, 4,500 hp; 3 props; 11,700 hp

REMARKS: Re-engined with German diesels in 1976. Have one U.S. Mk 51 gun director. Similar *Folgore* (P-490) stricken 1977, while the surviving ex-U.S. *Higgins* and World War II-vintage Italian torpedo boats were discarded 1977-79.

MINE WARFARE SHIPS

◆ **4 Lerici-class minehunter/minesweepers** Bldr: Intermarine, La Spezia

	Laid down	L	In serv.
M . . . LERICI	. . .	. . .	12-80
M . . . SAPRI	. . .	. . .	1981
M . . . MILAZZO	. . .	. . .	1982
M . . . VIESTE	. . .	. . .	1983

D: 485 tons (502 fl)   **S:** 15 kts   **Dim:** 49.98 (45.5 pp) × 9.56 × 2.63
A: 1/20-mm AA   **Electron Equipt:** Radar: 1/3ST7/DG   **Sonar:** SQQ-14
Man: 39 men   **Range:** 2,500/12, 1,500/14   **Electric:** 887 kva
M: 1 GMT B230-8M diesel; 1 prop; 1,840 hp (2 retractable auxiliary thrusters; 470 hp)

REMARKS: Ordered 4-78. Glass-reinforced, shock-resistant plastic construction throughout. To carry two PAP-104 remote-controlled minehunting devices as well as conventional sweep gear. SQQ-14 is a high-frequency minehunting sonar with a retractable transducer. While minehunting, speed is 7 knots, using the two drop-down, shrouded thrusters. Range at 12 knots can be extended to 4,000 nautical miles by using the passive roll stabilization tanks to carry fuel. Ten were originally planned, and a total of sixteen may ultimately be built.

◆ **4 ex-U.S. Agile-class fleet minesweepers**

	Bldr	In serv.
M 5340 SALMONE (ex-MSO-507)	Martinolich, San Diego	6-56
M 5431 STORIONE (ex-MSO-506)	Martinolich, San Diego	2-56
M 5432 SGOMBRO (ex-MSO-517)	Tampa Marine	2-57
M 5433 SQUALO (ex-MSO-518)	Tampa Marine	6-57

D: 665 tons (750 fl)   **S:** 14 kts   **Dim:** 52.27 × 10.71 × 4.0 (fl)
A: 1/40-mm AA   **Electron Equipt:** Radar: 1/3ST7/DG   **Sonar:** UQS-1
Man: 7 officers, 44 men   **Range:** 3,000/10   **Fuel:** 46 tons
M: 2 GM 8-278ANW diesels; 2 controllable-pitch props; 1,600 hp

Sgombro   1978

MINE WARFARE SHIPS (continued)

◆ 30 U.S. Adjutant-class minesweepers

	Bldr:	In serv.
M 5504 CASTAGNO (ex-MSC-74)	H. Grebe, New York	7-53
M 5505 CÉDRO (ex-MSC-88)	Berg SY, Wash.	10-53
M 5507 FAGGIO (ex-MSC-81)	Lake Union DD, Wash.	10-53
M 5508 FRASSINO (ex-MSC-89)	Berg SY, Wash.	1-54
M 5509 GELSO (ex-MSC-75)	H. Grebe, New York	2-54
M 5510 LARICE (ex-MSC-82)	Lake Union DD, Wash.	12-53
M 5511 NOCE (ex-MSC-90)	Berg SY, Wash.	5-54
M 5512 OLMO (ex-MSC-133)	Bellingham BY, Wash.	3-54
M 5513 ONTANO (ex-MSC-76)	H. Grebe, New York	10-54
M 5514 PINO (ex-MSC-134)	Bellingham BY, Wash.	5-54
M 5516 PLATANO (ex-MSC-136)	Bellingham BY, Wash.	9-54*
M 5517 QUERCIA (ex-MSC-137)	Bellingham BY, Wash.	11-54
M 5519 MANDORLO (ex-MSC-280)	Tacoma BY, Wash.	12-60*
M 5521 BAMBU (ex-MSC-214)	CRDA, Monfalcone	11-56
M 5522 EBANO (ex-MSC-215)	CRDA, Monfalcone	11-56
M 5523 MANGO (ex-MSC-216)	CRDA, Monfalcone	12-56
M 5524 MOGANO (ex-MSC-217)	CRDA, Monfalcone	1-57
M 5527 SANDALO (ex-MSC-240)	CRDA, Monfalcone	4-57
M 5531 AGAVE	CRDA, Monfalcone	12-55
M 5532 ALLORO	CRDA, Monfalcone	4-56
M 5533 EDERA	CRDA, Monfalcone	7-56
M 5534 GAGGIA	Baglietto, Varezze	2-56
M 5535 GELSOMINO	Baglietto, Varezze	5-56
M 5536 GIAGGIOLO	Picchiotti, Viareggio	6-56
M 5537 GLICINE	Picchiotti, Viareggio	2-56
M 5538 LOTO	Celli, Venice	9-56*
M 5540 TIMO	Costaguta, Voltri	8-56
M 5541 TRIFOGLIO	CN, Taranto	12-55
M 5542 VISCHIO	C. Mediterraneo, Piera	8-56

(minehunters:*)

D: 375 tons (405 fl) **S:** 13.5 kts **Dim:** 43.9 (42.1 pp) × 8.2 × 2.5
A: 2/20-mm AA (II × 1) **Electron Equipt:** Radar: 1/3ST7/DG
                                                    Sonar: UQS-1
Man: 5 officers, 33 men **Range:** 2,500/10 **Fuel:** 40 tons
M: 2 GM 8-268A diesels; 2 props; 1,200 hp (see Remarks)

REMARKS: M-5531 to M-5542 were built with "offshore procurement" funds and thus did not receive MSC-series hull numbers; the others were built under the U.S. Military Aid Program. M-5519 is of a later design than the others, with a lower bridge and larger stack; she was converted as a minehunter in 1975, while M-5516 and M-5538 have been similarly altered. An additional five are to become minehunters by 1981. All have wooden hulls and nonmagnetic fittings. M-5521 to M-5527 have Fiat diesels. Five more units have been scrapped: *Acacia* (M-5502), *Betulla* (M-5503), *Ciciegio* (M-5506), and *Rovere* (M-5526) in 1974, and *Abete* (M-5501) in 1977. *Mirto* (ex-M-5539) and *Pioppo* (ex-M-5515) have been converted to survey ships.

Mandorlo—minehunter C. Martinelli, 1977

Noce C. Martinelli, 1977

Agave G. Arra, 1976

MINE WARFARE SHIPS (*continued*)

◆ **10 Aragosta-class inshore minesweepers**

	L		L
M 5450 ARAGOSTA	8-56	M 5462 PINNA	4-57
M 5452 ASTICE	1-57	M 5463 POLIPO	5-57
M 5457 GAMBERO	5-57	M 5464 PORPORA	6-57
M 5458 GRANCHIO	5-57	M 6465 RICCIO	5-57
M 5459 MITILO	6-57	M 5466 SCAMPO	5-57

Bldrs: Monfalcone; Baglietto, Varazze; Viareggio; Celle, Venice; Costaguta, Voltri; C. N. Carrera; Ancona; Breda, Venice

D: 120 tons (188 fl)   **S:** 14 kts   **Dim:** 32.5 × 6.4 × 1.9
A: none   **Electron Equipt:** Radar: 1/MLN-1A
Man: 14 men   **Range:** 2,000/9   **Fuel:** 15 tons   **Electric:** 340 kw
M: 2 Fiat/MTU MB8ZOD diesels; 1 props; 1,000 hp

REMARKS: Based on British "-ham" class. Ten others scrapped in 1974. All built with U.S. Military Assistance Program funds as MSI-55 to MSI-74. Wooden construction. Single 20-mm AA forward removed.

Porpora   G. Arra, 1976

AMPHIBIOUS WARFARE SHIPS

◆ **2 ex-U.S. de Soto County-class LSTs**

	Bldr	L
L 9890 GRADO	Boston NSY	28-2-57
(ex-*de Soto County*, LST-1171)		
L 9891 CAORLE	Newport News SB & DD	5-9-57
(ex-*York County*, LST-1175)		

D: 4,164 tons (7,804 fl)   **S:** 16/15 kts   **Dim:** 134.7 × 18.9 × 5.5
A: 6/76-mm 50-cal. DP (II × 3)   **Electron Equipt:** Radar: 1/3RM-20
Man: 15 officers, 173 men
M: 6 Fairbanks-Morse 38D8⅛ diesels; 2 controllable-pitch props; 14,000 hp

Grado   G. Arra, 1972

REMARKS: Quarters for 634 troops, including 30 officers. Two Mk 51 gunfire-control systems, one forward, one aft. Carry four LCVPs each. Transferred in 7-72.

◆ **1 assault transport**   Bldr: Todd, Tacoma

	Laid down	L	In serv.
L 9871 ANDREA BAFILE			
(ex-*St. George*, AV-16)	4-8-43	14-2-44	24-7-44

D: 8,510 tons (13,380 fl)   **S:** 17 kts   **Dim:** 149.96 (141.73 pp) × 21.18 × 7.24
A: 2/127-mm DP (I × 2)   **Electron Equipt:** 1/SPS-6, 1/3RM-20
Range: 13,400/13   **Electric:** 1,500 kw
Boilers: 2 Foster-Wheeler "D," 32.7 kg/cm² – superheat 393°C
M: 1 set Allis-Chalmers GT; 1 prop; 8,500 hp

REMARKS: Former U.S. seaplane tender transferred 12-68 and modified as support ship for special forces. In reserve at Taranto. Can carry four or more LCVPs.

◆ **18 U.S. LCM(3)-class landing craft**

MTM 9901	MTM 9909	MTM 9913	MTM 9918	MTM 9923	MTM 9926
MTM 9902	MTM 9911	MTM 9914	MTM 9920	MTM 9924	MTM 9927
MTM 9905	MTM 9912	MTM 9915	MTM 9922	MTM 9925	MTM 9929

D: 56 tons (fl)   **S:** 9 kts   **Dim:** 15.2 × 4.3 × 1.17
Range: 130/9   **M:** 2 Gray Marine 64 HN9 diesels; 2 props; 330 hp

REMARKS: Transferred 1953. Several are of the 17.1-meter, 62-ton LCM(6) version.

◆ **37 U.S. LCVP class**

MTP 9703	MTP 9710	MTP 9715	MTP 9723	MTP 9729
MTP 9707	MTP 9711	MTP 9719	MTP 9727	MTP 9730
MTP 9708	MTP 9714	MTP 9720	MTP 9728	MTP 9732-MTP 9754

D: 7 tons (11 fl)   **S:** 9 kts   **Dim:** 10.9 × 3.2 × 1.03
Range: 110/9   **M:** 1 Gray Marine 64 HN9 diesel; 165 hp

REMARK: Transferred 1953.

HYDROGRAPHIC SHIPS

◆ **1 Ammiraglio Magnaghi class**   Bldr: C. N. del Tirreno, Riva Trigoso

	Laid down	L	In serv.
A 5303 AMMIRAGLIO MAGNAGHI	13-6-73	11-9-74	2-5-75

HYDROGRAPHIC SHIPS (*continued*)

Ammiraglio Magnaghi   G. Arra, 1976

  D: 1,700 tons (fl)   **S:** 16 kts   **Dim:** 82.7 (76.8 pp) × 13.7 × 3.6
  A: 1/40-mm – 1/AB-212 helicopter   **Electron Equipt:** Radar: 1/2RM-20
Man: 10 officers, 125 men, 15 scientists   **Range:** 6,000/12, 4,200/16
  M: 2 GMT B306 SS diesels; 1 controllable-pitch prop; 3,000 hp; 1 electric auxiliary
      engine; 240 hp (4 kts)

REMARKS: Equipped for survey and oceanographic studies. Passive tank stabilization. Bow thruster. Part of 1972 program.

◆ **2 ex-U.S. Adjutant-class minesweepers**

	Bldr	In serv.
A 5306 MIRTO (ex-M-5539)	Breda, Marghera	4-8-56
A 5307 PIOPPO (ex-M-5515, ex MSC-135)	Bellingham SY, Washington	31-7-54

Mirto   G. Arra, 1976

Pioppo   C. Martinelli, 1974

REMARKS: Characteristics generally as for minesweeper version. Superstructure enlarged, stack raised on A-5306; A-5307 less extensively altered. Both carry two 20-mm AA (II × 1).

REPLENISHMENT OILERS

◆ **2 Stromboli-class oilers**   Bldr: C. N. del Tirreno, Riva Trigoso

	Laid down	L	In serv.
A 5327 STROMBOLI	1-10-73	20-2-75	10-75
A 5329 VESUVIO	1976	4-6-77	25-3-79

  D: 8,706 tons (fl)   **S:** 20 kts   **Dim:** 129.0 (118.5 pp) × 18.0 × 6.5
  A: 1/76-mm DP
Electron Equipt: Radars: 1/3RM7-250, 1/RTN-10X (Argo system)
  Man: 10 officers, 109 men   **Range:** 4,000/19   **Electric:** 2,350 kw
  M: 2 Fiat C428 SS diesels; 1 controllable-pitch prop; 11,400 hp

REMARKS: Cargo: 3,000 tons fuel oil, 1,000 tons diesel, 400 tons lube oil, 100 tons miscellaneous (torpedoes, missiles, projectiles, spare parts) with the possibility of extending the latter to 400 tons. Capable of serving two units simultaneously alongside while

Stromboli   1978

REPLENISHMENT OILERS (*continued*)

Stromboli   1978

Stromboli   1978

underway with constant-tension fueling rigs, each capable of pumping 430 m³/hr of fuel oil and 100 m³/hr of diesel fuel or lube oil. Can also refuel over the stern at the rate of 430 m³/hr. There are also constant-tension cargo transfer rigs on either side, each capable of transferring 1.6-ton loads, as well as two stations for lighter loads. The ships can also replenish via helicopters, although they do not have hangars. Two single 40-mm AA can be added abreast the stack. Twenty repair-party personnel can also be accommodated.

EXPERIMENTAL SHIPS

◆ **1 ex-landing ship** Bldr: Taranto Naval Base

	Laid down	L	In serv.
A 5314 QUARTO	19-3-66	18-3-67	3-68

    D: 764 tons (980 fl)   **S:** 13 kts   **Dim:** 69.0 × 9.55 × 1.81
    A: 2/Otomat Mk 2 Teseo SSM (I × 2)
    Electron Equipt: Radars: 1/SPQ-2, 1/RAN-3L
    Range: 1,300/13   **M:** 3 diesels; 3 props; 2,300 hp

REMARKS: Unsuccessful landing ship used as a trials ship since early 1970s. Blunt bow restricts speed and seaworthiness. Sisters *Marsala* (hull used as a pontoon) and *Caprara* canceled. Four 40-mm AA (II × 2) removed.

◆ **1 converted fishing boat**

A . . . BARBARA Bldr: Castracani, Ancona

    D: 195 tons   **S:** 12 kts   **Dim:** 30.0 × 6.3 × 1.5
    M: 2 diesels; 2 props; 600 hp

REMARKS: Purchased 1975. Used for oceanographic research.

SUPPORT TENDERS

◆ **1 supply ship** Bldr: Lake Washington SY, Houghton, Washington

	Laid down	L	In serv.
A 5301 PIETRO CAVEZZALE	17-4-42	23-5-43	17-11-43
(ex-AGP-6, ex-*Oyster Bay*, AVP-28)			

Pietro Cavezzale   C. Martinelli, 1973

    D: 1,766 tons (2,800 fl)   **S:** 16 kts   **Dim:** 94.6 × 12.58 × 3.7
    A: 1/76-mm 50-cal. DP–2/40-mm AA (II × 1)
    Electron Equipt: Radars: 1/3ST7, 1/SPS-6C
    Man: 210 men   **Range:** 10,000/11   **Fuel:** 400 tons   **Electric:** 600 kw
    M: 2 Fairbanks-Morse 38D8⅛ diesels; 2 props; 6,000 hp

REMARKS: Transferred at the end of 1957. Serves amphibious ships and small boats.

◆ **1 support ship for frogmen and commandoes**

A 5328 APE Bldr: Nav. Mec. Castellammare
    D: 670 tons (77. fl)   **S:** 15 kts   **Dim:** 64.8 × 8.7 × 2.72
    A: 2/20-mm AA   **Man:** 108 men   **Range:** 2,445/15   **Fuel:** 63 tons
    M: 2 Fiat MS 407 diesels; 2 props; 3,500 hp

REMARKS: Launched 22-11-42. Former corvette.

SALVAGE SHIPS

◆ 1 salvage ship

	Bldr	Laid down	L	In serv.
A 5309 ANTEO	C. N. Breda, Mestre	1977	11-11-78	1979

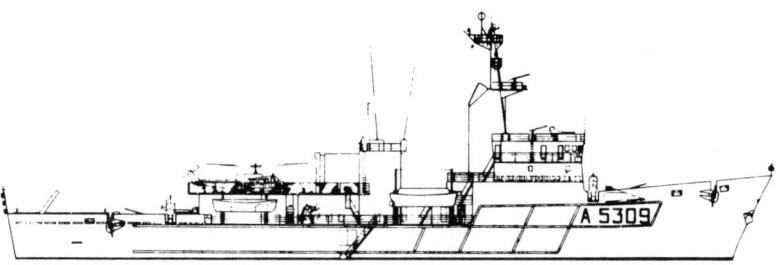

D: 2,178 tons (3,120 fl) **S:** 18.3 kts **Dim:** 98.4 (93.0 pp) × 15.8 × 5.8
A: 2/20-mm AA (II × 1) − 1/AB-212 helicopter **Range:** 4,000/16
Man: 120 men
M: 3 GMT A-230 diesels, electric drive (2 motors); 1 prop; 4,420 hp

REMARKS: Ordered 1977. Will carry U.S. Navy-style submarine rescue equipment, including a McCann rescue bell capable to 150 meters and two decompression chambers. A 13.2-ton salvage submersible will be carried also; 8.0 × 1.9 × 2.7 meters, it will submerge to 750 meters and will have 120-hour autonomous endurance. The ship will support saturation diving to 350 meters and will have a 27-ton bollard pull at 10 kts. A bow thruster is fitted.

◆ 1 U.S. AN-93-class former netlayer

	Bldr	Laid down	L	In serv.
A 5304 ALICUDI (ex-AN-99)	Ansaldo, Livorno	4-54	11-7-54	1955

Alicudi　　　　　　　　　　　　　　　　　　　G. Arra, 1976

D: 680 tons (832 fl) **S:** 13 kts **Dim:** 46.28 × 10.26 × 3.2
A: 1/40-mm AA − 4/20-mm AA (I × 4) **Electron Equipt:** Radar: MLN-1A
Fuel: 105 tons
M: 2 Maybach MBA 6H/D650/655 diesels, electric drive; 1 prop; 1,200 hp

REMARKS: Sister *Filicudi* (A-5305) stricken 1979. Used for salvage work and mooring-buoy laying.

◆ 1 salvage tug Bldr: C. N. Riuniti, Ancona

	Laid down	L	In serv.
A 5310 PROTEO (ex-*Perseo*)	1943	1950	24-8-51

Proteo　　　　　　　　　　　　　　　　　　　　　　　1968

D: 1,865 tons (2,178 fl) **S:** 16 kts **Dim:** 76.7 × 11.7 × 6.1
A: 2/20-mm AA (I × 2) **Range:** 7,500/13 **Man:** 10 officers, 120 men
M: 2 diesels; 1 prop; 4,800 hp

REMARKS: Will probably be scrapped soon after completion of *Anteo*. Used as submarine rescue ship and salvage ship.

WATER TANKERS

◆ 1 Piave class

	Bldr	L	In serv.
A 5354 PIAVE	Orlando, Livorno	1971	23-5-73

Piave　　　　　　　　　　　　　　　　　　　　　　　1973

WATER TANKERS (*continued*)

D: 4,973 tons   **S:** 13.6 kts   **Dim:** 86.7 × 13.4 × 5.9
A: 4/40-mm AA (II × 2)   **Electron Equipt:** Radar: 1/3RM7
Range: 1,500/12   **Cargo capacity:** 3,500 tons
M: 2 diesels; 2,560 hp

REMARK: Sister *Tevere* (A-5355) sold commercially, 1976.

◆ **3 Basento class**   Bldr: Inma, La Spezia, 1970-71

A 5356 BASENTO   A 5357 BRADANO   A 5358 BRENTA

Basento

D: 1,914 tons (fl)   **S:** 12.5 kts   **Dim:** 66.1 × 1.0 × 3.9
A: 2/20-mm AA (I × 2)   **Electron Equipt:** Radar: 1/3RM7
Range: 1,650/12.5   **Man:** 4 officers, 31 men   **Cargo Capacity:** 1,200 tons
M: 2 Fiat LA-230 diesels; 1,730 hp

◆ **3 ex-U.S. Army 327E class, 1943-44**

A 5369 ADIGE (ex-YW-92)   A 5376 TANARO (ex-YW-99)
A 5377 TICINO (ex-YW-97)

Ticino   C. Martinelli, 1974

D: 476 tons (1,517 fl)   **S:** 9 kts   **Dim:** 55.63 × 9.14 × 4.29
A: 3/20-mm AA (I × 3)   **Electron Equipt:** Radar: 1/3RM7
Man: 23 men   **Range:** 2,560/7   **Fuel:** 32 tons
Cargo Capacity: 1,000 tons
M: 2 Clark MD-4 diesels; 2 props; 700 hp

TRAINING SHIPS

◆ **1 Capitani Romani class**

	Bldr	Laid down	L	In serv.
D 562 SAN GIORGIO	C. N. del Tirreno,	23-9-39	28-8-41	24-6-43
(ex-*Pompeo Magno*)	Ancona			

San Giorgio   1978

D: 3,950 tons (4,450 fl)   **Dim:** 142.18 (138.75 pp) × 14.4 × 5.3
S: 27 kts   **Man:** 314 men, 130 midshipmen
A: 4/U.S. 127-mm 38-cal. DP (II × 2)—3/76-mm DP (I × 3) OTO Melara—Menon
triple ASW mortar—6/324-mm Mk 32 ASW TT (III × 2)
Electron Equipt: Radars: 1/SPS-6, 1/SPQ-2, 1/Mk 25, 3/Orion
Sonar: 1/SQS-4
Range: 4,800/20 (diesels)   **Fuel:** 500 tons
M: CODAG: 4 Fiat-Tosi 3012 RSS diesels, 4,000 hp each; 2 A.E.I. G6-2 gas turbines,
7,500 hp each; combined on 2 shafts (CODAG apparatus); 2 props

REMARKS: Sister ship of the *San Marco*, which was stricken from the active list in 1970.
Converted, with propulsion plant and armament, into a school ship for the naval
academy at Livorno in 1964-65.

A 5312 AMERIGO VESPUCCI   Bldr: Nav. Mec. Castellammare

D: 3,545 tons (4,186 fl)   **Dim:** 82.38 (70.72 pp) × 15.54 × 6.7
S: 10 kts   **Range:** 5,450/6.5
A: 4/40-mm AA (I × 4)-mm—1/20-mm AA   **Man:** 400 men, 150 cadets
M: 2 Tosi E6 diesels, electric drive; 1 prop; 1,900 hp

REMARK: Launched 22-3-30. Sail area: 2,100 m².

TRAINING SHIPS (*continued*)

Amerigo Vespucci   L. Fava

A 5311 PALINURO (ex-*Cdt Louis Richard*) Bldr: Dubigeon, 1920

D: 1,042 tons (1,351 fl)   S: 7.5 kts   Dim: 59.0 × 9.7 × 4.8
A: 2/76-mm (saluting battery)   **Range:** 5,300/7.5
M: 1 M.A.N. G8V23.5/33 diesel; 450 hp

Palinuro   A. Fraccaroli

REMARK: Former French cod-fishing craft bought in 1951. Steel hull.

A 5316 CONSARO II Bldr: Costaguta, Genoa, 1960

D: 41 tons   Dim: 20.9 × 4.7   M: 1 auxiliary engine; 96 hp

REMARK: Sailing ship, rigged as a yawl.

A 5313 STELLA POLARE Bldr: Sant. Germ., Chiavari, 1965

REMARK: 47 ton, RORC class cruising yacht

D: 47 tons   S: . . . kts   Dim: 20.9 × 4.7 × 2.9

SERVICE CRAFT

◆ 7 ex-British LCT(3)-class tenders

A 5331 MOC 1201	A 5335 MOC 1205
A 5332 MOC 1202	A 5337 MOC 1207
A 5333 MOC 1203	A 5338 MOC 1208
A 5334 MOC 1204	

MOC 1207   C. Martinelli, 1977

D: 640 tons (fl)   S: 10 kts   Dim: 58.5 × 9.4 × 2.0
Man: 3 officers, 21 men   M: 2 Paxman diesels; 1,000 hp

REMARKS: MOC-1201 is used for torpedo trials and torpedo-recovery; MOC-1207 and MOC-1208 are ammunition transports; the remainder serve as repair craft for mine-sweepers and small combatants. MOC-1201 has one torpedo tube.

◆ 2 ex-German MFP-D-class cargo lighters, former landing craft

MTC 1101   MTC 1102

MTC 1101   G. Arra, 1972

SERVICE CRAFT (*continued*)

D: 280 tons (fl)   **S:** 10 kts   **Dim:** 49.8 × 6.6 × 1.34
A: 2/20-mm AA   **Range:** 540/9
M: 3 Deutz diesels; 3 props; 450 hp

REMARKS: Built 1942. Can carry 150 tons cargo; beaching capability retained.

◆ 7 MZ-class cargo lighters

MTC 1004	MTC 1007	MTC 1010
MTC 1005	MTC 1008	
MTC 1006	MTC 1009	

D: 350 tons (fl)   **S:** 10.5 kts   **Dim:** 47.0 × 6.55 × 1.5
A: 2/20-mm AA   **M:** 3 Deutz diesels; 3 props; 450 hp

REMARKS: Former landing craft. Built 1942. Similar to MFP-D class but hull has sheer fore and aft. Can carry 150 tons cargo.

SEAGOING TUGS

◆ 2 Atlante class   Bldr: Visintini Donada

A 5317 ATLANTE   A 5318 PROMETEO

D: 478 tons (750 fl)   **S:** 13.5 kts   **Dim:** 38.8 × 9.6 × 4.1
Man: 23 men   **M:** 1 Tosi QT 320/8SS diesel; 1 controllable-pitch prop; 2,600 hp

REMARK: In service: 14-8-75.

◆ 1 Ciclope class

A 5319 CICLOPE

D: 1,200 tons (fl)   **S:** 8 kts   **Dim:** 47.9 × 9.8 × 3.61
M: 1 set triple-expansion reciprocating steam; 1,000 hp

REMARKS: In service: 1948. Sister *Titano* stricken.

◆ 2 U.S. Army 293-design class

A 5320 COLOSSO (ex-LT-214)   A 5321 FORTE (ex-LT-159)

D: 525 tons (835 fl)   **S:** 11 kts   **Dim:** 38.6 × 8.53 × 3.89
M: 2 Fairbanks-Morse 38D8⅛ diesels; 2 props; 1,690 hp
Range: 3,800/8   **Fuel:** 112 tons

Forte   G. Arra, 1974

REMARKS: Launched 1943-44. Transferred 1948. Sister *Tenace* (ex-LT-154) stricken. Wooden hulls.

◆ 1 San Giusto class   Bldr: CNR, Palermo, 1940

A 5326 SAN GIUSTO

D: 370 tons (486 fl)   **S:** 12 kts   **Dim:** 38.7 × 8.2 × 3.8
M: Triple-expansion reciprocating steam; 900 hp

◆ 4 Gagliardo class

	L		L
A 5322 GAGLIARDO	1938	A 5388 ERCOLE	1971
A 5323 ROBUSTO	1939	A 5394 VIGOROSO	1971

D: 389 tons (506 fl)   **S:** 8 kts   **Dim:** 33.2 × 7.1 × 3.6
M: Triple-expansion reciprocating steam; 850 hp

LARGE HARBOR TUGS

◆ 2 Favignana class

Y 424 FAVIGNANA   Y 448 USTICA

D: 270 tons   **S:** 13 kts   **Dim:** 35.0 × 9.0 × 4.0
M: Triple-expansion reciprocating steam; 1,200 hp

REMARK: Launched 1973.

◆ 2 Porto d'Ischia class   Bldr: CNR, Riva Trigoso, 1969-70

Y 436 PORTO D'ISCHIA   Y 443 RIVA TRIGOSO

D: 250 tons (296 fl)   **S:** 12 kts   **Dim:** 25.5 × 7.1 × 3.3
M: 1 diesel; 850 hp

MEDIUM HARBOR TUGS

◆ 8 Porto class

	L		L
Y 418 CAPRERA	1972	Y 438 PORTO PISANO	1937
Y 426 LEVANZO	1973	Y 441 PORTO RICANATI	1937
Y 432 PANTELLERIA	1972	Y 445 SALVORE	1927
Y 434 PIANOSA	1974	Y 447 TINO	1930

D: 226 tons (270 fl)   **S:** 9 kts   **Dim:** 27.1 × 6.7 × 3.1
M: Triple-expansion reciprocating steam; 600 hp

REMARK: Differ from one another in detail only.

◆ 2 U.S. Army 327E-design class

Y . . . MISENO (ex-ST-795)   Y . . . MONTE CRISTO (ex-ST-762)

D: 161 tons (729 fl)   **S:** 9.5 kts   **Dim:** 26.3 × 7.0 × 2.6
Range: 2,760/9.5   **M:** 1 GM 8-567 diesel; 700 hp

REMARK: Launched 1943-44; transferred 1948.

◆ 1 Ventimiglia class

Y . . . VENTIMIGLIA

D: 230 tons   **S:** 11 kts   **Dim:** 33.0 × 7.0 × 2.2
M: Triple-expansion reciprocating steam; 627 hp

ITALY (*continued*)

SMALL HARBOR TUGS

◆ **12 RP-101 class** Bldr: CN Visintini-Donado, Rovigo, 1972-75

Y 403 RP 101	Y 408 RP 105	Y 456 RP 109
Y 404 RP 102	Y 410 RP 106	Y 458 RP 110
Y 406 RP 103	Y 413 RP 107	Y 460 RP 111
Y 407 RP 104	Y 452 RP 108	Y 462 RP 112

D: 36 tons (75 fl) **S:** 12 kts **Dim:** 18.8 × 4.5 × 1.9
M: 1 diesel; 500 hp

◆ **18 miscellaneous tugs**

	L		L
Y 412 ALBENGA	1973	Y 435 MESCO	1933
Y 414 ARZACHENA	1931	Y 437 NISIDA	1943
Y 415 ASINARA	1934	Y 439 PASSERO	1934
Y 416 LAMPEDUSA	1972	Y 440 PLOMBINO	1969
Y 417 BOEO	1943	Y 446 SAN BENEDETTO	1941
Y 419 CARBONARA	1936	Y 454 SPERONE	1965
Y 422 POZZI	1912	Y 469 No. 78	1965
Y 430 LINARO	1913	Y 473 RIZZUTO	1956
Y 433 CIRCEO	1956	Y 474 No. 96	1962

IVORY COAST

PERSONNEL: 240 men

MERCHANT MARINE (1978): 65 ships — 156,749 grt

PATROL BOATS AND CRAFT

◆ **2 French Épée class** Bldr: Auroux, Arcachon

	Laid down	L	In serv.
L'ARDENT	15-4-77	21-7-78	10-78
L'INTREPIDE	7-7-77	21-7-78	10-78

D: 125 tons (148 fl) **S:** 26.3 kts **Dim:** 40.35 (38.5 pp) × 5.9 × 1.6
Man: 2 officers, 17 men **Range:** 750/20, 1,500/15, 1,750/10
A: 1/40-mm AA — 1/20-mm AA — 2/7.62-mm machine guns
M: 2 AGO V12CZ SHR diesels; 2 controllable-pitch props; 4,000 hp

REMARKS: Ordered 1-77 and 4-77, respectively. Do not carry SS-12 missiles.

L'Ardent   Auroux, 1978

◆ **2 PR-48 class** Bldr: S.F.C.N.

	Laid down	L	In serv.
VIGILANT	2-67	23-5-67	1968
LE VALEUREUX	28-10-75	8-3-76	25-9-76

D: 250 tons (fl) **S:** 23 kts **Dim:** 47.5 (45.5 pp) × 7.0 × 2.25
A: 2/40-mm AA (I × 2) **Man:** 4 officers, 30 men **Range:** 2,000/16
M: 2 MGO diesels with Masson reduction gear; 2 props; 4,200 hp

◆ **1 Perseverance class**

PERSEVERANCE (ex-P-759, VC-9)

D: 70 tons (80 fl) **S:** 28 kts **Dim:** 31.77 × 4.7 × 1.7
A: 2/20-mm AA **Man:** 15 men **Range:** 1,500/15
M: 2 Mercedes-Benz diesels; 12 cyl.; 2 props; 2,700 hp **Fuel:** 4 tons

REMARK: In service 25-2-58.

AMPHIBIOUS WARFARE SHIPS

◆ **1 French Batral-type medium landing ship** Bldr: Dubigeon, Normandy

	L	In serv.
ELEPHANT	. . .	2-2-77

D: 750 tons (1,330 fl) **S:** 16 kts **Dim:** 80.0 (68.0 pp) × 13.0 × 3.0 (max.)
A: 2/40-mm AA (I × 2) **Man:** 4 officers, 35 men **Range:** 3,500/13
M: 2 diesels; 2 props; 1,800 hp

REMARKS: Ordered 2-8-74. Similar to the French Navy's *Francis Garnier*. Helicopter platform aft.

◆ **1 Barracuda-type transport** Bldr: Halter, New Orleans, U.S.A., 1976

D: 6 tons (8.35 fl) **S:** 36 kts **Dim:** 11.0 × 3.8 × 0.6
M: 2 GM 6V-53PI diesels; 2 water jets; 540 hp **Capacity:** 20 men

◆ **2 LCVP** Bldr: Abidjan, 1970

D: 7 tons (9 fl) **S:** 9 kts **Dim:** 10.9 × 3.2 × 1.0
M: 1 Mercedes-Benz diesel

IVORY COAST (*continued*)

VARIOUS SHIPS

◆ **1 training and support ship**

LOCODJO   **D:** 450 tons

REMARK: Former coastal freighter built in West Germany in 1953, delivered in 1970.

◆ **4 small craft**   **Dim:** 7-10 meters

◆ **1 Arcoa-class small craft**

JAMAICA

MERCHANT MARINE (1978): 7 ships — 10,430 grt

Jamaica's naval force is similar to the U.S. Coast Guard. Its material is furnished by the United States under the Military Assistance Program.

PATROL BOAT AND CRAFT

◆ **1 Fort Charles-class boat**   Bldr: Teledyne Sewart, Berwick, La., U.S.A., 1974

P 7 FORT CHARLES

    D: 103 tons (fl)   **S:** 32 kts   **Dim:** 31.5 × 5.7 × 2.1
    A: 1/20-mm AA — 2/12.7-mm machine guns   **Man:** 15 men
    M: 2 MTU MB 16V538 TB90 diesels; 2 props; 7,000 hp   **Range:** 1,200/18

REMARK: Can carry twenty-four soldiers and serve as a floating hospital.

Discovery Bay

◆ **3 85-foot commercial cruisers**   Bldr: Sewart Seacraft, Berwick, La., U.S.A., 1966-67

P 4 DISCOVERY BAY   P 5 HOLLAND BAY   P 6 MANATEE BAY

    D: 60 tons   **S:** 30 kts   **Dim:** 25.9 × 5.68 × 1.83
    A: 3/12.7-mm machine guns   **Man:** 10 men   **Range:** 800/20
    M: 3 MTU 8V331 TC81 diesels; 3 props; 3,000 hp   **Fuel:** 13 tons

REMARK: Re-engined twice, most recently from 1975 to 1977, more than quadrupling the original horsepower.

JAPAN

PERSONNEL: approximately 41,000 men, including 8,300 officers

MERCHANT MARINE (1978): 9,321 ships — 39,182,079 grt
                      (tankers: 1,428 ships — 16,385,739)

The Maritime Self-Defense Force (MSDF), or Kaiso Jeitai, was created in 1954. In Article 9 of her constitution, Japan waived the right of belligerence and declared her peaceful intentions. Consequently, her armed forces are designed to carry out purely defensive tasks. The duties of the MSDF involve essentially the protection of coastal traffic and of Japan's sea lines of communication, both of which are vital to the economic survival of one of the world's most industrialized nations. For some years now, however, the MSDF has tended to look more and more like an oceangoing navy, as is evidenced by the construction of more important ships.

In addition to the MSDF, Japan has a rapidly expanding Maritime Safety Agency (Kaijo Hoancho) which, in function, is roughly comparable to the U.S. Coast Guard and which, in time of war, would come under the control of the Navy. Its ships are listed at the end of this section.

FIFTH DEFENSE PLAN: The Fifth Defense Plan, which covers the period from 1-4-77 to 31-3-82, called for:
    4 destroyers based on Nos. 143 and 144 of the Fourth Plan
    6 to 8 guided-missile destroyers, 2,500 to 3,000 tons, armed with Harpoon surface-to-surface missiles
    6 to 8 frigates, derived from the *Chikugo* design
    6 to 8 2,200-ton submarines

CONSTRUCTION PROGRAMS
1975-76 Budget:
    1 DDH (143 *Shirane*), 1 SS (572 *Yaeshio*), 3 MSC (646 *Okitsu*, 647 *Hashira*, 648 *Iwai*)
1976-77 Budget:
    1 DDH (144 *Kurama*), 1 MHC (649 *Hatsushima*), 1 AGS (5102 *Furami*)
1977-78 Budget:
    1 DDG (122 . . .), 1 frigate (226 *Ishikari*), 1 SS (573 *Yushio*), 2 MHC (650 *Ninoshima*, 651 *Miyajima*)

CONSTRUCTION PROGRAMS (*continued*)

1978-79 Budget:
1 DDG (170 . . .), 1 DDG (123 . . .), 1 SS (574 *Mochishio*), 2 MHC (652 . . ., 653 . . .)

1979-80 Budget (Requested):
3 DDG (124, 125, 126), 1 frigate (227), 1 SS (575), 2 MHC (654, 655), 2 LSU, 1 AGS (5103), and 6 service craft

NAVAL AVIATION: Naval air is an integral part of the Navy. The MSDF does not have any aircraft carriers: some 20 helicopters serve on board the destroyers and frigates. As of 1 March 1978, the naval air arm consisted of:

88 P-2V7 and P-2J patrol planes
28 S-2F ASW aircraft (some mothballed)
17 PS-1 ASW seaplanes
59 helicopters, 17 of which were HSS-2

Naval aviation is divided into two commands:

1. The Fleet Air Force, which consists of 8,000 men and 140 aircraft. Its headquarters are in Atsugi and it has twelve bases along the coasts of Japan.
2. The Air Training Command, which has several centers at Shimofusa.

Over the period 1980 through 1984, it is planned to acquire 37 Lockheed/Kawasaki P-3C long-range ASW aircraft (in addition to the 8 ordered in 1978 for delivery in 1982), 51 more Sikorsky/Mitsubishi SH-3B ASW helicopters (26 shipboard, 25 land-based), 6 RH-53E minesweeping helicopters, 2 Shin-Meiwa US-1 rescue amphibians, 18 Beech C-90 King Air trainers, 3 Fuji KM-2 trainers, 6 Hughes/Kawasaki OH-6J training helicopters, and 3 support craft. By 1984, the JMSDF plans to have 14 squadrons of long-range ASW patrol aircraft (P-3C, P-2J), 1 squadron of PS-1 ASW seaplanes, and five squadrons of SH-3A and SH-3B ASW helicopters in service.

It is also planned to acquire 18 aerial-minelaying versions of the C-130 Hercules, beginning in 1984. The 1979-80 budget included 1 PS-1 seaplane (to replace a lost aircraft), 8 HSS-2B ASW helicopters, 2 S-61A SAR helicopters, 3 Fuji KM-2 trainers, and 2 Beech TC-90 instrument trainers.

WARSHIPS IN SERVICE AND UNDER CONSTRUCTION AS OF 1 JANUARY 1980

	L	Tons (Surfaced)	Main armament
◆ 12 (+3) submarines			
0 (+3) YUSHIO	1979-	2,200	6/533-mm TT
7 UZUSHIO	1970-75	1,850	6/533-mm TT
5 OSHIO/ASASHIO	1964-68	1,650	8/533-mm TT
◆ 34 (+6) destroyers		Tons	
2 SHIRANE	1978-	5,200	2/127-mm DP, 3 helicopters
0 (+5) DDG	1980-	2,900	Harpoon missiles, Sea Sparrow
2 (+1) TACHIKAZE	1974-	3,850	1/Standard launcher, 2/127-mm, Asroc, 6 TT
2 HARUNA	1971-73	4,700	2/127-mm DP, 6/324-mm TT, Asroc, 3 helicopters
6 YAMAGUMO	1965-77	2,100	4/76-mm DP, 4/375-mm TT
3 MINEGUMO	1967-69	2,066	4/76-mm DP, 1 rocket launcher, 6/324-mm TT
4 TAKATSUKI	1966-69	3,200	2/127-mm DP, Asroc
1 AMATSUKAZE	1963	3,050	1/Standard launcher, 4/76-mm DP, Asroc
2 AKIKUZI	1959	2,300	3/127-mm AA, 4/76-mm DP
3 MURASAME	1958-59	1,800	3/127-mm DP, 4/76-mm DP, 6/324-mm TT
7 AYANAMI	1957-60	1,700	6/76-mm DP, 4/533-mm TT
2 HARUKAZE	1955	1;700	2-3/127-mm DP, 8/40-mm DP, ASW weapons
◆ 15 (+2) frigates			
0 (+2) ISHIKARI	1980-	1,200	Harpoon missiles, 1/76-mm DP
11 CHIKUGO	1970-76	1,470	2/76-mm DP, 2/40-mm AA, Asroc
4 ISUZU	1961-63	1,490	4/76-mm DP, ASW weapons
◆ 12 corvettes			
8 MIZUTORI	1959-65	420/440	2/40-mm, 6/ASW TT
4 UMITAKA	1959-63	490	2/40-mm, 6/ASW TT

◆ 5 torpedo boats

◆ 46 mine warfare ships

◆ 6 amphibious warfare ships

WEAPONS AND SYSTEMS

Until recently, most weapons and detection gear were of American design, built under license in Japan. However, the latest ships are being equipped with a Japanese-designed, long-range, air-search radar that has a short pulse, and with the 76-mm OTO Melara gun. The latter will be built under license.

In Japan, SPS-10 radar is referred to as OPS-1, SPS-6 as OPS-15, and SPS-12 as OPS-16.

SUBMARINES

◆ 3 Yushio class

		Bldr	Laid down	L	On serv.
573	YUSHIO	Mitsubishi, Kobe	3-12-76	29-3-79	3-80
574	MOCHISHIO	Kawasaki, Kobe	28-4-78	4-80	3-81
575	N . . .	Kawasaki, Kobe	. . .	. . .	. . .

D: 2,200 tons S: 20/13 kts Dim: 76.0 × 9.9 × 7.5
A: 6/533-mm TT M: Diesel-electric: 2 diesels, V8/V24; 1 prop; 7,200 hp

REMARKS: Deeper-diving than the *Uzushio* class and have more modern electronic equipment; otherwise, similar. This class will be ordered at the rate of one per year, 1980-84.

◆ 7 Uzushio class

		Bldr	Laid down	L	In serv.
566	UZUSHIO	Kawasaki, Kobe	25-9-68	11-3-70	21-1-71
567	MAKISHIO	Mitsubishi, Kobe	21-6-69	27-1-71	2-2-72
568	ISOSHIO	Kawasaki, Kobe	9-7-70	18-3-72	25-11-72
569	NARUSHIO	Mitsubishi, Kobe	8-5-71	22-11-72	28-9-73
570	KUROSHIO	Kawasaki, Kobe	5-7-72	22-2-74	27-11-74
571	TAKASHIO	Kawasaki, Kobe	6-7-73	30-6-75	30-1-76
572	YAESHIO	Kawasaki, Kobe	14-4-75	19-5-77	7-3-78

SUBMARINES (continued)

Narushio   1974

Makishio   *Ships of the World*

D: 1,850 tons, 3,600 submerged   **S:** 20/12 kts   **Dim:** 72.0 × 9.9 × 7.5
A: 6/533-mm TT   **Man:** 10 officers, 70 men
M: Diesel-electric propulsion; Kawasaki-M.A.N. V8424/30 diesels; 1 prop; 3,600 hp

REMARKS: Tear-drop hull. Double-hull construction, bow-sonar array, torpedo tubes amidships, as in modern U.S. Navy submarines. Maximum depth: 200 m.

◆ 5 Oshio/Asashio class

	Bldr	Laid down	L	In serv.
561 OSHIO	Mitsubishi, Kobe	29-6-63	30-4-64	31-3-65
562 ASASHIO	Kawasaki, Kobe	5-10-64	27-11-65	13-10-66
563 HARUSHIO	Mitsubishi, Kobe	12-10-65	25-2-67	1-12-67
564 MICHISIO	Kawasaki, Kobe	26-7-66	5-12-67	29-8-68
565 ARASHIO	Mitsubishi, Kobe	5-7-67	27-10-68	25-7-69

Asashio   *Ships of the World*

D: 1,650 tons   **S:** 18/14 kts   **Dim:** 88.0 × 8.2 × 4.9
A: 8/533-mm TT (6 fwd, 2 aft)   **Man:** 80 men
M: 2 Kawasaki diesels, 2,900 hp each; 2 electric motors, 3,150 hp each; 2 props

REMARKS: The *Oshio*, built during the 1961 program, was the prototype for the other four and is considered a separate class. She has a less elaborate sonar array and a more pointed bow.

NOTE: The three other submarines of the *Hayashio* and *Natsushio* classes were stricken: *Natsushio* (523) on 20-3-78, *Fuyushio* (524) on 20-6-78, and Wakashio (522) on 23-3-79.

HELICOPTER-CARRYING DESTROYERS

◆ 2 Shirane class

	Bldr	Laid down	L	In serv.
143 SHIRANE	Ishikawajima, Tokyo	25-2-77	18-9-78	3-80
144 KURAMA	Ishikawajima, Tokyo	1977	20-9-79	3-81

D: 5,200 tons (6,800 fl)   **S:** 32 kts   **Dim:** 158.8 × 17.5 × 5.3
A: 2/127-mm Mk 42 DP (I × 2)–1/Sea Sparrow SAM (VIII × 1)–1/Asroc–6/324-mm
  Mk 32 ASW TT (III × 2)–3/HSS-2B ASW helicopters   **Man:** 370 men
Electron Equipt: Radars: 1/OPS 12, 1/OPS 28, 1/WM 25 (HSA), 1/GFCS 1A
  Sonars: 1/OQS 101 (hull), 1/SQS 35 VDS
M: 2 sets GT; 2 props; 70,000 hp   **Boilers:** 2, 60 kg/cm² – superheat 480°C

REMARKS: Modified *Haruna* class. The Sea Sparrow system uses a U.S. Mk-25 launcher.

◆ 2 Haruna class

	Bldr	Laid down	L	In serv.
141 HARUNA	Mitsubishi, Nagasaki	19-3-70	12-71	22-3-73
142 HIEI	Ishikawajima-Harima	8-3-72	13-8-73	27-12-74

D: 4,700 tons (6,300 fl)   **S:** 32 kts   **Dim:** 153.0 × 17.5 × 5.1
A: 2/127-mm Mk 42 DP (I × 2)–6/324-mm Mk 32 ASW TT (III × 2)–1/Asroc ASW
  system–3/HSS-2 ASW helicopters
Electron Equipt: Radars: 1/OPS 11, 1/OPS 17, 2/GFCS 1
  Sonar: OQS 3 – URN 20A TACAN
Man: 36 officers, 304 men   **Boilers:** 2, 60 kg/cm² pressure – superheat 480°C
M: GT; 2 props; 70,000 hp

Hiei   *Ships of the World*

HELICOPTER-CARRYING DESTROYERS (*continued*)

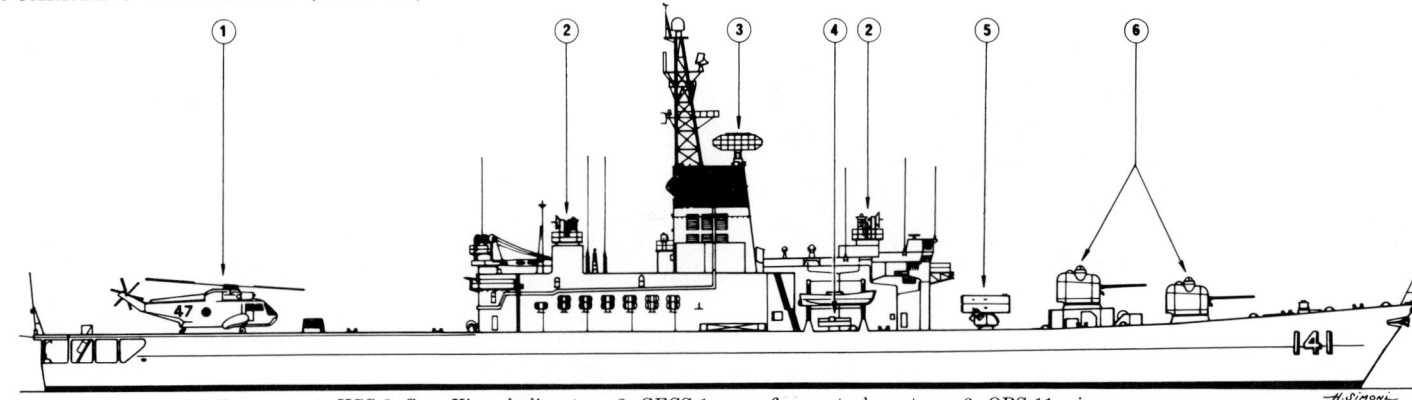

Haruna   1. HSS-2 Sea King helicopter 2. GFCS-1 gun fire-control system 3. OPS-11 air-search radar 4. Mk-32 ASW TT 5. Asroc ASW rocket launcher 6. 127-mm, 54-caliber, dual-purpose guns, Mk-42, mod 10

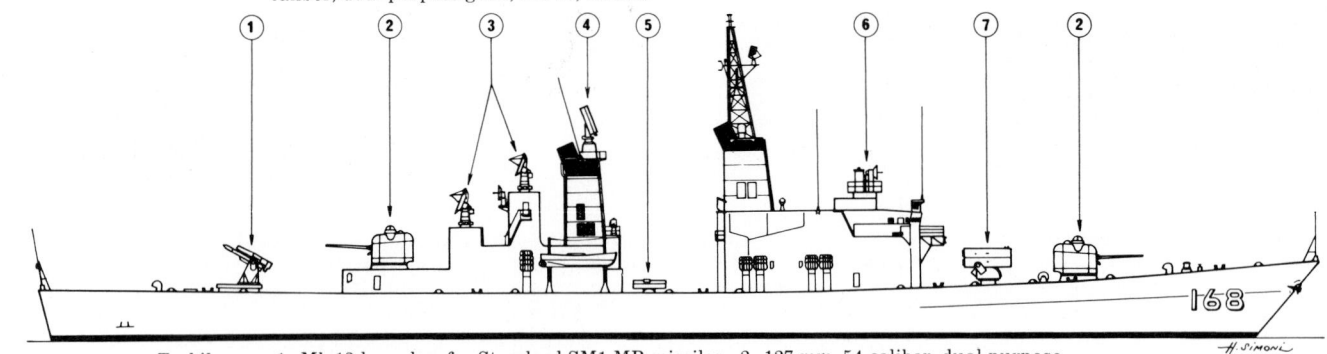

Tachikaze   1. Mk-13 launcher for Standard SM1-MR missiles 2. 127-mm, 54-caliber, dual-purpose guns, Mk-42, mod 10 3. SPG-51 missile-control radars 4. SPS-52B 3-D radar 5. Mk-32 ASW TT 6. GFCS-1 gun fire-control system 7. Asroc ASW rocket launcher

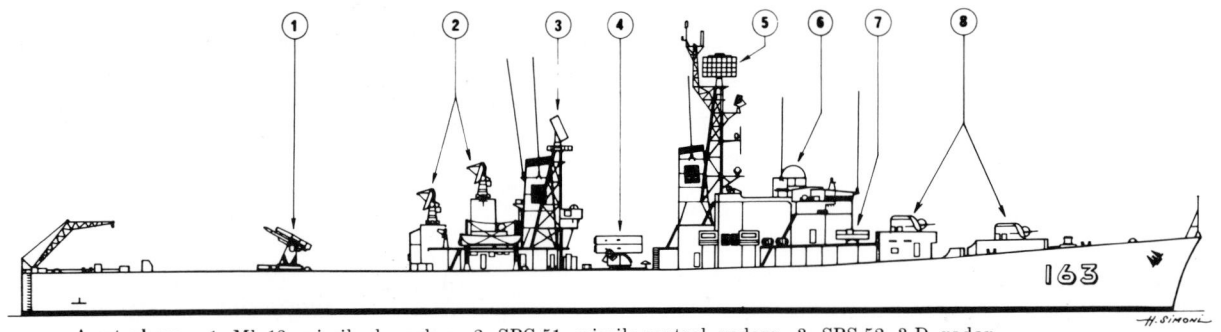

Amatsukaze   1. Mk-13 missile launcher 2. SPG-51 missile-control radars 3. SPS-52 3-D radar 4. Asroc ASW rocket launcher 5. SPS-29 air-search radar 6. Mk-63 gun fire-control director 7. Mk-32 ASW TT 8. 76-mm, 50-caliber, U.S. Mk-34, dual-purpose gun mounts

HELICOPTER-CARRYING DESTROYERS (*continued*)

Haruna *Ships of the World, 1973*

Haruna *Ships of the World*

GUIDED-MISSILE DESTROYERS

◆ 5 2,900-ton class

	Bldr	Laid down	L	In serv.
122 N . . .	Sumitomo, Uraga	. . .	10-80	3-82
123 N . . .	Hitachi, Maizuru	1-80	8-81	2-83
124 N . . .	Mitsubishi, Nagasaki	. . .	. . .	. . .
125 N . . .	Ishikawajima-Harima, Tokyo	. . .	. . .	. . .
126 N . . .	Mitsui, Tamano	. . .	. . .	. . .

D: 2,900 tons (3,700 fl)   **S:** 30 kts   **Dim:** 131.7 × 13.7 × 4.3

Man: 190 men   **Range:** . . .

A: 8/Harpoon SSM (IV × 2) – 1/Sea Sparrow SAM (VIII × 1) – 1/76-mm DP OTO Melara Compact – 1/Asroc rocket launcher (VIII × 1) – 6/324-mm Mk 32 ASW TT (III × 2) – 1/HSS-2B ASW helicopter

Electron Equipt: Radars: 1/OPS 18, 1/OPS 14A, 1/FCS 2, 1/GFCS 1
    Sonar: OQS 4

M: COGAG: 2 Kawasaki-Rolls-Royce Olympus TM-3B gas turbines, 28,390 hp each; 2 Tyne RM-1C gas turbines, 5,340 hp each; 2 controllable-pitch props

REMARKS: Will have fin stabilizers, and the Sea Sparrow launcher will be U.S. Mk-29 lightweight.

◆ 3 Tachikaze class

	Bldr	Laid down	L	In serv.
168 TACHIKAZE	Mitsubishi, Nagasaki	19-6-73	12-12-74	26-3-76
169 ASAKAZE	Mitsubishi, Nagasaki	27-5-76	15-10-77	27-3-79
170 . . .	Mitsubishi, Nagasaki	9-79	4-81	3-83

Tachikaze *Ships of the World, 1978*

Tachikaze *Ships of the World, 1976*

D: 3,850 tons (4,800 fl)   **S:** 32 kts   **Dim:** 143.0 × 14.3 × 4.6

A: 1/Mk 13 system (40 Standard SM1-MR SAM) – 2/127-mm Mk 42 DP (I × 2) – 1/Asroc ASW rocket launcher (VIII × 1) – 6/324-mm Mk 32 ASW TT (III × 2)

Electron Equipt: Radars: 1/OPS 17, 1/SPS 52B, 2/SPG 51, 1/GFCS 1
    Sonar: OQS 3

Man: 277 men   **Boilers:** 2, 60 kg/cm² pressure – superheat 480°C

M: 2 sets GT; 2 props; 70,000 hp

GUIDED-MISSILE DESTROYERS (*continued*)

REMARKS: The third unit may displace 3,950 tons standard and will have FCS-2 vice GFCS-1 gun fire-control radar. U.S. Vulcan/Phalanx Gatling guns are under consideration. The SPS-52B acts as the principal air-search radar. The missile-control system is Mk 73 and uses the two SPG-51 radars. The propulsion plant is identical to that of the *Haruna* class.

◆ 1 Amatsukaze class

	Bldr	Laid down	L	In serv.
163 AMATSUKAZE	Mitsubishi, Nagasaki	29-11-62	5-10-63	15-2-75

Amatsukaze   *Ships of the World*, 1978

D: 3,050 tons (4,000 fl)   **S:** 33 kts   **Dim:** 131.0 × 13.4 × 4.2
Man: 290 men   **Range:** 7,000/18   **Fuel:** 900 tons
A: 1/Mk 13 system (40 Standard SM1-MR SAM)—4/76-mm 50-cal. DP (II × 2)—1/Asroc ASW rocket launcher—6/324-mm Mk 32 ASW TT (III × 2)—2/Mk 15 trainable Hedgehog
Electron Equipt: Radars: 1/OPS 17, 1/SPS 29, 1/SPS 52, 2/SPG 51, 2/SPG 34
        Sonar: SQS 23
Boilers: 2 Ishikawajima-Foster-Wheeler, 38 kg/cm² pressure—superheat 438°C
Electric: 2,700 kw
M: 2 sets Ishikawajima-GE GT; 2 props; 60,000 hp

REMARKS: Refitted in 1967 with ASW TT and SPS-52 radar. Two U.S. Mk-63 fire-control systems for 76-mm guns, which have SPG-34 radars on the mounts. Guns may be replaced by two OTO Melara 76-mm compact mounts. Crane at stern handles boats stowed in a below-decks hangar.

DESTROYERS

◆ 4 Takatsuki class

	Bldr	Laid down	L	In serv.
164 TAKATSUKI	Ishikawajima, Tokyo	8-10-65	7-1-66	15-3-67
165 KIKIZUKI	Mitsubishi, Nagasaki	15-3-66	25-3-67	27-3-68
166 MOCHIZUKI	Ishikawajima, Tokyo	25-11-66	15-3-68	25-3-69
167 NAGATSUKI	Ishikawajima, Tokyo	2-3-68	19-3-69	12-2-70

Mochizuki—now has TACAN   *Ships of the World*

Takatsuki   *Ships of the World*

D: 3,200 tons (4,500 fl)   **S:** 32 kts   **Dim:** 136.0 (131.0 pp) × 13.4 × 4.4
Man: 270 men   **Range:** 7,000/20   **Fuel:** 900 tons
A: 2/127-mm Mk 42 DP (I × 2)—1/Asroc ASW rocket launcher—1/375-mm Bofors ASW rocket launcher (IV × 1)—6/324-mm Mk 32 ASW TT
Electron Equipt: Radars: 1/OPS 11, 1/OPS 17, 2/Mk 35 (Mk 56 GFCS)
        Sonars: No. 164, No. 165: SQS 23, SQS 35 (J), VDS (not in No. 166)
        No. 166, No. 167: OQS 3
        URN 20 TACAN (not on No. 165)

DESTROYERS (continued)

M: 2 sets Mitsubishi GT; 2 props; 60,000 hp
Boilers: 2 Mitsubishi-Combustion Eng.

REMARKS: Programmed for modernization in the early 1980s. Original three U.S. DASH drone helicopters stricken in 1977 and hangar not now used. Nos. 166 and 167 have a knuckle in the hull sides forward; the earlier two do not. No. 165 has fin stabilizers. No. 167 has two Japanese Mk-1 gun directors.

◆ 6 Yamagumo class

	Bldr	Laid Down	L	In serv.
113 YAMAGUMO	Mitsui, Tamano	23-3-64	27-2-65	29-1-66
114 MAKIGUMO	Uraga, Yokosuka	10-6-64	26-7-65	19-3-66
115 ASAGUMO	Maizuru, H.I.	24-6-65	25-11-66	29-8-67
119 AOKUMO	Sumitomo, Uraga	2-10-70	30-3-72	25-11-72
120 AKIGUMO	Sumitomo, Uraga	7-7-72	23-10-73	24-7-74
121 YUGUMO	Sumitomo, Uraga	4-2-76	31-5-77	24-3-78

Akigumo *Ships of the World*

Asagumo 1974

D: 2,100 tons (2,700 fl)   **S:** 27 kts   **Dim:** 114.9 × 11.8 × 4.0
A: 4/76-mm 50-cal. DP (II × 2) − 1/Asroc ASW rocket launcher (VIII × 1) − 1/375-mm Bofors ASW rocket launcher (IV × 1) − 6/324-mm Mk 32 ASW TT (III × 2)
Electron Equipt: Radars: 1/OPS 11, 1/OPS 17, 2/GFCS 2 (*see* Remarks)
　　　　　　　　　Sonars: Nos. 113-115: SQS 23; later: PQS 3; also SQS 35(J) (not in No. 115)
M: 6 Mitsubishi 12UEV 30/40N diesels; 2 props; 26,500 hp   **Range:** 7,000/20

REMARKS: Version of the *Minegumo* class with Asroc instead of DASH. May get OTO Melara 76-mm guns in place of U.S. Mk-34 mounts during refits in the 1980s. Nos. 113-115 and 119 were given U.S. Mk-46 gun director forward (Mk-35 radar) and Mk-63 GFCS aft (radar on after gun mount); Nos. 120 and 121 got two Japanese GFCS-1 systems instead. No. 113 has Mitsui diesels. Nos. 113 and 114 have raised sterns to house VDS; on Nos. 119-121 the VDS was installed during construction and, therefore, the stern was not raised.

◆ 3 Minegumo class

	Bldr	Laid down	L	In serv.
116 MINEGUMO	Mitsui, Tamano	14-3-67	16-12-67	21-8-68
117 NATSUGUMO	Uraga, Yokosuka	26-6-67	25-7-68	25-4-69
118 MURAKUMO	Maizuru, H.I.	19-10-68	15-11-69	21-8-70

Minegumo *Ships of the World*

D: 2,100 tons (2,750 fl)   **S:** 27 kts   **Dim:** 114.9 × 11.8 × 3.8
Man: 19 officers, 196 men   **Range:** 7,000/20
A: Nos. 116, 117: 4/76-mm 50-cal. DP (II × 2) − 1/375-mm Bofors ASW rocket launcher (IV × 1) − 6/324-mm Mk 32 ASW TT (III × 2)
　　　No. 118: 1/76-mm OTO Melara Compact − 2/76-mm DP (II × 1) − 1/Asroc ASW rocket launcher − 1/375-mm Bofors ASW rocket launcher (IV × 2) − 6/324-mm Mk 32 ASW TT (III × 2)
Electron Equipt: Radars: 1/OPS 11, 1/OPS 17, 1/Mk 35, 1/SPG 34
　　　　　　　　　　No. 118: 1/GFCS 2, 1/GFCS 1
　　　　　　　　　　No. 117: 1/GFCS 1, 1/SPG 34
　　　　　　　　　Sonars: OQS 3 − No. 118: SQS 35 (J) VDS also
M: 6 Mitsubishi 12UEV 30/40 diesels; 2 props; 26,500 hp

REMARKS: Originally differed from the *Yamagumo* class in having a DASH drone-helicopter facility instead of Asroc, but DASH is no longer carried. In 1976, No. 118 had an OTO Melara 76-mm gun and the prototype GFCS-2 radar director substituted for her after 76-mm twin mount and U.S. Mk-63 control system; in 1979, she received an Asroc launcher on what had been her DASH flight deck. All have a Mk-56 director forward. Nos. 116 and 117 are to receive Asroc, and all three will eventually carry two OTO Melara guns.

DESTROYERS (*continued*)

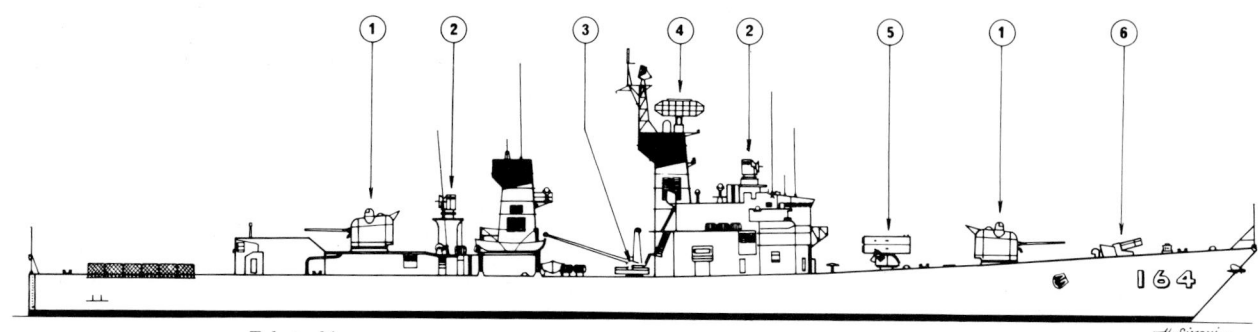

Takatsuki
1. 127-mm, 54-caliber, dual-purpose gun, Mk-42, mod 10 2. Mk-56 GFCS radar 3. Mk-32 ASW TT 4. OPS-11 air-search radar 5. Asroc rocket launcher 6. Bofors quadruple 375-mm ASW rocket launcher Note: Now carries a TACAN dome on tall lattice mast atop after stack.

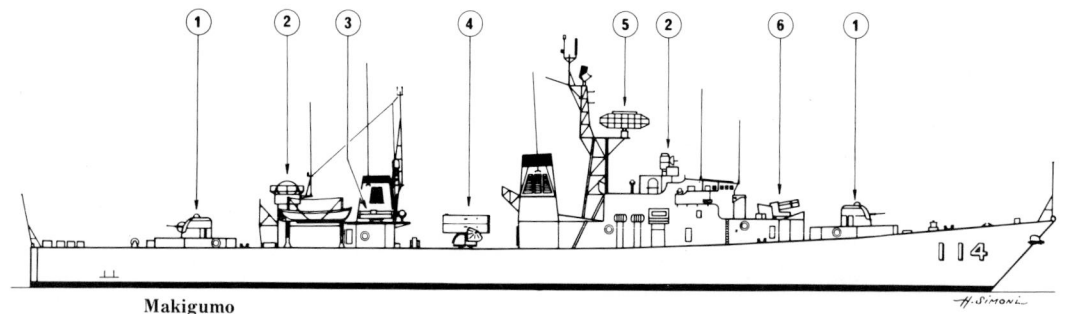

Makigumo
1. Twin 76-mm, 50-caliber, dual-purpose gun mounts, U.S. Mk-34 2. Mk-63 gun director (SPG-34 radar on after gun mount). 3. Mk-32 ASW TT 4. Asroc rocket launcher 5. OPS-11 air-search radar 6. Bofors quadruple 375-mm ASW rocket launcher

◆ **2 Akizuki class**

	Bldr	Laid down	L	In serv.
161 AKIZUKI	Mitsubishi, Nagasaki	31-7-58	26-6-59	13-2-60
162 TERUZUKI	Shin-Mitsubishi, Kobe	15-8-58	24-6-59	29-2-60

D: 2,300 tons (3,100 fl)   **S:** 32 kts   **Dim:** 118.0 (115.0 pp) × 12.0 × 4.02
A: 3/127-mm 54-cal. DP (I × 3) − 4/76-mm 50-cal DP (II × 2) − 4/533-mm TT (IV × 1) − 1/375-mm Bofors ASW rocket launcher (IV × 1) − 2/Mk 15 trainable Hedgehogs − 6/324-mm Mk ASW TT (III × 2)
Electron Equipt: Radars: 1/OPS 1, 1/OPS 15, 3/Mk 34
            Sonars: SQS 23, OQA 1 VDS
Man: 330 men   **Boilers:** 4, 43 kg/cm² pressure − superheat 454°C
M: No. 161: Mitsubishi-Escher-Wyss GT; No. 162: Westinghouse GT; 2 props; 45,000 hp

REMARKS: Weapons and ASW sensors modernized, for No. 162 in 1976-77 and No. 161 in 1977-78. The 127-mm guns they carry were removed from U.S. *Midway*-class car-

riers. Two Mk-57 and one Mk-63 gun fire-control systems are carried. Four reload 533-mm torpedoes are stowed on deck.

Akizuki   1970

DESTROYERS (continued)

◆ 3 Murasame class

		Bldr	Laid down	L	In serv.
107	MURASAME	Mitsubishi, Nagasaki	17-12-57	31-7-58	28-2-59
108	YUDACHI	Ishikawajima, Tokyo	16-12-57	29-7-58	25-3-59
109	HARUSAME	Uraga, Yokosuka	17-6-58	18-6-59	15-12-59

Harusame   *Ships of the World*

D: 1,800 tons (2,400 fl)   **S:** 30 kts   **Dim:** 109.73 × 10.97 × 3.7 (light)
Man: 250 men   **Range:** 6,000/18
A: 3/127-mm 54-cal DP (I × 3)—4/76-mm 50-cal. DP (II × 2)—1/Mk 15 trainable
    Hedgehog—6/324-mm Mk 32 ASW TT (III × 2)
Electron Equipt: Radars: 1/OPS 15, 1/OPS 1, 3/Mk 34—No. 109: 2/Mk 34, 1/GFCS 0
                Sonars: SQS 29—No. 109: OQA 1 VDS also
M: Nos. 107, 108: Kampon GT; No. 109: Mitsubishi-Escher-Wyss GT; 2 props; 35,000
    hp   **Boilers:** 2, 43 kg/cm² pressure—superheat 454°C

REMARKS: Hull and machinery spaces similar to those of the *Ayanami* class. No. 109
has Mitsubishi CE boilers, Nos. 107 and 108 have Foster-Wheeler-D boilers. All have
two Mk-57 and one Mk-63 gun-control systems. Nos. 107 and 108 retain one depth-
charge rack, two U.S. Mk-4 torpedo launchers (for Mk-32 ASW torpedoes), and a Y-gun
depth-charge mortar. The 127-mm gun mounts are Mk-39 versions that were removed
from the U.S. Navy's *Midway*-class carriers.

◆ 7 Ayanami class

103	AYANAMI	Mitsubishi, Nagasaki	20-11-56	1-6-57	12-2-58
104	ISONAMI	Mitsubishi, Kobe	14-12-56	30-9-57	14-3-58
105	URANAMI	Kawasaki, Kobe	1-2-57	29-8-57	27-2-58
106	SHIKINAMI	Mitsui, Tamano	24-12-56	25-9-57	15-3-58
110	TAKANAMI	Mitsui, Maizuru	8-11-58	8-8-59	30-1-60
111	ONAMI	Ishikawajima, Tokyo	20-3-59	13-2-60	29-8-60
112	MAKINAMI	Iino, Maizuru	20-3-59	25-4-60	30-10-60

D: 1,700 tons (2,400 fl)   **S:** 32 kts   **Dim:** 109.0 × 10.7 × 3.7 (light)
Man: 220-230 men   **Range:** 6,000/18
A: 6/76-mm DP (II × 3)—4/533-mm TT (IV × 1)—2/Mk 15 trainable Hedgehog—
    6/324-mm Mk 32 ASW TT (III × 2) (except Nos. 110 and 111: 2/Mk 4 torpedo
    launchers for Mk 32 ASW torpedoes)

Uranami   1978

Takanami

Electron Equipt: Radars: 1/OPS 15, 1/OPS 1 (Nos. 103-106: SPS 12) 2/Mk 34
                Sonars: OQS 12 or 14 (Nos. 103, 104, 110: OQA 1 VDS also)
M: No. 111: Hitachi-GE GT; Others: Mitsubishi-Escher-Wyss GT; 2 props; 35,000
    hp   **Boilers:** 2, 43 kg/cm² pressure—superheat 454°C

REMARKS: The boilers in Nos. 106 and 110 are Hitachi-Babcock, in the others, Mitsubishi. Nos. 104 and 106 are fitted as training ships; their trainable torpedo tubes
have been replaced by a classroom. There are two Mk-63 gun-control systems.

◆ 2 Harukaze class

		Bldr	Laid down	L	In serv.
101	HARUKAZE	Mitsubishi, Nagasaki	15-12-54	20-9-55	26-4-56
102	YUKIKAZE	Mitsubishi, Kobe	17-12-54	20-8-55	31-7-56

D: 1,700 tons (2,400 fl)   **S:** 30 kts   **Dim:** 106.3 × 10.5 × 4.4 (fl)
Man: 187 men   **Range:** 6,000/18   **Fuel:** 557 tons
A: 3 (No. 102: 2)/127-mm 38-cal. (I × 2 or 3)—8/40-mm AA (IV × 2)—2/Mk 10 Hedge-
    hog—2/Mk 4 ASW torpedo launchers
Electron Equipt: Radars: 1/SPS 5, 1/SPS 6, 2/Mk 34, 1/Mk 26
                Sonar: SQS 29 (*see* Remarks)
M: No. 101: Mitsubishi-Escher-Wyss GT; No. 102: Westinghouse GT; 2 props; 30,000
    hp   **Boilers:** 2, 43 kg/cm² pressure—superheat 435°C

DESTROYERS (*continued*)

Harukaze   A. Nakumo

REMARKS: Most of the hull is electric-welded and much of the superstructure is of light
alloys. The guns are American. Refitted, 1959-60. In 1976, No. 102 received provision
for a towed passive sonar array aft, in place of her after 127-mm gun and depth
charges; No. 101 has a Contraves fire-control system in place of Mk 52; both have two
Mk-63 control systems for their 40-mm guns.

GUIDED-MISSILE FRIGATES

◆ 2 Ishikari class

	Bldr	Laid down	L	In serv.
226 ISHIKARI	Mitsui, Tamano	3-78	4-80	1981
227 . . .	. . .	. . .	. . .	. . .

D: 1,200 tons **S:** . . kts **Dim:** . . . × . . . × . . .
A: 8/Harpoon SSM (IV × 2)−1/76-mm DP OTO Melara−1/375-mm Bofors ASW
rocket launcher (II × 1)−6/324-mm Mk 32 ASW TT
Electron Equipt: Radars: 1/OPS 28, 1/FCS 2
                              Sonar: . . .
M: CODOG: 1 Kawasaki-Rolls-Royce Olympus TM-3B gas turbine, 28,390 hp; 1
diesel, 5,000 hp; 2 controllable-pitch props

REMARKS: Smaller, more lightly armed, faster, and with fewer sensors than the preceding *Chikugo* class. Aluminum superstructure. Either the gas turbine *or* the single
diesel will drive both propellers. First unit in 1977-78 program, second requested
1979-80. As many as twenty more are planned, sixteen in the 1980-84 period.

FRIGATES

◆ 11 Chikugo class

	Bldr	Laid down	L	In serv.
215 CHIKUGO	Mitsui, Tamano	9-12-68	13-1-70	31-7-70
216 AYASE	Ishikawajima, Tokyo	5-12-69	16-9-70	20-7-71
217 MIKUMO	Mitsui, Tamano	17-3-70	16-2-71	26-8-71
218 TOKACHI	Mitsui, Tamano	11-12-70	25-11-71	17-5-72
219 IWASE	Mitsui, Tamano	6-8-71	29-6-72	12-12-72
220 CHITOSE	Hitachi, Maizuru	7-10-71	25-1-73	21-8-73
221 NIYODO	Mitsui, Tamano	20-9-72	28-8-73	8-2-74
222 TESHIO	Hitachi, Maizuru	11-7-73	29-5-74	10-1-75
223 YOSHINO	Mitsui, Tamano	28-9-73	22-8-74	6-2-75
224 KUMANO	Hitachi, Maizuru	29-5-74	24-2-75	19-11-75
225 NOSHIRO	Mitsui, Tamano	27-1-76	23-12-76	31-8-77

Chitose   *Ships of the World*, 1975

D: 1,470-1,530 tons (1,700-1,800 fl)   **S:** 25 kts
Dim: 93.0 × 10.8 × 3.5   **Man:** 165 men
A: 2/76-mm 50-cal. DP (II × 1)−2/40-mm AA (II × 1)−1/Asroc ASW launcher
(VIII × 1)−6/324-mm ASW TT
Electron Equipt: Radars: 1/OPS 16, 1/OPS 14, 1/GFCS 1
                              Sonars: OQS 3, SQS 35 (J) (*see* Remarks)
M: 4 Mitsubishi-Burmeister & Wain UEV 30/40 or Mitsui 28VBC-38 diesels; 2 props;
16,000 hp

REMARKS: SQS-35 (J) towed, variable-depth sonar has not yet been mounted in all units;
it is stowed in an open well at the stern, offset to starboard. These are the smallest
ships in any navy to carry Asroc. A Mk-51 director (no radar) controls the twin 40-mm
mounts.

Chitose   *Ships of the World*

FRIGATES *(continued)*

Noshiro   *Ships of the World*, 1977

◆ **4 Isuzu class**

	Bldr	Laid down	L	In serv.
211 ISUZU	Mitsui, Tamano	16-4-60	17-1-61	29-7-61
212 MOGAMI	Mitsubishi, Nagasaki	4-8-60	13-3-61	28-10-61
213 KITAKAMI	Ishikawajima, Tokyo	7-6-62	21-6-63	27-2-64
214 OHI	Maizuru H.I.	10-6-62	15-6-63	22-1-64

D: 1,490 tons (1,790 fl)   **S:** 25 kts   **Dim:** 94.0 × 10.4 × 3.5
A: 2/76-mm 50-cal. DP (II × 2)—1/375-mm Bofors ASW rocket launcher (IV × 1)—
     Nos. 213, 214: 6/324-mm Mk 32 ASW TT (III × 2)—1 depth-charge projector (not
     on Nos. 212 and 213)
Electron Equipt: Radars: 1/OPS 1, 1/OPS 16, 2/Mk 34
                  Sonars: OQS 12 or 14, Nos. 212, 213: OQA 1 VDS also
M: Diesels; 2 props; 16,000 hp   **Man:** 180 men

REMARKS: Each has a different diesel propulsion plant: No. 211: 4 Mitsui 35 VBU 45V;
No. 212: 2 Mitsubishi UET 52/65; No. 213: 4 Mitsubishi UEV 30/40; and No. 214: 4
Mitsui 28 VBU 38. No. 212, which has only two main engines, has a smaller stack.

Mogami   *Ships of the World*, 1975

Kitakami

CORVETTES

◆ **8 Mizutori class**

	Bldr:	Laid down	L	In serv.
311 MIZUTORI	Kawasaki, Kobe	13-3-59	22-9-59	27-2-60
312 YAMADORI	Fujinagata, Osaka	13-3-59	22-10-59	15-3-60
313 OTORI	Kure SY	16-12-59	27-5-60	13-10-60
314 KASASAGI	Fujinagata, Osaka	18-12-59	31-5-60	31-10-60
315 HATSUKARI	Sasebo DY	25-1-60	24-6-60	15-11-60
316 UMIDORI	Sasebo DY	15-2-62	15-10-62	30-3-63
319 SHIRATORI	Sasebo DY	29-2-64	8-10-64	26-2-65
320 HIYODORI	Sasebo DY	26-2-65	29-9-65	28-2-66

D: 420-440 tons (450-480 fl)   **S:** 20 kts   **Dim:** 60.0 × 7.1 × 2.35
Man: 75 men   **Fuel:** 24 tons
A: 2/40-mm AA (II × 1)—6/324-mm Mk 32 ASW TT (III × 2)—1/Mk 10 Hedgehog—
     1 depth-charge rack
Electron Equipt: Radars: Nos. 311, 312: 1/OPS 35, Nos. 313-316: OPS 36, Others:
                    OPS 16, All: 1/Mk 34
                Sonar: SQS 11A
M: Kawasaki-M.A.N. V8V diesels; 2 props; 3,800 hp

Yamadori

CORVETTES (*continued*)

◆ 4 Umitaka class

		Bldr:	Laid down	L	In serv.
309	UMITAKA	Kawasaki, Kobe	13-3-59	25-7-59	30-11-59
310	OTAKA	Kure SY	13-3-59	2-9-59	14-1-60
317	WAKATAKA	Kure SY	5-3-62	13-11-62	30-3-63
318	KUMATAKA	Fujinagata, Osaka	20-3-63	21-10-63	25-3-64

Umitaka   Kawasaki

D: 490 tons (530 fl)   **S:** 20 kts   **Dim:** 60.0 × 7.1 × 2.4
Man: 80 men   **Range:** 3,000/12
A: 2/40-mm AA (II × 1) — Nos. 317, 318: 6/324-mm Mk 32 ASW TT (III × 2) — Nos.
   309, 310: 2/Mk 4 launchers for Mk 32 torpedoes — 1/Mk 10 Hedgehog — 1 depth-
   charge rack
Electron Equipt: Radars: Nos. 309, 310: 1/OPS 35, No. 317: 1/OPS 36, No. 318:
   1/OPS 16, All: 1/Mk 34
   Sonar: SQS 11A
M: 2 Mitsui-Burmeister & Wain V8V diesels; 2 props; 4,000 hp

NOTE: The last units of the *Kari* and *Kamome* classes of corvettes were scrapped, 1977-
78. The *Hayabusa* (308) has been converted into a yacht (YAS-91).

TORPEDO BOATS

◆ 5 PT-11 class   Bldr: Mitsubishi

		L	In serv.			L	In serv.
811	PT 11	10-70	23-3-71	814	PT 14	...	10-7-73
812	PT 12	7-72	8-72	815	PT 15	...	8-1-75
813	PT 13	7-72	12-72				

D: 100 tons (125 fl)   **S:** 40 kts   **Dim:** 35.0 × 9.2 × 1.2
A: 2/40-mm AA (I × 2) — 4/533-mm TT (I × 4)
Electron Equipt: Radar: 1/OPS 13   **Man:** 26 men
M: CODAG: 2 Ishikawajima IM-300 gas turbines, 2 Mitsubishi 24 WZ-31MC diesels;
   3 props; 10,500 hp

PT-12   *Ships of the World*, 1973

PATROL CRAFT

◆ 9 PB type   Bldr: Ishikawajima, Yokohama, 1971-73
PB 19 to PB 27

D: 18 tons   **S:** 20 kts   **Dim:** 17.0 × 4.3 × 0.8
A: 1/20-mm AA   **Electron Equipt:** Radar: 1/OPS 29   **Man:** 5 men
M: 2 Isuzu 17T-MF RCOR diesels; 760 hp

REMARK: Fiberglass hulls.

MINE WARFARE SHIPS

◆ 1 minelayer   Bldr: Hitachi, Maizuru

		Laid down	L	In serv.
951	SOYA	9-7-70	31-3-71	30-9-71

Soya   *Ships of the World*, 1973

MINE WARFARE SHIPS (*continued*)

D: 2,150 tons (3,250 fl) **S:** 18 kts **Dim:** 99.0 × 15.0 × 4.2
A: 2/76-mm DP (II × 1)–2/20-mm AA (I × 2)–6/324-mm Mk 32 ASW TT (III × 2)–
200 mines **Man:** 185 men
Electron Equipt: Radars: 1/OPS 14, 1/OPS 16, 1/GFCS 1
  Sonar: SQS 11A
M: 4 Kawasaki-M.A.N. V6V 22/30 ATL diesels; 2 props; 6,400 hp

REMARKS: Platform for minesweeping-helicopter, six mine rails, two external, four through the transom stern.

◆ 1 mine-countermeasures support ship/minelayer

	Bldr	Laid down	L	In serv.
462 HAYASE	Ishikawajima, Haruna	16-9-70	21-6-71	6-11-71

Hayase   1974

D: 2,000 tons (3,050 fl) **S:** 18 kts **Dim:** 99.0 × 13.0 × 3.8
A: 2/76-mm 50-cal. DP (II × 1)–2/20-mm AA (I × 2)–6/324-mm Mk 32 ASW TT
(III × 2)–200 mines
Electron Equipt: Radars: 1/OPS 17, 1/Mk 34
  Sonar: SQS 11A
M: 4 Kawasaki-M.A.N. V6V 22/30ATL diesels; 2 props; 6,400 hp

REMARKS: The *Hayase* is similar to the *Soya* but has no forecastle, and has five mine rails existing through the transom stern. Her OPS-14 air-search radar has been removed. She has U.S. Mk-63 gun-control system. Fantail cleared as a helicopter platform.

◆ 1 Kasado class mine-countermeasures support ship

	Bldr	Laid down	L	In serv.
473 KOUZO	. . .	30-3-59	12-11-59	26-2-60

REMARKS: Former minesweeper converted in 1972 to support minesweeping boats. Hull has low knuckle forward, unlike the later *Kasado*-class units. Data as for *Kasado*-class minehunter/minesweeper.

◆ 7 Hatsushima-class minehunter/minesweepers

	Bldr	Laid down	L	In serv.
649 HATSUSHIMA	Nippon Kokan, Tsurumi	6-12-77	30-10-78	30-3-79
650 NINOSHIMA	Hitachi, Kanagawa	. . .	7-8-79	1-80
651 MIYAJIMA	Nippon Kokan, Tsurumi	11-78	18-9-79	3-80
652 N . . .	Nippon Kokan, Tsurumi	. . .	8-80	2-81
653 N . . .	Hitachi, Kanagawa	. . .	6-80	11-80
654 N . . .	Hitachi, Kanagawa	. . .	. . .	. . .
655 N . . .	Nippon Kokan, Tsurumi	. . .	. . .	. . .

D: 440 tons **S:** 14 kts **Dim:** 55.0 × 9.4 × 2.4
A: 1/20-mm AA **Electron Equipt:** Radar: OPS 9 **Man:** 45 men
M: 2 Mitsubishi YV12ZC-15/20 diesels; 2 controllable-pitch props; 1,440 hp

REMARKS: Expansion of the *Takami* design. Will be equipped with Type-54 mobile mine-hunting devices, which carry and lay their own disposal charges.

◆ 19 Takami-class minehunter/minesweepers

630 TAKAMI (15-7-69)	640 TAKANE (8-3-74)
631 IOU (12-8-69)	641 MUZUKI (5-4-74)
632 MIYAKE (3-6-70)	642 YOKOSE (21-7-75)
633 UTONE (6-4-70)	643 SAKATE (5-8-75)
634 AWAJI (11-12-70)	644 OUMI (28-5-72)
635 TOUSHI (13-12-70)	645 FUKUE (12-7-76)
636 TEURI (10-72)	646 OKITSU (4-3-77)
637 MUROTSU (10-72)	647 HASHIRA (8-11-77)
638 TASHIRO (2-4-73)	648 IWAI (8-11-77)
639 MIYATO (3-4-73)	

Bldrs: Odd-numbered ships: Nippon Kokan, Tsurumi; even-numbered ships: Hitachi, Kanagawa

Murotsu   1978

MINE WARFARE SHIPS (*continued*)

Awaji   *Ships of the World*

D: 380 tons   **S:** 14 kts   **Dim:** 52.0 × 8.8 × 2.4
A: 1/20-mm AA   **Electron Equipt:** Radar: OPS 9 — Sonar: ZQS 2
M: Mitsubishi YV12ZC-15/20 diesels; 2 controllable-pitch props; 1,440 hp
Man: 45-47 men

REMARKS: ZQS-2 sonar is a license-built version of the British Type 193-M minehunting sonar. OPS-9 radar, used in conjunction with a Mk-20 plotter, is a Japanese version of the British Type 978. These ships are of wooden construction, and they carry four divers for mine-clearance.

◆ **11 Kasado-class minehunter/minesweepers**

		L			L
619	MUTSURE	16-12-63	625	AMAMI	31-10-66
620	CHIBURI	29-11-63	626	URUME	12-11-66
621	OTSU	5-11-64	627	MINASE	10-1-67
622	KUDAKO	8-12-64	628	IBUKI	2-12-67
623	RISHIRI	22-11-65	629	KATSURA	18-9-67
624	REBUN	7-12-65			

Bldrs: Odd-numbered ships: Nippon Kokan, Tsurumi; even-numbered ships: Hitachi, Kanagawa

D: 330 tons (360 fl)   **S:** 14 kts   **Dim:** 45.7 × 8.38 × 2.3
A: 1/20-mm AA   **Man:** 40 men
Electron Equipt: Radar: OPS 9 — Sonar: ZQS 2
M: Mitsubishi YV10Z-DE diesels; 2 props; 1,200 hp

Hario — surviving units similar   *Shbldg. and Sh. Record*

REMARKS: Wooden construction. Fifteen earlier units of the class (Nos. 604-618) have been converted to auxiliary duties. All surviving units have ZQS-2 sonar in place of the earlier ZQS-1 (Japanese version UQS-1D).

◆ **6 inshore minesweepers**

	In serv.		In serv.		In serv.
MSB 707	30-3-73	MSB 709	28-3-74	MSB 711	10-5-75
MSB 708	27-3-73	MSB 710	29-3-74	MSB 712	24-4-75

MSB-708   *Ships of the World*, 1973

Bldrs: Odd-numbered craft: Hitachi, Kanegawa; even-numbered craft: Nippon Kokan, Tsurumi

D: 58 tons (fl)   **S:** 10 kts   **Dim:** 22.5 × 5.4 × 1.1
A: None   **Man:** 10 men   **M:** 2 Mitsubishi 4ZV20 Diesels; 2 props; 480 hp

AMPHIBIOUS WARFARE SHIPS

◆ **3 LSTs**   Bldr: Ishikawajima Harima, Tokyo

		Laid down	L	In serv.
4151	MIURA	26-11-73	13-8-74	29-1-75
4152	OJIKA	10-6-74	2-9-75	27-3-76
4153	SATSUMA	26-5-75	12-5-76	17-2-77

AMPHIBIOUS WARFARE SHIPS (continued)

Miura   1975

D: 2,000 tons (3,200 fl)   **S:** 14 kts   **Dim:** 98.0 (94.0 pp) × 14.0 × 3.0
A: 2/76-mm 50-cal. DP, No. 4153: 1/76-mm OTO Melara—2/40-mm AA (II × 1)
Man: 118 men
Electron Equipt: Radars: 1/OPS 14, 1/OPS 16, 1/GFCS 1
M: 2 Kawasaki-M.A.N. V8V 22/30 AMTL diesels; 2 props; 4,400 hp

REMARKS: Carry 180 troops, 1,800 tons cargo. No. 4153 carries prototype OTO Melara Compact gun at bow. All have two LCVP in davits and two LCM (6) on deck, the latter served by a traveling gantry.

◆ **3 Atsumi-class LSTs**   Bldr: Sasebo

	Laid down	L	In serv.
4101 ATSUMI	7-12-71	13-6-72	27-11-72
4102 MOTOBU	23-4-73	3-8-73	21-12-73
4103 NEMURO	18-11-76	16-6-77	27-10-77

D: 1,480 tons (2,400 fl)   **S:** 14 kts   **Dim:** 89.0 × 13.0 × 2.7
A: 4/40-mm AA (II × 2)   **Man:** 100 men   **Range:** 4,300/12
Electron Equipt: Radar: 1/OPS 9
M: 2 Kawasaki-M.A.N. V8V 22/30 AMTL diesels; 2 props; 4,400 hp

REMARKS: Can carry 120 men and 20 vehicles. No. 4102 is 1,550 tons standard, No. 4103 is 1,500. Have a Mk-51 gun-control system, two LCVP in davits, and one LCVP on deck, admidships.

Nemuro   *Ships of the World*, 1977

◆ **2 utility landing ships**   .D: 500 tons

REMARKS: Requested in 1979-80 budget. No data available.

◆ **15 U.S. LCM (6)-class landing craft**

◆ **22 LCVPs**

HYDROGRAPHIC SHIPS

◆ **1 Futami class**

	Bldr	Laid down	L	In serv.
5102 FUTAMI	Mitsubishi, Shimoneseki	20-1-78	9-8-78	27-2-79

D: 2,050 tons   **S:** 16 kts   **Dim:** 96.8 (90.0 pp) × 15.0 × 4.3
A: None   **Electron Equipt:** Radar: 1/OPS 18   **Man:** 105 men
M: 2 Kawasaki-M.A.N. V8V 22/30 ATL diesels; 2 controllable-pitch props; 4,400 hp

REMARKS: Configured for both hydrographic-surveying and cable-laying. Bow thruster. Has three diesel and one gas-turbine generator sets. Carries on RCV-225 remote-controlled unmanned submersible.

◆ **1 Akashi class**

	Bldr	Laid down	L	In serv.
5101 AKASHI	Nippon Kokan, Tsurumi	21-9-68	30-5-69	25-10-69

D: 1,420 tons   **S:** 16 kts   **Dim:** 74.0 × 12.9 × 4.3
A: None   **Electron Equipt:** Radar: OPS 9   **Man:** 70 men, 10 scientists
M: 2 Kawasaki-M.A.N. V8V 22/30 ATL diesels; 2 controllable-pitch props; 3,800 hp
Range: 16,500/14

REMARKS: Bow thruster. Two cranes: one 5-ton and one 1-ton.

◆ **5 Kasado-class converted minesweepers**   Bldr: Hitachi, Kanagawa, 1958-62

5111 AGS-1 (ex-*Kasado*, 604)	5114 AGS-4 (ex-*Hirado*, 614)
5112 AGS-2 (ex-*Habuchi*, 608)	5115 AGS-5 (ex-*Hario*, 618)
5113 AGS-3 (ex-*Tatara*, 610)	

D: 340 tons (355 fl)   **S:** 14.5 kts   **Dim:** 45.7 × 8.38 × 2.3
A: None   **Electron Equipt:** Radar: OPS 4   **Man:** 30 men
M: 2 Mitsubishi YV10ZC diesels; 2 props; 1,200 hp

CABLE-LAYERS

◆ **1 Muroto class**

	Bldr	Laid down	L	In serv.
482 MUROTO	Mitsubishi, Shimoneseki	. . .	. . .	3-80

D: 4,500 tons   **S:** . . . kts   **Dim:** . . . × . . . × . . .
A: None   **Electron Equipt:** Radar: 1/OPS . .   **Man:** . . .
M: . . .

REMARKS: Intended to replace the *Tsugaru*. Will be able to lay cable over bow or stern at 2-6 knots. Bow thruster. Similar to commercial *Kuroshio Maru*. Will have extensive facilities for oceanographic research.

◆ **1 Tsugaru class**

	Bldr	Laid down	L	In serv.
481 TSUGARU	Yokohama SY	18-12-54	19-7-55	15-12-55

D: 2,150 tons   **S:** 13 kts   **Dim:** 103.0 × 14.6 × 4.9

CABLE-LAYERS (continued)

Tsugaru   1971

A: 2/20-mm AA (I × 2)   **Electron Equipt:** Radar: 1/OPS 16
M: 2 Sulzer diesels; 2 props; 3,200 hp   **Man:** 103 men

REMARKS: Originally completed as a minelayer/cable-layer, between 10-7-69 and 30-4-70 she was lengthened and the amidships part of her hull was widened by 2.2 meters. Also, her cable facilities were greatly enlarged.

SUBMARINE-RESCUE SHIPS

◆ **1 Fushimi class**

402 FUSHIMI   Bldr: Sumitomo, Uraga

D: 1430 tons   **S:** 16 kts   **Dim:** 76.0 × 12.5 × 3.8
M: 1 Kawasaki-M.A.N. V6V 22/30 ATL diesel; 1 prop; 3,000 hp   **Man:** 102 men

REMARKS: Launched 10-9-69 and in service since 10-2-70. Has one rescue bell, two decompression chambers; one 12-ton crane.

Fushimi   *Ships of the World, 1975*

◆ 401 CHIHAYA   Bldr: Mitsubishi

D: 1,340 tons (1,800 fl)   **S:** 15 kts   **Dim:** 73.0 × 12.0 × 3.9
Man: 90 men   **Range:** 5,000/12
M: 1 Yokohama-M.A.N. G6Z S170 diesel, 2,700 hp

REMARKS: Launched 4-10-60 and in service since 15-3-61. Has a McCann rescue bell for six persons.

Chihaya   *Ships of the World*

REPLENISHMENT OILERS

◆ **1 Sagami class**

	Bldr	Laid down	L	In serv.
421 SAGAMI	Hitachi, Maizuru	28-9-77	4-9-78	30-3-79

D: 5,000 tons (11,600 fl)   **S:** 22 kts   **Dim:** 146.0 (140.0 pp) × 19.0 × 7.3
A: None   **Electron Equipt:** Radar: 1/OPS . . .   **Man:** . . .
M: 2 12 DRV diesels; 2 props; 18,600 hp

REMARKS: Has three stations per side, two for liquid transfers, one for solid. Large helicopter deck but no hangar. In addition to fuel oil, diesel fuel, and JP-5 aviation fuel, carries food and ammunition. 1975-76 budget.

◆ **1 Hamana class**

	Bldr	Laid down	L	In serv.
411 HAMANA	Uraga DY	17-4-61	24-10-61	10-3-62

Hamana   Uraga

REPLENISHMENT OILERS (*continued*)

D: 2,900 tons (7,550 fl)   **S:** 16 kts   **Dim:** 128.0 × 15.7 × 6.3
A: 2/40-mm AA (II × 1)   **Man:** 100 men
M: 1 Yokohama-M.A.N. KGZ 6D/150C diesel; 1 prop; 5,000 hp

REMARKS: Refitted, 1978-79, with two fueling positions per side. No solid-transfer capability. Mk 51, mod. 2, director for guns.

TRAINING SHIP

◆ **1 cadet-training ship**

	Bldr	Laid down	L	In serv.
3501 KATORI	Ishikawajima, Harima, Tokyo	8-12-67	19-11-68	10-9-69

D: 3,372 tons (4,100 fl)   **S:** 25 kts   **Dim:** 127.5 (122.0 pp) × 15.0 × 4.35
Man: 295 + 165 cadets   **Range:** 7,000/18
A: 4/76-mm DP Mk 34 (II × 2)−1/375-mm Bofors ASW rocket launcher (IV × 1)−
6/324-mm Mk 32 ASW TT (III × 2)
Electron Equipt: Radars: 1/SPS 12, 1/OPS 15, 1/Mk 34
Sonar: OQS 3
M: 2 sets Ishikawajima GT; 2 props; 20,000 hp   **Boilers:** 2

Katori   J.-C. Bellonne, 1974

REMARKS: After superstructure contains an auditorium. Helicopter deck is also used for ceremonial functions and calisthenics. An Intelset satellite communications system was added in mid-1979. The *Katori* could serve as an ASW frigate in wartime.

AUXILIARY SHIPS

	Bldr	Laid down	L	In serv.
ATS 4201 AZUMA	Maizuru	15-7-68	14-4-69	26-11-69

D: 1,950 tons (2,400 fl)   **S:** 18 kts   **Dim:** 98.0 (94.0 pp) × 13.0 × 3.8
Man: 185 men   **Electric:** 700 kw
A: 1/76-mm DP−2/Mk 4 launchers for Mk 32 ASW torpedoes
Electron Equipt: Radars: 1/OPS 15, 1/SPS 40
Sonar: SQS 11A
M: 2 Kawasaki-M.A.N. V8V 23/30 ATL diesels; 2 props; 4,000 hp

REMARKS: Has ten KD2R-5 and three BQM-34 drones. Portable ramp on helicopter

Azuma   1970

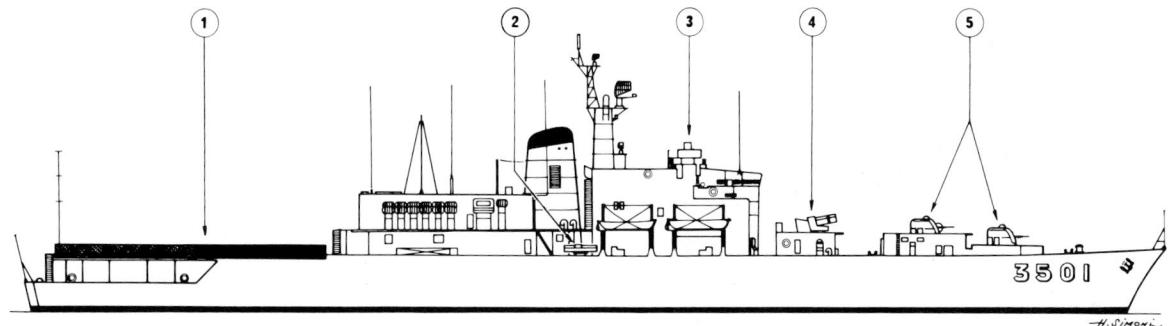

1. Helicopter and ceremonial deck   2. Mk-32 triple ASW TT   3. Mk-63 gun fire-control
director (radar on upper 76-mm mount)   4. Bofors 375-mm quadruple ASW rocket
launcher   5. Twin 76-mm, dual-purpose, gun mounts

AUXILIARY SHIPS (*continued*)

deck for launching. Hangar is used for drone check-out and storage. Special drone-tracking radar above the bridge. Has the only SPS-40 in Japanese service. Mk-51 director for gun.

◆ 5 target-support craft

	In serv.		In serv.
ASU 81 (ex-YAS-101)	30-3-68	ASU 84 (ex-YAS-104)	9-72
ASU 82 (ex-YAS-102)	31-3-69	ASU 85 (ex-YAS-105)	1974
ASU 83 (ex-YAS-103)	9-71		

ASU-85 — wearing former number   1974

D: 490 tons (543 fl)   **S:** 14.5 kts   **Dim:** 51.5 × 10.0 × 2.6
Man: 26 men + 14 passengers   **Range:** 2,500/12
Electron Equipt: Radar: OPS 10 (ASU-84: OPS 29; ASU-85: OPS 19)
M: 2 Akasaka UH-527-42 diesels; 2 props; 1,600 hp

REMARKS: ASU-82 is configured as a rescue ship. The others are intended to carry, control, recover, and service up to six KD2R-5 drone target aircraft.

◆ 1 navigational training tender   Bldr: Ando Iron Works

YTE 11

D: 120 tons (170 fl)   **S:** 13 kts   **Dim:** 33.0 × 7.0 × 1.5
M: 2 Shinko-Zoki SG175/CM diesels; 2 props; 1,400 hp

REMARKS: In service since 31-3-73. Attached to Etajima First Technical School. Can carry 25 cadets.

◆ 1 experimental trials ship

	Bldr	Laid down	L	In serv.
ASE KURIHAMA	Sasebo Heavy Industries	. . .	20-9-79	3-80

D: 900 tons   **S:** 15 kts   **Dim:** 68.0 × 11.6 × 3.3
A: Various   **Man:** 42 men + 13 scientists
M: 2 diesels; 2 props; 1,600 hp (2 auxiliary propulsors; 400 hp)

REMARKS: For testing mines, torpedoes, and sonars. In the 1979-80 budget.

◆ 1 mine-warfare trials ship

YAL 01

D: 240 tons (265 fl)   **S:** 12 kts   **Dim:** 37.0 × 2.0 × 1.9
A: Mine rails   **Man:** 16 men
M: 2 Type 6H19-E-4A diesels; 2 props; 800 hp

REMARK: In service since 1971.

◆ 1 icebreaker   Bldr: Nippon Kokan, Tsurumi

	Laid down	L	In serv.
5001 FUJI	28-8-64	18-3-65	15-7-65

Fuji   J.-C. Bellonne, 1974

D: 5,299 tons (8,566 fl)   **S:** 16.5 kts   **Dim:** 100.0 (90.0 pp) × 22.0 × 8.3
A: None   **Man:** 200 men + 45 scientists   **Range:** 15,000/15
Electron Equipt: Radars: 1/OPS 4, 1/OPS 16, 1/weather
Sonar: SQS 11A — URN-20 TACAN
M: 4 Mitsubishi-M.A.N. 48V30/42 AL diesels, electric drive; 2 props; 12,000 hp
Fuel: 1,900 tons

REMARKS: Carries three Sikorsky S-61 and one Bell 47G helicopters. Intended for Antarctic exploration and support. Cargo capacity in forward hold: 450 tons. Can break 2.5-meter ice. Passive tank roll stabilization. Hull plating up to 45 mm thick.

◆ 1 explosive-ordnance disposal diving tender

	Bldr	Laid down	L	In serv.
YAS 69 ERIMO	Uraga	1955	12-7-55	28-12-55

D: 630 tons (670 fl)   **S:** 18 kts   **Dim:** 64.0 × 7.93 × 2.95
A: 2/40-mm AA (II × 1) — 2/20-mm AA (I × 2)   **Man:** 74 men
M: 2 diesels; 2 props; 2,500 hp

REMARKS: Former minelayer (491), converted 1975-76.

AUXILIARY SHIPS (continued)

◆ 10 support ships

YAS 56 ATADA (ex-MSC-601)	YAS 65 KANAWA (ex-MSC-606)
YAS 58 YASHIRO (ex-MSC-603)	YAS 66 MIKURA (ex-MSC-612)
YAS 62 SHISAKA (ex-MSC-605)	YAS 67 TSUKUMI (ex-MSC-619)
YAS 63 KOSHIKI (ex-MSC-615)	YAS 70 HOTAKA (ex-MSC-616)
YAS 64 SAKITO (ex-MSC-607)	YAS 71 KARATO (ex-MSC-617)

REMARKS: Ex-Kasado-class minesweepers. YAS-66 and YAS-67 are designated gunnery school ships. YAS-71 is a support ship for mine-disposal divers. For characteristics, *see* Mine Warfare Ships.

◆ 1 yacht Bldr: Mitsubishi, Nagasaki

	Laid down	L	In serv.
YAS 91 HAYABUSA (ex-PC-308)	23-5-56	20-11-56	10-6-57

D: 400 tons (450 fl) **S:** 13 kts **Dim:** 57.0 (54.1 pp) × 7.9 × 3.2
M: 2 diesels; 2 props; 1,000 hp **Man:** 125 men

REMARKS: Originally a corvette similar to the *Umitaka* class but with an experimental gas turbine on the centerline shaft (removed 1970) and two 2,000-hp diesels. Re-engined on conversion to yacht and long deckhouse added aft. Armament removed.

TUGS

◆ 6 YT class

YT 53   YT 55 to YT 59

D: 195 tons **S:** 11 kts **Dim:** 25.7 × 7.0 × 2.3 **M:** 2 diesels; 1,500 hp

REMARK: In service 1975-79.

◆ 1 YT-50 class

YT 52

D: 22 tons **S:** 10 kts **Dim:** 17.0 × 4.2 × 0.7
M: 2 Gray Marine 64HN9 diesels; 2 props; 450 hp

REMARKS: In service since 1956. Former U.S. Navy LCM (6)-class landing craft converted in 1973.

◆ 8 YT-38 class

YT 35	YT 37	YT 40	YT 41	YT 44	YT 45	YT 46	YT 48

D: 100 tons **S:** 10 kts **Dim:** 23.8 × 5.4 × 1.8
M: 2 diesels; 400 hp

REMARK: In service 1963-68.

◆ 12 YT-34 class

YT 34	YT 36	YT 38	YT 39	YT 42	YT 43	YT 47	YT 49
YT 51	YT 54	YT 58	YT 59				

D: 30 tons **S:** 9 kts **Dim:** 14.5 × 4.0 × 1.0
M: 2 diesels; 320 hp

REMARKS: In service 1963-65, 1980. YT-34 is 28 tons standard, draws 0.9 meters, and has 330 hp.

◆ 9 YT-25 class

YT 25 to YT 33

D: 25 tons **S:** 11 kts **Dim:** 14.0 × 4.0 × 1.0
M: 2 diesels; 320 hp

REMARK: In service since 1955.

WATER LIGHTERS

◆ 5 YW-12 class

YW 12 to YW 16

D: 16 dwt **S:** 8 kts **Dim:** 30.5 × 5.7 × 2.2 **M:** 1 diesel; 180 hp

REMARK: In service 1964-67.

◆ 1 YW-11 class

YW 11

D: 310 dwt **S:** 10 kts **Dim:** 36.7 × 6.8 × 2.8
M: 2 diesels; 2 props; 360 hp

REMARK: In service since 1964.

◆ 1 YW-10 class

YW 10

D: 100 dwt **S:** 8 kts **Dim:** 23.5 × 5.1 × 1.0 **M:** 1 diesel; 160 hp

REMARK: In service since 1963.

◆ 7 YW-03 class

YW 03 to YW 09

D: 150 dwt **S:** 8 kts **Dim:** 27.0 × 5.5 × 2.1 **M:** 1 diesel; 75 hp

REMARK: In service since 1954.

◆ 1 YW-02 class

YW 02

D: 150 dwt **S:** 9 kts **Dim:** 27.0 × 5.5 × 2.1 **M:** 1 diesel; 90 hp

FUEL-OIL LIGHTERS

◆ 2 YO-14 class

YO 14   YO 15

D: 490 dwt **S:** 9 kts **Dim:** 45.0 × 7.8 × 2.9
M: 2 diesels; 2 props; 460 hp

REMARK: In service 1976 and 1980.

◆ 4 YO-10 class

YO 10 to YO 13

D: 290 dwt **S:** 9 kts **Dim:** 36.5 × 6.8 × 2.6
M: 2 diesels; 360 hp

REMARK: In service 1965, 1966, and 1972.

FUEL-OIL LIGHTERS (*continued*)

◆ **3 YO-07 class**

D: 490 dwt   **S:** 9 kts   **Dim:** 43.9 × 7.8 × 3.1
M: 2 diesels; 400 hp

REMARK: In service 1963-65.

◆ **4 YO-03 class**

YO 03 to YO 06

D: 300 dwt   **S:** 7 kts   **Dim:** 33.0 × 7.0 × 2.6
M: 2 diesels; 150 hp

REMARK: In service 1955-56.

◆ **1 YO-02 class**

YO 02

D: 100 dwt   **S:** 8 kts   **Dim:** 23.0 × 5.0 × 2.0   **M:** 1 diesel; 75 hp

REMARK: In service since 1954.

◆ **1 YO-01 class**

D: 100 dwt   **S:** 9 kts   **Dim:** 23.0 × 5.0 × 2.0   **M:** 1 diesel; 90 hp

REMARK: In service since 1953.

DIESEL-FUEL LIGHTERS

◆ **2 YG-07 class**

YG 07   YG 08

D: 270 dwt   **S:** 10 kts   **Dim:** 36.7 × 6.8 × 2.6
M: 1 diesel; 350 hp

REMARK: In service 1973 and 1977.

◆ **1 YG-06 class**

YG 06

D: 270 dwt   **S:** 9 kts   **Dim:** 34.4 × 6.8 × 2.8
M: 2 diesels; 330 hp

REMARK: In service since 1963.

◆ **4 YG-01 class**

YG 01 to YG 04

D: 100 dwt   **S:** 8 kts   **Dim:** 23.0 × 5.0 × 2.0   **M:** 1 diesel; 90 hp

CARGO LIGHTERS

◆ **1 YL-08 class**

YL 08

D: 50 dwt   **S:** 8 kts   **Dim:** 22.4 × 5.1 × 1.2
M: 1 diesel; 180 hp

REMARK: In service since 1967.

◆ **6 YL-02 class**

YL 02 to YL 07

D: 50 dwt   **S:** 8 kts   **Dim:** 20.0 × 5.1 × 1.2   **M:** 1 diesel; 100 hp

REMARK: In service since 1954.

◆ **1 YL-01 class**

D: 50 dwt   **S:** 7 kts   **Dim:** 20.0 × 5.1 × 1.2   **M:** 1 diesel, 90 hp

REMARK: In service since 1952.

SELF-PROPELLED FLOATING CRANES

◆ **1 YC-09 class**

Y 09

D: 260 tons   **S:** 6 kts   **Dim:** 26.0 × 14.0 × 0.9
M: 2 diesels; 2 props; 280 hp

REMARK: In service since 1974.

◆ **3 YC-06 class**

YC 06 to YC 08

D: 156 tons   **S:** 5 kts   **Dim:** 24.0 × 10.0 × 0.8
M: 2 diesels; 2 props; 240 hp

REMARK: In service 1969-72.

◆ **1 YC-05 class**

D: 110 tons   **S:** 5 kts   **Dim:** 22.0 × 10.0 × 0.9
M: 2 diesels; 180 hp

REMARK: In service since 1967.

SLUDGE-REMOVAL LIGHTER

◆ **1 YB 01 class**

D: 177 tons   **S:** 9 kts   **Dim:** 27.5 × 5.2 × 1.9   **M:** 1 diesel; 230 hp

REMARK: In service since 1975.

TENDERS

◆ **74 miscellaneous communications boats (YF series)**

REMARKS: YF-2048, YF-2097 to YF-2109, and YF-2075 are U.S. LCM (6) landing craft. YF-2066 to YF-2074, YF-2078 to YF-2081, YF-2083 to YF-2087, YF-2091, YF-2096, YF-2110, and YF-2116 are all LCVPs. The remainder are small passenger launches of various designs.

◆ **2 trials craft**

YD 01   YD 02

REMARK: Date from 1975.

BUOY TENDERS

◆ **3 YV-01 class**

YV 01 to YV 03

BUOY TENDERS (continued)

D: 45 tons **S:** 10 kts **Dim:** 20.0 × 4.4 × 1.0
M: 2 diesels; 2 props; 240 hp

REMARKS: In service 1968-70. Intended to service seaplane fairway buoy arrays in support of PS-1 Type ASW seaplanes.

◆ 1 catamaran

YS 01

D: 80 tons **S:** 9 kts **Dim:** 22.0 × 7.8 × 1.4
M: 2 diesels; 2 props; 460 hp **Man:** 6 men

REMARK: In service since 30-3-79.

FIREBOATS

◆ 1 YE-01 class

YE 01 (ex-*Kosuko*, 6)

D: 40 tons **S:** 19 kts **Dim:** 23.1 × 5.6 × 1.0
M: 3 diesels; 3 props; 1,300 hp

REMARKS: In service since 1964. Reclassified and re-engined in 1977. Originally made 30 knots on 2,800 hp.

BARGES, NON-SELF-PROPELLED

◆ 3 fuel barges

YO 106 to YO 108

◆ 7 cargo barges

YL 113 to YL 119

MOTOR BOATS

◆ 12 miscellaneous

B 4002 to B 4013

MARITIME SAFETY AGENCY
(*Kaijo Hoancho*)

PERSONNEL: Approximately 11,000 men

The Maritime Safety Agency, which was organized in 1948, is undergoing a massive expansion, which by 1982, it will make it the world's largest and best-equipped coast guard, by far. In peacetime, it is directed by the Department of Transportation and, although most of its ships are armed, they are not considered part of the Navy; they fly only the national colors (a red disk on a white background), not the flag flown by naval ships. In wartime, the ships would be under naval control.

AVIATION: In 1979, the MSA operated nineteen fixed-wing aircraft (5 YS-11A transports, 2 SC-7 Skyvan, 11 Beech light transports, and 1 Cessna SA 790/185C) and twenty-seven helicopters (1 Sikorsky S-62A, 14 Bell 212, 4 Bell 206B, 6 Bell 47G, and 2 Hughes 369-HS). More helicopters will be required for the Soya-class cutters.

HIGH-ENDURANCE CUTTERS

◆ 4 (+2) Soya class

	Bldr	Laid down	L	In serv.
PL 01 SOYA	Nippon Kokan, Tsurumi	12-9-77	3-7-78	22-11-78
PL 02 TSUGARU	Nippon Kokan, Tsurumi	18-4-78	6-12-78	17-4-79
PL 03 OOSUMI	. . .	1-9-78	6-79	18-10-79
PL 04 N . . .	. . .	14-3-79	10-79	12-10-79

D: 3,137 tons (3,562 fl) **S:** 23 kts **Dim:** 105.4 × 14.6 × 4.8
Man: 71 men **Range:** 5,700/18 **Fuel:** 650 tons **Electric:** 1,500 kva
A: 1/40-mm AA − 1/20-mm AA − 1/Bell 212 helicopter
M: 2 Pielstick 12PC2-5V400 diesels; 2 controllable-pitch props; 15,600 hp

REMARKS: The *Soya* was built under the 1977 program, the *Tsugaru*, P1-03, and PL-04 under the 1978 program. Two more are planned. The *Soya* has an icebreaking bow and will operate in the north; the others have normal bows. Fitted with both passive tank and fin stabilization. Data for the *Soya* are: **D:** 3,803 fl; **Dim:** 98.6 × 15.6 × 5.2; **S:** 20 kts.

◆ 24 Shiretoko class

	Bldr	L	In serv.
PL 101 SHIRETOKO	Mitsui	13-7-78	16-11-78
PL 102 ESAN	Sumitomo	8-78	16-11-78
PL 103 WAKASA	Kawasaki	8-78	29-11-78
PL 104 YAHIKO	Mitsubishi	8-78	16-11-78
PL 105 MOTOBU	Sasebo	8-78	29-11-78
PL 106 RISHIRI	Shikoku DY	27-3-79	8-79
PL 107 MATSUSHIMA	Tohoku	11-4-79	9-79
PL 108 IWAHI	Hitichi, Usumi	28-3-79	10-8-79
PL 109 SHIKINE	Usugine	27-4-79	9-79
PL 110 SURUGA	. . .	20-4-79	9-79
PL 111 REBUN	Narazaki	6-79	11-79
PL 112 CHOKAI	Nichokal	6-79	11-79
PL 113 ASHIZURI	Sanoyasu	6-79	10-79
PL 114 OKI	Tsuneishi	6-79	11-79
PL 115 N . . .	Miho	7-79	11-79
PL 116 YONAKUNI	Hiyashikane	6-79	31-10-79
PL 117 DAISETSU	Hakodate Dock	22-8-79	1-80
PL 118 N . . .	. . .	9-79	3-80
PL 119 SUZUKA	. . .	4-10-79	3-80
PL 120 KUNASAKI	. . .	8-10-79	2-80
PL 121 N . . .	. . .	9-79	1-80
PL 122 N . . .	. . .	10-79	2-80
PL 123 N . . .	. . .	9-79	1-80
PL 124 N . . .	. . .	11-79	3-80

D: 961 tons (1,279 fl) **S:** 20 kts **Dim:** 77.8 (73.6 pp) × 9.6 × 3.42
Man: 41 men **Range:** 5,800/16 **Fuel:** 191 tons
A: 1/40-mm AA − 1/20-mm AA **Electric:** 625 kva
M: 2 Niigata 8MA 40 diesels; 2 props; 7,000 hp

REMARKS: All twenty-four are programmed to be completed by 1980. Resemble the *Erima* class. Intended to patrol the 200-nautical-mile economic zone. PL-102 and PL-103 have Fuji 8540B diesels, also of 3,500 hp each.

HIGH-ENDURANCE CUTTERS (*continued*)

◆ **2 Izu class**   Bldrs: PL-31: Hitachi, Zosen; PL-32: Maizuru

PL 31 Izu   PL 32 Miura

   D: 2,081 tons (2,200 fl)   **S:** 24.6 kts   **Dim:** 95.5 (86.45 pp) × 11.6 × 3.8
   A: 1/40-mm AA   **Man:** 72 men   **Range:** 5,000/20.5, 14,500/12.7
   M: 2 diesels; 2 props; 10,400 hp

REMARKS: Launched 1-67 and 11-68, respectively. Large weather radar in dome aft removed in 1978 and gun added forward.

Miura   1972

◆ **4 Erimo class**

	Bldr	L	In serv.
PL 13 Erimo	Hitachi, Mukaishima	14-8-65	30-11-65
PL 14 Satsuma	Hitachi, Mukaishima	4-66	30-7-66
PL 15 Daio	Hitachi, Maizuru	19-6-73	28-9-73
PL 16 Muroto	Naikai, Taguma	5-8-74	30-11-74

Daio   1974

   D: 1,009 tons   **S:** 19.5 kts   **Dim:** 76.6 (73.0 pp) × 9.2 × 3.0
   A: 1/76-mm DP—1/20-mm AA   **Range:** 6,000/18
   M: 2 diesels; 2 props, 4,800 hp

REMARKS: The hull of PL-13 is reinforced against ice. PL-15 and PL-16: **D:** 1,170 tons; **Dim:** beam 9.6, draft 3.18; **A:** 1/40-mm AA—1/20-mm AA; **M:** 7,000 hp for 20.4 knots; **Range:** 6,600/18.

◆ **2 Nojima class**   Bldr: Uraga Dock Co., Ltd.

	L	In serv.
PL 11 Nojima	12-2-62	30-4-62
PL 12 Ojika	. . .	10-6-63

Nojima   E. Aoki

   D: 869 tons (1,009 fl)   **S:** 18.1 kts   **Dim:** 69.0 × 9.18 × 3.2
   A: None   **Man:** 73 men   **Range:** 8,000/14   **Electric:** 310 kva
   M: 2 Uraga-Sulzer 6 MD 42 diesels; 2 props; 3,000 hp

REMARKS: Used for meteorological reporting. Passive tank stabilization.

◆ **1 Kojima class**   Bldr: Kure, Zosen

Kojima   1972

HIGH-ENDURANCE CUTTERS (*continued*)

D: 1,066 tons (1,206 fl)   **S:** 17.3 kts   **Dim:** 69.6 × 10.3 × 3.53
Man: 59 men + 55 midshipmen   **Range:** 6,120/13   **Electric:** 550 kva
A: 1/76-mm DP – 1/40-mm AA – 1/20-mm AA
M: 1 Uraga-Sulzer 7 MD 51 diesel; 1 prop; 2,600 hp

REMARKS: In service since 21-5-64. Used as a training ship at Kure Academy.

MEDIUM-ENDURANCE CUTTERS

◆ **3 new construction 500-ton class**

	Bldr	L	In serv.
PM . . . N . . .	. . .	. . .	. . .
PM . . . N . . .	. . .	. . .	. . .
PM . . . N . . .	. . .	. . .	. . .

D: 540 tons (fl)   **S:** 18 kts   **Dim:** 66.5 × 7.9 × . . .
A: 1/20-mm AA   **M:** 2 diesels; 2 props; . . . hp

REMARKS: Authorized in 1979. Intended to replace the *Tokachi* (PM-51), *Tatsuta* (PM-52), and *Teshio* (PM-53) on completion, 1980-81.

◆ **2 Takatori class**

	Bldr	L	In serv.
PM 89 TAKATORI	Naikai, Taguma	8-12-77	24-3-78
PM 94 KUMANO	Naikai, Taguma	2-11-78	23-2-79

D: 477 tons (631 fl)   **S:** 15.7 kts   **Dim:** 46.5 (44.2 pp) × 9.2 × 3.9
A: None   **Man:** 34 men   **Range:** 750/15   **Electric:** 200 kva
M: 2 Niigata 6M31EX diesels; 1 prop; 3,000 hp

REMARKS: Rescue-tug types. Equipped for fire-fighting and salvage duties. Two water cannon.

◆ **20 Bihoro class**

	Bldr	In serv.
PM 73 BIHORO	Tohoku Zosen	28-2-74
PM 74 KUMA	Usuki	28-2-74
PM 75 FUJI	Usuki	7-2-75
PM 76 KABASHIMA	Usuki	25-3-75
PM 77 SADO	Tohoku Zosen	1-2-75
PM 78 ISHIKARI	Tohoku Zosen	13-3-76
PM 79 ABAKUMA	Tohoku Zosen	30-1-76
PM 80 ISUZU	Nakai, Taguma	10-3-76
PM 81 KIKUCHI	Usuki	6-2-76
PM 82 KUZURYU	Usuki	18-3-76
PM 83 HOROBETSU	Tohoku Zosen	21-1-77
PM 84 SHIRAKAMI	Tohoku Zosen	3-3-77
PM 85 SAGAMI	Utsumi	30-11-76
PM 86 TONE	Usuki	30-11-76
PM 87 YOSHINO	Usuki	28-1-77
PM 88 KUROBE	Shikoku DY	15-2-77
PM 90 CHIKUGO	Nakai, Taguma	1-78
PM 91 YAMAKUNI	Usuki	1-78
PM 92 KATSURA	Shikoku DY	2-78
PM 93 SHINANO	Tohoku Zosen	2-78

Sado   1978

D: 636 tons (657 fl)   **S:** 18 kts   **Dim:** 63.4 × 7.8 × 2.53
A: 1/20-mm AA   **Man:** 34 men   **Range:** 3,260/16
M: 2 Niigata GM31EX diesels; 2 controllable-pitch props; 3,000 hp

◆ **7 Kunashiri class**

	Bldr	In serv.
PM 65 KUNASHIRI	Maizuru DY	28-3-69
PM 66 MINABE	Maizuru DY	28-3-70
PM 67 SAROBETSU	Maizuru DY	30-3-71
PM 68 KAMISHIMA	Usuki	31-1-72
PM 70 MIYAKE	Tohoku Zosen	25-1-73
PM 71 AWAJI	Usuki	25-1-73
PM 72 YAEYAMA	Usuki	20-12-72

Yaeyama   1975

D: 498 tons (574 fl)   **S:** 17.5 kts   **Dim:** 58.0 × 7.4 × 2.4
A: 1/20-mm AA   **Man:** 40 men   **Range:** 3,040/16
M: 2 Niigata 6MF32H diesels; 2 props; 2,600 hp

REMARKS: PM-70 to PM-72 have GM31EX diesels, 3,000 hp. PM-72 has controllable-pitch propellers.

MEDIUM-ENDURANCE CUTTERS (continued)

◆ **5 Matsuura class** Bldrs: PM-60, PM-61: Osaka SB; Others: Hitachi, Zosen

	In serv.		In serv.
PM 60 MATSUURA	18-3-61	PM 63 NATORI	20-1-66
PM 61 SENDAI	14-4-62	PM 64 KARATSU	29-3-67
PM 62 AMAMI	29-3-65		

D: 425 tons **S:** 16.5 kts; PM-64: 18 kts; PM-63: 16.8 kts
Dim: 55.3 × 7.0 × 2.3 **Man:** 37-40 men **Range:** 3,500/12
A: 1/20-mm AA **M:** Diesels; 2 props; 1,400 hp; PM-63: 1,800 hp; PM-64: 2,600 hp

◆ **7 Yahagi class** Bldrs: Niigata; PM-69: Usuki

	In serv.		In serv.
PM 54 YAHAGI	31-7-56	PM 58 YUBARI	15-3-60
PM 55 SUMIDA	30-6-57	PM 59 HORONAI	11-2-61
PM 56 CHITOSE	30-4-58	PM 69 OKINAWA	8-10-69
PM 57 SORACHI	31-3-59		

D: 376 tons (430 fl) **S:** 15.5 kts **Dim:** 50.27 × 7.3 × 2.16
A: 1/40-mm AA **Man:** 44 men **Range:** 4,350/12
M: 2 Ikegai 6-MSB 31S diesels; 2 props; 1,400 hp

REMARK: PM-69 was originally built for Okinawa, transferred to MSA in 1972.

◆ **1 Teshio class** Bldr: Uraga

PM 53 TESHIO

Teshio — Yahagi class similar   1978

D: 421 tons **S:** 15.7 kts **Dim:** 50.3 × 7.0 × 2.5
A: 1/40-mm AA **Man:** 37 men **Range:** 3,800/12
M: 2 Niigata 6MSB 31S diesels; 2 props; 1,400 hp

REMARK: In service 19-3-55.

◆ **2 Tokachi class** Bldr: Ishikawajima Harima, Kure

	In serv.		In serv.
PM 51 TOKACHI	31-7-54	PM 52 TATSUTA	10-9-54

D: 370 tons (381 fl) **S:** 15.9 kts **Dim:** 51.8 × 6.6 × 2.15
A: 1/40-mm AA **Man:** 37 men **Range:** 3,820/12
M: 2 Ikegai 9-MSB 31 diesels; 2 props; 1,500 hp

◆ **4 Chifuri class**

	Bldr	In serv.		Bldr	In serv.
PM 18 CHIFURI	Nihonkai	30-4-52	PM 20 KOZU	Niigata	9-12-51
PM 19 KUROKAMI	Nihonkai	31-3-52	PM 22 DAITO	Niigata	25-2-52

D: 407 tons (490 normal) **S:** 16.1 kts **Dim:** 55.7 × 7.7 × 2.6
A: 1/76-mm DP – 1/20-mm AA **Man:** 45 men **Range:** 4,450/12
M: 2 RE 6 diesels; 1,300 hp **Electric:** 120 kw

◆ **13 Rebun class**

	Bldr	In serv.
PM 04 REBUN	Hitachi	28-2-51
PM 05 IKI	Hitachi	5-4-51
PM 06 OKI	Mitsui, Tamano	19-2-51
PM 08 HACHISO	Chu Nippon Juko	6-3-51
PM 09 AMAKUSA	Chu Nippon Juko	8-3-51
PM 10 OKUSHIRI	Hitachi	27-6-51
PM 11 KUSAKAKI	Hitachi	30-7-51
PM 12 RISHIRI	Fujinagata	30-6-51
PM 13 NOTO	Fujinagata	25-8-51
PM 14 HEKURA	Harima Zasen	30-6-51
PM 15 MIKURA	Harima Zasen	19-7-51
PM 16 KOSHIKI	Nishinihon	31-8-51
PM 17 HIRADO	Nishinihon	4-9-51

Iki   1978

D: 387 tons (503 fl) **S:** 14.6 kts **Dim:** 52.4 (47.5 pp) × 8.1 × 2.65
A: 1/76-mm DP – 1/20-mm AA **Man:** 40 men **Range:** 3,340/12
M: 2 M.A.N. G6V 37/50 diesels; 1,300 hp **Electric:** 120 kw

REMARK: The *Genkai* (PM-07) was stricken in 1978.

PATROL BOATS

◆ 1 new construction 130-ton class

		Bldr	In serv.
PS . . .	N . . .	. . .	. . .

D: 180 tons (fl) **S:** 28 kts **Dim:** 35.0 × 6.3 × . . .
A: 1/12.7-mm machine gun **M:** 2 diesels; 2 props; . . . hp

REMARKS: Authorized in 1979. Intended to replace the *Akagi* (PS-40), but much larger.

◆ 3 Bizan-class, aircraft-rescue

	Bldr	In serv.
PS 42 BIZAN	Mitsubishi, Shimonoseki	28-3-66
PS 47 ASAMA	Mitsubishi, Shimonoseki	31-1-69
PS 48 SHIRAMINE	Mitsubishi, Shimonoseki	15-12-69

D: 42-48 tons (83-85 fl) **S:** 21.6 kts; PS-48: 25 kts
Dim: 26.0 × 5.6 × 1.0 **Man:** 14 men **Range:** 400/18, PS-48: 250/25
A: 1/12.7-mm machine gun
M: 2 Mitsubishi 12 HD 2 OMTK diesels; 2 props; 1,140 hp; PS-48: 2 MTU diesels; 2,200 hp

◆ 1 Akagi-class, aircraft-rescue

PS 40 AKAGI Bldr: Hitachi, Kanagawa

D: 44 tons (64 fl) **S:** 28 kts **Dim:** 24.0 × 5.4 × 1.0
A: 1/12.7-mm machine gun **Man:** 14 men **Range:** 350/21
M: 2 MTU diesels; 2 props; 2,200 hp

REMARK: In service 24-3-65.

◆ 1 Tsukuba-class, aircraft-rescue

PS 31 TSUKUBA Bldr: Hitachi, Kanegawa

D: 65 tons (fl) **S:** 18 kts **Dim:** 24.5 × 6.5 × 1.0
A: 1/12.7-mm machine gun **Man:** 14 men **Range:** 230/15
M: 2 Niigata diesels; 2 props; 1,800 hp

REMARK: In service 30-3-62.

◆ 14 Hidaka class

	Bldr	In serv.
PS 32 HIDAKA	Azuma	23-4-62
PS 33 HIYAMA	Hitachi	13-3-63
PS 34 TSURUGI	Mukajima	13-3-63
PS 35 ROKKO	Shikoku	31-1-64
PS 36 TAKANAWA	Hayashikane	27-1-64
PS 37 AKIYOSHI	Hashihama	29-2-64
PS 38 KUNIMI	Hayashikane	15-2-65
PS 39 TAKATSUKI	Kurashima	30-3-65
PS 41 KAMUI	Hayashikane	15-2-66
PS 43 ASHITAKA	Usuki	10-2-67
PS 44 KURAMA	Usuki	28-2-67
PS 45 IBUKI	Usuki	5-3-68
PS 46 TOUMI	Usuki	20-2-68
PS 49 NOBARU	Hitachi	10-12-68

D: 130 tons (169.4 fl) **S:** 13.7 kts **Dim:** 33.72 (30.5 pp) × 6.3 × 1.8

Akiyoshi E. Aoki

A: 1/12.7-mm machine gun (usually not mounted) **Man:** 17 men
M: 1 6MSB 31S diesel; 700 hp **Range:** 1,100/12 **Electric:** 60 kva

COASTAL PATROL BOATS

◆ 12 (+7) Murakomo class

	Bldr	In serv.
PC 201 MURAKOMO	Mitsubishi, Shimonoseki	24-3-78
PC 202 KITAGUMO	Hitachi, Kanagawa	17-3-78
PC 203 YUKIGUMO	Hitachi, Kanagawa	27-9-78
PC 204 ASAGUMO	Mitsubishi, Shimonoseki	21-9-78
PC 205 HAYAGUMO	Mitsubishi, Shimonoseki	30-1-79
PC 206 AKIGUMO	Hitachi, Kanagawa	28-2-79
PC 207 YAEGUMO	Mitsubishi, Shimonoseki	16-3-79
PC 208 NATSUGUMO	Hitachi, Kanagawa	22-3-79
PC 209 YAMAGIRI	Hitachi, Kanagawa	26-6-79
PC 210 KAWAGIRI	. . .	7-79
PC 211 TERUZUKI	. . .	6-79
PC 212 NATSUZUKI	Maizuru Heavy Ind.	26-7-79
PC 213 N . . .	. . .	. . .
PC 214 N . . .	. . .	. . .
PC 215 N . . .	. . .	. . .
PC 216 N . . .	. . .	. . .
PC 217 N . . .	. . .	. . .
PC 218 N . . .	. . .	. . .
PC 219 N . . .	. . .	. . .

D: 85 tons (125 fl) **S:** 30 kts **Dim:** 31.0 (28.5 pp) × 6.3 × 1.2
A: 1/12.7-mm machine gun **Man:** 13 men **Range:** 350/28
M: 2 MTU 16V652 TB 81 diesels; 2 props; 4,400 hp **Electric:** 40 kva

REMARK: PC-201 to PC-204 built under 1977 program, remainder under 1978-80 program.

◆ 10 Akizuki class Bldr: Mitsubishi, Shimonoseki

	In serv.		In serv.
PC 64 AKIZUKI	28-2-74	PC 76 HAMAYUKI	2-76
PC 65 SHINONOME	25-2-74	PC 77 HAMAZUKI	11-76
PC 72 URAYUKI	31-5-75	PC 78 ISOZUKI	3-77
PC 73 ISEYUKI	31-7-75	PC 79 SHIMANAMI	12-77
PC 75 HATAYUKI	2-75	PC 80 YUZUKI	3-79

COASTAL PATROL BOATS (*continued*)

Hatayuki   F. Lauga, 1976

D: 76 tons (fl)   **S:** 22.1 kts   **Dim:** 26.0 × 6.3 × 1.12
Man: 10 men   **Range:** 290/21.5
M: 2 Mitsubishi 12 DM 20 MTK diesels; 2 props; 3,000 hp

◆ **17 Shikinami class**

	Bldr	In serv.
PC 54 SHIKINAMI	Mitsubishi, Shimonoseki	24-2-71
PC 55 TOMONAMI	Mitsubishi, Shimonoseki	20-3-71
PC 56 WAKANAMI	Mitsubishi, Shimonoseki	30-10-71
PC 57 ISENAMI	Hitachi, Kanegawa	29-2-72
PC 58 TAKANAMI	Mitsubishi, Shimonoseki	30-11-71
PC 59 MUTSUKI	Hitachi, Kanegawa	18-12-72
PC 60 MOCHIZUKI	Hitachi, Kanegawa	18-12-72
PC 61 HARUZUKI	Mitsubishi, Shimonoseki	30-11-72
PC 62 KIYOZUKI	Mitsubishi, Shimonoseki	18-12-72

Urazuki   1975

PC 63 URAZUKI	Mitsubishi, Shimonoseki	30-1-73
PC 66 URANAMI	Hitachi, Kanegawa	22-12-73
PC 67 TAMANAMI	Mitsubishi, Shimonoseki	25-12-73
PC 68 MINEGUMO	Mitsubishi, Shimonoseki	30-11-73
PC 69 KIYONAMI	Mitsubishi, Shimonoseki	30-10-73
PC 70 OKINAMI	Hitachi, Kanegawa	8-2-74
PC 71 WAKAGUMO	Hitachi, Kanegawa	25-3-74
PC 74 ASOYUKI	Hitachi, Kanegawa	16-6-75

D: 46 tons (64 fl)   **S:** 25.8 kts   **Dim:** 21.0 × 5.3 × 1.22
A: 1/12.7-mm machine gun (usually not mounted)   **Man:** 10 men
M: 2 Mercedes-Benz MB820Db diesels; 2 props; 2,200 hp   **Range:** 240/23.8

◆ **1 Matsunami class**   **Bldr:** Hitachi, Kanegawa

PC 53 MATSUNAMI

D: 59 tons (84 fl)   **S:** 20.7 kts   **Dim:** 24.96 × 6.0 × 1.33
Man: 30 men   **Range:** 270/18
M: 2 Mercedes-Benz MB820Db diesels; 2 props; 2,200 hp

REMARKS: In service 30-3-71. Especially configured for Emperor Hirohito for oceanographic research.

◆ **1 Hamanami class**   **Bldr:** Sumidagawa

PC 52 HAMANAMI

D: 60 tons (fl)   **S:** 20.9 kts   **Dim:** 21.0 × 5.1 × 1.22
Man: 10 men   **Range:** 290/20.9
M: 2 Mercedes-Benz MB820Db diesels; 2 props; 2,200 hp

REMARK: In service 22-3-71.

◆ **1 Hamagiri class**   **Bldr:** Sumidagawa

PC 48 HAMAGIRI

D: 51 tons (fl)   **S:** 14.6 kts   **Dim:** 21.0 × 5.1 × 1.11
Man: 10 men   **Range:** 270/12.9
M: 2 Mitsubishi 12DH 20TK diesels; 2 props; 1,140 hp

◆ **5 Umigiri class**   **Bldr:** Hitachi, Kanagawa

	In serv.			In serv.
PC 46 UMIGIRI	15-3-68		PC 50 SETOGIRI	5-3-70
PC 47 ASAGIRI	15-3-68		PC 51 HAYAGIRI	5-3-70
PC 49 SAGIRI	31-3-70			

Sagiri   1975

COASTAL PATROL BOATS (continued)

    D: 42 tons (59 fl)   **S:** 26.9 kts   **Dim:** 21.0 × 5.1 × 0.95
    A: 1/12.7-mm machine gun (usually not mounted)   **Man:** 10 men
    M: 2 Mercedes-Benz MB820Db diesels; 2 props; 2,200 hp   **Range:** 270/25.9

◆ **5 Matsuyuki class** Bldr: Hitachi, Kanegawa

	In serv.			In serv.
PC 40 MATSUYUKI	28-3-64		PC 44 YAMAYUKI	15-3-67
PC 41 SHIMAYUKI	31-1-66		PC 45 KOMAYUKI	15-3-67
PC 43 HAMAYUKI	24-3-66			

    D: 39 tons (64 fl)   **S:** 26.5 kts   **Dim:** 21.0 × 5.1 × 0.95
    A: 1/12.7-mm machine gun   **Man:** 10 men   **Range:** 240/25
    M: 2 Mercedes-Benz MB820Db diesels; 2 props; 2,200 hp

REMARKS: Sister *Tamayuki* (PC-42) down-rated to CL-305 on 11-1-79. Others will probably follow on completion of *Murakomo* class.

PATROL CRAFT

◆ **22 Yamayuri class** Bldr: Ishihara, Takasago, 1978-79

CL 201 YAMAYURI	CL 212 HIMAWARI
CL 202 TACHIBANA	CL 213 HAZAKURA
CL 203 KOMAKUSA	CL 214 HINAGIKU
CL 204 SHIRAGIKU	CL 215 HAMAGIKU
CL 205 YAGURUMA	CL 216 FUYUME
CL 206 HAMANASU	CL 217 TSUBAKI
CL 207 SUZURAN	CL 218 SAZANKA
CL 208 ISOGIKU	CL 219 AOI
CL 209 ISEGIKU	CL 220 SUISEN
CL 210 AYAME	CL 221 YAEZAKURA
CL 211 AJISAI	CL 222 AKEBI

    D: 27 tons (40.3 fl)   **S:** 19 kts   **Dim:** 18.0 × 4.3 × 0.82
    Man: 6 men   **Range:** . . .   **M:** 2 diesels; 2 props; 900 hp

REMARK: Three water cannon for fire-fighting.

◆ **4 Nogekaze class** Bldr: Sumidagawa, 1972

CL 99 NOGEKAZE	CL 107 ITOKAZE
CL 105 KUSUKAZE	CL 128 KAWAKAZE

    D: 22.5 tons (29 fl)   **S:** 16.6 kts   **Dim:** 16.0 × 4.1 × 0.8
    Man: 6 men   **Range:** 150/14.7
    M: 2 Type UDV816 diesels; 2 props; 500 hp

◆ **95 Chiyokaze class**

    Bldrs: Ishihara, Nobotuka, Yokohama Yacht, Sumidagawa, 1968-76

CL 44 CHIYOKAZE	CL 89 KISHIKAZE	CL 125 TONEKAZE
CL 50 SUZUKAZE	CL 90 MAYAKAZE	CL 126 SHIZUKAZE
CL 51 URAKAZE	CL 91 KIKUKAZE	CL 127 MUROKAZE
CL 53 SUGIKAZE	CL 92 HIROKAZE	CL 129 YAMAKAZE
CL 54 FUJIKAZE	CL 93 KIBIKAZE	CL 130 HIKOKAZE
CL 55 MIYAKAZE	CL 94 ASHIKAZE	CL 131 TAKAKAZE
CL 57 CHINUKAZE	CL 95 OTOKAZE	CL 132 MURAKAZE
CL 59 NACHIKAZE	CL 96 KURIKAZE	CL 133 NOMOKAZE

CL 65 TOMAKAZE	CL 97 IMAKAZE	CL 134 KUMOKAZE
CL 66 HIBAKAZE	CL 98 TERUKAZE	CL 135 YANAKAZE
CL 67 YURIKAZE	CL 100 TOKITSUKAZE	CL 136 YURAKAZE
CL 68 SUMIKAZE	CL 101 TSUKIKAZE	CL 137 WASHIKAZE
CL 69 KASHIMA	CL 102 AWAKAZE	CL 138 KUSHIKAZE
CL 70 TAKEKAZE	CL 104 MIOKAZE	CL 139 HOSHIKAZE
CL 71 KINUKAZE	CL 106 KILKAZE	CL 140 GETTŌ
CL 72 SHIGIKAZE	CL 108 TAMATSUKAZE	CL 141 IWAKAZE
CL 73 UZUKAZE	CL 109 MIYOKAZE	CL 142 MATSUKAZE
CL 74 AKIKAZE	CL 110 AYAKAZE	CL 143 OITSUKAZE
CL 75 SETOKAZE	CL 111 MITSUKAZE	CL 144 ARAKAZE
CL 76 KUREKAZE	CL 112 HATAKAZE	CL 145 TANIKAZE
CL 77 MOJIKAZE	CL 113 NUMAKAZE	CL 146 KOCHIKAZE
CL 78 SATAKAZE	CL 114 SOYOKAZE	CL 147 OKIKAZE
CL 79 KIRIKAZE	CL 115 MINEKAZE	CL 148 SUWAKAZE
CL 80 KAMIKAZE	CL 116 OKITSUKAZE	CL 149 SACHIKAZE
CL 81 UMIKAZE	CL 117 DEIGO	CL 150 NATSUKAZE
CL 82 YUMEKAZE	CL 118 YUUNA	CL 151 HARUKAZE
CL 83 MAKIKAZE	CL 119 ADAN	CL 152 RINDŌ
CL 84 HAKAZE	CL 120 HOROKAZE	CL 153 SAWAKAZE
CL 85 SHACHIKAZE	CL 121 SOMAKAZE	CL 154 KAIDŌ
CL 86 HIMEKAZE	CL 122 HATSUKAZE	CL 155 NADESHIKO
CL 87 ISEKAZE	CL 123 SASAKAZE	CL 156 YAMAZAKURA
CL 88 KOMAKAZE	CL 124 HAGIKAZE	

    D: 19.5 tons (27 fl)   **S:** 18.4 kts   **Dim:** 15.0 × 4.1 × 0.76
    Man: 6 men   **Range:** 180/16.1
    M: 2 Mitsubishi DH24MK diesels; 2 props; 500 hp

REMARKS: The *Nomakaze* (CL-103) was lost in 1978. CL-69 is named for her home port; CL-117 to CL-119 are homeported in Okinawa.

Takekaze   1975

PATROL CRAFT (*continued*)

◆ **31 Yakaze class** Bldrs: Yokohama Yacht, Sumidagawa, Hishihara, 1964-69

CL 26 Yakaze	CL 37 Amatsukaze	CL 48 Toyokaze
CL 27 Kiyokaze	CL 38 Kukikaze	CL 49 Tokikaze
CL 28 Iyokaze	CL 39 Sagikaze	CL 52 Mutsukaze
CL 29 Fusakaze	CL 40 Shiokaze	CL 56 Yoshikaze
CL 30 Tachikaze	CL 41 Nikaze	CL 58 Sukikaze
CL 31 Kotokaze	CL 42 Tomokaze	CL 60 Tatsukaze
CL 32 Kitakaze	CL 43 Wakakaze	CL 61 Umekaze
CL 33 Isokaze	CL 45 Tamakaze	CL 62 Yumikaze
CL 34 Kisokaze	CL 46 Nadakaze	CL 63 Mihokaze
CL 35 Michikaze	CL 47 Kunikaze	CL 64 Koshikaze
CL 36 Tsurukaze		

Isokaze   1975

D: 17.9 tons (24 fl)   **S:** 18.7 kts   **Dim:** 15.0 × 4.1 × 0.74
Man: 6 men   **Range:** 190/15.5, 320/12
M: 2 Mitsubishi DH24MK diesels; 2 props; 500 hp

◆ **5 Yukikaze class** Bldr: Yokohama Yacht, 1962-63

CL 21 Yukikaze	CL 23 Yukaze	CL 25 Asakaze
CL 22 Shimakaze	CL 24 Yodokaze	

D: 16.5 tons (24 fl)   **S:** 18.6 kts   **Dim:** 15.0 × 4.2 × 0.6
Man: 6 men   **Range:** 320/12   **M:** 2 DH24Mk diesels; 2 props; 500 hp

◆ **1 Matsuyuki class** Bldr: Sumidagawa

CL 305 Tamayuki (ex-PC-42)

REMARKS: In service 3-31-59. Reclassified 11-1-79. Data as for *Matsuyuki*-class coastal patrol boats.

◆ **5 Hamakaze class** Bldrs: Various, 1948-50

CL 306 Fubuki	CL 312 Akishimo	CL 317 Hatsugiku
CL 311 Asanagi	CL 314 Shirayuki	

D: 14 tons   **S:** 16.3 kts   **Dim:** 15.0 × 3.5 × . . .
Man: 5 men   **Range:** 270/15.7
M: 2 Isuzu DH100T diesels; 2 props; 350 hp

REMARK: Reclassified from PCs, 1966-70.

◆ **8 Asashimo class** Bldrs: Various, 1949-58

CL 304 Sawayuki	CL 313 Shiratae	CL 318 Hatsuharu
CL 307 Hatsuyuki	CL 315 Meiryu Maru	CL 319 Yuunagi
CL 308 Miyuki	CL 316 Hayate	

D: 13 tons (20 fl)   **S:** 15.2 kts   **Dim:** 17.0 × 3.5 × . . .
Man: 5 men   **Range:** 290/13.4   **M:** 1 Mitsubishi DH24Mk diesel; 250 hp

REMARKS: Reclassified from PCs, 1966-70. *Asashimo* (CL-302) stricken in 1978.

◆ **1 Kiyoshimo class** Bldr: Tsuboi, 1949

CL 310 Kiyoshimo

D: 14.9 tons   **S:** 15.5 kts   **Dim:** 17.0 × 3.5 × . . .
Man: 5 men   **Range:** 280/15   **M:** 2 diesels; 2 props; 360 hp

REMARK: Reclassified from PC, 3-15-69.

SMALL PATROL CRAFT

◆ **6 Shiragiku class** Bldrs: Various, 1948-57

CS 107 Kisaragi	CS 120 Matsuzakura	CS 123 Yamabuki
CS 108 Yayoi	CS 122 Yuguruma	CS 124 Shiraito

D: 7.7 tons (12 fl)   **S:** 14.3 kts   **Dim:** 12.0 × 3.2 × 0.72
Man: 4 men   **Range:** 160/13.5   **M:** 1 diesel; 175 hp

HYDROGRAPHIC SHIPS

◆ **1 Shoyo class** Bldr: Hitachi, Maizuru

HL 01 Shoyo

D: 2,044 tons   **S:** 17.4 kts   **Dim:** 80.0 (78.6 pp) × 12.3 × 4.2
Man: 73 men   **Range:** 12,000/14
M: 2 Fuji 12VM 32 H2F diesels; 4,800 hp

REMARK: In service 26-2-72.

◆ **1 Meiyo class** Bldr: Magoya, Zosen

HL 03 Meiyo

D: 486 tons   **S:** 12 kts   **Dim:** 44.8 (40.5 pp) × 8.05 × 2.88
Man: 40 men   **Range:** 5,280/11   **M:** 1 diesel; 1 prop; 700 hp

REMARK: In service 15-3-63.

HYDROGRAPHIC SHIPS (continued)

Meiyo 1975

◆ **1 Takuyo class** Bldr: Niigata

HL 02 TAKUYO

D: 867 tons (930 fl) **S:** 14 kts **Dim:** 62.4 (58.75 pp) × 9.48 × 3.25
Man: 50 men **Range:** 9,600/12 **M:** 2 MD6 diesels; 2 props; 1,300 hp

REMARK: In service 12-3-57.

COASTAL HYDROGRAPHIC SHIPS

◆ **1 Kaiyo class** Bldr: Ishikawajima Harima, Nagoya

HM 06 KAIYO

D: 378 tons **S:** 12 kts **Dim:** 44.53 × 8.05 × 2.39
Man: 31 men **Range:** 3,160/10 **M:** 1 diesel; 1 prop; 450 hp

REMARK: In service 14-5-64.

◆ **1 Tenyo class** Bldr: Yokohama Yacht

HM 05 TENYO

D: 121 tons (171 fl) **S:** 10 kts **Dim:** 30.2 (28.00 pp) × 5.8 × 1.96
Man: 28 men **Range:** 3,160/10 **M:** 1 MDF5-26 diesel; 1 prop; 230 hp

REMARK: In service 30-3-61.

◆ **1 Heiyo class** Bldr: Shimizu

HM 04 HEIYO

D: 77 tons **S:** 10.6 kts **Dim:** 23.3 × 4.4 × 1.45
Man: 12 men **Range:** 670/9 **M:** Diesel; 1 prop; 150 hp

REMARK: In service 22-3-55.

INSHORE HYDROGRAPHIC CRAFT

◆ **1 Kerama class** Bldr: Ho SB

HS 32 KERAMA

D: 23.2 tons (fl) **S:** 11 kts **Dim:** 15.0 × 4.0 × 0.86
Man: 7 men **Range:** 450/10 **M:** 1 diesel; 250 hp

REMARK: In service 28-11-73.

◆ **4 Akashi class** Bldrs: Various, 1973-77

HS 31 AKASHI   HS 33 HAYATOMO   HS 34 KURIHAMA   HS 35 KURUSHIMA

D: 21 tons (26 fl) **S:** 10.2 kts **Dim:** 15.0 × 4.0 × 0.84
Man: 7 men **Range:** 630/9.7 **M:** 1 MTU UD626 diesel; 180 hp

◆ **11 Hamashio class** Bldr: Nichihi, 1969-72

HS 01 HAMASHIO   HS 07 TAKASHIO
HS 02 ISESHIO   HS 08 WAKASHIO
HS 03 SETOSHIO   HS 09 YUKISHIO
HS 04 UZUSHIO   HS 10 OYASHIO
HS 05 HAYASHIO   HS 11 KUROSHIO
HS 06 ISOSHIO

D: 6 tons (fl) **S:** 8.9 kts **Dim:** 10.15 × 2.65 × 0.81
Man: 7 men **Range:** 343/8.5 **M:** 1 MTU UD326 diesel; 90 hp

NAVIGATIONAL AID TENDERS

◆ **1 Tsushima class** Bldr: Mitsui, Tamano

	Laid down	L	In serv.
LL 01 TSUSHIMA	10-6-76	7-4-77	9-9-77

D: 1,834 tons (1,865 normal) **S:** 16 kts (17.6 on trials)
Dim: 75.0 (70.0 pp) × 12.5 × 4.15 **Man:** 54 men **Range:** 10,000/15
M: 1 Fuji 8 S 40C diesel; 4,000 hp **Electric:** 900 kva

REMARKS: Intended for use as a lighthouse-supply ship. Has flume-type passive tank roll stabilization. Bow thruster. Replaced the original LL-01, the *Wakagusa*.

◆ **1 Hokuto-class buoy tender**

	Bldr	Laid down	L	In serv.
LL 11 HOKUTO	. . .	19-10-78	20-3-79	6-79

D: 800 tons (fl) **S:** 13 kts **Dim:** 55.0 × 10.6 × 2.7
M: 2 Hanshin 6L 24SH diesels; 2 props; 1,300 hp

REMARK: Replaces the old *Hokuto* (LL-11), which was stricken in 1979.

◆ **1 Kaio class** Bldr: Namura

LL 13 KAIO

D: 512 tons (700 normal) **S:** 11.9 kts **Dim:** 50.2 × 10.1 × 2.45
Man: 35 men **Range:** 6,730/10.9 **Electric:** 120 kw
M: 2 MS-6 diesels; 2 props; 560 hp

REMARK: In service 24-3-55.

◆ **1 Ginga class** Bldr: Osaka Zosen

LL 12 GINGA

D: 500 tons **S:** 11 kts **Dim:** 41.3 × 4.5 × 2.42
Man: 38 men **Range:** 4,500/10.7 **M:** 2 diesels; 2 props; 420 hp

REMARK: In service 30-6-54.

NAVIGATIONAL AID TENDERS (continued)

◆ 1 Miyojo-class buoy tender   Bldr: Asano DY

LM 11 Miyojo

> **D:** 248 tons (303 normal)   **S:** 11 kts   **Dim:** 27.0 × 12.0 × 2.58
> **Man:** 18 men   **Range:** 1,360/10   **Electric:** 135 kva
> **M:** 2 6MG 16HS diesels; 2 controllable-pitch props; 600 hp

REMARKS: In service 25-3-74. Has catamaran hull. Replaced a very similar ship with same name and number, which was lost in 4-72.

Miyojo   F. Lauga, 1976

◆ 2 Hakuun class   Bldr: Sumidagawa

LM 106 Hakuun   LM 107 Toun

> **D:** 57.6 tons (92.7 fl)   **S:** 15 kts   **Dim:** 24.0 (23.0 pp) × 6.0 × 1.0
> **Man:** 10 men   **Range:** 400/14
> **M:** 2 GM 12V71 TI diesels; 2 props; 1,080 hp

REMARKS: LM-106 in service 28-2-78, LM-107 1-79. Prototypes of a new class to replace earlier medium (LM) navigational aid tenders.

◆ 1 Ayabane class   Bldr: Shimoda

LM 112 Ayabane

> **D:** 187 tons   **S:** 12.3 kts   **Dim:** 32.7 × 6.5 × 1.8
> **Man:** 14 men   **Range:** 2,000/12   **M:** 1 diesel; 500 hp

REMARK: In service 25-12-72.

◆ 1 Zuiun class   Bldr: Nihonkai

LM 101 Zuiun

> **D:** 160 tons   **S:** 11.4 kts   **Dim:** 32.12 × 5.8 × 1.81
> **Man:** 21 men   **Range:** 3,330/12   **M:** 1 diesel; 260 hp

REMARK: In service 21-12-62.

◆ 8 23-meter group   Bldrs: Various, 1955-71

LM 102 Reiun	LM 107 Akatsuki	LM 109 Shoun	LM 111 Houn
LM 105 Sekiun	LM 108 Reimei	LM 110 Seiun	LM 113 Genun

> **D:** 67-74 tons (normal)   **S:** 9.7-10.5 kts   **Dim:** 22.1 × 4.65 × 1.4
> **Man:** 11-12 men   **Range:** 760-1,060/9.5   **M:** 1 diesel; 120-200 hp

REMARK: Minor variations but all similar.

◆ 3 Hatsunikari class

LS 204 Hatsunikari   LS 205 Nahahikari   LS 206 Matsuhikari

> **D:** 25 kts (35 fl)   **S:** 15 kts   **Dim:** 17.5 × 4.3 × . . .
> **Man:** 8 men   **Range:** 230/14.5   **M:** 2 diesels; 2 props; 560 hp

REMARK: In service since 1979.

◆ 6 Himehikari class

LS 212 Himehikari	LS 214 Akihikari	LS 216 Miohikari
LS 213 Kotohikari	LS 215 Wakahikari	LS 217 Tamahikari

> **D:** 27 tons (40 fl)   **S:** 9.7   **Dim:** 17.0 × 3.9 × . . .
> **Man:** 6 men   **Range:** 380/9   **M:** 1 3LD diesel; 75 hp

REMARK: In service 1965-69.

◆ 7 Urahikari class

LS 115 Fusahikari	LS 201 Haruhikari
LS 124 Urahikari	LS 202 Takahikari
LS 156 Sekihikari	LS 203 Setohikari
LS 184 Tomohikari	

> **D:** 16 tons (20 fl)   **S:** 17.2 kts   **Dim:** 17.0 × 3.5 × . . .
> **Man:** 10 men   **Range:** 320/5   **M:** 1 MTU UD 626 diesel; 180 hp

REMARK: In service 1969-75.

◆ 8 Taiko class

LS 122 Meiko	LS 152 Taiko	LS 171 Myoko	LS 218 Choko
LS 151 Kyoko	LS 153 Suiko	LS 183 Hakuko	LS 219 Saiko

> **D:** 8 tons (12 fl)   **S:** 14.8 kts   **Dim:** 12.0 × 3.2 × . . .
> **Man:** 6 men   **Range:** 130/12.5   **M:** 1 MTU UD 626 diesel; 180 hp

REMARK: In service 1970-73.

◆ 6 No. 1 Yoko class

LS 114 No. 3 Yoko	LS 182 No. 2 Yoko	LS 142 No. 5 Yoko
LS 180 No. 1 Yoko	LS 141 No. 4 Yoko	LS 143 No. 6 Yoko

> **D:** 3 tons (5 fl)   **S:** 16.2 kts   **Dim:** 7.3 × 2.45 × 0.5
> **Man:** . . . men   **Range:** 100/12   **M:** 1 GM 3-53N diesel; 112 hp

REMARKS: In service 1974-79. This design, built of fiberglass, will probably replace the older, small LS-boats in the early 1980s.

NAVIGATIONAL AID TENDERS (*continued*)

◆ 4 Shitoko class

LS 181 KEIKO	LS 185 SHITOKO	LS 186 TOKO	LS 187 SANHOKO

    D: 10 tons (14 fl)   **S:** 13 kts   **Dim:** 12.0 × 3.2 × 0.7
    Man: 6 men   **Range:** 120/12.5   **M:** 1 diesel; 210 hp

REMARKS: In service in 1979. Prototypes of a series to replace older, 12-meter series, LS-boats, Fiberglass hulls.

◆ 20 miscellaneous small navigational aid tenders

LS 102, LS 103, LS 105, LS 106, LS 112, LS 113, LS 116, LS 117, LS 118, LS 123, LS 125, LS 137, LS 146, LS 155, LS 163, LS 174, LS 175, LS 176, LS 191, LS 196

FIREBOATS

NOTE: Most patrol ships, boats, and craft are fitted for fire-fighting.

◆ 5 Hiryu class   Bldr: Asano DY

	In serv.			In serv.
FL 01 HIRYU	4-3-69		FL 04 KAIRYU	18-3-77
FL 02 SHORYU	4-3-70		FL 05 SUIRYU	3-78
FL 03 NANRYU	4-3-71			

Hiryu   1975

    D: 199 tons (251 normal)   **S:** 13.5 kts   **Dim:** 27.5 × 10.4 × 2.1
    Man: 14 men   **Range:** 400/13   **Electric:** 70 kva
    M: 2 MTU MB820Db diesels; 2,200 hp

REMARKS: Catamaran hulls. For fighting fires on board supertankers. 14.5m³ tank for fire-fighting chemicals. One 45-meter-range chemical sprayer; seven 60-meter-range water cannon.

◆ 8 Ninobiki class

    Bldrs: FM-02, FM-06, FM-08: Sumidagawa; Others: Yokohama Yacht

FM 01 NINOBIKI	FM 03 OTOWA	FM 05 KOTOBIKI	FM 07 KEGON
FM 02 YODO	FM 04 SHIRAITO	FM 06 NACHI	FM 08 MINOO

Otowa   1975

    D: 89 tons (99 normal)   **S:** 13.4 kts   **Dim:** 23.0 × 6.0 × 1.55
    Man: 12 men   **Range:** 234/13.4   **Electric:** 40 kva
    M: 1 MTU MB820Db and 2 Nissan diesels; 3 props; 1,400 hp

REMARKS: In service 1974-78. Four fire pumps: one of 6,000 l³/min., two of 3,000 l³/min., and one of 2,000 l³/min.

ENVIRONMENTAL-PROTECTION CRAFT

◆ 1 Katsuren-class   Bldr: Ishihara

MS 03 KATSUREN

    D: 30 tons (46 fl)   **S:** 12.3 kts   **Dim:** 16.5 × 5.5 × 1.1
    Man: 9 men   **Range:** 190/10.8   **M:** 2 UDV 816 diesels; 2 props; 500 hp

REMARK: In service 13-12-75. Used for monitoring radiation.

◆ 2 Kinagusa-class   Bldr: Sumidagawa

MS 01 KINAGUSA	MS 02 SAIKAI

    D: 16 tons (23 fl)   **S:** 8.1 kts   **Dim:** 10.5 × 5.0 × 0.63
    Man: 8 men   **Range** 170/7.6   **M:** 2 UD 326 diesels; 2 props; 180 hp

REMARK: MS-01 in service 25-9-70; MS-02, 1-10-70. Used for monitoring radiation.

◆ 29 Orion-class craft   Bldr: Yokohama Yacht

SS 01 ORION	SS 12 SPICA	SS 23 PERSEUS
SS 02 PEGASUS	SS 13 SIRIUS	SS 24 CENTAURUS
SS 04 NEPTUNE	SS 14 VEGA	SS 25 ANDROMEDA
SS 05 JUPITER	SS 16 PROCYON	SS 26 ALTAIR
SS 06 VENUS	SS 17 LEO	SS 27 HERCULES

JAPAN (*continued*)

ENVIRONMENTAL-PROTECTION CRAFT (*continued*)

SS 07 CASSIOPEIA	SS 18 POLARIS	SS 28 GEMINI
SS 08 PHOENIX	SS 19 RIGEL	SS 29 ERIZU
SS 09 SERPENS	SS 20 CYGNUS	SS 30 COMET
SS 10 CARINA	SS 21 DENEB	SS 31 REGULUS
SS 11 CAPELLA	SS 22 MERCURY	

    D: 2.1 tons (5 fl)   **S:** 28.0 kts   **Dim:** 5.99 × 2.44 × . . .
    Man: 6 men   **Range:** 85/25   **M:** 1 inboard/outboard motor; 130 hp

REMARK: In service 1972-78. Used for oil-spill surveillance.

◆ **1 Antares-class craft** Bldr: Sajima

SS 15 ANTARES

    D: 1.6 tons   **S:** 31.5 kts   **Dim:** 5.7 × 2.6 × . . .
    Man: 6 men   **M:** Water-jet drive

REMARK: In service 1-7-75. Used for oil-spill surveillance.

◆ **5 Shirasagi-class boats** Bldr: Sumidagawa

OR 01 SHIRASAGI	OR 03 . . .	OR 05 ISOSHIGI
OR 02 . . .	OR 04 CHIDORI	

    D: 78.5 tons (153 fl)   **S:** 6.8 kts   **Dim:** 22.0 × 6.4 × 0.9
    Man: 11 men   **Range:** 100/6   **M:** 2 UD 626 diesels; water-jet drive; 390 hp

REMARK: In service 1977-78. Used for clearing oil spills.

◆ **3 Uraga-class oil-skimmer boats** Bldr: Lockheed, U.S.A.

OS 01 URAGA	OS 02 BISAN	OS 03 NARUTO

    D: 6.4 grt   **S:** 5 kts   **Dim:** 8.25 × 5.0 × 0.7
    Man: 4 men   **Range:** 90/5   **M:** 2 diesels; 2 props; 2 props; 86 hp

REMARK: In service 1975-76.

◆ **19 M-101-class oil-boom-extender barges**

OX 01 to OX 19 (M-101 to M-119)

    D: 48 tons   **Dim:** 20.0 × 7.0 × 0.45

OX-01   1975

JORDAN

COASTAL GUARD

PERSONNEL: 300 men, including those at the base at Aqaba and frogmen

MERCHANT MARINE (1978): 31 ships—2,295 grt

◆ **4 U.S.-supplied small craft** Bldr: Bertram, Miami

FAYSAL	HAN	HASAYU	MUHAMMED

    D: 8 tons   **S:** 25 kts   **Dim:** 11.6 × 4.0 × 0.5
    A: 1/12.7-mm machine gun—2/7.62-mm machine guns

◆ **2 U.S.-supplied small craft** Bldr: Bertram, Miami

ALI	ABD ALLAH

    D: 6.5 tons   **S:** 25 kts   **Dim:** 9.26 × 3.26 × 0.46
    A: 1/12.7-mm machine gun—1/7.62-mm machine gun   **Man:** 8 men

---

KAMPUCHEA

(Cambodia, ex-Khmer Republic)

NOTE: The composition of Kampuchea's afloat forces, if any, is not known. Most of her large ships and craft fled in 1975 and, as of 1979, Vietnam apparently controlled coastal waters. A few small patrol craft, U.S. PBR Mk-I or Mk-II classes, may survive in Khmer Rouge river service.

KENYA

PERSONNEL: 360 men
MERCHANT MARINE (1978): 20 ships—15,224 grt
                           (tankers: 3 ships—2,704 grt)

PATROL BOATS

◆ **3 32-meter coastal surveillance boats** Bldr: Brooke Marine, Lowestoft, G.B.

P 3121 MADARAKA	P 3122 JAMHURI	P 3123 HARAMBEE

KENYA (*continued*)

PATROL BOATS (*continued*)

Jamhuri   1978

D: 120 tons (145 fl)   **S:** 25.5 kts   **Dim:** 32.6 × 6.1 × 1.7
A: 2/40-mm Mk 7 AA (I × 2)   **Man:** 21 men   **Range:** 2,300/12
M: 2 Paxman Valenta diesels; 5,400 hp

REMARK: The *Madaraka* was launched 28-1-75, the *Jamhuri* 14-3-76, and the *Harambee* 2-5-75.

◆ **1 37.5-meter coastal surveillance boat**   Bldr: Brooke Marine, Lowestoft, G.B.

P 3100 MAMBA

Mamba   1975

D: 130 tons (160 fl)   **S:** 25 kts   **Dim:** 37.5 × 6.86 × 1.78
A: 2/40-mm Mk 7 AA (I × 2)   **Man:** 3 officers, 22 men   **Range:** 3,500/13
M: 2 Paxman Valenta diesels; 4,000 hp

REMARK: Launched 6-11-73.

◆ **3 Vosper 31-meter coastal security craft**   Bldr: Vosper Portsmouth, G.B.

P 3110 SIMBA   P 3112 CHUI   P 3117 NDOVU (ex-*Twigg*)

Simba   Vosper

D: 96 tons (109 fl)   **Dim:** 31.25 (28.95 pp) × 5.95 × 1.65
S: 24/23 kts   **Man:** 3 officers, 21 men
A: 2/40-mm AA Mk 7 (I × 2)
Range: 1,500/16   **Fuel:** 14 tons
M: 2 Paxman Ventura 12-cyl. diesels; 2 props; 2,900 hp

REMARKS: Welded hull, similar to the Malaysian SRA class. The *Simba* was launched 9-9-65, the *Chui* 25-11-65, and the *Ndovu* 22-12-65.

KOREA
North

PERSONNEL: Approximately 9,000 men

MERCHANT MARINE (1976): 20 ships — 89,811 grt
                            (tankers: 3 — 21,734 grt)

The North Korean Navy is composed mainly of ships received from the U.S.S.R. and the People's Republic of China. *See* those sections for ship characteristics.

SUBMARINES

◆ **10 Soviet Romeo class**
    D: 1,330 tons (surfaced), 1,700 tons (submerged)
    S: 15/13 kts
    Dim: 77.0 × 6.7 × 4.95   **Man:** 56 men
    A: 8/533-mm TT (6 fwd, 2 aft) — 14/torpedoes or 28/mines
    Range: 14,000/9   **Endurance:** 60 days
    M: 2 diesels of 2,000 hp; electric drive; 2 props; 2,500 hp

REMARKS: Seven are of Chinese construction, transferred in 1973 (two), 1974 (two), and 1975 (three). The others were built in North Korea with Chinese assistance; construction may be continuing.

SUBMARINES *(continued)*

◆ **4 Soviet Whiskey class**

    D: 1,050 tons (surfaced), 1,350 (submerged)
    S: 16/17 kts   **Dim:** 76.0 × 6.3 × 4.8
    A: 6/533-mm TT (4 fwd, 2 aft) — 12/torpedoes or 24/mines
    Man: 60 men   **Range:** 4,000/5 (snorkel)   **Endurance:** 60 days
    M: 2 diesels of 2,000 hp, diesel-electric drive; 2 props; 2,500 hp

REMARK: Transferred from the U.S.S.R.

FRIGATES

◆ **3 Najin class**   Bldr: North Korea, 1973, 1975, 1977

    D: 1,200 tons   **S:** 25 kts   **Dim:** 100.0 × 10.0 × 2.7
    A: 2/100-mm DP — 4/57-mm AA (II × 2) — 4/25-mm AA (II × 2) — 4/depth-charge projectors — 30/mines
    M: 2 diesels; 2 props; 15,000 hp   **Man:** 155 men

CORVETTES

◆ **4 Sariwan class**   Bldr: North Korea, 1965

    D: 475 tons   **S:** 21 kts   **Dim:** 62.1 × 7.3 × 2.4
    A: 1/76-mm AA — 2/57-mm AA (II × 2) — 4/25-mm AA (II × 2) — depth-charge projectors
    M: 2 diesels; 2 props; 3,000 hp

REMARKS: Data dubious.

GUIDED-MISSILE PATROL BOATS

◆ **8 Soviet Osa-I class**

◆ **10 Soviet Komar class**

PATROL BOATS

◆ **4 Chinese Hainan class**

    D: 360 tons (400 fl)   **S:** 24 kts   **Dim:** 59.0 × 7.3 × 2.4
    A: 4/57-mm AA (II × 2) — 4/25-mm AA (II × 2) — 4/RBU-1200 ASW rocket launchers (V × 4) — 2/depth-charge projectors — 2/depth-charge racks — mines
    M: 4 diesels; 4 props; 8,000 hp

REMARK: Two transferred in 1975; two in 1976.

◆ **60 Chaho class**   Bldr: North Korea

    D: 80 tons (fl)   **S:** 40 kts   **Dim:** 27.7 × 6.1 × 1.8
    A: 4/14.5-mm AA (II × 2) — 1/200-mm artillery rocket launcher, (40 tubes)
    M: 4 M50 diesels; 4 props; 4,800 hp

REMARK: Based on P-6 design, but have steel hull.

◆ **30 Chong Jin class**   Bldr: North Korea

REMARKS: Data as for Chaho class except armaments include: one 85-mm tank gun and four 14.5-mm anti-aircraft guns (II × 2).

◆ **8 Chinese Shanghai class**, acquired since 1967

◆ **8 Soviet SO-1 class**

◆ **8 Chinese Swatow class**, transferred in 1968

◆ **4 Chodo class**   Bldr: North Korea

    D: 130 tons   **S:** 24 kts   **Dim:** 42.7 × 5.8 × 2.6
    A: 1/76-mm AA — 3/37-mm AA (I × 3) — 4/25-mm AA (II × 2)
    M: Diesels, 2 props, 6,000 hp   **Man:** 24 men

◆ **4 K-48 class**   Bldr: North Korea, 1951-54

    D: 110 tons (fl)   **S:** 24 kts   **Dim:** 38.1 × 5.5 × 1.5
    A: 1/76-mm AA — 3/37-mm AA (I × 3) — 4/14.5-mm AA (II × 2)
    M: 2 diesels; 2 props; 5,000 hp

◆ **20 Soviet M.O. IV class**

    D: 56 tons (fl)   **S:** 25 kts   **Dim:** 27.0 × 4.0 × 1.5
    A: 1/37-mm AA — 2/14.5-mm AA (I × 2)   **Man:** 20 men
    M: 2 diesels; 2 props; 2,600 hp

REMARKS: Built 1945-47, wooden construction. Transferred 1950.

TORPEDO BOATS

◆ **4 Soviet Shershen class**

◆ **80 Soviet P-4 class and P-6 class**

◆ **15 Iwon class**   Bldr: North Korea

    D: 40 tons (fl)   **S:** 45 kts   **Dim:** 19.2 × 3.7 × 1.5
    A: 2/25-mm AA (II × 2) — 2/533-mm TT
    M: 3 diesels; 3 props; 3,600 hp

◆ **6 An Ju class**   Bldr: North Korea

    D: 35 tons (fl)   **S:** 50 kts   **Dim:** 19.8 × 3.7 × 1.8
    A: 2/25-mm AA (II × 2) — 2/533-mm TT   **Man:** 20 men
    M: 4 M50 diesels; 4 props; 4,800 hp

◆ **60 Sin Hung class**   Bldr: North Korea

    D: 25 tons (fl)   **S:** . . .   **Dim:** 18.3 × 3.4 × 1.7
    A: 2/14.5-mm (II × 1) — 2/450-mm TT
    M: 2 diesels; 2 props; 2,400 hp

AMPHIBIOUS CRAFT

◆ **70 Nampo class**   Bldr: North Korea

    D: 82 tons (fl)   **S:** 40 kts   **Dim:** 27.7 × 6.1 × 1.8
    A: 6/14.5-mm AA (II × 3)   **Man:** 19 men   **Range:** 375/40
    M: 4 M50 diesels; 4 props; 4,800 hp

REMARKS: A version of the Chaho-class gunboat with a bow ramp and troop accommodations forward.

KOREA
South

PERSONNEL: Approximately 32,000 men, plus 20,000 Marines

MERCHANT MARINE (1978): 1,148 ships – 2,975,389 grt

(tankers: 64 ships – 1,065,562 grt)

◆ **3 ex-U.S. Gearing class, FRAM I**

	Bldr	L	In serv.
922 KANG WON			
(ex-*William R. Rush*, DD-714)	Federal SB, Newark	8-7-45	21-9-45
921 KUANG JU			
(ex-*Richard E. Kraus*, DD-849)	Consolidated Steel	2-3-46	23-5-46
919 TAEJON (ex-*New*, DD-818)	Bath Iron Works	18-8-45	5-4-46

D: 2,425 tons (3,500 fl) **S:** 30 kts **Dim:** 119.0 × 12.4 × 5.8
A: 8/Harpoon SSM (IV × 2) – 4/127-mm DP (II × 2) – 6/324-mm Mk 32 ASW TT (III × 2)
Electron Equipt: Radars: 1/SPS-10, 1/SPS-40 (922: SPS-29), 1/Mk 25
    Sonar: SQS-23
Man: 274 men **Range:** 4,800/15, 2,400/25 **Fuel:** 640 tons
Boilers: 4 Babcock & Wilcox, 39.8 kg/cm² pressure – superheat 454°C
M: 2 sets GT; 2 props; 60,00 hp

REMARKS: 919, 921 were transferred 25-2-77; 922 on 1-7-79. Asroc retained on 922 and 923. All to carry one Alouette III helicopter. Have one Mk 37 director. Harpoon added 1979.

◆ **2 ex-U.S. Gearing class, FRAM II** Bldr: Bath Iron Works

	L	In serv.
915 CHUNG BUK		
(ex-*Chevalier*, DDR-805)	29-10-44	8-9-44
916 JEONG BUK		
(ex-*Everett F. Larson*, DDR-830)	28-1-45	6-4-45

D: 2,400 tons (3,500 fl) **S:** 30 kts **Dim:** 119.17 × 12.45 × 5.8
A: 8/Harpoon (IV × 2) – 6/127-mm DP (II × 3) – 6/324-mm Mk 32 ASW TT (KKK × 2) – 2/Mk 11 Hedgehog – 1/Alouette III helicopter
Electron Equipt: Radars: 1/SPS-10, 1/SPS-40, 1/Mk 25
    Sonar: SQS-29 series
Man: 14 officers, 260 men **Range:** 4,800/15, 2,400/25 **Fuel:** 640 tons
Boilers: 4 Babcock & Wilcox, 39.8 kg/cm² pressure – superheat 454°C
M: 2 sets GT; 2 props; 60,000 hp

REMARKS: Transferred on loan 5-7-72 and 30-10-72; sold outright 31-1-77. One Mk 37 director for 127-mm guns.

◆ **2 ex-U.S. Allen M. Sumner class, FRAM II**

	Bldr	L	In serv.
917 DAE GU			
(ex-*Wallace L. Lind*, DD-703)	Federal SB, Kearney	14-6-44	8-9-44
918 INCHON (ex-*De Haven*, DD-727)	Bath Iron Works	9-1-44	31-3-44

D: 2,350 tons (3,320 fl) **S:** 34 kts **Dim:** 114.8 × 12.4 × 5.2
A: 8/Harpoon SSM (IV × 2) – 6/127-mm AA (II × 3) – 4/40-mm AA (II × 2) – 6/324-mm Mk 32 ASW TT (III × 2) – 2/Mk 11 Hedgehogs – 1/Alouette III helicopter
Electron Equipt: Radars: 1/SPS-10, 1/SPS-40 (918: SPS-29), 1/Mk 25
    Sonars: 1/SQS-29 series, 1/SQA-10 VDS (917 only)
Boilers: 4 Babcock & Wilcox, 39.8 kg/cm² pressure – superheat 454°C
M: 2 sets GE GT; 2 props; 60,000 hp

REMARKS: Transferred 12-73. Eight Harpoons added 1978-79 (IV × 2), helicopter deck and hangar enlarged to accommodate Alouette III, 1978.

◆ **3 ex-U.S. Fletcher class**

	Bldr	L	In serv.
911 CHUNG MU (ex-*Erben*, DD-631)	Bath Iron Works	21-3-43	28-5-43
912 SEOUL			
(ex-*Halsey Powell*, DD-686)	Bethlehem, Staten Isl.	30-6-43	25-10-43
913 PUSAN (ex-*Hickox*, DD-673)	Federal SB, Kearney	4-7-43	10-9-43

D: 2,050 tons (2,850 fl) **S:** 35 kts **Dim:** 114.85 (wl) × 12.03 × 5.5
A: 5/127-mm 38-cal. (I × 5) – 10/40-mm AA (IV × 2, II × 2, none in 912) – 6/324-mm Mk 32 ASW TT (IV × 2) – 2/Hedgehog
Electron Equipt: Radars: 1/SPS-10, 1/SPS-6C, 1/Mk 25
    Sonar: 1/SQS-4
Range: 4,500/12, 900/35 **Man:** 303 men **Fuel:** 650 tons
Boilers: 4 Babcock & Wilcox, 39.8 kg/cm² pressure – superheat 454°C
Electric: 540 kw **M:** GE GT; 2 props; 60,000 hp

REMARKS: The *Chung Mu* transferred 1-5-63, the *Seoul* on 27-4-68, the *Pusan* on 15-11-68; all purchased outright 31-1-77. The *Seoul* may by now have been given 40-mm anti-aircraft. Have one Mk 37 director for 127-mm mount; one Mk 51 mod 2 director for each 40-mm mount.

FRIGATES

◆ **1 new construction** Bldr: Hayundai, Korea

	Laid down	L	In serv.
. . . N . . .	. . .	. . .	. . .

D: 1,600 tons **S:** 35 kts **Dim:** . . . × . . . × . . .
A: 8/Harpoon SSM (IV × 2) – . . .
Electron Equipt: . . . **Man:** . . . **Range:** . . .
M: CODOG: 2 GE LM 2500 gas turbines, 40,000 hp; 2 MTU 16V538 diesels, 7,200 hp; 2 controllable-pitch props

◆ **1 ex-U.S. Rudderow class**

	Bldr	L	In serv.
DE 73 CHUNG NAM (ex-*Holt*, DE-706)	Defoe SB	15-12-43	9-6-44

D: 1,650 tons (2,230 fl) **S:** 23 kts **Dim:** 93.3 × 11.8 × 4.3
A: 2/127-mm DP (I × 2) – 4/40-mm AA (II × 2) – 6/20-mm AA – 6/324-mm Mk 32 ASW TT (III × 2) – 2/Hedgehog – 1/depth-charge rack
Electron Equipt: Radars: 1/SPS-5, 1/SPS-6, 1/Mk 34
    Sonar: SQS-11
Boilers: 2 Foster-Wheeler "D"-express, 30.6 kg/cm² pressure – superheat 399°C
Range: 5,000/15 **Fuel:** 360 tons
M: 2 sets GE GT, turbo-electric drive; 2 props; 12,000 hp

REMARKS: Loaned 19-6-63; sold outright 15-11-74.

FRIGATES *(continued)*

◆ **4 ex-U.S. Crosley class, ex-APD (high-speed transports)**

	Bldr	L	In serv.
821 KYONG NAM	Defoe SB, Bay city	15-6-44	13-3-45
(ex-*Cavallaro*, APD-128)			
822 AH SAN	Bethlehem, Hingham, Mass.	1-3-44	5-6-45
(ex-*Harry L. Corl*, APD-108)			
823 UNG PO	Bethlehem, Hingham, Mass.	3-3-44	28-6-45
(ex-*Julius A. Raven*, APD-110)			
827 CHE JU	Charleston Navy Yard	11-2-44	4-4-45
(ex-*William M. Hobby*, APD-95)			

D: 1,650 tons (2,130 fl)   **S:** 23.6 kts   **Dim:** 9313 × 11.3 × 3.2
A: 2/127-mm DP (I × 2) – 6/40-mm AA (II × 3) – 2/depth-charge projectors, Mk 6 – 2/depth-charge racks
Electron Equipt: Radars: 1/SPS-5, 1/SPS-6, 1/Mk 26
                    Sonar: QCU-2
Man: 200 men   **Range:** 4,800/12, 2,300/22
Boilers: 2 Foster-Wheeler "D"-express, 30.6 kg/cm² pressure – superheat 399°C
M: 2 sets GE GT, turbo-electric drive; 2 props; 12,000 hp

REMARKS: Transferred on loan 10-59, 6-66, 6-66, and 8-67; purchased outright 15-11-74. Second 127-mm gun added aft, as on Taiwanese sisters. Have low bridge compared to ex-*Charles Lawrence* ships, below. Can still carry 160 troops; two LCVPs and two LCPLs stowed beneath quadrantial davits. One Mk 52 director for 127-mm gun; three Mk 51 mod 2 for 40-mm anti-aircraft.

◆ **2 ex-U.S. Charles Lawrence class, ex-APD (high-speed transports)**

Bldr: Charleston Navy Yard

	L	In serv.
825 KYONG PUK (ex-*Kephart*, APD-61)	6-9-43	7-1-44
826 JON NAM (ex-*Hayter*, APD-80)	11-11-43	4-4-45

REMARKS: All data essentially the same as for the *Crosley* class, above. Loaned in 8-67; purchased outright 15-11-74. Have high bridge as compared to the *Crosley* class. All APDs of both classes were laid down originally as DE-destroyer escorts.

CORVETTES

◆ **3 ex-U.S. Auk class, ex-fleet minesweepers**

	Bldr	L	In serv.
PCE 1001 SHIN SONG	Savannah Mach.	15-7-44	15-1-45
(ex-*Ptarmigan*, MSF-376)			
PCE 1002 SUN CHONKE	American SB, Lorain	6-6-42	15-10-42
(ex-*Speed*, MSF-116)			
PCE 1003 KOJE HO	Gulf SB, Madisonville, Tenn.	17-1-43	8-9-43
(ex-*Dextrous*, MSF-341)			

D: 890 tons (1,250 fl)   **S:** 18 kts   **Dim:** 67.2 (65 pp) × 9.75 × 3.3
A: 2/76-mm DP (I × 2) – 4/40-mm AA (II × 2) – 4/20-mm AA (II × 2) – 1/Hedgehog – 3/324-mm Mk 32 ASW TT (III × 1) – 2/depth-charge racks
Man: 110 men   **Fuel:** 200 tons
M: 2 GM 12-278 diesels, electric drive; 2 props; 3,532 hp

REMARKS: Converted to corvettes before transfer. Minesweeping gear deleted and replaced by additional ASW equipment and second 76-mm Mk 22 gun aft.

NOTE: All units of the U.S. PCE-821 class have been stricken.

GUIDED-MISSILE PATROL BOATS

◆ **8 PSMM-5 class** Bldrs: PGM-102 to PGM-105: Tacoma Boatbuilding Co.; Others: Korea-Tacoma, Chinhae

	Laid down	In serv.
PGM 102 PAEK KU-12	1-75	14-3-75
PGM 103 PAEK KU-13	2-75	14-3-75
PGM 105 PAEK KU-15	. . .	1-2-76
PGM 106 PAEK KU-16	. . .	1-2-76
PGM 107 PAEK KU-17	. . .	1977
PGM 108 PAEK KU-18	. . .	1977
PGM 109 PAEK KU-19	. . .	1977
PGM 110 PAEK KU-20	. . .	1978

Paek Ku   1975

D: 240 tons (268 fl)   **S:** 40 kts   **Dim:** 53.6 (50.3 pp) × 8.0 × 1.6
A: 8/Harpoon SSM (IV × 2) – 1/76-mm DP – 1/40-mm AA – 2/12.7-mm machine guns
Electron Equipt: Radars: 1/LN-66, 1/SPG-50
Man: 5 officers, 27 men
M: 6 AVCO TF-35 gas turbines; 2 controllable-pitch props; 16,800 hp

REMARK: Ships built in Korea may have OTO Melara 76-mm Compact or no SPG-50 radar.

◆ **1 ex-U.S. Asheville class** Bldr: Tacoma Boat, Wash.

	L	In serv.
PGM 101 PAEK KU 11 (ex-*Benicia*, PG-96)	20-12-69	25-4-70

D: 225 tons (249 fl)   **S:** 40 kts   **Dim:** 50.14 × 7.28 × 2.9
A: 1/76-mm DP – 1/40-mm AA – 4/12.7-mm machine guns (II × 2)
Electron Equipt: Radars: 1/LN-66, 1/SPG-50
Range: 1,700/16, 390/35   **Man:** 29 men
M: CODOG: 1GE LM-1500-PE102 gas turbine, 12,500 hp; 2 Cummins VT12-875M diesels, 1,450 hp; 2 controllable-pitch props

REMARKS: May have eight Harpoon (IV × 2) or four Standard anti-ship missiles. Mk 63 radar fire control for 76-mm Mk 34 gun. Transferred 15-10-71; purchased 1977.

GUIDED-MISSILE PATROL BOATS *(continued)*

◆ **2 PGF type**

PKM 121   PKM 122

   D: 120 tons   **S:** 40 kts   **Dim:** 30.0 × 7.5 × 1.1
   A: 2/Exocet SSM – 1/40-mm AA – 1/20-mm AA
   M: 3 MTU MB 518D diesels; 3 props; 10,500 hp

REMARK: Built in Korea, 1971-72.

PATROL BOATS

◆ **1 U.S. CPIC type**   **Bldr:** Tacoma Boat, Wash.

	L	In serv.
PKM 123	3-5-73	1-8-75 (In Korea)

PKM 123   Tacoma Boatbuilding Co.

   D: 71 tons (fl)   **S:** 43 kts   **Dim:** 30.44 × 5.65 × 1.8
   A: 2/30-mm Emerlec AA (II × 1) – 1 recoilless rifle   **Man:** 11 men
   M: CODOG: 3 AVCO-Lycoming TF25A gas turbines; 3 props; 6,000 hp; 2 diesels,
      2 fold-down props; 440 hp

◆ **20 PK type** **Bldr:** South Korea

PK 151 to PK 170

   D: 78 tons   **S:** 40 kts   **Dim:** 23.6 × 3.8 × 1.2
   A: 1/20-mm Vulcan – 3/20-mm Mk 36 – 8/rocket launchers (IV × 2)
   M: 2 MTU 16V538 diesels; 2 props; 5,200 hp

◆ **8 ex-USCG Cape class**

PB 3 (ex-*Cape Rosier*, WPB-95333)	PB 9 (ex-*Cape Falcon*, WPB-95330)
PB 5 (ex-*Cape Sable*, WPB-95334)	PB 10 (ex-*Cape Trinity*, WPB-95331)
PB 6 (ex-*Cape Providence*, WPB-95335)	PB 11 (ex-*Cape Darby*, WPB-95323)
PB 8 (ex-*Cape Porpoise*, WPB-95327)	PB 12 (ex-*Cape Kiwanda*, WPB-95329)

   D: 105 tons (fl)   **S:** 18 kts   **Dim:** 28.95 × 5.8 × 1.55
   A: 1/81-mm mortar combined with 12.7-mm machine gun – 2/76-mm machine guns
   Man: 15 men   **Range:** 1,500
   M: 4 Cummins VT-12M diesels; 2 props; 2,200 hp

REMARK: PB-7 (ex-*Cape Florida*) was lost in 1971.

◆ **9 U.S. 65-foot commercial cruiser class**

   Bldr: Sewart Seacraft, Berwick, La., 1967

FB 1-3, 5-10

   D: 35 tons (fl)   **S:** 25 kts   **Dim:** 19.8 × 5.5 × 1.5
   A: 2/20-mm AA (I × 2) – 3/12.7-mm machine guns
   Man: 5 men   **Range:** 1,200/17   **Fuel:** 7 tons
   M: 3 GM 12V71 diesels; 3 props; 1,590 hp

MINE WARFARE SHIPS

◆ **5 U.S. MSC-289-class coastal minesweepers**

   Bldr: Peterson Builders, Sturgeon Bay, Wis.

	In serv.
MSC 526 NAM YANG (ex-MSC-295)	8-63
MSC 527 HA DONG (ex-MSC-296)	11-63
MSC 528 SAM KOK (ex-MSC-316)	7-68
MSC 529 YONG DONG (ex-MSC-320)	2-10-75
MSC 530 OK CHEON (ex-MSC-321)	2-10-75

   D: 315 tons (380 fl)   **S:** 14 kts   **Dim:** 44.32 × 8.29 × 2.7
   A: 2/20-mm AA (II × 1)   **Man:** 40 men   **Fuel:** 33 tons
   M: 4 GM 6-71 diesel; 2 props; 1,020 hp   **Electric:** 1,260 kw

REMARKS: Wooden construction. Built under Military Aid Program. Gas-turbine sweep generator. Lower superstructure than on the MSC-268 class, below.

◆ **3 U.S. MSC-268-class coastal minesweepers**

   Bldr: Harbor Boat Bldg., Terminal Isl., Cal.

	In serv.
MSC 522 KUM SAN (ex-MSC-284)	6-59
MSC 523 KO HUNG (ex-MSC-285)	8-59
MSC 525 KUM KOK (ex-MSC-286)	10-59

   D: 320 tons (370 fl)   **S:** 14 kts   **Dim:** 43.0 (41.5 pp) × 7.95 × 2.55
   A: 2/20-mm AA (II × 2)   **Electron Equipt:** Radar: Decca 45
                                            Sonar: UQS-1
   Man: 40 men   **Range:** 2,500/16   **Fuel:** 40 tons
   M: 2 GM 8-268A diesels; 2 props; 1,200 hp

REMARKS: Built under Military Aid Program. Wooden hulls.

◆ **1 ex-U.S. minesweeping boat**

MSB 1 PI BONG (ex-MSB-2)

   D: 44 tons (fl)   **S:** 12 kts   **Dim:** 17.0 × 4.6 × 1.5
   M: 2 GM 6-71 diesels; 2 props; 600 hp
   Range: 300/6   **Fuel:** 5 tons

REMARK: Launched 1946; transferred 1961.

AMPHIBIOUS WARFARE SHIPS

◆ 8 ex-U.S. LST-1 and U.S. LST-542-class landing ships

	Bldr	L
LST 807 UN-BONG (ex-LST-1010)	Bethlehem, Fore River	29-3-44
LST 808 TUK-BONG (ex-LST-227)	Chicago Bridge, Seneca, Ill.	21-9-43
LST 809 BI-BONG (ex-LST-218)	Chicago Bridge, Seneca, Ill.	20-7-43
LST 810 KAE-BONG (ex-LST-288)	American Bridge, Pa.	7-11-43
LST 812 WEE-BONG (ex-*Johnson County*, LST-849)	American Bridge, Pa.	30-12-43
LST 813 SU-YONG (ex-*Kane County*, LST-853)	Chicago Bridge, Seneca, Ill.	17-11-44
LST 815 BUK-HAN (ex-*Linn County*, LST-900)	Dravo, Pittsburgh	9-12-44
LST 816 HWA-SAN (ex-*Pender County*, LST-1080)	Bethlehem, Hingham, Mass.	2-5-45

Tuk-Bong

D: 1,653 tons (4,080 fl)   **S:** 10 kts   **Dim:** 100.04 × 15.24 × 4.3
A: 7/40-mm AA – 20/20-mm AA   **Man:** 70 men   **Electric:** 300 kw
M: 2 GM 12-567A or 12-278A diesels; 2 props; 1,800 hp

REMARKS: Transferred 1955-58; all purchased outright 15-11-74. LST-1 class had elevators from upper deck to tank deck; later ships had a ramp.

◆ 11 ex-U.S. LSM medium landing ships

Bldrs: Brown SB, Houston, Tex., except LSM-602: Federal SB, Newark; LSM 612: Pullman Standard Car Co., Chicago

LSM 601 TAE CHO (ex-LSM-546)	LSM 609 WOLMI (ex-LSM-57)
LSM 602 TYO TO (ex-LSM-268)	LSM 610 KI RIN (ex-LSM-19)
LSM 605 KA TOK (ex-LSM-462)	LSM 611 NUNG RA (ex-LSM-84)
LSM 606 KO MUN (ex-LSM-30)	LSM 612 SIN MI (ex-LSM-316)
LSM 607 PI AN (ex-LSM-96)	LSM 613 UL RUNG (ex-LSM-17)

D: 520 tons (1,095 fl)   **S:** 13 kts   **Dim:** 62.0 × 10.52 × 2.53
A: 2/40-mm AA (II × 1) – 4/20-mm AA (I × 4)   **Man:** 75 men
M: 2 Fairbanks-Morse 38D8⅛ × 10 diesels; 2 props; 2,880 hp

◆ 1 ex-U.S. amphibious fire-support ship

	Bldr	L
SI HUNG (ex-*St. Joseph River*, LSMR-527)	Brown SB, Houston, Tex.	19-5-45

D: 994 tons (1,084 fl)   **S:** 14 kts   **Dim:** 62.94 × 10.52 × 2.0
A: 1/127-mm DP – 2/40-mm AA (II × 2) – 4/20-mm AA (II × 2) – 8/127-mm Mk 105 twin rocket launchers (II × 8)

Range: 3,000/12   **Electric:** 480 kw
M: 2 GM 16-278A diesels; 2 props; 2,800 hp

◆ 1 ex-U.S. LCU-501-class utility landing craft

	Bldr	L
LCU 1 (ex-LCU-531)	Bison SB, Buffalo	5-9-43

D: 309 tons (fl)   **S:** 10 kts   **Dim:** 36.3 × 10.0 × 1.14
A: 2/20-mm AA (I × 2)   **Man:** 12 men
M: 3 Gray Marine 6-71 diesels; 2 props; 675 hp

REMARK: Transferred 1960.

◆ 10 ex-U.S. Army LCM(8)-class landing craft

D: 95-115 tons (fl)   **S:** 9-12 kts   **Dim:** 22.7 × 6.4 × 1.4
M: 4 GM 6-71 diesels; 2 props; 600 hp

REMARK: Transferred 9-78.

◆ 1 ex-Norwegian oiler

AO 2 CHUN JI (ex-*Birk*)   Bldr: Bergens Mekauske Verksteder, Norway, 1957

D: 1,400 tons (4,160 fl)   **S:** 12 kts   **Dim:** 90.65 (84.0 pp) × 13.56 × 5.35
A: 1/40-mm AA – 2/20-mm AA   **Man:** 73 men
M: 1 Sulzer 6 TD 48 diesel; 1 prop; 1,800 hp

REMARKS: Bought in 1953. The *Puchon* of the same class was lost 5-71. Can replenish alongside while underway.

◆ 2 ex-U.S. 174-foot class

YO 1 KU KYONG (ex-YO-118)   YO 6 N. . . (ex-YO-179)

D: 1,400 tons (fl)   **S:** 7 kts   **Dim:** 53.0 × 10.0 × 4.0
Man: 36 men   **M:** 1 diesel; 1 prop; 560 hp   **Cargo capacity:** 900 tons

REMARKS: Launched 1943. YO-1 transferred 1946, YO-6 in 9-71.

◆ 1 ex-U.S. YO-55 class

Bldr: R.T.C. SB, Camden, N.J., 1942

HWA CHON (ex-*Derrick*, YO-59)

D: 800 tons (2,700 fl)   **S:** 10 kts   **Dim:** 71.65 × 11.3 × 4.8
Man: 46 men   **Range:** 4,600/8   **Cargo capacity:** 1,600 tons
M: 2 Fairbanks-Morse 37E14-5 diesels; 2 props; 1,150 hp

REMARKS: Transferred 4-55. Sister in the French Navy.

◆ 6 ex-U.S. Army FS 331-design class

	Bldr
AKL 902 IN CHON (ex-Army FS-198)	Higgins Ind., New Orleans
AKL 905 CHI NAM PO (ex-Army FS-356)	J. K. Welding, Brooklyn
AKL 907 MOK PO (ex-U.S.C.G. *Trillium*, WAK-170, ex-Army FS-397)	Ingalls, Decatur, Ala.
AKL 908 KU SAN (ex-*Sharps*, AKL-10, ex-AG-139, ex-Army FS-385)	Ingalls, Decatur, Ala.
AKL 909 MA SAN (ex-AKL-35, ex-*Lt. Thomas W. Weigle*, FS-383)	Ingalls, Decatur, Ala.
AKL 910 UL SAN (ex-*Brule*, AKL-28, ex-Army FS-370)	Sturgeon Bay SB, Wis.

KOREA—SOUTH (continued)

AMPHIBIOUS WARFARE SHIPS (continued)

D: 520 tons (860 fl)   **S:** 13.5 kts   **Dim:** 53.95 (50, 3 pp) × 10.06 × 3.0
A: 2/20-mm AA (I × 2)   **Range:** 4,300/9.5, 3,000/12.5   **Man:** 20 men
Fuel: 57 tons   **Electric:** 275 kw
M: 2 GM 6-278A diesels; 2 props; 1,230 hp

REMARKS: Cargo plus passengers, 595 cubic meters. Launched 1943-44. Transferred: AKL-902 and AKL-905 in 1951; AKL-907 in 3-56; AKL-908 in 4-56; AKL-909 in 9-56; and AKL-910 on 1-11-71.

◆ **2 ex-U.S. Diver-class salvage ships**   Bldr: Basalt Rock Co., Napa, Cal.

	L	In serv.
ARS 5 CHANG WON (ex-*Grasp*, ARS-24)	31-7-43	22-8-44
ARS 6 GUM I (ex-*Deliver*, ARS-23)	25-9-43	18-7-44

D: 1,530 tons (1,970 fl)   **S:** 14.8 kts   **Dim:** 65.1 × 12.5 × 4.0
A: 2/20-mm AA   **Electric:** 460 kw   **Fuel:** 300 tons
M: 2 Cooper-Bessemer diesels, electric drive; 2 props; 2,440 hp

REMARKS: ARS-5 transferred 31-3-78; ARS-6 on 15-8-79; both by sale.

◆ **2 U.S. Sotoyomo-class auxiliary tugs**

	Bldr	L	In serv.
ATA 3 DO BANG	Gulfport Boiler Wks,	14-12-44	10-2-45
(ex-*Pinola*, ATA-206)	Port Arthur, Tex.		
ATA 2 YONG MUN	Levingston SB,	17-1-45	19-3-45
(ex-*Keosangua*, ATA-198)	Orange, Tex.		

D: 835 tons (fl)   **S:** 13 kts   **Dim:** 43.6 (40.7 pp) × 10.3 × 4.0
A: 1/76-mm Mk 22 DP—4/20-mm AA (II × 2)   **Man:** 45 men
Electric: 120 kw   **Fuel:** 158 tons
M: 2 GM 12-278A diesels, electric drive; 1 prop; 1,500 hp

REMARKS: Transferred 2-62. ATA-3 is used in salvage work. There are also about nine harbor tugs, including YTL-13 (ex-U.S.N. YTL-550), YTL-22 (ex-Army ST-2097), YTL-23 (ex-Army ST-2099), YTL-25 (ex-Army YT-2106), YTL-26 (ex-Army ST-2065), and YTL-30 (ex-Army ST-2101). All transferred 1968-72.

◆ **There are also about 35 yard and service craft.**

KOREAN HYDROGRAPHIC SERVICE

Subordinate to the Ministry of Transport.

◆ **2 ex-Belgian Herstal-class inshore minesweepers**

	L
SURO 5 (ex-*Temse*, ex-MSI-470)	6-8-56
SURO 6 (ex-*Tournai*, ex-MSI-481)	18-5-57

D: 160 tons (190 fl)   **S:** 15 kts   **Dim:** 34.5 × 6.6 × 2.1
Range: 2,300/10   **Man:** 10 men   **M:** 2 diesels; 2 props; 630 hp

REMARKS: Built in Belgium with U.S. funds. Transferred 3-70. Wooden hulls.

◆ **1 ex-U.S. YMS-class minesweeper**

SURO 3 (ex-U.S. Coast Geodetic Survey *Hodgson*)

D: 289 tons (fl)   **S:** 15 kts   **Dim:** 44.6 × 8.1 × 3.0
M: 2 GM 8-268 diesels; 2 props; 1,000 hp

REMARKS: Converted post-World War II as a coastal survey ship. Wooden hull. Launched 1943, transferred 1968.

◆ **3 inshore survey craft**

SURO 7, SURO 8: 30 tons
SURO 2: 145 tons

COAST GUARD

The Republic of Korea Coast Guard operates about 25 patrol boats and crafts. Most are very old, including a number of ex-Imperial Japanese Navy tugs and seaplane tenders.

KUWAIT

PERSONNEL: 200 men

MERCHANT MARINE (1978): 251 ships—2,240,030 grt
(tankers: 17 ships—1,218,912 grt)

NOTE: Despite continued rumors of orders for up to 10 missile-armed fast patrol boats, no orders had been announced as of late 1979.

PATROL BOATS

◆ **10 coastal boats**   Bldrs: Thornycroft, Woolston, 2; Vosper-Thornycroft, 8

	L		L
AL SALEMI	30-6-66	MARZOOK	1969
AL MUBARAKI	16-7-66	MASHHOOR	1969
MAYMOON	4-68	MURSHED	1970
AMAN	3-68	WATHAH	1970
AL SHURTI	1972	INTISAR	1972

Intisar   Vosper, 1972

KUWAIT *(continued)*

PATROL BOATS *(continued)*

    D: 40 tons   **S:** 20 kts   **Dim:** 27.78 × 4.73 × 1.38
    Man: 5 officers, 7 men   **Range:** 700/15
    M: 2 Rolls-Royce 8-cyl. diesels; 2 props; 1,340 hp
    Electron Equipt: Radar: Decca 202

PATROL CRAFT

◆ **4 56-foot boats** Bldr: Vosper Thornycroft Private, Ltd., Singapore

    D: 25 tons (fl)   **S:** 29 kts   **Dim:** 17.0 × . . . × . . .
    A: 2/20-mm AA (I × 2)   **M:** 2 MTU diesels; 2 props; 1,800 hp

REMARKS: Two ordered 10-3-77, two 7-78. In service 12-77, 1979.

◆ **6 36-foot boats** Bldr: Vosper Thornycroft Private, Ltd., Singapore

    D: 6.8 tons (fl)   **S:** 22 kts   **Dim:** 11.0 × 3.3 × 0.6
    A: 4/76-mm machine guns (II × 2)   **Man:** 4 men
    M: 2 Sabre 210 diesels; 2 props; 420 hp

REMARKS: Three ordered 26-3-77, in service 2-12-77; three ordered 7-78. Launched 1977, 1979.

◆ **2 56-foot boats** Bldr: Vosper Thornycroft Private, Ltd., Singapore, 1974

DASTOR   KASAR

    D: 25 tons   **S:** 21 kts   **Dim:** 16.8 × . . . × . . .
    A: 1/20-mm − 2 machine guns   **Man:** 8 men
    M: 2 MTU MB 6V331 diesels; 1,350 hp   **Range:** 320/20

◆ **7 50-foot craft** Bldr: Thornycroft Ltd., Singapore, 1977-78

◆ **1 46-foot craft** Bldr: Thornycroft Ltd., Singapore

MAHROOS

    D: 12 tons   **S:** 21 kts   **Dim:** 14.0 × . . . × . . .
    A: 2/20-mm AA (I × 2) − 2/7.6-mm machine guns
    M: 2 Rolls-Royce C8M-410 diesels; 780 hp

Mahroos   Vosper, 1975

◆ **8 35-foot craft** Bldr: Vosper Thornycroft Private Ltd., Singapore, 1972-73

    S: 24 kts   **M:** 2 Perkins diesels

◆ **5 landing craft** Bldr: Vosper Thornycroft Private Ltd., Singapore, 1971, 1979

WAHEED   REGGA   FAREED   N . . .   N . . .

Regga   Vosper, 1971

    D: 88 tons   **S:** 10 kts   **Dim:** 27.0 × 6.9 × 1.3
    M: 2 Rolls-Royce C8M-410 diesels; 752 hp   **Man:** 8 men

REMARKS: The two additional craft were ordered 7-78 and are 5 meters longer.

◆ **1 fireboat** Bldr: Vosper Thornycroft Private, Ltd., Singapore, 1978

WAHEED

    D: 112.6 grt   **S:** 26.6 kts   **Dim:** 26.2 × 5.8 × . . .   **Man:** 16 men
    M: 2 diesels; 2 props; 2,200 hp

LEBANON

PERSONNEL: 200 men

MERCHANT MARINE (1977): 189 ships − 277,846 grt
                  (tankers: 2 ships − 22,633 grt)

PATROL BOATS

NOTE: Attempts are being made to rejuvenate the aged and worn-out Lebanese Navy. Two 37-meter gunboats, *Jihad* and *Salam*, were ordered from Müller SY, Hameln, West Germany, in 1975 but were sold to Libya on completion in 1-78.

LEBANON *(continued)*

PATROL BOATS *(continued)*

Tarablous   1959

	Bldr	L
TARABLOUS	Estérel NSY	6-59

D: 105 tons   **S:** 27 kts   **Dim:** 38.0 × 5.5 × 1.75
A: 2/40-mm AA (I × 2)   **Range:** 1,500   **Man:** 3 officers, 16 men
M: 2 Mercedes-Benz diesels; 2 props; 2,700 hp

◆ **3 Biblos-class**   Bldr: Estérel NSY, 1954-55

11 BIBLOS   12 SIDON   13 BEYROUTH (ex-*Tir*)

D: 28 tons   **S:** 18 kts   **Dim:** 20.1 × 4.1 × 1.3
A: 1/20-mm AA – 2 machine guns
M: 2 General Motors diesels; 2 props; 530 hp

REMARK: In poor condition.

AMPHIBIOUS CRAFT

◆ **1 ex-U.S. LCU-1466-class landing craft**

SOUR (ex-LCU-1474)

D: 180 tons (347 fl)   **S:** 8 kts   **Dim:** 35.05 × 10.36 × 1.6 (aft)
A: 2/20-mm AA (I × 2)   **Cargo capacity:** 167 tons
M: 3 Gray Marine 64YTL diesels; 3 props; 675 hp

REMARKS: Transferred 11-58. Bow ramp.

LIBERIA

PERSONNEL: Approximately 225 men

MERCHANT MARINE (1978): 2,523 ships – 80,191,329 grt
(tankers: 821 ships – 49,778,422 grt)

PATROL BOAT

◆ **1 U.S. PGM-71-class**   Bldr: Peterson Builders, Sturgeon Bay, Wis.

102 ALERT (ex-PGM-102)

D: 130 tons (147 fl)   **S:** 17 kts   **Dim:** 30.8 × 6.45 × 2.3
A: 1/40-mm AA – 5/12.7-mm machine guns   **Man:** 2 officers, 13 men
Fuel: 15 tons   **Range:** 1,000/12
M: 8 GM 6-71 diesels; 2 props; 2,200 hp

REMARK: In service 2-12-66.

PATROL CRAFT

◆ **2 U.S. 65-foot class**   Bldr: Swiftships, Morgan City, La.

103 CAVILLA   104 MANO

D: 38 tons (fl)   **S:** 24 kts   **Dim:** 19.8 × 5.8 × 0.8
A: 1/81-mm mortar combined with 12.7-mm machine gun – 2/12.7-mm machine guns (I × 2)   **Man:** 2 officers, 18 men   **Range:** 600/21.5
M: 2 GM 12 V-71-TI diesels; 2 props; 1,920 hp

REMARK: In service 22-7-76.

◆ **1 U.S. 42-foot class**   Bldr: Swiftships, Morgan City, La.

101 ST. PAUL

D: 11 tons (12 fl)   **S:** 20 kts   **Dim:** 12.8 × 3.7 × 0.6
A: 2/12.7-mm machine guns (I × 2)   **Man:** 4 men
M: 2 GM 8 V-71 diesels; 2 props; 870 hp

LIBYA

PERSONNEL: Approximately 2,000 men
MERCHANT MARINE (1978): 75 ships – 885,362 grt
(tankers: 15 ships – 795,693 grt)

NAVAL AVIATION: 12 French Alouette-III helicopters are in service for naval use.

SUBMARINES

◆ **3 Soviet Foxtrot class**

AL BADR   AL FATEH   AL AHAD

D: 1,950 tons surfaced, 2,400 submerged   **S:** 18/16 kts
Dim: 96.0 × 7.5 × 6.0   **Man:** 8 officers, 70 men   **Range:** 9,000/7
A: 10/533-mm TT (6 fwd, 4 aft) – 22 torpedoes or 44 mines

SUBMARINES *(continued)*

Libyan Foxtrot   1978

M: Diesels and electric motors; 3 props; 6,000 hp
Endurance: 70 hours, submerged

REMARKS: One transferred in 12-76, two in 1978. Three more are expected.

FRIGATE

◆ **1 Vosper Mk 7** Bldr: Vosper Thornycroft

	Laid down	L	In serv.
F 211 DAT ASSAWARI	27-9-68	9-69	1-2-73

Dat Assawari—wearing old number   1976

D: 1,325 tons (1,650 fl) **Dim:** 101.6 (94.5 pp) × 11.08 × 3.36
S: 37/17 kts **Man:** 132 men **Range:** 5,700/17
A: 1/114-mm Mk 8 DP—1/Sea Cat SAM (III × 1)—2/40-mm (I × 2)—2/35-mm Oerlikon AA (II × 1)—1/Mk 10 Limbo ASW mortar (III × 1)
Electron Equipt: Radars: 1/AWS 1, 1/navigational, 1/NA 10
                      Sonars: 1/170B, 1/174—RDL 1 intercept
M: CODOG: 2 Rolls-Royce TM 2A Olympus gas turbines, 24,000 hp each; 2 Paxman-Ventura diesels, 1,900 hp each; 2 controllable-pitch props **Fuel:** 300 tons

REMARK: To be refitted in Italy, 1979-80.

CORVETTES

◆ **4 Wadi Mragh class** Bldr: CNR, Riva Trigoso, Italy

	L	In serv.		L	In serv.
WADI MRAGH	29-4-77	. . .	WADI MERCIT	4-12-78	. . .
WADI MAJER	20-4-78	. . .	WADI MEGRAWA	4-79	. . .

Wadi Mragh—on trials   CNR, 1979

Wadi Mragh—on trials   A. Fraccaroli, 1978

CORVETTES (*continued*)

D: 547 tons (fl) **S:** 33 kts **Dim:** 61.7 × 9.3 × 2.7
Man: 56 men **Range:** 1,200/31, 3,900/16, 4,400/14
A: 4/Otomat SSM – 1/76-mm OTO Melara – 2/35-mm Oerlikon AA (II × 1) – 6/324-mm Mk 32 ASW TT (III × 2) – 16 mines
Electron Equipt: Radars: 1/RAN 11 LX, 1/Decca TM 1226, 1/NA 10
  Sonar: Thomson-CSF Diodon
Fuel: 126 tons **Electric:** 480 kw
M: 4 MTU 16V956 TB 91 diesels; 4 props; 18,000 hp

REMARKS: Ordered in 1974. Completion delayed by prolonged trials. The ASW torpedo tubes have not yet been installed.

◆ **1 Vosper Mk-1B** Bldr: Vosper, Ltd., Portsmouth

TOBRUK

Tobruk *Shbldg. and Sh. Record*, 1966

D: 440 tons (500 fl) **S:** 18 kts **Dim:** 53.95 (48.77 pp) × 8.68 × 4.0
A: 1/102-mm – 4/40-mm AA (I × 4) **Man:** 5 officers, 58 men
Range: 2,900/14 **Fuel:** 60 tons
M: 2 Paxman YJCM Ventura diesels; 2 props; 3,800 hp

REMARKS: Launched in 1965. Anti-rolling devices, air-conditioned living spaces. No ASW equipment. Can be used as a yacht.

GUIDED-MISSILE PATROL BOATS

◆ **10 French La Combattante-II class** Bldr: CMN, Cherbourg

	L	In serv.		L	In serv.
BEIR-GRASSA	28-6-79	3-80	N . . .	3-81	9-81
N . . .	4-80	12-80	N . . .	5-81	11-81
N . . .	7-80	3-81	N . . .	7-81	1-82
N . . .	9-80	5-81	N . . .	9-81	3-82
N . . .	12-80	7-81	N . . .	11-81	5-82

Libyan La Combattante-II – artist's rendering Thomson-CSF, 1979

D: 311 tons (350 fl) **S:** 39 kts **Dim:** 49.0 × 7.6 × 2.4
Man: . . . **Range:** . . .
A: 4/Otomat SSM (II × 2) – 1/76-mm OTO Melara DP – 2/40-mm Breda/Bofors AA
Electron Equipt: Radars: 1/Triton search, 1/Castor track, 1/Vega II
  fire-control – all Thomson CSF
M: 4 MTU 20V538 TB 92 diesels; 4 props; 20,000 hp

REMARKS: Ordered in 5-77. The *Beir-Grassa* was laid down on 13-3-78 and the second unit on 19-6-78. Deliveries may be accelerated over above schedule by two to three months per unit.

◆ **6 Soviet Osa-II class**

205 AL KATUM	. . . AL RWAE	. . . AL NARHAA
. . . AL OWAKH	. . . AL BAIDA	. . . N . . .

D: 240 tons (fl) **S:** 36 kts **Dim:** 39.0 × 7.7 × 1.8
A: 4/SS-N-2 Styx SSM (I × 4) – 4/30-mm AA (II × 2) **Range:** 430/34, 700/20

Libyan Osa-II 1978

GUIDED-MISSILE PATROL BOATS *(continued)*

Electron Equipt: Radars: 1/Square Tie, 1/Drum Tilt
IFF: 2/Square Head, 1/High Pole
M: 3 M-504 diesels; 3 props; 15,000 hp

REMARKS: One transferred in 1976, four in 1977, and one in 1978. Six more may be delivered. Reportedly, the original order was reduced from twenty-four to twelve.

◆ **3 Sölöven class** Bldr: Vosper, Ltd., Portsmouth

	L	In serv.		L	In serv.
P 01 SUSA	31-8-67	8-68	P 03 SEBHA (ex-*Sokna*)	29-2-68	1-69
P 02 SIRTE	10-1-68	4-68			

Susa – firing a missile   Vosper, 1968

D: 95 tons (115 fl)   **S:** 50 kts   **Dim:** 30.38 (27.44 pp) × 7.3 × 2.15
A: 8/SS-11 or SS-12 SSM (II × 4) – 2/40-mm AA (I × 2)   **Man:** 20 men
M: CODOG: 3 Bristol-Siddeley Proteus gas turbines; 3 props; 12,750 hp; 2 GM B-71 cruising diesels, 190 hp

REMARKS: Modeled on the Danish *Sölöven* class. All-wood construction, nylon sheathing to hull. Missiles are wire-guided and are not very accurate, particularly at high speeds. Cruise diesels are on outboard propeller shaft. These ships will probably be discarded 1980-81.

PATROL BOATS AND CRAFT

◆ **3 customs patrol boats** Bldr: Müller, Hameln, West Germany

JIHAD   SALAM   N . . .

D: 120 tons (fl)   **S:** 27 kts   **Dim:** 37.0 × 6.2 × . . .
A: None   **Man:** . . .   **M:** MTU diesels; . . . props; . . . hp

REMARK: Ordered for Lebanon but, when that country could not pay, sold to Libya 1-78.

◆ **4 Brooke type** Bldr: Brooke Marine, Lowestoft, G.B., 1968-70

PC 1 GARIAN   PC 3 MERAWA
PC 2 KHAWLAN   PC 4 SABRATHA

D: 100 tons (125 fl)   **S:** 23.5 kts   **Dim:** 36.58 × 7.16 × 1.75
A: 1/40-mm – 1/20-mm AA   **Man:** 22 men   **Range:** 1,800/13
M: 2 Paxman 10 YJCM Ventura diesels; 2 props; 3,600 hp

Khawlan   1970

REMARKS: Have the same engines as the *Tobruk* and the *Zeltin*. At least one has a Soviet BM-21 multiple 122-mm rocket launcher (XX × 1) in place of the 20-mm AA gun.

◆ **3 security craft** Bldr: Vosper Thornycroft, Portsmouth, 1967-69

BENINA   MISURATA   HOMS

D: 100 tons   **S:** 20/18 kts   **Dim:** 30.5 × 6.4 × 1.7
A: 1/20-mm   **Man:** 15 men   **Range:** 1,800/14
M: 3 Rolls-Royce diesels; 1,740 hp

REMARKS: Used for customs and fishery protection. Sisters *Ar Rakib*, *Farwa*, and *Akrama* ceded to Malta, 1978.

AMPHIBIOUS WARFARE SHIPS

◆ **3 Soviet Polnocny-C class**

112 IBN AL HADRANI   . . . IBN AMIA   . . . IBN EL TARAT

D: 1,050 tons (fl)   **S:** 18 kts   **Dim:** 82.0 × 10.0 × 2.0
A: 4/30-mm AA (II × 2) – 2/122-mm artillery rocket launchers (XV × 2)
Electron Equipt: Radars: 1/Spin Trough, 1/Drum Tilt
M: 2 diesels; 2 props; 5,000 hp

REMARKS: One transferred in 12-77 and two in 6-79. Like the Iraqi examples of this Polish-built class of medium landing ships, these export versions have a raised helicopter deck forward of the superstructure. A fourth Libyan unit, the *Ibn Al Qyis* (113), was lost on 14 or 15 September 1978 through fire at sea.

◆ **2 Ibn Ouf-class LSTs** Bldr: C.N.I.M., La Seyne

	Laid down	L	In serv.
130 IBN OUF	1-4-76	5-77	11-3-77
131 IBN HARISSA	18-4-77	3-78	10-3-78

D: 2,800 tons (fl)   **S:** 15 kts   **Dim:** 100.0 × 15.65 × 2.6
A: 6/40-mm Breda-Bofors AA (II × 3) – 1/81-mm mortar

AMPHIBIOUS WARFARE SHIPS *(continued)*

Ibn Ouf   J. C. Bellonne, 1977

Man: 35 men + 240 passengers
M: 2 SEMT-Pielstick diesels; 2 controllable-pitch props; 5,340 hp
Range: 4,000/14

REMARKS: Cargo: 570 tons, including up to eleven tanks. Helicopter platform aft.

AUXILIARY SHIPS

◆ **2 support ships for small craft**

	Bldr	Laid down	L	In serv.
711 ZELTIN	Vosper Thornycroft, Woolston	1967	29-2-68	23-1-69

Zeltin   1968

D: 2,200 tons (2,470 fl)   **S:** 15 kts   **Dim:** 98.72 (91.44 wl) × 14.64 × 3.05
Man: 15 officers, 86 men   **Electric:** 800 kw
A: 2/40-mm AA (I × 2)   **Range:** 3,000/14
M: 2 Paxman 16 YSCM, Ventura diesels; 2 props; 3,500 hp

REMARKS: The well deck, 41 × 12, can receive small craft that draw up to 2.3 m. Hydraulically controlled stern gate. A moveable crane (3-ton loading capacity) is available for the well deck, and a 9-ton crane on the port side is available for the workshops.

Zeltin—showing well deck   1972

ZLEITEN (ex-British MRC-1013)

     D: 650 tons (900 fl)   **S:** 10/11 kts   **Dim:** 70.4 × 11.8 × 1.6
     M: 4 Paxman diesels; 2 props; 1,840 hp

REMARKS: Former LCT converted to a repair barge while in British service. Bought 5-9-66. Now a hulk.

◆ **1 ex-Italian Expresso-class ro-ro carrier**

EL TIMSAH

     D: 3,100 tons (fl)   **S:** 20 kts   **Dim:** 117.5 (108.7 pp) × 17.5 × 4.9
     M: 2 Fiat diesels, 18 cyl. in V; 9,000 hp

REMARKS: Has stabilizers. Used as a military transport and possibly as a minelayer.

◆ **4 Ras El Helal-class tugs**   Bldr: Mondego, Foz, Portugal

	In serv.		In serv.
RAS EL HELAL	22-10-77	AL KERIAT	17-2-78
AL SHWEIREF	17-2-78	AL TABKAH	. . .

     D: 200 grt   **S:** 14 kts   **Dim:** 34.8 × 9.0 × . . .
     M: 2 diesels; 2 props; 2,300 hp

LIBYA *(continued)*

AUXILIARY SHIPS *(continued)*

◆ **1 Soviet Nyryat-1-class diving tender**

VM 917 (Soviet number)

   D: 135 tons   **S:** 9 kts   **Dim:** 29.3 × 5.0 × 1.3

REMARK: Transferred 19-12-77.

MALAGASY REPUBLIC

PERSONNEL: Approximately 300 men

MERCHANT MARINE (1977): 45 ships—40,303 grt
                   (tankers: 3 ships—1,324 grt)

PATROL BOATS

◆ **1 PR-48-type coastal patrol boat**

	Bldr	Laid down	L	In serv.
MALAIKA	C.N. Franco-Belges	11-66	22-3-67	12-67

   D: 250 tons (fl)   **S:** 18.5 kts   **Dim:** 47.5 (45.5 pp) × 7.1 × 2.25
   A: 2/40-mm AA   **Man:** 3 officers, 22 men   **Range:** 2,000/15
   M: 2 MGO diesels; 2 props; 2,400 hp

REMARK: Sisters with more powerful propulsion plants in the Senegalese and Tunisian navies.

◆ **1 former trawler**

	Bldr	L
FANANTENANA (ex-*Richelieu*)	A.G. Weser, Bremen	1959

   D: 1,040 tons (1,200 fl)   **Dim:** 62.9 (56 pp) × 9.15 × 4.52
   S: 12 kts   **A:** 2/40-mm AA   **Man:** . . .
   M: 2 Deutz diesels ("father-mother" system); 1 prop; 1,060 + 500 hp

REMARKS: 691 grt. Bought and modified, 1966-67. Can carry 300 tons of freight and up to 120 military passengers. Used primarily as a training ship.

AMPHIBIOUS WARFARE SHIPS

◆ **1 LSM**

	Bldr	Laid down	L	In serv.
TOKY	Diego Suarez SY	1972	1973	10-74

   D: 810 tons (avg)   **S:** 13 kts   **Dim:** 66.37 (56.0 pp) × 12.5 × 1.9
   Man: 27 men   **Range:** 3,000/12   **Electric:** 240 kw
   A: 1/76-mm—2/20-mm AA—1/81-mm mortar
   M: 2 MGO diesels; 2 props; 2,400 hp

REMARKS: Similar to a French EDIC. Used as a transport and support ship. Forward ramp can be folded upon itself. Transport capacity: 250 tons. Quarters for 30 passengers; 120 soldiers can be carried for short distances. Financed by the French government under the military cooperation pact.

MARITIME POLICE

◆ **5 coast surveillance craft**

   D: 46 tons   **S:** 22 kts   **Dim:** 24.0 × . . . × . . .
   A: 1/40-mm AA   **M:** 2 diesels; 2 props; . . . hp

REMARK: Delivered by West Germany in 1962.

MALAYSIA

PERSONNEL: Approximately 5,500 men

MERCHANT MARINE (1979): 182 ships—552,456 grt
                   (tankers: 10 ships—4,750 grt)

NOTE: The names of all Malaysian warships are preceded by "KD" (Kapal Diraja).

FRIGATES

◆ **1 Yarrow class**

	Bldr	Laid down	L	In serv.
F 24 RAHMAT	Yarrow, Glasgow	2-66	18-12-67	3-71

   D: 1,290 tons (1,600 fl)   **S:** 27 kts (16.5, on diesels alone)
   Dim: 93.87 (91.44 pp) × 10.36 × 3.05   **Man:** 120 men
   A: 1/114-mm Mk 4 DP—2/40-mm 70-cal. Bofors AA (I × 2)—1/Sea Cat system
      (IV × 1)—1/Mk 10 Limbo triple ASW mortar
   Electron Equipt: Radars: 1/LWO 2, 1/Decca . . . , 1/M 22, 1/M 44
                Sonars: 1/170B, 1/174

FRIGATES (continued)

Rahmat 1973

M: CODOG: 1 Rolls-Royce Olympus TM-3 gas turbine, 19,500 hp; 2 Crossley-Pielstick 8-cyl. diesels, 3,850 hp; 2 controllable-pitch props; 22,000 hp
Range: 1,000/27, 5,200/16.5

REMARKS: Ordered in 1966. Advanced automation. Mk-22 fire-control radar atop the
mast for the 114-mm gun and Mk-44 on the stern for the Sea Cat system. The 114-mm
mount has 102-mm flare rocket launchers on the sides of the shield. The ASW mortar
is covered by a hatch that serves as a helicopter platform.

◆ **1 British built** Bldr: Yarrow, Glasgow

	Laid down	L	In serv.
F 76 HANG TUAH (ex-*Mermaid*, F-76)	1965	29-12-66	16-5-73

D: 2,300 tons (2,520 fl) **S:** 24/23 kts **Dim:** 103.4 × 12.2 × 4.8
Man: 200-210 men **Range:** 4,800/15 **Fuel:** 230 tons
A: 2/102-mm DP (II × 1)—2/40-mm AA (I × 2)—1/Mk 10 Limbo triple ASW mortar
Electron Equipt: Radars: 1/AWS 1, 1/978 Sonars: 1/174, 1/170B
M: 8 16-cyl. Admiralty Standard Range-I high-speed diesels with reduction gear
hydraulically linked, 4 by 4; 2 props; 14,400

Hang Tuah as the Mermaid 1975

REMARKS: Ordered for Ghana in 1964. Because of the political situation, the ship was
not delivered and, at the end of 1971, was purchased by the British government.
Transferred to Malaysia in 5-77. Lead-computing STD Mk-1 sight for the Mk-19 twin
102-mm mount, but no fire-control radar. Helicopter pad. Replaces the "Loch"-class
Hang Tuah as training ship.

GUIDED-MISSILE PATROL BOATS

◆ **4 Modified Spica Class** — Bldr: Karlskrona, Sweden

P 3511 HANDALAN   P 3513 PENDIKAR
P 3512 PERKASA   P 3514 GEMPITA

D: 240 tons (268 fl) **S:** 37.5/34.5 kts
Dim: 43.62 × 7.0 × 2.4 (aft) **Man:** 5 officers, 34 men
A: 4/MM 38 Exocet SSM (II × 2)—1/57-mm Bofors AA **Range:** 1,850/14
Electron Equipt: Radars: 1/DO Philips air-search, 1/CT Saab-Scania
M: 3 MTU MD 16V538 TB91 diesels; 3 props; 10,800 hp **Electric:** 200 kw

REMARKS: Contract signed 13-8-56. In service in 1979. Given the names of the four
Perkasa-class torpedo/patrol boats that were stricken in 1977. Will have six 103-mm
rocket flare launchers on the 57-mm mount.

◆ **4 French La Combattante-II 4AL class** Bldr: CMN, Cherbourg

	L	In serv.		L	In serv.
P 3501 PERDANA	31-5-72	31-12-72	P 3503 GANAS	26-10-72	28-2-73
P 3502 SERANG	22-12-71	31-2-73	P 3504 GANYANG	16-3-72	20-3-73

Ganyang 1973

GUIDED-MISSILE PATROL BOATS *(continued)*

Perdana   1978

> **D:** 234 tons (265 fl)   **S:** 36.5 kts   **Dim:** 47.0 × 7.1 × 2.5 (fl)
> **Man:** 5 officers, 30 men   **Range:** 800/25   **Fuel:** 39 tons
> **A:** 2/MM 38 Exocet SSM (I × 2) – 1/57-mm Bofors AA – 1/40-mm Bofors AA
> **Electron Equipt:** Radars: 1/Decca 1226, 1/Triton, 1/Pollox – 1/Vega C.T.
> **M:** 4 MTU MB 870 diesels; 4 props; 14,000 hp

REMARKS: Steel hulls. Superstructures in alloyed metal. Six 103-mm rocket flare launchers on the 57-mm mount, four on the 40-mm mount.

PATROL BOATS

◆ **6 Jerong class** Bldr: Hong Leong-Lürssen, Butterworth, Malaysia

		L	In serv.			L	In serv.
P 3505	JERONG	28-7-75	23-3-76	P 3508	YU	17-7-76	15-11-76
P 3506	TUDAK	16-3-76	16-6-76	P 3509	BAUNG	5-10-76	11-7-77
P 3507	PAUS	2-6-76	18-8-76	P 3510	PARI	1-77	23-3-77

> **D:** 210 tons (255 fl)   **S:** 32 kts   **Dim:** 44.9 × 7.0 × 2.5 (fl)
> **A:** 1/57-mm AA – 1/40-mm Bofors AA   **Man:** 35 men   **Range:** 2,000/15
> **Electron Equipt:** Radar: Decca 1226
> **M:** 3 MTU MB 870 diesels; 3 props; 9,900 hp

REMARKS: Reduced version of La Combattante-II design. No missiles. Rocket flare launchers are fitted on both gun mounts.

◆ **22 103-foot Vosper type** Bldr: Vosper Ltd., Portsmouth

Ordered in 1965

P 34	KRIS (11-3-66)	P 36	SUNDANG (22-5-66)
P 37	BADEK (8-5-66)	P 38	RENCHONG (22-6-66)
P 39	TOMBAK (20-6-66)	P 40	LEMBING (22-8-66)
P 41	SERAMPANG (15-9-66)	P 42	PANAH (10-10-66)
P 43	KERAMBIT (20-11-66)	P 44	BALADAU (11-1-67)
P 45	KELEWANG (31-1-67)	P 46	RENTAKA (15-3-67)
P 47	SRI PERLIS (26-5-67)	P 48	SRI JOHORE (21-8-67)

Sri Kedah (P-3138) – since stricken

Ordered in March 1963

P 3114	SRI SABAH (30-12-63)	P 3145	SRI SARAWAK (20-1-64)
P 3146	SRI NEGRI SEMBILAN (17-9-64)	P 3147	SRI MELAKA (25-2-64)

Ordered in September 1961

P 3140	SRI PERAK (30-8-62)	P 3139	SRI SELANGOR (17-7-62)
P 3142	SRI KELANTAN (8-1-63)	P 3143	SRI TRENGGANU (12-12-62)

> **D:** 96 tons (109 fl)   **S:** 27/23 kts
> **Dim:** 31.39 (28.95 pp) × 5.95 × 1.65   **Man:** 3 officers, 19-20 men
> **A:** 2/40-mm AA (I × 2) – 2 machine guns   **Range:** 1,400/14
> **Electron Equipt:** Radar: Decca
> **M:** 2 Bristol-Siddeley or Maybach MD 655/18 diesels; 2 props; 3,550 hp

REMARKS: Welded hulls. Vosper anti-roll stabilizers. The Malaysian prototype was delivered in February 1963 and was soon followed by many others. The middle group have greater range: 1,660 /14. The class prototype, the *Sri Kedah* (P-3138), and the *Sri Pahang* (P-3141) were stricken in 1976.

MINE WARFARE SHIPS

◆ **5 ex-British "-ton"-class coastal minesweepers**

		Bldr:	L	Trans.
M 1127	MAHAMIRU (ex-*Darlaston*)	Cook, Whelton & Gemmell	25-9-53	1960
M 1143	LEDANG (ex-*Keston*)	Cook, Whelton & Gemmell	1954	10-63
M 1134	KINABALU (ex-*Essington*)	Camper & Nicholson	9-54	1964
M 1163	TAHAN (ex-*Lullington*)	Harland & Wolff	31-8-55	4-66
M 1172	BRINCHANG (ex-*Thankerton*)	Camper & Nicholson	4-9-56	5-66

> **D:** 360 tons (425 fl)   **S:** 15 kts   **Dim:** 46.33 (42.68 pp) × 8.76 × 2.5
> **A:** 1/40-mm AA – 2/20-mm AA (II × 1)   **Man:** 39 men   **Fuel:** 45 tons
> **Range:** 2,300/13, 3,000/8
> **M:** 2 Napier Deltic 18A 7A diesels; 2 props; 3,000 hp

REMARKS: Sister *Jerai* (M-1168, ex-*Dilston*) stricken in 1977. All were refitted, 1972-73, by Vosper Thornycroft in Singapore. Wood-planked hulls with aluminum-alloy framing.

MINE WARFARE SHIPS (continued)

Ledang   1973

AMPHIBIOUS WARFARE SHIPS

◆ 3 ex-U.S. LST-542 class

		L	In serv.
A 1500 SRI LANGKAWI (ex-*Sutter County*, ex-LST-1150)		8-11-44	4-12-44
A 1501 SRI BANGG (ex-*Hunterdon County*, AGP-838, ex-LST-838)		8-11-44	30-11-44
A 1502 RAJAH JEROM (ex-*Sedgewick County*, LST-1123)		29-1-45	19-2-45

Bldrs: A-1500: American Bridge, Pa;
      A-1501: Missouri Valley Bridge & Iron, Evansville, Ind.;
      A-1502: Chicago Bridge & Iron, Seneca, Ill.

D: 1,653 tons (4,080 fl)   **S:** 11.6 kts   **Dim:** 100.0 (96.31 pp) × 15.24 × 4.26
A: 8/40-mm AA (II × 2, I × 4)   **Fuel:** 568 tons
M: 2 GM 12-567A diesels; 2 props; 1,700 hp

REMARKS: A-1500 was transferred 1-7-71, and the other two, 7-10-76. A-1500 was converted to a small-craft tender while still in U.S. Navy service; some of her tank deck was converted to machine shops and store rooms, and a kingpost and boom were added on her upper deck. The other pair are used as logistics support tenders and have a 2,100-ton cargo capacity. All have a helicopter pad amidships and bow doors.

◆ 2 Jernih-class utility landing craft   Bldr: Brooke DY, Malaysia

A . . . JERNIH   A . . . TERIJAH

D: 290 (fl)   **S:** 8 kts   **Dim:** 38.0 (35.2 pp) × . . . × 1.4
M: 2 Caterpillar D343T diesels; 2 props; 730 hp

REMARKS: In service in 1977 and 1978. Capacity: 170 tons of dry cargo or 240 tons of fresh water. Intended as supply craft for Sarawak.

◆ 1 Meleban-class utility landing craft   Bldr: Brooke DY, Malaysia

A . . . MELEBAN

D: . . .   **S:** 8 kts   **Dim:** 50.0 (43.5 pp) × . . . × 1.37
M: 2 Caterpillar D343T diesels; 2 props; 730 hp

REMARK: Launched 15-10-77.

HYDROGRAPHIC SHIP

◆ 1 seagoing oceanographic research and hydrographic survey ship

A 152 MUTIARA   Bldr: Hong Leong-Lürssen, Butterworth, Malaysia

D: 1,905 tons (fl)   **S:** 16 kts   **Dim:** 70.0 (64.0 pp) × 13.0 × 4.0
A: 2/20-mm AA (I × 2)   **Man:** 156 men   **Range:** 4,500/16
M: 1 Deutz SBA-12M-528 diesel; 1 controllable-pitch prop; 2,000 hp

REMARKS: Ordered 1975. In service 18-11-77. Carries six small survey launches and has a helicopter deck. White bull, buff stack. Replaces the *Perantau* (A-151, ex-British *Myrmidon*).

SUPPORT SHIP

	Bldr	L	In serv.
◆ A 1109 DUYONG	Kall Teck, Singapore	18-8-70	5-1-71

D: 140 tons (fl)   **S:** 10 kts   **Dim:** 33.0 × 6.3 × 1.7
A: 1/20-mm AA   **Man:** 23 men   **M:** 2 Cummins diesels; 2 props; 500 hp

REMARKS: Used as a support ship for divers. Originally configured as a torpedo-retriever.

ROYAL MALAYSIAN MARINE POLICE

PATROL BOATS

◆ 6 PZ class   Bldr: Hong Leong-Lürssen, Butterworth, Malaysia

	L		L		L
P 21 N . . .	. . .	P 23 N . . .	. . .	P 25 N . . .	. . .
P 22 N . . .	. . .	P 24 N . . .	. . .	P 26 N . . .	. . .

D: . . .   **S:** 30 kts   **Dim:** 38.0 × . . . × . . .
A: 2/40-mm AA (I × 2)   **Man:** . . .   **Range:** . . .
M: 2 diesels, 2 props; . . . hp

REMARK: Ordered in 1979.

◆ 6 PX-26 class   Bldr: Hong Leong-Lürssen, Butterworth, Malaysia, 1973

PX 25 N . . .	PX 27 SRI TAWAU	PX 29 N . . .
PX 26 Sri Kudat	PX 28 N . . .	PX 30 N . . .

D: 62.5 tons   **S:** 25 kts   **Dim:** . . . × . . . × . . .
A: 1/20-mm AA   **Man:** . . .   **Range:** . . .
M: 2 MTU diesels; 2 props; . . . hp

◆ 6 improved PX-class   Bldr: Vosper Thornycroft Private, Singapore, 1972-73

PX 19 ALOR STAR	PX 22 JOHORE BAHRU
PX 20 KOTA BAHRU	PX 23 SRI MENANTI
PX 21 KUALA TRENGGANU	PX 24 KUCHING

D: 92 tons (fl)   **S:** 25 kts   **Dim:** 27.3 × 5.8 × 1.5

MALAYSIA *(continued)*

PATROL BOATS *(continued)*

   A: 2/20-mm AA (I × 2)   **Man:** 18 men   **Range:** 750/15
   M: 2 MTU diesels; 2 props; 2,460 hp

◆ **18 PX class**   Bldr: Vosper Thornycroft Private, Singapore, 1963-70

PX 1 MAHKOTA	PX 7 BENTARA	PX 13 PEKAN
PX 2 TEMENGGONG	PX 8 PERWIRA	PX 14 KELANG
PX 3 HULUBALANG	PX 9 PERTANDA	PX 15 KUALA KANGSAR
PX 4 MAHARAJESETIA	PX 10 SHAHBANDAR	PX 16 ARAU
PX 5 MAHARAJELELA	PX 11 SANGSETIA	PX 17 SRI GUMANTONG
PX 6 PAHLAWAN	PX 12 LAKSAMANA	PX 18 SRI LABUAN

Shahbandar and Sangsetia   1975

   D: 85 tons (fl)   **S:** 25 kts   **Dim:** 26.29 × 5.7 × 1.45
   A: 2/20-mm AA (I × 2)   **Man:** 15 men   **Range:** 700/15
   M: 2 MTU diesels; 2 props; 2,700 hp

REMARKS: PX-17 and PX-18 are operated by the Sabah government.

NOTE: The Royal Malaysian Marine Police operate a large number of smaller patrol and support craft.

MALDIVES REPUBLIC

PERSONNEL: Approximately 150, total

MERCHANT MARINE (1978): 45 ships—110,681 grt

PATROL BOATS AND CRAFT

◆ **1 ex-British RTTL Mk-2-class target-towing launch**

N . . .

   D: 34.6 tons   **S:** 30 kts   **Dim:** 20.7 × 5.8 × 1.8
   A: Machine guns   **Man:** 9 men
   M: 2 Rolls-Royce Griffon gasoline engines; 2 props; 11,000 hp

REMARK: Transferred in 1976 by the departing Royal Air Force.

◆ **1 ex-British 1300-class pinnace**

N . . .

   D: 28.3 tons   **S:** 13 kts   **Dim:** 19.2 × 4.9 × 1.5
   A: . . .   **Man:** 5 men   **Cargo:** 5 tons
   M: 2 Rolls-Royce C6 diesels; 2 props; 190 hp

REMARK: Transferred by the departing Royal Air Force.

◆ **3 ex-Taiwanese trawlers**

REMARKS: Approximately 600 tons (fl). Fitted with 2/25-mm AA guns (II × 1) by the U.S.S.R. after confiscation for poaching in 1976.

◆ **4 ex-British 19.5-meter landing craft**

REMARK: Transferred in 1976.

◆ **1 customs launch**   Bldr: Fairey Marine, G.B., 1975

MALTA

MERCHANT MARINE (1978): 47 ships—101,541 grt
(tankers: 3 ships—5,339 grt)

◆ **2 ex-U.S. Swift-class PCF**   Bldr: Sewart Seacraft, 1967

C 23 (ex-U.S. 6823)   C 24 (ex-U.S. 6824)

   D: 22.5 tons (fl)   **S:** 25 kts   **Dim:** 15.6 × 4.12 × 1.5
   Man: 6-8 men   **Endurance:** 24-36 hours
   A: 3/12.7-mm machine guns (II × 1 and 1 combined with 1/81-mm mortar)
   M: GM 12-V-71T diesels; 2 props; 960 hp

REMARK: Transferred 1-71.

MALTA (*continued*)

◆ **3 ex-Libyan customs patrol craft** Bldrs: C-30 and C-32: Thornycroft, Woolston; C-31: Vosper Thornycroft

C 30 (ex-*Farwa*)   C 31 (ex-*Akrama*)   C 32 (ex-*Ar Rakib*)

   D: 100 tons (fl)   **S:** 18 kts   **Dim:** 30.5 × 6.4 × 1.7
   A: 1/20-mm AA   **Man:** 15 men   **Range:** 1,800/14
   M: 3 Rolls-Royce diesels; 3 props; 1,740 hp

REMARK: Transferred in 1978.

◆ **1 ex-German customs launch**

C 29 (ex-*Kondor*) Bldr: Lürssen, Bremen, 1953

   D: 100 tons (fl)   **S:** 10 kts   **Dim:** 28.0 × 5.25 × 2.0
   A: 1/12.7-mm machine gun   **Man:** 9 men
   M: 1 Deutz RT 8M33 diesel; . . . hp

REMARK: Purchased in 1974.

◆ **1 ex-German customs launch**

C 28 (ex-*Geier*) Bldr: Bremen Burg, 1955

   D: 125 tons (fl)   **S:** 12 kts   **Dim:** 28.0 × 5.0 × 2.0
   A: None   **Man:** 7 men   **M:** 2 Mercedes-Benz MB846 diesels

REMARK: Purchased in 1974.

◆ **1 ex-German customs launch**

C 27 (ex-*Brunsbuttel*) Bldr: Buschmann, Hamburg, 1953

C 27

   D: 105 tons (fl)   **S:** 16 kts   **Dim:** 29.5 × 5.2 × 1.6
   A: 1/12.7-mm machine gun   **Man:** 9 men
   M: 2 MWM TRM 134S diesels; 2 props; . . . hp

REMARK: Purchased in 1974.

◆ **2 ex-Libyan customs launches**

C 25   C 26 Bldr: Mosir SY, Trogir, Yugoslavia, 1963

   D: 86.2 tons (100 fl)   **S:** 20 kts   **Dim:** 35.0 × 5.0 × 1.7

   A: 1/12.7-mm machine gun   **Man:** 12 men   **Range:** 1,400/12
   M: 2 MTU 12V493 diesels; 2 props; 1,800 hp

REMARK: Transferred 16-1-74.

◆ **1 customs launch**

C 21 Bldr: Malta Drydocks, 1960

   D: 25 tons   **S:** 19 kts   **Dim:** 16.3 × 4.1 × 2.3
   A: 2/12.7-mm machine guns   **Man:** 8 men
   M: 2 Fiat 521-SH diesels; 2 props; 500 hp

REMARK: Purchased in 1973.

MAURITANIA

PERSONNEL: 200 men

MERCHANT MARINE (1978): 3 ships — 489 grt

PATROL BOATS AND CRAFT

◆ **3 Spanish Barcelo class** Bldr: Bazán, San Fernando

	In serv.		In serv.		In serv.
P 361 N . . .	12-79	P 362 EL BEG	5-79	P 363 N . . .	6-80

   D: 134 tons (fl)   **S:** 36.5 kts   **Dim:** 36.2 × 5.8 × 1.75
   Man: 3 officers, 16 men   **Range:** 1,200/17   **Fuel:** 18 tons
   A: 1/40-mm AA — 2/20-mm   **Electron Equipt:** Radar: Raytheon 1620
   M: 2 MTU MD 16V538 TB-90 diesels; 6,000 hp   **Electric:** 330 kva

REMARKS: Delivery of the first two was greatly delayed by the fact that they collided on trials, 12-78. The third unit was ordered in 1979.

◆ **2 ex-Soviet Mirnyi-class whaling ships** Bldr: Nosenko SY, Nikolaev, 1956

IDINI   BOULANOUAR

   D: 1,300 tons (fl)   **S:** 17.5 kts   **Dim:** 63.6 × 9.5 × 4.5
   A: 2/25-mm AA (II × 1) — 1/12.7-mm machine gun   **Range:** 18,700/11
   M: 4 6-cyl. diesels, electric drive; 1 prop; 3,100 hp

MAURITANIA (continued)
PATROL BOATS AND CRAFT (continued)

Idini 1975

REMARK: Used as fisheries-protection vessels and as tenders for the *Tichitt* class and smaller craft.

◆ **2 ex-Spanish trawlers** Bldr: Astano, El Ferrol, 1953

N . . . (ex-*Centinela*, W-33) N . . . (ex-*Serviola*, W-34)

 D: 255 tons (282 fl) **S:** 12 kts **Dim:** 36.0 × 6.8 × 3.0
 A: 2/37-mm (I × 2) **M:** 1 diesel; 450 hp

REMARK: Transferred 5-3-77.

◆ **2 Tichitt-class craft** Bldr: Chantiers Navals de l'Esterel

TICHITT DAR EL BARKA

Tichitt l'Esterel, 1969

 D: 80 tons (fl) **S:** 28 kts **Dim:** 32.0 × 5.75 × 1.7
 A: 1/20-mm – 1/12.7-mm machine gun **Range:** 1,500/15 **Fuel:** 15 tons
 M: 2 Mercedes-Benz MB820 Db/h diesels; 2 props; 2,700 hp

REMARKS: In service 4-69. Identical to the Tunisian *Istiklal* and the Moroccan *El Sabiq* classes of patrol craft.

◆ **2 security craft** Bldr: Chantiers Navals de l'Esterel

IMRAG'NI SLOUGHI

 D: 20 tons (fl) **S:** 21 kts (22.7, on trials)
 Dim: 18.15 (17.03 pp) × 4.03 × 1.1 **Man:** 8 men **Range:** 400/15
 A: 1/12.7-mm machine gun **M:** GM 671 diesels; 2 props; 512 hp

REMARK: In service 11-65 and 5-68, respectively.

MAURITIUS

MERCHANT MARINE (1978): 18 ships – 40,732 grt

PATROL BOAT

◆ **1 ex-Indian Ajay-class patrol boat** Bldr: Calcutta, 1961

AMAR

 D: 120 tons (160 fl) **S:** 18 kts **Dim:** 35.7 (33.52 pp) × 6.1 × 1.5
 A: 1/40-mm AA **Range:** 1,000/8, 500/12 **Fuel:** 23 tons
 M: 2 Paxman YHAXM diesels; 2 props; 1,000 hp; 1 Foden FD 6 cruise diesel; 100 hp

REMARKS: Retained original name on transfer 4-74. Indian version of British "Ford"-class seaward defense boat.

Amar 1976

MEXICO

PERSONNEL: 11,000 men, including 1,300 Marines

MERCHANT MARINE (1978): 336 ships – 727,201 grt
(tankers: 29 ships – 383,006 grt)

NAVAL AVIATION: The Mexican Navy operates 4 HU-6 Albatros amphibious patrol planes, 4 DC-3 transports, and 18 light fixed-wing aircraft, including 1 Learjet 24D and 3 T-34B Mentor trainers. Helicopters include four Alouette III, five Hughes 269 A, and three Bell 47G/J.

DESTROYERS

NOTE: Plans to transfer two ex-U.S. Navy *Gearing* FRAM 1-class destroyers to Mexico in 1979-80 have been postponed.

◆ 2 ex-U.S. Fletcher class   Bldr: Consolidated Steel, Orange, Tex.

	Laid down	L	In serv.
IE 01 CUAUHTEMOC (ex-*Harrison*, DD-573)	25-7-41	7-5-42	9-2-43
IE 02 CUITLAHUAC (ex-*John Rodgers*, DD-574)	25-7-41	7-5-42	25-1-43

D: 2,050 tons (2,850 fl)   **S:** 30 kts   **Dim:** 114.73 × 12.06 × 5.5
A: 5/127-mm Mk 30 DP (I × 5) – 14/40-mm AA (IV × 2, II × 3)
Electron Equipt: Radar: 1/Kelvin-Hughes 14/9, 1/Kelvin-Hughes 17/9, 1/Mk 12/22 f.c.
Boilers: 4 Babcock & Wilcox, 39.8 kg/cm² pressure – superheat 454° C
Fuel: 650 tons   **Range:** 4,400/15, 1,260/30   **Electric:** 590 kw
M: 2 sets GE GT; 2 props; 60,000 hp

REMARKS: Transferred 8-70. All ASW capability, torpedo tube mount, and obsolete U.S. electronics systems now deleted. Have one Mk 37 director for 127-mm guns; five Mk mod 2 directors for 40-mm guns. Could make 35 knots when new.

◆ 1 ex-U.S. Charles Lawrence and 3 Crosley class

	Bldr	L	In serv.
IB 02 COAHUILA (ex-*Rednour*, APD-102, ex-DE-592)	Bethlehem, Hingham, Mass.	12-2-44	30-12-44
IB 05 TEHUANTEPEC (ex-*Joseph M. Auman*, APD-117, ex-DE-674)	Consolidated Steel, Orange, Tex.	5-2-44	25-4-45
IB 06 USUMACINTA (ex-*Don O. Woods*, APD-118, ex-DE-721)	Consolidated Steel, Orange, Tex.	19-2-44	28-5-45
IB 08 CHIHUAHUA (ex-*Barber*, APD-57, ex-DE-161)	Norfolk NY, Va.	20-5-43	10-10-43

D: 1,450 tons (2,130 fl)   **S:** 23 kts   **Dim:** 93.26 × 11.28 × 3.83
A: 1/127-mm Mk 30 DP – 6/40-mm AA (II × 3)
Electron Equipt: Radar: 1/Kelvin-Hughes 14/9   **Man:** 204 men
Range: 5,000/15   **Electric:** 680 kw   **Fuel:** 350 tons
Boilers: 2 "D"-Express, 30.6 kg/cm² pressure – superheat 399°C
M: 2 sets GE GT, turbo-electric drive; 2 props; 12,000 hp

Tehuantepec – with old number

REMARKS: Former high-speed transports. IB-05 and IB-06 transferred 12-63; IB-02 and IB-08, 17-2-69. Used primarily as patrol ships; no longer carry the four landing craft that were once stowed amidships. Converted to APD while being built. IB-08, with a high bridge and lattice mast aft, is a member of the *Charles Lawrence* class; the others each have a low bridge and a tripod aft to support the 10-ton capacity cargo boom. The 127-mm gun has no director, while there are three Mk 51 mod 2 directors for the 40-mm anti-aircraft. Two others have been lost: *California* (B-3, ex-*Belet*, APD-109) went aground 16-1-72, and *Papaloapan* (B-4, ex-*Earheart*, APD-113) in 1976.

CORVETTES

◆ 18 ex-U.S. Auk-class former fleet minesweepers

	Bldr	L
IG 01 LEANDRO VALLE (ex-*Pioneer*, MSF-105)(1)	A	26-7-42
IG 02 GUILLERMO PRIETO (ex-*Symbol*, MSF-123)(2)	B	2-7-42
IG 03 MARIANO ESCOBEDO (ex-*Champion*, MSF-314)(3)	C	12-12-42
IG 04 PONCIANO ARRIAGA (ex-*Competent*, MSF-316)(3)	C	9-1-43
IF 05 MANUEL DOBLADO (ex-*Defense*, MSF-317)(3)	C	18-2-43
IG 06 SEBASTIAN LEIDO DE TEJADA (ex-*Devastator*, MSF-318)(3)	C	19-4-43
IG 07 SANTOS DEGOLLADO (ex-*Gladiator*, MSF-319)(3)	C	7-5-43
IG 08 IGNACIO DE LA LLAVE (ex-*Spear*, MSF-322)(2)	D	25-2-43
IG 09 JUAN N. ALVAREZ (ex-*Ardent*, MSF-340)(3)	C	22-6-43
IG 10 MELCHIOR OCAMPO (ex-*Roselle*, MSF-379)(4)	E	29-8-45
IG 11 VALENTIN G. FARIAS (ex-*Starling*, MSF-64)(5)	C	15-2-42
IG 12 IGNACIO ALTAMIRANO (ex-*Sway*, MSF-120)(2)	F	29-9-42
IG 13 FRANCISCO ZARCO (ex-*Threat*, MSF-124)(2)	B	15-8-42
IG 14 IGNACIO L. VALLARTA (ex-*Velocity*, MSF-128)(2)	E	19-4-42
IF 15 JÉSUS G. ORTEGA (ex-*Chief*, MSF-315)(3)	C	5-1-43
IG 16 GUTIERRIEZ ZAMORA (ex-*Scoter*, MSF-381)(4)	E	26-9-45
IG 18 JUAN ALDARMA (ex-*Pilot*, MSF-104)(1)	A	5-7-42
IG 19 HERMENEGILDO GALEANA (ex-*Sage*, MSF-111)(1)	G	21-11-42

Bldrs: *A*, Pennsylvania Shipyard, Beaumont, Tex.; *B*, Savannah Machine & Foundry Co., Savannah, Ga.; *C*, General Engineering and Drydock Co., Alameda, Cal.; *D*, Associated Shipbuilders; *E*, Gulf Shipbuilding; *F*, J. H. Mathis, Camden, N.J.; *G*, Winslow Marine Railway and Shipbuilding, Seattle, Wash.

CORVETTES (continued)

Ignacio L. Vallarta—bulwarks amidships　　　　　　　1974

Juan Aldarma—no bulwarks　　　　　　　　　　　　1975

D: 890 tons (1,250 fl)　　**S:** 17/18 kts　　**Dim:** 67.4 (65.5 wl) × 9.8 × 3.28
A: 1/76-mm Mk 22 DP—4/40-mm AA (II × 2)
Electron Equipt: Radars: 1/SPS-5 or 1/Kelvin-Hughes 14/9, 1/SO-13
Man: 9 officers, 96 men　　**Fuel:** 216 tons　　**Electric:** 300-360 kw
M: 2 diesels, electric drive (see Remarks); 2 props; 2,976, 3,118, or 3,532 hp

REMARKS: The numbers in parentheses after the ships' names refer to five different
diesels used in propulsion plants: (1) Busch-Sulzer 539; (2) GM 12-278; (3) Baldwin
VO-8; (4) GM 12-278A; (5) Alco 539. Diesels (1) and (5) produce 3,118 hp, (2) and (4)
3,532 hp, and (3) 2,976 hp.
　　All transferred in 1973. All minesweeping and ASW equipment removed. One other
unit, *Mariano Metamoros* (ex-*Herald*, MSF-101), was converted for use as a surveying
ship. Some have a small deckhouse between the stacks; some have no main deck bulwarks. New radars have been added to ships transferred without SPS-5.

◆ **16 ex-U.S. Admirable-class former fleet minesweepers**

	Bldrs	L
ID-01 DM 01 (ex-*Jubilant*, MSF-255)	American SB, Lorain, Oh.	20-2-43
ID-02 DM 02 (ex-*Hilarity*, MSF-241)	Winslow, Seattle, Wash.	30-7-44
ID-03 DM 03 (ex-*Execute*, MSF-232)	Puget Sound, Seattle, Wash.	22-1-44
ID-04 DM 04 (ex-*Specter*, MSF-306)	Associated Shipbldrs.	15-2-44
ID-05 DM 05 (ex-*Scuffle*, MSF-298)	Winslow, Seattle, Wash.	8-8-43
ID-06 DM 06 (ex-*Eager*, MSF-224)	American SB, Lorain, Oh.	10-6-44
ID-10 DM 10 (ex-*Instill*, MSF-252)	Savannah Mach., Ga.	5-3-44
ID-11 DM 11 (ex-*Device*, MSF-220)	Tampa SB, Fla.	21-5-44
ID-12 DM 12 (ex-*Ransom*, MSF-283)	General Eng. & DD	18-9-43
ID-13 DM 13 (ex-*Knave*, MSF-256)	American SB, Lorain, Oh.	13-3-43
ID-14 DM 14 (ex-*Rebel*, MSF-284)	General Eng. & DD	28-10-43
ID-15 DM 15 (ex-*Crag*, MSF-214)	Tampa SB, Fla.	21-3-43
ID-16 DM 16 (ex-*Dour*, MSF-223)	American SB, Lorain, Oh,	25-3-44
ID-17 DM 17 (ex-*Diploma*, MSF-221)	Tampa SB, Fla.	21-5-44
ID-18 DM 18 (ex-*Invade*, MSF-254)	Savannah Mach., Ga.	6-2-44
ID-19 DM 19 (ex-*Intrigue*, MSF-253)	Savannah Mach., Ga.	8-4-44

DM 02　　　　　　　　　　　　　　　　　　　　　1975

D: 650 tons (945 fl)　　**S:** 15 kts　　**Dim:** 56.24 (54.86 wl) × 10.06 × 2.97
A: 1/76-mm Mk 22 DP—2/40-mm AA (I × 2)—6/20-mm AA (I × 6)
Man: 9 officers, 86 men　　**Fuel:** 138 tons　　**Electric:** 240 or 280 kw
M: 2 Cooper-Bessemer GSB-8 diesels; 2 props; 1,710 hp

REMARKS: All minesweeping and ASW equipment deleted. Three more units were
scrapped and DM-20 was converted into a hydrographic survey ship. DM-04 was
transferred 2-73; all others, 1-10-62.

PATROL BOATS

◆ **31 Azteca class**

	Bldr	In serv.
P-01 ANDRES QUINTANA ROO	Ailsa	1-11-74
P-02 MATIAS DE CORDOVA	Scott	22-10-74
P-03 MIGUEL RAMOS ARIZPE	Ailsa	23-12-74
P-04 JOSÉ MARIA IZAZAGO	Ailsa	19-12-74
P-05 JUAN BAUTISTA MORALES	Scott	19-12-74
P-06 IGNACIO LOPEZ RAYON	Ailsa	19-12-74
P-07 MANUEL CRESCENCIO REJON	Ailsa	4-7-75
P-08 ANTONIO DE LA FUENTE	Ailsa	4-7-75
P-09 LEON GUZMAN	Scott	7-4-75
P-10 IGNACIO RAMIREZ	Ailsa	17-7-75
P-11 IGNACIO MARISCAL	Ailsa	23-9-75
P-12 HERIBERTO JARA CORONA	Ailsa	7-11-75
P-13 JOSÉ MARIA MATA	Lamont	13-10-75
P-14 FELIX ROMERO	Scott	23-6-75
P-15 FERNANDO LIZARDI	Ailsa	24-12-75
P-16 FRANCISCO J. MUJICA	Ailsa	21-11-75
P-17 PASTOR ROUAIX JOSÉ MARIA	Scott	7-11-75
P-18 JOSE MARIA DEL CASTILLO VELASCO	Lamont	14-1-75
P-19 LUIS MANUEL ROJAS	Lamont	3-4-76
P-20 JOSÉ NATIVIDAD MACIAS	Lamont	2-9-76
P-21 ESTEBAN BACA CALDERON	Lamont	18-6-76
P-22 IGNACIO ZARAGOZA	Vera Cruz	1-6-76
P-23 TAMAULIPAS	Vera Cruz	1978
P-23 YUCATAN	Vera Cruz	1978
P-24 N . . .	Vera Cruz	1978
P-25 TABASCO	Vera Cruz	1-1-79
P-26 VERACRUZ	Vera Cruz	1-1-79
P-27 CAMPECHE	Vera Cruz	1-1-79
P-28 N . . .	Vera Cruz	1-1-79
P-29 MAJA	Salina Cruz	1-79
P-30 VICARIO	Salina Cruz	1-79
P-31 ORTIZ	Salina Cruz	1-79

Andres Quintana Roo   1975

D: 130 tons   **S:** 24 kts   **Dim:** 34.06 (30.94 pp) × 8.6 × 2.0
A: 1/40-mm — 1/20-mm   **Man:** 2 officers, 22 men   **Electric:** 80 kw
M: 2 Ruston-Paxman-Ventura 12-cyl. diesels; 7,200 hp

REMARKS: Original order for 21 placed 27-3-73 with Associated British Machine Tool Makers, Ltd., which subcontracted the actual construction and assisted with the construction of another 11 in Mexico.

PATROL CRAFT

◆ **1 (+ . . .) Olmeca class**   Bldr: Mexico, 1979-80

D: . . .   **S:** . . . kts   **Dim:** 15.0 × . . . × . . .
A: 1/20-mm AA   **Man:** 7 men
M: 1 Cummins VT-series diesel; 400 hp

REMARK: Glass-reinforced plastic construction.

◆ **4 Polimar class**   Bldrs: Astilleros de Tampico (IF-01, IF-04); Iscacas SY, Guerrero (IF-02, IF-03)

	L		L
IF 01 POLIMAR 1	1962	IF 03 POLIMAR 3	1966
IF 02 POLIMAR 2	1966	IF 04 POLIMAR 4	1968

Polimar 1   1962

D: 57 tons (fl)   **S:** 16 kts   **Dim:** 20.5 × 4.5 × 1.3
A: 2/13.2-mm machine guns (II × 1)
M: 2 diesels; 2 props; 450 hp

◆ **2 Azueta class**   Bldr: Astilleros de Tampico

	L		L
IF 06 AZUETA	1959	IF 07 VILLAPANDO	1960

D: 80 tons (85 fl)   **S:** 12 kts   **Dim:** 26.0 × 4.9 × 2.1
A: 2/13.2-mm machine guns (II × 1)   **M:** 2 Superior diesels; 2 props; 600 hp

RIVER PATROL CRAFT

◆ **8 AM 1 class**   Bldrs: Astilleros de Tampico (4); Vera Cruz SY (4)

IF-11 to IF-18   AM-1 to AM-8

D: 37 tons (fl)   **S:** 6 kts   **Dim:** 17.7 × 5.0 × . . .
A: . . .   **M:** diesels

REMARK: Launched 1960-62.

AUXILIARIES

HYDROGRAPHIC SURVEY SHIPS

◆ **1 ex-U.S. Admirable-class former minesweeper** Bldr: Willamette Iron & Steel, Ore.

H 2 OCEANOGRAFICO (ex-DM-20, ex-*Harlequin*, MSF-365)

REMARKS: Launched 3-6-44. Data as for corvettes, except for displacement, which is approximately 900 tons (full load); no armament. Converted 1976-78.

◆ **1 ex-U.S. Auk-class former minesweeper** Bldr: General Eng. & DD, Alameda, Cal.

H 1 MARIANO METAMOROS (ex-*Herald*, MSF-101)

Mariano Metamoros 1975

REMARKS: Launched 4-7-42. Data generally as for corvette version in Mexican Navy. Has Busch-Sulzer BS539 diesels; 3,118 hp. No armament. Large deckhouse built around after stack with a portable facility for aerological balloon launching atop it. Oceanographic crane at stern. Radars used are one SPS-5 and one Kelvin-Hughes 14/9.

REPAIR SHIP

◆ **1 ex-U.S. Fabius-class former aircraft repair ship**

	Bldr	L	In serv.
IA 05 GENERAL VINCENTE GUERRERO	American Bridge, Pa.	25-3-45	27-6-45
(ex-*Megara*, ARVA-6, ex-LST-1095)			

General Vincente Guerrero 1974

D: 4,100 tons (fl) **S:** 11.6 kts **Dim:** 100.0 (96.3 wl) × 15.24 × 3.4
A: 8/40-mm AA (IV × 2) **Man:** 250 men **Range:** 10,000/10
Electric: 520 kw **Fuel:** 474 tons
M: 2 GM 12-567A diesels; 2 props; 1,700 hp

REMARKS: Transferred 1-10-73. Originally intended for repairing aircraft airframes. One 10-ton boom.

TRANSPORTS

◆ **1 Mexican built** Bldr: Ulua SY, Vera Cruz, 1959

B 2 ZACATECAS

D: 780 tons **S:** 10 kts **Dim:** 47.5 × 8.2 × 2.8
A: 1/40-mm AA − 2/20-mm AA (I × 2) **Man:** 13 officers, 37 men
M: 1 M.A.N. diesel; 1 prop; 560 hp

◆ **2 U.S. LST-511-class former landing ships**

	Bldr	L	In serv.
IA 01 RIO PANUCO	Bethlehem Steel,	9-3-44	31-3-44
(ex-*Park Co.*, LST-1077)	Hingham, Mass.		
IA 02 MANZANILLO	Chicago Bridge &	18-4-45	8-5-45
(ex-*Clearwater Co.*, LST-602)	Iron, Seneca, Ill.		

D: 1,625 tons (4,100 fl) **S:** 11.6 kts **Dim:** 100.0 × 96.3 × 15.24 × 3.4
A: 8/40-mm AA (II × 2, I × 4) − IA-02: none
Man: 130 men, 170 troops/passengers **Range:** 6,000/11 **Electric:** 300 kw

Rio Panuco 1975

MEXICO (*continued*)

TRANSPORTS (*continued*)

REMARKS: Transferred 20-9-71 and 25-5-72. Intended as disaster relief ships. IA-02 has been used in Arctic Supply by the Military Sealift Command and has two cargo king posts, no armament, and an ice-reinforced waterline forward.

TRAINING SHIP

◆ **1 ex-U.S. Edsall class**   Bldr: Brown SB, Houston, Tex.

	Laid down	L	In serv.
IA 06 MANUEL AZUETA (ex-*Hurst*, DE-250)	27-1-43	14-4-43	30-8-43

D: 1,200 tons (1,590 fl)   **S:** 21 kts   **Dim:** 93.26 × 11.15 × 3.73
A: 3/76-mm Mk 22 DP (I × 3)−8/40-mm AA (IV × 1, II × 2)
Electron Equipt: Radar: 1/Kelvin-Hughes 14/9, 1/Kelvin-Hughes 17/9, 1/Mk 26
Electric: 680 kw
Man: 15 officers, 201 men   **Range:** 13,000/12   **Fuel:** 258 tons
M: 4 Fairbanks-Morse 38D⅛, 10-cyl. diesels; 2 props; 6,000 hp

REMARKS: Transferred 1-10-73. Former destroyer escort. Used as training ship for the Gulf Fleet. Has one Mk 52 radar fire-control director and one Mk 51 range-finder for the 76-mm guns, and three Mk 51 mod 2 directors for the 40-mm anti-aircraft.

TUGS

◆ **4 ex-U.S. Abnaki-class fleet tugs**   Bldrs: IA-17, United Engineering, Alameda, Cal.; others, Charleston SB & DD, S.C.

	L	In serv.
IA 17 OTUMI (ex-*Molala*, ATF-106)	23-12-42	29-9-43
IA 18 YAQUI (ex-*Hitichi*, ATF-103)	29-1-44	27-5-44
IA 19 SERI (ex-*Abnaki*, ATF-96)	22-4-43	15-11-43
IA 20 CORA (ex-*Cocopa*, ATF-101)	5-10-43	25-3-44

D: 1,325 tons (1,675 fl)   **S:** 16.5 kts   **Dim:** 62.48 × 11.73 × 4.67
A: . . .   **Electron Equipt:** Radar: 1/LN-66   **Man:** 85 men
Range: . . .   **Fuel:** 304 tons   **Electric:** 400 kw
M: 4 Busch-Sulzer BS-539 diesels, electric drive; 1 prop; 3,000 hp

REMARKS: IA-17 transferred 1-8-78, the others on 30-9-78. Unarmed on delivery.

◆ **4 ex-U.S. Maritime Administration V-4 class**

Bldr: Pendleton SY, New Orleans, 1943-44.

IA 11 R-1 (ex-*Farallon*)	IA 13 R-3 (ex-*Point Vicente*)
IA 12 R-2 (ex-*Montauk*)	IA 15 R-5 (ex-*Burnt Island*)

D: 1,825 tons (fl)   **S:** 14 kts   **Dim:** 58.22 × 11.3 × 5.5
A: 1/76-mm Mk 22 DP−2/20-mm AA   **Man:** 90 men   **Range:** 19,000/14
M: 2 Enterprise diesels; 2 Kort-nozzle props; 2,250 hp

REMARKS: Transferred 9-78. Sister R-4 lost in 1973; R-6 discarded in 1970.

SERVICE CRAFT

◆ **2 ex-U.S. 174-foot-class harbor oilers**

	Bldr	L
IA 03 AGUASCALIENTES (ex-YOG-6)	J. H. Mathis, Camden, N.J.	1943
IA 04 TLAXCALA (ex-YO-107)	G. Lawley, Neponset, Mass.	1943

D: 440 tons (1,480 fl)   **S:** 8 kts   **Dim:** 53.0 × 9.75 × 2.5
A: 1/20-mm AA   **Man:** 5 officers, 21 men
Cargo capacity: 980 tons (6,570 bbl)
M: 1 or 2 diesels; 1 prop; 500-600 hp

REMARK: Transferred 8-64.

◆ **2 yard tugs**

PRAGMAR   PATRON

REMARK: Bought in 1973.

◆ **1 ex-U.S. ARD-12-class floating dry dock**

N . . . (ex-ARD-15)

Lift capacity: 3,500 tons   **Dim:** 149.87 × 24.69 × 1.73 (light)

REMARKS: Launched 1944; transferred 4-71.

◆ **2 ex-U.S. ARD-2-class floating dry docks**

N . . . (ex-ARD-2)   N . . . (ex-ARD-11)

Lift capacity: 3,500 tons   **Dim:** 148.0 × 21.64 × 1.6 (light)

REMARKS: Launched 1942-43; transferred 8-63 and 6-74.

◆ **1 ex-U.S. small auxiliary floating dry dock**

N . . . (ex-AFDL-28)

Lift capacity: 1,000 tons   **Dim:** 60.96 × 19.51 × 1.04 (light)

REMARKS: Launched 1944; transferred 1-73.

◆ **7 ex-U.S. floating cranes**

(ex-YD-156)	(ex-YD-179)	(ex-YD-183)	(ex-YD-203)
(ex-YD-157)	(ex-YD-180)	(ex-YD-194)	

REMARK: Transferred 1964-71.

◆ **1 ex-U.S. pile driver**

N . . . (ex-YPF-48)

REMARK: Transferred 8-68.

MOROCCO

PERSONNEL: 1,800 men, including 58 officers and 260 petty officers

MERCHANT MARINE (1978): 117 ships−341,410 grt
(tankers: 6 ships−109,128 grt)

FRIGATE

◆ **1 Spanish Descubierta class** Bldr: Bazán, El Ferrol

	Laid down	L	In serv.
F . . . N . . .	. . .	. . .	. . .

D: 1,270 tons (1,520 fl)   **S:** 28 kts
Dim: 88.88 (85.8 pp) × 10.4 × 3.1 (3.7 fl)
Man: 100 men   **Range:** 6,100/17 (one engine)   **Fuel:** 250 tons
A: 4-8/SSM – 1/NATO Sea Sparrow system (24 missiles) – 1/76-mm OTO Melara DP – 2/40-mm AA (I × 2) – 1/375-mm Bofors ASW rocket launcher (II × 1, 24 reloads) – 6/324-mm Mk 32 ASW TT (III × 2)
Electron Equipt: Radars: 1/DA 05, 1/WO 06, 1/WM 25
      Sonar: Raytheon DE 1160B – ELT 715 intercept/jammer
M: 4 Bazán-MTU 16V956 TB91 diesels; 2 controllable-pitch props; 16,000 hp
Electric: 1,810 kw

REMARKS: Ordered 14-6-77. The type of anti-ship missile to be installed has not yet been determined; either eight Harpoon or four Exocet could be accommodated.

PATROL BOATS

◆ **4 Spanish Lazaga class** Bldr: Bazán, Cadiz

	L	In serv.		L	In serv.
N . . .	. . .	1980	N . . .	. . .	1981
N . . .	. . .	1980	N . . .	. . .	1981

D: 134 tons (fl)   **S:** 36 kts   **Dim:** 36.2 × 5.8 × 1.75
A: 4/Exocet SSM – 1/76-mm OTO Melara DP   **Man:** . . .
Range: 1,200/17
Electron Equipt: Radar: 1/WM 25
M: 2 Bazán MTU MA 16V538 TB 90 diesels; 2 props; 6,000 hp

REMARK: Ordered 14-6-77.

◆ **2 French PR-72 type** Bldr: S.F.C.N., France

	L	In serv.		L	In serv.
OKBA	10-10-75	16-12-76	TRIKI	2-2-76	2-77

Okba   S.F.C.N., 1976

D: 370 tons (440 fl)   **S:** 28 kts (at 413 tons)
Dim: 57.0 (54.0 pp) × 7.6 × 2.5   **Man:** 5 officers, 48 men
A: 1/76-mm OTO Melara DP – 1/40-mm Bofors AA   **Range:** 2,500/16
M: 4 AGO 16ASHR diesels; 2 props; 11,040 hp   **Electric:** 360 kw

REMARK: Ordered in 6-73 from the Société Française de Construction Navale (ex-C.N. Franco-Belges).

◆ **1 Al Bachir class** Bldr: Constr. Méc. de Normandie

	Laid down	L	In serv.
22 AL BACHIR	6-65	25-2-67	4-67

Al Bachir – wearing old number

D: 124.5 tons (light) (153.5 fl)   **S:** 25.5 kts
Dim: 40.6 (38.0 pp) × 6.35 × 1.4   **Man:** 3 officers, 20 men
A: 2/40-mm – 2 machine guns   **Range:** 2,000/15   **Fuel:** 21 tons
M: 2 SEMT-Pielstick 12 PA diesels; 2 props; 3,600 hp

◆ **1 French Fougueux class** Bldr: Constr. Méc. de Normandie

	Laid down	L	In serv.
32 LIEUTENANT RIFFI	5-63	1-3-64	5-64

D: 311 tons (374 fl)   **S:** 19 kts   **Dim:** 52.95 (51.82 pp) × 7.04 × 2.01
Man: 4 officers, 55 men   **Range:** 2,000/15, 3,000/12
A: 1/76-mm – 2/40-mm AA – 2 depth-charge projectors – 2 depth-charge racks
M: 2 SEMT-Pielstick diesels; 2 controllable-pitch props; 3,600 hp

◆ **1 ex-French patrol boat** Bldr: Chantiers Navals de l'Esterel

11 EL SABIQ (ex-P-762, VC-12)

D: 60 tons (80 fl)   **S:** 28 kts   **Dim:** 31.77 × 4.7 × 1.7
A: 2/20-mm AA   **Man:** 17 men   **Range:** 1,500/15
M: 2 Mercedes-Benz diesels; 2 props; 2,700 hp

REMARKS: Launched 13-8-57. Transferred 15-11-60.

PATROL CRAFT

◆ **6 French P-92 type** Bldr: C.M.N., Cherbourg

	L	In serv.		L	In serv.
EL WACIL	12-6-75	9-10-75	EL KHAFIR	21-1-76	16-4-76
EL JAIL	10-10-75	3-12-75	EL HARIS	31-3-76	30-6-76
EL MIKDAM	1-12-75	30-1-76	ESSAHIR	2-6-76	16-7-76

MOROCCO (*continued*)
PATROL CRAFT (*continued*)

El Wacil   C.M.N., 1975

> **D:** 89 tons   **S:** 28 kts   **Dim:** 32.0 × 4.7 × 1.7
> **A:** 2/20-mm AA (I × 2)   **Electron Equipt:** Radar: 1/Decca
> **M:** 2 MGO 12 V BZSHR diesels; 1,270 hp   **Range:** 1,200/15

REMARKS: Contract, 2-74. Laminated-wood hull.

MINESWEEPER

◆ 1 French Sirius class

TAWFIC (ex-*Aries*, M-758)

> **D:** 365 tons (440 fl)   **S:** 15 kts   **Dim:** 46.3 × 8.5 × 2.2
> **A:** 1/40-mm AA—1/20-mm AA   **Man:** 38 men   **Range:** 3,000/10
> **M:** 2 diesels; 2 props; 2,000 hp   **Fuel:** 48 tons

REMARKS: Loaned by the French Navy 28-11-74 for a period of four years. Wood-planked hull on aluminum-alloy framing.

AMPHIBIOUS WARFARE SHIPS

◆ 3 French Champlain-class medium landing ships   Bldr: Dubigeon, Normandy

		In serv.
42	DAOUD BEN AICHA	28-5-77
43	AHMED ES SAKALI	9-77
44	ABOU ABDALLAH EL AYACHI	12-78

> **D:** 1,305 tons   **S:** 16 kts   **Dim:** 80.0 (68.0 pp) × 13.0 × 3.0
> **A:** 2/40-mm AA (I × 2)—2/81-mm mortars (I × 2)   **Man:** 30 officers, 54 men
> **M:** 2 diesels; 2 props; 1,800 hp   **Range:** 4,500/13

REMARKS: Can carry 133 troops and about 12 vehicles. Helicopter platform aft.

◆ 1 French EDIC-class utility landing craft

21 LIEUTENANT MALGHAGH   Bldr: C.N. Franco-Belges

Lieutenant Malghagh—wearing old number   1977

> **D:** 292 tons (642 fl)   **S:** 8 kts   **Dim:** 59.0 × 11.95 × 1.3
> **A:** 2/20-mm AA (I × 2)—1/120-mm mortar (fwd)   **Man:** 16 men
> **M:** 2 MGO diesels; 2 props; 1,000 hp   **Range:** 1,800/8

REMARK: In service in 1965.

TRAINING SHIP

ESSAOUIRA

> **D:** 60 tons

REMARKS: Yacht presented by Italy in 1967. Used for training watchstanders.

MOZAMBIQUE

CORVETTE

◆ 1 ex-British Bangor class   Bldr: North Vancouver Ship Repairs, Canada

N . . . (ex-Portuguese *Almirante Lacerda*, ex-Canadian *Caroquet*)

> **D:** 656 tons (825 fl)   **S:** 15.5 kts   **Dim:** 54.86 × 8.69 × 2.94
> **Man:** 49 men   **Range:** 2,600/10   **Fuel:** 150 tons
> **A:** 1/76-mm Mk 22 DP—2/20-mm AA   **Boilers:** 2, three-drum
> **M:** 2 sets triple-expansion reciprocating steam; 2 props; 2,600 hp

REMARKS: Launched 2-6-41. Purchased by Portugal in 1946 and later converted to a hydrographic survey ship for East African waters, carrying two inshore survey launches. Ceded to Mozambique when it gained its independence as not worth returning to Portugal.

MOZAMBIQUE (*continued*)

PATROL CRAFT

◆ **2 Portuguese Jupiter class**

  D: 32 tons   **S:** 20 kts   **A:** 1/20-mm AA (1964)

REMARK: Operates on Lake Malawi.

◆ **2 Portuguese Bellatrix class**

  D: 23 tons   **S:** 15 kts   **A:** 1/20-mm AA (1961-63)

REMARK: Operates on Lake Malawi.

AMPHIBIOUS WARFARE CRAFT

◆ **1 Portuguese Alfange-class landing craft**

  D: 285 tons (635 fl)   **S:** 10 kts   **Dim:** 59.0 × 11.91 × 1.6
  A: 2/20-mm AA (I × 2)   **Man:** 20 men   **Range:** 1,800/8
  M: 2 MTU MD225 diesels; 2 props; 1,000 hp

◆ **2 Portuguese LDM-100-class landing craft**

  D: 50 tons

NETHERLANDS

PERSONNEL: Approximately 18,000 men, including 3,000 Marines
MERCHANT MARINE (1978): 1,238 ships—5,180,392 grt
              (tankers: 84 ships—2,221,475 grt)

NAVAL AVIATION: The Navy's aircraft are divided into four administrative groups: three maritime patrol squadrons at Valkenburg and one helicopter squadron at Dekoog. A detachment for maritime surveillance (PH-25 Neptune) is stationed at Curaçao. Principal types include:
  13 PH-25 Neptune
   8 BR-1050 Atlantique
  12 Wasp helicopters
  24 WG-13 Lynx helicopters
The WG-13 Lynx are of the following subtypes: 6 SH-14A search-and-rescue, delivered in 1976; 10 SH-14B with dipping sonar, ordered in 1976; and 8 SH-14C with MAD gear, ordered in 1978. Twelve more Lynx will be ordered to replace the Wasps.
On 8-12-78, the Dutch Navy announced that the Lockheed P-3C Orion would be acquired to replace the PH-25 Neptune. The first two will be operational in 1981 and the last of a total of thirteen will be operational in 1984.

WARSHIPS IN SERVICE, UNDER CONSTRUCTION OR AUTHORIZED AS OF 1 JANUARY 1980

	L	Tons (surfaced)	Main armament
◆ **6 (+2) submarines**			
(2) WALRUS	1981-82	2,300	6/TT
2 ZWAARDVIS	1970-71	2,370	6/TT
4 DOLFIJN	1959-65	1,494	8/TT
◆ **10 destroyers**		Tons	
2 TROMP	1973-74	3,665	1/Standard, 8/Harpoon, and 1/Sea Sparrow systems, 2/120-mm DP, 6/ASW TT, 1/ASW helicopter
8 FRIESLAND	1953-56	2,496	4/120-mm DP, ASW weapons
◆ **18 (+5) frigates**			
0 (+4) M CLASS	1983 (?)	2,300	8/Harpoon and 1/Sea Sparrow systems, 1/76-mm DP, 6/ASW TT, 1/helicopter
12 (+1) KORTENAER	1976-	3,000	8/Harpoon and 1/Sea Sparrow systems, 2/76-mm DP, 4/ASW TT, 2/helicopters
6 VAN SPEIJK	1965-67	2,200	2/Sea Cat systems, 2/114-mm or 1/76-mm DP, ASW weapons, 1/helicopter (8 Harpoon being added)
◆ **6 corvettes**			
6 ROOFDIER	1953-54	808	1/76-mm DP, 4/40-mm AA
◆ **5 patrol boats**			
5 BALDER	1954	150	1/40-mm AA
◆ **34 (+15) mine warfare ships**			
0 (+15) ALKMAAR	1980-	511	1/20-mm AA
18 DOKKUM	1954-56	373	2/40-mm AA
16 VAN STRAELEN	1959-61	151	1/20-mm AA

WEAPONS AND SYSTEMS

A. MISSILES

◆ *surface-to-air*

  U.S./SM1-MR on the *Tromp*-class destroyers and on the thirteenth *Kortenaer*-class frigate
  U.S. Sea Sparrow on the *Tromp*-class destroyers and *Kortenaer*-class frigates.
  British Sea Cat on the *Van Speijk*-class frigates.

WEAPONS AND SYSTEMS (continued)

◆ *surface-to-surface*

U.S. Harpoon on the *Tromp, Kortenaer,* and modernized *Van Speijk* classes.

B. GUNS

120-mm twin-barreled automatic in the *Friesland-* and *Tromp*-class destroyers:
Weight: 65 tons
Arc of elevation: 10° to +85°
Muzzle velocity: 850 m/sec.
Direction rate: 25°/s in train, 40°/s in elevation
Rate of fire: 45 rounds/min/barrel
Maximum effective range in surface fire: 13,000 m
Maximum effective range in antiaircraft fire: 7,000 m

114-mm Mk 6 (*see* section on Great Britain) on unmodernized *Van Speijk*-class frigates.

76-mm OTO Melara Compact on the *Kortenaer* and modernized *Van Speijk*-class frigates.

40-mm Bofors automatic

NOTE: The Dutch Navy is studying the SEM-30 quadruple, 30-mm, close-in, defense, AA gun system (3,200 rounds per minute), which uses an Emerson mounting, HSA fire-control radar, and Rheinmetal guns.

C. ANTISUBMARINE WEAPONS

375-mm Bofors quadruple rocket launchers

U.S. Mk 44 and Mk 46 torpedoes on ships and aircraft

U.S. Mk 37 and Mk 48 torpedoes on submarines

D. RADARS

All designed and manufactured by Hollandse Signaal Apparaaten (HSA), a division of Philips:

Name	Type	Band
ZW-06	Navigation/surface search	. . .
LWO-2/3	Long-range air-search	D
LWO-4	Long-range air-search	D
LWO-8	Long-range air-search	D
DA-05	Combined surveillance	E/F
SPS-01	3-D	F
WM-20/25	Missile- and gunfire-control	. . .
M-44/45	Missile- and gunfire-control	. . .
STIR*	Missile- and gunfire-control	. . .

*U.S. design, built under license

E. SONARS

CWE-610, LF, hull-mounted: On the *Tromp*-class destroyers

SQS-505, 2 MF, Canadian: On the *Kortenaer*-class frigates

Type 184, MF, hull-mounted: On the *Van Speijk*-class frigates

F. DATA-PROCESSING

SEWACO (Sensoren Wapens Commando), built by Hollandse Signaal Apparaaten and centrally directed by a Daisy 1, 2, 3, 4, or 5 digital computer system. It exists in four versions (SEWACO I, II, II, and IV) tailored to the sensors and weapon systems of the ships that carry it.

SUBMARINES

◆ 2 Walrus class

		Bldr	Laid down	L	In serv.
S . . .	WALRUS	Rotterdam DDM	1-79	. . .	1982
S . . .	N . . .	Rotterdam DDM	1-80	. . .	1983

D: 1,900 tons, 2,300 surfaced, 2,500 submerged   S: 12/20 kts
Dim: 66.9 × 8.5 × 7.0   Man: 49 men
A: 6/533-mm TT fwd (20 torpedoes)—Sub-Harpoon capability
M: Diesel-electric: 3 generator groups; 1 motor; 1 7-bladed prop; 5,000 hp

REMARKS: The first ordered 19-6-78, the second in 1979. Design developed from *Zwaardvis* class, with more automation, smaller crew, more modern electronics, and a deeper-diving capability. Second ship may be named *Zeeleeuw*.

◆ 2 Zwaardvis class

		Bldr	Laid down	L	In serv.
S 806	ZWAARDVIS	Rotterdam DDM	7-67	2-7-70	18-2-72
S 807	TIJGERHAAI	Rotterdam DDM	7-67	25-5-71	20-10-72

Tijgerhaai   1977

D: 2,370 tons surface, 2,572 submerged   S: 12/20 kts
Dim: 66.92 × 8.4 × 7.0   Man: 8 officers, 59 men
A: 6/533-mm TT fwd—20 torpedoes
M: Diesel-electric: 3 sets of diesel generators, 900 kw each; 1 3,800-kw motor; 5,000 hp

REMARKS: Ordered 24-12-65 and 14-7-66. Based on the U.S. Navy's *Barbel* class, which has a teardrop hull. Use of Dutch equipment necessitated modifications to the original design. The torpedo-firing system uses a digital computer that permits the simultaneous launching of two torpedoes, one of which may be wire-guided. For silent running, all noise-producing machinery is mounted on a false deck with spring suspension.

SUBMARINES *(continued)*

◆ **4 Dolfijn/Potvis class**

	Bldr	Laid down	L	In serv.
S 804 POTVIS	Wilton-Fijenoord	17-9-62	12-1-65	2-11-65
S 805 TONIJN	Wilton-Fijenoord	28-11-62	14-6-65	24-2-66
S 808 DOLFIJN	Rotterdam DDM	30-12-54	20-5-59	16-12-60
S 809 ZEEHOND	Rotterdam DDM	30-12-54	20-2-60	16-3-61

Tonijn   1968

Dolfijn   1974

D: 1,140 tons, 1,494 surfaced, 1,826 submerged   **S:** 14.5/17 kts
Dim: 79.5 × 8.84 × 5.0   **Man:** 7 officers, 57 men
A: 8/533-mm TT (4 fwd, 4 aft)   **Electron Equipt:** Radar: 1/British 1001
M: Diesel-electric: 2 M.A.N. 12-cyl. diesels, 1,550 hp each; 2 electric motors; 2 props; 2,200 hp

REMARKS: S-804 and S-805 authorized in 1962, S-808 and S-809 in 1949. The exterior hull has three parallel interior pressure cylinders, one of which is placed on top of a pair of slightly shorter ones. The crew and the armament occupy the top cylinder, and the batteries and diesel engines are mounted in the other two. The *Tonijn* received SEMT-Pielstick PA4, 750-kw diesel generators during 1978; the *Potvis* was given new engines in 1979. The other pair will not be refitted, because they are to be stricken on completion of the *Walrus* class.

GUIDED-MISSILE DESTROYERS

◆ **2 Tromp class**   Bldr: Kon. Mij. De Schelde, Flushing

	Laid down	L	In serv.
F 801 TROMP	4-8-71	2-6-73	9-10-75
F 806 DE RUYTER (ex-*Heemskerck*)	22-12-71	9-3-74	3-6-76

Tromp   1978

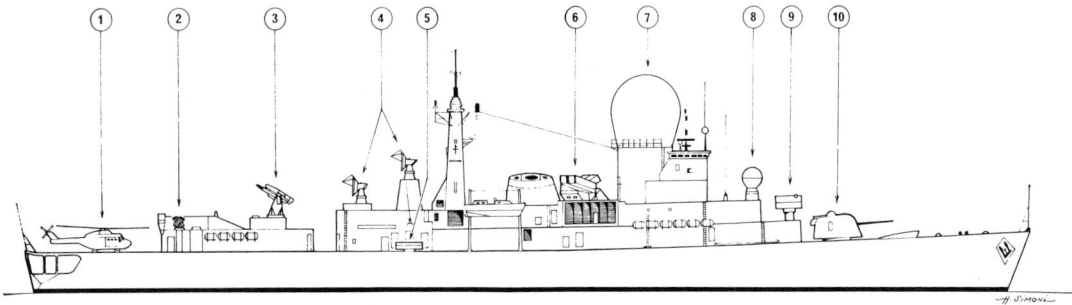

Scale 1/1000

Tromp
1. Lynx helicopter 2. Knebworth Corvus chaff launchers 3. MK-13 launcher
4. SPG-51C radars 5. MK-32 torpedo tubes 6. Harpoon launchers 7. SPS-01 3-D radar 8. WM-25 fire-control radar 9. Sea Sparrow system 10. 120-mm gun mount

GUIDED-MISSILE DESTROYERS (continued)

De Ruyter   1976

De Ruyter   1978

D: 3,665 tons (4,308 fl)   **S:** 28 kts
Dim: 138.2 (131.0 pp) × 14.8 × 4.6 (6.6 max.)   **Man:** 34 officers, 271 men
Range: 5,000/18   **Fuel:** 600 tons
A: 8/Harpoon missiles (IV × 2)—1 Mk-13 missile launcher (I × 1, 40 SM1-MR
   missiles)—1/NATO Sea Sparrow system (VII × 1, Mk 29, 60 missiles)—2/120-mm
   Bofors DP (II × 1)—6/324-mm Mk 32 ASW TT (III × 2)—1/WG-13 Lynx ASW
   helicopter

Electron Equipt: Radars: 1/SPS-01 3-D, 1/ZW 05, 1/WM 25, 2/SPG 51C
                       Sonars: 1/CWE 610, 1/162−2 Knebworth Corvus chaff launch-
                                ers, SEWACO-I data system
M: COGOG: 2 Rolls-Royce Olympus TM-3B gas turbines, 27,000 hp each; 2 Tyne
         RM-1C gas turbines, 4,100 hp each, for cruising (18 kts); 2 controllable-pitch,
         4-bladed props; 54,000 hp
Electric: 4,000 kw

REMARKS: Although the Dutch Navy designates them as frigates, these ships, by virtue
of their armament and size, are more closely related to guided-missile destroyers.
They have fin stabilizers and are excellent sea boats. Equipped with an admiral's
cabin and command facilities, they can act as flagships. Berthing for enlisted men is
in 6-, 9-, or 12-man compartments. The propulsion machinery is arranged in three
compartments, forward to aft: 2 Olympus gas turbines, 2 generator sets, and the
auxiliary boilers; 2 Tyne gas turbines; 2 generator sets. The 450-V, 3-phase, 60-Hz current is produced by four groups of 1,000-kw generators, each driven by a SMIT/Pax-
man Valenta RP 200, 12-cylinder diesel; two sets are sufficient for full combat power.
There are three auxiliary boilers for heating. Reduction gears were made by De
Schelde. Both fitted with Harpoon missiles by 1979.

DESTROYERS

◆ 8 Friesland class, 47-B type

		Bldr	Laid down	L	In serv.
D 812	FRIESLAND	Nederlandsche DSM	17-12-51	21-2-53	22-3-56
D 813	GRONINGEN	Nederlandsche DSM	4-2-52	9-1-54	19-9-56
D 814	LIMBURG	Kon. Mij. De Schelde	28-11-53	5-9-55	31-10-56
D 815	OVERIJSSEL	Wilton-Fijenoord	15-10-53	8-7-56	4-10-57
D 816	DRENTHE	Nederlandsche DSM	9-1-54	26-3-55	1-8-57
D 817	UTRECHT	Kon. Mij. De Schelde	15-2-54	2-6-56	1-10-57
D 818	ROTTERDAM	Rotterdam DDM	7-4-54	26-1-56	28-2-57
D 819	AMSTERDAM	Nederlandsche DSM	26-3-55	25-8-56	10-8-58

Groningen   1978

DESTROYERS (continued)

Limburg   G. Arra, 1976

Drenthe   G. Arra, 1972

D: 2,496 tons (3,100 fl)   **S:** 36 kts   **Dim:** 116.0 (112.8 pp) × 11.77 × 5.2
Man: 284 men   **Range:** 4,000/18   **Electric:** 1,350 kw
A: 4/120-mm DP (II × 2)−4/40-mm AA (I × 4)−2/375-mm Bofors ASW rocket
    launchers−1/depth-charge rack
Electron Equipt: Radars: 1/LWO 2, 1/DA 05, 1/Decca 1229, 1/M 45
               Sonar: 1/CWE 610
M: 2 sets Parsons GT; 2 props; 60,000 hp
Boilers: 4 Babcock & Wilcox, 39.8 kg/cm² −superheat 454°C

REMARKS: Two authorized in 1947, six in 1949. Same building program as the now-stricken *Holland* class, of which they are an improved version. The two forward 40-mm AA were removed around 1965; fire-control radar for the remaining 40-mm AA guns was removed 1977-78. The sonar was modernized in the early 1970s. The propulsion plant duplicates that of a U.S. *Gearing*-class destroyer. Two units will be retained through the early 1980s for patrol duties in the North Sea, while the others will be scrapped, as additional units of the *Kortenaer*-class frigates are completed.

NOTE: The *Zeeland* (D-809), the surviving unit of the *Holland* class, was stricken 29-9-78. The *Holland* (D-808) was sold to Peru in 1-78. The *Noord Brabant* (D-810) was in a col-lision on 9-1-74 and was too badly damaged to be worth repair. In 1973, the *Gelderland* (D-811) was stripped for use as a barracks and training hulk.

GUIDED-MISSILE FRIGATES

◆ **4 M class**

	Bldr	Laid down	L	In serv.
F . . . N . . .		. . .	. . .	. . .
F . . . N . . .	. . .	. . .	. . .	. . .
F . . . N . . .	. . .	. . .	. . .	. . .
F . . . N . . .	. . .	. . .	. . .	. . .

D: 2,300 tons   **S:** 26 kts   **Dim:** 100.0 × . . . × . . .
A: 8/Harpoon SSM (IV × 2)−1/NATO Sea Sparrow (VIII × 1, 16 spare missiles,
    Mk 29 launcher)−1/76-mm OTO Melara DP−4/30-mm AA SEM-30 (IV × 1)−
    6/324-mm Mk 32 ASW TT (III × 2)−1/WG-13 Lynx helicopter
M: CODOG: 1 gas turbine, 2 diesels; 1 controllable-pitch prop; . . . hp
Man: 79 men

REMARKS: These four ships were to be requested in the 1980 program as replacements for the Roofdier-class corvettes for fisheries-protection, North Sea, and the 200-nautical-mile economic zone patrols. With a crew of 79 men, they will require a high degree of automation. They will offer almost the same armament as the *Kortenaer*-class frigates and have a speed of only 4 knots less.

◆ **12 (+1) Kortenaer class**   Bldrs: F-823 and F-824: Wilton-Fijenoord; Others: De Schelde

	Laid down	L	In serv.
F 807 KORTENAER	8-4-75	18-12-76	26-10-78
F 808 CALLENBURGH	30-6-75	26-3-77	26-7-79
F 809 VAN KINSBERGEN	2-9-75	16-4-77	6-80
F 810 BANCKERT	25-2-76	30-9-78	12-80
F 811 PIET HEIN	28-4-77	3-6-78	1981
F 812 PIETER FLORESZ	1-7-77	. . .	1981
F 813 WITTE DE WITH	28-4-77	. . .	1982
F 816 ABRAHAM CRIJNSSEN	15-10-78	. . .	1982
F 823 PHILIPS VAN ALMONDE	3-10-77	11-8-79	1982
F 824 BLOIS VAN TRESLONG	27-4-78	. . .	1983
F 825 JAN VAN BRAKEL	1979	. . .	1983
F 826 WILLEM VAN DER ZAAN	25-10-78	. . .	1984
F . . . N . . .	1980	. . .	1984

Kortenaer   1978

GUIDED-MISSILE FRIGATES (continued)

D: 3,000 tons (3,750 fl) **S:** 30 kts (20, on 2 Tyne turbines)
Dim: 130.2 (121.8 pp) × 14.4 × 4.4 (5.8, props) **Electric:** 3,000 kw
Man: 18 officers, 182 men **Range:** 4,700/16 (on 1 Tyne turbine)
A: 8/Harpoon SSM (IV × 2)—1/NATO Sea Sparrow system (VIII × 2, 16 spare missiles, Mk 29 launcher)—2/76-mm OTO Melara DP (I × 2), *see* Remarks—4/324-mm Mk 32 ASW TT (II × 2)—2/WG-13 Lynx ASW helicopters
Electron Equipt: Radars: 1/LWO 8, 1/ZW 06, 1/WM 25 with STIR
  Sonar: 1/SQS 505—SEWACO-II data system, 2 Knebworth Corvus chaff launchers, 1 Spinx intercept
M: COGOG: 2 Rolls-Royce Olympus TM-3B gas turbines, 25,800 hp each; 2 Rolls-Royce Tyne RM-1C cruise gas turbines, 4,900 hp each; 2 LIPS controllable-pitch props; 51,600 hp

REMARKS: F-807 to F-810 ordered 31-8-74; F-811 to F-816 ordered 28-11-74; F-823 to F-826 ordered 29-12-76; final unit (to a modified design) to be ordered 1980. The thirteenth unit is to be equipped as a flagship so that, along with the two *Tromp*-class guided-missile destroyers, it will be possible to have three task groups; the ship will have a Mk-13 launcher for SM1-MR Standard missiles in place of the helicopter facility, and will have two SEM-30 AA mounts. F-807 and F-808 will have, initially, two 76-mm guns. The after 76-mm mount may be substituted for by a twin 40-mm Bofors AA in F-809 to F-816. In F-823 and later ships, the mount atop the hangar will be replaced by a SEM-30 quadruple, close-defense, AA gun with integral fire-control radar. Ultimately, all will carry SEM-30 aft.

The engineering plant is distributed in four compartments, forward to aft: auxiliaries; Olympus gas turbines; Tyne gas turbines plus reduction gears; auxiliaries. The 450-volt, 3-phase, 60-hertz electric current is supplied by four generators driven by four SEMT-Pielstick PA4, 750-kw diesels. There are two auxiliary boilers and two evaporators.

The hull is divided by fifteen watertight bulkheads. One pair of Denny-Brown, non-retracting, fin stabilizers is fitted. Officers are berthed in one- or two-man staterooms, while petty officers are in 1-, 2-, or 4-man cabins, and nonrated men are in 6-, 9-, or 12-bunk berthing compartments. Particular attention has been paid to habitability.

Kortenaer   1978

Kortenaer   1978

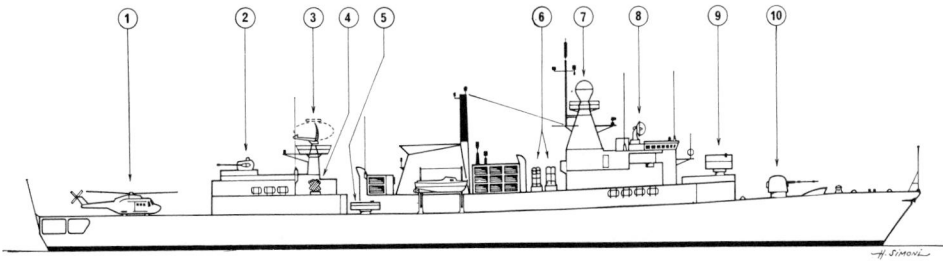

Scale 1/1000

Kortenaer
1. Lynx helicopter 2. 76-mm OTO Melara or SEM-30 gun mount 3. LWO-8 radar
4. Knebworth Corvus chaff launchers 5. Mk-32 ASW torpedo tubes 6. Harpoon launchers 7. WM-25 fire-control radar 8. STIR tracking radar 9. NATO Sea Sparrow Mk-29 launcher 10. 76-mm OTO Melara gun mount

GUIDED-MISSILE FRIGATES *(continued)*

Kortenaer   1978

Kortenaer   1978

◆ **6 Van Speijk class**

	Bldr	Laid down	L	In serv.
F 802 VAN SPEIJK	Nederlandsche DSM	1-10-63	5-3-65	14-2-67
F 803 VAN GALEN	Kon. Mij. De Schelde	25-7-63	19-6-65	1-3-67
F 804 TJERK HIDDES	Nederlandsche DSM	1-6-64	17-12-65	16-8-67
F 805 VAN NES	Kon. Mij. De Schelde	25-7-63	26-3-66	9-8-67
F 814 ISAAC SWEERS	Nederlandsche DSM	5-5-65	10-3-67	15-5-68
F 815 EVERTSEN	Kon. Mij. De Schelde	6-7-65	18-6-66	21-12-67

    D: 2,200 tons (2,835 fl)   **S:** 28.5 kts
    Dim: 113.42 (109.75 pp) × 12.48 × 4.57 (fl)
    Man: 19 officers, 228 men (180, after refit)   **Range:** 4,500/12
    A: After refit: 8/Harpoon SSM (IV × 2) − 2/Sea Cat systems (IV × 2) − 1/76-mm OTO
              Melara DP − 6/324-mm Mk 32 ASW TT (III × 2) − 1/WG-13 Lynx ASW
              helicopter
        Before refit: 2/114-mm Mk 6 (II × 1) − 2/Sea Cat systems (IV × 2) − 1 Mk 10
              Limbo ASW mortar (III × 1) − 1/Wasp ASW helicopter

Van Speijk — after refit   1978

GUIDED-MISSILE FRIGATES *(continued)*

Van Nes   1977

Van Nes   1977

Evertsen   S. Terzibaschitsch, 1978

REMARKS: Derived from the British *Leander* class with a few modifications and with Dutch electronic equipment. Undergoing 18-month-long refits, which began in 1977 with the *Van Speijk* and *Van Galen;* the former was recommissioned 3-1-79, and the latter in 7-79. The *Tjerk Hiddes* and *Van Nes* followed, 1979-80. In addition to the installation of new armament and electronics, the hangar has been made to telescope, in order to accommodate the SH-14B, a version of the WG-13 Lynx helicopter equipped with dipping sonar. The ASW mortar and its associated sonars are being removed. Full-load displacement of unmodified units is 2,787 tons.

Electron Equipt: Radars: 1/SGR 105 (after refit: 1/DA 05), 1/LWO 3, 1/Kelvin Hughes 14/9 (after refit: Decca 1229), 2/M 44 (for Sea Cat), 1/M 45 (for 114-mm)
Sonars: 1/CWE 610, 1/PDE 700 (before refit: 1/162, 1/170B, also) −2 Knebworth Corvus chaff launchers−after refit: SEWACO-V data system
Boilers: 2 Babcock & Wilcox, 38.7 kg/cm² pressure−superheat 450°C
M: 2 sets Werkspoor-English-Electric double-reduction GT; 2 props; 30,000 hp
Electric: 1,900 kw

CORVETTES

◆ **6 Roofdier (ex-U.S. PCE-821) class**

	L	In serv.
F 817 WOLF (ex-PCE-1607)	2-1-54	26-3-54
F 818 FRET (ex-PCE-1604)	30-7-53	4-5-54
F 819 HERMELIJN (ex-PCE-1605)	6-3-54	5-8-54
F 820 VOS (ex-PCE-1606)	1-5-54	2-12-54
F 821 PANTHER (ex-PCE-1608)	30-1-54	11-6-54
F 822 JAGUAR (ex-PCE-1609)	20-3-54	11-6-54

CORVETTES (continued)

Fret   1968

Bldrs: F-817, F-821, F-822: Avondale, New Orleans; F-818 to F-820: General
   Shipbldg. & Eng., Boston

D: 808 tons (878 fl)   **S:** 14 kts   **Dim:** 56.27 × 10.29 × 3.96 (max.)
Man: 96 men   **Range:** 9,000/10
A: 1/76-mm Mk 22 DP – 4/40-mm AA (II × 2) – 4/20-mm AA (II × 2) – 1/Mk 10 Hedge-
   hog – 2/MK 6 depth-charge projectors – 2/depth-charge racks
Electron Equipt: Radar: 1/Decca 1229 – Sonar: QCU 2
M: 2 GM 12-567ATL diesels; 2 props; 1,800 hp

REMARKS: Built with U.S. "offshore" funds. F-817 and F-822 are active in fisheries-
protection. The others are in reserve and may retain an additional twin 40-mm AA on
the stern and up to eight 20-mm AA (II × 4). All are to be stricken in the early 1980s,
the active units being temporarily replaced by *Friesland*-class destroyers and, ultimately, by the new M-class frigates.

PATROL BOATS

◆ **5 Balder class**   Bldr: Rijkswerf Willemsoord, Den Helder

	Laid down	L	In serv.
P 802 BALDER (ex-SC-1627)	8-53	24-2-54	6-8-54
P 803 BULGIA (ex-SC-1628)	10-53	24-4-54	9-8-54
P 804 FREYR (ex-SC-1629)	2-54	17-7-54	1-12-54
P 805 HADDA (ex-SC-1630)	4-54	2-10-54	3-2-55
P 806 HEFRING (ex-SC-1631)	8-54	1-12-54	23-3-55

D: 150 tons (170 fl)   **S:** 15.5 kts   **Dim:** 36.35 (35.0 pp) × 6.21 × 1.8
Man: 3 officers, 24 men   **Range:** 1,000/13
A: 1/40-mm AA – 3/20-mm AA (I × 3)
Electron Equipt: Radar: 1/Kelvin Highes 14/9
M: Diesels; 2 props; 1,050 hp

REMARKS: Built with U.S. "offshore" funds. P-805 and P-806 are active; the others, in
reserve, may retain two Mousetrap ASW rocket launchers, two depth-charge throwers, and two depth-charge racks.

Hefring   S. Terzibaschitsch, 1971

MINE WARFARE SHIPS

◆ **15 Alkmaar-class minehunters (Tripartite design)**

	L	In serv.		L	In serv.
M 850 ALKMAAR	...	...	M 858 SCHEVENINGEN	...	...
M 851 DELFZIJL	...	...	M 859 SCHIEDAM	...	...
M 852 DORDRECHT	...	...	M 860 URK	...	...
M 853 HAARLEM	...	...	M 861 VEERE	...	...
M 854 HARLINGEN	...	...	M 862 VLAARDINGEN	...	...
M 855 HELLEVOETSLUIS	...	...	M 863 WILLEMSTAD	...	...
M 856 MAKKUM	...	...	M 864 MAASLUIS	...	...
M 857 MIDDELBURG	...	...			

Bldr: van der Giessen de Noord, Alblasserdam

D: 511 tons (544 fl)   **S:** 15 kts
Dim: 51.6 (47.1 pp) × 8.96 × 2.45 (2.6 max.)
Man: 34 men   **Range:** 3,000/12   **Electric:** 880 kw

Model of Alkmaar   1977

MINE WARFARE SHIPS *(continued)*

A: 1/20-mm AA – 2/PAP-104 remote-controlled minehunting devices

Electron Equipt: Radar: 1/Decca 1229   Sonar: 1/DUBM 21A

1 EVEC 20 plot table, autopilot, Toran and Syledis radio navaids, Decca HiFix precision navigation system

M: 1 Brons-Werkspoor A-RUB 215 × 12 diesel; 1 controllable-pitch prop; 1,900 hp; bow thruster; 2 active rudders

REMARKS: Hull made of a compound of glass and polyester resin. The *Alkmaar* was laid down 15-12-78. The last unit will not be laid down until 1985. These ships can tow mechanical drag sweep.

Staphorst – minehunter   1975

◆ **18 Dokkum class**

4 Minehunters:

	Bldr	Laid down	L	In serv.
M 801 DOKKUM (ex-MSC-172)	Wilton-Fijenoord	15-6-53	12-10-54	26-7-55
M 818 DRUNEN (ex-MSC-181)	Gusto/F.A. Smulders	8-1-55	24-3-56	30-8-56
M 828 STAPHORST (ex-MSC-185)	Gusto/F.A. Smulders	2-5-55	21-7-56	23-1-57
M 842 VEERE (ex-MSC-188)	L. Smit & Son	30-3-55	9-2-56	27-9-56

11 Coastal Minesweepers:

M 802 HOOGEZAND (ex-MSC-173)	Gusto/F.A. Smulders	18-7-53	22-3-55	7-11-55
M 809 NAALDWIJK (ex-MSC-175)	De Noord	2-11-53	1-2-55	8-12-55
M 810 ABCOUDE (ex-MSC-176)	Gusto/F.A. Smulders	10-11-53	2-9-55	18-5-56
M 812 DRACHTEN (ex-MSC-177)	Niestern SB	9-12-53	24-3-55	27-1-56
M 813 OMMEN (ex-MSC-178)	J. & K. Smits	22-12-53	5-4-55	19-4-56
M 815 GIETHOORN (ex-MSC-179)	L. Smit & Son	22-12-53	30-3-55	29-3-56
M 817 VENLO (ex-MSC-180)	Arnhemse SB	10-2-54	21-5-55	26-4-56
M 823 NAARDEN (ex-MSC-183)	Wilton-Fijenoord	28-10-54	27-1-56	18-5-56
M 827 HOOGEVEEN (ex-MSC-184)	De Noord	1-2-55	8-5-56	2-11-56
M 830 SITTARD (ex-MSC-186)	Niestern SB	10-3-55	26-4-56	19-12-56
M 841 GEMERT (ex-MSC-187)	J. & K. Smits	5-4-55	13-3-56	7-9-56

3 Support Ships for Mine-demolition Divers:

M 806 ROERMOND (ex-MSC-174)	Wilton-Fijenoord	19-9-53	13-8-55	29-12-55
M 820 WOERDEN (ex-MSC-182)	Haarlemse SB	10-8-54	28-11-56	24-4-57
M 844 RHENEN (ex-MSC-189)	Arnhemse SB	18-4-55	31-5-56	7-12-56

Hoogezand   1974

D: 373 tons (453) fl)   **S:** 14 kts   **Dim:** 46.62 × 8.78 × 2.28

A: 2/40-mm AA (I × 2)   **Man:** 38 men   **Range:** 2,500/10

Electron Equipt: Radar: 1/Decca 1229 or ZW 04
Sonar: 1/193M (hunters only)

M: 2 Fijenoord-M.A.N. diesels; 2 props; 2,500 hp

MINE WARFARE SHIPS *(continued)*

REMARKS: Similar to the French *Sirius* and British "-ton" classes. The highly automated minehunters are equipped with the ARNAS system, which displays dropped marker buoys on the radar screen. The similar *Wildervank* class had all been scrapped by 1976.

◆ **16 Van Straelen-class inshore minesweepers**

		Bldr	Laid down	L	In serv.
M 868 ALBLAS (ex-MSI-3)		Noord	26-2-58	26-9-59	12-3-60
M 869 BUSSEMAKER (ex-MSI-4)		DVL	28-8-58	27-2-60	19-8-60
M 870 LACOMBLE (ex-MSI-5)		ASM	24-9-58	6-2-60	22-8-60
M 871 VAN HAMEL (ex-MSI-6)		DVL	27-4-59	28-5-60	14-10-60
M 872 VAN STRAELEN (ex-MSI-7)		ASM	28-11-58	17-5-60	20-12-60
M 873 VAN MOPPES (ex-MSI-8)		Noord	16-4-59	10-5-60	19-12-60
M 874 CHÖMPFF (ex-MSI-9)		Noord	29-6-59	10-5-60	19-12-60
M 875 VAN WELL GROENEVELD		ASM	29-12-59	1-10-60	28-4-61
M 876 SCHUILING (ex-MSI-10)		DVL	26-6-56	30-6-60	5-4-61
M 877 VAN VERSENDAAL		Noord	27-3-61	4-12-61	11-4-62
M 878 VAN DER WEL		DVL	30-5-60	3-5-61	6-10-61
M 879 VAN'T HOFF		Noord	8-6-60	15-3-61	6-10-61
M 880 MAHU		Noord	8-6-60	15-3-61	6-10-61
M 881 STAVERMAN		DVL	8-7-60	30-8-61	21-2-62
M 882 HOUTEPEN		ASM	19-9-60	26-8-61	21-3-62
M 883 ZOMER		ASM	6-5-60	4-3-61	6-10-61

Bldrs: De Noord, Alblasserdam; De Vries-Lentsch, Amsterdam; Arnhem Scheepsbouw Mij.

Van Versendaal

D: 151 tons (169 fl)   **S:** 13 kts   **Dim:** 33.08 × 6.87 × 1.8
A: 1/20-mm AA   **Electron Equipt:** Radar: Decca 12
M: 2 Werkspoor diesels; 2 props; 1,100 hp   **Man:** 14 men

REMARKS: Eight of these ships were built with U.S. "offshore" funds. Although similar, the Dutch designs differ from the French and British "-ham" classes. Wooden hulls. Named for officers, petty officers, and nonrated men who died for their country during World War II.

AMPHIBIOUS WARFARE SHIPS

◆ **10 personnel landing craft (LCA)**   Bldr: Rijkswerf Willemsoord, Den Helder, 1962-64

L 9510	L 9512	L 9514	L 9517	L 9520
L 9511	L 9513	L 9515	L 9518	L 9522

D: 8.5 tons (13.6 fl)   **S:** 11.6 kts   **Dim:** 14.45 × 3.82 × 1.3
A: 1/7.62-mm machine gun   **Man:** 3 men
M: 1 Rolls-Royce diesel; 1 Schöttel prop; 200 hp

REMARKS: Polyester plastic hulls. L-9510 is 14.5 × 3.62, and displaces 12.6 tons (fl).

HYDROGRAPHIC SHIPS

◆ **1 Tydeman class**   Bldr: B. V. De Merwede, Hardinxveld-Giessendam

	Laid down	L	In serv.
A 906 TYDEMAN	29-4-75	18-12-75	10-11-76

D: 2,950 tons (fl)   **S:** 15 kts   **Dim:** 90.19 × 14.43 × 4.75
Man: 63 men, 14 civilians   **Range:** 10,300/13.5, 15,700/10.3
M: 3 Stork-Werkspoor 8-FCHD-240 diesels, electric drive; 1 prop; 2,730 hp; 2 bow thrusters; 1 active rudder   **Electric:** 1,400 kw

REMARKS: Assigned to civilian and military research. Hangar and flight deck for one Wasp helicopter. Eight laboratories. Any two of the three main diesels power the propulsion motors, the other then provides ship's service power.

Tydeman   1976

HYDROGRAPHIC SHIPS *(continued)*

◆ **2 Blommendal class** Bldr: Boele S & M, Bolnes

	Laid down	L	In serv.
A 904 BUYSKES	31-1-72	11-7-72	9-3-73
A 905 BLOMMENDAL	1-8-72	21-11-72	22-5-73

Buyskes   1973

D: 1,050 tons (fl)   **S:** 13 kts   **Dim:** 59.0 × 11.3 × 3.5
M: 3 diesels, electric drive; 1 prop; 1,050 hp   **Man:** 45 men

REMARKS: Carry two survey launches and two chain-clearance drag boats. Automated data-logging system.

REPLENISHMENT SHIPS

◆ **1 improved Poolster class** Bldr: Verolme, Alblasserdam

	Laid down	L	In serv.
A 832 ZUIDERKRUIS	16-7-43	15-10-74	27-6-75

Zuiderkruis   1975

Zuiderkruis — refueling the **Tromp**   1975

D: 17,357 tons   **S:** 21 kts   **Dim:** 169.59 × 20.3 × 8.4 (max.)
Man: 17 officers, 26 petty officers, 130 men   **Electric:** 3,000 kw
A: 2/20-mm AA (I × 2)   **Electron Equipt:** Radar: 1/Decca 1226 — 2 Knebworth Corvus chaff launchers
M: 2 Werkspoor TM 410 16-cyl. diesels; 2 props; 21,000 hp

REMARKS: Cargo capacity: 9,000 tons fuel, 400 tons TR-5, 200 tons fresh water, spare parts, ammunition. Hangar for three helicopters. Can carry ASW torpedoes for launch by own helicopters. Two fueling stations per side, amidships, and one sliding-stay, constant-tension, solid transfer station each side, forward.

◆ **1 Poolster class**

	Bldr	Laid down	L	In serv.
A 835 POOLSTER	Rotterdam DDM	18-9-62	16-10-63	10-9-64

D: 16,836 tons (fl)   **S:** 21 kts   **Dim:** 168.3 (157.0 pp) × 20.3 × 8.2
A: 2/40-mm AA (I × 2) — 2/depth-charge racks
Electron Equipt: Radars: 1/Kelvin Hughes 14/9, 1/ZW 04
                    Sonar: 1/CWE 610
M: 2 sets GT; 1 prop; 22,500 hp   **Boilers:** 2

Poolster   1964

REPLENISHMENT SHIPS (continued)

REMARKS: Cargo capacity: 10,300 tons, including 8,000 tons of fuel. Hangar for three helicopters. This tanker is also a combat supply ship capable of participating effectively in antisubmarine warfare with a hunter/killer group, thanks to her ability to handle five helicopters, if required. For short distances, she can carry 300 soldiers as well as her own crew.

TENDERS

◆ 3 U.S. Agile-class mine-countermeasures support ships

	Laid down	L	In serv.
A 855 ONBEVREESD (ex-M-885, ex-MSO-481)	8-12-52	7-11-53	21-9-54
A 858 ONVERVAARD (ex-M-888, ex-MSO-482)	14-4-52	6-3-54	31-1-55
A 859 ONVERDROTEN (ex-M-889, ex-MSO-485)	17-2-52	22-8-53	22-11-54

Bldrs: A-859: Peterson Bldrs., Sturgeon Bay, Wisc; Others: Astoria Marine, Astoria, Ore.

D: 735 tons (780 fl)   **S:** 14.5 kts   **Dim:** 52.7 × 10.75 × 3.7
Man: 67 men   **Range:** 3,000/10   **Fuel:** 47 tons   **Electric:** 560 kw
A: 1/40-mm AA — 2/depth-charge racks — A-855 and A-858: mine rails
Electron Equipt: Radar: 1/Kelvin Hughes 14/9   Sonar: QCU 2
M: 2 GM 8-278A diesels; 2 controllable-pitch props; 1,600 hp

REMARKS: Former ocean minesweepers. A-855 and A-858 are typed "escort ships" and are intended to serve as flagships for the mine-countermeasures force and to lay mines in exercises. A-859 was reclassified 1-1-69 as a mine-countermeasures support ship. A-858 and A-859 are in reserve. Sister *Onversaagd* was stricken in 1976.

◆ 1 U.S. Agile-class torpedo-trials ship   Bldr: Peterson Bldrs., Sturgeon Bay, Wisc.

	Laid down	L	In serv.
A 856 MERCUUR	19-2-52	17-1-53	22-7-54

(ex-*Onverschrokken*, M-886, ex-MSO-483)

REMARKS: Former ocean minesweeper. Data as for ships above, except that she carries one 40-mm AA gun. Converted to a torpedo-trials and servicing ship in 1972.

◆ 1 torpedo-trials ship   Bldr: Zaanlandse SM, Zaandam

	Laid down	L	In serv.
A 923 VAN BOCHOVE	6-12-61	20-7-62	3-8-62

D: 140.8 tons (fl)   **S:** 8 kts   **Dim:** 29.79 × 5.53 × 1.8
A: 2/533-mm TT (submerged, at bow)   **Man:** 8 men
M: 1 Kromhout diesel; 1 Schöttel prop; 140 hp

TUGS

◆ 2 Westgat-class coastal tugs   Bldr: Naval Dockyard, Den Helder

	Laid down	L	In serv.
A 872 WESTGAT	3-4-67	22-8-67	10-1-68
A 873 WIELINGEN	28-8-67	6-1-68	31-5-68

D: 206 tons (fl)   **S:** 12 kts   **Dim:** 27.18 × 6.97 × 2.34
A: None   **Man:** 9 men   **M:** 1 Bolnes diesel; 1 prop; 720 hp

◆ 1 Wamandai-class coastal tug   Bldr: Naval Dockyard, Den Helder

	Laid down	L	In serv.
A 870 WAMANDAI (ex-Y-8035)	27-8-58	28-5-60	1-62

D: 201 tons (fl)   **S:** 11 kts   **Dim:** 27.25 × 6.98 × 2.8
A: 2/20-mm AA (I × 2)   **Man:** 10 men
M: 1 Werkspoor diesel; 1 prop; 500 hp

◆ 1 Wambrau-class coastal tug   Bldr: Naval Dockyard, Den Helder

	Laid down	L	In serv.
A 871 WAMBRAU (ex-Y-8036)	24-7-56	27-8-56	8-1-57

D: 179.4 tons (fl)   **S:** 10.8 kts   **Dim:** 26.38 × 6.6 × 2.45
A: None   **Man:** 10 men   **M:** 1 Werkspoor diesel; 1 prop; 500 hp

◆ 4 Berkel-class harbor tugs   Bldr: H. H. Bodewes, Millingen

	Laid down	L	In serv.
Y 8037 BERKEL	27-4-56	29-9-56	27-12-57
Y 8038 DINTEL	22-5-56	17-11-56	23-1-57
Y 8039 DOMMEL	29-8-56	22-12-56	27-2-57
Y 8040 IJSSEL	17-9-56	19-1-57	20-3-57

D: 163.4 tons (fl)   **S:** 10-6 kts   **Dim:** 25.09 × 6.27 × 2.45
M: 1 Werkspoor diesel; 1 Kort-nozzle prop; 500 hp   **Man:** 5 men

◆ 2 Bambi-class harbor tugs   Bldr: Naval Dockyard, Den Helder

Y 8016 BAMBI   Y 8017 DOMBO

D: 43 tons (fl)   **S:** . . . kts   **Dim:** 16.58 × 4.63 × 1.9
M: 1 Bolnes diesel; 1 prop; 200 hp   **Man:** 4 men

REMARK: Y-8016 launched 12-5-53; Y-8017, 25-5-57.

◆ 3 small harbor tugs

Y 8014 (ex-A-857, ex-RS-17, ex-OZD-4, ex-*Jade*)

D: 75 tons (fl)   **S:** . . . kts   **Dim:** 20.0 × 5.25 × 1.8
M: 1 diesel; 1 prop; 75 hp   **Man:** 3 men

Y 8022 (ex-A-867, ex-RS-27, ex-KM-4, ex-*Gejo*, ex-*Figuas*)

D: 70 tons (fl)   **S:** . . . kts   **Dim:** 18.5 × 4.4 × 1.6
M: 1 Brons diesel; 1 prop; 150 hp   **Man:** 3 men

Y 8028 (ex-A-868, ex-RS-28, ex-KM-15, ex-*Eems*).

D: 70 tons (fl)   **S:** . . . kts   **Dim:** 19.5 × 5.1 × 2.3
M: 1 Bolnes diesel; 1 prop; 200 hp   **Man:** 7 men

REMARK: Y-8014 was in service in 1942, Y-8022 and Y-8028 in 1938.

DIVING TENDERS

◆ 3 Triton class   Bldr: Naval Dockyard, Den Helder

	Laid down	L	In serv.
A 848 TRITON (ex-Y-8125)	3-2-64	27-2-64	5-8-64
A 849 NAUTILUS (ex-Y-8126)	17-3-64	1-5-64	20-4-65
A 850 HYDRA (ex-Y-8127)	21-5-64	1-7-64	20-4-65

D: 69.3 tons (fl)   **S:** 9 kts   **Dim:** 23.28 × 5.15 × 1.35
M: 1 Volvo Penta diesel; 1 prop; 105 hp   **Man:** 8 men

◆ 1 training tender for divers   Bldr: Naval Dockyard, Den Helder

	Laid down	L	In serv.
A 847 ARGUS (ex-Y-8124, ex-Y-8651, ex-A-950, ex-RD-10, ex-MOD IV, ex-D1)	18-5-38	6-12-38	10-5-39

DIVING TENDERS (continued)

D: 445 tons (fl)   **S:** 8 kts   **Dim:** 23.0 × 4.68 × 1.05
M: 1 Kromhout diesel; 1 prop; 144 hp   **Man:** 8 men

TRAINING SHIPS

◆ **1 former pilot ship**

	Bldr	Laid down	L	In serv.
A 903 ZEEFAKEL	J. & K. Smit, Kinderijk	28-11-49	21-7-50	16-3-51

D: 303 tons (384 fl)   **S:** 12 kts   **Dim:** 45.38 × 7.5 × 2.2
A: 1/76-mm Mk 22 DP − 1/40-mm AA   **Man:** 26 men
M: 2 Smit-M.A.N. diesels; 2 props; 640 hp

REMARK: Used for seamanship training at Den Helder.

◆ **1 sail training ketch**   Bldr: Haarlemse SM, Haarlem

Y 8050 URANIA (ex-*Tromp*)

D: 76.4 tons (fl)   **S:** 5 kts (10, under sail)   **Dim:** 23.94 × 5.29 × 3.15
M: 1 Kromhout diesel; 1 prop; 65 hp (625m² sail area)   **Man:** 17 men

REMARK: Launched in 1929; in service 23-4-38.

◆ **1 former Holland-class destroyer**

	Bldr	Laid down	L	In serv.
D 811 GELDERLAND	Wilton Fijenoord Schiedam	10-3-51	19-9-53	17-8-55

D: 2,215 tons (2,765 fl)   **S:** 32 kts   **Dim:** 111.3 × 11.33 × 3.88
A: None   **Electric:** 1,350 kw   **Boilers:** 4 Babcock & Wilcox
M: 2 sets Parsons GT; 2 props; 45,000 hp

REMARKS: Since 1973 used for technical training. Does not get under way.

NOTE: There are also 25 small sports and training sail yachts under naval control.

ACCOMMODATIONS SHIP

◆ **1 non-self-propelled**   Bldr: Voorwarts SY, Hoogezand

	Laid down	L	In serv.
A 886 CORNELIUS DREBBEL	18-5-70	19-11-70	30-11-71

D: 775 tons (fl)   **Dim:** 63.22 × 11.82 × 1.1   **Man:** 201 men

SERVICE CRAFT

There are approximately 50 small service craft, of which 18 are non-self-propelled barges, 5 are salvage pontoons, and others fill such roles as tank-cleaning vessels, torpedo transports, water and fuel-oil lighters and barges, floating workshops, floating cranes, and generator barges. All have NATO pendant numbers in the Y-8000 to Y-8700 series.

NETHERLANDS PILOT SERVICE

NOTE: This organization is under naval control, and funds for its ships come out of defense appropriations. Until recently, most of the older pilot ships carried one 76-mm Mk 22 DP and two 20-mm AA (I × 2). In wartime all could act as patrol ships. The listed pendant numbers are not borne in peacetime.

PILOT SHIPS

◆ **2 Mirfak class**   Bldr: A. Vuyk & Sons, Capelle-on-Ijssel

		Laid down	L	In serv.
A . . .	MIRFAK	. . .	. . .	-78
A . . .	MENKAR	. . .	. . .	-78

D: 1,080 tons (fl)   **S:** 13 kts   **Dim:** 59.0 (56.33 pp) × 10.6 × 3.8
Man: 38 men + 18 pilots   **Electric:** 540 kw
M: 3 Stork-Werkspoor DRO 216K diesels, electric drive; 1 prop; 1,400 hp

REMARKS: Helicopter platform aft. 864.17 grt/233.90 nrt. Provision for two 40-mm AA (I × 2).

◆ **Altair class**   Bldr: C. Amels B.V., Makkum

		Laid down	L	In serv.
A 805	ALTAIR	8-5-73	26-1-74	15-3-74
A 808	FOMELHAUT	31-10-73	14-8-74	12-9-74
A 909	SPICA	22-1-73	15-9-73	22-1-74

D: 1,000 tons (fl)   **S:** 13 kts   **Dim:** 59.0 × 10.69 × 3.66
M: 3 Paxman RPHXZ, 540-hp diesels, electric drive; 1 prop; 1,000 hp
Man: 44 men

REMARKS: Helicopter deck. Provision for two 40-mm AA (I × 2).

◆ **2 Capella class**

	Bldr	Laid down	L	In serv.
A 809 CAPELLA	Boele S & M, Bolnes	19-4-67	28-12-67	17-6-68
A 819 WEGA	A. Vuyk & Sons, Capelle	2-10-67	14-3-68	23-7-68

D: 1,000 tons   **S:** 13 kts   **Dim:** 59.0 (53.95 pp) × 10.67 × 3.7
M: 3 Paxman RPHXZ 540-hp diesels, electric drive, 1 prop; 1,200 hp
Man: 28 men

REMARKS: Helicopter deck. Provision for two 40-mm AA (I × 2).

◆ **6 Castor class**

	BLDR	Laid down	L	In serv.
A 804 ANTARES	Boele S & M, Bolnes	5-5-49	17-3-50	9-5-51
A 806 BELLATRIX	Boele S & M, Bolnes	24-2-49	17-4-50	24-4-51
A 807 BETELGEUZE	Pot Bros., Bolnes	1950	31-3-51	29-10-51
A 810 CASTOR	Pot Bros., Bolnes	1949	2-12-49	1-8-50
A 817 POLLUX	Pot Bros., Bolnes	1949	11-2-50	2-1-51
A 821 SIRIUS	Boele S & M, Bolnes	15-2-49	4-3-50	29-9-50

D: 503-525 tons (fl)   **S:** 12.5-13.2 kts   **Dim:** 45.95 × 8.43 × 3.13-3.18
M: 1 Smit-M.A.N. diesel; 1 prop; 650 hp   **Man:** 24 men   **Fuel:** 53 tons

REMARKS: A-817 is in reserve. Minor differences between individual ships. Provision for one 76-mm Mk 22 DP, two 20-mm AA (I × 2). No helicopter deck.

PILOT BOATS

◆ **2 Zeemeeuw class**   Bldr: Le Comte, Vianen

A 803 ZEEMEEUW   A 816 ZEEZWALUW

D: 41 tons (fl)   **S:** 15 kts   **Dim:** 23.37 × 5.37 × 1.12
M: 2 Rolls-Royce diesels; 2 Schöttel props; 760 hp

REMARK: A-803 in service 23-11-70; A-816, 12-2-71.

PILOT BOATS (continued)

◆ **2 Aalscholver class** Bldr: Le Comte, Vianen

A 827 AALSCHOLVER   A 828 JAN VAN GENT

    D: 41 tons (fl)   **S:** 15 klts   **Dim:** 23.3 × 5.35 × 1.12
    M: 2 Rolls-Royce diesels; 2 Schöttel props; 760 hp

REMARK: A-827 in service 5-11-69; A-828, 11-8-69.

◆ **2 Albatros class**

	Bldr	L	In serv.
A 921 ALBATROS	De Noord, Alblasserdam	12-2-64	29-11-64
A 922 ALK	G. de V. Leuntsch, Amsterdam	23-12-64	12-3-65

    D: 35 tons   **S:** 14 kts   **Dim:** 23.4 × 5.3 × 1.61
    M: 2 GM 6-71 diesels; 2 Schöttel props; 616 hp

◆ **1 Zeekoet class** Bldr: Naval Dockyard, Den Helder

A 826 ZEEKOET

    D: 229 tons   **S:** 11 kts   **Dim:** 33.6 × 7.27 × 2.25
    M: 1 Bolnes diesel; 1 prop; 480 hp

REMARK: In service 10-3-64.

◆ **2 Stormvogel class** Bldr: Naval Dockyard, Den Helder

A 913 STORMVOGEL   A 914 ZILVERMEEUW

    D: 235 tons (fl)   **S:** 11.9-12.2 kts   **Dim:** 31.88 × 6.85 × 2.65
    M: 1 Werkspoor diesel; 1 prop; 430 hp

REMARK: A-913 in service 28-9-54; A-914, 11-4-54.

PILOT LAUNCHES

◆ **2 Stern class** Bldr: Le Comte, Vianen

A 828 STERN   A 919 KLUT

    D: 11.5 tons (fl)   **S:** 19 kts   **Dim:** 12.5 × 3.6 × 1.0
    M: 2 Cummins diesels; 2 Schöttel props; 420 hp

REMARK: In service in 1976.

◆ **2 Walvis class** Bldr: Naval Dockyard, Den Helder

A 917 WALVIS   A 918 BRUINVIS

    D: 37 tons (fl)   **S:** 14 kts   **Dim:** 21.57 × 4.46 × 1.3
    M: 2 GM diesels; 2 props; 800 hp

REMARK: A-917 in service 25-8-65; A-918, 13-9-65.

◆ **4 Kabeljauw class** Bldr: Naval Dockyard, Den Helder

	In serv.		In serv.
A 924 KABELJAUW	2-6-50	A 930 ROG	12-8-50
A 929 MAKREEL	10-7-50	A 931 GEEP	10-50

    D: 38 tons (fl)   **S:** 10.4 kts   **Dim:** 19.75 × 5.04 × 1.1
    M: 1 Kromhout diesel; 160 hp

REMARK: Also in service are: A-933, *Poon* (12 tons), *Pampas* (1.5 tons), and A-915 (4 tons), the last being a workboat.

SEAGOING BUOY TENDERS

◆ **1 Breeveertien class** Bldr: Amels N.V., Makkum

A 908 BREEVEERTIEN

    D: 1,000 tons (fl)   **S:** 12 kts   **Dim:** 61.25 × 11.4 × 3.4
    M: Bolnes diesels; 1,230 hp

REMARKS: Launched, 21-10-72; in service, 16-2-73. One 12-ton crane.

◆ **1 Vlissingen class** Bldr: Naval Dockyard, Den Helder

A 815 VLISSINGEN

    D: 410 tons (fl)   **S:** 11.1 kts   **Dim:** 40.5 × 7.96 × 2.65
    M: 1 Bolnes diesel; 480 hp

REMARK: Launched, 5-10-68; in service, 5-5-69.

◆ **1 Terschelling class** Bldr: Zaanlandse S.M., Zaandam

A 948 TERSCHELLING

    D: 370 tons (fl)   **S:** 11.5 kts   **Dim:** 40.5 × 7.96 × 2.5
    M: 1 Bolnes diesel; 480 hp

REMARK: Launched, 21-9-63; in service, 30-1-64.

◆ **1 Delfshaven class** Bldr: Van Diepen SY, Waterhuizen

A 916 DELFSHAVEN

    D: 363 tons (fl)   **S:** 11.3 kts   **Dim:** 40.6 × 7.96 × 2.45
    M: 1 Bolnes diesel; 400 hp

REMARK: Launched, 4-2-59; in service, 28-4-59.

◆ **1 Frans Naerebout class** Bldr: E.J. Smit & Sons, Westerbroek

A 812 FRANS NAEREBOUT

    D: 432 tons (fl)   **S:** 11.2 kts   **Dim:** 40.5 × 7.96 × 2.75
    M: 1 Bolnes diesel; 400 hp

REMARK: Launched, 24-5-56; in service, 1-9-56.

◆ **1 Terneuzen class** Bldr: Haarlemse S.M., Haarlem

A 911 TERNEUZEN

REMARK: Launched, 2-12-53; in service, 15-7-54.

◆ **1 Zaandam class** Bldr: Haarlemse S.M., Haarlem

A 949 ZAANDAM

    D: 430 tons (fl)   **S:** 11.4 kts   **Dim:** 41.61 × 7.53 × 2.74
    M: 1 Werkspoor diesel; 430 hp

REMARK: Launched, 2-9-52; in service, 25-7-53.

MEDIUM BUOY TENDERS

◆ **2 Krammer class** Bldr: Stapel SY, Spaardam

A 831 KRAMMER   A 839 GREVELINGEN

    D: 192 tons (fl)   **S:** 9.2 kts   **Dim:** 30.63 × 6.43 × 1.68
    M: 1 Werkspoor diesel; 200 hp

REMARK: A-831 in service, 1-9-50; A-839, 20-1-50.

NETHERLANDS (continued)

SMALL BUOY TENDERS

◆ **5 Honte class** Bldr: Naval Dockyard, Den Helder

	In serv.		In serv.
A 814 HONTE	13-6-61	A 945 IJSELMEER	21-3-62
A 935 EEMS	14-7-61	A 947 HARINGVLIET	20-9-61
A 944 VLIESTROOM	4-12-61		

   D: 126-146 tons (fl) **S:** 9.2 kts **Dim:** 28.8 × 5.86 × 1.4-1.52
   M: 1 Bolnes diesel; 200 hp

REMARK: Beam for A-944 and A-945 is 5.8 m.

◆ **1 Textelstroom class** Bldr: Naval Dockyard, Den Helder

A 941 TEXTELSTROOM

   D: 100 tons (fl) **S:** 8 kts **Dim:** 24.1 × 5.56 × . . .
   M: 1 Kromhout diesel; 140 hp

REMARK: Launched, 1-4-59; in service, 11-7-59.

◆ **1 Waddenzee class** Bldr: Naval Dockyard, Den Helder

A 943 WADDENZEE

   D: 129 tons (fl) **S:** 9.5 kts **Dim:** 28.5 × 5.96 × 1.5
   M: 1 Bolnes diesel; 200 hp

REMARK: Launched, 1-11-58; in service, 27-1-59.

◆ **1 Lauwers class** Bldr: Akerboom Bros. N.V., Oegstgeest

A 940 LAUWERS

   D: 94 tons (fl) **S:** 7.5 kts **Dim:** 24.1 × 5.5 × 1.15
   M: 1 Kromhout diesel; 88 hp

REMARK: Launched, 19-8-52; in service, 17-11-52.

LIGHTSHIPS

◆ **1 No. 12 class** Bldr: De Waal N.V., Zaltbommel

A 824 No. 12

   D: 510 tons (fl) **Dim:** 45.09 × 8.38 × 3.15

REMARK: Launched, 23-3-63; in service, 18-10-63.

◆ **2 No. 10 class** Bldr: Naval Dockyard, Den Helder

A 833 No. 10   A 834 No. 11

   D: 493 tons (fl) **Dim:** 45.5 × 7.92 × 2.95

REMARK: A-833 launched 11-8-51, and in service 30-9-52; A-834 launched 29-9-51, and in service 9-1-53.

◆ **1 No. 9 class** Bldr: Naval Dockyard, Den Helder

A 823 No. 9

   D: 424 tons (fl) **Dim:** 42.6 × 7.67 × 2.82

REMARK: Launched in 1933, and in service, 6-9-33.

NETHERLANDS NATIONAL POLICE FORCE

NOTE: This organization operates a small number of patrol boats and craft, of which only RP-15, listed below, is seagoing. A number of other jurisdictions, including the Customs Service, the Rotterdam City Police, and the Department of Communications, also operate patrol craft.

RP 15 DE RUITER

   D: 27 tons (fl) **S:** 18.5 kts **Dim:** 19.13 × 4.27 × 1.3
   M: 2 12-cyl. diesels; 2 controllable-pitch props; 680 hp **Man:** 3-4 men

REMARK: In service in 5-79.

RP 17 Bldr: Le Comte, Vianen, 1974

   D: 29 tons **S:** 15 kts **Dim:** 15.75 × 3.83 × 1.05
   M: 1 MTU OM403 diesel; 1 Schöttel prop; 250 hp

RP 26 and 6 others Bldr: Le Comte, Vianen, 1970

   D: 8.5 tons **S:** 14.5 kts **Dim:** 10.8 × 3.22 × 1.2
   M: 1 MTU OM346 diesel; 1 Schöttel prop; 165 hp

RP 10 Bldr: Schuiten, Muiden, 1968

   D: 70 tons (fl) **S:** 14 kts **Dim:** 23.0 × . . . × . . .
   M: 1 Bolnes GDNL diesel; 600 hp

RP 3 Bldr: Koopman, Dordrecht, 1967

   D: 60 tons (fl) **S:** 12.7 kts **Dim:** 22.0 × 5.3 × 1.5
   M: 2 GM 12V71 diesels; 2 props; 670 hp

NEW ZEALAND

PERSONNEL: Approximately 2,700 men (plus 236 reserves)
MERCHANT MARINE: (1978): 109 ships — 211,112 grt
(tankers: 2 ships — 32,442 grt)
NAVAL AVIATION: Wasp helicopters are carried on the two *Leander*-class frigates and on the survey ship *Monowai*. Five P3-B Orion patrol planes belong to the Royal New Zealand Air Force.

FRIGATES

◆ **2 British Leander class**

	Bldr	Laid down	L	In serv.
F 55 WAIKATO	Harland & Wolff	10-1-65	18-2-65	16-9-66
F 421 CANTERBURY	Yarrow	12-4-69	6-5-70	22-10-71

FRIGATES *(continued)*

Canterbury   1977

Waikato   1972

D: F-55: 2,450 tons (2,850 fl); F-421: 2,470 tons (2,990 fl)
S: F-55: 30 kts; F-421: 28 kts
Dim: 113.38 (109.73 pp) × 12.5 (F-421: 13.12) × 5.49
A: 2/114-mm Mk 6 DP (II × 1) − 1/Sea Cat system (IV × 1) − 2/20-mm AA (I × 2) − 6/324-mm Mk 32 ASW TT (III × 2) − 1/Wasp ASW helicopter
Electron Equipt: Radars: 1/965, 1/993, 1/978, 1/903, 1/904
                Sonars: 1/177, 1/162B, 1/170
Man: 14 officers, 229 men   **Range:**   4,500/12
Fuel: F-55: 460 tons; F-421: 500 tons
Electric: F-55: 1,900 kw; F-421: 2,500 kw
Boilers: 2 Babcock & Wilcox, 38.7 kg/cm² pressure − superheat 450°C
M: 2 sets English-Electric GT; 2 props; 30,000 hp

REMARKS: F-55 originally had a Mk 10 Limbo triple ASW mortar and no ASW TT; she was refitted in 1977 when the Type 170B sonar was also removed. F-421 has exten-

sions for her smoke pipes from the top of the stack and is a unit of the final, "broad-beam" version of the class. The Sea Cat system is GWS 22 with a modified MRS-3 radar director.

◆ **2 British Rothesay class**

	Bldr	Laid down	L	In serv.
F 111 OTAGO	J. Thornycroft	1957	11-12-58	22-6-60
(ex-*Hastings*)				
F 148 TARANAKI	J. Samuel White	1957	19-8-59	28-3-61

Otago

D: 2,144 (2,557 fl)   **S:**   30 kts   **Dim:**   112.8 (109.7 pp) × 12.5 × 5.3
A: F-111: 2/114-mm Mk 6 DP (II × 1) − 1/Sea Cat system (IV × 2) − 2/20-mm AA (I × 2) − 2/Mk 10 Limbo ASW mortars (III × 2) − 6/324-mm Mk 32 ASW TT (III × 2)
       F-148: 2/114-mm Mk 5 DP (II × 1) − 2/40-mm Mk 5 AA (II × 1) − 2/20-mm AA (I × 2) − 6/324-mm Mk 32 ASW TT (III × 2)
Electron Equipt: Radars: 1/993, 1/277, 1/978, 1/275 fire-control, 1/262 (F-111 only)
                Sonars: 1/177, 1/170B, 1/162B
Man: 31 officers, 227 men   **Range:**   4,500/12   **Fuel:**   400 tons
Electric: 1,460 kw
Boilers: 2 Babcock & Wilcox, 37.5 kg/cm² pressure − superheat 450°C
M: 2 sets English-Electric GT; 2 props; 30,000 hp

REMARKS: F-148 was recommissioned from the ready reserve in 1979 as a combination training ship and patrol ship for the 200-nautical mile economic zone. Her ASW mortars and Sea Cat SAM system were removed, the latter being replaced by a twin 40-mm anti-aircraft. Both ships carried two 40-mm anti-aircraft (I × 2) from 1968-69 to the early 1970s and were originally fitted with 12 533-mm ASW TT (II × 2, I × 8). The Sea Cat system on F-111 is GWS 21 with a modified MRS-8 director and Type 262 radar.

PATROL CRAFT

◆ **4 Pukaki class**   Bldr: Brooke Marine, Lowestoft

PATROL CRAFT (continued)

	L	In serv.
P 3568 PUKAKI	1-3-74	24-2-75
P 3569 ROTOITI	8-3-74	24-2-75
P 3570 TAUPO	25-7-74	29-7-75
P 3571 HAWEA	9-9-74	29-7-75

D: 105 tons (135 fl) **S:** 22 kts **Dim:** 32.6 × 6.1 × 1.7
A: 1/81-mm mortar combined with 12.7-mm machine gun—2/12.7-mm machine guns (II × 1)
Electron Equipt: Radar: Decca 916 **Man:** 3 officers, 18 men
Range: 2,500/12 **M:** 2 Ruston-Paxman 12 YCJM diesels; 2 props; 3,000 hp

◆ **4 British HDML class**

	Bldr	In serv.
P 3552 PAEA (ex-Q-1184)	Hadden & Lewis, Sausalito, Cal.	21-12-42
P 3563 KUPARU (ex-Pegasus, ex-Q-1349)	Ackerman Boatyard, Cal.	19-1-44
P 3564 KOURA (ex-Toroa, ex-Q-1350)	Ackerman Boatyard, Cal.	19-1-44
P 3567 MANGA (ex-Q-1185)	Hadden & Lewis, Sausalito, Cal.	21-12-42

Paea

D: 46 tons (54 fl) **S:** 11-12 kts **Dim:** 21.95 × 4.83 × 1.45
Man: 9 men **Range:** 900/10 **Electron Equipt:** Radar: Decca 45
M: 2 Gray Marine 64HN9 diesels; 2 props; 320 hp

REMARKS: The *Paea* and the *Manga* originally had two Hercules diesels; 240 hp. All used for naval reserve training. Six sisters scrapped 1972-77. Two others, the *Takapu* (P-3556) and the *Tarapunga* (P-3566) were used as inshore survey craft until 1979. Wooden hulls.

HYDROGRAPHIC SURVEY SHIPS

◆ **1 converted passenger-cargo ship** Bldr: Grangemouth DY, 1960

A 06 MONOWAI (ex-*Moana Roa*)

D: 4,027 tons (fl) **S:** 13.5 kts **Dim:** 90.33 (82.3 pp) × 14.02 × 5.21
Fuel: 300 tons **Man:** 120 men **Range:** . . .
M: 2 Clark-Sulzer 7-cyl. diesels; 2 controllable-pitch props; 3,640 hp—bow thruster

REMARKS: Taken over from the government-run commercial service in 1974 and converted at Scott-Lithgow, Greenock, Scotland, 9-97 to 4-10-77. Telescoping hangar fitted for one Wasp helicopter. Two 10.36-meter and one 8.84-meter survey craft carried, as well as one Rotork "Sea Truck" workboat. Decca Hifix positioning system and Omega radio navigational aids installed, as well as a navigational satellite receiver. One 4-ton crane. Side-scanning mapping sonar and other sophisticated survey equipment carried.

◆ **2 new construction inshore survey craft** Bldr: Whangarei Eng. Ltd.

N . . . N . . .

D: 90 tons (fl) **S:** 12 kts **Dim:** 27.0 × . . . × . . .
Man: 1 officer, 10 men **M:** 2 diesels; 2 props; 730 hp

REMARKS: Ordered 30-11-77. Similar to diving tender *Manawanui*. To replace HDML-class survey craft *Takapu* (P-3556) and *Tarapunga* (P-3566).

OCEANOGRAPHIC RESEARCH SHIP

◆ **1 ex-U.S. Robert D. Conrad class** Bldr: Christy Corp., Sturgeon Bay, Wis.

	Laid down	L	In serv.
A 02 TUI (ex-*Charles H. Davis*, T-AGOR-5)	15-6-61	30-6-62	25-1-63

Tui 1972

D: 1,200 tons (1,380 fl) **S:** 12 kts **Dim:** 63.7 × 11.4 × 4.7
Man: 8 officers, 16 men, 15 scientists **Range:** 12,000/12 **Fuel:** 211 tons
M: 2 Caterpillar D-378 diesels, electric; 1 prop; 1,000 hp—175-hp bow thruster

REMARKS: Transferred 28-7-70. Used in acoustics research for the New Zealand Defense Research Establishment, which has modified the ship since it was loaned by the U.S. Navy, so that it may be used to lay and tow hydrophone arrays.

SERVICE CRAFT

◆ **1 tug** Bldr: Steel Ships, Ltd., Auckland

ARATAKI

NEW ZEALAND (*continued*)

SERVICE CRAFT (*continued*)

    D: 190 tons   **S:** 10 kts   **Dim:** 22.9 × 5.8 × 2.44   **Man:** 8 men
    M: 1 Atlas diesel; 1 prop; 320 hp

REMARK: Launched in 1947.

◆ **1 diving tender** Bldr: Whangarei Eng., Ltd.

MANAWANUI

    D: 90 tons   **S:** 12 kts   **Dim:** 27.0 × . . . × . . .
    M: 2 diesels; 2 props; 730 hp

REMARKS: Launched 8-12-78. Two inshore survey craft of the same basic design were ordered 30-11-78.

NICARAGUA

PERSONNEL: Approximately 200 men
MERCHANT MARINE (1978): 30 ships — 34,588 grt
          (tankers: 4 ships — 5,237 grt)

PATROL CRAFT

◆ **4 Israeli Dabur class** Bldr: Israeli Aircraft Industries

GC 10   GC 11   GC 12   GC 13

    D: 25 tons (35 fl)   **S:** 25 kts   **Dim:** 19.8 × 5.8 × 0.8
    A: 2/20-mm AA (I × 2)   **Man:** 6 men   **Range:** 1,200/17
    M: 2 GM diesels; 2 props; 960 hp

REMARKS: In service in 5-78. Two larger *Dvora*-class patrol craft were also ordered from Israel, but their delivery was embargoed in 1979 at the request of the U.S. government.

◆ **1 U.S. 65-foot cruiser class** Bldr: Sewart Seacraft, La.

GC 7 RIO KURINGWAS

    D: 60 tons   **S:** 26.5 kts   **Dim:** 25.9 × 5.6 × 1.8
    A: 2/20-mm AA (I × 2)   **Man:** 10 men   **Range:** 1,000/20
    M: 3 GM 8V71 diesels; 3 props; 2,000 hp

REMARK: In service since 1962.

◆ **6 U.S. Hatteras-class cabin cruisers**

    Dim: 11.6 oa

NIGERIA

PERSONNEL: 120 officers, 1,700 men
MERCHANT MARINE (1978): 101 ships — 324,024 grt
          (tankers: 8 ships — 143,999 grt)

FRIGATES

◆ **1 MEKO 360-H class** Bldr: Blohm & Voss, Hamburg

	Laid down	L	In serv.
F . . . N . . .	. . .	12-79	7-81

    D: 3,600 tons (fl)   **S:** 30.5 kts
    Dim: 125.9 (119.0 pp) × 14.0 × 4.32 (5.8 props)
    Man: 26 officers, 169 men, 35 cadets   **Range:** 4,500/18   **Fuel:** 440 tons
    A: 8/MM 40 Exocet SSM (IV × 2) — 1/127-mm OTO Melara DP — 1/Aspide SAM system, Mk 2, mod. 9 (VIII × 1, 24 missiles) — 8/40-mm Breda AA (II × 4) — 6/324-mm Mk 32 ASW TT (III × 2, 18 torpedoes) — 1/WG-13 Lynx ASW helicopter
    Electron Equipt: Radars: 1/AWS 5, 1/Decca 1226, 1/HSA WM 25, 1/HSA STIR
                  Sonar: 1/HSA PHS-32 — Decca intercept equipt — 2/SCLAR 105-mm chaff launchers
    M: CODOG: 2 Rolls-Royce Olympus TM-3B gas turbines, 50,000 hp; 2 MTU 20V956 TB 92 diesels, 11,070 hp; 2 controllable-pitch props   **Electric:** 4,120 kva

REMARKS: Ordered late 1977. Six similar ships (but with COGOG propulsion, two helicopters, and different electronics) ordered 11-12-78 for Argentina. Will make use of modular containers for electronics and weapon systems. Will carry 460 rounds of 127-mm ammunition, 10,752 rounds of 40-mm ammunition, and 120 chaff rounds for the Elsag/Breda chaff-rocket launchers.

	Bldr	Laid down	L	In serv.
F 87 NIGERIA	Wilton-Fijencord, Netherlands	4-64	9-65	9-66

    D: 1,724 tons (2,000 fl)   **S:** 25 kts   **Dim:** 109.85 (104.0 pp) × 11.3 × 3.35
    Man: 216   **Range:** 3,500/15
    A: 2/102-mm Mk 19 DP (II × 1) — 4/40-mm AA (I × 4) — 1/Squid ASW mortar (III × 1)
    Electron Equipt: Radars: 1/293B, 1/navigational
                    Sonars: 1/162B, 1/177

Nigeria   1966

FRIGATES *(continued)*

REMARKS: Helicopter platform. Refit by Cammell Laird, 1970-71, and again at Schiedam, the Netherlands, in 1977. Only a simple lead-computing director is fitted for the 102-mm guns.

CORVETTES

◆ **2 Erin'mi class, Mk 9** Bldr: Vosper Thornycroft, Portsmouth

	Laid down	L	In serv.
F 83 ERIN'MI	14-10-75	20-1-77	12-79
F 84 ENYMIRI	11-2-77	9-2-78	1980

Erin'Mi—on trials Vosper Thornycroft, 1979

D: 850 tons (fl) **S:** 27 kts **Dim:** 69.0 (64.0 pp) × 9.6 × 3.0 (3.6 max.)
Man: 90 men **Range:** 2,200/14 **Endurance:** 10 days
Electric: 889 kw
A: 1/76-mm OTO Melara DP—1/Sea Cat system (III × 1)—1/40-mm Bofors AA—
2/20-mm AA (I × 2)—1/375-mm Bofors ASW rocket launcher (II × 1)
Electron Equipt: Radars: 1/AWS 2, 1/Decca TM 1226, 1/HSA WM-24
  Sonar: 1/Plessey MS 26—Decca intercept—2/50-mm flare launchers
M: 4 MTU 20V956 TB 92 diesels; 2 controllable-pitch props; 20,512 hp

REMARKS: Can sustain 20 kts on two diesels. Uses three MTU 6V51 diesel generator sets of 260 kw each and one 109-kw emergency generator. Carries 750 rounds of 76-mm ammunition. Trials of the F-83 began 12-78. Both names are local words for "hippopotamus."

◆ **2 Dorina class, Mk 3** Bldr: Vosper Thornycroft, Portsmouth

	Laid down	L	In serv.
F 81 DORINA	26-1-70	16-9-70	6-72
F 82 OTOBO	28-9-70	25-5-71	11-72

D: 650 tons (fl) **S:** 22/23 kts **Dim:** 61.57 (55.4 pp) × 7.45 × 3.35
Man: 7 officers, 13 petty officers, 46 men **Range:** 3,500/14
A: 2/102-mm Mk 19 DP (II × 1)—2/40-mm Bofors AA (I × 2)—2/20-mm AA (I × 2)

Dorina Vosper Thornycroft, 1972

Electron Equipt: Radars 1/ASW 1, 1/Decca TM 626, 1/HSA M-22
Electric: 176 kw **Fuel:** 68 tons
M: 2 M.A.N. V8V 24/30-B diesels; 2 props; 3,400 hp (4,430 max.)
REMARKS: Can carry a flag officer and his staff. Living spaces air-conditioned. Fin stabilizers. The 102-mm guns are hand-loaded. Twelve watertight compartments. Refitted, 1975-76.

GUIDED-MISSILE PATROL BOATS

◆ **3 La Combattante-IIIB class** Bldr: CMN, Cherbourg, France

	Laid down	L	In serv.
P . . N . . .	. . .	. . .	. . .
P . . N . . .	. . .	. . .	. . .
P . . N . . .	. . .	. . .	. . .

D: 385 tons (425 fl) **S:** 37 kts **Dim:** 56.2 × 8.0 × 2.1
Man: 42 men **Range:** 2,000/15
A: 4/MM 38 Exocet SSM (II × 2)—1/76-mm OTO Melara DP—2/40-mm Breda-Bofors AA (II × 1)—4/30-mm Emerlec AA (II × 2)
Electron Equipt: Radars: . . .
M: 4 MTU 16V956 TB 92 diesels; 4 props; 20,000 hp

REMARKS: Ordered 1977. Very similar to the Lürssen-built boats listed below.

◆ **3 FPB-57 class** Bldr: Lürssen, Vegesack, West Germany

	Laid down	L	In serv.
P . . N . . .	. . .	. . .	. . .
P . . N . . .	. . .	. . .	. . .
P . . N . . .	. . .	. . .	. . .

D: 373 tons (436 fl) **S:** 35 kts **Dim:** 58.1 (54.4 wl) × 7.62 × 2.83 (props)
Man: 40 men **Range:** 1,600/32, 3,300/16 **Electric:** 405 kva
A: 4/MM 38 Exocet SSM (II × 2)—1/76-mm OTO Melara DP—2/40-mm Breda-Bofors (II × 1)—4/30-mm Emerlec AA (II × 2)
Electron Equipt: Radars: 1/navigational, 1/HSA WM-28
M: 4 MTU 16V956 TB 92 diesels; 4 props; 20,000 hp

REMARKS: Ordered late 1977. Very similar to *La Combattante*-IIIB class but with Dutch, vice French, electronics.

PATROL BOATS

◆ **4 Makurdi class**   Bldr: Brooke Marine Ltd., Lowestoft, G.B.

	In serv.			In serv.
P 167 MAKURDI	14-8-74		P 171 JEBBA	29-4-77
P 168 HADEJIA	14-8-74		P 172 OGUTA	29-4-77

Hadejia   1975

D: 115 tons (143 fl)   **S:** 20.5 kts   **Dim:** 32.6 × 6.1 × 3.5
A: 2/40-mm AA (I × 2)   **Man:** 4 officers, 20 men   **Range:** 2,300/12
M: 2 Ruston-Paxman YJCM diesels; 2 props; 3,000 hp   **Fuel:** 18 tons

◆ **4 Argundu class**   Bldr: Abeking & Rasmussen, West Germany

	L	In serv.		L	In serv.
P 165 ARGUNDU	4-7-73	10-74	P 169 BRAS	12-1-76	3-76
P 166 YOLA	12-6-73	10-74	P 170 EPE	9-2-76	3-76

D: 90 tons   **S:** 20 kts   **Dim:** 32.0 × 6.0 × 1.7
A: 1/40-mm AA – 1/20-mm AA   **Man:** 25 men   **Range:** . . .
M: 2 MTU diesels; 2,070 hp

Argundu   1975

◆ **1 British "-ford" class**   Bldr: J. Samuel White, Cowes, G.B.

P 09 SAPELE (ex-*Dubford*)

D: 120 tons (160 fl)   **S:** 15 kts   **Dim:** 35.76 × 6.1 × 1.68
A: 1/40-mm AA – 2/20-mm AA (I × 2)   **Man:** 26 men
Range: 500/12, 1,000/8
M: 2 Davey-Paxman YHAMX diesels; 2 props; 1,000 hp; 1 Foden FD-6 cruise diesel: 100 hp
Fuel: 23 tons

REMARKS: Transferred in 1968. Survivor of a group of five sisters. Used primarily for training. Sister *Ibadan* lost 1967; *Ibadan* II, *Bonny*, and *Enugu* stricken 1977-78.

AMPHIBIOUS WARFARE SHIPS

◆ **2 West German Type-502 landing ships**   Bldr: Howaldtswerke, Kiel

	L	In serv.
L . . . AMBE	7-78	11-5-79
L . . . OFIOM	7-12-78	6-79

D: 1,190 tons (1,350 fl)   **S:** 18 kts   **Dim:** 86.0 × 14.0 × 2.25
A: 1/40-mm AA – 2/20-mm AA (I × 2)   **Man:** 6 officers, 51 men
Range: 4,000/12
M: 2 MTU 16-cyl. diesels; 4 props; 7,000 hp   **Electric:** 880 kw

REMARKS: Cargo: 400 tons vehicles or other material plus berths for 1,000 troops. Bow and stern ramps. Each diesel engine drives two propellers.

◆ **2 French EDIC-class utility landing craft**   Bldr: La Manche, Dieppe

	In serv.			In serv.
L . . . N . . .	. . .		L . . . N . . .	. . .

D: 250 tons (670 fl)   **S:** 9 kts   **Dim:** 60.0 × 12.6 × 1.8 (props)
A: . . .   **M:** 2 diesels, 2 props; 800 hp

REMARK: Ordered 6-77.

HYDROGRAPHIC SHIPS

◆ **1 British Bulldog class**   Bldr: Brooke Marine Ltd., Lowestoft, G.B.

	Laid down	L	In serv.
LANA	5-4-74	4-3-76	9-76

Lana   G. Arra, 1976

NIGERIA *(continued)*

HYDROGRAPHIC SHIPS *(continued)*

D: 800 tons (1,100 fl)   **S:** 15 kts   **Dim:** 60.95 (57.8 pp) × 11.43 × 3.7
A: 2/20-mm AA (I × 2)
M: 4 Lister-Blackstone ERS-8M diesels; 2 controllable-pitch props; 2,000 hp
Range: 4,000/12   **Man:** 38 men   **Electric:** 880 kw

◆ **1 coastal survey craft**   Bldr: Akerboom, Leiden, Netherlands

Murtula Muhamed

D: 13 tons   **S:** 9 kts   **Dim:** 11.75 × 3.5 × 1.0
M: 1 Perkins 6-354M diesel; 1 prop; 75 hp

REMARK: In service in 1978.

TRAINING SHIP

◆ **1 training ship**   Bldr: Van Lent, Kaag, Netherlands

A 497 Ruwan Yaro (ex-*Ogina Bereton*)

Ruwan Yaro

D: 400 tons (fl)   **S:** 17 kts   **Dim:** 50.0 (44.2 pp) × 8.0 × 2.0
A: None   **Man:** 31 + 11 in officers' training   **Range:** 3,000/15
Electron Equipt: Radar: 1/Decca TM 626   **Fuel:** 64 tons
M: 2 Deutz SBA 12M528 diesels; 1 controllable-pitch prop; 3,000 hp

REMARKS: In service 10-5-75. An inspection ship with a glass-reinforced plastic hull and a bow thruster.

TUGS

◆ **1 harbor**   Bldr: De Hoop SY, Hardinxveld, Netherlands

A . . . Kain Ji-dam

REMARKS: Launched 15-11-77. 90 grt.

◆ **1 coastal**   Bldr: Oelkers, Hamburg

A 486 Ribadu

D: 147 tons   **S:** 12 kts   **Dim:** 28.5 × 7.2 × 3.7
M: 1 diesel; 1 prop; 800 hp.

REMARK: In service 19-5-73.

NIGERIAN COAST GUARD

PATROL CRAFT

◆ **15 glass-reinforced, plastic-hulled**   Bldr: Intermarine, Italy

D: 21 tons (fl)   **S:** 37 kts   **Dim:** 18.2 × 4.5 × 0.85
A: 1/20-mm AA − 2/7.62-mm machine guns   **Range:** 300/33
M: 2 diesels; 2 water jets; 2,000 hp

REMARK: Ordered 10-78.

NORWAY

PERSONNEL: Approximately 8,000 men, 1,600 of whom in the coast artillery
MERCHANT MARINE (1978): 2,646 ships − 26,128,428 grt
(tankers: 216 ships − 13,893,821 grt)
NAVAL AVIATION: The Norwegian Navy does not have an air arm, as such. However, two of the Air Force's formations are assigned to naval missions, usually reconnaissance and ASW patrol: a squadron of 10 SH-3 Sea King search-and-rescue and 11 UH-1 helicopters; a group of 5 P-3 Orion patrol aircraft and 4 De Havilland Twin Otter utility aircraft.
NAVAL PROGRAM: The long-term program, drawn up in 1973, was to replace the following ships before the end of the 1980s:
German 207-type submarines
Oslo-class frigates and *Sleipner*-class corvettes
Tjeld-class torpedo boats (i.e., with the *Hauk* class beginning to enter service in 1979)
Sauda/Tana-class minesweepers
The first increment of new construction was scheduled for 1974-78. Built or converted during this period were:
14 *Snögg*-class guided-missile patrol boats
2 minelayers, the *Vidar* and *Vale*
1 logistic-support ship for submarines, the *Horten*
1 glass-reinforced, plastic-hulled minehunter (delayed)
1 minesweeper, the *Tana*, converted to a minehunter
The long-range program is likely to be modified by the creation of a Coast Guard to protect offshore oil installations and patrol the 200-mile economic zone. The Coast Guard program provides for seven 2,000-ton escort ships, each carrying a helicopter; three Orion-type patrol aircraft; and six Westland WG-13 Lynx helicopters, which are on order for delivery in 1981.

WARSHIPS IN SERVICE OR UNDER CONSTRUCTION AS OF 1 JANUARY 1980

	L	Tons (surfaced)	Main armament
◆ **15 submarines**			
15 GERMAN 207 TYPE	1964-67	370	8/533-mm TT
◆ **5 frigates**			
5 OSLO	1964-66	1,450	4-6/Penguin SSM, 1/Sea Sparrow system, 4/76-mm DP, 1/Terne ASW system, 6/324-mm ASW TT
◆ **3 corvettes**			
2 SLEIPNER	1963-65	600	1/76-mm DP, 1/Terne ASW system, 6/324-mm ASW TT
1 VASDØ	1951	600	1/40-mm AA
◆ **49 (+ 6) missile and torpedo boats (some in reserve)**			
8 (+ 6) HAUK	1977-80	130	6/Penguin SSM, 1/40-mm AA, 2/533-mm TT
6 SNÖGG	1970-71	115	4/Penguin SSM, 1/40-mm AA, 4/533-mm TT
20 STORM	1963-67	100	6/Penguin SSM, 1/76-mm SSM
15 TJELD	1960-66	70	1 or 2/40-mm AA, 2 or 4/533-mm TT

WEAPONS AND SYSTEMS

The Norwegian Navy uses mostly British, American, and Swedish weapons and systems, but it has built two interesting systems of its own, the Terne automatic ASW defense system and the Penguin surface-to-surface missile, which are described below. Submarines are equipped with Swedish T 61 (45 kts, 20,000 m) or American Mk 37 (20,000 m) wire-guided torpedoes. Norway has also developed its own radar and electro-optical gun and missile fire-control systems.

Terne Mk III (ASW)

Maximum range: 900 m
1 search sonar (U.S. AN/SQS-36)
1 attack sonar ("Terne Mk 3" for range/depth determination)
1 computer
1 sextuple launcher mount with a rapid-reloading system.

The sextuple mount weighs a little less than 3 tons. Firing is done between 45° and 75° of elevation, the latter for minimum range. Six rounds are ripple-fired at a time. Reloading is done automatically in 40 seconds, as the carriage is returned to a vertical position, in which ready-service racks reload the launchers. The rocket is 1.97 m in length, 0.2 m in diameter, 120 kg in weight (warhead: 48 kg), and has a combination timed and proximity fuse.

Penguin (Anti-ship)

Length: 0.3 m
Wingspan: 1.4 m
Diameter: 0.28
Weight: 330 kg

Maximum range: 20,000 m
Speed: Mach 0.7
Guidance: infrared homing

The missile is protected by a fiberglass container that also serves as a launcher. Penguin II, with increased range, is under development in conjunction with the Swedish Navy.

76-mm Bofors gun

Single-barreled automatic gun mounted on the *Storm*-class patrol boats. Not intended for AA.

Turret weight (no ammunition): 6.5 tons
Length: 50 calibers
Muzzle velocity: 825 m/sec
Rate of train: 25°/sec
Rate of elevation: 25°/sec
Arc of elevation: −10° to +30°
Rate of fire: 30 rounds/min—100 rounds immediately available in the ready-firing station
Cartridge weight: 11.3 kg
Shell weight: 5.9 kg
Warhead weight: 0.54 kg
Maximum range, surface mode: 8,000 m

SUBMARINES

◆ **15 German 207 Type**   Bldr: Rheinstahl-Nordseewerke, Emden

	L	In serv.		L	In serv.
S 300 ULA	19-12-64	7-5-65	S 308 STORD	2-9-66	9-2-67
S 301 UTSIRA	11-3-65	1-7-65	S 309 SVENNER	27-1-67	1-7-67
S 302 UTSTEIN	19-5-65	9-9-65	S 315 KAURA	16-10-64	5-2-65
S 303 UTVAER	30-6-65	1-12-65	S 316 KINN	30-11-63	8-4-64
S 304 UTHAUG	8-10-65	16-2-66	S 317 KYA	20-2-64	15-6-64
S 305 SKLINNA	21-1-66	17-8-66	S 318 KOBBEN	25-4-64	17-8-64
S 306 SKOLPEN	24-3-66	17-8-66	S 319 KUNNA	16-7-64	1-10-64
S 307 STADT	10-6-66	15-11-66			

D: 370 tons surfaced, 482 submerged   **S:** 13.5/17 kts
Dim: 45.41 (S-309: 46.41) × 4.6 × 4.58   **Man:** 17 men
A: 8/533-mm TT, fwd
M: 2 Mercedes-Benz MB 820Db diesels, 2 405-kw generators, 1 1,100-kw motor; 1 prop (2.3 m diameter); 1,700 hp

Kya   1975

SUBMARINES *(continued)*

REMARKS: Based on the West German type 205, but with a stronger hull. They are fitted with new sensors, new batteries, and wire-guided U.S. Mk-37 torpedoes. MSI-700 torpedo fire-control is used. The *Svenner* is equipped for training, has a second periscope, and is one meter longer than the others.

NOTE: The West Germany Navy has given IKL, Lübeck, a contract to study a 750-ton submarine, to be designated type 210. This boat is expected to replace the above submarines, but not before the mid-1980s.

GUIDED-MISSILE FRIGATES

◆ **5 Oslo class** Bldr: Marinens Hovedverft (Naval Dockyard), Horten

	Laid down	L	In serv.
F 300 OSLO	1963	17-1-64	29-1-66
F 301 BERGEN	1963	23-8-65	15-6-67
F 302 TRONDHEIM	1963	4-9-64	2-6-66
F 303 STAVANGER	1964	4-2-66	1-12-67
F 304 NARVIK	1964	8-1-65	30-11-66

Narvik   G. Arra, 1977

Penguin anti-ship missile, NATO Sea Sparrow point-defense SAM, and ASW torpedo tubes. In the Sea Sparrow system, the Mk-91 radar director is on a pylon atop the missile-reload magazine; the launcher is a U.S. Mk 29.

CORVETTES

◆ **2 Sleipner class** Bldr: Nylands Verksted, Oslo

	L	In serv.		L	In serv.
F 310 SLEIPNER	9-11-63	29-4-65	F 311 AEGER	24-9-65	31-3-67

Narvik   G. Arra, 1977

D: 1,450 tons (1,850 fl) **S:** 25 kts **Dim:** 96.62 (93.87 pp) × 11.17 × 4.4
Man: 11 officers, 19 petty officers, 120 men **Range:** 4,500/15
A: 4-6/Penguin SSM−1/NATO Sea Sparrow system (VIII × 1, 24 missiles)−4/76-mm DP (II × 2)−1/Terne-III ASW rocket launcher (VI × 1)−6/324-mm Mk 32 ASW TT (III × 2)−1/depth-charge rack
Electron Equipt: Radars: 1/DRBV 22, 1/Decca TM 1226, 1/HSA M 24, 1/U.S. Mk 91
   Sonars: 1/Terne Mk 3 attack, 1/SQS 36
Boilers: 2 Babcock & Wilcox, 42.18 kg/cm² pressure−superheat 454°C
M: 1 set de Laval-Ljungstrom PN 20 GT; 1 prop; 20,000 hp **Electric:** 1,100 kw

REMARKS: Based on the U.S. *Dealey*-class destroyer escorts, but with higher freeboard forward and many European subsystems. Rebuilt during the late-1970s with the

Sleipner   1977

D: 600 tons (790 fl) **S:** 20+ kts **Dim:** 69.33 × 7.9 × 2.5
A: 1/76-mm Mk 34 DP−1/40-mm AA−1/Terne-III ASW rocket launcher (VI × 1)−6/324-mm Mk 32 ASW TT (III × 2)−1/depth-charge rack
Electron Equipt: Radars: 1/Decca 707, 1/Decca TM 1226
   Sonars: 1/Terne Mk 3 attack, 1/SQS 36
M: 4 Maybach diesels; 2 props; 9,000 hp **Man:** 61 men

REMARKS: From the 1960 program. Now employed primarily for training.

◆ **1 former whale-catcher** Bldr: Stord Verft

P 340 VADSØ

D: 600 tons (905 fl) **S:** 12 kts **Dim:** 51.0 × 9.0 × 4.1

CORVETTES (continued)

  A: 1/40-mm AA − 1/depth-charge rack   Man: 22 men   Range: 15,000/12
  Electron Equipt: Radars: 2/navigational   Sonar: . . .
  M: 1 M.A.K. 8M451 diesel; 1 prop; 1,400 hp

REMARKS: Launched in 1951. Purchased in 1976 and refitted for local patrol duties. The AA gun is mounted on what was the harpoon-gun platform at the extreme bow; the depth-charge rack is on a platform extending aft from the superstructure.

GUIDED-MISSILE PATROL BOATS

◆ **14 Hauk class** Bldr: Bergens Mekaniske Verksteder

		L	In serv.
P 986	HAUK	2-77	8-78
P 987	ØRN	2-78	22-1-79
P 988	TERNE	5-78	15-3-79
P 989	TJELD	8-78	29-5-79
P 990	SKARV	10-78	17-7-79
P 991	N . . .	. . .	. . .
P 992	JO	. . .	. . .
P 993	N . . .	. . .	. . .
P 994	N . . .	. . .	. . .
P 995	N . . .	. . .	. . .
P 996	N . . .	. . .	. . .
P 997	N . . .	. . .	. . .
P 998	N . . .	. . .	. . .
P 999	N . . .	. . .	. . .

  D: 130 tons (155 fl)   S: 35 kts   Dim: 36.53 × 6.3 × 1.65
  Man: 22 men   Range: 440/34
  A: 6/Penguin SSM (I × 6) − 1/40-mm AA − 1/20-mm AA − 2/533-mm TT for T-61 wire-guided torpedoes
  Electron Equipt: Radars: 2/Decca TM 1226   Sonar: Simrad SQ 30/SF
  M: 2 MTU 16V538 TB 92 diesels; 2 props; 7,340 hp

REMARKS: Four subcontracted to Westermöen, Alta. MSI-805 fire-control system, developed by Kongsberg, uses two Decca radars plus a TVT-300 electro-optical tracker and a laser range-finder. Will eventually have Penguin-II missiles.

◆ **6 Snögg class** Bldr: Båtservice Verft, Mandal, 1970-71

P 980	SNÖGG (ex-*Lyr*)	P 982	SNARR	P 984	KVIK
P 981	RAPP	P 983	RASK	P 985	KJAPP

Snarr   J.-C. Bellonne, 1974

  D: 115 tons (140 fl)   S: 36 kts   Dim: 36.53 × 6.3 × 1.65
  A: 4/Penguin SSM (I × 4) − 1/40-mm AA − 4/533-mm TT for T-61 wire-guided torpedoes   Man: 3 officers, 17 men   Range: 550/36
  M: 2 MTU 16V538 TB 92 diesels; 2 props; 7,200 hp

◆ **20 Storm class** Bldrs: P-963, P-966, P-969, P-972, P-975, and P-978: Westermöen, Mandal; Others: Bergens MV

		L			L			L
P 960	STORM	19-3-63	P 967	SKUDD	25-3-66	P 974	BROTT	27-1-67
P 961	BLINK	28-6-65	P 968	ARG	24-5-66	P 975	ODD	7-4-67
P 962	GLIMT	27-9-65	P 969	STEIL	20-9-66	P 976	PIL	29-3-67
P 963	SKJOLD	17-2-66	P 970	BRANN	3-7-66	P 977	BRASK	27-5-67
P 964	TRYGG	25-11-65	P 971	TROSS	29-9-66	P 978	ROKK	1-6-67
P 965	KJEKK	27-1-66	P 972	HVASS	20-12-66	P 979	GNIST	15-8-67
P 966	DJERV	28-4-66	P 973	TRAUST	18-11-66			

Gnist   R. Nerlich, 1974

  D: 100 tons (125 fl)   S: 37 kts   Dim: 36.53 × 6.3 × 1.55
  Man: 4 officers, 9 petty officers, 13 men   Range: 550/36
  A: 6/Penguin SSM (I × 6) − 1/76-mm − 1/40-mm AA
  Electron Equipt: Radars: 1/Decca TM 909, 1/HSA WM 26 fire-control
  M: Maybach MB 872A diesels; 2 props; 7,200 hp

REMARKS: Being backfitted with TVT-300 electro-optical tracker and laser range-finder, in a tub abaft the radar mast. Diesels are essentially the same as those in the *Hauk* and *Snögg* classes above. The number of missiles carried can be as high as six but, on occasion, only four are seen.

GUIDED-MISSILE PATROL BOATS (continued)

Hvass   1978

TORPEDO BOATS

◆ **15 Tjeld class** Bldr: Båtservice, Mandal

	In serv.			In serv.
P 345 TEIST	12-60		P 383 HVAL	3-64
P 347 LOM	4-61		P 384 LAKS	5-64
P 348 STEGG	6-61		P 385 KNURR	1966
P 350 FALK	9-61		P 387 LYR	1966
P 357 RAVN	12-61		P 388 GRIBB	3-62
P 380 SKREI	1962		P 389 GEIR	8-62
P 381 HAI	7-64		P 390 ERLE	6-62
P 382 SEL	5-63			

   D: 70 tons (82 fl)   **S:** 45 kts (40, cruising)   **Dim:** 24.5 × 7.5 × 1.95
   Man: 4 officers, 4 petty officers, 12 men   **Range:** 450/40, 600/25
   A: As a torpedo boat: 1/40-mm AA—1/20-mm AA—4/533-mm TT
         As a gunboat: 2/40-mm AA—2/533-mm TT
   M: 2 Napier-Deltic T18-37 turbo-charged diesels; 2 props; 6,280 hp
   Fuel: 10 tons

REMARKS: Designed by Jan H. Linge of Boat Service, Ltd., Oslo. Mahogany hull, engines and fittings imported from Great Britain. Two were delivered in 1962 to the
West German Navy, which later sold them to Turkey. Twenty-two were transferred

to the U.S.A., 1963-68. Six were built for Greece. Most, or all, of this class are in reserve, and the names of three (Tjeld, Hauk, and Skarv) have been used for new ships,
probably indicating that they have been, or soon will be, stricken.

MINE WARFARE SHIPS

◆ **2 Vidar-class minelayers** Bldr: Mjellem & Karlsen, Bergen

	Laid down	L	In serv.
N 52 VIDAR	1-3-76	18-3-77	21-10-77
N 53 VALE	1-2-76	5-8-77	10-2-78

Vidar   1978

   D: 1,500 tons (1,722 fl)   **S:** 15 kts   **Dim:** 64.8 (60.0 pp) × 12.0 × 4.0
   Man: 50 men   **Fuel:** 247 tons   **Electric:** 1,000 kw
   A: 2/40-mm AA (I × 2)—6/324-mm Mk 32 ASW TT (III × 2)—2/depth-charge racks—
         320 mines
   Electron Equipt: Radars: 2/Decca 1226   Sonar: . . .
   M: 2 Wichman 7AX diesels; 2 props; 4,200 hp

REMARKS: Capable of serving as minelayers (mines carried on three decks, automatic
hoist, three minelaying rails), torpedo-recovery ships, personnel and cargo transports,
fisheries-protection ships, and ASW escorts. Bow thruster fitted.

◆ **1 inshore mine-planter**

	Bldr	L
N 51 BORGEN	Marinens Hovedverft, Horten	29-4-60

   D: 282 tons (fl)   **S:** 9 kts   **Dim:** 31.28 × 8.0 × 3.35
   A: 2/20-mm AA (I × 2)—2 mine rails
   M: 2 GM 3-71 diesels; 2 Voith-Schneider cycloidal props; 330 hp

REMARKS: Patterned on the Swedish MUL-12 class. Designed to "plant" mines by crane.

◆ **1 prototype Swedish Gasten-class minesweeper** Bldr: Karlskrona, Sweden

   D: 120 tons (135 fl)   **S:** 11 kts   **Dim:** 23.0 × 6.6 × 2.0
   A: 1/40-mm AA   **M:** 2 diesels; 1 prop

REMARKS: Experimental plastic and fiberglass ship. May not have been completed.

MINE WARFARE SHIPS *(continued)*

◆ 10 U.S. Falcon-class coastal minesweepers

	In serv.
M 311 SAUDA (ex-MSC-102)	25-8-53
M 312 SIRA (ex-MSC-132)	28-11-55
M 313 TANA (ex-*Roeslaere*, ex-MSC-103)	9-53
M 314 ALTA (ex-*Arlon*, ex-MSC-104)	10-53
M 315 OGNA	5-3-55
M 316 VOSSO	16-3-55
M 317 GLOMMA (ex-*Bastogne*, ex-MSC-151)	12-53
M 331 TISTA	27-4-55
M 332 KVINA	12-7-55
M 334 UTLA	15-11-55

Bldrs: M-315, M-332, M-334: Båtservice Verft, Mandal
M-316: Skåluren, Rosendal
M-331: Forenede Båtbyggeri, Risŏr
M-311, M-313, M-314, M-317: Hodgdon Bros., Gowdy & Stevens, Boothbay, Maine
M-312: C. Hiltebrant DD, Kingston, New York

D: 300 tons (372 fl)   **S:** 13 kts (8, sweeping)   **Dim:** 43.0 × 7.95 × 2.55
Man: 38 men   **Range:** 2,500/10   **Fuel:** 40 tons
A: 1/12.7-mm machine gun — M-313: 2/20-mm AA
Electron Equipt: Radars: 1/Decca 707 (M-313: Decca 1226)
Sonar: 1/UQS 1 (M-313: 1/193M)
M: 2 GM 8-268A diesels; 2 props; 1,200 hp

REMARKS: The *Tana, Alta,* and *Glomma* were transferred by Belgium in 1966 in ex-change for two ocean minesweepers, the *Lagen* and *Namsen.* In 1977, the *Tana* was converted to a prototype minehunter, with British type 193M sonar, two PAP-104 remote-controlled minehunting devices, and divers' facilities in a large deckhouse aft. She was armed with 2/20-mm Rheinmetal AA guns (I × 2), which may be back-fitted into the others. At the waterline, across the stern, she has a platform for diver-recovery; this extends her overall length by more than one meter.

AMPHIBIOUS WARFARE SHIPS

◆ 5 Reinøysund-class utility landing craft   Bldr: Mjellem & Karlsen, Bergen, 1972-73

L 4502 REINØYSUND	L 4504 MAURSUND	L 4506 BORGSUND
L 4503 SØRØYSUND	L 4505 ROTSUND	

D: 596 tons (fl)   **S:** 11 kts   **Dim:** 51.4 × 10.3 × 1.85
A: 3/20-mm (I × 3) — 4/12.7-mm machine guns — rails for 120 mines
M: 2 MTU diesels; 2 props; . . . hp   **Man:** 2 officers, 7 men

REMARKS: Double-folding bow ramp door. Cargo capacity: 5 Leopard tanks, 80-180 men. Similar to class below, but superstructure is farther forward.

◆ 2 Kvalsund-class utility landing craft   Bldr: Mjellem & Karlsen, Bergen, 1970

L 4500 KVALSUND	L 4501 RAFTSUND

D: 590 tons (fl)   **S:** 11 kts   **Dim:** 50.0 × 10.2 × 1.8
A: 2/20-mm AA — rails for 120 mines   **Man:** 2 officers, 7 men
M: 2 MTU diesels; 2 props; . . . hp

REMARK: Cargo capacity: 5 Leopard tanks, 80-180 men.

Kvalsund — wearing old number   1971

AUXILIARY SHIPS

◆ 1 logistic-support ship   Bldr: Horten SY

	Laid down	L	In serv.
A 530 HORTEN	28-1-77	12-8-77	9-6-78

Horten   1978

D: 2,500 tons (fl)   **S:** 16.5 kts   **Dim:** 87.0 (82.0 pp) × 13.7 × . . .
A: 2/40-mm AA (I × 2) — mines   **Man:** 86 men
M: 2 Wichman 7AX diesels; 2 props; 4,200 hp

REMARKS: Used to support submarines and small combatants. Can accommodate up to 190 additional personnel. Helicopter deck. Bow thruster.

◆ 1 oceanographic-research ship   Bldr: Orens MV, Trondheim, 1960

H. U. SVERDRUP (ex-AGOR-2)

D: 400 tons   **S:** 11.5 kts   **Dim:** 38.9 × 7.6 × 4.0
M: 1 Wichman diesel; 1 prop; 600 hp   **Man:** 10 men + 9 scientists

AUXILIARY SHIPS *(continued)*

REMARKS: Strictly speaking, not naval, because she operates for the Norwegian Defense Research Establishment and has a civilian crew. Trawler hull. Purchase and outfitting financed by the U.S.A. under the Offshore Procurement Program.

◆ **1 royal yacht** Bldr: Camper & Nicholson's, Gosport, G.B.

A 533 NORGE (ex-*Philante*)

Norge   1971

> D: 1,686 tons   S: 14 kts   Dim: 76.27 × 8.53 × 4.65
> M: 2 8-cyl. diesels; 2 props; 3,000 hp

REMARKS: Launched 17-2-37 and used by the Royal Navy as an ASW escort from 1940 to 1943, then as a training ship. Purchased by Norway in 1947. Displacement listed is in Thames Yacht Measurement.

SERVICE CRAFT

◆ **1 torpedo-recovery and oil-spill cleanup ship** Bldr: Fjellstrand, Hardinger

VSD 1 VERNØY

> D: 150 grt   S: 12 kts   Dim: 31.3 × 6.76 × 2.0
> M: 2 MWM diesels; 2 Schöttel props; . . . hp

REMARK: In service 10-78.

◆ **7 Torpen-class support tenders**

	Bldr	In serv.
VSD 4 TORPEN	Båtservice, Mandal	12-77
ØSD 2 WISTING	Voldnes, Fosnavåg	1-78
TSD 5 TAUTRA	Båtservice, Mandal	2-78
NSD 35 ROTVAER	Båtservice, Mandal	3-78
RSD 23 FJØLØY	Voldnes, Fosnavåg	4-78
HSD 15 KRØTTØY	Voldnes, Fosnavag	6-78
TRSD 4 KARLSØY	P. Høivolds, Kristinstad	7-78

> D: 215 tons (300 fl)   S: 11 kts   Dim: 29.0 × 6.4 × 2.57
> A: 1/12.7-mm machine gun   Man: 6 men + 100 passengers
> Range: 1,200/11
> M: 1 MWM TBD 601-6K diesel; 1 controllable-pitch prop; 530 hp   Fuel: 11 tons

REMARKS: Basically similar craft tailored to a variety of duties, including logistics support, ammunition transport, personnel transport, and divers' support.

◆ **2 navigational training craft** Bldr: Fjellstrand, Omastrand

VSD 6 KVARVAN   VSD 2 MARSTEINEN

> D: 40 tons   S: 22 kts   Dim: 23.2 × 5.0 × 1.1
> M: 2 GM 12V71 diesels; 2 props; 1,800 hp   Man: 5 men + 8 cadets

REMARKS: In service 1-78. Aluminum construction. For use at the naval academy.

◆ **2 tenders for combat divers** Bldr: Nielsen, Harstad

SKV 10 DRAUG   SKV 11 SARPEN

> D: 250 tons   S: 12 kts   Dim: 29.0 × 6.7 × 2.5
> M: 1 diesel; 1 prop; 530 hp

REMARK: In service in 1972.

COAST GUARD (KYSTVAKT)

The Norwegian Coast Guard was established in 1976 to perform fisheries-protection duties, patrol the waters in the vicinity of offshore oil rigs, and maintain surveillance over the 200-nautical-mile economic zone. To begin with, six former naval fisheries-protection ships were transferred to it; then seven miscellaneous seagoing trawlers and oilfield-supply ships were leased from their owners. The latter will presumably be relinquished when the new-construction ships begun in 1978 are completed. The Coast Guard will also operate three P-3B Orion long-range reconnaissance aircraft and six WG-13 Lynx helicopters, the latter to be delivered for service aboard ships, beginning in 1981.

PATROL SHIPS

◆ **4 (+3) new construction**

	Bldr	Laid down	L	In serv.
W 318 N . . .	Bergens MV	9-78	. . .	. . .
W 319 N . . .	Horten SY	1-79	. . .	. . .
W 320 N . . .	. . .	. . .	. . .	. . .
W 321 N . . .	. . .	. . .	. . .	. . .

> D: 1,860 tons (2,800 fl)   S: 23 kts   Dim: 105.0 × 13.8 × 4.2
> A: 1/57-mm Bofors AA − 4/20-mm AA − 1/WG-13 Lynx helicopter
> Electron Equipt: Radar: 1/Plessey AWS 4   Sonar: . . .
> M: Diesels; 2 props; . . . hp   Man: 46 men   Range: 4,000/14

REMARKS: Program delayed by design changes and lack of funding; three additional units have had to be deferred. The first was to have been delivered in 11-80, with the fourth entering service in late 1982. One of the first four will be reinforced for service in Arctic waters and will displace 2,920 tons. Intended to serve as ASW escorts in wartime, provision being made for the installation of 6/324-mm Mk-32 ASW torpedo tubes (III × 2) and Penguin anti-ship missiles.

CHARTERED PATROL SHIPS

◆ **1 former stern-haul trawler** Bldr: Rickmers Werft, West Germany, 1962

W 311 KR. TØNDER

> D: 984 grt   S: 11 kts   Dim: 67.08 (58.73 pp) × 9.63 × 5.11
> A: 1/40-mm AA   Man: . . .
> M: 1 Klöckner-Humboldt-Deutz 8-cyl. diesel, electric drive; 1 prop; 1,665 hp

CHARTERED PATROL SHIPS *(continued)*

Kr. Tønder 1977

REMARKS: Chartered in 1977 from A/S Nordtrål. Ice-strengthened hull. Bow thruster.

◆ **1 former purse seiner**   Bldr: Hall-Russell, Aberdeen, Scotland

W 312 SØRFOLD (ex-*Olafur Jöhannesson*, ex-*Andvan*)

> D: 773 grt   S: 12 kts   Dim: 61.37 (55.06 pp) × 9.2 × 4.88
> A: 1/40-mm AA   Man: . . .   Fuel: 80 tons   Electric: 175 kw
> M: 1 Werkspoor 8-cyl. diesel; 1 controllable-pitch prop; 2,660 hp

REMARKS: In service 3-51. Chartered from Oddvar Jöhannesson in 1977. Side thrusters forward and aft.

◆ **1 former trawler**   Bldr: Kvina Verft/Flekkefjord MV

W 313 MØGSTERFJORD

> D: 768 grt   S: 12 kts   Dim: 60.86 (55.01 pp) × 12.0 × 3.9
> A: 1/40-mm AA   Man: . . .   Electric: 786 kw
> M: 1 Wichman 9-cyl. diesel; 1 prop; 2,500 hp

REMARKS: In service 11-55. Chartered from Kommandittelskapel Møgster in 1977. Bow thruster.

◆ **1 former purse seiner**   Bldr: Beliard, Crighton & Cie., France, 1955

W 314 STÅLBAS (ex-*Trålbas*, ex-*Cdt. Charcot*, ex-*Jean Charcot*)

> D: 498 grt   S: . . .   Dim: 58.76 × 9.41 × 4.51
> A: 1/40-mm AA   Man: . . .
> M: 1 Klöckner-Humboldt-Deutz 8-cyl. diesel; 1 prop; 1,500 hp

REMARK: Side thrusters fitted, forward and aft.

◆ **1 former factory stern trawler**   Bldr: Lübecker Flender-Werke, West Germany

W 315 NORVIKING (ex-*Vikings*)

> D: 1,798 grt   S: 15 kts   Dim: 80.05 (70.0 pp) × 12.52 × 5.0
> A: 1/40-mm AA   Man: . . .   Fuel: 590 tons   Electric: 800 kw

> M: 3 M.A. N. 12-cyl. diesels, electric drive (2 motors); 1 prop; 2,900 hp

REMARKS: In service 5-65. Built as a packing ship for processing fish fillets. Chartered in 1977.

◆ **1 former whale-catcher**   Bldr: Fredrikstad MV, 1950

W 316 VOLSTAD JR. (ex-XIV)

> D: 617 grt   S: . . .   Dim: 51.39 (45.32 pp) × 9.05 × 5.67
> A: 1/40-mm AA   Man: . . .   Electric: 224 kw
> M: 1 Klöchner-Humboldt-Deutz NE-66 8-cyl. diesel; 1 controllable-pitch prop; 1,200 hp

REMARKS: Chartered from Einar Volstad Partrederi in 1977. Built as a side-haul trawler, converted to a whaler in 1966, and well deck filled in.

◆ **1 former oilfield-supply ship**   Bldr: Belsønes Verft, Molde, Norway, 1973

W 317 RIG TUGGER

Rig Tugger 1977

> D: 498 grt   S: 15 kts   Dim: 57.61 (50.98 pp) × 11.03 × 4.55
> A: 1/40-mm AA   Man: . . .   Electric: 399 kw
> M: 2 Polar 12-cyl. diesels; 2 controllable-pitch props; . . . hp

REMARKS: Chartered from Sandøy Supply A/S Co. in 1977. Powerful tug- and pipe-carrier. 820 dwt/195 nrt. Ice-strengthened hull.

◆ **1 former naval fisheries-protection ship**   Bldr: Mjellem & Karlsen, Bergen

W 300 NORNEN

> D: 1,060 tons (fl)   S: 17 kts   Dim: 61.5 × 10.0 × 3.8
> A: 1/76-mm Mk 26 DP   Man: . . .   M: 4 diesels; 1 prop; 3,700 hp

REMARKS: Launched 20-8-62. Considerably altered, 1976-77: bridge enlarged, stack heightened, mast moved aft, hull side openings plated up, two new radars added, gun enclosed

◆ **2 former naval fisheries-protection ships**

W 301 FARM (ex-A-532)   W 302 HEIMDAL (ex-A-534)

Bldrs: W-301: Ankerlokken Verft, Fredrikstad; W-302: Bolsones Verft, Molde

NORWAY *(continued)*
CHARTERED PATROL SHIPS *(continued)*

Farm 1978

 D: 488 grt (600 fl) **S:** 16.5 kts **Dim:** 54.28 (49.0 pp) × 8.2 × 3.2
 A: 1/76-mm Mk 26 DP **Electric:** 150 kva
 M: 2 Wichman 9ACAT diesels; 2 controllable-pitch props, 2,400 hp

◆ **3 former naval fisheries-protection ships** Bldr: Netherlands, 1957

W 303 ANDENES W 304 SENJA W 305 NORDKAPP

 D: 500 tons (fl) **S:** 16 kts **Dim:** 56.7 × 9.45 × 4.9
 A: 1/76-mm Mk 26 DP **Man:** 29 men
 M: 1 M.A.N. diesel; 1 controllable-pitch prop; 2,300 hp

REMARKS: Modified whale-hunters, purchased in 1965. Considerably modified in the early 1970s: full forecastle added, pilothouse lowered one deck, new foremast, and gun enclosed.

OMAN

PERSONNEL: 600 officers and men
MERCHANT MARINE (1978): 11 ships—5,630 grt

CORVETTE

	Bldr	In serv.
AL SAID	Brooke Marine Ltd., Lowestoft, G.B.	1971

Al Said

 D: 785 tons (930 fl) **S:** 17 kts **Dim:** 57.4 × 10.7 × 3.05
 A: 1/40-mm AA **Man:** 11 officers, 23 men + 37 passengers
 M: 2 Paxman 12-YJCM diesels; 1,500 rpm; 2 props; 3,350 hp

REMARKS: Also used as a yacht. Helicopter deck added on first refit. Carries one Fairey Spear-class patrol craft: **D:** 10 tons **S:** 30 kts **Dim:** 9.1 × 2.75 × 0.84

PATROL BOATS

◆ **6 37.5-meter class** Bldr: Brooke Marine Ltd. Lowestoft, G.B., 1972-76

	In serv.		In serv.		In serv.
B 2 AL MANSUR	26-3-73	B 4 AL WAFI	24-3-77	B 6 AL AUL	8-77
B 3 AL NEJAH	13-5-73	B 5 AL FULK	24-3-77	B 7 AL JASBBAR	8-77

Al Fulk 1977

 D: 166 tons (fl) **S:** 25 kts **Dim:** 37.5 × 6.86 × 1.78
 Man: 27 men **Range:** 3,250/12
 A: B-2, B-3: 2/MM 38 Exocet SSM (I × 2)—2/40-mm Bofors-Breda AA (II × 1)
    B-4 to B-7: 1/76-mm OTO Melara DP—1/20-mm AA—2/7.62-mm machine guns
     (I × 2)

OMAN (continued)

PATROL BOATS (continued)

> **Electron Equipt:** Radar: 1/Decca TM-916
> **M:** 2 Paxman Ventura 16 RP-200 diesels; 2 props; 4,800 hp

REMARKS: B-1 to B-3 were rearmed with Exocet missiles and Sperry Sea Archer fire-control systems by builders, 1978-79. *Al Bushra* (B-1) were lost 11-78 when she was washed off the delivery ship while in the Bay of Biscay. A replacement will probably be ordered. B-4 to B-7 carry 130 rounds of 76-mm ammunition.

◆ **2 ex-Dutch Wildervank-class former coastal minesweepers**

P 1 AL NASSIRI (ex-*Axel*, M-808)   P 2 AL SALIHI (ex-*Aalsmeer*, M-811)

> **D:** 373 tons (417 fl)   **S:** 14 kts   **Dim:** 46.63 × 8.78 × 2.28
> **A:** 3/40-mm AA (I × 3)   **Electron Equipt:** Radar: 1/Decca TM-916
> **M:** 2 Werkspoor diesels; 2 props; 2,500 hp   **Man:** 40 men

REMARKS: Launched in 1955. Purchased in 1974, air-conditioned, and fitted as patrol boats by van der Giessen de Noord. Similar to the Birtish "-ton" class. Their minesweeping equipment has been removed and a third 40-mm AA placed on the main deck aft.

PATROL CRAFT Police-subordinated

◆ **4 fiberglass-hulled**   Bldr: Vosper Thornycroft, Singapore

HARAS 1   HARAS 2   HARAS 3   HARAS 4

> **D:** 45 tons (fl)   **S:** 24.5 kts   **Dim:** 22.9 × 6.0 × 1.5
> **A:** 2/20-mm AA   **Man:** 11 men   **Range:** 600/20, 1,000/11
> **M:** 2 Caterpillar D348 diesels; 2 props; 1,840 hp

REMARK: In service, 22-12-75.

◆ **3 customs launches**   Bldr: Cheverton, Cowes, G.B.

W 1   W 2   W 3

> **D:** 3.3 tons (fl)   **S:** 15 kts   **Dim:** 8.23 × 2.74 × 0.81
> **M:** 1 diesel; 150 hp

REMARK: In service, 4-75.

AMPHIBIOUS WARFARE SHIPS

◆ **1 for logistic support**

	Laid down	L	In serv.
AL MUNASSIR	4-7-77	25-7-78	3-4-79

> **D:** 2,000 tons (fl)   **S:** 12 kts   **Dim:** 84.0 (81.25 pp) 15.0 × 2.15 (max.)
> **Man:** 7 officers, 38 men, 188 troops   **Range:** 2,000/12
> **A:** 1/76-mm OTO Melara DP–2/20-mm AA (I × 2)
> **Electron Equipt:** Radar: 1/Decca TM 1229
> **M:** 2 Mirrlees-Blackstone ESL8MGR diesels; 2 controllable-pitch props; 2,400 hp

REMARKS: Cargo: 550 tons of stores or 8 heavy tanks. Has bow doors and ramp for beaching. Large helicopter deck aft can accommodate Westland Sea King or Commando helicopters and is spanned by a 16-ton-capacity traveling crane. Unusually bluff-bowed hull form. Sperry Sea Archer optical fire-control director.

◆ **5 utility landing craft**   Bldr: Impala Marine, Twickenham, G.B., 1977

KHASAB   KUMZAR   N . . .   N . . .   N . . .

> **D:** 122 grt   **S:** 9 kts   **Dim:** 25.6 × 7.6 × . . .
> **M:** 2 Caterpillar 3406 diesels; 2 props; 520 hp

◆ **2 75-foot Loadmaster-class landing craft**   Bldr: Cheverton, Cowes, G.B.

AL SANSOOR   KINZEER AL BAHR

> **D:** 64 tons (130 fl)   **S:** 8.75 kts   **Dim:** 22.86 × 6.1 × 1.07 (max.)
> **M:** 2 diesels; 2 props; 300 hp

REMARK: In service, 1-75.

◆ **1 45-foot Loadmaster-class landing craft**   Bldr: Cheverton, Cowes, G.B., 1975

SULHAFA AL BAHR

> **D:** 45 tons   **S:** 8.5 kts   **Dim:** 13.7 × 4.6 × 0.9
> **M:** 2 Perkins 4-236 diesels; 2 props; 240 hp

AUXILIARY SHIPS

◆ **1 supply ship**   Bldr: Conoship, Groningen, Netherlands

AL SULTANA

> **D:** 900 tons (1,380 dwt)   **S:** 11 kts   **Dim:** 65.4 × 10.7 × 4.2
> **M:** 1 Mirrlees-Blackstone diesel; 1,150 hp

REMARKS: Launched 18-5-75, in service 4-6-75. Traveling crane serves all holds.

◆ **1 training ship**

DHOFAR

> **D:** 1,500 tons   **S:** 10.5 kts   **Dim:** 66.8 × 10.4 × 4.0
> **M:** 1 M.A.K. diesel; 1 prop; 1,500 hp   **Man:** 22 men

REMARK: Ex-cargo ship.

◆ **1 sail training craft**

YOUTH OF OMAN

REMARK: Purchased in 1978.

PAKISTAN

PERSONNEL: Approximately 11,000 men

MERCHANT MARINE (1978): 80 ships—442,401 grt

NAVAL AVIATION. The naval air arm consists of: 3 Atlantic patrol aircraft, 6 Sea King helicopters (in 1976) armed with AM-39 anti-ship missiles, 4 Alouette-III helicopters, and 2 Cessna liaison aircraft.

WARSHIPS IN SERVICE AND UNDER CONSTRUCTION AS OF 1 JANUARY 1980

	L	Tons (Surfaced)	Main armament
◆ 5 (+1) submarines			
1 (+1) AGOSTA	1977-79	1,490	4/550-mm TT
4 DAPHNÉ	1968-70	869	12/550-mm TT
◆ 1 training cruiser			
1 MODIFIED DIDO	1942	5,900	8/133.5-mm DP, 6/533-mm TT
◆ 6 destroyers			
2 GEARING	1945	2,425	4/127-mm DP, 6/324-mm ASW TT
1 BATTLE	1945	2,325	4/114-mm DP, 8/533-mm TT
3 CLASS C	1944-45	1,710	3/114-mm DP, 4/533-mm TT
◆ 1 frigate			
1 CLASS O	1941	1,800	2/102-mm DP, 4/533-mm TT

◆ 19 patrol and torpedo boats

SUBMARINES

◆ 1 (+1) French Agosta class Bldr: Dubigeon, Nantes

	Laid down	L	In serv.
S 135 HASHMAT (ex-*Astraut*)	15-9-76	14-12-77	1979
S 136 HURMAT (ex-*Adventurous*)	. . .	3-79	1980

D: 1,230 tons, 1,490 surfaced, 1,740 submerged   **S:** 20 kts (submerged)
Dim: 67.57 × 6.8 × 5.4   **Man:** 55 men
Range: 8,500/9 (snorkel), 178/3.5 (submerged)
A: 4/550-mm TT, fwd (20 torpedoes)   **Fuel:** 200 tons
M: 2 SEMT-Pielstick A16 PA 4 185 diesels, electric drive (1 3,500-kw motor); 1 prop; 4,600 hp; 1 30-hp cruise motor

REMARKS: Originally ordered for South Africa but sale canceled in 1977 by arms embargo and completion slowed. Sold to Pakistan in 11-78. Very quiet, highly automated submarines.

◆ 4 French Daphné class

	Bldr	Laid down	L	In serv.
S 131 HANGOR	Arsenal de Brest	1-12-67	30-6-69	12-1-70
S 132 SHUSHUK	C. N. Ciotat, Le Trait	1-12-67	30-7-69	12-1-70
S 133 MANGRO	C. N. Ciotat, Le Trait	8-7-68	7-2-70	8-8-70
S 134 GHAZI (ex-*Cachalote*)	Dubigeon, Normandy	27-10-66	16-2-68	25-1-69

D: 700 tons, 869 surfaced, 1,043 submerged   **S:** 13.5/16 kts
Dim: 57.75 × 6.75 × 4.56   **Man:** 5 officers, 45 men
A: 12/550-mm TT (8 fwd, 4 aft), no reloads

Shushuk   J.-C. Bellonne, 1970

Mangro   1970

Electron Equipt: Radar: DRUA 31 (on periscope with passive ECM)
Sonar: DUUA−1 active, DSUV passive

REMARKS: S-134 purchased in 12-75 from Portugal. S-131 sank the Indian frigate *Khukri* in 1971.

◆ 5 SX-404-class midget submarines Bldr: Cosmos, Livorno, Italy

D: 40 tons, 70 submerged   **S:** 11/6.5 kts   **Dim:** 16.0 × 1.8 × . . .
A: 2/533-mm torpedoes or 6-8 mines   **Man:** 4 men
Range: 1,200/11 surfaced, 60/6.5 submerged

REMARKS: Used for the transport of up to twelve raiders. A sixth sank 27-12-76 following an accident at sea.

CRUISER

◆ 1 British modified Dido class

	Bldr	Laid down	L	In serv.
84 BABUR (ex-*Diadem*)	Hawthorn, Leslie & Co.	15-11-39	26-8-42	6-1-44

CRUISER (continued)

D: 5,900 tons (7,560 fl)   **S:** 18-20 kts
Dim: 165.05 (154.23 pp) × 15.7 × 5.7
Man: Peacetime: 590 men   **Range:** 3,800/20, 7,400/12
A: 8/133.5-mm DP (II × 4)−12/40-mm (II × 3, I × 6)−6/533-mm TT (III × 2)−
     4/47-mm (saluting battery)
Armor: Belt: 52-76   Deck: 52   Turret: 25   Bridge: 25
Boilers: 4 Admiralty, three-drum   **Fuel:** 1,100 tons
M: 4 sets Parsons GT; 4 props; 62,000 hp (when new)

REMARKS: Purchased 29-2-56. Adapted for use as training cruiser during refit in 1961. In poor condition and no longer able to make original speed of 32 kts. Now used primarily as a floating antiaircraft battery.

DESTROYERS

◆ **2 (+4) ex-U.S. Gearing-class, FRAM-I**   Bldr: Federal SB & DD Co., Newark, N.J.

	Laid down	L	In serv.
165 TARIQ (ex-*Wiltsie*, DD-716)	13-3-45	31-8-45	12-1-46
166 TAIMUR (ex-*Epperson*, DD-719)	20-6-45	29-12-45	19-3-49

D: 2,425 tons (3,500 fl)   **S:** 30 kts   **Dim:** 119.0 × 12.45 × 5.8 (max.)
A: 4/127-mm DP (II × 2)−1/Asroc ASW system (VIII × 1)−6/324-mm Mk 32 ASW
     TT (III × 2)
Electron Equipt: Radars: 1/SPS 10, 1/SPS 40, 1/Mk 25
                 Sonar: SQS 23
Boilers: 4 Babcock & Wilcox, 39.8 kg/cm² pressure−superheat 454°C
M: 2 sets GE GT; 2 props; 60,000 hp   **Fuel:** 600 tons

REMARKS: Sold to Pakistan 29-4-77, then extensively overhauled at Puget Sound Navy Yard, No. 165 being completed 2-6-78, and No. 166 on 16-2-78. As many as four more units may be transferred 1980-81.

◆ **1 ex-British Battle class**

	Bldr	Laid down	L	In serv.
161 BADR (ex-*Gabbard*)	Swan Hunter	2-2-44	16-3-45	10-12-46

D: 2,325 tons (3,360 fl)   **S:** 31 kts   **Dim:** 115.32 (108.2 pp) × 12.95 × 4.1
Man: 300 men   **Range:** 6,000/20   **Fuel:** 680 tons

Badr   1974

A: 4/114-mm DP (II × 2)−8/40-mm AA (II × 2, I × 4)−8/533-mm TT (IV × 2)−1/Mk 4
     Squid ASW mortar (III × 1)
Electron Equipt: Radars: 1/975, 1/293, 1/Marconi air-search, 1/275 fire-control
                  Sonars: 1/170, 1/174
M: 2 Parsons GT; 2 props; 50,000 hp   **Boilers:** 2 Admiralty, three-drum

REMARKS: Transferred 29-2-56. Sister ship *Khaibar* was sunk during the Indo-Pakistani conflict, 1971.

◆ **3 ex-British C class**

	Laid down	L	In serv.
160 ALAMGIR (ex-*Creole*)	3-8-44	22-11-45	14-10-46
162 JAHANGIR (ex-*Crispin*)	1-2-44	23-6-45	10-7-46
164 SHAH JAHAN (ex-DD-962, ex-*Charity*)	9-7-43	30-11-44	19-11-45

     Bldrs: No. 160, No. 162: J. Samuel White, Cowes; No. 164: J. I. Thornycroft, Woolston

Shah Jahan

D: 1,710 tons (2,500 fl)   **S:** 31 kts   **Dim:** 110.55 (106.07 pp) × 10.88 × 3.8
Man: 200 men   **Range:** 1,000/30, 2,800/20   **Fuel:** 580 tons
A: 3/114-mm DP (I × 3)−6/40-mm AA (II × 1, I × 4)−4/533-mm TT (IV × 1)−
     2/Squid ASW mortars (III × 2)
Electron Equipt: Radars: 1/975, 1/293, 1/275 fire-control
                   Sonars: 1/174, 1/170
M: 2 sets Parsons GT; 2 props; 40,000 hp   **Boilers:** 2 Admiralty, three-drum

REMARKS: From two groups within the C class, CH and CR. Minor differences. No. 164 was purchased by the U.S. from Great Britain in 1958 (hence DD-962 hull number), then turned over to Pakistan on 16-12-58. The other two were turned over directly in 1956 and then modernized with U.S. funds.

FRIGATE

◆ **1 British O-class former destroyer**   Bldr: John Brown, Clydebank

	Laid down	L	In serv.
260 TIPPU SULTAN (ex-*Onslow*)	1-7-40	31-3-41	8-10-41

D: 1,800 tons (2,300 fl)   **S:** 31 kts
Dim: 105.15 (103.2 wl) × 10.67 × 4.7 (props)
Range: 1,700/20, 2,700/12   **Fuel:** 472 tons
A: 2/102-mm Mk 19 DP (II × 1)−5/40-mm AA (II × 1, I × 3)−4/533-mm TT (IV × 1)−
     2/Squid ASW mortars

FRIGATE (continued)

Tippu Sultan 1973

    Electron Equipt: Radars: 1/293, 1/975 Sonars: 1/174, 1/170
    M: 2 sets Parsons GT; 2 props; 40,000 hp   **Boilers:** 2 Admiralty, three-drum

REMARKS: Transferred 30-9-49 and rebuilt as a Type-16 frigate, 1958-59. Sister *Tughril* (261) was disarmed in 1977 and is used for instructing midshipmen from the naval academy; she no longer gets under way. Sister *Terig* was stricken in 1959.

PATROL BOATS

◆ **2 Hainan class** Bldr: People's Republic of China

155 BALUCHISTAN   159 SIND

Baluchistan 1978

    D: 360 tons (400 fl)   **S:** 28 kts   **Dim:** 60.0 × 7.4 × 2.1
    Man: 60 men   **Range:** 1,000/10
    A: 4/57-mm AA (II × 2)−4/25-mm AA (II × 2)−4/RBU-1200 ASW rocket launchers
        (V × 4)−2/depth-charge throwers−2/depth-charge racks−mines
    Electron Equipt: Radar: 1/Pot Head   Sonar: . . .
    M: 4 diesels; 4 props; 8,000 hp

REMARKS: Transferred in 1976. Three more units were expected but have not materialized. Very primitive ships.

◆ **12 Shanghai-II class** Bldr: People's Republic of China

141 LAHORE	145 PISHIN	149 SAHIVAL
142 MULTAN	146 KALAT	150 BANNU
143 GUILGIT	147 SUKKUR	151 LARKANA
144 MARDAN	148 QUETTA	152 BAHAWALPUR

Quetta 1974

    D: 120 tons (155 fl)   **S:** 28 kts   **Dim:** 38.8 × 5.4 × 1.6
    A: 4/37-mm AA (II × 2)−4/25-mm AA (II × 2)−mines   **Man:** 28 men
    Electron Equipt: Radar: 1/Pot Head
    M: 4 MSO diesels; 4 props; 4,800 hp

REMARKS: Eight transferred in 1972, four in 1973. Very primitive ships.

◆ **1 10-foot class** Bldr: Brooke Marine, Lowestoft, 1965

140 RAJSHAHI

    D: 115 tons (143 fl)   **S:** 24 kts   **Dim:** 32.62 (30.48 pp) × 6.1 × 1.55
    A: 2/40-mm AA (I × 2)   **M:** 2 MTU 12V538 diesels; 2 props; 3,400 hp

REMARKS: Almost worn out. Welded construction, light metal used in the superstructure. Sister ships *Jessore*, *Comilla*, and *Sylhet* were sunk during the Indo-Pakistani conflict, 1971.

TORPEDO BOATS

◆ **4 Huchwan-class hydrofoils** Bldr: People's Republic of China

HDF 01   HDF 02   HDF 03   HDF 04

    D: 39 tons   **S:** 54 kts
    Dim: 21.8 × 4.9 (7.5 over foils) × 1.0 (0.31 foilborne)
    A: 4/14.5-mm AA (II × 2)−2/533-mm TT

HDF-03 1973

TORPEDO BOATS (*continued*)

Electron Equipt: Radar: 1/Skin Head
M: 3 M50F diesels; 3 props; 3,600 hp

REMARK: Maintained in land storage to prevent corrosion.

MINE WARFARE SHIPS

◆ **7 ex-U.S. coastal minesweepers** Bldrs: Various

Ex-MSC-289 class:

	In serv.			In serv.
161 MOMIN (ex-MSC-293)	7-62	167 MOSHAL (ex-MSC-294)		6-63

Ex-Falcon class:

	In serv.
160 MAHMOOD (ex-MSC-267)	4-57
162 MURABAK (ex-MSC-262)	1-57
164 MUJAHID (ex-MSC-261)	10-56
165 MUKHTAR (ex-MSC-274)	7-59
166 MUNSIF (ex-MSC-273)	6-59

Mukhtar   1974

D: 320 tons (372 fl)   **S:** 13 kts (8, sweeping)   **Dim:** 43.0 × 7.95 × 2.55
A: 4/23-mm AA ZSO-23 (IV × 1)   **Man:** 39 men   **Range:** 2,500/10
Electron Equipt: Radar: 1/Decca 45   Sonar: UQS 1D
M: 2 GM 8-268A diesels; 2 props; 1,200 hp

REMARKS: Nos. 161 and 167 have low bridges, the others have high, open bridges. Wooden hulls. All built under the Military Assistance Program

AUXILIARY SHIPS

◆ **1 hydrographic ship** Bldr: Smith's Dock, G.B.

	Laid down	L	In serv.
262 ZULFIQUAR (ex-Indian *Dhanush*, ex-British *Deveron*)	18-6-42	12-10-42	2-3-43

D: 1,370 tons (2,100 fl)   **S:** 19 kts   **Dim:** 91.84 × 11.17 × 4.34
Man: 150 men   **Range:** 7,500/15, 11,900/10   **Fuel:** 646 tons

A: 1/102-mm DP—2/40-mm AA (I × 2)   **Boilers:** 2 Admiralty, three-drum
M: 2 sets triple-expansion; 2 props; 5,500 hp

REMARKS: A former River-class frigate transferred to India during World War II and to Pakistan after the war. Very little altered from frigate configuration; charthouse and 2/40-mm antiaircraft mounts in place of after 102-mm gun.

◆ **1 ex-U.S. T-2-class replenishment oiler** Bldr: Marinship Corp., Sausalito, Calif.

41 DACCA (ex-*Mission Santa Clara*, TAO-132)

Dacca—with **Hangor** alongside   1975

D: 5,730 tons light (22,380 fl)   **S:** 15 kts   **Dim:** 159.56 × 20.73 × 9.4
A: 6/40-mm AA (I × 6)   **Man:** 15 officers, 145 men   **Fuel:** 1,300 tons
Electron Equipt: Radar: 1/RCA CRM-NIA-75   **Electric:** 1,150 kw
Boilers: 2 Combustion Engineering "D"; 42 kg/cm² pressure—superheat 440°C
M: 1 set GE FT, electric drive; 1 prop; 10,000 hp

REMARKS: In service 21-6-44. Loaned 17-1-63, after conversion to permit under-way replenishment alongside, one station each side. Bought outright 31-5-74. Cargo: 15,300 tons

◆ **1 ex-U.S. Cherokee-class ocean tug** Bldr: Commercial Iron Works, Portland, Ore.

	Laid down	L	In serv.
42 MADADGAR (ex-*Yuma*, ATF-94)	13-2-43	17-7-43	31-8-43

D: 1,325 tons (1,675 fl)   **S:** 16.5 kts   **Dim:** 62.48 (59.44 pp) × 11.73 × 4.67
Man: 85 men   **Electric:** 260 kw   **Fuel:** 295 tons
A: 2/40-mm AA (I × 2)
M: 4 GM 12-278 diesels, electric drive; 1 prop; 3,000 hp

REMARK: Employed as a salvage and rescue tug.

◆ **1 large harbor tug** Bldr: Worstd Dutmer, Meppel, Netherlands

RUSTOM

D: 530 tons (fl)   **S:** 9.5 kts   **Dim:** 32.0 × 9.1 × 3.3
Man: 21 men   **Range:** 3,000/8   **M:** 1 Crossley diesel; 1 prop; 1,000 hp

REMARK: Launched 29-11-55.

◆ **2 small harbor tugs**

GAMA (ex-YTL-754)   BHOLU (ex-YTL-755)

PAKISTON (continued)

AUXILIARY SHIPS (continued)

REMARKS: Built in Italy under the U.S. Offshore Procurement Program, and completed in 1958. 300 hp.

◆ **1 harbor oiler** Bldr: Trieste, Italy

46 ATTOCK (ex-U.S. YO-249)

D: 600 tons (1,225 fl) **S:** 8 kts **Dim:** 54.0 × 9.8 × 4.6
A: 2/20-mm AA (I × 2) **M:** 1 diesel; 800 hp

REMARKS: Built under the U.S. Offshore Procurement Program, and completed in 5-60. Cargo: 6,500 barrels of liquid.

◆ **1 water tanker** Bldr: Italy, 1957

15 ZUM ZUM

REMARK: Characteristics very similar to those of small oiler *Attock* above.

◆ **1 U.S. ARD-2-class floating dry dock**

PESHAWAR (ex-ARD-6)

Dim: 148.03 × 21.64 × 1.6 (light) **Lift capacity:** 3,500 tons

REMARK: Built in 1942 and transferred in 6-61.

◆ **1 small floating dry dock**

FD II

Lift capacity: 1,200 tons

REMARK: Built in 1974.

PANAMA

MERCHANT MARINE (1978): 3,640 ships—20,748,696 grt
(tankers: 317 ships—6,337,292 grt)

NATIONAL GUARD

PATROL BOATS AND CRAFT

◆ **2 103-foot boats** Bldr: Vosper Thornycroft, Portsmouth, G.B.

GC 10 PANQUIACO GC 11 LIGIA ELENA

D: 96 tons (123 fl) **S:** 24 kts **Dim:** 31.25 × 6.02 × 1.98
A: 2/20-mm AA (I × 2) **Man:** 23 men **Electric:** 80 kva
Electron Equipt: Radar: 1/Decca 916
M: 2 Paxman Ventura 12-YJCM diesels; 2 props; 2,800 hp

REMARK: Launched 22-7-70 and 25-8-70, respectively.

◆ **2 ex-U.S. Coast Guard 40-foot Mk-1-class utility boats**

GC 14 MARTI GC 15 JUPITER

D: 13 tons (fl) **S:** 18 kts **Dim:** 12.3 × 3.4 × 1.0
A: 1/12.7-mm machine gun **Man:** 4 men **Range:** 160/8
M: 2 GM 6-71 diesels; 2 props; 300 hp

REMARKS: In service in 1950 and transferred in 1962.

◆ **2 ex-U.S. 63-foot AVR class**

GC 12 AYANASI GC 13 ZARTI

D: 35 tons (fl) **S:** 22.5 kts **Dim:** 19.3 × 4.7 × 1.0
A: 2/12.7-mm machine guns (I × 2) **Man:** 8 men
Electron Equipt: Radar: 1/Raytheon 1500B
M: 2 GM 8V-71 diesels; 2 props; 900 hp

REMARKS: In service in 1943 and transferred 1965-66.

AUXILIARY SHIPS AND CRAFT

◆ **1 ex-U.S. LSMR-class rocket-assault ship** Bldr: Brown SB Co., Houston

TIBURON (ex-*Smokey Hill River*, LSMR-531)

D: 2,084 tons (fl) **S:** 12 kts **Dim:** 62.87 × 10.52 × 2.18
A: None **Man:** . . . **Electric:** 440 kw
M: 2 GM 16-278A diesels; 2 props; 2,800 hp

REMARKS: Launched 7-7-45. Purchased from a commercial source 14-3-75 and used for logistics-support duties. May have had bow doors added, although, as completed, she had none and had her well deck plated over. Cargo: approximately 400 tons.

◆ **2 logistics-support landing craft** Bldr: France, 1978

GN . . . GN . . .

D: 60 tons (fl) **S:** 9 kts **Dim:** 12.6 × . . . × . . .
M: 2 SKL 8NVD26 diesels; 2 props; 400 hp

◆ **3 ex-U.S. Army LCM (8)-class landing craft**

GN 1 GN 2 GN 3

D: 115 tons (fl) **S:** 9 kts **Dim:** 22.7 × 6.4 × 1.4
A: None **Man:** 6 men **M:** 4 GM 6-71 diesels; 2 props; 600 hp

REMARKS: Transferred 1972. Used for logistics-support duties. Two-level superstructure aft.

◆ **1 ex-U.S. YF-852-class cargo lighter** Bldr: Defoe SB, Bay City, Michigan, 1945

N . . . (ex-YF-886)

D: 590 tons (fl) **S:** 11 kts **Dim:** 40.23 × 9.1 × 2.7
Man: 11 men **M:** 2 GM 6-71 diesels; 2 props; 600 hp

REMARKS: Transferred 5-75. Cargo: 250 tons

PANAMA (*continued*)

AUXILIARY SHIPS AND CRAFT (*continued*)

◆ **1 former shrimp boat**

GN 8

   S: 11 kts   **Capacity:** 150 passengers

REMARK: Used for logistics-support duties.

PAPUA NEW GUINEA

MERCHANT MARINE (1978): 67 ships—16,718 grt
                (tankers: 3 ships—1,276 grt)

PATROL BOATS

◆ **5 ex-Australian Attack class**

   Bldrs: Nos. 84, 92: Walker's, Maryborough; Nos. 85, 93, 94: Evans, Deakin & Co., Queensland

84 AITAPE   85 SAMARAI   92 LAVADA   93 LAE   94 MADANG

   D: 146 tons (fl)   **S:** 21-24 kts   **Dim:** 32.76 (30.48 pp) × 6.2 × 1.9
   A: 1/40-mm AA—2/7.62-mm machine guns   **Man:** 18 men
   Electron Equipt: Radar: 1/975
   M: 2 Davey-Paxman Ventura 16-YJCM diesels; 3,500 hp   **Fuel:** 20 tons

REMARK: Transferred in 1975.

AMPHIBIOUS WARFARE SHIPS

◆ **2 ex-Australian Balikpapan-class utility landing craft** Bldr: Walker's, Maryborough

131 SALAMAUA   132 BUNA

   D: 310 tons (503 fl)   **S:** 8 kts   **Dim:** 44.5 × 12.2 × 1.9
   Man: 2 officers, 11 men   **Range:** 3,000/10
   A: 2/12.7-mm machine guns (I × 2)   **M:** 3 GM diesels; 3 props; 675 hp

REMARK: In service in 1972 and transferred 1975.

◆ **7 Kokuba-class personnel landing craft** Bldr: Australia, 1975

KOKUBA   KUTUBA   KIAIPIT   KANDEP
KUNIAWA   KIUNGA   KUKIPI

   D: 12 tons (fl)   **S:** 9 kts   **Dim:** 12.0 × 4.0 × 1.0
   M: 2 Gardner diesels; 2 props; 150 hp

◆ **1 ex-Australian tug** Bldr: Perrin, Brisbane, 1972

. . . (ex-503)

   D: 47.5 tons   **S:** 9 kts   **Dim:** 15.4 × 4.6 × . . .
   M: 2 GM diesels; 2 props; 340 hp   **Man:** 3 men

REMARK: Transferred in 1974.

PARAGUAY

MERCHANT MARINE (1978): 26 ships—21,930 grt
                (tankers: 3 ships—2,935 grt)

RIVER GUNBOATS

◆ **6 ex-Argentinian Bouchard-class minesweepers**

	Bldr	L
M 1 NANAWA (ex-*Bouchard*)	Rio Santiago NY	20-3-36
M 2 CAPITÁN MEZA (ex-*Parker*)	Sanchez, San Fernando	2-5-37
M 3 TENIENTE FARINA (ex-*Py*)	Rio Santiago NY	30-3-38

   D: 450 tons (650 fl)   **S:** 16 kts   **Dim:** 59.5 × 7.3 × 2.6
   Man: 70 men   **Range:** 3,000/12
   A: 4/40-mm AA (II × 2)—2/12.7-mm machine guns—mines
   M: 2 M.A.N. diesels; 2 props; 2,000 hp

REMARK: Transferred between 1964 and 1967.

◆ **2 Paraguay class** Bldr: Odero, Genoa, 1930

C 1 PARAGUAY (ex-*Comodoro Meya*)   C 2 HUMAITÁ (ex-*Capitan Cabral*)

   D: 636 tons, 745 avg. (865 fl)   **S:** 17.5 kts   **Dim:** 70.15 × 10.7 × 1.65
   Man: 86 men   **Range:** 1,700/16   **Fuel:** 170 tons
   A: 4/120-mm (II × 2)—3/76-mm AA (I × 3)—2/40-mm AA (I × 2)—6 mines
   M: 2 sets Parsons GT; 2 props; 3,800 hp   **Boilers:** 2

REMARK: In service in 5-31.

A 1 CAPITÁN CABRAL (ex-*Adolfo Riquelme*) Bldr: Werf Conrad, Haarlem, 1908

   D: 206 tons (fl)   **S:** 9 kts   **Dim:** 30.5 × 7.0 × 2.9
   A: 1/76-mm—2/37-mm   **Man:** 47 men   **M:** Reciprocating; 300 hp

REMARK: Wooden hull, former tug, used for riverine patrol.

PARAGUAY (continued)

PATROL CRAFT

◆ **6 small craft**   Bldr: Sewart Seacraft, Berwick, La.

| PT 101 | PT 102 | PT 103 | PT 104 | PT 105 | PT 106 |

    D: 15 tons (fl)   **S:** 20 kts   **Dim:** 13.1 × 3.9 × 0.9
    A: 2/12.7-mm machine guns   **Man:** 7 men
    M: 2 GM G-71 diesels; 2 props; 500 hp

REMARK: PT-101 and PT-102 were in service in 12-67; PT-103, PT-104, and PT-105, in 9-70; and PT-106, in 3-71.

AUXILIARY SHIPS

◆ **1 repair/headquarters ship**   Bldr: Brown SB, Houston

	L	In serv.
PH 1 TENIENTE PRATT GIL (ex-*Corrientes*, ex-LSM-86)	15-9-44	13-10-44

    D: 743 tons (1,095 fl)   **S:** 12.6 kts   **Dim:** 61.88 × 10.51 × 2.54
    A: 2/40-mm AA (II × 1)   **Man:** . . .   **Electric:** 240 kw
    M: 2 Fairbanks-Morse 38D8⅛ × 10 diesels; 2 props; 2,800 hp

REMARKS: An ex-U.S. LSM-1-class landing ship donated by Argentina on 13-1-72, after conversion to a command and repair ship. Well deck plated over to create a helicopter deck aft; superstructure enlarged and moved to the centerline.

◆ **1 cargo and training ship**   Bldr: Ruiz de Velasco, Bilboa, Spain

GUARANI

    D: 714 grt   **S:** 12.2 kts   **Dim:** 73.6 × 11.9 × 3.7
    M: 1 diesel; 1 prop; 1,300 hp

REMARKS: In service since 2-68. Purchased and refitted in 1974 to provide seagoing experience for naval cadets and to engage in commercial voyages to raise revenue for running the navy. Cargo: approximately 1,000 tons.

◆ **2 ex-U.S. LCU-501-class landing craft**

| BT 1 (ex-YFB-82, ex-LCU-. . .) | BT 2 (ex-YFB-86, ex-LCU-. . .) |

    D: 143 tons (309 fl)   **S:** 10 kts   **Dim:** 36.3 × 9.8 × 1.2 (aft)
    M: 3 Gray Marine 64YTL diesels; 3 props; 675 hp

REMARKS: Transferred in 6-70. Used for logistics duties. Cargo: 125 tons.

◆ **2 ex-U.S. 64-foot YTL-class tugs**

| R 5 (ex-YTL-211) | R 6 (ex-YTL-567) |

    D: 84 tons   **S:** 9 kts   **Dim:** 20.2 × 5.2 × 2.6
    M: 1 diesel; 300 hp   **Man:** 5 men

REMARK: Transferred in 3-67 and 4-74.

◆ **1 ex-U.S. floating dry dock**

N . . . (ex-AFDL-26)

Dim: 60.96 × 19.5 × 1.04 (light)   **Lifting capacity:** 1,000 tons

REMARK: Transferred in 3-65.

◆ **1 ex-U.S. floating workshop**

N . . . (ex-YR-37)

    D: 600 tons (fl)   **Dim:** 45.72 × 10.36 × . . .

REMARK: Transferred in 3-63.

◆ **1 dredge**

TENIENTE O CARRERAS SAGUIER

PERU

PERSONNEL: Approximately 14,000 men, including 1,200 officers and 1,000 Marines

MERCHANT MARINE (1978): 686 ships − 574,718 grt
               (tankers: 13 ships − 97,556 grt)

NAVAL AVIATION: The air arm consists of the following helicopters and fixed-wing aircraft: 6 SH-3D Sea King, 6 Agusta-Bell AB 212, 10 Bell 206 Jetranger, 20 Bell UH-1, 2 Bell 47G, and 2 Alouette-III helicopters; 9 Grumman S-2 Tracker ASW aircraft, 6 C-47 transports, 1 Piper Aztec liaison aircraft, and 2 Beech T-34 trainers. The Air Force operates 4 aging HU-16B Albatross patrol amphibians.

WARSHIPS IN SERVICE AND UNDER CONSTRUCTION AS OF 1 JANUARY 1980

	L	Tons (surfaced)	Main armament
◆ **8 (+4) submarines**			
2 (+4) TYPE 209	1973-. . .	980	8/533-mm TT
4 DOS DE MAYO	1953-57	825	6/533-mm TT, 1/127-mm DP (in two units)
2 GUPPY IA	1944	1,830	10/533-mm TT
◆ **3 cruisers**			
1 AGUIRRE	1950	9,850	4/152-mm DP, 6/57-mm AA, 4/40-mm AA, 3 helicopters
1 ALMIRANTE GRAU	1944	9,529	8/152-mm DP, 8/57-mm AA
1 COLONIES	1942	8,781	9/152-mm, 8/102-mm DP
◆ **5 destroyers**			
2 DARING	1949-52	2,800	8/MM 38 Exocet, 4/114-mm
1 HOLLAND	1953	2,215	4/120-mm DP, 1/40-mm AA
2 FLETCHER	1942-43	2,050	4/127-mm DP, 6/76-mm DP, 5/533-mm TT
◆ **4 frigates**			
4 LUPO TYPE	1976-. . .	2,208	8/Otomat, 1/Albatros system, 1/127-mm DP

SUBMARINES

◆ 2 (+4) German Type 209 Bldr: Howaldtswerke, Kiel

	L	In serv.		L	In serv.
S 45 ISLAY	1973	23-1-75	S 48 N . . .	. . .	. . .
S 46 ARICA	8-74	4-4-75	S . . N . . .	. . .	. . .
S 47 N . . .	. . .	. . .	S . . N . . .	. . .	. . .

Islay   1975

D: 980 tons surfaced, 1,230 submerged   **Dim:** 55.0 × 6.6 × 5.9
S: 21 kts for 5 minutes, submerged, 12 with snorkel
A: 8/533-mm TT — 6 torpedoes in reserve   **Man:** 5 officers, 26 men
M: 4 MTU Type 12V-493-TY60 diesels, each linked to a 450-kw AEG generator, single Siemans electric motor; 3,600 hp

REMARKS: S-47 and S-48 were ordered 12-8-76, and two more in 3-77. Completion may be delayed by lack of funding.

◆ 4 Dos de Mayo class Bldr: General Dynamics, Groton, Conn.

	Laid down	L	In serv.
S 41 DOS DE MAYO (ex-*Lobo*)	12-5-52	6-2-54	14-6-54
S 42 ABTAO (ex-*Tiburon*)	12-5-52	27-10-53	20-2-54
S 43 ANGAMOS (ex-*Atun*)	27-10-55	5-2-57	1-7-57
S 44 IQUIQUE (ex-*Merlin*)	27-10-55	5-2-57	1-10-57

D: 825 tons, 1,400 submerged   S: 16/10 kts   **Dim:** 74.1 × 6.7 × 4.2
Man: 40 men   **Range:** 5,000/10 (snorkel)   **Fuel:** 45 tons

Angamos

A: S-41, S-42: 1/127-mm DP — 6/533-mm TT (4 fwd, 2 aft)
M: 2 GM 12-278A diesels; 2 electric motors; 2,400 hp

REMARKS: Patterned after the U.S. *Marlin* class of 1941. These were the last U.S. submarines to be built for a foreign customer. S-41 and S-42 were refitted in 1965, S-43 and S-44 in 1968. The 127-mm gun carried by S-41 and S-42 is a 25-caliber U.S. W.E.T. model and is mounted abaft the sail.

◆ 2 ex-U.S. Guppy-IA class Bldr: Portsmouth NSY, N.H.

	Laid down	L	In serv.
S 49 PEDRERA (ex-*Sea Poacher*, SS-406)	23-2-44	20-5-44	31-7-44
S 50 PACOCHA (ex-*Atule*, SS-403)	2-12-43	6-3-44	21-6-44

D: 1,830 tons surfaced, 2,440 submerged   S: 17/15 kts
Dim: 93.57 × 8.23 × 5.18   **Man:** 82 men   A: 10/533-mm TT (6 fwd, 4 aft)
M: 4 Fairbanks-Morse 38D8⅛ diesels; 2 electric motors; 2 props; 4,610 hp

REMARKS: Purchased in 7-74. Both were converted to Guppy-IA configuration during 1951. They can maintain 15 kts for half an hour while submerged, 3 kts for thirty-six hours. Snorkel speed is 7.5 kts. A third submarine of this class, ex-*Tench* (SS-417), was towed out in 11-76 for cannibalization.

CRUISERS

◆ 1 ex-Dutch, guided-missile cruiser Bldr: Rotterdam DDM

	Laid down	L	In serv.
84 AGUIRRE (ex-*De Zeven Provincien*)	19-5-39	22-8-50	17-12-53

D: 9,850 tons (12,250 fl)   S: 32 kts   **Dim:** 185.7 (182.4 pp) × 17.25 × 6.7
Man: 856 men   **Armor:** Belt: 76-102 Decks (2): 20-25
A: 4/152-mm DP (II × 2) — 6/57-mm AA (II × 3) — 4/40-mm AA (I × 4) — 3 SH-3D Sea King helicopters
Electron Equipt: Radars: 1/LWO 2, 1/SGR-103, 1/DA 02, 1/ZW 03, 2/M 25, 2/M 45
M: Parsons GT; 2 props; 80,000 hp   **Boilers:** 4 Yarrow, three-drum

REMARKS: Purchased in 8-76. The Terrier missile system was replaced by a hangar (20.4 × 16.5) and a helicopter platform (35.0 × 17.0) at Rotterdam. Recommissioned on 31-10-77. The helicopters are intended to carry French anti-ship missiles. Four MM-38 Exocet missiles may be added.

◆ 1 ex-Dutch cruiser Bldr: Wilton-Fijenoord, Schiedam

	Laid down	L	In serv.
81 ALMIRANTE GRAU (ex-*de Ruyter*)	5-9-39	24-12-44	18-11-53

Almirante Grau   1977

CRUISERS (continued)

D: 9,529 tons (11,850 fl)   **S:** 32 kts   **Dim:** 187.32 (182.4 pp) × 17.25 × 6.7
Man: 926 men   **Armor:** Belt: 76-102   Decks (2): 20-25
A: 8/152-mm DP (II × 4)−8/57-mm AA (II × 4)−8/40-mm AA (II × 4)
Electron Equipt: Radars: 1/LWO 1, 1/LWO 2, 1/SGR 105, 1/SGR 103, 1/SGR 104,
            2/M 45, 4/M 44
M: 2 sets Parsons GT; 2 props; 85,000 hp   **Boilers:** 4 Yarrow, three-drum

REMARK: Purchased 7-3-73.

◆ **1 ex-British Colonies class**   Bldr: Alexander Stephen & Sons, Glasgow, Scotland

	Laid down	L	In serv.
82 CORONEL BOLOGNESI (ex-*Ceylon*)	27-4-39	30-7-42	13-7-43

Coronel Bolognesi   1974

D: 8,781 tons (11,110 fl)   **S:** 29 kts (max.)   **Dim:** 169.31 × 18.9 × 6.25
Man: 766 men   **Range:** 2,300/29, 6,800/20, 11,400/12   **Fuel:** 1,600 tons
A: 9/152-mm (III × 3)−8/102-mm Mk-19 DP (II × 4)−18/40-mm (II × 5, I × 8)
Electron Equipt: Radars: 1/960, 1/277, 1/293, 1/274, 2/Mk 34
Armor: Belt: 76-102   Deck: 52   Turret: 25-52   Conning tower: 102
M: 4 sets Parsons GT; 4 props; 72,500 hp   **Boilers:** 4 Admiralty, three-drum

REMARKS: Modernized 1955-56, and transferred 9-2-60. U.S. Mk-34 fire-control radars on
two of the 102-mm mounts. Can land a small helicopter at the stern. Sister *Capitán
Quiñones* (ex-*Almirante Grau*, ex-British *Newfoundland*) stricken in 5-78.

GUIDED-MISSILE DESTROYERS

◆ **2 ex-British Daring class**   Bldr: Yarrow, Glasgow, Scotland

	Laid down	L	In serv.
73 PALACIOS (ex-*Diana*)	3-4-47	8-5-52	29-3-54
74 FERRÉ (ex-*Decoy*)	22-9-46	29-3-49	28-4-53

Palacios—before most recent reconstruction   1973

D: 2,800 tons (3,700 fl)   **S:** 30 kts   **Dim:** 118.87 (111.55 pp) × 13.1 × 5.5
Man: 297 men   **Range:** 3,000/20   **Fuel:** 584 tons
A: 8/MM 38 Exocet SSM (II × 4)−4/114-mm Mk-6 DP (II × 2)−4/40-mm Breda
      Dardo AA (II × 2)−1/AB-212 ASW helicopter
Electron Equipt: Radars: 1/Plessey ASW 1, 1/Decca 1226, 1/903, 1/NA 10, 1/Triton
            Sonar: Removed
Boilers: 2 Foster-Wheeler, 45.7 kg/cm² pressure−superheat 454°C
M: 2 sets English-Electric GT; 2 props; 54,000 hp

REMARKS: Purchased in 1969. Welded hull. Refit by Cammell Laird & Co. completed at
the end of 1973. In 1975 a helicopter deck was added over the stern. In 1977-78 a telescoping hangar replaced the after 114-mm gun mount, the after stack was enlarged
and heightened, and a Selenia NA-10 radar director was added abaft the new second
stack to control two enclosed, twin automatic Dardo 40-mm mounts, which replaced
the single 40-mm AA abreast the bridge. These lightly built, much-modified ships now
have no ASW capability other than the embarked helicopter. They carry a complex
and unique mixture of British, French, and Italian electronics and weapons.

DESTROYERS

◆ **1 ex-Dutch Holland class**   Bldr: Rotterdam DDM

	Laid down	L	In serv.
75 GARCIA Y GARCIA (ex-*Holland*)	21-4-50	11-4-53	31-12-54

D: 2,215 tons (2,765 fl)   **S:** 32 kts   **Dim:** 111.3 × 11.3 × 4.86
Man: 247 men   **Range:** 4,000/18   **Electric:** 1,350 kw
A: 4/120-mm DP (II × 2)−1/40-mm AA−2/375-mm Bofors ASW rocket launchers
      (IV × 2)−1/depth-charge rack
Electron Equipt: Radars: 1/LWO 2, 1/DA 05, 2/M 45
            Sonars: 1/CWE 10, 1/170B, 1/162

DESTROYERS (continued)

Garcia y Garcia—as the **Holland**   A. D. Baker, 1976

Boilers: 4 Babcock & Wilcox, 39.8 kg/cm² pressure—superheat 454°C
M: 2 sets Parsons GT; 2 props; 45,000 hp

REMARKS: Transferred 5-1-78 without refit. Commissioned 21-1-78 in Peruvian Navy.
Purchase of sister *Zeeland* no longer contemplated.

◆ **2 ex-U.S. Fletcher class** Bldr: Bethlehem Steel, Staten Island

	Laid down	L	In serv.
71 VILLAR (ex-*Benham*, DD-796)	3-4-43	30-8-43	20-12-43
72 GUISE (ex-*Isherwood*, DD-520)	12-5-42	24-11-42	12-4-43

Villar—with Bell-47G helicopter   1975

D: 2,050 tons (3,050 fl)   **S:** 30 kts
Dim: 114.73 (112.5 wl) × 12.07 × 5.49 (4.27 hull)
Man: 15 officers, 260 men   **Range:** 1,260/30, 4,400/15   **Fuel:** 650 tons
A: 4/127-mm DP (I × 4)—6/76-mm DP (II × 3)—5/533-mm TT (V × 1)—2/Hedgehogs
—1/helicopter
Electron Equipt: Radars: 1/SPG 10, 1/SPS 6, 1/Mk 25, 2/Mk 34, 1/Mk 35
Sonar: SQS-29 series
Boilers: 4 Babcock & Wilcox, 39.8 kg/cm² pressure—superheat 454°C
M: GE GT; 2 props; 60,000 hp   **Electric:** 580 kw

REMARKS: Transferred 1960-61 under MAP. Have one Mk-37 director for 127-mm, two
Mk-63 gun fire-control systems for 76-mm, and one Mk-56 for either 127-mm or 76-mm.
Helicopter platform added in 1975. Two sister ships, *La Valette* (DD-448) and *Terry*
(DD-513), were transferred in 1974 for cannibalization.

GUIDED-MISSILE FRIGATES

◆ **4 Italian Lupo type**
Bldrs: No. 51, No. 52: CNTR, Riva Trigoso; No. 53, No. 54: CNTR, Callao

	Laid down	L	In serv.
51 CARVAJAL	8-10-74	17-11-76	3-2-79
52 VILLAVICENCIO	6-10-76	7-2-78	8-79
53 N . . .	1977	. . .	. . .
54 N . . .	1977	. . .	. . .

Carvajal   A. Fraccaroli, 1978

D: 2,208 tons (2,500 fl)   **S:** 32 kts   **Dim:** 108.4 (106.0 pp) × 11.28 × 3.66
Man: 185 men   **Range:** 4,350/16 (1 diesel)   **Electric:** 3,120 kw
A: 8/Otomat Mk-2 Teseo (I × 8)—1/127-mm OTO Melara DP—1/Albatros system
(VIII × 1)—4/40-mm Breda Dardo AA (II × 2)—6/324-mm Mk 32 ASW TT
(III × 2)—1/AB-212 ASW helicopter
Electron Equipt: Radars: 1/SMA 3RM20, 1/RAN 10S air-search, 1/RAN 11LX
surface-search, 1/SPQ 2F, 2/NA-10 Mod. 2, 2/Dardo
Sonar: Edo 610E—IPN-10 data system, 2 SCLAR chaff
launchers
M: CODOG: 2 Fiat-GE LM-2500 gas turbines, 25,000 hp each; 2 GMT A230-20M
diesels, 3,900 hp each; 2 controllable-pitch props

REMARKS: Italian technicians were to assist in the building of Nos. 53 and 54 at Callao.
Differ from the Italian Navy's version in having a fixed (vice telescoping) hangar and
a step down to the hull at the stern; the Dardo 40-mm mounts are one deck higher.

GUIDED-MISSILE CORVETTES

◆ **6 French PR-72-560 class**

	Bldr	L	In serv.
21 VELARDE	Lorient DY	11-9-78	1979
22 SANTILLANA	SFCN	16-9-78	1979
23 DE LOS HEROES	Lorient DY	. . .	. . .
24 HERRERA	SFCN	. . .	. . .
25 LARREA	Lorient DY	. . .	. . .
26 SANCHEZ CARRION	SFCN	. . .	. . .

GUIDED-MISSILE CORVETTES (*continued*)

D: 465 tons (536 fl)   **S:** 37 kts   **Dim:** 64.0 (59.0 pp) × 8.35 × 2.6
Man: 45 men   **Range:** 700/30, 2,000/16   **Electric:** . . . kw
A: 4/MM 38 Exocet SSM (II × 2)—1/76-mm OTO Melara DP—2/40-mm Breda-
   Bofors AA (II × 1)—2/20-mm AA
Electron Equipt: Radars: 1/Thomson-CSF Triton, 1/Vega fire-control
M: 4 SACM AGO 240 V-16 diesels; 4 props; 20,000 hp

REMARKS: These ships, designed by SFCN, Villeneuve-la-Garonne, have been given
the names of the Vosper patrol boats that were transferred to the Coast Guard.

RIVER GUNBOATS

◆ **2 Marañon class**   Bldr: John I. Thornycroft

	Laid down	L	In serv.
13 MARAÑON	4-50	23-4-51	7-51
14 UCAYALI	4-50	7-3-51	7-51

Marañon   1975

D: 350 tons (365 fl)   **S:** 12 kts   **Dim:** 47.22 × 9.75 × 1.22
Man: 4 officers, 36 men   **Range:** 5,000/10
A: 2/76-mm DP (I × 2)—4/20-mm (II × 2)
M: 2 British Polar 441 diesels; 2 props; 800 hp

REMARKS: Based at Iquitos and in service on the Upper Amazon. Forced ventilation.
Superstructure of aluminum alloy.

◆ **2 Amazonas class**   Bldr: Electric Boat Co., Groton, 1934

11 AMAZONAS   12 LORETO

D: 250 tons   **S:** 15 kts   **Dim:** 46.7 × 6.7 × 1.2
Man: 5 officers, 20 men   **Range:** 4,000/10
A: 2/76-mm DP (I × 2)—2/40-mm AA (I × 2)—2/20-mm AA (I × 2)
M: 2 diesels; 2 props; 750 hp

Loreto   1975

◆ **14 America**   Bldr: Tranmere Bay Development Co., Birkenhead, 1904

D: 185 tons (240 fl)   **S:** 12 kts   **Dim:** 40.5 × 5.9 × 1.4
A: 2/40-mm AA (I × 2)—4/20-mm AA (I × 4)   **Man:** 26 men
M: Reciprocating; 1 prop; 350 hp   **Fuel:** 42 tons

America   1975

PATROL CRAFT

◆ **3 Rio Zarumilla class**   Bldr: Viareggio, Italy

PL 250 RIO ZARUMILLA   PL 251 RIO TUMBES   PL 252 RIO PIURA

D: 37 tons (fl)   **S:** 18 kts   **Dim:** 20.27 × 5.25 × 2.75
A: 2/40-mm AA (I × 2)   **Man:** . . .   **Range:** 1,000/14
M: 2 GM diesels; 2 props; 1,200 hp

REMARKS: In service 5-9-60. Patrol the Salto River border with Ecuador. Possibly now
in the Coast Guard.

PATROL CRAFT (*continued*)

◆ **4 ex-U.S. Coast Guard 40-foot utility boats**

PL 230 La Punta   PL 231 Rio Chillon   PL 232 Rio Sanra   PL 233 Rio Majes

    D: 16 tons (fl)   **S:** 18 kts   **Dim:** 12.3 × 3.4 × 1.0
    A: 2/12.7-mm machine guns (I × 2)   **Man:** 5 men   **Range:** 160/18
    M: 2 GM 6-71 diesels, 2 props; 300 hp

REMARK: Possibly now in the Coast Guard.

◆ **4 Rio Ramis class**

PL 290 Rio Ramis   PL 292 Rio Coata
PL 291 Rio Illave   PL 293 Rio Huancané

    D: 12-14 tons (fl)   **A:** 1/12.7-mm machine gun   **Man:** 4 men

REMARK: Serve on Lake Titicaca.

AMPHIBIOUS WARFARE SHIPS

◆ **2 ex-U.S. LST-1-class landing ships**

	Bldr	L	In serv.
141 Paita (ex-*Burnett County*, LST-512)	Chicago B & I	10-12-43	8-1-44
142 Chimbote (ex-*Rawhiti*, ex-LST-283)	American Bridge	10-10-43	18-11-43

    D: 1,625 tons (4,080 fl)   **S:** 10 kts   **Dim:** 100.0 × 15.24 × 4.29
    Man: 16 officers, 106 men   **Range:** 9,500/9   **Fuel:** 600 tons
    A: No. 141: 6/20-mm AA (I × 6) No. 142: 2/40-mm AA (I × 2)–8/20-mm (I × 8)
    M: 2 GM 12-567A diesels; 2 props; 1,700 hp   **Electric:** 300 kw

REMARKS: No. 142 was purchased in 1947, No. 141 in 1957. The latter is assigned to the naval academy; her 01-level superstructure has been extended forward to increase accommodations. Both have helicopter-landing positions amidships.

◆ **2 ex-U.S. LSM-1-class landing ships**   Bldr: Charleston NY

	Laid down	L	In serv.
36 Lomas (ex-LSM-396)	13-12-44	2-1-45	24-3-45
37 Atico (ex-LSM-554)	3-3-45	22-3-45	14-9-45

    D: 513 tons (1,095 fl)   **S:** 12.5 kts   **Dim:** 62.02 × 10.52 × 2.24
    A: 2/40-mm AA (II × 1)–4/20-mm AA (I × 4)   **Fuel:** 165 tons
    Range: 5,000/7   **Electric:** 240 kw
    M: 2 GM 16-278A diesels; 2 props; 2,800 hp

REMARKS: Purchased in the U.S.A. and transferred in 7-59. Living spaces for 116 men.

HYDROGRAPHIC SURVEY SHIPS

◆ **1 new construction**   Bldr: SIMA, Callao

	Laid down	L	In serv.
Humboldt	3-1-77	1979	1980

    D: 1,200 tons (fl)   **S:** 14 kts   **Dim:** 76.0 × 12.0 × . . .
    M: Diesels

◆ **1 ex-U.S. Sotoyomo-class tug**   Bldr: Levingston SB, Orange, Texas

	Laid down	L	In serv.
136 Unanue (ex-*Wateree*, ATA-174)	5-10-43	18-11-43	20-7-44

    D: 534 tons (835 fl)   **S:** 13 kts   **Dim:** 43.59 × 10.31 × 4.01
    M: 2 GM 12-278A diesels, electric drive; 1 prop; 1,500 hp   **Electric:** 120 kw

REMARK: Sold to Peru in 11-61.

◆ **3 inshore survey craft**

API 171 Cardenas (ex-YP-99)   API 173 N . . . (ex-YP-243)
API 172 N . . . (ex-YP-242)

    D: 19 tons   **S:** . . .   **Dim:** . . . × . . . × . . .

REMARK: Ex-U.S. patrol craft, purchased in 11-58.

◆ **1 river research craft**

N . . .   **Dim:** 23.5 oa   **Man:** 16 men

REMARK: Operated on the Amazon by the Navy for the Oceanographic Institute.

REPLENISHMENT OILERS

◆ **2 Talara class**   Bldr: SIMA, Callao

	Laid down	L	In serv.
152 Talara	1975	9-7-76	3-77
153 Bayovar	9-7-76	18-7-77	2-78

    D: 30,000 tons (fl)   **S:** 16.25 kts   **Dim:** 171.18 (161.55 pp) × 25.38 × 9.53
    M: 1 Burmeister & Wain 6K 47EF diesel; 1 prop; 11,600 hp   **Electric:** 1,890 kw

REMARKS: 16,633 grt, 25,648 dwt. Cargo: 35,642 m³. Sister *Trompeteros* is operated by Petroperu, the state fuel monopoly, which transferred these two ships to the Navy upon their completion. One under-way fueling station per side.

◆ **2 Parinas class**   Bldr: SIMA, Callao

	L	In serv.
155 Parinas	12-6-67	13-6-68
156 Pimental	5-4-68	27-6-69

Pimental   1977

    D: 13,600 tons (fl)   **S:** 14.25 kts   **Dim:** 134.19 (124.82 pp) × 18.98 × 7.27
    Electric: 464 kw   **Fuel:** 610 tons
    M: 1 Burmeister & Wain 7-cyl. diesel; 1 prop; 4,900 hp

REMARKS: 7,121 grt, 10,140 dwt. Cargo: 13,851 m³. Normally used by Petroperu for commercial purposes, but have naval crews and can refuel ships from one rig on either beam. No. 156 had her commercial certification withdrawn 19-6-77 pending repairs.

REPLENISHMENT OILERS (continued)

◆ **2 Sechura class**   Bldr: SIMA, Callao

		Laid down	L	In serv.
158	ZORRITOS	8-10-55	8-10-58	1959
159	LOBITOS	1964	5-65	1966

Lobitos   C. Dragonette, 1979

D: 8,700 tons (fl)   **S:** 12 kts   **Dim:** 116.82 (109.73 pp) × 15.91 × 6.63
Electric: 750 kw   **Fuel:** 549 tons
M: 1 Burmeister & Wain 562-VTF-115 diesel; 1 prop; 2,400 hp

REMARKS: 4,297 grt, 5,732 dwt. Cargo: 7,488 m³. Sister *Sechura*, built in England 1952-55 and fully equipped for under-way replenishment, was stricken in 1968. Nos. 158 and 159 are used for commercial cargoes for Petroperu, but have one fueling station on either beam.

◆ **1 ex-Danish commercial tanker**   Bldr: Hitachi Zosen, Osaka, Japan

151 MOLLENDO (ex-*Amalienborg*)

D: 6,084 tons light (25,670 fl)   **S:** 15 kts
Dim: 170.69 (163.0 pp) × 22.05 × 9.06   **Range:** 19,800/15   **Fuel:** 1,480 tons
M: 1 Hitachi-B & W 674-VTFS-160 diesel; 1 prop; 7,500 hp   **Electric:** 540 kw

REMARKS: 12,490 grt, 19,900 dwt. Cargo: 26,073 m³. In service in 9-62. Purchased in 4-67. Used primarily for commercial cargoes for Petroperu, but can refuel under way from one station on each beam.

CARGO SHIPS

◆ **1 Ilo-class transport**   Bldr: SIMA, Callao

131 ILO

D: 18,400 tons (fl)   **S:** 15.6 kts   **Dim:** 153.85 (144.53 pp) × 20.4 × 9.2
M: 1 B & W 6K 47EF diesel; 1 prop; 11,600 hp   **Electric:** 1,140 kw

REMARKS: In service 15-12-71. Cargo: 13,000 tons. Sister *Rimac* is in commercial service for the state shipping company. The *Ilo* is also used to carry commercial cargo.

Ilo   J. Jedrlinic, 1975

◆ **1 ex-U.S. Bellatrix-class attack cargo ship**   Bldr: Tampa SB, Tampa, Fla.

31 INDEPENDENCIA (ex-*Bellatrix*, AKA-3, ex-*Raven*, AK-20)

Independencia   1974

D: 6,200 tons (14,225 fl)   **S:** 15 kts   **Dim:** 140.0 × 19.2 × 7.95
Man: 19 officers, 220 men   **Range:** 18,000/14
A: 1/127-mm DP−4/76-mm 50-cal. DP−10/20-mm AA (I × 10)
Electron Equipt: Radars: 1/SPS 6, 1/Decca, 1/Mk 26
M: 1 Nordberg TSM diesel; 1 prop; 6,000 hp

REMARKS: In service 14-6-41. Former U.S. C2-T-class cargo ship. Refitted in 1954, and transferred under MAP in 2-63. Used for training midshipmen as well as for carrying military and commercial cargo (4,500 tons). Has one Mk-52 radar gunfire-control system and three Mk-51 gunfire-control systems. Normally carries two LCVP.

HOSPITAL SHIPS

◆ **3 Morona class**   Bldr: SIMAI, Iquitos, 1976-77

| MORONA | N . . . | N . . . |

D: 150 tons (fl)   **S:** 12 kts   **Dim:** 30.0 × 6.0 × 0.6
M: Diesels; . . . hp

REMARK: Serves on the rivers.

HOSPITAL SHIPS (continued)

◆ **1 former river gunboat** Bldr: Yarrow, Scotstoun, 1921

NAPO

D: 98 tons **S:** 12 kts **Dim:** 30.94 × 5.49 × 0.91
Man: 22 men **Boilers:** 2 Yarrow
M: 2 sets triple-expansion; 2 props; 250 hp

REMARKS: With the above craft, operates in the Upper Amazon Flotilla as a mobile dispensary. Converted in 1968.

TUGS

◆ **1 ex-U.S. Cherokee-class ocean tug** Bldr: Cramp SB, Philadelphia, Pa.

	Laid down	L	In serv.
123 GUARDIAN RIOS (ex-*Pinto*, ATF-90)	10-8-42	5-1-43	1-4-43

D: 1,235 tons (1,675 fl) **S:** 16.5 kts **Dim:** 62.48 × 11.73 × 4.67
Man: 85 men **Electric:** 260 kw
M: 4 GM 12-278 diesels, electric drive; 1 prop; 3,000 hp

REMARKS: Transferred in 12-60. Unarmed. Used for salvage and rescue.

SERVICE CRAFT

◆ **2 Selendon-class harbor tugs** Bldr: Ruhrorter, Duisburg, West Germany, 1967

SELENDON   OLAYA

D: 80 grt **S:** 10 kts **Dim:** 61.3 × 20.3 × 2.3
M: 1 diesel; 1 prop; 600 hp

◆ **1 river tug** Bldr: SIMAI, Iquitos, 1973

CONTRAESTRE NAVARRO

D: 50 tons

◆ **1 ex-U.S. medium tug** Bldr: City Point Iron Works, Boston, 1892

124 FRANCO (ex-*Tigre*, ex-*Iwana*, YTM-2)

Franco   1975

D: 192 tons (fl) **S:** 9 kts **Dim:** 29.26 × 6.4 × 2.59
M: 1 set single-expansion, reciprocating steam; 1 prop; 400 hp

REMARKS: Transferred in 3-46. The oldest operational tug in any navy. Converted to burn oil. Has push-bar built across bows for handling barges. Operates in the Upper Amazon Flotilla.

◆ **1 ex-U.S. 174-foot-class yard oiler** Bldr: Jeffersonville Boat & Machinery, Ind.

N . . . (ex-YO-221)

D: 1,400 tons (fl) **S:** 10 kts **Dim:** 53.04 × 9.75 × 4.0
M: 2 diesels; 1 prop; 540 hp **Range:** 2,000/8 **Man:** 20 men

REMARKS: Transferred in 2-75. Cargo: approximately 900 tons (6,570 barrels).

◆ **1 ex-U.S. 174-foot water tanker** Bldr: Henry C. Grebe, Inc., Chicago, Ill., 1945

110 MANTILLA (ex-YW-122)

D: 1,235 tons (fl) **S:** 8 kts **Dim:** 53.04 × 9.75 × 4.0
M: 1 diesel; 600 hp

REMARKS: Transferred in 3-63. Cargo: 900 tons

ABA 113   **D:** 330 tons Bldr: Peru, 1972

ABA 091   Barge with 800-ton capacity. Blt: 1972

REMARK: Serves in the Amazon Flotilla.

◆ **1 new construction floating dry dock** Bldr: West Germany

AFD . . .
  Dim: 195.0 × 42.0 × . . . **Lift capacity:** 15,000 tons

REMARKS: In service in 7-79. Lift capacity can be increased to 18,000 tons by use of extension sections, bringing total length to 225 meters.

◆ **1 ex-U.S. ARD-2-class floating dry dock**

AFD 112 (ex-WY-20, ex-ARD-8)
  Dim: 148.03 × 21.64 × 1.6 (light) **Lift capacity:** 3,500 tons

REMARKS: In service in 1943. Transferred in 2-61.

◆ **1 ex-U.S. AFDL-7-class floating dry dock**

AFD 111 (ex-WY-19, ex-AFDL-33)
  Dim: 87.78 × 19.51 × 0.99 (light) **Lift capacity:** 1,900 tons

REMARKS: In service in 10-44. Transferred in 7-59.

◆ **1 small floating dry dock** Bldr: Thornycroft, Southampton, 1951

AFD 108
  Dim: 59.13 × 18.7 × . . . **Lift capacity:** 600 tons

REMARK: Serves the Amazon Flotilla.

◆ **1 ex-U.S. YR-24-class floating workshop** Bldr: DeKom SB, Brooklyn, NY, 1943

RC 105 (ex-YR-59)
  D: 600 tons **Dim:** 45.72 × 10.36 × . . .

REMARK: Transferred 8-8-61.

SERVICE CRAFT *(continued)*

◆ **1 floating crane**

Capacity: 120 tons

REMARK: Serves at Callao.

COAST GUARD

The Peruvian Coast Guard was established in 1975 and is intended to patrol to the extent of the 200-nautical-mile economic zone.

PATROL SHIPS

◆ **2 ex-U.S. Auk-class former minesweepers** Bldr: Gulf SB Corp., Chickasaw, Ala.

	Laid down	L	In serv.
GALVEZ (ex-*Ruddy*, MSF-380)	24-2-44	29-10-44	28-4-45
DIEZ CANSECO (ex-*Shoveler*, MSF-382)	1-4-44	10-12-44	28-6-45

Diez Canseco—in naval colors

D: 890 tons (1,250 fl)   **S:** 18 kts   **Dim:** 67.39 × 9.8 × 3.28
Man: 100 men   **Range:** 4,300/10   **Fuel:** 216 tons
A: 1/76-mm Mk 22 DP—4/40-mm AA (II × 2)—4/20-mm AA (II × 2)
Electron Equipt: Radar: 1/SPS 5   **Electric:** 360 kw
M: 2 GM 12-278A diesels, electric drive; 2 props; 3,532 hp

REMARKS: Loaned by the U.S. on 1-11-60. Purchased outright in 1974. Transferred to the Coast Guard in 1975. All minesweeping and ASW gear now removed. "Guarda-costa" painted in large letters on hull sides.

PATROL BOATS

◆ **1 Rio Cañete class** Bldr: SIMA, Callao

	L	In serv.
234 RIO CAÑETE	8-10-74	31-3-76

D: 300 tons (fl)   **S:** 21 kts   **Dim:** 50.62 (49.1 pp) × 7.4 × 1.7
A: 1/40-mm AA—1/20-mm AA   **Man:** 6 officers, 33 men
M: 4 MTU V-8 diesels; 2 props; 5,640 hp   **Electric:** 170 kw

REMARKS: Intended as the first of a class of six for the Navy. The design is evidently not a success. Endurance: 20 days.

◆ **2 ex-U.S. PGM-71 class**

	Bldr	In serv.
222 RIO SAMA (ex-PGM-78)	Peterson, Sturgeon Bay, Wisc.	9-66
223 RIO CHIRA (ex-PGM-111)	SIMA, Callao	6-72

D: 130 tons (145 fl)   **S:** 17 kts   **Dim:** 30.8 (30.2 wl) × 6.4 × 1.85
Man: 27 men   **Range:** 1,000/12
A: 1/40-mm AA—4/20-mm AA (II × 2)—2/12.7-mm machine guns (I × 2)
Electron Equipt: Radar: 1/Raytheon 1500 Pathfinder
M: 8 GM 6-71 diesels; 2 props; 2,200 hp

REMARKS: Transferred to the Coast Guard in 1975. The *Rio Chira* was built with U.S. aid and equipment.

◆ **6 110-foot class** Bldr: Vosper, Portsmouth, G.B.

	L
224 RIO CHICAWA (ex-*De Los Heroes*)	18-11-64
225 RIO PATIVILCA (ex-*Herrera*)	26-10-64
226 RIO HUAORA (ex-*Larrea*)	18-2-65
227 RIO LOCUMBA (ex-*Sanchez Carrion*)	18-2-65
228 RIO ICA (ex-*Santillana*)	24-8-64
229 RIO VITOR (ex-*Velarde*)	10-7-64

Rio Ica—as the **Santilla**   *Shbldg. and Sh. Record,* 1965

PERU (*continued*)

PATROL BOATS (*continued*)

D: 100 tons (130 fl)   **S:** 30 kts   **Dim:** 33.4 (31.46 wl) × 6.4 × 1.7
A: 2/20-mm AA   **Man:** 4 officers, 27 men   **Range:** 1,100/15
Electron Equipt: Radar: 1/Decca TM 707
M: 2 Napier Deltic T38-37 diesels; 2 props; 6,280 hp

REMARKS: All delivered under own power by 10-65. Never fully equipped with armament, although fittings for four 533-mm torpedo tubes were installed in the decks. Air-conditioned. Steel hull, aluminum-alloy superstructure. Transferred to the Coast Guard in 1975 and renamed, their old names going to a new class of naval guided-missile corvettes.

PHILIPPINES

PERSONNEL (1978): 20,000 men, including a brigade of Marines

MERCHANT MARINE (1978): 577 ships—1,264,995 grt
(tankers: 57 ships—301,522 grt)

NAVAL AVIATION: Ten Philippine-built Brittain-Norman BN-2 Defender light maritime patrol aircraft and 10 MBB BO-105 helicopters are in service.

FRIGATES

◆ 1 ex-U.S. Savage class

	Bldr	Laid down	L	In serv.
PS 4 RAJAH LAKANDULA (ex-*Tran Hung Dao*, ex-*Camp*, DER-251)	Brown SB, Houston	27-1-43	16-4-43	16-9-45

Rajah Lakandula   1977

D: 1,590 tons (1,850 fl)   **S:** 19 kts   **Dim:** 93.27 × 11.15 × 4.27
A: 2/76.2-mm DP Mk 34 (I × 2)—4/20-mm AA (II × 2)—1/81-mm mortar combined with 1/12.7-mm machine gun—2/12.7-mm machine guns—6/324-mm Mk 32 ASW TT (III × 2)
Electron Equipt: Radars: 1/SPS-10, 1/SPS-28, 1/Mk 34
               Sonar: SQS-31
Man: 150 men   **Range:** 11,500/11   **Fuel:** 300 tons
M: 4 Fairbanks-Morse 38D⅛ × 10 diesels; 2 props; 6,080 hp

REMARKS: Transferred to Vietnam 6-2-71; to the Philippines, 5-4-75. Converted to radar picket in the late 1950s, but most electronic gear and ASW ordnance was removed in 1971. Has one Mk 63 and one Mk 51 gunfire-control system.

◆ 4 ex-U.S. Barnegat-class former seaplane tenders
     Bldr: Lake Washington SY, Houghton, Wash.

	Laid down	L	In serv.
PS-7 ANDRES BONIFACIO (ex-*Ly Thoung Kiet*, ex-*Chincoteague*, WHEC-375, ex-AVP-24)	23-7-41	15-4-42	12-4-43
PS-8 GREGORIO DE PILAR (ex-*Ngo Kuyen*, ex-*McCulloch*, WHEC-386, ex-*Wachapreague*, AGP-8, ex-AVP-56)	1-2-43	10-7-43	17-5-44
PS-9 DIEGO SILANG (ex-*Tran Quang Khai*, ex-*Bering Strait*, WHEC-382, ex-AVP-34)	7-6-43	15-1-44	19-7-44
PS-10 FRANCISCO DAGAHOY (ex-*Tran Binh Trong*, ex-*Castle Rock*, WHEC-383, ex-AVP-35)	12-7-43	11-3-44	8-10-44

D: 1,766 tons (2,800 fl)   **S:** 17 kts   **Dim:** 95.72 (91.44 wl) × 12.55 × 4.27
A: 1/127-mm DP—4/40-mm AA (II × 1, I × 2)—2/20-mm AA (I × 2)—2/12.7-mm machine guns—1/BO-105 helicopter
Electron Equipt: 1/SPN-21, 1/SPS-29, 1/Mk 26 (fire control)
Man: 160 men   **Fuel:** 400 tons   **Range:** 18,000/15   **Electric:** 600 kw
M: 4 Fairbanks-Morse 38D8⅛ × 10 diesels; 2 props; 6,080 hp

Andres Bonifacio   1977

FRIGATES (continued)

REMARKS: Transferred to U.S. Coast Guard in 1946-48, PS-8 having served as a motor torpedo-boat tender and the others as seaplane tenders. Transferred to South Vietnam in 1971-72 after extensive overhauls. Escaped from Vietnam 4-75 to Philippines, to which they were formally sold 5-4-76. Two other escapees, ex-*Yakutat* (WHEC-380) and *Cook Inlet* (WHEC-383) were in too poor condition to refit and have been used for cannibalization spares. PS-7–PS-10 received helicopter decks at the 01 level aft in 1978-79; a twin 40-mm mount was added in a tub projecting over the stern, adding 1 meter to the original length. Have Mk 52 GFCS with Mk 26 radar for the 127-mm gun.

◆ **3 ex-U.S. Cannon class** Bldr: Federal SB & DD Co., Newark, N.J.

	Laid down	L	In serv.
PS 76 DATU KALANTIAW (ex-*Booth*, DE-170)	30-1-43	21-6-43	18-9-43
PF-5 DATU SIKATUNA (ex-*Asahi*, ex-*Amick*, DE-168)	30-11-42	27-5-43	26-7-43
PF-6 RAJAH HUMABON (ex-*Hatsuhi*, ex-*Atherton*, DE-169)	14-1-43	27-5-43	29-8-43

D: 1,240 tons (1,620 fl) **S:** 20 kts
Dim: 93.27 (91.44 wl) × 11.15 × 3.56 (hull)
A: 3/76-mm DP (I × 3)—6/40-mm AA (II × 3)—2/20-mm AA (I × 2)—6/324-mm Mk 32 ASW TT (III × 2)—1/Hedgehog—1 depth-charge rack
Electron Equipt: Radar: 1/SPS-5, 1/SPS-6, 1/Mk 26 **Sonar:** . . .
Man: 165 men **Electric:** 680 kw **Fuel:** 260 tons **Range:** 11,600/11
M: 4 GM 16-278A diesels, electric drive; 2 props; 6,000 hp

REMARKS: Ex-*Asahi* and ex-*Hatsuhi* were transferred to Japan on 14-6-55 and stricken 6-75, reverting to U.S. ownership; they were sold to the Philippines 23-12-78 but remained laid up in Japan until towed to South Korea for overhaul in 1979. PS-76 was transferred on 15-12-67, purchased outright 31-8-78, having hitherto been on loan. The others were transferred on 13-9-76. Equipment and armament above are on PS-76, but the others are likely to be similar upon recommissioning. PS-76 has a tripod mast. All have one Mk 52 radar GFCS and one Mk 51 range-finder for 76-mm gun control, plus three Mk 51 mod. 2 GFCS for the 40-mm guns.

CORVETTES

◆ **2 ex-U.S. Auk-class former minesweepers**

	Bldr	Laid down	L	In serv.
PS 69 RIZAL (ex-*Murrelet*, MSF-372)	Savannah Mach. & Foundry, Ga.	24-8-44	29-12-44	21-8-45
PS 70 QUEZON (ex-*Vigilance*, MSF-324)	Associated SB, Seattle, Wash.	28-11-42	5-4-43	28-2-44

D: 890 tons (1,250 fl) **S:** 18 kts **Dim:** 67.39 (65.53 wl) × 9.8 × 3.28
A: 2/76-mm DP (I × 2)—4/40-mm AA (II × 2)—4/20-mm AA (II × 2)—3/324-mm Mk 32 ASW TT (III × 2)—1/Hedgehog—2/Mk 6 depth-charge throwers—2/depth-charge racks
Electron Equipt: Radar: 1/SPS-5 Sonar: SQS-17 **Man:** 100 men
Fuel: 216 tons **Electric:** 360 kw
M: 2 GM 12-278 (PS-70: 12-278A) diesels, electric drive; 2 props; 3,532 hp

Rizal

◆ **7 ex-U.S. PCE-821 and PCER-848 classes**

	Bldr	Laid down	L	In serv.
PS 19 MIGUEL MALVAR (ex-*Ngoc Hoi*, ex-*Brattleboro*, EPCER-852)	A	28-10-43	1-3-44	26-5-44
PS 22 SULTAN KUDARAT (ex-*Dong Da II*, ex-*Crestview*, PCE-895)	B	2-12-42	18-5-43	30-10-44
PS 23 DATU MARIKUDO (ex-*Van Kiep II*, ex-*Amherst*, PCER-853)	A	16-11-43	18-3-44	16-6-44
PS 28 CEBU (ex-*PCE-881*)	C	11-8-43	10-11-43	31-7-44
PS 29 NEGROS OCCIDENTAL (ex-*PCE-885*)	C	25-2-44	20-6-44	30-4-45
PS 31 PANGASINAN (ex-*PCE-891*)	B	28-10-42	24-4-43	15-6-44
PS 32 ILOILO (ex-*PCE-897*)	B	16-12-42	3-8-43	6-1-45

Bldrs: *A:* Pullman Standard Car Co., Chicago; *B:* Willamette Iron & Steel Corp. Portland, Ore.; *C:* Albina Eng. & Machine Works, Portland, Ore.

Leyte—lost 1979   G. Arra, 1977

CORVETTES (continued)

D: 903 tons (fl) **S:** 15 kts **Dim:** 56.24 (54.86 wl) × 10.08 × 2.87
A: PS-19–23: 1/76-mm DP−2/40-mm AA (I × 2)−8/20-mm AA (II × 1)
PS-28–32: 1/76-mm DP−6/40-mm AA (II × 3)−4/20 mm AA (I × 4)
Electron Equipt: Radar: 1/SPN-21 (PS-19–23: 1/LN-66)
Man: 100 men **Range:** 9,000/10 **Fuel:** 125 tons
Electric: 240−280 kw
M: 2 GM 12-278A diesels; 2 props; 2,000 hp (PS-19, 28, 31: 2 GM 12-567A diesels; 2 props; 1,800 hp)

REMARKS: PS-28 through PS-32 were transferred 7-48; a fifth, *Leyte*, (PS-30, ex-PCE-885), was lost by grounding in 1979. PS-19 through-23 were transferred to South Vietnam on 11-7-66, 29-11-61, and 6-70, and escaped Vietnam in 5-75; they were sold to the Philippines 11-75 (PS-23: 5-4-76). All ASW equipment is now deleted from all units. Ex-PCER and EPCER originally had longer forecastles as rescue ships; they were brought to standard PCE configuration before transfer to South Vietnam.

◆ 1 ex-U.S. Admirable-class former minesweeper
Bldr: Winslow Marine Railway, Seattle, Wash.

	Laid down	L	In serv.
PS 20 MAGAT SALAMAT (ex-*Chi Lang II*, ex-*Gayety*, MSF-239)	14-11-43	19-3-44	23-9-45

Magat Salamat 1977

D: 650 tons light (905 fl) **S:** 14 kts **Dim:** 56.24 (54.86 wl) × 10.06 × 2.75
A: 1/76-mm DP−2/40-mm (I × 2)−8/20-mm AA (II × 4)
Electron Equipt: Radar: 1/LN-66 **Electric:** 280 kw **Fuel:** 140 tons
M: 2 Cooper-Bessemer GSB-8 diesels; 2 props; 1,710 hp

REMARKS: Transferred to Vietnam and escaped to the Philippines 4-75. Acquired by the latter in 11-75.

◆ 3 ex-U.S. PC-461-class former submarine chasers

	Bldr	Laid down	L	In serv.
PS 24 BATANGAS (ex-PC-1134)	Defoe, Bay City, Mich.	4-12-42	18-1-43	11-9-43
PS 29 NEGROS ORIENTAL (ex-E-312, ex-*L'Inconstant*, ex-PC-1171)	L. D. Smith, Sturgeon Bay, Wis.	12-3-43	15-5-43	24-9-43
PS 80 NUEVA VISCAYA (ex-USAF *Altus*, ex-PC-568)	Brown SB, Houston, Tex.	15-9-41	25-4-42	13-7-42

D: 280 tons (450 fl) **S:** 18 kts **Dim:** 52.93 × 7.01 × 2.31 (hull)
A: 1/76-mm DP−1/40-mm AA− 3 or 5/20-mm AA (I × 3 or 5)
Man: 70 men **Electric:** 120 kw **Fuel:** 62 tons
M: 2 GM 16-278A diesel; 2 props; 2,880 hp

REMARKS: The EC-312 escaped from Cambodia to the Philippines and was acquired by the latter in 1976; She had previously been transferred to France in 1951, then to Cambodia in 1956. PS-80 served the U.S. Air Force 1963-68, transferring to the Philippines in 3-68. PS-24 was transferred in 7-48. All originally had different diesels, but now have been standardized. Several others have been stricken, including the *Capiz* (PS-27, ex-PC-1564) in 1979.

PATROL BOATS

◆ 5 (+ . . .) Katapangan class
Bldrs: W. Müller, Hameln, West Germany; Cavite NY; and Boseco, Bekan

	In serv.		In serv.
P 101 KATAPANGAN	9-2-79	P 102 BAGONG LAKAS	9-2-79
P 103 N . . .	. . .	P 104 N . . .	. . .
P 105 N . . .	. . .		

D: 135 tons (150 fl) **S:** 29 kts **Dim:** 37.0 × 6.2 × 1.7
A: 4/30-mm AA Emerlec (II × 2)
M: 2 MTU diesels; 2 props; 5,000 hp

REMARKS: Designed in West Germany. Prototype delivered for trials 11-10-78. Up to nine more may be built.

◆ 1 ex-U.S. PGM-71 class Bldr: Peterson Builders, Sturgeon Bay, Wis.

PG 60 BASILAN (ex-*Hon Troc*, ex-PGM-83)

D: 130 tons (145 fl) **S:** 17 kts **Dim:** 30.8 (30.2 wl) × 6.4 × 1.85
A: 1/40-mm AA−4/20-mm AA (II × 2)−4/12.7-mm machine guns (III × 2)
Electron Equipt: Radar: 1/Raytheon 1500B
Range: 1,000/12 **Man:** 27 men
M: 8 GM 6-71 diesels; 2 props; 2,200 hp

REMARKS: In service 4-67. Escaped from Vietnam 4-75, the only one of her class to do so out of 20 transferred; acquired officially by the Philippines 12-76.

◆ 4 ex-U.S. PGM-39 class Bldr: Tacoma Boat, Tacoma, Wash.

	In serv.		In serv.
PG 61 AGUSAN (ex-PGM-39)	3-60	PG 63 ROMBLON (ex-PGM-41)	6-60
PG 62 CATANDUANES (ex-PGM-40)	3-60	PG 64 PALAWAN (ex-PGM-42)	6-60

D: 122 tons **S:** 17 kts **Dim:** 30.6 × 6.4 × 2.1 (props)
A: 2/20-mm AA (I × 2) **Electron Equipt:** Radar: 1/Raytheon 1500

PATROL BOATS (continued)

Catanduanes—in Coast Guard Service   G. Arra, 1977

Man: 15 men
M: 2 MTU MB 820 Db diesels; 2 props; 1,900 hp

REMARKS: PG-62 has served in the Coast Guard but may now be naval again.

PATROL CRAFT

◆ **80 fiberglass-hulled** Bldr: Marcelo, Manila, 1976-. . .

PSB 411   PSB 414   PSB 417-434   PSB . . .

PSB-411   G. Arra, 1977

D: 21.75 (fl)   **S:** 42 kts   **Dim:** 14.07 × 4.32 × 1.04 (1.48 props)
A: 4/12.7-mm machine guns (II × 1, I × 2)
Electric: 7.5 kva   **Man:** 6 men   **Range:** 200/36
M: 2 MTU 8V-331 TC80 diesels; 2 props; 1,800 hp

REMARKS: Eighty were ordered 8-75, but of 25 hulls completed during 1975, 15 were destroyed by fire. Twin machine-gun mount is recessed into the forecastle.

◆ **6 Australian fiberglass-hulled** Bldr: De Havilland Marine, Sydney

PC 326-331

D: 16.5 tons (fl)   **S:** 25 kts   **Dim:** 14.0 × 4.6 × 1.0
A: 2/12.7-mm machine guns   **Man:** 8 men   **Range:** 500/12
M: 2 Caterpillar D348 diesels; 2 props; 740 hp

REMARK: In service 20-11-74 to 8-2-75.

◆ **14 U.S. Swift Mk III class** Bldr: Sewart, La.

PCF 318-323   PCF 333-340

PCF-335   G. Arra, 1977

D: 28 tons (36.7 fl)   **S:** 30 kts   **Dim:** 19.78 × 5.5 × 1.8
A: 2/12.7-mm machine guns (I × 2)−2/7.6-mm machine guns (I × 2)
Range: 500/30   **Man:** 5 men
M: 3 GM 8V 71 TI diesels; 3 props; 1,950 hp

REMARKS: Aluminum construction. Pilothouse offset to starboard. Some or all have served in the Philippine Coast Guard. In service 1972-76.

◆ **3 Abra class**

	Bldr	In serv.
FB 83 ABRA	Vosper, Singapore	8-1-70
FB 84 BUKINDON	Cavite NY	1971
FB 85 TABLAS	Cavite NY	1975

PATROL CRAFT (continued)

D: 40 tons   **S:** 25 kts   **Dim:** 26.7 × 5.8 × 1.5
A: 2/20-mm AA   **Man:** 3 officers, 12 men
M: 2 MTU diesels; 2 props; 2,400 hp

REMARKS: Wooden hulls, aluminum superstructure. Construction financed by Australia. Have served in the Coast Guard.

◆ **13 U.S. Swift Mk I and II class**   Bldr: Sewart, Berwick, La.

PCF 300   PCF 301   PCF 306-PCF 316

PCF-308 – Swift Mk II type   G. Arra, 1977

D: 17.5 tons (22.1 fl)   **S:** 24 kts   **Dim:** 15.66 × 4.55 × 1.8 (props)
A: 2/12.7-mm machine guns (II × 1)   **Electric:** 6 kw
Range: 400/22   **Man:** 6 men
M: 2 GM 12 V 71 N diesels; 2 props; 850 hp

REMARKS: In service 1966-70. PCF-300 and PCF-301, transferred 1966, are *Swift* Mk I class, 15.3 overall and with flush-decked hulls. All-aluminum construction. PCF-303, PCF-324, PCF-325, and PCF-317 (the latter of ferro-concrete construction and used as a yacht) were discarded in 1976; PCF-304, PCF-305, and one other were written-off in 1976.

NOTE: The *Camiguin*-class hydrofoil patrol craft *Camiguin* and *Siquijor* are now used as personnel launches; the similar *Bontoc* and *Balek* have been discarded.

MINE WARFARE SHIPS

◆ **2 ex-U.S. Falcon-class coastal minesweepers**   Bldr: Bellingham SY, Wash.

	In serv.
M 55 ZAMBALES (ex-MSC-218)	7-3-56
M 56 ZAMBOANGA DEL NORTE (ex-MSC-219)	23-4-56

D: 320 tons (372 fl)   **S:** 13 kts (8 sweeping)   **Dim:** 43.0 × 7.95 × 2.55
A: 2/20-mm AA (II × 1)   **Man:** 39 men   **Range:** 2,500/10
M: 2 GM 8-268A diesels; 2 props; 1,200 hp

REMARKS: Wooden construction. The two U.S. *Agile*-class ocean minesweepers were transferred in 1972; the *Davao del Norte* (ex-*Firm*, MSO-444) and *Davao del Sur* (ex-*Energy*, MSO-436) were stricken in 1976.

AMPHIBIOUS WARFARE SHIPS

◆ **21 ex-U.S. LST-1 and LST-542-class landing ships**

	Bldr	In serv.
LT 54 AGUSAN DEL SUR (ex-*Nha Trang*, ex-*Jerome Cty.*, LST-848)	A	20-1-45
LT 85 BATAAN (ex-*Caddo Parish*, LST-515)	B	28-1-44
LT 86 CAGAYAN (ex-*Hickman Cty.*, LST-825)	C	8-12-44
LT 87 COTABATO DEL SUR (ex-*Thi Nai*, ex-*Cayuga Cty.*, LST-529)	D	29-2-44
LT 93 MINDORO OCCIDENTAL (ex-T-LST-222)	B	10-9-43
LT 94 SURIGAO DEL NORTE (ex-T-LST-488)	E	24-5-43
LT 95 SURIGAO DEL SUR (ex-T-LST-546)	C	27-3-44
LT 97 ILOCOS NORTE (ex-*Madera Cty.*, LST-905)	F	20-1-45
LT 500 TARLAC (ex-T-LST-47)	F	8-11-43
LT 501 LAGUNA (ex-T-LST-230)	B	3-11-43
LT 502 SAMAR ORIENTAL (ex-T-LST-287)	A	15-12-43
LT 503 LANAO DEL SUR (ex-T-LST-491)	C	3-12-43
LT 504 LANAO DEL NORTE (ex-T-LST-566)	C	29-5-44
LT 505 LEYTE DEL SUR (ex-T-LST-607)	B	24-4-44
LT 506 N . . . (ex-*Oosumi*, ex-*Daggett Cty.*, LST-689)	D	2-5-44
LT 507 BENGUET (ex-*Davies Cty.*, T-LST-692)	D	10-5-44
LT 508 AURORA (ex-*Harris Cty.*, T-LST-822)	C	23-11-44
LT 509 N . . . (ex-*Shimokita*, ex-*Hillsdale Cty.*, LST-835)	A	20-11-44
LT 510 N . . . (ex-*Shiretoko*, ex-*Nansemond Cty.*, LST-1064)	G	12-3-45
LT 511 COTABATO DEL NORTE (ex-*Orleans Parrish*, T-LST-1069, ex-MCS-6, ex-LST-1069)	G	31-3-45
LT 512 TAWI-TAWI (ex-T-LST-1072)	G	12-4-45

Bldrs: *A*, American Bridge, Ambridge, Pa.; *B*, Chicago Bridge & Iron Co., Seneca, Ill.; *C*, Missouri Valley Bridge & Iron Co., Evansville, Ind.; *D*, Jeffersonville Boat and Machinery Co., Jeffersonville, Ind.; *E*, Kaiser Co., Richmond. Cal.; *F*, Dravo Corp., Pittsburgh, Pa.; *G*, Bethlehem Steel, Hingham, Mass.

D: 1,620 tons (4,080 fl)   **S:** 11 kts   **Dim:** 99.98 (96.32 wl) × 15.24 × 4.29
A: 7–8/40-mm AA (II × 1 or 2, I × 4–6)–2–4/20-mm AA
Electric: 300 kw   **Man:** 60–100 men   **Fuel:** 570 tons
M: 2 GM 12-567A diesels (LT 510, 511, 512: 2 GM 12-278A); 2 props; 1,700 hp

REMARKS: LT-54 and LT-87 escaped from Vietnam (to which they had been transferred in 4-70 and 12-63, respectively) in 4-75; they were officially transferred to the Philippines on 17-11-75. LT-85, LT-86, and LT-97 were transferred in 11-69. LT-93, LT-94, and LT-95 were transferred unarmed in 7-72 but may since have received guns. LT-500–LT-505, LT-507, LT-508, LT-511, and LT-512 were purchased in 1976, having previously been stricken by the USN and laid up in Japan. LT-506, LT-509, and LT-510 had been transferred to Japan 4-61 and stricken in 1975; They were purchased in 1978. All the LT-500 series were refitted and thoroughly overhauled in Japan, recommissioning in 1978-79. Armament: Some ex-T-LSTs carry only 4 20-mm AA (I × 4), while others received a single 40-mm forward after transfer, plus several 20-mm AA. LT-87 has four sets of Welin davits for LCVP landing craft, the others only two; ex-T-LSTs do not carry LCVPs.

◆ **4 ex-U.S. LSM-1-class landing ships**

	Bldr	In serv.
LP 41 ISABELA (ex-LSM-463)	Brown SB, Houston	7-3-45
LP 65 BATANES (ex-*Huong Giang*, ex-*Oceanside*, ex-LSM-175)	Charleston NY	25-9-44

AMPHIBIOUS WARFARE SHIPS *(continued)*

LP 66 WESTERN SAMAR (ex-*Hat Giang*, ex-9011,   Pullman, Chicago   9-12-44
ex-LSM-335)

LP 68 MINDORO ORIENTAL (ex-LSM-320)   Pullman, Chicago   19-8-44

D: 513 tons (1,095 fl)   **S:** 12 kts   **Dim:** 62.02 × 10.52 × 2.24
A: 2/40-mm AA (II × 1) − 4/20-mm AA (I × 4)   **Electric:** 240 kw
Man: 39 men   **Fuel:** 165 tons   **Range:** 5,000/7
M: 2 GM 16-278A (LP 41: Fairbanks-Morse 38D8⅛ × 10) diesels; 2 props; 2,800 hp

REMARKS: LP-41 transferred 3-61, LP-68 in 4-62. LP-65 and LP-66 escaped from Vietnam (to which they had been transferred in 8-61 and 10-55, respectively, LP-65 having served in the French Navy from 1-54 to 10-55) in 4-75 and were officially transferred on 17-11-75. LP-66 was equipped with hospital facilities in a deckhouse filling much of her tank deck while in Vietnamese service, but retained guns. Ex-*Han Giang*, ex-LSM-110, which also escaped, was transferred also on 17-11-75, but used for cannibalization.

◆ **3 ex-U.S. LSSL-1-class gunfire-support landing ships**

Bldr: Lawley & Sons, Neponset, Mass.; LS-49: Commercial Iron Works, Portland, Ore.

In serv.
LF 48 CAMARINES SUR (ex-*Nguyen Duc Bong*, ex-LSSL-129)   31-12-44
LF 49 SULU (ex-*Nguyen Ngoc Long*, ex-LSSL-96)   24-1-45
LF 50 LA UNION (ex-*Doan Ngoc Tang*, ex-*Hallebarde*, ex-LSSL-9)   6-9-44

D: 250 tons (387 fl)   **S:** 14.4 kts   **Dim:** 48.15 × 7.21 × 1.73
A: 1/76-mm DP − 4/20-mm AA (II × 2) − 4/12.7-mm machine guns (I × 4)
Electric: 120 kw   **Fuel:** 84 tons   **Range:** 5,000/12
M: 8 GM 6-71 diesels; 2 controllable-pitch props; 1,320 hp

REMARKS: These are ex-Vietnamese ships (transferred 1965-66) that took refuge in the Philippines and were acquired by the latter 17-11-75. LS-50 had earlier served in the French (1951-55) and Japanese (1956-64) navies. Four additional ex-Japanese sisters were to have been transferred in 1978, but the sale was canceled.

◆ **4 ex-U.S. LSIL-351-class personnel landing ships**   Bldr: New Jersey SB Corp., Barber, NJ. (LS-52: G. Lawley & Sons, Neponset, Mass.)

In serv.
LF 36 MARINDUQUE (ex-P-111, ex-LSIL-875)   16-10-44
LF 37 SORSOGON (ex-*Thien Kich*, ex-L9038, ex-LSIL-872)   11-10-44
LF 52 CAMARINES NORTE (ex-*Loi Cong*, ex-L9034, ex-LSIL-699)   25-6-44
LF 53 MISAMIS OCCIDENTAL (ex-*Tam Set*, ex-L9033, ex-LSIL-871)   10-10-44

D: 227 tons (387 fl)   **S:** 14.4 kts   **Dim:** 48.46 (46.63 wl) × 7.21 × 1.73
A: 1/76-mm DP − 1/40-mm AA − 2/20-mm AA (I × 2) − 2/81-mm mortars − 2/60-mm mortars − 4/12.7-mm machine guns (I × 4)
Electric: 40 kw   **Range:** 5,000/12   **Man:** 40 men   **Fuel:** 113 tons

REMARKS: LF-36 served in the Cambodian Navy from 5-62 to 4-75, where she escaped to the Philippines, being incorporated officially into the Philippine Navy on 17-11-77, as were IF-37, LF-52, IF-53; the latter had served in the French Navy from 1951-55, when they were turned over to South Vietnam. All have bow doors and can transport about 200 troops.

◆ **3 ex-U.S. LCU-1466-class utility landing craft**   Bldr: Japan

L . . . N . . . (ex-LCU-2002, ex-LCU-1603)
L . . . N . . . (ex-LCU-2003, ex-LCU-1604)
L . . . N . . . (ex-LCU-2005, ex-LCU-1606)

D: 180 tons (347 fl)   **S:** 8 kts   **Dim:** 35.05 × 10.36 × 1.6 (aft)
A: 2/20-mm AA (I × 2)   **Man:** 6 men plus 8 troops
Cargo capacity: 167 tons
M: 3 GM Gray marine 64YTL diesels; 3 props; 675 hp

REMARKS: Built in Japan under the offshore procurement plan; in service 3-55, stricken 1975. Purchased by the Philippines in 1975 while laid up, then refitted and recommissioned in 1979.

◆ **9 U.S. LCM(8)-class landing craft**

LCM 257   LCM 258   LCM 260-LCM 266

D: 118 tons (fl)   **S:** 9 kts   **Dim:** 22.43 × 6.42 × 1.4 (aft)
M: 4 GM 6-71 diesels; 2 props; 600 hp   **Cargo capacity:** 54 tons

REMARKS: Transferred 19-73-75. The similar *Bagong Pilipino* (TK-81) and *Dakila* (TK-82), built in the Philippines, have been stricken.

◆ **75 ex-U.S. LCM(6)-class landing craft**

D: 56 tons (fl)   **S:** 10 kts   **Dim:** 17.1 × 4.4 × 1.2 (aft)
Cargo capacity: 30 tons
M: 2 GM Gray Marine 64HN9 diesels; 2 props; 330 hp

REMARKS: Transferred 1955-78. Twenty-five ex-Japanese craft were purchased in 1978; the remainder came directly from the U.S. Navy.

AUXILIARY SHIPS

YACHTS

◆ **1 new construction**   Bldr: Vosper-Thornycroft, Singapore

N . . .

D: . . . tons   **S:** 28.5 kts   **Dim:** 64.7 × 11.6 × 1.8
A: . . .   **Man:** . . .   **Range:** . . .
M: 3 MTU 12V 538 TB91 diesels; 3 props; 7,500 hp

REMARKS: In service 12-77. Low freeboard hull with forecastle, large stack, and lattice mast; used as a "command ship" for the president.

◆ **1 former transport**   Bldr: Ishikawajima, Harima, Japan, 1958

TP 777 ANG PANGULO (ex-*The President*, ex-*Roxas*, ex-*Lapu-Lapa*)

Ang Pangulo   G. Arra, 1977

AUXILIARY SHIPS (continued)

D: 2,230 tons (2,750 fl)   **S:** 18 kts   **Dim:** 83.84 × 13.01 × 6.4
A: 2/20-mm AA   **Electric:** 820 kw   **Man:** 81 men plus 48 passengers
M: 2 Mitsui-Burmeister & Wain DE 642 VBF 75 diesels; 2 props; 5,000 hp

REMARKS: Built as war reparations. Can be converted for use as a troop transport.

TENDERS

◆ **3 ex-U.S. Achelous-class repair ships** Bldr: Chicago Bridge & Iron Co., Seneca, Ill.
(AR-67: Bethlehem Steel, Hingham, Mass.)

		L	In serv.
AE 517 YAKAL (ex-*Satyr*, ARL-23, ex-LST-852)		13-11-44	24-11-44
AR 67 KAMAGONG (ex-*Aklan*, ex-*Romulus*, ARL-22, ex-LST-926)		15-11-44	9-12-44
AR 88 NARRA (ex-*Krishna*, ARL-38, ex-LST-1149)		25-5-45	3-12-45

D: 3,960 tons (fl)   **S:** 11.6 kts   **Dim:** 99.98 (96.32 wl) × 15.24 × 3.71
A: 8/40-mm AA (IV × 2)   **Electric:** 420 kw   **Fuel:** 620 tons
Man: 250 men
M: 2 GM 12-567A diesels (AR-67: GM 12-278A); 2 props; 1,800 hp

REMARKS: AE-517, transferred 24-1-77, may be in use as an ammunition transport,
based on the hull number, but was equipped for repair duties on delivery. AR-67 was
transferred in 11-61 and AR-88 on 31-10-71. All have a 60-ton capacity A-frame lift
boom to port and one 10-ton derrick and one 20-ton derrick.

◆ **2 ex-U.S. LST-542-class small craft tenders**

	Bldr	In serv.
AL 57 SIERRA MADRE (ex-*Dumagat*, ex-*My Tho*, ex-*Harnett County*, AGP-821, ex-LST-821)	Missouri Valley B & I, Evansville, Ind.	14-11-44
AE 516 APAYAO (ex-*Can Tho*, ex-*Garrett County*, AGP-786, ex-LST-786)	Dravo Corp., Pittsburgh, Pa.	28-8-44

D: 1,620 tons (4,080 fl)   **S:** 11.6 kts
Dim: 99.98 (96.32 wl) × 15.24 × 4.29 (max.)
A: 8/40-mm AA (II × 2, I × 4)–4/20-mm AA (II × 2)
Electric: 500 kw   **Man:** 160 men   **Range:** 19,000/10   **Fuel:** 370 tons
M: 2 GM 12-567A diesels; 2 props; 1,700 hp

REMARKS: Converted in the mid-1960s to act as tenders to riverine-warfare craft. Retain bow doors, but much of the tank deck is filled with repair shops and bins for spare
parts. Helicopter deck amidships, tripod masts, 10-ton derrick, and enlarged hatch.
Transferred to South Vietnam 10-70 and 4-71; both escaped 4-75 and purchased
outright on 13-9-77. Different hull numbers (and change of letter-designator and name
for AL-57 from AE-57) may indicate new roles.

CARGO TRANSPORTS

◆ **1 ex-U.S. Alamosa class** Bldr: Froemming Bros. Inc., Milwaukee, Wis.

TK 90 MACTAN (ex-*Kukui*, WAK-186, ex-*Colquitt*, AK-174)

D: 4,900 tons (7,450 fl)   **S:** 12.5 kts   **Dim:** 103.18 (97.54 wl) × 15.24 × 6.43
A: 2/20-mm AA   **Man:** 85 men   **Fuel:** 830 tons

REMARKS: In service 22-9-45; 6,071 dwt. Built for U.S. Maritime Commission, taken
over by the Navy upon completion, then transferred to the U.S. Coast Guard 24-9-45.

First platform deck in cargo-hold area converted to personnel accommodations.
Transferred to the Philippines 1-3-72 and used as a military transport, supply ship,
and lighthouse tender.

◆ **3 ex-U.S. Army FS-381 class** Bldr: Ingalls, Pascagoula, Miss., 1943-44

TK 79 LIMASAWA (ex-*Nettle*, WAK 129, ex-FS-169)
TK . . . N . . . (ex-*Miho*, ex-FS-524)
TK . . . N . . . (ex-*Nasami*, ex-FS-408)

D: 473 tons light (950 fl)   **S:** 13 kts   **Dim:** 53.8 (50.27 pp) × 9.75 × 3.05
A: 2/20-mm AA (I × 2)   **Electric:** 225 kw   **Man:** . . .
Fuel: 67 tons   **Range:** 4,150/10, 3,700/11   **Cargo Capacity:** 345 tons
M: 2 GM 6-278A diesels; 2 props; 1,000 hp

REMARKS: The *Limasawa* was loaned in 1-68 and purchased outright 31-8-78. The other
two were purchased 24-9-76 after having served in the Japanese Navy as an inshore
minesweeper depot ship and a mine countermeasures support ship; they were to be
refitted and should have been recommissioned during 1979. All were to serve as buoy
tenders and lighthouse supply ships.

◆ **2 ex-U.S. Army FS-330 class** Bldr: Higgins, Inc., New Orleans, 1943-44

TK 45 LAUIS LEDGE (ex-FS-185)
TK 46 CAPE BOJEADOR (ex-FS-203)

Cape Bojeador—in Coast Guard colors   G. Arra, 1977

D: 420 tons light (742 fl)   **S:** 10 kts   **Dim:** 51.77 (48.77 pp) × 9.75 × 2.43
A: 2/20-mm AA (I × 2)   **Electric:** 225 kw   **Man:** . . .
Range: 1,370/10   **Fuel:** 18 tons   **Cargo Capacity:** 150 tons
M: 4 Buda-Lanova 6 DHMR-1879 diesels; 2 props; 680 hp

REMARKS: TK-45 transferred 11-47; TK-46 transferred 2-50. Can carry up to 50 tons of

CARGO TRANSPORTS *(continued)*

fuel for a range of 3,830/10. Used as navigational buoy tenders and lighthouse supply ships.

◆ **1 ex-Australian motor stores lighter** Bldr: . . ., 1944

TK . . . PEARL BANK (ex-U.S. Army LO-4, ex-. . .)

D: 140 tons light (345 fl)   **S:** 8 kts   **Dim:** 37.26 × 7.47 × 2.07
A: 2/20-mm AA   **Man:** 35 men   **Range:** 2,000/6   **Fuel:** 20 tons
Cargo Capacity: 170 tons
M: 2 Fairbanks-Morse 35F8¼ diesels; 2 props; 240 hp

REMARKS: Transferred 1947. Used as a navigational buoy tender and lighthouse supply ship.

◆ **1 ex-U.S. Admirable-class minesweeper** Bldr: Gulf SB Corp., Madisonville, La.

	Laid down	L	In serv.
TK 21 MOUNT SAMAT (ex-*Pagasa*, ex-*Santa Maria*, ex-*Quest*, MSF-281)	24-11-43	16-3-44	25-10-44

Mount Samat   G. Arra, 1977

D: 650 tons (945 fl)   **S:** 14.8 kts   **Dim:** 58.0 (54.86 wl) × 10.06 × 2.97
A: 2/20-mm AA   **Electric:** 280 kw   **Man:** 60 men   **Fuel:** 138 tons
M: 2 Cooper-Bessemer GSB-8 diesels; 2 props; 1,710 hp

REMARKS: Transferred 2-7-48 and then converted to presidential yacht with considerable additions to superstructure and increased rake to bow. Now primarily used as a lighthouse supply ship.

◆ **1 ex-U.S. Coast Guard Balsam-class buoy tender**

Bldr: Marine Iron & SB Corp., Duluth, Minn.

TK 89 KALINGA (ex-*Redbud*, WAGL-398, ex-T-AKL-398, ex-AG-398)

D: 935 tons (1,020 fl)   **S:** 13 kts   **Dim:** 54.86 × 11.28 × 3.96
A: 1/20-mm AA   **Man:** 50 men   **Range:** 3,500/7.5
M: 2 Cooper-Bessemer GSD-8 diesels, electric drive; 1 prop; 1,200 hp

Kalinga—in Coast Guard colors   1977

REMARKS: In service 2-5-44. Built for U.S. Coast Guard, transferred to the U.S. Navy on 25-3-49 as AG-398, to Military Sealift Command on 10-49 as T-AKL-398, and returned 20-11-70 to the U.S. Coast Guard. Transferred to the Philippines 1-3-72. Has helicopter platform and ice-breaking bow—the latter, a useful feature in Philippine waters.

SERVICE CRAFT

TANKERS

◆ **3 ex-U.S. 174-foot YO and YOG-class small tankers**

Bldr: R.T.C. SB, Camden, N.J. (YO-78: Puget Sound NY)

		L
YO 35 LAKE MAINIT (ex-YO-116)		1943
YO 43 LAKE NAUJAN (ex-YO-173)		1944
YO 78 LAKE BUHI (ex-YOG-73)		1944

D: 445 tons light (1,420 fl)   **S:** 8 kts   **Dim:** 53.04 × 10.01 × 4.27
A: 2/20-mm AA   **Man:** . . .   **Cargo Capacity:** 985 tons
M: 2 Union diesels; 2 props; 560 hp (YO 78: 2 GM 8-278A diesel; 2 props; 640 hp)

REMARKS: YO-35 was transferred in 7-75, YO-43 in 7-48, and YO-78 (formerly used as a gasoline tanker) in 7-67. Ex-U.S. YOG-33 and YOG-80, which escaped from Vietnam, were used for cannibalization spares.

◆ **2 ex-U.S. 174-foot YW-class water tankers** Bldr: L. D. Smith SB, Sturgeon Bay, Wis. (YW-111: Marine Iron & SB Co., Duluth, Minn.)

	L	Transferred
YW 33 LAKE BOLUAN (ex-YW-111)	1943	16-7-75
YW 34 LAKE PAOAY (ex-YW-130)	1943	16-7-75
YW 42 LAKE LANAO (ex-YM-125)	1943	7-78

D: 445 tons light (1,235 fl)   **S:** 8 kts   **Dim:** 53.04 × 10.01 × 4.0
A: 2/20-mm AA (I × 2)   **Man:** . . .   **Cargo Capacity:** 743 tons

REMARKS: One other unit, which escaped from Vietnam, ex-U.S. YO-103, was cannibalized.

TUGS

◆ **1 ex-U.S. Army tug**

YQ 58 TIBOLI (ex-LT-1976)

REMARK: Transferred, 3-76.

◆ **5 ex-U.S. YTL-442 class** Bldr: Everett-Pacific Co., Everett, Wash. (YQ-222: Winslow Marine Railway & SB, Winslow, Wash.)

YQ 222 IGOROT (ex-YTL-572)	YQ 226 TASADAY (ex-YTL-425)
YQ 223 TAGBANUA (ex-YTL-429)	YQ 271 AGNO RIVER (ex-YAS-3,
YQ 225 ILONGOT (ex-YTL-427)	ex-YTL-750)

D: 70 tons (80 fl) **S:** 9 kts **Dim:** 20.17 × 5.18 × 1.5
M: 1 Hamilton 685A diesel; 300 hp

REMARKS: Built 1944-45. Transferred 7-48, 5-63, 12-69, 8-71, 11-75, and 9-76 — the latter two transferred from Japan, which had received them from the U.S. in 1-55. Two others, the *Maranao* (YQ-221, ex-YTL-554) and the *Aeta* (YQ-224, ex-YTL-449) have been scrapped. The ex-Japanese craft were overhauled and arrived in the Philippines during 1979.

FLOATING DRY DOCKS

◆ **1 ex-U.S. AFDL** Bldr: V.P. Loftis, Wilmington, N.C., 1944

YD 205 (ex-AFDL-44, ex-ARDC-. . .)

Lift Capacity: 2,800 tons **Dim:** 118.6 × 25.6 × 3.1 (light)

REMARK: Transferred, 9-69.

◆ **2 ex-U.S. AFDL-1 class**

	Bldr	L	Transferred
YD 200 (ex-AFDL-24)	Doullet & Ewin, Mobile, Ala.	1944	7-48
YD 204 (ex-AFDL-20)	G.D. Auchter, Jacksonville, Fla.	1944	10-61

Lift Capacity: 1,000 tons **Dim:** 60.96 × 19.51 × 1.04 (light)

◆ **2 ex-U.S. Army**

	L	Transferred
YD 201 (ex-AFDL-3681)	1943	5-52
YD 203 (ex-AFDL-3682)	1943	8-55

Lift Capacity: 150 tons **Dim:** 30.63 × 15.83 × 1.0 (light)

FLOATING CRANES

◆ **1 ex-U.S. floating crane**

	L	Transferred
YU 206 (ex-YD-163)	1943	1-71

D: 650 tons (fl) **Lift Capacity:** 30 tons **Dim:** 36.58 × 13.72 × 2.13

◆ **1 ex-U.S. floating crane**

	L	Transferred
YU 207 (ex-YD-191)	1944	8-71

D: 920 tons (fl) **Lift Capacity:** 60 tons **Dim:** 36.58 × 18.24 × 2.13

FLOATING REPAIR BARGES

◆ **1 ex-U.S. Army 230 class**

	L	Transferred
YD 202 (ex-. . .)	1943	7-49

D: 2,100 tons (fl) **Dim:** 64.0 × 12.5 × 3.4 **A:** 2/20-mm AA

BARGES

◆ **1 ex-U.S. YCV-3-class former aircraft transport lighter**

Bldr: City Lumber Co., Bridgeport, Conn., 1943

YB 206 (ex-YCV-7)

Dim: 33.53 × 9.14 × . . . **Lift Capacity:** 250 tons

REMARK: Transferred, 5-63.

◆ **2 ex-U.S. Navy barges**

	Transferred
YC 207 (ex-YC-1402)	8-59
YC 301 (ex-YC-1403)	8-71

Dim: 24.38 × 8.73 × 1.22

COAST GUARD

The size of the Philippine Coast Guard has fluctuated widely since its establishment in the early 1970s. At one time it had responsibility for maintaining navigational aids and included many of the tenders now returned to the Navy. The majority of the patrol craft operated by the Coast Guard have been back under naval control since 1977, leaving only a few small craft and the larger ships described below still under Coast Guard control.

◆ **2 Bessang Pass-class search and rescue boats**
Bldr: Sumidagawa, Tokyo, Japan, 1976-77

SAR 99 BESSANG PASS SAR 100 TIRAD PASS

D: 275 tons (fl) **S:** 30 kts **Dim:** 44.0 × 7.4 × 1.5
A: machine guns **Man:** 32 men
M: 2 diesels; 2 props; . . . hp

Bessang Pass   G. Arra, 1977

PHILIPPINES (*continued*)

COAST AND GEODETIC SURVEY

The ships listed below are subordinate to the Ministry of Defense and are used for hydrographic survey.

◆ **1 survey ship** Bldr: Walker, Maryborough, Australia, 1969

ATYIMBA

Atyimba   G. Arra, 1977

D: 611 tons (686 fl)   **S:** 11 kts   **Dim:** 49.08 (44.3 pp) × 10.14 × 2.74
Electric: 175 kw   **Range:** 5,000/8   **Man:** 54 men
M: Mirrlees-Blackstone 6-cyl. diesels; 1,620 hp

◆ **2 Arinya-class coastal survey ships** Bldr: Walker, Maryborough, Australia

	L
ARINYA	1962
ALUNYA	1964

D: 245 tons (fl)   **S:** 10 kts   **Dim:** 30.64 (27.44 pp) × 6.76 × 2.43
Man: 33 men   **M:** 2 GM 6-71 diesels; 2 props; 336 hp

◆ **1 ex-U.S. coast & geodetic survey ship** Bldr: Lake Washington SY, Houghton, Wash.

	Laid down	In serv.
PATHFINDER (ex-*Pathfinder*, OSS-30, ex-AGS-1)	3-9-42	31-8-42

D: 2,175 tons (fl)   **S:** 14 kts   **Dim:** 69.9 (63.8 wl) × 11.89 × 4.88
Electric: 145 kw   **Boilers:** 2 Babcock & Wilcox, 22 kg/cm² − superheat 330°C
Man: 150 men   **Fuel:** 340 tons
M: 2 sets GT; 2 props; 2,000 hp

REMARKS: Served in the U.S. Navy during World War II, transferred to the Philippines in the mid-1970s.

POLAND

PERSONNEL (1978): 25,000 men

MERCHANT MARINE (1978): 796 ships − 3,490,587 grt (tankers: 32 ships − 562,597 grt)

NAVAL AVIATION: About 40 fixed-wing aircraft, including MIG-17 Fresco fighters and IL-28 Beagle bombers, and about 20 Hare and Hound helicopters. All are of Soviet origin and in need of being replaced.

WEAPONS AND SYSTEMS

Most weapons and systems in use in the Polish Navy are of Soviet origin.

SUBMARINES

◆ **4 ex-Soviet Whiskey class**

ORZEL   SOKOL   KONDOR   BIELIK

Orzel

D: 1,050 tons surfaced, 1,350 submerged   **S:** 17/16 kts
Dim: 76.0 × 6.3 × 4.8   **Man:** 60 men   **Range:** 13,000
A: 6/533-mm TT (4 fwd, 2 aft) − 14 torpedoes or 28 mines
M: 2 diesels, diesel-electric drive; 2 props; 4,000/2,500 hp

REMARK: Transferred after 1962.

GUIDED-MISSILE DESTROYER

◆ **1 ex-Soviet SAM Kotlin class**

275 WARSZAWA (ex-*Spravedlivy*)

Warszawa   1973

GUIDED-MISSILE DESTROYER (continued)

D: 2,850 tons (3,500 fl)　　**S:** 34 kts　　**Dim:** 127.0 × 12.75 × 4.25
Man: 300 men　　**Range:** 1,200/30, 4,100/18
A: 1/SA-N-1 SAM system (II × 1) – 2/130-mm DP (II × 1) – 4/45-mm AA (IV × 1) –
　　2/RBU-2500 ASW rocket launchers (XVI × 2) – 5/533-mm TT (V × 1)
Electron Equipt: Radars: 1/Head Net A, 1/Don 2, 1/Sun Visor, 1/Hawk Screech,
　　　　　　　　　　　　　　　1/Peel Group
　　　　　　　　Sonar: 1/Herkules or Pegas
M: 2 sets GT; 2 props; 72,000 hp　　**Boilers:** 4

REMARK: Built in the U.S.S.R. in 1958, and transferred in 1970.

GUIDED-MISSILE PATROL BOATS

◆ **13 Osa-I class**

D: 175 tons (210 fl)　　**S:** 36 kts　　**Dim:** 39.0 × 7.7 × 1.8
A: 4/SS-N-2 Styx missile launchers (I × 4) – 4/30-mm AA (II × 2)
Electron Equipt: Radars: 1/Square Tie, 1/Drum Tilt
　　　　　　　　　　IFF: 2/Square Head, 1/High Pole
M: 3 M503A diesels; 3 props; 12,000 hp　　**Man:** 25 men

REMARK: Built in the U.S.S.R., 1960 –, and transferred since 1966.

TORPEDO BOATS

◆ **15 Wisla class**　Bldr: Poland, 1970-

Wisla class

Wisla class

D: 70 tons (fl)　　**S:** 34 kts　　**Dim:** 25.0 × 5.4 × 1.8
A: 2/30-mm AA – 4/533-mm TT
Electron Equipt: Radar: 1/Pot Head　　IFF: 1/High Pole A
M: 4 diesels; 4 props; 4,800 hp

◆ **1 or more Pilica class**

REMARKS: Built in Poland since 1973. At least one *Pilica*-class patrol craft of the Border
　　Guard (WOP) has been equipped with two 533-mm torpedo tubes taken from discarded
　　P-6-class torpedo boats. For details, *see* Border Guard.

PATROL BOATS

◆ **5 modified Obluze class**　Bldr: Oksywie SY, 1970-72
NO. 349 to NO. 353

Modified Obluze class – wearing old pendant number

REMARKS: Almost identical to the Border Guard's *Obluze* class but have Drum Tilt
fire-control radar for their 30-mm AA. For details, *see* Border Guard.

MINE WARFARE SHIPS

◆ **12 Krogulec-class minesweepers** Bldr: Stocznia Gdynska, Gdynia, 1963-67

PELIKAN	KORMORAN	KANIA	ZURAW
KROGULEC	JASTRAB	TUKAN	CZAPLA
ORLIK	ALBATROS	JASKOLKA	CZALDA

Krogulec class—with six 25-mm AA

Krogulec class—with four 23-mm AA   1978

    D: 450 tons   **S:** 16 kts   **Dim:** 58.0 × 8.4 × 2.5
    A: 6/25-mm AA (II × 3)—mines   **M:** 2 diesels; 2 props; 2,200 hp

REMARKS: Some of these ships have four 23-mm rapid-fire AA (II × 2) mounted aft in place of the original four 25-mm AA.

◆ **12 Soviet T-43-type minesweepers** Bldr: Stocznia Gdynska, Gdynia, 1957-62

ZUBR	LOZ	BIZON	ROZMAK	FOKA	RYS
TUR	DZIK	BOBR	DELFIN	MORS	ZBIK

Polish T-43

    D: 500 tons (580 fl)   **S:** 14 kts   **Dim:** 60.0 × 8.4 × 2.3
    A: 4/37-mm AA (II × 2)—4/25-mm AA (II × 2)—8/14.5-mm machine guns—2/depth-charge projectors—mines
    Electron Equipt: Radar: 1/Don 2   IFF: 1/Square Head, 1/High Pole A
    M: 2 diesels; 2 props; 2,200 hp

REMARKS: Some have twin 23-mm AA in place of the twin 25-mm AA. The first four completed are 58.0 m overall, the *Zubr, Tur, Loz,* and *Dzik.* Two have been converted into radar pickets.

◆ **28 K-8-class inshore minesweepers** Bldr: Poland, 1954-59.

    D: 26 tons (fl)   **S:** 12 kts   **Dim:** 16.9 × 3.2 × 0.8
    A: 2/14.5-mm machine guns   **M:** 2 3D6 diesels; 2 props; 600 hp

REMARKS: Wooden hulls; simple wire sweeps only.

AMPHIBIOUS WARFARE SHIPS

◆ **23 Soviet Polnocny-class landing ships** Bldr: Poland, 1964-71

BALAS	JANOW	NARWIK	. . .
GRUNWALD	LENIN	WARTA	

    D: 800-850 tons (fl)   **S:** 18 kts   **Dim:** 72.5 × 8.5 × 1.8
    A: 4/30-mm AA (II × 2)—2/140-mm rocket launchers (XVIII × 2)
    Electron Equipt: Radars: 1/Drum Tilt, 1/Don 2
                      IFF: 1/Square Head, 1/High Pole A
    M: 2 diesels; 2 props; 4,000 hp

AMPHIBIOUS WARFARE SHIPS *(continued)*

REMARKS: The *Narwik* is 82.0 × 10.0 × 2.0 and 1,150 tons, full load. Others are either A version or B version (74.0 m. overall). Cargo: 200 tons.

◆ **15-16 Marabut-class and Eichstaden-class landing craft**

Marabut class

Marabut class

D: 60 tons (fl)   **S:** . . . kts   **Dim:** 21.0 × . . . × . . .
A: 1/14.5-mm machine gun (*Marabut* only)   **M:** 2 diesels; 2 props; . . . hp

REMARKS: The *Marabut* class has plastic hull, ramped bow, and can carry light vehicles. The *Eichstaden* class has steel hull, pointed bow, and carries personnel only.

HYDROGRAPHIC SHIP

◆ **1 Soviet Moma class**   Bldr: Polnocny SY, Gdansk, 1973

KOPERNIK

Kopernik   1976

D: 1,260 tons (1,540 fl)   **S:** 17 kts   **Dim:** 73.3 × 10.8 × 3.8
Man: 56 men   **Range:** 8,700/11   **Endurance:** 35 days
Electron Equipt: Radars: 2/RN 231
M: 2 Zgoda-Sulzer 6TD48 diesels; 2 controllable-pitch props; 3,600 hp

REMARKS: Sisters in Bulgarian and Yugoslav navies. *Piast*-class salvage ships and *Wodnik*-class training ships are very similar. Two others, the *Nawigator* and *Hydrometr*, serve as intelligence collectors. The *Kopernik* has 35 m² of laboratory deck area. She can also be used as a buoy tender.

AUXILIARY SHIPS

◆ **3 Moskit-class coastal oilers**   Bldr: Poland, 1971-72

Z 1 KRAB   Z 2 MEDUSA   Z 3 SLIMAK

Moskit class — now renumbered   1973

AUXILIARY SHIPS (*continued*)

D: 900 tons (fl)   **A:** 4/25-mm AA (II × 2)   **M:** Diesel

◆ **5 Type-5-class coastal oilers**

Z 5   Z 6   Z 7   Z 8   Z 9

REMARKS: Approximately 300 tons capacity. Similar to Soviet *Toplivo-3* class. No armament.

◆ **2 Piast-class salvage ships**   Bldr: Polnocny SY, Gdansk, 1974

PIAST   LECH

Piast   1974

D: 1,560 tons (1,732 fl)   **S:** 16.5 kts   **Dim:** 73.2 (67.2 pp) × 10.8 × 4.0
Electron Equipt: Radars: 2/RN 231   **Range:** 3,000/12

M: 2 Zgoda-Sulzer 6TD48 diesels; 2 controllable-pitch props; 3,600 hp

REMARKS: Variation of *Moma* design for salvage and rescue duties. Equipped to mount eight 25-mm AA in wartime (II × 4). Carry submarine rescue bell to port, can tow, and have extensive pump and fire-fighting facilities. Sister *Otto von Guericke* is in the East German Navy.

INTELLIGENCE COLLECTORS

◆ **2 modified Moma class**   Bldr: Polnocny SY, Gdansk, 1975-76

HYDROMETR   NAWIGATOR

REMARKS: Data as for hydrographic ship *Kopernik* above. Crane removed, superstructure lengthened, lattice mainmast as on *Piast* class, two large radomes. Euphemistically described as "navigational training ships."

◆ **1 B-1-class trawler**   Bldr: Gdansk SY, 1954

BALTYK

Baltyk—now has large deckhouse before bridge   1970

D: 1,200 tons   **S:** 11 kts   **Dim:** 58.3 × 8.74 × 4.2
M: Steam; 1,200 hp

TRAINING SHIPS

◆ **2 Wodnik class**   Bldr: Polnocny SY, Gdansk

WODNIK   GRYF

Wodnik   1976

D: 1,800 tons (fl)   **S:** 16.8 kts   **Dim:** 74.0 × 13.0 × 4.2
Man: 60 men + 13 instructors and 87 cadets   **Range:** 7,500/11
A: 4/30-mm AA (II × 2)—4/25-mm AA (II × 2)
Electron Equipt: Radars: 2/RN 231, 1/Drum Tilt
M: 2 Zgoda-Sulzer 6TD48 diesels; 2 controllable-pitch props; 3,600 hp

REMARKS: Launched 29-11-75 and 13-3-76, respectively. Identical to the East German Navy's *Wilhelm Pieck* and similar to the *Luga* and *Oka* in the Soviet Navy. Developed from the *Moma* design. Have latest navigational systems from the West and the U.S.S.R.

◆ **4 Bryza class**

BRYZA   ELEW   KADET   PODCHORAZY

TRAINING SHIPS (continued)

Podchorazy   1976

    D: 150 tons   **S:** 10 kts   **Dim:** 30.0 × 7.0 × 2.0
    Man: 11 men, 26 midshipmen   **M:** Diesels

◆ **2 Pajak-class torpedo-recovery ships**

◆ **18 tugs of various types**

◆ **3 Mrowka-class degaussing ships**

◆ **8 diving tenders**

BORDER GUARD (WOP)

PATROL BOATS

◆ **8 Obluze class** Bldr: Oksywie SY, 1965-68

    D: 150 tons (fl)   **S:** 24 kts   **Dim:** 41.0 × 6.0 × 2.1
    A: 4/30-mm AA (II × 2) − 2/depth-charge racks
    Electron Equipt: Radar: 1/RN 231   Sonar: Tamir 11
                    IFF: 2/Square Head, 1/High Pole A
    M: 2 diesels; 2 props; 5,000 hp

REMARKS: Five additional units with Drum Tilt fire-control radars for the 30-mm AA serve in the Polish Navy. *See* photo in naval section.

◆ **9 Gdansk class** Bldr: Poland, 1960 –

    D: 140 tons (fl)   **S:** 20 kts   **Dim:** 41.0 × 6.0 × 1.9
    A: 2/37-mm AA (I × 2) − 2/12.7-mm machine guns (II × 1) − 2/depth-charge racks
    Electron Equipt: Radar: 1/RN 231   Sonar: Tamir 11
    M: 2 diesels; 2 props; 5,000 hp

Gdansk class

◆ **3 Oksywie class** Bldr: Poland, late 1950s

Oksywie class   1972

    D: 170 tons   **S:** 24 kts   **Dim:** 41.0 × 6.0 × 2.0
    A: 2/37-mm AA (I × 2) − 4/14.5-mm machine guns (II × 2) − 2/depth-charge racks
    Electron Equipt: Radar: 1/RN 231   Sonar: Tamir 10
    M: 2 diesels; 2 props; 5,000 hp

REMARKS: Based on German R-boat design. One scrapped.

PATROL CRAFT

◆ **5 Wisloka class** Bldr: Poland, 1975 –

    D: 100 tons   **S:** 10 kts   **Dim:** . . .
    A: 2/14.5-mm machine guns (II × 1)   **M:** Diesels

POLAND (*continued*)

PATROL CRAFT (*continued*)

◆ **7 Pilica class**   Bldr: Poland, 1973–

KP 162 to KP 168

   D: . 100 tons   **S:** 15 kts   **Dim:** . . .
   A: 2/25-mm AA (II × 1)   **M:** 2 diesels

REMARK: At least one has had two 533-mm torpedo tubes added and is now naval.

NOTE: There are a number of smaller launches under WOP control.

PORTUGAL

PERSONNEL: Approximately 12,000, including 3,000 Marines

MERCHANT MARINE (1978): 342 ships – 1,234,963 grt
          (tankers: 22 ships – 646,041 grt)

NAVAL AVIATION: A new Air Force P2-V Neptune maritime patrol aircraft are at the disposal of the Navy.

WARSHIPS IN SERVICE OR UNDER CONSTRUCTION AS OF 1 JANUARY 1980

	L	Tons (surfaced)	Main armament
◆ **3 submarines**			
3 DAPHNÉ	1966-68	869	12/550-mm TT
		Tons	
◆ **17 frigates**			
4 BAPTISTE DE ANDRADE	1973-74	1,252	1/100-mm DP, ASW weapons
6 JOÃO COUTINHO	1969-70	1,252	2/76-mm DP, ASW weapons
4 COMMANDANT RIVIÈRE	1966-68	1,760	3/100-mm DP, ASW weapons
3 ALMIRANTE PEREIRA DA SILVA	1963-65	1,450	4/76-mm DP, ASW weapons

WEAPONS AND SYSTEMS

Many of the recently acquired systems are of French origin. Some radars and armament come from the United States, Italy, the United Kingdom, and Sweden.

SUBMARINES

◆ **3 Daphné class**   Bldr: Dubigeon, Normandy

	Laid down	L	In serv.
S 163 ALBACORA	6-9-65	15-10-66	1-10-67
S 164 BARRACUDA	19-10-65	24-4-68	4-5-68
S 166 DELFIM	14-5-67	23-9-68	1-10-69

Albacora

   D: 869 tons surfaced, 1,043 submerged   **S:** 13.5/16 kts
   Dim: 57.75 × 6.76 × 4.5   **Man:** 5 officers, 45 men
   A: 12/550-mm TT (8 fwd, 4 aft, no reloads)
   Electron Equipt: Radar: 1/DRUA 31 (with ECM)
          Sonar: DUUA-1 active, DSUV passive
   M: Diesel-electric propulsion: SEMT-Pielstick diesels (450 kw); 2 props; 1,300-1,600 hp

REMARKS: Purchased in 1964. *See* remarks on the *Daphné* class in the French section. Have DUU-61 radio direction-finders. Sister *Cachalote* (S-165) was purchased by the Pakistani Navy in 1975.

FRIGATES

◆ **4 Baptiste de Andrade class**   Bldr: Bazan, Spain

	Laid down	L	In serv.
F 486 BAPTISTE DE ANDRADE	1972	3-73	19-11-74
F 487 JOÃO ROBY	1972	3-6-73	18-3-75
F 488 AFONSO CERQUEIRA	1973	6-10-73	26-6-75
F 489 OLIVEIRA E CARMO	1973	2-74	2-76

Oliveira e Carmo   1976

FRIGATES *(continued)*

D: 1,252 tons (1,401 fl)   **S:** 24.4 kts   **Dim:** 84.59 (81.0 pp) × 10.3 × 3.3
Man: 113 men   **Range:** 5,900/18   **Electric:** 1,110 kva
A: 1/100-mm DP, French Model 1968 – 2/40-mm AA (I × 2) – 6/324 mm Mk 32 ASW
   TT (III × 2) – 2/depth-charge racks
Electron Equipt: Radars: 1/Decca TM 626, 1/Plessey AWS 2, 1/Thomson CSF
                   Pollux
                  Sonar: 1/Diodon
M: 2 OEW-Pielstick 12PC2V diesels; 2 props; 10,560 hp

REMARKS: Developed version of the *João Coutinho* class with more modern weapons
and electronics. Helicopter platform. Can carry 34 troops. Planned sale to Colombia
in 1977 canceled.

◆ 6 João Coutinho class

	Laid down	L	In serv.
F 475 JOÃO COUTINHO	9-68	2-5-69	7-3-70
F 476 JACINTO CANDIDO	4-68	16-6-69	10-6-70
F 477 GENERAL PEREIRA D'ECA	10-68	26-7-69	10-10-70
F 484 AUGUSTO CASTILHO	8-68	5-7-69	14-11-70
F 485 HONORIO BARRETO	7-68	11-4-70	15-4-71
F 471 ANTONIO ENES	4-68	1-8-69	18-6-71

Bldrs: F-475 to F-477: Blohm & Voss, Germany; F-484 to F-471: Bazan, Spain

João Coutinho

D: 1,252 tons (1,401 fl)   **S:** 24.4 kts   **Dim:** 84.59 (81.0 pp) × 10.3 × 3.3
Man: 9 officers, 84 men   **Range:** 5,900/18   **Electric:** 900 kw
A: 2/76-mm Mk 33 DP (II × 1) – 2/40-mm AA (II × 1) – Mk 10 Hedgehog – 2/Mk
   6 depth-charge projectors – 2/Mk 9 depth-charge racks
Electron Equipt: Radars: 1/Decca TM 626, 1/MLA 1B, 1/SPG 50
                  Sonar: 1/QCU 2
M: 2 OEW-Pielstick 12PC2V diesels; 2 props; 10,560 hp

REMARKS: The engines for these ships were ordered from Chantiers de l'Atlantique,
St. Nazaire, France, in 1967. The ships can carry thirty-four Marines, and have Mk-

General Pereira d'Eca

63 fire-control system for 76-mm guns, Mk-51, mod. 2, for 40-mm. Modernization
planned.

◆ 4 French Commandant Rivière class   Bldr: A. C. de Bretagne

	Laid down	L	In serv.
F 480 COMANDANTE JOÃO BELO	5-65	22-3-66	1-7-67
F 481 COMANDANTE HERMEGILDO CAPELO	5-66	29-11-66	26-4-68
F 482 COMANDANTE ROBERTO IVENS	1-67	11-8-67	23-11-68
F 483 COMANDANTE SACADURA CABRAL	8-67	15-3-68	25-11-69

Comandante João Belo

D: 1,760 tons (2,250 fl)   **S:** 25 kts (26.6 max.)
Dim: 103.0 (98.0 pp) × 11.5 × 3.8
Man: 214 men   **Range:** 2,300/25, 4,500/15   **Electric:** 1,280 kw
A: 3/100-mm DP, Model 1953 (I × 3) – 2/40-mm AA (I × 2) – 1/305-mm ASW mortar
   (IV × 1) – 6/550-mm ASW TT (III × 2)
Electron Equipt: Radars: 1/Decca RM 316, 1/DRBV 22A, 1/DRBV 50, 1/DRBR-C
                   31D
                  Sonars: 1/DUBA, 1/SQS 17A
M: 4 SEMT-Pielstick diesels; 2 props; 16,000 hp

REMARKS: *See* Remarks on Commandant Rivière class in French section. Modernization planned.

FRIGATES *(continued)*

◆ **3 Almirante Pereira da Silva class**

	Laid down	L	In serv.
F 472 ALMIRANTE PEREIRA DA SILVA	14-6-62	2-12-63	20-12-66
F 473 ALMIRANTE GAGO COUTINHO	2-12-63	13-8-65	29-11-67
F 474 ALMIRANTE MAGALHAES CORREA	30-8-63	26-4-65	4-11-68

Bldrs: F-472 and F-473: Est. Nav. Lisnave, Lisbon; F-474: Est. Nav de Viana do Castelo

Almirante Pereira da Silva   1972

Almirante Gago Coutinho   J.-C. Bellonne, 1973

D: 1,450 tons (1,950 fl)   **S:** 26 kts
Dim: 95.86 (93.88 wl) × 11.18 × 4.04 (hull)
Man: 11 officers, 154 men   **Range:** 1,600/25, 4,400/11   **Fuel:** 360 tons
A: 4/76-mm DP (II × 2)—2/375-mm Bofors ASW rocket launchers (IV × 2)—6/324-mm Mk 32 ASW TT (III × 2)

Electron Equipt: Radars: 1/Decca RM 316P, 1/978, 1/MLA 1B, 2/Mk 34 fire-control
                Sonars: SQS 30 series, DUBA 3A, 1/SQA 10 (VDS)
Boilers: 2 Foster-Wheeler, 42 kg/cm² pressure—superheat 510°C
M: 1 set GT; 1 prop; 20,000 hp   **Electric:** 700 kw

REMARKS: Based on U.S. *Dealey*-class escorts and funded as U.S. DE-1039, DE-1042, and DE-1046, respectively. Two Mk-63 gunfire-control systems. Search sonars are SQS-30, SQS-31, and SQS-32 respectively, to avoid interference. To be modernized.

PATROL BOATS

◆ **10 Cacine class**

P 1140 CACINE (1968)	P 1144 QUANZA (30-5-69)	P 1160 LIMPOPO (9-4-73)
P 1141 CUNENE (1968)	P 1145 GEBA (21-5-69)	P 1161 SAVE
P 1142 MANDOVI (1968)	P 1146 ZAIRE (28-11-70)	
P 1143 ROVUMA (1968)	P 1147 ZAMBEZE (1971)	

Bldrs: P-1140 to P-1143: Arsenal do Alfeite; others: Est. Nav. do Mondego

Cacine   1970

D: 292 tons (310 fl)   **S:** 20 kts   **Dim:** 44.0 × 7.67 × 2.2
Man: 3 officers, 30 men   **Range:** 4,400/12
A: 2/40-mm AA (I × 2)—1/37-mm rocket launcher (XXXII × 1)
Electron Equipt: Radar: 1/975
M: 2 Maybach 12V538 diesels; 2 props; 4,400 hp

PATROL CRAFT

◆ **2 Dom Aleixo class**   Bldr: San Jacintho Aveiro

P 1148 DOM ALEIXO   P 1149 DOM JEREMIAS

Dom Aleixo

PATROL CRAFT (continued)

D: 62.6 tons (67.7 fl) **S:** 16 kts **Dim:** 25.0 × 5.2 × 1.6
Man: 2 officers, 8 men **Electron Equipt:** Radar: Decca RM 316P
A: 1/20-mm **M:** 2 Cummins diesels; 2 props; 1,600 hp

REMARKS: Both launched in 12-67. P-1149 is used for inshore surveys.

◆ **6 Albatroz class** Bldr: Arsenal do Alfeite, 1974

P 1162 ALBATROZ	P 1164 ANDORHINA	P 1166 CONDOR
P 1163 ACOR	P 1165 AGUIA	P 1167 CISNE

D: 45 tons (fl) **S:** 20 kts **Dim:** 23.6 (21.88 pp) × 5.25 × 1.6
A: 1/20-mm AA — 2/12.7-mm machine guns **Man:** 8 men
Range: 450/18, 2,500/12
Electron Equipt: Radar: 1/Decca RM 316P
M: 2 Cummins diesels; 2 props; 1,100 hp

REMARK: Eight additional units may have been built.

◆ **1 river patrol craft** Bldr: Arsenal do Alfeite, 1957

P 1170 RIO MINHO

D: 14 tons **S:** 9 kts **Dim:** 15.0 × 3.2 × 0.7
A: 2/7.62-mm machine guns **Man:** 7 men
M: 2 Alfa-Romeo diesels; 2 props; 130 hp

MINE WARFARE SHIPS

◆ **4 São Roque-class minesweepers** Bldr: Estaleiros Navais da C.U.F., Lisbon

M 401 SÃO ROQUE	M 403 LAGOA
M 402 RIBEIRA GRANDE	M 404 ROSARIO

D: 394 tons (452 fl) **S:** 15 kts **Dim:** 46.33 (42.68 pp) × 8.75 × 2.5
Man: 4 officers, 43 men **Range:** 2,300/13, 3,000/8 **Fuel:** 45 tons
A: 2/20-mm AA (II × 1) **M:** 2 Mirrlees JVSS-12 diesels; 2 props; 2,500 hp

REMARKS: Ordered early in 1954 and all launched in 1955. M-401 and M-403 built with U.S. "offshore" funds as MSC-241 and MSC-242. Similar in appearance to the British "-ton" class. Wooden hulls, fin stabilizers. One 40-mm AA removed in 1972.

AMPHIBIOUS WARFARE CRAFT

◆ **2 Bombarda-class landing craft** Bldr: Mondego SY, 1969-71

LDG 201 BOMBARDA	LDG 202 ALABARDA

D: 285 tons (635 fl) **S:** 11 kts **Dim:** 59.0 (52.88 pp) × 11.91 × 1.6
Man: 2 officers, 18 men **Range:** 1,800/8
M: 2 MTU MD 225 diesels; 2 props; 1,000 hp

◆ **3 LDM-100-class landing craft** Bldr: Mondego SY, 1965

LDM 119	LDM 120	LDM 121

D: 50 tons (fl) **S:** 9 kts **Dim:** 15.25 × . . . × . . .
M: 2 GM diesels; 2 props; 450 hp

◆ **7 LDM-400-class landing craft**

LDM 406	LDM 420	LDM 422	LDM 424
LDM 418	LDM 421	LDM 423	

D: 56 tons (fl) **S:** 9 kts **Dim:** 17.0 × 5.0 × 1.2
A: 1/20-mm **M:** 2 Cummins diesels; 2 props; 450 hp

REMARK: Date from 1967.

HYDROGRAPHIC SHIPS

◆ **1 ex-U.S. Kellar class** Bldr: Marietta SB Co., Pt. Pleasant, W. Va.

	Laid down	L	In serv.
A 527 ALMEIDA CARVALHO (ex-*Kellar*, T-AGS-25)	20-11-62	30-7-64	31-1-69

D: 1,200 tons (1,400 fl) **S:** 13.5 kts **Dim:** 63.7 (58.0 pp) × 11.4 × 4.7
Man: 5 officers, 25 men **Fuel:** 211 tons
Electron Equipt: 1/RCA CRM-N2A-30, 1/Decca TM 829
M: 2 Caterpillar D-378 diesels, electric drive; 1 prop; 1,000 hp

REMARKS: Transferred on loan 21-1-72. Similar to U.S. *Robert D. Conrad*-class T-AGOR.

◆ **1 ex-British Bay-class converted frigate** Bldr: Wm. Pickersgill & Sons, Sunderland

	Laid down	L	In serv.
A 526 AFONSO DE ALBUQUERQUE (ex-*Dalrymple*, ex-*Luce Bay*)	8-2-44	12-4-45	10-2-49

D: 1,590 tons (2,230 fl) **S:** 19.5 kts **Dim:** 93.57 (87.17 pp) × 11.76 × 4.32
Man: 9 officers, 100 men **Range:** 7,055/9.1
Boilers: 2 Admiralty, three-drum
M: 2 sets triple-expansion reciprocating steam; 2 props; 5,500 hp

REMARKS: Converted while under construction. Purchased in 1966.

◆ **1 inshore survey craft**

A 5200 MIRA (ex-*Fomalhaut*, ex-*Arrabile*)

D: 23 tons (30 fl) **S:** 15 kts **Dim:** 19.2 (18.9 pp) × 4.6 × 1.2
Man: 16 men **Range:** 650/8 **M:** 3 Perkins diesels; 300 hp

REMARKS: Dates from 1961. The *Dom Aleixo*-class patrol craft *Dom Jeremias* (P-1149) is also used for survey duties.

AUXILIARY SHIPS

◆ **1 replenishment oiler** Bldr: Est. Nav. de Viana do Castelo

	L	In serv.
A 5206 SÃO GABRIEL	1961	3-63

São Gabriel

PORTUGAL *(continued)*
AUXILIARY SHIPS *(continued)*

D: 9,000 tons (14,200 fl)   **S:** 17 kts   **Dim:** 146.0 (138.0 pp) × 18.22 × 8.0
Man: 9 officers, 93 men   **Range:** 6,000/15
Electron Equipt: Radars: 1/975, 1/MLN-1A   **Boilers:** 2
M: Pamtreda GT; 1 prop; 9,500 hp

REMARKS: Cargo: 9,000 tons. Two liquid- and one solid-stores replenishment stations per side. Former oiler *Sam Bras* is now an accommodations hulk.

◆ **1 lighthouse tender and tug**

	Laid down	L	In serv.
A 54 SCHULTZ XAVIER	2-70	1972	14-7-72

Schultz Xavier   J.-C. Bellonne, 1973

D: 900 tons   **S:** 14 kts   **Dim:** 56.1 × 10.0 × 3.8
Man: . . .   **Range:** 3,000/12.5   **M:** 2 diesels; 1 prop; 2,400 hp

◆ **1 U.S. 174-foot-class yard oiler**   Bldr: Brunswick Marine, Georgia, 1944

BC 3 (ex-YO-194)

D: 1,470 tons (fl)   **S:** 9 kts   **Dim:** 53.04 × 9.75 × . . .
M: 2 GM diesels; 2 props; 560 hp

REMARKS: Transferred in 4-62. Cargo: 1,000 tons.

◆ **3 Spartacus-class coastal tugs**   Bldr: Argibay, Lisbon

SPARTACUS   ULISSES   N . . .

D: 194 grt   **S:** 12 kts   **Dim:** 28.65 (25.0 pp) × 8.53 × 2.0
M: 2 Stork-Werkspoor G-FCHD-240 diesels; 2 cycloidal props; 2,400 hp

REMARK: The *Spartacus* was launched 18-2-77 and the *Ulisses* 9-3-77.

◆ **2 ex-U.S. Army harbor tugs**

RB 1 (ex-ST-1994)   RB 2 (ex-ST-1996)

REMARK: Transferred in 1961 and 1962.

QATAR

MERCHANT MARINE (1978): 28 ships—87,767 grt
(tankers: 2 ships—72,570 grt)

PATROL BOATS AND CRAFT

◆ **6 103-foot boats**   Bldr: Vosper Thornycroft

	In serv.		In serv.
Q 11 BARZAN	13-1-75	Q 14 AL WUSSAIL	28-10-75
Q 12 HWAR	30-4-75	Q 15 AL KHATAB	22-1-76
Q 13 THAT ASSUARI	3-10-75	Q 16 TARIQ	1-3-76

D: 120 tons   **S:** 27 kts   **Dim:** 32.4 (31.1 pp) × 6.3 × 1.6
A: 2/30-mm AA (II × 1)—2/20-mm AA   **Man:** 25 men
M: 2 Paxman Valenta diesels; 2 props; 6,250 hp

◆ **2 75-foot craft**   Bldr: Whittingham & Mitchell, Chertsey, 1969

D: 60 tons (fl)   **Dim:** 22.5 × . . . × . . .   **A:** 2/20-mm
M: 2 diesels; 1,420 hp

◆ **2 45-foot craft**   Bldr: Vosper

D: 13 tons   **S:** 26 kts   **Dim:** 13.5 × 3.8 × 1.1
A: 1/12.7-mm machine gun—2/7.62-mm machine guns
M: 2 Caterpillar diesels; 2 props; 800 hp

◆ **25 Spear-class craft**   Bldr: Fairey Marine, 1974-77

D: 4.3 tons   **S:** 26 kts   **Dim:** 9.1 × 2.8 × 0.8   **Man:** 4 men
A: 3/7.62-mm machine guns   **M:** 2 diesels; 2 props; 290 hp

ROMANIA

PERSONNEL: 10,000 men, 2,000 of whom are in the Border Guard

MERCHANT MARINE (1978): 239 ships—1,428,041 grt
(tankers: 10 ships—246,927 grt)

CORVETTES

◆ 3 ex-Soviet Poti class

V 31   V 32   V 33

> **D:** 500 tons (fl)   **S:** 34 kts   **Dim:** 60.3 × 8.0 × 3.0
> **A:** 2/57-mm AA (II × 1) – 2/RBU-2500 rocket launchers – 2/533-mm ASW TT (I × 2)
> **Man:** 50 men
> **Electron Equipt:** Radars: 1/Don 2, 1/Strut Curve, 1/Muff Cob
>   IFF: 1/High Pole B
> **M:** CODAG: 2 M503A diesels (4,000 hp each); 2 GT (20,000 hp each); 2 props

REMARKS: Transferred 1964-67. Have simpler systems than the Soviet units: open, nonautomatic 57-mm gun mount, 533-mm vice 400-mm torpedo tubes, RBU-2500 vice RBU-6000 rocket launchers, etc.

◆ 3 ex-Soviet Kronstadt class   Bldr: U.S.S.R., 1950

V 1   V 2   V 3

> **D:** 300 tons (330 fl)   **S:** 18 kts   **Dim:** 52.1 × 6.5 × 2.2
> **Man:** 40 men   **Range:** 3,500/14   **Fuel:** 20 tons
> **A:** 1/85-mm DP – 2/37-mm AA   **M:** 3 diesels; 3 props, 3,300 hp

GUIDED-MISSILE PATROL BOATS

◆ 5 ex-Soviet Osa-I class

Osa-I type   1974

> **D:** 175 tons (210 fl)   **S:** 36 kts   **Dim:** 39.0 × 7.7 × 1.8
> **A:** 4/SS-N-2 missile launchers – 4/20-mm AA (II × 2)
> **Electron Equipt:** Radars: 1/Square Tie, 1/Drum Tilt
> **M:** 3 M503A diesels; 3 props; 12,000 hp

REMARK: Transferred since 1960.

PATROL BOATS

◆ 1 new construction hydrofoil   Bldr: Dobreta, Turnu

> **D:** 50 tons (fl)   **S:** . . .   **Dim:** 25.0 × 6.0 × . . .
> **A:** 1/57-mm AA – 2/14.5-mm AA (II × 1) – 1/81-mm mortar
> **M:** 2 gas turbines; 2,400 hp

REMARK: The existence of this boat cannot be confirmed.

◆ 17 Shanghai-II class   Bldr: Mangalia, Romania, 1972-76

VS 41 to VS 44   VS 52   VP 20 to VP 31

> **D:** 120 tons (155 fl)   **S:** 28 kts   **Dim:** 38.8 × 5.4 × 1.6
> **A:** VS-41 to VS-44, VS-52: 1/37-mm AA – 2/14.5-mm machine guns (II × 1) 2/RBU-1200 rocket launchers
> VP-20 to VP-31: 6/14.5-mm machine guns (II × 3)
> **M:** 4 M50 diesels; 4 props; 4,800 hp

REMARKS: Units with VP pendants serve the Border Guard; some have only two 14.5-mm machine guns and have a large deckhouse aft.

TORPEDO BOATS

◆ 12 Huchwan-class hydrofoils

VT 51 to VT 62

VT-53

> **D:** 39 tons (fl)   **S:** 54 kts   **Dim:** 21.8 × 4.9 × 1.0; foilborne: 7.5 × 0.31
> **A:** 4/14.5-mm AA (II × 2) – 2/533-mm TT   **Range:** 500/20
> **M:** 3 M50 diesels; 3 props; 3,600 hp

◆ 14 ex-Soviet P-4 class

P-4 class

ROMANIA *(continued)*

TORPEDO BOATS *(continued)*

D: 19.3 tons (22.4 fl)   **S:** 55 kts   **Dim:** 19.3 × 3.7 × 1.0
A: 2/14.5-mm AA (II × 1) − 2/450-mm TT (one on each side)
Electron Equipt: Radar: Skin Head   **M:** 2 M50 diesels; 2 props; 2,400 hp

REMARKS: Launched before 1954. The torpedo tubes have been removed from some of these boats.

MINE WARFARE SHIPS

◆ **4 Democratia-class minesweepers (German M-40 class)**   Bldr: Galati, 1943-1951

DB 13 DEMOCRATIA   DB 15 DESROBIREA
DB 14 DESCATUSARIA   DB 16 DREPTATEA

D: 643 tons (775 fl)   **S:** 17 kts   **Dim:** 62.3 × 8.5 × 2.6
Man: 80 men   **Range:** 4,000/10   **Fuel:** 152 tons oil
A: 6/37-mm AA (II × 3) − 2 depth-charge projectors − mines
M: 2 triple-expansion engines, each driving an exhaust turbine; 2 props; 2,400 hp
Boilers: 2, three-drum

◆ **18 ex-Soviet T-301-class minesweepers**

DR 4 to DR 9   DR 17 to DR 19   DR 21 to DR 29

D: 145.8 tons (160 fl)   **S:** 12.5 kts   **Dim:** 38.0 × 5.1 × 1.6
A: 1/45-mm AA − 4/12.7-mm machine guns (II × 2) − mines   **Man:** 32 men
M: 3 diesels; 3 props; 1,440 hp

REMARK: Transferred 1956-60.

◆ **8 Polish TR-40-class inshore minesweepers**

VD 241 to VD 248

D: 70 tons (fl)   **S:** 18 kts   **Dim:** 27.7 × 4.1 × 0.6
A: 2/25-mm AA − 2/14.5-mm AA (II × 1) − mines
M: 2 3D6 diesels; 2 props; 600 hp

REMARK: Transferred 1956-60.

AUXILIARY SHIPS

◆ **3 coastal tankers**

◆ **4 Soviet Roslavl-class ocean tugs**   Bldr: Galati, 1953-54

RM 101 VITEAZUL   RM . . . VOINICUL   RM . . . N . . .   RM . . . N . . .

D: 750 tons (fl)   **S:** 11 kts   **Dim:** 44.5 × 9.5 × 3.5
M: Diesel-electric; 2 props; 1,200 hp   **Man:** 28 men

◆ **1 sail training ship**   Bldr: Blohm & Voss

MIRCEA CEL BATRIN

D: 1,630 tons (fl)   **S:** 6 kts   **Dim:** 81.78 × 12.5 × 5.2
Man: 20 men + 120 cadets   **M:** 1 diesel; 1,100 hp   **Sail area:** 1,750 m²

REMARKS: Launched in 9-38. Refitted in Germany, 1966-67. Name means *"Mircea the Old."*

◆ **3 ex-French Friponne-class former minesweepers**
   Bldrs: Lorient and Brest Dockyards, 1916-17

NH 111 STIHI (ex-*Mignonne*)   ND 113 GHICULESCU (ex-*Impatiente*)
NH 112 DUMITRESCU (ex-*Friponne*)

D: 330 tons (400 fl)   **S:** 12 kts   **Dim:** 60.9 × 7.0 × 2.5
Man: 50 men   **Range:** 3,000/10   **Fuel:** 30 tons
A: 1/37-mm AA − 4/14.5-mm AA (II × 2)
M: 2 Sulzer diesels; 2 props; 1,800 hp

REMARKS: ND-113 used as a headquarters ship, the others as survey ships. All recently modernized with streamlined superstructures, new armament, etc.

DANUBE FLOTILLA

◆ **7 monitors**

VB 76 to VB 82

D: 85 tons   **S:** 17 kts   **Dim:** 32.0 × 4.8 × 0.9
A: 1/85-mm − 4/14.5-mm AA (II × 2) − 2/81-mm mortars (I × 2)
M: 2 diesels; 2 props; 2,400 hp   **Man:** 25 men

◆ **10 VG-class patrol craft**   Bldr: Galati

D: 40 tons (fl)   **S:** 18 kts   **Dim:** 16.0 × 4.4 × 1.2
A: 2/12.7-mm machine guns   **Man:** 10 men
M: 2 3D12 diesels; 2 props; 600 hp

SABAH

PATROL BOATS

◆ **2 55-foot boats**   Bldr: Vosper Thornycroft, Singapore

SRI SEMPORNA   SRI BANGJI

D: 50 tons (fl)   **S:** 20 kts   **Dim:** 16.8 × 4.6 × 0.9
A: 1/12.7-mm machine gun   **Man:** 11 men   **Range:** 300/15
M: 2 diesels; 2 props; 1,200 hp

REMARK: Launched in 2-75.

SABAH (*continued*)

PATROL BOATS (*continued*)

◆ **2 91-foot boats** Bldr: Vosper Thornycroft, Singapore

SRI GUMANGTONG   SRI LABUAN

   D: 80 tons (fl)   **S:** 29 kts   **Dim:** 26.29 × 5.7 × 1.45
   A: 2/20-mm AA   **Range:** 700/15   **Man:** 15 men
   M: 2 Mercedes-Benz MB820Db diesels; 2 props; 2,700 hp

REMARKS: The *Sri Gumangtong* was launched on 18-8-69 and the *Sri Labuan* later the same year. On detachment from the Royal Malaysian Marine Police.

◆ **1 yacht** Bldr: Vosper Thornycroft, Singapore

PUTRI SABAH

   D: 117 tons   **S:** 22 kts   **Dim:** 27.3 × 9.5 × 1.65

REMARK: In service in 7-71.

AMPHIBIOUS WARFARE CRAFT

◆ **1 utility landing craft** Bldr: Chung Wah SY, Hong Kong

GAYA 2

   D: 220 grt   **S:** 8 kts   **Dim:** . . . × . . . × . . .
   M: 2 Caterpillar D3406TA diesels; 2 props; 275 hp

REMARK: In service on 28-1-78.

ST. KITTS

MERCHANT MARINE (1978): 1 ship — 256 grt

PATROL CRAFT

◆ **1 Spear class** Bldr: Fairey Marine, G.B.

   D: 4.3 tons (fl)   **S:** 30 kts   **Dim:** 9.1 × 2.8 × 0.8
   A: 2/7.62-mm machine guns   **Man:** 2 men   **M:** 2 diesels; 2 props; 360 hp

REMARK: In service 10-9-74.

ST. LUCIA

MERCHANT MARINE (1978): 3 ships — 928 grt

◆ **1 small craft** Bldr: Brooke Marine Ltd., Lowestoft, G.B.

CHATOYER

   D: 15 tons (fl)   **S:** 22 kts   **Dim:** 13.7 × 4.0 × 1.2
   A: 2/7.62-mm machine guns   **M:** 2 Cummins diesels; 2 props; 370 hp

ST. VINCENT

MERCHANT MARINE (1978): 25 ships — 8,428 grt

◆ **1 small craft** Bldr: Brooke Marine Ltd., Lowestoft, G.B.

HELEN

   D: 15 tons (fl)   **S:** 22 kts   **Dim:** 13.7 × 4.0 × 1.2
   A: 2/7.62-mm machine guns (I × 2)   **M:** 2 Cummins diesels; 2 props 370 hp

SAUDI ARABIA

PERSONNEL: 750 men + 350 in the coast guard

MERCHANT MARINE (1978): 154 ships — 1,246,112 grt
               (tankers: 47 ships — 1,021,656 grt)

GUIDED-MISSILE CORVETTES

◆ **4 U.S. PCG-class** Bldr: Tacoma Boatbuilding, Tacoma, Wash.

	Laid down	L	In serv.
612 BADR (ex-PCG-1)	9-4-79	6-8-79	8-80
614 AL-YARMOOK (ex-PCG-2)	20-8-79	26-12-79	1-81
616 HITTEN (ex-PCG-3)	7-1-79	3-80	4-81
618 TABUK (ex-PCG-4)	3-80	6-80	7-81

D: 720 tons (fl) **S:** 30 kts gas turbines, 20 kts diesels
Dim: 71.4 × 8.4 × 2.65 **Man:** 5 officers, 48 men
A: 8/Harpoon (IV × 2)—1/76-mm OTO Melara Compact—2/20-mm AA (I × 2)—1/81-mm mortar—2/40-mm army grenade launchers—6/Mk 32 ASW TT (III × 2)
Electron Equipt: Radars: 1/SPS 40A, 1/SPS 60, 1/Mk 92 fire-control system
  Sonar: SQS 56
M: CODOG: 1 GE gas turbine (16,500 hp); 2 MTU diesels (2,000 hp); 2 props

REMARK: Ordered 30-8-77.

GUIDED-MISSILE PATROL BOATS

◆ **9 U.S. PGG class** Bldr: Peterson Builders, Sturgeon Bay, Wisc.

	Laid down	L	In serv.
511 AS-SIDDIQ (ex-PGG-1)	30-9-78	6-7-79	10-80
513 AL-FAROUQ (ex-PGG-2)	12-3-79	12-79	6-81
515 ABDUL-AZIZ (ex-PGG-3)	4-6-79	1-80	8-81
517 FAISAL (ex-PGG-4)	8-79	4-80	10-81
519 KHALID (ex-PGG-5)	11-79	8-80	1982
521 AMR (ex-PGG-6)	3-80	. . .	1982
523 TARIQ (ex-PGG-7)	6-80	. . .	1982
525 OQBAH (ex-PGG-8)	9-80	. . .	1982
527 ABU OBAIDAH (ex-PGG-9)	12-80	. . .	1982

D: 320 tons (fl) **S:** 38 kts gas turbines, 18 kts diesels
Dim: 56.2 × 4.6 × 1.75 **Man:** 35 men
A: 4/Harpoon (II × 2)—1/76-mm OTO Melara Compact—2/20-mm AA (I × 2)—1/81-mm mortar—2/40-mm army grenade launchers
Electron Equipt: Radars: 1/SPS 60, 1/Mk-92, fire-control system
M: CODOG: 1 GE gas turbine (16,500 hp); 2 MTU diesels (2,000 hp); 2 props

REMARK: Ordered 16-2-77.

TORPEDO BOATS

◆ **3 ex-German Jaguar class (Type 141)** Bldr: Lürssen, Vegesack, 1969

DAMMAM KHABAR MACCAH

1975

D: 170 tons **S:** 40 kts **Dim:** 42.8 × 7.15 × 2.2
A: 2/40-mm—4/533-mm TT **Man:** 3 officers, 33 men
M: 4 diesels; 4 props; 12,000 hp

MINE WARFARE SHIPS

◆ **4 U.S. MSC-322 class** Bldr: Peterson Builders, Sturgeon Bay, Wisc.

	Laid down	L	In serv.
412 ADDIRIYAH (ex-MSC-322)	12-5-76	20-12-76	6-7-78
414 AL-QUYSUMAH (ex-MSC-323)	24-8-76	26-5-77	15-8-78
416 AL-WADEEAH (ex-MSC-324)	28-12-76	6-9-77	7-9-78
418 SAFWA (ex-MSC-325)	5-3-77	7-12-77	20-10-78

D: 320 tons (375 fl) **S:** 14 kts **Dim:** 46.33 × 8.29 × 2.5
A: 2/20-mm AA (II × 1) **Man:** 4 officers, 35 men **Electric:** 200 kw
M: 2 Waukesha E1616 DSIN diesels; 2 props; 1,200 hp

REMARK: Ordered 30-9-75.

AMPHIBIOUS WARFARE SHIPS

◆ **4 U.S. LCU-1646 class** Bldr: Newport SY, Rhode Island, 1976

212 AL-QIAQ (ex-SA-310)   216 AL-ULA (ex-SA-312)
214 AS-SULAYEL (ex-SA-311)   218 AFIF (ex-SA-313)

D: 173 tons (396 fl) **S:** 11 kts **Dim:** 41.07 × 9.07 × 2.08
A: 1/12.7-mm machine gun **Man:** 8 men **Range:** 1,200/10
M: 4 GM 6-71 diesels; 2 props; 1,200 hp **Electric:** 80 kw

AUXILIARY SHIPS

◆ **1 training ship** Bldr: Bayerische Schiffsbau, Erlenbach, West Germany
TEBUK

D: 585 grt **S:** 20 kts **Dim:** 60.0 (pp) × 10.0 × 1.8
A: . . . **Man:** 60 men **M:** 2 MTU diesels; 2 props, 5,260 hp

REMARK: In service in 12-77.

◆ **1 royal yacht** Bldr: C. Van Lent & Sons, Kaag, Netherlands
AL RIYADH

D: 670 tons (fl) **S:** 20 kts **Dim:** 64.64 (59.22 pp) × 9.7 × 3.0
A: None **Man:** 16 men **Range:** 1,750/18
Electron Equipt: Radar: 1/Decca RM-916 **Electric:** 370 kw
M: 2 MTU 16V956 diesels; 2 props; 5,720 hp

REMARKS: In service in 1-78. Fin stabilizers and Schöttel bow thruster fitted.

◆ **1 salvage tug** Bldr: Hayashikane, Shimonoseki, 1978
13 JEDDAH

D: 350 tons **S:** 12 kts **Dim:** 34.4 × . . . × . . .
M: 2 diesels; 800 hp

◆ **2 U.S. YTB-752 class**
EN 111 TUWAIG (ex-YTB-837)   EN 112 DAREEN (ex-YTB-838)

D: 291 tons (352 fl) **S:** 12 kts **Dim:** 33.05 × 9.3 × 4.5
M: 2 diesels; 1 prop; 2,000 hp **Man:** 12 men **Range:** 2,000/10

REMARK: Transferred 15-10-75.

SAUDI ARABIA *(continued)*

COAST GUARD

PATROL BOAT

◆ **1 U.S. Coast Guard Cape class**

RIYADH

> **D:** 102 tons (fl) **S:** 18 kts **Dim:** 28.95 × 5.8 × 1.55
> **A:** 1/40-mm AA **Man:** 15 men **Range:** 1,500/12
> **M:** 4 Cummins VT-12-M diesels; 2 props; 2,324 hp **Electric:** 40 kw

REMARK: Transferred in 1969.

PATROL CRAFT

◆ **8 French P-32 class** Bldr: CMN, Cherbourg

> **D:** 90 tons (fl) **S:** 29 kts **Dim:** 32.0 × 5.3 × 2.9
> **A:** 2/20-mm AA (II × 1) **Man:** 17 men **Range:** 1,500/15
> **M:** 2 MGO V-12 diesels; 2 props; 2,700 hp

REMARKS: Ordered in 1-76. Wooden hull, sheathed in fiberglass. Sisters to Moroccan *El Wacil.* Delivery uncertain.

◆ **15 Scorpion class**
Bldrs: 10 units: Bayerische Schiffsbau; 5 units: Werft Union, West Germany, 1979

> **D:** . . . **S:** 30 kts **Dim:** 17.0 × 4.9 × 1.25
> **A:** . . . **Man:** 12 men **Range:** 350/30
> **M:** 2 GM 12V-71TI diesels; 2 props; 1,300 hp

◆ **12 Rapier class** Bldr: Halter Marine, New Orleans, La., 1976-77

Rapier class   Halter Marine, 1976

> **D:** 24 tons (light) **S:** 28 kts **Dim:** 15.24 × 4.57 × 1.35
> **A:** 2/7.62-mm machine guns (I × 2) **Man:** 1 officer, 8 men
> **M:** 2 GM 12V-71TI diesels; 2 props; 1,300 hp **Electric:** 20 kw

◆ **50 C-80 class** Bldr: Northshore Yacht Yard, G.B., 1975-77

> **D:** 2.8 tons (fl) **S:** 20 kts **Dim:** 8.9 × 2.9 × 0.6
> **A:** 1/7.62-mm machine gun **Man:** 3 men
> **M:** 1 Caterpillar diesel; Castoldi water jet; 210 hp

◆ **10 Huntress class** Bldr: Fairey Marine, Hamble, G.B., 1976

> **D:** . . . **S:** 20 kts **Dim:** 7.1 × 2.7 × 0.8
> **A:** 1/7.62-mm machine gun **Man:** 4 men **Range:** 150/20
> **M:** 1 diesel; 180 hp

◆ **8 SRN-6-class hovercraft** Bldr: British Hovercraft, 1970

> **D:** 10 tons **S:** 58 kts **Dim:** 14.8 × 7.7 × 4.8 (high)
> **A:** 1/7.62-mm machine gun **M:** 1 Rolls-Royce Gnome gas turbine

◆ **8 harbor patrol craft** Bldr: Yokohama Yacht, Japan, 1972

> **D:** . . . **S:** 20 kts **Dim:** 10.5 × 3.0 × . . .
> **M:** 2 diesels, 2 props; 280 hp

SENEGAL

PERSONNEL: 350 men

MERCHANT MARINE (1978): 80 ships—29,404 grt
(tankers: 3 ships—1,911 grt)

PATROL BOATS

◆ **3 PR-48 class** Bldr: S.F.C.N., Villeneuve-la-Garonne

	Laid down	L	In serv.
SAINT LOUIS	20-4-70	5-8-70	1-3-71
POPENGUINE	12-73	22-3-74	10-8-74
PODOR	12-75	20-7-76	13-7-77

Saint Louis   1971

SENEGAL *(continued)*

PATROL BOATS *(continued)*

> **D:** 240 tons (avg.) **S:** 23 kts **Dim:** 47.5 (45.5 pp) × 7.1 × 2.5
> **A:** 2/40-mm AA (I × 2) − 2/7.62-mm machine guns **Man:** 3 officers, 22 men
> **M:** 2 AGO V12 CZSHR diesels; 2 props; 6,240 hp **Range:** 2,000/16

PATROL CRAFT

◆ **3 fisheries craft** Bldr: Turbec, St. Catherine, Canada

SENEGAL II   SINÉ SALOUM II   CASAMANCE II

> **D:** 52 tons (62 fl) **S:** 32 kts **Dim:** 26.5 × 5.81 × . . .
> **A:** . . . **M:** 2 diesels; 2 props; 2,700 hp

REMARK: In service 2-79, 7-79, and 10-79, respectively.

◆ **4 harbor craft** Bldr: ARESA, Arenys de Mar, Spain, 1979

> **D:** 3.5 tons (fl) **S:** 18 kts **Dim:** 8.5 × . . . × . . .

REMARKS: Subordinate to the Senegal Police. Fiberglass hulls.

◆ **3 Lance class** Bldr: Fairey Marine, Hamble, G.B., 1974-77

DJIBRILL   DJILOR   GORÉE

> **D:** 15.7 tons **S:** 24 kts **Dim:** 14.8 × 4.7 × 1.3
> **A:** 2/7.62-mm machine guns **Man:** 7 men
> **M:** 2 GM 8V71 diesels; 2 props; 850 hp

REMARK: Subordinate to the Senegal Police.

◆ **12 45-foot class** Bldr: Vosper Thornycroft

> **D:** 10 tons (fl) **S:** 25 kts **Dim:** 13.7 × 4.0 × 1.1
> **A:** 1/12.7-mm machine gun − 2/7.62-mm machine guns (I × 2)
> **M:** 2 diesels; 2 props; 920 hp **Man:** 6 men

REMARK: Subordinate to the Senegal Police.

◆ **2 Huntress class** Bldr: Fairey Marine, Hamble, G.B., 1974

> **D:** . . . **S:** 29 kts **Dim:** 7.1 × 2.7 × 0.6
> **A:** 1/7.62-mm machine gun **Man:** 2 men **M:** 1 diesel; 180 hp

REMARK: Subordinate to the Customs Service.

AMPHIBIOUS WARFARE SHIPS

◆ **1 ex-French EDIC-class landing craft**

FALEME (ex-EDIC-9095)

> **D:** 250 tons (670 fl) **S:** 8 kts **Dim:** 59.0 × 11.95 × 1.3
> **A:** 2/20-mm AA (I × 2) **Man:** 16 men **Range:** 1,800/8
> **M:** MGO diesels; 2 props; 1,000 hp

REMARKS: Launched 11-4-58, and transferred 7-1-74. Can carry eleven trucks or five LVT landing craft.

◆ **2 ex-U.S. LCM-6-class landing craft**

DJOMBOSS   DOULOULOU

> **D:** 26 tons (52 fl) **S:** 10 kts **Dim:** 17.1 × 4.4 × 1.2
> **M:** 2 Gray Marine 64 HN9 diesels; 2 props; 330 hp

REMARK: Transferred in 1968.

AUXILIARY SHIPS

◆ **1 training ship**

RAYMOND SARR

> **D:** 18 tons

REMARK: A former fishing vessel, in service since 1978.

◆ **1 tug**

IBIS

> **D:** 200 tons (fl) **S:** 9 kts **Dim:** 18.4 × 5.7 × 2.5
> **M:** 1 Poyaud diesel; 250 hp **Range:** 1,700/9

REMARK: On loan from the French Navy.

SEYCHELLES

MERCHANT MARINE (1978): 10 ships − 53,646 grt

PATROL BOAT

◆ **1 ex-French Sirius-class former minesweeper** Bldr: Seine Maritime

P . . . TOPAZ (ex-*Croix du Sud*, P-658)

> **D:** 400 tons (440 fl) **S:** 15 kts **Dim:** 46.4 (42.7 pp) × 8.55 × 2.5
> **A:** 1/40-mm AA − 1/20-mm AA **Man:** 2 officers, 35 men **Fuel:** 48 tons
> **M:** 2 SEMT-Pielstick diesels; 2 props; 2,000 hp **Range:** 3,000/10

REMARK: Launched 13-6-56.

AMPHIBIOUS WARFARE SHIP

◆ **1 medium landing ship** Bldr: A.C. de la Perrière

	Laid down	L	In serv.
5 JUIN	7-4-78	19-9-78	11-1-79

> **D:** 350 tons (855 fl) **S:** 9 kts **Dim:** 58.2 × 11.37 × 1.9
> **A:** . . . **Range:** 2,000/9 **M:** 2 Poyaud A12 150M diesels; 2 props; 880 hp

REMARK: Owned by the government but operated in local commercial service. Bow ramp. Cargo: 272 tons.

SIERRA LEONE | SINGAPORE

MERCHANT MARINE (1978): 11 ships — 4,689 grt

PATROL BOATS

◆ **3 Chinese Shanghai-II class**

001 N . . .   002 N . . .

001 and 002

D: 120 tons (155 fl)   **S:** 28 kts   **Dim:** 38.8 × 5.4 × 1.6
A: 4/37-mm AA (II × 2) — 4/25-mm AA (II × 2) — 8 depth charges
Electron Equipt: Radar: Pot Head   **Man:** 28 men
M: 4 M50 diesels; 4 props; 4,800 hp

REMARK: Transferred in 6-73.

PERSONNEL (1978): 3,000 men

MERCHANT MARINE (1978): 954 ships — 7,489,205 grt
                        (tankers: 144 ships — 3,155,150 grt)

GUIDED-MISSILE PATROL BOATS

◆ **8 Lürssen type**

P 76 SEA WOLF   P 78 SEA DRAGON   P 80 SEA HAWK   P 82 N . . .
P 77 SEA LION   P 79 SEA TIGER   P 81 SEA SCORPION   P 83 N . . .

Bldrs: P-76 and P-77: Lürssen, Vegesack; others: Singapore SB & Eng. Co., Jurong,
    Singapore, with German technical assistance

Sea Dragon — without missiles   1979

Sea Tiger — without missiles   G. Arra, 1977

D: 280 tons (fl)   **S:** 38 kts   **Dim:** 44.9 × 7.0 × 2.3
A: 5/Israeli Gabriel missiles (III × 1, I × 2) — 1/57-mm AA — 1/40-mm AA
Electron Equipt: Radars: 1/HSA WM 28, 1/Decca TM 626
M: 4 MTU 16V538 diesels; 4 props; 14,400 hp   **Man:** 40 men

GUIDED-MISSILE PATROL BOATS (continued)

REMARKS: Six units ordered in 1970, in service 1972-80. Two additional units ordered in 1977. Frequently seen without missiles. Two multiple 57-mm flare launchers on 57-mm mount.

PATROL BOATS AND CRAFT

◆ 3 110-foot, "Type A"

	Bldr	L	
P 69 INDEPENDENCE	Vosper, Portsmouth	. . .	
P 70 FREEDOM	Vosper, Singapore	. . .	
P 72 JUSTICE	Vosper, Singapore	. . .	. . .

Independence   G. Arra, 1977

D: 100 tons (130 fl)   **S:** 30 kts   **Dim:** 33.4 (31.46 pp) × 6.4 × 1.71
Man: 3 officers, 16 men   **Range:** 1,100/15   **Electric:** 100 kw
A: 1/40-mm Bofors AA – 1/20-mm Oerlikon AA
Electron Equipt: Radar: 1/Decca TM 626
M: 2 MTU 16V538 diesels; 2 props; 7,200 hp

REMARK: Ordered 21-5-68.

◆ 3 110-foot, "Type B"

	Bldr	L	In serv.
P 71 SOVEREIGNTY	Vosper, Portsmouth	25-11-69	2-71
P 73 DARING	Vosper, Singapore	1970	18-9-71
P 74 DAUNTLESS	Vosper, Singapore	6-5-71	7-71

Sovereignty   Thornycroft, 1971

D: 100 tons (130 fl)   **S:** 32 kts   **Dim:** 33.4 × 6.4 × 1.71
A: 1/76-mm Bofors – 1/20-mm Oerlikon   **Man:** 3 officers, 16 men
Electron Equipt: Radars: 1/HSA M-26, 1/Decca TM 626   **Range:** 1,000/15
M: 2 MTU 16V538 diesels; 2 props; 7,200 hp

REMARK: Gun and fire-control system as on the Norwegian Storm class.

◆ 1 British Ford class   Bldr: United Engineers, Singapore, 1956

P 48 PANGLIMA

D: 119 tons (131 fl)   **S:** 14 kts   **Dim:** 35.76 × 6.1 × 1.68
A: 1/40-mm AA – 1/20-mm AA   **Man:** 15 men   **Fuel:** 15 tons
M: 2 Paxman YHAXM diesels; 2 props; 1,000 hp

REMARK: Transferred by Malaysia in 1967, and used for training.

◆ 1 ex-Dutch craft   Bldr: Schiffswerf Oberwinter, West Germany, 1955

P 75 ENDEAVOR

D: 250 tons (fl)   **S:** 20 kts   **Dim:** 40.9 × 7.6 × 2.4
A: 2/20-mm AA (I × 2)   **Man:** 24 men   **Range:** 800/8
M: 2 Maybach diesels; 2 props; 2,000 hp

REMARKS: Purchased on 30-9-70. Low freeboard. Used for training.

MINE WARFARE SHIPS

◆ 2 ex-U.S. Bluebird-class minesweepers

	L	In serv.
M 101 JUPITER (ex-Thrasher, MSC-203)	6-10-54	16-8-55
M 102 MERCURY (ex-Whippoorwill, MSC-207)	13-8-54	20-10-55

D: 300 tons (372 fl)   **S:** 13 kts   **Dim:** 43.0 × 7.95 × 2.55
A: 2/20-mm (II × 1)   **Man:** 39 men   **Range:** 2,500/10
Electron Equipt: Radar: 1/SPS 5   Sonar: UQS 1D
M: 2 GM 8-268A diesels; 2 props; 1,200 hp   **Fuel:** 40 tons

REMARK: Transferred on 5-12-75.

AMPHIBIOUS WARFARE SHIPS

◆ 6 ex-U.S. LST-542 class

	Laid down	L	In serv.
L 201 ENDURANCE (ex-Holmes City, LST-836)	11-9-44	29-10-44	25-11-44
L 202 EXCELLENCE (ex-T-LST-629)	13-4-44	8-7-44	28-7-44
L 203 INTREPID (ex-T-LST-579)	4-5-44	22-6-44	21-7-44
L 204 RESOLUTION (ex-T-LST-649)	19-7-44	6-10-44	26-10-44
L 205 PERSISTENCE (ex-T-LST-614)	28-1-44	6-5-44	22-5-44
L 206 PERSEVERANCE (ex-T-LST-623)	13-3-44	12-6-44	21-6-44

Bldrs: L-201: American Bridge, Pa.; L-202, L-204, L-205, L-206: Chicago Bridge & Iron, Seneca, Ill.; L-203: Missouri Valley Bridge & Iron, Evansville, Ind.

D: 1,653 tons, light (4,080 fl)   **S:** 11.6 kts
Dim: 99.98 (96.32 pp) × 15.24 × 4.29
A: 2 or 4/40-mm AA (I × 2 or 4)   **Man:** 120 men   **Range:** 19,000/9
M: 2 GM 12-567A diesels; 2 props; 1,800 hp   **Electric:** 300 kw

REMARKS: Originally numbered A-81 to A-86. L-201 loaned 1-7-71 and sold outright 5-12-75; originally had eight 40-mm AA (II × 2, I × 4); chartered in 1976 for commercial service at which time guns may have been removed. Others purchased 4-6-76.

SINGAPORE (continued)

AMPHIBIOUS WARFARE SHIPS (continued)

Endurance   G. Arra, 1977

L-202 has two 40-mm AA (I × 2) forward; L-203 is unarmed; both are active. L-204 to L-206 are in reserve and may be unarmed. Three more ex-Military Sealift Command T-LSTs (ex-T-LST-117, ex-T-LST-276, and ex-*Chase County*, T-LST-532) were purchased 4-6-76 but later sold commercially.

◆ **4 Ayer Chawan-class landing craft** Bldr: Vosper Thornycroft, Singapore, 1968-69

RPL . . . AYER CHAWAN   RPL . . . N . . .
RPL . . . AYER MERBAN   RPL . . . N . . .

Ayer Chawan class   G. Arra, 1977

 D: 150 tons (fl) **S:** 10 kts **Dim:** 27.0 × 6.9 × 1.3
 M: 2 diesels; 2 props; 650 hp

◆ **2 Brani-class landing craft** Bldr: Australia, 1955-56

RPL . . . BRANI   RPL . . . BERLAYER

 D: 56 tons (fl) **S:** 9 kts **Dim:** 17.0 × 4.3 × 1.4
 M: 2 diesels; 2 props; 460 hp

MARINE POLICE

PATROL CRAFT

◆ **12 craft** Bldr: De Havilland Marine, Homebush Bay, Australia, 1980-81

 D: 40 tons (fl) **S:** 35 kts **Dim:** 22.5 × 6.0 × 1.6
 A: 1/20-mm AA − 2/12.7-mm machine guns **Range:** 960/20
 M: 2 diesels; 2 props; . . . hp

◆ **20 PC-32 class** Bldr: Vosper Thornycroft, Singapore, 1978-79

PC 32 to PC 51

 D: 2 tons (fl) **S:** 35 kts **Dim:** 6.5 × 2.5 × 0.46
 A: Small arms **Man:** 4 men **M:** 2 Johnson outboards; 280 hp

◆ **4 PX class** Bldr: Vosper Thornycroft, Singapore, 1969

PX 10 PX 11 PX 12 PX 13

 D: 80 tons (fl) **S:** 29 kts **Dim:** 26.29 × 5.7 × 1.45
 A: 2/20-mm AA **Man:** 15 men **Range:** 700/15
 M: 2 MTU diesels; 2 props; 2,700 hp

SOLOMON ISLANDS

MERCHANT MARINE (1978): 10 ships − 2,018 grt

PATROL CRAFT

◆ **1 Carpentaria class** Bldr: De Havilland Marine, Homebush Bay, Australia

 D: 27 tons (fl) **S:** 30 kts **Dim:** 16.0 × 5.0 × 1.2
 A: 2/7.62-mm machine guns **M:** 2 MTU diesels; 2 props; 1,440 hp

REMARK: Launched in 12-78.

SOMALI REPUBLIC

MERCHANT MARINE (1978): 19 ships – 72,961 grt
(tanker: 1 ship – 10,458 grt)

GUIDED-MISSILE PATROL BOATS

◆ 2 ex-Soviet Osa-II class

Osa-II class – under tow to Somalia   1976

D: 205 tons (240 fl)   **S:** 36 kts   **Dim:** 39.0 × 7.7 × 1.8
A: 4/SS-N-2 Styx missile launchers – 4/30-mm AA (II × 2)   **Man:** 30 men
Range: 450/34, 700/20
Electron Equipt: Radars: 1/Square Tie, 1/Drum Tilt
IFF: 2/Square Head, 1/High Pole B
M: 3 M504 diesels; 3 props; 15,000 hp

REMARK: Transferred 1975-76.

TORPEDO BOATS

◆ 4 ex-Soviet MOL class

D: 170 tons (220 fl)   **S:** 40 kts   **Dim:** 39.0 × 7.7 × 1.8
A: 4/30-mm AA (II × 2) – 4/533-mm TT (I × 4)   **Man:** 25 men
Electron Equipt: Radars: 1/Pot Head, 1 /Drum Tilt
IFF: 1/Square Head, 1/High Pole B
M: 3 M504 diesels; 3 props; 15,000 hp

REMARKS: Transferred in 1976. Two did not have torpedo tubes.

MOL class – without torpedo tubes   1976

MOL class – with torpedo tubes   1976

◆ 4 ex-Soviet P-6 class

D: 56 tons (66.5 fl)   **S:** 43 kts   **Dim:** 25.3 × 6.1 × 1.7
A: 4/25-mm AA (II × 2) – 2/533-mm TT   **Man:** 20 men
M: 4 M50-F4 diesels; 4 props; 4,800 hp   **Range:** 450/30

REMARK: Transferred in 1968.

PATROL BOATS

◆ 5 ex-Soviet Poluchat class

D: 80 tons (90 fl)   **S:** 18 kts   **Dim:** 29.86 × 5.8 × 1.5
A: 2/14.5-mm AA (II × 1)   **M:** 2 M50 diesels; 2 props; 2,400 hp

AMPHIBIOUS WARFARE SHIPS

◆ 1 ex-Soviet Polnocny-class landing ship

D: 900 tons (fl)   **S:** 18 kts   **Dim:** 72.5 × 8.5 × 2.0
A: 2/25-mm AA (II × 1) – 2/140-mm rocket launchers (XVIII × 2)
Electron Equipt: Radar: 1/Don 2   **Man:** 40 men
M: 2 diesels; 2 props; 4,000 hp

REMARK: Transferred in 12-76.

◆ 4 ex-Soviet T-4-class landing craft

D: 70 tons (fl)   **S:** 10 kts   **Dim:** 19.0 × 4.3 × 1.0
M: 2 diesels; 2 props; 600 hp

REMARK: Transferred 1968-69.

SOUTH AFRICA
Republic of

PERSONNEL (1978): 3,950, including 560 officers

MERCHANT MARINE (1978): 295 ships – 660,735 grt
(tankers: 3 ships – 27,355 grt)

NAVAL AVIATION: An air force detachment is available to the navy. Shackleton and Piaggio aircraft are used for patrol and Wasp helicopters are embarked on the ships.

SUBMARINES

◆ **3 Daphné class** Bldr: Dubigeon, Nantes

	Laid down	L	In serv.
S 97 MARIA VAN RIEBEECK	14-3-68	18-3-69	22-6-70
S 98 EMILY HOBHOUSE	18-11-68	24-10-69	25-1-71
S 99 JOHANNA VAN DER MERWE	24-4-69	21-7-70	21-7-71

Emily Hobhouse   M. Bar, 1971

D: 869 tons surfaced, 1,043 submerged   **S:** 13/15.5 kts
Dim: 57.75 × 6.75 × 4.5   **Man:** 6 officers, 41 men
A: 12/550-mm TT (8 fwd, 4 aft) – no reloads
M: 2 SEMT-Pielstick 450-kw diesels, electric drive; 2 props; 1,300/1,600 hp

REMARK: *See* French *Daphné* class. Two embargoed *Agosta*-class submarines ordered from France in 1975 were sold by France to Pakistan.

FRIGATES

◆ **3 British Whitby class**
Bldrs: F-145 and F-150: Yarrow, Scotstoun F-147: Alex. Stephen, Govan

	Laid down	L	In serv.
F 145 PRESIDENT PRETORIUS	21-11-60	28-9-62	4-3-64
F 147 PRESIDENT STEYN	20-5-60	23-11-61	25-4-63
F 150 PRESIDENT KRUGER	6-4-59	20-10-60	1-10-62

D: 2,250 tons (2,800 fl)   **S:** 29 kts
Dim: 112.77 (100.73 pp) × 12.5 × 5.2 (fl)

President Kruger   1970

President Steyn   J. Jedrlinic, 1976

Man: 13 officers, 190 men   **Range:** 2,100/26, 4,500/12
A: 2/114-mm Mk 6 DP (II × 1) – 2/40-mm AA (I × 2) – 6/324-mm Mk 32 ASW TT
(III × 2) – 1/Mk 10 Limbo mortar (III × 1) – 1/Wasp helicopter (Mk 44 torpedoes)
Electron Equipt: Radars: 1/293 M, 1/Thomson CSF Jupiter, 1/Elsag NA 9C fire-control
Sonars: 1/177, 1/174
Boilers: 2 Babcock & Wilcox, 38.7 kg/cm² – superheat 454°C
M: 2 double-reduction GT; 2 props; 30,000 hp

REMARKS: F-147 and F-150 modernized at Simonstown, 1968-70 and 1969-71; F-145 in 1971-77. F-150 again refitted in 1979 when old fire-control system was replaced.

NOTE: The two French A-69-class corvettes, *Transvaal* and *Good Hope*, ordered in 1976 were embargoed and sold instead to Argentina. The two Loch-class frigates of the same names were stricken in 1976.

GUIDED-MISSILE PATROL BOATS

◆ 12 Israeli Reshef type

	Bldr	In serv.		Bldr	In serv.
P 1561 FRANZ ERASMUS	Haifa	1978	P 1567 N . . .	Durban	. . .
P 1562 OSWALD PIRO	Haifa	1978	P 1568 N . . .	Durban	. . .
P 1563 JIM FOUCHE	Haifa	1978	P 1569 N . . .	Durban	. . .
P 1564 N . . .	Durban	1979	P 1570 N . . .	Durban	. . .
P 1565 N . . .	Durban	. . .	P 1571 N . . .	Durban	. . .
P 1566 N . . .	Durban	. . .	P 1572 N . . .	Durban	. . .

D: 415 tons (450 fl) **S:** 32 kts **Dim:** 58.1 × 7.6 × 2.4
Man: 7 officers, 40 men **Range:** 1,500/30, 5,000/15
A: 6/Gabriel Mk 2 SSM (I × 6) − 2/76-mm OTO Melara DP (I × 2) − 2/20-mm AA
(I × 2)
Electron Equipt: Radar: 1/Thompson-CSF Vega system
M: 4 MTU MD87 diesels; 4 props; 14,000 hp

REMARKS: Six were ordered in 1974 and six on 15-11-77. Armament presumably being fitted, although the three delivered from Israel arrived unarmed. South Africa has announced development of its own anti-ship missile, which may be a licence-built version of Gabriel.

PATROL BOATS AND CRAFT

◆ 5 British Ford class

	Bldr	In serv.
P 3105 GELDERLAND (ex-*Brayford*)	A. & J. Inglis, Glasgow	30-8-54
P 3120 NAULTILUS (ex-*Glassford*)	R. Dunstan, Thorne	23-8-55
P 3125 RIJGER	Vosper, Portsmouth	1958
P 3126 HAERLEM	Vosper, Portsmouth	1959
P 3127 OOSTERLAND	Vosper, Portsmouth	1959

Haerlem−as a hydrographic ship

D: 120 tons (160 fl) **S:** 15 kts **Dim:** 35.7 × 6.1 × 2.1
A: 1/40-mm AA **Man:** 19 men **Fuel:** 23 tons
M: 2 Paxman YHAXM diesels, 500 hp each, 1 Foden FD-6 diesel, 100 hp; 3 props

REMARKS: P-3126 has been fitted as a hydrographic ship and disarmed. P-3125 and P-3127 still carry two depth-charge racks. P-3120 is manned by the Citizens Force.

◆ 4 ex-British "-ton"-class former minesweepers

	Bldr	L
P 1556 PRETORIA (ex-*Dunkerton*)	Goole SB Co.	8-3-54
P 1557 KAAPSTAD (ex-*Hazleton*)	Cook, Welton & Gemmell	6-2-54
P 1559 WALVISBAAI (ex-*Packington*)	Harland & Wolff	3-7-58
P 1560 DURBAN	Camper & Nicholson	12-6-57

REMARKS: Data as for minesweepers below, except that P-1556 and P-1557 have 2 Mirrlees JVSS-12 diesels of 1,250 hp each. Manned by Citizens Force, having been redesignated 1977-78. Retain most sweep gear and could be used to sweep moored and mechanical mines. All carry Gemini inspection dinghys.

◆ 1 harbor patrol craft Bldr: South Africa, 1976

P 1558 N . . .

D: . . . **S:** . . . **Dim:** . . . × . . . × . . .
A: 1/40-mm AA − 2/20-mm AA (I × 2) **M:** 2 diesels; 2 props; . . . hp

REMARKS: The first South African-designed warship. Prototype for a new class of local patrol craft.

MINE WARFARE SHIPS

◆ 6 British "-ton"-class minesweepers and minehunters*

	Bldr	L
M 1207 JOHANNESBURG (ex-*Castleton*)	J.S. White	26-8-58
M 1210 KIMBERLEY (ex-*Stratton*)*	Dorset Yacht	29-7-57
M 1212 PORT ELIZABETH (ex-*Dumbleton*)	Harland & Wolff	8-11-57
M 1213 MOSSELBAAI (ex-*Oakington*)*	Harland & Wolff	10-12-58
M 1215 EAST LONDON (ex-*Chilton*)	Cook, Welton & Gemmell	15-7-57
M 1498 WINDHOEK	Thornycroft	28-6-57

Windhoek

D: 370 tons (425 fl) **S:** 15 kts (cruising)
Dim: 46.33 (42.68 pp) × 8.76 × 2.5
A: 1/40-mm AA − 2/20-mm AA (II × 1) **Man:** 27 men (*36)
Electron Equipt: Radar: 1/978 (*1/1006) Sonar: (*only): 1/193M
Range: 2,300/13, 3,000/8 **Fuel:** 45 tons
M: 2 Paxman Deltic 18A-7A; 2 props; 3,000 hp

MINE WARFARE SHIPS *(continued)*

REMARKS: Four have been redesignated as patrol boats, *see above*. M-1210 and M-1213 have been converted as minehunters, with Type 193M minehunting sonar, Type 1000 radar, two PAP-104 remote-controlled minehunting devices, and mine-disposal diver facilities. All now have enclosed bridges and tripod masts.

AUXILIARY SHIPS

◆ 1 British Hecla-class hydrographic ship

	Bldr	Laid down	L	In serv.
PROTEA	Yarrow	20-7-70	14-7-71	23-5-72

D: 2,750 tons (fl)   **S:** 15.5 kts   **Dim:** 71.6 × 14.9 × 4.6
Man: 123 men   **Range:** 12,000/11   **Fuel:** 500 tons
M: 4 Paxman-Ventura diesels; 1 controllable-pitch prop; 4,800 hp

REMARKS: Ordered 7-11-69. Hull reinforced for navigating in ice. Bow thruster and anti-roll tanks fitted. Helicopter hangar and flight deck for one Wasp.

◆ 1 fleet replenishment ship

A 243 TAFELBERG (ex-Danish tanker *Annam*)

Tafelberg   1974

D: 12,499 get   **S:** 15 kts   **Dim:** 170.6 × 21.9 × 9.2
M: 1 B & W diesel; 8,420 hp   **Man:** 100 men

REMARKS: Launched 20-6-58. Purchased and refitted in Durban, 1965-67. 18,980 dwt. Two refueling stations and one solid-stores transfer station per side.

◆ 1 British "Bar-"-class net-tender   Bldr: Blyth Dry Dock & SB Co.

P 285 SOMERSET (ex-*Barcross*)

D: 750 tons (960 fl)   **S:** 11.7 kts   **Dim:** 52.96 × 9.8 × 4.62 (aft)
Range: 3,100/10   **Fuel:** 214 tons   **Boilers:** 2
M: 1 set triple-expansion reciprocating steam; 1 prop; 850 hp

REMARK: Launched 21-10-41.

◆ 1 torpedo-recovery and diver-training ship   Bldr: Dorman Long, Durban, 1969

P 3148 FLEUR

Fleur   1970

D: 220 tons (257 fl)   **S:** 14 kts   **Dim:** 35.0 × 7.5 × 3.4
M: 2 Paxman-Ventura diesels; 2 props; 1,400 hp   **Man:** 22 men

◆ 1 training craft   Bldr: Fred Nicholls, Durban, 1964

NAVIGATOR

D: 75 tons (fl)   **S:** 9.5 kts   **Dim:** 19.2 × 6.0 × . . .
M: 2 Foden FD-6 diesels; 2 props; 200 hp

REMARKS: Wooden-hulled fishing cutter type. Serves as tender at Naval College, Gordon's Bay.

◆ 3 tugs

DE MIST   Bldr: Dorman Long, Durban

     S: 12 kts   **Dim:** . . . × . . . × . . .

REMARK: Launched 21-12-78.

DE NEYS   Bldr: Globe Eng., Capetown

     D: 180 tons   **Dim:** 30.8 × 8.7 × 5.2
     M: 2 Lister-Blackstone diesels; 608 hp

REMARK: Launched 7-69.

DE NOORDE   Bldr: Globe Eng., Capetown

     D: 170 tons   **Dim:** 34.2 × 8.2 × 4.9.
     M: 2 Lister-Blackstone diesels; 608 hp

REMARK: Launched 12-61.

◆ 1 harbor launch

Y 1501 NAMACURA

     D: 5 tons   **S:** 30 kts   **Dim:** 9.0 × . . . × . . .
     A: 1/12.7-mm machine gun – 2/7.62-mm machine guns   **M:** Diesels

AIR SEA RESCUE BOATS

◆ 2 Fairey Tracker class   Bldr: Groves & Gutteridge, Cowes, G.B.

P 1554   P 1555

     D: 31 tons (fl)   **S:** 29 kts   **Dim:** 19.25 × 4.98 × 1.45
     Man: 11 men   **Range:** 650/20
     M: 2 GM 12V71 TI diesels; 2 props; 1,120 hp

SOUTH AFRICA (*continued*)

AIR SEA RESCUE BOATS (*continued*)

◆ **2 German-built** Bldr: Krogerwerft, Rendsburg, 1961-62

P 1551   P 1552

> **D:** 87 tons (fl)   **S:** 30 kts   **Dim:** 23.9 × 5.8 × 1.2
> **M:** 2 MTU diesels; 2 props; 4,480 hp

DEPARTMENT OF TRANSPORT

◆ **1 Antarctic survey and supply ship**

	Bldr	Laid down	L	In serv.
AGULHAS	Mitsubishi, Shimonoseki	14-6-77	30-9-77	31-1-78

> **D:** 3,035 dwt   **S:** 14 kts   **Dim:** 109.2 (100.0 pp) × 18.0 × 5.8
> **Man:** 40 men + 92 scientists/passengers   **Range:** 8,200/14
> **M:** 2 Mirrlees-Blackstone K-6 Major diesels; 1 prop; 6,000 hp

REMARKS: Manned by the South African Navy. Twin helicopter hangar. Red hull, white upper works.

SPAIN

PERSONNEL (1977): 46,000, including 4,000 officers, 650 Marine officers, and 5,200 Marine enlisted.

MERCHANT MARINE (1978): 2,753 ships — 8,056,080 grt
(tankers: 119 ships — 5,079,240 grt)

WARSHIPS IN SERVICE OR UNDER CONSTRUCTION AS OF 1 JANUARY 1980

	L	Tons	Main armament
◆ **1 aircraft carrier**			
DEDALO	1943	13,000	26/40-mm, 20 aircraft

	L	Tons (surfaced)	
◆ **8 (+4) submarines**			
0 (+4) AGOSTA	1979-	1,490	4/550-mm TT
4 DAPHNÉ	1972-74	870	12/550-mm TT
3 GUPPY IIA	1943-44	1,848	10/533-mm TT
1 BALAO	1944	1,827	10/533-mm TT

		Tons	
◆ **12 destroyers**			
2 ROGER DE LAURIA	1967-68	3,012	6/127-mm DP, ASW weapons
1 ALAVA	1946	1,841	3/76-mm DP, ASW weapons
5 GEARING (FRAM I)	1945	2,425	4/127-mm, 1/Asroc system
4 FLETCHER	1942-44	2,080	4 or 5/127-mm, 0 or 6/76-mm, ASW weapons
◆ **10 (+11) frigates**			
0 (+3) OLIVER HAZARD PERRY	. . .	. . .	1/76-mm, 1 Standard system, 2 helicopters
4 (+8) DESCUBIERTA	1975-	1,270	1/76-mm, 1/Sea Sparrow, 8/Harpoon
5 BALÉARES	1970-72	3,015	1/127-mm, 1/Asroc system, 1/Standard system, ASW weapons
1 PIZARRO	1945	1,924	2/127-mm, ASW weapons
◆ **2 corvettes**			
2 ATREVIDA	1955-56	977	1/76-mm DP, 3/40-mm, ASW weapons

◆ **12 (+18) torpedo and patrol boats**

◆ **15 minesweepers**

◆ **14 amphibious warfare ships**

NAVAL AVIATION: Five single-seat AV-8A and two two-seat TAV-8A were delivered in 1976 for service in the *Dedalo;* subsequently, two of the aircraft, named Matador in Spanish service, were lost. Five more AV-8A were ordered for delivery in 1977-80. Another increment of five may follow.

AV-8A Matador on Dedalo

NAVAL AVIATION (continued)

The Arma Aerea de la Armada also operates 10 Agusta-Bell 204-B (with SS-12 missiles), 11 Bell 47G, 9 Sikorsky SH3-D Sea King, 5 AH-1G Huey, and 12 Hughes 316-HM Cayuse helicopters plus 2 Piper Comanche and 2 Piper Twin Comanche liaison aircraft. Purchase of six more SH3-D is planned.

The search and rescue service (Servicio de Búsqueda y Salvamento) received 3 Fokker F-27 SAR aircraft in 1979 for coastal surveillance; they carry Litton APS-504V radar.

The Spanish Air Force performs a maritime surveillance role, using three Grumman UH-16B Albatross amphibians and two Lockheed P-3A Orion. Purchase of five or six more Orion is planned.

WEAPONS AND SYSTEMS

Except for naval guns, which are domestically designed and manufactured, most of the weapon systems in use are of American or French make. However, an advanced antiaircraft/anti-missile point-defense system of Spanish origin is in development. Called Meroka, it consists of two six-barreled, 20-mm Oerlikon guns, whose characteristics are:

Length: 120 calibers
Muzzle velocity: 1,250m/sec
Maximum rate of fire: 3,600 rounds/minute
Maximum effective range: 2,000 m
Fire control: Lockheed "sharp shooter" with Doppler radar and stabilized optical sights

Two prototypes are undergoing firing tests, and twenty units may be produced to equip the aircraft carrier *Dedalo*, the *Roger de Lauria*-class destroyers, the *Baléares*-class and *Descubierta*-class frigates, and the programmed new carrier.

AIRCRAFT CARRIERS

◆ 1 new construction

	Bldr	Laid down	L	In serv.
PA 11 N . . .	Bazán, el Ferrol	1980	. . .	. . .

D: 14,300 tons (fl)   **S:** 26.28 kts
Dim: 195.1 × 24.4 (30.0 flight deck) × 9.1
Man: 750-780 men, including air group   **Range:** 7,500/20
A: 4/Meroka 20-mm gun systems—19 aircraft (AV-8A and SH-3D)
Electron Equipt: Radars: 1/SPS 55, 1/SPS 52B—URN 22 TACAN
M: 2 GE LM-2500 gas turbines; 1 prop; 40,000 hp

REMARKS: Ordered 29-6-77. Originally to have been named *Almirante Carrero Blanco* but will probably be named *Dedalo* to commemorate the ship she is replacing. Design is essentially that of the final version of the U.S. Navy's Sea Control Ship concept. The flight deck is 175 × 30 m and is served by two elevators, one at the extreme aft end. Takeoff pattern angled to starboard. No "ski-jump" takeoff ramp is planned.

◆ 1 ex-U.S. light aircraft carrier   Bldr: New York SB

	Laid down	L	In serv.
PA 01 DEDALO (ex-*Cabot*, AVT-3, ex-CVL-28, (ex-*Wilmington*, CL-79)	16-3-42	4-4-43	24-7-43

D: 13,000 tons (16,416 fl)   **S:** 31 kts (trials)
Dim: 188.35 (182.9 wl) × 20.11 (hull) 31.7 (flight deck) × 7.2
Man: 1,112 men = air group   **Range:** 7,200/15   **Electric:** 2,400 kw
A: 26/40-mm (IV × 2, II × 9)—about 20 aircraft, 5 of which are Matadors

Dedalo   1974

Electron Equipt: Radars: 1/SPS 10, 1/SPS 40A, 1/SPS 8, 1/SPS 6C, 4/Mk 34 fire-control—URN 22 TACAN—ECM: WLR-1
Armor: Partial belt: 37-127
Boilers: 4 Babcock & Wilcox, 39.8 kg/cm² pressure—superheat 454°C
M: GT; 4 props; 100,000 hp   **Fuel:** 1,800 tons

REMARKS: Ended service in the U.S. Navy as an aviation transport (AVT-3). Transferred on five-year loan on 30-8-67 and purchased in 12-73. Redesignated from PH (portahelicópteros) to PA (portaaviones) on 28-9-76, when AV-8A V/STOL fighters were added to her complement. The flight deck is 166.1 × 32.9 m (max.). Two elevators. Four Mk-63 radar gunfire-control systems and seven Mk-51, mod. 2, optical gunfire control installed. Did not receive SPS-52B radar in place of SPS-8, as planned; the SPS-52B is to be installed in PA-11. She is supposed to be given the Meroka point-defense gun system, but will probably be retired on completion of PA-11.

SUBMARINES

◆ 4 Agosta class   Bldr: Bazán, Cartagena

	Laid down	L	In serv.		Laid down	L	In serv.
S 70 N . . .	1975	1979	1980	S 72 N . . .	1977	1981	1982
S 71 N . . .	1976	1980	1981	S 73 N . . .	1978	1982	1983

D: 1,230 standard, 1,490 surfaced, 1,740 submerged   **S:** 20 kts (submerged)
Dim: 67.57 × 6.8 × 5.4   **Man:** 6 officers, 49 men   **Fuel:** 200 tons
A: 4/550-mm TT (rapid reload)—20 reloads   **Range:** 8,500/9 (snorkeling)
Electron Equipt: Radar: 1/Calypso   Sonar: 2/DUUA 1, active, DSUV, passive
M: 2 SEMT-Pielstick A16 PA4 185 diesel generator sets, 850 kw each; 4,600-hp main engine; 1 23-kw cruising engine; 1 prop

REMARKS: *See Agosta* class in section on France. As with the *Daphné* class, will be built with French technical assistance. Agreement signed 6-2-74; first two ordered 9-5-74, second pair 29-6-77.

◆ 4 Daphné class   Bldr: Bazán, Cartagena

	Laid down	L	In serv.
S 61 DELFIN	13-8-68	25-3-72	3-5-73
S 62 TONINA	1969	3-10-72	10-7-73
S 63 MARSOPA	19-3-71	15-3-74	12-4-75
S 64 NARVAL	1972	14-12-74	22-11-75

D: 870 tons surfaced, 1,040 submerged   **S:** 13/15.5 kts
Dim: 57.75 × 6.76 × 4.62   **Man:** 6 officers, 41 men

SUBMARINES (continued)

Tonina   G. Arra, 1976

Marsopa   Pradignac & Leo, 1976

Isaac Peral   1971

A: 12/550-mm TT (8 fwd, 4 aft)—no reloads
Electron Equipt: Radar: 1/Thomson-CSF DRUA 31 (with ECM)
    Sonars: DUUA 1, active, DSUV, passive
M: 2 SEMT-Pielstick diesel generators of 450 kw each; 2 props; 2,000 hp

REMARKS: Built with French technical assistance. Agreement made on 16-7-66.

◆ **3 ex-U.S. Guppy-IIA class**
  Bldrs: S-32, S-34: Portsmouth NSY; S-35: Manitowoc SB, Wisc.

	Laid down	L	In serv.
S 32 ISAAC PERAL (ex-*Ronquil*, SS-396)	9-9-43	27-1-44	22-4-44
S 34 COSME GARCIA (ex-*Bang*, SS-385)	30-4-43	30-8-43	4-12-43
S 35 N . . . (ex-*Jallao*, SS-368)	29-9-43	12-3-44	8-7-44

D: 1,525 tons standard, 1,848 surfaced, 2,440 submerged   **S:** 17/14.1 kts
Dim: 93.57 × 8.23 × 5.18   **Man:** 74 men   **Range:** 10,000/10
A: 10/533-mm TT (6 fwd, 4 aft)—22 torpedoes   **Fuel:** 404 tons (S-35: 472)
Electron Equipt: Radar: 1/SS-2   Sonars: BQS 2, BQR 3, BQR 2
M: Diesel-electric propulsion: 3 Fairbanks-Morse 38D8¼ (S-35: GM 16-278A) diesels;
    2 electric motors; 2 props; 3,430 hp

REMARKS: S-32 transferred on 1-7-71, S-34 on 1-10-72, and S-35 on 26-6-74. Two 126-cell batteries. Modernized, 1952-53. Diving depth is 137 m. Sister *Narciso Monturiol* (S-33, ex-*Picuda*, SS-382) was stricken on 30-4-77. Reason for not naming S-35 has not been given.

◆ **1 ex-U.S. Balao class** Bldr: Manitowoc SB, Wisc.

	Laid down	L	In serv.
S 31 ALMIRANTE GARCIA DE LOS REYES (ex-*Kraken*, SS-370)	14-12-43	30-4-44	8-9-44

Almirante Garcia de los Reyes

D: 1,525 tons standard, 1,827 surfaced, 2,400 submerged   **S:** 18.5/10 kts
Dim: 95.10 × 8.23 × 5.18   **Man:** 80 men   **Range:** 10,000/10
A: 10/533-mm TT (6 fwd, 4 aft)—22 torpedoes   **Fuel:** 472 tons
Electron Equipt: Radar: 1/SS 2   Sonars: BQR 2, BQS 2
M: Diesel-electric propulsion: 4 GM 16-278A diesels; 2 electric motors; 4,610 hp

REMARKS: "Fleet Snorkel" conversion, transferred 24-10-59. Complete modernization in Philadelphia, 1965-66. Was to have been stricken in 1975 because of her poor condition, but was refitted as a replacement for the *Narciso Monturiol*.

NOTE: The two midget submarines, SA-51 and SA-52, were stricken on 5-3-79.

DESTROYERS

◆ **2 Roger de Lauria class** Bldr: Bazán, el Ferrol, Cartagena

	Laid down	L	In serv.
D 42 Roger De Lauria	4-9-51	22-8-67	30-5-69
D 43 Marques De La Ensenada	4-9-51	22-2-68	10-9-70

Roger de Lauria   1973

Roger de Lauria   1974

D: 3,012 tons (3,785 fl)   **S:** 28 kts
Dim: 116.68 (110.8 pp) × 12.5 × 6.5 (max.)
Man: 20 officers, 235 men   **Range:** 4,500/15   **Fuel:** 673 tons
A: 6/127-mm DP (II × 3)—6/324-mm Mk 32 ASW TT (III × 2)—2/ASW fixed Mk 25
     TT for Mk 37 torpedoes—1/Hughes 316-HM ASW helicopter
Electron Equipt: Radars: 1/SPS 10B, 1/SPS 40, 1 Mk 25, 1/Mk 35
     Sonars: 1/SQS 32, 1/SQA 10 VDS—ECM: WLR-1
Boilers: 3 three-drum, 35 kg/cm² pressure—superheat 375°C
M: 2 sets Rateau-Bretagne GT; 2 props; 60,000 hp   **Electric:** 1,900 kw

REMARKS: Widened and lengthened during construction in order to eliminate defects
found in the *Oquendo* prototype; completion consequently delayed. U.S. semiautomatic, 38-caliber guns, 1 Mk-37 and 1 Mk-56 radar gun-control system. The *Oquendo*
was stricken on 2-11-78.

◆ **1 Alava class** Bldr: Bazán, Cartagena

	Laid down	L	In serv.
D 51 Liniers	1-1-45	1-5-46	27-1-51

Liniers   1969

D: 1,841 tons (2,270 fl)   **S:** 28 kts   **Dim:** 101.15 (97.52 pp) × 9.65 × 3.1
Man: 15 officers, 207 men   **Range:** 4,500/14   **Fuel:** 540 tons
A: 3/76-mm DP (I × 3)—3/40-mm AA (I × 3)—2/Hedgehogs—8/depth-charge pro-
     jectors—2/ASW TT racks (6 Mk 32 torpedoes)—2/depth-charge racks
Electron Equipt: Radars: 1/SG 6B, 1/Decca TM 626, 1/MLA 1B, 2/Mk 34
     Sonar: SQS 30
M: 2 sets Parsons GT; 2 props; 31,500 hp   **Boilers:** 4 three-drum Yarrow

REMARKS: Ordered in 1936. Rearmed with U.S. weapons in 1964. Used for training midshipmen at the Naval Academy. Two Mk 63 gunfire-control radars for 76-mm guns.
Sister *Alava* (D-52) stricken on 2-11-78.

DESTROYERS (continued)

♦ 5 ex-U.S. Gearing FRAM-I

	Bldr	Laid down	L	In serv.
D 61 CHURRUCA (ex-Eugene A. Greene, DD-711)	Federal SB, Newark,	17-8-44	18-3-45	8-6-45
D 62 GRAVINA (ex-Furse, DD-882)	Consolidated, Orange, Tex.	23-9-44	9-3-45	10-7-45
D 63 MENDEZ NUÑEZ (ex-O'Hare DD-889)	Consolidated, Orange, Tex.	27-1-45	22-6-45	29-11-45
D 64 LANGARA (ex-Leary, DD-879)	Consolidated, Orange, Tex.	11-8-44	20-1-45	7-5-45
D 65 BLAS DE LEZO (ex-Noa, DD-841)	Bath Iron Works	26-3-45	30-7-45	2-11-45

Churruca   1974

D: 2,425 tons (light)(3,540 fl)   **S:** 31 kts
Dim: 119.02 × 12.45 × 6.4 (max.) 4.45 (hull)
Man: 17 officers, 257 men   **Range:** 2,400/25, 4,800/15
A: 4/127-mm 38-cal. (II × 2) − 1/Asroc system (VIII × 1) − 6/324-mm Mk 32 ASW TT ASW TT (III × 2) − 1/ASW helicopter
Electron Equipt: Radars: 1/SPS 10, 1/SPS 29 (D-61, D-62: SPS 40), 1/Mk 25
              Sonar: 1/SQS 23
Boilers: 4 Babcock & Wilcox, 39.8 kg/cm² pressure − superheat 454°C
M: GT; 2 props; 60,000 hp   **Fuel:** 650 tons   **Electric:** 1,100 kw

REMARKS: D-61 and D-62 were loaned on 31-8-72, and D-63 to D-65 on 31-10-73. All purchased outright on 17-5-78. D-65 has both her 127-mm mounts forward and no Asroc. Mk-37 fire-control system for guns. Carry manned helicopter in place of original drones.

♦ 4 ex-U.S. Fletcher class

	Bldr	Laid down	L	In serv.
D 21 LEPANTO (ex-Capps, DD-550)	Gulf SB, Chickasaw, Ala.	12-6-41	31-5-42	23-6-43
D 23 ALMIRANTE VALDES (ex-Converse, DD-509)	Bath Iron Works, Me.	23-2-42	30-8-42	20-11-42
D 24 ALCALA GALIANO (ex-Jarvis, DD-799)	Todd, Seattle, Wash.	7-6-43	14-2-44	3-6-44
D 25 JORGE JUAN (ex-McGowan, DD-678)	Federal SB, Kearny, N.J.	30-6-43	14-11-43	20-12-43

Lepanto

Almirante Valdes

D: 2,850 tons (3,050 fl)   **S:** 30-32 kts   **Dim:** 114.85 × 12.03 × 5.5
Man: 17 officers, 273 men   **Range:** 1,260/32, 4,400/15   **Fuel:** 650 tons
A: D-21: 5/127-mm DP (I × 5) − 6/40-mm AA (II × 3) − 6/20-mm AA − 6/324-mm Mk 32 ASW TT (III × 2) − 2/Mk 11 Hedgehogs − 6/depth-charge mortars − 2/depth-charge racks
         D-23 to D-25: 4/127-mm DP (I × 4) − 6/76-mm AA (II × 3) − 5/533-mm TT (V × 1) − 6/324-mm Mk 32 ASW TT (III × 2) − 2/Mk 11 Hedgehogs − 1/depth-charge rack
Electron Equipt: Radars: 1/SPS 10, 1/SPS 6C, 1/Mk 25, 1/Mk 35, 2/Mk 34
                Sonars: SQS-29 series
Boilers: 4 Babcock & Wilcox, 39.8 kg/cm² pressure − superheat 454°C
M: 2 sets GT; 2 props; 60,000 hp   **Electric:** 580 kw

REMARKS: D-21 was transferred on 15-5-57, D-23 on 1-7-59, D-24 on 3-11-60, and D-25 on 1-12-60. Sister Almirante Ferrandiz (D-22, ex-David W. Taylor, DD-551) was stricken on 2-11-78. D-21 and D-23 have high, "early Fletcher" bridges, the others low bridges. All have one Mk-37 gunfire-control system; D-23 to D-25 also have one Mk-56 and two Mk-63 gunfire-control systems.

FRIGATES

◆ 3 U.S. Oliver Hazard Perry class   Bldr: Bazán, el Ferrol

	Laid down	L	In serv.
F 1 NAVARRA	1980	...	...
F 2 MURCIA	1981	...	...
F 3 LEÓN	1982	...	...

D: 3,537 tons (fl)   **S:** 30 kts   **Dim:** 135.64 (125.9 wl) × 13.72 × 7.47 (max.)
Man: 11 officers, 152 men   **Range:** 5,000/18   **Electric:** 3,000 kw
A: 1/Mk 13, mod. 4, missile launcher (40 Harpoon and Standard SM1-MR) — 1/76-mm OTO Melara DP — 2/Meroka 20-mm AA systems — 6/324-mm Mk 32 ASW TT — 2/ASW helicopters
Electron Equipt: Radars: 1/SPS 55, 1/SPS 49, 1/Mk 92 fire-control system (with STIR)
  Sonar: SQS 56
M: 2 GE LM-2500 gas turbines; 1 controllable-pitch prop; 40,000 hp (2/325-hp electric auxiliary propulsion motors)

REMARKS: Although officially ordered on 29-6-77, little or no progress has been made on construction, the new carrier PA-11 taking precedence. Will duplicate U.S. version except for close-defense AA gun system. Type of helicopter to be carried has not been decided, which may be contributing to the delay.

◆ 4 improved Descubierta class   Bldr: ...

	Laid down	L	In serv.		Laid down	L	In serv.
F...N...	...	...	...	F...N...	...	...	...
F...N...	...	...	...	F...N...	...	...	...

D: 1,900 tons (fl)   **S:** 32 kts   **Dim:** 98.0 × 10.4 × 3.4
A: 8/Harpoon SSM (IV × 2) — 1/Sea Sparrow SAM system (VIII × 1) — 1/76-mm OTO Melara DP — 2/Meroka 20-mm AA systems — 6/324-mm Mk 32 ASW TT
Electron Equipt: Radar: ...
  Sonars: Raytheon 1160B, Raytheon 1167 VDS
M: 2 gas turbines; 2 controllable-pitch props; ... hp

REMARKS: To commence construction in sequence on completion of *Descubierta* class. Raytheon-1160B is a commercial version of the U.S. SQS-56 sonar.

◆ 8 Descubierta class

	Bldr	Laid down	L	In serv.
F 31 DESCUBIERTA	Bazán, Cartagena	16-11-74	8-7-75	18-11-78
F 32 DIANA	Bazán, Cartagena	8-7-75	26-1-76	30-6-79
F 33 INFANTA ELENA	Bazán, Cartagena	26-1-76	14-9-76	11-79
F 34 INFANTA CRISTINA	Bazán, Cartagena	14-9-76	25-4-77	5-80
F 35 CAZADORA	Bazán, el Ferrol	14-12-77	17-10-78	1981
F 36 VENCEDORA	Bazán, el Ferrol	5-78	27-4-79	1981
F 37 CENTINELLA	Bazán, el Ferrol	31-10-78	6-7-79	1981
F 38 SERVIOLA	Bazán, el Ferrol	-79	-80	1982

D: 1,270 tons (1,520 fl)   **S:** 26 kts   **Dim:** 88.88 (85.8 pp) × 10.4 × 3.7
Man: 10 officers, 106 men   **Range:** 6,100/18   **Fuel:** 250 tons
A: 8/Harpoon SSM (IV × 2) — 1/Sea Sparrow SAM system (VIII × 1) — 1/76-mm OTO Melara — 2/40-mm AA (I × 2) — 1/375-mm Bofors ASW rocket launcher (II × 1) — 6/324-mm Mk 32 ASW TT (III × 2)
Electron Equipt: Radars: 1/HSA ZW-06, 1/HSA DA-05/2, 1/HSA WM 22/41 fire-control

Descubierta   1978

Descubierta   Bazan, 1978

Descubierta — final configuration, less Meroka

  Sonars: Raytheon 1160B, Raytheon 1167 (VDS last four)
M: 4 MTU-Bazán 16V956 TB91 diesels; 2 controllable-pitch props; 16,000 hp
Electric: 1,810 kw

REMARKS: Design evolved from the Portuguese Navy's *João Coutinho* class, built by same yard. The first four were ordered on 7-12-73, the others on 25-5-76. All later to

FRIGATES (continued)

receive one Meroka multi-barreled 20-mm AA gun aft. F-35 to F-38 to have Raytheon 1167 VDS on completion; others to back-fit. Have fin stabilization plus "Maslar" bubble system to reduce radiated noise below the waterline. Can accommodate thirty troops. Carry sixteen reloads for Sea Sparrow, which may be the Italian Selenia Albatros version in later ships. Have Elettronica SpA Beta ECM suit. Four improved units with gas turbine propulsion are to follow.

◆ **5 Baléares class** Bldr: Bazán, el Ferrol

	Laid down	L	In serv.
F 71 BALEARES	31-10-68	20-8-70	24-9-73
F 72 ANDALUCIA	2-7-69	30-3-71	23-5-74
F 73 CATALUÑA	20-8-70	3-11-71	16-1-75
F 74 ASTURIAS	30-3-71	13-5-72	2-12-75
F 75 EXTREMADURA	3-11-71	21-11-72	10-11-76

Baléares   1976

Asturias   A. D. Baker III, 1976

D: 3,015 tons (4,177 fl)   **S:** 27/28 kts   **Man:** 15 officers, 241 men
Dim: 133.6 (126.5 pp) × 14.3 × 4.6 (7.55 over sonar)   **Fuel:** 750 tons
A: 1/Mk 22 guided-missile launcher (16 Standard SM1-MR) – 1/127-mm Mk 42 DP – 1/Asroc ASW system – 4/324-mm Mk 32 fixed ASW TT (I × 4) – 2/fixed Mk 25 ASW TT for Mk 37 torpedoes

Electron Equipt: Radars: 1/SPS 10, 1/SPS 52A, 1/SPG 51C, 1/SPG 53B
    Sonars: 1/SQS 23 (hull), 1/SQS 35V (VDS)
Boilers: 2 Combustion-Engineering, 84 kg/cm² pressure – superheat 510°C
M: 1 set Westinghouse GT; 1 prop; 35,000 hp   **Electric:** 3,000 kw

REMARKS: Built with American aid (agreement of 31-5-66) as U.S. DEG-7 to DEG-11. The Mk-74 missile-fire-control system can use both the Mk-73 director (with SPG-51C radar) and Mk-68 director (with PSG-53B) to control two Standard missiles; the Mk-68 is also used to control the 127-mm gun. The ships have the Mk-114 digital ASW computer to control Asroc and ASW-torpedo firing. No less than forty-one ASW torpedoes of the Mk-44/46 and Mk-37 wire-guided types can be accommodated. The Mk-32 torpedo tubes are built into the port and starboard sides of the after superstructure and are oriented to a 45-degree angle outboard of the centerline. The two Mk-25 tubes are built into the stern, facing aft. The Meroka 20-mm AA gun system was to be installed during 1979, and it is planned to install Harpoon missiles. The ships have non-retractable gyrofin stabilizers. Three 750-kw steam turbogenerators and one 750-kw diesels generator are installed.

◆ **1 Pizarro class** Bldr: Bazán, el Ferrol

	Laid down	L	In serv.
F 41 VICENTE YANEZ PINZON	9-44	8-8-45	5-8-49

D: 1,924 tons (2,228 fl)   **S:** 18.5 kts (20 on trials)
Dim: 95.2 (87.54 pp) × 12.15 × 3.4 (5.4 over sonar)
Man: 16 officers, 239 men   **Range:** 3,000/15
A: 2/127-mm 38-cal DP (I × 2) – 4/40-mm AA (I × 4) – 2/Mk 11 Hedgehogs – 8/depth-charge projectors – 2/fixed ASW torpedo launchers (6 Mk 32 torpedoes) – 2/depth-charge racks
Electron Equipt: Radars: 1/Decca TM 626, 1/SPS 5B, 1/MLA 1B, 1/Mk 29
    Sonar: QHB A
Boilers: 2 Yarrow, 25 kg/cm² pressure   **Fuel:** 402 tons (max.), 386 (normal)
M: 2 sets Parsons GT; 2 props; 6,000 hp

REMARK: Exceptionally seaworthy ship, modernized in 1960. Six that were not modernized have been taken out of service since 1965. Although modernized, the *Herman Cortes* (F-32) and *Sarmiento de Gamboa* (F-36) were stricken in 1971 and 1973, and the *Legazpi* (F-42) on 4-11-78. F-41 will probably be stricken shortly.

CORVETTES

◆ **2 Atrevida class**

	Bldr	Laid down	L	In serv.
F 62 PRINCESA	Bazán, Cartagena	18-3-53	31-3-55	2-10-59
F 64 NAUTILUS	Bazán, Cadiz	27-7-53	23-8-56	10-12-59

D: 977 tons (1,136 fl)   **S:** 18 kts   **Dim:** 75.5 (68.0 pp) × 10.2 × 2.64
Man: 9 officers, 123 men   **Range:** 8,000/10   **Fuel:** 100 tons
A: 1/76-mm DP – 3/40-mm AA (I × 3) – 2/Mk 11 Hedgehogs – 8/depth-charge projectors – 2/depth-charge racks
Electron Equipt: Radar: 1/SPS 5B combination search
    Sonar: QHB 2
M: 2 Sulzer diesels; 2 props; 3,000 hp

REMARKS: Tandem machinery arrangement. Electronic equipment and weapons modernized with U.S. aid. Can carry twenty mines. The *Diana* (F-63) stricken in 1972, *Atrevida* (F-61) and *Villa de Bilboa* (F-65) in 1979.

CORVETTES (continued)

Princesa   1971

PATROL BOATS

◆ **8 Cormorán class**   Bldr: Bazán, San Fernando, Cadiz

	L			L
P . . . N . . .	. . .	P . . . N . . .	. . .
P . . . N . . .	. . .	P . . . N . . .	. . .
P . . . N . . .	. . .	P . . . N . . .	. . .
P . . . N . . .	. . .	P . . . N . . .	. . .

    D: 300 tons (355 fl)   **S:** 36 kts   **Dim:** 51.93 (49.0 pp) × 7.53 × 1.86
    Man: . . .   **Range:** 2,500/15   **Electric:** 405 kva
    A: Guided missiles (?) – 1/76-mm OTO Melara DP – 1/40-mm AA
    Electron Equipt: Radars: 1/Raytheon 1620/6, 1/HSA WM 22
    M: 3 MTU MA-16V596 TB91 diesels; 3 props; 13,500 hp   **Fuel:** 52 tons

REMARKS: To have been ordered during 1979. A faster but shorter-ranged version of the *Lazaga* class, to which it is very similar, except for a deeper chine line to the hull forward and hard, versus round, turns to the bilge.

◆ **10 PVM class**   Bldr: Bazán, San Fernando, Cadiz

	L	In serv.		L	In serv.
PVM 1 N . . .	. . .	1980	PVM 6 N . . .	. . .	1982
PVM 2 N . . .	. . .	1980	PVM 7 N . . .	. . .	1982
PVM 3 N . . .	. . .	1980	PVM 8 N . . .	. . .	1982
PVM 4 N . . .	. . .	1980	PVM 9 N . . .	. . .	1982
PVM 5 N . . .	. . .	1982	PVM 10 N . . .	. . .	1982

    D: 350 tons (fl)   **S:** 20 kts   **Dim:** 44.4 × 6.6 × 2.1
    Man: 21 men   **Range:** 4,000/15
    A: 1/76-mm Mk 22 DP – 1/20-mm AA   **M:** 2 diesels; 2 props; 4,800 hp

REMARKS: Fisheries-protection craft resembling fishing boats with long forecastle. First unit laid down in 4-79.

◆ **4 LVE-1 class**   Bldr: Bazán, San Fernando, Cadiz, 1979-80

LVE 1   LVE 2   LVE 3   LVE 4

    D: 85 tons (fl)   **S:** 25 kts   **Dim:** 32.1 × 4.8 × 1.4
    A: 2/40-mm Breda-Bofors AA   **Range:** 1,200/15
    M: 2 diesels; 2 props; 2,800 hp

◆ **6 Lazaga class**   Bldrs: P-01: Lürssen; others: Bazán, La Carraca, Cadiz

	L	In serv.		L	In serv.
P 01 LAZAGA	30-9-74	16-7-75	P 04 VILLAMIL	24-5-74	26-4-77
P 02 ALSEDO	8-1-75	28-2-77	P 05 BONIFAZ	24-5-74	11-7-77
P 03 CADARSO	8-1-75	10-7-76	P 06 RECALDE	9-11-75	15-12-77

Alsedo   1976

    D: 275 tons (399 fl)   **S:** 29.6 kts   **Dim:** 58.1 (54.4 pp) × 7.6 × 2.64
    Man: 4 officers, 35 men   **Range:** 2,260/27, 4,200/17   **Fuel:** 112 tons
    A: 1/76-mm OTO Melara DP – 1/40-mm Breda-Bofors AA – 2/20-mm AA (I × 2)
    Electron Equipt: Radars: 1/Raytheon 1620/6, 1/HSA M 22
    M: 2 MTU MA-16V956 TB91 diesels; 2 props; 7,780 hp   **Electric:** 405 kva

REMARKS: P-01 and P-03 were commissioned with a U.S. Mk-22, 76-mm instead of an OTO Melara 76-mm. Space reserved for addition of six 324-mm Mk-32 ASW torpedo tubes and a small, high-frequency sonar. Carry 300 rounds of 76-mm, 1,472 rounds of 40-mm, and 3,000 rounds of 20-mm.

◆ **6 Barcelo class**   Bldrs: P-11 Lürssen; others: Bazán, La Carraca, Cadiz

	L	In serv.		L	In serv.
P 11 BARCELO	10-10-75	26-3-75	P 14 ORDONEZ	10-9-76	7-6-77
P 12 LAYA	18-12-75	21-12-76	P 15 ACEVEDO	10-9-76	14-7-77
P 13 JAVIER QUIROGA	18-12-75	1-4-77	P 16 CANDIDO PEREZ	3-3-77	25-11-77

Barcelo   1976

PATROL BOATS (continued)

D: 110 tons (134 fl)   **S:** 36.5 kts   **Dim:** 36.2 (34.0 pp) × 5.8 × 1.75
Man: 3 officers, 16 men   **Range:** 1,200/17   **Electric:** 110 kva
A: 1/40-mm Breda-Bofors AA – 1/20-mm AA – 2/12.7-mm machine guns
Electron Equipt: Radar: 1/Raytheon 1620/6
M: 2 MTU MD-16V538 TB90 diesels; 2 props; 5,760 hp   **Fuel:** 18 tons

PATROL CRAFT

◆ **20 LVC-1 class** Bldr: Aresa, Arenys del Mar, 1978-80

LVC 1 through LVC 20

D: 22 tons (fl)   **S:** 26 kts   **Dim:** 16.0 × 4.36 × 1.3
A: 1/12.7-mm machine gun   **Man:** 6 men   **Range:** 400/18
M: 2 Baudouin DNP-8 MIR diesels; 2 props; 700 hp

◆ **30 LVI-1 class** Bldr: Rodman, Vigo, 1978-80

D: 3 tons (4.2 fl)   **S:** 18 kts   **Dim:** 9.0 × 3.1 × 0.8
A: 1/7.62-mm machine gun   **Man:** 6 men   **Range:** 120/18
M: 2 inboard/outboard diesels; 240 hp

◆ **2 ex-fishing boats**

NÉCORA   PERCEBE

D: 300 grt   **S:** 12.7 kts   **Dim:** 31.44 (29.0 pp) × 6.5 × . . .
A: . . .   **M:** 1 diesel; 550 hp

REMARKS: In service since 1963. Purchased in 1979 to replace the *Centinela* and *Serviola*, which were sold to Mauritania. Used as fisheries-patrol craft in the Canary Islands.

◆ **1 ex-trawler** Bldr: Juliana, Gijon, 1948

W 32 SALVORA (ex-*Virgen de la Almudena*, ex-*Mendi Eder*)

Salvora   1969

D: 270 tons (fl)   **S:** 12 kts   **Dim:** 31.0 × 6.1 × 2.5
A: 1/20-mm AA   **Man:** 31 men   **Fuel:** 25 tons
M: 1 Sulzer diesel; 400 hp

REMARK: Fisheries-patrol vessel, purchased on 25-9-54.

◆ **1 ex-smuggling launch**

W 01 GAVIOTA

D: 104.2   **S:** . . .   **Dim:** 27.5 × 5.2 × 1.7
A: 2/12.7-mm machine guns   **Man:** 14 men   **M:** . . .

REMARK: Built in 1944, captured in 1970, and used as a fisheries-patrol craft.

◆ **5 LPI class** Bldr: Bazán, La Carraca, Cadiz, 1965

LPI 1   LPI 2   LPI 3   LPI 4   LPI 5

LPI-5   1969

D: 17.2 tons (25 fl)   **S:** 13 kts   **Dim:** 14.0 × 4.7 × 1.0
A: 2/7.62-mm machine guns (II × 1)   **Man:** 8 men
M: 2 Gray Marine 64HN9 diesels; 2 props; 450 hp

REMARK: Copy of U.S. "45-foot picket boat."

◆ **3 83-foot craft** Bldr: Bazán, Cadiz, 1962-64

LAS 10   LAS 20   LAS 30

LAS-20   1969

PATROL CRAFT (continued)

D: 49 tons (63 fl)   **S:** 15 kts   **Dim:** 25.4 (23.8 pp) × 4.9 × 2.0

A: 1/20-mm AA—2/13.7-mm machine guns—2 Mk 20 Mousetrap ASW rocket launchers

Electron Equipt: Radar: Decca 978   Sonar: QCU   **Man:** 15 men

M: 2 diesels; 2 props; 800 hp

REMARKS: Wooden hull. Based on U.S.C.G. WPBs.

◆ **1 river craft** Bldr: Bazán, La Carraca, Cadiz, 1966

V 22 CABO FRADERA

D: 28 tons (fl)   **S:** 16 kts   **Dim:** 14.05 × 4.67 × 0.99

A: 2/machine guns   **M:** Diesel; 280 hp

REMARK: For use on the Miño River.

◆ **11 miscellaneous local patrol craft**

V 1 (ex-*Azor*)   **D:** 112 tons   **Dim:** 31.1 × 5.7 × 2.1   **Man:** 16 men

V 4 ALCATRAZ   **D:** 65 tons   **S:** 8 kts   **Dim:** 19.0 × 4.6 × 2.1

    Man: 13 men

V 5	**D:** 5 tons	**S:** 5 kts	**Dim:** 8.2 × 2.9 × 1.1	**Man:** 7 men
V 6	**D:** 42 tons	**S:** 19 kts	**Dim:** 22.0 × 4.8 × 1.6	**Man:** 4 men
V 11	**D:** 11.7 tons	**S:** 8 kts	**Dim:** 14.8 × 3.0 × 1.0	**Man:** 7 men
V 31	**D:** 3.3 tons	**S:** 27 kts	**Dim:** 9.1 × 3.2 × 0.8	
V 32	**D:** 5 tons	**Man:** 4 men		
V 33	**D:** 25 tons	**S:** 25 kts	**Man:** 7 men	
V 34	**D:** 25 tons	**S:** 25 kts	**Man:** 7 men	

REMARKS: V-1 was built in 1926 and is a tender to the Naval School, Maran. V-4 and V-5 were built in 1947 and 1968, respectively. V-32 was built in 1974 and V-31, V-33, and V-34 in 1977. V-31 to V-34 are commercial cabin cruisers. V-5 to V-11 are wooden craft likely to be stricken soon.

MINE WARFARE SHIPS

◆ **4 ex-U.S. Aggressive-class minesweepers**

	Bldr	In serv.
M 41 GUADELETE (ex-*Dynamic*, MSO-432)	Colbert BW, Stockton, Cal.	15-12-53
M 42 GUADALMEDINA (ex-*Pivot*, MSO-463)	Wilmington BW, Cal.	12-7-54
M 43 QUADALQUIVIR (ex-*Persistent*, MSO-491)	Tacoma Boat, Wash.	3-2-56
M 44 GUADIANA (ex-*Vigor*, MSO-473)	Burgess Boat, Manitowoc, Wisc.	8-11-54

D: 665 tons (750 fl)   **S:** 14 kts   **Dim:** 52.3 × 10.36 × 4.2

Man: 6 officers, 65 men   **Range:** 2,000/12, 3,000/10

A: 2/20-mm AA (II × 1)—2/12.7-mm machine guns (I × 2)

Electron Equipt: Radars: 1/SPS 5C, 1/Decca TM 626   Sonar: SQQ 14

M: 4 Packard diesels; 2 controllable-pitch props; 2,280 hp

REMARKS: Modernized, 1969-70. Loaned 1-7-71, except M-44 on 4-4-72. All purchased in 8-74. Equipped for mechanical, magnetic, and acoustic sweeping.

Guadalmedina   1977

Guadalquivir   1977

◆ **11 ex-U.S. Adjutant-, MSC-268(*)-, and Redwing (**)-class minesweepers**

	Bldr	In serv.
M 21 NALON (ex-MSC-139)	South Coast Co. Newport Beach, Cal.	2-54
M 23 JUCAR (ex-MSC-220)	Bellingham SY, Wash.	6-56
M 24 ULLA (ex-MSC-265)	Adams Yacht, Mass.	7-58
M 25 MIÑO (ex-MSC-266)	Adams Yacht, Mass.	10-56
M 26 EBRO (ex-MSC-269)*	Bellingham SY, Wash.	12-58
M 27 TURIA (ex-MSC-130)	Hiltebrand DD, Kingston, NY	1-55
M 28 DUERO (ex-*Spoonbill*, MSC-202)**	Tampa Marine Corp., Fla.	1-59
M 29 SIL (ex-*Redwing*, MSC-200)**	Tampa Marine Corp., Fla.	1-59
M 30 TAJO (ex-MSC-287)*	Tampa Marine Corp., Fla	7-59
M 31 GENIL (ex-MSC-279)*	Tacoma BB, Wash.	9-59
M 32 ODIEL (ex-MSC-288)*	Tampa Marine Corp., Fla.	10-59

MINE WARFARE SHIPS *(continued)*

Ebro   1977

D: 355 tons (384 fl)	**S:** 13 kts (sweeping)	**D:** 43.0 (41.5 pp) × 7.95 × 2.55
Man: 2 officers, 35 men	**Range:** 2,500/10	**Fuel:** 40 tons

A: 2/20-mm AA (II × 1)
Electron Equipt: Radar: 1/Decca TM 626 or RM 914   Sonar: UQS 1D
M: 2 GM 8-268A diesels; 2 props; 1,200 hp

REMARKS: Transferred under MAP: two in 1954, one in 1955, three in 1956, one in 1958, two in 1959, and three in 1960. The *Llobregat* (M-22, ex-MSC-143) was stricken on 4-7-79 after a fire. M-21 through M-25 and M-27 through M-29 have a mast well astern of the stack. The others have only a small davit behind the stack. MSC-268 class have only 900 hp, four GM diesels. M-24 has been used for patrol duties.

NOTE: All remaining German M-40-class minesweepers were stricken 1978-79.

AMPHIBIOUS WARFARE SHIPS

◆ **2 ex-U.S. Paul Revere-class transports**   Bldr: New York SB Corp. Camden, N.J.

	L	In serv.
TA . . . N . . . (ex-*Paul Revere*, LPA-248, ex-*Diamond Mariner*)	13-2-54	3-9-58
TA . . . N . . . (ex-*Francis Marion*, LPA-249, ex-*Prairie Mariner*)	11-4-53	6-7-61

D: 10,709 tons light (16,838 fl)	**S:** 22 kts	**Dim:** 171.9 × 23.2 × 7.3

Man: 28 officers, 424 men + troops: 96 officers, 1,561 men
A: 8/76-mm Mk 33 DP (II × 4)   **Electron Equipt:** Radars: 1/SPS 10, 1/SPS 40
M: 1 set GE GT; 1 prop; 22,000 hp   **Boilers:** 2 Combustion Engineering

REMARKS: Mariner-class C4-S-1A merchant ships converted to troop transports, LPA-248 by Todd Shipyard, San Diego, and LPA-249 by Bethlehem Steel, Baltimore. Can carry seven LCM(6) and sixteen LCVP. Four Mk-63 gunfire-control systems removed between 1977 and 1978, but intercept and jamming equipment retained. In recent years had served the Naval Reserve Force. Were to be sold to Spain on decommissioning: LPA-248 on 1-10-79 and LPA-249 on 14-3-80, subject to congressional approval.

ex-Francis Marion – in U.S. Navy   W. Simms, USN, 1978

NOTE: The two *Paul Revere*-class transports were to replace the attack transports *Aragón* (TA-11, ex-*Noble*, APA 218) and *Castilla* (TA-21, ex-*Achernar*, AKA-53), which were to be stricken on their receipt.

◆ **1 ex-U.S. landing ship, dock**   Bldr: Philadelphia Navy Yard

	Laid down	L	In serv.
TA 31 GALICIA (ex-*San Marcos*, LSD-25)	1-9-44	10-1-45	15-4-45

Galicia   1978

D: 4,790 tons (9,375 fl)	**S:** 15 kts	**Dim:** 139.0 × 21.9 × 4.0

Man: 18 officers, 283 men + 137 troops   **Range:** 8,000/15
A: 12/40-mm AA (IV × 2, II × 2)   **Electron Equipt:** Radars: 1/Decca TM 626, 1/SPS 10
M: GT; 2 props, 7,000 hp   **Boilers:** 2 two-drum, 17.6 kg/cm² pressure

AMPHIBIOUS WARFARE SHIPS (continued)

Galicia   1978

REMARKS: Loaned 1-7-71 and sold outright 8-74. Well deck is 103.0 × 13.3 m. Platform for three helicopters. Can carry eighteen LCMs with one LCVP nested in each in the well. Cargo capacity: 1,347 tons. Four Mk-51, mod. 2, lead computing gun directors (no radar).

◆ **3 ex-U.S. tank landing ships**
Bldrs: L-11 and L-13: Bath Iron Works, Me.; L-12: Christy Corp.

	In serv.
L 11 VELASCO (ex-*Terrebonne Parish*, LST-1156)	21-11-52
L 12 MARTIN ALVAREZ (ex-*Wahkiakum County*, LST-1162)	15-6-54
L 13 CONDE DEL VENADITO (ex-*Tom Green County*, LST-1159)	12-9-53

Martin Alvarez   1978

D: 2,590 tons (5,786 fl)   S: 13 kts   Dim: 117.35 × 16.7 × 3.7
Man: 115 men   Range: 6,000/9   Fuel: 1,060 tons
A: 6/76-mm AA (II × 3)
Electron Equipt: Radars: 1/Decca TM 626, 1/SPS 10, 2/Mk 34
M: 4 GM diesels; 2 props; 6,000 hp

REMARKS: L-11 and L-12 transferred on 29-10-71, and L-13 on 5-1-72. All purchased outright on 1-11-76. Accommodations for 395 troops. Carry two LCVP to starboard and one LCPL to port. Two Mk-63 radar gun-control systems.

◆ **3 French EDIC-type landing craft**   Bldr: Bazán, La Carraca, Cadiz

BDK 6   BDK 7   BDK 8

BDK-6   1970

D: 279 tons (665 fl)   S: 9.5 kts   Dim: 56.94 (52.9 pp) × 11.57 × 1.36
Man: 14 men + 35 troops   Range: 1,500/9   Electric: 25 kw
A: 2/20-mm AA (I × 2)—2/12.7-mm machine guns
Electron Equipt: Radar: 1/Decca 404   M: 2 MGO diesels; 2 props; 1,040 hp

REMARKS: In service in 12-66. Cargo: 300 tons.

◆ **3 landing ships**   Bldr: Bazán, el Ferrol

BDK 3   BDK 4   BDK 5
D: 602 tons (fl)   S: 8.5 kts   Dim: 56.6 × 11.6 × 1.7
A: 2/20-mm AA   Man: 1 officer, 19 men   Range: 1,000/7
M: 2 MGO V8AS diesels; 2 props; 1,000 hp

REMARKS: In service on 15-6-59. Cargo: 300 tons.

◆ **2 ex-U.S. LCU-1466 class**

LCU 1 (ex-PCU-1471)   LCU 2 (ex-LCU-1491)
D: 180 tons (347 fl)   S: 8 kts   Dim: 35.05 × 10.36 × 1.6
A: 2/20-mm AA   Man: 6 men + 8 troops
M: 3 Gray Marine 64YTL diesels; 3 props; 675 hp

REMARKS: Transferred in 6-72. Cargo: 160 tons.

◆ **6 U.S. LCM(8)-class landing craft**   Bldr: Spain, 1975

E 81   E 82   E 83   E 84   E 85   E 86

E-81   1975

AMPHIBIOUS WARFARE SHIPS (*continued*)

D: 115 tons (fl)   **S:** 10 kts   **Dim:** 22.7 × 6.4 × 1.4 (aft)
M: 4 GM 6-71 diesels; 2 props; 600 hp   **Man:** 5 men

◆ **5 ex-U.S. LCM(6)-class landing craft**

D: 24 tons (57 fl)   **S:** 10.2 kts   **Dim:** 17.07 × 4.37 × 1.17
M: 2 Gray Marine 64HN9 diesels; 2 props; 330 hp

REMARKS: Transferred in 9-71. Cargo: 30 tons.

◆ **7 ex-U.S. LCM (3)-class landing craft**

D: 20 tons (50 fl)   **S:** 10.2 kts   **Dim:** 15.24 × 4.37 × 1.17
M: 2 Gray Marine 64HN9 diesels; 2 props; 330 hp

REMARKS: Transferred in 12-57. Cargo: 25 tons

◆ **16 ex-U.S. LCP(L)**

D: 10.2 tons (fl)   **S:** 19 kts   **Dim:** 10.91 × 3.42 × 1.07 (aft)
M: 1 GM 8V71N diesel; 1 prop; 350 hp

REMARK: Transferred in 10-58 and 1971.

◆ **49 ex-U.S. LCVP**

D: 13 tons (fl)   **S:** 5 kts   **Dim:** 11.0 × 3.2 × 1.1 (aft)
M: 1 Gray Marine 64HN9 diesel; 1 prop; 225 hp

NOTE: Above totals reflect landing craft on hand before the transfer of LPA-248 and LPA-249, which may have retained their nine LCM(6) and eleven LCVP each. Most LCP(L) and LCVP are aboard larger ships.

AUXILIARY SHIPS

◆ **4 Castor-class survey ships**   Bldr: Bazán, La Carraca, Cadiz

	L	In serv.		L	In serv.
A 21 CASTOR	5-11-65	10-11-66	A 23 ANTARES	3-73	21-11-74
A 22 POLLUX	5-11-65	15-12-66	A 24 RIGEL	3-73	21-11-74

Antares   1974

D: 354.5 tons (383.4 fl)   **S:** 11.5 kts   **Dim:** 38.33 (33.8 pp) × 3.85 × 2.61
Man: 38 men   **Range:** 3,000/11.5   **Fuel:** 22.5 tons

Electron Equipt: Radar: 1/Raytheon 1620
M: 1 Echevarria-B & W Alpha 408-26VO diesel; 1 prop; 800 hp

REMARKS: Produced in pairs, the later units having full main-deck bulwarks. A-21 and A-22 have one Sulzer diesel, one prop, and 720 hp. Have Raydist navigation system, Omega receivers, three echo-sounders, and a Hewlett-Packard 2100A computer.

◆ **2 Malaspina-class hydrographic ships**   Bldr: Bazán, La Carraca, Cadiz

	L	In serv.		L	In serv.
A 31 MALASPINA	15-8-73	21-2-75	A 32 TOFIÑO	21-12-73	1-5-75

D: 820 tons (1,090 fl)   **S:** 15 kts   **Dim:** 57.7 (51.4 pp) × 11.7 × 3.64
A: 2/20-mm AA   **Man:** 63 men   **Range:** 3,140/14.5, 4,000/12
Electron Equipt: Radar: 1/Raytheon 1620   **Fuel:** 115 tons
M: 2 San Carlos-MWM TbRHS-345-6I diesels; 2 controllable-pitch props; 2,700 hp
Electric: 780 kva

REMARK: Have Magnavox satellite navigation system, Omega, Raydist, three echo-sounders, side-scanning mapping sonar Mk 8, and a Hewlett-Packard 2100AC computer.

◆ **1 oiler**   Bldr: Bazán, Cartagena

	Laid down	L	In serv.
BP 11 TEIDE	11-11-54	20-6-55	20-10-56

Teide

D: 2,750 tons (8,030 fl)   **S:** 12 kts   **Dim:** 117.5 × 14.78 × 6.2
M: Diesels

REMARK: Fitted for underway replenishment.

◆ **1 netlayer**   Bldr: Penhoët-Loire, 1954

CR 1 (ex-G-6)

D: 770 tons (850 fl)   **S:** 12 kts   **Dim:** 46.28 (44.5 pp) × 10.2 × 3.2
A: 1/40-mm AA – 1/20-mm AA   **Man:** 45 men   **Range:** 5,200/12
M: Diesel-electric propulsion (2 SEMT-Pielstick diesels); 1 prop; 1,600 hp
Fuel: 125m³ diesel

REMARKS: Same characteristics as the French *Scarabée*. Transferred in 1955 under MAP.

AUXILIARY SHIPS (continued)

CR-1

◆ **1 salvage ship and diving tender**   Bldr: Bazán, La Carraca, Cadiz

BS 1 POSEIDÓN (ex-RA-6)

Poseidón   1977

D: 951 tons (1,098 fl)   **S:** 15 kts   **Dim:** 55.9 (49.8 pp) × 10.0 × 4.0
A: 4/20-mm AA (II × 2)   **Man:** 60 men   **Range:** 4,640/14
Electron Equipt: Radar: 1/Decca TM 626
M: 2 Sulzer diesels; 1 controllable-pitch prop; 3,200 hp

REMARKS: In service on 8-8-64. Near sister to RA-4 and RA-5. Can support a frogman group and has a 300-meter-depth diving bell. Equipped for fire-fighting, towing, and has salvage pumps.

◆ **2 RA-4-class ocean tugs**   Bldr: Bazán, La Carraca, Cadiz

RA 4   RA 5

   D: 951 tons (1,069 fl)   **S:** 15 kts   **Dim:** 55.9 (49.8 pp) × 10.0 × 4.0
   A: 4/20-mm AA (II × 2)   **Man:** 49 men   **Range:** 4,640/14
   Electron Equipt: Radar: 1/Decca TM 626
   M: 2 Sulzer diesels; 1 controllable-pitch prop; 3,200 hp

REMARKS: RA-4 in service on 25-3-64 and RA-5 on 11-4-64. Improved version of RA-1 design, similar to BS-1. Can carry and lay twenty-four mines.

◆ **2 RA-1 class ocean tugs**   Bldr: Bazán, Cartagena

RA 1   RA 2

RA-2

   D: 757 tons (1,039 fl)   **S:** 15 kts   **Dim:** 56.1 (49.8 pp) × 10.0 × 4.0
   A: 2/20-mm AA (I × 2)   **Man:** 49 men   **Range:** 5,500/15
   M: 2 Sulzer diesels; 1 controllable-pitch prop; 3,200 hp   **Fuel:** 142 tons

REMARKS: RA-1 in service on 9-7-55, RA-2 on 12-9-55. Can carry and lay twenty-four mines on two rails.

◆ **1 ex-British "Empire"-class ocean tug**   Bldr: Clelands Ltd., Willington, G.B.

RA 3 (ex-*Metinda III*, ex-*Empire Jean*)

   D: 762 tons (1,080 fl)   **S:** 10 kts   **Dim:** 43.59 (41.45 pp) × 10.1 × 4.5
   M: Triple-expansion; 1 prop; 3,200 hp   **Boilers:** 2, Scotch type

REMARKS: In service in 4-45. Purchased on 26-5-61.

AUXILIARY SHIPS *(continued)*

◆ **1 royal yacht** Bldr: Bazán, el Ferrol

WO 1 Azor

Azor   J. Taibo, 1970

D: 442 tons (486 fl)   **S:** 13.3 kts   **Dim:** 47.0 × 7.7 × 3.8
M: 2 diesels; 2 props; 1,200 hp   **Electron Equipt:** Radar: 1/Decca TM 626

REMARK: In service on 20-7-49.

◆ **1 sail training ship** Bldr: Ast. Echevarrieta, Cadiz

	Laid down	L	In serv.
JUAN SEBASTIAN DE ELCANO	24-11-25	5-3-27	28-2-28

Juan Sebastian de Elcano   1972

D: 3,420 tons (3,754 fl)   **S:** 10 kts   **Dim:** 94.11 × 13.6 × 6.95
Electron Equipt: Radars: 2/Decca TM 626   **Man:** 224 men, 80 cadets
M: 1 Sulzer diesel; 1 prop; 1,500 hp   **Range:** 13,000/8   **Fuel:** 230 tons

REMARKS: Four-masted schooner, 2,467m² sail area. Carries two 37-mm saluting cannon.

SERVICE CRAFT

◆ **1 new-construction large yard oiler** Bldr: Bazán, Cartagna, 1979

PP 6

D: 535 grt   **S:** 10.8 kts   **Dim:** 34.0 × 7.0 × 3.0
M: 1 diesel; 1 prop; 600 hp

◆ **3 PP-3 class large yard oilers** Bldr: Bazán, Cartagena

PP 3   PP 4   PP 5

D: 510 grt   **S:** 10 kts   **Dim:** 37.0 × 6.8 × 3.0
M: 1 diesel; 1 prop; . . . hp

◆ **1 new-construction small yard oiler** Bldr: Bazán, Cadiz, 1979

PP 23

D: 214 grt   **S:** 10.7 kts   **Dim:** 24.0 × 5.5 × 2.2
M: 1 diesel; 1 prop; 400 hp   **Cargo:** 100 tons

◆ **3 PB-20 class small yard oilers** Bldr: Bazán, . . ., 1965

PB 20   PB 21   PB 22

D: 200 grt   **S:** 10 kts   **Dim:** 34.0 × 6.0 × 2.7
M: 1 diesel; 1 prop; . . . hp   **Cargo:** 193 tons

◆ **3 PB-4 class small yard oilers** Bldr: Bazan, . . ., 1960-65

PB 4   PB 5   PB 6

D: . . .   **S:** 9 kts   **Dim:** . . . × . . . × . . .   **Cargo:** 300 tons

◆ **2 PB-1 class small yard oilers** Bldr: Bazan, . . ., 1960

PB 2   PB 3

D: . . .   **S:** 9 kts   **Dim:** . . . × . . . × . . .   **Cargo:** 100 tons

◆ **1 new-construction large water tanker** Bldr: Bazán, Cadiz, 1979

A . . .

D: 895 tons (fl)   **S:** 10.8 kts   **Dim:** 48.8 × 7.5 × 3.4
M: 1 diesel; 1 prop; 700 hp   **Cargo:** 600 tons

◆ **1 new-construction large water tanker** Bldr: Bazán, Cadiz, 1979

A . . .

D: 535 tons (fl)   **S:** 10.8 kts   **Dim:** 34.0 × 7.0 × 3.0
M: 1 diesel; 1 prop; 600 hp   **Cargo:** 300 tons

◆ **4 A-7-class large water tankers** Bldr: Bazán, La Carraca

A 7   A 8   A 9   A 10

D: 610 tons (fl) (A-7, A-8: 706 fl)   **S:** 9 kts   **Dim:** 44.8 × 7.6 × 3.0
M: 1 diesel; 1 prop; 700 hp   **Range:** 1,000/9   **Man:** 16 men
Cargo: 300 tons

REMARK: A-7 dates from 1952, A-8 to A-10 from 1-63.

SERVICE CRAFT (*continued*)

◆ **5 miscellaneous small water tankers**

AB 1   AB 3   AB 10   AB 17   AB 18   **Cargo:** 100 tons

◆ **3 gate craft**

PBP 1   PBP 2   PBP 3

    D: 140 tons (fl)   **Dim:** 22.3 × 8.7 × 0.8   **M:** Non-self-propelled

REMARK: Date from 1959-60.

◆ **5 netlaying barges**

PR 1   PR 2   PR 3   PR 4   PR 5

    D: 140 tons (fl)   **Dim:** 22.3 × 8.7 × 0.8   **M:** Non-self-propelled

REMARK: Date from 1959-60.

◆ **8 harbor-defense support tugs**

    D: . . .   **S:** . . .   **Dim:** 28.0 × 8.5 × 0.7
    M: 1 diesel; 1 prop; . . . hp

REMARK: Built, 1959-60, to handle the PBP-series gate craft and PR-series netlaying barges.

◆ **6 torpedo-recovery craft/harbor minelayers**

BTM 1   BTM 2   BTM 3   BTM 4   BTM 5   BTM 6

BTM-5   1974

REMARKS: Built, 1961-63. Most of 190 tons (fl), diesel-powered.

◆ **2 submarine-support torpedo retrievers**

LRT 3   LRT 4

    D: 58.2 tons   **S:** . . .   **Dim:** 17.7 × 2.2 × . . .

REMARKS: Built, 1956. Ramp at stern; can stow six torpedoes.

◆ **1 torpedo-tracking launch:** ST 5   **Dim:** 11-m overall.

◆ **5 diving tenders**

BZL 1   BZL 3   BZL 9   NEREIDA (BXL) 10)   BL 13

REMARK: All of 50 tons, self-propelled except BL-13, a barge.

◆ **8 floating cranes**

GR 1 SAMSON (100 tons capacity)
GR 3, GR 4, GR 5 (30 tons capcity)
GR 6, GR 7, GR 8, GR 9 (15 tons capacity)

◆ **1 floating dry dock**

◆ **2 new-construction coastal tugs**   Bldr: Bazán, el Ferrol, 1979

RR . . .   RR . . .

    D: 422 tons (fl)   **S:** 12.4 kts   **Dim:** 28.0 × 8.0 × 3.8
    M: 1 diesel; 1 prop; 1,600 hp

◆ **3 RR-53-class coastal tugs**   Bldr: Bazán, Cartagena, 1967

RR 53   RR 54   RR 55

    D: 227 tons (320 fl)   **S:** 12 kts   **Dim:** 27.8 × 7.0 × 2.6
    M: 1 diesel; 1 prop; 1,400 hp   **Man:** 13 men

◆ **3 RR-50-class coastal tugs**   Bldr: Bazán, Cartagna, 1963

RR 50   RR 51   RR 52

    D: 205 tons (300 fl)   **S:** 10 kts   **Dim:** 27.8 × 7.0 × 2.5
    M: 1 diesel; 1 prop; 800 hp   **Man:** 13 men

◆ **1 coastal tug**   Bldr: Bazán, La Carraca

RR 16

    D: 200 tons   **S:** 10 kts   **Dim:** 27.0 × . . . × . . .
    M: 1 diesel; 1 prop; . . . hp

REMARK: In service in 4-62.

◆ **2 new-construction large harbor tugs**   Bldr: Bazán, Cartagena, 1979

RP . . .   RP . . .

    D: 229 tons (fl)   **S:** 11 kts   **Dim:** 28.0 × 7.5 × 3.4
    M: 1 diesel; 1 prop; 950 hp

◆ **1 medium harbor tug**

RP 40

    D: 150 tons (fl)   **S:** . . .   **Dim:** 21.3 × 5.9 × . . .
    M: 1 diesel; 1 prop; 600 hp

REMARK: In service in 12-61.

◆ **1 medium harbor tug**

RP 18

    D: 160 tons (fl)   **S:** . . .   **Dim:** 24.7 × 5.4 × 2.1
    M: Triple-expansion; 1 Kort-nozzle prop; . . . hp

REMARK: Built in 1952.

SPAIN (*continued*)

SERVICE CRAFT (*continued*)

◆ **12 RP-1-class small harbor tugs**

RP 1 through RP 12

    D: 65 tons (fl)   **S:** . . .   **Dim:** 18.5 × 4.7 × . . .
    M: 1 diesel; 1 prop; 200 hp

REMARK: Built, 1965-67.

◆ **5 miscellaneous launch-type small tugs**

LR 47   LR 51   LR 67   LR 68   LR 69

CUSTOMS SERVICE

(Servicio Especial de Vigilancia Fiscal)

PATROL BOATS

◆ **5 Carabo class** **Bldr:** . . ., 1978-79

CARABO   N . . .   N . . .
N . . .   N . . .

    D: 53 tons (fl)   **S:** 18 kts   **Dim:** 24.4 × 5.15 × . . .
    A: 1/20-mm AA   **M:** 2 diesels; 2 props; . . . hp

REMARK: *Carabo* in service in 9-78.

◆ **3 Aguilucho class** **Bldr:** J. Roberto Rodriguez, Vigo, 1973-76

AGUILUCHO   GAVILAN-I   GAVILAN-II

    D: 45 tons (fl)   **S:** 30 kts   **Dim:** 26.1 × 5.1 × 1.3
    A: 1/20-mm AA   **Range:** 750/30
    M: 2 MTU 820Db diesels; 2 props; 2,750 hp   **Man:** 14 men

◆ **3 Albatros class** **Bldr:** CMN, Cherbourg, 1968

ALBATROS-I   ALBATROS-II   ALBATROS-III

    D: 82 tons (fl)   **S:** 28 kts   **Dim:** 31.8 × 4.7 × 1.7
    A: 1/20-mm AA   **Man:** 15 men
    M: 2 MTU 820Db diesels; 2 props; 2,750 hp

◆ **3 miscellaneous patrol boats**

AGUILA   BASANTE SILVA   SACRE

    S: 17 kts (*Aguila:* 30)   **Dim:** 32.0 × . . . × . . .   **A:** 1/20-mm AA

PATROL CRAFT

◆ **4 22-meter patrol craft**

ALCA   GERIFALTE   MILANO   NEBLI-II   **S:** 17 kts (*Alca:* 10, *Gerifalte:* 12)

◆ **1 16.5-meter patrol craft:** COLIMBO   **S:** 20 kts

◆ **1 14.5-meter patrol craft:** ROQUERO   **S:** 14 kts

◆ **6 LVR-class patrol craft:** LVR 1 to LVR 6   **Dim:** 11.4 × . . . × . . .   **S:** 14 kts

SRI LANKA

PERSONNEL (1978): 2,600 men, including 230 officers

MERCHANT MARINE (1978): 37 ships — 92,581 grt (tankers: 6 ships — 21,302 grt)

PATROL BOATS

◆ **1 Soviet MOL class**

SAMUDRA DEVI

Samudra Devi

    D: 170 tons (210 fl)   **S:** 40 kts   **Dim:** 39.0 × 7.7 × 1.8
    A: 4/30-mm AA (II × 2)   **Electron Equipt:** Radar: 1/Pot Drum
    M: 3 M-504 diesels; 3 props; 15,000 hp   **Man:** 25 men

REMARKS: Does not have four 533-mm torpedo tubes, Drum Tilt gunfire-control radar, or IFF gear, as do the Somali units. Hull and propulsion same as Osa-II-class missile boat.

◆ **5 Chinese Shanghai-II class**

SURAYA   WEERAYA   BALAWATHA   DAKSAYA   RAMAKAMI

    D: 155 tons (fl)   **S:** 28 kts   **Dim:** 38.8 × 5.4 × 1.6
    A: 4/37-mm AA (II × 2) — 4/25-mm AA (II × 2)   **Range:** 800/17
    M: 4 diesels; 4 props; 4,800 hp   **Man:** 28 men

REMARK: Transferred in February 1972 and in 1975.

PATROL CRAFT

◆ **3 (+5) Pradeepa class** **Bldr:** Colombo DY, 1976-78

PRADEEPA   N . . .   N . . .

    D: 44 tons (fl)   **S:** 19 kts   **Dim:** 19.5 × 4.9 × 1.1
    A: 2/20-mm AA (I × 2)   **Man:** 12 men   **Range:** 1,200/14
    M: 2 GM 8V-71TI diesels; 2 props; 1,240 hp

REMARK: Five more with a speed of 22 knots were ordered in 1979.

SRI LANKA (*continued*)

PATROL CRAFT (*continued*)

◆ **1 craft**   Bldr: Colombo DY, 1977

N . . .

D: 15 tons (fl)	**S:** 16 kts	**Dim:** 13.7 × 3.6 × 0.9
A: 1/12.7-mm machine gun	**Man:** 8 men	**Range:** 250/16

◆ **5 Belikawa class**   Bldr: Cheverton, Cowes, G.B.

421 BELIKAWA	423 KORAWAKKA	425 TARAWA
422 DIYAKAWA	424 SERUWA	

D: 22 tons (fl)	**S:** 23.6 kts	**Dim:** 17.0 × 4.5 × 1.2
A: 3/7.62-mm machine guns	**Man:** 7 men	**Range:** 790/18, 1,000/12.2
M: 2 GM 8V-71TI diesels; 2 props; 800 hp		

REMARKS: In service between 4-77 and 10-77. Plastic construction. Originally intended for customs duties but used as patrol craft.

◆ **19 101 class**   Bldr: Thornycroft, Singapore, 1966-68

No. 103 to No. 110   No. 201 to No. 211

D: 15 tons	**S:** 25 kts	**Dim:** 13.86 × 3.65 × 0.92
A: 1/machine gun	**Man:** 6 men	**M:** 2 GM 6-71 diesels; 2 props; 500 hp

REMARKS: Two are employed as inshore-survey craft. Wooden construction. *No. 102* was lost in 1979.

SUDAN

PERSONNEL: 600 men

MERCHANT MARINE (1978): 13 ships — 43,375 grt

PATROL BOATS

◆ **2 Yugoslav Kraljevica class**   Bldr: Yugoslavia, 1968-69

522 EL FASHER   523 EL KHARTOUM

D: 190 tons (202 fl)	**S:** 18 kts	**Dim:** 41.0 × 6.3 × 2.2
A: 2/40-mm AA — 4/20-mm AA — 2/Mk 22 Mousetrap ASW rocket launchers — 2/Mk 6 depth-charge throwers — 2/depth-charge racks		
Electron Equipt: Radar: 1/Decca 45		Sonar: QCU-2
Range: 1,000/12	**Man:** 4 officers, 40 men	
M: 2 M.A.N. W8V 30/38 diesels; 2 props; 3,300 hp		

REMARKS: One 76.2-mm U.S. Mk 22 DP forward replaced by a 40-mm Bofors L76 before transfer; after 40-mm is a U.S. Mk 3.

El Khartoum   1974

◆ **4 El Gihad class**   Bldr: Mosor, Yugoslavia 1961-62

PB 1 EL GIHAD	PB 3 EL ISTIQLAL
PB 2 EL HORRIYA	PB 4 EL SHAAB

El Horriya   L. V. Pujo

D: 86 tons (100 fl)	**S:** 20 kts	**Dim:** 31.4 × 4.9 × 1.45
A: 2/40-mm AA (I × 2) — 2/12.7-mm machine guns		**Man:** 17 men
M: 2 Mercedes-Benz diesels; 2 props; 1,820 hp		**Range:** 1,200/12

◆ **6 ex-Yugoslav modified 101 class**

D: 60 tons (fl)	**S:** 36 kts	**Dim:** 23.8 × 6.5 × 2.4
A: 2/40-mm AA (I × 2) — 2/20-mm AA		**Man:** 14 men **Range:** 1,500/10
M: 3 dunkers diesels; 3 props; 5,000 hp		

REMARKS: Yugoslav copy of the U.S. *Higgins* 78-foot motor torpedo boat, equipped as a gun boat. Built 1949-53; transferred 4-70. Wooden hull, ex-German engines.

PATROL CRAFT

◆ **3 ex-Iranian**   Bldr: Abeking & Rasmussen, West Germany, 1970

SHEKAN (ex-*Gohar*)	KADER (ex-*Shahpar*)	KARARI (ex-*Shahram*)

D: 80 tons (fl)	**S:** 28 kts	**Dim:** 22.9 × 5.0 × 1.8
A: 1/12.7-mm machine gun	**Electron Equipt:** Radar: 1/Decca 202	
Man: 3 officers, 16 men	**Range:** 1,220/21	

SUDAN (*continued*)

PATROL CRAFT (*continued*)

REMARKS: Built for the Iranian Navy, transferred to the Iranian Coast Guard in 1975 and to Sudan the same year.

◆ **4 ex-Iranian 40-foot class**   Bldr: Sewart, Morgan City, La., 1970

D: 10 tons (fl)   **S:** 30 kts   **Dim:** 12.2 × 3.4 × 1.1
A: 2/7.62-mm machine guns   **M:** 2 GM 6-71 diesels; 2 props; 600 hp

REMARKS: Transferred from the Iranian Coast Guard in 1975.

AMPHIBIOUS CRAFT

◆ **2 ex-Yugoslav DTK-221-class LCUs**

SOBAT   DINDER

D: 410 tons   **S:** 10 kts   **Dim:** 49.8 × 6.0 × 2.1
A: 5/20-mm AA (III × 1, I × 2) — 100 mines
Man: 2 officers, 25 men   **Range:** 500/9
M: 3 Gray Marine 64 MN 9 diesels; 3 props; 495 hp

REMARKS: Transferred 1970. Copy of German MFP-D3 class. Can carry 200 tons cargo or 250 troops.

AUXILIARIES

◆ **1 small oiler**   Bldr: Yugoslavia

FASHODA

D: 400 tons   **S:** 7 kts   **Dim:** 43.6 × 7.0 × 4.2
M: 1 Burmeister & Wain diesel; 1 prop; 300 hp   **Cargo:** 250 tons

REMARK: Transferred in 1969.

◆ **1 water tanker**   Bldr: Yugoslavia

BARAKA

D: 125 dwt   **S:** 7 kts   **Dim:** 32.2 × . . . × . . .
M: 1 diesel; 1 prop; . . . hp

REMARK: Transferred in 1969.

◆ **1 survey ship**

TIRHAGA

D: 240 tons   **S:** . . . kts   **Dim:** 30.0 × . . . × . . .

SURINAM

MERCHANT MARINE (1978): 21 ships — 8,847 grt

PATROL BOATS AND CRAFT

◆ **3 32-meter**   Bldr: De Vries, Aalsmeer, Netherlands, 1976-77

S 401   S 402   S 403

D: 127 tons (fl)   **S:** 17.5 kts   **Dim:** 32.0 × 6.5 × 1.7
A: 2/40-mm AA (I × 2)   **Man:** 15 men   **Range:** 1,200/13.5
M: 2 Paxman 12 YHCM diesels; 2 props; 2,110 hp

◆ **3 22-meter**   Bldr: Schottel, Netherlands, 1976

S . . .   S . . .   S . . .

D: 70 tons (fl)   **S:** 24 kts   **Dim:** 22.0 × . . . × . . .
A: 1/40-mm AA   **Man:** . . . men
M: 2 Paxman 12 YHCM diesels; 2 props; 2,110 hp

◆ **3 12.6-meter**   Bldr: Schottel, Netherlands, 8-75

S . . .   S . . .   S . . .

D: 20 tons (fl)   **S:** 14 kts   **Dim:** 12.6 × . . . × . . .
A: . . .   **M:** 1 Dorman 8JT diesel; 280 hp

◆ **1 10-meter**   Bldr: Schottel, Netherlands, 8-75

S . . .

D: 10 tons   **S:** 14 kts   **Dim:** 10.0 × . . . × . . .
A: . . .   **M:** 1 Dorman 8JT diesel; 280 hp

SWEDEN

PERSONNEL: 4,800 men of the regular navy, including officers, petty officers, enlisted men, and civilians with permanent status, plus 7,000 national service men available for immediate service and 3,100 reserves. Additionally, some 8,000 conscripts receive annual naval training.

MERCHANT MARINE (1978): 696 ships — 6,508,255
(tankers: 106 ships — 3,075,005)

NAVAL AVIATION: Consists of some 25 helicopters: Alouette II (HKP-2) for training, 10 Agusta Bell 206-A (HKP-6), and 10 Vertol 107 (HKP-4B) for minesweeping and rescue.

WARSHIPS IN SERVICE OR UNDER CONSTRUCTION AS OF 1 JANUARY 1980

	L	Tons (surfaced)	Main armament
◆ **14 submarines**			
3 NÄCKEN	1978	980	6/533-mm TT
5 SJÖORMEN	1967-68	1,125	4/533-mm TT, 2 ASW TT
6 DRAKEN	1960-61	835	4/533-mm TT

WARSHIPS IN SERVICE OR UNDER CONSTRUCTION *(continued)*

◆ **6 destroyers**		Tons	
4 ÖSTERGÖTLAND	1956-57	2,150	4/120-mm DP, 1 Sea Cat, 5/533-mm
2 HÅLLAND	1952	2,650	4/120-mm DP, SSM system
◆ **2 frigates**			
2 VISBY	1942-43	1,150	2/57-mm AA, ASW weapons
◆ **11 (+6) guided-missile patrol boats**			
11 (+6) HUGIN	1972-80	120	1/57-mm, 6 Penguin
◆ **22 torpedo boats**			
12 SPICA II	1972-76	230	1/57-mm, 6/533-mm TT
6 SPICA	1966-67	190	1/57-mm, 6/533-mm TT
4 T-42	1956-59	44.5	1/40-mm, 2/533-mm TT

In peacetime, the fleet is used primarily for training recruits, and not all the ships are manned.

WEAPONS AND SYSTEMS

Most of the electronic equipment in use in the Swedish Navy is French construction and Dutch design (for example, LWO-3 air-search radars, HSA fire-control radars) but was locally manufactured.

A. Missiles

The SAAB 08-A, a surface-to-surface missile based on the CT-30 of the SNIAS, is in use on both the *Hålland*-class destroyers and in the coastal batteries.

    Length: 5.7 m
    Diameter: 0.65 m
    Wingspan: 3.6 m
    Weight: 9,000 kg
    Max. range: 30 nautical miles (on destroyers), 70 nautical miles (in coastal batteries)

The infrared homing Norwegian Penguin Mk 2 missile is in use on board the *Hugin*-class patrol boats, where it is called the RB-12. It has a 120-kg warhead.

    Length: 3.0 m
    Diameter: 280 mm
    Wingspan: 1.4 m
    Weight: 340 kg
    Speed: Mach 0.7
    Max. range: 30 km at an altitude of 60–100 m

The SAAB RBS-15 is being developed for installation in the Spica-II class, becoming operational by 1985. The missile will have a solid rocket booster and a turbojet sustainer. A sea-skimmer, it will have a terminal-homing guidance system.

    Length: 4.5 m
    Diameter: 0.5 m
    Wingspan: 0.85 m (folded) 1.2 (extended)
    Weight: 550 kg (+ 700 kg booster)
    Speed: Mach 0.8
    Range: 80–100 km at an altitude of 10–20 m

B. Guns

The Swedish Bofors firm furnishes the guns, the principal ones being:

120-mm twin automatic

    Installed on the *Hålland*-class destroyers
        Mount weight: 55 tons
        Length of barrel: 46 calibers
        Muzzle velocity: 850 m/sec (projectile weight 23.5 kg)
        Elevation: +80°
        Firing rate: 40 rounds/min/barrel
        Max. effective range, surface target: 12,000–13,000 m
        Max. effective range, anti-aircraft fire: 7,000–8,000 m

Each barrel can fire 26 rounds at a time, after which the magazine must be reloaded. Water-cooled. Used with Hollandse Signaal Apparaten (HSA) LA-01 fire-control radar.

120-mm twin semi-automatic

    Installed on the *Östergötland*-class destroyers
        Mount weight: . . . tons
        Length of barrel: 46 calibers
        Muzzle velocity: 850 m/sec
        Elevation: +80°
        Firing rate: 20 rounds/min/barrel

57-mm twin automatic

    Installed on the *Hålland*-class destroyers
        Mount weight: 20 tons
        Muzzle velocity: 850 m/sec
        Maximum rate of fire: 120/rounds/barrel
        Max. effective range, surface target: 13,000 m
        Max. effective range, anti-aircraft fire: 5,000 m

57-mm single-barrel automatic

    Installed on the *Hugin*-class missile boats, the *Spica* and *Spica II* torpedo boats and the *Visby*-class frigates
        Mount weight (without ammunition): 6 tons
        Train speed: 55°/sec
        Elevation speed: 20°/sec
        Elevation: −10° +75°
        Max. rate of fire: 200/rounds/min

C. Torpedoes

The wire-guided Type 61 is used for anti-surface duties from surface ships and submarines.

    Length: 7,025 mm
    Diameter: 533.4 mm
    Weight: 1,765 kg
    Warhead: 250 kg

The Type 42 torpedo is wire-guided and has acoustic homing, for use by submarines, surface ships, and aircraft against submarines. It was developed from the similar Type 41, which is still in service.

    Length: 2,600 mm (2,440 mm minus wire-guidance attachment)
    Diameter: 400 mm
    Weight: 300 kg

D: ASW Weapons

The 375-mm Bofors ASW rocket launcher is used in a quadruple mount on the *Hålland*-class destroyers and the *Visby*-class frigates.

The British Mk 3 Squid ASW mortar is used in the *Östergötland*-class destroyers.

SUBMARINES

◆ 4 Type A-17 (projected)

REMARKS: A lengthened, even more highly automated improvement of the Type A-14 (*Näcken*) design is being developed by Karlskrona/Kockums for construction during the mid-1980s. Crew will be 19 men. Exotic forms of propulsion (i.e., Sterling engines, fuel cells, hydrogen peroxide) appear to have been ruled out, and the craft will probably be similar to the A-14.

◆ 3 Näcken (Type A-14) class

	Bldr	Laid down	L	In serv.
NÄK NÄCKEN	Kockums, Malmö	11-72	17-4-78	1979
NAJ NAJAD	Karlskrona	9-73	. . .	. . .
NEP NEPTUN	Kockums, Malmö	3-74	6-12-78	. . .

Näcken—being launched by crane   1978

   D: 980 tons surfaced; 1,125 tons submerged   **S:** 20/20 kts
   Dim: 49.5 × 6.1 × 4.1
   A: 6/533-mm TT (fwd)—2/400-mm TT (fwd)—12 torpedoes
   Man: 5 officers, 14 men
   M: Diesel-electric: 2 Hedemora-Pielstick 12-PA-4 diesel generator groups, 2,100 hp; 1 5-bladed prop; 1,500 hp

REMARKS: Ordered at the end of 1972. The electric battery installation is mounted on shock absorbers. Single periscope. A central computer furnishes, in addition to tactical information, data on the main engines. Will be able to lay mines. Stern planes are x-configuration; bow planes on the sail.

◆ 5 Sjöormen (Type 11-B) class

	Bldr	Laid down	L	In serv.
SOR SJÖORMEN	Kockums, Malmö	1965	25-1-67	31-7-67
SLE SJÖLEJONET	Kockums, Malmö	1966	29-6-67	16-12-68
SHU SJÖHUNDEN	Kockums, Malmö	1966	21-3-68	25-6-69
SBJ SJÖBJÖRNEN	Karlskrona	1967	6-8-68	28-2-69
SHÄ SJÖHÄSTEN	Karlskrona	1966	9-1-68	15-9-69

   D: 1,125 tons surfaced; 1,400 tons submerged   **S:** 15/20 kts
   Dim: 51.0 × 6.1 × 5.1
   A: 4/533-mm TT fwd—2/400-mm TT fwd for ASW torpedoes or mines
   Endurance: 21 days   **Man:** 7 officers, 11 men
   M: Diesel-electric: 4 Hedemora-Pielstick 12-PA-4 diesel generator groups, 2,100 hp; 1 electric motor; 1 5-bladed prop; 3,500 hp

REMARKS: Maximum diving depth 150 meters (the Baltic Sea is quite shallow). Four battery compartments. Stern planes are x-configuration; bow planes on the sail.

Sjöormen

◆ 6 Draken (A-11) class

	Bldr	Laid down	L	In serv.
DEL DELFINEN	Karlskrona	1959	7-3-61	7-6-62
DRA DRAKEN	Kockums, Malmö	1958	1-4-60	4-4-62
GRI GRIPEN	Karlskrona	1959	31-5-60	28-4-62
NOR NORDKAPAREN	Kockums, Malmö	1959	8-3-60	4-4-62
SPR SPRINGAREN	Kockums, Malmö	1960	21-8-61	7-11-62
VGN VARGEN	Kockums, Malmö	1958	20-5-60	15-11-61

Nordkaparen

SUBMARINES *(continued)*

D: 770 tons; 835 surfaced; 1,110 submerged   **S:** 17/20 kts
Dim: 69.0 × 5.1 × 5.0   **A:** 4/533-mm TT fwd – 12 torpedoes
Man: 36 men
M: Diesel-electric: 2 SEMT-Pielstick diesels, 1,660 bhp; 2 electric motors; 1 prop; 1,500 hp

REMARKS: Snorkel-equipped; 1 periscope. All to be modernized. Six similar sisters with two propellers, *Hajen, Sälen, Valen, Bävern, Illern,* and *Uttern,* were stricken in 1978.

◆ **3 URF-class salvage and rescue submersibles**   Bldr: Kockums, Malmö

URF 1   URF 2   URF 3

D: 50 tons (surfaced)   **S:** 3 kts   **Dim:** 13.5 × 4.3 × 2.9

REMARKS: URF-1 launched 8-78. Has a depth capability of 460 meters and can accommodate up to 25 persons rescued from a bottomed submarine. To be based at the Naval Diving Center, Berga. Can be towed at up to 10 kts to the scene of an accident. Lock-out capability to support two divers to 300 meters. Pressure hull of HY 130 steel; collapse depth 900 meters.

DESTROYERS

◆ **4 Östergötland**

	Bldr	Laid down	L	In serv.
J 20 ÖSTERGÖTLAND	Götaverken, Göteborg	1-9-55	8-5-56	3-3-58
J 21 SÖDERMANLAND	Eriksberg, Göteborg	1-6-55	28-5-56	27-6-58
J 22 GÄSTRIKLAND	Götaverken, Göteborg	1-10-55	6-6-56	14-6-59
J 23 HÄLSINGLAND	Kockums, Malmö	1-10-55	14-1-57	17-6-59

Gästrikland

D: 2,150 tons (2,600 fl)   **Dim:** 115.8 (112.0 pp) × 11.2 × 3.7
S: 35 kts   **Man:** 18 officers, 226 men
Range: 2,200/20   **Fuel:** 330 tons

A: 4/120-mm DP (II × 2) – 4/40-mm AA – 1/Sea Cat system (IV × 1) – 5/533-mm TT (V × 1) – 1 Squid ASW mortar (III × 1) – 60 mines
Electron Equipt: Radars: 1/Thomson-CSF Saturn, 1/navigational, 2/HSA M45 (fire control), 1/HSA M44
    Sonars: 1/search, 1/attack
Boilers: 2 Babcock & Wilcox
M: 2 sets De Laval GT; 2 props; 40,000 hp

REMARKS: Modernized 1965-69. J-20 to be discarded in 1979-80; J-21 and J-23 (in reserve) to be stricken by 1983. J-22 active 1978-79. Have one 57-mm and four 103-mm rocket flare launchers.

◆ **2 Hålland class**

	Bldr	Laid down	L	In serv.
J 18 HÅLLAND	Götaverken, Göteborg	1949	16-7-52	8-6-55
J 19 SMÅLAND	Eriksberg, Göteborg	1949	23-10-52	12-1-56

Hålland   1972

D: 3,400 tons (fl)   **S:** 35 kts   **Dim:** 121.05 (116.0 pp) × 12.4 × 4.7
A: 1/launcher for SAAB RB-08A SSM – 4/120-mm DP (II × 2) – 2/57-mm AA (II × 1) – 6/40-mm AA – 8/533-mm TT (V × 1, III × 1) – 2/375-mm Bofors ASW rocket launchers (IV × 2) – mines
Electron Equipt: Radars: 1/HSA LWO-3, 1/Thomson-CSF Saturn, 1/navigational, 1/HSA M22, 1/HSA M45
    Sonars: 1/search, 1/attack
Range: 3,000/20   **Fuel:** 524 tons   **Man:** 18 officers, 272 men
Boilers: 2 Penhöet/Motala
M: 2 sets De Laval double-reduction GT; 2 props; 55,000 hp

REMARKS: Both modernized in 1962. Magazine for RB-08A missiles is beneath the after superstructure and the launcher is atop the after (triple) torpedo tube mount. Two sisters were built for Columbia. J-18 in reserve in 1979, J-19 active.

FRIGATES

◆ **2 Visby class**

	Bldr	L	In serv.
F 11 VISBY	Götaverken, Göteborg	16-10-42	10-8-43
F 12 SUNDSVALL	Eriksberg, Göteborg	20-10-42	17-9-43

Sundsvall

D: 1,150 tons (1,320 fl)   **S:** 35 kts   **Dim:** 98.0 × 9.1 × 3.8
Man: 140 men   **Range:** 1,600/20
A: 2/57-mm AA (I × 2)−1/375-mm Bofors ASW rocket launcher (IV × 1)−2/depth-charge racks
Electron Equipt: Radars: 1/Thomson-CSF Saturn, 1/navigational, 1/HSA M24
Boilers: 3 3-drum   **Fuel:** 150 tons
M: 2 sets De Laval GT; 2 props; 36,000 hp

REMARKS: Both converted from small destroyers during the 1960s; now in reserve. Helicopter platform. Unconverted sisters *Hälsingborg* (F-13) and *Kalmar* (F-14) stricken in 1978, as were the former destroyers *Öland* and *Uppland*−the *Öland* is to be a museum.

GUIDED-MISSILE PATROL BOATS

◆ **17 Hugin class**

	In serv.		In serv.
P 150 JÄGAREN	8-6-72	P 159 KAPAREN	8-79
P 151 HUGIN	3-6-77	P 160 VÄKTAREN	11-79
P 152 MUNIN	1-4-78	P 161 SNAPPHANEN	. . .
P 153 MAGNE	15-6-78	P 162 SPEJAREN	. . .
P 154 MODE	9-1-78	P 163 STYRBJÖRN	. . .
P 155 VALE	8-8-78	P 164 STARKODDER	. . .
P 156 VIDAR	11-11-78	P 165 TORDÖN	. . .
P 157 MJÖLNER	3-2-79	P 166 TIRFING	. . .
P 158 MYSING	5-79		

Bldrs: Bergens Mekanske Verksted, Norway; 5 subcontracted to Westermoen, Mandal, Norway

Munin   1978

Jägaren−with old number and six Penguin Mk 1 missiles   1975

D: 120 tons (150 fl)   **S:** 35 kts   **Dim:** 36.4 (33.6 pp) × 6.3 × 1.5
A: 6 Penguin Mk 2 (I × 6)−1/57-mm AA Bofors−24 mines (in lieu of missiles)−2/depth-charge racks
Electron Equipt: Radars: 1/Terma navigational, 1/PEAB 2LV200 Mk 2 (fire control)
   Sonar: 1/Simrad SQ3D/SF
Range: 550/35   **Man:** 18 men   **Electric:** 200 kva
M: 2 MTU 20V672 TB90 diesels; 2 props; 7,000 hp

REMARKS: Prototype *Jägaren*, renumbered from P-151, has new engines; those in the others came from discarded *Plejad*-class torpedo boats. Carry 103-mm rocket flare launchers on either side of the 57-mm gun mount. The PEAB 2LV200 Mk 2 fire-control system employs separate search and tracking radars.

TORPEDO BOATS

◆ **12 Spica-II class**   Bldrs: Karlskronavarvet and Götaverkem

	L	In serv.
T 131 NÖRRKÖPING	16-11-72	5-11-73
T 132 NYNÄSHAMN	24-4-73	8-9-73
T 133 NORTÄLJE	18-9-73	1-8-74
T 134 VARBERG	2-2-74	13-6-74
T 135 VÄSTERAS	15-5-74	25-10-74
T 136 VÄSTERVIK	2-9-74	15-1-75
T 137 UMEA	13-1-75	15-5-75
T 138 PITEA	12-5-73	13-9-75
T 139 LULEA	19-8-75	28-11-75
T 140 HALMSTAD	28-11-75	9-4-76
T 141 STRÖMSTAD	26-4-76	13-9-76
T 142 YSTAD	3-9-76	10-12-76

D: 230 tons (fl)   **S:** 40.5 kts   **Dim:** 43.6 × 7.1 × 1.6
A: 1/57-mm AA — 6/533-mm TT
Electron Equipt: Radars: 1/Terma navigational, 1/PEAB 9LV200 Mk 1
Man: 7 officers, 20 men
M: 3 Rolls-Royce Proteus gas turbines; 3 props; 12,900 hp

REMARKS: All are to be re-equipped with the SAAB RBS-15 cruise missile by 1985. Eight missiles will be carried, plus two 533-mm torpedo tubes for wire-guided Type 61 torpedoes. The fire-control system is an analog version of the digital system used in the *Hugin* class. The gas turbines exhaust through the stern transom to provide residual thrust. Mines can be substituted for the torpedo tubes, the forwardmost of which must be swung out several degrees before firing.

Nörrköping   1978

◆ **6 Spica class**

	Bldr	L
T 121 SPICA	Götaverken	26-4-66
T 122 SIRIUS	Götaverken	26-4-66
T 123 CAPELLA	Götaverken	26-4-66
T 124 CASTOR	Karlskronavarvet	7-6-67
T 125 VEGA	Karlskronavarvet	7-6-67
T 126 VIRGO	Karlskronavarvet	7-6-67

D: 190 tons (235 fl)   **S:** 40 kts   **Dim:** 42.5 × 7.3 × 1.6
A: 1/57-mm AA — 6/533-mm TT   **Man:** 7 officers, 21 men
Electron Equipt: Radars: 1/Decca navigational, 1/HSA M22
M: 3 Bristol-Siddeley Proteus 1274 gas turbines; 3 Ka-Me-Wa controllable-pitch props; 12,720 hp

REMARKS: In service 1966-67. To be re-equipped with eight RBS-15 missiles by 1985, retaining two 533-mm torpedo tubes. Carry four 103-mm (I × 4) and six 57-mm (VI × 1) rocket flare launchers. Mines can be substituted for the torpedo tubes, the forward-most of which must be swung out several degrees before firing. There are two Rover IS90 gas-turbine generators.

Sirius   1970

Spica—note mine rails and gas turbine exhausts at stern

TORPEDO BOATS *(continued)*

Capella   1972

NOTE: The eleven *Plejad*-class torpedo boats were discarded in 1978-79; their MB 518 (MTU 20V672) diesels were used in constructing the *Hugin*-class guided-missile patrol boats.

◆ **4 T-42 class** Bldr: Karlskronavarvet, 1958-59

T 53   T 54   T 55   T 56

T 56   1974

D: 44.5 tons (fl)   **S:** 40 kts   **Dim:** 23.0 × 5.9 × 1.4
A: 1/40-mm AA – 2/533-mm TT
M: 3 Isotla-Fraschini gasoline engines; 3 props; 4,500 hp

REMARKS: Steel hull, welded construction. One 57-mm rocket flare launcher (VI × 1). T-42 to T-45 were converted 1976-77 to *Skanör*-class patrol boat configuration. T-46 to T-52 were stricken in 1978.

PATROL BOATS

◆ **4 Skanör class** Bldr: Kockums, Malmö, 1956-58

V 01 SKANÖR (ex-T-42)   V 03 ARILD (ex-T-44)
V 02 SMYGE (ex-T-43)   V 04 VIKEN (ex-T-45)

Skänor   1978

D: 44.5 tons (fl)   **S:** 27 kts   **Dim:** 42.5 × 5.6 × 1.6
A: 1/40-mm AA   **Electron Equipt:** Radar: 1/Terma navigational
M: 2 MTU diesels; 2 props; 1,600 hp

PATROL BOATS (continued)

REMARKS: Converted at Karlskrona for service as surveillance boats; original three gasoline engines replaced for safety and economy. Have one six-railed 57-mm rocket flare launcher on the bow.

◆ **6 Hanö-class former minesweepers**   Bldr: Karlskrona

M 51 HANÖ	M 53 TJURKÖ	M 55 ORNÖ
M 52 TÄRNÖ	M 54 STURKÖ	M 56 UTÖ

Tärnö   1978

Utö   1972

D: 270 tons   **S:** 14.5 kts   **Dim:** 42.0 (40.0 pp) × 7.0 × 2.7
A: 2/40-mm AA (I × 2) (M-56: 1/40-mm AA)   **Man:** 25 men
M: 2 Nohab diesels; 2 props; 910 hp

REMARKS: In service since 1954. Redesignated as patrol craft on 1-1-79. Have steel hulls. M-56 had been equipped as a mine-disposal divers' support ship and had a deckhouse aft for accommodations and a decompression chamber. May be renumbered with P-series pendants. Each has one six-railed 57-mm rocket flare launcher.

PATROL CRAFT

◆ **5 SKV-1 class**

SKV 1	SKV 2	SKV 3	SKV 4	SKV 5

D: 19 tons   **S:** 10 kts   **Dim:** 16.0 × 3.7 × 1.2
A: 1/20-mm AA   **M:** 1 diesel; 100-135 hp   **Man:** 12 men

REMARKS: Built 1944. Maintained for training the Naval Reserve (Sjövarnskarens).

MINE WARFARE SHIPS

◆ **1 new construction minelayer**   Bldr: Karlskrona

	Laid down	L	In serv.
M 04 KARLSKRONA	1978	. . .	1980

D: 3,100 tons (fl)   **S:** 20 kts   **Dim:** 105.0 (100.0 pp) × 15.0 × 4.0
A: 2/57-mm AA (I × 2)—2/40-mm AA (I × 2)—105 mines
Electron Equipt: Radars: 1/Thomson-CSF Saturn, 2/navigational, 2/PEAB 2LV200 Mk 2
Man: 95 men, 185 cadets
M: 2 Hohab-Polar diesels; 2 props; 10,560 hp

REMARKS: Ordered 25-11-77. Intended to replace the *Älvsnabben* as cadet training ship as well as acting as a fleet minelayer in wartime. Similar to the *Älvsborg* class. Helicopter deck aft.

◆ **2 Älvsborg-class minelayers**   Bldr: Karlskronavarvet

	Laid down	L	In serv.
M 02 ÄLVSBORG	11-68	11-11-69	10-4-71
M 03 VIBORG	16-10-73	22-1-75	6-2-76

Älvsborg   1971

MINE WARFARE SHIPS (continued)

D: 2,660 tons (fl) (M-03: 2,450 (fl)) **S:** 16 kts
Dim: 92.4 (83.8 pp) × 14.7 × 4.0
A: 3/40-mm AA (I × 3)—300 mines **Man:** 97 men **Electric:** 1,200 kw
M: 2 Nohab-Polar 12-cyl. diesels; 1 controllable-pitch prop; 4,200 hp

REMARKS: M-02 is used as a submarine tender in peacetime and has accommodations for 205 submarine crew members. M-03 is equipped as Flag Ship, Coastal Fleet, and has accommodations for 158 flag staff. Each has a helicopter deck.

◆ **1 converted merchant ship minelayer** Bldr: Eriksberg, Göteborg

	Laid down	L	In serv.
M 01 ÄLVSNABBEN	31-10-42	19-1-43	8-5-43

Älvsnabben 1975

D: 4,250 tons **S:** 14 kts **Dim:** 102.0 (96.8 pp) × 13.6 × 4.9
A: 2/152-mm (I × 2)—2/57-mm AA (I × 2)—2/40-mm AA (I × 2)— at least 300 mines
Man: 255 men, 63 cadets
Electron Equipt: Radars: 2/navigational, 1/Thomson-CSF Saturn, 1/HSA M45
M: Diesel; 1 prop; 3,000 hp

REMARKS: Former cargo ship modified while under construction. Will be replaced by the M-04. Used as a training ship since 1953. Has the last 152-mm guns on an active Western European naval ship, mounted aft. Eight 103-mm rocket flare rails (four per 152-mm mount) and one six-railed 57-mm rocket flare launcher are carried.

◆ **12 Arkö-class coastal minesweepers**

	L			L
M 57 ARKÖ	21-1-57		M 63 ASPÖ	1962
M 58 SPÅRÖ	1957		M 64 HASSLÖ	1962
M 59 KARLSÖ	1957		M 65 VINÖ	1962
M 60 IGGÖ	1958		M 66 VALLÖ	1962
M 61 STYRSÖ	1961		M 67 NÄMDÖ	1964
M 62 SKAFTÖ	1961		M 68 BLIDÖ	1964

Bldrs: Odd numbers—Karlskrona; even numbers—Hälsingborg

D: 285 tons (300 fl) **S:** 14.5 kts **Dim:** 44.0 × 7.0 × 2.5
A: 1/40-mm AA **Man:** 25 men
M: 2 MTU 12V493 diesels; 1,000 hp

Iggö—early version 1972

Aspö—late version

REMARKS: Wooden-hulled construction. M-61 through M-68 have a curved rubbing strake line along the hull side; in earlier ships there are two strakes, paralleling the hull sheer. Each of the twelve ships has one six-railed 57-mm rocket flare launcher. Because of their high magnetic signature, the six steel-hulled Hanö class were re-designated as patrol boats in 1979.

◆ **3 Gåssten-class inshore minesweepers**

	Bldr	L	In serv.
M 31 GÅSSTEN	Knippla SY	11-72	16-11-73
M 32 NORSTEN	Hellevikstrands SY	4-73	12-10-73
M 33 VIKSTEN	Karlskrona	18-4-74	1-7-74

D: 120 tons (M-33: 130 tons) **S:** 11 kts **Dim:** 23.0 (M-33: 25.3) × 6.6 × 3.7
A: 1/40-mm AA **M:** 1 diesel; 1 prop; 460 hp

REMARKS: The hull of M-31 is made of glass-reinforced plastic; she was intended to serve as the prototype for a new class of 300-ton, 43-meter coastal minesweepers,

MINE WARFARE SHIPS *(continued)*

Viksten

which were not built for lack of funds. The other two are built of wood. These are the latest in a long series of Swedish inshore minesweepers built on fishing-boat designs.

◆ **7 Hisingen-class inshore minesweepers**

	L		L
M 43 HISINGEN	1960	M 47 GILLÖGA	1964
M 44 BLACKAN	1960	M 48 RÖDLÖGA	1964
M 45 DÄMMAN	1960	M 49 SVARTLÖGA	1964
M 46 GALTEN	1960		

Hisingen—early version

D:	140 tons	**S:**	9 kts	**Dim:**	22.0 × 6.4 × 1.4
A:	1/40-mm	**M:**	1 diesel; 1 prop; 380 hp		

Gillöga—late version   1975

REMARKS: Wooden-hulled fishing boats. M-47 through M-49 have higher bridges and bluffer bow lines. The older *Örust* (M-41) and *Tjörn* were discarded in 1977.

◆ **8 M-15-class inshore minesweepers**

M 15   M 16   M 21 to M 26

M-15   1975

MINE WARFARE SHIPS (continued)

D: 70 tons **S:** 12-13 kts **Dim:** 26.0 × 5.05 × 1.4
A: 1/20-mm AA **Man:** 10 men
M: Diesels; 1 prop; 320-430 hp

REMARKS: Wooden hulls. M-21, M-22, and M-25 are used as tenders for mine clearance divers. M-17, M-18, and M-20 are now support tenders.

AUXILIARIES

◆ **1 coastal tanker**

A 228 BRANNAREN (ex-*Indio*)

Bldr: D. W. Kremer Son, Elmshorn, West Germany, 1965

Brannaren   1972

D: 857 tons (fl) **S:** 11 kts **Dim:** 61.71 (56.76 pp) × 8.6 × 3.57
M: 1 Mak 6 Mu 51 diesels; 1 prop; 800 hp

REMARKS: Eight cargo tanks totaling 1170 m³. Purchased in 1972.

◆ **1 submarine rescue and salvage ship** Bldr: . . .

	L	In serv.
A 211 BELOS	15-11-61	29-5-63

Art

D: 1,000 tons **S:** 13 kts **Dim:** 62.3 × 11.2 × 3.65
M: 2 diesels; 2 props; 1,200 hp

REMARKS: Well-equipped for underwater search: decompression chamber, active rudder, underwater television, and a small helicopter deck. Being modernized in 1979-80.

Belos   1970

SERVICE CRAFT

◆ **1 water tanker**

A 217 FRYKEN

D: 307 tons **S:** 10 kts **Dim:** 34.4 (32.0 pp) × 6.1 × 2.9
M: 1 diesel; 1 prop; 370 hp

REMARK: Launched 1959.

◆ **1 water tanker**

A 216 UNDEN

D: 540 tons **S:** 9 kts **Dim:** 39.8 (36.5 pp) × 7.6 × 3.2
M: 1 set reciprocating triple-expansion steam; 1 prop; 225 hp

REMARK: Launched 1946.

◆ **1 new construction cargo lighter** Bldr: Marinteknik Verkstad

REMARKS: Ordered in 1978. No data available.

◆ **1 provisions lighter** Bldr: Kroger, Rendsburg, West Germany, 1953

A 221 FREJA

D: 415 tons (465 fl) **S:** 11 kts **Dim:** 49.0 × 8.5 × 3.7
M: 1 diesel; 1 prop; 600 hp

◆ **1 torpedo and missile recovery craft**

Bldr: Lundevarv-Ooverkstads AB, Kramfors

	L	In serv.
A 248 PINGVINEN	26-9-73	3-75

D: 191 tons **S:** 13 kts **Dim:** 33.0 × 6.1 × 1.8
M: 2 MTU 12V493 diesels; 2 props; 1,040 hp

REMARKS: Similar to A-247 but has superstructure aft, 2 articulated cranes, and bow bulwarks.

◆ **1 torpedo and missile recovery craft**

A 247 PELIKANEN

D: 130 tons **S:** 15 kts **Dim:** 33.0 × 5.8 × 1.8

SERVICE CRAFT (continued)

Pelikanen — with RB-O8A missile   1974

M: 2 MTU 12V493 diesels; 2 props; 1,040 hp

REMARK: Launched 9-63.

◆ 1 torpedo-recovery craft

A 246 HÄGERN

D: 50 tons   S: 10 kts   Dim: 29.0 × 5.4 × 1.6
M: 2 diesels; 2 props; 240 hp

REMARK: Launched in 1951.

◆ 1 trials craft

A 241 URD (ex-*Capella*)

D: 63 tons (90 fl)   S: 8 kts   Dim: 27.0 × 5.6 × 2.8
M: 2 diesels; 200 hp

REMARK: Launched in 1969.

◆ 2 mine-transport lighters

	L		L
A 236 FÄLLAREN	1941	A 237 MINÖREN	1940

D: 165 tons   S: 9 kts   Dim: 31.5 × 6.1 × 2.1
M: 2 diesels; 1 prop; 240 hp

◆ 1 laundry ship

A 256 SIGRUN

Sigrun   1974

D: 250 tons   S: 11 kts   Dim: 32.0 × 6.8 × 3.6
M: 1 diesel; 1 prop; 320 hp

REMARKS: Launched 1961. Probably the world's only camouflaged laundry, and certainly the fastest.

◆ 3 M-15-class general-purpose tenders, former minesweepers

A 231 LOMMEN (ex-M-17)   A 232 SPOVEN (ex-M-18)   A 242 SKULD (ex-M-20)

D: 70 tons   S: 13 kts   Dim: 26.0 × 5.0 × 1.4
M: 2 diesels; 2 props; 410 hp

REMARKS: Launched 1941. Wooden hulls. Used as personnel, mail, and stores transports for mine trials (except A-242).

◆ 5 L-51-class stores lighters

L 51   L 52   L 53   L 54   L 55

D: 32 tons   S: 7 kts   Dim: 14.0 × 4.8 × 1.0
M: 1 diesel; 140 hp

REMARKS: Launched 1947-48. Steel-hulled former landing craft, bow ramps.

◆ 2 sail training schooners

	L		L
S 01 GLADAN	1947	S 02 FALKEN	1948

D: 220 tons   S: . . . kts   Dim: 42.5 (28.3 pp) × 7.27 × 4.2
M: 1 diesel auxiliary; 50 hp

REMARK: Sail area, 512 m².

SERVICE CRAFT (continued)

Gladan   1974

TUGS

◆ **2 Herkules-class icebreaking tugs**

	L		L
A 323 HERKULES	1969	A 324 HERA	1971

D: 127 tons   S: 11.5 kts   Dim: 21.4 × 6.9 × 3.7
M: diesels; 615 hp

◆ **2 Achilles-class icebreaking tugs**

A 251 ACHILLES   A 252 AJAX

Ajax   1974

D: 450 tons   S: 12 kts   Dim: 35.5 (33.15 pp) × 9.5 × 3.9
M: diesels; 1,650 hp

REMARK: The *Achilles* launched in 1962.

◆ **3 Hermes-class icebreaking tugs**

A 253 HERMES   A 321 HECTOR   A 322 HEROS

D: 185 tons   S: 11 kts   Dim: 24.5 (23.0 pp) × 6.8 × 3.6
M: diesel; 600 hp

REMARK: Launched 1953-57.

◆ **13 harbor tugs**

A 326 HEBE	A 330 ATLAS	A 342 ATB-2
A 327 PASSOP	A 332 MÄRSGARN	A 343 ATB-3
A 328 RAN	A 336 VITSGARN	A 345 GRANATEN
A 329 HENRIK	A 341 ATB-1	A 347 EDDA
		A 349 GERDA

REMARKS: Five new tugs ordered in 1978 from Lundevarv.

MINISTRY OF TRANSPORT

ICEBREAKERS

NOTE: All Swedish icebreakers are owned by the Ministry of Transport but are manned and administered by the Swedish Navy. Most have provision for arming in wartime.

ICEBREAKERS *(continued)*

◆ **3 Finnish Urho class**   Bldr: Wärtsilä, Helsinki

	Laid down	L	In serv.
ATLE	10-5-73	27-11-73	21-10-74
FREJ	. . .	3-6-74	30-9-75
YMER	12-2-76	3-9-76	25-10-77

Atle   1975

D: 7,800 tons   **S:** 19 kts   **Dim:** 104.6 (99.0 pp) × 23.8 × 7.8
M: 5 Wärtsilä-Pielstick 5,000-bhp diesels; Diesel-electric drive: 4 props; 22,000 hp
Man: 16 officers, 38 men

REMARKS: Two props forward, two aft. Helicopter platform. All personnel live and, normally, work above the main deck.

◆ **1 Ale class**   Bldr: Wärtsilä, Helsinki

	L	In serv.
ALE	1-6-73	12-12-73

D: 1,488 tons   **S:** 14 kts   **Dim:** 46.0 × 13.0 × 5.0
M: Diesels; 2 props; 4,750 hp   **Man:** 21 men

REMARKS: Built for service on Lake Vänern in central Sweden; also used for surveying in summer.

◆ **1 modified Tor class**   Bldr: Wärtsilä, Helsinki

	L	In serv.
NJORD	2-10-68	10-69

D: 5,150 tons (5,686 fl)   **S:** 18 kts   **Dim:** 86.45 (79.45 pp) × 21.18 × 6.9
M: Diesel-electric propulsion: 4 Sulzer 9MH-51 diesels; Stromberg electric motors, 2 fwd (3,400 kw each), 2 aft (2,200 kw each); 4 props; 13,620 hp

REMARK: Can be armed with four 40-mm anti-aircraft (II × 1, I × 2).

◆ **1 Tor class**   Bldr: Wärtsilä, Turku

	L	In serv.
TOR	25-5-63	31-1-64

Njord   1970

D: 4,980 tons (5,290 fl)   **S:** 18 kts   **Dim:** 84.4 × 20.42 × 6.2
M: Diesel-electric propulsion; 4 props; 11,200 hp. Same motors as the *Njord*.

REMARKS: The Finnish *Tarmo* is similar. Can be armed with four 40-mm anti-aircraft (II × 1, I × 2).

◆ **1 Oden class**   Bldr: Sandviken, Helsinki

	L	In serv.
ODEN	16-10-56	1958

D: 4.950 tons (3,370 light)   **S:** 17 kts   **Dim:** 83.35 (78 pp) × 19.4 × 6.9
Man: 75 men   **Fuel:** 740 tons
M: Diesel-electric; 4 props (2 fwd, 2 aft); 10,500 hp

REMARKS: Very similar to the Finnish *Voima* and the three Soviet *Kapitan Belousov* class.

◆ **1 Thule class**   Bldr: Karlskronavarvet

	L	In serv.
THULE	10-51	1953

D: 2,200 tons   **S:** 14 kts   **Dim:** 57.0 × 16.07 × 5.9
M: Diesel-electric; 3 props (1 fwd, 2 aft); 4,800 hp   **Man:** 43 men

HYDROGRAPHIC SHIPS

NOTE: Swedish hydrographic ships are operated by the Navy but are owned by the Ministry of Transport. The icebreaker *Ale* also performs survey tasks.

◆ **6 survey ships**

	Laid down	L	In serv.
N . . .	. . .	1980	10-3-80

HYDROGRAPHIC SHIPS *(continued)*

D: . . .   **S:** 15 kts   **Dim:** 73.0 (64.0 pp) × 14.0 × 3.8
Man: 66 men
M: 2 Hedemora diesels; 1 controllable-pitch prop; 3,520 hp

REMARKS: New construction. One 700-hp bow thruster. Can make 13 knots on one engine. Will carry nine survey launches, placed in the water by three sets of davits per side.

JOHAAN MÅNSSON

Johaan Månsson

D: 977 tons (1,030 fl)   **S:** 15 kts   **Dim:** 56.0 × 11.0 × 2.6
Man: 85 men   **M:** Nohab-Polar diesel; 3,300 hp

REMARKS: Launched 14-1-66. Survey boats are stowed in a hangar aft and launched/recovered via a ramp.

GUSTAF AF KLIMT

D: 750 tons   **S:** 10 kts   **Dim:** 52.0 × 8.7 × 4.7
M: 2 diesels; 2 props; 640 hp   **Man:** 66 men

REMARKS: Launched 1941. Lengthened by 5 meters and modernized in 1963.

RAN

D: 285 tons   **S:** 9 kts   **Dim:** 30.0 × 7.0 × 2.6
M: 1 diesel; 1 prop; 260 hp   **Man:** 37 men

REMARK: Launched 1945.

ANDERS BURE (ex-*Rali*)

D: 54 tons   **S:** 15 kts   **Dim:** 24.6 × 5.9 × 2.0
M: 2 diesels; 2 props; . . . hp   **Man:** 11 men

REMARK: Former boat dating from 1968 and bought in 1971.

NILS STRÖMKRONA

D: 140 tons   **S:** 9 kts   **Dim:** 26.6 × 5.1 × 2.5
M: 1 diesel; 300 hp   **Man:** 14 men

REMARK: Launched in 1894 and rebuilt in 1952.

COASTAL ARTILLERY SERVICE

PATROL CRAFT

◆ **1 coastal patrol craft**   Bldr: Stockholm Naval Dockyard, 1953

V 57

D: 115 tons (135 fl)   **Dim:** 29.9 × 5.3 × 2.2
S: 13.5 kts   **Man:** 12 men
A: 1/20-mm AA – mines   **M:** Nohab-Polar diesel; 1 prop; 500 hp

◆ **22 61 class**

61 to 77

D: 30 tons (fl)   **S:** 19 kts   **Dim:** 21.0 × 4.6 × 1.2
A: 1/20-mm AA   **M:** 2 diesels; 2 props; . . . hp

REMARKS: Built in two series, nos. 61 to 70 in 1960-61 and nos. 71 to 77 in 1966-67.

PATROL CRAFT (continued)

◆ **Minelayers 8 Mul-12-class mine planters**

MUL 12 to MUL 19

MUL 19   1970

D:	245 tons	**S:** 10.5 kts	**Dim:** 31.18 (29.0 pp) × 7.62 × 3.1
A:	1/40-mm AA−... mines		**M:** 2 Nohab diesels; 2 props; 460 hp

REMARKS: Launched 1952-56. A new coastal mineplanter, MUL-20, is planned. These craft are used for placing and maintaining controlled mine fields.

◆ **1 coastal mine planter**

MUL 11

D:	200 tons	**S:** 10 kts	**Dim:** 30.1 (27.0 pp) × 7.21 × 3.65
A:	... mines		**M:** 2 Atlas diesels; 1 prop; 300 hp

REMARK: Launched 1946.

◆ **36 501-class minelaying launches**

501 through 536

D:	15 tons	**S:** 14 kts	**Dim:** ... × ... × ...
A:	12 mines	**Man:** 7 men	**M:** Diesels

REMARKS: Launched 1969-71. Nine more are planned.

LANDING CRAFT

◆ **3 Grim-class utility landing craft**   Bldr: Åsiguerken

BORE   GRIM   HEIMDAL

D:	340 tons (fl)	**S:** 12 kts	**Dim:** 36.0 × 8.5 × 2.6
A:	none		**M:** 2 diesels; 2 props; 800 hp

REMARKS: The *Grim* was launched in 1962, the *Bore* and the *Heimdal* in 1967. Car ferry design; bow hinges upward to permit extending ramp.

Bore   1969

◆ **2 Sleipner-class utility landing craft**

SKAGUL   SLEIPNER

D:	335 tons	**S:** 10 kts	**Dim:** 35.0 × 8.5 × 2.9
A:	none		**M:** 2 diesels; 2 props; 640 hp

REMARKS: The *Skagul* was launched in 1960, the *Sleipner* in 1959. Similar to the *Grim* class.

◆ **4 Ane-class utility landing craft**

ANE   BALDER   LOKE   RING

D:	135 tons	**S:** 8.5 kts	**Dim:** 28.0 × 8.0 × 1.8
A:	1/20-mm AA		**M:** Diesels

REMARK: Launched 1943-45.

◆ **81 201-series large personnel landing craft**

Bldrs: Lundevarv Verkstads and Marinteknik, Oregrund, 1957-77

201 to 276   280 to 284

220   1960

SWEDEN *(continued)*

LANDING CRAFT *(continued)*

D: 31 tons (fl) **S:** 17 kts **Dim:** 21.4 × 4.2 × 1.3
A: 2 or 3/6.5-mm machine guns (II × 1, I × 1)
Man: 5 men, 40 troops
M: 3 SAAB-Scania 6 DS 11 diesels; 3 props; 705 hp

REMARKS: Nos. 266 through 269 have Volvo Penta diesels. Early units were 20 meters overall and had three 200-hp diesels. Patrol-boat-like bow opens to permit extension of ramp from troop compartment below decks. Twin machine gun to port, plus single-mount aft in some.

◆ **54 personnel landing craft**

		L						
337 through 354	1970-73	**D:**	6 tons	**S:**	21 kts	**M:**	225 hp	
332 through 336	1967	**D:**	5.4 tons	**S:**	25 kts	**M:**	225 hp	
331	1965	**D:**	6 tons	**S:**	20 kts			
301 through 330	1956-59	**D:**	4 tons	**S:**	9.5 kts	**Dim:**	9.5 × 2.5 × 0.9	

309   1972

◆ **5 cargo lights** Bldr: Lundevarv

REMARK: Ordered in 1978.

◆ **3 coastal personnel transports**

Bldrs: Farösund Naval SY (2) and Marinteknik, Oregrund (1)

REMARK: Ordered in 1978.

COAST GUARD

PATROL BOATS

◆ **2 Tv-71 class** Bldr: Karlskrona

Tv 71   Tv 72

D: 300 tons (fl) **S:** 20 kts **Dim:** 43.5 × 8.5 × 2.4
A: none **Man:** 14 men **Endurance:** 14 days
M: 2 diesels; 2 props; 5,000 hp

REMARKS: Tv-71 to be launched in 1980, Tv-72 in 1981. Helicopter platform, bow thruster. Glass-reinforced plastic sandwich hull construction, originally developed for the not-built M-70-class naval minesweeper.

◆ **5 Tv-103 class** Bldr: Karlskrona, 1969-

TV 103   Tv 104   Tv 105   Tv 106   Tv 107

D: 50 tons **S:** 25 kts **Dim:** 26.7 × 5.2 × 1.1
Man: 8 men **Range:** 1,000/15
M: 2 diesels; 2 props; 1,800 hp

◆ **1 oil-spill pollution control craft** Bldr: . . ., 1978

Tv 04

D: . . . tons **S:** 12 kts **Dim:** 35.5 × 8.0 × . . .
M: 2 diesels; 2 props; 1,200 hp

◆ **1 oil-spill pollution control craft** Bldr: Djupriks SY, 1976

MAJEKAR

D: 76 tons **S:** 12 kts **Dim:** 25.0 × 6.0 × 1.5
M: 2 Volvo-Penta diesels; 2 props; 550 hp

NOTE: There are a number of other coast guard craft, assigned to customs patrol and rescue duties. All are painted white and have a broad and a narrow red diagonal stripe on the hull side, as on U.S. Coast Guard units. Hull numbers are all in the "Tv" series. None is armed.

SYRIA

PERSONNEL: Approximately 2,500

MERCHANT MARINE (1978): 41 ships—26,518 grt

NAVAL AVIATION: Several Soviet Mi-8 helicopters.

FRIGATES

◆ **2 ex-Soviet Petya class**

12 N . . .   14 N . . .

D: 950 tons (1,100 fl) **S:** 30 kts **Dim:** 82.3 × 9.1 × 3.2
Man: 80 men
A: 4/76.2-mm DP (II × 2)—4/RBU 2500 ASW rocket launchers (XV × 4)—3/533-mm TT (III × 1)
Electron Equipt: Radars: 1/Don-2, 1/Strut Curve, 1/Hawk Screech—IFF: 2/Square Head, 1/High Pole B
  Sonar: Hull-mounted HF
M: CODAG: 2 gas turbines (15,000 hp each); 1 diesel (6,000 hp); 3 props; 36,000 hp

REMARK: Transferred: 1975.

SYRIA (continued)

GUIDED-MISSILE PATROL BOATS

◆ **2 ex-Soviet OSA-II class**

D: 240 tons (fl)   **S:** 36 kts   **Dim:** 39.0 × 7.7 × 1.8
A: 4/SS-N-26 Styx SSM (I × 4) − 4/30-mm AA (II × 2)
Electron Equipt: Radar: 1/Square Tie, 1/Drum Tilt − IFF: 2/Square Head, 1/High Pole B
M: 3 M504 diesels; 3 props; 15,000 hp   **Range:** 450/34, 700/20

REMARK: Transferred 1978.

◆ **6 ex-Soviet Osa-I class**

21   22   23   24   25   26

Syrian Osa-I   1976

D: 175 tons (210 fl)   **S:** 36 kts   **Dim:** 39.0 × 7.7 × 1.8
A: 4/SS-N-20 Styx (I × 4) − 4/30-mm AA (II × 2)
Electron Equipt: Radars: 1/Square Tie, 1/Drum Tilt − IFF: 2/Square Head, 1/High Pole B
M: 3 M503A diesels; 3 props; 12,000 hp   **Range:** 450/34, 700/20

REMARK: Two transferred earlier were sunk during the Arab-Israeli War, October 1973.

◆ **6 ex-Soviet Komar class**

41   42   43   44   45   46

D: 71 tons (82 fl)   **S:** 40 kts   **Dim:** 25.3 × 7.0 × 2.0
A: 2/SS-N-2a Styx (I × 2) − 2/25-mm AA (II × 1)   **Man:** 20 men
Electron Equipt: Radar: 1/Square Tie
M: 4 M50 diesels; 4 props; 4,800 hp   **Range:** 400/32, 700/15

REMARKS: Transferred 1963-66. Survivors of a group, three of which were sunk in the Arab-Israeli War, October 1973. Probably in poor condition due to age. Wooden hulls.

TORPEDO BOATS

◆ **1 ex-Soviet P-6 class**

76

D: 66.5 tons (fl)   **S:** 43 kts   **Dim:** 25.3 × 6.1 × 1.7
A: 4/25-mm AA (II × 2) − 2/533-mm TT (I × 2) − 6/depth charges
Electron Equipt: Radar: 1/Skin Head   **Man:** 12 men
Range: 400/32, 700/15
M: 4 M50 diesels; 4 props; 4,800 hp

◆ **12 ex-Soviet P-4 class**

D: 19.3 tons (22.4 fl)   **S:** 55 kts   **Dim:** 19.3 × 3.7 × 1.0
A: 2/14.5-mm machine guns (II × 1) − 2/450-mm TT (I × 2)
M: 2 M50 diesels; 2 props; 2,400 hp   **Man:** 12 men

REMARK: Transferred 1958-60. The remaining units in service of a group of at least 17; one was sunk during the Arab-Israeli War, October 1973.

MINE WARFARE AND VARIOUS SHIPS

◆ **1 Soviet-T-43 class fleet minesweeper**

504 YARMOUK

D: 500 tons (580 fl)   **S:** 14 kts   **Dim:** 58.0 × 8.4 × 2.3
A: 4/37-mm AA (II × 2) − 8/12.7-mm machine guns (II × 4) − 2/depth-charge mortars − mines
Electron Equipt: Radar: 1/Ball End   **Man:** 75 men   **Range:** 3,200/10
M: 2 diesels; 2 props; 2,200 hp

REMARKS: One sister lost in the October 1973 war.

◆ **2 ex-Soviet Vanya-class coastal minesweepers**

D: 200 tons (245 fl)   **S:** 18 kts   **Dim:** 40.0 × 7.6 × 1.8
A: 2/30-mm AA (II × 1) − mines   **Electron Equipt:** Radar: 1/Don-2
Man: 30 men   **M:** 2 diesels; 2 props; 2,200 hp

REMARK: Transferred 12-72.

◆ **1 Soviet Nyryat-1-class diving tender**

TAIWAN

Republic of China

PERSONNEL (1978): 74,000 men, including 39,000 Marines

MERCHANT MARINE (1978): 443 ships − 1,558,713 grt
(tankers: . . . ships)

NAVAL AVIATION: Nine elderly S-2A Tracker ASW aircraft remain in inventory. Twelve Hughes-500 MO/ASW helicopters were ordered during 1979 for use from destroyers.

WARSHIPS IN SERVICE OR UNDER CONSTRUCTION
AS OF 1 JANUARY 1980

	L	Tons (Surfaced)	Main armament
◆ **2 submarines**			
2 GUPPY II	1944-45	1,870	10/533-mm TT
		Tons	
◆ **22 destroyers**			
8 GEARING FRAM I	1945-46	2,425	4/127-mm, 0-4/40-mm, ASW weapons
2 GEARING FRAM II	1945	2,425	4-6/127-mm, 4-8/40-mm, ASW weapons
2 ALLEN M. SUMNER FRAM II	1944	2,350	6/127-mm, ASW weapons
6 ALLEN M. SUMNER	1943-44	2,200	6/127-mm, Gabriel SSM, ASW weapons
4 FLETCHER	1942-43	1,680	2/127-mm, ASW weapons

◆ **10 frigates**
1 RUDDEROW
6 CROSLEY
3 CHARLES LAWRENCE

◆ **3 corvettes**
3 AUK

◆ **12 guided-missile patrol boats**

◆ **14 minesweepers**

◆ **50 amphibious ships and craft**

NOTE: Hull numbers were altered in 1976 and now are not usually worn. The latest known are given, but ships are listed in alphabetical order.

SUBMARINES

◆ **2 ex-U.S. Guppy II class**

	Bldr	Laid down	L	In serv.
736 HAI SHIH (ex-*Cutlass*, SS-478)	Portsmouth NSY	22-7-44	5-11-44	17-3-45
794 HAI PAO (ex-*Tusk*, SS-426)	Cramp SB, Philadelphia	23-8-43	8-7-45	11-4-46

Hai Pao—as the **Tusk**   1967

D: 1,517 tons standard, 1,870 surfaced, 2,440 submerged   **S:** 18/13.5 kts
Dim: 93.6 × 8.2 × 5.2   **Man:** 11 officers, 70 men
A: 10/533-mm TT (6 fwd, 4 aft)   **Range:** 10,000/10
M: Diesel-electric propulsion: 4 Fairbanks-Morse 38D8⅛ diesels; 2 electric motors; 4,610 hp

REMARKS: Transferred, 12-4-73 and 18-10-73, for ASW training. British Mk-24 Tigerfish torpedoes ordered in 1979 to arm them. Four 126-cell batteries.

DESTROYERS

◆ **8 ex-U.S. Gearing Fram-I class**

	Bldr	Laid down	L	In serv.
921 CHIEN YANG (ex-*James E. Kyes*, DD-787)	Todd, Seattle	27-12-44	4-8-45	8-2-46
978 HAN YANG (ex-*Herbert J. Thomas*, DD-833)	Bath Iron Wks.	30-10-44	25-3-45	29-5-45
. . . KAI YANG (ex-*Richard B. Anderson*, DD-786)	Todd, Seattle	1-12-44	7-7-45	26-10-45
981 LAI YANG (ex-*Leonard F. Mason*, DD-852)	Bethlehem, Quincy		4-1-46	28-6-46
. . . LAO YANG (ex-*Shelton*, DD-790)	Todd, Seattle		8-3-46	21-6-46
938 LIAO YANG (ex-*Hanson*, DD-832)	Bath Iron Wks.	7-10-44	11-3-45	11-5-45
932 SHEN YANG (ex-*Power*, DD-839)	Bath Iron Wks.	26-2-45	30-6-45	13-9-45
925 TE YANG (ex-*Sarsfield*, DD-837)	Bath Iron Wks.	15-1-45	27-5-45	31-7-45

Lai Yang—as the **Leonard F. Mason**   PH3 H. Burgess, 1976

D: 2,425 tons (3,465-3,540 fl)   **S:** 32 kts
Dim: 119.03 (116.74 wl) × 12.52 × 4.61 (6.5 over sonar)
Man: 275 men   **Range:** 1,500/31, 5,800/12   **Fuel:** 720 tons
A: 4/127-mm DP (II × 2)—*Han Yang, Kai Yang:* 4/40-mm AA (II × 2)—4 or 6/12.7-mm machine guns—1/Asroc (not in *Han Yang* and *Kai Yang*)—6/324-mm Mk 32 ASW TT (III × 2)—1/Hughes-500 ASW helicopter
Electron Equipt: Radars: 1/SPS 10, 1/SPS 29 (*Chien Yang, Te Yang:* SPS 40), 1/Mk 25
     Sonar: SQS 23—ECM: WLR 1, WLR 3 (ULQ 6 also in some)

DESTROYERS (continued)

Han Yang—as the **Herbert J. Thomas**. Now has no Asroc   1965

Boilers: 4 Babcock & Wilcox, 43.3 kg/cm² pressure—superheat 454°C
M: 2 sets GE GT; 2 props; 60,000 hp   **Electric:** 1,200 kw

REMARKS: *Chien Yang*, *Lao Yang*, and *Liao Yang* transferred 18-4-73; *Han Yang*, 6-5-74; *Kai Yang*, 10-6-77; *Te Yang*, *Shen Yang*, 1-10-77; *Lai Yang*, 10-3-78. A ninth unit, *Chao Yang* (ex-*Rowan*, DD-782) was lost 22-8-77 while on tow to Taiwan. *Kai Yang* and *Lao Yang* both have 127-mm twin mounts forward and the Mk-32 ASW torpedo tubes abreast the after stack. *Han Yang* has extra superstructure, as she was converted for NBC-warfare defense trials 1963-64; she has an extra gas-turbine generator to run additional air-conditioning systems. She and *Kai Yang* had no Asroc on delivery and have received two twin 40-mm antiaircraft guns, each with a Mk-51, mod. 2, director in the Asroc location. All have Mk-37 gunfire-control radars for the 127-mm guns.

◆ 2 ex-U.S. Gearing FRAM-II class

	Bldr	Laid down	L	In serv.
966 DANG YANG	Bethlehem,	26-3-44	5-10-45	21-3-47
(ex-*Lloyd Thomas*, DD-764)	San Francisco			
963 FU YANG	Bath Iron	30-1-45	14-6-45	21-8-45
(ex-*Ernest G. Small*, DD-838)	Works			

Fu Yang—wearing old number   1973

D: 2,425 tons (3,477 fl)   **S:** 32 kts
Dim: 119.03 (116.74 wl) × 12.52 × 4.61 (6.54 over sonar)
Man: 275 men   **Range:** 1,600/31, 6,100/12   **Fuel:** 720 tons
A: 963: 6/127-mm DP (II × 3)—8/40-mm AA (II × 4)—4/12.7-mm machine guns (I × 4)—2/Mk 11 Hedgehog—6/324-mm Mk 32 ASW TT (III × 2)—1/depth-charge rack
    966: 4/127-mm DP (II × 2)—4/40-mm AA (II × 2)—4/12.7-mm machine guns (I × 4)—1/Mk 15 trainable Hedgehog—6/324-mm Mk 32 ASW TT (III × 2)—1/Hughes-500 ASW helicopter
Electron Equipt: Radars: 963: 1/SPS 10, 1/SPS 37, 1/Mk 25—1/URN-6 TACAN—ECM: WLR 1
           966: 1/SPS 10, 1/SPS 6B, 1/Mk 25—ECM: WLR 1, WLR 3, ULQ 6
        Sonars: SQS-23 series (hull); 963 only: SQA 10 (VDS)
Boilers: 4 Babcock & Wilcox, 43.3 kg/cm² pressure—superheat 454°C
M: 2 sets GE GT; 2 props; 60,000 hp   **Electric:** 1,200 kw

REMARKS: *Dang Yang*, completed as an ASW destroyer (DDE), finished FRAM-I modernization in 11-61 and was transferred to Taiwan on 12-10-72. *Fu Yang*, transferred in 2-71, completed FRAM-II modernization as a radar picket destroyer in 8-61; her SPS-30 height-finder was removed before transfer. Both received 40-mm and 12.7-mm guns in Taiwan. One Mk-37 radar gunfire control for 127-mm, one Mk-51, mod. 2, optical gunfire control per 40-mm mount.

◆ 2 ex-U.S. Allen M. Sumner FRAM-II class

	Bldr	Laid down	L	In serv.
949 LO YANG	Bethlehem,	30-8-43	25-1-44	20-5-44
(ex-*Taussig*, DD-746)	Staten I.			
954 NAN YANG	Bethlehem,	21-11-43	30-9-44	11-10-45
(ex-*John W. Thomason*, DD-760)	San Francisco			

D: 2,350 tons (3,220 fl)   **S:** 33 kts
Dim: 114.63 (112.52 wl) × 12.52 × 4.4 (5.9 over sonar)
Man: 275 men   **Range:** 1,000/32   **Fuel:** 500 tons
A: 6/127-mm DP (II × 3)—4/12.7-mm machine guns (I × 4)—2/Mk 11 Hedgehogs—6/324-mm Mk 32 ASW TT (III × 2)—1/Hughes-500 ASW helicopter
Electron Equipt: Radars: 1/SPS 10, 1/SPS 29, 1/Mk 25
        Sonars: SQS-29 series, SQA 10 (VDS)
Boilers: 4 Babcock & Wilcox, 43.3 kg/cm² pressure—superheat 454°C
M: 2 sets GT; 2 props; 60,000 hp   **Electric:** 1,200 kw

REMARKS: Both transferred on 6-5-74, having completed FRAM-II modernization in 9-62 and 1-60, respectively. Have Mk-37 radar fire control for the 127-mm guns and Mk-5 target-designation system.

◆ 6 ex-U.S. Allen M. Sumner class

	Bldr	Laid down	L	In serv.
976 HENG YANG	Bethlehem,	30-9-43	23-2-44	24-6-44
(ex-*Samuel N. Moore*, DD-747)	Staten Isl.			
986 HSIANG YANG	Bethlehem,	30-7-43	28-12-43	17-4-44
(ex-*Brush*, DD-745)	Staten Isl.			
988 HUA YANG	Bethlehem,	5-5-44	29-10-44	17-3-45
(ex-*Bristol*, DD-857)	San Pedro			

DESTROYERS (continued)

972 HUEI YANG	Federal,	19-10-43	27-2-44	4-5-44
(ex-*English*, DD-696)	Kearny			
928 PO YANG	Bath Iron	28-10-43	19-3-44	2-6-44
(ex-*Maddox*, DD-731)	Wks.			
944 YUEN YANG	Federal,	16-12-43	15-4-44	22-6-44
(ex-*Haynsworth*, DD-700)	Kearny			

Heng Yang—wearing old number   1972

D: 2,200 tons (3,300 fl)   **S:** 33 kts
Dim: 114.63 (112.52 wl) × 12.52 × 4.4 (5.9 over sonar)
Man: 275 men   **Range:** 1,000/32, 4,400/11   **Fuel:** 500 tons
A: *Hsiang Yang, Hua Yang, Yueng Yang:* 5/Gabriel SSM (III × 1, II × 1)—6/127-
   mm DP (II × 3)—4/40-mm AA (II × 2)—
   4/12.7-mm machine guns (I × 4)—2/Mk
   11 Hedgehogs—6/324-mm Mk 32 ASW
   TT (III × 2)—1/depth-charge rack
   Heng Yang: 6/127-mm DP (II × 3)—8/40-mm AA (IV × 1, II × 2)—4/12.7-mm
   machine guns (I × 4)—2/Mk 11 Hedgehogs—6/324-mm Mk 32 ASW
   TT (III × 2)—1/depth-charge rack
   Huei Yang, Po Yang: 6/127-mm DP (II × 3)—4/76-mm DP (II × 2)—4/12.7-mm
   machine guns—2/Mk 11 Hedgehogs—6/324-mm Mk 32
   ASW TT—1/depth-charge rack
Electron Equipt: Radars: 1/SPS 10, 1/SPS 6C (*Po Yang:* SPS 40), 1/Mk 25 (*Huei
   Yang, Po Yang:* 1/Mk 35 also, Gabriel ships: 1/. . .)
   Sonars: SQS-29 series—ECM: WLR 1
Boilers: 4 Babcock & Wilcox, 43.3 kg/cm² pressure—superheat 454°C
M: 2 sets GT; 2 props; 60,000 hp   **Electric:** 1,000 kw

REMARKS: *Heng Yang* transferred in 2-70; *Hsiang Yang* and *Hua Yang* on 9-12-69;
Huei Yang in 9-70; *Po Yang* on 6-7-72; *Yuen Yang* on 12-5-70. All unmodified units of
the class. *Hsiang Yang* had four 76-mm DP before Gabriel conversion. Those that
have 40-mm antiaircraft guns had them added in Taiwan; each mount has one Mk-51,
mod. 2, gunfire control. All have Mk-37 radar gunfire control for the 127-mm guns;
those with 76-mm also have Mk-56 radar gunfire control. The Gabriel-equipped units
have an extra fire-control radar on the after side of the tripod mast.

◆ **4 ex-U.S. Fletcher class**

Bldrs: *An Yang:* Bethlehem Steel, Staten Island; others: Bethlehem, San Francisco

	Laid down	L	In serv.
997 AN YANG (ex-*Kimberly*, DD-521)	27-7-42	4-2-43	24-5-43
947 CHIANG YANG (ex-*Mullany*, DD-528)	15-1-42	12-10-42	23-4-43
934 KUN YANG (ex-*Yarnell*, DD-541)	5-12-42	25-7-43	30-12-43
956 KWEI YANG (ex-*Twining*, DD-540)	21-11-42	11-7-43	1-2-43

Kun Yang—wearing old number   1970

D: 2,100 tons (3,036 fl)   **S:** 35 kts
Dim: 114.65 (112.52 wl) × 11.99 × 4.39 (5.38 over sonar)
Man: 275 men   **Range:** 860/35, 4,700/13   **Fuel:** 512 tons
A: *Chiang Yang:* 4/127-mm DP (I × 4)—6/76-mm DP (II × 2)—2/Mk 11 Hedgehogs—
   6/324-mm Mk 32 ASW TT (III × 2)—1/depth-charge rack
   Kun Yang: 5/127-mm DP (I × 5)—1/Sea Chaparral system (VI × 1)—4/40-mm
   AA (II × 2)—5/533-mm TT (V × 1)—2/Mk 11 Hedgehogs—mines
   Others: 5/127-mm DP (I × 5)—1/Sea Chaparral system (VI × 1)—4/40-mm AA—
   2/Mk 11 Hedgehogs—6/324-mm Mk 32 ASW TT (III × 2)—1/depth-
   charge rack
Electron Equipt: Radars: 1/SPS 10, 1/SPS 6C, 1/Mk 25 (*Chiang Yang:* 1/Mk 35,
   2/Mk 34, also)
   Sonars: SQS 4 or SQS-29 series—ECM: BLR 1
Boilers: 4 Babcock & Wilcox, 43.3 kg/cm² pressure—superheat 454°C
M: 2 sets GT; 2 props; 60,000 hp   **Electric:** 880 kw

REMARKS: *An Yang* transferred in 6-67; *Chiang Yang* in 10-71; *Kun Yang* in 6-68; *Kwei
Yang* in 10-71. All have Mk-37 gunfire-control radars for the 127-mm guns, while
Chiang Yang also has one Mk-56 and two Mk-63 gunfire-control radars for her 76-mm
guns. Sea Chaparral is a manned mounting for launching Redeye, heat-seeking,
short-range SAMs; it replaced a twin 40-mm antiaircraft mount in three ships.

FRIGATES

◆ **1 ex-U.S. Rudderow class**   Bldr: Bethlehem Steel, Hingham, Mass.

	Laid down	L	In serv.
959 TAI YUAN (ex-*Riley*, DE-579)	20-10-43	29-12-43	13-3-44

FRIGATES (continued)

Tai Yuan—wearing old number   1968

D: 1,450 tons (1,950 fl)   **S:** 24 kts
Dim: 93.27 × 11.24 × 3.43 (4.3 over sonar)
Man: 200 men   **Range:** 1,100/24, 5,000/12   **Fuel:** 354 tons
A: 2/127-mm DP (I × 2)—4/40-mm AA (II × 2)—4/20-mm AA (I × 4)—1/Mk 11 Hedgehog—6/324-mm Mk 32 ASW TT (III × 2)—2/Mk 9 depth-charge racks—mines
Electron Equipt: Radars: 1/SPS 5, 1/SPS 6, 1/Mk 26 fire-control
                 Sonar: . . .
Boilers: 2 Foster-Wheeler D-type, 31.7 kg/cm² pressure—superheat 399°C
M: 2 sets GE turbo-electric drive; 2 props; 12,000 hp   **Electric:** 1,140 kw

REMARKS: Transferred, after modernization, on 10-7-69; purchased outright in 3-74. Has one Mk-52 gunfire-control radar and two Mk-51, mod. 2, gunfire-control radars. Minelaying capability added in Taiwan.

◆ **9 former high-speed transports**

6 ex-U.S. Crosley class:

	Bldr	Laid down	L	In serv.
838 FU SHAN (ex-*Truxtun*, APD-98, ex DE-282)	Charleston NY	13-12-43	9-3-44	3-7-44
854 HUA SHAN (ex-*Donald W Wolf*, APD-129, ex-DE 713)	Defoe, Bay City	17-4-44	22-7-44	13-4-45
893 SHOU SHAN (ex-*Kline*, APD-120, ex-DE 687)	Bethlehem, Quincy	27-5-44	27-6-44	18-10-44
878 TAI SHAN (ex-*Register*, APD-92, ex-DE-233)	Charleston NY	27-10-43	20-1-44	11-1-45
615 TIEN SHAN (ex-*Kleinsmith*, APD-134, ex-DE-718)	Defoe, Bay City	30-8-44	27-1-45	12-6-45
. . . YU SHAN (ex-*Kinzer*, APD-91, ex-DE-232)	Charleston NY	9-9-43	9-12-43	1-11-44

Fu Shan—wearing old number   *Ships of the World*, 1975

3 ex-U.S. Charles Lawrence class:

	Bldr	Laid down	L	In serv.
845 CHUNG SHAN (ex-*Blessman*, APD-48, ex-DE-69)	Bethlehem, Hingham	22-3-43	19-6-43	19-9-43
821 LU SHAN (ex-*Bull*, APD-APD-78, ex-DE-693)	Defoe, Bay City	14-12-42	25-3-43	12-8-43
834 WEN SHAN (ex-*Gantner*, APD-42, ex-DE-60)	Bethlehem, Hingham	21-12-42	17-4-43	23-7-43

D: 1,680 tons (2,150 fl)   **S:** 22 kts   **Dim:** 93.27 × 11.24 × 3.96 (hull)
Man: 200 men + 160 troops   **Range:** 1,800/22, 5,000/13   **Fuel:** 346 tons
A: 2/127-mm DP (I × 2)—6/40-mm AA (II × 3)—4/20-mm AA (I × 4)—2/Mk 9 depth-charge racks—*see also* Remarks
Electron Equipt: Radars: 1/SPS 5, 1/Decca 707, some: 1/Mk 26
                 Sonar: . . .
Boilers: 2, Babcock & Wilcox, Foster-Wheeler, or Combustion Engineering; 31.7 kg/cm² pressure—superheat 399°C
M: 2 sets GE turbo-electric drive; 2 props; 12,000 hp   **Electric:** 1,140 kw

REMARKS: *Yu Shan* transferred in 4-62; *Hua Shan* in 5-65; *Fu Shan* and *Shou Shan* in 3-66; *Wen Shan* in 5-66; *Lu Shan* in 8-66; *Tai Shan* in 10-66; *Tien Shan* in 6-67, and *Chung Shan* in 8-67. All were sold outright except *Tien Shan* which, because she was on loan, was not modified by the addition of a second 127-mm mount aft until after her purchase in 1974; the others all received the second gun in lieu of a cargo hold and derrick, beginning about 1970. ASW armaments vary, with *Fu Shan* having two Mk-11 Hedgehogs on her main deck forward and several (but not all) carrying six 324-mm Mk-32 ASW torpedo tubes (III × 2); all have two Mk-9 depth-charge racks, and *Hua Shan* has four *twin* 20-mm antiaircraft guns. Most have only a Mk-51 range-finder for 127-mm fire control forward and a Mk-51 optical gunfire-control system aft, plus three Mk-51, mod. 2, for the 40-mm antiaircraft guns. Welin davits are retained amidships, but only two (vice the original four) landing craft are carried, to save top weight. The former *Crosley*-class ships have low navigating bridges, the other ships have high ones. Sisters *Heng Shan* (ex-*Raymond W. Herndon*, APD-121) and *Lung Shan* (ex-*Schmitt*, APD-76) were stricken in 1976, and *Kang Shan* (ex-*George W. Ingram*, APD-43) was stricken in 1978.

CORVETTES

◆ **3 ex-U.S. Auk-class former minesweepers**

Bldrs: *Wu Sheng:* Savannah Machine & Foundry, Ga; others: American SB, Cleveland, O.

	Laid down	L	In serv.
896 CHU YUNG (ex-*Waxwing*, MSF-389)	24-5-44	10-3-45	6-8-45
867 PING JIN (ex-*Steady*, MSF-118)	17-11-41	6-6-42	16-11-42
884 WU SHENG (ex-*Redstart*, MSF-378)	14-6-44	18-10-45	4-4-45

D: 890 tons (1,250 fl)   **S:** 18 kts   **Dim:** 67.39 (65.53 pp) × 9.8 × 3.3
Man: 80 men   **Fuel:** 216 tons   **Electric:** 360 kw
A: 2/76-mm DP (I × 2)—4/40-mm AA (II × 2)—4/20-mm AA (II × 2)—1/Mk 11 Hedgehog—3/324-mm Mk 32 ASW TT (III × 1)—2/depth-charge racks
Electron Equipt: Radar: 1/SPS 5   Sonar: SQS 17
M: 2 GM 12-278A diesels; 2 props; 3,532 hp

REMARKS: After conversion to corvettes, transferred as follows: *Chu Yung* in 11-65, *Ping Jin* in 3-68, and *Wu Sheng* in 7-65. *Chu Yung* was fitted with mine rails in 1975.

GUIDED-MISSILE PATROL BOATS

◆ **12 Lung Chiang class**   Bldrs: 1st unit: Korea-Tacoma SY; others: Taiwan

587 LUNG CHIANG	. . . N . . .	. . . N . . .	. . . N . . .
. . . N . . .	. . . N . . .	. . . N . . .	. . . N . . .
. . . N . . .	. . . N . . .	. . . N . . .	. . . N . . .

D: 218 tons (250 fl)   **S:** 40 kts   **Dim:** 50.14 (46.94 pp) × 7.25 × 2.26
Man: 5 officers, 30 men
Range: 700/40 (gas turbines), 1,900/30 (3 diesels), 2,700/12 (1 diesel)
A: 4/Hsiung Feng SSM—1/76-mm OTO Melara DP—2/30-mm Emerlec AA (II × 1)—2/12.7-mm machine guns (I × 2)
Electron Equipt: Radars: 1/navigational, 1/RAN 11LX (NA 10 system)
M: CODOG: 3 GM 12V-149TI diesels (3,600 hp), 3 AVCO-Lycoming TF-40A gas turbines; 3 controllable-pitch props

REMARKS: *Lung Chiang* was in service on 15-5-78. Design is a variation of Tacoma Boatbuilding (U.S.) PSMM Mk-5. The Hsiung Feng missile is reported to be indigenous design. Prototype built in Korea, with follow-on units to be built in Taiwan.

PATROL CRAFT

◆ **10 or more**

D: 12 tons   **S:** 25 kts   **Dim:** 15.0 × . . . × . . .
A: 1/40-mm AA   **M:** 2 diesels; water-jet drive

REMARKS: Date from 1971. There are believed to be a number of other small patrol craft of Taiwanese construction, for which no details are available. The six remaining torpedo boats are believed to have been stricken.

MINE WARFARE SHIPS

◆ **14 ex-U.S. and ex-Belgian Adjutant, MSC-268*, and MCS-289** classes of coastal minesweepers**

	Bldr	In serv.
. . . YUNG AN (ex-MSC-123)	. . .	6-55
. . . YUNG CHEN (ex-*Maaseick*, ex-MSC-78)	Quincy Adams Yacht, Mass.	7-53
. . . YUNG CHI (ex-*Charleroi*, ex-MSC-152)	Hodgdon Bros., Me.	2-54
. . . YUNG CHING (ex-*Eakloo*, ex-MSC-101)	Hodgdon Bros., Me.	5-53
. . . YUNG CHOU (ex-MSC-278)*	Tacoma Boat, Wash.	7-59
. . . YUNG FU (ex-*Diest*, ex-*Macaw*, MSC-77)	Quincy Adams Yacht, Mass.	5-53
. . . YUNG HSIN (ex-MSC-302)**	Dorchester Bldrs., N.J.	3-65
. . . YUNG JEN (ex-*St. Nicholas*, ex-MSC-64)	H. B. Nevins, N.Y.	2-54
. . . YUNG JU (ex-MSC-300)**	Tacoma Boat, Wash.	3-65
. . . YUNG LO (ex-MSC-306)**	Dorchester Bldrs., N.J.	4-66
. . . YUNG NIEN (ex-MSC-277)*	Tacoma Boat, Wash.	5-59
. . . YUNG PING (ex-MSC-140)	. . .	9-55
. . . YUNG SHAN (ex-*Lier*, ex-MSC-63)	H. B. Nevins, N.Y.	7-53
. . . YUNG SUI (ex-*Diksmude*, ex-MSC-65)	H. B. Nevins, N.Y.	2-54

Yung Chi—Adjutant class, ex-Belgian, wearing old number   1970

Yung Chou—MSC-268 class, wearing old number   1970

D: 320 tons (378 fl)   **S:** 12.5 kts   **Dim:** 43.0 (41.5 wl) × 7.95 × 2.55
Man: 40 men   **Range:** 2,500/12   **Fuel:** 40 tons
A: 2/20-mm AA (II × 1)   **Electron Equipt:** Radar: 1/Decca 45 or 707   Sonar: UQS 1D
M: 2 GM 8-268A diesels; 2 props; 1,200 hp (MSC-268 class: 4 GM 6-71 diesels; 2 props; 890 hp)

MINE WARFARE SHIPS *(continued)*

Yung Lo — MSC-289 class, wearing old number   1970

REMARKS: Wooden hulls. All, except ex-Belgian ships, transferred in 11-69. Have a variety of configurations, the ex-MSC-268 having a different propulsion scheme and the ex-MSC-289 class having a lower bridge and taller stack.

◆ **1 ex-U.S. minesweeping boat**

MSB 12 (ex-U.S. Navy MSB-4, ex-U.S. Army . . .)

D: 39 tons (fl)   **S:** 12 kts   **Dim:** 17.5 × 4.6 × 1.25
M: 2 Packard diesels; 2 props; 600 hp   **Man:** 6 men

REMARKS: Built in 1945 and transferred in 12-61. Wooden hull. Sister to South Korean MSB-1.

◆ **8 ex-U.S. minesweeping launches**

MSML 1   MSML 3   MSML 5   MSML 6   MSML 7   MSML 8   MSML 11   MSML 12

D: 24 tons (fl)   **S:** 8 kts   **Dim:** 15.29 × 3.96 × 1.31
M: 1 diesel; 1 prop; 60 hp   **Range:** 800/8   **Man:** 4 men

REMARKS: Built between 1943 and 1945, and converted from personnel launches before transfer in 3-61. Wooden hulls.

AMPHIBIOUS WARFARE SHIPS

◆ **1 command ship**   Bldr: Dravo Corp., Neville I., Pittsburgh, Pa.

	L	In serv.
663 KAO HSIUNG (ex-*Chung Hai*, LST-229, ex-*Dukes County*, LST-735)	11-3-44	26-4-44

D: 1,650 tons (4,080 fl)   **S:** 11 kts   **Dim:** 99.98 × 15.24 × 3.4
A: 8/40-mm AA (II × 2, I × 4) – 4/20-mm AA (II × 2)   **Range:** 15,000/9
Electron Equipt: Radars: 1/SPS 10, 1/SPS 12
M: 2 GM 12-567A diesels; 2 props; 1,700 hp

Kao Hsiung — wearing old number   1968

REMARKS: Transferred in 5-57, converted to command ship in 1964, with additional communications gear and radars. Retains bow doors.

◆ **1 ex-U.S. Cabildo-class dock landing ship**   Bldr: Gulf SB, Chickasaw, Ala.

	Laid down	L	In serv.
618 CHEN HAI (ex-*Fort Marion*, LSD-22)	15-9-44	22-5-45	29-1-46

D: 4,790 tons (9,375 fl)   **S:** 15.6 kts   **Dim:** 139.52 (138.38 wl) × 22.0 × 5.49
Man: 326 men + several hundred troops   **Range:** 8,000/15
A: 12/40-mm AA (IV × 2, II × 2)   **Electron Equipt:** Radars: 1/LN 66, 1/SPS 5
Boilers: 2, 30.6 kg/cm² pressure – superheat 393°C
M: 2 sets GT; 2 props; 9,000 hp   **Fuel:** 1,758 tons

REMARKS: Transferred by sale on 15-4-77, having been stricken from the U.S. Navy in 10-74. Modernized under FRAM-II program 12-59 to 4-60. Helicopter platform over 119.5 × 13.4 meter docking well, which can accommodate three LCUs, eighteen LCMs, or thirty-two amphibious armored troops carriers.

◆ **1 ex-U.S. Ashland-class dock landing ship**   Bldr: Moore DD Co., Oakland, Cal.

	Laid down	L	In serv.
639 CHUNG CHENG (ex-*Tung Hai*, ex-*White Marsh*, LSD-8)	7-4-43	19-7-43	29-1-44

Chung Cheng — wearing old number

AMPHIBIOUS WARFARE SHIPS *(continued)*

D: 4,032 tons (8,700 fl)   **S:** 15 kts   **Dim:** 139.52 (138.38 wl) × 22.0 × 5.49
A: 12/40-mm AA (IV × 2, II × 2)   **Electron Equipt:** Radar: 1/SPS 5
Boilers: 2, two-drum, 17.6 kg/cm² pressure   **Range:** 8,000/15
Fuel: 1,758 tons   **Electric:** 400 kw
M: 2 sets Skinner Uniflow reciprocating steam; 2 props; 7,400 hp

REMARKS: Transferred on loan on 17-11-60, purchased in 5-76. Generally similar to *Chen Hai,* above, except for propulsion.

◆ **21 ex-U.S. LST-1- and LST-542-class tank landing ships**

		Bldr.	In serv.
. . .	CHUNG CHENG (ex-*Lafayette County,* LST-859)	Chicago B & I, Seneca, Ill.	29-12-44
. . .	CHUNG CHI (ex-LST-1017)	Bethlehem, Fore River, Mass.	12-5-44
. . .	CHUNG CHIANG (ex-*San Bernardino County,* LST-1110)	Missouri Valley B & I, Evansville, Ind.	7-3-45
. . .	CHUNG CHIEN (ex-LST 716)	Jeffersonville B & M, Ind.	18-8-44
. . .	CHUNG CHIH (ex-*Sagadahoc County,* LST-1091)	American Br., Ambridge, Pa.	6-4-45
. . .	CHUNG CHUAN (ex-LST-1030)	Boston Navy Yd.	19-7-44
619	CHUNG FU (ex-*Iron County,* LST-840)	American Br., Ambridge, Pa.	11-12-44
697	CHUNG HAI (ex-LST-755)	American Br., Ambridge, Pa.	29-7-44
. . .	CHUNG HSING (ex-LST-557)	Missouri Valley B & I, Evansville, Ind.	5-5-44
. . .	CHUNG KUANG (ex-LST-503)	Jeffersonville B & M, Ind.	14-12-43
691	CHUNG LIEN (ex-LST-1050)	Dravo, Pittsburg, Pa.	3-4-45
. . .	CHUNG MING (ex-*Sweetwater County,* LST-1152)	Dravo, Pittsburg, Pa.	13-4-45
. . .	CHUNG PANG (ex-LST-578)	Missouri Valley B & I, Evansville, Ind.	15-7-44
. . .	CHUNG SHENG (ex-LST(H)-1033)	Chicago B & I, Seneca, Ill.	. . . -4-44
. . .	CHUNG SHU (ex-LST-520)	Chicago B & I, Seneca, Ill.	28-2-44
624	CHUNG SHUN (ex-LST-732)	Dravo, Pittsburg, Pa.	10-4-44
. . .	CHUNG SUO (ex-*Bradley County,* LST-400)	Newport News SB, & DD, Va.	7-1-43
. . .	CHUNG TING (ex-LST-537)	Missouri Valley B & I, Evansville, Ind.	9-2-44
. . .	CHUNG WAN (ex-LST-535)	Missouri Valley B & I, Evansville, Ind.	4-2-44
. . .	CHUNG YEH (ex-*Sublette County,* LST-1144)	Chicago B & I, Seneca, Ill.	28-5-45
. . .	CHUNG YUNG (ex-LST-574)	Missouri Valley B & I, Evansville, Ind.	26-6-44

D: 1,653 tons (4,080 fl)   **S:** 11.6 kts   **Dim:** 99.98 × 15.24 × 3.4
Man: 100-125 men   **Range:** 15,000/9   **Fuel:** 569 tons
A: Several: 2/76-mm DP (I × 2)—6-8/40-mm AA (II × 2, I × 2 or 4)—4-8/20-mm AA
M: 2 GM 12-567A diesels; 2 props; 1,700 hp   **Electric:** 300 kw

REMARKS: Six transferred in 1946, two in 1947, *Chung Shu* in 1948, seven in 1958, *Chung Yung* in 1959, *Chung Kuang* in 1960, *Chung Yeh* in 1961, and two subsequently. All extensively rebuilt during the late 1960s, in many cases becoming almost new ships; re-engined at the same time. Most have four pairs of Welin davits, while *Chung Chih,*

Chung Kuang—wearing old number   1969

Chung Yung, Chung Sheng, and *Chung Shu* have six, and *Chung Chien* has two; each pair of davits handles one MCVP. Five or more have two 76-mm guns. *Chung Chih* (ex-216, ex-LST-279) was stricken in 1978.

◆ **4 ex-U.S. LSM-1-class medium landing ships**

		Bldr	In serv.
637	MEI LO (ex-LSM-362)	Brown SB, Houston, Tex.	11-1-45
659	MEI PING (ex-LSM-471)	Brown SB, Houston, Tex.	23-2-45
694	MEI SUNG (ex-LSM-457)	Western Pipe & Steel, San Pedro, Cal.	28-3-45
649	MEI TSENG (ex-LSM-431)	Dravo, Wilmington, Del.	25-2-45

Mei Tseng—wearing old number   1969

D: 1,095 tons (fl)   **S:** 12.5 kts   **Dim:** 62.03 (59.89 wl) × 10.52 × 2.54 (max.)
Man: 60 men   **Fuel:** 161 tons   **Electric:** 240 kw
A: 2/40-mm AA—4 or 8/20-mm AA (I or II × 4)—4/12.7-mm machine guns (I × 4)
2 props; 2,800 hp

REMARK: *Mei Sung* and *Mei Tseng* transferred in 1946, *Mei Ping* in 11-56, and *Mei Lo* in 5-62.

AMPHIBIOUS WARFARE SHIPS (continued)

◆ **6 ex-U.S. LCU-1466-class utility landing craft** Bldr: Ishikawajima, Harima, Japan

. . . Ho SHAN (ex-LCU-1596)	. . . Ho MENG (ex-LCU-1599)
. . . Ho CHUAN (ex-LCU-1597)	. . . Ho MOU (ex-LCU-1600)
. . . Ho SENG (ex-LCU-1598)	. . . Ho SHOU (ex-LCU-1601)

Ho Mou—wearing old number   1955

D: 347 tons (fl)   **S:** 8 kts   **Dim:** 35.08 × 10.36 × 1.6 (max.)
A: 4/20-mm AA (II × 2)   **Man:** 14 men   **Range:** 1,200/6
Fuel: 11 tons
M: 3 Gray Marine 64/65YTL diesels; 3 props; 675 hp

REMARKS: Built under Offshore Procurement Program. In service in 3-55. Cargo: 167 tons.

◆ **16 ex-U.S. LCU-501-(LCT-(6)) class utility landing craft**

	In serv.		In serv.
. . . Ho CHANG (ex-LCU-512)	7-9-43	. . . Ho DENG (ex-LCU-1367)	12-10-44
. . . Ho CHAO (ex-LCU-1429)	8-12-44	. . . Ho FENG (ex-LCU-1397)	26-10-44
. . . Ho CHENG (ex-LCU-1145)	11-5-44	. . . Ho HOEI (ex-LCU-1218)	25-8-44
. . . Ho CHI (ex-LCU-1212)	16-8-44	. . . Ho SHUN (ex-LCU-1225)	4-9-44
. . . Ho CHIE (ex-LCU-700)	18-5-44	. . . Ho TENG (ex-LCU-1452)	20-10-44
. . . Ho CHIEN (ex-LCU-1278)	22-7-44	. . . Ho TSUNG (ex-LCU-1213)	17-8-44
. . . Ho CHUN (ex-LCU-892)	27-7-44	. . . Ho YAO (ex-LCU-1244)	22-9-44
. . . Ho CHUNG (ex-LCU-849)	7-8-44	. . . Ho YUNG (ex-LCU-1271)	19-8-44

D: 143 tons (309 fl)   **S:** 10 kts   **Dim:** 36.3 (32.0 wl) × 9.96 × 1.14
A: 2/20-mm AA (I × 2)—2/12.7-mm machine guns   **Man:** 10 men
M: 3 GM 6-71 diesels; 3 props; 675 hp   **Electric:** 20 kw

REMARK: Six transferred between 1946 and 1948, the others between 1958 and 1959.

◆ **several hundred U.S. LCM (3)- and LCM (6)-class landing craft**

Bldrs: U.S. and Taiwan

D: 62 tons (fl)   **S:** 9 kts   **Dim:** 17.07 × 4.37 × 1.07
A: 1/20-mm AA or 12.7-mm machine gun in some   **Man:** 5 men
M: 2 Gray Marine 64HN9 diesels; 2 props; 450 hp   **Range:** 130/9

REMARKS: LCM (3) are 56 tons (fl), 15.38 m. overall. Cargo: LCM (3): 30 tons, LCM (6): 34 tons.

◆ **about 100 U.S. LCVP class**

D: 13 tons (fl)   **S:** 9 kts   **Dim:** 10.9 × 3.21 × 1.04
A: 2/7.62-mm machine guns   **Man:** 3 men   **Range:** 110/9
M: 1 Gray Marine 64HN9 diesel; 225 hp

REMARKS: Most attached to LSTs and former APDs. Wooden construction. Cargo: 36 troops or 4 tons.

HYDROGRAPHIC SHIPS

◆ **1 ex-U.S. Cl-M-AV1-class former transport**

398 CHIU HUA (ex-Sgt. George D. Keithley, T-AGS-35, ex-T-APc-117)

Chiu Hua—wearing old number   1972

D: 6,090 tons (fl)   **S:** 11.5 kts   **Dim:** 103.18 (97.54 wl) × 15.24 × 5.33
A: 1/40-mm AA—2/20-mm AA   **Man:** 72 men
M: 1 Nordberg TSM6 diesel; 1 prop; 1,750 hp

REMARKS: Completed in 1945 as a Maritime Commission cargo ship and taken over by the U.S. Army as a personnel transport. Transferred to the U.S. Navy in 1950 and converted for hydrographic-survey duties in 1966-67. Loaned to Taiwan on 29-3-72 and sold outright on 19-5-76.

◆ **1 ex-U.S. Sotoyomo-class former auxiliary tug**

Bldr: Gulfport Boiler & Welding Works, Port Arthur, Tex.

	Laid down	L	In serv.
563 CHIU LIEN (ex-Geronimo, ATA-207)	10-11-44	4-1-45	1-3-45

HYDROGRAPHIC SHIPS (continued)

Chiu Lien
1969

D: 835 tons (fl)   **S:** 13 kts   **Dim:** 43.59 (40.74 wl) × 10.31 × 4.01
A: 1/20-mm AA   **Man:** 45 men   **Fuel:** 158 tons   **Electric:** 120 kw
M: 2 GM 12-278A diesels, electric drive; 1 prop; 1,500 hp

REMARKS: Transferred in 2-69. Operated for the Institute of Oceanology and equipped with various oceanographic winches and laboratories.

♦ **1 ex-U.S. LSIL-351-class former landing craft**

Bldr: Albina Eng. & Mach. Works, Portland Ore.

	Laid down	L	In serv.
466 LIEN CHANG (ex-LSIL-1017)	31-1-44	14-3-44	12-4-44

D: 387 tons (fl)   **S:** 14.4 kts   **Dim:** 48.46 (46.63 wl) × 7.21 × 1.73
A: 1/40-mm AA−4/20-mm AA (I × 4)   **Man:** 40 men   **Fuel:** 113 tons
M: 8 GM 6-71 diesels; 2 props; 2,320 hp

REMARKS: Transferred in 5-58. Retains LSIL appearance.

AUXILIARY SHIPS

♦ **1 offshore-island support tanker**

	Bldr	In serv.
512 WAN SHOU	Ujina SB, Hiroshima, Japan	1-11-69

Wan Shou
1970

D: 1,049 tons light (4,150 fl)   **S:** 13 kts   **Dim:** 86.5 × 16.5 × 5.5
A: 2/40-mm AA (I × 2)−2/20-mm AA (I × 2)   **Man:** 70 men
M: 1 diesel; 1 prop; 2,100 hp   **Fuel:** 230 tons

REMARKS: No underway-replenishment capability. Cargo: 2,600 tons.

♦ **3 ex-U.S. Patapsco-class support tankers**   Bldr: Cargill Inc., Savage, Minn.

	Laid down	L	In serv.
378 CHANG PEI (ex-*Pecatonica*, AOG-57)	6-12-44	17-3-45	28-11-45
389 HSIN LUNG (ex-*Elkhorn*, AOG-7)	7-9-42	15-5-43	12-2-44
342 LUNG CHUAN (ex-*Endeavor*, ex-*Namakagon*, AOG-53)	1-8-44	4-11-44	10-5-45

D: 1,850 tons light (4,335 fl)   **S:** 14 kts
Dim: 94.72 (89.0 wl) × 14.78 × 4.78
A: 2/76-mm DP (I × 2)−4/20-mm AA (I × 4)   **Man:** 124 men
Fuel: 295 tons
M: 2 GM 16-278A diesels; 2 props; 3,300 hp   **Electric:** 460 kw

REMARKS: Former gasoline tankers. Cargo: 2,040 tons. *Chang Pei* transferred on 24-4-61, *Hsin Lung* on 1-7-72, and *Lung Chuan* on 29-6-71 after serving in the New Zealand Navy as antarctic supply ship since 5-10-62. All used for supplying offshore islands.

♦ **1 transport**

	Bldr	L	In serv.
522 LING YUEN	Taiwan SB, Keelung	27-1-75	15-8-75

D: 4,000 tons (fl)   **S:** . . .   **Dim:** 100.2 ×14.6 × 5.0
A: 2/20-mm AA (I × 2)−2/12.7-mm machine guns (I × 2)   **Man:** 55 men
M: 1 6-cylinder diesel; 1 prop; . . . hp

REMARKS: 2,510 dwt/3,040 grt. Can carry 500 troops. There is also a slightly smaller Taiwanese-built transport, name not available.

♦ **1 ex-U.S. Achelous-class transport**   Bldr: Kaiser Co., Vancouver, Wash.

	Laid down	L	In serv.
520 WU TAI (ex-*Sung Shan*, ex-*Agenor*, ARL-3, ex-LST-490)	24-1-43	3-4-43	20-8-43

D: 4,100 tons (fl)   **S:** 11.6 kts   **Dim:** 99.98 × 15.24 × 3.4
A: 8/40-mm AA (IV × 2)   **Man:** 100 men + 600 troops   **Electric:** 500 kw
M: 2 GM 12-567A diesels; 2 props; 1,800 hp

REMARKS: Converted to a repair ship while building. Transferred to France in 1951, then to Taiwan on 15-9-57. Converted to transport, 1973-74.

♦ **1 ex-U.S. Army small transport**   Bldr: Higgins, New Orleans, La.

359 YUNG KANG (ex-*Mark*, AKL-12, ex-AG-143, ex-Army FS-214)

D: 640 tons (930 fl)   **S:** 13 kts   **Dim:** 54.86 (52.37 wl) × 9.75 × 3.05
A: 2/20-mm AA (I × 2)   **Man:** 37 men   **Range:** 3,700/11
Fuel: 100 tons
M: 2 GM 6-278A diesels; 2 props; 1,000 hp   **Electric:** 225 kw

REMARKS: Built as a training version of the U.S. Army FS-381 class, with lengthened forecastle for more accommodations. In service on 21-12-44. Transferred to the U.S. Navy on 30-9-47 and to Taiwan on 1-6-71. Sold outright on 19-5-76. Now has intelligence-gathering equipment. Cargo: 210 tons.

AUXILIARY SHIPS *(continued)*

Yung Kang — wearing old number   1971

◆ **1 ex-U.S. Amphion-class repair ship**   Bldr: Tampa SB, Tampa, Fla.

	Laid down	L	In serv.
358 Yu Tai (ex-*Cadmus*, AR-14)	30-10-44	5-8-45	23-4-46

D: 7,826 tons light (14,490 fl)   **S:** 16.5 kts
Dim: 149.96 (141.73 pp) × 21.18 × 8.38
A: 1/127-mm DP (*see* Remarks)   **Man:** 920 men   **Fuel:** 2,430 tons
Boilers: 2 Foster-Wheeler D-type, 30.6 kg/cm² pressure—superheat 399°C
M: 1 set Westinghouse GT; 1 prop; 8,500 hp   **Electric:** 3,600 kw

REMARKS: Transferred on 15-1-74. Additional antiaircraft armament has probably been added over that listed on transfer date.

◆ **1 ex-U.S. Diver-class salvage ship**   Bldr: Basalt Rock Co., Napa, Cal.

	Laid down	L	In serv.
. . . Tai Hu (ex-*Grapple*, ARS-7)	8-9-42	31-12-42	16-12-43

D: 1,530 tons (1,900 fl)   **S:** 14.8 kts
Dim: 65.08 (63.09 wl) × 11.89 × 4.29
A: 2/20-mm AA (I × 2)   **Man:** 85 men   **Fuel:** 283 tons
Electric: 460 kw
M: 2 Cooper-Bessemer GSB-8 diesels, electric drive; 2 props; 3,000 hp

REMARK: Transferred on 1-12-77.

◆ **3 ex-U.S. Cherokee- and Abneki-class fleet tugs**
Bldrs: *Ta Wan*: Charleston SB & DD, S.C.   others: United Eng., Alameda, Cal.

	Laid down	L	In serv.
. . . Ta Han (ex-*Tawakoni*, ATF-114)	19-5-43	28-10-43	15-9-44
548 Ta Tung (ex-*Chickasaw*, ATF-83)	14-2-42	23-7-42	4-2-43
550 Ta Wan (ex-*Apache*, ATF-67)	8-11-41	8-5-42	12-12-42

D: 1,235 tons (1,675 fl)   **S:** 15 kts   **Dim:** 62.48 (59.44 wl) × 11.73 × 4.67
A: 1/76-mm DP—2/12.7-mm machine guns   **Man:** 85 men
Fuel: 295 tons
M: 4 GM 12-278 diesels, electric drive; 1 prop; 3,000 hp   **Electric:** 260 kw

REMARKS: *Ta Tung* transferred in 1-66 (sold on 19-5-75), *Ta Wan* on 30-6-74, and *Ta Han* on 1-6-78. *Ta Han* has Busch-Sulzer BS-539 diesels and only a small exhaust pipe.

◆ **3 ex-U.S. Sotoyomo-class ocean tugs**   Bldr: Levingston SB, Orange, Tex.

	Laid down	L	In serv.
395 Ta Peng (ex-*Mohopac*, ATA-196)	24-11-44	21-12-44	6-3-45
357 Ta Sueh (ex-*Tonkawa*, ATA-176)	30-1-44	1-3-44	19-8-44
367 Ta Teng (ex-*Cahokia*, ATA-186)	16-8-44	18-9-44	24-11-44

D: 435 tons (835 fl)   **S:** 13 kts   **Dim:** 43.59 (40.74 wl) × 10.31 × 4.01
A: 1/76-mm DP—2/20-mm AA (I × 2)   **Man:** 45 men   **Fuel:** 158 tons
M: 2 GM 12-278A diesels, electric drive; 1 prop; 1,500 hp   **Electric:** 120 kw

REMARKS: *Ta Peng* transferred on 1-7-71, *Ta Sueh* in 4-62, and *Ta Teng* on 29-3-72 after serving the U.S. Air Force since 1971. Sister *Chiu Lien* is an oceanographic research ship.

SERVICE CRAFT

◆ **1 ex-U.S. 174-foot yard oiler**   Bldr: Manitowoc SB, Wisc.
504 Szu Ming (ex-YO-198)

D: 650 tons (1,595 fl)   **S:** 10.5 kts   **Dim:** 53.04 × 9.75 × . . .
A: 1/40-mm AA—5/20-mm AA (I × 5)   **Man:** 65 men
M: 1 Union diesel; 1 prop; 560 hp

REMARKS: Built in 1945 and transferred in 12-49. In reserve.

◆ **1 ex-U.S. Army large tug**
373 Ta Yu (ex-LT-310)

Ta Yu — wearing old number

REMARK: Transferred in 4-49.

◆ **6 ex-U.S. Navy YTL-422 class**

YTL 8 (ex-ST-2002)	YTL 10 (ex-ST-2008)	YTL 12 (ex-YTL-584)
YTL 9 (ex-ST-2004)	YTL 11 (ex-YTL-454)	YTL 14 (ex-YTL-585)

D: 75 tons (fl)   **S:** 8 kts   **Dim:** 20.3 × 5.18 × 1.5
M: 1 diesel; 1 prop; 300 hp

REMARK: YTL-8 to YTL-10 transferred in 3-62, YTL-11 in 8-63, YTL-12 and YTL-14 in 7-64.

TAIWAN – REPUBLIC OF CHINA *(continued)*

SERVICE CRAFT *(continued)*

♦ **1 ex-U.S. ARD-12-class floating dry dock**

FO WU 6 (ex-*Windsor*, ARD-22)

    Dim: 149.86 × 24.69 × 1.73 (light)   **Capacity:** 3,500 tons

REMARK: Built in 1944, transferred on 19-5-76.

♦ **1 ex-U.S. ARD-2-class floating dry dock**

FO WU 5 (ex-ARD-9)

    Dim: 148.03 × 21.64 × 1.75 (light)   **Capacity:** 3,500 tons

REMARK: Built in 1943, transferred on 12-1-77.

♦ **2 ex-U.S. floating dry docks**

HAY TAN (ex-AFDL-36)   HAN JIH (ex-AFDL-34)

    Dim: 73.15 × 19.69 × 1.3 (light)   **Capacity:** 1,000 tons

REMARK: Built in 1943, transferred in 3-47 and 7-59.

♦ **1 ex-U.S. floating dry dock**

KIM MEN (ex-AFDL-5)

    Dim: 60.96 × 19.5 × 1.04   **Capacity:** 1,000 tons

REMARK: Built in 1944, transferred in 1-48.

CUSTOMS SERVICE

Subordinate to the Ministry of Finance

PATROL SHIPS

♦ **2 ex-U.S. Admirable-class former minesweepers**

	Bldr	L	In serv.
HUNG HSING (ex-*Embattle*, MSF-226)	American SB, Lorain, O.	17-9-44	25-4-45
N . . . (ex-*Improve*, AM-247)	Savannah Mach., Ga.	26-9-43	29-2-44

    D: 945 tons (fl)   **S:** 14.8 kts   **Dim:** 56.24 × 10.06 × 2.97
    A: 2/20-mm AA   **M:** 2 Cooper-Bessemer GSB-8 diesels; 2 props; 1,710 hp

REMARK: Transferred to Taiwan in late 1940s and handed over to the Customs Service in early 1970s.

♦ **3 ex-U.S. PC-461-class submarine chasers**

	Bldr	In serv.
N . . . (ex-*Tung Kiang*, ex-*Placerville*, PC-1087)	G. Lawley, Neponset, Mass.	22-5-44
N . . . (ex-*Hsi Kiang*, ex-*Susanville*, PC-1149)	Defoe, Bay City, Mich.	22-6-44
N . . . (ex-*Pei Kiang*, ex-*Hanford*, PC-1142)	Defoe, Bay City, Mich.	3-6-44

    D: 280 tons (450 fl)   **S:** 20 kts   **Dim:** 52.93 × 7.01 × 2.72
    A: 2/20-mm AA (I × 2)   **M:** 2 GM 16-278A diesels; 2 props; 2,880 hp
    Fuel: 62 tons

REMARK: Transferred in 7-57 and turned over to the Customs Service in early 1970s.

PATROL CRAFT

♦ **2 aluminum-hulled**   Bldr: Halter Marine, New Orleans, 1977

    D: 70 tons   **S:** . . .   **Dim:** 23.77 × . . . × . . .
    A: . . .   **M:** 2 GM diesels; 2 props; . . . hp

TANZANIA

PERSONNEL: Approximately 700 men

MERCHANT MARINE (1978): 26 ships – 39,968 grt
                       (2 tankers – 497 grt)

PATROL BOATS

♦ **7 Chinese Shanghai-II class**

JW 9861 to JW 9867

JW 9862   1975

    D: 120 tons (155 fl)   **S:** 28 kts   **Dim:** 38.8 × 5.8 × 1.6
    A: 4/37-mm AA (II × 2) – 4/25-mm AA (II × 2)
    Electron Equipt: Radar: 1/Pot Head   **Man:** 28 men
    M: 4 diesels; 4 props; 4,800 hp

REMARK: Transferred 1970-71.

TORPEDO BOATS

♦ **4 Chinese Hu Chwan class**

JW 9841 to JW 9844

TANZANIA (*continued*)

TORPEDO BOATS (*continued*)

JW 9842   1976

D: 39 tons   **S:** 54 kts   **Dim:** 21.8 × 4.9 × 1.0
A: 4/14.5-mm machine guns (II × 2) − 2/533-mm TT (I × 2)
Electron Equipt: Radar: 1/Skin Head
M: 3 M50 diesels; 3 props; 3,600 hp

REMARKS: Transferred 1975. Unlike Chinese Navy Hu Chwans, these craft have no hydrofoils. Gun mounts are fore and aft, while on most units of this class both mounts are aft.

COASTAL PATROL CRAFT

◆ **3 Soviet P-6-class former torpedo boats**

D: 62 tons (fl)   **S:** 43 kts   **Dim:** 25.3 × 6.1 × 1.6
A: 4/25-mm AA   **Electron Equipt:** Radar: 1/Pot Head
Man: 12 men   **Range:** 400/32, 700/15
M: 4 M50 diesels; 4 props; 4,800 hp

REMARKS: Transferred from East Germany in 1974-75. Torpedo tubes removed before transfer. Bridges enclosed. Wooden construction.

◆ **2 East German Schwalbe-class former inshore minesweepers**

ARAKA   SALAAM

D: 70 tons (fl)   **S:** 14 kts   **Dim:** 26.0 × 4.5 × 1.4
A: 2/25-mm AA (II × 2)   **M:** 2 diesels; 2 props; 600 hp

REMARKS: Transferred in 1-66 and 1-67. Minesweeping gear removed. No radar.

◆ **4 Chinese Yu Lin-class craft**

D: 27 tons   **S:** 20 kts   **Dim:** 13.0 × 4.0 × 1.2
A: 1/12.7-mm machine gun   **M:** 2 diesels; 2 props; 600 hp

REMARKS: Transferred by the Chinese People's Republic in 11-66. These craft operate on Lake Victoria.

◆ **2 aluminum-hulled craft**   Bldr: Bayerische Schiffsbau, West Germany, 1967

RAFIKI   UHURU

D: 40 tons   **S:** 14 kts   **Dim:** 24.0 × 5.0 × 1.3

Rafiki or Uhuru

A: 1/40-mm AA − 2/machine guns
M: 2 Caterpillar diesels; 2 props; . . . hp

◆ **1 Soviet Poluchat-1 class**

D: 90 tons (fl)   **S:** 19 kts   **Dim:** 29.6 × 5.8 × 1.6
A: 2/14.5-mm AA   **Electron Equipt:** Radar: 1/Skin Head
Man: 15 men   **Range:** 460/17
M: 2 M50 diesels; 2 props; 2,400 hp

REMARKS: May be of the torpedo retriever variant, armed. Transferred sometime in the 1970s.

HYDROGRAPHIC SHIPS

◆ **1 coastal survey craft**   Bldr: Bayerische Schiffsbau, West Germany, 1979

UTAFITI

D: 33 tons (fl)   **S:** 14 kts   **Dim:** 19.05 × . . . × 1.0
Electron Equipt: Radar: 1/Decca 060   **Range:** 250/12   **Man:** 6 men
M: 2 Caterpillar diesels; 2 props; 456 hp

REMARKS: Has Atlas DESO 10 echo-sounder. Steel hull, aluminum superstructure.

◆ **2 ex-Chinese landing craft for logistics duties.**

THAILAND

PERSONNEL (1978): Navy: approximately 13,000 men − Marines: 7,000 men

MERCHANT MARINE (1978): 117 ships − 335,116 grt
(tankers: 35 ships − 151,220 grt)

NAVAL AVIATION: Available are: 9 Grumman S-2F land-based ASW aircraft, 2 SU-16 amphibians, 12 C-46 and C-47 transports (plus 12 more in mothballs), 21 Cessna 0-1 Birddog observation aircraft, 4 U-17 Skywagon utility aircraft, 2 Lake L-A4 Skimmer training amphibians, and 3 Bell UH-1H and 10 Bell 212 helicopters.

FRIGATES

◆ 1 "Yarrow frigate" class   Bldr: Yarrow, Scotstoun, Glasgow, Scotland

	Laid down	L	In serv.
7 MAKUT RAJAKUMARN	11-1-70	18-11-71	7-5-73

Makut Rajakumarn   Yarrow, 1975

D: 1,650 tons (1,900 fl)   **S:** 26 kts (gas turbine)/18 kts (diesel)
Dim: 97.56 (92.99 pp) × 10.97 × 5.5   **Man:** 16 officers, 124 men
A: 2/114-mm DP Mk 8 − 1/Sea Cat Mk 10 − 2/40-mm AA (I × 2) − 1/Limbo ASW mortar (III × 1) − 2/depth-charge projectors, 1/depth-charge rack
Electron Equipt: Radars: 1/HSA LWO-4, 1/Decca 626, 1/HSA WM.22, 1/HSA WM.44
            Sonars: 1/170B, 1/162, 1/Plessey MS27
Range: 1,000/25, 4,000/18   **Electric:** 2,200 kw
M: CODOG: 1 Rolls-Royce Olympus TBM 3B gas turbine (23,125 hp), 1 Crossley-Pielstick 12 PC2 diesel; 6,000 hp; 2 controllable-pitch props

REMARKS: Similar to the Malaysian *Rahmat* but longer and more heavily armed. Highly automated. The WM.22 track-while-scan radar controls the 114-mm guns; the WM.44 controls the Sea Cat missiles.

◆ 2 ex-U.S. PF-103 class

	Bldr	Laid down	L	In serv.
5 TAPI (ex-PF-107)	American SB, Toledo, Oh.	1-4-70	17-10-70	1-11-71
6 KHIRIRAT (ex-PF-108)	Norfolk SB & DD, Va.,	18-2-72	2-6-73	10-8-74

D: 864 tons light (1,143 fl)   **S:** 20 kts
Dim: 84.04 × 10.06 × 3.05 (4.27 sonar)
A: 2/76.2-mm DP Mk 34 (I × 2) − 2/40-mm AA (II × 1) − 1/Mk 11 Hedgehog − 6/324-mm Mk 32 ASW TT (III × 2) − 1/Mk 9 depth-charge rack
Electron Equipt: Radars: 1/Raytheon navigational, 1/SPS-6, 1/SPG-34
            Sonar: 1/SQS-17A
Fuel: 110 tons   **Electric:** 750 kw   **Range:** 2,400/18
Man: 15 officers, 135 men
M: 2 Fairbanks-Morse 38D8⅛-10 diesels; 2 props; 5,300 hp

REMARKS: Patterned after the Italian-built *Pattimura* class for Indonesia; four sisters in the Iranian Navy. Mk 63 radar GFFCS forward for 76.2-mm guns (radar on forward

Khirirat   1974

Khirirat   1977

gun mount); Mk 51 mod 2 GFCS aft for the 40-mm anti-aircraft. Transferred on completion.

◆ 1 ex-U.S. escort   Bldr: Western Pipe and Steel, Los Angeles

	Laid down	L	In serv.
3 PIN KLAO (ex-*Hemminger*, DE-746)	8-5-43	27-12-43	30-5-44

D: 1,240 tons (fl)   **S:** 20 kts   **Dim:** 93.27 (91.44 wl) × 11.15 × 4.3 (sonar)
A: 3/76.2-mm DP Mk 22 (I × 3) − 6/40-mm AA (II × 3) − 1/Mk 10 Hedgehog − 6/324-mm Mk 32 ASW TT (III × 2) − 8/Mk 6 depth-charge projectors − 2/Mk 9 depth-charge racks

FRIGATES (continued)

Pin Klao 1967

Electron Equipt: Radar: 1/SG, 1/SPS-5, 1/SC-2, 1/Mk 26, 1/MK 32
Sonar: . . .
Range: 11,500/11 **Fuel:** 260 tons **Electric:** 680 kw **Man:** 220 men
M: 2 GM 16-278A diesels, electric drive; 2 props; 6,000 hp

REMARKS: Transferred 7-59; sold outright 6-6-75, at which time the ship underwent extensive overhaul in Guam. Has Mk 52 radar GFCS for 76.2-mm guns, one Mk 63 radar GFCS and two Mk 51 mod 2 optical GFCS for the 40-mm anti-aircraft.

◆ **2 ex-U.S. patrol frigates** Bldr: Consolidated Steel, Los Angeles

	Laid down	L	In serv.
1 TAHCHIN (ex-*Glendale*, PF-36)	6-4-43	28-5-43	1-10-43
2 PRASAE (ex-*Gallup*, PF-47)	18-8-43	17-9-43	29-2-44

Prasae 1977

D: 1,430 tons (2,100 fl) **S:** 19 kts
Dim: 92.63 (87.02 pp) × 11.43 × 4.17 (hull)
A: 3/76.2 DP (I × 3) − 2/40-mm AA (I × 2) − 9/20-mm AA (I × 9) − 1/Mk 10 Hedgehog −
8/Mk 6 depth-charge projectors − 2/Mk 9 depth-charge racks

Electron Equipt: Radars: 1/SPS-5, 1/SPS-6 Sonar: QCU
Man: 180 men **Range:** 5,600/16, 7,800/12
Boilers: 2, 3-drawn Express; 16.9 kg/cm² **Fuel:** 685 tons
M: 2 sets triple-expansion steam; 2 props; 5,500 hp

REMARKS: Transferred 29-10-57. Both refitted at Guam in the early 1970s, but the *Prasae* was damaged in a collision in 1-72, and never fully repaired. Last "active" examples of a class that once numbered 102 ships.

GUIDED-MISSILE PATROL BOATS

◆ **3 Ratcharit class** Bldr: Breda, Venice, Italy

	L	In serv.
4 RATCHARIT	31-7-78	1979
5 WITTHAYAKOM	. . .	1979
6 UDOMET	. . .	1979

D: 235 tons normal (270 fl) **S:** 36 kts **Dim:** 49.8 (47.25 pp) × 7.5 × 1.68
A: 4/MM 38 Exocet (II × 2) − 1/76-mm DP OTO Melara − 2/40-mm AA Breda (II × 1)
Electron Equipt: 1/navigational, 1/HSA M 25
Range: 650/36, 2,000/15 **Man:** 7 officers, 38 men **Electric:** 440 kw
M: 3 MTU MD20 V538 TB91 diesels; 3 controllable-pitch props; 13,500 hp

REMARKS: Ordered 23-7-76. Can make 20 kts on one engine.

◆ **3 Prabrarapak class** Bldr: Singapore SB & Eng. Co., Jurong, Singapore

	L	In serv.
1 PRABRARAPAK	29-7-75	28-7-76
2 HANHAK SATTRU	28-10-75	6-11-76
3 SUPHAIRIN	20-2-76	1-2-77

D: 224 tons (260 fl) **S:** 34 kts **Dim:** 44.9 × 7.0 × 2.1
A: 5/Gabriel (III × 1, I × 2) − 1/57-mm AA Bofors − 1/40-mm AA Bofors
M: 4 MTU diesels; 4 props; 14,400 hp **Man:** 40 men

REMARK: Similar to the Singapore Navy's Lürssen-designed boats; built under license.

PATROL BOATS

◆ **3 T 91 class** Bldr: Royal Thai Naval Dockyard, Bangkok

T 91 T 92 T 93

T 92 G. Arra

PATROL BOATS (continued)

D: 87.5 tons   **S:** 25 kts   **Dim:** 31.8 × 5.36 × 1.5
A: 2/40-mm AA – 1/12.7-mm machine guns   **Man:** 21 men
M: 2 MTU diesels; 2 props; 3,300 hp   **Range:** 770/21

REMARKS: T 91 launched in 1965; others, 1973. T 93 reported 36.0 × 5.7 × 1.7. T 91 has a longer superstructure and no spray strakes on the hull sides forward, and only one 40-mm anti-aircraft.

◆ **10 ex-U.S. PGM-71 class**   Bldr: Peterson Builders, Sturgeon Bay, Wis.

	L		L
T 11 (ex-PGM-71)	22-5-65	T 16 (ex-PGM-115)	24-4-69
T 12 (ex-PGM-79)	18-12-65	T 17 (ex-PGM-116)	3-6-69
T 13 (ex-PGM-107)	13-4-67	T 18 (ex-PGM-117)	24-6-69
T 14 (ex-PGM-113)	3-6-69	T 19 (ex-PGM-123)	4-5-70
T 15 (ex-PGM-114)	24-6-69	T 20 (ex-PGM-124)	22-6-70

T 11   G. Arra, 1976

D: 130 tons (144 fl)   **S:** 17 kts   **Dim:** 30.81 × 6.45 × 2.3
A: 1/40-mm AA – 4/20-mm AA (II × 2) – 2/12.7-mm machine guns
M: 8 GM 6-71 diesels; 2 props; 2,040 hp
Man: 30 men   **Range:** 1,000/12

◆ **1 Klongyai class**   Bldr: Royal Thai Naval Dockyard, Bangkok

	Laid down	L	In serv.
8 SATTAHIP	21-11-56	28-10-57	1958

Sattahip   1957

D: 110 tons (135 fl)   **S:** 18 kts   **Dim:** 42.0 × 4.6 × 1.5
A: 1/40-mm AA – 2/20-mm AA (II × 1) – 2/457-mm TT
Man: 31 men   **Range:** 475/15   **Fuel:** 18 tons
Boilers: 2 Yarrow watertube
M: 2 sets GT; 2 props; 2,000 hp

REMARK: Survivor of a class of eight, the others of which were all built in Japan in the late 1930s.

◆ **4 ex-U.S.C.G. Cape-class**   Bldr: U.S. Coast Guard, Curtis Bay, Md., 1953

T 81   T 82   T 83   T 84

T 84 – with old number   1967

PATROL BOATS (continued)

D: 105 tons (fl)   **S:** 18 kts   **Dim:** 28.95 × 5.8 × 1.55
A: 1/20-mm AA−2/Mk 20 Mousetrap ASW RL−2/depth-charge racks
Electron Equipt: Radar: 1/SPN-21   Sonar: QCO
Man: 15 men   **Range:** 2,600/9   **Electric:** 40 kw
M: 4 Cummins VT-12-M diesels; 2 props; 2,200 hp

REMARKS: Transferred in 1954. Previously numbered 13 through 16.

◆ **7 ex-U.S. PC-461 class**

			L	In serv.
1	SARASIN (ex-PC-495)	Dravo, Pittsburgh	30-12-41	23-4-42
2	THAYANCHON (ex-PC-575)	Dravo, Pittsburgh	5-5-42	8-8-42
4	PHALI (ex-PC-1185)	Gibbs, Jacksonville, Fla.	27-8-43	24-4-44
5	SUKRIP (ex-PC-1218)	Luders, Stamford, Conn.	24-10-43	29-5-44
6	TONGPLIU (ex-PC-616)	G. Lawley, Neponset, Mass.	4-7-42	19-8-42
7	LIULOM (ex-PC-1253)	Brown, Houston, Tex.	14-10-42	1-4-43
8	LONGLOM (ex-PC-570)	Albina, Portland, Ore.	11-9-41	9-5-42

Tongpliu−outboard **Thayanchon**

D: 280 tons (450 fl)   **S:** 19 kts   **Dim:** 52.93 × 7.01 × 2.31 (3.31 sonar)
A: 1/76.2-mm DP−1/40-mm AA−5/20-mm AA−2/324-mm Mk 32 ASW TT (I × 2)−
2/Mk 6 depth-charge projectors−2/depth-charge racks
Man: 62-71 men   **Range:** 6,000/10   **Fuel:** 60 tons   **Electric:** 120 kw
M: 2 Hoover, Owens, & Rentschler RB-99DA diesels; 2 props; 2,560 hp

REMARKS: In poor condition. Transferred 1947-52. The *Sarasin* does not have the two
fixed ASW torpedo tubes. The *Tongpliu*, the *Liulom*, and the *Longlom* have two
Fairbanks-Morse 38D8⅛ diesels; 2,880 hp.

PATROL CRAFT

◆ **12 ex-U.S. Swift Mk II-class inshore patrol craft**   Bldr: Swiftships, La.

T 27 to T 35   T 210 to T 212

D: 20 tons (fl)   **S:** 25 kts   **Dim:** 15.64 × 4.14 × 1.06
A: 3/12.7-mm machine guns (II × 1, and 1 combined with an 81-mm mortar)
Man: 1 officer, 7 men   **Range:** 400/24
M: 2 GM 12-V 71 N diesels; 2 props; 860 hp

REMARK: Transferred 1967-75.

◆ **37 ex-U.S. PBR Mk II river patrol boats**

D: 8 tons (fl)   **S:** 24 kts   **Dim:** 9.73 × 3.53 × 0.6   **Man:** 4 men
Range: 150/23
A: 3/12.7-mm machine guns (II × 1, I × 1)−1/60-mm mortar
M: 2 Detroit 6-V-53N diesels; 2 Jacuzzi waterjets; 430 hp

REMARK: Transferred: 20 in 1957-67; 10 in 1972; 7 in . . . .

◆ **3 ex-U.S. 36-foot RPC class**

T 21   T 22   T 23

T 21   G. Arra, 1976

D: 10.4 tons (13 fl)   **S:** 14 kts   **Dim:** 10.9 × 3.15 × 1.0
A: 4/12.7-mm machine guns (II × 2)−2/7.62-mm machine guns (I × 2)
M: 2 Gray Marine 64 HN9 diesels; 2 props; 450 hp   **Man:** 6 men

REMARKS: Transferred 3-67. Survivors of six. Unsuccessful design, supplanted by PBR
in the U.S. Navy.

MINE WARFARE SHIPS

◆ **2 Bangrachan-class minelayers**   Bldr: C. R. del Adriatico, Monfalcone, Italy

		Laid down	L	In serv.
1	BANGRACHAN	20-1-36	22-7-36	28-11-36
2	NHONG SARHAI	20-1-36	12-7-36	28-11-36

Nhong Sarhai   1967

MINE WARFARE SHIPS *(continued)*

D: 319 tons (408 fl)   **S:** 12 kts   **Dim:** 49.0 × 7.96 × 2.2
Man: 55 men   **Range:** 2,690/10   **Fuel:** 33.5 tons
A: 1/76-mm AA – 1/40-mm AA – 2/20-mm AA (I × 2) – 142 mines
M: 2 Burmeister & Wain diesels; 2 props; 540 hp

◆ **1 mine countermeasures support ship**   Bldr: Mitsubishi, Shimonoscki

		L	In serv.
11	RANG KWIEN (ex-*Yumihari Mara*)	16-12-44	12-3-45

Rang Kwien   1968

D: 586 tons (883 fl)   **S:** 12 kts   **Dim:** 51.8 (48.8 pp) × 9.5 × 3.5
A: 2/20-mm AA (I × 2)   **Electron Equipt:** Radar: 1/Decca 707
Boilers: 2
M: 2 sets vertical triple-expansion steam; 2 props; 2,200 hp

REMARKS: Former Imperial Japanese Navy *Miura*-class salvage tug, acquired 6-9-67 and converted to serve as headquarters and support ship for mine warfare units. Hull has no compound curves in form and no camber.

◆ **4 ex-U.S. MSC-289-class coastal minesweepers**

		Bldr	In serv.
5	LADYA (ex-MSC-297)	Peterson, Sturgeon Bay, Wis.	14-12-63
6	BANGKEO (ex-MSC-303)	Dorchester SB, Camden, N.J.	9-7-65
7	TADINDENG (ex-MSC-301)	Tacoma Boat, Wash.	23-8-65
8	DON CHEDI (ex-MSC-313)	Peterson, Sturgeon Bay, Wis.	17-9-65

Bangkeo   1967

D: 330 tons (362 fl)   **S:** 13 kts   **Dim:** 44.32 × 8.29 × 2.6
A: 2/20-mm AA (II × 1)
Electron Equipt: Radar: 1/Decca 707   Sonar: UQS-1D
Man: 7 officers, 36 men   **Range:** 2,500/10
M: 4 GM 6-71 diesels; 2 props; 1,000 hp

REMARKS: Transferred on completion. Wooden construction. Four new minesweepers are projected.

◆ **5 ex-U.S. 50-foot motor-launch minesweepers**

MLMS 6 to MLMS 10

D: 21 tons (fl)   **S:** 8 kts   **Dim:** 15.29 × 4.01 × 1.31
A: Small arms only   **Man:** 6 men   **Range:** 150/8
M: 1 Navy DB diesel

REMARKS: Transferred 1963-66. Wooden-hulled former personnel launches, converted before transfer.

◆ **5 ex-U.S. 40-foot motor-launch minesweepers**

MLMS 1 to MLMS 5

MLMS 5   1968

D: 12.5 tons (fl)   **S:** 8 kts   **Dim:** 12.23 × 3.46 × 0.76
A: Small arms only   **Man:** 4 men   **Range:** 150/8
M: 1 Navy DB diesel; 60 hp

REMARKS: Transferred 7-61. Wooden-hulled former personnel launches, converted before transfer. Wire sweep only.

AMPHIBIOUS WARFARE SHIPS

◆ **4 ex-U.S. LST-542-class tank-landing ships**

		Bldr	L	In serv.
2	CHANG (ex-*Lincoln Cty.*, LST-898)	Dravo, Pittsburgh	25-11-44	29-12-44
3	PANGAN (ex-*Stark Cty.*, LST-1134	Chicago Br. & Iron, Ind.	16-3-45	7-4-45
4	LANTA (ex-*Stone Cty.*, LST-1141)	Chicago Br. & Iron, Ind.	18-4-45	9-5-45
5	PRATHONG (ex-*Dodge Cty.*, LST-722)	Jeffersonville Br. & Mach. Co., Ind.	21-8-44	13-9-44

AMPHIBIOUS WARFARE SHIPS *(continued)*

D: 1,625 tons (4,080 fl)   **S:** 11 kts   **Dim:** 99.98 × 15.24 × 4.36
A: 8/40-mm AA (II × 2, I × 4)   **Cargo Capacity:** 2,100 tons
M: 2 GM 12-567A diesels; 1,700 hp

REMARKS: The *Chang* was transferred in 8-62, the *Pangan* in 5-66, the *Lanta* on 12-3-70, and the *Prathong* on 17-12-75. Sister *Angthong* (ex-LST-294) was deleted in 1978. The *Chang* has a reinforced bow and waterline, originally intended for arctic navigation.

◆ 3 ex-U.S. LSM-1-class medium landing ships

Bldrs: Pullman Standard Car Mfg. Co., Chicago (3: Brown SB, Houston, Tex.)

		Laid down	L	In serv.
1	KUT (ex-LSM-338)	17-8-44	5-12-44	10-1-45
2	PHAI (ex-LSM-333)	13-7-44	27-10-44	25-11-44
3	KRAM (ex-LSM-469)	27-1-45	17-2-45	17-3-45

Kram   1967

D: 743 tons (1,095 fl)   **S:** 12.5 kts   **Dim:** 62.03 × 10.52 × 2.54
A: 2/40-mm AA (II × 1) (1, 2: 1/40-mm AA) – 4/20-mm AA (I × 4)
Electron Equipt: Radar: 1/SO-8 (3: 1/SPS-5)   **Range:** 2,500/12
M: 2 Fairbanks-Morse 38D8⅛ diesels; 2 props; 2,800 hp

REMARKS: The *Kut* and the *Phai* were transferred in 10-46, the *Kram* on 25-5-62. The *Kram* has a Mk 51 mod 2 optical lead-computing director for the 40-mm anti-aircraft.

◆ 1 ex-U.S. LCI(M)-351-class infantry-landing ship

Bldr: Commercial Iron Works, Portland, Ore.

		Laid down	L	In serv.
2	SATAKUT (ex-LSIM-739)	30-1-44	27-2-44	6-3-44

D: 231 tons (381 fl)   **S:** 14 kts   **Dim:** 48.46 × 7.21 × 1.73
A: 1/40-mm AA – 4/20-mm AA (I × 4)   **Electron Equipt:** Radar: 1/SO-8
Man: 53 men   **Fuel:** 113 tons   **Electric:** 40 kw
M: 8 GM 6-71 diesels; 2 controllable-pitch props; 1,320 hp

REMARKS: Originally one of 60 LCIL (later LSIL) converted to carry three 107-mm chemical mortars, removed before transfer in 5-47. Now used as personnel-landing craft. Sister *Prab* (ex-LCI(M)-739) exists as a hulk.

◆ 1 ex-U.S. LSSL-1-class support-landing craft

Bldr: Commercial Iron Works, Portland, Ore.

		Laid down	L	In serv.
3	NAKHA (ex-*Himiwari*, ex-LSSL-102)	13-1-45	3-2-45	17-2-45

D: 233 tons (387 fl)   **S:** 14 kts   **Dim:** 48.16 × 10.52 × 2.54
A: 1/76.2-mm DP Mk 22 – 4/40-mm AA (II × 2) – 4/20-mm AA (I × 4) – 4/12.7-mm machine guns (I × 4) – 4/81-mm mortars (I × 4)
Electron Equipt: Radar: 1/Raytheon 1500B Pathfinder
Electric: 120 kw   **Fuel:** 84 tons
M: 8 GM 6-71 diesels; 2 controllable-pitch props; 1,320 hp

REMARKS: Transferred to Japan in 7-59 and to Thailand in 10-66 on return to U.S. control. Used mainly as a tender to small patrol craft.

◆ 6 ex-U.S. LCU-501-class utility-landing craft

		Bldr	L	In serv.
1	MATAPHON (ex-LCU-1260)	Quincy Barge, Ill.	29-7-44	8-9-44
2	RAWI (ex-LCU-800)	Mt. Vernon Br. Co., Oh.	14-6-44	16-6-44
3	ADANG (ex-LCU-861)	Darby, Kansas City, Kans.	15-2-44	22-2-44
4	PHE TRA (ex-LCU-1089)	Quincy Barge, Ill.	10-5-44	20-6-44
5	KOLUM (ex-LCU-904)	Missouri Valley, Kans.	13-5-44	17-5-44
6	TALIBONG (ex-LCU-753)	Quincy Barge, Ill.	30-3-44	10-5-44

Mataphon   1967

D: 134 tons (309 fl)   **S:** 10 kts   **Dim:** 36.3 × 9.96 × 1.14
A: 2/20-mm AA (I × 2)   **Man:** 10 men   **Fuel:** 10.5 tons
M: 3 GM 6-71 diesels; 3 props; 675 hp

REMARKS: Transferred 10-46 to 11-47. Used as logistics transports on the Chao Phyra river.

◆ 25 ex-U.S. LCM(6)-class landing craft

D: 56 tons (fl)   **S:** 9 kts   **Dim:** 17.11 × 4.27 × 1.17
Man: 5 men   **Range:** 130/9   **Cargo Capacity:** 34 tons

REMARK: Transferred 2-65 to 4-69.

◆ 8 ex-U.S. LCVP-class landing craft

AMPHIBIOUS WARFARE SHIPS *(continued)*

D: 12 tons (fl)   **S:** 9 kts   **Dim:** 10.9 × 3.21 × 1.04
Range: 110/9   **Cargo Capacity:** 39 men
M: 1 Gray Marine 64 HN 9 diesels; 225 hp

REMARKS: Transferred 3-63. Eight LCVPs are carried aboard the four Thai LSTs.

◆ **1 personnel-landing craft**   Bldr: Royal Thai Dockyard, Bangkok, 11-68

D: 10 tons (fl)   **S:** 25 kts   **Dim:** 12.0 × 3.0 × 1.0
Cargo Capacity: 35 troops
M: 2 Chrysler diesels; 2 Castoldi model 6 waterjets; . . . hp

REMARKS: Built with U.S. aid. Glass-reinforced plastic construction. Additional units may have been constructed.

HYDROGRAPHIC SHIPS

◆ **11 Chandhara**   Bldr: C. Melchers, Bremen, West Germany

Chandhara   1966

D: 870 tons (997 fl)   **S:** 13 kts   **Dim:** 70.0 (61.0 pp) × 10.5 × 3.0
A: 1/20-mm AA   **Range:** 10,000/12   **Man:** 72 men
M: 2 Deutz diesels; 2 props; 1,000 hp

REMARKS: Launched 17-12-60. Used in oceanography but built as a training ship.

◆ **2 inshore survey craft**   Bldr: Lürssen, Vegasack, West Germany, 1956

D: 96 tons (fl)   **S:** 12 kts   **Dim:** 29.0 × 5.5 × 1.5
M: 2 diesels; 2 props; . . . hp   **Man:** 8 men

AUXILIARIES

◆ **1 ex-Japanese 2TM-class support tanker/supply ship**

Bldr: Mitsubishi, Japan, 1944

3 MATRA (ex-*Wakakasa Maru*)

D: 2,395 tons (4,750 fl)   **S:** 11.5 kts   **Dim:** 98.8 (93.0 pp) × 13.8 × 6.0
A: 4/20-mm AA (I × 4)   **Boilers:** 2, watertube   **Range:** 5,000/11
M: 1 set steam turbines; 1,100 hp

REMARKS: Sister *Chula* (2) survives as a fuel-storage hulk. This class was built as an emergency measure and had no compound curves to the hull form or chamber to the decks. Acquired in 1946.

◆ **1 personnel and cargo transport**   Bldr: Ishikawajima, Harima, Japan, 10-11-37

1 SICHANG

Sichang   1978

D: 815 tons (1,369 fl)   **S:** 15 kts   **Dim:** 48.77 × 8.54 × 4.9
A: 2/40-mm AA (I × 2) – 1/20-mm AA   **Man:** 66 men
M: 2 diesels; 2 props; 550 hp

REMARK: In service since 1-38.

TRAINING SHIPS

◆ **1 ex-British Algerine-class former fleet minesweeper**

Bldr: Redfern Const. Co., Toronto, Canada

	Laid down	L	In serv.
1 PHOSAMTON (ex-*Minstrel*)	27-6-44	5-10-44	9-6-45

Phosamton   1967

TRAINING SHIPS (continued)

D: 1,010 tons (1,300 fl) **S:** 16 kts **Dim:** 68.58 × 10.82 × 3.28
A: 1/102-mm DP – 6/20-mm AA (II × 2, I × 2)
Electron Equipt: Radar: 1/Decca 45 **Boilers:** 2, 3-drum
Fuel: 235 tons **Range:** 10,000/10 **Man:** 103 men
M: 2 sets triple-expansion steam; 2 props; 2,400 hp

REMARKS: Transferred 4-47. Now mainly relegated to static training. Retains moored mechanical minesweeping equipment.

◆ **1 ex-British modified flower-class corvette**

Bldr: Ferguson Bros., Port Glasgow, Scotland

	Laid down	L	In serv.
4 BANGPAKONG (ex-*Burnet*, ex-*Gondwana*)	2-11-42	31-5-43	23-9-43

Bangpakong 1967

D: 980 tons (1,350 fl) **S:** 16.5 kts **Dim:** 63.48 × 10.11 × 5.14 (aft)
A: 1/76.2-mm DP – 1/40-mm AA – 6/20-mm AA (I × 6) – 4/depth-charge throwers – 2/depth-charge racks
Electron Equipt: Radar: 1/SG-1 **Range:** 4,500/14, 7,400/10
Boilers: 2, 3-drum **Fuel:** 337 tons **Man:** 100 men
M: 1 set triple-expansion reciprocating steam; 1 prop; 2,750 hp

REMARKS: Built for the British Navy; loaned to the Indian Navy on completion and returned in 1945; transferred to Thailand 15-5-47. Now mainly immobile.

◆ **1 Tachin-class former frigate** Bldr: Uraga Dockyard, Japan

	Laid down	L	In serv.
4 MAEKLONG	24-7-36	27-11-36	6-37

D: 1,400 tons (2,000 fl) **S:** 14 kts **Dim:** 112.5 × 10.5 × 3.2
A: 4/76-mm DP (I × 4) U.S. Mk 22 – 3/40-mm AA (I × 3) – 3/20-mm AA (I × 3) – mines
Boilers: 2, watertube **Fuel:** 487 tons
Range: 8,000/12 **Man:** 155 men
M: 2 sets triple-expansion reciprocating steam; 2 props; 2,500 hp

REMARKS: Sister *Tachin* bombed in 1945 and discarded circa 1950. Formerly carried four 102-mm guns (replaced in 1974) and four 450-mm torpedo tubes (II × 2). Now mainly immobile.

SERVICE CRAFT

◆ **1 navigational buoy tender** Bldr: Royal Thai Navy DY, Bangkok

. . . SURIYA

D: 690 tons light (960 fl) **S:** 12 kts **Dim:** 54.2 (47.3 pp) × 10.0 × 3.0
A: 2/20-mm AA (I × 2) **Electric:** 300 kw **Man:** 14 officers, 46 men
Range: 3,000/12 **Cargo Capacity:** 270 tons
M: 2 MTU diesels; 1 prop; 1,310 hp

REMARKS: In service since 18-1-79. One 10-ton crane.

◆ **2 Proet-class harbor oilers** Bldr: Royal Thai Navy DY, Bangkok

		In serv.
9	PROET	16-1-70
11	SAMED	15-12-70

Samed – while fitting out 1967

D: 360 tons (465 fl) **S:** 9 kts **Dim:** 39.0 (36.6 pp) × 6.1 × 3.1
A: 2/20-mm AA (I × 2) **M:** 1 diesel; 500 hp

◆ **1 provisions transport** Bldr: . . .

7 KLED KEO

Kled Keo 1967

SERVICE CRAFT (continued)

D: 382 tons (450 fl) **S:** 12 kts **Dim:** 46.0 × 7.6 × 4.3
A: 3/20-mm AA (I × 3) **Man:** 54 men
M: 1 diesel; 600 hp

REMARKS: Former trawler. Acquired in 1967.

◆ **2 Charn-class water tankers** Bldr: Royal Thai Navy DY

	L
6 CHARN	1965
8 CHUANG	14-1-65

Chuang   1967

D: 355 tons (485 fl) **S:** 11 kts **Dim:** 42.0 × 7.5 × 3.1
A: . . . **Man:** 29 men **M:** 1 GM diesel; 500 hp

◆ **2 new construction coastal tugs**

REMARKS: Ordered in 1979. Three hundred tons.

◆ **1 ex-British coastal tug** Bldr: Cochrane & Sons, Selby, England, 1944

1 SAMAE SAN (ex-*Empire Vincent*)

D: 274 grt (503 fl) **S:** 10.5 kts **Dim:** 34.14 (32.0 pp) × 8.23 × 4.0
A: . . . **Man:** 27 men **Boilers:** 2, watertube
M: 1 set triple-expansion reciprocating steam; 1 prop; 850 hp

REMARK: Acquired in 1947.

◆ **2 ex-Canadian small harbor tugs** Bldr: Central Bridge Co., Trenton, Ontario, 1943-44

2 KLUENG BADEN 3 MARIN VICHAI

D: 63 grt **S:** 8 kts **Dim:** 19.8 × 5.0 × 1.8
M: 1 diesel; 240 hp

REMARK: Acquired in 1953.

◆ **1 ex-U.S. 66-foot YTL-class small harbor tug** Bldr: Pearl Harbor NY, 1942

4 RAD (ex-YTL-340)

Rad   1967

D: 52 tons **S:** 8 kts **Dim:** 20.17 × 5.18 × 1.5
M: 1 diesel; 240 hp

REMARK: Transferred in 5-55.

ROYAL THAI MARINE POLICE

This organization performs duties analogous to those of a coast guard and operates a large number of patrol boats and craft. A number of the newer and larger units are listed below.

PATROL BOATS AND CRAFT

◆ **8 new construction** Bldr: Captain Co., Thailand, 1978-79

D: 18 tons **S:** 22 kts **Dim:** 16.5 × 3.8 × . . .
A: 2/12.7-mm machine guns **M:** 2 Cummins diesels; 400 hp

◆ **3 U.S. Cutlass class** Bldr: Halter Marine, New Orleans, La., 1978

807 PHRA ONG CHAO KHAMROP 808 PICHARN PHOLAKIT 809 RAM INTHRA

Phra Ong Chao Khamrop—with old number   Halter, 1978

THAILAND (*continued*)

PATROL BOATS AND CRAFT (*continued*)

> **D:** 34 tons (fl)   **S:** 25 kts   **Dim:** 19.66 × 5.18 × 1.12
> **A:** 2/12.7-mm machine guns   **Man:** 15 men   **Fuel:** 2.7 tons
> **M:** 2 GM 12 V-71 TI diesels; 2 props; 960 hp

REMARKS: Up to eight additional units of this size (but not necessarily of this design) are programmed.

◆ **1 seagoing patrol boat**   Bldr: Yokohama Yacht, Japan, 1975

1802 DAMRONG RACHANUPHAT (ex-112)

> **D:** 200 grt   **S:** 31 kts   **Dim:** 37.0 × 6.5 × . . .
> **A:** 1/76.2-mm DP – 2/20-mm AA
> **M:** 4 diesels; 2 props; 2,200 hp

◆ **2 seagoing patrol boats**

102 N . . .   103 N . . .

Police 103   1973

> **D:** Approx. 400 tons (fl)   **A:** 1/76-mm DP – 2/20-mm AA
> **M:** Diesel-powered

NOTE: There are a number of other craft, mostly armed with either one 20-mm anti-aircraft or two 12.7-mm machine guns. Most craft are Japanese-built.

Three small police launches   1973

TOGO

PERSONNEL: 200 men

MERCHANT MARINE (1978): 4 ships – 15,498 grt

PATROL BOATS

◆ **2 32-meter boats**   Bldr: C. N. de l'Estérel, Cannes, France

KARA   MONO

> **D:** 80 tons (fl)   **S:** 30 kts   **Dim:** 32.0 × 5.8 × 1.5
> **A:** 1/40-mm AA – 1/20-mm AA   **Electron Equipt:** Radar: 1/Decca 916
> **Man:** 1 officer, 17 men   **Range:** 1,500/15
> **M:** 2 MTU 12 V 493 diesels; 2,700 hp

Kara   1976

TONGA

MERCHANT MARINE (1978): 14 ships – 20,663 grt

MARITIME DEFENSE DIVISION
TONGAN DEFENSE SERVICE

PATROL CRAFT

◆ **2 fiberglass-hulled**   Bldr: Brooke Marine, Lowestoft, G.B.

P 101 NGAHAU KOULA   P 102 NGAHAU SILIVA

> **D:** 15 tons (fl)   **S:** 21 kts   **Dim:** 13.7 × 4.0 × 1.2
> **A:** 2/12.7-mm machine guns   **Electron Equipt:** Radar: 1/Decca 101
> **M:** 2 Cummins diesels; 2 props; . . . hp   **Man:** 7 men   **Range:** 800/21

REMARK: In service 10-3-73 and 10-5-74, respectively.

TRINIDAD AND TOBAGO

PERSONNEL: 280 men

MERCHANT MARINE (1978): 39 ships — 15,890 grt (1 tanker — 1,766 grt)

PATROL BOATS AND CRAFT

◆ **2 CG-40 class**   Bldr: Karlskrona, Sweden, 1980

CG 5 N . . .   CG 6 N . . .

  D: 200 tons (fl)   **S:** 31 kts   **Dim:** 40.6 × 6.7 × 1.6
  A: 1/40-mm AA — 1/20-mm AA   **Man:** 22 men   **Range:** 2,000/15-20
  M: 2 Paxman 16RP200 Valenta diesels; 2 props; 8,000 hp

REMARKS: Ordered in 8-78. The hull form is a diminutive of the *Spica* design. Will have two 50-mm rocket-flare launchers and one fire-fighting water cannon.

◆ **4 103-foot**   Bldr: Vosper, Portsmouth

	L	In serv.		L	In serv.
CG 1 TRINITY	14-4-64	20-2-65	CG 3 CHAGUARAMAS	29-3-71	18-3-72
CG 2 COURLAND BAY	20-5-64	20-2-65	CG 4 BUCCO REEF	1971	18-3-72

Courland Bay   1968

  D: 96-100 tons (123-125 fl)   **S:** 23 kts   **Dim:** 31.29 (28.95 pp) × 5.94 × 1.68
  Man: 3 officers, 14 men   **Range:** 1,800/13.5   **Fuel:** 18 tons
  A: CG-1 and CG-2: 1/40-mm; CG-3 and CG-4: 1/20-mm AA
  M: 2 Paxman 12 YJCM Ventura diesels; 2 props; 2,900 hp

REMARKS: Second pair are heavier and have slightly longer range, 2,000/13; their super-structures are broader and they do not have an enclosed pilothouse. All are air-conditioned and have roll-damping fins.

◆ **2 Sword class**   Bldr: Fairey Marine, Hamble, G.B.

CG . . . SEA SPRAY   CG . . . N . . .

  D: 15.5 tons (fl)   **S:** 28 kts   **Dim:** 13.7 × 4.1 × 1.32
  A: 1/7.62-mm machine gun   **Man:** 6 men   **Range:** 500/. . .
  M: 2 GM 8V71 TI diesels; 2 props; 850 hp

REMARK: In service in 1-78 and 1979, respectively.

◆ **1 coastal patrol craft**   Bldr: Tugs & Lighters, Ltd., Port-of-Spain, Trinidad

CG NAPARIMA

  D: 20 tons   **S:** 20 kts   **Dim:** 16.4 × 5.2 × 2.6
  M: 2 GM 6V71 diesels; 2 props; 460 hp

REMARK: In service on 15-8-76.

◆ **1 fiberglass patrol launch**   Bldr: Trinidad

  D: . . .   **S:** 27 kts   **Dim:** 7.0 × . . . × . . .
  M: 1 Caterpillar diesel; . . . hp

◆ **1 sail training ketch**   Bldr: Trinidad, 1966

HUMMINGBIRD II

REMARKS: 12 meters overall, one 3-cylinder Lister auxiliary diesel.

TUNISIA

PERSONNEL: 2,600 men

MERCHANT MARINE (1978): 41 ships — 112,303 grt (tankers: 2 ships — 27,030 grt)

FRIGATE

◆ **1 ex-U.S. Savage-class former radar picket**   Bldr: Consolidated Steel, Orange, Tex.

	Laid down	L	In serv.
E 7 PRESIDENT BOURGUIBA (ex-*Thomas J Gary*, DER-326, ex-DE-326)	15-6-43	21-8-43	27-11-43

FRIGATE *(continued)*

President Bourguiba   J.-C. Bellonne, 1974

    D: 1,590 tons (2,100 fl)   **S:** 19 kts   **Dim:** 93.26 (91.5 pp) × 11.22 × 4.0
    A: 2/76-mm DP−2/20-mm AA−6/324-mm Mk 32 ASW TT   **Man:** 160-170 men
    M: 4 Fairbanks-Morse 38D8⅛ diesels; 2 props; 6,000 hp   **Range:** 11,500/11

REMARKS: Modified as a radar picket ship in 1957, transferred on 27-10-73. SPS-8 height-finding radar, TACAN, and Hedgehog removed about 1968.

PATROL BOATS AND CRAFT

◆ **3 French P-48 class**   Bldr: SFCN, Villeneuve-la-Garenne

	L	In serv.
P 301 BIZERTE	20-11-69	10-7-70
P 302 EL HORRIA (ex-*Liberté*)	19-2-70	10-70
P 304 MONASTIR	25-6-74	25-3-75

El Horria   J.-C. Bellonne, 1973

    D: 250 tons (fl)   **S:** 22 kts   **Dim:** 48.0 (45.5 pp) × 7.1 × 2.25
    A: 2/40-mm AA (I × 2)−8/SS-12 missiles (IV × 2)   **Man:** 4 officers, 30 men
    M: 2 MGO MB-839 Bb diesels; 2 props; 4,000 hp   **Range:** 2,000/16

◆ **1 French Le Fougueux class**   Bldr: Dubigeon, 1956
P 303 SAKIET SIDI YOUSSEF (ex-UW-12, ex-PC-1618)

Sakiet Sidi Youssef   1970

    D: 325 tons (402 fl)   **S:** 18.7 kts   **Dim:** 53.1 × 6.4 × 2.1
    Man: 4 officers, 59 men   **Range:** 3,300/15, 6,350/12   **Electric:** 60 kw
    A: 1/40-mm−2/20-mm−2/Mk 20 Mousetrap ASW rocket launchers−4/depth-charge projectors−2/depth-charge racks
    M: 4 SEMT-Pielstick 14-cyl. diesels; 2 controllable-pitch props; 3,240 hp

REMARKS: Begun as P-7 for the French Navy, using U.S. "offshore" funds. Transferred to West Germany and went into service on 12-3-57 and used as a training ship at the Underwater Weapons School. Purchased by Tunisia on 16-6-70.

◆ **2 ex-U.S. Adjutant-class former coastal minesweepers**

	Bldr	In serv.
P . . . HANNIBAL (ex-*Coquelicot*, ex-MSC-48)	Steven Bros., Cal.	10-53
P . . . SOUSSE (ex-*Marjolaine*, ex-MSC-66)	Harbor Boat, Cal.	4-53

Hannibal   J.-C. Bellonne, 1973

PATROL BOATS AND CRAFT *(continued)*

D: 300 tons (372 fl)   **S:** 13 kts   **Dim:** 43.0 (41.5 pp) × 7.95 × 2.55
Man: 3 officers, 35 men   **Range:** 2,500/10   **Fuel:** 40 tons
A: 2/20-mm AA (II × 1)   **Electron Equipt:** Radar: 1/DRBN 31
                                  Sonar: 1/UQS 1D

M: 2 GM 8-268A diesels; 2 props; 1,200 hp

REMARKS: Loaned in 1973 and 1977. Minesweeping gear removed. Used in fisheries-
protection duties.

◆ **2 103-foot class**   Bldr: Vosper Thornycroft, Portchester, G.B.

	L	In serv.
P 205 TAZARKA	19-7-76	27-10-77
P 206 MENZEL BOURGUIBA	19-7-76	27-10-77

Menzel Bourguiba   1977

D: 100 tons (125 fl)   **S:** 27 kts   **Dim:** 31.29 (28.95 pp) × 6.02 × 1.98
A: 2/20-mm AA (I × 2)   **Electron Equipt:** Radar: 1/Decca 916
Man: 24 men
M: 2 MTU diesels; 2 props; 4,000 hp   **Range:** 1,500/. . .

◆ **2 ex-Chinese Shanghai-II class**

P 305 GAFSA   P 306 AMILCAR

Gafsa   1978

D: 120 tons (155 fl)   **S:** 28 kts   **Dim:** 38.8 × 5.4 × 1.6
A: 4/37-mm AA (II × 2) — 4/25-mm AA (II × 2) — depth charges
Electron Equipt: Radar: 1/Pot Head   **Man:** 25 men   **Range:** 800/17
M: 4 diesels; 4 props; 4,800 hp

REMARK: Transferred on 2-5-77.

◆ **4 French 32-meter class**   Bldr: CN de l'Estérel, Cannes

	In serv.
P 201 ISTIKLAL (ex-French V-11)	1957
P 202 JOUMHOURIA	1-61
P 203 AL JALA	11-63
P 204 REMADA	7-67

Istiklal   1970

D: 60 tons (82 fl)   **S:** 28 kts   **Dim:** 31.45 × 5.75 × 1.7
A: 2/20-mm   **Man:** 3 officers, 14 men   **Range:** 1,400/15
M: 2 MTU 12V493 diesels; 2 props; 2,700 hp

REMARKS: Wooden construction. P-201 was launched on 25-5-57 and transferred in 3-59.

TUNISIA (*continued*)

PATROL BOATS AND CRAFT (*continued*)

◆ **6 French 25-meter class**   Bldr: CN de l'Estérel, Cannes, 1961-63

V 101 to V 106

V-101 class

D: 38-39 tons   **S:** 23 kts   **Dim:** 25.0 × 4.75 × 1.25
A: 1/20-mm AA   **Man:** 10 men   **Range:** 900/16
M: 2 GM 12V71 TI diesels; 2 props; 940 hp

REMARK: V-107 and V-108 were transferred to the Fisheries Administration, disarmed, in 1971, as *Sabeq el Bahr* (T-2) and *Jaouel el Bahr* (T-3).

AUXILIARY SHIPS

◆ **1 ex-U.S. Sotoyomo-class oceangoing tug**

Bldr: Gulfport Boilers & Welding Works, Port Arthur, Tex.

	Laid down	L	In serv.
. . . RAS ADAR (ex-*Zeeland*, ex-*Pan America*, ex-*Ocean Pride*, ex-*Oriana*, ex-BAT-1)	16-3-42	15-8-42	13-12-42

D: 570 tons (835 fl)   **S:** 13 kts   **Dim:** 43.59 (41.0 pp) × 10.31 × 4.01
A: None   **Man:** 45 men   **Fuel:** 171 tons   **Electric:** 90 kw
M: 2 GM 12-278A diesels, electric drive; 1 prop; 1,500 hp

REMARKS: Built under Lend-Lease, transferred to Great Britain on 22-12-42. Returned and sold commercially in 1946. Purchased for Tunisia from Dutch company in late 1960s. BAT series had larger superstructure than standard *Sotoyomo* class and were considered to be ocean rescue tugs.

TURKEY

PERSONNEL (1978): 45,000 men

MERCHANT MARINE (1978): 460 ships — 1,358,779 grt
(tankers: 55 ships — 356,558 grt)

NAVAL AVIATION: A small naval air arm, organized in 1972, consists of sixteen S-2E Tracker ASW airplanes, three AB-204 helicopters, and six AB-212 helicopters.

WARSHIPS IN SERVICE OR UNDER CONSTRUCTION AS OF 1 JANUARY 1980

	L	Tons (surfaced)	Main armament
◆ **13 (+1) submarines**			
4 (+ 1) TYPE 209	1974	990	8/533-mm TT
2 GUPPY III	1945	1,975	10/533-mm TT
7 GUPPY II-A	1943-44	1,848	10/533-mm TT
		Tons	
◆ **12 destroyers**			
3 GEARING FRAM-I	1945-46	2,425	4/127-mm, 1 Asroc, 6/ASW TT
	1944		
2 GEARING FRAM-II	1945	2,390	4/127-mm, 1/Hedgehog, 6/ASW TT
1 ALLEN M. SUMNER FRAM-II	1944	2,200	6/127-mm, 6/ASW TT
1 ROBERT H. SMITH	1944	2,250	6/127-mm, mines
5 FLETCHER	1942-43	2,050	4/127-mm, 6/76.2-mm, 6/ASW TT
◆ **2 frigates**			
2 BERK	1971-72	1,450	4/76.2-mm, 6/ASW TT

◆ **47 patrol and torpedo boats**

◆ **43 mine warfare ships and craft**

◆ **54 amphibious warfare ships**

WEAPONS AND SYSTEMS

Most weapons and systems are furnished by the U.S.A., some by West Germany. For characteristics, *see* the sections on the U.S.A. and Germany, Federal Republic.

SUBMARINES

◆ **5 German Type 209**

Bldrs: S-347, S-348, S-349: Howaldtswerke, Kiel; S-350, S-351; Gölcük NSY

	Laid down	L	In serv.
S 347 ATILAY	2-8-72	23-10-74	29-7-75
S 348 SALDIRAY	1972	14-2-75	15-1-77
S 349 BATIRAY	11-6-75	1977	26-7-78
S 350 YILDIRAY	1977	. . .	. . .
S 351 N . . .	1977	. . .	. . .

D: 990 tons surfaced, 1,230 submerged   **S:** 10/21 max. kts
Dim: 55.0 × 6.6 × 5.9   **Man:** 6 officers, 27 men
A: 8/533-mm TT — 6 torpedoes in reserve
M: 4 MTU 12V-493-TY60 diesels; 1 Siemens electric motor, 3,600 hp

REMARKS: For further details, *see* sections on Argentina and Greece. S-350 and S-351 are being built in Turkey with German assistance. Have HSA M8 torpedo-fire control.

NOTE: A number of stricken U.S. Navy submarines have been proposed for transfer to Turkey over the last few years, all of which have been deferred by congressional

SUBMARINES *(continued)*

action. Two additional Guppy-III conversions, *Clamagore* (SS-343) and *Tiru* (SS-416), have been retained on the possibility of transfer, while sale of the *Sailfish* (SS-572) and *Salmon* (SS-573) has also been proposed. Most recently, in mid-1979, it was proposed to *lease* the *Tang* (SS-563), whose sale to Iran had been canceled. Due to the uncertainty of the political climate, no details of any of those ships are presented here.

◆ 2 ex-U.S. Guppy-III class Bldr: Electric Boat Co., Groton, Conn.

	Laid down	L	In serv.
S 333 IKINCI INONU (ex-*Corporal*, SS-346)	27-4-44	1-4-45	8-8-45
S 341 CANAKKALE (ex-*Cobbler*, SS-344)	3-4-44	1-4-45	9-11-45

D: 1,975 tons surfaced, 2,450 submerged   **S:** 17.2/14.5 kts
Dim: 99.52 × 8.23 × 5.18   **Man:** 86 men
Range: 10,000-12,000/10, 95/5 (submerged)
A: 10/533-mm TT (6 fwd, 4 aft) — 24 torpedoes
Electron Equipt: Radar: 1/SS 2A   Sonar: BQG 4 (PUFFS), BQR 2B
M: 4 GM 16-278A diesels (1,625 hp each), electric drive

REMARKS: Transferred on 21-11-73. Lengthened by 3.6 meters in 1962 at Philadelphia (S-341) and Charleston (S-333). Two 126-cell batteries.

◆ 7 ex-U.S. Guppy II-A

Bldrs: S-345: Electric Boat Co., Groton, Conn.; others: Portsmouth NSY

	Laid down	L	In serv.
S 335 BURAK REIS (ex-*Sea Fox*, SS-402)	2-11-43	28-3-44	13-6-44
S 336 MURAT REIS (ex-*Razorback*, SS-394)	9-9-43	27-1-44	3-4-44
S 337 ORUÇ REIS (ex-*Pomfret*, SS-391)	17-7-43	27-10-43	19-2-44
S 338 ULUÇ ALI REIS (ex-*Thornback*, SS-418)	5-4-44	7-7-44	13-10-44
S 340 CERBE (ex-*Trutta*, SS-421)	22-5-44	18-8-44	16-11-44
S 345 PREVEZE (ex-*Entemedor*, SS-340)	3-2-44	17-12-44	6-4-45
S 346 BIRINCI İNÖNÜ (ex-*Threadfin*, SS-410)	18-3-44	26-6-44	30-8-44

Murat Reis   1976

D: 1,525 tons, 1,848 surfaced, 3,440 submerged   **S:** 17.4/14 kts, 9.4 snorkel
Dim: 93.36 × 8.32 × 5.04   **Man:** 8-9 officers, 76 men
Range: 10,000/10, 95/5 (submerged)   **Fuel:** 330 tons
A: 10/533-mm TT (6 fwd, 4 aft) — 24 torpedoes or 40 mines, which can be laid through the tubes
Electron Equipt: Radar: 1/SS 2A   Sonar: BQR 2B, BQS 4
M: 3 Fairbanks-Morse 38D8⅛ (S-345: GM 16-278A) diesels, electric drive

REMARKS: S-335 was transferred in 12-70, S-336 in 11-70, S-337 on 3-5-72, S-338 and S-345 on 24-8-73, S-340 in 6-72, and S-346 on 15-8-73. S-336 and S-338 were at one time while in U.S. service equipped as "hard" targets for ASW training. All have high sails.

NOTE: The Guppy-IA class *Dumlupinar* (S-339, ex-*Caiman*, SS-323) was stricken in 1977, as were the Fleet Snorkel Class *Turgut Reis* (S-342, ex-*Bergall*, SS-320) and *Hizir Reis* (S-344, ex-*Mero*, SS-378).

DESTROYERS

◆ 3 ex-U.S. Gearing FRAM-I class

Bldrs: D-351: Bethlehem Steel, Quincy, Mass.; D-352: Todd Pacific SY, Seattle, Wash.; D-353: Bethlehem Steel, Staten I., N.Y.

	L	In serv.
D 351 M. FEVZI CAKMAK (ex-*Charles H. Roan*, DD-853)	15-5-46	12-9-46
D 352 GAYRET (ex-*Eversole*, DD-789)	8-1-46	10-7-46
D 353 ADATEPE (ex-*Forrest Royal*, DD-872)	17-1-45	28-6-46

Adatepe — before addition of 40-mm AA gun mounts   G. Arra, 1973

D: 2,425 tons (3,600 fl)   **S:** 32 kts
Dim: 119.03 × 12.49 × 4.56 (6.4 over sonar)
Man: 14 officers, 260 men   **Range:** 2,400/25, 4,800/15   **Fuel:** 720 tons
A: 4/127-mm 38-cal. AA (II × 2) — 4/40-mm AA (II × 1, I × 2) — 6/324-mm Mk 32 ASW TT (III × 2) — 1 Asroc system (VIII × 1) — 1/depth-charge rack
Electron Equipt: Radars: 1/SPS 10, 1/SPS 40, 1/Mk 25   Sonar: SQS 23
Boilers: 4 Foster-Wheeler and/or Babcock & Wilcox, 43.3 kg/cm² pressure — superheat 454°C
M: 2 sets GT; 2 props; 60,000 hp   **Electric:** 1,200 kw

REMARKS: D-351 was transferred on 29-9-73, D-352 on 11-7-73, and D-353 on 27-3-71. Received a twin 40-mm mount just before the bridge (with Mk-51, mod. 2, optical director) and two single 40-mm antiaircraft guns on the former DASH drone helicopter deck in the mid-1970s. D-351 has four Babcock & Wilcox boilers, while the other pair have two Babcock & Wilcox and two Foster-Wheeler boilers. D-353 has two 35-mm (II × 1) Oerlikon guns on former helicopter deck vice two single 40-mm. All have Mk-37 gunfire-control radar. All are to be modernized.

◆ 2 ex-U.S. Gearing FRAM-II class

Bldrs: D-354: Bethelehem Steel, San Pedro, Cal.; D-355: Bethlehem Steel, San Francisco, Cal.

DESTROYERS (continued)

		L	In serv.
D 354 KOCATEPE (ex-Norris, DD-859)		25-2-45	9-6-45
D 355 TINAZTEPE (ex-Keppler, DD-765)		24-6-45	23-5-47

Tinaztepe G. Arra, 1976

D: 2,390 tons (3,480 fl) **S:** 32 kts
Dim: 119.03 × 12.49 × 4.6 (6.54 over sonar)
Man: 14 officers, 260 men **Range:** 2,400/25, 4,800/15 **Fuel:** 720 tons
A: 4/127-mm DP (II × 2) − 6/40-mm AA (II × 2, I × 2) − 1/Mk 15 trainable Hedgehog − 6/324-mm Mk 32 ASW TT (III × 2) − 1/depth-charge rack
Electron Equipt: Radars: 1/SPS 10, 1/SPS 6B, 1/Mk 25
　　　　　　　　　 Sonar: 1/SQS 23
Boilers: 4 Babcock & Wilcox and/or Foster Wheeler, 43.3 kg/cm² pressure − superheat 454°C
M: 2 sets GT; 2 props; 60,000 hp **Electric:** 1,200 kw

REMARKS: A previous *Kocatepe* (ex-*Harwood*, DD-861) was lost on 21-7-74 when mistakenly bombed by the Turkish Air Force. She was replaced by the *Norris* (DD-859), which had been transferred on 7-7-74 for cannibalization spares. D-355 was transferred on 30-6-72. Two single 40-mm AA mounted on former DASH drone helicopter deck in 1974, and two twin 40-mm AA (with two Mk-51, mod. 2, directors) added on upper deck between stacks in 1977. Both have Mk-37 gunfire-control radar. D-354 has Babcock & Wilcox boilers, while D-355 has two Babcock & Wilcox and two Foster-Wheeler.

◆ 1 ex-U.S. Allen M. Sumner FRAM-II class Bldr: Federal SB, Kearney, N.J.

	Laid down	L	In serv.
D 356 ZAFER (ex-*Hugh Purvis*, DD-709)	23-5-44	17-12-44	1-3-45

Zafer 1978

D: 2,200 tons (3,300 fl) **S:** 33 kts
Dim: 114.76 × 12.49 × 4.39 (5.79 over sonar)
Range: 800/32, 4,300/11 **Fuel:** 650 tons **Electric:** 1,200 kw
A: 6/127-mm DP (II × 3) − 6/40-mm AA (II × 2, I × 2) − 2/Mk 11 Hedgehogs − 6/324-mm Mk 32 ASW TT − 1/depth-charge rack
Electron Equipt: Radars: 1/SPS 10, 1/SPS 29, 1/Mk 25
　　　　　　　　　 Sonars: SQS-29 series − ECM: ULQ 6
Boilers: 4 Babcock & Wilcox, 43.3 kg/cm² pressure − superheat 454°C
M: GT; 2 props; 60,000 hp

REMARKS: Transferred on 15-2-72. Unlike Turkish Gearing FRAM-1 and FRAM-II has complete ECM/ESM suit. In 1977 40-mm AA with two Mk-52, mod. 2, optical directors for the twin mounts were added amidships; also has Mk-37 gunfire-control radar for 127-mm DP. The large deckhouse atop the hangar, which she had while in the U.S. Navy (as ASW radar and sonar trials ship), was removed well prior to transfer.

◆ 1 ex-U.S. Robert H. Smith-class destroyer minelayer

Bldr: Bethlehem Steel, San Pedro, Cal.

	Laid down	L	In serv.
DM 357 MUAVENET (ex-*Gwin*, MMD-33, ex-DD-772)	31-10-43	9-4-44	30-9-44

D: 2,250 tons (3,375 fl) **S:** 34 kts **Dim:** 114.76 × 12.49 × 4.4 (hull)
Man: 274 men **Range:** 4,600/15 **Fuel:** 494 tons
A: 6/127-mm DP (II × 3) − 16/40-mm AA (IV × 3, II × 2) − 80 mines
Electron Equipt: Radars: 1/SPS 10, 1/SPS 6, 1/Mk 25, 2/Mk 34
　　　　　　　　　 Sonar: Probably none
Boilers: 4 Babcock & Wilcox, 43.3 kg/cm² pressure − superheat 454°C
M: 2 sets GT; 2 props; 60,000 hp **Electric:** 900 kw

REMARKS: Transferred on 22-10-71 after reactivation and modernization. Has no ASW equipment. Fire control includes 1 Mk-37 radar for 127-mm guns, two Mk-63 radars, and two Mk-51, mod. 2, optical controls for 40-mm AA. Mine rails on either side of main deck of what is basically an *Allen M. Sumner*-class destroyer. Last survivor of a class of twelve.

DESTROYERS *(continued)*

◆ 5 ex-U.S. Fletcher class

Bldrs: D-340: Federal SB, Kearney, N.J.; DD-341: Gulf SB, Chickasaw, Ala.; DD-342: Bath Iron Works, Me.; DD-343, DD-344: Bethlehem Steel, San Pedro, Cal.

	Laid down	L	In serv.
D 340 ISTANBUL (ex-*Clarence K. Bronson,* DD-668)	9-12-42	18-4-43	11-6-43
D 341 IZMIR (ex-*Van Valkenburgh,* DD-656)	15-11-42	19-12-43	2-8-44
D 342 IZMIT (ex-*Cogswell,* DD-651)	1-2-43	5-6-43	17-8-43
D 343 ISKENDERUN (ex-*Boyd,* DD-544)	2-4-42	29-10-42	8-5-43
D 344 IÇEL (ex-*Preston,* DD-795)	13-6-43	12-12-43	20-3-44

Iskenderun

D: 2,050 tons (3,036 fl)   **S:** 35 kts
Dim: 114.74 × 12.09 × 4.29 (5.79 over sonar)
Man: 15 officers, 247 men   **Range:** 1,260/30, 4,400/15   **Fuel:** 530 tons
A: 4/127-mm DP (I × 4) — 6/76.2-mm DP (II × 3) — 2/Mk 11 Hedgehogs — 6/324-mm Mk 32 ASW TT (III × 2) — 1/depth-charge rack
Electron Equipt: Radars: 1/SPS 10, 1/SPS 6C, 1/Mk 25, 1/Mk 35
             Sonars: SQS-29 series
Boilers: 4 Babcock & Wilcox, 43.3 kg/cm² pressure — superheat 454°C
M: 2 sets GT; 2 props; 60,000 hp   **Electric:** 880 kw

REMARKS: D-340 transferred on 14-1-67, D-341 on 28-2-67, D-342 and D-343 on 1-10-69, and D-344 on 15-11-69. All have one Mk-37 and one Mk-56 gunfire-control radar; two Mk-63 gunfire-control radars amidships were removed before transfer. D-344 has a "flat-faced" bridge like West German units of the class.

FRIGATES

◆ 2 Berk class   Bldr: Gölçük NSY

	Laid down	L	In serv.
D 358 BERK	9-3-67	25-6-71	12-7-72
D 359 PEYK	18-1-68	7-6-72	24-7-75

D: 1,450 tons (1,950 fl)   **S:** 25 kts
Dim: 95.15 × 11.82 × 4.4 (5.5 over sonar)
A: 4/76.2-mm DP (II × 2) — 2/Mk 11 Hedgehogs — 6/324-mm Mk 32 ASW TT (III × 2) — 1/depth-charge rack
Electron Equipt: Radars: 1/SPS 10, 1/SPS 40, 2/SPG 34
             Sonar: 1/SQS 11

Berk   G. Arra, 1977

M: 4 Fiat-Tosi 3-016-RSS diesels; 1 prop; 24,000 hp

REMARKS: Based on the U.S. *Claud Jones* class, but more heavily armed. The 16-cylinder, 800-rpm engines (300 mm × 610 mm) are similar to those installed in the Italian training ship, *San Giorgio.* Can carry a helicopter but have no hangars. Two Mk-63 gunfire-control with SPG-34 radars mounted on the guns.

GUIDED-MISSILE PATROL BOATS

◆ 4 FPB-57 class

Bldrs: P-340: Lürssen, Vegesack, W. Germany; others: Taskizak NDY, Istanbul

	L	In serv.		L	In serv.
P 340 DOGAN	16-6-76	15-6-77	P 342 TAYFUN	...	...
P 341 MARTI	30-6-77	27-7-78	P 343 VOLKAN	...	...

Dogan   1977

D: 436 tons (fl)   **S:** 35 kts   **Dim:** 58.1 (54.4 pp) × 7.62 × 2.83
Range: 1,600/32.5, 3,300/16   **Electric:** 405 kva
A: 8/Harpoon SSM (IV × 2) — 1/76-mm OTO Melara Compact DP — 2/35-mm AA (II × 1) — 2/7.62-mm machine guns
Electron Equipt: Radars: 1/Decca navigational, 1/HSA WM28-41
             ECM: Susie 1
M: 4 MTU diesels; 4 props; 14,400 hp

GUIDED-MISSILE PATROL BOATS *(continued)*

REMARKS: Carry 300 rounds 76-mm, 2,750 rounds 35-mm. Steel hulls, aluminum superstructures.

◆ **9 Kartal-class guided-missile and torpedo boats** Bldr: Lürssen, Vegesack, 1967-71

P 321 DENIZKUSU	P 324 KARTAL	P 327 ALBATROS
P 322 ATMACA	P 325 MELTEN	P 328 SIMSEK
P 323 SAHIN	P 326 PELIKAN	P 329 KASIRGA

Kartal   1970

D: 184 tons (210 fl)   S: 42 kts   Dim: 42.8 × 7.14 × 2.21
Man: 39 men   Range: 500/39, 1,000/32
A: 2/40-mm AA (I × 2) − 4/533-mm TT (P-325 to P-328: 4/Norwegian Penguin missiles and only 2 TT)
M: 4 MTU 16V538 diesels; 4 props; 12,000 hp

REMARKS: Similar to the German Jaguar class. Wooden hull; steel and light-metal keel and frames; light-metal superstructure. Can be fitted as fast gunboats or minelayers (four mines).

TORPEDO BOATS

◆ **7 ex-German Jaguar class (Type 140)**

Bldrs: P-330 and P-336: Krögerswerft, Rendsburg; others: Lürssen, Vegesack

	L		L
P 330 FIRTINA (ex-*Pelikan*)	12-12-59	P 334 YILDIZ (ex-*Wolf*)	21-9-57
P 331 TUFAN (ex-*Storch*)	16-11-59	P 335 KALKAN (ex-*Löwe*)	8-11-58
P 332 KILIÇ (ex-*Pinguin*)	4-7-60	P 336 KARAYEL (ex-*Tiger*)	21-4-58
P 333 MIZRAK (ex-*Häher*)	9-1-60		

D: 184 tons (210 fl)   S: 42 kts   Dim: 42.62 × 7.1 × 2.21
Man: 39 men   Range: 500/39, 1,000/32
A: 2/40-mm AA (I × 2) − 4/533-mm TT or 2/TT and mines
M: 4 MTU 16V538 diesels; 4 props; 12,000 hp

REMARKS: Transferred, 1975-76. The *Alk*, *Iltis*, and *Reiher* were transferred at the same time to be cannibalized for the maintenance of the seven in service. Similar to *Kartal* class but shorter deckhouse with stepped face.

PATROL BOATS AND CRAFT

◆ **1 PB-57 class** Bldr: Taskizak NDY, Istanbul

P 140 GIRNE

D: 341 tons (399 fl)   S: 29.5 kts   Dim: 58.1 (54.4 pp) × 7.6 × 2.8
Man: 3 officers, 27 men   Range: 2,200/28, 4,200/16
A: 3/40-mm AA (II × 1, I × 1) − 4/Mk 20 Mousetrap ASW rocket launchers − 2/depth-charge projectors − 2/depth-charge racks
Electron Equipt: Radar: 1/navigational
M: 2 MTU MA15 TB91 diesels; 2 props; 9,000 hp   Electric: 405 kva

REMARKS: In service on 30-10-76. Same basic design as the Spanish *Lazaga*-class patrol boats, but with lighter armament. Design by Lürssen. Construction program canceled after one unit. INTELSAT satellite-communications antenna mounted on superstructure in 1978. U.S. Mk-51, mod. 2, optical director for twin 40-mm aft.

◆ **2 ex-U.S. Asheville class** Bldr: Peterson Builders, Sturgeon Bay, Wisc.

	L	In serv.
P 338 YLDIRIM (ex-*Defiance*, PG-95)	24-8-68	17-10-69
P 339 BORA (ex-*Surprise*, PG-97)	15-11-68	24-9-69

D: 225 tons (240 fl)   S: 40 kts (16 on diesels)
Dim: 50.14 (46.94 pp) × 7.28 × 2.9
Man: 25 men   Range: 325/35, 1,700/16   Fuel: 50 tons
A: 1/76.2-mm DP − 1/40-mm AA − 4/12.7-mm machine guns (II × 2)
Electron Equipt: Radars: 1/LN 66, 1/SPG 50
M: CODAG: 1 LM 1500 Mk-7 gas turbine (12,500 hp); 2 Cummins 875 V-12 diesels (1,450 hp); 2 props

REMARKS: P-338 transferred on 11-6-73 and P-339 on 28-2-73. P-338 was formerly P-340. Mk-63 gunfire-control radar with SPG-50 on 76-mm gun.

◆ **10 AB-25 class** Bldrs: Gölçük NSY, 1967-70

P 1225 AB 25	P 1229 AB 29	P 1232 AB 32
P 1226 AB 26	P 1230 AB 30	P 1233 AB 33
P 1227 AB 27	P 1231 AB 31	P 1234 AB 34
P 1228 AB 28		

AB-26 − wearing old number   1969

D: 170 tons (fl)   S: 22 kts   Dim: 40.24 × 6.4 × 1.65
A: 1/40-mm AA − 2/Mk 20 Mousetrap ASW rocket launchers − 1/depth-charge rack
M: SACM-AGO V16CSHR diesels; 2 props; 4,800 hp; 2 cruise diesels; 300 hp

REMARKS: Twenty others are assigned to the Gendarmerie. Built with French assistance.

PATROL BOATS AND CRAFT *(continued)*

◆ **4 ex-U.S. PGM-71 motor gunboats** Bldr: Peterson Builders, Sturgeon Bay, Wisc.

	L	In serv.
P 1221 (ex-P-117) AB 21 (ex-PGM-104)	4-5-67	8-67
P 1222 (ex-P-118) AB 22 (ex-PGM-105)	25-5-67	9-67
P 1223 (ex-P-119) AB 23 (ex-PGM-106)	7-7-67	10-67
P 1224 (ex-P-120) AB 24 (ex-PGM-108)	14-9-67	5-68

AB-23—wearing old number   1969

D: 104 tons (144 fl)   **S:** 17 kts   **Dim:** 30.81 × 6.45 × 1.83
Man: 30 men   **Range:** 1,000/12   **Fuel:** 16 tons
A: 1/40-mm AA—4/20-mm AA (II × 2)—4/12.7-mm machine guns—2/Mk 22 double
   Mousetrap ASW rocket launchers—2/depth-charge racks
Electron Equipt: Radar: 1/Raytheon 1500B   Sonar: SQS 17A
M: 8 GM 6-71 diesels; 2 props; 2,040 hp   **Electric:** 30 kw

◆ **6 ex-U.S. PC-1638 class**

Bldrs: P-116: Gölçük, NSY; others: Gunderson, Portland, Ore.

	L	In serv.
P 111 Sultan Hisar (ex-PC-1638)	1964	5-64
P 112 Demirhisar (ex-PC-1639)	9-7-64	4-65
P 113 Yarhisar (ex-PC-1640)	14-5-64	9-64
P 114 Akhisar (ex-PC-1641)	14-5-64	12-64
P 115 Sivrihisar (ex-PC-1642)	5-11-64	6-65
P 116 Kochisar (ex-PC-1643)	12-64	7-65

D: 325 tons (477 fl)   **S:** 19 kts   **Dim:** 52.9 × 7.0 × 3.1 (hull)
Man: 5 officers, 60 men   **Range:** 5,000/10   **Fuel:** 60 tons
A: 1/40-mm AA—4/20-mm AA (II × 2)—1/Mk 15 trainable Hedgehog—4/Mk 6 depth-
   charge projectors—1/depth-charge rack
Electron Equipt: Radar: 1/Decca 707   Sonar: SQS 17A
M: 2 Alco 16 9 × 10½T diesels; 2 props; 4,800 hp

REMARK: Based on the PC-471 class of World War II.

Demirhisar   1970

◆ **4 ex-U.S. Coast Guard 83-foot class** Bldr: U.S.C.G. Yard, Curtis Bay, Md.

P 1209 LS 9   P 1210 LS 10   P 1211 LS 11   P 1212 LS 12

LS-12—wearing old number   1969

D: 63 tons   **S:** 18 kts   **Dim:** 25.3 × 4.25 × 1.55
A: 1/20-mm AA—2/Mk 20 Mousetrap ASW rocket launchers   **Man:** 15 men
Electron Equipt: Radar: 1/SO 2   Sonar: QBE 3
M: 4 GM 6-71 diesels; 2 props; 900 hp

REMARKS: Transferred on 25-6-53. Former Turkish hull numbers P-339, P-308, P-309,
and P-310. Wooden hulls.

MINE WARFARE SHIPS

◆ **1 Danish Falster class minelayer** Bldr: Frederikshaven NDY

	Laid down	L	In serv.
N 110 Nusret (ex-N-108, ex-MMC-16)	1962	1964	16-9-64

D: 1,880 tons   **S:** 16.5 kts   **Dim:** 77.0 (72.5 pp) × 12.8 × 3.4
A: 4/76-mm AA (II × 2)—400 mines   **Man:** 130 men   **Fuel:** 130 tons

MINE WARFARE SHIPS (continued)

Nusret — wearing old number

Electron Equipt: Radars: 1/navigational, 1/RAN 7S, 2/SPG 34
M: 2 GM 16-567D3 diesels; 2 controllable-pitch props; 4,800 hp

REMARKS: Ordered by the U.S.A. under MAP. Two Mk-63 gunfire-control radar systems.

◆ **5 minelayers** Bldr: Brown SB, Houston, Tex.

	Laid down	L	In serv.
N 101 MORDOGAN (ex-MMC-11, ex-LSM-484)	17-2-45	10-3-45	15-4-45
N 102 MERIC (ex-MMC-12, ex-LSM-481)	17-2-45	10-3-45	8-4-45
N 103 MARMARIS (ex-MMC-10, ex-LSM-490)	3-3-45	24-3-45	28-4-45
N 104 MERSIN (ex-Vale, ex-MMC-13, ex-LSM-492)	28-5-44	22-6-44	4-8-44
N 105 MUREFTE (ex-Vidar, ex-MMC-14, ex-MSC-493)	10-3-45	30-3-45	4-5-45

Mersin

D: 743 tons (1,100 fl) **S:** 12.5 kts **Dim:** 62.0 × 10.52 × 2.54
Man: 70 men **Range:** 2,500/12 **Fuel:** 60 tons
A: 6/40-mm AA (II × 3) – 5/20-mm AA (I × 5) – 400 mines
Electron Equipt: Radar: 1/SO 8 **M:** 2 GM 16-278A diesels; 2 props; 2,800 hp

REMARKS: Ex-U.S. LSM-1 medium landing ships. In 10-52, after a complete overhaul, the first three were transferred to Turkey, the other two to Norway. They were returned to the U.S.A. in 1960, then all reassigned to Turkey. Four booms, two forward, two aft, for the loading of mines. Two minelaying rails. Originally had four twin 40-mm AA and six 20-mm AA. N-104 has two Fairbanks-Morse 38D8⅛ diesels.

◆ **1 mine-planter** Bldr: Higgins, New Orleans, La.

N 115 MEHMETCIK (ex-YMP-3)

D: 540 tons (fl) **S:** 10 kts **Dim:** 39.62 × 10.67 × 3.05
A: 1/40-mm AA **Man:** 22 men **Electron Equipt:** Radar: 1/Decca 12
M: 2 diesels; 2 props

REMARKS: An ex-U.S. coastal minelayer launched in 1958 and transferred that same year under MAP. Used to place controlled minefields. Gun not normally mounted.

◆ **5 ex-German French Mercure-class coastal minesweepers**

Bldr: Amiot (C.M.N.), Cherbourg

	Laid down	L	In serv.
M 520 KARAMÜRSEL (ex-Worms)	19-3-58	30-1-60	30-4-60
M 521 KEREMPE (ex-Detmold)	19-2-58	17-11-59	20-2-60
M 522 KILIMLI (ex-Siegen)	18-4-58	29-3-60	9-7-60
M 523 KOZLU (ex-Hameln)	20-1-58	20-8-59	15-10-59
M 524 KUSADASI (ex-Vegesack)	20-12-57	21-5-59	19-9-59

Kilimli 1976

D: 366 tons (383 fl) **S:** 14.5 kts **Dim:** 44.62 (42.5 pp) × 8.41 × 2.55
A: 2/20-mm AA (II × 1) **Man:** 40 men **Electric:** 520 kw

MINE WARFARE SHIPS *(continued)*

Electron Equipt: Radar: 1/Decca 707
M: Mercedes-Benz MB-820-EB diesels; 2 controllable-pitch props; 4,000 hp

REMARKS: These ships were built for the German Navy, placed in reserve in 1963, and stricken on 31-12-73. Transferred to Turkey between 6-75 and 10-75. German sister *Passau* scrapped on 31-8-77; French sister *Mercure* now a fisheries-protection ship. Wooden construction.

◆ **12 ex-U.S. Adjutant-, MSC-268(*)-, and MSC-294(**)-class coastal minesweepers**

		L	In serv.
M 507 SEYMEN (ex-*De Panne*, ex-MSC-131)		. . .	28-10-55
M 508 SELÇUK (ex-*Pavot*, ex-MSC-124)		. . .	6-54
M 509 SEYHAN (ex-*Renoncule*, ex-MSC-142)		. . .	8-54
M 510 SAMSUN (ex-MSC-268)*		6-9-57	30-9-58
M 511 SINOP (ex-MSC-270)*		4-1-58	2-59
M 512 SÜRMENE (ex-MSC-271)*		1958	27-3-59
M 513 SEDDUL BAHR (ex-MSC-272)*		1958	5-59
M 514 SILIFKE (ex-MSC-304)**		21-11-64	9-65
M 515 SAROS (ex-MSC-305)**		1-5-65	2-66
M 516 SIGAÇIK (ex-MSC-311)**		12-6-64	6-65
M 517 SAPANCA (ex-MSC-312)**		14-9-64	26-7-65
M 518 SARIYER (ex-MSC-315)**		21-4-66	8-9-67

Bldrs: M-507: Hiltebrant DD, Kingston, N.Y.; M-508: Stephen Bros.; M-509: South Coast Co., Newport Beach, Cal.; M-510 to M-513: Bellingham SY, Bellingham, Wash.; M-514, M-515: Dorchester Builders, Dorchester, N.J.; M-516 to M-518: Peterson Builders, Sturgeon Bay, Wisc.

Selçuk — J.-C. Bellonne, 1970

D: 300 tons (392 fl)   **S:** 14 kts   **Dim:** 43.0 (41.5 pp) × 7.95 × 2.55
A: 2/20-mm AA (II × 1)   **Man:** 4 officers, 34 men   **Range:** 2,500/10
M: 2 GM 8-268A diesels; 2 props; 1,200 hp

REMARKS: M-507 was returned to the U.S.A. by Belgium in 1970, and M-508 and M-509 were returned by France on 23-3-70, then transferred to Turkey. The MSC-268 class have 4 GM 6-71 diesels; 2 props; 880 hp. The MSC-294 class have lower superstructure, taller stacks, and 2 Waukesha L-1616 diesels of 600 hp each; **Dim:** 44.32 × 8.29 × 2.55.

◆ **4 ex-Canadian Bay-class coastal minesweepers**   Bldr: Davie SB, Lauzon, Quebec

	L		L
M 530 TRABZON (ex-*Gaspé*)	20-5-53	M 532 TIREBOLU (ex-*Comax*)	24-4-52
M 531 TERME (ex-*Trinity*)	31-7-53	M 533 TEKIRDAG (ex-*Ungava*)	12-11-51

Trabzon — wearing old number   1969

D: 390 tons (412 fl)   **S:** 16 kts   **Dim:** 50.0 (46.05 pp) × 9.21 × 2.8
A: 1/40-mm   **Man:** 44 men   **Range:** 4,500/11   **Fuel:** 52 tons
Electron Equipt: Radar: 1/Sperry Mk 2
M: 2 GM 8-268A diesels; 2 props; 2,400 hp

REMARKS: Transferred under U.S. MAP on 19-5-58. Wood-planked skin on steel frame.

◆ **4 ex-U.S. Cape-class inshore minesweepers**

Bldr: Peterson Builders, Sturgeon Bay, Wisc.

	L	In serv.
M 500 FOCA (ex-MSI-15)	23-8-66	8-67
M 501 FETHIYE (ex-MSI-16)	7-12-66	9-67
M 502 FATSA (ex-MSI-17)	11-4-67	10-67
M 503 FINIKE (ex-MSI-18)	11-67	12-67

D: 203 tons (239 fl)   **S:** 12.5 kts   **Dim:** 34.06 × 7.14 × 2.4
A: 1/12.7-mm machine gun   **Man:** 20 men   **Range:** 1,000/9
M: 4 GM 6-71 diesels; 2 props; 960 hp   **Fuel:** 20 tons   **Electric:** 120 kw

REMARKS: Transferred on completion, under MAP. Wooden construction.

MINE WARFARE SHIPS (continued)

Fethiye 1970

◆ 2 ex-U.S. 64-foot distribution-box minefield tenders

Y 1148 SAMANDIRA L 1   Y 1149 SAMANDIRA L 2

D: 72 tons (fl)   **S:** 9.5 kts   **Dim:** 19.58 × 5.72 × 1.83
M: 1 Gray Marine 64HN9 diesel; 1 prop; 225 hp   **Man:** 6 men

REMARK: Transferred in 1959.

◆ 9 mine-disposal diving tenders   Bldr: G.B., 1942

P 311 MTB 1   P 314 MTB 4   P 318 MTB 8
P 312 MTB 2   P 316 MTB 6   P 319 MTB 9
P 313 MTB 3   P 317 MTB 7   P 320 MTB 10

D: 70 tons   **S:** 20 kts   **Dim:** 21.8 × 4.2 × 2.6
M: 2 diesels; 2,000 hp

AMPHIBIOUS WARFARE SHIPS AND CRAFT

◆ 1 Cakabey-class tank landing ship   Bldr: Taskizak NDY, Istanbul

	L	In serv.
L 405 CAKABEY	30-6-77	1979

D: 1,600 tons (fl)   **S:** 14 kts   **Dim:** 77.3 × 12.0 × 2.3
A: 2/40-mm AA (I × 2)—2/20-mm AA (I × 2)   **M:** 3 diesels; 3 props; 4,320 hp

REMARKS: First of a planned four units. Can carry sixteen tanks and has a helicopter
pad amidships. Resembles U.S. LST-1 class but has higher freeboard and less sheer.

◆ 2 ex-U.S. Terrebonne Parish-class tank landing ships

Bldr: Christy Corp., Sturgeon Bay, Wisc.

	L	In serv.
L 401 ERTUGRUL (ex-*Windham County*, LST-1170)	22-5-54	15-12-54
L 402 SERDAR (ex-*Westchester County*, LST-1167)	18-4-53	10-3-54

D: 2,590 tons (5,786 fl)   **S:** 15 kts   **Dim:** 117.35 (112.77 pp) × 17.06 × 5.18
Man: 116 men + 395 troops   **Fuel:** 874 tons   **Electric:** 600 kw
A: 6/76.2-mm DP (II × 3)   **Electron Equipt:** Radars: 1/SPS 21, 2/Mk 34
M: 4 GM 16-268A diesels; 2 controllable-pitch props; 6,000 hp

REMARKS: L-401 transferred in 6-73 and L-402 in 8-74. Cargo: 2,200 tons. Can carry four
LCVPs in Welin davits. Two Mk-63 gunfire-control radars.

◆ 2 ex-German U.S. LST-542-class tank landing ships/minelayers

Bldrs: L-403: Missouri Valley Bridge & Iron, Evansville, Ind.; L-404: American
Bridge Co., Ambridge, Pa.

	Laid down	L	In serv.
L 403 BAYRAKTAR (ex-*Bottrop*, ex-*Saline County*, LST-1101)	22-11-44	3-1-45	26-1-45
L 404 SANCAKTAR (ex-*Bochum*, ex-*Rice County*, LST-1089)	20-12-44	17-2-45	14-3-45

Sancaktar—as the **Bochum**

D: 3,640 tons (4,140 fl)   **S:** 11 kts   **Dim:** 101.37 × 15.28 × 3.98 (max.)
Man: 60 men   **Range:** 15,000/9   **Electric:** 860 kw
A: 6/40-mm AA (II × 2, I × 2)—790 mines, as minelayers
Electron Equipt: Radar: 1/Kelvin-Hughes 14/9
M: 2 GM 16-567A diesels; 2 props; 1,700 hp

REMARKS: L-403 was transferred to West Germany on 6-2-64 and to Turkey on 13-12-72;
L-404 to West Germany on 23-1-64 and to Turkey on 12-12-72. Converted to minelayers
while in German service, with six rails on the upper deck, tapering to two at the stern,
and four rails below decks, exiting through a broadened stern. Four two-ton mine-
handling cranes added. Bow doors retained. Redesignated as amphibious ships 1974-
75 and mine rails possibly removed.

◆ 28 utility landing ships   Bldr: Taskizak NDY, Istanbul, 1966-

Ç 107 to Ç 134

D: 280 tons (580 fl)   **S:** 10 kts   **Dim:** 57.07 × 11.79 × 1.3 (aft)
A: 2/20-mm AA (I × 2)   **Man:** 15 men   **Range:** 600/10, 1,100/8
M: 2 diesels; 2 props; 1,000 hp

REMARKS: Built on the British LCT (4) design. Construction continues, with Ç-132 and
Ç-133 launched in 8-78 and Ç-134 in 7-79. Up to 350 tons cargo. Cargo deck is 28.5 ×
7.9 m.

AMPHIBIOUS WARFARE SHIPS AND CRAFT *(continued)*

◆ **5 ex-British LCT (4)-class utility landing ships**

Ç 101   Ç 103   Ç 104   Ç 105   Ç 106

   D: 280 tons (600 fl)   **S:** 9.5 kts   **Dim:** 57.07 × 11.79 × 1.3 (aft)
   A: 2/20-mm AA (I × 2)   **Man:** 15 men   **Range:** 500/9.5, 1,100/8
   M: 2 Paxman diesels; 2 props; 1,000 hp

REMARKS: Transferred on 25-9-47. Cargo: 350 tons. Considerably modernized since transfer.

◆ **12 utility landing craft**   Bldr: Taskizak, Istanbul, 1965-66

Ç 205 to Ç 216

Ç-211   1973

   D: 320 tons (405 fl)   **S:** 10 kts   **Dim:** 43.3 × 8.5 × 1.7
   A: 2/20-mm AA (I × 2)   **M:** 2 GM 6-71 diesels; 3 props; 675 hp

◆ **4 ex-U.S. LCU-501 (LCT (6))-class utility landing craft**
   Bldr: Pidgeon-Thomes Iron Co., Memphis, Tenn.

Ç 201 (ex-LCU-588)   Ç 202 (ex-LCU-608)   Ç 203 (ex-LCU-666)   Ç 204 (LCU-667)

Ç-201   1976

   D: 143 tons (309 fl)   **S:** 8 kts   **Dim:** 36.68 × 9.75 × 1.22 (aft)
   A: 2/20-mm AA   **Man:** 12 men   **Range:** 700/7   **Fuel:** 11 tons
   M: 3 Gray Marine 64HN9 diesels; 3 props; 675 hp   **Electric:** 20 kw

REMARKS: Launched on 8-10-43, 12-12-43, 5-2-44, and 9-2-44, respectively. Transferred in 7-67. Cargo: 150 tons + 8 troops.

◆ **20 U.S. LCM (8)-class landing craft**   Bldr: Taskizak, Istanbul, 1965-66

Ç 301 to Ç 320

   D: 56 tons (118 fl)   **S:** 9 kts   **Dim:** 22.43 × 6.42 × 1.6
   A: 2/12.7-mm machine guns   **Man:** 5 men
   M: 4 GM 6-71 diesels; 2 props; 590 hp

HYDROGRAPHIC SHIPS

◆ **1 new construction oceanographic ship**   Bldr: Turkey, 1979

PIRI REIS

REMARK: No data available.

◆ **2 ex-British Catherine-class former minesweepers**
   Bldrs: A-593: Assoc. SB, Lake Washington, Wash; A-594: Gulf SB, Mobile, Ala.

	L	In serv.
A 593 ÇANDARLI (ex-*Frolic*, ex-BAM-29)	20-6-43	18-5-44
A 594 ÇARSAMBA (ex-*Tattoo*, ex-BAM-32)	27-1-43	29-10-43

Çandarli   G. Arra, 1972

   D: 1,010 tons (1,185 fl)   **S:** 18 kts   **Dim:** 67.31 × 9.75 × 3.2
   A: 1/76.2-mm DP — 4/20-mm AA   **Man:** 105 men
   Range: 3,500/17, 8,500/11
   Electron Equipt: Radar: 1/Decca 707   **Fuel:** 210 tons   **Electric:** 360 kw
   M: 4 GM 12-278A diesels, electric drive; 2 props; 3,532 hp

REMARKS: Lend-lease version of the U.S. *Auk* class, transferred to Great Britain on

HYDROGRAPHIC SHIPS *(continued)*

completion. Survivors of a group of seven transferred to Turkey in 3-47. Converted later for service as survey ships. Charthouse added between stacks.

◆ **2 ex-U.S. 52-foot inshore-survey craft**

MESAHA 1 to MESAHA 4

    D: 31.7 tons (37.6 fl)   **S:** 10 kts   **Dim:** 15.9 × 4.45 × 1.3
    M: 2 GM 6-71 diesels; 2 props; 330 hp   **Man:** 10 men   **Range:** 600/10

AUXILIARY SHIPS

◆ **1 Turkish-designed replenishment oiler** Bldr: Taskizak NDY, Istanbul

A 573 BINBASI SAADETTIN GÜRÇAN

    D: 1,505 tons (4,680 fl)   **S:** 16 kts   **Dim:** 89.7 × 11.8 × 5.4
    A: 1/40-mm AA − 2/20-mm AA (I × 2)
    M: 4 GM 16-567A diesels, electric drive; 2 props; 4,400 hp

REMARKS: Launched on 1-7-69. One liquid-replenishment station on each side. Primarily a tanker.

◆ **1 Turkish-designed replenishment oiler** Bldr: Gölçük NSY, 1964

A 572 ALBAY HAKKI BURAK

    D: 1,800 tons (3,740 fl)   **S:** 16 kts   **Dim:** 83.73 × 12.25 × 5.49
    A: 2/40-mm AA (I × 2)   **Electron Equipt:** Radar: 1/Decca 707
    Man: 88 men
    M: 4 GM 16-567A diesels, electric drive; 2 props; 4,400 hp

REMARKS: One liquid-replenishment station on each side. Primarily a tanker.

◆ **1 ex-West German Bodensee-class replenishment oiler** Bldr: Lindenau-Werft, Kiel

	Laid down	L	In serv.
A 575 ÜNÄBOLU (ex-*Bodensee*, ex-*Unkas*)	24-8-55	19-11-55	11-2-56

Ünäbolu – as the **Bodensee**   1975

    D: 1,237 tons (1,840 fl)   **S:** 13.5 kts   **Dim:** 67.1 (61.2 pp) × 9.84 × 4.27
    A: . . .   **Man:** 21 men   **Range:** 6,240/12   **Electric:** 238 kva
    Electron Equipt: Radar: 1/Kelvin-Hughes 14/9
    M: 1 MAK 6-cyl. diesel; 1 prop; 1,050 hp

REMARKS: Former merchant tanker acquired on 26-3-59 for the West German Navy; transferred to Turkey on 25-8-77. Cargo: 1,231 tons. One replenishment station.

◆ **1 Turkish-designed replenishment oiler** Bldr: Taskizak NDY, Istanbul

A 571 YUZBASI TOLÜNAY (ex-*Taskizak*)

    D: 2,500 tons (3,500 fl)   **S:** 14 kts   **Dim:** 79.0 × 12.4 × 5.9
    A: 2/40-mm AA (I × 2)   **M:** 2 Atlas-Polar diesels; 2 props; 1,900 hp

REMARKS: Launched on 22-8-50. Has one alongside replenishment station and can replenish over the stern.

◆ **1 ex-U.S. Mettawee-class former gasoline tanker** Bldr: East Coast SY, Bayonne, N.J.

	Laid down	L	In serv.
A 574 AKPINAR (ex-*Chiwaukum*, AOG-26)	2-4-44	5-5-44	22-7-44

    D: 700 tons (2,270 fl)   **S:** 14 kts   **Dim:** 67.21 (64.77 pp) × 11.28 × 3.99
    A: 1/76.2-mm DP − 1/40-mm AA − 2/20-mm AA   **Fuel:** 29 tons
    M: 1 Fairbanks-Morse 37E16 diesel; 1 prop; 800 hp   **Electric:** 155 kw

REMARKS: Transferred in 5-48. Cargo: 1,365 tons. Very low freeboard restricts use to sheltered waters.

◆ **2 tenders, ex-West German Angeln-class cargo ships**

    Bldr: Ateliers et Chantiers de Bretagne, Nantes, France

	Laid down	L	In serv.
A 586 ÜLKÜ (ex-*Angeln*, ex-*Borée*)	17-5-54	9-10-54	20-1-55
A 588 UMERBEY (ex-*Dithmarschen*, ex-*Hebé*)	20-10-54	7-5-55	17-11-55

Ülkü – as the **Angeln**

    D: 2,998 tons (4,089 fl)   **S:** 19 kts   **Dim:** 90.53 (84.5 pp) × 13.32 × 6.2
    A: . . .   **Man:** 57 men   **Range:** 3,660/15   **Electric:** 335 kw
    M: 2 SEMT-Pielstick 6-cyl. diesels; 1 prop; 3,000 hp

REMARKS: Former French cargo ships acquired for the West German Navy on 27-11-59 and 19-12-59, respectively. A-586 was transferred to Turkey on 28-3-72 and A-588 on

AUXILIARY SHIPS *(continued)*

6-10-76. A-586 is used as a patrol-boat tender and A-588 as a submarine tender. A-588's displacement is: 3,098 tons (4,189 fl). Cargo: A-586, 2,665 tons; A-588, 2,670 tons. Six 2.5-ton derricks, three holds.

◆ **1 ex-U.S. Portunus-class patrol-boat tender** Bldr: Bethlehem Steel, Hingham, Mass.

	Laid down	L	In serv.
A 581 ONARAN (ex-*Alecto*, AGP-14, ex-LST-977)	12-12-44	15-1-45	8-2-45

Onaran   G. Arra, 1971

D: 4,100 tons (fl)   **S:** 11.6 kts   **Dim:** 99.98 × 15.24 × 3.4
Man: 291 men   **Range:** 9,000/9   **Fuel:** 590 tons   **Electric:** 500 kw
A: 8/40-mm AA (IV × 2)−8/20-mm AA (II × 4)
M: 2 GM 12-278A diesels; 2 props; 1,800 hp

REMARKS: Transferred in 11-52. Retains bow doors. Superstructure enlarged after transfer.

◆ **1 ex-U.S. Achelous-class submarine tender** Bldr: Bethlehem Steel, Hingham, Mass.

	Laid down	L	In serv.
A 582 BASARAN (ex-*Patroclus*, ARL-19, ex-LST-955)	22-9-44	22-10-44	13-11-44

REMARKS: Former landing-craft repair ship. Data as for *Onaran*, above, except: **Electric:** 420 kw; **Fuel:** 621 tons. Has less superstructure than *Oneran*.

◆ **1 ex-U.S. Aegir-class submarine tender** Bldr: Ingalls, Pascagoula, Miss.

	Laid down	L	In serv.
A 583 DONATAN (ex-*Anthedon*, AS-24)	1943	15-10-43	15-9-44

Donatan   1970

D: 16,500 tons (fl)   **S:** 18.4 kts (trials)
Dim: 149.96 (141.73 pp) × 21.18 × 8.23
Man: 1,460 men   **Fuel:** 3,045 tons   **Electric:** 1,200 kw
A: 3/76.2-mm DP (I × 3)−8/40-mm AA (II × 1, I × 6)−8/20-mm AA (I × 8)
Boilers: 2 Foster-Wheeler "D", 37.2 kg/cm² pressure−superheat 407°C
M: 1 set Westinghouse GT; 1 prop; 8,500 hp

REMARKS: Transferred on 7-2-69. Had been in U.S. Navy Reserve Fleet since 21-9-46. Unarmed at transfer. A helicopter platform has been added over the stern.

◆ **1 submarine tender** Bldr: Nakskov SY, Nakskov, Denmark

A 599 ERKIN (ex-*Trabzon*, ex-*Imperial*)

Erkin−wearing old number   G. Arra, 1972

D: 9,900 tons (fl)   **S:** 16 kts   **Dim:** 134.25 (125.0 pp) × 17.8 × 7.2
A: 2/40-mm AA (II × 1)   **Man:** 128 men   **Range:** 15,950/16
Electron Equipt: Radars: 1/Decca 707, 1/SG 1   **Fuel:** 1,380 tons
M: 1 Fiat B-680-S diesel; 1 prop; 6,560 hp   **Electric:** 720 kw

REMARKS: Built as the Chilean passenger-cargo ship *Imperial;* acquired by the U.S. Army on 30-8-43 as a troop transport with same name. Sold to Turkey in 1948 as commercial ship *Trabzon;* taken over by the Turkish Navy for conversion to a submarine-support ship in 1968 and commissioned in 1970. Can carry more than 500 passengers.

◆ **1 ex-U.S. AN-103-class net-tender** Bldr: Kröger, Rendsburg, West Germany

	Laid down	L	In serv.
P 305 AG 5 (ex-AN-104)	1960	20-10-60	5-2-61

D: 680 tons (960 fl)   **S:** 12 kts   **Dim:** 52.5 × 10.5 × 4.05
A: 1/40-mm AA−3/20-mm AA (I × 3)   **Man:** 48 men   **Range:** 8,000/12
M: 4 M.A.N. 67V 40/60 diesels; 2 props; 1,450 hp

REMARKS: Sister to the netlayer *Thetis* in the Greek Navy. Built with U.S. Offshore Procurement funds.

◆ **1 ex-U.S. AN-93-class net-tender** Bldr: Bethlehem Steel, Staten Island, N.Y.

	L	In serv.
P 306 AG 6 (ex-*Cerberus*, ex-AN-93)	5-52	10-11-52

D: 780 tons (902 fl)   **S:** 12.8 kts   **Dim:** 50.29 (44.5 pp) × 10.20 × 3.2
A: 1/76.2-mm DP−4/20-mm AA (I × 4)   **Man:** 48 men   **Range:** 5,200/12
M: 2 GM 8-268A diesels, electric drive; 1 prop; 1,500 hp

AUXILIARY SHIPS *(continued)*

REMARKS: Prototype of a class also built in France and Italy. Transferred to the Netherlands in 12-52 and returned 17-9-70; transferred to Turkey the same day.

◆ **1 ex-U.S. Aloe-class net-tender** Bldr: Marietta Mfg. Co., Pt. Pleasant, W. Va.

	Laid down	L	In serv.
P 304 AG 4 (ex-*Larch*, AN-21, ex-YN-16)	18-10-40	2-7-41	13-12-41

D: 560 tons (805 fl)   **S:** 12.5 kts   **Dim:** 49.73 (44.5 wl) × 9.3 × 3.56
A: 1/76.2-mm DP – 4/20-mm AA (I × 4)   **Man:** 48 men   **Fuel:** 80 tons
M: 2 Alco 538-6 diesels, electric drive; 1 prop; 620 hp   **Electric:** 120 kw

REMARK: Transferred in 5-46.

◆ **1 ex-British "Bar"-class net-tender** Bldr: Blyth DD & SB Co., G.B.

	Laid down	L	In serv.
P 301 AG 2 (ex-*Barbarian*)	10-6-37	21-10-37	16-4-38

D: 750 tons (1,000 fl)   **S:** 11.7 kts   **Dim:** 52.96 × 9.8 × 4.62
A: 1/76.2-mm DP   **Man:** 32 men   **Fuel:** 214 tons
Boilers: 2, single-end, three-drum
M: 1 set triple-expansion; 1 prop; 850 hp   **Range:** 3,100/10

REMARKS: Transferred in 1947. Sisters *AG-2* (ex-*Barbette*) and *AG-3* (ex-*Barfair*) were stricken in 1975.

◆ **1 ex-U.S. Bluebird-class submarine-rescue ship**

Bldr: Charleston SB & DD Co., Charleston, S.C.

	Laid down	L	In serv.
A 584 KURTARAN (ex-*Bluebird*, ASR-19, ex-*Yurok*, ATF-164)	23-6-45	15-2-46	28-5-46

Kurtaran   1970

D: 1,294 tons (1,760 fl)   **S:** 16 kts   **Dim:** 62.48 (59.44 pp) × 12.19 × 4.88
A: 1/76.2-mm DP   **Man:** 100 men   **Fuel:** 300 tons   **Electric:** 600 kw
M: 4 GM 12-278A diesels, electric drive; 1 prop; 3,000 hp

REMARKS: Begun as an *Achomawi*-class fleet tug but altered while under construction, wooden fenders adding 5 meters to the beam. Carries McCann rescue diving bell and four marker buoys. Transferred on 15-8-50.

◆ **1 ex-U.S. Chanticleer-class submarine-rescue ship**

Bldr: Moore SB & DD Co., Oakland, Cal.

	Laid down	L	In serv.
A 585 AKIN (ex-*Greenlet*, ASR-10)	15-10-41	12-7-42	29-5-43

D: 1,770 tons (2,321 fl)   **S:** 15 kts   **Dim:** 76.61 (73.15 pp) × 12.8 × 4.52
Man: 85 men   **Fuel:** 235 tons   **Electric:** 460 kw
A: 1/40-mm AA – 4/20-mm AA (II × 2)   **Electron Equipt:** Radar: 1/SPS 5
M: 4 Alco 539 diesels, electric drive; 1 prop; 3,000 hp

REMARKS: Loaned on 12-6-70 and purchased outright on 15-2-73. Carries McCann rescue diving bell and four marker buoys.

◆ **1 ex-U.S. Diver-class salvage ship** Bldr: Basalt Rock Co., Napa, Cal.

	Laid down	L	In serv.
A 589 ISIN (ex-*Safeguard*, ARS-25)	5-6-43	20-11-43	31-10-44

D: 1,480 tons (1,970 fl)   **S:** 14.8 kts   **Dim:** 65.08 (63.09 pp) × 12.5 × 4.0
A: 2/20-mm AA (I × 2)   **Man:** 97 men   **Fuel:** 300 tons
Electric: 460 kw
M: 4 Cooper-Bessemer GSB-8 diesels, electric drive; 2 props; 3,000 hp

REMARKS: Purchased on 28-9-79. Wooden fenders add .6 meters to beam.

◆ **1 training ship** Bldr: Schlieker, Hamburg, West Germany

	Laid down	L	In serv.
A 579 CEZAYIRLI GAZI HASAN PASA (ex-*Ruhr*)	1959	18-8-60	2-5-64

Cezayirli Gazi Hasan Pasa – as the **Ruhr**

D: 2,370 tons (2,740 fl)   **S:** 20 kts   **Dim:** 98.18 × 11.8 × 3.9
Man: 120 men   **Range:** 1,600/16   **Fuel:** 113 tons   **Electric:** 2,250 kw

AUXILIARY SHIPS (continued)

A: 2/100-mm French Model 1953 DP (I × 2) – 4/40-mm AA (I × 4) – 70 mines
Electron Equipt: Radars: 1/HSA SGR 105, 1/HSA SGR 103, 2/HSA M 45
M: 6 Maybach 16-cyl. diesels; 2 controllable-pitch props; 11,400 hp

REMARKS: Ex-German Rhein-class former patrol-boat tender. Transferred on 15-11-76, having served primarily as a training ship in the West German Navy until placed in reserve on 20-12-71. Two radar directors for the 100-mm guns.

◆ **1 training ship** Bldr: Blohm & Voss, Hamburg, West Germany

A 578 SAVARONA (ex-*Gunes Dil*)

Savarona   J.-C. Bellonne, 1973

D: 5,750 tons   **S:** 18 kts   **Dim:** 123.0 × 16.1 × 5.6
A: 2/75-mm (I × 2) – 2/40-mm AA (I × 2) – 2/20-mm (I × 2)
Electron Equipt: Radars: 2/Sperry Mk 2   **Man:** 132 men, 80 midshipmen
M: 2 sets GT; 2 props; 8,000 hp   **Boilers:** 4   **Range:** 9,000/15

REMARKS: A former state yacht, launched on 28-2-31 and converted to a cadet-training ship in 1952. Pendant number not painted on. White hull, buff stacks. Has 75-mm guns for saluting.

◆ **1 ex-U.S. Cherokee-class fleet tug** Bldr: United Eng. Co., Alameda, Cal.

	Laid down	L	In serv.
A 587 GAZAL (ex-*Sioux*, ATF-75)	14-2-42	27-5-42	6-12-42

D: 1,235 tons (1,675 fl)   **S:** 16.5 kts   **Dim:** 62.48 (59.44 pp) × 11.73 × 4.67
A: 1/76.2-mm DP   **Man:** 85 men   **Fuel:** 300 tons   **Electric:** 260 kw
M: 4 GM 12-278 diesels, electric drive; 1 prop; 3,000 hp

REMARKS: Transferred on 30-10-72 and purchased outright on 15-8-73. Can be used for salvage. Similar to submarine-rescue ship *Kurtaran* (A-584).

SERVICE CRAFT

◆ **1 yard oiler** Bldr: Gölçük NSY

Y 1207 GÖLÇÜK

   D: 1,250 tons   **S:** 12.5 kts   **Dim:** 56.4 × 9.55 × 3.05
   A: . . .   **M:** 1 Burmeister & Wain diesel; 700 hp

REMARKS: Launched on 4-11-53. Cargo: 760 tons of fuel oil. Former number A-573.

◆ **3 small yard oilers** Bldr: Taskizak NDY, Istanbul

Y 1233   Y 1234   Y 1235

   D: 300 tons   **S:** 11 kts   **Dim:** 33.6 × 8.5 × 1.8
   M: 1 GM 6-71 diesel; 1 prop; 225 hp   **Cargo:** 150 tons

◆ **2 Van-class water tankers** Bldr: Gölçük NSY, 1969-70

Y 1208 VAN   Y 1209 ULABAT

   D: 900 tons (1,250 fl)   **S:** 10 kts   **Dim:** 53.1 × 9.0 × 3.0
   M: 1 diesel; 1 prop; 650 hp   **Cargo:** 700 tons

◆ **1 ex-German FW-1-class water tanker** Bldr: Schichau, Bremerhaven

	Laid down	L	In serv.
Y 1217 SÖGÜT (ex-FW-2)	5-4-63	3-9-63	4-1-64

   D: 598 tons (626 fl)   **S:** 9.5 kts   **Dim:** 44.03 (41.1 pp) × 7.8 × 2.63
   Man: 12 men   **Range:** 2,150/9   **Fuel:** 15 tons   **Electric:** 130 kva
   M: 1 MWM 12-cyl. diesel; 1 prop; 230 hp

REMARKS: Transferred on 3-12-75. Cargo: 343 tons of fresh water.

◆ **6 small water tenders** Bldr: Taskizak NDY, Istanbul

Y 1211   Y 1212   Y 1213   Y 1214   Y 1215   Y 1216

   D: 300 tons   **S:** 11 kts   **Dim:** 33.6 × 8.5 × 1.8
   M: 1 GM 6-71 diesel; 1 prop; 225 hp   **Cargo:** 150 tons

◆ **3 Kanarya-class cargo lighters** Bldr: Taskizak NDY, Istanbul, 1972-74

Y 1155 KANARYA   Y 1156 SARKÖY   Y 1165 ECEABAD

Kanarya – at launch   1972

SERVICE CRAFT (*continued*)

D: . . .   **S:** 10 kts   **Dim:** . . . × . . . × . . .
A: 1/20-mm AA   **M:** 1 diesel; 1 prop; . . . hp

◆ **4 transport ferries** Bldr: Great Britain, 1940-42

Y 1163 LAPSEKI   Y 1164 ERDEK   Y 1166 KILYA   Y 1168 TUZLA

Lapseki

D: 700 tons (1,012 grt)   **S:** 9.5 kts   **Dim:** 56.0 × 12.2 × 2.7
A: 1/20-mm AA   **M:** 1 set reciprocating steam; 1 prop; 700 hp

REMARKS: Survivors of a class of eleven. Used as personnel and vehicle ferries in the Dardanelles. Ramps at both ends. Can quickly convert to minelayers.

◆ **3 ex-U.S. non-self-propelled gate craft** Bldr: Weaver SY, Orange, Texas, 1960-61

Y 1201 (ex-YNG-45)   Y 1202 (ex-YNG-46)   Y 1203 (ex-YNG-47)

D: 325 tons (fl)   **Dim:** 33.5 × 10.4 × 1.5

◆ **2 ex-U.S. APL-41-class barracks barges**

	Bldr	L
Y 1204 (ex-APL-47)	Puget Sound Bridge & Dredge, Seattle, Wash.	5-1-45
Y 1205 (ex-APL-53)	Tampa SB, Tampa, Fla.	3-3-45

D: 2,660 tons (fl)   **Dim:** 79.6 × 14.99 × 2.59
Man: 650 men   **Electric:** 300 kw

REMARK: Y-1204 was transferred in 10-72, Y-1205 in 12-74.

◆ **2 Oncü-class coastal tugs** Bldr: Gölçük NSY, 1953

Y 1120 ONCÜ   Y 1124 ÖNDER

D: 500 tons   **S:** 12 kts   **Dim:** 40.0 × 9.1 × 4.0   **M:** Diesel

◆ **3 ex-U.S. Army 254-design coastal tugs** Bldr: U.S.A., 1943-44

Y 1118 AKBAS (ex-. . .)   Y 1119 KEPEZ (ex-. . .)   Y 1120 ONDEV (ex-. . .)

D: 570 tons (967 fl)   **S:** 12 kts   **Dim:** 45.42 (42.67 pp) × 10.06 × 4.12
Man: 28 men   **Fuel:** 400 tons   **Electric:** 50 kw   **Boilers:** 2
M: 1 set Skinner Uniflow reciprocating steam; 1 prop; . . . hp

REMARK: Transferred in 1963.

◆ **1 ex-U.S. coastal tug**

Y 1122 KUVVET (ex-. . .)

D: 390 tons   **S:** . . .   **Dim:** 32.1 × 7.9 × 3.6

REMARK: Transferred in 2-62.

◆ **1 ex-U.S. Army 320-design small harbor tug**

Y 1134 ERSEN BAYRAK

D: 30 tons   **S:** 9 kts   **Dim:** 13.8 × 3.9 × 1.6
M: 1 diesel; 1 prop; 175 hp

REMARK: Transferred in 6-71.

◆ **2 Turkish-designed harbor tugs** Bldr: Denizcilik, Bancusi, 1976

Y . . .   Y . . .

D: 300 grt   **S:** . . .   **Dim:** 32.8 × 8.9 × . . .   **M:** Diesels; 250 hp

◆ **2 ex-U.S. small harbor tugs**

Y 1117 SONDUREN (ex-YTL-751)   Y 1121 YEDEKCI (ex-YTL-155)

D: 100 tons (120 fl)   **S:** 12 kts   **Dim:** 21.34 × 5.89 × 2.21
M: 1 Atlas diesel; 1 prop; 500 hp   **Fuel:** 18 tons

REMARK: Transferred in 4-54 and 11-57.

◆ **1 ex-U.S. floating crane**

Y 1023 ALGARNA III (ex-YD-185)

REMARK: Transferred in 9-63.

◆ **1 ex-U.S. ARD-12-class floating dry dock**

Y 1087 (ex-ARD-12)

Dim: 149.86 × 24.69 × 1.73 (light)   **Lift capacity:** 3,500 tons

REMARK: Launched in 1943 and transferred in 11-71.

◆ **6 miscellaneous floating dry docks**

Y 1081 (16,000-ton capacity)	Y 1084 (4,500-ton capacity)
Y 1082 (12,000-ton capacity)	Y 1085 (400-ton capacity)
Y 1083 (2,500-ton capacity)	Y 1086 (3,000-ton capacity)

REMARKS: Y-1083 was built in Turkey in 1958 with U.S. funds. These docks are named in sequence *Havuz I* to *Havuz VI*.

TURKEY (*continued*)

MARINE POLICE FORCE
(GENDARMERIE)

PATROL BOATS

◆ **3 SAR-33 class**

Bldrs: J-61: Abeking & Rasmussen, Lemwerder, West Germany; others: Taskizak NDY, Istanbul

J 61   J 62   J 63

    D: 150 tons (170 fl)   **S:** 40 kts   **Dim:** 33.5 (29.0 wl) × 8.6 × 1.85
    A: 1/40-mm AA − 2/12.7-mm machine guns (I × 2)   **Man:** 23 men
    Range: 450/35, 1,000/. . .   **Fuel:** 18 tons   **Electric:** 300 kw
    M: 3 SACM-AGO V16CSHR diesels; 3 controllable-pitch props; 12,000 hp

REMARKS: J-61 was launched on 12-12-77 and J-62 in 7-78; date for J-63 not available. Prototype built in Germany. Wedge-shaped hull design of remarkable seaworthiness and steadiness at high speeds in heavy weather. Turkey will build fourteen units of this class for Libya. The same design can accommodate guns of up to 76-mm bore, missiles, and a propulsion plant of up to twice the power of the above. The 40-mm AA is in a Mk-3 mount.

◆ **23 AB-25 class**   Bldr: Taskizak NDY, Istanbul, 1972-78

J 21 to J 34   J 41 to J 49

J-28   1976

    D: 170 tons (fl)   **S:** 22 kts   **Dim:** 40.24 × 6.4 × 1.65
    A: 2/40-mm AA (I × 2) − 2/12.7-mm machine guns
    M: 2 SACM-AGO V16CSHR diesels; 2 props; 4,800 hp; 2 cruise diesels; 300 hp

REMARKS: Ten sisters are operated by the Turkish Navy. Some have one 40-mm AA aft and one 20-mm AA forward. Built with French assistance.

◆ **8 German KW-15 class**   Bldr: Schweers, Bardenfleth, West Germany, 1961-62

J 12 to J 16   J 18 to J 20

J-16   1970

    D: 59.5 tons (69.6 fl)   **S:** 25 kts   **Dim:** 28.9 × 4.7 × 1.42
    A: 1/40-mm AA − 2/20-mm AA (I × 2)   **Man:** 15 men   **Fuel:** 8 tons
    M: 2 MTU 12-cyl. diesels; 2 props; 2,000 hp   **Range:** 1,500/19

REMARK: Will probably be replaced by the SAR-33 class.

U.S.S.R.

Today, our country has a powerful oceangoing fleet capable beyond any question of doubt of serving its interests at sea.

          ADMIRAL GORSHKOV
          Commander in Chief of the
          Soviet Navy

Demonstrating economic and military power abroad; showing readiness for action; deterring potential enemies and encouraging friends; being so equipped that probable enemies see the futility of combat — this is a situation that has often in the past led to the settlement of political ends without recourse to military operations.

          ADMIRAL GORSHKOV
          Commander in Chief of the
          Soviet Navy

Submarines play an important role in the Soviet Navy's missions. Of all types of combatants, they are the most able to fullfill the needs of modern warfare.

ADMIRAL SMIRNOV
First Deputy Commander in Chief
of the Soviet Navy

Although surface ships have ceded the primary role to submarines and naval aviation, they are still an essential component of the navy.

ADMIRAL GORSHKOV
Commander in Chief of the
Soviet Navy

The advent of jet aircraft carrying long-range missiles has increased significantly the military usefulness of naval aviation. Not even the most modern surface ships of our potentional enemy could withstand the weaponry of our naval aviation.

ADMIRAL SMIRNOV
First Deputy Commander in Chief
of the Soviet Navy

Kiev

1978

PERSONNEL: 431,000 men and women: 57,000 officers, 84,000 petty officers, and 290,000 sailors (nearly all conscripts).

MERCHANT MARINE (1978): 7,991 ships—22,261,927 grt
(tankers: 495 ships—4,693,173 grt)

WARSHIPS IN SERVICE OR UNDER CONSTRUCTION AS OF 1 JANUARY 1980

	L	Tons	Main armament
◆ 2 (+2) VTOL carriers			
2 (+2) KIEV	1972-	36,000	Missile launchers, guns, helicopters, VTOL aircraft
		Tons (surfaced)	
◆ 355 (+) submarines			
90 (+) ballistic-missile:			
0 (+1) TYPHOON (nuclear)	. . .	. . .	. . .
10 (+. . .) DELTA III (nuclear)	1975-	13,250 (submerged)	16/SS-N-18, 6/TT
2 DELTA II (nuclear)	1975	9,700	16/SS-N-8, 6/TT
16 DELTA I (nuclear)	1972-77	8,100	12/SS-N-8, 6/TT
34 YANKEE (nuclear)	1967-74	7,900	16/SS-N-6, 6/TT
1 HOTEL III (nuclear)	1965	4,500	3/SS-N-8, 8/TT
8 HOTEL II (nuclear)	1960-63	4,500	3/SS-N-5, 8/TT
1 GOLF IV (diesel)	1958-61	2,500	6/SS-N-8, 10/TT
1 GOLF III (diesel)	1958-61	2,300	3/SS-N-6, 10/TT
13 GOLF II (diesel)	1958-61	2,300	3/SS-N-5, 10/TT
4 GOLF I (diesel)	1958-61	2,300	3/SS-N-4, 10/TT
65 (+) cruise-missile attack:			
1 PAPA (nuclear)	1970	6,580 (submerged)	10/SS-N-7, 8/TT
4 (+) CHARLIE II (nuclear)	1973-	4,300	8/SS-N-7, . ./SS-N-15, 6/TT
10 CHARLIE I (nuclear)	1968-72	4,000	8/SS-N-7, 6/TT
29 ECHO II (nuclear)	1960-68	4,800	8/SS-N-3 or SS-N-12, 10/TT
16 JULIETT (diesel)	1961-68	2,800	4/SS-N-3, 10/TT
5 WHISKEY LONG BIN (diesel)	1961-63	1,200	4/SS-N-3, 4/TT
200 (+) attack:			
2-3 ALFA (nuclear)	1972-	3,900	. ./SS-N-15, . ./TT
8 (+) VICTOR II (nuclear)	1972-	4,500	. ./SS-N-15, 8/TT
14 VICTOR I (nuclear)	1967-74	4,300	. ./SS-N-15, 8/TT
5 ECHO (nuclear)	1960-68	4,600	10/TT
13 NOVEMBER (nuclear)	1958-62	4,000	12/TT
10 (+) TANGO (diesel)	1972-	3,000	. ./SS-N-15, . ./TT

WARSHIPS IN SERVICE OR UNDER CONSTRUCTION (*continued*)

		Tons	
4 Bravo (diesel)	1968-72	2,400	6/TT
60 Foxtrot (diesel)	1957-74	1.950	10/TT
1 Mod. Golf (diesel)	1958-61	2,300	10/TT
12 Romeo (diesel)	1960	1,330	8/TT
15 Zulu IV (diesel)	1952-55	1,900	10/TT
50 Whiskey (diesel)	1949-57	1,050	6/TT
4 Whiskey Canvas Bag (diesel)	1949-57	1,080	4/TT
2 Quebec (diesel)	1954-57	460	4/TT

◆ 39 (+5) cruisers

2 helicopter:

2 Moskva	1964-66	14,500	4/SA-N-3, 1/SUW-N-1, 16/helicopters, ASW weapons

25 (+5) guided-missile:

0 (+3?) . . .	1979	7,900	. . .
0 (+2) Kirov	1977-	25,000	. . .
6 (+1) Kara	1971-78	8,200	8/SS-N-14, 4/SA-N-3, 4/SA-N-4, 4/76.2-mm DP, 10/TT, 1/helicopter
10 Kresta II	1967-76	6,000	8/SS-N-14, 4/SA-N-3, 4/57-mm, 10/TT, 1/helicopter
4 Kresta I	1965-66	6,000	4/SS-N-3, 4/SA-N-1, 4/57-mm, 10/TT, 1/helicopter
4 Kynda	1961-65	4,400	8/SS-N-3, 2/SA-N-1, 4/76.2-mm DP, 6/TT
1 Mod. Sverdlov	1951	12,900	2/SA-N-2, 9/152-mm, 12/100-mm DP, 16/37-mm AA

12 conventional:

2 Mod. Sverdlov	1950-54	12,900	2/SA-N-4, 6 or 9/152-mm, 12/100-mm DP
9 Sverdlov	1950-60	12,900	12/152-mm, 12/100-mm DP
1 Chapaev	1947	12,000	12/152-mm, 8/100-mm DP

◆ 90 + destroyers

39 guided-missile:

5 Mod. Kashin	1963-72	3,950	4/SS-N-2C, 4/SA-N-1, 4/76.2-mm DP, 5/TT
14 Kashin	1963-72	3,750	4/SA-N-1, 4/76.2-mm DP, 5/TT
8 Kanin	1958-60	3,700	2/SA-N-1, 8/57-mm, 10/TT
3 Mod. Kildin	1958	3,100	4/SS-N-2C, 4/76.2-mm DP, 16/45- or 57-mm AA, 4/TT
1 Kildin	1958	2,900	1/SS-N-1, 16/57-mm, 4/TT
8 Sam Kotlin	1955-57	2,850	2/SA-N-1, 2/130-mm DP, 12/45-mm AA, 5/TT

51 conventional:

18 Kotlin and Mod. Kotlin	1954-57	2,850	4/130-mm DP, 16/45-mm AA, 4 or 8/25-mm AA, 5 or 10/TT
33 Skory and Mod. Skory	1949-54	2,240	4/130-mm DP, 2/85-mm or 5/57-mm AA, 5 or 10/TT

◆ 123 (+) frigates

24 (+ . .) Krivak II, I	1970-	3,300	4/SS-N-14, 4/SA-N-4, 2/100-mm DP or 4/76.2-mm DP, 8/TT
44 Petya II, I	1962-69	950	4/76.2-mm DP, 5 or 10/TT
18 Mirka II, I	1964-66	950	4/76.2-mm DP, 5 or 10/TT
37 Riga	1952-58	1,000	3/100-mm DP, 2 or 3/TT

◆ 128 (+) corvettes

1 (+ . .) Tarantul	1978	750 (fl)	4/SS-N-2C, 1/76.2-mm DP
21 Nanuchka III, I	1969-76	780	6/SS-N-9, 2/SA-N-4, 1/76.2-mm DP or 2/57-mm AA
6 Grisha II	1974-76	950	4/57-mm AA, 4/TT
27 Grisha III, I	1968-	950	2/SA-N-4, 2/57-mm, 4/TT
65 Poti	1961-67	500	2/57-mm AA, 2 or 4/TT
16 T-58	1957-61	790	4/57-mm AA, 2/RBU-1200

SOVIET SHIPS

Submarines

Although progress has been made in reducing radiated noise from the newest units, all types of Soviet nuclear submarines are still noisier than their Western counterparts. They can dive to considerable depths but, in spite of the strides that have been made in that area, their detection equipment still cannot match the sonars of American nuclear submarines.

The Delta I, II, and III submarines are the biggest in the world, and the U.S. Navy will not match them in size until the *Ohio* class goes into service in the early 1980s. Delta-Is and Delta-IIs deploy the SS-N-8 ballistic missile, whose range is 4,200 nautical miles. Delta-IIIs carry SS-N-18 MIRV-type missiles with a similar range. Overall, the ballistic missiles of Soviet submarines are seen as being less sophisticated than those of their American opposite numbers. For example, with the exception of the SS-N-17, they still have liquid propellants, which the West has abandoned as being too vulnerable.

The latest nuclear attack submarines have high speed and are well armed. Some of them have tactical missiles that can be launched from underwater at longer range than

SOVIET SHIPS (*continued*)

the active sonars of their adversaries can reach, a feature that constitutes a serious threat.

Finally, the most recent Tango-class conventional submarines are at least the equals of such submarines in the West.

Surface ships

Soviet surface combatants carry a multiplicity of weapon systems. They are generally more heavily armed than are ships of similar tonnage in other navies. An effort has apparently been made to build ships that would be able to deal with any threat. While habitability standards are lower than in the West, life aboard is perfectly tolerable by Soviet standards. Endurance has not been made to suffer in favor of armament, and most Soviet surface combatants have ranges equivalent to those of their Western counterparts. Damage-control equipment and training in Soviet surface ships seems to be less developed than in the West, although the ships are particularly well equipped to fight in an NBC (nuclear, biological, and/or chemical) warfare environment.

Most Soviet cruisers and destroyers are very seaworthy and fin stabilizers have been fitted to all classes of over 1,000 tons since the 1950s.

Considerable advances have been made in gas-turbine propulsion, both when it is used alone and when it is combined with other machinery. The Soviet Union continues to be a leader in the manufacture of high-performance marine propulsion diesels. Nuclear propulsion for surface warships will become a reality in 1980, when the first of a new class of very large nuclear-powered cruisers goes to sea.

Sonars, too, have been improved, as has their employment. Most new ships have both medium- and low-frequency sonars. The Soviet Navy employs considerable numbers of towed variable-depth sonars in larger ships and has also developed novel tactics for the use of helicopter dipping sonars from surface ships.

It seems that in the future radars in the whole gamut of frequencies will be used extensively. The use of varying pulse-repetition rates, frequency agility, phased antenna arrays, and digital processing is now commonplace.

For lack of sufficiently sophisticated and rugged computers, the Soviet Navy has not, it seems, been able to produce a satisfactory tactical data system.

WEAPONS AND SYSTEMS

A. MISSILES

◆ ballistic missiles

NOTE: All have liquid-fuel propulsion, except the SS-N-17 which has solid-fuel propulsion.

SS-N-4

Range: 300 nautical miles. Nuclear warhead. Fitted in Golf-I diesel-powered fleet ballistic-missile submarines. Can be launched only from the surface.

SS-N-5

Range: 900 nautical miles. Nuclear warhead of about 800 kilotons. Fitted in Hotel II nuclear-powered submarines and in Golf-II diesel-powered strategic submarines. Can be launched while submerged. Range has been increased from its original 700 nautical miles.

SS-N-6

Range: 1,300 nautical miles. Nuclear warhead of about 1 metaton. Fitted in Yankee-class nuclear submarines. Can be launched while submerged. A more recent version has a 1,600 nautical-mile range and an MRV-type warhead.

SS-N-8 (NATO code name: Sawfly)

Range: 4,200 miles. Nuclear warhead of about 1 megaton. Fitted in Delta I and Delta II nuclear submarines.

SS-N-13

Range: 370 nautical miles. Nuclear warhead. Tactical ballistic missile. Program suspended in 1973 due to inadequate technology, but the concept may yet be revived in a new program.

SS-N-17

Range: 1,800 nautical miles. Nuclear warhead. First ballistic missile with solid-fuel propulsion. Aboard one experimental Yankee-class submarine.

SS-N-18

Two stage missile with range of 4,000 nautical miles. Triple nuclear MRV-type warhead. Believed to be aboard Delta-III submarines. Circular error probable (CEP): 700 – 1,000-m.

◆ surface-to-surface cruise missiles

NOTE: Liquid-fuel propulsion, except for SS-N-7, which has a solid-propellant engine.

SS-N-1 (NATO code name: Scrubber)

Range: 25 nautical miles on surface targets, 120 to 130 miles on land targets. Subsonic turbojet engine. Radio-directed for initial trajectory, then active automatic radar guidance to the target. Nuclear or conventional warhead. Fitted in the remaining Kildin-class destroyer, *Neulovimyy*. No longer produced.

SS-N-2 A and B (NATO code name: Styx)

Maximum range: 25 nautical miles. Practical range: 16 nautical miles. Liquid propulsion. I-band active radar guidance in targeting, with infrared homing in the most recent version, SS-N-2B. Altitude can be preset at 100, 150, 200, 250, or 300 m. 400 to 450 kg conventional warhead. Installed in Osa-I and Osa-II guided-missile boats. The SS-N-2B has folding wings.

SS-N-2C (formerly SS-N-11)

Maximum range: 45 nautical miles. Liquid propulsion. Altitude can be preset at 100, 150, 200, 250, or 300 m. Combined radar and infrared terminal homing. During its final approach to the target, the missile descends to an altitude of 2 to 5 m. In order to employ fully the over-the-horizon maximum range of the SS-N-2C, it is necessary to have a forward observer. The SS-N-2C is carried by the destroyers of the Modified Kashin and Modified Kildin classes, by the Tarantul guided-missile corvette, and by the Nanuchka-II-class guided-missile corvettes of the Indian Navy.

SS-N-3 (NATO code name: Shaddock)

Maximum range: 250 nautical miles. Inertial guidance with mid-course correction by radio, active radar homing to target. Turbojet propulsion. Conventional or nuclear warhead. Fitted in Kynda (quadruple launcher) and Kresta-I (twin launcher) cruisers, and Whiskey Long Bin, Juliett, and Echo-II submarines. Launched from the surface by submarines.

WEAPONS AND SYSTEMS (*continued*)

SS-N-7

Maximum range: 30 nautical miles. Conventional warhead, can be launched while submerged. Charlie-I and Charlie-II class nuclear-powered attack submarines have eight per ship and the Papa class has ten.

SS-N-9

Maximum range: 30 miles, but can reach 150 miles with an aerial relay (aircraft fitted with a Video Data Link system), inertial guidance, and active radar homing to the target. Turbojet propulsion. Conventional or nuclear warhead. Installed in Nanuchka-class guided-missile corvettes and the Sarancha-class hydrofoil.

SS-N-12

Maximum range: 300 nautical miles. Conventional or nuclear warhead. Replacing the SS-N-3 on submarines and is aboard the *Kiev*.

◆ surface-to-air missiles

SA-N-1 (NATO code name: Goa)

Twin-launcher. Range: 30,000 m, interception altitude: 1,000 to 50,000 feet. Guidance: radar/command. Conventional warhead, 60 kg. Fitted on Kynda and Kresta-I cruisers, as well as on Kashin, Kanin, and Kotlin destroyers. Also has a surface-to-surface capability.

SA-N-2 (NATO code name: Guideline)

Twin-launcher. Range: 40,000 m, interception altitude: 1,000 to 80,000 feet. Guidance: radar/command. Conventional warhead, 150 kg. Fitted on the cruiser *Dzerzhinskiy* only. Obsolescent.

SA-N-3 (NATO code name: Goblet)

Twin launcher. Range: 30,000 m, interception altitude: 500 to 80,000 feet. Guidance: radar/command. Conventional warhead, 60 kg. Fitted on Kresta-II and Kara cruisers as well as the *Moskva*-class helicopter cruisers. An improved version has a range of 55,000 m and is on the *Kiev*. Goblet has an anti-surface target capability.

SA-N-4 (short-range system)

Twin launcher, retracting into a vertical drum. Range: 9,000 m, interception altitude: 30 to 10,000 feet. Guidance: radar/command. Conventional warhead. Fitted in Kara cruisers, two *Sverdlov* cruisers, Krivak guided-missile frigates, Grisha and Nanuchka guided-missile corvettes, the Sarancha hydrofoil, and the replenishment ship *Berezina*.

SA-N-5 (very-short-range system)

Naval version of SA-7 Strela. Fitted on some Osa-class guided-missile patrol boats, some Polnocnyy-class landing ships, and some auxiliaries.

NOTE: Both a vertically launched naval surface-to-air missile and a new missile fired from a single-armed launcher have been reported as under development.

◆ air-to-surface missiles

AS 1 (NATO code name: Kennel)

Range: 50 to 55 nautical miles. Turbojet propulsion. Semi-active radar guidance. Conventional warhead. No longer used by the U.S.S.R.

AS 2 (NATO code name: Kipper)

Range: 100 nautical miles. Solid-fuel propulsion. Inertial guidance or automatic pilot with radar homing head. 900-1,000 kg. Conventional or nuclear warhead. Launched from Badger-C aircraft.

AS 4 (NATO code name: Kitchen)

Range: 170 nautical miles. Nuclear warhead. Inertial guidance with radar terminal homing. In service on Backfire and Blinder aircraft.

AS 5 (NATO code name: Kelt)

Range: 100 nautical miles. Solid-fuel propulsion. Inertial or autopilot guidance with radar terminal homing. Conventional and nuclear warheads. In service on Badger-C and Badger-G aircraft.

AS 6 (NATO code name: Kingfish)

Range: over 100 nautical miles. Conventional or nuclear warhead. In service on Badger-C aircraft, two on each.

AS 7

Range: 6 nautical miles. Mach. 1. Tactical weapon. Solid-fuel propulsion. Pencil-beam radar terminal homing. 100 kg. Conventional warhead. Used on Forger aircraft aboard the *Kiev*.

AS 9

Range: 55 nautical miles. Anti-radar missile. Turbojet propulsion. Passive homing on electromagnetic radiation. 150 kg. Conventional warhead. In use on Badger, Backfire, and Fitter-C and Fitter-D aircraft.

AS 10

Range: 6 nautical miles. Mach 1.2. Solid propulsion. Electro-optical guidance. Conventional warhead of 100 kg. Carried by Fitter-D.

B. GUNS

152-mm

Fitted in triple turrets on *Sverdlov* and *Chapaev* cruisers. Individual barrels can be loaded and elevated separately.

  barrel length: 57 calibers
  muzzle velocity: 915 m/sec
  altitude arc: −5° to +50°
  maximum rate of fire: 4 to 5 rounds/min/barrel
  maximum range: 27,000 m
  effective range: 18,000 m
  projectile weight: 50 kg
  fire control: Top Bow or Egg Cup radars in the upper turrets forward and aft, or 8-m range-finder in each turret

130-mm twin

Semi-automatic for surface and air targets. Fitted on Kotlin and SAM-Kotlin destroyers. Mechanically triaxially stabilized. Twin mount with electric or hydraulic-electric pointing system.

  barrel length: 58 calibers
  muzzle velocity: 900 m/sec
  arc of elevation: −5° to +80°

WEAPONS AND SYSTEMS (*continued*)

SUW-N-1 system with FRAS-1 missile

SA-N-3 launcher with Goblet missile

SS-N-2C launchers (SA-N-1 system at right) on a Modified Kashin-class destroyer

SS-N-2B launcher on an Osa-II-class patrol boat

Kiev

1. Top Sail 3-D radar 2. Top Knot radome with High Pole B atop 3. Top Steer 3-D radar 4. Rum Tub ESM antennas 5. Bell Bash jammer antennas 6. Bell Thump jammer radome 7. Tee Plinth electro-optical device with conical Pert Spring radome just below it 8. Side Globe radomes

WEAPONS AND SYSTEMS (*continued*)

100-mm dual-purpose guns on the Krivak-II-class frigate Neukrotimyy

Head Lights missile-control and tracking radar on a Kara-class cruiser

Towed variable-depth sonar partially deployed from a Krivak-class frigate

Helicopter-type dipping sonar being deployed from a Mirka-II-class frigate. Note the circular covers over gas-turbine exhausts.

Top Sail (left) and Head Net-C search radars and Side Globe radomes aboard an early Kresta-II-class cruiser. Two Gatling AA guns are visible at lower center, below the tub for their director.

WEAPONS AND SYSTEMS (*continued*)

maximum rate of fire: 10 rounds/min/barrel
maximum range, surface target: 28,000 m
effective range, surface target: 16,000 to 18,000 m
maximum vertical range: 13,000 m
projectile weight: 27 kg
fire control: stabilized Wasp Head director, with a Sun Visor tracking radar.
Egg Cup ranging radar on each mount (being removed)

130-mm twin

Semi-automatic type fitted on *Skoryy*-class destroyers.
barrel length: 50 calibers
muzzle velocity: 875 m/sec
arc of elevation: −5° to + 45°
maximum rate of fire: 10 rounds/min/barrel
maximum range: 24,000 m
effective range: 14,000 to 15,000 m
projectile weight: 27 kg
fire control: Four Eyes optical director and associated Top Bow or Post Lamp radars.

100-mm twin

Mechanically triaxially stabilized mounts installed on *Sverdlov* and *Chapaev* cruisers.
barrel length: 50 calibers
weight: approx. 40 tons
muzzle velocity: 900/sec
arc of elevation: −15° to 85°
maximum rate of fire: 15 rounds/min/barrel
maximum range, surface target: 20,000 m
effective range, surface target: 10,000 to 12,000 m
maximum range, AA fire: 15,000 m
effective range, AA fire: 8,000 to 9,000 m
projectile weight: 16 kg
fire control: Round Top stabilized director with Sun Visor tracking radar and/or associated Top Bow or Post Lamp radars.
Egg Cup ranging radar on each mount (being removed)

100-mm single

Gun mount with a shield. Installed on Riga frigates, and Don-class submarine tenders.
barrel length: 56 calibers
muzzle velocity: 850 m/sec
arc of elevation: −5° to + 40°
maximum rate of fire: 15 rounds/min
maximum range: 16,000 m
effective range: 10,000 m
projectile weight: 13.5 kg
fire control: stabilized Wasp Head director fitted with Sun Visor radar

100-mm automatic AA

A single-barreled, water-cooled gun in an enclosed mounting found on Krivak-III-class frigates.
rate of fire: 40 rounds/min

maximum theoretical range: 15,000 m
maximum effective range: 8,000 m
fire control: Kite Screech radar director

85-mm AA

Twin-barreled gun mount on some *Skoryy* destroyers.
barrel length: 50 calibers
muzzle velocity: 850 m/sec
arc of elevation: −5° to +70°
maximum rate of fire: 10 rounds/min/barrel
maximum range, surface target: 15,000 m
effective range, surface target: 8,000 to 9,000 m
practical maximum range, AA fire: 6,000 m
fire control: Cylinder Head optical director (no radar).

76.2-mm twin

Installed on Kara and Kynda cruisers, Kashin destroyers and Krivak-I, Petya and Mirka frigates, *Smolny*-class training ships and *Ivan Susanin*-class icebreakers.
length of barrel: 60 calibers
muzzle velocity: 900 m/sec
maximum rate of fire: 60 rounds/min/barrel
arc of elevation: +80°
maximum range, AA fire: 10,000 m
effective range, AA fire: 6,000 to 7,000 m
projectile weight: 16 kg
fire control: Owl Screech or Hawk Screech radar director.

76.2-m single

Fully automatic, dual-purpose gun with on-mount crew. Carried by Nanuchka-III- and Tarantul-class corvettes, Matka-class guided-missile hydrofoils, and the Slepen-class patrol boat.
rate of fire: 120 rounds/min
theoretical maximum range against surface target: 14,000 m
practical range against aerial target: 6,000 to 7,000 m

57-mm

Single-barrel gun mount (Mod. *Skoryy* destroyers and some Sasha minesweepers), twin-barrel (several classes), and quadruple on Kanin and Kildin destroyers; in the latter case the guns are mounted in superimposed pairs.
length of barrel: 70 calibers
muzzle velocity: 900 to 1,000 m/sec
arc of elevation: 0° to +90°
maximum rate of fire: 150 rounds/min/gun
effective vertical range: 4,500 m
fire control: by Hawk Screech or Muff Cob radar directors

57-mm twin automatic

This equipment, which appears to be entirely automatic from the ammunition-handling room to the gun mount, is installed on *Moskva*, Kresta-I, and Kresta-II cruisers, Poti and Grisha corvettes, Nanuchka-I guided-missile corvettes, Turya torpedo boats, Ropucha LSTs, *Ugra* submarine tenders, and the replenishment ship *Berezina*. Now, removed from *Boris Chilikin* replenishment ships and *Manych*-class oilers.
length of barrel: 70 calibers?
water-cooling system

WEAPONS AND SYSTEMS (*continued*)

maximum rate of fire: 120 rounds/min/barrel
maximum effective vertical range: 5,000 to 6,000 m
fire control: by Muff Cob or Bass Tilt radar directors.

45-mm

Quadruple-barreled installations in SAM-Kotlin, Kotlin and one Mod. Kildin destroyers; single on some Sasha minesweepers. The quadruple-mounted guns are in two superimposed pairs.

length of barrel: 85 calibers
muzzle velocity: 900 m/sec
arc of elevation: 0° to +90°
rate of fire: 300 rounds/min/mount
effective maximum vertical range: 4,000 m
fire control: Hawk Screech radar director (visually in Sasha)

37-mm Model 39

Installed in twin-barreled mounts in *Sverdlov* and *Chapaev* cruisers, *Skoryy* destroyers, Riga frigates, and T-43-class minesweepers.

length of barrel: 60 calibers?
muzzle velocity: 900 m/sec
arc of elevation: 0° to +80°?
maximum rate of fire: 160 rounds/min/gun
fire control: on-mount lead-computing sights

30-mm twin automatic

Installed in a light mount on several classes of ships—cruisers, destroyers, guided-missile boats, supply ships, etc. Water-cooling system.

length of barrel: 60 calibers
muzzle velocity: 1,000 m/sec
maximum rate of fire: 240 rounds/min/barrel
effective maximum range, AA fire: 2,500 to 3,000 m
fire control: by Drum Tilt radar director or remote optical director.

30-mm Gatling gun

This gun is in service on *Kiev*-class carriers, Kara and Kresta-II cruisers, and several other classes. It is installed in mounts similar to those of the 30-mm AA double-barreled automatic guns, and is designed to fire a great number of rounds at an extremely high rate in order to intercept a cruise missile at a comparatively short distance. It has six 30-mm barrels.

minimum rate of fire: 3,000 rounds/min/mount
fire control: Bass Tilt radar director or remote visual director

25-mm twin

Found on many ships and made up of two superimposed guns.

length of barrel: 60 calibers
muzzle velocity: 900 m/sec
maximum rate of fire: 150-200 rounds/min/barrel
fire control: on-mount ring sights

C. ANTISUBMARINE WEAPONS

◆ **missiles**

FRAS 1

Rocket-propelled weapon similar to the U.S. Navy's ASROC. Installed on *Kiev*-class carriers and *Moskva*-class helicopter cruisers. Maximum range: 16 miles. Nuclear warhead. Twin SUW-N-1 system.

SS-N-14

A weapon conceptually resembling the French Malafon, using a solid-propelled aerodynamic cruise missile that drops a parachute-retarded homing torpedo. Maximum range: 25 nautical miles (4 nautical miles minimum). Carried by Kara- and Kresta-II-class cruisers and Krivak-I- and Krivak-II-class frigates. Can also be used against surface ships.

SS-N-15

ASW missile similar to the U.S. Navy's SUBROC. Maximum range: 25 miles. Nuclear warhead. Submerged-launched from submarine torpedo tubes.

SS-N-16

Derived from the SS-N-15 system but using a homing torpedo payload in lieu of the nuclear depth bomb. Maximum range: 65 nautical miles.

◆ **rockets**

RBU-1200

Formerly MBU-1800. Made up of two horizontal rows of short, superimposed barrels, three on two. Tube diameter: 0.250 m; length: 1.400 m; the 70-kg (34-kg warhead) rocket is somewhat shorter. Range: 1,200 m. Tubes elevate but are fixed in train. Installed in S.O.-1 patrol boats and Natya and T-58 minesweepers.

RBU-2500

Formerly MBU-2500. Made up of two horizontal rows of eight barrels each, approximately 1.600 m in length, which can be trained and elevated. Manual reloading. Range: 2,500 m. 21-kg warhead. Carried by Kildin and Mod. Kildin, one SAM Kotlin, most Mod. Kotlin, and all *Mod. Skoryy* destroyers, and Petya and Riga frigates.

RBU-6000

Formerly MBU-2500A. Made up of twelve barrels, approximately 1,600 m in length, arranged in a horseshoe and fired in paired sequence. Vertical automatic loading system, barrel by barrel. Can be trained and elevated. Range: 6,000 m. Installed in *Kiev*-class carriers, *Moskva*, Kynda, Kresta-I, and Kresta-II cruisers, Kashin and Kanin guided-missile destroyers, Krivak frigates, the smaller Mirka and Petva frigates, and the Poti and Grisha corvettes.

RBU-600

Formerly MBU-4500. Made up of six barrels, 0.300 m in diameter and 1,500 in length, superimposed in two rows and fired simultaneously. Trainable. Range: 600 m. 90-kg rocket with 55-kg warhead. Used only in Mod. Kotlin destroyers.

RBU-1000

Formerly MBU-4500A. Made up of six barrels arranged in two vertical rows of three and fired in order, with vertical automatic loading. Trainable, Tube diameter: approx.

WEAPONS AND SYSTEMS (*continued*)

0.300 m. Length: approx. 1.800 m. Range: 1,000 m. 90-kg rocket with 55-kg warhead. Installed in Kara, Kresta-I, and Kresta-II cruisers and Kashin destroyers.

◆ torpedoes

The Soviet Navy uses 533-mm antisurface and ASW torpedoes, and short 400-mm ASW homing torpedoes.

D. RADARS

NOTE: Designations are NATO code names.

◆ navigation

The most widely used are the I-band Neptune, Ball End, various Don types, and Spin Trough.

◆ surface search

Most common on surface ships are Square Tie (also used for cruise-missile target-designation), Pot Head, and Pot Drum. Older equipment such as Skin Head and Ball End is being phased out. Submarines carry Snoop Tray, Snoop Slab, and Snoop Plate.

◆ long-range air search

Cross Bird, carried by some *Skoryy*-class destroyers.
Head Net A
Head Net B, consisting of 2 Head Net A antennae, mounted back-to-back in a horizontal plane (found only on *Desna*-class missile range ships).
Head Net C, consisting of 2 Head Net A antennae, mounted back-to-back, one in a horizontal plane, the other inclined.
These radars use a band that gives a 60- to 70-mile detection range on an attack bomber flying at high altitude.
Big Net, a large C-band radar fitted on Kresta-I and a few *Sverdlov* cruisers, and some Kashin destroyers. Its detection range on an aircraft is probably over 100 miles.
Slim Net (E band), early model radar fitted on some cruisers and destroyers.
Hair Net (E band), early model radar now only on one Riga frigate.
Top Trough (C band), on some *Sverdlov* cruisers.
Sea Gull (A band), copy of British WW2 Type 193.
Knife Rest (A band), antenna resembles a large television antenna.
Strut Curve (F band), mounted on the Petya and Mirka frigates and Poti and Grisha corvettes.
Strut Pair (F band), mounted on one Mod. Kildin destroyer. Employs pulse-compression.
Boat Sail, carried only by Whiskey Canvas Bag submarines. Has folding antenna.
Low Sieve, carried by *Chapaev* and some *Sverdlov* cruisers.
High Sieve. Carried by some *Sverdlov* cruisers and *Skoryy* destroyers.

◆ height-finding

Top Sail (C band), three-dimensional radar installed in *Moskva*, Kresta-II, and Kara cruisers.
Top Steer, (F band) three-dimensional radar found with Top Sail on the *Kiev;* possibly for air-controlling.

◆ tracking

Trap Door, in a retractable mount. Used for SS-N-12 on *Kiev*-class carriers.
Peel Group, mounted on Kynda and Kresta-I cruisers as well as Kashin, Kanin and SAM Kotlin destroyers. Consists of a tracking radar for high altitudes (I-band) and a missile-guidance radar at lower altitudes (E-band). The assembly is made up of two groups of large and small reflectors, in both horizontal and vertical position, with parabolic design. Maximum range approximately 30 to 40 miles. Used for guidance of the Goa missile in the SA-N-1 system.
Head Lights (F, G, H, and D bands), mounted in *Kiev* carriers and *Moskva*, Kresta-II and Kara cruisers. Similar to the Peel Group with an assembly of tracking radar for the target and guidance radar for the missile. Used for guidance for the Goblet missile of the SA-N-3 system and for the surface-to-underwater missiles of the SS-N-14 system. In several versions, designated "A", "B" and "C".
Scoop Pair (E band), guidance radar for the Shaddock missile of the SS-N-3 system on board Kynda and Kresta-I cruisers.
Pop Group (F, H, and I bands), missile guidance for the SA-N-4 system.
Eye Bowl (F band), smaller version of Head Lights, installed in Krivak frigates, missile-guidance radar for the SS-N-14 system.
Fan Song E, installed in the *Dzerzhinskiy;* used with the Guideline missile of the SA-N-2 system. Consists of two antennae made up of parabolic reflectors in the form of troughs, one vertical and one horizontal, plus three circular reflectors, two side-by-side, and a third mounted on an arm at the extreme end of the horizontal reflector. Detection range: at least 80 miles on a bomber-size aircraft.
Band Stand, On Nanuchka corvettes and the Sarancha hydrofoil for missile-tracking and control. In large radome.
Plinth Net (F band?), on Kynda and Kresta-I cruisers, possibly for SS-N-3 missile tracking.

◆ fire-control

Half Bow
Post Lamp } (I band), mounted on various older classes of ships.
Top Bow, 152-mm gun.
Sun Visor, 130-mm DP, 100-mm DP guns.
Hawk Screech, 45-mm and 76.2-mm AA guns.
Owl Screech, 76.2-mm DP.
Kite Screech, 100-mm DP.
Muff Cob (H Band), 57-mm AA twin automatic guns.
Egg Cup (E band), installed in turrets for 152-mm, 130-mm, and 100-mm AA guns.
Drum Tilt (H and I bands), installed on Osa patrol boats and ships fitted with 30-mm twin-barrel AA.
Bass Tilt (H band), used with Gatling gun fitted in *Kiev* carriers, Kara and Kresta-II cruisers, and Mod. Kildin destroyers, as well as in Grisha-III corvettes, where it also controls the twin 57-mm, and on Nanuchka-III corvettes and Matka guided-missile hydrofoils, where it also controls the 76.2-mm gun.
Front Piece and **Front Door,** used with submarine-launched missiles.

E. SONARS

Until a few years ago, the Soviet Navy showed little interest in antisubmarine warfare or, of course, submarine detection. Most of its ships were equipped with high-frequency sonar (Tamir, Pegas, Herkules). New or modernized ships appear to have better sensors.
Medium-frequency hull sonar, on Kresta-II cruisers, Kanin destroyers, Krivak frigates, and Grisha corvettes.
Medium-frequency, towed, variable-depth sonar, on *Kiev* carriers, *Moskva* and Kara cruisers, Mod. Kashin destroyers, and Krivak frigates.
Low-frequency hull sonar, on *Kiev* carriers and *Moskva* cruisers.

WEAPONS AND SYSTEMS (*continued*)

Helicopter dipping sonar, on Mirka frigates, Stenka and Pchela patrol boats, Turya torpedo boats and others.

Most submarines still have old equipment (active-passive Hercules, passive Feniks), but recent nuclear submarines have modern low-frequency sonar.

F. ELECTRONIC WARFARE

The increasing number of radomes of every description that can be seen on Soviet ships, especially on the newest and most important types (helicopter and guided-missile cruisers, for example) is an indication of the attention the Soviet Navy gives to electronic warfare. NATO code names for the antenna arrays for intercept or for jamming radars include: Side Globe, Top Hat A and B, Bell Clout, Bell Shroud, Bell, Squat, Cage Pot, Watch Dog, and Rum Tub.

Many of the more modern ships are equipped with twin-tubed chaff rocket launchers (*Kiev, Moskva*, Kresta I and II, Kara, *Berezina*) or 16-tubed fixed chaff rocket launchers (Mod. Kashin, Krivak I and II, Nanuchka, Matka, etc.).

IFF (Identification Friend or Foe) is taken care of by High Pole A and B transponders and by Square Head or other interrogators. The modern radars have integral IFF interrogation.

VTOL CARRIERS

NOTE: Rumors of the building of a nuclear-powered, Western-style, conventional air-craft carrier of 60,000 tons full-load displacement and equipped with catapults and arresting gear have appeared in the West. Both Severodvinsk and Nikolayev have been mentioned as construction sites. Completion in the near future is unlikely.

◆ **4 Kiev class**

	Bldr	Laid down	L	In serv.
KIEV	Black Sea SY, Nikolayev	9-70	12-72	5-75
MINSK	Black Sea SY, Nikolayev	12-72	5-75	2-78
KHARKOV	Black Sea SY, Nikolayev	10-75	12-78	. . .
NOVOROSSIYSK	Black Sea SY, Nikolayev	1978	. . .	. . .

Kiev

D: 36,000 tons (44,000 fl)   **S:** 32 kts   **Range:** 4,000/30, 13,500/18
Dim: 275.0 (249.5 wl) × 50.0 (38.0 wl) × 9.0   **Man:** 1,700 men
A: 8/SS-N-12 (II × 4)–2/SA-N-3 systems (II × 2) with 72 Goblet missiles–4/launch-ers for SA-N-4 (II × 2)–4/76.2-mm DP (II × 2)–8/30-Gatling AA (VI × 8)–

10/533-mm TT (V × 2)–2/SUW-N-1 systems (II × 1)–2/RBU-6000 rocket launch-ers–23/Hormone A and Hormone B helicopters–12/Forger aircraft
Electron Equipt: Radars: 1/Don Kay, 2/Don 2, 1/Top Sail, 1/Top Steer, 2/Head Lights, 2/Pop Group, 2/Owl Screech, 4/Bass Tilt, 1/Trap Door
 Sonars: 1/low-frequency, hull mounted, 1/medium-frequency, towed VDS
 ECM: 8/Side Globe, 4/Top Hat A, 4/Top Hat B, 4/Rum Tub, 2/Bell Clout–4/chaff launchers (II × 2)
M: 4 sets GT; 4 props; 140,000 hp   **Boilers:** . . .   **Fuel:** 7,000 tons

Minsk   1979

Kiev

REMARKS:

General: The Soviet Navy's designation for the *Kiev* class is Tyazholyy Protivolo-dochyy Kreuzer (heavy ASW cruiser) but it obviously has capabilities for sea-control and sea-denial missions. The hull is unusual in having a counter stern that sweeps up several meters above the waterline before meeting the transom. The vari-able-depth sonar is deployed through doors on the centerline of the transom stern; the function of the black-painted, ribbed recess to port of the VDS has not yet been determined, but it definitely is *not* a door for launching amphibious vehicles. For their size and function, the ships carry very small crews.

Aviation installations: The flight-deck portion of the upper deck is inclined about 4.5° to port of the centerline axis of the ship and is about 185 m long by 20 m wide. To protect against the hot exhaust of the Forger aircraft, it is partially covered with a mosaic of refractory tiles. There are two elevators to the hangar deck: one (19.20 m × 10.35 m) beside the stack; the other (18.50 m × 4.70 m) abaft the island. Five small ammunition elevators are connected by an on-deck rail system.

VTOL CARRIERS (continued)

Aviation: It is possible to stow a maximum of 30 Forger or 35 Hormone A/B to the exclusion of the other.

Armament: The SS-N-12 missiles are launched from four twin elevating tubes that are fixed in train. In order to use the full range of the missiles over the horizon, a forward-located, target-designation platform has to be used. On the *Kiev,* that re-

quirement is met by the Hormone-B, which carries a long-range radar giving a range of 100 nautical miles with the helicopter at an altitude of 4,000 feet. It is also not impossible that the ship uses target information relayed by a satellite. There are eight missiles in the launch tubes, plus sixteen reloads raised from a below-decks magazine by a centerline elevator between the launch-tube sets and aligned with the launchers for loading by a traversing system.

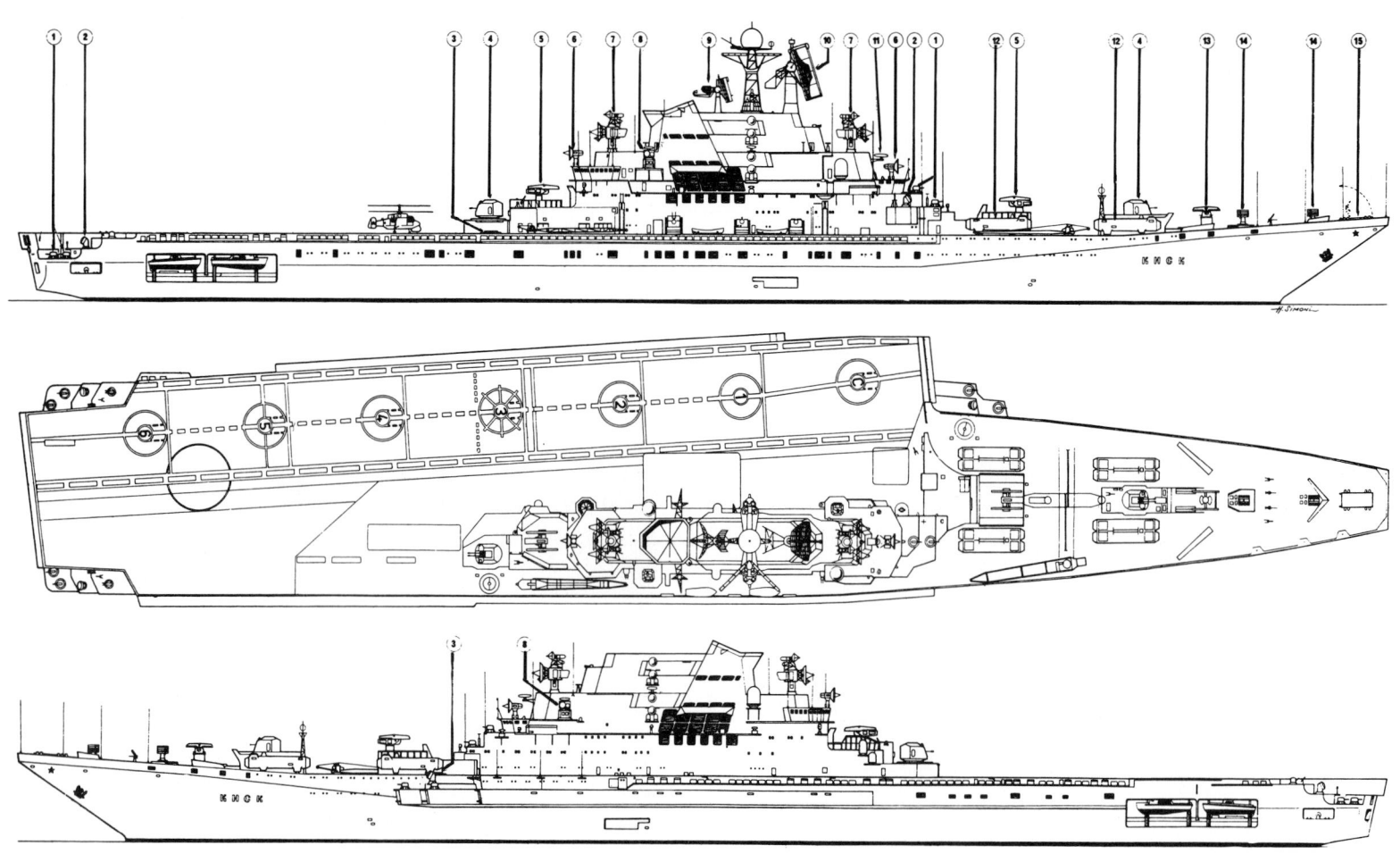

1. 30-mm Gatling guns 2. Bass Tilt radar 3. SA-N-4 system 4. Twin 76.2-mm DP mount 5. SA-N-3 system 6. Owl Screech radar 7. Head Lights radar 8. Pop Group radar 9. Top Steer radar 10. Top Sail radar 11. Don-2 radar 12. Twin launchers for SS-N-12 system 13. SUW-N-1 system 14. RBU-6000 15. Trap Door radar

VTOL CARRIERS (continued)

Island of the Kiev   1979

Island of the Minsk   1979

Kiev   1978

Minsk   1979

NAVAL AVIATION

Naval aviation, which dates from 1919, is an integral part of the Soviet Navy in which approximately 65,000 men are involved, but its organization and ranks are the same as those of the air forces. Aircraft are part of the four naval fleets (Northern, Baltic, Black Sea, and Pacific) and are under the direct control of the commanders of those fleets. The air arm has some 1,300 aircraft, including:

75 Bear, C, D, and F ⎫
60 Badger, E, F, and J ⎬ fitted for reconnaissance, electronic warfare, etc.
60 Blinder-A ⎭
40 Forger, A and B, shipboard VTOL fighters
40 Fitter, C and D, ground-attack
350 Badger, A, C, and G, bombers
40 Backfire bombers
80 Badger-A, aerial-refueling
90 Mail ASW amphibians
50 May ASW patrol bombers
250 Haze, Hound, and Hormone, A and B, helicopters

Backfire—with AS-4 missile   1979

Forger-A   1976

Bear-D—reconnaissance   1972

Hormone-A   1971

Badger-A—tanker   1972

NAVAL AVIATION (*continued*)

Badger-C—bomber   1972

Mail—ASW seaplane   1972

May—ASW patrol   1972

Bear-F   1979

Badger

COMBAT AIRCRAFT

NATO code name and builder	Mission	Year put in serv.	Weight	Wing-span	Length	Engine	Speed max. cruising	Operational radius[1]	Armament	Fitted with	Remarks
◆ **FIXED-WING**											
Backfire TU-22M (Tupoler)	Reconnaissance and ship attack	1975	130 t	34 m	38 m	2 Kuznetsov NK 144 turbo-jets of 20,000 kg thrust each	Mach 2.2 at 50,000 ft; Mach 1.3 at 3,000 ft	Supersonic: 3,485/2,250 km with/without refueling Subsonic: 6,300/5,320 km with/without refueling	4/23-mm cannon, 9 tons of bombs (nuclear or conventional), 1-2 AS 4 Kitchen or AS 9	1 navigation and bombing radar; 1 optical bomb sight; 1 tail radar; IFF.	The naval version of Backfire B has ECM and ECCM equipment.
Blinder A TU 22 (Tupolev)	Reconnaissance	1963	84 t	24 m	38 m	2 turbojets, 20,000-kg thrust each (13,000-kg thrust without using after burners)	Mach 1.6 at 36,000 ft	Supersonic speeds: 1,000 km without refueling; 1,600 km with refueling Subsonic speeds: 1,500 km without refueling, 2,000 km with refueling	2/23-mm cannon	1 navigation radar; 1 tail radar; IFF; 7 cameras.	
Bear C, D, F TU 20 (Tupolev)	Reconnaissance and electronic warfare	1955	165 t	50 m	44 m	4 turboprops of 12,500 hp each; 4 bladed, contrarotating props	550 kts at 25,000 ft 440 kts at sea level	8,000 km without refueling; 9,500 km with	6/23-mm cannon	Radomes and tail radar; well equipped with electronic countermeasures.	Bear F, the ASW version, has sono-buoys, depth charges, and torpedoes.
Badger A TU 16 (Tupolev)	Bombardment and ship attack	1953	75 t	33 m	35 m	2 RD 3 M turbojets, 9,550-kg thrust each	540 kts at 22,000 ft 445 kts at sea level	3,000 km without refueling; 4,500 km with	7/23-mm cannon, 9 tons of bombs	1 navigation and bombing radar; 1 rail radar; Some electronic warfare equipment.	A modified version is used for in-flight fueling.
Badger C TU 16 (Tupolev)	Ship attack	. . .	75 t	33 m	35 m	2 RD 3 M turbojets, 9,550-kg thrust each	540 kts at 22,000 ft 445 kts at sea level	3,000 km without refueling; 4,500 km with	6/23-mm cannon, 1 AS 2 Kipper or 2 AS 6 King-fish	1 navigation and bombing radar; 1 Doppler radar; 1 tail radar.	
Badger G TU 16 (Tupolev)	Ship attack	. . .	75 t	33 m	35 m	2 RD 3 M turbojets, 9,550-kg thrust each	540 kts at 22,000 ft 445 kts at sea level	3,000 km without refueling; 4,500 km with	8/23-mm cannon, 2 AS 5 Kelt or 2 AS 6 King-fish	1 navigation and bombing radar; 1 Doppler radar; 1 tail radar.	
Badger D, E, F, J TU 16 (Tupolev)	Reconnaissance and electronic warfare	. . .	75 t	33 m	35 m	2 RD 3 M turbojets 9,550-kg thrust each	540 kts at 22,000 ft 445 kts at seal level	3,000 km without refueling; 4,500 km with	6-7/23-mm cannon	1 navigation and bombing radar; electronic warfare equipment; 1 tail radar; IFF.	Different versions for ELINT, photo reconnaissance, etc.
Forger A, B YAK-36 (Yakolev)	Attack and reconnaissance	1976	10 t	7 m	15 m	1/7,650 kg thrust main engine; 2/2,520 kg lift engines	Mach 1.1 at 30,000 ft	125 nautical miles low-low-low; 240 n.m. low-high-low	16 or 32 rockets, 2/23-mm cannon, 2/AS-7 or AS-10 missiles	Ranging radar; passive warning system; inertial navigation; laser range-finder	Vertical take off and land-ing. Forger-B, the two-seat training version, is also carried aboard ship.

COMBAT AIRCRAFT (cont.)

NATO code name and builder	Mission	Year put in serv.	Weight	Wing-span	Length	Engine	Speed max. cruising	Operational radius[1]	Armament	Fitted with	Remarks
Fitter C, D **SU-20** (Sukhoi)	Ship attack	1976	18 t	14 m	18 m	1/12,000 kg thrust Turbojet	Mach 2.6 at 50,000 ft	220 nautical miles low-low-low; 435 n.m. high-low-high	32/57-mm rockets, 2/ 30-mm cannon, 727 kg bombs, nuclear or conventional	Ranging radar; tail warning radar; laser range-finder; automatic control.	Used by Naval Air Force in Baltic area. Can also carry AA-2 Atoll or AA-8 Aphid air-air or AS-7 or AS-10 air-ground-missiles.
May **IL-38** (Ilyushin)	ASW	1969	64 t	37 m	40 m	4 turboprops, 4,000 hp each	380 kts at 30,000 ft 315 kts at sea level	3,000 km endurance: 12 hours	4 tons of bombs, depth charges, torpedoes	Radomes, MAD,[2] sonobuoys	
Mail **BE 12** (Beriev) (Amphibian)	ASW	1967	38 t	27 m	25 m	2 AI 20 K turboprops, 4,000 hp each	310 kts at 30,000 ft 240 kts at sea level	1,300 km	Bombs, charges, mines	Radomes, MAD,[2] sonobuoys.	
◆ **HELICOPTERS**											
Haze **MI 14**	ASW	1976	12 t	rotor dia. 21 m	24 m	2 Isotov TV 2 117A turboprops, 1,500 hp each	140 kts 122 kts	305 km endurance: 2.5 hours	Depth bombs and torpedoes: 2,000 kg total	Sonobuoys and dipping sonar.	Based (initially) in the Baltic
Hormone A, B **KA 25** (Kamov)	A: ASW B: Targeting	1967	7.3 t	rotor diam. 16 m	10 m	2 GTD 3 F turbo-shafts, 905 hp each	120 kts 105 kts	300 km endurance: 1.5 to 2 h.	Depth charges or torpedoes: 1,000 kg total	Sonobuoys and dipping sonar.	Carried on board *Kiev*, *Moskva*, Kara and Kresta classes. The B version has a Video Data Link system.
Hound **MI 4** (Mil)	ASW	1953	7.2 t	rotor diam. 21 m	17 m	1 ASH 82V piston engine, 1,700 hp	97 kts 86 kts	230 km	1/12.7-mm machine gun, Depth charges, 4 × 16 depth charges, 57-mm rockets.	Sonobuoys and towed MAD[2]	Land-based. Obsolescent and being phased out.

(1) The operational radius is roughly 60% of the radius given by one-half of the range
(2) MAD = Magnetic Anomaly Detection

SUBMARINES

Most modern Soviet submarines have an anechoic hull coating that absorbs the echoes of sonars and, thus, reduces the intensity of reflected echoes.

BALLISTIC-MISSILE SUBMARINES (NUCLEAR-POWERED)

NOTE: Nuclear-powered submarines are built or modernized in the Severodvinsk (formerly, Molotovsk) Naval Shipyard on the White Sea, near Arkhangelsk; at Komsomolsk-on-Amur in the Far East; in the Gorki Shipyard on the Volga; and in the Admiralty Shipyard in Leningrad.

◆ **1 Typhoon class** Bldr: Severodvinsk

This ballistic-missile submarine is a derivation of the Delta-III and is a response to the U.S. *Ohio* class with its Trident-1 C-4 missiles. Its existence is not confirmed; it was not mentioned during the testimony of the director of naval intelligence in his annual report to Congress (14-2-79).

◆ **10 Delta-III class** Bldr: Severodvinsk

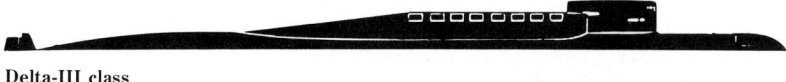

Delta-III class

D: 13,250 tons (submerged)   **S:** 24 kts   **Dim:** 155.5 × 12.0 × 8.7
A: 16/SS-N-18—6/533-mm TT (12 torpedoes)   **Man:** 120 men

BALLISTIC-MISSILE SUBMARINES (NUCLEAR-POWERED) *(continued)*

Electron Equipt: Radar: 1/Snoop Tray
M: 1 nuclear reactor, steam turbines; 2 five-bladed props

REMARKS: Two went into service in 1975, four in 1976, two in 1977, and two in 1978. Construction continues.

◆ **2 Delta-II** Bldr: Severodvinsk, 1975

Delta-II class

D: 9,700 tons surfaced, 11,300 submerged   **S:** 24 kts
Dim: 152.5 × 12.0 × 8.7
Man: 100 men
A: 16/SS-N-8 — 6/533-mm TT (18 torpedoes)
Electron Equipt: Radar: 1/Snoop Tray
M: 1 nuclear reactor, steam turbines; 2 five-bladed props

◆ **16 Delta-I class** Bldrs: Severodvinsk and Komsomolsk, 1973-76

Delta-I class   1973

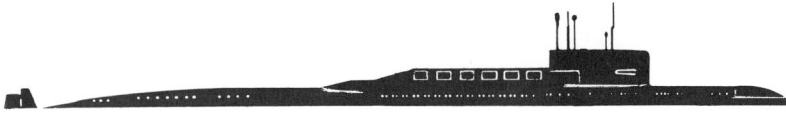

Delta-I class

D: 8,100 tons surfaced, 9,700 submerged   **S:** 25 kts
Dim: 137.0 × 12.0 × 8.7
A: 12/SS-N-8 — 6/533-mm TT (18 torpedoes)   **Man:** 100 men
Electron Equipt: Radar: 1/Snoop Tray
M: 1 nuclear reactor, steam turbines; 2 five-bladed props

REMARK: One was in service in 1972, four in 1973, six in 1974, two in 1975, two in 1076, and one in 1977.

◆ **34 Yankee class** Bldrs: Severodvinsk and Komsomolsk

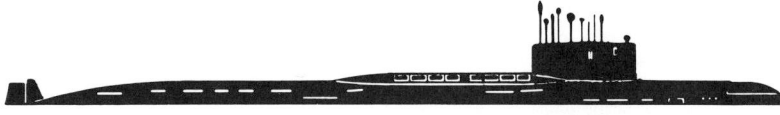

Yankee-I class

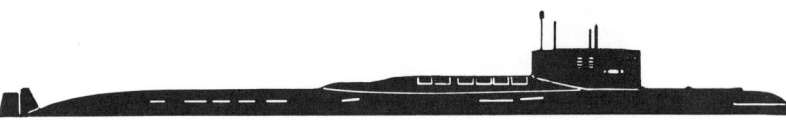

Yankee-II class

D: 7,900 tons surfaced, 9,500 submerged   **S:** 27 kts
Dim: 128.0 × 12.0 × 8.7
A: 16/SS-N-6 — 6/533-mm TT (18 torpedoes)   **Man:** 100 men
Electron Equipt: Radar: 1/Snoop Tray
M: 1 nuclear reactor, steam turbines; 2 five-bladed props

Yankee class

REMARKS: In one experimental unit, Yankee-II, SS-N-6 has been replaced by SS-N-17

BALLISTIC-MISSILE SUBMARINES (NUCLEAR-POWERED) (continued)

Yankee class

Hotel-II class   1972

Hotel-II class

with twelve tubes. Two were in service in 1967, four in 1968, six in 1969, eight in 1970, six in 1971, five in 1972, two in 1973, and one in 1974.

♦ **1 Hotel-III class** Bldr: Severodvinsk, 1965

> **D:** 4,500 tons surfaced, 5,500 submerged   **S:** 20/25 kts
> **Dim:** 116.0 × 9.0 × 7.0
> **A:** 3/SS-N-8 – 6/533-mm TT – 2/400-mm TT   **Man:** 80 men
> **Electron Equipt:** Radar: 1/Snoop Tray
> **M:** 1 nuclear reactor, steam turbines; 2 six-bladed props

REMARK: Used as trial ship for SS-N-8 missiles.

♦ **8 Hotel II class** Bldrs: Severodvinsk and Komsomolsk, 1960-63

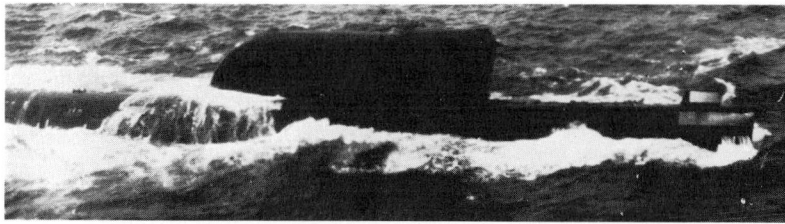

Hotel-II class   1972

> **D:** 4,500 tons surfaced, 5,500 submerged   **S:** 20/23 kts
> **Dim:** 116.0 × 9.0 × 7.0
> **A:** 3/SS-N-5 – 6/533-mm TT – 2/400-mm TT   **Man:** 80 men
> **Electron Equipt:** Radar: 1/Snoop Tray
> **M:** 1 nuclear reactor, steam turbines; 2 six-bladed props

BALLISTIC-MISSILE SUBMARINES (DIESEL-ELECTRIC-POWERED)

♦ **1 Golf-IV class** Bldr: Severodvinsk, 1958-61

> **D:** 2,500 tons surfaced, 2,900 submerged   **S:** 12 kts (submerged)
> **Dim:** 118.0 × 8.5 × 6.6   **Range:** 9,000/5   **Endurance:** 70 days
> **A:** 6/SS-N-8 – 10/533-mm TT (6 fwd, 4 aft)
> **Electron Equipt:** Radar: 1/Snoop Tray
> **M:** Diesel-electric drive; 3 props

REMARKS: Around 1970 the sail was lengthened and six missile tubes were installed in order to conduct trials with the SS-N-8 system. Originally a Golf-I. Hull also lengthened.

♦ **1 Golf-III class** Bldr: Severodvinsk, 1958-61

> **D:** 2,500 tons surfaced, 2,700 submerged   **S:** 12 kts (submerged)
> **Dim:** 100.0 × 8.5 × 6.6   **Range:** 9,000/5   **Endurance:** 70 days
> **A:** 3/SS-N-6 – 10/533-mm TT (6 fwd, 4 aft)
> **Electron Equipt:** Radar: 1/Snoop Tray
> **M:** Diesel-electric drive; 3 props

REMARK: Converted before 1967 as a trials ship for the SS-N-6.

♦ **13 Golf II class** Bldr: Severodvinsk, 1958-61

> **D:** 2,300 tons surfaced, 2,700 submerged   **S:** 12 kts (submerged)
> **Dim:** 100.0 × 8.5 × 6.6   **Range:** 9,000/5   **Endurance:** 70 days

BALLISTIC-MISSILE SUBMARINES
(DIESEL-ELECTRIC-POWERED) (continued)

Golf-II class   1976

Golf-II class   1976

Golf-II class

A: 3/SS-N-5—10/533-mm TT (6 fwd, 4 aft)   **Man:** 75 men
M: Diesel-electric drive; 3 props

REMARKS: These submarines continue to be active and a number of them have been stationed in the Baltic. The range of the SS-N-5 has been extended from the original 700 nautical miles to 900. All Golf-IIs are conversions from Golf-I.

◆ **4 Golf-I class**   Bldr: Severodvinsk, 1958-61

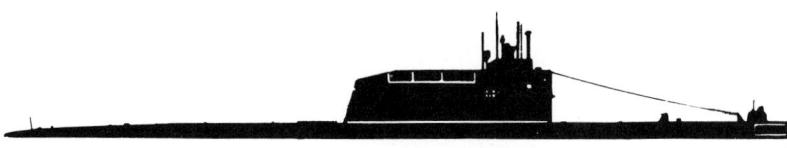

Golf-I class

D: 2,300 tons surfaced, 2,700 submerged   **S:** 12 kts (submerged)
Dim: 100.0 × 8.5 × 6.6   **Man:** 75 men   **Range:** 9,000/5
A: 3/SS-N-4—10/533-mm TT (6 fwd, 4 aft)   **Endurance:** 70 days
Electron Equipt: Radar: 1/Snoop Tray   **M:** Diesel-electric drive; 3 props

REMARKS: SS-N-4 can be fired only while the submarine is surfaced. These obsolescent submarines will probably be retired or converted for other purposes (see Modified Golf class under Attack Submarines-Diesel-Electric-Powered).

CRUISE-MISSILE ATTACK SUBMARINES (NUCLEAR-POWERED)

◆ **1 Papa class**   Bldr: Gorki (?), 1970

Papa class

D: 6,500 tons submerged   **S:** 28 kts   **Dim:** 109.0 × 11.5 × 7.6
A: 10/SS-N-7—8/533-mm TT   **Man:** 85 men
M: 1 nuclear reactor, steam turbines; 2 five-bladed props

REMARK: Possibly, the prototype for submerged-launch cruise-missile submarines.

◆ **4 Charlie-II class**   Bldr: Gorki

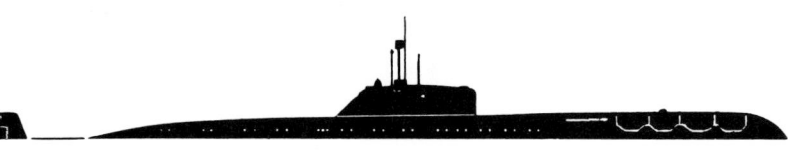

Charlie-II class

CRUISE-MISSILE ATTACK SUBMARINES
(NUCLEAR-POWERED) (continued)

Charlie-II class 1975

D: 4,300 tons surfaced, 5,100 submerged   **S:** 26 kts
Dim: 103.0 × 10.0 × 8.0
A: 8/SS-N-7—. ./SS-N-15—6/533-mm TT   **Man:** 80 men
Electron Equipt: Radar: 1/Snoop Tray   ECM: 1/Stop Light
M: 1 nuclear reactor, steam turbines; 1 five-bladed prop

REMARKS: One in service in each of the years 1973, 1974, 1977, and 1979. Construction continues.

◆ **10 Charlie-I class** Bldr: Gorki

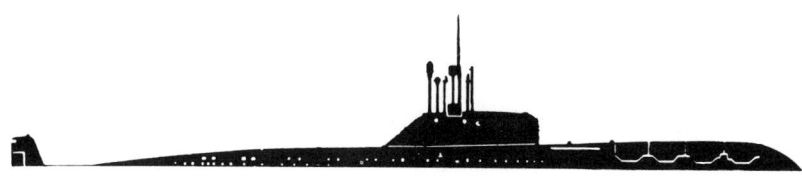

Charlie-I class

Charlie-I class 1971

D: 4,000 tons surfaced, 4,900 submerged   **S:** 27 kts
Dim: 94.0 × 10.0 × 8.0
A: 8/SS-N-7—6/533-mm TT   **Man:** 80 men
Electron Equipt: Radar: 1/Snoop Tray
M: 1 nuclear reactor, steam turbines; 1 five-bladed prop

REMARK: In service at the rate of about two a year between 1968 and 1972.

◆ **29 Echo-II class** Bldr: Severodvinsk and Komsomolsk, 1960-68

Echo-II class

Charlie-I class 1974

CRUISE-MISSILE ATTACK SUBMARINES (NUCLEAR-POWERED) *(continued)*

Echo class

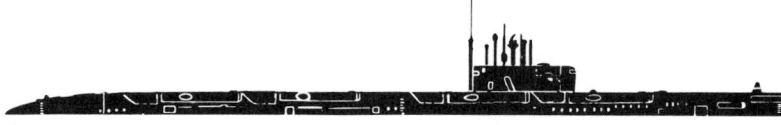

Echo-II class

D: 4,800 tons surfaced, 5,800 submerged   **S:** 20/23 kts
Dim: 120.0 × 9.0 × 7.5
A: 8/SS-N-3 or SS-N-12 – 6/533-mm TT (fwd) – 4/400-mm TT (aft)
Man: 80-85 men
Electron Equipt: Radars: 1/Snoop Tray, 1/Front Piece, 1/Front Door
M: 1 nuclear reactor, steam turbines; 2 four-bladed props

Echo-II class

CRUISE-MISSILE ATTACK SUBMARINES (DIESEL-ELECTRIC-POWERED)

◆ **16 Juliett class**   Bldr: Leningrad, 1961-68

Juliett class

D: 2,800 tons surfaced, 3,550 submerged   **S:** 19/8 kts
Dim: 87.0 × 10.0 × 7.0
A: 4/SS-N-3 – 6/533-mm TT (fwd) – 4/400-mm TT (aft)   **Range:** 9,000/7
Electron Equipt: Radars: 1/Snoop Slab, 1/Front Piece, 1/Front Door
M: Diesel-electric; 2 props   **Endurance:** 70 days

Juliett class

Juliett class

REMARK: In view of great beam in relation to length and blunt hull form, surface speed is likely to be well below that listed.

CRUISE-MISSILE ATTACK SUBMARINES (DIESEL-ELECTRIC-POWERED) *(continued)*

Juliett class

◆ **5 Whiskey Long Bin class** Bldr: Baltic, Leningrad, 1961-63

Whiskey Long Bin class   1968

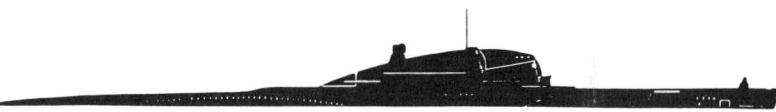

Whiskey Long Bin class

    D: 1,200 tons surfaced, 1,500 submerged   **S:** 13.5/8
    Dim: 83.0 × 6.1 × 5.0
    A: 4/SS-N-3 — 4/533-mm TT (fwd)   **Man:** 60-65 men   **Range:** 6,000/5
    M: 2 2,000-hp diesels, electric drive; 2 props; 2,500 hp   **Endurance:** 40 days

REMARKS: Converted from attack submarines by being lengthened and having a section containing four missile tubes inserted in a greatly broadened sail and fixed at elevation of 15°. Stern torpedo tubes removed. All of the less-elaborate Whiskey Twin Cylinder class are believed to have been scrapped, and the remaining Long Bin conversions are probably retained for training.

ATTACK SUBMARINES (NUCLEAR-POWERED)

◆ **2 or 3 Alfa class** Bldr: Sudomekh, Leningrad, 1972-

Alfa class

    D: 3,900 tons surfaced, 4,250 submerged   **S:** 40 kts
    Dim: 80.0 × 10.0 × . . .
    A: . . SS-N-15 —. ./533-mm TT   **Electron Equipt:** Radar: 1/Snoop Tray
    M: 1 nuclear reactor, steam turbines; 1 prop   **Man:** . . .

ATTACK SUBMARINES (NUCLEAR-POWERED) (continued)

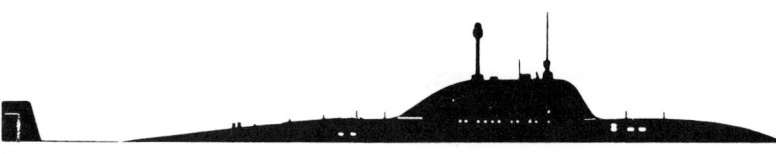

Alfa class

REMARKS: The prototype, shown above, has been scrapped, but the class has now entered production as the world's fastest and deepest-diving combatant submarine. The pressure hull is constructed of titanium and the ships are extremely quiet and highly automated. Construction continues.

◆ **8 Victor-II class** Bldr: Admiralty, Leningrad

Victor-II class

D: 4,500 tons surfaced, 5,700 submerged **S:** 28 kts
Dim: 100.0 × 10.0 × 7.0
A: . ./SS-N-15—8/533-mm TT **Man:** 80 men
M: 1 nuclear reactor, steam turbines; 1 five-bladed prop

REMARK: One went into service in each of the years 1972, 1973, 1974, and 1975, two in 1976, and one each in 1977 and 1979. Construction continues. The most recent are again longer (Victor-III).

◆ **14 Victor-I class** Bldr: Admiralty, Leningrad, 1967-74
50 LET SSR 13 others

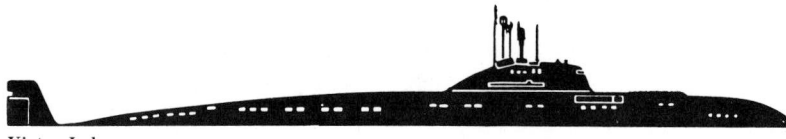

Victor-I class

D: 4,300 tons surfaced, 5,100 submerged **S:** 30 kts
Dim: 93.0 × 10.0 × 7.0
A: . ./SS-N-15—8/533-mm TT
M: 1 nuclear reactor, steam turbines; 1 five-bladed prop + 2 small, two-bladed props for slow speeds

Victor-I class — sail

Victor-I class

1974

ATTACK SUBMARINES (NUCLEAR-POWERED) (*continued*)

Victor-I class 1975

◆ **5 Echo class** Bldr: . . ., 1960-68

Echo class 1975

Echo class

D: 4,600 tons surfaced, 5,600 submerged **S:** 25/20 kts
Dim: 114.0 × 9.0 × 7.5
A: 6/533-mm TT (fwd) — 4/400-mm TT (aft) **Man:** 75 men
Electron Equipt: Radar: 1/Snoop Tray
M: 1 nuclear reactor, steam turbines; 2 five-bladed props

REMARKS: Formerly, cruise-missile submarines that carried six SS-N-3. Probably built at Komsomolsk, as all are in the Pacific.

◆ **13 November class** Bldr: Severodvinsk, 1958-62

LENINETS   LENINSKIY KOMSOMOL   11 others

November class

November class

D: 4,000 tons surfaced, 4,800 submerged **S:** 30 kts
Dim: 109.0 × 9.0 × 7.7
A: 8/533-mm TT (fwd) — 4/400-mm TT (aft) — 32 torpedoes or mines
Electron Equipt: Radar: 1/Snoop Tray **Man:** 75-80 men
M: 1 nuclear reactor, steam turbines; 2 props; (four- or six-bladed)

REMARK: One of this class was lost off Cape Finisterre in 1970.

ATTACK SUBMARINES (DIESEL-ELECTRIC-POWERED)

◆ **10 Tango class**   Bldr: Gorki (?)

Tango class

Tango class

Tango class   1976

D: 3,000 tons surfaced, 3,500 submerged   **S:** 20/16 kts
Dim: 96.0 × 9.0 × 6.5
A: . ./SS-N-15−. ./533-mm TT   **Man:** 72 men   **Endurance:** . . .
Electron Equipt: Radar: 1/Snoop Tray
M: Diesels and electric motors; 3 props; 6,000 hp

Tango class

REMARK: One was in service in 1972, two in 1974, two in 1975, one in 1976, two in 1977, and two in 1978. Construction continues.

◆ **4 Bravo class**   Bldr: . . ., 1968-72

D: 2,400 tons surfaced, 2,900 submerged   **S:** 14/16 kts
Dim: 70.1 × 9.8 × 7.3
A: 6/533-mm TT (fwd)   **Man:** 65 men
M: Diesels and electric motors; 1 prop; 4,000 hp

ATTACK SUBMARINES (DIESEL-ELECTRIC-POWERED) (*continued*)

Bravo class

REMARK: Training and target submarines.

◆ **60 Foxtrot class** Bldr: Leningrad, 1957-74

CHELYABINSKIY KOMSOMOLETS
KOMSOMOLETS KAZAKHSTANA
KUIBISHEVSKIY KOMSOMOLETS
PSKOVSKIY KOMSOMOLETS

UL'YANOVSKIY KOMSOMOLETS
VLADIMIRSKIY KOMSOMOLETS
YAROSLAVSKIY KOMSOMOLETS
53 others

Foxtrot class   1976

Foxtrot class   1978

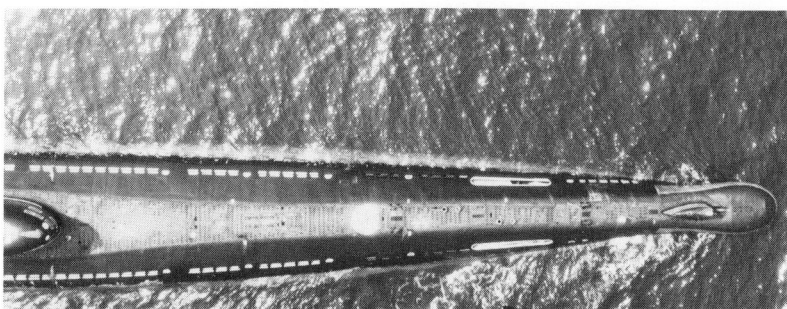

Foxtrot class—aerial view of bow   1974

D: 1,950 tons surfaced, 2,400 submerged   **S:** 16/15.5 kts
Dim: 96.0 × 7.5 × 6.0
A: 10/533-mm TT (6 fwd, 4 aft)—22 torpedoes or 44 mines
Man: 8 officers, 70 men

Foxtrot class   1974

ATTACK SUBMARINES (DIESEL-ELECTRIC-POWERED) (continued)

Foxtrot class

Range: 11,000/8 (snorkel), 350/2 (submerged)   **Endurance:** 70 days
M: Diesels and electric motors; 3 props; 6,000 hp

REMARKS: These submarines seem to be strongly built. Eight of the class have been transferred to India, three to Libya, and one to Cuba (with more apparently to follow). Two, temporarily named *Sirius* and *Saturn*, have been used in "oceanographic research."

◆ **1 Modified Golf class**

Modified Golf class   1978

Modified Golf class

D: 2,300 tons surfaced, 2,700 submerged   **S:** 12 kts (submerged)
Dim: 100.0 × 8.5 × 6.6   **Man:** . . .
A: 10/533-mm TT (6 fwd, 4 aft)   **M:** Diesels and electric motors; 3 props

REMARKS: Three missile tubes removed. Apparently converted in 1978 as a submersible command ship. Structure aft supports folding whip antennas; there are similar whips on either side of the sail. Sail extension possibly to house buoy antenna.

◆ **12 Romeo class**   Bldr: Leningrad, 1960

Romeo class   1967

ATTACK SUBMARINES (DIESEL-ELECTRIC-POWERED) *(continued)*

D: 1,330 tons surfaced, 1,700 submerged   **S:** 15.5/13 kts
Dim: 77.0 × 6.7 × 4.9
A: 8/533-mm TT (6 fwd, 2 aft) — 14 torpedoes or 28 mines   **Man:** 60 men
Range: 14,000/9   **Endurance:** 45 days
M: 2 2,000-hp diesels, electric motors; 2 props; 2,500 hp

REMARKS: Diving depth: 270-300 meters. Six transferred to Egypt, and two to Bulgaria. Also built in China and North Korea.

◆ **15 Zulu-IV class**   Bldrs: Various, 1952-55

Zulu-IV class   1974

D: 1,900 tons surfaced, 2,350 submerged   **S:** 18/16 kts
Dim: 90.0 × 7.5 × 6.0
A: 10/533-mm TT (6 fwd, 4 aft) — 22 torpedoes or 44 mines   **Man:** 70 men
Electron Equipt: Radar: 1/Snoop Plate   **Range:** 12,400/8 (snorkel)
M: 3 2,000-hp diesels, electric drive; 3 props   **Endurance:** 70 days

REMARKS: Between 1956 and 1957, several (since scrapped) were converted as Zulu-V ballistic-missile submarines, the world's first of their type. Each had two tubes for surface launch of SS-N-4. Nine other Zulu-IVs have been scrapped and the class will probably soon disappear. Earlier configurations (Zulu-I to Zulu-III) had deck guns, AA guns in the sail, and no snorkel; all later updated to Zulu-IV standard. Some of the fifteen survivors are in reserve.

◆ **50 Whiskey class**   Bldrs: Various, 1949-57

D: 1,050 tons surfaced, 1,350 submerged   **S:** 17/13.5 kts
Dim: 76.0 × 6.3 × 4.8
A: 6/533-mm TT (4 fwd, 2 aft) — 12 torpedoes or 24 mines   **Man:** 50 men
Electron Equipt: Radar: 1/Snoop Plate   **Range:** 8,300/8 (snorkel)
M: 2 Type 37D 2,000-hp diesels, electric motors; 2 props; 2,500 hp
Endurance: 40-45 days

REMARKS: Built in prefabricated sections, these strong, uncomplicated boats have proven quite satisfactory. Twelve were converted to cruise-missile boats. Four were

Whiskey class

modified as radar-picket submarines. As many as eighty additional Whiskey-class units are now in reserve; the others are used for training. Some have been transferred to Egypt, Poland, Albania, Communist China, and Indonesia. Many of the 240 built have been stricken.

◆ **4 Whiskey Canvas Bag class**

D: 1,080 tons surfaced, 1,450 submerged   **S:** 17/13.5 kts
Dim: 76.0 × 6.3 × 4.8
A: 4/533-mm TT (fwd) — 8 torpedoes   **Man:** 50 men

Whiskey Canvas Bag class   1965

ATTACK SUBMARINES (DIESEL-ELECTRIC-POWERED) (*continued*)

Range: 8,300/8 (snorkel)
Electron Equipt: Radars: 1/Snoop Plate, 1/Boat Sail
M: 2 Type 37D 2,000-hp diesels, electric motors; 2 props; 2,500 hp

REMARKS: Converted from standard Whiskey class to radar pickets about 1960. One has since had the folding Boat Sail radar removed from the top of her lengthened sail and an unidentified housing built on her stern.

◆ **2 Quebec class** Bldr: Sudomekh, Leningrad, 1954-57

Quebec class

D: 460 tons surfaced, 540 submerged   **S:** 18/16 kts
Dim: 57.0 × 5.1 × 3.8
A: 4/533-mm TT (fwd)—8 torpedoes or 16 mines   **Man:** 30 men
Range: 4,500/6   **Endurance:** 30 days
M: 3 1,000-hp diesels, electric motors; 3 props; 2,200 hp

REMARKS: Especially designed for operations in the Baltic and Black Sea. Most now stricken; some additional may be in reserve. Some or all had Kreislauf closed-cycle diesel propulsion systems.

HELICOPTER CRUISERS

◆ **2 Moskva class**

	Bldr	Laid down	L	In serv.
MOSKVA	Black Sea SY, Nikolayev	1962	1964	7-67
LENINGRAD	Black Sea SY, Nikolayev	1964	1966	1968

D: 14,500 tons (19,200 fl)   **S:** 30 kts
Dim: 190.0 × 34.0 (flight deck) 26.0 (wl) × 7.6
Man: 850 men   **Range:** 2,500/30, 7,000/15
A: 2/SA-N-3 systems (II × 2) with 44 Goblet missiles—1/SUW-N-1 system—4/57-mm AA (II × 2)—2/RBU 6000 rocket launchers—16/Hormone-A helicopters
Electron Equipt: Radars: 3/Don 2, 1/Top Sail, 1/Head Net-C, 2/Head Lights, 2/Muff Cob

Leningrad   1974

Sonars: 1/low-frequency hull-mounted, 1/medium-frequency towed VDS
ECM: 8/Side Globe, 2/Top Hat, several Bell series, 4/chaff launchers (II × 2)
IFF: High Pole B
M: 2 sets GT; 2 props; 100,000 hp   **Boilers:** 4

REMARKS: Russian type designation: Protivolodochnyy Kreyser (ASW cruiser). Flight deck 86 × 34 m. Hangar beneath flight deck, with small hangar between stack uptakes in superstructure. Two elevators on the flight deck. The *Moskva* was modified for a time to permit the testing of VTOL Forger-A aircraft, which were to go aboard the *Kiev* carriers. Both ships have now had their ten 533-mm ASW TT removed and the side embrasures plated in.

Moskva—torpedo tubes since deleted   1969

HELICOPTER CRUISERS (*continued*)

Leningrad—torpedo embrasures abaft the companionway-opening in hull side now deleted

1974

GUIDED-MISSILE CRUISERS

◆ 3 or more . . . class

	Bldr	Laid down	L	In serv.
N . . .	Zhdanov, Leningrad	. . .	1979	. . .
N . . .	Zhdanov, Leningrad	. . .	. . .	. . .
N . . .	Zhdanov, Leningrad	. . .	. . .	. . .

D: 7,900 tons   S: . . .   **Dim:** 160.0 × . . . × . . .
A: . . .   **Electron Equipt:** Radars: . . .   **Man:** . . .   **M:** . . .

REMARKS: Possibly replacements for the *Sverdlov*-class cruisers. Yet another class of larger guided-missile cruiser has been reported in the U.S. press as under construction at Nikolayev. Of a reported 14,000 tons, it has supplanted the Kara class in production.

◆ 2 Kirov class

	Bldr	Laid down	L	In serv.
KIROV	Baltic SY, Leningrad	1975	12-77	1980
N . . .	Baltic SY, Leningrad	12-77	. . .	. . .

D: 25,000 tons   S: 30 kts   **Dim:** 240.0 × 28.0 × 8.0
A: . . .   **Man:**
Electron Equipt: Radars: at least, 1/Top Sail, 1/Top Steer
                 Sonars: bow-mounted, hull; towed VDS
M: Nuclear reactors, steam turbines; . . props; . . . hp

REMARKS: The first Soviet nuclear-powered surface combatants. Will carry surface-to-surface, surface-to-air, and ASW missile systems, several gun mounts, short-range ASW ordnance, and one or more helicopter. The Top Sail radar is a new variant incorporating a Big Net. Massive superstructure, with two tower masts, both surmounted by a forest of radar, communications, and ECM antennas.

◆ 7 Kara class

	Bldr	Laid down	L	In serv.
NIKOLAYEV	Nikolayev	1969	1971	1973
OCHAKOV	Nikolayev	1970	1972	1974
KERCH	Nikolayev	1971	1973	1975
AZOV	Nikolayev	1972	1974	1977
PETROPAVLOVSK	Nikolayev	1973	1975	1978
TASHKENT	Nikolayev	1975	1977	1979
N . . .	Nikolayev	1976	1978	. . .

Azov   *Military Herald*, 1979

Petropavlovsk   1979

Petropavlovsk—At right is a Pop Group radar director, at center are two Gatling AA guns below their Bass Tilt radar director, and at extreme left is the ship's after Head Lights radar tracker-illuminator for the SA-N-3 system. Above the ship's launch is the cupola for a backup director for the AA guns, while at the extreme right are two of the Side Globe ECM radomes.

GUIDED-MISSILE CRUISERS (*continued*)

Petropavlovsk—Side Glove and Rum Tub electronic-warfare antenna arrays

Ochakov   1979

D: 8,200 tons (10,000 fl) **S:** 30 kts **Dim:** 173.8 × 18.3 × 6.2

Man: 30 officers, 490 men **Range:** 2,000/30, 8,000/15

A: 8/SS-N-14 (IV × 2) with 8 missiles—2/SA-N-3 systems (II × 2) with 44 Goblet missiles—4/SA-N-4 (II × 2) with 36 missiles—4/76.2-mm DP (II × 2)—4/Gatling AA (I × 4)—2/RBU 6000 rocket launchers—2/RBU 1000 rocket launchers—10/533-mm TT (V × 2)—1/Hormone-A helicopter

Electron Equipt: Radars: 2/Don Kay, 1/Top Sail, 1/Head Net-C, 2/Head Lights, 2/Pop Group, 2/Owl Screech, 2/Bass Tilt

Sonars: 1/low-frequency hull-mounted, 1/medium-frequency towed VDS

ECM: 8/Side Globe, 2/Bell Clout, several other Bell series, 2/chaff launchers

IFF: 1/High Pole B (interrogation by search radars)

M: Gas turbines; 2 props; 120,000 hp

REMARKS: Russian type designation: Bol'shoy Protivolodochnyy Korabl' (large ASW ship). The *Petropavlovsk* has Rum Tab ECM antennas and two cylindrical radomes abreast the helicopter hangar, which is higher than on the other ships; she has no RBU-1000 rocket launchers. She and the *Tashkent* joined the Pacific Fleet in 1979. The *Azov* has been reported as a trials ship for vertically launched surface-to-air missiles and has only one SA-N-3 launcher, forward; a new type of missile radar director is mounted aft.

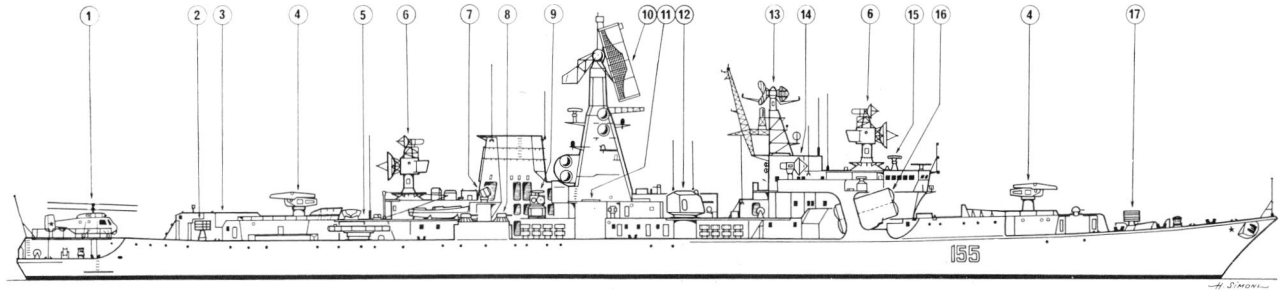

1. Hormone-A 2. RBU-1000 3. Helicopter hangar 4. SA-N-3 5. 533-mm TT 6. Head Lights
7. Bass Tilt 8. Gatling AA guns 9. Pop Group 10. Top Sail 11. SA-N-4 12. 76.2-mm guns
13. Head Net-C 14. Owl Screech 15. Don Kay 16. SS-N-14 17. RBU-6000

GUIDED-MISSILE CRUISERS (*continued*)

Tashkent   1979

Ochakov   1979

GUIDED-MISSILE CRUISERS (continued)

◆ **10 Kresta-II class**

	Bldr	L	In serv.
KRONSHTADT	Zhdanov, Leningrad	1967	1970
ADMIRAL ISAKOV	Zhdanov, Leningrad	1968	1971
ADMIRAL NAKHIMOV	Zhdanov, Leningrad	1969	1972
ADMIRAL MAKAROV	Zhdanov, Leningrad	1970	1973
MARSHAL VOROSHILOV	Zhdanov, Leningrad	1971	1973
ADMIRAL OKTYABR'SKIY	Zhdanov, Leningrad	1972	1974
ADMIRAL ISACHENKOV	Zhdanov, Leningrad	1973	1975
MARSHAL TIMOSHENKO	Zhdanov, Leningrad	1974	1976
VASILIY CHAPAEV	Zhdanov, Leningrad	1975	1977
ADMIRAL YUMASHEV	Zhdanov, Leningrad	1976	1978

D: 6,000 tons (7,600 fl)   **S:** 34 kts   **Dim:** 158.0 × 17.0 × 5.5 (avg.)

Man: 380 men   **Range:** 1,600/34, 7,000/14   **Fuel:** 1,100 tons

A: 8/SS-N-14 (IV × 2) with 8 missiles—2/SA-N-3 systems (II × 2) with 44 Goblet missiles—4/57-mm AA (II × 2)—2/RBU 6000 rocket launchers—2/RBU 1000 rocket launchers—10/533-mm TT (V × 2)—4/Gatling AA (I × 4)—1/Hormone-A helicopter

Electron Equipt: Radars: 2/Don Kay, 1/Top Sail, 1/Head Net-C, 2/Head Lights, 2/Muff Cob, 2/Bass Tilt
Sonar: 1/medium-frequency hull-mounted
ECM: 8/Side Globe, several Bell series
IFF: 1/High Pole B (interrogation by search radars)

M: 2 sets GT; 2 props; 100,000 hp   **Boilers:** 4

REMARKS: Russian type designation; Bol'shoy Protivolodochnyy Korabl' (large ASW ship). The first three units do not have Bass Tilt. Late units have larger forward superstructure, the area between the tower foremast and the bridge being filled in by a two-level deckhouse.

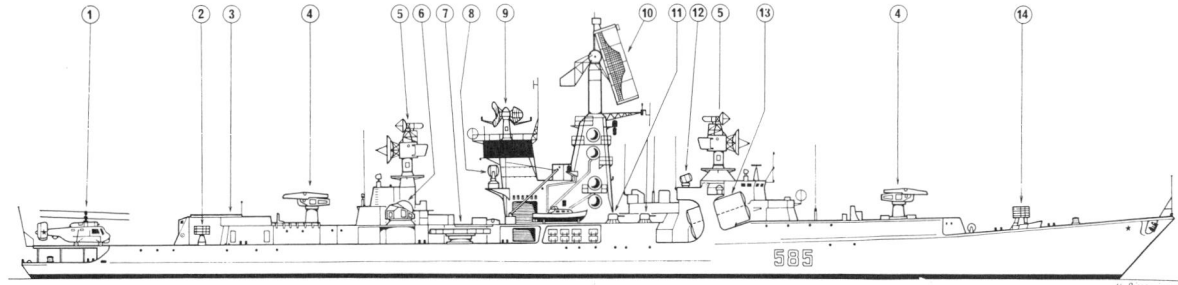

1. Hormone-A 2. RBU-1000 3. Helicopter hangar 4. SA-N-3 5. Head Lights 6. 57-mm AA
7. 533-mm TT 8. Muff Cob 9. Head Net-C 10. Top Sail 11. Gatling AA guns 12. Bass Tilt
13. SS-N-14 14. RBU-6000

Admiral Oktyabr'skiy   1974

GUIDED-MISSILE CRUISERS (*continued*)

Vasiliy Chapaev   1977

Vasiliy Chapaev   1977

◆ **4 Kresta-I class**

	Bldr	L	In serv.
VITSE ADMIRAL DROZD	Zhdanov, Leningrad	1965	1967
SEVASTOPOL	Zhdanov, Leningrad	1965	1967
ADMIRAL ZOZULYA	Zhdanov, Leningrad	1966	1968
VLADIVOSTOK	Zhdanov, Leningrad	1966	1968

Vitse Admiral Drozd   1976

GUIDED-MISSILE CRUISERS (*continued*)

D: 6,000 tons (7,500 fl) **S:** 34 kts **Dim:** 155.0 × 17.0 × 5.5 (avg.)

Man: 380 men **Range:** 1,600/34, 7,000/14

A: 4/SS-N-3 (II × 2) with 4 Shaddock missiles—2/SA-N-1 systems (II × 2) with 44 Goa missiles—4/57-mm AA (II × 2)—*Vitse Admiral Drozd:* 4/Gatling AA (I × 4)—2/RBU 6000 rocket launchers—2/RBU 1000 rocket launchers—10/533-mm TT (V × 2)—1/Hormone-B helicopter

Electron Equipt: Radars: 2/Don 2, 1/Big Net, 1/Head Net-C, 2/Plinth Net, 1/Scoop Pair, 2/Peel Group, 2/Muff Cob—*Vitse Admiral Drozd:* 2/Bass Tilt

Sonar: 1/medium-frequency hull-mounted (Herkules)

ECM: 8/Side Globe, several Bell series

IFF: 2/High Pole B

M: 2 sets GT; 2 props; 100,000 hp **Boilers:** 4

REMARKS: Russian type designation: Raketnyy Kreyser (missile cruiser). Based on the Kynda class cut has a better mixture of weapons. The surface-to-surface launchers, fitted on each side of the superstructure, forward under the bridge wings, can be elevated, not trained. No Shaddock missile reloads. Installation of Gatling guns abaft the Shaddock launchers and construction of a new deckhouse between the Gatling guns has altered the silhouette of the *Vitse Admiral Drozd* (*see* photos).

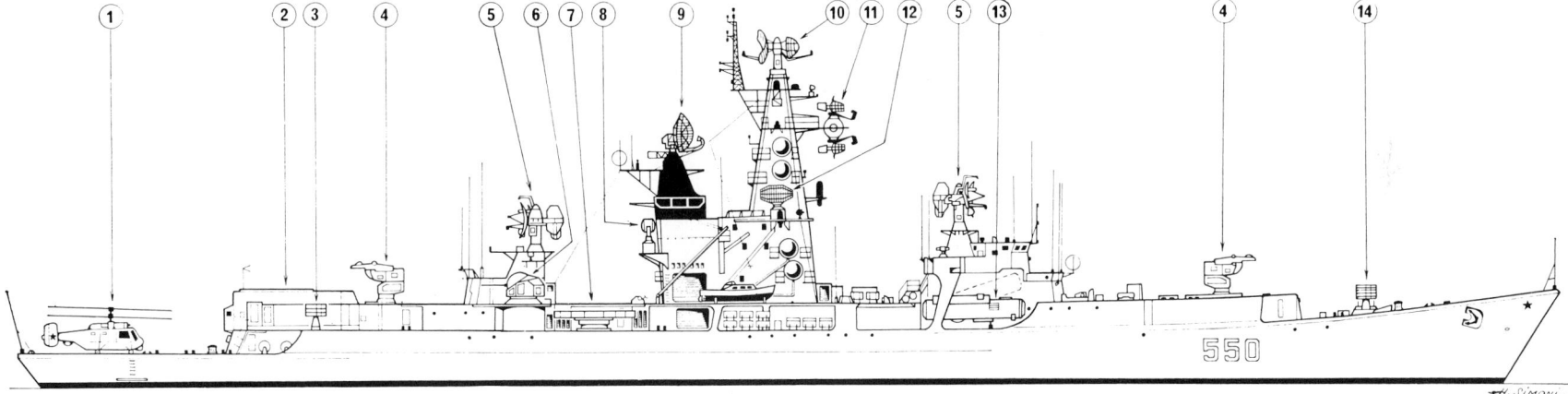

1. Hormone-B 2. Helicopter hangar 3. RBU-1000 4. SA-N-1 5. Peel Group 6. 57-mm AA
7. 533-mm TT 8. Muff Cob 9. Big Net 10. Head Net-C 11. Scoop Pair 12. Plinth Net 13. SS-N-3 14. RBU-6000

Vitse Admiral Drozd 1976

GUIDED-MISSILE CRUISERS (*continued*)

Admiral Zozulya

1968

♦ **4 Kynda class**

	Bldr	Laid down	L	In serv.
GROZNYY	Zhdanov, Leningrad	6-60	4-61	6-62
ADMIRAL FOKIN	Zhdanov, Leningrad	. . .	11-61	8-62
ADMIRAL GOLOVKO	Zhdanov, Leningrad	. . .	. . .	1965
VARYAG	Zhdanov, Leningrad	. . .	. . .	1965

D: 4,400 tons (5,600 fl)   **S:** 34 kts   **Dim:** 141.7 × 15.8 × 5.3 (avg.)
Man: 375 men   **Range:** 1,100/32, 6,800/15
A: 8/SS-N-3 (IV × 2) with 16 Shaddock missiles—1/SA-N-1 system (II × 1) with 22 Goa missiles—4/76.2-mm DP (II × 2)—2/RBU 6000 rocket launchers—6/533-mm TT (III × 2)

Admiral Golovko

1978

GUIDED-MISSILE CRUISERS (continued)

Electron Equipt: Radars: 2/Don 2, 2/Head Net-A, 2/Scoop Pair, 1/Peel Group, 1/Owl Screech—*Grozny, Varyag:* 2/Plinth Net
Sonar: 1/high-frequency hull-mounted (Herkules)
IFF: 2/High Pole B
M: GT; 2 props; 100,000 hp

REMARKS: Russian type designation: Raketnyy Kreyser (missile cruiser). Eight Shaddock missiles are loaded in the trainable and elevatable quadruple tubes; reloading from the handling rooms requires some time. The *Varyag* now has one Head Net-A, one Head Net-C, and two Plinth Net; the *Groznyy* received two Plinth Net around 1973.

Admiral Golovko   1978

Admiral Golovko   1978

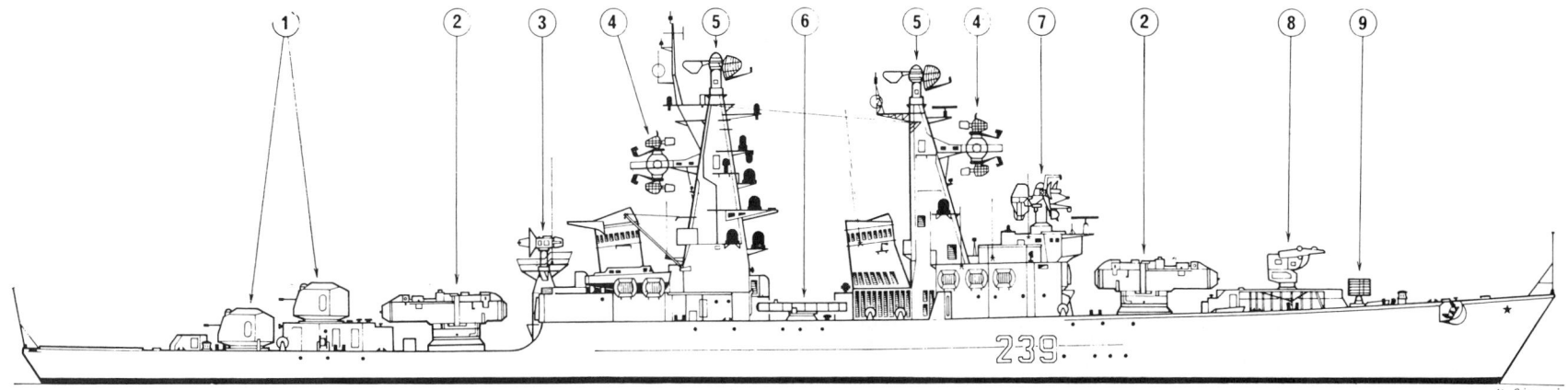

1. 76.2-mm DP 2. SS-N-3 3. Owl Screech 4. Scoop Pair 5. Head Net-A 6. 533-mm TT 7. Peel Group 8. SA-N-1 9. RBU-6000

GUIDED-MISSILE CRUISERS (continued)

◆ 1 Modified Sverdlov class

	Bldr	Laid down	L	In serv.
DZERZHINSKIY	Marti, Nikolayev	5-49	1951	11-52

Dzerzhinskiy   1976

For characteristics of hull and machinery, see *Sverdlov*-class light cruisers
    A: 1/SA-N-2 system (II × 1) with Guideline missiles—9/152-mm guns (III × 3)—
      12/100-mm DP (II × 6)—16/37-mm AA (II × 8)—mines   **Man:** 1,040 men
  Electron Equipt: Radars: 1/Neptune, 1/Low Sieve, 1/Big Net, 1/Slim Net, 1/Fan
      Song-E, 1/Top Brow, 2/Sun Visor, 6/Egg Cup

REMARKS: Russian type designation: Kreyser (cruiser). In 1961 the *Dzerzhinskiy* completed refit, during which her No. 3 152-mm turret was replaced by an SA-N-2 system (twin launcher aft), making her the only ship to carry the system. Her High Lune height-finding radar was removed in 1976.

COMMAND CRUISERS

◆ 2 Modified Sverdlov class

	Bldr	Laid down	L	In serv.
ADMIRAL SENYAVIN	Severodvinsk	. . .	. . .	1955
ZHDANOV	Baltic SY, Leningrad	10-49	12-50	1952

Admiral Senyavin   1973

Zhdanov   1973

For characteristics of hull and machinery, see *Sverdlov*-class light cruisers
    A: 6 (*Admiral Senyavin*) or 9/152-mm (III × 2 or 3)—12/100-mm DP (II × 6)—
      1/SA-N-4 system (II × 1)—16/37-mm AA—8 (*Zhdanov*) or 16/30-mm AA (II × 4
      or 8)
  Electron Equipt: Radars: 2/Top Bow, 1/Top Trough, 2/Sun Visor, 6/Egg Cup, 1/Pop
      Group—*Zhdanov:* 2/Drum Tilt, *Admiral Senyavin:*
      4/Drum Tilt

REMARKS: Russian type designation: Kreyser (cruiser). Both completed modernization in 1972. Excellent long-range communications, including a Vee Cone antenna, which can be seen on the after tripod mast. The 30-mm guns are divided on each side of the forward stack and, on the *Admiral Senyavin*, of the after deckhouse as well. Her two after turrets have been replaced by a hangar and platform for one Hormone helicopter. Both ships have had their mine rails removed.

LIGHT CRUISERS

◆ 9 Sverdlov class   Bldrs: Baltic SY, Leningrad; Marti SY, Nikolayev; Severodvinsk

	L		L
ADMIRAL LAZAREV	. . .	MIKHAIL KUTUZOV	5-54
ADMIRAL USHAKOV	5-52	MURMANSK	. . .
ALEXANDR NEVSKIY	7-51	OKTYABRSKAYA REVOLUTSIYA (ex-*Molotovsk*)	1954
ALEXANDR SUVOROV	6-52		
DMITRI POZHARSKIY	. . .	SVERDLOV	7-50

Dmitri Pozharskiy   1975

LIGHT CRUISERS (continued)

D: 12,900 tons (17,200 fl) **S:** 32 kts **Dim:** 210.0 (199.95 pp) × 21.6 × 7.2
Man: 70 officers, 940 men **Range:** 2,200/32, 8,400/15 **Fuel:** 3,800 tons
A: 12/152-mm (III × 4) − 12/100-mm DP (II × 6) − 32/37-mm AA (II × 16) − mines −
Oktyabrskaya Revolutsiya, Admiral Ushakov, Alexandr Suvorov: 16/30-mm AA
(II × 8) also
Electron Equipt: Radars: 1/Neptune or Don 2, 1/Low Sieve or High Sieve, 1/Big
Net or Top Trough, 1/Slim Net, 2/Top Bow, 2/Sun Visor,
8/Egg Cup − Knife Rest in some − ships with 30-mm AA:
4/Drum Tilt
  ECM: 2/Watch Dog   IFF: 1/High Pole

Oktyabrskaya Revolutsiya   1977

Armor: 152-mm turret: 76-100   **Deck:** 25-50 and 50-75 100-mm   gun shields: 25
M: 2 sets GT; 2 props; 100,000 hp   **Boilers:** 6

REMARKS: Russian type designation: Kreyser. Based on the *Chapaev* class. Fourteen
put in service between 1951 and 1956; others were laid down but construction was
suspended in 1956 and canceled in 1960. Slight differences in profile, the merging of
the forward stack with the bridge structure being noticeable. The *Admiral Nakhimov*
was scrapped in 1961; the *Ordzhonikidze* was transferred to Indonesia in 1962 and has
since been scrapped. By 1961 the *Dzerzhinskiy* had been converted to a guided-missile
cruiser; two others, the *Zhdanov* and *Admiral Senyavin*, completed conversion to command cruisers in 1972. In 1977 the *Oktyabrskaya Revolutsiya* completed overhaul,
during which eight twin 30-mm AA and four Drum Tilt radars were added, the Egg
Cup radars were removed from her 100-mm mounts, and her bridge was enlarged.
Radar suits vary widely. In 1979 the *Admiral Ushakov* and *Alexandr Suvorov* appeared with similar alterations; all three ships have had four of their 37-mm AA
(II × 2) removed. The Soviets evidently intend to continue this class in operation for
some time; the ships provide excellent command facilities and their powerful gunnery
batteries give the U.S.S.R. the world's finest shore-bombardment capability.

◆ **1 Chapaev class**

	Bldr	Laid down	L	In serv.
KOMSOMOLETS (ex-*Chlakov*)	Baltic SY, Leningrad	1939	11-47	8-50

D: 12,000 tons (15,000 fl) **S:** 34 kts **Dim:** 201.2 × 18.9 × 7.3 (mean)
Man: 900 men **Range:** 1,200/34, 5,400/15 **Fuel:** 2,500 tons
A: 12/152-mm (III × 4) − 8/100-mm DP (II × 4) − 24/37-mm AA (II × 12) − 200 mines
Electron Equipt: Radars: 1/Neptune, 1/Low Sieve, 1/Slim Net, 1/Knife Rest,
1/Top Bow, 2/Sun Visor, 6/Egg Cup
  ECM: 2/Watch Dog   IFF: 1/High Pole, 1/Square Head
M: 2 sets GT; 2 props; 120,000 hp   **Boilers:** 6

REMARKS: Russian type designation: Kreyser (cruiser). Training ship. Survivor of a
class of seven. Construction interrupted by World War II. Very little armor, no belt.
Has never operated outside the Baltic.

Zheleznyakov − similar to **Komsomolets**   1975

GUIDED-MISSILE DESTROYERS

◆ **5 Modified Kashin class**

	Bldr		Bldr
OGNEVOY	Zhdanov, Leningrad	SMELYY	Nikolayev
SLAVNYY	Zhdanov, Leningrad	SMYSHLENNYY	Nikolayev
SDERZHANNYY	Nikolayev		

Ognevoy   1974

D: 3,950 tons (4,950 fl)   **S:** 35 kts   **Dim:** 146.0 × 15.8 × 4.8

A: 4/SS-N-2C (I × 4) − 2/SA-N-1 systems (II × 2) with 44 Goa missiles − 4/76.2-mm DP (II × 2) − 4/Gatling AA (I × 4) − 5/533-mm TT (V × 1) − *Ognevoy* only: 2/RBU 6000 rocket launchers

Sderzhannyy   1975

Electron Equipt: Radars: 2/Don Kay, 1/Head Net-C (*Ognevoy* only: Head Net-A) and 1/Big Net, 2/Peel Group, 2/Owl Screech, 2/Bass Tilt
Sonars: 1/towed, 1/medium-frequency hull-mounted VDS

M: 4 gas turbines; 2 props; 96,000 hp   **Range:** 900/35, 5,000/18

REMARKS: Russian type designation: Bol'shoy Raketnyy Korabl' (large missile ship). Conversions completed from 1973 onward. Several have a new ECM array; all have four 16-tubed chaff launchers and a helicopter platform.

Sderzhannyy   1975

Smyshlennyy

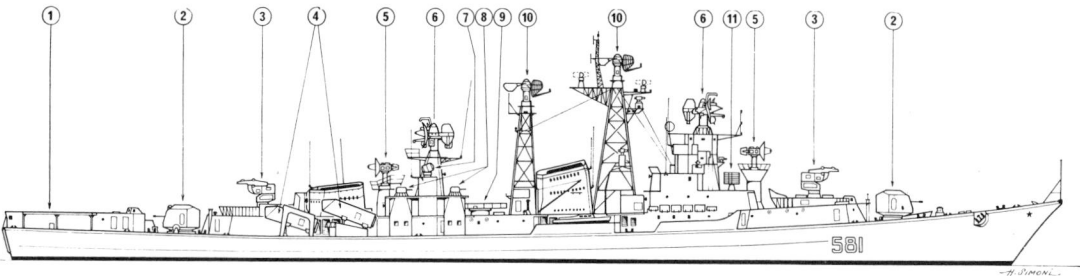

1. Towed sonar fittings 2. 76.2-mm 3. SA-N-1 4. SS-N-2C 5. Owl Screech 6. Peel Group 7. Bass Tilt 8. Gatling guns 9. 533-mm TT 10. Head Net-A 11. RBU-6000

GUIDED-MISSILE DESTROYERS (*continued*)

◆ 14 Kashin class

Bldrs: *Obraztsovyy, Odarennyy, Steregushchiy:* Zhdanov, Leningrad, 1963-66; others: Nikolayev, 1963-72

OBRAZTSOVYY	KRASNYY KAVKAZ	SKORYY	STROYNYY
ODARENNYY	KRASNYY KRYM	SMETLIVYY	STROGIY
STEREGUSHCHIY	PROVORNYY	SOOBRAZITELNYY	
KOMSOMOLETS UKRAINYY	RESHITELNYY	SPOSOBNYY	

Komsomolets Ukrainyy   1972

Steregushchiy   1973

Reshitelnyy

Provornyy   *Military Herald,* 1979

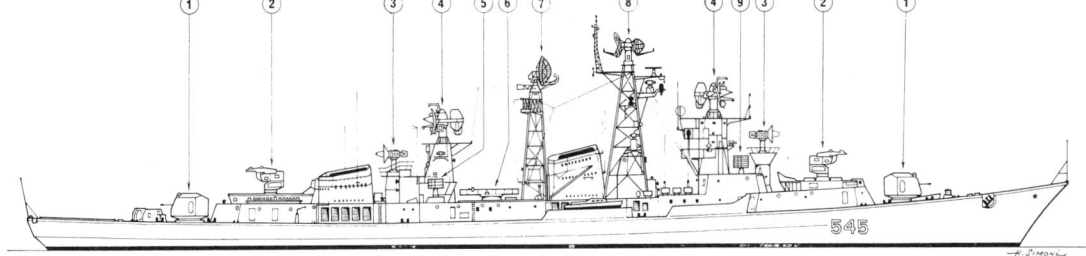

1. 76.2-mm   2. SA-N-1   3. Owl Screech   4. Peel Group   5. RBU-1000   6. 533-mm TT
7. Big Net   8. Head Net-C   9. RBU-6000

GUIDED-MISSILE DESTROYERS (*continued*)

Obraztsovyy   1974

Skoryy   1978

Krasnyy Krym   1976

D: 3,750 tons (4,750 fl)   **S:** 35 kts   **Dim:** 144.0 × 15.8 × 4.8 (mean)
Man: 280 men   **Range:** 900/35, 4,500/18
A: 2/SA-N-1 systems (II × 2) and 44 Goa missiles — 4/76.2-mm DP (II × 2) — 2/RBU 6000 rocket launchers — 2/RBU 1000 rocket launchers — 5/533-mm TT (V × 1) — mines

Electron Equipt: Radars: 2/Don 2, 2/Head Net-A or 1/Head Net-C and 1/Big Net, 2/Peel Group, 2/Owl Screech
Sonar: 1/high-frequency hull-mounted
ECM: 2/Watch Dog   IFF: 2/High Pole B
M: 4 gas turbines; 2 props; 96,000 hp

REMARKS: Russian type designation: Bol'shoy Protivolodochnyy Korabl' (large ASW ship). One of this class, the *Otvazhnyy*, was sunk 31-8-74 following an explosion: five others have been converted to Modified Kashin configuration. All have a helicopter pad on the fantail. In 1979, the *Provornyy* appeared with a single-armed SAM launcher aft in place of SA-N-1, but no similar weapon appears in place of the missing forward SA-N-1. Top steer radar is atop a new after mast, while Head Net-C has replaced Peel Group atop the bridge. She appears to be a trials ship for the new SAM system.

◆ **8 Kanin class**

Bldrs: Zhdanov, Leningrad; Severodvinsk; and Nikolayev, 1958-60

BOIKIY	GNEVNYY	GREMYASHCHIY	ZHGUCHIY
DERZKIY	GORDYY	UPORNYY	ZORKIY

Zhguchiy   1977

Zhguchiy   1977

D: 3,700 tons (4,700 fl)   **S:** 34 kts   **Dim:** 141.0 × 14.6 × 5.0 (avg.)
Man: 350 men   **Range:** 1,000/30, 4,500/18
A: 1/SA-N-1 system (II × 1) and 22 Goa missiles — 8/57-mm AA (IV × 2) — 8/30-mm AA (II × 4) — 3/RBU 6000 rocket launchers — 10/533-mm TT (V × 2)
Electron Equipt: Radars: 2/Don Kay, 1/Head Net-C, 1/Peel Group, 1/Hawk Screech, 2/Drum Tilt

GUIDED-MISSILE DESTROYERS (*continued*)

Sonar: 1/medium-frequency hull-mounted
ECM: . . .   IFF: 1/High Pole
M: GT; 2 props; 80,000 hp

REMARKS: Russian type designation: Bol'shoy Protivolodochnyy Korabl' (large ASW ship). Helicopter platform. Converted at Zhdanov, Leningrad, and a yard in the Far East, 1968-77.

◆ 3 Modified Kildin class

	Bldr	L
BEDOVYY	Nikolayev	1958
NEUDERZHIMYY	Komsomolsk	1958
PROZORLIVYY	Zhdanov, Leningrad	1958

Bedovyy   1977

D: 3,100 tons (4,150 fl)   **S:** 34 kts   **Dim:** 126.5 × 12.9 × 4.7 (avg.)
Man: 300 men   **Range:** 1,000/30, 4,000/18
A: 4/SS-N-2C (I × 4)−4/76.2-mm DP (II × 2)−16/57-mm AA (IV × 4) except *Bedovyy*: 16/45-mm AA (IV × 4)−2/RBU 2500 rocket launchers−4/533-mm TT (II × 2)
Electron Equipt: Radars: 1/Don 2, 1/Head Net-C, 1/Owl Screech, 2/Hawk Screech
    Sonar: 1/high-frequency-hull-mounted (Herkules or Pegas)
    ECM: 2/Watch Dog   IFF: 1/High Pole B
M: 2 sets GT; 2 props; 72,000 hp   **Boilers:** 4

REMARKS: Russian type designation: Bol'shoy Raketnyy Korabl' (large missile ship). The *Bedovyy* has broader stacks than her sisters and has Strut Pair radar in place of Head Net-C. Conversions completed at Nikolayev, 1973-75.

◆ 1 Kildin class

	Bldr	L
NEULOVIMYY	Zhdanov, Leningrad	1958

D: 2,900 tons (3,950 fl)   **S:** 34 kts   **Dim:** 126.5 × 12.9 × 4.6 (avg.)
Man: 285 men   **Range:** 1,000/30, 4,000/18

A: 1/SS-N-1 (I × 1) and 6 Scrubber missiles − 16/57-mm AA (IV × 4) − 2/RBU 2500 rocket launchers − 4/533-mm TT (II × 2)
Electron Equipt: Radars: 1/Slim Net, 1/Flat Spin, 1/Top Bow, 2/Hawk Screech
    Sonar: 1/Herkules
    ECM: 2/Watch Dog   IFF: 1/High Pole, 2/Square Head
M: 2 sets GT; 2 props; 72,000 hp   **Boilers:** 4

REMARKS: Russian type designation: Bol'shoy Raketnyy Korabl' (large missile ship). The SS-N-1 launcher and reload hangar are aft. Design modified from that of the Kotlin class. Unlikely to be converted because of age. In the Pacific Fleet.

◆ 8 SAM Kotlin class   Bldrs: Various, 1955-57

BRAVYY	NASTOCHIVYY	SKROMNYY	SOZNATEL'NYY
NAKHODCHIVYY	NESOKRUSHIMYY	SKRYTNYY	VOZBUZHDENNY

Bravyy−conversion prototype   1970

Soznatel'nyy   1977

GUIDED-MISSILE DESTROYERS (continued)

D: 2,850 tons (3,950 fl) S: 34 kts Dim: 126.5 × 12.9 × 4.6 (avg.)
Man: 300 men Range: 1,000/30, 4,000/18
A: *Bravyy:* 1/SA-N-1 system (II × 1) − 2/130-mm DP (II × 1) − 12/45-mm AA (IV × 3) − 5/533-mm TT (V × 1) − 2/RBU 2500 rocket launchers
Others: 1/SA-N-1 system (II × 1) − 2/130-mm DP (II × 1) − 4/45-mm AA (IV × 1) − 5/533-mm TT (V × 1) − 2/RBU 6000 rocket launchers (two have RBU 2500, *see* Remarks)
Electron Equipt: Radars: 1 or 2/Don 2, 1/Head Net-C, 1/Peel Group, 1/Sun Visor, 1/Hawk Screech, 1/Egg Cup
  Sonar: 1/high-frequency (Herkules or Pegas)
  ECM: 2/Watch Dog IFF: 1/High Pole B
M: 2 sets GT; 2 props; 72,000 hp Boilers: 4

Skromnyy 1973

Nakhodchivyy

REMARKS: Russian type designation: Eskadrennyy Minonosets (destroyer). The *Neso-krushimyy, Soznatel'nyy,* and *Vozbuzhdennyy* have eight 30-mm AA (II × 4) in addition to the above, with two Drum Tilt fire-control radars. The *Nastochivyy* has no Egg Cup radar. The *Bravyy* has Head Net-A, two extra quadruple 45-mm AA mounts and, as does the *Skromnyy,* RBU 2500 vice RBU 6000. The *Bravyy,* which served as the SA-N-1 trials ship, completed conversion in 1962, the others 1966-72.

Nastochivyy 1974

DESTROYERS

◆ **18 Kotlin and Modified Kotlin**(*) **classes** Bldrs: Leningrad and Nikolayev, 1954-57

BESSLEDNYY	MOSKOVSKIY KOMSOMOLETS*	SVETLYY
BLAGORODNYY*	NAPORISTIY*	VESKIY
BLESTYASHCHIY*	PLAMENNYY*	VDOKHNOVENNYY*
BURLIVYY*	SPESHNYY	VLIYATEL'NYY
BYVALYY*	SPOKOYNYY	VOZMUSHCHYENNYY
DAL'NEVOSTOCHNYY KOMSOMOLETS	SVEDUSHCHIY*	VYDERZHANNYY*
		VYZYVAYUSHCHIY*

Speshnyy

D: 2,850 tons (3,800 fl) S: 34 kts Dim: 126.5 × 12.9 × 4.6
Man: 36 officers, 300 men Range: 1,000/32, 4,000/18
A: Kotlin: 4/130-mm DP (II × 2) − 16/45-mm AA (IV × 4) − 4/25-mm AA (II × 2) − 10/533-mm TT (V × 2) − 6/depth-charge projectors − 6/depth-charge racks − 70 mines may be carried
  Mod. Kotlin: 4/130-mm DP (II × 2) − 16/45-mm AA (IV × 4) − 8/25-mm AA (II × 4) − 5/533-mm TT (V × 1) − 2/RBU 2500 rocket launchers − 2/RBU 600 − 70 mines
Electron Equipt: Radars: 1/Neptune or Don 2, 1/Slim Net, 1/Sun Visor, 2/Hawk Screech, 2/Egg Cup, 1/Post Lamp or Top Bow
  Sonar: 1/high-frequency (Herkules)
  ECM: 2/Watch Dog IFF: 1/High Pole, 2/Square Head
M: 2 sets GT; 2 props; 72,000 hp Boilers: 4

DESTROYERS (continued)

Svetlyy   1974

Dal'nevostochny Komsomolets   1974

Speshnyy   1974

REMARKS: Russian type designation: Eskadrennyy Minonosets (destroyer). Eleven were modified between 1960 and 1962, receiving two RBU-2500 forward and two RBU-600 in place of their depth-charge equipment, the after bank of five 533-mm TT being

removed. Later, most of these ships got eight more 25-mm AA (II × 4). The *Moskovskiy Komsomolets* got RBU-6000 forward, nothing aft; in 1978 she received a variable-depth sonar on her stern. Most of those that were not modified received four 25-mm AA (II × 2) additional. The *Svetlyy* has a helicopter platform in place of depth-charge gear and thus has no ASW armament. Helicopter decks were removed from the other two ships that had them. Many have had their Egg Cup radars removed.

◆ 33 Skoryy and Modified Skory(*) classes

Bldrs: Severodvinsk; Zhdanov, Leningrad; Nikolayev; Komsomolsk
Possible names:

BESSMENNYY	OTCHETLIVYY*	STATNYY
BESSTRASHNYY	OTMENNYY	STEPENNYY
BEZBOYAZNENYY	OTVETSTVENNYY	STOYKIY*
BEZUDERZHNYY	OZHESTOCHENNYY	STREMITEL'NYY
BEZUKORIZNENNY	OZHIVLYENNYY	SUROVYY
BUYNYY	SERDITYY	SVOBODNYY*
OGNENNYY*	SER'YEZNYY	VDUMCHIVYY
OKRYLENNYY	SMOTRYASHCHIY	VNEZAPNYY
OSTOROZHNYY*	SOKRUSHITEL'NYY	VNIMATEL'NYY
OSTRYY	SOLIDNYY	VOL'NYY*
OTCHAYANNYY	SOVERSHENNYY	VRAZUMITEL'NYY

Modified Skoryy class   1961

D: 3,240 tons (3,130 fl)   S: 34 kts
Dim: 130.5 (116.0 pp) × 12.0 × 4.3
Man: 280 men   Range: 940/33, 3,550/14
A: Standard: 4/130-mm (II × 2) − 2/85-mm AA (II × 1) − 7/37-mm AA (I × 7) or 8 (II × 4) − 4 or 6/25-mm AA (II × 2 or 3) − 10/533-mm TT (V × 2) − 2/depth-charge projectors − 2/depth-charge racks − 50 mines
     Modified: 4/130-mm DP (II × 2) − 5/57-mm AA (I × 5) − 2/RBU 2500 rocket launchers − 5/533-mm TT (V × 1) − 50 mines
Electron Equipt: Radars: Standard: 1/High Sieve, 1/Top Bow or Half Bow or Post Lamp, 1/Cross Bird, 1 or 2/Don 2 (also 1/Knife Rest on a few)
     Modified: 1/Slim Net, 1/Top Bow, 1 or 2/Don 2, 2/Hawk Screech
Sonar: 1/high-frequency (Tamir or Pegas)
ECM: 2/Watch Dog   IFF: 2/Square Head, 1/High Pole A
M: 2 sets GT; 2 props; 60,000 hp   Boilers: 4

DESTROYERS (*continued*)

Skoryy class—with seven 37-mm AA   1978

Skoryy class—with eight 37-mm AA   1968

REMARKS: Russian type designation: Eskadrennyy Minonosets (destroyer). Went into service 1949-54. Survivors of seventy-two built, derived from prewar *Ognevoyy* design. A small number were modernized around 1960 to *Modified Skoryy* configuration. Only those with eight 37-mm AA have been given two or three twin 25-mm AA. Nineteen ships are believed still active. Several *Skory* class were transferred to Egypt (only four remain), Poland, and Indonesia. Now of little value.

FRIGATES

◆ **7 Krivak-II class**   Bldr: Kaliningrad, 1976-

GROMKIY	NEUKROTIMYY	RAZITEL'NYY	REZVYY
GROZYASHCHIY	PYLKYY	REZKIY	

Razitel'nyy   1978

Neukrotimyy—with VDS deployed   1979

Rezkiy   1976

FRIGATES (continued)

D: 3,300 tons (3,600 fl)   S: 33 kts   Dim: 122.0 × 14.3 × 5.0
Man: 200 men   Range: 700/30
A: 4/SS-N-14 (IV × 1) with no reloads — 2/SA-N-4 systems (II × 2) with 36 missiles —
2/100-mm DP (I × 2) — 2/RBU 6000 rocket launchers — 8/533-mm TT (IV × 2) —
mines
Electron Equipt: Radars: 1/Don 2 or Spin Trough, 1/Head Net-C, 2/Eye Bowl,
1/Kite Screech, 2 /Pop Group
Sonars: 1/hull-mounted, 1/medium-frequency, towed VDS
ECM: 4/chaff launchers (XVI × 4)   IFF: 1/High Pole B

M: COGOG: 2 cruise and 2 boost gas turbines; 2 props; . . .–50,000 hp

REMARKS: Russian type designation: Storozhevoy Korabl' (patrol ship). Construction
continues. The VDS housing at the stern is somewhat larger than on the Krivak-Is,
but the principal difference is substitution of a single 100-mm for twin 76.2-mm gun.

◆ 17 Krivak-I class   Bldrs: Zhdanov, Leningrad; Kaliningrad; Kamish-Burun, Kerch

BEZZEVETNIY	LENINGRADSKIY KOMSOMOLETS	STOROZHEVOY
BDITEL'NYY	LETOCHIY	SVIREPYY
BODRYY	RAZUMNYY	ZADORNYY
DEYATEL'NYY	RAZYASHCHIY	ZHARKYY
DOBLESTNYY	RETIVYY	. . .
DRUZHNYY	SIL'NYY	

![Krivak-I class — with quadruple SS-N-14 launcher elevated and trained to starboard]

Krivak-I class — with quadruple SS-N-14 launcher elevated and trained to starboard

D: 3,300 tons (3,600 fl)   S: 33 kts   Dim: 122.0 × 14.3 × 5.0
Man: 200 men   Range: 700/30
A: 4/SS-N-14 (IV × 1) with no reloads — 2/SA-N-4 systems (II × 2) with 36 missiles —
4/76.2-mm DP (II × 2) — 2/RBU 6000 rocket launchers — 8/533-mm TT (IV × 2) —
mines
Electron Equipt: Radars: 1/Don 2 or Spin Trough, 1/Head Net-C, 2/Eye Bowl,
1/Owl Screech, 2 Pop Group
Sonars: 1/hull-mounted, 1/towed VDS (both medium-frequency)
ECM: 4/chaff launchers (XVI × 4)   IFF: High Pole B

M: COGOG: 2 cruise and 2 boost gas turbines; 2 props; . . .–50,000 hp

Bditel'nyy   1971

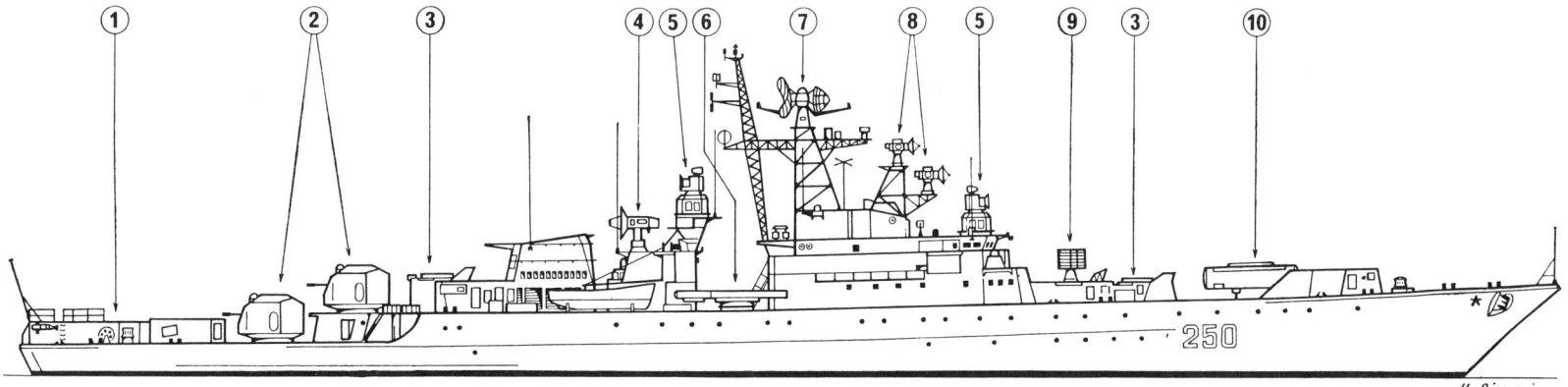

1. Towed sonar fittings 2. 76.2-mm 3. SA-N-4 4. Owl Screech 5. Pop Group
6. 533-mm TT 7. Head Net-C 8. Eye Bowl 9. RBU-6000 10. SS-N-14

FRIGATES (continued)

Krivak-I class—amidships detail   1979

Razyashchiy   1976

REMARKS: Russian type designation: Storozhevoy Korabl' (patrol ship). Construction began in 1970 and continues. In 1978 Krivak-I and Krivak-II classes were rerated from BPK (Bol'shoy Protivolodochnyy Korabl'—large ASW ship) to SKR (Storozhevoy Korabl'—patrol ship), a demotion prompted perhaps by their limited endurance at high speeds, speed, and size.

NOTE: The Koni class, described in the previous edition, now appears to have been intended for export only, although it is reported that one unit, named *Timofey Ol'-yantsev*, may be in Soviet service. The class is described under Germany, Democratic Republic, which operates two units, the *Berlin* and the *Rostock*.

◆ 1 Modified Petya-II class

Modified Petya-II class   1978

A: 4/76.2-mm DP—2/RBU 6000 rocket launchers—5/400-mm ASW TT (V × 1)—mines

REMARKS: Conversion in 1978 similar to Modified Petya-I, but new VDS deckhouse at stern does not extend to the sides of the ship, which permits retention of mine rails. One quintuple ASW torpedo-tube mounting has been removed.

◆ 8 Modified Petya-I class

A: 4/76.2-mm DP (II × 2)—2/RBU 2500 rocket launchers—5/400-mm ASW TT (V × 1)—1/depth-charge rack

Modified Petya-I class   1976

REMARKS: Conversions began in 1973. Petya-I class altered by the addition of a medium-frequency towed sonar in a new raised stern deckhouse. The designation "Modified Petya I" is also applied to several trials units, one with a very large VDS exposed at her stern (no raised stern); another with a deckhouse abaft her stack and a complex towing array, reels, and winch on her stern; still another with a small, boxlike deckhouse at her extreme stern.

FRIGATES (*continued*)

◆ **23 Petya-II class**   Bldrs: Various, 1964-69

Petya-II   1976

Petya-II   1976

REMARK: Russian type designation: Storozhevoy Korabl' (patrol ship).

◆ **12 Petya-I class**   Bldrs: Various, 1962-64

Petya-I class—under way on diesels and gas turbines

D: 950 tons (1,100 fl)   **S:** 30 kts   **Dim:** 82.3 × 9.1 × 3.2
Man: 80-90 men   **Range:** 850/30 (diesel + gas turbine), 4,000/10 (diesel),
A: Petya-I: 4/76.2-mm DP (II × 2) — 4/RBU 2500 rocket launchers — 5/400-mm ASW
     TT (V × 1) — 2/depth-charge racks — mines
    Petya-II: 4/76.2-mm DP (II × 2) — 2/RBU 6000 rocker launchers — 10/400-mm
     ASW TT (V × 2) — 2/depth-charge racks — mines

Electron Equipt: Radars: 1/Don 2, 1/Slim Net (Petya-II: Strut Curve), 1/Hawk
                  Screech
           Sonar: 1/high-frequency (Herkules)
           ECM: 2/Watch Dog   IFF: 1/High Pole B
M: CODAG: 2 15,000-hp gas turbines + 1 6,000-hp diesel; 3 props

REMARKS: Russian type designation: Storozhevoy Korabl' (patrol ship). Both versions are being gradually modernized (*see above*). Some carry helicopter dipping sonars in temporary installations amidships. Petya-I has two Square Head IFF interrogators. A version with two RBU-2500 rocket launchers and three 533-mm torpedo tubes (III × 1) has been exported to India, Syria, and Vietnam.

◆ **9 Mirka-I class**

◆ **9 Mirka-II class**

Mirka-I class

Mirka-II class—with Slim Net and dipping sonar   1977

D: 950 tons (1,100 fl)   **S:** 34 kts   **Dim:** 82.3 × 9.1 × 3.2
Man: 98 men   **Range:** 500/30 (gas turbine), 4,000/10 (diesel)
A: Mirka-I: 4/76.2-mm DP (II × 2) — 4/RBU 6000 rocket launchers — 5/400-mm
     ASW TT (V × 1) — 1/depth-charge rack

FRIGATES (continued)

Mirka-II: 4/76.2-mm DP (II × 2) — 2/RBU 6000 rocket launchers — 10/400-mm
ASW TT (V × 2)
Electron Equipt: Radars: 1/Don 2, 1/Slim Net or Strut Curve, 1/Hawk Screech
Sonars: 1/high-frequency (Herkules or Pegas), Mirka-II also:
1/dipping
ECM: 2/Watch Dog   IFF: 1/High Pole B, 2/Square Head
M: CODAG: 2 15,000-hp gas turbines + 2 6,000-hp diesels; 2 props

Mirka-II class — with Strut Curve and dipping sonar   1977

REMARKS: Russian type designation: Storozhevoy Korabl' (patrol ship). Built at various
yards, 1964-66. All Mirka-Is have Slim Net, while a few late Mirka-IIs have Strut
Curve. The latter have been modernized with a new type of dipping sonar in place of
the internal depth-charge rack.

◆ **37 Riga class** Bldrs: Various, 1952-58

Possible names:

ASTRAKHAN'SKIY KOMSOMOLETS	KOBCHIK	PANTERA
ARKHANGEL'SKIY KOMSOMOLETS	KOMSOMOLETS GRUZIY	ROSOMAKHA
BARS	KOMSOMOLETS LITVIY	SHAKAL
BARSUK	KRASNODARSKIY KOMSOMOLETS	TIGR
BOBR	KUNITSA	TURMAN
BUYVOL	LEOPARD	VOLK
BYK	LEV	VORON
GEPARD	LISA	YAGUAR
GIENA	MEDVED'	

D: 1,000 tons (1,320 fl)   **S:** 28 kts   **Dim:** 91.0 × 11.0 × 3.4
Man: 175 men   **Range:** 2,000/10
A: 3/100-mm DP (I × 3) — 4/37-mm AA (II × 2) — 4/25-mm AA (II × 2) — 2 or 3/533-mm
ASW TT (II or III × 1) — 2/depth-charge racks — 2/RBU 2500 rocket launchers
(a few have 1/RBU 600 Hedgehog and 4/depth-charge projectors vice RBU 2500)
— mines
Electron Equipt: Radars: 1/Neptune or Don 2, 1/Slim Net, 1/Sun Visor
Sonar: 1/high-frequency (Herkules or Pegas)
ECM: 2/Watch Dog   IFF: 1/High Pole, 2/Square Head
M: 2 sets GT; 2 props; 20,000 hp   **Boilers:** 2

Riga class — with flare launcher on the forecastle   1974

Riga class — only one of class with extra radomes, tall stack cap   1972

Riga class

REMARKS: Russian type designation: Storozhevoy Korabl' (patrol ship). One ship has a
Hawk Screech radar director forward and the main gun director aft. Some have been
transferred to other countries, including Indonesia, Finland, Bulgaria, China, and
East Germany.

GUIDED-MISSILE CORVETTES

◆ **1 Tarantul class** Bldr: Petrovskiy SY, Leningrad, 1979

> **D:** 750 tons (fl)   **S:** 35 kts   **Dim:** 56.5 × 10.5 × 2.5
> **A:** 4/SS-N-2C (II × 2)−1/76.2-mm DP−2/Gatling AA (VI × 2)
> **Electron Equipt:** Radars: 1/Spin Trough, 1/Bass Tilt, 1/Square Tie
> IFF: 1/High Pole, 1/Square Head
> **M:** CODAG: 2 20,000-hp gas turbines, 1 cruise diesel; 3 props

REMARKS: Russian type designation: Raketnyy Korabl' (missile ship). The function of this class is uncertain, because in many respects, particularly weapons, it is not as up to date as the Nanuchka class, which continues in production. It may be for export.

◆ **3 Nanuchka-III class** Bldr: Petrovskiy SY, Leningrad, 1977-

> **D:** 780 tons (930 fl)   **S:** 34 kts   **Dim:** 60.3 × 12.2 × 3.1
> **Man:** 60 men   **Range:** . . .
> **A:** 6/SS-N-9 (III × 2)−1/SA-N-4 system (II × 1) with 18 missiles−1/76.2-mm DP−
> 1/Gatling AA (VI × 1)
> **Electron Equipt:** Radars: 1/Peel Pair, 1/Band Stand, 1/Bass Tilt
> ECM: . . .   IFF: 1/High Pole, 1/Square Head
> **M:** 6 diesels; 3 props; 30,000 hp

REMARKS: Russian type designation: Raketnyy Korabl' (missile ship). Construction continues. The single 76.2-mm DP was substituted for the twin 57-mm AA aft, the Gatling gun is in the position occupied by Muff Cob in the Nanuchka-I, and Bass Tilt is situated atop a new deckhouse abaft the mast. The pilothouse is higher and the superstructure is enlarged.

◆ **18 Nanuchka-I class** Bldr: Petrovskiy SY, Leningrad, 1969-76

GRAD   RADUGA   16 others

Nanuchka-I class   1976

> **D:** 780 tons (930 fl)   **S:** 34 kts   **Dim:** 60.3 × 12.2 × 3.1
> **Man:** 60 men   **Range:** . . .
> **A:** 6/SS-N-9 (II × 3)−1/SA-N-4 system (II × 1) with 18 missiles−1/76.2-mm DP or
> 2/57-mm AA (II × 1)
> **Electron Equipt:** Radars: 1/Peel Pair, 1/Pop Group, 1/Muff Cob, 1/Band Stand
> ECM: . . .   IFF: 1/High Pole, 1/Square Head
> **M:** 6 diesels; 3 props; 30,000 hp

Nanuchka-I class   1975

Nanuchka-I class   1976

REMARK: Russian type designation: Raketnyy Korabl' (missile ship). These are reported to be poor sea boats with very unreliable engines (paired M-504 diesels). Three of them, modified with four SS-N-2C missiles, have been sold to India (Nanuchka-II).

CORVETTES

◆ 12 Grisha-III class

Grisha-III class   1978

Grisha-III class — Gatling-gun installation   1976

A: 1/SA-N-4 system (II × 1) with 18 missiles — 2/57-mm AA (II × 1) — 2/RBU 6000 rocker launchers — 4/533-mm TT (II × 2) — 2/depth-charge racks or mines

REMARKS: Russian type designation: Mal'yy Protivolodochnyy Korabl' (small ASW ship). Started building in 1975 and construction continues. Bass Tilt, which is atop a small deckhouse to port on the aft superstructure, has been substituted for Muff Cob radar fire control, while a Gatling gun has been mounted in the space occupied by Muff Cob in the Grisha I and II. Depth-charge racks can be mounted on the aft end of the mine rails.

◆ 6 Grisha-II class

AMETIST	IZUMRUD	SAFFIR
BRILLIANT	RUBIN	ZHEMCHUG

Brilliant

A: 4/57-mm AA (II × 2) — 2/RBU 6000 rocket launchers — 4/533-mm TT (II × 2) — 2/depth-charge racks or mines

REMARKS: Russian type designation: Pogranichniy Storozhevoy Korabl' (border patrol ship). Built between 1974 and 1976 and manned by the KGB Maritime Border Guard. A second twin 57-mm has replaced SA-N-4 forward and the Pop Group missile-control radar is not carried.

◆ 15 Grisha-I class   Bldrs: Various, 1968-74

Grisha-I class   1977

D: 950 tons (1,100 fl)   **S:** 34 kts   **Dim:** 73.0 × 9.7 × 3.7
Man: 60 men   **Range:** 450/30, 4,000/12

CORVETTES (*continued*)

A: 1/SA-N-4 system (II × 1) with 18 missiles—2/57-mm AA (II × 1)—2/RBU 6000 rocket launchers—4/533-mm TT (II × 2)—depth-charge racks—mines

Electron Equipt: Radars: 1/Don 2, 1/Strut Curve, 1/Pop Group, 1/Muff Cob
Sonars: 1/medium-frequency, 1/dipping
ECM: 2/Watch Dog   IFF: 1/High Pole

M: CODAG: 2 diesels, 1 gas turbine; 3 props; 24,000 hp

Grisha-I class   1977

REMARKS: Russian type designation: Mal'yy Protivolodochnyy Korabl' (small ASW ship). Although of the same size as the Petya and Mirka classes, the Grisha is typed here as a corvette because the Soviet Navy gives it a different designation. A plate has been added forward of the Muff Cob fire-control radar to protect people on the bridge from its radiation.

◆ **65 Poti class**   Bldrs: Various, 1961-67

Poti class

D: 500 tons (580 fl)   **S:** 36 kts   **Dim:** 60.3 × 8.0 × 3.0

A: 2/57-mm AA (II × 1)—2/RBU 6000 rocket launchers—2 or 4/400-mm TT (I × 2 or 4)

Electron Equipt: Radars: 1/Don 2, 1/Strut Curve, 1/Muff Cob
Sonars: 1/high-frequency (Herkules), 1/Hormone dipping
ECM: 2/Watch Dog   IFF: 1/High Pole B

M: CODAG: 2 M503A diesels (8,000 hp) + 2 gas turbines (40,000 hp); 2 props

Poti class—amidships detail, showing Muff Cob fire-control radar, twin 57-mm AA gun, and port 400-mm torpedo tube

Poti class—gas-turbine installation, showing canvas-covered air intakes and circular covers over exhausts

CORVETTES (continued)

REMARKS: Russian type designation: Mal'yy Protivolodochnyy Korabl' (small ASW ship). Several have old-style open 57-mm AA mounts and two RBU 2500. This class has been exported to Romania and Bulgaria.

◆ **16 T-58-class ex-minesweepers, 1957-61**

DZERZHINSKIY   KOMSOMOLETS LATVIY
KALININGRADSKIY KOMSOMOLETS   SOVETSKIY POGRANICHNIK
12 others

T-58 class   1975

D: 790 tons (900 fl)   **S:** 18 kts   **Dim:** 70.0 × 9.1 × 2.5
A: 4/57-mm AA (II × 2) − 2/RBU 1200 rocket launchers − mines
Electron Equipt: Radars: 1/Don 2, 1/Muff Cob   **M:** 2 diesels; 2 props; 4,000 hp

REMARKS: Reclassified as Storozhevoy Korabl' (patrol ship) in 1978 and portable mine-sweeping gear offloaded. Several are operated by the KGB Border Guard. One has been transferred to Guinea, one to Yemen, and another has been converted as a radar picket with a Big Net radar aft.

GUIDED-MISSILE PATROL BOATS

◆ **1 Sarancha class**   Bldr: Petrovsky SY, Leningrad, 1977

D: 300 tons (fl)   **S:** 50 kts
Dim: 50.6 (45.0 hull) × 23.5 (11.0 hull) × 7.3 (2.8 hull)
A: 4/SS-N-9 (II × 2) − 1/SA-N-4 system (II × 1) − 1/Gatling AA (VI × 1)
Electron Equipt: Radars: 1/Band Stand, 1/Pop Group, 1/Bass Tilt
M: 2 gas turbines; 4 props; 20,000 hp

REMARKS: Too large and complex to be a successor to the Osa class. Essentially, a reduced, high-speed Nanuchka. Folding-foil system similar to U.S. Navy's PHM. Stepped hydroplane hull bottom.

◆ **6 Matka class**   Bldr: Izhora SY, Leningrad, 1978-

D: 215 tons (250 fl)   **S:** 40 kts   **Dim:** 40.0 × 12.0 (7.7 hull) × 1.9 (hull)
Man: 30 men   **Range:** 400/36, 650/20
A: 2/SS-N-2C (I × 2) − 1/76.2-mm DP − 1/Gatling AA (VI × 1)

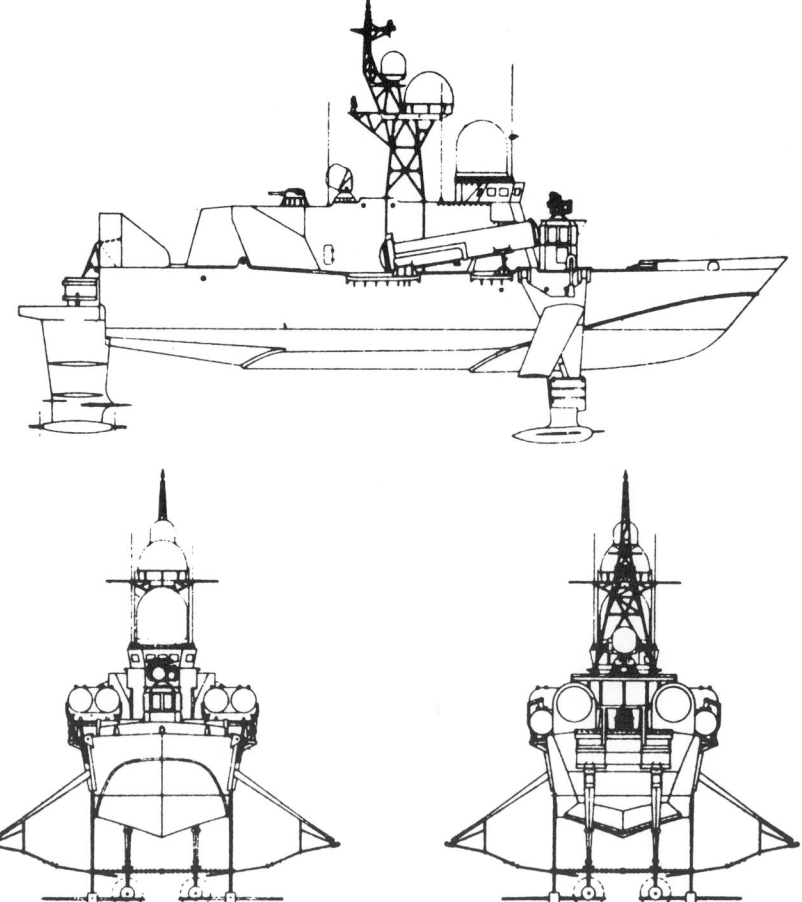

Sarancha class   House Armed Services Committee, U.S. Congress, 1979

Electron Equipt: Radars: 1/navigational, 1/Square Tie, 1/Bass Tilt
                      ECM: 2/chaff launchers (XVI × 2)   IFF: 1/High Pole B, 1/Square Head
M: 3 M504 diesels; 3 props; 15,000 hp

REMARKS: Essentially, a missile-armed version of the Turya-class hydrofoil torpedo boat, with larger superstructure, 76.2-mm gun forward, and missiles and Gatling gun aft. Believed intended to replace the Osa-I class. Construction continues.

◆ **45 Osa-II class, 1966-70**

KIROVSKIY   TAMBOVSKIY   KRONSHTADTSKIY
   KOMSOMOLETS   KOMSOMOLETS   KOMSOMOLETS
42 others

GUIDED-MISSILE PATROL BOATS (*continued*)

Osa-II class   1971

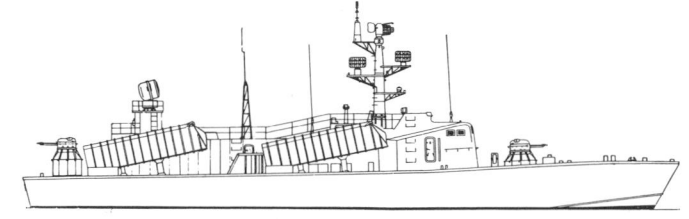

Osa-II class   S. Breyer

Osa-II class—with SA-N-5 aft   1976

Osa-II class   1976

D: 215 tons (245 fl)   **S:** 36 kts   **Dim:** 39.0 × 7.7 × 1.9
Man: 30 men   **Range:** 450/34, 700/20
A: 4/SS-N-2B Styx (I × 4)—4/30-mm AA (II × 2)
Electron Equipt: Radars: 1/Square Tie, 1/Drum Tilt
                IFF: 1/High Pole B, 2/Square Head
M: 3 M504 diesels; 3 props; 15,000 hp

REMARK: Russian type designation: Raketnyy Kater (missile cutter). Some units have been given SA-N-5 systems aft. Algeria, Cuba, Finland and Iraq have received some Osa-IIs.

◆ **70 Osa-I class**   Bldrs: Various, 1959-66

D: 175 tons (210 fl)   **S:** 36 kts   **Dim:** 39.0 × 7.7 × 1.8
Man: 30 men   **Range:** 450/34, 700/20
A: 4/SS-N-2 Styx (I × 4)—4/30-mm AA (II × 2)
Electron Equipt: Radars: 1/Square Tie, 1/Drum Tilt
                IFF: 1/High Pole B, 2/Square Head
M: 3 M503A diesels; 3 props; 12,000 hp

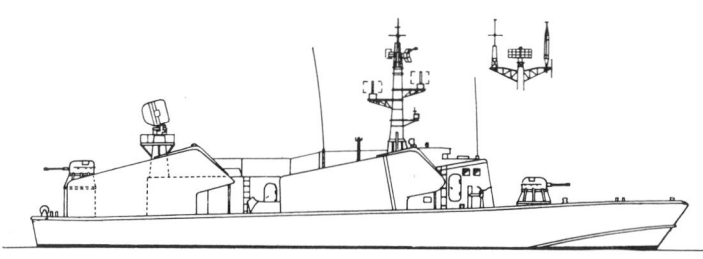

Osa-I class   S. Breyer

GUIDED-MISSILE PATROL BOATS (continued)

Osa-I class   1970

REMARKS: Russian type designation: Raketnyy Kater (missile cutter). These small craft can launch their missiles in a Force-4 sea (2-m waves). Many of them have been transferred to other navies. Some have been built as, or converted to, targets. Stenka, Matka, Turya, and Mol (an export torpedo boat, *see* Somalia and Sri Lanka) all use Osa hulls and propulsion plants.

PATROL BOATS

◆ **1 Babochka class**   Bldr: . . ., 1978

Babochka class   1978

D: 400 tons (fl)   **S:** 45 kts   **Dim:** 50.0 × 13.0 (8.5 hull) × . . .
A: 8/400-mm ASW TT (IV × 2) − 2/Gatling AA (VI × 2)
Electron Equipt: Radars: 1/Don 2, 1/new-type surveillance, 1/Bass Tilt
M: CODAG: 2 cruise diesels, 3 gas turbines; 3 props; 30,000 hp

REMARKS: A prototype ASW hydrofoil with fixed, fully submerged foils fore and aft. The torpedo tubes are mounted, two on two, on either side of the forecastle between the forward Gatling gun and the superstructure.

◆ **1 Slepen class**   Bldr: Petrovskiy SY, Leningrad

D: 205 tons (230 fl)   **S:** 36 kts   **Dim:** 39.0 × 7.7 × 1.8
A: 1/76.2-mm DP − 1/Gatling gun   **Man:** 30 men

Electron Equipt: Radars: 1/Don 2, 1/Bass Tilt
           ECM: 2/chaff launchers (XVI × 2)   IFF: 1/High Pole B,
                2/Square Head
M: 3 M504 diesels; 3 props; 15,000 hp

REMARKS: The Soviet Navy's only high-speed gunboat is a trials craft for systems for small combatants. Twin 57-mm AA replaced by single 76.2-mm DP forward in 1975. Resembles a Matka but does not have missiles or hydrofoils.

◆ **70 Stenka class**   Bldrs: Various, 1967-

Stenka class   S. Breyer

D: 170 tons (210 fl)   **S:** 36 kts   **Dim:** 39.5 × 7.7 × 1.8
A: 4/30-mm AA (II × 2) − 4/400-mm ASW TT − 2/depth-charge racks
Electron Equipt: Radars: 1/Pot Drum, 1/Drum Tilt
                 Sonar: 1/Hormone-helicopter dipping
                 IFF: 1/High Pole B, 2/Square Head
M: 3 M503A diesels; 3 props; 12,000 hp   **Range:** 450/34, 700/20

Stenka class

PATROL BOATS (continued)

REMARKS: Russian type designation: Pogranichnyy Storazhevoy Korabl' (border-patrol ship). Recent units have a new navigational radar via Pot Drum. Manned by the Maritime Border Guard of the KGB.

◆ **47 S.O.-1 class**   Bldrs: Various, 1958-64

S.O.-1 class   S. Breyer

    D: 170 tons (215 fl)   **S:** 28 kts   **Dim:** 42.0 × 6.1 × 1.9
    A: 4/25-mm AA (II × 2)−4/RBU 1200 rocket launchers−2/depth-charge racks−
        mines   Some ships: 2/400-mm ASW TT replacing the 25-mm mount aft
    Electron Equipt: Radar: 1/Pot Head   Sonar: 1/high-frequency (Tamir)
                  IFF: 1/Dead Duck, 1/High Pole A
    M: 3 diesels; 3 props; 7,500 hp   **Man:** 3 officers, 27 men

REMARKS: Poor sea boats. Class being scrapped. Several have been transferred to East Germany, North Vietnam, Algeria, Iraq, Cuba, South Yemen, etc.

HYDROFOIL TORPEDO BOATS

◆ **30 Turya class**   Bldr: . . ., 1974-

Turya class

    D: 205 tons (240 fl)   **S:** 42 kts
    Dim: 39.0 × 7.7 (12.0 over foils) × 1.8 (without foils)
    Man: 14 men   **Range:** 400/38, 650/20
    A: 2/57-mm AA aft (II × 1)−2/25-mm AA (II × 1)−4/533-mm TT (I × 4)

Turya class

Turya class−dipping sonar on starboard quarter

Turya class

    Electron Equipt: Radars: 1/Pot Drum, 1/Muff Cob
                  Sonar: 1/Hormone-helicopter dipping
                  IFF: 1/High Pole B, 1/Square Head
    M: 3 M504 diesels; 3 props; 15,000 hp

HYDROFOIL TORPEDO BOATS (continued)

REMARKS: Fixed hydrofoils foward only, stern planes on water surface. Has Osa-II hull and propulsion. Two of this class, without dipping sonar, were delivered to Cuba in 1-79.

TORPEDO BOATS

◆ **40 Shershen class**   Bldr: . . ., 1963-70

    D: 150 tons (180 fl)   **S:** 45 kts   **Dim:** 34.0 × 7.2 × 1.5
    A: 4/30-mm AA (II × 2)—4/533-mm TT (I × 4)—2/depth-charge racks
    Electron Equipt: Radars: 1/Pot Drum, 1/Drum Tilt
                      IFF: 1/High Pole A, 1/Square Head
    M: 3 M503A diesels; 3 props; 12,000 hp   **Range:** 450/34, 700/20

Shershen class   Skyfotos, Ltd., 1978

REMARKS: Contemporaneous with the Osa-I class, and have the same propulsion but a smaller hull. Have been exported to Egypt, North Korea, East Germany, Angola, Cape Verde Islands, Guinea, and Vietnam. Yugoslavia has built some under licence.

NOTE: A torpedo boat of a new design, Mol, based on the Osa class but with Shershen armament, has been built for export only, units having gone to Sri Lanka (no TT) and Somalia (TT and no TT). All operational units of the older P-6 and P-4 classes of torpedo boats are believed to have been discarded.

PATROL CRAFT

◆ **20 or more Zhuk class**   Bldr: . . ., 1975-

    D: 50 tons (fl)   **S:** 30 kts   **Dim:** 22.9 × 4.9 × 1.5
    A: 2/14.5-mm AA (II × 1)   **Electron Equipt:** Radar: 1/Spin Trough
    M: 2 M50 diesels; 2 props; 2,400 hp

REMARKS: Some carry four 14.5-mm AA (II × 2). Probably manned by the KGB Border Guard. A number have been exported to Cuba, Vietnam, and several African states.

◆ **20 Pchela-class hydrofoils**   Bldr: . . ., 1964-65

    D: 70 tons (83 fl)   **S:** 45 kts   **Dim:** 25.3 × 5.8 × 1.3 (without foils)
    A: 4/14.5-mm AA (II × 2)—4/depth-charge racks   **Man:** 12 men
    Electron Equipt: Radar: 1/Pot Drum
                         Sonar: On a few: 1/Hormone-helicopter dipping
    M: Diesels; 2 props; 6,000 hp

Pchela class—with ECM radomes atop bridge

Pchela class—without ECM radomes

REMARKS: Simple, fixed, surface-piercing hydrofoils. Aircraft-type machine-gun mountings. Manned by the KGB Border Guard.

PATROL CRAFT (*continued*)

◆ **34 Poluchat-I class** Bldr: . . ., 1953-56

D: 90 tons (fl)   **S:** 18 kts   **Dim:** 29.6 × 5.8 × 1.5
A: 2/14.5-mm AA (II × 1)   **Man:** 20 men   **Range:** 450/17, 900/10
M: 2 M50 diesels; 2 props; 2,400 hp

Poluchat-I-class torpedo-retriever—patrol version similar

REMARKS: Modified version of a standard Soviet Navy torpedo-retriever, with stern ramp decked over, a boat carried aft, and a twin machine-gun mount. Probably operated by the KGB Border Guard.

RIVERINE CRAFT

NOTE: The U.S.S.R. maintains a number of river gunboats on the Lower Danube, on the Amur and Ussuri river systems in the Far East, and possibly elsewhere. In addition to gunboats, the riverine forces have a few support craft, including the administrative craft PS-10 on the Danube.

◆ **75-80 Shmel-class patrol gunboats** Bldr: . . ., 1967-74

Shmel class—no rocket launcher, unarmored 25-mm mount aft

Shmel class—Austrian gunboat in background   J. Meister, 1975

D: 60 tons (fl)   **S:** 22 kts   **Dim:** 28.3 × 4.6 × 1.0
A: 1/76.2-mm, 48 cal., fwd in a tank turret—2/25-mm AA (II × 1) aft—1/18-tube, 122-mm rocket launcher—mines
M: 2 M50 diesels; 2 props; 2,400 hp   **Man:** 15 men

REMARKS: Russian type designation: AK—Artilleriyskiy Kater (artillery cutter); earlier classes were BK—Bronovoy Kater (armored cutter). Not all these craft have a rocket launcher. An earlier version has a twin machine-gun mount aft that resembles a tank turret. A few of the older BK-IV-class river monitors may still be in service; similar in size to the Shmel, they had an undulating deckline, were more heavily armed, slower, and carried one 85-mm and four 14.5-mm AA (II × 2).

MINE WARFARE SHIPS

◆ **3 Alesha-class minelayers** Bldr: . . ., 1967-69

Alesha class   1969

MINE WARFARE SHIPS (*continued*)

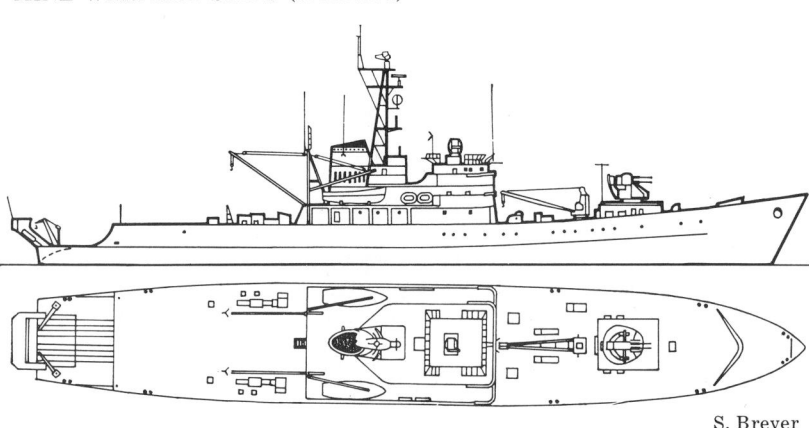

S. Breyer

D: 2,900 tons (3,500 fl)   **S:** 20 kts   **Dim:** 98.0 × 14.5 × 4.8
A: 4/57-mm (IV × 1)—400 mines   **Man:** 190 men
Electron Equipt: Radars: 1/Don 2, 1/Strut Curve, 1/Muff Cob
                  IFF: 1/High Pole B
M: 4 diesels; 2 props; 8,000 hp

REMARK: Can also be used as netlayers, minesweeper tenders, and command ships.

◆ **30 Natya-class fleet minesweepers** Bldr: . . ., 1970-77

ADMIRAL PERSHIN   DMITRI LYSOV   KONTRADMIRAL HOROSHKIN SEMEN ROSHAL'
26 others

Natya class   1978

D: 650 tons (750 fl)   **S:** 20 kts   **Dim:** 61.0 × 9.6 × 2.7
A: 4/30-mm AA (II × 2)—4/25-mm AA (II × 2)—2/RBU 1200 rocket launchers—
      mines   **Man:** 50 men
Electron Equipt: Radars: 1/Don 2, 1/Drum Tilt
                  IFF: 1/High Pole B, 2/Square Head
M: 2 diesels; 2 props; 8,000 hp

Natya class   1978

REMARKS: Russian type designation: Morskoy Tral'shchik (seagoing minesweeper).
Equipped to serve as ASW escorts. Early units have rigid davits aft; on later units
they are articulated. Four have been built for India.

◆ **48 Yurka-class fleet minesweepers** Bldr: . . ., 1964-70
GAFEL'   EVGENIY NIKONOV   46 others

Yurka class

D: 400 tons (460 fl)   **S:** 18 kts   **Dim:** 52.0 × 9.3 × 2.0
A: 4/30-mm AA (II × 2)—20 mines   **Man:** 45 men
Electron Equipt: Radars: 1/Don 2, 1/Drum Tilt
                  IFF: 1/High Pole B, 3/Square Head
M: 2 diesels; 2 props; 4,000 hp

REMARKS: Russian type designation: Morskoy Tral'shchik (seagoing minesweeper).
Aluminum-alloy hull. Four transferred to Egypt.

MINE WARFARE SHIPS (continued)

◆ **62 T-43-class fleet minesweepers** Bldr: . . ., 1947-57

IVAN FIOLETOV	KONTRADMIRAL YUROKOUSKIY	NIKOLAY MARKIN
KOMSOMOLETS	KOMSOMOLETS KALMYKIY	SAKHALINSKIY
BYELORUSSIY	MEZHADIY AZIZBAKOV	KOMSOMOLETS
KOMSOMOLETS		STEPAN SAUMYAN
ESTONIY		

53 others

T-43 class—long-hull version   1975

D: 500 tons (550 fl)   **S:** 14 kts   **Dim:** 58.0 × 8.4 × 2.3
Man: 65 men   **Range:** 3,200/10
A: 4/37-mm AA (II × 2) — 4/25-mm AA (II × 2) or 4-8/14.5-mm or 12.7-mm AA (II × 2 or 4) — 2/depth-charge projectors — mines
M: 2 diesels; 2 props; 2,200 hp

REMARKS: Russian type designation: Morskoy Tral'shchik (seagoing minesweeper). Many of the T-43 class have been transferred to Poland, Egypt, Algeria, China, etc. The version armed with four 25-mm AA amidships is 60 m long and displaces 600 tons (fl). Most Soviet units have no machine guns. A few operated by the KGB Border Guard have two 45-mm AA (I × 2) vice four 37-mm AA. Also built on the T-43 hull were radar pickets, noise-measurement ships, diving tenders, and trials ships. Well over 200 were built. Rapidly being disposed of.

◆ **30 Sonya-class coastal minesweepers** Bldr: . . ., 1973-

D: 350 tons (400 fl)   **S:** 18 kts   **Dim:** 48.5 × 8.8 × 2.1
A: 2/30-mm AA (II × 1) — 2/25-mm AA (II × 1)   **Man:** 43 men
Electron Equipt: Radar: 1/Spin Trough   **IFF:** 1/High Pole B, 2/Square Head
M: 2 diesels; 2 props; 2,400 hp

REMARKS: Russian type designation: Bergovoy Tral'shchik (coastal minesweeper). Wooden hull with plastic sheathing.

Sonya class

◆ **4 Zhenya-class coastal minesweepers** Bldr: . . ., 1972

Zhenya class

D: 220 tons (300 fl)   **S:** 18 kts   **Dim:** 42.7 × 7.5 × 1.8
A: 2/30-mm AA (II × 1)   **Electron Equipt:** Radar: 1/Spin Trough
M: 2 diesels; 2 props; 2,400 hp   **Man:** 40 men

REMARKS: Russian type designation: Beregovoy Tral'shchik (coastal minesweeper). Plastic hull. Apparently not successful, as similar but larger, wooden-hulled Sonya class went into production instead.

◆ **70 Vanya-class coastal minesweepers** Bldr: . . ., 1961-73

D: 200 tons (245 fl)   **S:** 18 kts   **Dim:** 39.9 × 7.3 × 1.8
A: 2/30-mm AA (II × 1)   **Man:** 30 men
Electron Equipt: Radar: 1/Don 2   **IFF:** 1/High Pole B, 1/Dead Duck
M: 2 diesels; 2 props; 2,200 hp

MINE WARFARE SHIPS (*continued*)

Vanya class

REMARKS: Russian type designation: Beregovoy Tral'shchik (coastal minesweeper). Wooden construction. At least one was built or has been converted as a minehunter, armed with two 25-mm AA (II × 1) – more accurate than 30-mm for mine-disposal?, and with one Don Kay in place of Don-2; has two boats in davits on the fantail. Some, Vanya-II, are one meter longer and have a large exhaust pipe amidships.

◆ **8 Sasha-class coastal minesweepers**   Bldr: . . ., 1954-59

    D: 250 tons (280 fl)   **S:** 18 kts   **Dim:** 45.7 × 6.2 × 1.8
    A: 1/45- or 57-mm AA – 4/25-mm AA (II × 2) – mines   **Man:** 25 men
    Electron Equipt: Radar: 1/Ball End   IFF: 1/High Pole A, 1/Dead Duck
    M: 2 diesels; 2 vertical cycloidal props; 2,200 hp

Sasha class

REMARKS: Russian type designation: Reydovoy Tral'shchik (roadstead minesweeper). Steel hull. Also used as patrol boats. Ships with 57-mm AA have shorter masts. Class being scrapped.

◆ **30 Yevgenya-class inshore minesweepers**   Bldr: . . ., 1970-

Yevgenya class   1976

    D: 70 tons (80 fl)   **S:** 12 kts   **Dim:** 26.1 × 5.8 × 1.2
    A: 2/14.5-mm AA (II × 1)
    Electron Equipt: Radar: 1/Spin Trough   IFF: 1/High Pole B
    M: 2 diesels; 2 props; 600 hp

REMARKS: Plastic hull. Several transferred abroad. Some Soviet and foreign ships have two 25-mm AA (II × 1).

◆ **3 Andryusha-class special minesweepers**   Bldr: . . ., 1975

    D: 320 tons (360 fl)   **S:** 15 kts   **Dim:** 44.9 × 8.2 × 3.0
    A: None   **Electron Equipt:** Radar: 1/Spin Trough   IFF: 1/High Pole B
    M: 2 diesels; 2 props; 2,200 hp   **Man:** 40 men

REMARKS: Wooden or plastic hulls. Large cable ducts running down both sides indicate probable role in sweeping magnetic mines. Prominent stack for gas-turbine generator; diesel engines exhaust through hull sides.

◆ **10 Olya-class minesweeping boats**   Bldr: . . ., 1976-

    D: 50 tons (70 fl)   **S:** 15 kts   **Dim:** 25.5 × 4.5 × 1.4
    A: 2/25-mm AA   **Electron Equipt:** Radar: 1/Spin Trough
    M: 2 diesels; 2 props; 600 hp   **Man:** 15 men

◆ **10 Ilyusha-class minesweeping boats**

    D: 50 tons (70 fl)   **S:** 12 kts   **Dim:** 24.4 × 4.9 × 1.4
    A: None   **Electronic Equipt:** Radar: 1/Spin Trough IFF: 1/High Pole B
    M: 1 diesel; 450 hp   **Man:** 10 men

REMARK: Apparently radio-controlled while operating, but can be manned for transit.

◆ **45 K-8-class minesweeping boats**   Bldr: Poland, 1954-59

    D: 26 tons (fl)   **S:** 12 kts   **Dim:** 16.9 × 3.2 × 0.8
    A: 2/14.5-mm (II × 1)   **Electron Equipt:** None
    M: 2 diesels; 2 props; 300 hp   **Man:** 6 men

RADAR PICKET SHIPS

◆ **1 T-58-class converted fleet minesweeper**

D: 700 tons (900 fl)   **S:** 18 kts   **Dim:** 70.0 × 9.1 × 2.5
A: 2/57-mm AA (II × 1) — 4/30-mm AA (II × 2)
Electron Equipt: Radars: 1/Big Net, 1/Strut Curve, 1/Don 2, 1/Muff Cob
                    IFF: . . .
M: 2 diesels; 2 props; 4,000 hp

REMARKS: Converted at Izhora, Leningrad, in 1979. Evidently successor to the T-43 class. Originally completed between 1957 and 1961. Other units may also be converted.

◆ **6 T-43 class**   Bldr: . . ., 1952-54

T-43-class radar picket — Big Net radar aft   1966

D: 500 tons (580 fl)   **S:** 14 kts   **Dim:** 58.0 × 8.4 × 2.3
A: 4/37-mm AA (II × 2) — 2/25-mm AA (II × 1) — 2/depth-charge projectors — mines
Man: 77 men
Electron Equipt: Radars: 1/Don, 1/Big Net or 2/Knife Rest
                    ECM: 2/Watch Dog
M: 2 diesels; 2 props; 2,200 hp

REMARKS: Configured as radar pickets; otherwise similar to the short-hulled minesweeper version. Not likely to last much longer.

AMPHIBIOUS-WARFARE SHIPS AND CRAFT

◆ **2 Ivan Rogov-class landing ships**   Bldr: Kaliningrad

	In serv.		In serv.
IVAN ROGOV	1978	N . . .	. . .

D: 11,000 tons (14,000 fl)   **S:** 20 kts   **Dim:** 158.0 × 24.0 × 8.0
Man: 200 men + 600 troops   **Range:** . . .
A: 1/SA-N-4 system (II × 1), 18 missiles — 2/76.2-mm DP (II × 1) — 4/Gatling AA (VI × 4) — 1/automatic bombardment rocket launcher (XL × 1) for BM-21 rockets — 4/Hormone helicopters — 2-3/Lebed air-cushion landing craft

Ivan Rogov   1978

Ivan Rogov — showing stern and helicopter-hangar doors   1979

Electron Equipt: Radars: 2/Don Kay, 1/Head Net-C, 1/Owl Screech, 1/Pop Group, 2/Bass Tilt
                    ECM: Rum Tub, numerous other radomes
                    IFF: High Pole B
M: Gas turbines; 2 props; 40,000 hp

REMARKS: Russian type designation: Bol'shoy Desantnyy Korabl' (large landing ship). Equipped with bow doors and a ramp evidently leading to a vehicle cargo deck in the forward part of the hull, while a massive stern door provides access to a floodable docking well intended to accommodate Gus- or Lebed-air-cushion landing craft. The massive superstructure incorporates a helicopter hangar, with a steep ramp leading

AMPHIBIOUS-WARFARE SHIPS AND CRAFT (*continued*)

Ivan Rogov — showing helicopter-landing position, rocket launcher to starboard, forward, and SA-N-4 to port, aft

1979

Ropucha class — note blunt bow plan at upper-deck level

1977

AMPHIBIOUS-WARFARE SHIPS AND CRAFT (*continued*)

downward to a helicopter pad on the foredeck, and doors aft leading to a second heli-copter platform over the stern. There are also hydraulically raised ramps leading from the upper deck forward of the superstructure to both the bow doors and the docking well. The *Ivan Rogov* is probably capable of transporting an entire naval infantry battalion and its vehicles, including tanks, armored personnel carriers, and trucks. Her ability to use helicopters, to beach, and to deploy air-cushion vehicles gives her a versatility unmatched by any other amphibious-warfare ship; this is combined with an organic shore-fire-bombardment capability and very extensive com-mand, control, and surveillance facilities.

◆ **12 Ropucha-class tank landing ships**   Bldr: Gdansk, Poland, 1975-78

Ropucha class   1976

Ropucha class   1976

D: 3,450 tons (4,400 fl)   **Dim:** 110.0 × 14.5 × 3.6 (aft) 2.0 (fwd)
S: 17 kts   **Man:** 70 men + 230 troops
A: 4/57-mm AA (II × 2)
Electron Equipt: Radars: 1/Don-2, 1/Strut Curve, 1/Muff Cob
                             IFF: 1/High Pole B
M: 4 diesels; 2 props; 10,000 hp

REMARKS: Russian type designation: Srednyy Desantnyy Korabl' (medium landing ship). Bow and stern doors permit roll-on/roll-off loading. Mounting positions forward for two bombardment rocket launchers. Cargo capacity: 1,000 tons; usable deck space: 600 m². The later units have angled hances to the corners of the main-deck super-structure and reinforcing gussets around the forward 57-mm AA platform.

Ropucha class   1976

◆ **14 Alligator-class tank landing ships**   Bldr: U.S.S.R., 1964-77

ALEKSANDR TORTSEV	NIKOLAY FIL'CHENKOV	SERGEI LAZO
DONETSKIY SHAKHTER	NIKOLAY VILKOV	TOMSKIY KOMSOMOLETS
KRASNAYA PRESNYA	NIKOLAY OBYEKOV	VORONEZHSKIY KOMSOMOLETS
KRYMSKIY KOMSOMOLETS	PETR IL'ICHYEV	50 LET SHEFSTVA V.L.K.S.M.
2 others		

Alligator class — late unit, no rocket launcher   1969

AMPHIBIOUS-WARFARE SHIPS AND CRAFT (*continued*)

Alligator class — late unit with rocket launcher forward   1976

Alligator class — early unit   1971

D: 3,400 tons (4,500 fl)   **S:** 18 kts   **Dim:** 114.0 × 15.6 × 3.7 (aft)
Man: 75 men + 400 troops   **Range:** 6,000/16
A: 2/57-mm AA (II × 1) — See Remarks
Electron Equipt: Radars: 2/Don-2 and/or Spin Trough   **IFF:** 1/High Pole B
M: 2 diesels; 8,000 hp

REMARKS: Russian type designation: Bol'shoy Desantnyy Korabl' (large landing ship). The design evolved continually during the time these ships were built. They have ramps fore and aft. Their hoisting equipment varies (one or two 5-ton cranes, one 15-ton crane), as does their armament: later ships also have a rocket launcher forward for shore bombardment, the last two have four 25-mm AA (II × 2) aft, and some are equipped with SA-N-5 short-range SAM missiles.

◆ **58 Polnocny-class medium landing ships**   Bldr: Gdansk, Poland, 1961-1973

A version:

D: 900 tons (fl)   **S:** 18 kts   **Dim:** 72.5 × 8.5 × 2.0 (fl)
A: 2/14.5-mm AA (II × 1) or 2/30-mm AA (II × 1) or none — 2/140-mm multiple rocket launchers (XVIII × 2) — 2 or 4/SA-N-5 systems (or none)
M: 2 diesels; 2 props; 4,000 hp   **Man:** 40 men

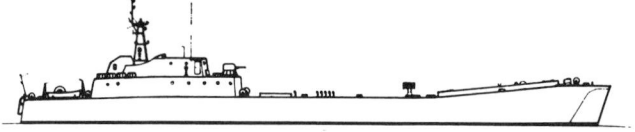

Polnocny-A — with twin 14.5-mm AA   1974

B version:

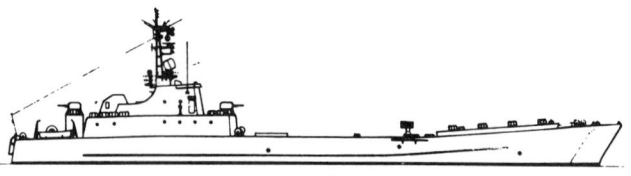

Polnocny-B — with high stack and 30-mm AA aft   1971

D: 950 tons (fl)   **S:** 18 kts   **Dim:** 74.0 × 8.5 × 2.0
A: 2 or 4/30-mm AA — 2/140-mm multiple rocket launchers (XVIII × 2) — 4/SA-N-5 systems
M: 2 diesels; 2 props; 4,000 hp   **Man:** 40 men

AMPHIBIOUS-WARFARE SHIPS AND CRAFT (*continued*)

Polnocny-B—with low stack and no 30-mm aft   1974

C version:

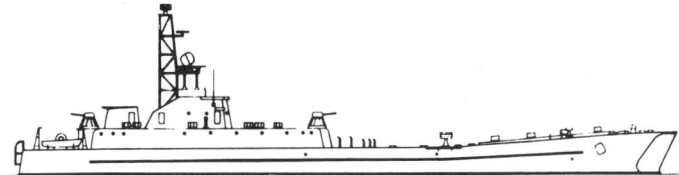

Polnocny-C   1974

D: 1,150 tons (fl)   **S:** 18 kts   **Dim:** 82.0 × 10.0 × 2.0
A: 4/30-mm AA (II × 2)—2/140-mm multiple rocket launchers (XVIII × 2)—4/SA-N-5 systems
M: 2 diesels; 2 props; 5,000 hp   **Man:** 60 men

REMARKS: Russian type designation: Srednyy Desantnyy Korabl' (medium landing ship). Most have now been equipped with two or four SA-N-5 systems. The Polnocny-Bs that have 30-mm aft have heightened stacks. Very few Polnocny-Cs were built. Radars: 1/Spin Trough, 1/Drum Tilt (30-mm AA ships), IFF: 1/High Pole B, 1/Square Head. This class delivered to India, Iraq, Indonesia, Egypt, Angola, etc.

◆ **13 Vydra-class utility landing craft**   Bldr: U.S.S.R., 1967

    D: 425 tons (600 fl)   **S:** 11 kts   **Dim:** 54.8 × 8.1 × 2.0
    A: None   **Electron Equipt:** Radar: 1/Spin Trough   IFF: 1/High Pole
    M: 2 diesels; 2 props; 800 hp

◆ **5 SMB-I-class utility landing craft**   Bldr: U.S.S.R., 1959-64

    D: 180 tons (335 fl)   **S:** 10 kts   **Dim:** 48.2 × 6.5 × 2.0
    Man: 16 men   **Range:** 400/8   **Cargo:** 180 tons
    A: None   **Electron Equipt:** Radars: None   IFF: 1/High Pole
    M: 2 diesels; 2 props; 600 hp

◆ **5 Lebed-class surface-effects landing craft**

    D: 85 tons (fl)   **S:** 60 kts   **Dim:** 24.0 × 12.0 × . . .
    A: 2/30-mm AA (II × 1)   **M:** 3 turbofans; 2 props

REMARKS: Broad bow ramp, ducted props, control cab to starboard, gun to port. Can carry one or two PT-76 light tanks or 120 troops or about 45 tons of cargo.

◆ **7 Aist-class surface-effects landing craft**

Aist class—on cushion   1978

    D: 220 tons (fl)   **S:** 65 kts   **Dim:** 47.8 × 17.5 × . . .
    A: 4/30-mm AA (II × 2)
    Electron Equipt: Radars: 1/Spin Trough, 1/Drum Tilt
                 IFF: 1/High Pole B, 1/Square Head
    M: 4 turbofans; 4 props; 2 lift fans

AMPHIBIOUS-WARFARE SHIPS AND CRAFT (*continued*)

Aist class—at rest   1978

REMARK: Can carry five PT-76 light tanks or four PT-76 tanks and 150 troops.

◆ **32 Gus-class surface-effects landing craft**

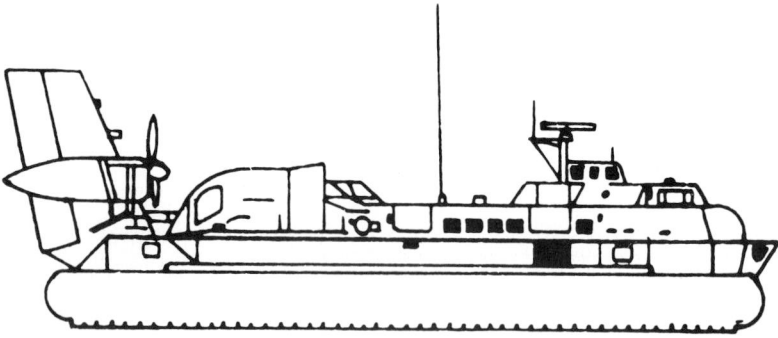

Gus class

D:	27 tons (fl)	S: 57.5 kts	Dim: 21.3 × 8.2 × . . .
A:	None	M: 2 turbofans; 2 props; 1 lift fan; 2,340 hp	

REMARKS: Can carry twenty-four troops. Drawing shows training version with two pilot positions.

SUBMARINE TENDERS

◆ **6 Ugra-class command tenders** Bldr: Nikolayev, 1963-72

IVAN KOLYSHKIN	IVAN VAKHRAMEEV	VOLGA
IVAN KUCHERENKO	TOBOL	N . . .

D: 6,750 tons (9,500 fl)   S: 20 kts   Dim: 141.4 × 17.7 × 6.5
A: 8/57-mm AA (II × 4)   **Man:** 300 men   **Range:** 10,000/12
Electron Equipt: Radars: 1-3/Don 2, 1/Strut Curve, 2/Muff Cob
                  ECM: 4/Watch Dog
                  IFF: 1/High Pole B, 1/High Pole A, 2/Square Head
M: 4 diesels; 2 props; 8,000 hp

Volga—Vee Cone communications antenna aft   1976

Ivan Kolyshkin—helicopter hangar aft   1978

REMARKS: Russian type designation: Plavuchaya Baza (floating base). One modified version was built for India, as *Amba*. The *Ivan Kolyshkin* has a tall helicopter hangar. The *Volga* has a Vee Cone communications antenna. Can support eight to twelve submarines at sea with supplies, fuel, provisions, water, and spare torpedoes and can offer repair services. This class and the Don class are frequently used as flagships. Two 6-ton and one 10-ton cranes are fitted. Sisters *Gangut* and *Borodino* are configured as training ships for naval officer cadets and do not serve submarines—*see* Training Ships.

◆ **6 Don-class command tenders** Bldr: Nikolayev, 1958-61

DMITRIY GALKIN	KAMCHATSKIY KOMSOMOLETS	MAGOMED GADZIEV
FYEDOR VIDYAEV	MAGADANSKIY KOMSOMOLETS	VIKTOR KOTEL'NIKOV

D: 6,730 tons (9,000 fl)   S: 21 kts   Dim: 137.0 × 16.8 × 5.2
A: 4/100-mm AA (I × 4)—4/57-mm AA (II × 2)   **Man:** 300 men
Electron Equipt: Radars: 1-2/Don 2, 1/Slim Net, 1/Sun Visor, 2/Hawk Screech
                  ECM: 2/Watch Dog   IFF: 1/High Pole B, 2/Square Head
M: 4 diesels; 2 props; 8,000 hp

REMARKS: Russian type designation: Plavuchaya Baza (floating base). Can serve as logistic support for a flotilla of eight to twelve submarines. The *Viktor Kotel'nikov's* after 100-mm mount has been replaced by a helicopter platform, while the *Magadanskiy Komsomolets* has always had a very large helicopter platform aft in place of a 100-mm. The *Dmitriy Galkin* and *Fyedor Vidyaev* have eight 25-mm (II × 4) also, no

SUBMARINE TENDERS (*continued*)

Don class—original mast arrangement   1970

Dmitriy Galkin—Vee Cone communications antenna aft   1974

Hawk Screech, and have been fitted with a Vee Cone antenna for long-range communications. A bow lift-hook of 100-ton capacity is fitted, as are one 10-ton, two 5-ton, and two 1-ton cranes. All are used as flagships. One other unit was transferred to Indonesia.

◆ **6 Atrek class** Bldr: East Germany, 1955-57

ATREK	BAKHMUT	EVGENIY OSIPOV
AYAT	DVINA	MURMAT

D: 3,413 tons (5,386 fl)   **S:** 13 kts   **Dim:** 102.4 × 14.4 × 5.5
M: 1 triple-expansion engine, 1 turbine; 1 prop; 2,400 hp   **Range:** 6,900/13

REMARKS: Russian type designation: Plavuchaya Baza (floating base). Modified Kolomna-class cargo ships. Several carry six 37-mm AA (II × 3). Two 5-ton cranes forward.

Atrek   1970

MISSILE TRANSPORTS

◆ **2 Amga class** Bldr: U.S.S.R., 1973 and 1976

AMGA   VETLUGA

Amga   1973

D: 4,800 tons (5,800 fl)   **S:** 12 kts   **Dim:** 102.0 × 18.0 × 4.5
A: 4/25-mm AA (II × 2)   **Range:** 4,500/12
Electron Equipt: Radar: 1/Don 2   IFF: 1/High Pole B
M: 2 diesels; 2 props; 4,000 hp

REMARKS: One 55-ton crane with a reach of 34 meters. Intended to transport ballistic missiles for Delta-class submarines. The *Vetluga* may be slightly longer than her sister.

◆ **7 Lama class** Bldr: . . ., 1963-79

GENERAL RIYABAKOV	PM 44	PM 131	PB 625
VORONEZH	PM 93	PM 150	

D: 6,000 tons (fl)   **S:** 14 kts   **Dim:** 113.0 × 15.0 × 5.0
A: 4 or 8/57-mm AA (IV × 1 or 2, or II × 2)
Electron Equipt: Radars: 1/Don 2, 1/Slim Net or Strut Curve, 1 or 2/Hawk Screech or 2/Muff Cob
IFF: 1/High Pole B, 2/Square Head

MISSILE TRANSPORTS (*continued*)

PM-44 — with eight 57-mm AA and two Hawk Screech radars

Lama class — missile-boat tender version, wearing old number

Lama class — missile-boat tender version

REMARKS: PM = Plavuchaya Masterskaya (floating workshop) and PB = Plavuchaya Baza (floating base). Vary greatly in equipment. Intended to transport cruise missiles for submarines and surface units. Two have larger missile-stowage areas and smaller cranes, and carry four 57-mm AA (IV × 1) and four 25-mm AA (II × 2), but have no fire-control radar. These apparently serve Nanuchka-class corvettes and Osa-class patrol boats. Two 20-ton (10-ton on missile-boat tenders) precision cranes.

◆ **2 Modified Andizhan class**

VENTA   VILYUY

D:	4,500 tons (fl)	**S:** 13.5 kts	**Dim:** 104.0 × 14.4 × 5.2
A:	None	**Electron Equipt:**	Radars: 2/Don 2
			IFF: 1/High Pole B, 1/Square Head
M:	1 diesel; 1,890 hp	**Range:** 6,000/13	

REMARKS: Built in the 1950s. Converted from cargo ships during the 1970s. Large crane forward, two small cranes and a helicopter deck aft.

REPAIR SHIPS

◆ **19 Amur class**   Bldr: Szczecin, Poland, 1968-78

PM 9	PM 40	PM 52	PM 64	PM 81	PM 129	PM 139	PM 156	PM 164	PM . . .
PM 34	PM 49	PM 56	PM 73	PM 94	PM 138	PM 140	PM 161	PM . . .	

PM-56   1977

D: 5,000 tons (6,500 fl)	**S:** 14 kts	**Dim:** 120.0 × 17.4 × 5.2
A: None	**Electron Equipt:** Radar: 1/Don 2	**IFF:** 1/High Pole B
M: 2 diesels; 1 prop; 9,000 hp		

REMARKS: PM = Plavuchaya Masterskaya (floating workshop). Enlarged version of the Oskol class. Later units have crews of more than 220 men. Two 5-ton cranes.

◆ **12 Oskol class**   Bldr: Szczecin, Poland, 1964-67

PM 20	PM 24	PM 28	PM 68	PM 148	PM . . .
PM 21	PM 26	PM 51	PM 146	PM 447	PM . . .

D: 2,500 tons (3,000 fl)	**S:** 14 kts	**Dim:** 91.4 × 12.2 × 4.0
Electron Equipt: Radar: 1/Don 2	**IFF:** 1/High Pole A	
M: 2 diesels; 1 prop; 4,000 hp	**Man:** 60 men	

REMARKS: PM = Plavuchaya Masterskaya (floating workshop). Most have a well deck forward of the bridge. One unit has two 57-mm AA (II × 1), four 25-mm AA (II × 2); no fire-control radar. All have one or two 3.4-ton cranes.

REPAIR SHIPS (continued)

PM-146—flush-decked Oskol class   1970

PM-26—well-deck Oskol class   1975

◆ **5 Dnepr class**   Bldr: U.S.S.R., 1960-64

PM 17   PM 22   PM 30   PM 130   PM 135

PM-17   1960

D: 4,500 tons (5,300 fl)   **S:** 11 kts   **Dim:** 113.3 (100.0 pp) × 16.5 × 4.4
Electron Equipt: Radar: 1/Don or Don 2   **IFF:** 1/High Pole A
M: 1 diesel; 2,000 hp   **Man:** 420 men   **Range:** 6,000/8.3

REMARKS: PM = Plavuchaya Masterskaya (floating workshop). Have one 150-ton bow
hoist, one kingpost, and one crane. Equipment varies from ship to ship. The last two
units (Modified Dnepr class) are flush-decked.

GENERATOR SHIPS

◆ **4 Tomba class**   Bldr: Szczecin, Poland, 1975-

ENS 244   ENS 254   ENS 348   ENS 357

ENS-244   1976

D: 3,500 tons (4,900 fl)   **S:** 14 kts   **Dim:** 96.5 × 15.5 × 5.0
A: None   **Electron Equipt:** Radar: 1/Don 2   **IFF:** 1/High Pole B
M: 1 diesel; 1 prop; 4,500 hp   **Man:** 50 men

REMARKS: ENS = Elektrostantsiye Nalivatel'noye Sudno (electric-power station and
steam-source ship). Two stacks and a "mack" on the forecastle, all containing diesel-
engine exhausts, while the stack amidships also has the uptake from a large boiler.
Two 3-ton cranes.

SUBMARINE-RESCUE SHIPS

◆ **1 Nepa class**   Bldr: . . ., 1970

KARPATY

Karpaty   1971

D: 9,500 tons (fl)   **S:** 18 kts   **Dim:** 130.0 × 19.0 × 6.5
A: None   **Electron Equipt:** Radars: 2/Don 2   **IFF:** 1/High Pole B
M: 2-4 diesels; 2 props; 8,000 hp   **Man:** 270 men

REMARKS: Has a 600-ton lift hook supported by horns extending over the stern, others
beneath the hull. Very large all-purpose salvage ship with submarine-rescue equipment, including several rescue bells and observation chambers.

SUBMARINE-RESCUE SHIPS (*continued*)

◆ **9 Prut class** Bldr: U.S.S.R., 1960-68

| ALTAY | VLADIMIR TREFOLEV | SS 21 | SS 26 | SS 83 |
| BESHTAU | ZHIGULI | SS 23 | SS 44 | |

Beshtau   1969

SS-21   1978

D: 2,120 tons (2,640 fl) **S:** 18 kts **Dim:** 86.9 × 13.4 × 4.3
Electron Equipt: Radars: 1-2/Don 2 and/or Don
M: 4 diesels; 2 props; 8,000 hp

REMARKS: SS = Spasitel'noye Sudno (rescue ship). One derrick, two or three special carriers for rescue chambers, submersible decompression chambers for divers, and salvage observation bells. Four anchor buoys are stowed on inclined racks on the after deck. One unit was armed for a while with four 57-mm AA (IV × 1) controlled by a Muff Cob radar director, long since removed.

◆ **12 Modified T-58-class minesweepers** Bldr: . . ., late 1950s

| KAZBEK | VALDAY | SS 30 | SS 40 | SS 48 | SS 53 |
| KHIBINY | ZANGEZUR | SS 35 | SS 47 | SS 50 | SS . . |

Valday

D: 725 tons (840 fl) **S:** 18 kts **Dim:** 72.0 × 9.1 × 2.5
Electron Equipt: Radars: 1/Don 2, 1/Spin Trough
                      Sonar: 1/Tamir IFF: 1/Dead Duck
M: 2 diesels; 2 props; 4,000 hp **Man:** 60 men

REMARKS: SS = Spasitel'noye Sudno (rescue ship). Altered while under construction. Lift rig overhanging the stern to handle divers' gear and submersible decompression chamber. Rescue diving chamber to port, amidships. Can be armed with one 37-mm AA. One sister, *Gidrolog*, has served as an intelligence-collector; another was transferred to India.

FLEET REPLENISHMENT SHIPS

Kara-class cruiser Ochakov fueling from the Boris Chilikin   1978

FLEET REPLENISHMENT SHIPS (*continued*)

NOTE: In the field of seagoing replenishment, the Soviet Navy has made great progress. With the acquisition of such classes as the *Berezina*, *Boris Chilikin*, and *Dubna* and the modernization of a great many older oilers to enable them to perform alongside fueling under way, the Soviets have made great strides in achieving a large and thoroughly modern afloat logistics force. Furthermore, the navy continues to call on the resources of the Soviet merchant marine, particularly tankers, which still supply a large, if declining, proportion of deployed refuelings. Most of the naval units are now civilian-manned and fly the flag of the Auxiliary Service; for this reason, those that were armed have had their guns and fire-control systems removed or demilitarized.

Boris Chilikin passing a hose to a Modified Kashin-class destroyer
to starboard while continuing to supply the Ochakov to port   1979

◆ 1 Berezina class   Bldr: GI Kommuna SY, Nikolayev, 1978

BEREZINA

Berezina   1979

Berezina   1979

> D: 40,000 tons (fl)   S: 20-22 kts   Dim: 208.7 × 24.0 × 11.0
> Man: 600 men   Range: 12,000/18
> A: 1/SA-N-4 system (II × 1), 18 missiles—4/57-mm DP (II × 2)—4/Gatling AA
>   (VI × 4)—2/RBU 1000 rocket launchers—2/Hormone helicopters
> Electron Equipt: Radars: 1/Don 2, 2/Don Kay, 1/Strut Curve, 1/Pop Group, 1/Muff
>   Cob, 2/Bass Tilt
>   Sonar: . . .
>   ECM: 2/chaff launchers (II × 2)   IFF: 1/High Pole
> M: 2 diesels; 2 props; 54,000 hp

REMARKS: Russian type designation: Voyenyy Transport (naval transport). The largest multipurpose under-way replenishment ship yet built for the Soviets and the only one

Berezina—replenishment stations amidships   1979

FLEET REPLENISHMENT SHIPS (*continued*)

Berezina—after superstructure with twin stacks, SA-N-4 system,
four Gatling AA guns, and helicopter facilities   1979

Berezina—with a Foxtrot submarine alongside and a helicopter
on the flight deck   1979

currently to be armed. Can refuel over the stern and from single constant-tensions on either side, amidships. Solid replenishment is by two sliding-stay, constant-tension transfer rigs on either side. Vertical replenishment is by two specially configured Hormone helicopters hangared in the after superstructure. There are four 10-ton stores-handling cranes to supply ships moored alongside. Cargo: approx. 16,000 tons of fuel oil and diesel fuel, 500 tons fresh water, and 2,000-3,000 tons of provisions, munitions, and combat spares. The very large crew may be accounted for, in part, by a capability to transport spare submarines, for which mooring packets are provided along the ship's sides. This unusually sophisticated and well equipped ship marks the maturation of Soviet naval logistics at sea.

◆ **6 Boris Chilikin class**   Bldr: Baltic Yd., Leningrad, 1971-78

BORIS BUTOMA	DNESTR	IVAN BUBNOV
BORIS CHILIKIN	GENRIKH GASANOV	VLADIMIR KOLYACHITSKIY

Boris Chilikin   1978

Ivan Bubnov   1975

D: 24,500 tons (fl)   **S:** 17 kts   **Dim:** 162.3 × 21.4 × 8.9
A: Removed   **Range:** 10,000/16.6
Electron Equipt: Radars: 2/Don Kay   **IFF:** 1/High Pole B
M: 1 diesel; 9,600 hp

REMARKS: Russian type designation: Voyenyy Tanker (naval tanker). Naval version of the merchant *Velikiy Oktyabr* class. 16,300 dwt. Equipment varies: early units had solid-stores, constant-tension rigs on both sides forward; later units, only to starboard, with liquids to port. All have port and starboard liquid-replenishment stations amidships and can replenish liquids over the stern. Cargo: 13,500 tons liquid (fuel oil, diesel, water); 400 tons ammunition; 400 tons provisions; 400 tons stores. The *Ivan Bubnov* and *Genrikh Gasanov* were completed in merchant colors, without guns, Strut Curve, or Muff Cob; that equipment has now been removed from the other ships, although several retain their gun houses.

FLEET REPLENISHMENT SHIPS (*continued*)

◆ **4 Dubna class** Bldr: Rauma-Repola, Rauma, Finland

	In serv.		In serv.
DUBNA	1974	PECHENGA	1978
IRKUT	1975	SVENTA	1979

Irkut—refueling over stern   1976

Irkut

D: 13,500 tons (fl) **S:** 16 kts **Dim:** 130.0 (120.0 pp) × 20.0 × 7.2
A: None **Man:** 66 men **Electric:** 1,485 kva
Electron Equipt: Radar: 1/Don 2
M: 1 Russkiy diesel; 6,000 hp

REMARKS: Russian type designation: Voyenyy Tanker (naval tanker). 6,022 grt/6,500 dwt. Cargo: 2,100 tons fuel oil, 2,080 tons diesel, 120 tons lube oil, 50 tons refrigerated stores, 50 tons dry stores, 300 tons water. Can transfer one-ton loads from constant-tension stations forward. Liquid replenishment from one station on port and starboard, amidships, and over the stern.

◆ **5 Altay class** Bldr: Rauma-Repola, Rauma, Finland, 1969-73

ILIM	IZHORA	KOLA	YEGORLIK	YEL'NYA

Izhora   1975

D: 7,400 tons (fl) **S:** 14.2 kts **Dim:** 106.0 × 15.0 × 6.7
Man: 60 men **Range:** 8,600/12
Electron Equipt: Radars: 2/Don 2 IFF: 1/High Pole A
M: 1 Burmeister & Wain diesel; 2,900 hp

REMARKS: 3,670 grt/5,045 dwt. All have had an under-way replenishment, A-frame kingpost added forward since 1975, permitting them to refuel one ship at a time on either beam. Also able to replenish over stern. More than two dozen sisters in the Soviet merchant marine.

◆ **1 Sofia class** Bldr: U.S.S.R., 1969

AKHTUBA (ex-*Khanoi*)

Akhtuba—as the merchant ship Khanoi   1969

D: 62,600 tons (fl) **S:** 17 kts **Dim:** 230.6 × 31.0 × 11.8
Man: 70 men **Range:** 20,900/17
M: Steam turbine; 1 prop; 19,000 hp **Boilers:** 2

REMARKS: 32,840 grt/49,385 dwt. Largest ship in the Soviet Navy. Carries 44,500 tons of liquid cargo. Can refuel over the stern.

◆ **3 Olekhma and Pevek classes** Bldr: Rauma-Repola, Rauma, Finland

OLEKHMA	IMAN	SOLOTOI ROG

D: 6,700 tons (fl) **S:** 14 kts **Dim:** 105.0 × 14.8 × 6.8
Man: 40 men **Range:** 7,900/13.6 **Electron Equipt:** Radar: 1/Don 2
M: 1 Burmeister & Wain diesel; 2,900 hp

REMARKS: The *Zolotoi Rog* belongs to the *Pevek* class. All built in the mid-1960s. 3,300 grt/4,400 dwt. The *Olekhma* was modernized in 1978 with A-frame abaft the bridge to permit under-way fueling of one ship at a time on either beam. The other two may

FLEET REPLENISHMENT SHIPS (continued)

Olekhma—modified for under-way replenishment   1978

have been similarly upgraded. Predecessor to the *Altay* design but with conventional "three-island" tanker layout. The *Zolotoi Rog* differs very slightly. All can refuel over the stern.

◆ 6 Uda class   Bldr: . . ., 1962-64

| DUNAY | KOIDA | LENA | SHEKSNA | TEREK | VISHERA |

Terek

D: 7,100 tons (fl)   **S:** 17 kts   **Dim:** 122.0 × 15.8 × 6.3
A: Removed   **Man:** 85 men
Electron Equipt: Radars: 1/Don, 1/Don 2 (or 2/Don 2)   **IFF:** High Pole A
M: 2 diesels; 2 props; 8,000 hp

REMARKS: Russian type designation: Voyenyy Tanker (naval tanker). Equipped to carry eight 57-mm AA (IV × 2). The *Vishera* and one other have been equipped with a second A-frame kingpost for liquid replenishment, amidships. Three transferred to Indonesia.

◆ 3 Kazbek class

| ALATYR' | DESNA | VOLKHOV |

D: 16,250 tons (fl)   **S:** 14 kts   **Dim:** 145.5 × 19.24 × 8.5
A: None   **Man:** 46 men   **Range:** 18,000/14

Desna—replenishing the Kara-class cruiser Nikolayev and,
aft, a Kashin-class destroyer   1973

Desna   1978

Electron Equipt: Radars: 2/Don 2   **IFF:** 1/High Pole A
M: 2 Russkiy diesels; 2 props; 4,000 hp

REMARKS: Russian type designation: Voyenyy Tanker (naval tanker). Built in the mid-1950s. 8,230 grt/11,800 dwt. Carry 11,600 tons of fuel. The three naval units can be distinguished from their civilian sisters because they have, before the bridge, two tall kingposts and an A-frame kingpost to support fueling hoses and working decks added over the cargo decks before and abaft the bridge. Merchant units of this class are among those most frequently used to support naval forces.

◆ 1 ex-German, ex-Dutch   Bldr: C. van den Giessen, Krimpen, Netherlands

POLYARNIK (ex-*Kärnten*, ex-*Tankboot-I*)

D: 12,500 tons (fl)   **S:** 17.1 kts   **Dim:** 132.1 (125.0 pp) × 16.15 × 7.6
M: 2 Werkspoor 8-cyl. diesels; 2 props; 7,000 hp   **Man:** 57 men

FLEET REPLENISHMENT SHIPS (*continued*)

REMARKS: Launched, 3-5-41. War reparations, 30-12-45. Oldest replenishment oiler in any navy. 5,709 grt/6,640 dwt. Liquid cargo 5,600 tons; solid stores and provisions. In the Pacific Fleet.

OILERS

◆ **2 or more Baskunchak class** Bldr: U.S.S.R.

IVAN GOLUBETS   UKHTA

> **D:** 2,920 tons (fl)   **S:** 13 kts   **Dim:** 83.6 × 12.0 × 4.9
> **Man:** 30 men   **Range:** 5,000/13   **Electron Equipt:** Radar: 1/Don 2
> **M:** 2 diesels; 2,000 hp

REMARKS: 1,756 grt/1,660 dwt. One sister, *Usedom*, in East German Navy; others in Soviet merchant marine.

◆ **4 Konda class** Bldr: Sweden

KONDA   ROSSOCH'   SOYANA   YAKHROMA

> **D:** 1,980 tons (fl)   **S:** 12 kts   **Dim:** 69.0 × 10.0 × 4.3
> **Man:** 26 men   **Range:** 2,470/10
> **Electron Equipt:** Radar: 1/Neptune or Don 2
> **M:** 1 diesel; 1,600 hp

REMARKS: Built in the mid-1950s. 1,117 grt/1,265 dwt. Can refuel over the stern.

◆ **3 Nercha class** Bldr: Finland, 1952-55

KLYAZ'MA   NARVA   NERCHA

Nercha   1967

> **D:** 1,800 tons (fl)   **S:** 11.3 kts   **Dim:** 63.5 × 10.0 × 4.5
> **Man:** 25 men   **Range:** 2,000/10   **Electron Equipt:** Radar: 1/Don
> **M:** 1 diesel; 1,000 hp

REMARKS: 1,081 grt/1,127 dwt. Can refuel over the stern.

◆ **11 (approx.) Khobi class** Bldr: U.S.S.R.

Possible names:

CHEREMSHAN	KHOBI	ORSHA	SHELON'	TUNGUSKA
INDIGA	LOVAT'	SEYM SHACHA	SOS'VA	

Lovat'   1978

> **D:** 1,525 tons (fl)   **S:** 12 kts   **Dim:** 62.0 × 10.0 × 4.4
> **Man:** 29 men   **Electron Equipt:** Radars: 1/Don 2, 1/Spin Trough
>   IFF: High Pole A
> **M:** 2 diesels; 2 props; 1,600 hp

REMARKS: Built in the early 1950s, now being discarded. 795 grt. Refuel over bows while being towed by receiving ship. *Linda* and one other went to Albania in 1959; others to Indonesia.

◆ **1 ex-German Dora class** Bldr: D. W. Kremer Sohn, Elmshorn

IZHMA (ex-. . .)

> **D:** 973 tons (fl)   **S:** 12 kts   **Dim:** 61.0 (56.5 pp) × 9.0 × 2.75
> **A:** None   **Man:** 26 men   **Range:** 1,200/12   **Fuel:** 17.5 tons
> **Electron Equipt:** Radar: . . .   **M:** 2 M.W.M. 6-cyl diesels; 2 props; 900 hp

REMARKS: Built between 1941 and 1943. One of a group of four Luftwaffe aviation-fuel tankers: *Dora*, *Else*, *Grete*, and *Hanna*, all of which passed into British hands in 5-45 and went to the U.S.S.R. in 1946. The others may also remain in service. 638 grt. Cargo: 331 tons of liquid petroleum.

◆ **1 ex-German Usedom class** Bldr: Howaldtswerke, Hamburg

FEOLENT (ex-*Empire Tegadea*, ex-*Jeverland*)

> **D:** 5,250 tons (fl)   **S:** 15.5 kts   **Dim:** 96.16 × 13.8 × 5.56
> **A:** None   **Man:** 64 men   **Electron Equipt:** Radar: . . .
> **M:** 2 Schichau diesels; 2 props; 3,500 hp

REMARKS: Launched on 15-6-38. Completed by Burmeister & Wain in 5-42. Turned over to Great Britain in 5-45, later to the U.S.S.R. 2,579 grt. Cargo: 2,600 tons of fuel oil. In Black Sea Fleet.

WATER TANKERS

◆ **2 Manych class** Bldr: U.S.S.R., 1971 and 1977

MANYCH   TAYGIL

> **D:** 6,500 tons (8,600 fl)   **S:** 18 kts   **Dim:** 115.0 × 15.5 × 7.0
> **A:** Removed   **Man:** 90 men
> **Electron Equipt:** Radars: 2/Don Kay; *Manych:* 2/Muff Cob
> **M:** 2 diesels; 2 props; 9,000 hp

WATER TANKERS (*continued*)

Manych — when armed   1974

Taygil   1977

REMARKS: Originally intended to be small replenishment oilers to carry fuel and solid stores for submarines. Reported in the Soviet press as unsuccessful, the *Manych* was assigned as a water tender to support the Mediterranean Squadron. Her four 57-mm guns were removed in 1975. The appearance of a second unit may indicate that the earlier difficulties with the design have been overcome. The *Taygil* was completed without armament.

◆ **14 Voda class**   Bldr: . . ., 1950s

ABAKAN	VODOLEY-3	MVT 10	MVT 18	MVT 134
SURA	MVT 6	MVT 16	MVT 20	MVT 138
VODOLEY-2	MVT 9	MVT 17	MVT 21	

Voda class   1972

D: 2,100 tons (3,100 fl)   **S:** 12 kts   **Dim:** 81.5 × 11.5 × 4.3
Man: 40 men   **Electron Equipt:** Radar: 1/Neptune
M: 2 diesels; 2 props; 1,600 hp

REMARK: MVT = Maloye Vodoloye Tanker (small water tanker).

SPECIAL-LIQUIDS TANKERS

◆ **1 Ural class**   Bldr: . . ., 1970 (?)

URAL

D: 2,000 tons (fl)   **S:** 12 kts   **Dim:** 80.0 × 12.0 × 4.5
Electron Equipt: Radar: 1/Spin Trough   **M:** 2 diesels; 1 prop; 1,200 hp

REMARKS: Transports liquid nuclear waste. High freeboard, superstructure aft, traveling crane.

◆ **9 Luza class**

ALAMBAY	BARGUZIN	KANA	SASIMA	YENISEY
ARAGUY	DON	OKA	SELENGA	

D: 1,500 tons (fl)   **S:** 12 kts   **Dim:** 62.0 × 10.5 × 4.2
Electron Equipt: Radar: 1/Don 2   **M:** 1 diesel; 1,000 hp

REMARKS: Built in the 1960s. Carry volatile liquids, probably missile fuel.

◆ **5 Vala class**

D: 3,100 tons (fl)   **S:** 14 kts   **Dim:** 76.2 × 12.5 × 5.0
Range: 2,000/11   **M:** 1 diesel; 1,000 hp

REMARK: Carry waste liquids from nuclear-propulsion plants.

TRANSPORT

◆ **1 Mikhail Kalinin class**

Bldr: Mathias Thesen Werft, Wismar, East Germany, 1963

KUBAN (ex-*Nadezhda Krupskaya*)

TRANSPORT (*continued*)

Kuban

D: 6,400 tons (fl)   **S:** 18 kts   **Dim:** 122.2 × 16.0 × 5.1
A: None   **Range:** 8,100/17   **Electron Equipt:** Radars: 2/Don 2
M: 2 M.A.N. 6-cyl. diesels; 2 props; 8,000 hp

REMARKS: Former passenger-cargo ship used to rotate crews on ships in the Mediterranean Squadron. 5,260 grt/1,354 dwt. Can carry 340 passengers, 1,000 tons of cargo.

CARGO SHIPS

NOTE: Cargo ships are usually referred to as Voyenyy Transport (naval transport).

◆ **1 Amguema class**   Bldr: U.S.S.R., 1975

YAUZA

Yauza   1976

D: 15,100 tons (fl)   **S:** 15 kts   **Dim:** 133.1 × 18.9 × 9.1
Electron Equipt: Radars: 2/Don 2   **Range:** 10,000/15
M: 4 1,800-hp diesels, electric drive; 1 prop; 7,200 hp

REMARKS: 7,900 grt/9,045 dwt. Icebreaking passenger-cargo ship. Cargo: 6,600 tons. Numerous merchant sisters.

◆ **4 Yuny Partizan class**   Bldr: Romania, 1975-78

PECHORA   PINEGA   TURGAY   UFA

Turgay   1977

D: 2,840 tons (fl)   **S:** 12.9 kts   **Dim:** 88.75 (80.25 pp) × 12.8 × 5.2
A: None   **Man:** 25 men   **Range:** 4,000/12
Electron Equipt: Radar: 1/Don 2   **IFF:** 1/High Pole
M: 1 diesel; 2,080 hp

REMARKS: 2,079 grt/2,150 dwt. Small container ships. Three 10-ton cranes, one of which can be rigged to lift 28 tons. Cargo: 3,200 m³. Originally intended to be able to carry fifty-eight standard cargo containers. Twenty sisters are civilian.

◆ **8 Vytegrales class**   Bldr: Zhdanov SY, Leningrad, 1963-66

APSHERON (ex-*Toonales*)   DONBASS (ex-*Kirishi*)
BASKUNCHAK (ex-*Vostok-4*)   SEVAN (ex-*Vyborgles*)
DAURIYA (ex-*Suzdal*)   TAMAN' (ex-*Vostok-3*)
DIKSON (ex-*Vagales*)   YAMAL (ex-*Svirles*)

Yamal—with Hormone helicopter on deck   1979

CARGO SHIPS (continued)

Sevan   1979

D: 9,650 tons (fl)   **S:** 16 kts   **Dim:** 121.9 × 16.7 × 7.3
A: None   **Man:** 90 men   **Range:** 7,380/14.5
Electron Equipt: Radars: 2/Don 2   **IFF:** 1/High Pole B
M: 1 Burmeister & Wain 950 VTBF 110 diesel; 1 prop; 5,200 hp

REMARKS: Originally built as merchant timber-carriers, then converted as space-event support ships by the addition of more communications facilities and a helicopter platform over the stern—consequently losing access to the after hold. They carry one Hormone helicopter but have no hangar. Now used as fleet supply ships. The *Donbass* has a Big Net air-search radar, as may others. All retain three holds forward, except the *Dikson*, which has a deckhouse over hold number three. Seven sisters were converted to serve the Academy of Sciences as satellite-tracking ships.

◆ **8 Keyla class** Bldr: Hungary, 1960-66

MEZEN'   PONOY   TERIBERKA   UNZHA
ONEGA   RITSA   TULOMA   YERUSLAN

D: 2,000 tons (fl)   **S:** 12 kts   **Dim:** 78.5 × 10.5 × 4.6
A: None   **Man:** 26 men   **Range:** 4,200/10.7
Electron Equipt: Radar: 1/Don 2 or Spin Trough   **M:** 1 diesel; 1,000 hp

REMARKS: 1,296 grt/1,280 dwt. Carry 1,100 tons of cargo. The *Ritsa* has a deckhouse over her after hatch and numerous communications antennas.

◆ **5 MP-6 ckass former landing ships** Bldr: Hungary, 1959-60

BIRA   BUREYA   IRGIZ   KHOPER   VOLOGDA

D: 2,100 tons (fl)   **S:** 12 kts   **Dim:** 75.0 × 11.3 × 4.4
M: 1 diesel; 1,000 hp

REMARK: Unsuccessful as landing ships, bow doors welded closed.

◆ **2 Andizhan class** Bldr: East Germany, 1959

ONDA   POSET

D: 6,739 tons (fl)   **S:** 13.5 kts   **Dim:** 104.2 × 14.4 × 6.6
A: None   **Man:** 43 men   **Range:** 6,000/13.5
Electron Equipt: Radar: 1/Don 2   **M:** 1 diesel; 1,890 hp

REMARKS: 3,368 grt/4,324 dwt. 3,954 tons of cargo. Two naval sisters are now missile transports; other sisters are in the merchant service.

◆ **4 Chulym class** Bldr: Poland, 1950s

INSAR   KAMCHATKA   LENINSK-KUZNETSKIY   SEVERODONETSK

D: 5,050 tons (fl)   **S:** 12 kts   **Dim:** 101.9 × 14.6 × 6.0
A: None   **Man:** 41 men   **Range:** 5,000/11.5
Electron Equipt: Radar: 1/Don 2
M: Reciprocating plus auxiliary GT; 1 prop; 1,650 hp

REMARKS: 2,135 grt/3,120 dwt. 2,240 tons of cargo. Coal-burners.

◆ **1 Donbass class** Bldr: East Germany, 1950s

SVIR

Donbass class

D: 7,200 tons (fl)   **S:** 12 kts   **Dim:** 108.2 × 14.6 × 7.2
A: None   **Electron Equipt:** Radar: 1/Neptune   **Range:** 9,800/12
M: Reciprocating steam; 1 prop; 2,300 hp

REMARKS: 3,561 grt/4,864 dwt. 3,570 tons of cargo. Coal-burner.

◆ **4 Kolomna class** Bldr: East Germany, 1950s

KRASNOARMEYSK   KUZNETSK   MEGRA   SVANETIYA

D: 6,700 tons (fl)   **S:** 13 kts   **Dim:** 102.3 × 14.4 × 6.6
Man: 44 men   **Range:** 6,890/13
Electron Equipt: Radars: 1/Don 2, 1/Neptune   **IFF:** 1/High Pole A
M: Reciprocating steam plus GT; 1 prop; 2,450 hp

CARGO SHIPS (continued)

Svanetiya   1976

REMARKS: 3,758 grt/4,355 dwt. 3,634 tons of cargo. Coal-burners. Six sisters serve as *Atrek*-class submarine tenders.

◆ **3 Telnovsk class**   Bldr: Hungary, 1949-57

BUREVESTNIK   LAG   MANOMETR

> **D:** 1,700 tons (fl)   **S:** 11 kts   **Dim:** 70.0 × 10.0 × 4.2
> **Man:** 40 men   **Range:** 3,300/9.7   **M:** 1 diesel; 800 hp

REMARKS: 1,194 grt/1,133 dwt. Several others serve as survey ships. Being discarded.

◆ **up to 25 Khabarovsk class**   Bldr: U.S.S.R., 1950s

> **D:** 600 tons (fl)   **S:** 9.5 kts   **Dim:** 46.4 × 8.0 × 3.2
> **Electron Equipt:** Radar: 1/Neptune or Don   **M:** 1 diesel; 600 hp

REMARKS: 402 dwt. Some are civilian, others may be degaussing tenders.

PROVISION SHIPS

◆ **8 Mayak class**   Bldr: U.S.S.R., 1970s

BUZULUK	LAMA	NEMAN	ULMA
ISHIM	MIUS	RIONI	VYTEGRA

Buzuluk   1978

> **D:** 1,050 tons (fl)   **S:** 11 kts   **Dim:** 54.3 × 9.3 × 3.6
> **A:** None   **Man:** 29 men   **Range:** 9,400/11
> **Electron Equipt:** Radar: 1/Spin Trough   **M:** 1 diesel; 800 hp

REMARKS: 690 grt. Former trawlers. Refrigerated fish holds are used to carry provisions. Other naval sisters operate as intelligence-collectors.

AMMUNITION SHIPS

◆ **9 Muna class**

Muna class

> **D:** 680 tons (fl)   **S:** 11 kts   **Dim:** 51.0 × 8.5 × 2.7
> **Man:** 40 men
> **Electron Equipt:** Radar: 1/Spin Trough   IFF: 1/High Pole A
> **M:** 1 diesel; 600 hp

REMARKS: When deployed, carry VTR — Voyenyy Transport (naval transport) numbers, but in home waters are listed as MBSS — Morskaya Barzha Samokhodnaya Sukhogruznaya (seagoing self-propelled dry-cargo lighter). Specialized transports for torpedoes and perhaps also surface-to-air missiles.

MOORING TENDERS

◆ **10 Sura class**   Bldr: Neptun Werft, Rostock, East Germany, 1965-72, 1976-78

KIL 1	KIL 21	KIL 23	KIL 29	KIL 32
KIL 2	KIL 22	KIL 27	KIL 31	KIL 33

> **D:** 2,370 tons (3,150 fl)   **S:** 13 kts   **Dim:** 87.0 (68.0 pp) × 14.8 × 5.0
> **A:** None   **Range:** 4,000/10   **Electron Equipt:** Radar: 1
> **M:** 4 diesels, electric drive; 2 props; 2,240 hp

REMARKS: KIL = Kilektor (mooring tender). 2,366 grt. 890 tons of cargo in hold amidships. Stern rig, which can lift 60 tons, is used for buoy-handling and salvage. Can also carry several hundred tons of cargo fuel.

MOORING TENDERS (continued)

KIL-23

KIL-22

◆ **14 Neptun class**   Bldr: Neptun Werft, Rostock, East Germany, 1957-60

| KIL 3 | KIL 6 | KIL 12 | KIL 15 | KIL 17 | KIL . . | KIL . . |
| KIL 5 | KIL 9 | KIL 14 | KIL 16 | KIL 18 | KIL . . | KIL . . |

   D: 700 tons (1,240 fl)   **S:** 12 kits   **Dim:** 57.3 (46.5 pp) × 11.4 × 3.4
   M: 2 triple-expansion; 1,000 hp   **Man:** 41 men   **Range:** 1,000/11

Neptun class

REMARKS: KIL = Kilektor (mooring tender). Most burn coal. 80-ton bow lift for buoy-handling and salvage.

CABLE-LAYERS

◆ **8 Klazma class**   Bldr: Wärtsilä SY, Turku, Finland, 1962-78

| DONETS | INGURI | TAVDA | YANA |
| INGUL | KATUN' | TSNA | ZEYA |

Klazma class—later unit

   D: 6,920 tons (fl)   **S:** 14 kts   **Dim:** 130.4 (120.0 pp) × 16.0 × 5.75
   Man: 110 men   **Range:** 12,000/14   **Electron Equipt:** Radars: 2/Don 2
   M: 5 1,000-hp Wärtsilä 624TS diesels, electric drive; 2,150 hp

REMARKS: 5,760 grt/3,750 dwt. The *Ingul* and *Yana*, the first built, have four diesels, a longer forecastle, and are 5,645 grt/3,400 dwt. All have ice-strengthened hulls and can carry up to 3,000 km of cable. The diesel engines drive five 680-kw generators, which provide power for propulsion and for all auxiliary functions. Two more under construction.

FLEET TUGS

◆ **4 Goryn class**   Bldr: Rauma-Repola, Rauma, Finland, 1977-78

| BAYKALSK | BEREZINSK | BILBINO | BOLSHEVETSK |

Baykalsk   1978

FLEET TUGS (*continued*)

D: 2,600 tons (fl)   **S:** 13.5 kts   **Dim:** 63.5 × 14.3 × 5.1
Man: 40 men   **Electron Equipt:** Radar: 1/Don 2
M: 1 Russkiy 67N diesel; 3,500 hp

REMARKS: Also have MB—Morskoy Buksir (ocean tug) numbers. 1,600 grt. 35-ton pull. For ocean towing, salvage, and fire-fighting.

◆ **11 or more Sorum class**   Bldr: U.S.S.R., 1874-7

| AMUR | KAMCHATKA | PRIMORYE | MB 105 | MB 119 | MB . . . |
| BREST | PRIMORSK | SAKHALIN | MB 115 | MB . . . |

Sakhalin—armed KGB unit   1975

D: 1,210 tons (1,656 fl)   **S:** 14 kts   **Dim:** 58.3 × 12.6 × 4.6
A: Named units only: 4/30-mm (II × 2)   **Man:** 35 men
Range: 6,720/13
Electron Equipt: Radars: 2/Don 2   IFF: 1/High Pole B
M: 2 5-2D42 diesels, electric drive; 1 prop; 1,500 hp   **Fuel:** 322 tons

REMARKS: Units with names are manned by the KGB and are typed PSKR—Pogranichny Storozhevoy Korabl' (border-patrol ship); MB in naval units means Morskoy Buksir (ocean tug).

◆ **57 Okhtensky class**   Bldr: U.S.S.R., 1960s

D: 700 tons (950 fl)   **S:** 13.3 kts   **Dim:** 47.3 × 10.3 × 5.5
Electron Equipt: Radar: 1/Don 2 or Spin Trough   IFF: 1/High Pole
M: 2 diesels; 1 prop; 1,500 hp   **Range:** 7,800/7

REMARKS: Several have two 57-mm AA (II × 1) and are probably manned by the KGB for use as patrol ships. Units with names are civilian; naval units have MB—Morskoy Buksir (ocean tug) or SB—Spastel'noye Buksir (rescue tug) hull numbers.

◆ **12-16 Roslavl class**   Bldr: U.S.S.R., 1950s

D: 750 tons (fl)   **S:** 11 kts   **Dim:** 44.5 × 9.5 × 3.5
M: Diesel-electric; 2 props; 1,200 hp   **Man:** 28 men

REMARK: All have MB pendants—Morskoy Buksir (ocean tug).

◆ **10-12 Zenit class**   Bldr: Finland, 1948-55

D: 800 tons (fl)   **S:** 10 kts   **Dim:** 47.9 × 10.0 × 4.3
M: Reciprocating steam; 2 props; 800 hp   **Range:** 10,000/8

Okhtensky class   1965

REMARKS: Well over one hundred of this class were built as war reparations. A number remain in service with the merchant marine, also.

SALVAGE AND RESCUE SHIPS

◆ **1 Pioneer Moskvy-class salvage ship**   Bldr: . . . , 1979

MIKHAIL RUDNITSKIY

D: 10,000 tons (fl)   **S:** 15.4 kts   **Dim:** 130.3 (119.0 pp) × 17.3 × 6.93
A: None   **Man:** 120 men   **Electron Equipt:** Radars: 2/Don 2
M: 1 5DKRN 62/140-3 diesel; 1 prop; 6,100 hp   **Electric:** 1,500 kw

REMARKS: Modification of a standard merchant timer-carrier/container ship design, retaining two holds. The after hold has two superstructure levels built over it and the small hold forward has been plated over. Retains two 40-ton and two 20-ton beams and has had heavy cable fairleads cut in the bulwarks fore and aft and a number of boat booms added to starboard. Carries the ensign of the Naval Salvage and Rescue Service.

◆ **2 Ingul class**   Bldr: Admiralty, Leningrad, 1975-77

PAMIR   MASHUK

D: 3,200 tons (4,050 fl)   **S:** 20 kts   **Dim:** 92.8 × 15.4 × 5.8
Electron Equipt: Radars: 2/Don-2   IFF: 1/High Pole B, 1/Square Head
Man: 120 men   **Range:** 9,000/18.7
M: 2 type 58D-4R diesels; 2 props; 9,000 hp

REMARKS: Two sisters, *Yaguar* and *Bars*, are in the Merchant Marine. Very powerful

SALVAGE AND RESCUE SHIPS (continued)

Pamir   1975

tugs with constant-tension highline personnel rescue system, salvage pumps, fire-fighting equipment, and complete diving gear. Large bulbous bow.

◆ **2 Pamir class** Bldr: Gävle, Sweden, 1958

AGATAN   ALDAN

Agatan

D: 1,443 tons (2,240 fl)   **S:** 17.5 kts   **Dim:** 78.0 × 12.8 × 4.0
Electron Equipt: Radar: 1-2/Don and/or Don-2   **Range:** 15,200/17.5, 21,800/12
M: 2 M.A.N. G10V 40/60 diesels; 2 controllable-pitch props; 4,200 hp

REMARKS: 1,443 grt. One 10-ton and two 1.5-ton booms. Carries fixed fire pumps with 2,600 tons/hour capacity and portable pumps with 1,650 tons/hour capacity. Can support divers to a depth of 90 m, and have decompression chambers and powerful air-compressors. Two sisters, the *Gidrograf* and *Peleng*, are intelligence collectors.

◆ **3 Orel class** Bldr: Finland

Orel class

D: 1,200 tons (1,760 fl)   **S:** 15 kts   **Dim:** 61.3 × 11.9 × 4.5
Man: 37 men   **Range:** 13,000/13.5
Electron Equipt: Radar: 1/Don or Don 2
M: 1 M.A.N. G5Z52/70 diesel; 1,700 hp

REMARKS: Built in the late 1950s. Several civilian sisters, including the *Stremitel'nyy,* serve the fishing fleet.

SEAGOING FIRE BOATS

◆ **5 Katun class** Bldr: U.S.S.R., 1970-78

PDS 96   PDS 98   PDS 123   PDS 124   PDS 209

Katun class

D: 1,016 tons (fl)   **S:** 17 kts   **Dim:** 62.6 × 10.2 × 3.6
Man: 32 men   **Range:** 2,200/16
Electron Equipt: Radar: 1/Don 2   IFF: 1/High Pole B
M: 2 40DM diesels; 2 props; 4,000 hp

REMARKS: PDS = Pozharno-Degazatsionnoye Sudno (fire-fighting and decontamination ship); this designation is being revised to PS = Pozharnoye Sudno (fire-fighting ship).

SEAGOING FIRE BOATS (continued)

Extensive fire-fighting gear, including extendable boom. Powerful pumps. There are several civilian sisters, including the *General Gamidov*.

INTELLIGENCE COLLECTORS (AGI)

NOTE: Many of the Soviet ships of this type, often designated ELINT (electronic intelligence) or SIGINT (signal intelligence), look like trawlers; others, such as the *Primorye* class, are obviously configured for their roles. No pretense is made that the AGIs are anything but intelligence collectors, which detect and analyze radioelectric and electromagnetic signals. Some of them patrol offshore from the home ports of strategic submarines, others follow Western fleets.

◆ **6 Primor'ye class**

KAVKAZ	PRIMOR'YE	ZAKARPAT'YE
KRYM	ZABAYKAL'YE	ZAPOROZH'YE

Primor'ye

Zaporozh'ye

D: 3,400 tons (4,500 fl) **S:** 12 kts **Dim:** 84.7 × 14.0 × 7.0
Man: 117 men **Electron Equipt:** Radars: 2/Don Kay **ECM:** Various
M: 2 diesels; 1 prop; 2,000 hp

REMARKS: Although these ships resemble small passenger liners, they are in fact modified versions of *Mayakovsky*-class stern-haul factory trawlers. They have the most extensive arrays and are the newest and largest of the Soviet ELINT/SIGINT ships.

◆ **6 Moma class** Bldr: Gdansk, Poland, 1968-72

ARKHIPELAG	NAKHODKA	SELIGER
IL'MEN	PELORUS	YUPITER

Yupiter 1976

D: 1,260 tons (1,540 fl) **S:** 17 kts **Dim:** 73.3 × 10.8 × 3.8
Electron Equipt: Radars: 2/Don 2 **ECM:** Various **Range:** 8,000/11
M: 2 Sgoda 6TD48 diesels; 2 props; 3,600 hp

REMARKS: Ex-survey ships/buoy tenders. The *Yupiter* (see photo) and *Arkhipelag* have new superstructures in the area forward of the bridge and new masts (the *Arkhipelag* has a larger deckhouse). The others are much less modified, most having only a few canvas-covered antennas atop the bridge.

◆ **8 Mayak class** Bldr: . . ., 1967-70

ANEROYD	KHERSONES	KURSOGRAF	GS 239
GIRORULEVOY	KURS	LADOGA	GS 242

GS-242—with extended main-deck superstructure and parabolic antenna aft 1978

INTELLIGENCE COLLECTORS (*continued*)

Kurs   1975

GS-239   1975

D: 1,050 tons (fl)   **S:** 11 kts   **Dim:** 54.2 × 9.3 × 3.6
Electron Equipt: Radars: 1-2/Don 2 and/or Spin Trough   **ECM:** Various
M: 1 8NVD48 diesel; 800 hp   **Range:** 9,400/11

REMARKS: GS = Gidrograficheskoye Sudno (survey ship), an interesting euphemism. These ships vary greatly in appearance and equipment carried.

◆ **2 Nikolai Zubov class**   Bldr: Poland

KHARITON LAPTEV   GAVRIL SARYCHEV

Gavril Sarychev   1978

D: 2,200 tons (3,100 fl)   **S:** 16.5 kts   **Dim:** 90.0 × 13.0 × 4.7
Electron Equipt: Radars: 2/Don 2   IFF: 1/High Pole B   ECM: Various
M: 2 Sgoda 85D48 diesels; 2 props; 4,800 hp   **Range:** 11,000/14

REMARKS: Ex-oceanographic ships. Similar to oceanographic sisters, but have a collection of antenna arrays. The *Gavril Sarychev* has been extensively reconstructed: her forecastle has been extended to her stern and an extra deck has been added to her superstructure.

◆ **2 Pamir class**   Bldr: Gävle, Sweden, 1958

GIDROGRAF   PELENG (ex-*Pamir*)

Gidrograf   1976

D: 1,443 tons (2,300 fl)   **S:** 17.5 kts   **Dim:** 78.0 × 12.8 × 4.0
Electron Equipt: Radars: 2/Don 2   ECM: Various   **Man:** 70 men
M: 2 M.A.N. G10V 40/60 diesels; 2 controllable-pitch props; 4,200 hp
Range: 15,200/17.5, 21,800/12

INTELLIGENCE COLLECTORS (*continued*)

REMARKS: Ex-rescue tugs. Both heavily modified: extra deckhouse levels, extended forecastle, numerous collection antenna arrays, etc. Their extremely long endurance makes them invaluable in the Pacific and Indian oceans. Sisters *Agatan* and *Aldan* are salvage ships.

◆ **4 Mirny class**

BAKAN   LOTSMAN   VAL   VERTIKAL

Val 1972

D: 850 tons (1,300 fl)   S: 17.5 kts   Dim: 63.0 × 9.5 × 4.5
Electron Equipt: Radars: 2/Don 2   ECM: Various   Man: 31 men
M: 4 diesels, electric drive; 1 prop; 4,000 hp   Range: 18,700/11

REMARKS: Ex-whalers. Differ in detail. Very low freeboard amidships.

◆ **15 Okean class**   Bldr: East Germany, 1960s

ALIDADA	DEFLEKTOR	LINZA	TEODOLIT
AMPERMETR	EKHOLOT	LOTLIN'	TRAVERS
BAROGRAF	GIDROFON	REDUKTOR	ZOND
BAROMETR	KRENOMETR	REPITER	

Alidada 1975

Zond 1976

D: 700 tons (fl)   S: 11 kts   Dim: 50.8 × 8.9 × 3.7
M: 1 diesel; 540 hp   Range: 7,900/11   Man: 32 men

REMARKS: Ex-trawlers. Appearances vary greatly, many having had their poop deck extended well forward of the bridge superstructure and their port sides plated in (*see* photo of the *Zond*).

◆ **2 Dnepr class**   Bldr: Japan

IZERMETEL'   PROTRAKTOR

D: 750 tons (fl)   S: 11 kts   Dim: 52.7 × 9.2 × 3.5
M: 2 Burmeister & Wain diesels; 1 prop; 1,210 hp

REMARK: Ex-tuna boats built in the late 1960s.

OCEANOGRAPHIC-RESEARCH SHIPS

NOTE: The only units included are those known to be subordinate to the Soviet Navy. There are in addition nearly 300 research ships under the control of civilian agencies, primarily the Ministry of Science and the Ministry of Fisheries. Some of the civilian ships may from time to time perform research in support of military aims, but their purpose is primarily peaceful and, because of their number and variety, they cannot be described here. Such ships include the seven-unit *Akademik Kurchatov* expeditionary ships, the nine *Passat*-class weather ships, and the large and complex *Yuriy Gagarin, Kosmonaut Vladimir Komorov, Akademik Sergey Korolev*, as well as the 20 or more Finnish-built *Dimitriy Ovtsyn* arctic oil survey ships, which operate under the Ministry of the Merchant Marine. All naval units are painted white.

◆ **10 Yug class**   Bldr: Gdansk, Poland, 1978-79

GIDROLOG	PERSEY	SENESH	TAYGA	ZODIAK
PEGAS	PLUTON	STRELETS	YUG	N . . .

OCEANOGRAPHIC-RESEARCH SHIPS (*continued*)

Yug   1979

Strelets   1979

> **D:** 2,500 tons (fl)   **S:** 16 kts   **Dim:** 82.5 × 13.5 × 3.9
> **Electron Equipt:** Radars: 2/Don 2   IFF: 1/High Pole B   **Man:** 54 men
> **M:** 2 Sgoda-Sulzer 6TD48 diesels; 2 controllable-pitch props; 3,600 hp
> **Range:** 8,700/11

REMARKS: Developed from the Moma design and Wodnik training ships. Equipped with a stern ramp and quadrantal-gallows crane for trailing towed equipment. Deck reinforcements for six 25-mm AA (II × 3).

◆ **6 Akademik Krylov class**   Blrs: Szczecin SY, Poland, 1974-79

| ADMIRAL VLADIMIRSKY | IVAN KRUZHENSTERN | LEONID SOBELYEV |
| AKADEMIK KRYLOV | LEONID DEMIN | MIKHAIL KRUSKIY |

Akademik Krylov   1975

> **D:** 6,600 tons (9,100 fl)   **S:** 20.4 kts   **Dim:** 147.0 × 18.6 × 6.3
> **Man:** 90 men   **Range:** 23,000/15.4   **Endurance:** 90 days
> **Electron Equipt:** Radars: 3/Don 2   IFF: 1/High Pole B
> **M:** 4 diesels; 2 props; 16,000 hp

REMARKS: The largest ships of their type in any navy. Equipped with helicopter hangar and flight deck, two survey launches, and twenty-six laboratories totaling 900 m². The *Leonid Demin* and *Mikhail Kruskiy* were delivered in 1978 and 1979, respectively.

◆ **1 Vladimir Kavrayskiy class**   Bldr: Admiralty SY, Lenigrad, 1973

VLADIMIR KAVRAYSKIY

> **D:** 3,900 tons (fl)   **S:** 15.4 kts   **Dim:** 70.0 × 18.0 × 6.4
> **Range:** 13,900/9.4   **Endurance:** 60 days
> **M:** 3 13D100 diesels, electric drive; 2 props; 4,800 hp

REMARKS: Greatly modified version of the *Dobrynya Nikitich* icebreaker class for arctic research. Has helicopter deck but no hangar, a survey launch, nine laboratories, totaling 180 m², one 8-ton crane, two 3-ton booms, and a hold capacity of 200 m³. The *Otto Schmidt*, completed in 1979 and subordinate to the Academy of Sciences, differs in appearance but is of similar design. The civilian icebreakers *Georgiy Sedov* and *Petr Pakhtusov*, also subordinate to the Academy of Science, are units of the *Dobrynya Nikitich* class with very few external alterations.

◆ **4 Abkhaziya class**   Bldr: Mathias Thesen Werft, Wismar, East Germany 1971-73

| ABKHAZIYA | ADZHARIYA | BASHKIRIYA | MOLDAVIYA |

Abkhaziya

> **D:** 5,460 tons (7,500 fl)   **S:** 21 kts   **Dim:** 124.7 × 17.0 × 6.4
> **Man:** 85 men   **Range:** 20,000/16   **Endurance:** 60 days
> **Electron Equipt:** Radars: 3/Don 2
> **M:** 2 M.A.N. K6Z 57/80 diesels; 2 props; 8,000 hp

REMARKS: Military version of the *Akademik Kurchatov* class with helicopter deck, telescoping hangar, Vee Cone communications antenna, stern-mounted A-frame lift gear, two survey launches, and twenty-seven laboratories totaling 460 m².

OCEANOGRAPHIC-RESEARCH SHIPS (continued)

◆ **9 Nikolay Zubov class** Bldr: Szczecin, Poland, 1963-68

ALEKSEY CHIRIKOV   NIKOLAY ZUBOV
ANDREY VIL'KITSKIY   SEMYEN CHELYUSHKIN
BORIS DAVYDOV   SEMYEN DEZHNYEV
FADDEY BELLINGSGAUZEN   VASILIY GOLOVNIN
FYEDOR LITKE

Aleksey Chirikov—no survey launches aboard   1979

D: 2,200 tons (3,020 fl)   **S:** 16.5 kts   **Dim:** 90.0 × 13.0 × 4.7
Man: 50 men   **Range:** 11,000/14   **Endurance:** 60 days
Electron Equipt: Radars: 2/Don 2   IFF: 1/High Pole
M: 2 Sgoda-Sulzer 85D48 diesels; 4,800 hp

REMARKS: Considerable variation from ship to ship. Can carry four survey launches but usually have only two. Small deck aft for weather balloons, not for helicopters. Nine laboratories, totaling 120 m². Two 7-ton and two 5-ton booms, nine .5- to 1.2-ton oceanographic-equipment davits, 600 m³ capacity total in two holds. The *Andrey Vil'kitskiy* carries a Strut Curve radar antenna on her equipment pedestal forward of her stack. The after platform, *not* for helicopters, is larger in the later ships.

◆ **1 Nevel'skoy class** Bldr: U.S.S.R., 1962

NEVEL'SKOY

Nevel'skoy   1979

D: 2,350 tons (fl)   **S:** 18 kts   **Dim:** 83.0 × 15.2 × 3.6
Electron Equipt: Radars: 2/Don 2   **Man:** 45 men
M: 2 diesels; 2 props; 4,000 hp

REMARKS: The only naval oceanographic-research ship, other than the *Vladimir Kavrayskiy*, built in the Soviet Union; apparently the prototype for the *Nikolay Zubov* design. In the Pacific Fleet.

◆ **3 Polyus class** Bldr: Neptun Werft, Rostock, East Germany, 1962-64

BAYKAL   BALKHASH   POLYUS

Baykal

D: 4,560 tons (6,900 fl)   **S:** 14.2 kts   **Dim:** 111.6 × 14.4 × 6.3
Electron Equipt: Radars: 2/Don 2   **Range:** 25,000/12.3
M: 4 diesels, electric drive; 2 props; 4,000 hp   **Endurance:** 75 days

REMARK: Seventeen laboratories, totaling 290 m².

HYDROGRAPHIC-SURVEY SHIPS

NOTE: Ships of the Finik, Moma, Biya, Kamenka, and Samara classes are used as hydrographic-survey ships and navigation tenders, handling buoys, marking channels, etc. They set and retrieve the 2,000 buoys and 4,000 spar buoys that are taken up for the winter months. Most can carry from two to six navigation buoys. In addition, they are equipped to take basic oceanographic and meteorological samplings. The Soviet Navy's Hydrographic Service has the task not only of surveying Soviet and overseas waters, but of maintaining no less than 600 lighthouses, 150 noise beacons, and 3,000 navigation buoys.

◆ **4 or more Finik class** Bldr: Gdansk, Poland, 1979-

GS 272   GS 278   GS . . .   GS . . .

D: . . .   **S:** . . .   **Dim:** . . .
Electron Equipt: Radars: . . .   **Man:** . . .
M: 2 diesels; 2 props; . . . hp

REMARKS: GS = Gidrograficheskoye Sudno (survey ship). A new design, similar to Moma, but has a larger, higher superstructure. One 5-ton crane forward.

HYDROGRAPHIC-SURVEY SHIPS (*continued*)

◆ 22 **Moma class** Bldr: Poland, 1967-74

AL'TAYR	ARTIKA	KIL'DIN	MORZHOVETS	VEGA
ANADYR'	ASKOL'D	KOLGUEV	OKEAN	ZAPOLAR'E
ANDROMEDA	CHELEKEN	KRIL'ON	RYBACHIY	
ANTARES	EKVATOR	LIMAN	SEVER	
ANTARTIKA	EL'TON	MARS	TAYMYR	

Cheleken   1977

El'ton

D: 1,260 tons (1,540 fl)   **S:** 17 kts   **Dim:** 73.3 × 10.8 × 3.8
Man: 56 men   **Range:** 8,700/11   **Endurance:** 35 days
Electron Equipt: Radars: 2/Don 2   IFF: 1/High Pole A
M: 2 Sgoda 6TD48 diesels; 2 controllable-pitch props; 3,600 hp

REMARKS: Carry one survey launch and a 7-ton crane, and have four laboratories, totaling 35 m². The *Rybachiy* (ex-*Odograf*) has a deckhouse in place of the crane and may be involved in oceanographic research. Sisters in Polish and Yugoslav navies.

◆ 13 **Biya class** Bldr: Gdansk, Poland, 1972-76

GS 186	GS 194	GS 202	GS 206	GS 210	GS 271	GS 275
GS 193	GS 198	GS 204	GS 208	GS 214	GS 273	

D: 750 tons (fl)   **S:** 13 kts   **Dim:** 55.0 × 9.2 × 2.6
Man: 25 men   **Range:** 4,700/11   **Endurance:** 15 days
Electron Equipt: Radar: 1/Don 2
M: 2 diesels; 2 controllable-pitch props; 1,200 hp

REMARKS: GS = Gidrograficheskoye Sudno (survey ship). Similar to Kemenka class but have longer superstructure and less buoy-handling space; one survey launch; one 5-ton crane. Laboratory space: 15 m². One unit transferred to Guinea-Bissau.

◆ 10 **Kamenka class** Bldr: Gdansk, Poland, 1968-72

BEL'BEK	VERNIER	GS 74	GS 107	GS 203
SIMA	GS 66	GS 82	GS 108	GS 207

GS-108

D: 703 tons (fl)   **S:** 13.7 kts   **Dim:** 53.5 × 9.1 × 2.6
Electron Equipt: Radar: 1/Don 2   **Range:** 4,000/10
M: 2 diesels; 2 controllable-pitch props; 1,765 hp

REMARKS: GS = Gidrograficheskoye Sudno (survey ship). Similar to Biya class but have more facilities for stowing and handling buoys. No survey launch. One 5-ton crane. One sister in the East German Navy.

HYDROGRAPHIC-SURVEY SHIPS (continued)

◆ **16 Samara class** Bldr: Gdansk, Poland, 1962-64

AZIMUT	GLUBOMETR	KOMPAS	RUMB	VAYGACH	ZENIT
DEVIATOR	GORIZONT	PAMYAT'	TROPIK	VOSTOK	
GIGROMETR	GRADUS	MERKURIYA	TURA	YUG	

Gorizont   1976

D: 1,050 tons (1,276 fl)   **S:** 15.5 kts   **Dim:** 59.0 × 10.4 × 3.8
Man: 45 men   **Range:** 6,200/11   **Endurance:** 25 days
Electron Equipt: Radars: 2/Don 2
M: 2 Sgoda 5TD48 diesels; 2 controllable-pitch props; 3,000 hp

REMARKS: Have one survey launch and 15 m² of laboratory space. The *Tura* (ex-*Globus*) had her forecastle extended to her superstructure in 1978 and her 7-ton crane removed; she may no longer be a survey ship. The *Deviator* served briefly as a survey ship. The *Yug* has probably been renamed—possibly as GS-275, which has been reported.

◆ **5 Telnovsk class** Bldr: Hungary, 1949-57

AYTODOR	SIRENA	STVOR	SVIYAGA	ULYANA GROMOVA

D: 1,300 tons (1,700 fl)   **S:** 11 kts   **Dim:** 70.0 × 10.0 × 4.2
Electron Equipt: Radar: 1/Neptune, Don, or Don 2   **Man:** 50 men
M: 1 Ganz diesel; 800 hp   **Range:** 3,300/9.7

REMARKS: Similar in most respects to cargo-ship version. All carry one launch; 15 m² of laboratory space. The *Stvor* and *Ulyana Gromova* have lengthened poop decks.

◆ **3 Melitopol class** Bldr: U.S.S.R., 1950s

MAYAK	NIVILER	PRIZMA

Prizma

D: 1,200 tons (fl)   **S:** 11.3 kts   **Dim:** 57.6 × 9.0 × 4.3
Electron Equipt: Radar: 1/Don
M: 1 6DR30/40 diesel; 600 hp   **Range:** 2,500/10.5

REMARKS: Converted small, two-hatch, cargo ships with few modifications; 673 grt/776 dwt. Carry one survey launch on deck.

◆ **several GPB-480-class inshore-survey craft** Bldr: U.S.S.R., 1960s

GPB 480, etc.

D: 120 tons (fl)   **S:** 12 kts   **Dim:** 29.0 × 5.0 × 1.7
Electron Equipt: Radar: 1/Spin Trough   **Man:** 15 men
M: 1 diesel; 450 hp   **Range:** 1,600/10   **Endurance:** 10 days

REMARKS: GPB = Gidrograficheskoye Pribezhnyy Bot (coastal survey boat). VM on the diving-tender version stands for Vodolaznyy Morskoy (seagoing diving tender). Same hull and propulsion as the Nyryat-I-class diving tenders. The charthouse/laboratory is 6 m² and there are two 1.5-ton derricks. The smaller GPB-710 class is carried aboard the larger survey and oceanographic ships listed above: **D:** 7 tons (fl)
S: 10 kts for 150 nautical miles   **Dim:** 11.0 × 3.0 × 0.7.

MISSILE-RANGE INSTRUMENTATION SHIPS

◆ **2 Desna class** Bldr: Poland, 1963

CHAZHMA (ex-*Dangera*)	CHUMIKAN (ex-*Dolgeschtchel'ye*)

MISSILE-RANGE INSTRUMENTATION SHIPS (*continued*)

Chazhma   1978

   D: 14,065 tons (fl)   **S:** 15 kts   **Dim:** 139.9 × 18.0 × 7.9
   Electron Equipt: Radars: 2/Don 2, 1/Head Net-B, 1/Ship Globe (tracking)
      ECM: 2/Watch Dog
   M: 1 M.A.N. diesel; 5,400 hp   **Range:** 9,000/13

REMARKS: Heavily modified cargo ships. Tracking radar in large dome atop the bridge, with three tracking directors mounted forward. Hormone helicopter with hangar aft. Vee Cone communications antennas atop the stack. Based in the Pacific.

◆ **4 Sibir' class**   Bldr: East Germany

CHUKOTKA   SAKHALIN   SIBIR'   SPASSK (ex-*Suchan*)

Sakhalin   1976

   D: 7,800 tons (fl)   **S:** 12 kts   **Dim:** 108.2 × 14.6 × 7.2
   Electron Equipt: Radars: 2/Don 2, 1/Head Net, several tracking sets
   M: Triple-expansion; 1 prop; 2,300 hp   **Range:** 11,800/12

REMARKS: Converted Donbass-class cargo ships built since 1958. Carry Big Net radar for tracking, and two or three tracking directors forward. The *Chukotka* is flush-decked; the others have a well deck forward. All carry one Hormone helicopter, but have no hangar. All are in the Pacific Fleet.

NOISE-MEASUREMENT SHIPS

◆ **3 or more Onega class**   Bldr: . . . , 1973-

GKS 83   GKS . . .   GKS . . .

   D: 2,150 tons (2,500 fl)   **S:** 16 kts   **Dim:** 86.0 × 10.5 × 4.5
   M: 1 gas turbine; 1 prop; . . . hp   **Man:** 45 men

REMARKS: GKS = Gidroakusticheskoye Kontrol'noye Sudno (hydroacoustic monitoring ship) and indicates that these ships are successors to the T-43-class noise-monitoring ships. Helicopter deck aft, long forecastle, two pylon masts, and a low stack.

◆ **20 Modified T-43 class**   Bldr: . . . , 1950s

GKS 11	GKS 15	GKS 19	GKS 23	GKS 42
GKS 12	GKS 16	GKS 20	GKS 24	GKS 45
GKS 13	GKS 17	GKS 21	GKS 25	GKS 46
GKS 14	GKS 18	GKS 22	GKS 26	GKS 49

GKS-15

   D: 500 tons (570 fl)   **S:** 14 kts   **Dim:** 58.0 × 8.5 × 2.3
   Electron Equipt: Radar: 1/Neptune or Spin Trough   IFF: 1/High Pole
   M: 2 diesels; 2 props; 2,200 hp   **Man:** 77 men

REMARKS: GKS = Gidroakusticheskoye Kontrol'noye Sudno (hydroacoustic monitoring ship) and indicates that these ships measure the radiated noise of other ships, including submarines, by laying hydrophone arrays via the numerous small davits they carry aft.

ICEBREAKERS

NOTE: The Soviet Union has far and away the largest and most powerful icebreaker fleet in the world. Its civilian component includes the atomic-powered *Artika* and *Sibir'* the most powerful of all. The two types, patrol and support, that the navy operates are both based on the same civilian design and are among the very few con-

ICEBREAKERS (*continued*)

ventionally driven icebreakers in service to be designed and built in the U.S.S.R. The others were built in Finland.

◆ **6 Ivan Susanin-class patrol icebreakers**

AYSBERG	IMENI XXV SEZDA K.P.S.S.	NEVA
DUNAY	IVAN SUSANIN	RUSLAN

Ivan Susanin   1975

D: 3,400 tons (fl)   **S:** 14.5 kts   **Dim:** 67.6 × 18.3 × 6.4
A: 2/76-mm DP (II × 1) − 2/Gatling AA (VI × 2)   **Range:** 13,000/9.4
Electron Equipt: Radars: 2/Don Kay, 1/Strut Curve, 1/Owl Screech
                    IFF: 1/High Pole B
M: 3 13D100 diesels, electric drive; 2 props; 5,400 hp

REMARKS: Based on the *Dobrynya Nikitich* and *Vladimir Kavrayskiy* designs. All manned by the KGB Border Guard and typed PSKR − Pogranichnyy Storozhevoy Korabl' (border patrol ship). Helicopter deck aft, but no hangar. Gatling guns do not have Bass Tilt radar directors, as do those on other classes. The *Dunay* and *Neva* also carry two launch positions for SA-N-5 short-range AA missiles.

◆ **7 Dobrynya Nikitich-class support icebreakers**

Bldr: Admiralty SY, Leningrad, 1959-74

BURAN	IL'YA MUROMETS	PURGA	VYUGA
DOBRYNYA NIKITICH	PERESVET	SADKO	

D: 2,940 tons (fl)   **S:** 14.5 kts   **Dim:** 67.7 × 18.3 × 6.1
A: Four units: 2/57-mm AA (II × 1) − 2/25-mm AA (II × 1)
Electron Equipt: Radars: 1-2/Don 2   IFF: 1/High Pole   **Man:** 100 men
Range: 5,500/12
M: 3 13D100 diesels, electric drive; 3 props (1 fwd); 5,400 hp

REMARKS: More than twenty of this class were built, the remainder being civilian. The *Peresvet, Purga, Sadko,* and *Vyuga* are armed. Resemble the *Ivan Susanin* class, but have much less superstructure and an open fantail rigged for ocean towing. Later units do not have a bow propeller but have the same horsepower.

TRAINING SHIPS

◆ **3 Smol'ny class**   Bldr: Warski SY, Szczecin, Poland, 1976-78

KHASAN	PEREKOP	SMOL'NY

Smol'ny   1977

Perekop   Skyfotos, Ltd., 1979

D: 6,500 tons (fl)   **S:** 20 kits   **Dim:** 137.5 × 16.7 × 6.3
A: 4/76.2-mm DP (II × 2) − 4/30-mm AA (II × 2) − 2/RBU 2500 rocket launchers
Electron Equipt: Radars: 4/Don 2, 1/Head Net-C, 1/Owl Screech, 1/Drum Tilt
                 Sonar: 1/medium-frequency   ECM: 2/Watch Dog
                 IFF: 1/High Pole B
M: 4 diesels; 2 props; 16,000 hp

REMARKS: Presumably relieving the *Sverdlov*-class cruisers that were formerly used for cadet-training. Can carry more than 270 cadets. The *Perekop* substitutes one Don Kay radar for one of the four Don-2s. Carry six rowboats aft for exercising the cadets.

TRAINING SHIPS (*continued*)

◆ **2 Ugra class** Bldr: Nikolayev, 1970-71

BORODINO   GANGUT

Gangut   1974

D: 6,750 tons (9,500 fl)   S: 20 kts   Dim: 141.4 × 17.7 × 6.5
A: 8/57-mm AA (II × 4)   Man: 300 men + 400 cadets
Electron Equipt: Radars: 4/Don 2, 1/Strut Curve, 2/Muff Cob
                ECM: 4/Watch Dog   IFF: 1/High Pole B
M: 4 diesels; 2 props; 8,000 hp

REMARKS: Russian type designation: Uchebnoye Sudno (training ship). Similar to the submarine-tender version but have accommodations and training facilities in place of workshops, magazines, storerooms, etc. Enlarged after deckhouse incorporates navigation-training space, including numerous duplicate navigator's positions. No helicopter facilities.

◆ **2 Modified Wodnik class** Bldr: Poland, 1977

OKA   LUGA

D: 1,500 tons (1,800 fl)   S: 15 kts   Dim: 70.0 × 12.0 × 4.0
Electron Equipt: Radar: . . .   Man: 58 men + 90 cadets
Range: 8,000/11
M: 2 diesels; 2 controllable-pitch props; 3,600 hp

REMARKS: Used for navigation training. Similar to Polish and East German units of the Wodnik class, but have slightly larger superstructures, with pilothouse one deck higher, and are not armed. Based on the Moma design.

TARGET-SERVICE SHIPS AND CRAFT

◆ **2 or more Potok class** Bldr: . . . , 1978 (?)

OS 225   OS . . .

D: 750 tons (860 fl)   S: 18 kts   Dim: 71.0 × 9.1 × 2.5
A: 1/533-mm TT   Electron Equipt: Radar: 1/Don 2
M: 2 diesels; 2 props; 4,000 hp

REMARKS: OS = Opytnoye Sudno (experimental ship). The design closely resembles the T-58 class, but the forecastle extends well aft. The torpedo tube is on the bow. A large crane aft is probably used for retrieval. These ships are probably replacements for Modified T-43-class minesweepers, which have been used in torpedo trials since the 1950s.

◆ **9 target-control boats**

Osa target controller   1974

REMARKS: Have Osa hull and propulsion. Used to operate craft shown below by remote control. Carry Square Tie radar and a High Pole B IFF transponder. Communications antennas have been enhanced to provide for radio-control.

◆ **8 Modified Osa-class missile targets**

KTs-594, Osa target   1974

REMARKS: KTs = Kontrol'naya Tsel' (controlled target). Have Osa hull and propulsion. Crew departs when ship is in operation. Equipped with radar corner reflectors to strengthen the target and two heat-generator chimneys to attract infrared homing missiles.

◆ **several Shelon-class torpedo-retrievers** Bldr: . . . , 1978-

U.S.S.R. (*continued*)

TARGET-SERVICE SHIPS AND CRAFT (*continued*)

D: 300 tons (fl)   **S:** . . .   **Dim:** . . . × . . . × . . .
M: Diesels; 2 props; . . . hp

REMARKS: High-speed hull with a covered torpedo-recovery ramp aft and a lattice mast. May be replacing the Poluchat-I class.

◆ **60 or more Poluchat-I-class torpedo-retrievers**

D: 90 tons (fl)   **S:** 18 kts   **Dim:** 29.6 × 5.8 × 1.5
A: 2/14.5-mm AA (II × 1) in some   **Man:** 20 men   **Range:** 450/17,900/10
Electron Equipt: Radar: 1/Spin Trough   **IFF:** 1/High Pole A
M: 2 M50 diesels; 2 props; 2,400 hp

REMARKS: Carry numbers in the TL — Torpedolov (torpedo retriever) — series. Built in the 1950s. Recovery ramp aft. Also configured as patrol boats. Many exported abroad. *See* photo in section on Patrol Craft.

SERVICE CRAFT

NOTE: The Soviet Navy operates more than 1,000 service craft in many categories, but space and lack of comprehensive information prohibits their description here.

UNITED ARAB EMIRATES

NOTE: Primarily incorporating the former Defense Force Sea Wing of the Abu Dhabi National Defense Force, the UAE Navy was formed on 1 February 1978 as part of the federated forces of Abu Dhabi, Ajman, Dubai, Fujairah, Ras al Khaimah, Sharjah, and Umm al Qaiwan.

◆ **4 TNC-45 Jaguar-II-class guided-missile boats**   Bldr: Lürssen, Vegesack

P . . . N . . .   P . . . N . . .   P . . . N . . .   P . . . N . . .

D: 255 tons (fl)   **S:** 30 kts   **Dim:** 44.9 (42.3 pp) × 7.0 × 2.44
A: 4/MM-38 Exocet — 1/57-mm Bofors AA — 1/40-mm Breda AA — 2/7.62-mm machine guns (I × 2) -- Dagaie chaff launcher
M: 2 MTU 16V538 TB91 diesels; 2 props; 7,200 hp   **Range:** 1,670/16

REMARKS: Ordered in 1978 and first unit to be delivered in 4-80. CSEE DMQa fire control for guns.

◆ **6 110-foot patrol boats**   Bldr: Vosper Thornycroft, Portsmouth, G.B.

	L		L
P 1101 ARDHANA	7-3-75	P 1104 AL GHULIAN	16-9-75
P 1102 ZURARA	13-6-75	P 1105 RADOOM	15-12-75
P 1103 MURBAN	15-9-75	P 1106 GHANADHAH	1-3-76

Ardhana and Zurara   1976

D: 110 tons (140 fl)   **S:** 29 kts   **Dim:** 33.5 (31.5 pp) × 6.4 × 1.7
A: 2/30-mm AA (II × 1) — 1/20-mm AA   **Man:** 26 men   **Range:** 1,800/14
Electron Equipt: Radar: 1/Decca RM 916
M: 2 Ruston-Paxman Valenta RP200M diesels; 2 props; 5,400 hp

REMARK: The 30-mm mount is a BMARC/Oerlikon A32.

◆ **10 customs patrol craft**

REMARK: Ordered in 1978 in the U.S.A. Details not available.

◆ **5 customs patrol craft**   Bldr: Camcraft, New Orleans, La.

No. 21 through No. 25

D: 70 tons (fl)   **S:** 25 kts   **Dim:** 23.4 × 5.5 × 1.5
A: 2/20-mm AA (I × 2)   **Range:** 750/25
M: 2 GM 12V 71T diesels; 2 props; 1,400 hp

REMARKS: U.S. P-77A design. In service in 9-75.

◆ **2 50-foot customs patrol craft**   Bldr: Cheverton, Cowes, G.B.

AL SHAHEEN   AL AQAB

D: 20 tons   **S:** 23 kts   **Dim:** 15.2 × 4.3 × 1.4
A: 1/7.62-mm machine gun   **Man:** 8 men   **Range:** 1,000/20
M: 2 GM diesels; 2 props; 850 hp

REMARK: In service in 2-75.

◆ **3 Kawkab-class patrol craft**   Bldr: Keith Nelson, G.B.

	L		L		L
P 561 KAWKAB	1-69	P 562 THOABAN	1-69	P 563 BANIYAS	7-69

UNITED ARAB EMIRATES (*continued*)

Kawkab   1969

D: 25 tons (32 fl)   **Dim:** 17.52 (15.84 pp) × 4.72 × 1.37
A: 2/20-mm AA (I × 2)   **Man:** 2 officers, 9 men
Electron Equipt: Radar: 1/Decca RM 916   **Electric:** 24 kw
M: 2 Caterpillar diesels; 2 props; 750 hp   **Endurance:** 1 week

REMARKS: Fiberglass hull. Used for coastal patrol, hydrographic surveys, and surveillance of petroleum leases. Designed by Keith Nelson, a division of Vosper. Freshwater evaporator provides 900 liters daily.

◆ **6 Dhafeer-class patrol craft**   Bldr: Keith Nelson, G.B.

	L			L
P 401 DHAFEER	2-68	P 404 DURGHAM		9.68
P 402 GHADUNFAR	5-68	P 405 TIMSAH		9-68
P 403 HAZZA	5-68	P 406 MURAYJIB		2-70

D: 10 tons   **S:** 19 kts   **Dim:** 12.5 × 3.65 × 1.1
A: 1/12.7-mm machine gun   **Man:** 1 officer, 5 men   **Range:** 15/18, 350/15
M: 2 Cummins diesels; 2 props; 370 hp

REMARKS: Subordinate to Marine Police. Fiberglass hull.

◆ **6 Spear-class police patrol craft**   Bldr: Fairey Marine, Hamble, G.B.

D: 10 tons;   **S:** 26 kts   **Dim:** 9.1 × 2.75 × 0.84
A: 2/12.7-mm machine guns   **Man:** 3 men
M: 2 Perkins T 6-354 diesels; 2 props; 580 hp

REMARKS: In service in 8-74, 9-74, and 1-75. Fiberglass hull.

◆ **2 Cheverton motor launches**

A 271   A 272

D: 3.3 tons   **S:** 15 kts   **Dim:** 8.2 × 2.7 × 0.8
M: 1 Lister-Blackstone diesel; 150 hp

REMARK: In service in 1975.

U.S.A.

PERSONNEL: 63,200 officers, 460,500 enlisted, plus 189,000 marines and 87,000 ready naval reserves
MERCHANT MARINE (1978): 4,746 ships — 16,187,636 grt
(tankers: 311 ships — 6,657,942 grt)

NAVAL PROGRAM

The table lists new construction programs for fiscal years 1978 through 1985, including the supplemental FY 79 program, as reported to Congress in 1979, and changes reported later in the press. The annual five-year program has fluctuated drastically for many years and, because of changing political pressures, cannot be relied on as an accurate projection of what will actually be proposed, let alone authorized and appropriated by the Congress. It is nonetheless presented here as the best available forecast.

SHIPBUILDING PROGRAMS

New Construction	FY 78	FY 79	79 S	FY 80	FY 81	FY 82	FY 83	FY 84	FY 85
SSBN, *Ohio* class	2	—	—	1	1	1	1	1	2
SSN, *Los Angeles* class	1	2	—	2	1	1	1	2	—
SSN, new class	—	—	—	—	—	—	1	1	4
CVN, *Nimitz* class	—	—	—	1	—	—	—	—	—
CG, CG-47 class	1	—	—	1	2	3	3	4	4
DDG, new class	—	—	—	—	—	—	—	—	1
DDG, *Kidd* class	—	—	4	—	—	—	—	—	—
DD, *Spruance* class	1	—	—	—	—	—	—	—	—
FFG, *O. H. Perry* class	8	8	—	6	4	4	3	4	—
FF, new class	—	—	—	—	—	—	1	—	4
LSD, LSD-41 class	—	—	—	—	1	—	1	—	1
MCM, new class	—	—	—	—	—	1	—	4	4
AD, *Yellowstone* class	—	1	—	—	—	—	—	—	—
T-AGOS	—	2	—	1	5	4	—	—	—
T-AKX	—	—	—	—	2	3	3	3	3

Three Trident submarines: **Ohio** (SSBN-726)—in the launch basin; **Michigan** (SSBN-727)—on the quay; and a cylindrical hull section for **Georgia** (SSBN-729)   1979

SHIP BUILDING PROGRAMS (continued)

	FY 78	FY 79	79 S	FY 80	FY 81	FY 82	FY 83	FY 84	FY 85
AO, *Cimarron* class*	2	—	—	—	—	—	2	2	—
T-ARC, T-ARC-7 class	—	1	—	—	—	—	—	—	—
ARS, new class	—	—	—	—	1	2	1	—	—
T-ATF, *Powhatan* class	3	—	—	—	—	—	—	—	—
Total Conversions:**	18	14	4	12	17	19	17	21	23
CV-SLEP program	—	—	—	—	1	—	1	—	1
DD-963 Moderniza- tion	—	—	—	—	—	—	—	1	—
T-AK, Trident Support	—	—	—	—	1	—	—	—	—

*FY 83 and FY 84 ships to be T-AO, under Military Sealift Command.
**DDG-2 class modernization program cancelled in favor of performing similar work program on 13 ships over two successive overhaul periods, using operational vice ship-building funds.

MARINE CORPS

Created in 1775, the Marine Corps has three missions:
—to seize and/or defend advanced bases as needed for the operations of the fleet
—to furnish security detachments on board ships and at land bases
—to carry out any other operations that the president of the United States may assign.
The third mission permits the corps to be used in operations that are not purely naval (e.g., Belleau Wood in 1918 and Vietnam in the 1960s and 1970s).

Its total strength is about 189,000 men, and they form three divisions (one stationed in Okinawa/Japan, two in the United States), each of 18,000 men and three air wings, organized under two Fleet Marine Forces (FMF). These last also maintain heavy support elements for the divisions. A fourth division-wing team constitutes a reserve cadre. The total number of marines is to be reduced to 179,000 by 1981.

The Marine Corps has approximately 400 fighter and attack aircraft (A-4M, A-6, AV-8A, F-4), 600 assault and utility helicopters, more than 500 tanks, and some 450 amphibious landing vehicles.

The major operational unit is the Marine Amphibious Force (MAF), which consists of one division, one air wing, and Fleet Marine Forces augmentation, for a total of about 45,000 men.

Amphibious ships currently in service do not permit the rapid overseas deployment of MAFs, but only of two Marine Amphibious Brigades (MAB). An MAB consists of one Regimental Landing Team, a strong unit with two or more battalion landing teams of about 1,500 men each; one mixed air group of fighter, attack fixed-wing aircraft and/or helicopter squadrons; and some augmentation from the Fleet Marine Force. No new amphibious ships are programmed over the next decade.

WARSHIPS IN ACTIVE SERVICE, UNDER CONSTRUCTION, OR APPROPRIATED AS OF 1 JANUARY 1980

	L	Tons	Main armament
♦ **13 (+ 2) attack carriers**			
2 (+2) NIMITZ (CVN)	1972-	81,600	90-100 aircraft, 3/Sea Sparrow
1 ENTERPRISE (CVN)	1960	75,700	84-90 aircraft
1 JOHN F. KENNEDY (CV)	1967	61,000	80-90 aircraft, 3/Sea Sparrow
3 KITTY HAWK (CV)	1960-64	60,100	85-90 aircraft, 2-3/missile launchers
4 FORRESTAL (CV)	1954-58	59,600	85-90 aircraft, 2/Sea Sparrow
2 MIDWAY (CV)	1945-46	51,000	up to 72 aircraft, 0 or 2/Sea Sparrow
♦ **11 (+ 1) amphibious assault ships and helicopter carriers**			
4 (+1) TARAWA (LHA)	1972-78	39,000(fl)	3/127-mm DP, 2/Sea Sparrow, 26 helicopters
7 IWO JIMA (LPH)	1960-69	17,000	4/76.2-mm, 2/Sea Sparrow, 20 helicopters
♦ **41 (+ 8) nuclear-powered ballistic-missile submarines**			
		(surfaced)	
0 (+ 8) OHIO (SSBN)	1979-	15,750	24/Trident-I, 4/TT
31 LAFAYETTE (SSBN)	1962-66	7,250	16/Poseidon or Trident, 4/TT
5 ETHAN ALLEN (SSBN)	1960-62	6,300	16/Polaris, 4/TT
5 GEORGE WASHINGTON (SSBN)	1959-60	6,019	16/Polaris, 6/TT
♦ **74 (+ 24) nuclear-powered attack submarines**			
11 (+ 24) LOS ANGELES	1973-	6,000	4/TT
1 GLENARD P. LIPSCOMB	1973	5,813	4/TT
37 STURGEON	1966-74	3,640	4/TT
1 NARWHAL	1967	4,550	4/TT
13 PERMIT	1961-66	3,526	4/TT
1 TULLIBEE	1960	2,317	4/TT
5 SKIPJACK	1958-60	3,075	6/TT
4 SKATE	1957-58	2,570	8/TT
1 SEAWOLF	1955	3,765	6/TT
♦ **5 diesel/electric-powered submarines**			
3 BARBEL	1958-59	2,146	6/TT
1 DARTER	1956	1,720	8/TT
1 GRAYBACK	1957	2,670	8/TT
♦ **28 (+ 3) cruisers**			
8 (+ 1) nuclear-powered:		Tons	
3 (+ 1) VIRGINIA (CGN)	1974-78	10,400	2/missile launchers, 2/127-mm DP, 6/ASW TT
2 CALIFORNIA (CGN)	1971-72	10,400	2/missile launchers, 2/127-mm DP, 8/ASW TT
1 TRUXTUN (CGN)	1964	8,600	1/missile launcer, 1/127-mm DP, 6/ASW TT
1 BAINBRIDGE (CGN)	1961	8,600	2/missile launchers, ASROC, 6/ASW TT
1 LONG BEACH (CGN)	1959	15,500	2/missile launchers, 16/Harpoon, ASROC, 6/ASW TT

WARSHIPS IN ACTIVE SERVICE, UNDER CONSTRUCTION OR APPROPRIATED (continued)

20 (+ 2) conventional:

0 (+ 2) CG-47	1981-	. . .	2/missile launchers, 8 Harpoon, 2/127-mm DP, 6/ASW TT, 1/helicopter
9 BELKNAP (CG)	1963-65	6,570	1/missile launcher, 8/ Harpoon, 1/127-mm DP, 6/ASW TT
9 LEAHY (CG)	1961-63	6,070	2/missile launchers, ASROC, 6/ASW TT
2 ALBANY (CG)	1944-45	14,600	2/missile launchers, 2/127-mm DP, ASROC

◆ **86 (+ 10) destroyers**

0 (+ 4) KIDD	1979-80	8,140	2/missile launchers, 2/127-mm DP, 1/ or 2/ helicopters
25 (+ 6) SPRUANCE	1973-81	5,830	1/Sea Sparrow, 8/ Harpoon, 2/127-mm DP, ASROC, 6/ASW TT, 1/helicopter
23 CHARLES F. ADAMS	1959-63	3,370	1/missile launcher, 2/127-mm DP, ASROC, ASW TT
10 COONTZ	1958-60	4,700	1/missile launcher, 8/ Harpoon, 1/127-mm DP, ASROC, 6/ASW TT
4 DECATUR	1955-58	2,850	1/missile launcher, 1/127-mm DP, ASROC, 6/ASW TT
8 MOD. FORREST SHERMAN	1955-58	2,850	2/127-mm DP, ASROC, 6/ASW TT
6 FORREST SHERMAN	1955-58	2,780	3/127-mm DP, 6/ASW TT
2 CARPENTER	1945-46	2,425	2/127-mm DP, ASROC, 6/ASW TT
9 GEARING	1944-46	2,425	4/127-mm DP, ASROC, 6/ASW TT

◆ **67 (+ 37) frigates**

2 (+ 37) OLIVER HAZARD PERRY	1976-	. . .	1/missile launcher, 1/76.2-mm, 6/ASW TT, 2/ helicopters
46 KNOX	1966-73	3,011	0 or 1/Sea Sparrow, 1/127-mm DP, ASROC 4/ASW TT, 1/helicopter
6 BROOKE	1963-66	2,643	1/missile launcher, 1/127-mm DP, ASROC, 6/ASW TT, 1/helicopter
10 GARCIA	1963-65	2,624	2/127-mm DP, ASROC, 6/ASW TT, 1/helicopter
1 GLOVER	1965	2,650	1/127-mm DP, ASROC, 6/ASW TT
2 BRONSTEIN	1962	2,360	2/76.2-mm DP, ASROC, 6/ASW TT

WEAPONS AND SYSTEMS

NOTE: A number of weapon systems no longer in use have been dropped from this edition. It will be noted that not only is the number of U.S. ships and aircraft declining but the number of active weapon options available for use by them is also declining. Furthermore, available systems, particularly guns and fire-control systems, are being removed without replacement, while the development of new systems is being stretched out. Systems dropped include Polaris A-2, Standard RGM-66, Talos, Tartar, Terrier, 203-mm Mk-71 and Mk-15 guns, the 152-mm gun, the Mk-44 torpedo, and UUM-44 SUBROC.

A. MISSILES

◆ **fleet ballistic missiles**

NOTE: All are launched from submerged submarines.

Polaris A-3 (UGM 27C A-3) — Lockheed

Length:	9.5 m
Diameter:	1.4 m
Weight:	15,860 kg at launch
Propulsion:	solid propellant, two stages
Guidance:	inertial
Range:	2,500 nautical miles
Warhead:	1 MT or 3 independent but not individually controllable (MRV) of 200 kt each

Poseidon C-3 (UGM 73A) — Lockheed

Length:	10.4 m
Diameter:	1.8 m
Weight:	about 30 tons at launch
Propulsion:	solid propellant, two stages
Guidance:	inertial
Range:	2,500 or 3,200 nautical miles
Warhead:	14 warheads with independent and controllable trajectory, each of 50 kt (MIRV) to 2,500 nautical miles or 10 of 50 kt to 3,200 nautical miles

Trident-1 C-4 (UGM-96A) — Lockheed

New type missile, operational in 1978 and designed for the *Ohio*-class SSBN, which will carry 24, and for twelve *Lafayette* and *Benjamin Franklin* classes of SSBN, which will carry 16.

Length:	10.4 m
Weight:	more than 30 tons at launch
Propulsion:	solid propellant, three stages
Guidance:	inertial
Range:	about 4,000 nautical miles
Warhead:	8 MIRV of 100 kt, Mk 4

The Mk 500 Evader MARV-Maneuverable Re-entry vehicle with six 100-kt warheads is under development by Lockheed for procurement commencing in 1980.

Trident-2 D5 — Lockheed

In development for deployment in the 1990s.

Length:	13.9 m
Weight:	57 tons
Propulsion:	solid propellant, three stages

WEAPONS AND SYSTEMS (*continued*)

Range: 6,000 nautical miles
Warhead: 14 MIRV of 150 kt each or 7 MARV (Maneuverable Re-entry Vehicles)
             of 300 kt each

◆ **surface-to-surface missiles**

Tomahawk (BGM-109) – General Dynamics

Two versions are projected, strategic and tactical. The anti-ship tactical version will become operational in 1982.

Length: 6.17 m
Diameter: 0.52 m
Weight: 1,542 kg at launch (1,816 kg encapsulated for submarine launch)
Propulsion: solid booster, turbojet sustainer
Navigation/
  Guidance: TAINS (Tercom-Aided Inertial Navigation System) using prepro-
              grammed data plus TERCOM (Terrain Contour Matching)
Range: *Strategic version:* 600 nautical miles, operating at an altitude between
              15 and 100 meters, at a speed of Mach 0.7. For launching from sub-
              marines, the weapon will be fired from torpedo tubes in a special con-
              tainer, jettisoned on leaving the water.
              Tactical version: 350 nautical miles, approximately, thus requiring an
              external means of target designation. Warhead weight up to 454 kg

Harpoon (RGM-84A) – McDonnell-Douglas

An all-weather cruise missile that can be launched by aircraft, surface ships, or submarines. A total of 281 surface ships and submarines are programmed to receive it.

Length: 4.6 m, including 4-m booster
Diameter: 0.35 m
Weight: 694 kg from canister, 667 kg from trainable launcher
Propulsion: turbojet, with a rocket booster added to the ship- and submarine-
              launched versions
Guidance: inertial, then active homing on J band in the final trajectory
Range: 60 nautical miles
Warhead: 231 kg

AGM-84 is the 530-kg, air-dropped version, which does not require a solid rocket booster, and **UGM-84** is the submarine version. The submarine version is shrouded and is launched from the torpedo tubes while submerged. In order to reach the maximum range, it is necessary to use targeting systems external to the launching unit – heli-copters, for example.

Penguin Mk-II – Norway

The U.S. Navy is testing this weapon for potential use aboard small combatants, presumably for foreign sale, as there are no plans to build any craft to carry it for U.S. Navy usage.

◆ **surface-to-air missiles**

Standard SM-1 MR (RIM-66B) – General Dynamics
Single-stage missile to replace Tartar.
Length: 4.3 m
Diameter: 0.36 m
Weight: 590 kg
Guidance: semi-active homing
Range: 25 nautical miles, 150-60,000 ft

System comprises Mk-11 twin launcher or Mk-13 single launcher with a vertical ready-service magazine containing 40 missiles (on the FFG-1 class, Mk-22 with 16 missiles), a computer, an air-search radar, a three-dimensional SPS-39, SPS-48 or SPS-52 radar, and two SPG-51 guidance radars. A series of missiles of approximately the same size as the first RIM 24, Mod. 0, (U.S. military designation) but constantly improved propulsion, miniaturization of components, and missile-flight profile.

Standard SM-2 MR (RIM-66C) – General Dynamics

Single-stage missile for use with Aegis-equipped ships. Initial procurement of 30 in FY 80.

Length: 4.3 m
Diameter: 0.36 m
Weight: 590 kg
Guidance: semi-active homing, with mid-course guidance capability, inertial refer-
              ence, and improved ECCM
Range: more than 25 nautical miles

Standard SM-1 ER (RIM-67) – General Dynamics

Two-stage missile that replaced the Terrier family.
Length: 7.9 m
Diameter: 0.36 m
Weight: 1,317 kg
Guidance: semi-active homing
Range: 30-40 nautical miles

Standard SM-2 ER (RIM-67B) – General Dynamics

Two-stage missile to replace Talos. Will be employed in ships with Mk-10 or Mk-26 launch systems, and later in vertical launches. May have a nuclear warhead option. Initial procurement of 55 in FY 80.

Length: 7.9 m
Diameter: 0.36 m
Weight: 1,317 kg
Guidance: semi-active homing, with mid-course guidance capability, inertial refer-
              ence, and improved ECCM
Range: more than 75 nautical miles

Sea Sparrow (RIM-7) – Raytheon

Known at first as BPDMS (Basic Point Defense Missile System). Initial installations employed fixed-fin missiles launched from the eight-celled Mk-25 launcher and controlled by the Mk-115 radar-equipped fire-control system. A lightweight launcher, Mk-29, employing eight RIM-7F folding-fin missiles and the Mk-91 radar fire-control system, is now coming into use. In Europe this later system, IPDMS (Independent Point Defense Missile System), is also known as NATO Sea Sparrow and was first tested in the *Downes* (FF-1070).

Length: 3.657 m
Weight: 171 kg
Range: 8 nautical miles

Aegis (ex-Advanced Surface Missile System – ASMS)

Under study since 1964. A fire-control system based on the AN/SPY-1 "billboard" fixed-array radar to provide 360° coverage. It will employ SM-2 ER missiles to repel simultaneously a number of targets under the most adverse electronic countermeasures, including targets at extremely low altitude (sea skimmers). For precise response to threats, the Aegis system will be made of various components permitting the control

WEAPONS AND SYSTEMS (*continued*)

of all necessary steps from target-acquisition to missile-detonation against the target. Three clusters of four AN/UYK-7 computer systems will direct all these functions automatically, especially the detection and tracking of the closing targets, data distribution for target evaluation and designation through pre-programmed information retained in the system, integration of radar and other information sources in the ship, and the selection of missiles and distribution of fire.

The Mk-26 twin launcher, which can also handle the ASW ASROC system and Harpoon surface-to-surface missile, will be used. The various types of missiles are stowed vertically in ready-service magazines below the launcher. The Aegis system has been undergoing trials in the *Norton Sound* since 1974 and will first be operational in CG-47 in 1983.

RAM (Rolling Airframe Missile) — General Dynamics

A point-defense system intended to replace or supplement Sea Sparrow. Will use a 127-mm missile that employs spinning for stability (hence the name). Guidance may be by infrared homing, and either a new 24-missile launcher, modified ASROC/Sea Sparrow-type launchers, or even 127-mm guns may be used as the launcher. Project still in definition.

◆ antisubmarine warfare missiles

ASROC (RUR-5) — Honeywell

A solid-fuel rocket used with a parachute-retarded Mk-26 torpedo. Range is regulated by the combustion time of the rocket motor. Rocket-torpedo separation is timed. The Mk-112 launcher carries eight rockets that can be trained together and elevated in pairs. Fire control is made up of a computer linked with an SQS-23, SQS-26, or SQS-53 sonar.

Length:	4.6 m
Diameter:	0.3 m
Weight:	454 kg
Range:	9,200 m
Warhead:	Mk-46 torpedo or Mk-17 nuclear depth bomb
Rate of fire:	2 rockets/minute
Arc of elevation:	3°-85° — almost invariably launched at 45°

On some *Knox*-class escorts the launcher was modified to permit the launching of Standard SSM missiles (later: Harpoon) in place of some ASW weapons. Loading is slow because the rockets have to be manually transferred from the magazines. However, on some recently built escorts, a hoist brings the rocket up forward of the bridge for semiautomatic loading, while in the *Spruance* class the missiles are reloaded vertically.

ASROC may also be launched from the Mk-10 missile launchers in the CG-26 and CGN-35 classes and from the Mk-26 launchers in the CGN-38 and CG-47 classes.

◆ air-to-surface missiles

Bullpup B (AGM-12C/D) — Martin Marietta

Fixed cruciform wings and four control ailerons forward. Bullpup A is no longer in use.

Length:	4.07 m
Diameter:	0.44 m
Weight at launch:	812 kg
Propulsion:	liquid-propellant rocket
Range:	17,000 m

Warhead:	454 kg
Wingspan:	1.18 m

Standard-ARM (AGM-78) — General Dynamics

Air-launched version of Standard that homes on electromagnetic radiation. More versatile than Shrike.

Length:	4.57 m
Range:	35 natuical miles

Shrike (AGM-45) — Texas Instruments

An anti-radar missile.

Length:	3.048 m
Diameter:	0.2 m
Weight:	117 kg
Propulsion:	solid-propellant rocket motor
Range:	12,000 to 16,000 m
Speed:	Mach 2
Wingspan:	0.914 m

Walleye I and II (AGM-62) — Martin Marietta/Hughes

Glide bomb guided by television.

Length:	I: 3.5 m, II: 4.0 m
Diameter:	0.325 m
Weight:	I: 511 kg, II: 1,090 kg
Range:	I: 16 nautical miles, II: 35 nautical miles
Warhead:	conventional — I: 373 kg, II: 908 kg
Wingspan:	1.16 m

Harpoon (AGM-84)

See under surface-to-surface missiles.

HARM (AGM-88) — Naval Weapons Center, China Lake

HARM (High-Speed Anti-Radiation Missile) is in the final stages of development, with more than 80 missiles built to date. It will be employed by A-7E, A-6E, FA-18, and U.S. Air Force F-4E Wild Weasel aircraft to suppress or destroy ground defenses. Will replace the obsolescent Shrike.

Length:	4.17 m
Diameter:	. . .
Weight:	354 kg
Propulsion:	solid-propellant rocket
Guidance:	homes on electromagnetic radiation
Range:	. . .

TOW (MGM-71) — Hughes

Wire-guided, helicopter- or ground-launched anti-tank weapon that uses optical sight and tube launcher.

Length:	1.12 m
Weight:	21 kg
Propulsion:	solid-propellant rocket
Warhead:	3.6 kg hollow, shaped-charge

◆ air-to-air missiles

Sparrow III (AIM 7E, F) — Raytheon

Length:	3.65 m

WEAPONS AND SYSTEMS (*continued*)

Diameter: 0.20 m
Weight: 204 kg
Propulsion: solid propellant grains
Guidance: semi-active homing
Speed: Mach 2.5
Range: 15,000 m (AIM 7D version), 26,000 m (AIM 7E, F versions)
Warhead: 27 kg, proximity fuse

Sidewinder (AIM 9) – Raytheon

Sidewinder 1A

Length: 2.84 m
Diameter: 0.13 m
Wingspan: 0.61 m
Weight: 75 kg
Propulsion: solid propellant rocket
Guidance: infrared
Speed: Mach 2.5
Range: 6,000 m (3,500 m practical)

Sidewinder 1C

Length: 2.95 m
Weight: 85 kg
Propulsion: solid propellant rocket
Guidance: semi-active homing
Speed: Mach 3
Range: 18,000 m

Phoenix (AIM 54A, C) – Hughes

Length: 3.96 m
Diameter: 0.38 m
Wingspan: 0.914 m
Weight: 380 kg
Propulsion: solid propellant rocket
Range: over 80,000 m

AMRAAM-. . .

AMRAAM (Advanced Medium-Range Air-to-Air Missile) is intended to replace the AIM-7F Sparrow. In development.

B. GUNS

406-mm, Model 1936

Fitted in 1,700-ton triple turrets in *Iowa*-class battleships. Inactive. Requires a crew of 70 men per mount.

Length: 50 calibers
Muzzle velocity: 850 m/second
Rate of fire: 2 rounds/minute/barrel
Maximum range: armor-piercing shell: 36,700 m; high-capacity shell: 38,000 m
Weight of projectile: armor-piercing shell: 1,226 kg; high-capacity shell: 863 kg
Cartridge bags: 6 300-kg
Fire control: Mk-38 director with Mk-13 radar

203-mm, Mk-16, Mod. 0

Automatic weapon fitted in 451-ton triple turrets on *Des Moines*-class cruisers.

Length: 55 calibers
Muzzle velocity: 900 m/second
Arc of elevation: −5° to +41°
Rate of fire: 10 rounds/minute/barrel
Maximum range: armor-piercing shell: 27,500 m; high-capacity shell: 28,670 m
Weight of projectile: armor-piercing shell: 152 kg; high-capacity shell: 113 kg
Fire control: Mk-54 director with Mk-13 radar

203-mm, Mk-71

This model, which has been undergoing tests since the mid-1960s, can fire 75 projectiles in sequence without interference, at a rate of 12 rounds per minute. The evaluation ship was the destroyer *Hull*. The project was canceled on 25-7-78 and the weapon removed in 7-79, but some research is still being pursued in the hope that this highly effective weapon might be reinstated.

127-mm, twin barrel, Mk-12, Mod. 1

Semiautomatic, dual-purpose gun fitted in the Mk-32 series mounts of the *Iowa*-class battleships and *Des Moines*-class cruisers and in the Mk-38 series mounts of the *Gearing*-class destroyers.

Length: 38 calibers
Muzzle velocity: 792 m/sec
Elevation: −15° to +85°
Rate of fire: 18 rounds/minute/barrel with a well-trained crew
Maximum range on a surface target: 16,500 m
Maximum effective range on a ship target: 12,000 to 13,000 m
Maximum range in anti-aircraft fire: 11,400 m
Maximum effective range in anti-aircraft fire: 8,000 m
Weight of projectile: 25 kg
Fire control: Mk-37 director with Mk-25 radar; Mk-56 director in a few ships

127-mm, Mk-24, Mk-30, Mk-37

Single mounting, weighing between 15 and 20.4 tons, in open Mk-24 and Mk-37 series or enclosed Mk-30 series mountings on a few combatants and auxiliaries. Other data as for twin mounting.

127-mm, Mk-42

Single-barrel, dual-purpose gun fitted on ships built in the 1950s and 1960s. Most mounts converted to Mk-42, Mod. 10, configuration.

Length: 45 calibers
Muzzle velocity: 810 m/second
Mount weight: 65.8 tons, Mod. 10: 63.9 tons
Arc of elevation: −5° to +80°
Rate of train: 50°/second
Rate of elevation: 80°/second
Rate of fire: 40 rounds/minute
Weight of projectile: 32 kg
Range: 23,700 m horizontal/14,840 vertical
Fire control: Mk-68 system in most ships
Personnel: 13 men, with 2 in turret

Loading entirely automatic from two ammunition drums in the handling room up to the loading tray by means of a rotating hoist. Each drum contains twenty rounds.

WEAPONS AND SYSTEMS (*continued*)

The rate of fire can be maintained for only one minute, inasmuch as it is necessary to reload the drums.

127-mm, Mk-45

Single-barrel mount fitted on *California*- and *Virginia*-class cruisers, *Spruance*-class destroyers, and *Tarawa*-class amphibious assault ships.

Length: 54 calibers
Muzzle velocity: 810 m/second
Mount weight: 21.7 tons
Arc of elevation: −5° to +65°
Rate of fire: 20 rounds/minute
Range: 23,700 m horizontal/14,840 vertical
Fire control: 1 SPQ-9 search radar, 1 SPQ-60 tracking radar
Personnel: none on mount; 6 in handling room to reload ammunition drums

76.2-mm, Mk-22

Automatic dual-purpose gun in single (Mk-34) or twin (Mk-33) mounts. Mk-27 twin mounts in CA-134 and CA-139

Length: 50 calibers
Mount weight: 15 tons. Mk-33 open mount
Weight of projectile: 3.2 kg
Rate of fire: 45 rounds/minute/barrel
Maximum range: 12,840 m horizontal/8,950 vertical
Fire control: Mk-56 system or none in active ships

76.2-mm, Mk-21

Single-fire, dual-purpose gun on a few auxiliaries and some Coast Guard ships. Mk-26 mount. Being phased out.

Length: 50 calibers
Mount weight: 4.2 tons
Weight of projectile: 3.2 kg
Rate of fire: 20 rounds/minute
Maximum range: 12,840 horizontal/8,950 vertical
Fire control: ring sight only

76-mm, Mk-75

Single-barrel, license-built version of OTO Melara Compact, tested in the frigate *Talbot* and used in PHM and FFG-7 classes.

Length: 62 calibers
Mount weight: 6.2 tons
Weight of projectile: 6.4 kg
Rate of fire: 85 rounds/minute
Maximum range: 19,200 m horizontal/11,900 m vertical
Fire control: Mk-92 radar system
Personnel: 4 below decks

20-mm, Mk-10

Single-barrel, license-built Oerlikon mounting in minesweepers and auxiliaries.

Length: 70 calibers
Mount weight: 318-500 kg
Rate of fire: 450 rounds/minute
Maximum range: 4,390 m horizontal/3,050 m vertical
Fire control: ring sights on mount

20-mm, Mk-16, Mod. 5

Single-barrel Mk-67 or Mk-68 mounting in small combatants, amphibious ships, and auxiliaries.

Length: 80 calibers
Mount weight: . . .
Rate of fire: 800 rounds/minute
Maximum range: 3,000 m horizontal
Fire control: ring sights on mount

Vulcan/Phalanx, Mk-15

"Close-in" system designed to destroy missiles such as Styx and sea-skimmer missiles such as the French Exocet and the Israeli Gabriel. It consists of a multibarrel, M61A1 20-mm gun with a very high rate of fire, which is comounted with two radars, one of which follows the target and the other the projectile burst. A computer furnishes necessary corrections for train and elevation so that the two radar targets coincide, bringing heavy fire to bear on the target. Programmed to be fitted to 239 ships, beginning with the *Enterprise* (CVN-65). A total of 61 mounts requested under FY 80.

Mount weight: 5.4 tons
Rate of fire: 3,000 rounds/minute
Maximum range: 1,486 m horizontal

C. TORPEDOES

◆ submarine torpedoes

Mk 37, Mod. 2

Electric torpedo with a wire-guided plus active-passive guidance system. Used against surface and submarine targets.

Length: 4.1 m
Diameter: 0.485 m
Weight: 767 kg
Speed: 25 knots
Run duration: 20,000 m

Mk 37, Mod. 3

Similar to the Mk-37, Mod. 0, but is not wire-guided.

Length: 3.4 m
Weight: 649 kg

Mk-48, Mod. 1 and Mod. 3

Will replace or supplement the Mk-37, Mod. 2 and Mod. 3, torpedoes. Can be launched from a submarine against a surface target or a submarine. No surface ships are currently equipped to launch Mk-48, although that capability was originally intended. A total of 2,771 Mk-48s has been procured, plus 56 for Australia and 92 for the Netherlands; 144 additional for the U.S. Navy were appropriated under FY 80.

Length: 5.54 m
Diameter: 0.533 m
Weight: 1,633 kg

Can be launched with its own active-passive or acoustic homing system or with a wire-guidance system. High speed (40 knots?) and long run duration (50,000 m). An improvement program, ADCAP (Added Capability) is being instituted, with the first twenty-two conversion kits requested under FY 80.

WEAPONS AND SYSTEMS (*continued*)

◆ surface-launched torpedoes

Mk-46, Mod. 1 and Mod. 2

ASW torpedo using solid fuel (Monergol). Active-passive guidance. Launched from Mk-32 ASW torpedo tubes or as playload for the ASROC ASW missile system.

    Length: 2.59 m
    Diameter: 0.324 m
    Weight: 231 kg

The Mk-46, Mod. 1, is being upgraded to Mod. 5 NEARTIP (Near-Term Improvement Program) status with improved acoustic homing system and countermeasures resistance. Under FY 80, 576 conversion kits were requested, and 1,128 more will be requested under FY 82. The Mk-46, Mod. 4, is the payload for the Captor mine.

ALWT

The ALWT (Advanced Lightweight Torpedo) is being developed as a replacement for the Mk-46 series and will be supplied in surface-launched and air-droppable configurations. It will be roughly the same weight as the Mk-46 and of the same dimensions, but will be deeper-diving (600 m), faster (40 knots), and have better homing and counter-countermeasures capabilities. Will not be operational before the late 1980s.

◆ aircraft torpedoes

Mk-46, Mod. 0

Similar to the surface-launched weapon, but equipped with a retarding parachute, solid vice liquid propellant, and does not have a straight run-out before commencing helical search.

    Weight: 258 kg.

D. MINES

Mk-25

Aircraft-dropped. 907 kg (with 550-kg warhead). 2.13 m long by 571.5-mm diameter.

Mk-52, Mod. 2

Aircraft-dropped. 540 kg. 2.26 m long by 338-mm diameter. Magnetic-influence type.

Mk-55

Aircraft-dropped. 963 kg (with 500-kg warhead). 2.91 m long by 592-mm diameter.

Mk-56

Aircraft-dropped. 933 kg. 3.51 m long by 592-mm diameter.

Mk-57

Submarine-laid. 935 kg. 3.07 long by 533-mm diameter.

Mk-60 Captor (enCAPsulated TORpedo)

Submarine-laid or aircraft-dropped. Uses Mk-46, Mod. 4, acoustic-homing torpedo payload. Primarily ASW in function. 908 kg. 3.66 m long by 324-mm diameter. 44.5 kg warhead. In development since 1961. 260 requested under FY 80 in first major operational buy, with 660 programmed for FY 81. Moored mine, before torpedo launch.

Mk-67 SLMM (Submarine-Launched Mobile Mine)

Converted Mk-37, Mod. 0, torpedo. 754 kg. 4.09 m long by 483-mm diameter. Bottom mine.

IWD (Intermediate Water-Depth)

Formerly PRAM (Propelled Rocket Ascent Mine). Anti-surface and ASW mine for launch by submarines and aircraft. Moored mine. In development.

DST-36 Quickstrike

Aircraft dropped. Converted from 500-lb (227 kg) Mk-80 series standard aircraft bomb. Magnetic. Bottom mine. 87-kg explosive charge.

DST-40 Quickstrike

Aircraft-dropped. Converted from 1,000-lb (454 kg) Mk-80 series standard aircraft bomb. Magnetic. Bottom mine. Minelaying: No surface ships are capable of minelaying. Naval aircraft of the S-3, P-3, A-6, and A-7 types are capable of laying mines, as are some 80 operational Air Force B-52D bombers. Theoretically, any U.S. Navy submarine can lay mines from its torpedo tubes.

E. RADARS

Radars for active ships are:

◆ surface-search and navigation

SPS-10: Primary surface-search set before the introduction of SPS-55.

SPS-53: Navigational set for large ships and for MSOs and auxiliaries.

SPS-55: On *Spruance*-class destroyers and planned for the FFG-7 and others of this class. Will eventually replace the SPS-10.

SPS-65: A low-level, pulse-Doppler, threat-detection set that uses the same antenna as SPS-10 or SPS-58.

BPS-5, 11, 14, 15: Submarine search, navigational, and fire-control radars. Mounted on telescoping masts.

◆ air-search

LN-66: A small commercial navigational radar carried on large ships.

SPS-6: Being replaced.

SPS-12: On AVT-16, CA-139, and several amphibious warfare ships. Obsolescent.

SPS-29: On some of the older DDGs and DDs. Same antenna as SPS-37 and SPS-43A.

SPS-37: On CGN-25, some CVs, CGs, and DDGs. **SPS-37A** uses long SPS-43A antenna.

SPS-40: The most widely used air-search radar. Range against medium bombers: 150-180 miles. Earlier "A" models being modernized to **SPS-40D.** B band.

SPS-43A: Mounted in most aircraft carriers.

SPS-49: New type of search radar for the FFG-7 class and others. Will eventually replace SPS-37 in all ships so fitted.

SPS-58: Combined air-surface search radar, comounted with **SPS-65** low-level air search. Uses modified SPS-10 antenna.

◆ height-finding

SPS-39: Mod. A uses same antenna as SPS-52. In some DDGs. E band.

WEAPONS AND SYSTEMS (*continued*)

SPS-48A: Mounted on CG classes.

SPS-48B, C: Electronic frequency scanning in elevation.

SPS-52A: Mounted on some DDGs.

SPS-52B: Electronic frequency scanning in elevation.

SPY-1: Aegis system. Obtaining a directional effect by dipole radiation to secure an electronic sweep, it has four fixed aerials that provide instant 360° coverage. Long-range air-search, target-tracking, and missile-guidance.

◆ fire-control

Mk-13: Ranging set for Mk-38 director on *Iowa*-class battleships and on Mk-34 director on CA-134 and CA-139.

Mk-25: Mounted on Mk-37 GFCS directors on CA, old DD.

Mk-35: Mounted on Mk-56 GFCS director for 127-mm and 76.2-mm guns. On older FFGs and FFs. Removed from auxiliaries.

Mk-91: Technically, the fire-control *system* for the Sea Sparrow SAM system, used with the Mk-29 lightweight launcher. Either one or two radar directors per launcher.

Mk-92/94: U.S. Navy adaptation of Dutch H.S.A. (Hollandse Signaal Apparaten) WM-20 series track-while-scan gun/missile fire-control system. Used in FFG-7, PHM-1, and the Coast Guard's new WMEC classes. Antennas mounted in egg-shaped radome.

Mk-115: Technically the fire-control *system* for Sea Sparrow when launched from the Mk-25 heavy launcher. Older than Mk-91 and being phased out.

SPQ-9: Special surface-search and weapons-control for use with Mk-86 GFCS. Antenna mounted in spherical radome.

SPG-50: On 76.2-mm gun mount on PG; used with later Mk-63 GFCS. Being phased out. Earlier version, Mk-34/SPG-34, entirely phased out.

SPG-51B, C, D: Standard MR illuminator-tracker; used with Mk-74 missile fire-control system.

SPG-52: Mounted on twin 76.2-mm gun mounts in LPH-2 class only; used with Mk-70 GFCS.

SPG-53: Mounted on Mk-68 GFCS director on CG, DDG, and DD with 127-mm Mk-42 guns.

SPG-55A, B: Standard ER illuminator-tracker; used with Mk-76 missile fire-control system.

SPG-60: Standard MR illuminator-tracker with Mk-74 missile fire-control system in later CGN classes; also illuminates for guns in conjunction with Mk-86 GFCS. STIR version, used on FFG-7 class, is modified for use with Mk-92, Mod. 2, missile/gun control system.

SPG-62: Standard SM-2 illuminator; used with Aegis system, in CG-47 class. Slaved to SPY-1 radar.

◆ carrier-controlled approach systems

SPN-6: Formerly installed on aircraft carriers but now limited to AVT-16 and some LPH. Antennas in large radomes.

SPN-10: Aircraft landing aid, incorporating a radar set to determine aircraft position relative to the carrier. Antennas are two small conical dishes. Being replaced by SPN-42, which is less bulky. Other carrier aircraft landing aid/radar systems include SPN-41, SPN-43, and SPN-44.

F. SONARS

◆ on surface ships

SQQ-23: PAIR (Performance and Integration Refit). Modified SQS-23 using two transducer domes (except in CGN-9 and CG-16 classes, one dome); also in DDG-2, DDG-37 classes.

SQR-17: Passive classification device for processing data transmitted to CG-26, DD-963, FF-1052, and FFG-7 class ships by LAMPS helicopters from SSQ-53 DIFAR sonobuoys.

SQR-18: TACTAS (Tactical Towed Acoustic Sensor). For use on FF-1052 class equipped with SQS-35 VDS; array attaches to VDS towed body.

SQR-19: Improved TACTAS for use on CA-47, DD-963, FFG-7, and FF-1037 classes; deployed through port in stern on most.

SQS-23: Bow- or hull-mounted, low-frequency, active-passive. In CV-66, CGN-25, some CG, older DDG, DD-931, and DD-710 classes.

SQS-26: Bow-mounted, low-frequency set, in various versions. In older CGN, CG-26, FFG-1, FF-1037, FF-1040, FF-1052, FF-1098 classes.

SQS-35: Independent, variable-depth, towed, active-passive. In some DD-931 class, all FF-1052 class.

SQS-53: SQS-26 with digital computer interface, for use with Mk-116 UWFCS (Underwater Fire Control System) on DD-963, DDG-993, CG-47 classes.

SQS-56: Raytheon 1160B commercial active-passive, hull-mounted, medium-frequency set; used on FFG-7 class.

SQQ-14: High-frequency, minehunting, and classification set in housing transducer array on MSOs.

◆ on submarines

BQG-4: PUFFS (Passive Underwater Fire Control). Three-fin arrays, on SSN-597, SS-574, SS-563 classes.

BQQ-2: Active-passive system on SSN-594 class, SSN-597, SSN-637 class, SSN-671, SSN-685. Incorporates BQR-7 conformed hydrophone array and BQS-6 spherical hydrophone array. Being upgraded to BQQ-5 in most ships.

BQQ-5: Active-passive system on the SSN-688 class; being backfitted in SSN-594 and SSN-637 classes. Incorporates BQS-11, 12, or 13 spherical bow hydrophone array.

BQQ-6: Passive-only version of the BQQ-5 system, for SSBN-627 class.

WEAPONS AND SYSTEMS (*continued*)

BQR-15: Towed, passive array for SSBN-608, SSBN-616 classes.

BQR-19: Active, short-range, navigational set for SSBNs.

BQR-21: DIMUS (Digital Multi-Beam Steering). Passive array for SSBNs.

BQS-18, 11, 20: Under-ice and mine-avoidance, high-frequency set, mostly on later SSNs.

BQS-15: Under-ice set tailored to the requirements of the SSN-688 class.

G. PROCESSING OF TACTICAL DATA

The system now in use is the NTDS (Naval Tactical Data System). Thanks to its digital calculators (AN/UYK 20 and AN/UYK 7), it instantaneously gives an overall picture of a tactical situation—air, surface, and underwater—and enables the commander to employ the means necessary to oppose the enemy. Excellent automatic data transmission systems (Links-11 and Links-14) permit the exchange of tactical information with similarly equipped ships and aircraft carrying the ATDS (P-3C Orion and S-3A Viking) and amphibious landing forces equipped with NTDS.

By mid-1978, some 427 ships were equipped to receive SATCOMM (Satellite Communications) messages, while 259 could send ultrahigh-frequency messages via satellite and 6 (with another 25 programmed) could send superhigh-frequency messages.

NUCLEAR-POWERED AIRCRAFT CARRIERS

◆ **1 improved Nimitz class** Bldr: Newport News SB & DD

	Laid down	L	In serv.
CVN 71 N . . .	. . .	. . .	1988-89

D: 96,836 tons (fl) **S:** 30+ kts
Dim: 332.84(317.0 pp) × 40.85 (flight deck: 78.33) × 11.12
Man: 5,529 men
Electric: 64,000 kw + 8,000 kw emergency power from 4 diesel sets
A: 3/Mk-29 launchers (VIII × 3) for Sea Sparrow—4/Vulcan Phalanx 20-mm Gatling AA—90+ aircraft, including F-14, F/A-18, EA-6B, A-6E, A-7E, E-2C, 10/S-3A, and 6/SH-3D
Electron Equipt: Radars: 1/SPS-53, 1/SPS-55, 1/SPS-48C, 1/SPS-49, 1/SPS-65, 1/SPN-41, 1/SPN-35A, 1/SPN-44, 6/Mk-91
  ECM: WLR-8, SLQ-17, Super RBOC chaff—TACAN
M: 2 A4W/A1G pressurized-water reactors, 4 sets GT; 4 props; 280,000 hp

REMARKS: Appropriate for under FY 80. This badly needed ship was repeatedly delayed in favor of conventionally powered designs of inferior capabilities. Won out over both an administration-sponsored 62,427-ton (fl) paper CVV design and a compromise 82,561-ton repeat *John F. Kennedy* (CV-67) design. Will cost in excess of $2.1 billion (1980 dollars), exclusive of aircraft.

The hangar will have 7.6 m clear height. The angled deck will be 237.7 m long and will be equipped with four arrester wires and a barrier, as well as four Mk-13, Mod. 1, catapults (94.5 m long), and four elevators. An aviation payload of some 14,909 tons will be carried, and the aviation ordnance magazines will hold 1,954 tons. Aviation fuel capacity will be more than 9,000 tons. Kevlar armor will be fitted over vital spaces.

Other data under the *Nimitz* class will generally apply.

◆ **3 Nimitz class** Bldr: Newport News SB & DD

	Laid down	L	In serv.
CVN 68 NIMITZ	22-6-68	13-5-72	3-5-75
CVN 69 DWIGHT D. EISENHOWER	15-8-70	11-10-75	18-10-77
CVN 70 CARL VINSON	11-10-75	11-79	1982

Authorized: CVN-68 in FY 67, CVN-69 in FY 71, CVN-70 in FY 74.

D: 81,600 tons (96,351 fl) **S:** 30+ kts
Dim: 327.0 (over catapult bridle retrieval horns: 332.8, pp: 317.0) × 40.85 (flight deck: 77.11, max.: 89.4) × 11.3
Man: 6,286 men (569 officers), including aviation personnel (2,626 with 304 officers)
A: 90-100 airplanes and helicopters—3/Mk-25 launchers (VIII × 3) for Sea Sparrow
Electron Equipt: Radars: 1/SPS-10F, 1/SPS-43A, 1/SPS-48B, 1/SPN-41 (CVN-69 only), 2/SPN-42, 1/SPN-43A, 1/SPN-44
  ECM: WLR-8, SLQ-17
  NTDS—1/URN-20 TACAN
Electric: 64,000 kw + 8,000 kw emergency power from 4 diesel sets
M: 2 A4W/A1G pressurized-water reactors, 4 sets GT; 4 props; 280,000 hp

REMARKS: The *Nimitz* cost $685,800,000 to build, while her air wing and equipment cost $710,600,000. The offensive potential of these ships is remarkable; they carry 90% more aviation fuel and 50% more ammunition (3,000 tons) than the *Forrestal* class. They have an ASCAC (Antisubmarine Classification and Analysis Center), which permits instant sharing of target data between the carrier, its ASW aircraft, and escorting ships.

Armament: The *Carl Vinson* will be completed with three Mk-29 launchers (VIII × 3) for Sea Sparrow, six Mk-91 directors for the missile, and four Vulcan/Phalanx Gatling AA guns. The others are to be similarly refitted, but will get only three Vulcan/Phalanx.

Armor: Decks and hull are of extra-strong, high-tensile steel that can limit the impact of semi-armor-piercing bombs. Apart from the longitudinal bulkheads, there are twenty-three watertight transverse bulkheads (more than 2,000 compartments) and ten firewall bulkheads. Foam devices for fire-fighting are very well developed, and pumping equipment is excellent, a 1.5°-list being correctable in 20 minutes. Thirty damage-control teams are available at all times. *Nimitz*-class ships can withstand three times the severe pounding taken by the *Essex*-class aircraft carriers in 1944-45, and they can take impacts and shock waves in the same proportion. They are to be equipped with Kevlar armor over vital spaces during refits scheduled for 1982, 1987, and 1988 (in order of construction).

Machinery: The cores of these ships are expected to last 13 years in normal usage, for a cruising distance of 800,000 to 1,000,000 miles. The evaporators can produce 1,520 tons of fresh water per day.

Aircraft-handling installations: There are four side elevators: two forward, one aft of the island to starboard, and one on the stern to port. There are also four Mk-C13, Mod. 1, steam catapults, 94.5 m long. The *Dwight D. Eisenhower* has only the forward starboard bridle retrieval horn, because most aircraft in service do not require the bridle for launching. The 15,134 m³ of aviation magazine space can hold 1,954 tons of aviation ordnance, and the total aviation-associated payload is on the order of 15,000 tons. The hangar is 7.8 meters high and can accommodate only 35-40 per cent of the aircraft aboard. The angled part of the flight deck is 237.7 meters long and has four arrester wires and a barrier to halt aircraft. The aircraft complement normally includes ten S-3A ASW aircraft and six SH-3D ASW helicopters. Other aircraft are a mix of F-14 interceptors, C-2C early-warning, A-7E day and A-6E all-weather attack, and EA-6B electronics aircraft. Sufficient aviation fuel for 16 days' operations is carried.

NUCLEAR-POWERED AIRCRAFT CARRIERS (*continued*)

Dwight D. Eisenhower   1977

Dwight D. Eisenhower   1977

Nimitz   1977

NUCLEAR-POWERED AIRCRAFT CARRIERS (*continued*)

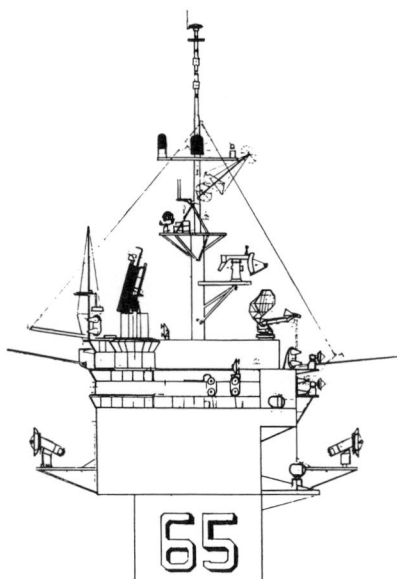

Enterprise—reconfigured island
LT P. Clayton, 1979

Enterprise   G. Arra, 1978

◆ **1 Enterprise class (SCB 160 type)**

	Bldr	Laid down	L	In serv.
CVN 65 ENTERPRISE	Newport News SB & DD	4-2-58	24-9-60	25-11-61

Authorized: FY 58

D: 75,700 tons (91,000 fl)   **S:** 33 kts
Dim: 335.75 (over catapult bridle horn: 342.3, wl: 317.0) × 40.54 (flight deck: 78.4) × 11.3

Enterprise   1976

Enterprise   1976

Man: 451 officers, 5,237 men (including 304/2,323 aviation personnel)
A: 84–90 airplanes and helicopters–3/Mk-29 launchers (VIII × 3) for Sea Sparrow
3/Vulcan Phalanx 20-mm Gatling guns
Electron Equipt: Radars: 1/SPS-10F (with SPS-65), 1/SPS-48C, 1/SPS-49, 1/SPN-41, 1/SPN-35A, 1/SPN-44, 3/Mk-91
ECM: WLR-8, SLQ-17A(V)2, chaff–1/URN-20 TACAN–NTDS
Electric: 40,000 kw + 8,000 kw emergency
M: 8 Westinghouse A2W reactors, supplying 32 Foster-Wheeler heat exchangers;
4 sets Westinghouse GT; 4 props; 280,000 hp

REMARKS: Began a two-year overhaul at Puget Sound NSY in 1-79, during which the radar and other electronics suits will be extensively renovated. The SPS-32 and SPS-33 "billboard" radar arrays are to be removed, as is the "beehive" dome atop the blockhouse superstructure. A new mast, resembling that on the *Nimitz*, will be installed atop the superstructure, and SPS-48C will be atop a new lattice mast abaft the island. Equipment and armament listed above is for the post-modernization configuration. There are four Mk-C13 steam catapults and four elevators, one on the port side of the angled deck, three to starboard, two of which are forward of and one abaft the island. Elevators are steel and alloy and weigh 105 tons; 26 m long, 16 m wide, lift 45 tons. The hangar is 7.62 m high and the flight deck is more than 20,000 m². Carries half again as much aviation fuel as the *Forrestal* class, which permits 12 days of intensive aerial operations without replenishment. Carries fuel oil to replenish other ships. Like the *Nimitz*, she has ASCAC. Since 1976 has carried two British SCOT satellite-communications antenna radomes on island.

CONVENTIONAL AIRCRAFT CARRIERS

◆ 1 John F. Kennedy class (SCB 127C type)   Bldr: Newport News SB & DD

	Laid down	L	In serv.
CV 67 John F. Kennedy	22-10-64	27-5-67	7-9-68

Authorized: FY 63

John F. Kennedy   1975

John F. Kennedy   1975

D: 61,000 tons (82,561 fl)   **S:** 32 kts
Dim: 320.7 (301.8 wl) × 39.32 (flight deck: 76.9, max.: 81.53) × 11.13
Man: 460 officer, 4,917 men (including aviation personnel)
A: 3/Mk-25 launchers (VIII × 3) for Sea Sparrow—80-90 aircraft
Electron Equipt: Radars: 1/SPS-10, 1/SPS-43A, 1/SPS-48C, 1/SPS-58, 1/SPN-35,
2/SPN-42, 3/Mk-115
ECM: WLR-8, SLQ-17, chaff—1/URN-20 TACAN—NTDS
M: 4 sets GE GT; 4 props; 280,000 hp
Boilers: 8 Foster-Wheeler, 83.4 kg/cm² pressure

REMARKS: Four side elevators, three to starboard (two forward of and one abaft the
island) and one on the port quarter. Completely automatic landing system, permitting
all-weather operation. Four arrester wires and a barrier on the 227-m angled flight
deck. Three 90-m Mk-C13 and one 94.5-m Mk-C13-1 catapults. Has PLAT, which fa-

John F. Kennedy   G. Arra

cilitates the control of launching and recovery operations. Stack angled to starboard.
The 11,808-m² aviation-ordnance magazine can accommodate 1,250 tons of amuni-
tions. Carries 5,919 tons of aviation fuel. The Mk-25 Sea Sparrow launchers are to be
replaced by Mk-29 launchers with six Mk-91 fire-control systems, and three 20-mm
Vulcan Phalanx Gatling AA are to be added. Equipped to carry SQS-23 sonar in bow
dome but it was not installed.

◆ 3 Kitty Hawk class (SCB 127A and SCB 127B types)

	Bldr	Laid down	L	In serv.
CV 63 Kitty Hawk	New York SB	27-12-56	21-5-60	29-4-61
CV 64 Constellation	Brooklyn NSY	14-9-57	8-10-60	27-10-61
CV 66 America	Newport News SB	9-1-61	1-2-64	23-1-65

Authorized: CV-63 in FY 56, CV-64 in FY 57, CV-66 in FY 61

D: 60,100 tons (80,300 fl, CV-66: 81,700)   **S:** 33 kts
Dim: 318.8 (CV-66: 319.25) (301.76 pp) × 39.62 (flight deck: 76.81) × 11.2 (CV-66: 11.3)
Man: approx. 5,400: 137 officers, 2,765 men + air group: 290 officers, 2,200 men
Range: 4,000/30, 8,000/20   **Fuel:** 7,800 tons
A: 85-90 aircraft—2 or 3/Mk-29 launchers (VIII × 2 or 3) for Sea Sparrow, see
Remarks
Electron Equipt: Radars: 1/SPS-10, 1/SPS-58, 1/SPS-43A, 1/SPS-48C, 1/SPN-35,
2/SPN-42, 4 or 6/Mk-91, see Remarks
ECM: WLR-8, SLQ-17, chaff—1/URN-20 TACAN—NTDS
M: 4 sets Westinghouse GT; 4 props; 280,000 hp

REMARKS: These ships are a great improvement over the *Forrestal* class, on which they
are based, and have one significant difference: three elevators on the starboard side,
two forward of and one abaft the island, and one to port, abaft the angled flight deck.
Aircraft can be landed and catapulted simultaneously, a difficult operation on the
earlier ships. Four Mk-C13 steam catapults, except on CV-66, on which one is of the
longer Mk-C13-1 type. Carry 5,882 tons of aviation fuel. CV-63 and CV-64 will receive

CONVENTIONAL AIRCRAFT CARRIERS (*continued*)

Kitty Hawk—with Mk-29 Sea Sparrow launchers PH1 A. Legare, USN, 1978

Constellation 1977

three 20-mm Vulcan-Phalanx. As of mid-1979, CV-66 retained two Mk-10 twin launchers for Standard SM-1 ER missiles and two SPQ-55B radar directors; she also had SPS-52B on her lattice mast instead of SPS-48C. She will replace her Standard systems with three Mk-29 Sea Sparrow systems during her next refit, at which time her SPS-52 will be replaced by SPS-48C. She was the first to have a special integrated CIC and airborne ASW control center (ASCAC). All will have Mk-36 Super RBOC chaff rocket systems (four launchers).

◆ **4 Forrestal class (CV-59: SCB 80 type, CV-60 to CV-62: SCB 80M type)**

	Bldr	Laid down	L	In serv.
CV 59 FORRESTAL	Newport News SB & DD	14-7-52	11-12-54	1-10-55
CV 60 SARATOGA	Brooklyn NSY	16-12-52	8-10-55	14-4-56
CV 61 RANGER	Newport News SB & DD	2-8-54	29-9-54	10-8-57
CV 62 INDEPENDENCE	Brooklyn, NSY	1-7-55	6-6-58	10-1-59

Authorized: CV-59 in FY 52, CV-60 in FY 53, CV-61 in FY 54, CV-62 in FY 55

Independence 1979

D: CV-59: 59,600 tons (79,250 fl); CV-60, CV-61: 60,000 tons (80,250 fl) CV-62: 60,000 tons (79,650 fl)

Dim: CV-59: 331.0; CV-60: 324; CV-61: 326.4; CV-62: 326.1 (319.13 flight deck, 301.8 pp) × 39.47 (CV-59, CV-60: 78.9; CV-61, CV-62: 77.7 flight deck) × 11.2

S: 33 kts **Range:** 4,000/30, 8,000/20 **Fuel:** 7,800 tons

Man: approx. 4,940: 145 officers, 2,645 enlisted + air group: 290 officers, 3,100 enlisted

A: 85-90 planes and helicopters—2/Mk-25 launchers (VIII × 2) for Sea Sparrow (CV-61, CV-62: 2/Mk-29 launchers)

Electron Equipt: Radars: 1/LN-66, 1/SPS-10, 1/SPS-43A, 1/SPS-48C, 1/SPS-58, 1/SPN-35, 2/SPN-42, 2/Mk-115 (CV-61, CV-62: 4/Mk-91)
ECM: WLR-8, SLQ-17, chaff—1/URN-20 TACAN—NTDS

Boilers: 8 Babcock & Wilcox; CV-59: 41.7 kg/cm² pressure, others: 83.4 kg/cm²; superheat 520° C

M: 4 sets GE or Westinghouse GT; 4 props; CV-59: 260,000 hp, others: 280,000

REMARKS: Hangar is 7.6 m high and 234-240 m long. The landing system permits safe landing on the darkest of nights. Four side elevators (15.95 × 18.9). Deck angled at 8°. Armored flight deck. Four-cable arresting gear. CV-59 and CV-60 have two Mk-C7 (75 m) and two Mk-C11 (65 m) steam catapults; the others have four Mk-C7. Carry 5,880 tons of aviation fuel. CV-59 has three rudders and four propellers, the two outboard being five-bladed, the two inboard, four-bladed. Deck protection and internal

CONVENTIONAL AIRCRAFT CARRIERS (continued)

Forrestal   S. Terzibaschitsch, 1976

Independence—Nimitz across pier   C. Dragonette, 1979

Saratoga   PH1 Deverman, USN, 1975

Ranger   1976

compartmentation are extensive (1,200 watertight compartments). Two longitudinal bulkheads are fitted from keel to waterline from stem to stern; there are transverse bulkheads about every 10 meters.

CV-59 will be the first to receive a major SLEP modernization, beginning in FY 81. The others will follow in order of their construction, the yard periods lasting about two years and adding fifteen years to their service lives. All will ultimately be armed with three Mk-29 Sea Sparrow launchers, each with two Mk-91 directors, three MK-15 Vulcan/Phalanx Gatling guns, and will carry SPS-43C and SPS-49 radars. All catapults will be replaced with longer and more powerful Mk-C13s. The ships will get Kevlar armor, improved data systems, and more habitability. All originally carried eight 127-mm/54, Mk-42 guns. CV-61 relinquished her last two guns in 1977, later than her sisters did, and retains her forward gun sponsons.

◆ **2 Midway class**   Bldr: Newport News SB & DD

		Laid down	L	In serv.
CV 41	MIDWAY	27-10-43	20-3-45	10-9-45
CV 43	CORAL SEA	10-7-44	2-4-46	1-10-47

Coral Sea—guns now removed   PH1 D. Hanson, USN, 1977

CONVENTIONAL AIRCRAFT CARRIERS (*continued*)

D: CV-41: 51,000 tons (64,100 fl) − CV-43: 52,500 tons (63,800 fl) **S:** 33 kts

Dim: 298.38 (293.91 pp) × 41.45 (flight deck: 72.54) × 10.9

Man: CV-41: 338 officers, 4,253 enlisted men (including 222/1,724 aviation personnel)

CV-43: 317 officers, 4,058 enlisted men (including 201/2,063 aviation personnel)

A: up to 72 aircraft − CV-41 only: 3/Mk-29 launchers (VIII × 3) for Sea Sparrow − 2/20-mm Vulcan-Phalanx AA

Electron Equipt: Radars: CV-41: 1/LN-66, 1/SPS-10F or SPS-65, 1/SPS-43C, 1/SPS-49, 1/SPN-35A, 1/SPN-41, 1/SPN-44, 6/Mk-91

CV-43: 1/LN-66, 1/SPS-10, 1/SPS-43C, 1/SPS-30, 1/SPN-10

ECM: WLR-8, SLQ-17 − 1/URN-20 TACAN − NTDS

Boilers: 12 Babcock & Wilcox, 41.7 kg/cm² pressure − superheat 454°C

M: 4 sets Westinghouse GT; 4 props; 212,000 hp

Midway   G. Arra, 1979

REMARKS: CV-43 does not have a regularly assigned air group and is maintained in an operationally contingent status, occasionally being used to train Naval Reserve and student aviators; she is expected to be stricken in 1985 and replaced in that role by CV-41. Despite her age, CV-41 is in superb condition and is one of the most effective U.S. carriers. Sister *Franklin D. Roosevelt* (CV-42) was stricken on 1-10-72. Machinery and ships' bottoms very similar to the *Iowa*-class battleships. Both have now had the last of their Mk-39 127-mm DP guns removed; CV-43 now has no defensive armament.

Two side elevators to starboard, one forward of and one abaft the island; one side elevator to port aft of the angled flight deck. The elevator platforms are of alloy construction. CV-41 has a considerably larger flight deck than does CV-43. During her deployment to the Indian Ocean in 11-79, CV-41 carried only 52 aircraft. CV-41 has two Mk-C13 steam catapults (both forward) and three arrester wires on the angled flight deck. CV-43 retains three C-11-1 catapults.

Refits: From 1954 to 1963, the ships underwent several overhauls: angled flight deck installed; flight deck lengthened; hydraulic catapults replaced with steam ones; side

armor removed and "bulges" added. reinforced arresting gear and barriers installed; centerline elevators replaced with side ones; aviation gasoline capacity increased; new jet-fuel bunkers installed. In October 1967 CV-41 began another major overhaul and returned to service in 1-70. Her angled flight deck was extended to port; her three elevators were enlarged; her forward port elevator was moved aft; her catapults were replaced by more powerful ones; and all her electronic equipment was replaced. She can launch the all-weather F-14 Tomcat interceptor. In 1979, during an overhaul at Yokosuka, CV-41's radar suit was updated. CV-43 was overhauled 11-78 to 10-79 at Puget Sound NSY, where her catapults were brought up to Mk-C13 capability.

RESERVE AIRCRAFT CARRIERS

◆ **6 Essex class**

	Bldr	Laid down	L	In serv.
CVS 11 INTREPID	Newport News SB	1-21-41	26-4-43	16-8-43
CVS 12 HORNET	Newport News SB	3-8-42	29-8-43	29-11-43
CVS 20 BENNINGTON	New York NSY	15-12-42	26-2-44	6-8-44
CVA 31 BON HOMME RICHARD	New York NSY	1-2-43	29-4-44	26-11-44
CV 34 ORISKANY	New York NSY	1-5-44	13-10-45	25-9-50
CVS 38 SHANGRI-LA	Norfolk NSY	15-1-43	24-2-44	15-9-44

Shangri-La   1966

D: approx. 33,000 tons (40,600 to 41,900 fl)   **S:** 30+ kts

Dim: 274.01 (CVS-38: 270.97) (249.94 wl) × 31.39 (CV-34: 32.46) (flight deck: approx. 58.5 × 9.45)

Man: None   **Range:** 18,000/12   **Fuel:** 6,750 tons

A: CV/CVA: 75 aircraft; CVS: 40 to 45 aircraft; − 4/127-mm DP (I × 4), except CV-34: 2/127-mm DP (I × 2)

Electron Equipt: Radars: 1/SPS-10, 1/SPS-30, 1/SPS-43 (CVS-11, CV-34: SPS-37), 1/SPN-10, 1/SPN-43, 1-2/Mk-25, 0-4 Mk-35

Sonars: CVS only; SQS-23 (bow-mounted) − TACAN

Boilers: 8 Babcock & Wilcox, 41.7 kg/cm² pressure − superheat 454°C

M: Westinghouse GT; 4 props; 150,000 hp

RESERVE AIRCRAFT CARRIERS (*continued*)

Bennington   1967

Oriskany   1969

REMARKS: CVS-11, CVA-31, CV-34, and CVS-38 are sometimes referred to as *Hancock*-class carriers. CV-34, the only unit with sufficiently modern equipment be to worth reactivating, was placed in reserve on 30-9-76; she carries NTDS. The *Lexington* (formerly CVT-16) was redesignated AVT-16 on 1-7-78 and is used for training in deck landing. She is the only operational unit of the class. CVS-11 was decommissioned on 15-3-74, CVS-12 on 15-1-70, CVS-20 on 30-6-69, CVA-31 on 2-7-71, and CVS-38 on 30-7-71. CVS-12 and CVS-20 have retained their Mk-H8 hydraulic catapults; the others have steam catapults. All have three elevators: one on the centerline between the catapults, one at the forward end of the angled deck, and one (vertically stowable) to starboard, abaft the island. Four arrester wires. CV-34 has two Mk-37 gun directors. The others have one Mk-37 and two or three Mk-56 directors.

NAVAL AND MARINE CORPS AVIATION

Aviation is an integral part of the U.S. Navy and Marine Corps. The approximately 5,300 aircraft (FY 1980) assigned to it include:
  1,053 attack planes
   713 fighters
   144 ship-based ASW planes
   381 patrol aircraft
  1,069 helicopters
   799 training aircraft

S-3A Viking ASW aircraft   1975

Air squadrons are designated by an alphanumerical system, the letter prefixes for the principal squadron types being:

Navy:

HC	Helicopter Combat Support (UH-46)
HM	Helicopter Mine Countermeasures (RH-533)
HS	Helicopter Antisubmarine (SH-3)
HSL	Light Helicopter Antisubmarine (SH-2)
HT	Helicopter Training (TH-57A, UH-1E, TH-1L)
VA	Attack (A-4, A-6, A-7)
VAQ	Tactical Electronic Warfare (EA-6B)
VAW	Carrier Airborne Early Warning (E-2C)
VC	Fleet Composite (utility aircraft)
VF	Fighter (F-4, F-14, F-18)
VFP	Light Photographic (RF-8G)
VP	Patrol (P-3)
VQ	Fleet Air Reconnaissance (EP-3, EA-3B), also: Communications Support (EC-130)
VR	Fleet Logistics Support (C-9, C-117D, C-118D, C-130, etc.)
VRC	Fleet Logistics Support-COD (Carrier on-board Delivery) (C-1A, C-2A)
VRF	Aircraft Ferry
VS	Air Antisubmarine (S-3A)
VT	Training (TA-4J, T-28, T-2C, T-39D, T-44A)
VX	Air Test and Evaluation
VXE	Antarctic Development (LC-130F, UH-1)
VXN	Oceanographic Development (RP-3A/D)

Marine Corps:

HMA	Marine Attack Helicopter (AH-1)
HMH	Marine Heavy Helicopter (CH-53)

NAVAL AND MARINE CORPS AVIATION (*continued*)

HML   Marine Light Helicopter (UH-1N)
HMM   Marine Medium Helicopter (CH-46)
VMA   Marine Attack (A-4M, A-6E, AV-8A)
VMAQ   Marine Electronic Warfare (EA-6B)
VMFA   Marine Fighter-Attack (F-4)
VMFP   Marine Photo Reconnaissance (RF-4B)
VMGR   Marine Refueler-Transport (KC-130F)
VMO   Marine Observation (OV-10A/D)

Letters may be placed in front of the letter that indicates an aircraft's mission, as follows:

G   Permanently grounded   X   Experimental
J   Temporary special test   Y   Prototype
N   Permanent special test   Z   Planning

Naval Aviation

The Navy has the following squadrons:

   60 attack and fighter
    1 reconnaissance
    5 helicopter
   23 ASW
   24 patrol
   41 various

The combination of all the aircraft on board an aircraft carrier is called a Carrier Air Wing (CAW), whose composition varies according to the carrier's mission. There are three basic types of air wing: one to project power or support landing operations; one to control the sea, with emphasis on antisubmarine warfare and the protection of ships; and one to perform the two previously mentioned missions at the same time. A typical wing would consist of: 24 all-weather fighters, 34-36 attack planes, 10 ASW aircraft, 6 ASW helicopters, 3 reconnaissance aircraft, 8 electronics-warfare aircraft, and 2 utility aircraft (COD). This combination would be modified according to mission.

Currently, twelve carrier air wings (CVW), twenty-four patrol squadrons (PatRon) and three Marine Corps air wings (MAW) are active, plus others for training and support and in reserve. Aircraft production of about 300 per year is mandatory to sustain the size of the current force, but recent and projected requests for procurement of aircraft have been:

	FY 78	FY 79	FY 80	FY 81
A-6E	12	12	--	--
EA-6B	6	6	6	--
A-7E	12	12	--	--
F-14A	44	36	24	24
F/A-18	--	9	15	36
CH-53E	--	14	15	14
AH-1J/T	8	--	--	--
P-3C	14	12	12	8
E-2C	6	6	6	6
C-9B	--	1	--	--
UC-12B	22	22	22	--
T-34C	13	--	--	--
T-44A	23	--	--	--
EC-130Q	--	1	3	3
Total	160	131	103	91

Marine Corps Aviation

The Marines operate a considerable air force. Their aircraft are intended to operate principally from amphibious-warfare ships, but their squadrons of attack, reconnaissance, and electronic-warfare aircraft frequently operate from carriers as well. The principal air complement is:

12 Fighter-Attack Squadrons with 12/F-4 Phantoms each
 5 Attack Squadrons with 16/A-6E Intruders each
 5 Attack Squadrons with 16/A-4M Skyhawks each
 3 Attack Squadrons with 20/AV-8A Harrier each
 3 Attack Helicopter Squadrons with 24/AH-1 Sea Cobra each
 6 Heavy Helicopter Squadrons with 21 CH-53D Sea Stallion each
 9 Medium Helicopter Squadrons with 18/CH-46D/F Sea Knight each
 3 Light Helicopter Squadrons with 24/UH-1N Iroquois (Huey) each

Aircraft Designations

Besides the name given to an aircraft—Phantom, Intruder, Orion, etc.—each type is designated by a group of letters and figures divided by a hyphen and made up in the following manner:

1. The letter immediately preceding the hyphen indicates the principal mission:

A — attack   P — patrol
B — bomber   S — antisubmarine
C — cargo/transport   T — training
E — airborne early warning   U — utility
F — fighter   V — VTOL/STOL, vertical or short
K — tanker, inflight refueling   takeoff and landing
O — observation   X — research

2. The figure that comes immediately after the hyphen is the design sequence number. When a letter follows this figure, its position in the alphabet indicates that the aircraft is the first, second, third, etc. modification to the original design.

Example: A-4E = an attack aircraft, the fourth attack plane design, the fifth modification

3. When an aircraft is assigned to duty that is not its principal mission, a second letter precedes the letter of that mission (see para. 1 above):

A — attack   M — missile carrier or mine-countermeasures
C — cargo/transport   Q — drone aircraft
D — direction or control of   R — reconnaissance
     drones, aircraft, or missiles   S — antisubmarine
E — special electronic installation   T — trainer
H — search and rescue   U — utility, general service
K — tanker, inflight refueling   V — staff
L — cold weather; for arctic regions   W — weather, meteorology

F-18A Hornet all-weather fighter   McDonnell-Douglas, 1978

NAVAL AND MARINE CORPS AVIATION (*continued*)

F-14A Tomcat, all-weather fighter   PHCS(A) R. Lawson, 1974

F-4B Phantom all-weather fighter

A-6E Intruder attack aircraft   1972

AV-8A Harrier attack aircraft (Marine Corps)   1971

A-4E Skyhawk attack aircraft   1974

RF-4B Phantom, reconnaissance-configured

A-7A Corsair attack aircraft   1968

NAVAL AND MARINE CORPS AVIATION (*continued*)

RF-8G Crusader reconnaissance aircraft

P-3B Orion patrol aircraft   1975

C-1A Trader COD aircraft   PHCS(A) R. Lawson, 1974

SH-3G Sea King ASW helicopter   1978

ASW helicopter SH-2D Sea Sprite (LAMPS-I)   1971

EA-6A Intruder, Marine electronics-warfare aircraft

NAVAL AND MARINE CORPS AVIATION (*continued*)

C-2A Greyhoud COD aircraft   1966

E-2C Hawkeye early-warning aircraft

EA-6B Prowler electronics-warfare aircraft   1974

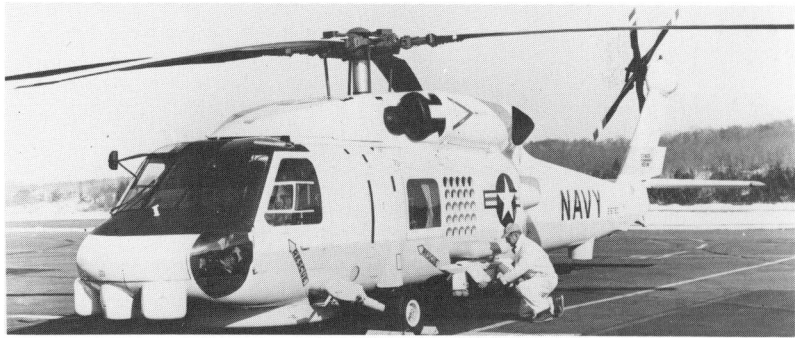

SH-60B LAMPS-III ASW helicopter—mock-up   Sikorsky, 1978

PRINCIPAL COMBAT AIRCRAFT

Class, builder	Mission	Wingspan in m	Length in m	Height in m	Weight in kg	Engine	Max speed mach/knots	Ceiling in feet	1) Ferry range (nautical miles) 2) Combat radius (nautical miles) 3) Range (hours)
SHIP-BASED FIXED WING									
F-18 Hornet (McDonnell-Douglas)	Multirole fighter (Navy)	11.43	17.07	4.67	15,247	2 GE F404-GE-400 6,800 kg thrust each	M 1.8	49,400	2,000 460 3

Armament: 5,900 kg of conventional or nuclear bombs; 2/Sidewinder; 4/Sparrow-III; 1/20-mm M61A1 cannon.

REMARKS: First aircraft to have a system using a microprocessor to control the various weapons. An A-18 version to be built by Northrop is being developed to replace the A-7. A two-seat TF-18 is also being built. A total of at least 800 A/F-18 aircraft is planned. Twenty-five to be procured under FY 80.

| **F-14A Tomcat** (Grumman) | Two-man, all-weather fighter with variable-geometry wing | 19.53/ 11.63 | 18.85 | 4.88 | 32,659 (17,010 empty) | 2 P&W TF30-P-412A 9,480 kg thrust each, with afterburners | M 2.34 | 60,000 | 2,000 500 2.50 to 3 |

Armament: 1/20-mm M61A1 Vulcan gun; 6/Phoenix, 4/Sidewinder missiles (standard weapons) or 3,856 kg of Sparrow and Sidewinder missiles or bombs, including nuclear bombs.

REMARKS: Primarily an interceptor. Max. landing speed: 120 knots. Thirty to be procured under FY 80. Production now scheduled to cease after FY 82, with 467 built instead of the planned 521. An RF-14 reconnaissance version was not proceeded with; 27 were planned. Instead, a reconnaissance pod for F-14A is being developed.

PRINCIPAL COMBAT AIRCRAFT (continued)

SHIP-BASED FIXED-WING (continued)

Class, builder	Mission	Wingspan in m	Length in m	Height in m	Weight in kg	Engine	Max speed mach/knots	Ceiling in feet	1) Ferry range (nautical miles) 2) Combat radius (nautical miles) 3) Range (hours)
F-4 Phantom (McDonnell-Douglas)	All-weather fighter (Navy) fighter-bomber (Marine Corps)	11.71	17.75	4.96	24,767 (12,700 empty)	2 GE J79-GE-10 8,120 kg thrust each, with afterburners	M 2.2	71,000	2,300 900 2.25

Armament: 4/Sparrow III and 4/Sidewinder missiles (standard weapons) or 6/Sparrow III or 7,258 kg of missiles, rockets, or bombs: 18/340-kg, 15/309-kg, 11/454-kg bombs; 7/smoke bombs; 11/napalm bombs; 4/Bullpup missiles; 15/air-to-surface rocket pods.

REMARKS: Several versions: B, J, G, and RF-4B (reconnaissance). Max. landing speed: 140 knots. The Marines are receiving older Navy F-4B as they are replaced by F-14s.

Class, builder	Mission	Wingspan in m	Length in m	Height in m	Weight in kg	Engine	Max speed mach/knots	Ceiling in feet	Range
A-4M Skyhawk (McDonnell-Douglas)	Attack (Navy Reserve and Marine Corps)	8.38	12.50	4.57	11,113 (4,747 empty)	1 P&W J52-P-408A 5,080 kg thrust	580 kts	42,000	2,055 355 2.12

Armament: 2/20-mm Mk-12 guns; 2,950 kg bombs, rockets, or Sidewinder or Bullpup missiles.

REMARKS: Nonfolding wings. Very strong; versatile. Can carry a nuclear bomb. Several verions: A-4E & M remain in active Marine squadrons, but Navy use is by Reserves and in support duties. Final units built 1979, after 25 years' production. A-4M has large hump on spine, for electronics. Two-seat TA-4F and J trainers also in use.

Class, builder	Mission	Wingspan	Length	Height	Weight	Engine	Max speed	Ceiling	Range
A-6E Intruder (Grumman)	All-weather attack (Navy and Marine Corps)	16.15	16.67	4.92	27,397 (11,627 empty)	2 P&W J52-P-8A/8B 4,218 kg thrust each	594 kts	44,600	2,400 300 . . .

Armament: 18,000 pounds of conventional or nuclear bombs, rockets, etc. Examples of ordnance: 46/250-pound, 30/450-pound, 15/900-pound, 5/2,000-pound bombs; 13 pods with 247 rockets; 52/Zuni rockets; 4/Sidewinder or 4/Bullpup missiles.

REMARKS: Very strong; versatile. Earlier versions are out of service. EA-6A is fitted for electronics warfare and has a four-man crew, a minimum of 30 sensors of various types and the ALQ-99 jammer. Four KA-6D tanker versions are aboard most carriers. Procurement of 45 new KA-6H tanker versions, beginning with six in FY 83, has been canceled in favor of converting S-3s.

Class, builder	Mission	Wingspan	Length	Height	Weight	Engine	Max speed	Ceiling	Range
A-7E Corsair II (Ling-Temco-Vought)	Attack	11.80	14.06	4.90	19,051 (8,973 empty)	1 Allison TF41-A-2 6,800 kg thrust	599 kts	42,600	2,800 700 2.25

Armament: 1/20-mm M61A1 Vulcan gun; up to 6,800 kg bombs, rockets, or missiles, according to the mission and the target distance. Examples of weapons: 24/113-kg Mk-81 bombs; 4/Zuni rockets; 28/2.75-inch rockets; 1/Shrike missile and 1/Walleye guided bomb; 12/Snakeye bombs; 2/Bullpup-B missiles; 2/Shrike missiles; 2/907-kg bombs. Normally carry two Sidewinder AAM for defense.

REMARKS: A-7E is the only version in use on carriers; earlier A, B, and C models are used by the Reserves. 81 TA-7C two-seat trainers are being converted from single-seat B&C models.

Class, builder	Mission	Wingspan	Length	Height	Weight	Engine	Max speed	Ceiling	Range
AV-8 Harrier (McDonnell-Douglas)	Attack (Marine Corps)	7.70	13.87	3.43	VTOL: 7,938 STOL: 9,747	1 RR Pegasus Mk-103 9,750 kg thrust	640 kts	50,000	2,000 VTOL: 160; STOL: 500 1

Armament: 2/30-mm guns; bombs, rockets, etc. to a total of 2,700 kg. Can carry two Sidewinder AAM for defense.

REMARKS: Eight two-seat TAV-8A and 108 single-seat AV-8A have been acquired. High loss rate through accidents. Two greatly improved AV-8B have been flown, but procurement has been held up by the Department of Defense. Under FY 80, $180 million were appropriated for continued AV-8B research and $5 million were appropriated for "AV-8B plus" R & D for a navy-subordinated version.

Class, builder	Mission	Wingspan	Length	Height	Weight	Engine	Max speed	Ceiling	Range
S-3 Viking (Lockheed)	ASW	20.93	16.26	6.94	23,832 (12,150 empty)	2 GE TF34-GE-2 9,207 kg thrust each	Max: 440 kts Cruise: 350 kts Patrol: 210 kts	40,000	3,000 2,300 6

Armament: 60/sonobuoys, 4/Mk-32 bombs; 4/Mk-57 depth charges; 4/Mk-53 depth charges or 4/Mk-53 mines or 2/Mk-46 torpedoes.

REMARKS: Fitted with a Univac AYK-10 digital computer to apply the information from the sensors on board. Four-man crew. Out of 180 total available, the Navy may have to convert 60 to KS-3 tankers and 24 to US-3 Carrier Onboard Delivery (COD) aircraft.

PRINCIPAL COMBAT AIRCRAFT (*continued*)
SHIP-BASED FIXED-WING (*continued*)

Class, builder	Mission	Wingspan in m	Length in m	Height in m	Weight in kg	Engine	Max speed mach/knots	Ceiling in feet	1) Ferry range (nautical miles) 2) Combat radius (nautical miles) 3) Range (hours)
RF-8G Crusader (Ling-Temco-Vought)	Photo reconnaissance	10.87	16.61	4.80	12,620 (7,619 empty)	1 P&W J57-P420 8,165 kg thrust with afterburner (5,190 kg without)	854 kts	51,800	... 640 2

Armament: None.

REMARKS: A few RF-8G are retained as the only carrier-operated photo reconnaissance aircraft owned by the Navy; all are very old, but have been refurbished. To be discarded 1980-81. Note: All RA-5C Vigilante reconnaissance aircraft have been retired.

Class, builder	Mission	Wingspan in m	Length in m	Height in m	Weight in kg	Engine	Max speed mach/knots	Ceiling in feet	
E-2C Hawkeye (Grumman)	Airborne early warning and air control	24.58	17.56	5.59	23,392 (17,091 empty)	2 Allison T56-A-422 turboprops, 4,591 shp each	326 kts (270 kts, cruise)	30,800	1,525 ... 6

REMARKS: APS-120 radar in 7.32-m circular, rotating radome. Five-man crew. A few E-2B remain, but will be replaced by 1981, when total of 85 E-2C will be available.

Class, builder	Mission	Wingspan in m	Length in m	Height in m	Weight in kg	Engine	Max speed mach/knots	Ceiling in feet	
EA-6B Prowler (Grumman)	Electronics warfare	16.15	18.11	4.95	29,536 (15,686 empty)	2 P&W J52-P-408, 5,080 kg thrust each	573 kts (410 kts, cruise)	37,800	2,400 710 ...

REMARKS: ECM version of A-6 Intruder; four-man crew. Five ALQ-99 jammer pods beneath wings and fuselage. Will replace two-seat Marine EA-6A Intruder, which carries five ALQ-31B jammer pods and can alternatively be used as an attack aircraft, with up to 8,160 kg of ordnance. Both aircraft are distinguished from the standard A-6E by a large streamlined electronics-equipment pod atop the vertical stabilizer.

Class, builder	Mission	Wingspan in m	Length in m	Height in m	Weight in kg	Engine	Max speed mach/knots	Ceiling in feet	
EA-3B Skywarrior (McDonnell-Douglas)	Electronics warfare	22.11	23.28	6.94	35,380 (18,685 empty)	2 P&W J57-P-10 5,625 kg thrust each	556 kts (400 kts, cruise)	41,300	5,000 1,100 6

REMARKS: The only type still used on carriers; will remain in service to 1985. EKA-3B is used by the Reserves for both flight refueling and electronics warfare, ERA-3B is used for reconnaissance.

Class, builder	Mission	Wingspan in m	Length in m	Height in m	Weight in kg	Engine	Max speed mach/knots	Ceiling in feet	
P-3C Orion (Lockheed)	Maritime patrol and ASW	30.37	35.61	10.28	64,411 (27,892 empty)	4 Allison T56-A-14 turboprops, 4,910 hp each	410 kts (205 kts patrol)	28,300	4,500 2,380 patrol 17

Armament: 6/908-kg mines; 2/Mk-101 nuclear depth charges; 4/Mk-46 torpedoes; 87/sonobuoys, 4/Harpoon anti-ship missiles, etc. Weapons vary. Can carry a total of 7,700 kg of disposable ordnance and sensors.

REMARKS: Crews of up to 15 men. The P-3C is fitted with an A-NEW central operations module built around the ASQ-114 miniaturized computer and with an Air Tactical Data System. ASQ-10 Magnetic Anomaly Detector (MAD), APS-115 radar, electronics countermeasures carried. EP-3B/E are for electronics warfare, RP-3A/D are for research, and WP-3D perform weather reconnaissance. Twelve P-3C to be procured under FY 80.

Class, builder	Mission	Wingspan in m	Length in m	Height in m	Weight in kg	Engine	Max speed mach/knots	Ceiling in feet	
C-1A Trader (Grumman)	Carrier Onboard Delivery (COD)	21.23	22.80	4.98	12,247	2 Wright R1820-82 piston; 1,525 hp each	290 kts	22,000	1,200 ... ...

REMARKS: Despite advanced obsolescence, retained for lack of a successor. Cargo version of out-of-service S-2 Tracker ASW aircraft. Two-man crew plus 9 passengers. To be replaced by US-3 Viking beginning in 1983, when some will be 30 years old.

Class, builder	Mission	Wingspan in m	Length in m	Height in m	Weight in kg	Engine	Max speed mach/knots	Ceiling in feet	
C-2A Greyhound (Grumman)	Carrier Onboard Delivery (COD)	24.57	17.27	4.85	24,668 (14,175 empty)	2 Allison T56-A-8A turboshaft; 4,050 shp each	306 kts (257 kts, cruise)	28,800	1,440

REMARKS: Unsuccessful variant of E-2 Hawkeye with large-diameter fuselage. Three-man crew plus 39 passengers or 20 litter patients or cargo. Stern ramp for loading. Must be retained until replaced by smaller US-3, beginning in 1983.

NAVAL AND MARINE CORPS AVIATION (*continued*)

CH-53 Sea Stallion minesweeping helicopter—with the
Mk-105 mine sled attached preparing to take off from the **Raleigh**   1975

UH-46 Sea Knight utility helicopter

AV-8B Advanced Harrier V/STOL fighter-bomber   McDonnell-Douglas, 1978

P3 Orion ASW patrol aircraft

PRINCIPAL COMBAT AIRCRAFT (*continued*)

Class, builder	Mission	Diameter (rotor)	Length (overall)	Height	Weight in kg	Engine	Max speed in knots	Ceiling in feet	1) Mission range (nautical miles) 2) Ferry range (nautical miles) 3) Endurance (hours)
HELICOPTERS **SH-3A, D, G Sea King** (Sikorsky)	ASW	18.9	22.16 (16.70, fuselage)	5.13	9,300 (5,302 empty)	2 GE T58-GE-10 turboshaft, 1,400 shp each	144 118, cruise	14,700	625 ... 4.50

Armament: Depth charges or two Mk-46 torpedoes.

REMARKS: Four-man crew. On CV aircraft carriers or land-based; can be carried on *Spruance*-class DD. SH-3H is a multipurpose version of the SH-3G utility model. Fitted with AZS-10 dipping sonar, ASQ-81 MAD. All 137 SH-3A and G models updating to SH-3H standard, carry APS-24 radar.

Class, builder	Mission	Diameter (rotor)	Length (overall)	Height	Weight in kg	Engine	Max speed in knots	Ceiling in feet	
SH-2D, F, LAMPS-I (Kaman)	ASW	13.42	16.04 (11.69, fuselage)	4.73	5,800 (3,154 empty)	2 GE T58-GE-8F turboshaft, 1,350 hp each	143 130, cruise	22,500	420 ... 2.50

Armament: 15/sonobuoys, 2/Mk-46 ASW torpedoes.

REMARKS: Found on FF, DD, and CG types. Approx. 105 in service. All conversions of UH-2 Sea Sprite utility helicopters.

Class, builder	Mission	Diameter (rotor)	Length (overall)	Height	Weight in kg	Engine	Max speed in knots	Ceiling in feet	
SH-60B LAMPS-III (Sikorsky)	ASW	16.36	19.76 (15.24, fuselage)	5.23	9,435	2 GE T700-GE-400 turboshaft, ... shp each	...	...	150 ... ...

Armament: 25/sonobuoys; 2/Mk-46 ASW torpedoes.

REMARKS: To replace SH-2D, F in 1980s. Introduction delayed because of excessive cost. Will carry APS-24 radar, ASQ-81 MAD, SSQ-53 DIFAR sonobuoys, SSQ-50 CASS active sonobuoys. Highly automated; all sensors display on ship, which controls the helicopter. Up to 200 to be procured.

Class, builder	Mission	Diameter (rotor)	Length (overall)	Height	Weight in kg	Engine	Max speed in knots	Ceiling in feet	
CH-46 A, D, E **Sea Knight** (Boeing Vertol)	Troop-carrying assault (Marine Corps)	15.56	25.72 (13.67 fuselage)	5.08	10,438 (5,947 empty)	2 GE T58-GE-10 turboshaft, 1,450 shp each	144	14,000	206 774 ...

REMARKS: Can carry 18 full equipped troops. The two cargo version (UH-46A and 46D) are Navy-subordinated and are usually assigned to vertical-replenishment duties in modern under-way replenishment ships. Can carry 1,360 kg of cargo internally or 4,536 kg in a sling beneath. CH-46E is updated version with automatic navigation system and armored seats; all earlier units will be modernized.

Class, builder	Mission	Diameter (rotor)	Length (overall)	Height	Weight in kg	Engine	Max speed in knots	Ceiling in feet	
CH-53 A, D, RH-53D **Sea Stallion** (Sikorsky)	Navy RH-53D: Minesweeping Marine Corps CH-53A, D: Assault transport	22.04	26.92 (20.48, fuselage)	7.59	19,050 (10,718 empty)	2 GE T64-GE-413 turboshaft, 3,925 hp each	170 150, cruise	21,000	540 886 3.50

REMARKS: Version A can carry 38 fully equipped troops or 24 occupied stretchers with 4 hospital corpsmen or 4 tons of freight (2 Hawk missiles, for example). CH-53E (three turboshafts totaling 11,570 hp) first flew in 1974 and will be used for amphibious support. The RH-53D version is equipped for aerial minesweeping and has T64-GE-415 engines, 2/12.7-mm machine guns, and points for towing Mk-103 cutters, Mk-104 magnetic minesweeping arrays. Mk-105 hydrofoil sled. Mk-106 acoustic sweep array, and SPU-1 shallow-water sweep rig.

Class, builder	Mission	Diameter (rotor)	Length (overall)	Height	Weight in kg	Engine	Max speed in knots	Ceiling in feet	
CH-53E Super Stallion (Sikorsky)	Troop-carrying assault (Marines) Heavy lift (Navy)	24.08	30.35 (27.94, fuselage)	8.44	31,700 (14,477 empty)	3 GE T64-GE-415 turboshaft; 4,380 shp each	170	21,000	50 with 14,500 kg cargo; 1,000 ...

REMARKS: Can carry 56 troops or 14,500 kg cargo. Three-man crew. Seven-bladed main rotor. One being rebuilt under FY 80 budget as MH-53E minesweeper prototype. Navy and Marines each have 35; Navy use is for cargo, aircraft-recovery, and heavy lift.

PRINCIPAL COMBAT AIRCRAFT (*continued*)
HELICOPTERS (*continued*)

Class, builder	Mission	Diameter (rotor)	Length (overall)	Height	Weight in kg	Engine	Max speed in knots	Ceiling in feet	1) Mission range (nautical miles) 2) Ferry range (nautical miles) 3) Endurance (hours)
UH-1E/N Iroquois (Bell)	Assault (Marine Corps)	14.70	17.47 (12.93, fuselage)	4.39	4,763 (2,517 empty)	2 United Aircraft PT6 turboshaft, 900 shp each	110	15,000	250 . . . 2

Armament: 2/7.62 machine guns and rockets.

REMARKS: Can carry 16 troops. UH-1N is replacing earlier UH-1E, which had 1 Lycoming T53 turboshaft of 1,100 shp. Navy uses UH-1 and TH-1 for utility and training duties.

Class, builder	Mission	Diameter (rotor)	Length (overall)	Height	Weight in kg	Engine	Max speed in knots	Ceiling in feet	
AH-1G, J, T Sea Cobra (Bell)	Attack (Marine Corps)	13.42	16.27 (13.60, fuselage)	4.17	4,536 3,000 empty	2 United Aircraft T400-CP-400 turboshaft; 1,800 shp each	180	10,500	360 . . . 2

Armament: 1/20-mm XM-197 Gatling gun, plus 76/2.75-in rockets or 2/7.62-mm minigun (AH-1T also: TOW anti-tank missiles).

REMARKS: The initial version, AH-1G, is identical to the Army Huey Cobra and has only 1 Lycoming T53-L5 engine of 1,100 shp; it is being replaced by the AH-1T.

Also in service with Navy and Marine Corps aviation are 23 F-SE/F fighters for "Top Gun" training to simulate Soviet aircraft, a few P-2-series Neptune for utility duties, OV-10A and OV-10D twin-engine observation/attack aircraft for the Marines, C-4 Gulfstream transports, C-9B transports (military DC-9) for the Marines and Naval Reserve, C-117D Skytrain (military DC-3) transports, C-118B Liftmaster (military DC-6), C-130 Hercules (in C-130, LC-130 arctic, DC-130 drone control, and EC-130 TACANO communications versions), C-131F, G Samaritan transports, T-2C Buckeye jet trainers, T-28B propeller trainers, T-34B/C student trainers, T-38A Talon jet test-pilot trainers, T-39D Sabreliner flight-officer trainers (and CT-39E/G light transport versions), T-44 twin-engine trainers, and TH-57A helicopter trainers. Two C-9B transports are to be procured under FY 80.

NUCLEAR-POWERED BALLISTIC-MISSILE SUBMARINES

◆ 8 (+ 3) **Ohio class** (SCB 304, 74 design) Bldr: General Dynamics, Groton, Conn.

	Program	Laid down	L	In serv.
SSBN 726 OHIO	FY 74	10-4-76	7-4-79	3-11-80
SSBN 727 MICHIGAN	FY 75	4-4-77	7-80	3-11-81
SSBN 728 N . . .	FY 75	9-6-77	1981	7-82
SSBN 729 GEORGIA	FY 76	7-4-79	1981	3-83
SSBN 730 N . . .	FY 77	. . .	1982	11-83
SSBN 731 N . . .	FY 78	. . .	1983	7-84
SSBN 732 N . . .	FY 78	. . .	1983	3-85
SSBN 733 N . . .	FY 80	. . .	. . .	. . .

Ohio   1976

Ohio—at launch

NUCLEAR-POWERED BALLISTIC-MISSILE SUBMARINES (*continued*)

D: 15,750 tons surfaced/18,750 submerged   **S:** 25 kts (submerged)
Dim: 170.69 × 12.8 × 11.13 (surfaced)   **Man:** 16 officers, 117 men
A: 24/Trident-1 missiles — 4/533-mm Mk-68 TT (fwd)   **Endurance:** 70 days
Electron Equipt: Radar: BPS-15   Sonar: BQQ-6   ECM: WLR-8(v)
M: 1 GE S8G pressured-water reactor; steam GT; 1 prop; 60,000 hp

REMARKS: SSBN-726 to run trials in 7-80, make first operational patrol in 8-81. Others to make first patrols, in order: 8-82, 4-83, 12-83, 8-84, etc. However, program continues to experience delays. The availability of this class as a whole is to be 66 per cent, using a planned schedule of 70-day patrols, followed by 25-day refit periods, and with a 12-month overhaul every nine years. Each ship has two crews. None ordered under FY 79 because of program delays and cost overruns; the FY 80 unit to cost more than $1.1 billion, *without* missiles. Planned to request one each under FY 81 to FY 84, with two under FY 85.

Will be able to submerge to 300 meters. Will carry two Mk-2 SINS (Ship's Inertial Navigational System) and have navigational satellite receivers. Mk-98 digital computer missile-fire-control system and Mk-118 torpedo-fire-control system are installed. Under current planning, will be backfitted with Trident-2 missiles in the 1990s.

◆ 31 Layfayette class (SCB 216 and SCB 216A types)

	Bldr	Laid down	L	In serv.
SSBN 616 LAFAYETTE	Gen. Dynamics	17-1-61	8-5-62	23-4-63
SSBN 617 ALEXANDER HAMILTON	Gen. Dynamics	26-6-61	18-8-62	27-6-63
SSBN 619 ANDREW JACKSON	Mare Island NSY	26-4-61	15-9-62	3-7-63
SSBN 620 JOHN ADAMS	Portsmouth NSY	19-5-61	12-1-63	12-5-64
SSBN 622 JAMES MONROE	Newport News	31-7-61	4-8-62	7-12-63
SSBN 623 NATHAN HALE	Gen. Dynamics	2-10-61	12-1-63	23-11-63
SSBN 624 WOODROW WILSON	Mare Island NSY	13-9-61	22-2-63	27-12-63
SSBN 625 HENRY CLAY	Newport News	23-10-61	30-11-62	20-2-64
SSBN 626 DANIEL WEBSTER	Gen. Dynamics	23-12-61	27-4-63	9-4-64
SSBN 627 JAMES MADISON*	Newport News	5-3-62	15-3-63	28-7-64
SSBN 628 TECUMSEH	Gen. Dynamics	1-6-62	22-6-63	29-5-64
SSBN 629 DANIEL BOONE*	Mare Island NSY	6-2-62	22-6-63	23-4-64
SSBN 630 JOHN C. CALHOUN*	Newport News	4-6-62	22-6-63	15-9-64
SSBN 631 ULYSSES S. GRANT	Gen. Dynamics	18-8-62	2-11-63	17-7-64
SSBN 632 VON STEUBEN*	Newport News	4-9-62	18-10-63	30-9-64
SSBN 633 CASIMIR PULASKI*	Gen. Dynamics	12-1-63	1-2-64	14-8-64
SSBN 634 STONEWALL JACKSON*	Mare Island NSY	4-7-62	30-11-63	26-8-64
SSBN 635 SAM RAYBURN	Newport News	3-12-62	20-12-63	2-12-64
SSBN 636 NATHANAEL GREENE	Portsmouth NSY	21-5-62	12-5-64	19-12-64
SSBN 640 BENJAMIN FRANKLIN*	Gen. Dynamics	25-5-63	5-12-64	22-10-65
SSBN 641 SIMON BOLIVAR*	Newport News	17-4-63	22-8-64	29-10-65
SSBN 642 KAMEHAMEHA	Mare Island NSY	2-5-63	16-1-65	10-12-65
SSBN 643 GEORGE BANCROFT*	Gen. Dynamics	24-8-63	20-3-65	22-1-66
SSBN 644 LEWIS AND CLARK	Newport News	29-7-63	21-11-64	22-12-65
SSBN 645 JAMES K. POLK	Gen. Dynamics	23-11-63	22-5-65	16-4-66
SSBN 654 GEORGE C. MARSHALL	Newport News	2-3-64	21-5-65	29-4-66
SSBN 655 HENRY L. STIMSON*	Gen. Dynamics	4-4-64	13-11-65	20-8-66
SSBN 656 GEORGE WASHINGTON CARVER	Newport News	24-8-64	14-8-65	15-6-66
SSBN 657 FRANCIS SCOTT KEY*	Gen. Dynamics	5-12-64	23-4-66	3-12-66
SSBN 658 MARIANO G. VALLEJO*	Mare Island NSY	7-7-64	23-10-65	16-12-66
SSBN 659 WILL ROGERS	Gen. Dynamics	20-3-65	21-7-66	1-4-67

Authorized: SSBN-616 to SSBN-626 in FY 61, SSBN-627 to SSBN-636 in FY 62, SSBN-640 to SSBN-645 in FY 63, and SSBN-654 to SSBN-659 in FY 64.

James Monroe   1970

Daniel Webster—Note the unique position of the diving planes, on the dome on the bow at the extreme lower right of the photograph   1972

John C. Calhoun

NUCLEAR-POWERED BALLISTIC-MISSILE SUBMARINES (*continued*)

D: 7,250 tons surfaced/8,250 submerged   **S:** 15/25 kts
Dim: 129.54 × 10.05 × 9.0
Man: 17 officers, 128 men   **Endurance:** 68 days
A: 16/Poseidon or Trident-1 missiles—4/533-mm TT (fwd)
Electron Equipt: Sonars: BQR-7, BQR-15, BQR-19, BQS-4
M: 1 Westinghouse SW5 pressurized-water reactor; 1 seven-bladed prop; 15,000 hp

REMARKS: The units marked with an asterisk are scheduled to receive Trident-1 missiles by 3-82. SSBN-640 and following units have quieter propulsion machinery and are officially designated the *Benjamin Franklin* class. Three Mk-2 SINS were installed during conversion. Submersion depth for all is more than 300 meters. Mk-88 missile-fire-control system and Mk-113 torpedo-fire-control system fitted. Conversion of both classes from Polaris A-3 to Poseidon missiles was completed between 1970 and 1977. Poseidon may be replaced by Trident-1. Funds were requested under FY 79 for conversion of the first SSBN and for three each year thereafter through FY 82. SSBN-657 commenced the first Trident-1 operational patrol on 20-10-79. All Trident-1 units are to be homeported at King's Bay, Georgia, and all ships in both classes belong to the Atlantic Fleet. They operate on a schedule of 68-day patrols, followed by 32-day refit periods; every six years a 16-month yard period is requested, giving an overall force availability of 55 per cent. Each ship has two crews.

◆ 5 Ethan Allen class (SCB 180 type)

	Bldr	Laid down	L	In serv.
SSBN 608 ETHAN ALLEN	Gen. Dynamics	14-9-59	22-11-60	8-8-61
SSBN 609 SAM HOUSTON	Newport News	28-12-59	2-2-61	6-3-62
SSBN 610 THOMAS A. EDISON	Gen. Dynamics	15-3-60	15-6-61	10-3-62
SSBN 611 JOHN MARSHALL	Newport News	4-4-60	15-7-61	21-5-62
SSBN 618 THOMAS JEFFERSON	Newport News	3-2-61	24-2-62	4-1-63

Authorized: SSBN-608 to SSBN-611 in FY 59, SSBN-618 in FY 61

D: 6,300 tons surfaced/7,880 submerged   **S:** 15/20 kts
Dim: 124.96 × 10.05 × 9.0
A: 16/Polaris A-3—4/533-mm TT (fwd)   **Man:** 12 officers, 128 men
Electron Equipt: Sonars: BQR-7, BQR-15, BQR-19, BQS-4
M: 1 Westinghouse SW5 pressurized-water reactor, GT; 1 seven-bladed prop; 15,000 hp

Ethan Allen

REMARKS: Two Mk-2, Mod. 3, SINS; Mk-84 missile-fire-control system; Mk-112, Mod. 1, torpedo-fire-control system. All in Pacific Fleet. Each has two crews. Will not be modernized to accommodate Poseidon missiles. Deeper-diving than the *George Washington* class. To be decommissioned in FY 81.

◆ 5 George Washington class (SCB 180A type)

	Bldr	Laid down	L	In serv.
SSBN 598 GEORGE WASHINGTON	Gen. Dynamics	1-11-57	9-6-59	30-12-59
SSBN 599 PATRICK HENRY	Gen. Dynamics	27-5-58	22-9-59	9-4-60
SSBN 600 THEODORE ROOSEVELT	Mare Island NSY	20-5-58	3-10-59	13-2-61
SSBN 601 ROBERT E. LEE	Newport News SB	25-8-58	18-12-59	16-9-60
SSBN 602 ABRAHAM LINCOLN	Portsmouth NSY	1-11-58	14-5-60	11-3-61

Authorized: SSBN-598 to SSBN-600 in FY 58, SSBN-601 and SSBN-602 in FY 59

George Washington

D: 6,019 tons surfaced/6,888 submerged   **S:** 15/20 kts
Dim: 115.82 × 10.05 × 8.8
A: 16/Polaris A-3—6/533-mm Mk-59 TT (fwd)
Electron Equipt: Sonars: BQS-4, BQR-7, BQR-19
M: 1 Westinghouse S5W pressurized-water reactor, GT; 1 seven-bladed prop; 15,000 hp

REMARKS: Conversion of *Skipjack* class attack submarines, stretched 39.62 m while building, in order to insert new section with sixteen missile tubes. During her first cruise (30-12-60 to 8-3-61), SSBN-599 remained submerged for 60 days and 22 hours, traveled 11,000 miles (20,400 km), and, in exercises, successfully launched eight Polaris missiles. From 6-64 to 6-67, SSBN-598 to SSBN-602 were overhauled; a new core and a Mk-84 missile-fire-control system were added and launching wells were modified to permit launch by steam of Polaris A-3 missiles in place of the original A-1. SSBN-598 to retire on completion of the *Ohio* (SSBN-726), others shortly thereafter. All in the Pacific Fleet. Each has two crews. To be decommissioned in FY 80, beginning with SSBN-600 and SSBN-602 in 5-80.

NUCLEAR-POWERED ATTACK SUBMARINES

◆ **34 (+ 4) Los Angeles class (SCB 303 type)**

	Bldr	Laid down	L	In serv.
SSN 688 LOS ANGELES	Newport News	8-1-72	6-4-74	13-11-76
SSN 689 BATON ROUGE	Newport News	18-11-72	18-4-75	25-6-77
SSN 690 PHILADELPHIA	Gen. Dynamics	12-8-72	19-10-74	25-6-77
SSN 691 MEMPHIS	Newport News	23-6-73	3-4-76	17-12-77
SSN 692 OMAHA	Gen. Dynamics	27-1-73	21-2-76	11-3-78
SSN 693 CINCINNATI	Newport News	6-4-74	19-2-76	10-6-78
SSN 694 GROTON	Gen. Dynamics	3-8-73	9-10-76	8-7-78
SSN 695 BIRMINGHAM	Newport News	26-4-75	15-10-77	20-12-78
SSN 696 NEW YORK CITY	Gen. Dynamics	15-12-73	18-6-77	10-3-79
SSN 697 INDIANAPOLIS	Gen. Dynamics	19-10-74	30-7-77	
SSN 698 BREMERTON	Gen. Dynamics	8-5-76	22-7-78	27-10-79
SSN 699 JACKSONVILLE	Gen. Dynamics	21-2-76	18-11-78	2-80
SSN 700 DALLAS	Gen. Dynamics	9-10-76	28-4-79	6-80
SSN 701 LA JOLLA	Gen. Dynamics	16-10-76	11-8-79	10-80
SSN 702 PHOENIX	Gen. Dynamics	30-7-77	17-11-79	81
SSN 703 BOSTON	Gen. Dynamics	11-8-78	3-80	81
SSN 704 BALTIMORE	Gen. Dynamics	21-5-79	11-80	82
SSN 705 N . . .	Gen. Dynamics	1-9-79	81	82
SSN 706 N . . .	Gen. Dynamics	8-12-79	81	82
SSN 707 N . . .	Gen. Dynamics	4-80	81	83
SSN 708 N . . .	Gen. Dynamics	11-80	82	83
SSN 709 N . . .	Gen. Dynamics	81	82	84
SSN 710 N . . .	Gen. Dynamics	81	83	84
SSN 711 SAN FRANCISCO	Newport News	26-5-77	27-10-79	12-80
SSN 712 ATLANTA	Newport News	17-8-78	6-80	81
SSN 713 HOUSTON	Newport News	29-1-79	11-80	82
SSN 714 N . . .	Newport News	1-8-79	81	82
SSN 715 N . . .	Newport News	2-80	81	83
SSN 716 N . . .	Newport News	7-80	82	83
SSN 717 N . . .	Newport News	81	82	84
SSN 718 N . . .	Newport News	81	83	84
SSN 719 N . . .	Gen. Dynamics	81	83	84
SSN 720 N . . .	Gen. Dynamics	82	83	85
SSN 721 N . . .	. . .	82	84	85
SSN 722 N . . .	. . .	. . .	. . .	. . .

Authorized: SSN-688 to SSN-690 in FY 70, SSN-691 to SSN-694 in FY 71, SSN-695 to SSN-700 in FY 72, SSN-701 to SSN-705 in FY 73, SSN-706 to SSN-710 in FY 74, SSN-711 to SSN-713 in FY 75, SSN-714 and SSN-715 in FY 76, SSN-716 to SSN-718 in FY 77, SSN-719 in FY 78, SSN-720 in FY 79, SSN-721 and SSN-722 in FY 80.

D: 6,000 tons surfaced/6,900 submerged **S:** 30+ kts (submerged)
Dim: 109.73 × 10.06 × 9.75 **Man:** 12 officers, 115 men
A: 4/533-mm TT (amidships) for Harpoon and Mk-48 torpedoes
Electron Equipt: Radars: 1/BPS-15
  Sonars: 1/BQQ-5-A(v)1, BQS-15, BQR-15 — ECM: BRD-7
M: GE S6G reactor, 2 GT; 1 prop; 30,000 hp

REMARKS: One per year planned FY 81 to FY 83 and two under FY 84. A new class is to be introduced, the prototype being under FY 83, with one in FY 84 and four under FY 85, and series-production commencing under FY 86. Mk-113, Mod. 10, torpedo-fire-

Los Angeles 1976

Groton A. Baker, 1978

control in SSN-688 to SSN-699, Mk-117 in later units. Harpoon began to be carried in 1978. Maximum diving depth is 450 m. Described as the finest ASW platforms now afloat. Bow is of fiberglass and there is a streamlined cover over the spherical BQQ-5-A(v)1 sonar array. There are two SINS. Construction program very far behind schedule because of labor problems and lack of shipyard capacity.

◆ **1 Glenard P. Lipscomb class**

	Bldr	Laid down	L	In serv.
SSN 685 GLENARD P. LIPSCOMB	Gen. Dynamics	5-6-71	4-8-73	21-12-74

Authorized: FY 68

D: 5,813 tons standard/6,480 submerged **S:** 25 kts (submerged)
Dim: 111.3 × 9.7 × 8.8
A: 4/533-mm TT (amidships) **Man:** 12 officers, 108 men
Electron Equipt: Radar: BPS-14 Sonar: BQQ-2
M: 1 Westinghouse S5W reactor, GE turboelectric drive; 1 prop; . . . hp

REMARKS: This TEDS (Turbo-Electric Drive Submarine) was an effort to make an exceptionally quiet submarine at the expense of some speed. Most other equipment is similar to the *Sturgeon* class. During the next overhaul, it is to be equipped to launch Harpoon, with BQQ-5 vice BQQ-2 sonar, and Mk-117 torpedo-fire-control vice Mk-113, Mod. 8.

NUCLEAR-POWERED ATTACK SUBMARINES (*continued*)

Glenard P. Lipscomb — Gneral Dynamics, 1974

◆ **37 Sturgeon class (SCB 188A and SCB 188M types)**

	Bldr	Laid down	L	In serv.
SSN 637 STURGEON	Gen. Dynamics	10-8-63	26-2-66	3-3-67
SSN 638 WHALE	Gen. Dynamics	27-5-64	14-10-66	12-10-68
SSN 639 TAUTOG	Ingalls SB	27-1-64	15-4-67	17-8-68
SSN 646 GRAYLING	Portsmouth NSY	12-5-64	22-6-67	11-10-69
SSN 647 POGY	New York SB	4-5-64	3-6-67	15-5-71
SSN 648 ASPRO	Ingalls SB	23-11-64	29-11-67	20-2-69
SSN 649 SUNFISH	Gen. Dynamics	15-1-65	14-10-66	15-3-69
SSN 650 PARGO	Gen. Dynamics	3-6-64	17-9-66	1-5-68
SSN 651 QUEENFISH	Newport News	11-5-64	25-2-66	6-12-66
SSN 652 PUFFER	Ingalls SB	8-2-65	30-3-68	9-8-69
SSN 653 RAY	Newport News	1-4-65	21-6-66	12-4-67
SSN 660 SANDLANCE	Portsmouth NSY	15-1-65	11-11-69	25-9-71
SSN 661 LAPON	Newport News	26-7-65	16-12-66	14-12-67
SSN 662 GURNARD	Mare Island NSY	22-12-64	20-5-67	6-12-68
SSN 663 HAMMERHEAD	Newport News	29-11-65	14-4-67	28-6-68
SSN 664 SEA DEVIL	Newport News	12-4-66	5-10-67	30-1-69
SSN 665 GUITARRO	Mare Island NSY	9-12-65	27-7-68	9-9-72
SSN 666 HAWKBILL	Mare Island NSY	12-9-66	12-4-69	4-2-71
SSN 667 BERGALL	Gen. Dynamics	16-4-66	17-2-69	13-6-69
SSN 668 SPADEFISH	Newport News	21-12-66	15-5-68	14-8-69
SSN 669 SEA HORSE	Gen. Dynamics	13-8-66	15-6-68	19-9-69
SSN 670 FINBACK	Newport News	26-6-67	7-12-68	4-2-70
SSN 672 PINTADO	Mare Island NSY	27-10-67	16-8-69	11-9-71
SSN 673 FLYING FISH	Gen. Dynamics	30-6-67	17-5-69	29-4-70
SSN 674 TREPANG	Gen. Dynamics	28-10-67	27-9-69	14-8-70
SSN 675 BLUEFISH	Gen. Dynamics	13-3-68	10-1-70	8-1-71
SSN 676 BILLFISH	Gen. Dynamics	20-9-68	1-5-70	12-3-71
SSN 677 DRUM	Mare Island NSY	20-8-68	23-5-70	15-4-72
SSN 678 ARCHERFISH	Gen. Dynamics	19-6-69	16-1-71	24-12-71
SSN 679 SILVERSIDES	Gen. Dynamics	13-12-69	4-6-71	5-5-72
SSN 680 WILLIAM H. BATES (ex-*Redfish*)	Ingalls SB	4-8-69	12-71	5-5-73
SSN 681 BATFISH	Gen. Dynamics	9-2-70	9-10-71	1-9-72
SSN 682 TUNNY	Ingalls SB	22-5-70	10-6-72	26-1-74
SSN 683 PARCHE	Ingalls SB	10-12-70	12-72	17-8-74
SSN 684 CAVALLA	Gen. Dynamics	4-6-70	19-2-72	9-2-73
SSN 686 MENDEL RIVERS	Newport News	26-6-71	2-6-73	1-2-75
SSN 687 RICHARD B. RUSSELL	Newport News	19-10-71	12-1-74	16-8-75

Authorized: SSN-637 to SSN-639 in FY 62, SSN-646 to SSN-653 in FY 63, SSN-660 to SSN-664 in FY 64, SSN-665 to SSN-670 in FY 65, SSN-672 to SSN-677 in FY 66, SSN-678 to SSN-682 in FY 67, SSN-683 and SSN-684 in FY 68, SSN-686 and SSN-687 in FY 69

D: 3,640 tons surfaced/4,640 submerged   **S:** 15/30 kts

Dim: 89.0 (SSN-678 and later: 92.1) × 9.65 × 8.8

A: 4/533-mm TT (amidships) for Mk-37 and Mk-48 torpedoes and Harpoon

Electron Equipt: Radar: 1/BPS-14

           Sonars: BQQ-2 (with BQS-6 active/BQR-7 passive) or BQQ-5, BQS-8, (SSN-637 to SSN-664: BQS-12; others: BQS-13

M: 1 Westinghouse S5W2 reactor, GE or de Laval GT; 1 prop; 20,000 hp

REMARKS: The construction contract of SSN-647 with New York Shipbuilding, Camden, N.J., was canceled in 4-67 and completion of the ship was given to Ingalls, Pascagoula,

NUCLEAR-POWERED ATTACK SUBMARINES (*continued*)

Pintado   G: Arra

Cavalla—note bow sonar dome.   General Dynamics, 1973

Pintado—with **Mystic** (DSRV-1) aboard   PH1 A. Legare, USN, 1977

Richard B. Russell   1976

Miss. Completion of SSN-665 was delayed twenty-eight months after ship sank while fitting out. The Mk-113 torpedo-fire-control system is being replaced by Mk-117. Later units (SCB-188M) were lengthened to permit installation of BQQ-5 sonar suit, now being backfitted in all; since that extra space is free-flooding it materially affects submerged displacement. Diving planes are 11.6 m wide. Maximum depth is about 400 m. SSN-666, SSN-672, and others have been modified to carry a DSRV (salvage submarine), which can be launched and recovered while submerged. The after hatch is so constructed that people can be transferred between the two ships while submerged.

◆ **1 Narwhal class (SCB-245)**

	Bldr	Laid down	L	In serv.
SSN 671 NARWHAL	Gen. Dynamics	17-1-66	9-9-67	12-7-69

Authorized: FY 64

D: 4,550 tons surfaced/5,350 submerged   **S:** 20/25 kts
Dim: 95.7 × 11.5 × 7.9   **A:** 4/533-mm TT (amidships)
Man: 12 officers, 108 men
Electron Equipt: Sonars: BQQ-2 (BQS-6 active/BQR-7 passive), BQS-8
M: 1 GE S5G reactor, 2 GT; 1 prop; 17,000 hp

REMARKS: Prototype seagoing reactor designed to study the cooling of the S5G reactor by free circulation, thus eliminating circulation pumps and their noise. In most other

NUCLEAR-POWERED ATTACK SUBMARINES (*continued*)

Narwhal   General Dynamics, 1969

Tinosa—4.6-meter long sail   1964

Gato—6.1-meter long sail   1967

respects, essentially a lengthened *Sturgeon*. Will receive Harpoon Mk-117 torpedo-fire-control system and BQQ-5 sonar suit.

♦ **13 Permit class (SSN-594 to SSN-612 and SSN-621 are SCB-188 type, SSN-613 to SSN-615 are SCB-188M type)**

		Bldr	Laid down	L	In serv.
SSN 594	PERMIT	Mare Island NSY	16-7-59	1-7-61	29-5-62
SSN 595	PLUNGER	Mare Island NSY	2-3-60	9-12-61	21-11-62
SSN 596	BARB (ex-*Pollack)*	Ingalls SB	9-11-59	12-2-62	24-8-63
SSN 603	POLLACK (ex-*Barb)*	New York SB	14-3-60	17-3-62	26-5-64
SSN 604	HADDO	New York SB	9-9-60	18-8-62	16-12-64
SSN 605	JACK	Portsmouth NSY	16-9-60	24-4-63	31-3-67
SSN 606	TINOSA	Portsmouth NSY	24-11-59	9-12-61	17-10-64
SSN 607	DACE	Ingalls SB	6-6-60	18-8-62	4-4-64
SSN 612	GUARDFISH	New York SB	28-2-61	15-5-65	20-12-66
SSN 613	FLASHER	Gen. Dynamics	14-4-61	22-6-63	22-7-66
SSN 614	GREENLING	Gen. Dynamics	15-8-61	4-4-64	3-11-67
SSN 615	GATO	Gen. Dynamics	15-12-61	14-5-64	25-1-68
SSN 621	HADDOCK	Ingalls SB	24-4-61	21-5-66	22-12-67

Authorized: SSN-594 to SSN-596 in FY 58, SSN-603 to SSN-607 in FY 59, SSN-612 to SSN-615 in FY 60, SSN-621 in FY 61

SSN-594 to SSN-604, SSN-606 to SSN-612, and SSN-621:

D: 3,526 tons surfaced, 4,310 submerged   **Dim:** 84.88 × 9.75 × 8.80

SSN-606:

D: 3,526 tons surfaced, 4,465 submerged   **Dim:** 90.11 × 9.65 × 8.80

SSN-613 to SSN-615:

D: 3,836 tons surfaced, 4,650 submerged   **Dim:** 89.0 × 9.65 × 8.80
A: 4/533-mm TT (Harpoon)   **S:** 15/30 kts   **Man:** 12 officers, 108 men
Electron Equipt: Sonar: BQQ-2 (BQS-6 active/BQR-7 passive)
M: 1 S5W Westinghouse reactor; GE or de Laval GT; 1 prop; 15,000 hp

REMARKS: The *Thresher* (SSN-593) was lost 10-4-63. SSN-605 has contrarotating props with a contrarotating turbine and no reduction gearing. SSN-613 to SSN-615 have taller sails (6.1 m vice 4.2 or 4.6 in other ships) heavier machinery, and had safety features built in that were later backfitted in the others. The BQR-7 spherical array is in the bow, necessitating placement of the tubes abreast the sail. These ships are being fitted to carry Harpoon, and therefore receiving Mk-117 torpedo-fire-control systems in place of Mk-113. SSN-594 conduct Harpoon trials during 1976. All are scheduled to receive the BQQ-5 sonar suit during refits. SSN-621 ran trials in 7-79 for the Sperry PASRAN (passive-ranging) sonar system, which is similar to the exported "Micro Puffs" concept, but with an array of six larger hydrophones.

♦ **1 Tullibee class (SCB 178 type)**

		Bldr	Laid down	L	In serv.
SSN 597	TULLIBEE	Gen. Dynamics	26-5-58	27-4-60	9-11-60

Authorized: FY 58

D: 2,490 tons normal/2,317 surfaced/2,640 submerged   **S:** 15/20 kts
A: 4/533-mm Mk-64 TT (amidships)   **Dim:** 83.15 × 7.31 × 6.1
Man: 6 officers, 50 men
Electron Equipt: Sonars: BQQ-2 (BQS-6 active/BQR-7 passive), BQG-4 (PUFFS)
M: 1 Combustion Engineering S2C reactor, turboelectric propulsion; 1 prop; 2,500 hp

REMARKS: The torpedo tubes have a 10° angle from the centerline. Original nuclear core changed in 1965. PUFFS hydrophones are mounted in three fins along the top of the hull. Mk-112, Mod. 1, torpedo-fire-control system.

NUCLEAR-POWERED ATTACK SUBMARINES (*continued*)

Tullibee   1975

◆ **1 Halibut class (SCB 137A type)**

	Bldr	Laid down	L	In serv.
SSN 587 HALIBUT	Mare Island NSY	4-57	9-1-59	4-1-60

Authorized: FY 57

D: 3,850 tons surfaced/5,000 submerged   **S:** 15/20 kts
Dim: 106.7 × 8.85 × 8.8
A: 6/533-mm TT (4 fwd, 2 aft)   **Man:** 10 officers, 88 men
Electron Equipt: Sonar: BQS-4
M: 1 Westinghouse S3W reactor, 2 GT; 2 props; 13,200 hp

Halibut—with DSRV aboard aft   1970

REMARKS: Ex-SSGN. Placed in reserve on 30-6-76. Forward watertight compartment is 27 m long and 7.6 m high, where four Regulus missiles were stowed. The missiles and the single, trainable launcher were removed in 1965 when the ship was reclassified as an SSN. Equipped to carry a DSRV.

◆ **1 Triton class (SCB 132 type)**

	Bldr	Laid down	L	In serv.
SSN 586 TRITON	Gen. Dynamics	29-5-56	19-8-58	10-11-59

Authorized: FY 56

Triton   1959

D: 5,940 tons surfaced/7,780 submerged   **S:** 27/20 kts
Dim: 136.25 × 11.3 × 7.6
A: 6/533-mm TT (4 fwd, 2 aft)   **Man:** 14 officers, 156 men
Electron Equipt: Sonar: BQS-4
M: 2 GE S4G reactors, 2 GT; 2 props; 34,000 hp

REMARKS: Ex-SSRN. Decommissioned since 3-5-69 as too unwieldy and uneconomical to operate. First submarine with three decks and only U.S. submarine with two reactors. In 1960 made a round-the-world cruise submerged, sailing 41,519 miles in 84 days at an average speed of 18 knots. In 1962 the original nuclear core, with which she had run 125,000 miles (231,500 km), was replaced. Unlike other U.S. nuclear-powered submarines, her speed on the surface is greater than her submerged speed. It was hoped that she would be able to operate as a radar picket with large surface-ship task forces. Reclassified as SSN on 1-3-61. Mk-101, Mod. 11, torpedo-fire-control system.

◆ **5 Skipjack class (SCB 154 type)**

	Bldr	Laid down	L	In serv.
SSN 585 SKIPJACK	Gen. Dynamics	29-5-56	26-5-58	15-4-59
SSN 588 SCAMP	Mare Island, NSY	23-1-59	8-10-60	5-6-61
SSN 590 SCULPIN	Ingalls	3-2-58	31-3-60	1-6-61
SSN 591 SHARK	Newport News SB	24-2-56	16-3-60	9-2-61
SSN 592 SNOOK	Ingalls	7-4-58	31-10-60	24-10-61

Authorized: SSN-585 in FY 56, SSN-588 and SSN-590 to SSN-592 in FY 57

D: 3,075 tons surfaced/3,513 submerged   **S:** 15/30 kts
Dim: 76.8 × 9.75 × 8.5
A: 6/533-mm TT (fwd)   **Man:** 8 officers, 85 men

NUCLEAR-POWERED ATTACK SUBMARINES (*continued*)

Scamp   G, Arra, 1976

Electron Equipt: Sonar: Modified BQS-4

M: 1 Westinghouse S5W reactor; SSN-585: 1 Westinghouse GT, others: 1 GE GT; 1 prop, 15,000 hp

REMARKS: The reactor compartment takes up 6.10 m. Between the reactor and the propeller, all engine fittings are duplicated (two heat exchangers, two pressurized-water coolers; two groups of turbines, two groups of turbo-generators). In case of emergency, submerged propulsion can take over by means of two electric motors linked directly on the propeller shaft and feeding off two electric batteries or two small diesel generators. Better hull form than later SSNs. Still considered first-line submarines. The *Scorpion* (SSN-589) disappeared in the Atlantic about 27-5-68. Mk-101, Mod. 17, torpedo-fire-control system.

◆ **4 Skate class (SCB 121 type)**

	Bldr	Laid down	L	In serv.
SSN 578 SKATE	Gen. Dynamics	21-7-55	16-5-57	23-12-57
SSN 579 SWORDFISH	Portsmouth NSY	25-1-56	27-8-57	15-9-58
SSN 583 SARGO	Mare Island NSY	21-2-56	10-10-57	1-10-58
SSN 584 SEADRAGON	Portsmouth NSY	20-6-56	16-8-58	5-12-59

Authorized: SSN-578 and SSN-579 in FY 55, SSN-583 and SSN-584 in FY 56

Swordfish   G. Arra, 1978

D: 2,570 tons surfaced/2,860 submerged   **S:** 15/19 kts
Dim: 81.4 × 7.62 × 6.1
A: 8/533-mm TT (6 fwd, 2 aft)   **Man:** 8 officers, 87 men
Electron Equipt: Sonar: BQS-4
M: 1 Westinghouse reactor—S3W in SSN-578 and SSN-583, S4W in SSN-579 and SSN-584; 2 GT; 2 props; 13,200 hp

REMARKS: SSN-578 passed under the North Pole twice (8-58), coming to the surface nine times while in ice-capped waters during this cruise. She ran 120,862 miles in 39 months with her first core. Mk-101, Mod. 19, torpedo-fire-control system. Now considered second-line submarines, due to be disposed of 1982-83.

◆ **1 Seawolf class (SCB 64A type)**

	Bldr	Laid down	L	In serv.
SSN 575 SEAWOLF	Gen. Dynamics	15-9-53	21-7-55	30-3-57

Authorized: FY 53

Seawolf   1977

D: 3,765 tons surfaced/4,287 submerged   **S:** 20/20 kts
Dim: 102.87 × 8.45 × 6.7   **A:** 6/533-mm TT (fwd)   **Man:** 11 officers, 90 men
M: 1 Westinghouse S2WA reactor; 2 GT; 2 props; 15,000 hp

REMARKS: The original propulsion, which was by an S2G reactor with sodium cooling, did not prove satisfactory and was replaced by an S2WA. Four side-thrusters, two forward and two aft, have been added to the casing above the pressure hull for precision maneuvering while submerged, and foundations have been added at the stern to permit a DSRV to be carried and to mate with the after rescue hatch. Mk-101, Mod. 8, torpedo-fire-control system. Now considered a second-line submarine and due to be disposed of 1982.

NOTE: The *Nautilus* (SSN-571), the world's first nuclear-powered ship, was placed in technical reserve on 30-9-79. In fact, she is being stripped of her reactor plant and will be taken to the Navy Yard in Washington, D.C., where she will serve as a memorial to her technical achievements.

CONVENTIONAL SUBMARINES

◆ 3 Barbel class (SCB 150 type)

	Bldr	Laid down	L	In serv.
SS 580 BARBEL	Portsmouth NSY	18-5-56	19-7-58	17-1-59
SS 581 BLUEBACK	Ingalls	15-4-57	16-5-59	15-10-59
SS 582 BONEFISH	New York SB	3-6-57	22-11-58	9-7-59

Authorized: FY 56

Barbel—in dry dock   1963

Bonefish   1962

D: 1,740 tons normal/2,146 surfaced/2,895 submerged   **S:** 15/25 kts
Dim: 66.75 × 8.84 × 5.8   **Man:** 8 officers, 70 men
A: 6/533-mm TT (fwd)   **Electron Equipt:** Sonar: BQS-4
M: 3 1,600-hp Fairbanks-Morse 38D8⅛ diesels, 1 Westinghouse electric motor; 1 prop; 3,150 hp

REMARKS: Teardrop hull design, as on the *Albacore*. Diving planes were moved to the sail structure in 1961-62. Dutch *Zwaardvis* class based on this design. Mk-101, Mod. 20, torpedo-fire-control system. Last conventional submarines built for the U.S. Navy.

NOTE: The *Sailfish* (SS-572) was stricken on 30-9-78. She and her sister *Salmon* (SS-573), stricken on 1-10-77, are being retained for possible foreign sale.

◆ 1 Darter class (SCB 116 type)

	Bldr	Laid down	L	In serv.
SS 576 DARTER	Electric Boat Co.	10-11-54	28-5-56	26-10-56

Authorized: FY 54

Darter

D: 1,590 tons standard/1,720 surfaced/2,372 submerged   **S:** 20/20 kts
Dim: 81.68 × 8.23 × 5.8   **Man:** 10 officers, 75 men
A: 8/533-mm TT (6 fwd, 2 aft)
Electron Equipt: Sonar: BQS-4, BQG-4 (PUFFS)
M: 3 Fairbanks-Morse diesels, 2 Westinghouse motors; 2 props; 5,500 hp

REMARKS: Very similar to the ultimate configuration of the *Tang* class. Mk-106, Mod. 11, torpedo-fire-control system. Homeported at Sasebo, Japan, in 3-79. To have been stricken in 9-79, but given at least one year's extension.

◆ 1 Grayback class (SCB 161 type)

	Bldr	Laid down	L	In serv.
SS 574 GRAYBACK	Mare Island NSY	1-7-54	2-7-57	5-58

Authorized: FY 53

D: 2,670 tons surfaced/3,650 submerged   **S:** 20/16.7 kts
Dim: 101.8 × 8.2 × 5.8   **A:** 8/533-mm TT (6 fwd, 2 aft)
Man: 7 officers, 60 men   **Electron Equipt:** Sonars: BQS-4, BQG-4 (PUFFS)
M: 3 Fairbanks-Morse 38D8⅛ diesels, 2 Elliot motors; 2 props; 5,500 hp

REMARKS: Designed as SSG, carrying two Regulus-II surface-to-surface missiles. Conversion to amphibious transport submarine, which took six years, was finished in 9-5-69. Redesignated SS in 1975, but retains capacity for 10 officers and 75 commandos

CONVENTIONAL SUBMARINES (*continued*)

Grayback　　　　　　　　　　　　　　　　PH3 B. Halbert, 1975

Grayback—with hangar doors open　　　　　　　G. Arra, 1978

with their equipment (including swimmer-delivery vehicles) stowed in the former missile hangars. Mk-106, Mod. 12, torpedo-fire-control system. Homeported at Sasebo, Japan.

GUIDED-MISSILE SUBMARINE

◆ 1 Grayback class (SCB 161 type)

	Bldr	Laid down	L	In serv.
SSG 577 GROWLER	Portsmouth NSY	10-11-54	28-5-56	30-8-58

Authorized: FY 55

D: 2,540 tons surfaced/3,515 submerged　　**S:** 20/12 kts
Dim: 96.8 × 8.2 × 5.8
A: 6/533-mm TT (4 fwd, 2 aft)　　**Man:** 9 officers, 87 men
M: 3 Fairbanks-Morse 38D8⅛, 1,500-hp diesels, 2 motors; 2 props; 5,500 hp

REMARKS: In reserve. Intended for Regulus-II cruise missiles, two of which were carried in her two hangars forward. Design is essentially a lengthened *Darter*, cut

Growler　　　　　　　　　　　　　　　　　　1958

in two to add missile features. Decommissioned 25-5-64. Planned conversion to amphibious transport submarine canceled in 1968 but retained because of her low usage and potential for conversion.

BATTLESHIPS

◆ 4 Iowa class

	Bldr	Laid down	L	In serv.
BB 61 IOWA	New York NSY	27-6-40	27-8-42	22-2-43
BB 62 NEW JERSEY	Philadelphia NSY	16-9-40	7-12-42	23-5-43
BB 63 MISSOURI	New York NSY	6-1-41	29-1-44	11-6-44
BB 64 WISCONSIN	Philadelphia NSY	25-1-41	7-12-43	16-4-44

New Jersey　　　　　　　　　　　　　　　　1968

D: 47,000 tons (57,540 fl)　　**S:** 30.5 kts
Dim: 270.57 (262.13 pp) × 33.0 × 11.43
Man: 70 officers, 1,556 men (after reactivation)　　**Range:** 9,600/25, 16,600/15
A: 9/406-mm (III × 3)—20/127-mm DP (II × 10)
Electron Equipt: Radars: 1/SPS-53A, 1/SPS-10F, 1/SPS-6C, 2/Mk-13, 4/Mk-25, 2/Mk-35
Armor: Belt: 406 3 armored decks with a total of 285 (one of which 200)
　　Turrets and Bridge: 457

BATTLESHIPS (continued)

New Jersey   1969

Boilers: 8 Babcock & Wilcox, 43.3 kg/cm² pressure—superheat 454°C
M: 4 sets GT; 4 props; 212,000 hp   **Electric:** 10,500 kw   **Fuel:** 8,800 tons

REMARKS: Data given apply to BB-62. The above battleships are being maintained in inactive reserve, one at Philadelphia and three, including BB-62, at Bremerton, as potential fire-support ships. BB-62, reactivated from 1966 to December 1969, underwent a partial overhaul that enabled her to be used for bombardment operations in Vietnam, where her 406-mm guns were very effective. Only one of these survivors of a long line of dreadnoughts, which for several decades were the keystone of the fleet, BB-62, could be returned to service. BB-63 went aground in 1950 and was not restored to her original condition and speed. A fire broke out near the No. 1 and No. 2 406-mm turrets of BB-64 during her last inactivation overhaul and her circuitry was not repaired. The electronics equipment of BB-61 is completely out of date, and she and BB-64 were cannibalized to refurbish BB-62. In the 1950s the 40-mm antiaircraft guns originally carried were removed, except from BB-63 which has 80 (IV × 20). All have two Mk-38 directors for the 406-mm guns, one Mk-40 director, and four Mk-37 fire-control systems for the 127-mm guns. BB-61 and BB-62 also have six Mk-56 fire-control systems (only two were activated in BB-62 for Vietnam) to control 127-mm guns. BB-63 has six Mk-57 and two Mk-63 radar fire-control systems for her 40-mm AA, while BB-64 has no light AA directors. BB-62 had ECM/ESM gear added during reactivation.

NUCLEAR-POWERED GUIDED-MISSILE CRUISERS

◆ **4 Virginia class**

	Bldr	Laid down	L	In serv.
CGN 38 VIRGINIA	Newport News SB	19-8-72	14-12-74	11-9-76
CGN 39 TEXAS	Newport News SB	18-8-73	9-8-75	10-9-77
CGN 40 MISSISSIPPI	Newport News SB	22-2-75	31-7-76	5-8-78
CGN 41 ARKANSAS	Newport News SB	17-1-77	21-10-78	8-80

Authorized: CGN-38 in FY 70, CGN-39 in FY 71, CGN-40 in FY 72, and CGN-41 in FY 75

D: 10,400 tons (fl)   **S:** 30+ kts   **Dim:** 177.3 × 19.2 × 9.0 (fwd)
A: 2/Mk-26 twin launchers (1/Mod. 1 fwd, 1/Mod. 0 aft), 68 total Standard SM-1-MR surface-to-air or ASROC ASW missiles—2/127-mm Mk-45 DP (I × 2)—2/324-mm Mk-32 ASW TT (III × 2), Mk-46 torpedoes
Electron Equipt: Radars: 1/navigational, 1/SPS-40B, 1/SPS-48A, 1/SPS-55, 2/SPG-51D, 1/Mk-86, Mod. 5, 1/SPQ-9A, 1/SPG-60
    Sonar: 1/SQS-53A
    ECM: SLQ-32(v)3, Mk-36 RBOC chaff—URN-20 TACAN—NTDS
M: 2 GE D2G reactors; 2 props; 60,000 hp   **Man:** 27 officers, 415 men

Mississippi   Newport News SB, 1978

REMARKS: The Standard SM-1-MR antiaircraft missiles and ASROC ASW missiles, stowed vertically, will be replaced by SM-2-MR beginning in 1983. Eventually, they will carry eight Harpoon SSM in canister launchers (IV × 2), and later the Tomahawk cruise-missile system. Harpoon was added to CGN-39 in 1979 and CGN-40 will get it in 1980. It is also planned to add two Vulcan-Phalanx 20-mm Gatling guns on the forward superstructure. A hangar is fitted beneath the fantail, the helicopters being raised to the main deck by elevator. These ships are no longer scheduled to carry UH-60B LAMPS-III helicopters. All four will eventually carry the Mk-36 RBOC chaff/flare rocket system (four launchers) and SLQ-32(v)3 threat-detection/classification/jamming system; CGN-38 was the first ship to carry the equipment, in 1978. The missile-fire-control system is Mk-74; ASW-fire-control is Mk-116. SQS-53A sonar is a greatly improved version of SQS-26. Kevlar plastic armor will be added over vital

NUCLEAR-POWERED GUIDED-MISSILE CRUISERS (*continued*)

topside and magazine spaces during sequential overhauls scheduled from FY 82 to FY 86.

NOTE: Future construction of nuclear-powered surface combatants for the U.S. Navy is in doubt because of the extraordinary initial costs. The building of the 12,000-ton, Aegis-equipped CGN-42 class, based on the *Virginia*-class design, has been canceled —at least through FY 85. Hull numbers in the block CGN-42 through CGN-46 are being "reserved" for future construction, CG-47 and above being the redesignated DDG-47 class.

Texas   Newport News, 1977

Texas   Newport News, 1977

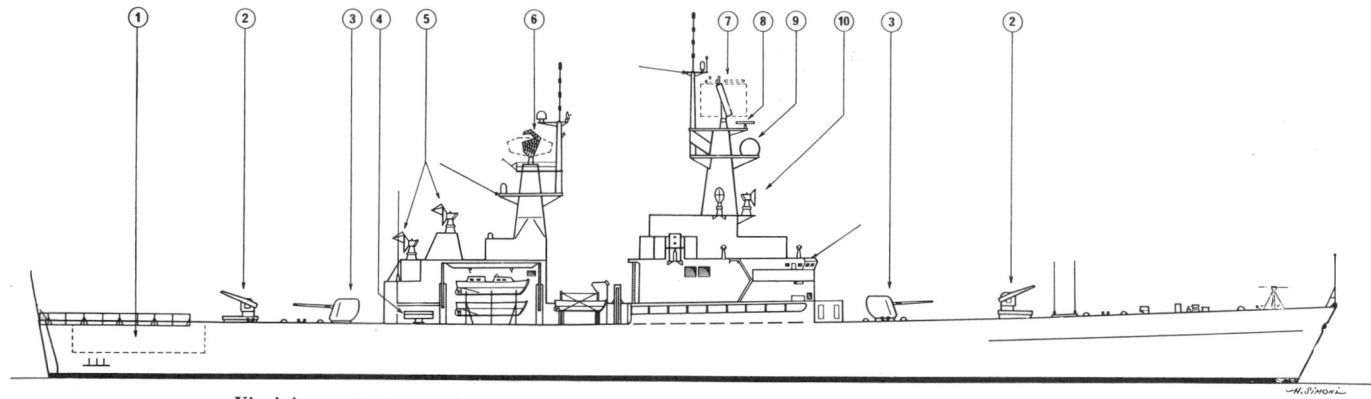

Virginia   1. Helicopter hangar   2. Mk-26 launcher   3. 127-mm Mk-45 mount   4. Mk-32 ASW TT 5. SPG-51D radar   6. SPS-40B radar   7. SPS-48A radar   8. SPS-55 radar   9. SPQ-9A radar   10. SPG-60 radar

NUCLEAR-POWERED GUIDED-MISSILE CRUISERS (*continued*)

Texas Newport News, 1977

Mississippi Newport News, 1978

Virginia G. Arra, 1976

◆ **2 California class (SCB 241.65 type)**

	Bldr	Laid down	L	In serv.
CGN 36 CALIFORNIA	Newport News SB	23-1-70	22-9-71	16-2-74
CGN 37 SOUTH CAROLINA	Newport News SB	1-12-70	1-7-72	25-1-75

Authorized: CGN-36 in FY 67, CGN-37 in FY 68

California JO2 R. Leonard, 1976

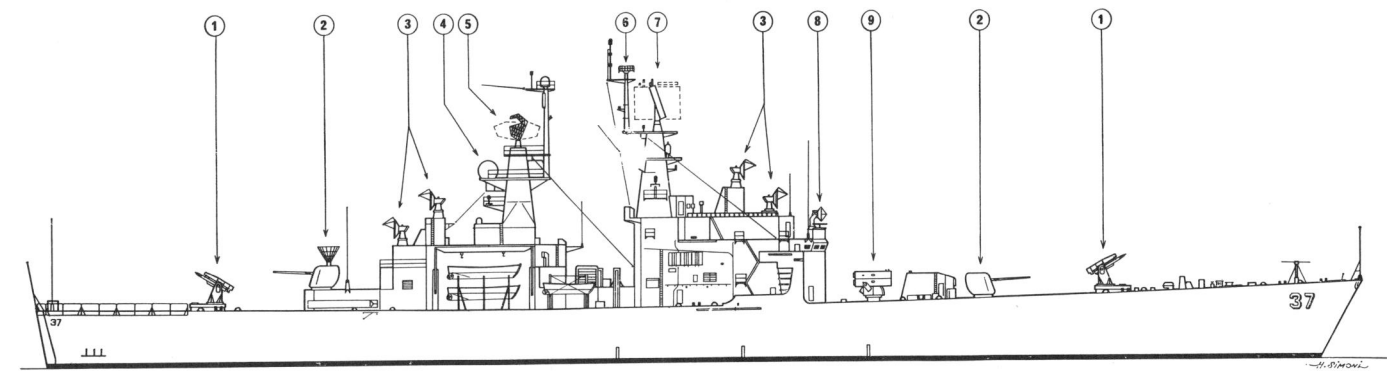

1. Mk-13 launcher 2. 127-mm Mk-45 mount 3. SPG-51D radar 4. SPQ-9A radar
5. SPS-40B radar 6. SPS-10 radar 7. SPS-48A radar 8. SPG-60 radar 9. ASROC launcher

NUCLEAR-POWERED GUIDED-MISSILE CRUISERS (*continued*)

South Carolina   JO2 R. Leonard, 1976

D: 10,400 tons (fl)   **S:** 30+ kts   **Dim:** 181.66 × 18.6 × 9.6 (fwd)
A: 2/Mk-13 launchers (II × 1) for 80 SM-1-MR missiles—2/127-mm Mk-45 DP
(I × 2)—1/ASROC ASW system (VIII × 1)—4/324-mm Mk-32 ASW TT (II × 2)
Electron Equipt: Radars: 1/navigational, 1/SPS 10, 1/SPS-40B, 1/SPS-48A, 4/SPG-
51D, 1/Mk-86, 1/SPQ-9A, 1/SPG-60
Sonar: 1/SQS-26CX
ECM: to receive SLQ-32(v)3—URN-20 TACAN—NTDS
M: 2 GE D2G reactors, 2 GT; 2 props; 60,000 hp   **Man:** 28 officers, 512 men

REMARKS: Each Mk-13 launcher magazine holds 40 vertically stowed missiles, and the
ASROC system includes automatic reloading from a magazine on deck, forward of
the launcher. The ships will eventually receive two Vulcan/Phalanx 20-mm AA,
Harpoon and Tomahawk ASMs, SLQ-32(v)3 ECM/ESM, and four Mk-36 Super RBOC
chaff/flare rocket launchers. They have no helicopter hangar. Weapons are controlled
by the Mk-11, Mod. 13, direction system, handling two Mk-74, Mod. 2, missile-fire-
control systems and the Mk-86, Mod. 3, gun-fire-control system. ASW fire is controlled
by a Mk-114 system. Kevlar plastic armor will be added over vital spaces in overhauls
scheduled for 1986 and 1987.

◆ **1 Truxtun class (SCB 222 type)**

	Bldr	Laid down	L	In serv.
CGN 35 TRUXTUN	New York SB, Camden, N.J.	17-6-63	19-12-64	27-5-67

Authorized: FY 62

D: 8,600 tons (fl)   **S:** 30+ kts   **Dim:** 171.91 × 17.67 × 9.45 (fwd)
Man: 36 officers, 465 men   **Electric:** 10,000 kw
A: 1/Mk-10 launcher (II × 1) for 40 Standard SM-1-ER and 20 ASROC missiles—
1/127-mm Mk-42, 54-cal. DP—2/76.2-mm Mk-34 DP (I × 2)—4/324-mm Mk-32
ASW TT (II × 2)—1/SH-2 LAMPS-II ASW helicopter
Electron Equipt: Radars: 1/SPS-10, 1/SPS-40, 1/SPS-48, 1/SPG-53A, 2/SPG-55B
Sonar: 1/SQS-26
ECM: WLR-6, 2/Mk-28 chaffroc—URN-20 TACAN—NTDS
M: 2 GE D2G reactors, 2 sets GT; 2 props; 60,000 hp

REMARKS: When next overhauled, will receive two Vulcan-Phalanx 20-mm AA in place

Truxtun   G. Arra, 1977

Truxtun   G. Arra, 1977

of the 76.2-mm DP and will be given eight Harpoon SSM (IV × 2). Two Mk-25 torpedo
tubes at stern removed. Eventually will carry the SM-2-ER missile. Has flag accommodations for six officers and twelve enlisted in addition to crew. Mk-76, Mod. 6,
missile-control system. Mk-68 fire-control system for the 127-mm gun. Two Mk-51 (no
radar) directors for the 76.2-mm have been removed. Mk-114 ASW-fire-control system.
The ECM system will be updated with the SLQ-32(v)3 system and four Mk-36 Super
RBOC chaff launchers in place of the two Mk-28 chaffroc.

◆ **1 Bainbridge class**

	Bldr	Laid down	L	In serv.
CGN 25 BAINBRIDGE	Bethlehem Steel, Quincy	5-59	15-4-61	6-10-62

Authorized: FY 59

D: 8,600 tons (fl)   **S:** 34 kts   **Dim:** 172.21 (167.65 wl) × 17.57 × 9.45
Man: 34 officers, 436 men   **Electric:** 14,500 kw
A: 4/Mk-10 launchers (II × 2), 80 Standard SM-1-ER missiles—8/Harpoon SSM
(IV × 2)—1/ASROC system (VIII × 1)—6/324-mm Mk-32 ASW TT (III × 2)
Electron Equipt: Radars: 1/navigational, 1/SPS-10, 1/SPS-48A, 1/SPS-37, 4/SPG-
55B

NUCLEAR-POWERED GUIDED-MISSILE CRUISERS (*continued*)

Bainbridge — with Harpoon system   PH2 P. Salesi, 1979

Bainbridge   G. Arra, 1978

Bainbridge   1977

      Sonar: 1/SQS-23
      ECM: WLR-6, 2/Mk-28 chaffroc – URN-20 TACAN – NTDS
M: 2 GE D2G reactors, 2 GT; 2 props; 60,000+ hp

REMARKS: In refit-modernization at Puget Sound NSY from 6-74 to 9-76 to improve AAW; refit completed at San Diego in 4-77. Obsolete 76-mm AA removed, temporarily replaced by two 20-mm AA, 1978-79. Two quadruple Harpoon canister launch groups replaced the 20-mm AA during 1979, those to port firing forward and those to starboard firing aft. Two Mk-15 Vulcan-Phalanx 20-mm AA will eventually be added. Large deckhouse added aft to house NTDS. SPS-37 radar will be replaced by SPS-49.

Still to be fitted with SLQ-32(v)3 ECM/ESM and Mk-36 RBOC chaff-flare system. Helicopter platform but no hangar. Will eventually carry Standard SM-2-ER SAM. Mk-111 ASW-fire-control system, two Mk-76, Mod. 1, missile-fire-control systems.

◆ **1 Long Beach class (SCB 169 type)**

	Bldr	Laid down	L	In serv.
CGN 9 LONG BEACH	Bethlehem Steel (Quincy)	2-12-57	14-7-59	9-9-61

Authorized: FY 57

D: 15,500 tons (17,500 fl)   **S:** 30.5 kts   **Dim:**   219.75 × 22.35 × 9.45 (over sonar)

Man: 79 officers, 1,081 men, + flag group: 10 officers, 58 men   **Electric:** 17,000 kw
A: 1/Mk-10, Mod. 0, and 1/Mk-10, Mod. 1, launchers (II × 2), 120 Standard SM-1-ER

Long Beach — before modernization   G. Arra, 1978

Long Beach — before modernization   G. Arra, 1978

NUCLEAR-POWERED GUIDED-MISSILE CRUISERS (*continued*)

missiles—16/Harpoon SSM (IV × 4)—2/127-mm 38-cal. DP (I × 2)—2/20-mm Mk-15 Vulcan-Phalanx AA (I × 2)—1/ASROC ASW system (VIII × 1)—6/324-mm ASW TT (III × 2)

Electron Equipt: Radars: 1/SPS-10-65, 1/SPS-48C, 1/SPS-49, 4/SPG-55D, 2/Mk-35
Sonar: 1/SQQ-23 PAIR (single-dome)
ECM: SLQ-32(v)3, 4/Mk-36 Super RBOC chaff—URN-20 TACAN

M: 2 Westinghouse C1W reactors, 8 Foster-Wheeler heat exchangers, 2 sets GE GT; 2 props; 80,000 hp

REMARKS: The first U.S. surface ship to have nuclear propulsion. Original number was CLGN-160, then CGN-160. Originally intended to carry Regulus-II cruise missiles and eight Polaris ballistic missiles. Under FY 77, Congress appropriated long-lead funds to equip the ship with Aegis radar/fire-control system, since it is planned to operate the ship into the twenty-first century; the radical modernization plans were, however, canceled in 12-76.

The *Long Beach* is to enter Puget Sound for a less extensive two-year modernization period in 1980; the equipment and armament listed above will be carried when she emerges in 1981. The Mk-12 launch system aft for Talos missiles (deactivated in 1978) was stripped out in 1979 and the pedestals on the after superstructure that formerly supported SPG-49B Talos missile-direction radars will carry the two Vulcan-Phalanx Gatling AA guns. Harpoon canister clusters, arranged to fire athwartships, will be situated before and abaft the superstructure, which will be surmounted by a tall lattice mast to support the antenna for the SPS-49C 3-D air-search radar. The "billboard" fixed-array antennas on the blockhouse-style forward superstructure will be removed but the structure will otherwise be little altered. SPS-49 will replace SPS-12 on the pole foremast. The obsolescent Mk-30, 127-mm, dual-purpose guns and their two equally aged Mk-56 directors (Mk-35 radars) will be retained, as will the original ASW weapons and the forward missile-launching arrangements. No helicopter hangar will be provided, only a pad on the stern. The Mk-10, Mod. 0, launcher for Standard missiles has two magazine drums, each holding 20 missiles; the Mk-10, Mod. 1, in the upper position has four magazine drums. Standard SM-2-ER will be substituted for SM-1-ER when available. The *Long Beach* will continue to have flagship facilities, and extensive satellite-communications facilities will be provided.

GUIDED-MISSILE CRUISERS

◆ 2 (+ . . .) . . . **class**

	Bldr	Laid down	L	In serv.
CG 47 N . . .	Ingalls, Pascagoula	3-80	4-81	1-83
CG 48 N . . .		. . .	. . .	. . .

Authorized: CG-47 in FY 78, CG-48 in FY 80

D: 8,910 tons (fl) **S:** 30+ kts **Dim:** 172.5 (161.24 wl) × 16.76 × 6.52 (9.57 over sonar)

Man: 33 officers, 327 men **Range:** 6,000/20 **Electric:** 6,000 kw

A: 2/Mk-26, Mod. 1, launchers (II × 2), 68 Standard SM-2-MR and 20 ASROC missiles—8/Harpoon SSM (IV × 2)—2/127-mm Mk-45 (I × 2)—2/20-mm Vulcan-Phalanx AA (I × 2)—6/324-mm Mk-32 ASW TT (III × 2)—2/SH-60B LAMPS-III ASW helicopters

Electron Equipt: Radars: 1/SPS-55, 1/SPS-49, 1/SPY-1A, 1/SPQ-9A, 4/Mk-99
Sonars: 1/SQS-53A, 1/SQR-19A TACTASS (towed passive array)
ECM: SLQ-32(v)3, 4/Mk-36 Super RBOC—URN-20 TACAN

M: 4 GE LM-2500 gas turbines; 2 five-bladed controllable-pitch props; 80,000 hp

REMARKS: Ex-DDG-47 class. Greatly revised version of the *Spruance*-class destroyers, using same hull and propulsion but incorporating the Aegis weapon system (SPY-1A phased-array radar, four Mk-99 missile illuminator radars, Mk-26 missile-launch system). Designation changed from DDG to CG in late 1979 to reflect size, importance, and combat capability. Future acquisition plans uncertain, as by FY 81 *each* unit will probably cost more than $1 billion. The FY 80 version of the five-year construction plan called for two in 1981, three per year in FY 82 and 83, with four each in FY 84/85.

Each Mk-26, Mod. 1, missile-launcher magazine holds 44 missiles, the forward magazine holding the 20 ASROC. A new vertical-launch system is planned to replace the Mk-26, possibly early enough for installation in CG-49. The Mk-86 fire-control system for the 127-mm guns provides no AA capability in this class, as no SPG-60 radar is carried. The R.C.A.-built Aegis Mk-7 system, which uses several UYK-7 and UYK-20 computers, uses the four fixed faces of the SPY-1A radar to detect and track up to several hundred targets simultaneously; the four Mk-99 illuminators are slaved to the system and can, through time-share switching, serve more than a dozen missiles

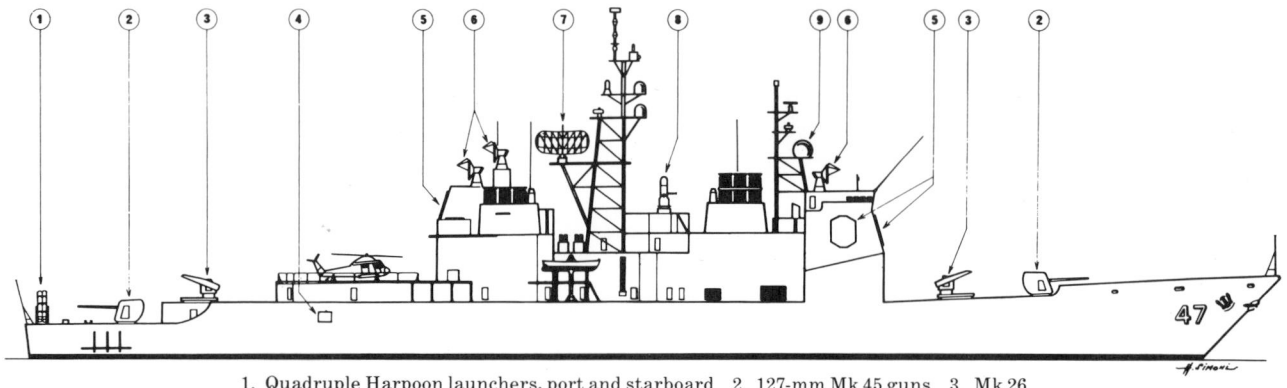

1. Quadruple Harpoon launchers, port and starboard 2. 127-mm Mk 45 guns 3. Mk 26 guided-missile launchers 4. Shutters over Mk 32 ASW TT 5. SPY-1A radar antennas 6. Mk 99 illuminators 7. SPS-49 radar 8. Vulcan-Phalanx 20-mm AA 9. SPQ-9A fire-control radar

GUIDED-MISSILE CRUISERS (*continued*)

CG-47 — model   R.C.A., 1978

CG-47 — model   R.C.A., 1978

in the air at once. The Harpoon missiles are in an exposed and vulnerable position at the extreme stern. Bow bulwarks were required to keep decks dry, as draft was increased about one meter over that of the original *Spruance* design. No fin stabilization is fitted.

◆ **9 Belknap class (SCB 212 type)**

		Bldr	Laid down	L	In serv.
CG 26	BELKNAP	Bath Iron Works	5-2-62	20-7-63	7-11-64
CG 27	JOSEPHUS DANIELS	Bath Iron Works	23-4-62	2-12-63	8-5-65
CG 28	WAINWRIGHT	Bath Iron Works	2-7-62	25-4-64	8-1-66
CG 29	JOUETT	Puget Sound NSY	25-9-62	30-6-64	3-12-66
CG 30	HORNE	San Francisco NSY	12-9-62	30-10-64	15-4-67
CG 31	STERRETT	Puget Sound NSY	25-9-62	30-6-64	8-4-67
CG 32	WILLIAM H. STANDLEY	Bath Iron Works	29-7-63	19-12-64	9-7-66
CG 33	FOX	Todd SY, San Pedro	15-1-63	21-11-64	28-5-66
CG 34	BIDDLE	Bath Iron Works	9-12-63	2-7-65	21-1-67

Authorized: Three in FY 61 and six in FY 62

Wainwright   G. Arra, 1979

D: 6,570 tons (8,250 fl)   **S:** 34 kts   **Dim:** 166.72 × 16.76 × 5.9 (8.8 over sonar)

Man: 31 officers, 387 men + flag group: 6 officers, 12 enlisted

Range: 2,500/30, 8,000/14   **Electric:** 6,800 kw

A: 1/Mk-10, Mod. 7, launcher (II × 1), 40 Standard SM-1-ER or SM-2-MR and 20 ASROC missiles — 8/Harpoon SSM (IV × 2) — 1/127-mm Mk-42 DP (aft) — 6/324-mm Mk-32 ASW TT (III × 2) — 1/SH-2D Sea Sprite LAMPS-I ASW helicopter

Electron Equipt: Radars: 1/LN-66, 1/SPS-10F, 1/SPS-40A (except CG-27, CG-28, and CG-30: 1/SPS-43), 1/SPS-48, 2/SPG-55D, 1/SPG-53A
         Sonar: 1/SQS-26 — URN-20 TACAN — NTDS
         ECM: WLR-6, 2/Mk-28 chaffroc *or* 4/Mk-36 Super RBOC

Boilers: CG-24, CG-28, CG-32, CG-34: 4 Foster-Wheeler; others: 4 Combustion Engineering, 84 kg/cm² pressure — superheat 520°C

M: 2 sets GT; 2 six-bladed props; 85,000 hp

REMARKS: Ex-DLG, classified CG on 1-7-75. CG-26, severely damaged in collision with CV-67 in Mediterranean in November 1975, will be out of commission for repairs at Philadelphia until late 1980. She will have her 76.2-mm guns replaced by two Vulcan-Phalanx 20-mm Gatling AA and will receive SPS-48C radar, Harpoon, SM-2-MR missiles, and improved electronics (including NTDS, Mod. 4) and communications gear. CG-31 was the first to lose her 76-mm, in 1976, to make way for eight Harpoon ASM (IV × 2), now also carried by the others (firing forward to port, aft to starboard). All will eventually receive Vulcan-Phalanx. CG-28 has been used as trials ship for SM-2-MR. SPS-49 will replace SPS-43 in CG-27, CG-28, and CG-30. The 127-mm gun is controlled by a Mk-68 director. Mk-114 ASW-fire-control system, one Mk-11 weapon-

GUIDED-MISSILE CRUISERS (continued)

Horne   G. Arra, 1978

Sterrett — with Harpoon   G. Arra, 1978

Sterrett — with Harpoon   PH3 C. Phelps, 1976

direction system, and two Mk-76 missile-fire-control systems. Two Mk-25 ASW torpedo tubes have been removed from all. CG-33 conducted trials with a twin box-type launcher for Tomahawk cruise missiles in 1977; all will receive the missile in about 1983. These ships will not receive the SH-60B LAMPS-III ASW helicopter.

Josephus Daniels   G. Arra, 1978

GUIDED-MISSILE CRUISERS (*continued*)

Biddle   1978

Jouett   G. Arra, 1978

Jouett   PH1 A. Lagare, 1978

◆ **9 Leahy class (SCB 172 type)**

	Bldr	Laid down	L	In serv.
CG 16 LEAHY	Bath Iron Works	3-12-59	1-7-61	4-8-62
CG 17 HARRY E. YARNELL	Bath Iron Works	31-5-60	9-12-61	2-2-63
CG 18 WORDEN	Bath Iron Works	19-9-60	2-6-62	3-8-63
CG 19 DALE	New York SB	6-9-60	28-7-62	23-11-63
CG 20 RICHMOND K. TURNER	New York SB	9-1-61	6-4-63	13-6-64
CG 21 GRIDLEY	Puget Sound B & DD Co.	15-7-60	31-7-61	25-5-63
CG 22 ENGLAND	Todd SY, Los Angeles	4-10-60	6-3-62	7-12-63
CG 23 HALSEY	San Francisco NSY	26-8-60	15-1-62	20-7-63
CG 24 REEVES	Puget Sound NSY	1-7-60	12-5-62	15-5-64

Authorized: 3 in FY 58, 6 in FY 59

Leahy   G. Arra, 1977

D: 6,070 tons (8,200 fl)   **S:** 34 kts   **Dim:** 162.46 × 16.15 × 5.9 (7.9 over sonar)
Man: 32 officers, 381 men + flag group: 6 officers, 12 enlisted
Range: 2,500/30, 8,000/14   **Fuel:** 1,800 tons   **Electric:** 6,800 kw
A: 2/Mk-10 launchers (II × 2), 80 Standard SM-1-ER missiles – 8/Harpoon SSM (IV × 2) – 1/ASROC ASW system – 6/324-mm Mk-32 ASW TT (III × 2)
Electron Equipt: Radars: 1/SPS-53, 1/SPS-10, 1/SPS-37 (CG-19: SPS-49), 1/SPS-48, 4/SPG-55B
    Sonar: 1/SQQ-23 PAIR (single-dome)
    ECM: WLR-6, 2/Mk-28 chaffroc or 4/Mk-36 Super RBOC – URN/20 TACAN – NTDS
Boilers: CG-16 to CG-20: 4 Babcock & Wilcox; others: 4 Combustion Engineering; 84 kg/cm² pressure – superheat 520°C
M: CG-16 to CG-19: 2 sets GE, CG-20 to CG-22: 2 sets de Laval, CG-23 and CG-24: 2 sets Allis Chalmers, GT; 2 five-bladed props; 85,000 hp

REMARKS: During their overhaul, 1967-72, the *Leahy*-class ships received an advanced version of the Mk-76 missile-fire-control system, permitting firing of Standard SM-1-ER missiles. CG-16 was the first to complete this overhaul and returned to active service on 17-8-68. These are former DLGs, classified CG on 1-7-75. All will receive SM-2-ER missiles commencing with CG-17. Two Vulcan-Phalanx 20-mm Gatling AA will be added. The four 76.2-mm (II × 2) guns have been removed from all and their

GUIDED-MISSILE CRUISERS (continued)

Dale—with SPS-49 radar   A. Baker, 1976

gun tubs are used as locations for Harpoon missile launchers. Like CGN-25, these ships are completely devoid of gun armament. CG-19 received SPS-49 in place of SPS-37 in 1976; the others will be similarly reequipped and all will get Mk-36 RBOC chaff/flare rocket launchers. Four Mk-76 missile-fire-control systems, with SPG-55B radar trackers/illuminators. Mk-114 ASW-fire control. Mk-11, Mod. 2, weapons-control system.

Halsey   PH3 C. Phelps, 1976

◆ **1 Albany class (SCB 002-66 conversion)**

	Bldr	Laid down	L	In serv.
CG 10 ALBANY (ex-CA-123)	Bethlehem, Quincy	6-3-44	30-6-45	15-6-46

Albany   1977

D: 14,600 tons (19,500 fl)   **S:** 32 kts   **Dim:** 205.25 (202.4 wl) × 21.27 × 7.8 (9.1 fwd)

Man: 72 officers, 1,150 men + flag group: 10 officers, 58 enlisted

Range: 7,000/15   **Fuel:** 2,500 tons   **Electric:** 3,000 kw

A: 2/Mk-11 launchers (II × 2), 80 Standard SM-1-MR missiles—2/127-mm Mk-24 DP (I × 2)—1/ASROC ASW system (VIII × 1)—6/324-mm Mk-32 ASW TT (III × 2)

Armor: Belt: 152-203   Upper deck: 100   Lower deck: 62

Electron Equipt: Radars: 1/LN-66, 1/SPS-10C, 1/SPS-43A, 1/SPS-48, 4/SPG-51C, 2/Mk-35

       Sonar: SQS-23

       ECM: WLR-6, 2/Mk-28 chaffroc—URN-20 TACAN—NTDS

Boilers: 8 Babcock & Wilcox, 43 kg/cm² pressure—superheat 465°C

M: 4 sets GE GT; 4 props; 120,000 hp

REMARKS: CG-10 was to have been stricken on 1-2-80 but has been retained as flagship of the Sixth Fleet in the Mediterranean because of a lack of suitable replacement. She is now scheduled to be stricken 29-8-80. CG-11 began her final cruise in the Western Pacific in 7-79 and was to be stricken on 1-3-80. The Talos missile systems in both were inactivated in 1978; the two Mk-12 launchers and four SPG-49B radars were left aboard but are not functional. Former *Baltimore*-class heavy cruisers. Reconversion took four years, CG-10 recommissioning on 2-11-62. Alloy superstructure; living spaces entirely air-conditioned. Old masts and stacks replaced by "macks," which allow the stack gases to vent through lateral conduits in the same structures on which the radar antennas are mounted. Two single-barrel 127-mm semiautomatic, 38-caliber, gun mounts were added in 1963, one on each side; each has a Mk-56 director. Sister *Columbus* (CG-12) was decommissioned at Norfolk on 31-1-75 and stricken on 9-8-76. CG-10 and CG-11 were to have been extensively refitted in 1978 and funds were appropriated but used for other purposes. The principal justification for retention of CG-10 is her extensive communications, including several different satellite systems.

NOTE: The *Galveston*-class guided-missile cruiser *Oklahoma City* (CG-5) was stricken on 15-12-79; her place as flagship of the Seventh Fleet has been taken by the *Blue Ridge* (LCC-19).

The *Providence*-class guided-missile cruisers *Providence* (CG-6) and *Springfield* (CG-7) were stricken on 30-7-78; both had been in reserve since 1973 or 1974.

HEAVY CRUISERS

◆ 2 Des Moines class

	Bldr	Laid down	L	In serv.
CA 134 DES MOINES	Bethlehem, Fore River	28-5-45	27-9-46	16-11-48
CA 139 SALEM	Bethlehem, Fore River	4-7-45	25-3-47	14-5-49

Des Moines   1960

D: 17,255 tons (21,470 fl)   **S:** 32 kts   **Dim:** 218.42 (213.36 wl) × 22.96 × 7.5
Man: 105 officers, 1,745 men (wartime)   **Range:** 8,000/15   **Fuel:** 2,600 tons
A: 9/203-mm (III × 3) – 12/127-mm DP (II × 6) – 20-22/76.2-mm DP (II × 10 or 11)
Armor: Belt: 102-152   Upper deck: 25   Lower deck: 85   Turrets:
     203 face, 95 sides, 102 roof   Barbettes: 160   Pilothouse: 102-160
     Steering: 96-160
Electron Equipt: Radars: 1/SG-6, 1/SPS-8, 1/SPS-6C (CA-139: SPS-12), 2/Mk-13,
     4/Mk-25, 4/Mk-35 (CA-139: 2/Mk-34 also) – URN-6
     TACAN

Boilers: 4 Babcock & Wilcox   **Electric:** 7,700 kw
M: 4 sets GT; 4 props; 120,000 hp

REMARKS: CA-139 to reserve on 30-1-59, CA-134 on 14-7-61. Sister *Newport News* (CA-148), in reserve since 27-6-75, was stricken on 30-6-78. The last "gun cruisers" on the Navy List, neither survivor is likely to see further active service; both have thoroughly antiquated sensors and communications systems. CA-134 has ten twin 76.2-mm Mk-34 DP mounts, her sister has eleven. Each has two Mk-54 directors (with Mk-13 radar) for the 203-mm guns, four Mk-37 fire-control systems for the 127-mm guns, and four Mk-56 and two Mk-63 fire-control systems for the 76.2-mm guns.

NOTE: The *Baltimore*-class cruisers *Canberra* (CA-70) and *Saint Paul* (CA-73) were stricken on 30-6-78; they had been in reserve since 1970 or 1971.

     The *Northampton* (CC-1) and *Wright* (CC-2) were stricken on 1-12-77; both were in reserve. The flagship for the Mid East Force, *La Salle* (AGF-3, ex-LPD-3) is described under Auxiliary Ships. The *Albany* (CG-10) serves as flagship of the Sixth Fleet in the Mediterranean, the *Mount Whitney* (LCC-20) is flagship of the Second Fleet on the East Coast, and her sister, the *Blue Ridge* (LCC-19), has replaced the *Galveston* (CG-5) as flagship of the Seventh Fleet in the Far East.

GUIDED-MISSILE DESTROYERS

◆ . . . DDX class

Originally scheduled for introduction under FY 84, this new program remains undefined after several years of study and may now be slipped to FY 86 or later. The ships are intended to replace the DD-931 class and were to be between 5,500 and 8,000 tons, full load, with gas-turbine propulsion. The weapons and sensor systems have not yet been specified, but vertically launched missiles may be incorporated.

◆ 4 Kidd class   Bldr: Ingalls, Pascagoula

	Laid down	L	In serv.
DDG 993 KIDD (ex-*Kouroush*)	26-6-78	28-8-79	1981
DDG 994 CALLAGHAN (ex-*Daryush*)	23-10-78	1-80	1981
DDG 995 SCOTT (ex-*Nader*)	12-2-79	4-80	1981
DDG 996 CHANDLER (ex-*Andushirvan*)	7-5-79	7-80	1981

Authorized: FY 79 Supplemental

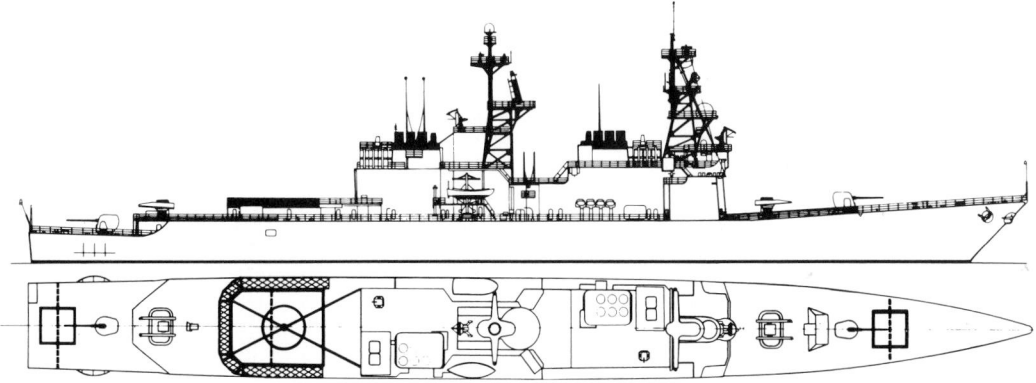

Kidd class   Ingalls Shipbuilding, 1979

GUIDED-MISSILE DESTROYERS (*continued*)

Kidd—artist's impression   Ingalls/Hamelrath, 1976

D: 8,140 tons (fl)   **S:** 30+ kts
Dim: 171.7 (161.23 wl) × 16.76 × 6.07 (9.11 over sonar)
Man: 34 officers, 299 men   **Range:** 3,300/30, 6,000/20   **Electric:** 6,000 kw
A: 1/Mk-26, Mod. 0, and 1/Mk-26, Mod. 1, launchers (II × 2), 52 Standard SM-1-MR
and 16 ASROC missiles—8/Harpoon SSM (IV × 2)—2/127-mm Mk-45 DP (I × 2)—
2/20-mm Vulcan-Phalanx AA (I × 2)—6/324-mm Mk-32 ASW TT (III × 2)—
1/SH-3 Sea King or 2/SH-60B LAMPS-III ASW helicopters
Electron Equipt: Radars: 1/SPS-53, 1/SPS-55, 1/SPS-48, 2/SPG-55D, 1/SPG-60,
1/SPQ-9A
Sonar: SQS-53
ECM: ULQ-32(v)3, 4/Mk-36 Super chaffroc—URN-20—TACAN
M: 4 GE LM-2500 gas turbines; 2 five-bladed controllable-pitch props; 80,000 hp

REMARKS: The original order for these superb ships placed with the U.S. Navy by Iran
in 1974 was for six; two were canceled before the order to Ingalls Shipbuilding for the
remaining four was issued on 23-3-78. DDG-993 and DDG-994 were canceled by the
new Iranian government on 3-2-79, and the other pair shortly thereafter. Their completion for the U.S. Navy was authorized by the U.S. Congress under a Fiscal 1979
Supplementary Appropriations Act. At approximately $510 million each, they repre-
sent a considerable bargain. The first two were to be numbered DD-995 and DD-996;
the new numbers do not fit in USN hull-numbering sequence for guided-missile destroyers.

Harpoon and Vulcan-Phalanx were not in the weapons suit ordered for Iran and
may not be fitted when the ships are first commissioned. Standard SM-2-MR missiles
will be backfitted at a later date. Two Mk-74 missile-fire-control systems (with SPG-
51D radar tracker/illuminators) are carried, as well as the Mk-86, Mod. 5, gun-fire-
control system, which uses the SPQ-9A radar for surface fire and the SPG-60 for AA
(the latter can also be used as a missile illuminator). There are two IR/TV tracker
directors. The ASROC missiles are carried in the larger Mk-26, Mod. 1, missile-launch
system's magazine, which is aft; the Mk-116 underwater battery fire-control system
is carried. SLQ-25 NIXIE towed, anti-torpedo decoys are fitted; the ships were not
intended to have the SQR-19A TACTASS towed passive sonar array, but it could be
backfitted.

These ships were given better air-intake filter systems than the U.S. *Spruance*
class has, in order to handle the dust and sand prevailing in Iranian operating areas.

They also have greater air-conditioning capacity. These features should make them
invaluable for duties in the Indian Ocean. The Iranian Navy planned to type them
as cruisers.

Kidd—just before launch   Ingalls, 1979

GUIDED-MISSILE DESTROYERS (continued)

◆ 23 Charles F. Adams class (SCB 155 type)

	Bldr	Laid down	L	In serv.
DDG 2 CHARLES F. ADAMS	Bath Iron Works	16-6-58	8-9-59	10-9-60
DDG 3 JOHN KING	Bath Iron Works	25-8-58	30-1-60	4-2-61
DDG 4 LAWRENCE	New York SB	27-10-58	27-2-60	6-1-62
DDG 5 CLAUDE V. RICKETTS (ex-Biddle)	New York SB	18-5-59	16-4-60	5-5-62
DDG 6 BARNEY	New York SB	18-8-59	10-12-60	11-8-62
DDG 7 HENRY B. WILSON	Defoe SB	28-2-58	22-4-59	17-12-60
DDG 8 LYNDE MCCORMICK	Defoe SB	4-4-58	9-9-60	3-6-61
DDG 9 TOWERS	Todd, Seattle	1-4-58	23-4-59	24-6-61
DDG 10 SAMPSON	Bath Iron Works	2-3-59	9-9-60	24-6-61
DDG 11 SELLERS	Bath Iron Works	3-8-59	9-9-60	28-10-61
DDG 12 ROBISON	Defoe SB	23-4-59	27-4-60	9-12-61
DDG 13 HOEL	Defoe SB	1-6-59	4-8-60	16-6-62
DDG 14 BUCHANAN	Todd, Seattle	23-4-59	11-5-60	7-2-62
DDG 15 BERKELEY	New York SB	1-6-60	29-7-61	15-12-62
DDG 16 JOSEPH STRAUSS	New York SB	27-12-60	9-12-61	20-4-63
DDG 17 CONYNGHAM	New York SB	1-5-61	19-5-62	13-7-63
DDG 18 SEMMES	Avondale SY	18-8-60	20-5-61	10-12-62
DDG 19 TATTNALL	Avondale SY	14-11-60	26-8-61	13-4-63
DDG 20 GOLDSBOROUGH	Puget Sound B & DD	3-1-61	15-12-61	9-11-63
DDG 21 COCHRANE	Puget Sound B & DD	31-7-61	18-7-62	21-3-64
DDG 22 BENJAMIN STODDERT	Puget Sound B & DD	11-6-62	8-1-63	12-9-64
DDG 23 RICHARD E. BYRD	Todd, Seattle	12-4-61	6-2-62	7-3-64
DDG 24 WADDELL	Todd, Seattle	6-2-62	26-2-63	28-8-64

Authorized: 8 in FY 57, 5 in FY 58, 5 in FY 59, 3 in FY 60, and 2 in FY 61

Buchanan   PHAN P. Tiffany, 1977

D: 3,370 tons (4,600 fl)   **S:** 31.5 kts
Dim: 133.19 (128.0 wl) × 14.32 × 6.1 (8.3 over sonar)
Man: 20-24 officers, 319-330 men   **Range:** 1,600/30, 6,000/14
Fuel: 900 tons

Towers   PH1 A. Lagare, 1976

GUIDED-MISSILE DESTROYERS (*continued*)

Tattnall   1978

A: 1/Mk-11 twin missile launcher or, beginning with DDG-16, 1/Mk-13, single
    launcher, 40 Standard SM-1-MR missiles—2/127-mm Mk-42 DP (I × 2)—1/
    ASROC system (VIII × 1)—6/324-mm Mk-32 ASW TT (III × 2)

Electron Equipt: Radars: 1/SPS-10, 1/SPS-37 (DDG-15 to DDG-24: SPS-40), 1/SPS-
39A, 2/SPG-51C, 1/SPG-53

Sonar: 1/SQS-23 (hull-mounted in DDG-2 to DDG-15; bow-
mounted in DDG-20 to DDG-24)

ECM: WLR-6—URN-20 TACAN

Boilers: 4, 84 kg/cm² pressure—superheat 520°C

M: 2 sets GT; 2 props; 70,000 hp   **Electric:** 2,000 kw

REMARKS: Although they have the lowest hull numbers, these are the newest of the
DDGs. Sisters DDG-25, DDG-26, and DDG-27, built at the Defoe Shipbuilding Company, Bay City, Michigan, were ordered by Australia; DDG-28; DDG-29, and DDG-30
were built at Bath Iron Works for the West German Navy. Ships with bow-mounted
sonars have stern-mounted anchors. All have been backfitted with an ASROC ASW
missile reload magazine beside the forward stack, to starboard. It was planned to
give these ships a badly needed modernization, beginning with DDG-3 under FY 80.
Costs rose enormously, and the program was cut to ten, permitting them to operate
for another fifteen to twenty years. Congressional reluctance to spend $221 million
per ship (equal to the cost of a new FFG-7-class frigate) forced postponement of even
the reduced program, which is now being reconsidered. Alterations planned included
updating the SPS-40 in DDG-15 to DDG-24 to SPS-40C of SPS-40D and replacing the
SPS-37 in the earlier ships with SPS-49. The SPS-10 will be updated to incorporate
SPS-65 (which uses the same antenna) and the SPS-39A 3-D height-finder will be converted to SPS-52B. The Mk-68 gun director in all will be replaced by Mk-86 (with SPQ-9
in a radome on the mast and SPG-60 atop the bridge), permitting control of three

missiles at a time. The missile-fire-control system will thus be upgraded to Mk-74,
Mod. 8, status. Harpoon SSM can be carried in the Mk-11 or Mk-13 missile-launcher
magazines, and is already carried by several, including DDG-11. Mk-13 weapons
direction will replace Mk-4, while the CIC will be greatly modernized with the SYS-1
small computerized Tactical Data System, which uses the UYA-4 NTDS. The SLQ-32-
(v)2 ECM system will replace existing gear. Mk-36 Super RBOC will be added, engineering and hull systems will be upgraded or overhauled, and generating capacity
will be increased to 3,000 kw. The original missile launchers and Mk-42 guns will be
retained, and the SQS-23 sonar will be converted to SQQ-23 PAIR with two sonar
domes (already done in several ships). The modernizations were to have required
from eighteen to twenty months per ship.

◆ **10 Coontz class (SCB 142/149 type)**

	Bldr	Laid down	L	In serv.
DDG 37 FARRAGUT (ex-DLG-6)	Bethlehem Steel (Quincy)	3-6-57	18-7-58	12-10-60
DDG 38 LUCE (ex-DLG-7)	Bethlehem Steel (Quincy)	1-10-57	11-12-58	20-5-61
DDG 39 MacDONOUGH (ex-DLG-8)	Bethlehem Steel (Quincy)	15-4-58	9-7-59	4-11-61
DDG 40 COONTZ (ex-DLG-9)	Puget Sound NSY	1-3-57	6-12-58	15-7-60
DDG 41 KING (ex-DLG-10)	Puget Sound NSY	1-3-57	6-12-58	17-10-61
DDG 42 MAHAN (ex-DLG-11)	San Francisco NSY	31-7-57	7-10-59	25-8-60
DDG 43 DAHLGREN (ex-DLG-12)	Philadelphia NSY	1-3-58	16-3-60	8-4-61
DDG 44 WILLIAM V. PRATT (ex-DLG-13)	Philadelphia NSY	1-3-58	16-3-60	4-11-61
DDG 45 DEWEY (ex-DLG-14)	Bath Iron Works	10-8-57	30-11-58	7-12-59
DDG 46 PREBLE (ex-DLG-15)	Bath Iron Works	16-12-57	23-5-59	9-5-60

Authorized: DDG-37 to 42 in FY 57, DDG-43 to 46 in FY 57

Farragut—ASROC reload magazine, taller mast   G. Arra, 1976

D: 4,700 tons (5,700-5,900 fl)   **S:** 34 kts   **Dim:** 156.21 × 16.0 × 7.6 (max.)

Man: 21 officers, 356 men + flag group: 7 officers, 12 enlisted   **Fuel:** 900 tons

Range: 1,500/30, 6,000/14   **Electric:** 4,000 kw

A: 1/Mk-10, Mod. 0, twin launcher (II × 1), 40 Standard SM-1-ER missiles—8/Har-
poon SSM (IV × 2)—1/127-mm Mk-42 automatic DP—1/ASROC system (VIII × 1)
—6/324-mm ASW TT (III × 2)

GUIDED-MISSILE DESTROYERS (*continued*)

Luce   IS1 Shaw, 1978

Dahlgren   PH1 F. Osborne, 1978

Electron Equipt: Radars: 1/SPS-53, 1/SPS-10B, 1/SPS-29C or 37, 1/SPS-48, 2/SPG-55B, 1/SPG-53A
 Sonar: SQQ-23 PAIR
 ECM: WLR-6 – URN-20 TACAN – NTDS
Boilers: 4 Foster-Wheeler (Babcock & Wilcox in DDG-40 to DDG-46), 84 kg/cm² pressure – superheat 520°C
M: DDG-37 to DDG-39, DDG-45: 2 sets de Laval GT others: 2 sets Allis-Chalmers; 2 props; 85,000 hp

REMARKS: Reclassified DDG from DLG-6 to DLG-15 in 1975. All modernized between 1970 and 1977 with Standard SM-1-ER missiles, NTDS (fitted earlier in DDG-40, DDG-41), SPS-48 radar, etc.; four 76.2-mm DP (II × 2) removed and Harpoon launchers are being installed in their former locations (firing forward to port, aft to starboard). DDG-37, the first to be modernized, received an ASROC reload magazine forward of the bridge and a taller after mast; to save weight and cost, the others were not similarly equipped. Missile-fire-control is Mk-76. A Mk-68 fire-control system is carried for the 127-mm gun. DDG-40 carried two Vulcan Gatling guns (*not* Phalanx) in 1975. DDG-41 conducted Vulcan-Phalanx 20-mm Gatling AA sea trials in 1973-74, before she was modernized. All will eventually receive two Vulcan-Phalanx, Harpoon ASM, four Mk-36 Super RBOC chaff launchers (in DDG-37, DDG-38, and DDG-44), and the SLQ-32 ECM system. SPS-49 will be substituted for the SPS-29C or SPS-37 radars.

Coontz – with Harpoon   1978

Mk-111, Mod. 8, ASW fire-control systems and satellite-communications antenna systems in all units. The SQQ-23 PAIR sonar installed uses two separate domes.

◆ 4 Decatur class (SCB 222-66 type)

	Bldr	Laid down	L	In serv.	After mod.
DDG 31 DECATUR (ex-DD-936)	Bethlehem Steel, Quincy	13-9-54	15-12-55	7-12-56	29-4-67
DDG 32 JOHN PAUL JONES (ex-DD-932)	Charleston NSY	18-1-54	7-5-55	5-4-56	23-9-67
DDG 33 PARSONS (ex-DD-949)	Ingalls, Pascagoula	17-6-57	19-8-58	29-10-59	3-11-67
DDG 34 SOMERS (ex-DD-947)	Bath Iron Works	4-3-57	30-5-58	3-4-59	2-10-68

Somers   G. Arra, 1977

GUIDED-MISSILE DESTROYERS (*continued*)

Decatur G. Arra, 1977

John Paul Jones PH3 T. Pfrang, 1977

D: 2,850 tons (4,200 fl) **S:** 32.5 kts **Dim:** 127.4 × 13.7 × 6.1 (fl)
Man: 25 officers, 339 men **Range:** 4,500/20 **Fuel:** 750 tons
A: 1/Mk-13 launcher, 40 Standard SM-1-MR missiles – 1/127-mm Mk-42 DP –
  1/ASROC (VIII × 1) – 6/324-mm Mk-32 ASW TT (III × 2)
Electron Equipt: Radars: 1/SPS-10, 1/SPS-29E (DDG-34: SPS-40), 1/SPS-48, 1/SPG-
  51C, 1/SPG-55B

Sonar: 1/SQS-23
ECM: WLR-6 – URN-20 TACAN – NTDS
Boilers: DDG-31 and DDG-33: 4 Foster-Wheeler; DDG-32 and DDG-34: 4 Babcock
  & Wilcox; 84 kg/cm² pressure – superheat 520°C
M: DDG-32: 2 sets Westinghouse GT; others: 2 sets GE GT; 2 props; 70,000 hp

REMARKS: Originally *Forrest Sherman-* and *Hull*-class destroyers. Mk-68, Mod. 9 or 10,
radar director forward can control gun *or* missiles. DDG-33 and DDG-34 have higher
freeboard forward. Alloy superstructure. All to receive Mk-36 RBOC chaff/flare
rocket system. Around 1976 some plating was removed from the covered passageway
at the ships' sides amidships, presumably to save top weight.

NOTE: The *Mitscher*-class guided-missile destroyer *Mitscher* (DDG-35) was stricken on
1-6-78 and her sister *John S. McCain* (DDG-36) on 24-4-78. Both were plagued with
engineering problems throughout their careers.

DESTROYERS

◆ **31 Spruance class (SCN 275 type)**

Bldr: Ingalls SB, Pascagoula, Miss. (Litton Industries)

	Laid down	L	In serv.
DD 963 SPRUANCE	17-11-72	10-11-73	20-9-75
DD 964 PAUL F. FOSTER	6-2-73	23-2-74	21-2-76
DD 965 KINKAID	19-4-73	25-5-74	10-7-76
DD 966 HEWITT	23-7-73	24-8-74	25-9-76
DD 967 ELLIOT	15-10-73	19-12-74	22-1-76
DD 968 ARTHUR W. RADFORD	14-1-74	1-3-75	16-4-77
DD 969 PETERSON	29-4-74	21-6-75	9-7-77
DD 970 CARON	1-7-74	24-6-75	1-10-77
DD 971 DAVID R. RAY	23-9-74	23-8-75	19-11-77
DD 972 OLDENDORF	27-12-74	21-10-75	4-3-78
DD 973 JOHN YOUNG	17-2-75	7-2-76	20-5-78
DD 974 COMTE DE GRASSE	4-4-75	26-3-76	5-8-78
DD 975 O'BRIEN	9-5-75	8-7-76	3-12-77
DD 976 MERRILL	16-6-75	1-9-76	11-3-78
DD 977 BRISCOE	21-7-75	15-12-76	3-6-78
DD 978 STUMP	25-8-75	29-1-77	19-8-78
DD 979 CONOLLY	29-9-75	19-2-77	14-10-78
DD 980 MOOSBRUGGER	3-11-75	23-7-77	16-12-78
DD 981 JOHN HANCOCK	16-1-76	29-10-77	10-3-79
DD 982 NICHOLSON	20-2-76	11-11-77	12-5-79
DD 983 JOHN RODGERS	12-8-76	25-2-78	14-7-79
DD 984 LEFTWICH	12-11-76	8-4-78	25-8-79
DD 985 CUSHING	2-2-77	17-6-78	22-9-79
DD 986 HARRY W. HILL	1-4-77	10-8-78	10-11-79
DD 987 O'BANNON	24-6-77	25-9-78	1-12-79
DD 988 THORN	29-8-77	22-11-78	12-1-80
DD 989 DEYO	14-10-77	20-1-79	2-80
DD 990 INGERSOLL	5-12-77	10-3-79	3-80
DD 991 FIFE	6-3-78	1-5-79	4-80
DD 992 FLETCHER	24-4-78	16-6-79	5-80
DD 997 N. . . .	-80	-81	-82

Authorized: DD 963-965 in FY 70, DD 966-971 in FY 71, DD 972-978 in FY 82, DD 979-
985 in FY 74, DD 986-992 in FY 75, DD 997 in FY 78

DESTROYERS (*continued*)

Spruance 1978

Nicholson Ingalls, 1979

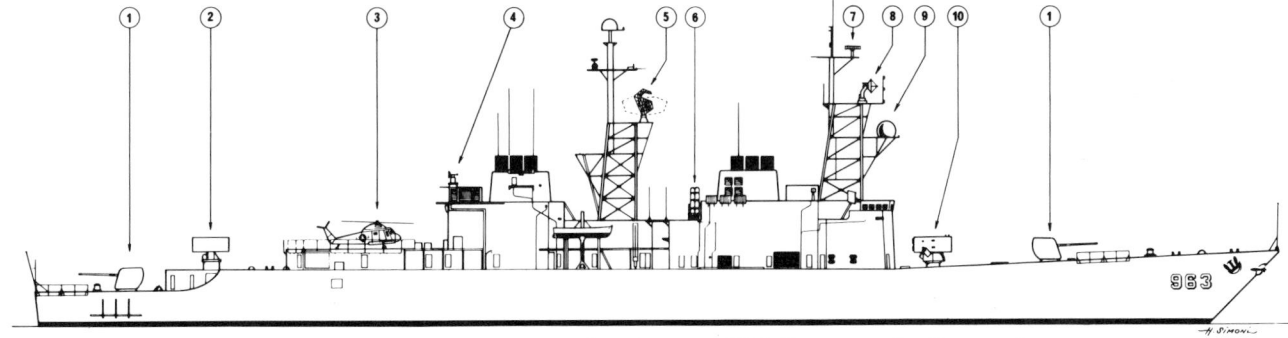

1. 127-mm mount 2. Sea Sparrow launcher 3. ASW helicopter 4. Sea Sparrow fire-control director 5. SPS-40 radar 6. Harpoon SSM launchers 7. SPS-55 radar 8. SPG-60 radar 9. SPQ-9A radar 10. ASROC launcher

DESTROYERS (continued)

D: 5,830 tons light (7,810 fl)   **S:** 30+ kts

Dim: 171.68 (oa) (161.25 pp) × 16.76 × 5.79 (8.84 over sonar)

Man: 24 officers, 272 men   **Range:** 3,300/30, 6,000/20   **Fuel:** 1,500+ tons

A: 8/Harpoon SSM (IV × 2) – 2/127-mm Mk-45 DP (I × 2) – 1/Mk-29 launcher (VIII × 1), 24 Sea Sparrow – 1/ASROC system (VIII × 1) – 6/324-mm Mk-32 ASW TT (III × 2) – 1/SH-3 Sea King or SH-2 Sea Sprite ASW helicopter

Electron Equipt: Radars: 1/SPS-55, 1/SPS-40, 1/SPQ-9A, 1/SPG-60, 1/Mk-91
                Sonar: 1/SQS-53
                ECM: WLR-8, 4/Mk-36 Super RBOC – URN-20 TACAN – NTDS

M: 4 GE LM-2500 gas turbines; 2 controllable-pitch props; 80,000 hp

Electric: 6,000 kw

Spruance   1978

Spruance   1978

REMARKS: After commissioning, the ships perform preliminary work-up and then enter a naval shipyard for installation of electronic-warfare equipment, the Mk-29 Sea Sparrow launcher, the Mk-91 fire-control system, and other gear. There are currently not enough helicopters to equip these ships and it is no longer planned to give all of them the new LAMPS-III ASW helicopter. Plans were announced in 1979 for backfitting them with vertical missile-launcher installations to replace the current Sea

Hewitt – note Harpoon canisters amidships   G. Arra, 1979

Sparrow and ASROC launchers, beginning with FY 84. Plans to replace the forward 127-mm gun mount with the 203-mm Mk-71 mount were canceled when the latter was canceled by DOD on 25-7-78, thus depriving the navy of a superb and highly successful new weapon. The Harpoon anti-ship cruise missiles amidships and electronics warfare suits are being added well after completion, making these ships still suitable only for ASW duties.

The hull is so constructed that standard prefabricated sections (modules) weighing 1,500 to 2,100 tons can be fitted out (small machinery and its components, piping, wiring, etc.) before they are joined. Once these elements are brought together, the ship is 92 per cent complete. The hull is transferred to a submersible pontoon for launching – there is no launching in the usual sense – and the ship is then fitted-out alongside a pier.

Considerable attention was given to the propulsion machinery from the viewpoint of silent operation and flexibility. Prarie-Masker bubbler systems are installed to enhance quietness. On each of the two shafts, two General Electric LM-2500 gas turbines are coupled to a reduction gear. Each shaft turns a controllable-pitch propeller (5.1 m in diameter, 168 rpm at 30 knots). Electric power is furnished by three gas turbines, each powering one 2,000-kw alternator and mounted in separate compartments. Full speed can be reached from 12 knots in only 53 seconds. All propulsion machinery is under the control of a single operator in a central control station (CCS). 30 knots was considerably exceeded on trials. Endurance can be extended greatly by using one engine on one shaft for cruising. The plant has been very successful, except for the exhaust-gas auxiliary boilers.

The hull conformations were carefully studied to minimize rolling and pitching. Habitability received particular attention, living spaces being divided by bulkheads and intended for no more than six men each, with a recreational area and good sanitary facilities. The crew is small for a ship the size of the *Spruance* class because all the machinery and systems have advanced automation.

The armament of these large destroyers will later be augmented by the installation of two Vulcan-Phalanx systems. All will be equipped with a four-launcher Mk-36 RBOC chaff-flare rocket system. ASW is handled by a Mk-116 fire-control system. The

DESTROYERS (*continued*)

Mk-32 torpedo tubes are standard triple trainable mountings fired through doors in the ships' sides. The Mk-91, Mod. 0, fire-control system for Sea Sparrow uses a single radar director. The Mk-86, Mod. 3, fire-control system for the 127-mm guns uses the SPG-60 radar for AA and the SPQ-9A for surface fire. Magazines hold 1,200 rounds 127-mm, 14 ASW torpedoes, and 16 reload ASROC missiles, the latter in vertical rotary stowage beneath the launcher. Kevlar plastic armor is to be added over vital spaces, beginning with four ships under FY 81; the entire class will be equipped by 1986.

NOTE: Under the FY 78 budget Congress appropriated $310 million for design and construction of an additional unit of the *Spruance* class to be equipped with an enlarged aircraft facility, ostensibly to increase the helicopter capacity, but also to be capable of handling a V/STOL ASW aircraft, should one be developed. The navy did not request the ship, did not want it, and has determined that the funded amount is sufficient to build only a standard ship of the class, which, after much delay, was contracted for in 9-79. The notional design for this DDG-997 envisaged enlarging the hangar and extending the flight deck aft to a point just forward of the after 127-mm gun.

Barry—bow sonar   1971

◆ **14 Forrest Sherman and Hull classes (SCB 240 type):**

8 ASW refits (1967-71) (SCB 221 modernization, except DD-933: SCB 251):

	Bldr	Laid down	L	In serv.
DD 933 BARRY	Mare Island NSY	15-3-54	1-10-55	31-8-56
DD 937 DAVIS	Bethlehem, Quincy	1-2-55	28-3-56	28-2-57
DD 938 JONAS INGRAM	Bethlehem, Quincy	15-6-55	8-7-56	19-7-57
DD 940 MANLEY	Bath Iron Works	10-2-55	12-4-56	1-2-57
DD 941 DUPONT	Bath Iron Works	11-5-55	8-9-56	1-7-57
DD 943 BLANDY	Bethlehem, Quincy	29-12-55	19-12-56	8-11-57
DD 948 MORTON	Ingalls, Pascagoula	4-3-57	23-5-58	26-5-59
DD 950 RICHARD S. EDWARDS	Puget Sound B & DD	20-12-56	21-9-57	5-2-59

6 unmodified:

	Bldr	down	L	In serv.
DD 931 FORREST SHERMAN	Boston NSY	27-10-53	5-2-55	9-11-55
DD 942 BIGELOW	Bath Iron Works	6-7-55	2-2-57	8-11-57
DD 944 MULLINIX	Bethlehem, Quincy	5-4-56	18-3-57	7-3-58
DD 945 HULL	Bath Iron Works	12-9-56	10-8-57	3-7-58
DD 946 EDSON	Bath Iron Works	3-12-56	1-1-58	7-11-58
DD 951 TURNER JOY	Puget Sound B & DD	30-9-57	5-5-58	3-8-59

Morton   G. Arra, 1978

Authorized: DD 931, 933 in FY 55, DD 937, 938 in FY 54, DD 940-944 in FY 55, others in FY 56

D: 2,780-2,850 tons (4,050-4,200 fl)   **S:** 32.5 kts
Dim: 127.51 (DD-933: 129.54; DD-945 to DD-951: 127.4) × 13.7 × 6.1
Man: ASW refits: 17 officers, 287 men; others: 17 officers, 275 men
Range: 4,500/20   **Fuel:** 750 tons
A: ASW refits: 2/127-mm Mk-42 DP (I × 2)—1 ASROC system—6/324-mm Mk-32 ASW TT (III × 2)
     Others: 3/127-mm Mk-42 DP (I × 3)—6/324-mm Mk-32 ASW TT (III × 2)
Electron Equipt: Radars: 1/SPS-10, 1/SPS-40 (DD-933, DD-937, DD-938, DD-942, DD-946, DD-951: SPS-32), 1/SPG-53A, 1/Mk-35
             Sonars: SQS-23; ASW refits: SQS-35 VDS also

Forrest Sherman   PH1 L. Sallions, 1978

DESTROYERS (*continued*)

ECM: WLR-2 or WLR-6—DD-945, DD-946, DD-951: URN-20
TACAN

Boilers: DD-937, DD-938, DD-943, DD-944, DD-948: 4 Foster-Wheeler;
Others: 4 Babcock & Wilcox; 84 kg/cm² pressure—superheat 520°C

M: GE (DD-931, DD-933: Westinghouse) GT; 2 props, 70,000 hp

REMARKS: DD-946 is assigned to the Naval Reserve Force for reserve training and as a training ship for the officer candidate school. From DD-937 on, the bows are somewhat higher than DD-931 and DD-933, while DD-945 and later are considered a separate class by reason of their different bow design. Four of the same series were rebuilt as DDGs. From 1974-78 DD-945 was used as the trials ship for the 203-mm Mk-71 gun mounted forward. All 127-mm Mk-42 guns modernized to Mod. 10 configuration. There are two gun-fire-control systems, Mk-68 forward and Mk-56 aft (positions reversed in DD-931, DD-937, DD-938, and DD-944). ASW refits have Mk-114 ASW-fire-control systems, the others Mk-105. All Hedgehog and depth charges removed in early 1970s. Originally had four 76.2-mm DP (II × 2) but they were removed from all by 1978. ECM equipment varies; most is older.

NAVAL RESERVE FORCE DESTROYERS

NOTE: The ships listed below, plus the *Forrest-Sherman*-class destroyer DD-946, are used for training by the Naval Reserve Force. They spend very little time at sea. Most of the crews are regular navy, with rotating crews of reservists to augment them. There are plans for a new class of "Reserve Corvettes" (FFX) to be constructed especially for manning by the Naval Reserve Force, with the first to be ordered under FY 83.

◆ 2 Carpenter class

	Bldr	Laid down	L	In serv.
DD 827 ROBERT A. OWENS	Bath Iron Works	29-10-45	15-7-46	5-11-49
DD 825 CARPENTER	Consolidated Steel	30-7-45	30-12-45	15-12-49

Carpenter—now stricken   1976

D: 2,425 tons (3,540 fl)   S: 34 kts   Dim: 119.0 × 12.4 × 5.8
Man: 12 officers, 176 men + Naval Reserve: 8 officers, 86 men   Fuel: 650 tons
A: 2/127-mm 38-cal. DP (II × 1)—1/ASROC system (VIII × 1)—6/324-mm Mk-32
ASW TT (III × 2)
Electron Equipt: Radars: 1/SPS-10, 1/SPS-40, 1/Mk-35
Sonar: SQS-23

Boilers: 4 Babcock & Wilcox; 43.3 kg/cm² pressure—superheat 454°C
M: 2 sets GE GT; 2 props; 60,000 hp   Electric: 1,200 kw

REMARKS: Ex-DDE. Variant of the *Gearing* class, with higher bridge, Mk-56 gun-fire-control system, tripod mainmast, and enlarged after superstructure. Mk-114 ASW-fire-control. FRAM-I modernization completed in 1962.

◆ 17 Gearing class, FRAM-I

	Bldr	Laid down	L	In serv.
DD 743 SOUTHERLAND	Bath Iron Works	27-5-44	5-10-44	22-12-44
DD 763 WILLIAM C. LAWE	Bethlehem, San Francisco	12-3-44	21-5-45	18-12-46
DD 784 MCKEAN	Todd, Seattle	15-9-44	31-3-45	9-6-45
DD 785 HENDERSON	Todd, Seattle	27-10-44	28-5-45	4-8-45
DD 817 CORRY	Consolidated Steel	5-4-45	28-7-45	26-2-46
DD 821 JOHNSTON	Consolidated Steel	6-5-45	19-10-45	10-10-46
DD 822 ROBERT H. MCCARD	Consolidated Steel	20-6-45	9-11-45	26-10-46
DD 842 FISKE	Bath Iron Works	9-4-45	8-9-45	28-11-45
DD 862 VOGELGESANG	Bethlehem, Staten Island	3-8-44	15-1-45	28-4-45
DD 863 STEINAKER	Bethlehem, Staten Island	1-9-44	13-2-45	26-5-45
DD 864 HAROLD J. ELLISON	Bethlehem, Staten Island	3-10-44	14-3-45	23-6-45
DD 866 CONE	Bethlehem, Staten Island	30-11-44	10-5-45	18-8-45
DD 871 DAMATO	Bethlehem, Staten Island	10-5-45	21-11-45	27-4-46
DD 876 ROGERS	Consolidated Steel	3-6-44	20-11-44	26-3-45
DD 880 DYESS	Consolidated Steel	17-8-44	26-1-45	21-5-45
DD 883 NEWMAN K. PERRY	Consolidated Steel	10-10-44	17-3-45	26-7-45
DD 886 ORLECK	Consolidated Steel	28-11-44	12-5-45	15-9-45

D: 2,425 tons (3,480-3,520 fl)   S: 30 kts
Dim: 119.03 (116.74 wl) × 12.52 × 4.45 (6.4 over sonar)
Man: 12 officers, 176 men + Naval Reserve: 7 officers, 112 men
Range: 2,400/25, 4,800/15
A: 4/127-mm 38-cal. DP (II × 2)—1/ASROC system (VIII × 1)—6/324-mm Mk-32
ASW TT (III × 2)

Fiske   G. Arra, 1976

NAVAL RESERVE FORCES DESTROYERS (*continued*)

McKean

PH3 J. Romesburg, 1974

Electron Equipt: Radars: 1/SPS-10, 1/SPS-29 or 37 (DD-817, DD-862, DD-866: SPS-40), 1/Mk-25

Sonar: SQS-23   ECM: WLR-3

Boilers: 4 Babcock & Wilcox, 43.3 kg/cm² pressure—superheat 454°C

M: 2 sets GE GT; 2 props; 60,000 hp   **Electric:** 1,200 kw

Fuel: 650 tons

William C. Lawe

1978

REMARKS: Survivors of some 79 *Gearing*-class destroyers which completed FRAM-I between 1960 and 1965. The remaining ships have been used for Naval Reserve Force training since 1973-75. Their wartime utility would be negligible. The DASH drone ASW helicopter, around which the modernization was designed, was retired in 1969. DD-763, DD-784, and DD-866, which were to have been stricken in late 1979, are instead to be refitted for further service, due to congressional action. DD-863, which underwent overhaul during 1979, has special stack caps to reduce the heat signature. All have a Mk-37 gun-fire-control system and Mk-114 ASW-fire-control system. Nine ASROC reload missiles can be carried. ULQ-6 electronics countermeasures gear has been removed from mast.

NOTE: The following have been stricken since the last edition: *Rich* (DD-820) on 15-12-77, *Bausell* (DD-845) on 30-5-78, *William R. Rush* (DD-714) on 1-7-79, *Agerholm* (DD-826) on 1-12-78, *Meredith* (DD-890) on 29-6-79, *Higbee* (DD-806) on 15-7-79, *John R. Craig* (DD-885) on 27-7-79 (after having sunk at her pier), *Hollister* (DD-788) on 31-8-79, and *Hamner* (DD-718), *Charles P. Cecil* (DD-835), and *Hawkins* (DD-873) on 1-10-79. Under the FY 80 budget, the U.S. Congress has extended the service of the following destroyers: *Southerland, Johnston, Robert H. McCard, Fiske, Harold J. Ellison, Damato, Rogers,* and *Dyess,* which were scheduled for striking on 1-10-79. Although essentially obsolete, they will probably continue in commission, serving the Naval Reserve Force, into the mid-1980s. The navy had hoped to use their regular navy crews to man new *Oliver Hazard Perry*-class frigates.

GUIDED-MISSILE FRIGATES

◆ 46+ Oliver Hazard Perry class (SCN 207/2081 type)

	Bldr	Laid down	L	In serv.
FFG 7 OLIVER HAZARD PERRY	Bath Iron Works	6-12-75	9-25-76	30-11-77
FFG 8 MCINERNEY	Bath Iron Works	16-1-78	4-11-78	-79
FFG 9 WADSWORTH	Todd, San Pedro	13-7-77	29-7-78	3-80
FFG 10 DUNCAN	Todd, Seattle	29-4-77	1-3-78	3-80
FFG 11 CLARK	Bath Iron Works	17-7-78	24-3-79	6-80
FFG 12 GEORGE PHILIP	Todd, San Pedro	14-12-77	16-12-78	7-80
FFG 13 SAMUEL ELIOT MORISON	Bath Iron Works	4-12-78	14-7-79	10-80
FFG 14 SIDES	Todd, San Pedro	7-8-78	19-5-79	11-80
FFG 15 ESTOCIN	Bath Iron Works	2-4-79	3-11-79	81
FFG 16 CLIFTON SPRAGUE	Bath Iron Works	30-7-79	2-80	81
FFG 19 JOHN A. MOORE	Todd, San Pedro	19-12-78	.20-10-79	81
FFG 20 ANTRIM	Todd, Seattle	21-6-78	27-3-79	81
FFG 21 FLATLEY	Bath Iron Works	12-79	5-80	81
FFG 22 FAHRION	Todd, Seattle	1-12-78	24-8-79	81
FFG 23 LEWIS B. PULLER	Todd, San Pedro	23-5-79	3-80	81
FFG 24 JACK WILLIAMS	Bath Iron Works	2-80	9-80	81
FFG 25 COPELAND	Todd, San Pedro	24-10-79	7-80	82
FFG 26 GALLERY	Bath Iron Works	6-80	12-80	82
FFG 27 MAHLON S. TISDALE	Todd, San Pedro	4-80	11-80	82
FFG 28 BOONE	Todd, Seattle	27-3-79	28-12-79	82
FFG 29 N . . .	Bath Iron Works	9-80	81	82
FFG 30 N . . .	Todd, San Pedro	7-80	81	82
FFG 31 STARK	Todd, Seattle	24-8-79	5-80	82
FFG 32 N . . .	Bath Iron Works	81	81	82
FFG 33 N . . .	Todd, San Pedro	11-80	81	83
FFG 34 N . . .	Bath Iron Works		81	82
FFG 36 N . . .	Bath Iron Works	81	82	83
FFG 37 N . . .	Todd, Seattle	6-80	81	83
FFG 38 N . . .	Todd, San Pedro	81	82	83
FFG 39 N . . .	Bath Iron Works	82	82	83
FFG 40 N . . .	Todd, Seattle	10-80	81	83
FFG 41 N . . .	Todd, San Pedro	81	82	83
FFG 42 N . . .	Bath Iron Works	82	82	83
FFG 43 N . . .	Todd, San Pedro	82	82	84
FFG 44 N . . .	. . .	. . .	. . .	84
FFG 45 N . . .	. . .	. . .	. . .	. . .
FFG 46 N . . .	. . .	. . .	. . .	. . .
FFG 47 N . . .	. . .	. . .	. . .	. . .
FFG 48 N . . .	. . .	. . .	. . .	. . .
FFG 49 N . . .	. . .	. . .	. . .	. . .
FFG 50 N . . .	. . .	. . .	. . .	. . .
FFG 51 N . . .	. . .	. . .	. . .	. . .
FFG 52 N . . .	. . .	. . .	. . .	. . .
FFG 53 N . . .	. . .	. . .	. . .	. . .
FFG 54 N . . .	. . .	. . .	. . .	. . .
FFG 55 N . . .	. . .	. . .	. . .	. . .

Authorized: FFG 7 in FY 73, FFG 8-10 in FY 74, FFG 11-16 in FY 75, FFG 19-26 in FY 76, FFG 27-34 in FY 77, FFG 36-43 in FY 78, FFG 44-49 in FY 79, FFG 50-55 in FY 80

Oliver Hazard Perry　　　　　　　　　　Bath Iron Works, 1977

Oliver Hazard Perry　　　　　　　　　　Bath Iron Works, 1977

GUIDED-MISSILE FRIGATES (*continued*)

Oliver Hazard Perry   Bath Iron Works, 1977

Oliver Hazard Perry   1977

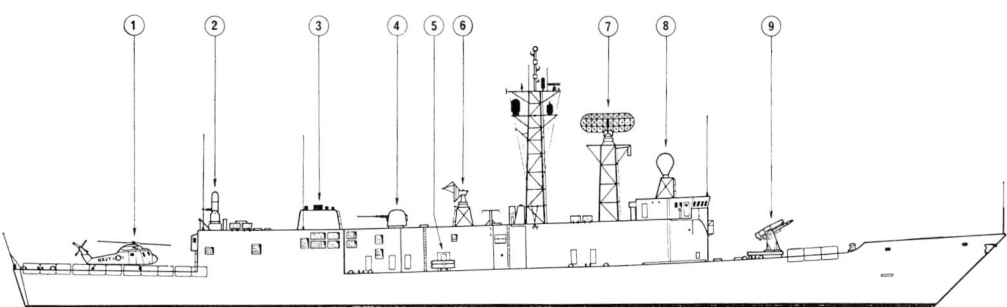

1. ASW helicopter 2. Vulcan-Phalanx system 3. Stack 4. 76-mm 5. ASW TT
6. STIR radar 7. SPS-49 radar 8. Mk 92 fire-control 9. Missile launcher

GUIDED-MISSILE FRIGATES (*continued*)

D: 3,605 tons (fl)   **S:** 30 kts
Dim: 135.64 (125.9 wl) × 13.72 × 4.52 (7.47 max.)
Man: 14 officers, 162 men   **Range:** 4,500/20   **Electric:** 3,000 kw
A: 1/Mk-13, Mod. 4, launcher, 40 Harpoon and Standard SM-1-MR missiles – 1/76-mm Mk-75 DP – 6/324-mm ASW TT (III × 2)
Electron Equipt: Radars: 1/SPS-55, 1/SPS-49, 1/Mk-92, Mod. 2, 1/STIR (SPG-6 Mod.)
   Sonar: 1/SQS-56
   ECM: SLQ-32(v)2, 4/Mk-36 Super RBOC – URN-26 TACAN
M: 2 GE LM-2500 gas turbines; 1 controllable-pitch prop, 5.5 m in diameter; 40,000 hp

REMARKS: Although these ships were intended to operate the LAMPS-III ASW helicopter, the first twenty-six of them lack the equipment necessary to handle helicopters safely and are not scheduled to begin receiving them until FY 85, which is when the Sikorsky SH-60B LAMPS-III helicopter is expected to be operationally available. Two of them can be accommodated. Beginning with the FY 79 ships (FFG-36 and later), helicopter support equipment will be aboard on completion: fin stabilizers, RAST (Recovery Assistance, Securing, and Traversing System), and other systems. Beginning with FFG-36, SQR-19 TACTASS towed passive hydrophone arrays will be aboard ships when they complete; earlier units will be backfitted. The Mk-15 CIWS (Close-In Weapon System) 20-mm Vulcan-Phalanx will be backfitted into all units eventually, as will the SLQ-32(v)2 ECM system and Mk-36 Super RBOC chaff system, which were not fitted to the ships as completed until FFG-27. Thus, it can be seen that at least the initial units of this class were not well equipped for most forms of war at sea when they were commissioned; despite this, they are, ton for ton, the most expensive ships being built for the navy at this time. FFG-7 was originally numbered PF-109. Plans now call for ordering four more each in FY 81 and FY 82, three in FY 83, and four in FY 84 to complete the class. FFG-17, FFG-18, and FFG-35, built at Todd, Seattle, are for Australia. Speed on one turbine is 25 knots; the auxiliary power system uses two retractable pods located well forward and can drive the ships at up to 6 knots. The Mk-92, Mod. 4, fire-control system controls missile- and 76-mm-gun fire; it uses a STIR (modified SPG-60) antenna and a U.S.-built version of the Hollandse Signaal Apparaten WM-28 radar forward, and can track four separate targets. The Mk-75 gun is a license-built version of the OTO Melara Compact. A Mk-13 weapons-direction system is fitted. Without the helicopters, the only ASW ordnance is the Mk-36 torpedoes in the two triple torpedo tubes. These ships are particularly well protected against splinter and fragmentation damage, with three 4-inch aluminum-alloy armor over magazine spaces, ⅝-in steel over the main engine-control room, and ¾-inch Kevlar plastic armor over vital electronics and command spaces.

◆ **6 Brooke class (SCR 199B type)**

	Bldr	Laid down	L	In serv.
FFG 1 BROOKE	Lockheed, Seattle	10-12-62	19-7-63	12-3-66
FFG 2 RAMSEY	Lockheed, Seattle	4-2-63	15-10-63	3-6-67
FFG 3 SCHOFIELD	Lockheed, Seattle	15-4-63	7-12-63	11-5-68
FFG 4 TALBOT	Bath Iron Works	4-5-64	6-1-66	2-4-67
FFG 5 RICHARD L. PAGE	Bath Iron Works	4-1-65	4-4-66	5-8-67
FFG 6 JULIUS A. FURER	Bath Iron Works	12-7-65	22-7-66	11-11-67

D: 2,643 tons (3,425 fl)   **S:** 27.2 kts
Dim: 126.33 (121.9 wl) × 13.47 × 7.9 (over sonar)

Brooke   PH3 J. Austin, 1977

Richard L. Page – hangar extended   1977

Man: 17 officers, 231 men   **Range:** 4,000/20   **Fuel:** . . . tons
A: 1/Mk-22 launcher (I × 1), 16 Standard SM-1-MR missiles – 1/127-mm 38-cal. DP – 1 ASROC system (VIII × 1) – 6/324-mm Mk-32 ASW TT (III × 2) – 1/SH-2 LAMPS-I ASW helicopter
Electron Equipt: Radars: 1/LN-66, 1/SPS-10F, 1/SPS-52, 1/SPG-51C, 1/Mk-35
   Sonar: 1/SQS-26AX
   ECM: WLR-6, Mk-33 or Mk-36 RBOC/Super RBOC
Boilers: 2 Foster-Wheeler, 84 kg/cm² pressure – superheat 510°C
M: 1 set Westinghouse (FFG-4 to FFG-6: GE) GT; 1 prop; 35,000 hp

REMARKS: Differ from the *Garcia* class in having their 127-mm aft replaced by a missile launcher. Excellent sea-keeping qualities. Anti-rolling stabilizers. The hangar, which was enlarged for the SH-2 LAMPS-I helicopter, is telescoping, as on the *Knox* class. FFG-4 through FFG-6 have an ASROC system with a reloading magazine. FFG-4 was used as an experimental ship for the weapons and systems of the *Oliver Hazard Perry* (FFG-7) but has now been restored to standard configuration. A Mk-56, Mod. 43, radar gunfire-control system is carried, while the missile system is Mk-74, Mod. 6; Mk-4, Mod. 2, weapons-direction system is fitted, as is the Mk-114 ASW-control system.

GUIDED-MISSILE FRIGATES (*continued*)

Richard L. Page   PH3 J. Barber, 1976

Ramsey   G. Arra, 1977

FRIGATES

◆ **46 Knox class (SCN 199C, 200 and 200-65 types)**

	Bldr	Laid down	L	In serv.
FF 1052 KNOX	Todd, Seattle	5-10-65	19-11-66	12-4-69
FF 1053 ROARK	Todd, Seattle	2-2-66	24-4-67	22-11-69
FF 1054 GRAY	Todd, Seattle	19-11-66	3-10-67	4-4-70
FF 1055 HEPBURN	Todd, San Pedro	1-6-66	25-3-67	3-7-69
FF 1056 CONNOLE	Avondale SY	23-3-67	20-7-68	30-8-69
FF 1057 RATHBURNE	Lockheed, Seattle	8-1-68	2-5-69	16-5-70
FF 1058 MEYERKORD	Todd, San Pedro	1-9-66	15-7-67	28-11-69
FF 1059 WILLIAM S. SIMS	Avondale SY	10-4-67	4-1-69	3-1-70
FF 1060 LANG	Todd, San Pedro	25-3-67	17-2-68	28-3-70
FF 1061 PATTERSON	Avondale SY	12-10-67	3-5-69	14-3-70
FF 1062 WHIPPLE	Todd, Seattle	24-4-67	12-4-68	22-8-70
FF 1063 REASONER	Lockheed, Seattle	6-1-69	1-8-70	31-7-71
FF 1064 LOCKWOOD	Todd, Seattle	3-11-67	5-9-68	5-12-70
FF 1065 STEIN	Lockheed, Seattle	1-6-70	19-12-70	8-1-72
FF 1066 MARVIN SHIELDS	Todd, Seattle	12-4-68	23-10-69	10-4-71
FF 1067 FRANCIS HAMMOND	Todd, San Pedro	15-7-67	11-5-68	25-7-70
FF 1068 VREELAND	Avondale SY	20-3-68	14-6-69	13-6-70
FF 1069 BAGLEY	Lockheed, Seattle	22-9-70	24-4-71	6-5-72
FF 1070 DOWNES	Todd, Seattle	5-9-68	13-12-69	28-8-71
FF 1071 BADGER	Todd, San Pedro	17-2-68	7-12-68	1-12-70
FF 1072 BLAKELY	Avondale SY	3-6-68	23-8-69	18-7-70
FF 1073 ROBERT E. PEARY (ex-*Conolly*)	Lockheed, Seattle	20-12-70	23-6-71	23-9-72
FF 1074 HAROLD E. HOLT	Todd, San Pedro	11-5-68	3-5-69	26-3-71
FF 1075 TRIPPE	Avondale SY	29-7-68	1-11-69	19-9-70
FF 1076 FANNING	Todd, San Pedro	7-12-68	24-1-70	23-7-71
FF 1077 OUELLET	Avondale SY	15-1-69	17-1-70	12-12-70
FF 1078 JOSEPH HEWES	Avondale SY	15-5-69	7-3-70	24-4-71
FF 1079 BOWEN	Avondale SY	11-7-69	2-5-70	22-5-71
FF 1080 PAUL	Avondale SY	12-9-69	20-6-70	14-8-71
FF 1081 AYLWIN	Avondale SY	13-11-69	29-8-70	18-9-71
FF 1082 ELMER MONTGOMERY	Avondale SY	23-1-70	21-11-70	30-10-71
FF 1083 COOK	Avondale SY	20-3-70	23-1-71	18-12-71
FF 1084 McCANDLESS	Avondale SY	4-6-70	20-3-71	18-3-72
FF 1085 DONALD B. BEARY	Avondale SY	24-7-70	22-5-71	22-7-72
FF 1086 BREWTON	Avondale SY	2-10-70	24-7-71	8-7-72
FF 1087 KIRK	Avondale SY	4-12-70	25-9-71	9-9-72
FF 1088 BARBEY	Avondale SY	5-2-71	4-12-71	11-11-72
FF 1089 JESSE L. BROWN	Avondale SY	8-4-71	18-3-72	17-2-73
FF 1090 AINSWORTH	Avondale SY	11-6-71	15-4-72	31-3-73
FF 1091 MILLER	Avondale SY	6-8-71	3-6-72	30-6-73
FF 1092 THOMAS C. HART	Avondale SY	8-10-71	12-8-72	28-7-73
FF 1093 CAPODANNO	Avondale SY	12-10-71	21-10-72	17-11-73
FF 1094 PHARRIS	Avondale SY	11-2-72	16-12-72	26-1-74
FF 1095 TRUETT	Avondale SY	27-4-72	3-2-73	1-6-74
FF 1096 VALDEZ	Avondale SY	30-6-72	24-3-73	27-7-74
FF 1097 MOINESTER	Avondale SY	25-8-72	12-7-73	2-11-74

Authorized: 10 in FY 64, 16 in FY 65, 10 in FY 66, 10 in FY 67

FRIGATES (*continued*)

Bagley—bow bulwarks and spray-suppressing strake
PH1 A. Legare, 1969

D: 3,011 tons light (4,200 fl)   **S:** 27+ kts
Dim: 133.5 (126.5 wl) × 14.25 × 4.6 (7.55 over sonar)
Man: 22 officers, 261 men   **Range:** 4,300/20
Fuel: 715 tons (+ 35 tons aviation)
A: Harpoon SSM—1/127-mm Mk-42 DP—1/Mk-25 Sea Sparrow on FF-1052 to FF-1069, FF-1071 to FF-1083 (FF-1070: 1/Mk-29 launcher)—1/ASROC system (VIII × 1)—4/324-mm Mk-32 fixed ASW TT—1/SH-2 LAMPS-I ASW helicopter
Electron Equipt: Radars: 1/SPS-10, 1/SPS-40, 1/SPG-53, 1/Mk-115

McCandless—with SLQ-32 ECM, URN-26 TACAN
C. Dragonette, 1979

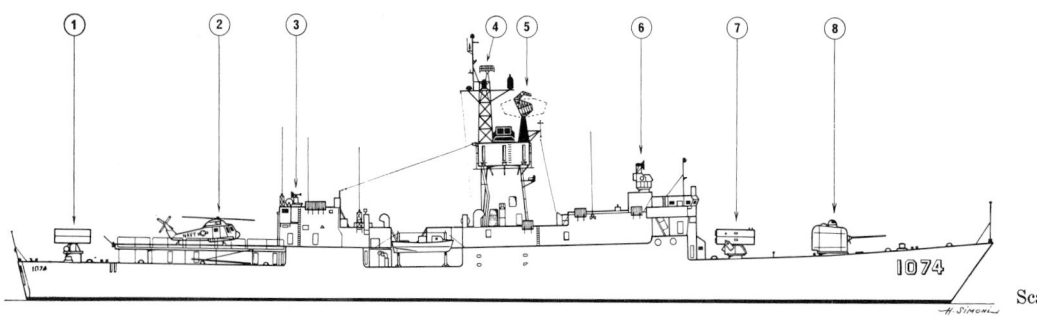

Scale 1/1000

1. Mk-25 BPDMS Sea Sparrow launcher   2. LAMPS-I ASW helicopter   3. Mk-115 Sea Sparrow director atop telescoping hangar   4. SPS-10 radar   5. SPS-40 radar   6. Mk-68 fire-control director   7. ASROC ASW system   8. 127-mm Mk 42 DP mount

FRIGATES (continued)

Bowen 1976

Rathburne—no VDS, LAMPS-I helicopter on deck G. Arra, 1977

Roark PH1 D. Hanson, 1977

Moinester—the final Knox PH1 D. Hanson, 1977

REMARKS: An additional ten ships of the FY 68 program (FF-1098 to FF-1107) were canceled. Bow bulwarks and a spray strake are being added forward to reduce deck wetness, a problem in this class—*see* photo pf the *Bagley*, the first to receive the modification. The ASROC system has an automatic reloading magazine beneath the bridge; it will be used to stow Harpoon missiles, which are launched from the port pair of eight launcher cells (FF-1091 first to receive Harpoon, 1976). FF-1084 to FF-1097 are not to receive Sea Sparrow but may later get a 24-missile General Dynamics RAM infrared-homing SAM launcher. FF-1070 has been used as NATO Sea Sparrow trials ship; she carries a Mk-29 NATO Sea Sparrow launcher and the two-director Mk-91, Mod. 1, fire-control system. The ASW torpedo tubes are fixed, in the forward end of the hangar superstructure, aimed outboard at an angle of 45°. In 1973 FF-1070 tested SPS-58 on a lattice mast aft, but since 1975 has carried SPS-40 aft and has the prototype radar for the Mk-23 Target Acquisition System on her mack. FF-1053 to FF-1055, FF-1057 to FF-1062, FF-1072, and FF-1077 do not have SQS-35 independent VDS. Beginning with twelve ships under FY 80, the SQS-35 towed VDS transducer body and hoist will be modified to permit towing the SQR-18A TACTASS. FF-1088 has acted as a trials ship and has a controllable-pitch prop; the large inflatable radome atop her hangar has been removed. All carry a Mk-68 gunfire-control system with SPG-53A, D, F, radar. In those ships not already equipped with Mk-33 RBOC, Mk-36 will be fitted. FF-1083 and FF-1084 have URN-26 TACAN, to be backfitted in the others. SLQ-32(v)2 is replacing WLR-6 as the ECM suit. A few ships retain LN-66 navigational radars and all have two satellite-communications antennas.

Sonars: 1/SQS-26CX, SQS-35 (except FF-1053 to FF-1055, FF-1057 to FF-1062, FF-1072, FF-1077), SQR-18A TACTASS on 12 ships
ECM: WLR-6, 4 Mk-33 RBOC or Mk-36 Super RBOC
Boilers: 2 Babcock & Wilcox or Foster-Wheeler, 84 kg/cm² pressure—superheat 510°C
M: 1 set Westinghouse GT; 1 prop; 35,000 hp **Electric:** 3,000 kw

FRIGATES (continued)

Ships with Sea Sparrow have a single Mk-115 missile-fire-control system (Mk-71 director). All have Mk-114 ASW-fire-control system. FF-1078 to FF-1097 have a TEAM (SM-5) system for the continual monitoring of ship's electronic equipment. Anti-rolling fin stabilizers fitted in all. Prarie-Masker bubble system fitted to hulls and propellers to reduce radiated noise.

◆ 10 Garcia class (SCB 199A type)

	Bldr	Laid down	L	In serv.
FF 1040 GARCIA	Bethlehem, San Francisco	16-10-62	31-10-63	21-12-64
FF 1041 BRADLEY	Bethlehem, San Francisco	17-1-63	26-3-64	15-5-65
FF 1043 EDWARD MCDONNELL	Avondale SY	1-4-63	15-2-64	15-2-65
FF 1044 BRUMBY	Avondale SY	1-8-63	6-6-64	5-8-65
FF 1045 DAVIDSON	Avondale SY	20-9-63	3-10-64	7-12-65
FF 1047 VOGE	Defoe SB, Michigan	21-11-63	4-2-65	25-11-66
FF 1048 SAMPLE	Lockheed, Seattle	19-7-63	28-4-64	23-3-68
FF 1049 KOELSH	Defoe SB, Michigan	19-2-64	8-6-65	10-6-67
FF 1050 ALBERT DAVID	Lockheed, Seattle	29-4-64	19-12-64	19-10-68
FF 1051 O'CALLAHAN	Defoe SB, Michigan	19-2-64	20-10-65	13-7-68

Authorized: 2 in FY 61, 3 in FY 62, 5 in FY 63

Albert David – no LAMPS capability   1975

D: 2,624 tons (3,403 fl)   **S:** 27 kts
Dim: 126.33 (121.9 wl) × 13.47 × 7.9 (over sonar)
Man: 16 officers, 231 men   **Range:** 4,000/20
A: 2/127-mm 38-cal. DP (I × 2) – 1/ASROC system (VIII × 1) – 6/324-mm Mk-32 ASW TT (III × 2) – 1/SH-2 LAMPS-I ASW helicopter (except FF-1048 and FF-1050)
Electron Equipt: Radars: 1/SPS-10, 1/SPS-40, 1/Mk-35
              Sonars: 1/SQS-26, FF-1048 and FF-1050: SQR-15 towed array, also
              ECM: WLR-6
Boilers: 2 Foster-Wheeler, 83.4 kg/cm² pressure – superheat 510°C
M: 1 set GE GT; 1 prop; 35,000 hp

Davidson   PH2 L. Foster, 1978

REMARKS: Anti-rolling stabilizers. FF-1047 and FF-1049 have a special ASW NTDS. The boilers are vertical and have pressure combustion. Hangar enlarged for SH-2 LAMPS-I helicopter, 1972-75, except for FF-1048 and FF-1050, which conduct trials for towed passive sonar array. Gunfire control is by a Mk-56 radar director and the Mk-114 ASW fire-control system is installed. FF-1047 and later have an ASROC re-load magazine beneath the bridge. Twin Mk-25 torpedo tubes at the stern have been removed from the ships that had them. FF-1041 carried Mk-25 Sea Sparrow launcher in 1967-68 for trials. Although these are relatively recent ships, there are no plans to modernize their obsolescent gun systems or to add Harpoon.

◆ 1 former experimental escort ship (SCB 198 type)

	Bldr	Laid down	L	In serv.
FF 1098 GLOVER	Bath Iron Works	7-63	17-4-65	11-65

Authorized: FY 61

Glover – with old number   G. Arra, 1976

D: 2,650 tons (3,500 fl)   **S:** 27 kts
Dim: 126.33 (121.9 wl) × 13.47 × 7.9 (over sonar)
A: 1/127-mm 38-cal. DP – 1/ASROC system (VIII × 1) – 6/324-mm Mk-32 ASW TT (III × 2)

FRIGATES (continued)

Man: 14 officers, 211 men
Electron Equipt: Radars: 1/SPS-10, 1/SPS-40, 1/Mk-35
Sonars: SQS-26AXD, SQS-35 VDS, SQR-13 PADLOC
ECM: WLR-6
Boilers: 2 Foster-Wheeler, 83.4 kg/cm² pressure – superheat 510°C
M: 1 set Westinghouse GT; 1 prop; 35,000 hp

REMARKS: Redesignated from AGFF on 1-10-79 because she now conducts operational cruises. "FF-1098" was previously used for a later-canceled *Knox*-class frigate; this is the first instance of a previously allocated hull number being reused. Basically a *Garcia*-class ship but with a pump-jet propeller and the after 127-mm gun omitted to provide accommodations for civilian technicians. Extreme stern raised during installation of SQS-35 VDS. Most systems similar to those of the *Garcia* class. SQR-13 PADLOC sonar is hull-mounted.

◆ 2 Bronstein class

	Bldr	Laid down	L	In serv.
FF 1037 BRONSTEIN	Avondale SY	16-5-61	31-5-62	16-6-63
FF 1038 McCLOY	Avondale SY	15-9-61	9-6-62	21-10-63

Bronstein   1975

McCloy   1977

D: 2,360 tons (2,650 fl)   **S:** 26 kts   **Dim:** 113.23 × 12.34 × 7.0
A: 2/76.2-mm Mk-33 (II × 1) – 1/ASROC system (VIII × 1) – 6/324-mm Mk-32 ASW TT (III × 2)
Man: 16 officers, 180 men

Electron Equipt: Radars: 1/SPS-10, 1/SPS-40, 1/Mk-35
Sonars: 1/SQS-26, 1/SQR-15 TASS   ECM: WLR-6
Boilers: 2 Foster-Wheeler, 83.4 kg/cm² pressure – superheat 510°C
M: 1 set de Laval GT; 1 prop; 20,000 hp

REMARKS: Only remaining U.S. frigates with 76.2-mm guns, controlled by a Mk-56 radar director. Single 76.2-mm aft replaced by TASS sonar. Have Mk-114, Mod. 7, ASW-fire-control system.

GUIDED-MISSILE PATROL BOATS

◆ 6 PHM (Patrol Hydrofoil Missile) class (SCB 602 type)

	Bldr	Laid down	L	In serv.
PHM 1 PEGASUS (ex-*Delphinus*)	Boeing, Seattle	10-5-73	9-11-74	9-7-77
PHM 2 HERCULES	Boeing, Seattle	30-5-74*	81	82
PHM 3 TAURUS	Boeing, Seattle	30-1-79	12-80	81
PHM 4 AQUILA	Boeing, Seattle	10-7-79	81	81
PHM 5 ARIES	Boeing, Seattle	28-11-79	81	81
PHM 6 GEMINI	Boeing, Seattle	3-80	81	82

Authorized: 2 in FY 73*, 4 in FY 75

*PHM-2 originally authorized under FY 73 and laid down on 30-5-74; her construction was suspended in 8-75, when 40.9 per cent complete, but will be laid down again in July 1980 with FY 76 funds.

Pegasus – note the Harpoon canisters on the stern   1975

D: 218 tons (239 fl)   **S:** 48 kts (12 on diesels)
Dim: 40.2 (45.0 with foils retracted) × 8.6 × 7.1 (1.9 with foils retracted)
A: 8/Harpoon SSM (IV × 2) – 1/76-mm Mk-76 DP (OTO Melara Compact)
Man: 4 officers, 17 men

GUIDED-MISSILE PATROL BOATS *(continued)*

Pegasus 1975

Electron Equipt: Radars: 1/LN-66, 1/Mk-92, Mod. 1, fire-control system
M: CODOG: 1 GE LM-2500 gas turbine; water jets; 18,000 hp; 2 MTU 8V331 TC80 diesels; 2 water jets; 1,340 hp

REMARKS: Originally projected as a class of thirty, also to be built by or for other NATO nations, but the additional cost over that of conventional missile craft with similar capabilities was prohibitive, and the U.S. Navy's interest in the type is minimal. PHM-1 began her protracted trials on 2-25-75. PHM-2 through PHM-6 were canceled on 15-4-77, then reinstated on 14-8-77 at the insistence of Congress, the contract going to Boeing on 20-10-77. No more are likely to be built. PHM-2 will be unarmed, as yet another hydrofoil trials craft. The others may be used in the Caribbean area. The Mk-92, Mod. 1, fire-control system is an Americanized version of the Hollandse Signaal Apparaten WM-28 system. PHM-1 has the earlier Mk-94, Mod. 1, variant. It was planned at one time to carry eight reload Harpoons, for a total of sixteen. All will have a simple threat-warning ESM set and Mk-34 chaff rocket launchers.

PATROL BOATS

◆ **4 Asheville class (SCB 229/600 type)**

	Bldr	Laid down	L	In serv.
PG 92 TACOMA	Tacoma Boat	24-7-67	13-4-68	14-7-69
PG 93 WELCH	Peterson Builders	8-8-67	25-7-68	8-9-69
PG 99 BEACON	Peterson Builders	. . .	68	21-11-69
PG 101 GREEN BAY	Peterson Builders	. . .	68	5-12-69

Authorized: FY 66

D: 225 tons (245 fl) **S:** 40 kts (16 cruising)
Dim: 50.14 (46.94 pp), × 7.28 × 2.9
Man: 3 officers, 22 men **Range:** 325/37, 1,700/16 **Fuel:** 50 tons
A: 1/76.2-mm Mk-34 DP – 1/40-mm AA – 4/12.7-mm machine guns (II × 2)
Electron Equipt: Radars: 1/LN-66, 1/SPG-50 **Electric:** 100 kw
M: CODOG: 1 GE 7LM-1500-PE102 GT, 12,500 hp (13,300 max.); 2 Cummins VT12-875M diesels, 725 hp each (875 max.); 2 controllable-pitch props

Tacoma G. Arra, 1975

REMARKS: Mk-63 gunfire control, with SPG-50 mounted on the 76.2-mm mount and the director atop the bridge. PG-92 and PG-93 are used at Little Creek, Virginia, to train Saudi Arabian crews for the Saudi Navy's new PGG and PCG classes. PG-99 and PG-101 were to have been transferred to Greece in 1977 but, when Congress objected, they were laid up in reserve on 1-4-77. Of the others, PG-84, PG-87, and PG-89 transferred to the Massachusetts Maritime Academy in 1977-78; PG-85, PG-86, and PG-90, stricken in 1977, are available for sale abroad; PG-88, with gas turbines removed, was transferred to the Environmental Protection Agency in 1977; PG-94 (now named *Athena*), PG-98 (*Athena-II*), and PG-100 (*Athena-III*) are operated as "boats," disarmed by the Naval Ships R & D Center (1975, 1977, and 1979, respectively); PG-95 and PG-97 transferred to Turkey in 1973; PG-96 to South Korea in 1971. None of these ships served the U.S. Navy for more than ten years.

NOTE: Of the PTF-23 ("Osprey")-class fast patrol boats, PTF-23, PTF-24, and PTF-26 were sold in 1979. PTF-25 has been converted as a gas-turbine-engine trials craft and disarmed. The hydrofoil submarine chaser *High Point* (PCH-1) was stricken on 30-9-79, having been extended in service for one year by Congress, over Defense Department objections.

PATROL CRAFT

◆ **13 PB Mk III class** Bldr: Peterson Bldrs., 1975

ART

D: 28 tons (36.7 fl) **S:** 30 kts **Dim:** 19.78 × 5.5 × 1.8
A: 5/12.7-mm machine guns (II × 1, I × 3) **Man:** 1 officer, 4 men
Electron Equipt: Radar: 1/LN-66
M: 3 G.M. 8V71 TI diesels; 3 props; 1,950 hp **Range:** 500/30

REMARKS: For Naval Reserve training. Winner in competition with Mk-I. Sisters were built for Iran and the Philippines. One may be used as trials craft for Norwegian Penguin II missiles.

PATROL CRAFT (*continued*)

PB Mk-III class   G. Arra, 1975

◆ **2 PB Mk-I class** Bldr: Sewart, Berwick, La, 1972

   D: 27 tons (36.3 fl)   **S:** 25 kts   **Dim:** 19.78 × 5.25 × 1.37
   Man: 2 officers, 6 men   **Range:** 30/26
   A: 2/20-mm AA (II × 1)—4/12.7-mm machine guns—1/81-mm mortar/12.7-mm
     machine gun combination
   M: 2 GM 12V71 TI diesels; 2 props; 1,200 hp

REMARKS: Used for Naval Reserve training.

◆ **5 PCF Mk-I class** Bldr: Swiftships, La, 1965-68

PCF Mk-I class

   D: 22.5 tons (fl)   **S:** 22 kts   **Dim:** 15.3 × 4.55 × 1.1
   A: 1/81-mm mortar/12.7-mm machine gun combination—2/12.7-mm machine guns
   Man: 6 men   **Range:** 400/22
   M: 2 GM 12V71 TI diesels; 2 props; 850 hp

REMARKS: Survivors of some 125 built. Aluminum alloy construction. Used for Naval
Reserve training.

RIVERINE WARFARE CRAFT

◆ **29 PBR (Patrol Boat, Riverine) Mk-II**

   D: 8.9 tons (fl)   **S:** 24 kts   **Dim:** 9.73 × 3.53 × 0.81
   Man: 4 men   **Range:** 150/23
   A: 3/12.7-mm machine guns (II × 1, I × 1)—1/60-mm mortar
   M: 2 GM 6V53N diesels; 2 Jacuzzi water jets; 430 hp

REMARKS: Built 1967-73. Fiberglass hull, plastic armor. Used for Naval Reserve
training.

MINE WARFARE SHIPS

NOTE: Except for MSO-443, MSO-448, and MSO-490, all minesweepers are assigned to
the Naval Reserve Force.

◆ **0 (+ 9) MCM-class oceangoing minehunters**

  Programmed: 1 in FY 82, 4 in FY 84, 4 in FY 85

   D: 1,100 tons (fl)   **S:** 18 kts   **Dim:** 61.0 × . . . × . . .
   A: 2/20-mm AA (I × 2)—2/12.7-mm machine guns (I × 2)
   Electron Equipt: Radar: SPS-55
                  Sonar: SQQ-14 Deep Mod.
   M: 2 diesels; 2 controllable-pitch props; . . . hp

REMARKS: This class was originally programmed for construction under FY 79-82 as a
group of nineteen ships of 2,200 tons (fl), some 80.0 × 12.1 × 3.4, with a 6,800-hp diesel
plant. The concept was obviously too large and expensive and has been recast as a

MCM class—artist's concept   1979

MINE WARFARE SHIPS (*continued*)

smaller number of smaller ships—in the face of an increasing threat. The MCMs would use a remote-controlled minehunting device similar to the French PAP-104 but would have much greater range and depth capability. They would be steel-hulled and have bow and stern side-thrusters for precision maneuvering at low speed. An SSN-2 precise-navigation system would be installed. These ships, if built, would be operated by the Naval Reserve Force.

◆ **2 Acme-class oceangoing minesweepers**
  Bldr: Frank L. Sample, Jr., Boothbay Harbor, Maine

	Laid down	L	In serv.
MSO 509 ADROIT	18-11-54	20-8-55	4-3-57
MSO 511 AFFRAY	24-8-55	18-12-56	8-8-58

  D: 720 tons (780 fl)   **S:** 14 kts   **Dim:** 52.73 × 10.97 × 4.3
  A: 2/12.7-mm machine guns (I × 2)
  Man: 7 officers, 37 men + 4 officers, 33 men Reserves
  Electron Equipt: Radar: 1/SPS-53   Sonar: SQQ-14   **Fuel:** 47 tons
  M: 4 Packard diesels; 2 controllable-pitch props; 2,280 hp   **Range:** 3,000/10

REMARKS: Similar to *Aggressive* and *Dash* class below, but slightly larger and originally equipped as Mine Division flagships. Not modernized. At 22-23 years of age, they are the U.S. Navy's newest minesweepers.

◆ **23 Aggressive and Dash* class oceangoing minesweepers**

	Bldr	Laid down	L	In serv.
MSO 427 CONSTANT	Fulton SY	16-8-51	14-2-53	8-9-54
MSO 428 DASH*	Astoria Marine	2-7-51	20-9-52	14-8-53
MSO 429 DETECTOR*	Astoria Marine	1-10-51	5-12-52	26-1-54
MSO 430 DIRECT*	C. Hiltebrant DD	2-2-52	27-5-53	9-7-54
MSO 431 DOMINENT*	C. Hiltebrant DD	23-4-52	5-11-53	8-11-54
MSO 433 ENGAGE	Colberg Boat Wks	7-11-51	18-6-53	29-6-54
MSO 437 ENHANCE	Martinolich SB	12-7-52	11-10-52	16-4-55
MSO 438 ESTEEM	Martinolich SB	1-9-52	20-12-52	10-9-55
MSO 439 EXCEL	Higgins, New Orleans	4-2-53	25-9-53	24-2-55
MSO 440 EXPLOIT	Higgins, New Orleans	28-12-51	10-4-53	31-3-54
MSO 441 EXULTANT	Higgins, New Orleans	22-5-52	6-6-53	22-6-54
MSO 442 FEARLESS	Higgins, New Orleans	23-7-52	17-7-53	22-9-54
MSO 443 FIDELITY	Higgins, New Orleans	15-12-52	21-8-53	19-1-55
MSO 446 FORTIFY	Seattle, SB & DD	30-11-51	14-2-53	16-7-54
MSO 448 ILLUSIVE	Martinolich SB	23-10-51	12-7-52	14-11-53
MSO 449 IMPERVIOUS	Martinolich SB	18-11-51	29-8-52	15-7-54
MSO 455 IMPLICIT	Wilmington Boat Wks.	29-10-51	1-8-53	10-3-54
MSO 456 INFLICT	Wilmington Boat Wks.	29-10-51	6-10-53	11-5-54
MSO 464 PLUCK	Wilmington Boat Wks.	31-3-52	6-2-54	11-8-54
MSO 488 CONQUEST	J. M. Martinac	26-3-53	20-5-54	20-7-55
MSO 489 GALLANT	J. M. Martinac	21-5-53	4-6-54	14-9-55
MSO 490 LEADER	J. M. Martinac	22-9-53	15-9-54	16-11-55
MSO 492 PLEDGE	J. M. Martinac	24-6-54	20-7-55	20-4-56

  D: 665 tons light (735 fl)   **S:** 14 kts   **Dim:** 52.42 × 10.97 × 4.2
  Man: 8 officers, 70 men (Naval Reserve Force ships: 3 officers, 36 men + 3 officers and 44 men Reserves)
  A: 2/12.7-mm machine guns (I × 2)   **Range:** 2,400/10 (*Dash* class: 3,000/10)

Direct   G. Arra, 1976

Pluck   PH3 H. Burgess, 1976

  Electron Equipt: Radar: SPS-53 E or L   Sonar: SQQ-14
  M: 4 Packard diesels; 2 controllable-pitch props; 2,280 hp; *Dash* class: 2 GM 8-268A diesels; 2 controllable-pitch props; 1,520 hp

REMARKS: Wooden construction; nonmagnetic, stainless-steel machinery. Except for MSO-443, MSO-448, and MSO-490, which are employed in experimental mine-warfare-related duties, all are operated for the Naval Reserve Force. Ninety-three of the MSO-421 to MSO-508 classes were built; many transferred abroad. Hoist machinery for the SQQ-14 minehunting sonar occupies the position of the former 40-mm AA gun. MSO-433, MSO-437, MSO-438, MSO-442, MSO-446, MSO-449, MSO-456, MSO-488, and MSO-490 were given very thorough rehabilitations; they have Waukesha diesels, improved accommodations, and new communications gear. All surviving units have received SQQ-14, semienclosed bridges, and enlarged superstructures abaft the bridge. In 1975 MSO-404 was equipped with the prototype SSN-2 precise-navigation system for the new MCM class.

MINESWEEPING BOATS

◆ **1 MSB-29 class** Bldr: Trumpy, Annapolis, 1954

D: 80 tons (fl) **S:** 12 kts **Dim:** 25.0 × 5.8 × 1.7

REMARKS: Enlarged MSB-5; only one built. Based at Charleston.

◆ **7 MSB-5 class**

MSB 15, MSB 16, MSB 25, MSB 28, MSB 41, MSB 51, MSB 52

D: 30 tons (39 fl) **S:** 12 kts **Dim:** 17.45 × 4.83 × 1.2
A: 1/12.7-mm machine gun **Man:** 6 men
M: 2 Packard diesels; 2 props; 600 hp

REMARKS: Survivors of a class of forty-seven built between 1952 and 1956. Wooden hulls; nonmagnetic machinery (including 2 sweep generators). All based at Charleston.

Mount Whitney C. Dragonette, 1979

MSB 15—in Vietnam 1970

AMPHIBIOUS WARFARE SHIPS

◆ **2 Blue Ridge-class amphibious command ships (SCN 400-65 type)**

	Bldr	Laid down	L	In serv.
LCC 19 BLUE RIDGE	Philadelphia NSY	27-2-67	4-1-69	14-11-70
LCC 20 MOUNT WHITNEY	Newport News SB & DD	8-1-69	8-1-70	16-1-71

Authorized: FY 65 and FY 66

D: 12,290 tons (fl) **S:** 21.5 kts **Dim:** 213.6 (183.2 pp) × 25.3 × 8.2
Man: 40 officers, 680 men + flag group: 200 officers, 500 men **Range:** 13,000/16
A: 4/76.2-mm DP (II × 2)−2/Mk-25 launchers for Sea Sparrow (VIII × 2)
Electron Equipt: Radars: 1/SPS-10, 1/SPS-48, 1/SPS-40, 2/Mk-115
　　　　　　　　 ECM: WLR-8, 4/Mk-36 Super RBOC−URN-20 TACAN−NTDS
Boilers: 2 Foster-Wheeler, 42.3 kg/cm² pressure−superheat 467°C
M: 1 set GE GT; 1 prop; 22,000 hp

Blue Ridge PH3 T. Pfrang, 1977

REMARKS: LCC-19 is the flagship of the Seventh Fleet; LCC-20 is the flagship of the Second Fleet. These ships have a good cruising speed (20 knots) and excellent satellite communications and analysis systems: ACIS (Amphibious Command Information System), NIPS (Naval Intelligence Processing System); photographic laboratories and document-publication facilities; four LCP and two LCVP landing craft are carried in davits. Liaison and transport helicopters (two UH-2 and one CH-46A). Same machinery and basic hull form as the *Iwo Jima*-class LPH. Air-conditioned; antirolling stabilizers. Two Mk-56 fire-control systems for the 76.2-mm guns deleted in 1978; two Mk-115 fire control for Sea Sparrow retained. They will eventually receive two Vulcan-Phalanx 20-mm AA. Kevlar plastic armor to be added.

AMPHIBIOUS WARFARE SHIPS (*continued*)

◆ **5 Tarawa-class amphibious assault ships (SCB 410 type)**

Bldr: Ingalls SB, Litton Ind., Pascagoula, Miss.

	Laid down	L	In serv.
LHA 1 TARAWA	15-11-71	1-12-73	29-5-76
LHA 2 SAIPAN	21-7-72	18-7-74	15-10-77
LHA 3 BELLEAU WOOD (ex-*Philippine Sea*)	5-3-73	11-4-77	23-9-78
LHA 4 NASSAU (ex-*Leyte Gulf*)	13-8-73	21-1-78	28-7-79
LHA 5 PELELIU (ex-*Da Nang*, ex-*Khe Sanh*)	12-11-76	25-11-78	3-80

Authorized: 1 in FY 69, 2 in FY 70, 2 in FY 71

Belleau Wood—with **John Young**   Ingalls, 1978

Saipan   Ingalls, 1977

D: 39,300 tons (fl)   **S:** 24 kts   **Dim:** 249.94 (237.14 pp) × 32.3 × 8.4

Man: 90 officers, 812 men + 172 officers, 1,731 troops   **Range:** 10,000/20

A: 2/Mk-25 Sea Sparrow launchers (VIII × 2)−3/127-mm 54-cal. Mk-45 DP (I × 3)−6/20-mm Mk-67 AA (I × 6)−19/CH-53 or 30/CH-46 helicopters

Electron Equipt: Radars: 1/SPS-53, 1/SPS-10F, 1/SPS-40B, 1/SPS-52B, 1/SPN-35, 1/SPG-60, 1/SPQ-9A, 2/Mk-115

ECM: LWR-8, 4/Mk-36 Super RBOC chaff−ITAWDS (Integrated Tactical Amphibious Warfare Data System)−URN-20 TACAN

Electric: 14,600 kw (4 × 2,500 kw, 2 × 2,000 kw, 4 × 150 kw)

Boilers: 2 Combustion Engineering V2M-VS, 49.3 kg/cm² pressure−superheat 482°C

M: 2 sets Westinghouse GT; 2 props, 140,000 hp

REMARKS: The LHA is a multipurpose assault transport, a combination of LPH and LPD. It has the general profile of an aircraft carrier, with its superstructure to starboard, flight deck, helicopter elevators to port (folding) and aft, and an 80 × 23.4-m well deck for landing craft (up to four LCU-1610 class). Two LCM(6) and two LCP are stowed on deck. The boilers are the largest ever installed in a U.S. Navy ship; the propulsion plant is highly automated. Communications systems include satellite antennas and a large, long-range, high-frequency, log-periodic array. Can carry AV-8A Harrier VTOL/STOL aircraft as well as the usual transport helicopters; may eventually carry one surface-effect landing craft of the JEFF A/B type. Very complete 300-bed hospital and mortuary facilities are fitted. All troops have bunks. Completely air-conditioned. Four additional units were canceled in 1971. The 127-mm guns are aboard primarily to provide shore fire support, but can also be used for AA; they are controlled by a Mk-86, Mod. 4, fire-control system with SPQ-9A radar for surface fire, SPG-60 for AA, and two unmanned electro-optical backup directors. Each Mk-25 Sea Sparrow launcher has an associated Mk-115 radar fire-control system with Mk-71 directors. All scheduled to receive two 20-mm Vulcan-Phalanx Gatling AA. Kevlar plastic armor to be added to all 1982-85.

AMPHIBIOUS WARFARE SHIPS (*continued*)

Tarawa   1976

AMPHIBIOUS ASSAULT HELICOPTER CARRIERS

◆ **7 Iwo Jima class (SCB P57, LPH-12: SCB 401-66)**

	Bldr	Laid down	L	In serv.
LPH 2 IWO JIMA	Puget Sound NSY	2-4-59	17-9-60	26-8-61
LPH 3 OKINAWA	Philadelphia NSY	1-4-60	14-8-61	14-4-62
LPH 7 GUADALCANAL	Philadelphia NSY	1-9-61	16-3-63	20-7-63
LPH 9 GUAM	Philadelphia NSY	15-11-62	22-8-64	16-1-65
LPH 10 TRIPOLI	Ingalls, Pascagoula	15-6-64	31-7-65	6-8-66
LPH 11 NEW ORLEANS	Philadelphia NSY	1-3-66	3-2-68	16-11-68
LPH 12 INCHON	Ingalls, Pascagoula	8-4-68	24-5-69	20-6-70

Authorized: 1 each year in FY 59-63, FY 65, FY 66

D: 17,000 tons (17,515-18,300 (fl)   **S:** 23 kts

Dim: 179.83 (180.18 pp) × 31.7 (25.6 wl) × 7.92

Man: 47 officers, 605 men + 190 officers, 1,900 troops

A: 4/76.2-mm DP (II × 2) — 2/Mk-25 Sea Sparrow launchers (VIII × 2) — 20-24/CH-46 helicopters — 4/CH-53 heavy helicopters — 4/HU-1 utility or AH-1 attack helicopters

Electron Equipt: Radars: 1/LN-66, 1/SPS-10, 1/SPS-40, 1/SPN-10 or 1/SPN-6

                 ECM: WLR-6, 4/Mk-36 Super RBOC — URN-20 TACAN

Boilers: 4 Combustion Engineering (LPH-9: Babcock & Wilcox), 42.3 kg/cm² pressure — superheat 467°C

M: 1 set GT; 1 prop; 23,000 hp

REMARKS: Congressional plans to convert one of these ships to a V/STOL fighter carrier have not been funded, which is perhaps fortunate, since there is no suitable aircraft (LPH-3 conducted V/STOL suitability trials during 1972 and for several years there-

Guam — no LCVP, SPN-10   1978

Inchon — with LCVP in davits aft, SPN-25, enclosed 76.2 guns   1977

AMPHIBIOUS ASSAULT HELICOPTER CARRIERS (*continued*)

after operated up to twelve AV-8A Harrier). The ships have also acted as carriers for RH-53 minesweeping helicopters. One folding side elevator forward, to port; one to starboard, aft of the island; 70-m hangar. Excellent medical facilities (300 beds). LPH-9 has an ASCAC (Air-Surface Classification and Analysis Center). LPH-12, to a slightly different design, carries two LCVP in davits. Two Mk-63 gunfire control being removed. Two 20-mm Vulcan-Phalanx AA to be added.

AMPHIBIOUS TRANSPORTS, DOCK

◆ 12 Austin class (SCB 187B type)

	Bldr	Laid down	L	In serv.
LPD 4 AUSTIN	New York NSY	4-2-63	27-6-64	6-2-55
LPD 5 OGDEN	New York NSY	4-2-63	27-6-64	19-6-65
LPD 6 DULUTH	New York NSY	18-12-63	14-8-65	18-12-65
LPD 7 CLEVELAND	Ingalls, Pascagoula	30-11-64	7-5-66	21-4-67
LPD 8 DUBUQUE	Ingalls, Pascagoula	25-1-65	6-8-66	1-9-67
LPD 9 DENVER	Lockheed SB, Seattle	7-2-64	23-1-65	26-10-68
LPD 10 JUNEAU	Lockheed SB, Seattle	23-1-65	12-2-66	12-7-69
LPD 11 CORONADO	Lockheed SB, Seattle	3-5-65	30-7-66	23-5-70
LPD 12 SHREVEPORT	Lockheed SB, Seattle	27-12-65	25-10-66	12-2-70
LPD 13 NASHVILLE	Lockheed SB, Seattle	14-3-66	7-10-67	14-2-70
LPD 14 TRENTON	Lockheed SB, Seattle	8-8-66	3-8-68	6-3-71
LPD 15 PONCE	Lockheed SB, Seattle	31-10-66	20-5-70	10-7-71

Authorized: 3 in FY 62, 4 in FY 63, 3 in FY 64, 2 in FY 65

Shreveport – flagship version   PH2 T. Baroody, 1977

Cleveland – two gun mounts, new life rafts   1978

Nashville – with LCM(6) and LCU in ducking well   PH3 W. Szymofelnik, 1977

D: 11,050 tons (16,550-17,000 fl)   **S:**   21 kts

Dim: 173.4 × 25.6 (hull) × 7.0-7.2

Man: 27 officers, 446 men (+ 90 staff in LPD-7 to LPD-13) + 940 troops (840 in LPD-7 to LPD-13)

A: 4/76.2-mm AA (II × 2)

Electron Equipt: Radars: 1/LN-66, 1/SPS-10, 1/SPS-40

                ECM: WLR-1 – URN-20 TACAN

Boilers: 2 Foster-Wheeler (LPD-5 and LPD-12: Babcock & Wilcox), 42.3 kg/cm² pressure – superheat 467°C

M: 2 sets de Laval GT; 2 props; 24,000 hp

REMARKS: Lengthened version of the *Raleigh* class. Combination LSD and assault transports; well deck 120 × 15.24; helicopter platform. Either one LCU and three LCM(6) or nine LCM(6) or four LCM(8) or twenty-eight LVT can be carried in the well deck. Six cranes, one 8.15-ton elevator, two forklifts. Up to six CH-46 helicopters can be carried for brief periods, but the small, telescoping hangar can accommodate only one utility helicopter. LPD-7 to LPD-13 are fitted for flagship duty and have one additional superstructure deck. All have lost their one Mk-56 and two Mk-63 gunfire control, leaving the 76.2-mm guns locally controlled. Two twin 76.2-mm DP removed 1977-78. Two 20-mm Vulcan-Phalanx AA to be added, as well as four Mk-36 Super RBOC chaff launchers.

AMPHIBIOUS TRANSPORTS, DOCK (*continued*)

◆ 2 Raleigh class

	Bldr	Laid down	L	In serv.
LPD 1 RALEIGH	New York NSY	6-60	17-3-62	8-9-62
LPD 2 VANCOUVER	New York NSY	11-60	15-9-62	11-5-63

Vancouver   G. Arra, 1977

D: 8,040 tons light (13,600 fl)   **S:** 21 kts
Dim: 159.0 (152.4 wl) × 25.60 (hull) × 6.7
A: 6/76-mm AA (II × 3)   **Man:** 30 officers, 460 men, + 930 troops
Electron Equipt: Radars: 1/LN-66, 1/SPS 10, 1/SPS-40 – URN-20 TACAN
M: 2 de Laval GT; 2 props; 24,000 hp
Boilers: 2 Babcock & Wilcox; 40.8 kg/cm² pressure

REMARKS: Sister *La Salle* (LPD-3), modified as flagship for CoMideastFor in the Indian Ocean and reclassified AGF-3, had an additional superstructure deck like LPD-7 to LPD-13. Docking well, 51.2 × 15.2 m, is shorter than on *Austin* class. Emphasis in LPD is on personnel capacity, in LSD on dock capacity; the flight deck, which forms the top of the well deck, can handle up to six CH-46 helicopters; there is no hangar. One twin 76.2-mm gun mount and all fire-control systems were removed 1977-78.

DOCK LANDING SHIPS

◆ . . . LSD-41 class

D: 10,976 tons light (15,774 fl)   **S:** 22 kts
Dim: 185.32 (176.79 pp) × 25.6 × 5.97
A: 2/20-mm Vulcan-Phalanx AA (I × 2)
Man: 22 officers, 379 men + 25 officers, 313 troops
Electron Equipt: Radars: 1/LN-66, 1/SPS-55, 1/SPS-65
                ECM: SLQ-32(v)1, 4/Mk-36 Super RBOC
M: 4 Colt-Pielstick 16PC2 5V400 diesels; 2 props; 41,600 hp
Electric: 3,000 kw

REMARKS: Originally planned to order LSD-41 under FY 79, then FY 80, but the Department of Defense deleted the entire class from the FY 80 – FY 84 construction program. Nonetheless, congressional pressure to build these replacements for the LSD-28 class is intense and one has been requested in FY 81 and one each in FY 83 and FY 85. The design was to have been a near-repeat of the LSD-36 class but a require-

LSD-41 – artist's rendering   1978

ment to accommodate four LCAC (Air-Cushion Landing Craft) caused considerable alteration and increase in size. The well deck is 134 × 15.24, and the helicopter deck above it is raised to provide ventilation. Will carry one LCM(6), two LCPL, and one LCVP. Helicopters of up to CH-53 size would be able to use the flight deck, but there will be no on-board support facilities. Without these ships, the navy's ability to perform amphibious warfare will seriously decline in the late 1980s.

◆ 5 Anchorage class (SCN 404-65 and 66 types)

	Bldr	Laid down	L	In serv.
LSD 36 ANCHORAGE	Ingalls, Pascagoula	13-3-67	5-5-68	15-3-69
LSD 37 PORTLAND	Gen'l Dynamics, Quincy	21-9-67	20-12-69	3-10-70
LSD 38 PENSACOLA	Gen'l Dynamics, Quincy	12-3-69	11-7-70	27-3-71
LSD 39 MOUNT VERNON	Gen'l Dynamics, Quincy	29-1-70	17-4-71	13-5-72
LSD 40 FORT FISHER	Gen'l Dynamics, Quincy	15-7-70	22-4-72	12-9-72

Authorized: 1 in FY 65, 3 in FY 66, 1 in FY 67

D: 8,600 tons light (13,600 fl)   **S:** 22 kts
Dim: 168.66 (162.8 wl) × 25.6 × 6.1
A: 6/76.2-mm DP (II × 3)   **Man:** 21 officers, 376 men + 28 officers, 348 troops
Electron Equipt: Radars: 1/SPS-10, 1/SPS-40
Boilers: 2 Foster-Wheeler (LSD-36: Combustion Engineering), 42.3 kg/cm² – superheat 467°C
M: 2 sets de Laval GT; 2 props; 24,000 hp

DOCK LANDING SHIPS (continued)

Fort Fisher   General Dynamics, 1972

Pensacola   1975

REMARKS: Carry assault landing craft in the well deck (113.28 × 15.24); can accommodate three LCU or eight LCM(8) or fifty LVT. One or two LCM(6) stowed on deck, handled by the two 50-ton cranes. The helicopter deck is removable. One twin 76.2-mm removed to allow later mounting of two 20-mm Vulcan-Phalanx. Mk-56 and Mk-63 directors removed in 1977. No ECM equipment.

◆ **8 Thomaston class (SCB-75 type)**   Bldr: Ingalls, Pascagoula, Miss.

		Laid down	L	In serv.
LSD 28	THOMASTON	3-3-53	9-2-54	17-9-54
LSD 29	PLYMOUTH ROCK	5-5-53	7-5-54	29-11-54
LSD 30	FORT SNELLING	17-8-53	16-7-54	24-1-55
LSD 31	POINT DEFIANCE	23-11-53	28-9-54	31-3-55
LSD 32	SPIEGEL GROVE	7-9-54	10-11-55	8-6-56
LSD 33	ALAMO	11-10-54	20-1-56	24-8-56
LSD 34	HERMITAGE	11-4-55	12-6-56	14-12-56
LSD 35	MONTICELLO	6-6-55	10-8-56	29-3-57

Authorized: 4 in FY 52, 2 in FY 54, 2 in FY 55

D: 6,880 tons (12,000 fl)   **S:** 22.5 kts   **Dim:** 155.45 × 25.6 × 5.8
A: 6/76.2-mm DP (II × 3)   **Man:** 21 officers, 379 men + 340 troops
Electron Equipt: Radars: 1/SPS-10, 1/SPS-6
Boilers: 2 Babcock & Wilcox, 40.8 kg/cm² pressure
M: 2 sets GE GT; 2 props; 24,000 hp   **Range:** 10,000/20

Plymouth Rock   G. Arra, 1975

REMARKS: Portable helicopter platform. Can carry three LCU or nine LCM(8) in 119.2 × 14.6 well deck. Two 50-ton cranes. Originally had sixteen 76.2-mm DP (II × 8). Now have one mount forward, to starboard, and two amidships. Two Mk-56 and Mk-63 gun-fire-control systems removed in 1977. Last active ships with SPS-6 air-search radar.

TANK LANDING SHIPS

◆ **20 Newport class (SCN 405-66 type)**

Bldrs: LST-1179: Philadelphia NSY; others: National Steel SB, San Diego

		Laid down	L	In serv.
LST 1179	NEWPORT	1-11-66	3-2-68	7-6-69
LST 1180	MANITOWOC	1-2-67	4-6-69	24-1-70
LST 1181	SUMTER	14-11-67	13-12-69	20-6-70
LST 1182	FRESNO	16-12-67	28-9-68	22-11-69
LST 1183	PEORIA	22-2-68	23-11-68	21-2-70
LST 1184	FREDERICK	13-4-68	8-3-69	11-4-70
LST 1185	SCHENECTADY	2-8-68	24-5-69	13-6-70
LST 1186	CAYUGA	28-9-68	12-7-69	8-8-70
LST 1187	TUSCALOOSA	23-11-68	6-9-69	24-10-70
LST 1188	SAGINAW	24-5-69	7-2-70	23-1-71
LST 1189	SAN BERNARDINO	12-7-69	28-3-70	27-3-71
LST 1190	BOULDER	6-9-69	22-5-70	4-6-71
LST 1191	RACINE	13-12-69	15-8-70	9-7-71
LST 1192	SPARTANBURG COUNTY	7-2-70	11-11-70	1-9-71
LST 1193	FAIRFAX COUNTY	28-3-70	19-12-70	16-10-71
LST 1194	LA MOURE COUNTY	22-5-70	13-2-71	18-12-71
LST 1195	BARBOUR COUNTY	15-8-70	15-5-71	12-2-72
LST 1196	HARLAN COUNTY	7-11-70	24-7-71	8-4-72
LST 1197	BARNSTABLE COUNTY	19-12-70	2-10-71	27-5-72
LST 1198	BRISTOL COUNTY	13-2-71	4-12-71	5-8-72

Authorized: 1 in FY 65, 8 in FY 66, 11 in FY 67

D: 4,164 tons light (8,342-8,450 fl)   **S:** 20 kts
Dim: 159.2 (171.3 over horns) × 21.18 × 5.3 (aft) × 1.80 (fwd)
A: 4/76.2-mm DP (II × 2)   **Man:** 12 officers, 174 men + 20/411 troops
Electron Equipt: Radars: 1/LN-66, 1/SPS-10
M: 6 Alco (LST-1179 to LST-1181: GM) diesels; 2 controllable-pitch props; 16,500 hp

REMARKS: Can carry 500 tons of cargo on 1,765 m² of deck space, and 431 troops. A side-thruster propeller forward helps when marrying to a causeway. There is a mobile aluminum ramp forward (34.15 tons), which is linked to the tank deck by a second

TANK LANDING SHIPS (continued)

Saginaw   1978

Barnstable County   Skyfotos, Ltd., 1978

Sumter—with pontoon sections   Skyfotos, Ltd., 1978

ramp. These ramps can carry 75 tons. Aft is a helicopter platform and a stern door for loading and unloading vehicles. Four pontoon causeway sections can be carried on the hull sides. Mk-63 radar gunfire-control systems removed 1977-78; two 20-mm Vulcan-Phalanx AA are intended to replace the 76.2-mm guns.

◆ **3 de Soto County class (SCB-119 type)**
Bldrs: LST-1173: Boston NSY, others: American SB, Lorain, Ohio

	Laid down	L	In serv.
LST 1173 SUFFOLK COUNTY	17-7-56	5-9-56	15-8-57
LST 1177 LORAIN COUNTY	9-8-56	22-6-57	3-10-59
LST 1178 WOOD COUNTY	1-10-56	14-12-57	5-8-59

D: 3,560 tons light (7,800 fl)   **S:** 16 kts
Dim: 135.7 (129.8 wl) × 18.9 × 5.3
A: 6/76-mm 50-cal. (II × 3)   **Man:** 15 officers, 173 men
Electron Equipt: Radar: 1/SPS-21   **Electric:** 900 kw
M: 6 Fairbanks-Morse 38D8⅛ (LST-1177 and LST-1178: Cooper Bessemer) diesels; 2 controllable-pitch props; 14,000 hp

Lorain County

REMARKS: All in reserve since 1972. Last U.S. Navy LSTs with bow doors. Air-conditioned. Can carry 700 troops. Special tanks for vehicle fuel. Four LCVP carried in davits; one LCU and two pontoons can be carried on board. Helicopter platform. Tank deck, 88-m long, can stow twenty-three tanks. *De Soto County* (LST-1171) and *York County* (LST-1175) transferred to Italy, *Grant County* (LST-1174) to Brazil. *Graham County* (LST-1176) scrapped in 1977. *Wood County* was to have been converted as a tender to the *Pegasus*-class PHM but plan was canceled in 1977.

AMPHIBIOUS CARGO SHIPS

◆ **5 Charleston class**

	Bldr	Laid down	L	In serv.
LKA 113 CHARLESTON	Newport News	5-12-66	2-12-67	14-12-68
LKA 114 DURHAM	Newport News	10-7-67	29-3-68	24-5-69
LKA 115 MOBILE	Newport News	15-1-68	19-10-68	29-9-69
LKA 116 ST. LOUIS	Newport News	3-4-68	4-1-69	22-11-69
LKA 117 EL PASO	Newport News	22-10-58	17-5-69	17-1-70

Authorized: 4 in FY 65, 1 in FY 66

D: 18,600 tons (fl)   **S:** 20 kts   **Dim:** 175.4 × 18.9 × 7.8
A: 6/76.2-mm DP (II × 3)   **Man:** 24 officers, 310 men + 15 officers, 211 troops

AMPHIBIOUS CARGO SHIPS (*continued*)

Charleston—with CH-46 helicopters   Pradignac & Leo, 1975

St. Louis   PH1 A. Lagare, 1976

St. Louis

Electron Equipt: Radars: 1/LN-66, 1/SPS-10
Boilers: 2 Combustion Engineering, 42.2 kg/cm² pressure
M: 1 set Westinghouse GT; 1 prop; 22,000 hp

REMARKS: Some or all of these ships may be employed, with partial Naval Reserve Force crews, as replacements for the stricken LPA-248, LPA-249, and LKA-112. Air-conditioned. Machinery control is automatic. Helicopter platform. Fittings include two 78-ton heavy-lift booms, two 40-ton booms, and eight 15-ton booms. Normally carry four LCM(8), four LCM(6), two LCVP, and two LCP. Two Mk-56 radar gunfire-control systems and one twin 76.2-mm gun mount removed 1977-78; to receive two 20-mm Vulcan-Phalanx AA.

NOTE: The *Mariner*-class amphibious cargo ship *Tulare* (LKA-112) was stricken on 15-2-80. The amphibious transport *Paul Revere* (LPA-248) was stricken on 1-10-79, and her sister *Francis Marion* (LPA-249) on 14-3-80; both were to be sold to Spain.

UTILITY LANDING CRAFT

◆ **60 LCU-1610 class (SCB 149, 149B, and 406 types)** Bldrs: Various, 1960-78

LCU 1613	LCU 1623	LCU 1637
LCU 1614	LCU 1624	LCU 1641
LCU 1616 to LCU 1619	LCU 1626	LCU 1644 to LCU 1651
LCU 1621	LCU 1628 to 1634	LCU 1653 to LCU 1685

LCU-1653   G. Arra, 1975

LCU-1618—used as trials craft for NAVSTAR global positioning system   LCdr. J. Strada, 1978

UTILITY LANDING CRAFT (*continued*)

D: 190 tons (390 fl)   **S:** 11 kts   **Dim:** 41.07 × 9.07 × 2.08
Man: 6 men + 8 troops   **Range:** 1,200/11   **Fuel:** 13 tons
A: 2/12.7-mm machine guns
M: 4 GM 6-71 diesels; 2 Kort-nozzle props; 1,200 hp

REMARKS: LCU-1621 has vertical, cycloidal propellers. LCU-1637 is constructed of aluminum, displaces 357 tons (fl), and draws 1.97 m. Cargo capacity is 143 tons; cargo space, 30.5 × 5.5 m. Usually unarmed; can be equipped with an LN-66 or other small navigation radar. Most of the missing hull numbers converted to other functions. Minor differences as construction progressed.

◆ **31 LCU-1466 class (SCB 25 type)**

LCU 1466 to LCU 1470	LCU 1484	LCU 1532	LCU 1554
LCU 1472	LCU 1485	LCU 1535 to LCU 1537	LCU 1558
LCU 1473	LCU 1487 to LCU 1490	LCU 1539	LCU 1559
LCU 1477	LCU 1492	LCU 1547	LCU 1563
LCU 1482	LCU 1505	LCU 1548	LCU 1564
		LCU 1552	LCU 1578

LCU-1468   1969

D: 180 tons (347 fl)   **S:** 8 kts   **Dim:** 35.08 × 10.36 × 1.6 (aft)
Man: 6 men + 8 troops   **Range:** 1,200/6   **Fuel:** 11 tons
M: 3 Gray Marine 64YTL diesels; 3 props; 675 hp

REMARKS: Built between 1953 and 1958. Can carry 167 tons. Engines and bridge aft. Improved version of LCU-501 class. Missing numbers have been either transferred, sunk, or converted to service craft (YFU). LCU-1473, LCU-1505, LCU-1532, LCU-1537, LCU-1548, LCU-1552, LCU-1554, LCU-1558, LCU-1563, LCU-1564, and LCU-1578 were reacquired from the U.S. Army in 9-78.

NOTE: The last twenty-two units of the LCU-501 class have been stricken.

MINOR LANDING CRAFT

NOTE: Exact totals not available.

◆ **. . . LCM(8) Mk-2 class**

D: 34 tons light (95 fl)   **S:** 12 kts   **Dim:** 22.7 × 6.41 × 1.37
M: 4 GM 6-71 diesels; 2 props; 590 hp   **Range:** 150/12

REMARKS: Began building in 1969. Aluminum version of LCM(8) Mk-1. Cargo: 58 tons. Some have two GM 12V71 diesels.

◆ **. . . LCM(8), Mod. 1 and Mod. 2, class**

LCM(8), Mod. 1, class

D: 56 tons light (116 fl)   **S:** 9 kts   **Dim:** 22.43 × 6.42 × 1.57
M: 4 GM 6-71 diesels; 2 props; 620 hp   **Range:** 140/9

REMARKS: Built between 1949 and 1976. Cargo: 54 tons. U.S. Army also uses large numbers of this class, which has now been in production for more than thirty years.

◆ **. . . LCM(6) class**

D: 24 tons (56 fl)   **S:** 10 kts   **Dim:** 17.07 × 4.37 × 1.17 (aft)
M: 2 Gray Marine 64NN9 diesels; 2 props; 330 hp   **Range:** 130/10

REMARKS: Designed during World War II and built between 1952 and 1977. Many used in utility roles. Cargo: 30 tons

◆ **. . . LCVP class**

D: 13 tons (fl)   **S:** 9 kts   **Dim:** 10.90 × 3.21 × 1.04 (aft)
M: 1 Gray Marine 64HN9 diesel; 225 hp   **Range:** 110/9

REMARKS: 1,552 built, 1950-62. Wooden or plastic hulls. Can carry 36 troops or 3.5 tons cargo.

◆ **. . . LCP(L) Mk-11 class**

D: 9.2 tons (fl)   **S:** 17 kts   **Dim:** 10.98 × 3.97 × 1.13
M: 1 GM 6-71 diesel; 270 hp   **Range:** 160/7

REMARKS: Plastic construction. For use as control craft. Carried aboard are LHA, LPD, LSD, LST classes etc. Twenty-six additional requested in FY 80 budget. A large number of the older, steel, Mk-4 version remain in service: 10.2 tons; one GM 8V71 diesel; 350 hp for 19 knots.

EXPERIMENTAL LANDING CRAFT

NOTE: The best features of the two AALC (Amphibious Assault Landing Craft) designs listed below were to be combined into a new production air-cushion vehicle intended to supplement the LCU classes beginning in the 1980s. They were to be carried in the *Tarawa*-class LHA and by the LSD-41 class. The goal is to carry a 54,446-kg payload at 50 knots. The prototypes will now be tested through FY 82 before any decision is made on production.

◆ **JEFF-A** Bldr: Aerojet General

Weight: 85.8 tons (166 loaded)   **Dim:** 31.5 × 15.7 × 7.5 (high)
S: 50 kts   **Range:** 200/50   **Man:** 6 men
M: 6 Avco T40 gas turbines (2 for lift); 4 shrouded air screws; 11,200 hp

REMARKS: Actually built at Todd Shipyards, Seattle, and delivered in 2-77. Aluminum construction.

EXPERIMENTAL LANDING CRAFT (*continued*)

◆ **JEFF-B** Bldr: Bell Aerosystems, New Orleans

Weight: 93 tons (147 loaded)   **Dim:** 26.4 × 14.3 × 7.1 (high)
S: 70 kts   **Range:** 200/50   **Man:** 6 men
M: 6 Avco T40 gas turbines (4 for lift); 2 shrouded propellers; 16,080 hp

Jeff-B   1979

Jeff-B   1979

REMARKS: Delivered in 1976. In this design, all six turbines are interconnected to provide power simultaneously to the two propellers and four lift fans.

AUXILIARY SHIPS

NOTE: This section includes only ships that are subordinate to the U.S. Navy proper.
Ships assigned to the civilian-manned Military Sealift Command are listed separately
in a following section. Below, ships are listed alphabetically by their U.S. Navy type
designation i.e., AD, AF, AG, etc.

◆ **3 (+2) Samuel Gompers-class destroyer tenders (SCB 244 type)**

Bldrs: AD-37 and AD-38, Puget Sound NSY; AD-41 to AD-44, National Steel, San
Diego

	Laid down	L	In serv.
AD 37 SAMUEL GOMPERS	9-7-64	14-5-66	1-7-67
AD 38 PUGET SOUND	15-2-65	16-9-66	27-4-68
AD 41 YELLOWSTONE	27-6-77	27-1-79	2-80
AD 42 ACADIA	14-2-78	28-7-79	12-80
AD 43 CAPE COD	27-1-79	5-80	81
AD 44 N . . .	81	82	83

Authorized: 1 in FY 64, 1 in FY 65, 1 in FY 75, 1 in FY 76, 1 in FY 77, 1 in FY 79

Samuel Gompers   G. Arra, 1977

Puget Sound—127-mm gun now removed   C. Dragonette, 1979

D: 20,500 tons (fl)   **S:** 20 kts   **Dim:** 196.29 × 25.91 × 6.86
A: 4/20-mm AA (I × 4)   **Man:** 135 officers, 1,671 men
Electron Equipt: Radar: 1/SPS-10   **Electric:** 12,000 kw
Boilers: 2 Combustion Engineering, 43.6 kg/cm² pressure—superheat 462°C
M: 1 set de Laval GT; 1 prop; 20,000 hp

AUXILIARY SHIPS (continued)

REMARKS: Similar to *L. Y. Spear*-class submarine tenders; AD-41 and later considered a separate class (SCB-700 type). Maintenance ships for guided-missile cruisers and destroyers. Two 30-ton cranes; two 3.5-ton traveling cranes. Helicopter deck. Excellent workshops for electronic equipment and surface-to-air missiles. No longer planned to carry Sea Sparrow in AD-41 and later, which will carry only two 20-mm AA (I × 2). One 127-mm DP removed from AD-38 in 1979. Also carry two 40-mm Mk-64 grenade launchers.

◆ 2 Klondike-class destroyer tenders

	Bldr	Laid down	L	In serv.
AD 24 EVERGLADES	Los Angeles SB	26-6-44	28-1-45	25-5-51
AD 36 BRYCE CANYON	Charleston NSY	. . .	7-3-46	15-9-50

Bryce Canyon   PHAN J. Mason, 1978

D: 8,165 tons (14,700 fl)   **S:** 18 kts   **Dim:** 149.96 (141.73 pp) × 21.25 × 8.3
A: AD-36: 1/127-mm 38-cal. DP   **Man:** 800-918 men   **Fuel:** 2,415 tons
Electron Equipt: Radar: 1/SPS-10   **Electric:** 3,600 kw
Boilers: 2 Foster-Wheeler, 30.6 kg/cm² pressure—superheat 393°C
M: 1 set Westinghouse GT; 1 prop; 8,500 hp

REMARKS: AD-24 is in reserve as an accommodations ship; AD-36, which underwent FRAM-II modernization, is active. Built on C-3 cargo hull. Helicopter deck; hangar

for DASH, now not used. Sister *Shenandoah* (AD-26) stricken on 1-4-80. AD-36 begun as a seaplane tender (AV-20).

◆ 5 Dixie-class destroyer tenders

	Bldr	Laid down	L	In serv.
AD 14 DIXIE	New York SB	17-3-38	25-5-39	25-4-40
AD 15 PRAIRIE	New York SB	7-12-38	9-12-39	5-8-40
AD 17 PIEDMONT	Tampa SB	1-12-41	7-12-42	5-1-44
AD 18 SIERRA	Tampa SB	31-12-41	23-2-43	20-3-44
AD 19 YOSEMITE	Tampa SB	19-1-42	16-5-43	25-3-44

Dixie—oldest active ship in the U.S. Navy   1976

Yosemite   1977

D: 9,450 tons (17,190 fl)   **S:** 18 kts   **Dim:** 161.7 × 22.33 × 7.8
A: 4/20-mm AA (I × 4)   **Man:** 1,131-1, 271 men   **Fuel:** 3,680 tons
Electron Equipt: Radar: 1/SPS-10   **Electric:** 3,600 kw
Boilers: 4 Babcock & Wilcox, 28.4 kg/cm² pressure—superheat 382°C
M: 2 sets GT; 2 props; 11,000 hp

REMARKS: The design of these support ships goes back to pre-1939 programs. Modernized under the FRAM program from 1959 to 1963 to serve as maintenance vessels for guided-missile ships, they have workshops, spare parts for missiles, and two 20-ton rotating cranes. Helicopter deck. 127-mm guns removed 1974-75.

AUXILIARY SHIPS (*continued*)

◆ 8 Kilauea-class ammunition ships (SCB 703 type)

	Bldr	Laid down	L	In serv.
AE 26 KILAUEA	Gen. Dynamics	10-3-66	9-8-67	10-8-68
AE 27 BUTTE	Gen. Dynamics	21-7-66	9-8-67	14-12-68
AE 28 SANTA BARBARA	Bethlehem, Sparrows Pt	20-12-66	23-1-68	11-7-70
AE 29 MOUNT HOOD	Bethlehem, Sparrows Pt	8-5-67	17-7-68	1-5-71
AE 32 FLINT	Ingalls, Pascagoula	4-8-69	9-11-70	20-11-71
AE 33 SHASTA	Ingalls, Pascagoula	10-11-69	3-4-71	26-2-72
AE 34 MOUNT BAKER	Ingalls, Pascagoula	10-5-70	23-10-71	22-7-72
AE 35 KISKA	Ingalls, Pascagoula	4-8-71	11-3-72	16-12-72

Authorized: 2 in FY 65, 2 in FY 66, 2 in FY 67, 2 in FY 68.

Mount Baker   1976

Butte

D: 88 tons (fl)   **S:** 20 kts   **Dim:** 171.9 × 24.7 × 8.5
A: 4/7 .2-mm DP (II × 2) – 2/UH-46 helicopters   **Man:** 28 officers, 37 men
Electron Equipt: Radar: 1/SPS-10
Boilers: 3 Foster-Wheeler, 42.3 kg/cm² pressure – superheat 467°C
M: GE GT; 1 prop; 22,000 hp

REMARKS: Sophisticated FAST rapid-replenishment system. Hangar and flight deck aft. Two twin 76.2-mm mounts amidships and both Mk-56 directors removed; two 20-mm Vulcan-Phalanx AA and Mk-36 Super RBOC chaff-flare launchers to be added.

◆ 3 Nitro-class ammunition ships (SCB 114A type)
Bldr: Bethlehem Steel Corp., Sparrows Point, Md.

	Laid down	L	In serv.
AE 23 NITRO	20-5-57	26-6-58	1-5-59
AE 24 PYRO	21-10-57	5-11-58	24-7-59
AE 25 HALEAKALA	10-3-58	17-2-59	3-11-59

Nitro   G. Arra, 1975

D: 10,000 tons (16,083 fl)   **S:** 20 kts   **Dim:** 156.1 × 22.0 × 8.8
A: 4/76-mm AA (II × 2)   **Man:** 20 officers, 330 men
Electron Equipt: Radar: 1/SPS-10   **Boilers:** 2 Combustion Engineering
M: 1 set Bethlehem GT; 1 prop; 16,000 hp

REMARKS: All had landing platforms for cargo helicopters added aft during the 1960s. Mk-63 gun directors removed, 1977-78. Mk-36 Super RBOC to be added; SPS-6 removed.

◆ 2 Suribachi-class ammunition ships (SCB 114 type)
Bldr: Bethlehem Steel Corp., Sparrows Point, Md.

	Laid down	L	In serv.
AE 21 SURIBACHI	16-5-55	3-5-56	30-3-57
AE 22 MAUNA KEA	31-1-55	2-11-55	17-11-56

Suribachi   1978

D: 10,000 tons (15,500 fl)   **S:** 1 kts   **Dim:** 156.1 × 22.0 × 8.8
A: 4/76.2-mm DP (II × 2)   **Man:** 16 officers, 370 men
Electron Equipt: Radar: SPS-10   **Boilers:** 2 Combustion Engineering
M: 1 set GT; 1 prop; 16,000 hp

AUXILIARY SHIPS (*continued*)

REMARKS: SPS-6 radar removed. Gun mounts superfiring, whereas AE-23 to AE-25 have them side by side. Mk-63 gunfire-control systems removed, 1977-78.

◆ **7 Mars-class combat stores ships (SCB 208 type)**

Bldr: National Steel & SB Co., San Diego

	Laid down	L	In serv.
AFS 1 MARS	5-5-62	15-6-63	21-12-63
AFS 2 SYLVANIA	18-8-62	10-8-63	11-7-64
AFS 3 NIAGARA FALLS	22-5-65	25-3-66	29-4-67
AFS 4 WHITE PLAINS	2-10-65	23-7-66	23-11-68
AFS 5 CONCORD	26-3-66	17-12-66	27-11-68
AFS 6 SAN DIEGO	11-3-67	13-4-68	24-5-69
AFS 7 SAN JOSE	8-3-69	13-12-69	23-10-70

Authorized: 1 in FY 61, 1 in FY 62, 1 in FY 64, 2 in FY 65, 1 in FY 66, 1 in FY 67

Mars—URN-6 TACAN   PH3 M. Markham, 1975

Sylvania   1979

D: 16,240 tons (fl)   **S:** 20 kts   **Dim:** 177.08 (161.54 pp) × 24.08 × 7.32
A: 4/76.2-mm DP (II × 2)   **Man:** 45 officers, 441 men
Electron Equipt: Radar: 1/SPS-10 – URN-20 TACAN (AFS-1: URN-6 TACAN)

Boilers: 3 Babcock & Wilcox, 40.8 kg/cm² pressure
M: 1 set GT; 1 prop; 22,000 hp

REMARKS: Two UH-46A (Sea Knight) cargo helicopters, with platform and hangar. Four M-shaped cargo masts with constant-tension equipment; transfer from the supply ship to the receiving ship takes 90 seconds. Five holds (1 and 5 for spare parts, 3 and 4 for provisions, 2 for aviation parts) have only two hatches. Eleven hoists, which raise up to 5.5 tons, link the decks; several others feed into the helicopter area. Ten loading areas (five on each side) and palletized cargo help in the control of replenishment. There are four refrigerated compartments, and three for the storage of dried provisions. Some 35,000 types of spare parts are divided between 40,000 bins and racks and are accounted for by five data-processing machines. Quarters air-conditioned. Draw 2.7 m more aft than forward. One boiler always in reserve. Three additional units no longer planned. SPS-40 radar fire-control directors and two twin 76.2-mm mounts amidships removed.

◆ **1 navigation-systems trials ship**   Bldr: Marine Ship Corp., Sausalito, Cal.

	L	In serv.
AG 194 VANGUARD (ex-T-AGM-19, ex-*Muscle Shoals*, ex-*Mission San Fernando*, T-AO-122)	23-11-43	21-10-47

Vanguard—as T-AGM-19   MSC, 1970

D: 21,626 tons (fl)   **S:** 16 kts   **Dim:** 181.4 × 22.9 × 7.6
Man: . . .   **Range:** 28,000/16   **Fuel:** 4,158 tons
Boilers: 2 Babcock & Wilcox "D," 42.25 kg/cm² pressure – superheat 440°C
M: 1 set GE turbo-electric drive; 1 prop; 10,000 hp

REMARKS: Former T-2-SE-A2-type tanker converted 1964-66 as a tracking and communications ship for NASA manned space flights. Stretched 22 meters and built up one deck-level amidships. Being converted under FY 80 as a replacement for *Compass Island* (AG-153) as trials ship for navigation systems for ballistic-missile submarines. Sister *Redstone* (T-AGM-20) remains in MSC service.

NOTE: AG-193 (ex-*Hughes Glomar Explorer*), transferred to Navy ownership in 9-76 and laid up at Suisun Bay, California, was chartered in June 1978 for thirteen months by Global Marine Corporation for deep-water mineral exploration. In late 1979 it was announced that she had been placed at the disposal of the National Science Foundation and would embark on a ten-year research program as a deep-sea drilling ship for the Ocean Margin Drilling Program. When conversion is completed in 10-82, the ship will be able to drill to depths of 7,000 meters beneath the sea floor while operating in 4,000 meters of water.

AUXILIARY SHIPS (continued)

◆ **1 auxiliary deep-submergence support ship**   Bldr: Maryland SB & DD

	L	In serv.
AGDS 2 POINT LOMA (ex-*Point Barrow*, T-AKD-1)	25-5-57	29-5-58

Point Loma   1977

D: 9,415 tons (14,094 fl)   **S:** 18 kts   **Dim:** 150.0 × 23.8 × 6.7
Electron Equipt: Radar: RCA CR-101-A
Man: 10 officers, 249 men, 8 scientists
M: 2 sets Westinghouse GT; 2 props; 6,000 hp   **Boilers:** 2 Foster-Wheeler

REMARKS: Built for Arctic supply and configured like a landing ship, dock (LSD). Served in MSC until 28-9-72, when placed in reserve. Transferred to the Navy on 28-2-74, renamed, renumbered, and reactivated as a tender for deep-submergence vehicles, particularly Trieste-II. Operates from San Diego. Carries 275 tons of gasoline as flotation liquid for Trieste-II. Two traveling cranes. Second stack added for diesel-generator exhausts.

NOTE: The experimental hydrofoil *Plainview* (AGEH-1) was stricken 30-9-78.

◆ **1 Raleigh-class auxiliary command ship**

	Bldr	Laid down	L	In serv.
AGF 3 LA SALLE (ex-LPD-3)	New York NSY	2-4-62	3-8-63	22-2-64

D: 8,040 tons (13,900 fl)   **S:** 21 kts   **Dim:** 158.4 (155.4 wl) × 25.6 × 6.4
A: 8/76.2-mm DP (II × 4)
Man: 18 officers, 369 men + flagstaff: 12 officers, 47 men
Electron Equipt: Radars: 1/SPS-10, 1/SPS-40
                    ECM: WLR-1 – URN-20 TACAN

La Salle   PH1 R. Green, 1975

Boilers: 2 Babcock & Wilcox, 42.2 kg/cm² pressure
M: 2 sets de Laval GT; 2 props; 24,000 hp

REMARKS: Ex-landing platform, dock (LPD). Since redesignated 1-7-72 employed as flagship of Commander, Middle East Force. Painted white. Well deck used for ship's boats. Helicopter hangar for one SH-3 built on flight deck, to port, with shelter for ceremonial activities to starboard. One Mk-56 and two Mk-63 gunfire-control systems removed 1977-78; will lose one gun mount but gain two 20-mm Vulcan-Phalanx during overhaul commencing 1980.

RESEARCH SUBMARINES

◆ **1 Dolphin class (SCB 207 type) research submarine**

	Bldr	Laid down	L	In serv.
AGSS 555 DOLPHIN	Portsmouth NSY	9-11-62	8-6-68	17-8-69
Authorized: FY 61				

Dolphin

AUXILIARY SHIPS (*continued*)

D: 860 tons surfaced/950 submerged   **S:** 7.5/10 or 15 (*see* Remarks)
Dim: 50.29 × 5.92 × 4.9   **Man:** 3 officers, 26 men, 5 scientists
Electron Equipt: Sonars: BQS 15, bow passive array, towed array, BQR 2
M: Diesel-electric, 2 GM 12V71 diesels; 1 prop; 1,650 hp
Endurance: 14 days (12 hours submerged)

REMARKS: The pressure hull is a perfect cylinder, 5.49 m in diameter, strongly braced and closed at the forward and after ends by two hemispheric bulkheads. Used for deep-diving tests as well as acoustic and oceanographic experiments. Single torpedo tube removed in 1970. Scientific payload of 12 tons. Using two 330-cell, 250-volt, lead-acid batteries, 10 knots can be reached when submerged; when silver-zinc batteries are substituted, the speed is 15 knots. Very quiet machinery. Has four minicomputers for scientific-data-processing. Several scientific, passive multihydrophone arrays are fitted at the bow, and acoustic arrays can be towed at up to 4,000 feet behind the craft. Most support is shore-based. Homeported at San Diego.

◆ **1 Albacore class (SCB 182A type) research submarine**

	Bldr	Laid down	L	In serv.
AGSS 569 ALBACORE	Portsmouth NSY	15-3-52	1-8-53	12-53

Authorized FY 62

D: 1,517 tons normal/1,265 surfaced/1,810 submerged   **S:** 25/33 kts
Dim: 60.95 × 8.33 × 5.65   **Man:** 5 officers, 47 men
M: 1 1,700-hp diesel; 1 electric motor (*see* Remarks); 1 five-bladed prop

REMARKS: In reserve since 9-72. Hydrodynamic, teardrop hull. Fittings reduced to a minimum. Forward planes not retractable, after planes in cruciform configuration. At 18 knots and an angle of 20°, can submerge 105 m per minute. In 1963, she was fitted with a new type of electric motor that drives counterrotating propellers. Batteries of a new type permitted higher speed and greater distances while submerged.

◆ **1 Tang class (SCB 2A type) research submarine**

	Bldr	Laid down	L	In serv.
SSAG 567 GUDGEON	Portsmouth NSY	20-5-50	11-6-52	21-11-52

Authorized: FY 49

Gudgeon   PH3 J. B. Land, 1970

D: 2,100 tons surfaced/2,700 submerged   ⌐5 16 kts
Dim: 84.73 × 8.3 × 5.7
A: 8/533-mm TT (6 fwd, 2 aft)   **Man:** 11 officers, 75 men
Electron Equipt: Sonars: BQS 4, BQG 4 (PUFFS)
M: 3 Fairbanks-Morse 38D8⅛ diesels; 2 Westinghouse Electric Motors; 2 props; 5,600 hp

REMARKS: Survivor of a class of six. Forward diving planes retractable. The pancake engines of the first four proved unsatisfactory and were replaced by the same Fairbanks-Morse high-speed diesels that were used in the last two built, which necessitated lengthening of the ship by 2.75 m (1957-58). All had FRAM-II modernization. Mk-106, Mod. 18, torpedo-fire-control system. The *Trigger* (SS-564) and *Harder* (SS-568) were transferred to Italy in 7-73 and 3-74, respectively. The *Gudgeon* (SS-567) replaced the *Tang* (SS-563) as AGSS on 1-4-79, when the latter began transfer overhaul. The *Trout* (SS-566) was handed over to Iran on 19-12-78 but was later returned and will be transferred abroad, reportedly to Greece. The Tang was also to have gone to Iran, but was instead leased to Turkey in 2-80. The *Wahoo* (SS-565), the third unit for Iran, may now go to Egypt. SS-563 and SS-565 were stricken on 31-12-79.

◆ **1 hospital ship**

	Bldr	Laid down	L	In serv.
AH 17 SANCTUARY	Sun SB & DD	. . .	15-8-44	20-6-45

Sanctuary   1974

D: 11,141 tons (15,400 fl)   **S:** 18.3 kts
Dim: 158.5 (151.18 pp) × 21.79 × 7.32
Man: 70 officers, 460 men   **Fuel:** 2,055 tons   **Electric:** 2,400 kw
Electron Equipt: Radars: 1/SPS-53, 1/SPS-10
Boilers: 2 Babcock & Wilcox, 31.7 kg/cm² pressure — superheat 396°C
M: 1 set GE GT; 1 prop; 9,000 hp

REMARKS: In reserve. Survivor of a class of six; built on C4-S-B2 cargo-ship hull. Converted 15-12-71 to 18-11-72 as a dependent support ship for service at Piraeus, Greece.

AUXILIARY SHIPS (continued)

Has 74-bed hospital that can be expanded to 300. In addition to medical facilities, had stores, entertainment facilities, etc. Could carry 50 officer and 120 enlisted medical personnel. Change in government in Greece canceled plan; decommissioned 28-3-74, having not fitted intended purpose. First naval ship to include women in regular crew.

◆ 5 (+4) Cimarron-class oilers (SCB 739 type)

	Bldr	Laid down	L	In serv.
AO 177 CIMARRON	Avondale SY	18-5-78	28-4-79	5-80
AO 178 MONONGAHELA	Avondale SY	15-8-78	4-8-79	9-80
AO 179 MERRIMACK	Avondale SY	16-7-79	4-80	81
AO 180 N . . .	Avondale SY	5-80	81	81
AO 186 N . . .	Avondale SY	11-80	81	82

Cimarron—at launch   Avondale, 1979

D: 27,500 tons (fl)   **Dim:** 180.2 (167.64 pp) × 26.8 × 10.2
S: 20 kts   **Man:** 11 officers, 124 men
A: 2/20-mm Vulcan/Phalanx AA (I × 2)   **Electric:** 8,250 kw
Boilers: 2; 42.25 kg/cm² pressure—superheat 454°C
M: 1 set GT; 1 prop; 24,000 hp

REMARKS: Will carry 72,000 barrels fuel oil, 48,000 barrels JP-5 gas turbine fuel, and will be able to replenish ships while making 15 knots. Mk 36 RBOC chaff/flare rocket system will be carried, and there will be a helicopter platform aft. Four constant-tension replenishment stations to port, three to starboard. Will be able to transfer 408,000 liters of fuel oil and 245,000 liters JP-5 per hour. Planned to request two each in FY 83 and FY 84, to be MSC-manned as T-AO-187 to T-AO-190.

◆ 3 Ashtabula class oilers (SCB 224 jumbo type)

Bldr: Bethlehem Steel, Sparrows Points, Md.

	L	In serv.
AO 51 ASHTABULA	22-5-43	7-8-43
AO 98 CALOOSAHATCHEE	6-7-45	3-12-45
AO 99 CANISTEO	2-6-45	10-10-45

Ashtabula   PH3 T. Pfrang, 1978

D: 34,750 tons (fl)   **S:** 18 kts   **Dim:** 196.3 × 22.9 × 9.6
A: 2/76.2-mm Mk-26 DP (I × 2)   **Man:** 13 officers, 287 men
Electron Equipt: Radar: 1/SPS-10
Boilers: 4 Foster-Wheeler "K," 31.7 kg/cm² pressure—superheat 399°C
M: GT; 2 props; 13,500 hp

REMARKS: Lengthened 27 m by insertion of new mid-body during 1960s. Two 76.2-mm being removed, 1977-78, along with one Mk-52 and two Mk-51 directors. Carry 143,000 barrels of fuel, 175 tons of ammunition, and 100 tons of provisions. No helicopter deck. Last World War II-built oilers in regular naval service; will probably strike on completion of AO-177 to AO-179.

◆ 4 Sacramento-class fast combat support ships (SCB 196 type)

	Bldr	Laid down	L	In serv.
AOE 1 SACRAMENTO	Puget Sound NSY	30-6-61	14-9-63	14-3-64
AOE 2 CAMDEN	New York SB	17-2-64	29-5-65	1-4-67
AOE 3 SEATTLE	Puget Sound NSY	1-10-65	2-3-68	5-4-69
AOE 4 DETROIT	Puget Sound NSY	29-11-66	21-6-69	28-3-70

Authorized: 1 in FY 61, 1 in FY 63, 1 in FY 65, 1 in FY 66

D: 19,200 tons light (53,600 fl)   **S:** 26 kts
Dim: 241.4 (215.8 pp) × 32.9 × 11.6
Man: 33 officers, 567 men   **Range:** 10,000/17
A: 1/Mk-29 launcher for Sea Sparrow (VIII × 1)—4/76.2-mm DP (II × 2)
Electron Equipt: Radars: 1/SPS-10, 1/SPS-53 (AOE-1 and AOE-2: 1/SPS-40, also)
ECM: WLR-1—URN-20 TACAN

AUXILIARY SHIPS (continued)

Sacramento   PH1 A. Legare, 1978

Sacramento   PH1 A. Legare, 1978

Boilers: 4 Combustion Engineering, 42.2 kg/cm² pressure – superheat 480°C
M: GE GT; 2 props; 100,000 hp

REMARKS: Sea Sparrow launcher and Mk-91 control system with two directors replacing two twin 76.2-mm DP; two Mk-56 directors removed. Will also receive two 20-mm Vulcan-Phalanx and Mk-36 RBOC chaff/flare rocket system. Carry 177,000 barrels fuel plus 2,150 tons ammunition, 750 tons provisions. Helicopter hangar and flight deck for two UH-46 Sea Knight vertical-replenishment helicopters. Plans to build AOE-5 under FY 68 were canceled in 11-69. Turbines in AOE-1 and AOE-2 are from battleship *Kentucky* (BB-66). SPS-6 radar removed from AOE-3 and AOE-4, which may receive SPS-58 in its stead.

◆ **7 Wichita-class replenishment oilers (SCB 707 type)**
Bldr: General Dynamics, Quincy, Mass.

	Laid down	L	In serv.
AOR 1 WICHITA	18-6-66	18-3-68	7-6-69
AOR 2 MILWAUKEE	29-11-66	17-1-69	1-11-69
AOR 3 KANSAS CITY	20-4-68	28-6-69	6-6-70
AOR 4 SAVANNAH	22-1-69	25-4-70	5-12-70
AOR 5 WABASH	21-1-70	6-2-71	20-11-71
AOR 6 KALAMAZOO	28-10-70	11-11-72	11-8-73
AOR 7 ROANOKE	19-1-74	7-12-74	30-10-76

Authorized: 2 in FY 66, 2 in FY 67, 2 in FY 68, 1 in FY 73

Kalamazoo – no hangar   A. Baker, 1976

Roanoke   1976

D: 37,360 tons (fl)   **S:** 20 kts   **Dim:** 200.9 × 29.3 × 10.1
Man: 27 officers, 363 men   **Range:** 6,500/20, 10,000/17
A: AOR-1, AOR-4 to AOR-6; 4/76.2-mm DP (II × 2); AOR-2: 4/20-mm AA (I × 4); AOR-3 and AOR-7: 1/Mk 29 launcher for Sea Sparrow (VIII × 1) – 4/20-mm AA (I × 4)
Electron Equipt: Radar: 1/SPS-10 (AOR-7: SPS-58, also)
M: General Electric GT; 2 props; 32,000 shp   **Boilers:** 3 Foster-Wheeler

AUXILIARY SHIPS (continued)

Savannah   1978

REMARKS: Carry 175,000 barrels fuel (90,000 distillate fuel), 600 tons ammunition, 575 tons provisions. AOR-1 and AOR-4 to AOR-6 have no hangars; others have hangars flanking stack—two UH-46 Sea Knight vertical-replenishment helicopters. AOR-3 and AOR-7 have single Sea Sparrow launcher with two Mk-76 directors (Mk-91 fire-control system) on lattice towers abreast the stack. AOR-2 may be similarly armed shortly. All are to receive two Vulcan-Phalanx Gatling AA and the Mk-36 RBOC system. Ships with four 76.2-mm DP have had two Mk-56 directors removed. All will be brought up to AOR-7 standard eventually. There are four stations for liquid transfer and two for solid transfer to port, three liquid and two solid to starboard; all have constant-tension devices.

◆ 4 Vulcan-class repair ships

	Bldr	Laid down	L	In serv.
AR 5 VULCAN	New York SB	26-12-39	14-12-40	16-6-41
AR 6 AJAX	Los Angeles SB & DD	7-5-41	22-8-42	30-10-42
AR 7 HECTOR	Los Angeles SB & DD	28-7-41	11-11-42	7-2-44
AR 8 JASON	Los Angeles SB & DD	9-3-42	3-4-43	19-6-44

Hector   PH2 M. Holliday, 1975

D: 9,140 tons (16,380 fl)   **S:** 19.2 kts
Dim: 161.37 (158.5 pp) × 22.35 × 7.11
A: 4/20-mm AA (I × 4)   **Man:** 63 officers, 1,273 men
Electron Equipt: Radars: 1/SPS-10, 1/SPS-53   **Fuel:** 3,800 tons
Boilers: 4 Babcock & Wilcox, 28.2 kg/cm² pressure—superheat 382°C
M: 2 sets GT; 2 props; 11,000 hp   **Electric:** 4,500 kw

REMARKS: Very elaborately equipped repair facilities. Four 127-mm DP (I × 4) removed from all. The *Jason*, typed ARH-1 (heavy hull-repair ship), was redesignated as AR-8 in 1957.

NOTE: The sole surviving converted landing-ship-type small repair ship, *Sphinx* (ARL-24), remains on the Navy List in reserve, earmarked for possible foreign transfer. Sister *Indra* (ARL-37) was stricken on 1-12-77, but has been retained as an accommodations hulk.

◆ 8 Diver- and Bolster-class salvage ships   Bldr: Basalt Rock Co., Napa, Calif.

	Laid down	L	In serv.
ARS 33 CLAMP	2-3-42	24-10-42	23-8-43
ARS 34 GEAR	2-3-42	24-10-42	24-9-43
ARS 38 BOLSTER	20-7-44	23-12-44	1-5-45
ARS 39 CONSERVER	10-8-44	27-1-45	9-6-45
ARS 40 HOIST	13-9-44	31-3-45	21-7-45
ARS 41 OPPORTUNE	13-9-44	31-3-45	5-10-45
ARS 42 RECLAIMER	11-11-44	25-6-45	20-12-45
ARS 43 RECOVERY	6-1-45	4-8-45	15-5-46

Opportune   G. Arra, 1974

D: 1,530 tons (1,970 fl) ARS-38 to ARS-43: 2,040 (fl)   **S:** 14.8 kts
Dim: 65.1 × 12.5 × 4.0 (ARS-38 to ARS-43: 13.4 beam)   **Fuel:** 300 tons
A: 2/20-mm AA (ARS-33 and ARS-34: none)   **Man:** 6 officers, 77 men
Electron Equipt: Radars: 1/LN-66, 1/SPS-53   **Range:** 9,000/14, 20,000/7
M: 4 Cooper-Bessemer GSB-8 diesels, electric drive; 2 props; 2,440 hp
Electric: 460 kw

REMARKS: Equipped for diver support, salvage, and towing. ARS-33 is in the Maritime Administration Reserve Fleet. ARS-34 is operated for the Navy by a private company. ARS-38, ARS-39, and ARS-42 reengined with Caterpillar diesels. The *Preserver* (ARS-8), stricken on 1-12-79, the *Deliver* (ARS-23) sold to South Korea on 15-8-79, and the *Safeguard* (ARS-25) sold to Turkey on 30-9-79. The first of a repeat *Bolster* class was requested under FY 81, with two for FY 82 and one for FY 83 planned.

AUXILIARY SHIPS (*continued*)

◆ 5 L. Y. Spear-class submarine tenders (SCB 702 and 737 types)

	Bldr	Laid down	L	In serv.
AS 36 L. Y. SPEAR	Gen. Dynamics, Quincy	5-5-66	7-9-67	28-2-70
AS 37 DIXON	Gen. Dynamics, Quincy	7-9-67	20-6-70	7-8-71
AS 39 EMORY S. LAND	Lockheed SB, Seattle	2-3-76	4-5-77	7-7-79
AS 40 FRANK CABLE	Lockheed SB, Seattle	2-3-76	14-1-78	13-10-79
AS 41 MCKEE	Lockheed SB, Seattle	14-1-78	2-80	-81

Authorized: 1 in FY 65, 1 in FY 66, 1 in FY 72, 1 in FY 73, 1 in FY 77

Emory S. Land   J. Davis, 1979

D: 13,000 tons AS-36 and AS-37: 22,640 (fl) AS-39 to AS-41: 23,000 (fl)   **S:** 20 kts
Dim: 196.29 × 25.91 × 7.77
Man: AS-36 and AS-37: 96 officers, 1,252 men
      AS-39 to AS-41: 50 officers, 1,108 men + flag staff: 75 officers, 44 men
A: 4/20-mm AA (I × 4)   **Electric:** 11,000 kw
Electron Equipt: Radar: 1/SPS-10
Boilers: 2 Combustion Engineering, 43.6 kg/cm² pressure — superheat 462°C
M: 1 set de Laval GT; 1 prop; 20,000 hp

REMARKS: Provide support to submarines (SSN), AS-39 to AS-41 being specifically tailored to the needs of the *Los Angeles* class. One 30-ton crane and two 5-ton traveling cranes. Helicopter deck, but no hangar. AS-36 and AS-37 have General Electric turbines and Foster-Wheeler boilers. No longer planned to fit Vulcan-Phalanx or Sea Sparrow in later ships. Two 127-mm DP (I × 2) removed from AS-36 and AS-37. AS-38 (FY 69) canceled 27-3-69. No other submarine tenders currently programmed.

◆ 2 Simon Lake-class submarine tenders (SCB 238 type)

	Bldr	Laid down	L	In serv.
AS 33 SIMON LAKE	Puget Sound NSY	7-1-63	8-2-64	7-11-64
AS 34 CANOPUS	Ingalls, Pascagoula	2-3-64	12-2-65	4-11-65

Authorized: 1 in FY 63, 1 in FY 64

Canopus   1966

D: 12,000 tons AS-33: 19,934 (fl) AS-34: 21,089 (fl)   **S:** 18 kts
Dim: 196.2 × 25.9 × 8.7   **Man:** AS-33: 90 officers, 1,338 men
                    AS-34: 95 officers, 1,326 men
A: 4/76.2-mm DP (II × 2)   **Electron Equipt:** Radar: 1/SPS-10
Boilers: 2 Combustion Engineering, 43.6 kg/cm² pressure — superheat 462°C
M: de Laval GT; 1 prop; 20,000 hp   **Electric:** 11,000 kw

REMARKS: Specifically equipped to support nuclear-powered, ballistic-missile submarines, with reload missiles stowed vertically amidships. Converted to carry Poseidon missiles, 1969-71. Both are to serve Trident-equipped SSBNs; AS-33 converted under FY 78, and AS-34 will convert under FY 84. Sister AS-35 canceled on 3-12-64. Two 30-ton cranes and four 5-ton traveling cranes. Helicopter deck aft, but no hangar. Two Mk-63 fire-control systems for guns removed.

◆ 2 Hunley-class submarine tenders (SCB 194 type)

	Bldr	Laid down	L	In serv.
AS 31 HUNLEY	Newport News SB	28-11-60	28-9-61	16-6-62
AS 32 HOLLAND	Ingalls, Pascagoula	5-3-62	19-1-63	7-9-63

Authorized: 1 in FY 60, 1 in FY 62

D: 10,500 tons (19,300 fl)   **S:** 19 kts   **Dim:** 182.6 × 25.3 × 7.4
Man: 144 officers, 2,424 men
A: 4/20-mm AA (I × 4)   **Electron Equipt:** Radar: 1/SPS-10
M: 10 Fairbanks-Morse 38D8⅛ diesels, electric drive; 1 prop, 15,000 hp
Electric: 12,000 kw

Holland   1971

AUXILIARY SHIPS (*continued*)

REMARKS: Intended to support SSBNs; converted to carry Poseidon missiles, 1973-75. Air-conditioned. Helicopter platform. Original 32.5-ton rotating crane removed around 1970 and replaced by two 30-ton cranes.

◆ **1 Proteus-class submarine tender (SCB 190 conversion type)**

Bldr: Moore SB & DD, Oakland, Cal.

	Laid down	L	In serv.	Conv.
AS 19 PROTEUS	15-9-41	12-11-42	31-1-44	8-7-60

Proteus—127-mm gun now removed   1963

D: 10,250 tons (19,200 fl)   **S:** 15.4 kts   **Dim:** 175.1 × 27.3 × 8.2
Man: 86 officers, 1,214 men
A: 4/20-mm AA (I × 4)   **Electron Equipt:** Radar: 1/SPS-10
M: 8 GM 16-248 diesels, electric drive; 2 props; 11,200 hp

REMARKS: Lengthened 13.4 m, 1959-60, as the first SSBN tender, carrying Polaris missiles in the new section, handled by an extendable gantry crane. Superstructure enlarged over that of former sisters in the *Fulton* class. Serves the *George Washington* and *Ethan Allen* class SSBNs in the Pacific.

◆ **6 Fulton-class submarine tenders**

	Bldr	Laid down	L	In serv.
AS 11 FULTON	Mare Island NSY	19-7-39	27-12-40	12-9-41
AS 12 SPERRY	Mare Island NSY	1-2-41	17-12-41	1-5-42
AS 15 BUSHNELL	Mare Island NSY	23-12-41	14-9-42	10-4-43
AS 16 HOWARD W. GILMORE (ex-*Neptune*)	Mare Island NSY	21-12-42	16-9-43	24-5-44
AS 17 NEREUS	Puget Sound NSY	11-10-43	12-2-45	27-10-45
AS 18 ORION	Moore SB, Oakland	31-7-41	14-10-42	30-9-43

D: 9,734 tons (18,000 fl)   **S:** 15.4 kts   **Dim:** 161.4 × 22.3 × 7.8
Man: 1,286 to 1,937 men   **Range:** 15,600/10   **Fuel:** 3,760 tons
A: AS-15 and AS-17: 2/127-mm DP (I × 2), AS-17 also: 4/20-mm AA (II × 2)
Others: 4/20-mm AA (I × 4)
M: 8 GM 16-248 diesels, electric drive; 2 props; 11,200 hp   **Electric:** 6,700 kw

REMARKS: AS-15, used as an accommodations ship at Norfolk, and AS-17 are in reserve. AS-16 to decommission in 1980. All received FRAM-II modernization and can support nuclear submarines. Foundry can cast pieces up to 250 kg. Two 20-ton rotating cranes (as in *Dixie*-class ADs) are fitted to all but AS-16, which has two kingposts and booms. AS-15 and AS-17 retain a Mk-37 fire-control system for their 127-mm guns.

Howard W. Gilmore   G. Arra, 1976

Bushnell   C. Dragonette, 1979

◆ **2 Pigeon-class submarine-rescue ships (SCB 721 type)**

Bldr: Alabama DD & SB, Mobile

	Laid down	L	In serv.
ASR 21 PIGEON	17-7-68	13-8-69	28-4-73
ASR 22 ORTOLAN	22-8-68	10-9-69	14-7-73

Authorized: 1 in FY 67, 1 in FY 68

D: 3,411 tons (fl)   **S:** 15 kts   **Dim:** 76.5 × 26.2 × 6.5
A: 2/20-mm AA (I × 2)   **Range:** 8,500/13
Electron Equipt: Radar: 1/SPS-53
Man: 6 officers, 109 men + staff: 4 officers, 10 men + DSRV crew: 4 officers, 20 men
M: 4 Alco high-speed diesels; 2 props; 6,000 hp

AUXILIARY SHIPS (continued)

Pigeon   PHAN B. Trombecky, 1976

Ortolan   1973

REMARKS: The catamaran hulls (7.925-m beam) are separated by 10.36 m. Diving bells and other salvage equipment are lowered between the two hulls by a moving crane. The ships can carry two small DSRV (Deep Submergence Rescue Vehicle) submarines, but as only two DSRV have been built, they normally have only one each—or none. Excellent lowering and handling equipment for up to 60 tons; divers to 260 m. Not considered to be successful ships.

◆ **4 Chanticleer-class submarine-rescue ships**
Bldr: Savannah Machine Foundry (ASR-9: Moore SB & DD, Oakland)

	Laid down	L	In serv.
ASR 9 FLORIKAN	30-9-41	14-6-42	5-4-43
ASR 13 KITTIWAKE	5-1-45	10-7-45	18-7-46
ASR 14 PETREL	26-2-45	29-9-45	24-9-46
ASR 15 SUNBIRD	2-4-45	3-4-46	28-1-47

Kittiwake   C. Dragonette, 1979

D: 1,653 tons (2,320 fl) **S:** 14.9 kts **Dim:** 76.7 × 13.4 × 4.9
A: 2/20-mm AA (I × 2) **Man:** 116-221 men **Electric:** 460 kw
M: 4 GM 12-278A diesels, electric drive; 1 prop; 3,000 hp

REMARKS: Carry a McCann rescue bell aft. All equipped for helium/oxygen diving. ASR-9 has Alco, Model 539, diesels.

◆ **6 Abnaki and Achomawi classes fleet ocean tugs**

	Bldr	L	In serv.
ATF 105 MOCTABI	Charleston SB&DD	25-3-44	25-7-44
ATF 110 QUAPAW	United Eng., Alameda	15-5-43	6-5-44
ATF 113 TAKELMA	United Eng., Alameda	18-9-43	3-8-44
ATF 159 PAIUTE	Charleston SB&DD	4-6-45	27-8-45
ATF 160 PAPAGO	Charleston SB&DD	21-6-45	3-10-45
ATF 162 SHAKORI	Charleston SB&DD	9-8-45	20-12-45

D: 1,235 tons (1,640 fl) **S:** 16.2 kts **Dim:** 62.48 (59.44 pp) × 11.73 × 4.67
A: None **Man:** 5 officers, 70 men **Range:** 6,500/16, 15,000/8
M: 4 diesels, electric drive; 1 prop; 3,000 hp **Electric:** 400 kw

Papago—gun now removed   A. Baker, 1976

AUXILIARY SHIPS (continued)

REMARKS: All operated by the Naval Reserve Force. Developed from pre-World War II *Apache* class. ATF-105, ATF-110, and ATF-113 have four Busch-Sulzer BS-539 diesels and a small-diameter funnel; the others have GM 12-278A diesels and a large funnel. Also operational are the *Atakapa* (T-ATF-149) and *Mosopelea* (T-ATF-158) of the *Achomawi* class, manned by the Military Sealift Command. Available in the Maritime Commission Reserve Fleet are the *Chippewa* (ATF-69), *Hopi* (ATF-71), *Moreno* (ATF-87), *Narragansett* (ATF-88), *Seneca* (ATF-91), *Tenino* (ATF-115), *Wenatchee* (ATF-118), and *Achomawi* (ATF-148). Three sisters serve in the U.S. Coast Guard, and the class can be found in many of the world's navies.

NOTE: The new-construction fleet ocean tugs of the *Powhatan* class are to be operated by the Military Sealift Command.

◆ 3 Edenton-class salvage and rescue ships   Bldr: Brooke Marine, G.B.

Authorized: 1 in FY 66; 2 in FY 67

	Laid down	L	In serv.
ATS 1 EDENTON	1-4-67	15-5-68	23-1-71
ATS 2 BEAUFORT	19-2-68	20-12-68	22-1-72
ATS 3 BRUNSWICK	5-6-68	14-11-69	19-12-72

Beaufort 1974

D: 2,650 tons (2,929 fl)   **S:** 16 kts   **Dim:** 88.0 (80.5 pp) × 1.53 × 4.6
A: 4/20-mm AA (II × 2)   **Man:** 9 officers, 91 men
Range: 12,000/. . .   **Electron Equipt:** Radar: 1/SPS-53
M: 4 Paxman 12 YLCM (900 rpm) diesels: 2 Escher-Wyss controllable-pitch props; 6,000 hp

REMARKS: ATS-4 (FY 72) and ATS-5 (FY 73) canceled in favor of *Powhatan* class T-ATF. Can tow ships up to AOE-1 class size. 272-ton dead lift over the bow. 20-ton crane aft; 10-ton boom forward. Can conduct dives to 260 m. Powerful pumps and complete fire-fighting equipment. Equipped with bow-thruster.

◆ 1 Currituck-class guided-missile ship   Bldr: Los Angeles SB & DD Co., San Pedro

	Laid down	L	In serv.
AVM 1 NORTON SOUND (ex-AV-11)	7-9-42	28-11-43	8-1-45

Norton Sound 1975

D: 9,106 tons light (15,170 fl)   **S:** 19 kts
Dim: 164.72 (158.5 wl) × 21.11 × 7.16   **A:** *See* Remarks
Fuel: 2,300 tons
Electron Equipt: Radars: 1/SPS-10, 1/SPS-40, 1/SPY-1A, 1/Mk-99
　　　　　　　　　URN-20 TACAN
Boilers: 4 Babcock & Wilcox Express, 28.2 kg/cm² pressure—superheat 366°C
M: 2 sets Allis-Chalmers GT; 2 props; 12,000 hp

REMARKS: Ex-seaplane tender. Has served as a guided-missile trials ship since 1948. The prototype Aegis system was installed in 1975, with only forward, starboard "face" of the SPY-1A phased-array radar operational. SPS-40 replaced the unique, large-antenna SPS-52 variant radar in 1975. Refit in 1979 included removal of the prototype Mk-26, Mod. 0, twin missile launcher. The ship will conduct trials with vertical-launch missile systems.

◆ 1 Intrepid-class auxiliary-training aircraft carrier

	Bldr	Laid down	L	In serv.
AVT 16 LEXINGTON	Bethlehem, Quincy	16-7-41	25-9-42	17-2-43

Lexington JO1 S. Auld, 1977

AUXILIARY SHIPS (*continued*)

D: Approx. 33,000 tons (39,000 fl)   **S:** 30 + kts
Dim: 270.97 (249.94 wl) × 31.39 (58.5 flight deck) × 9.4
Man: 75 officers, 1,365 men   **Range:** 18,000/12   **Fuel:** 6,750 tons
A: Removed (no aircraft permanently assigned)
Electron Equipt: Radars: 1/SPS-10, 1/SPS-12, 1/SPS-43, 1/SPN-6, 1/SPN-10
         URN-20 TACAN
Boilers: 8 Babcock & Wilcox, 41.7 kg/cm² pressure—superheat 454°C
M: 4 sets Westinghouse GT; 4 props; 150,000 hp

REMARKS: Employed in deck-landing training at Pensacola, Fla. Was to have been stricken in FY 80 and replaced by the *Coral Sea* (CV-43) but has been extended in service to FY 84. Refit 1978-79. On 29-12-68 number changed from CVS-16 to CVT-16; changed to AVT-16 on 15-7-78. Has two steam catapults, three elevators (one centerline, forward; one at the forward end of the angled deck; and one to starboard, abaft the island), and four arrester wires. All guns and fire-control equipment removed. SPS-12 has probably been replaced.

UNCLASSIFIED MISCELLANEOUS SHIPS

◆ **1 Admiral W. S. Benson-class barracks ship**   Bldr: Bethlehem Steel, Alameda, Cal.

	Laid down	In serv.
IX 507 GENERAL HUGH J. GAFFEY (ex-T-AP-121, ex-*Admiral W. L. Capps*, AP-121)	1942	18-9-44

D: 12,657 tons light (22,574 fl)   **S:** 19 kts
Dim: 185.6 (174.65 pp) × 23.01 × 8.05
Man: Berthing for 499 officers, 1,577 men   **Fuel:** 3,840 tons
Boilers: 4 Combustion Engineering "D," 42.3 kg/cm² pressure—superheat 449°C
M: 2 sets GE GT, electric drive; 2 props; 18,000 hp   **Electric:** 2,400 kw

REMARKS: Former troop transport transferred to the Army in 1946, reacquired by the Navy on 1-3-50 for MSC (then MSTS). Stricken on 9-1-69 and transferred to Maritime Commission Reserve Fleet. Partially reactivated and redesignated IX-507 on 1-11-78 for service at Bremerton NSY, Washington, as berthing ship for crew of CVN-65, undergoing overhaul. Will be in service into FY 83 Propulsion plant not reactivated.

◆ **1 YFU-71-class trials tender**   Bldr: Pacific Coast Eng. Co., Alameda

IX 506 (ex-YFU-82)

D: 400 tons (fl)   **S:** 8 kts   **Dim:** 38.1 × 10.97 × 2.29
M: 4 GM 6-71 diesels; 2 props; 1,000 hp

REMARKS: Ex-harbor utility craft. Reclassified on 1-4-78 for service with Naval Ocean Systems Center, San Diego, to replace IX-505 (ex-YTM-759). Can carry 300 tons of cargo. Craft is now permanently attached to former barge YFN-816 as a work platform.

◆ **3 Benewah-class barracks ships**   Bldr: Boston NSY

	Laid down	L	In serv.
IX 502 MERCER (ex-APB-39)	25-8-44	17-11-44	19-9-45
IX 503 NUECES (ex-APB-40)	2-1-45	6-5-45	30-11-45
IX 504 ECHOLS (ex-APB-37)	. . .	30-7-45	1-1-47

D: 2,189 tons light (4,080 fl)   **S:** 10 kts   **Dim:** 100.0 × 15.2 × 3.4
Man (when operational): 13 officers, 180 men + 26 officers, 1,200 troops
M: 2 GM 12-267ATL diesels; 2 props; 1,600 hp

REMARKS: IX-502 and IX-503 recommissioned 1968 for service in Vietnam, placed back in reserve 1969-71; activated again in 1-11-75 as barracks ships at Puget Sound NSY. IX-504, in reserve since completion in 1947, activated 1-2-76 as a barracks ship for *Ohio*-class SSBN crews at General Dynamics, Groton. Propulsion plant inactivated. Eight 40-mm AA (IV × 2) removed.

◆ **1 test range support ship (ex-LSMR)**   Bldr: Brown SB, Houston

	Laid down	L	In serv.
IX 501 ELK RIVER (ex-LSMR-501)	24-3-45	21-4-45	27-5-45

Elk River   1968

D: 1,785 tons (fl)   **S:** 11 kts   **Dim:** 70.0 × 15.2 × 2.8
Man: 25 men + 20 technicians   **Electron Equipt:** Radar: 1/SPS-53
M: 2 GM 16-278A diesels; 2 props; 2,800 hp

REMARKS: Former fire-support rocket ship converted 1967-68 at Avondale Shipyards, Westwego, Louisiana, to act as support ship at the San Clemente Island Range for the Navy deep-submergence diving program. 2.4-m bulges were added to her hull sides and a center well cut for lowering equipment through the hull. The well is straddled by a 65-ton traveling gantry crane. Thrusters added to allow accurate dynamic mooring. Tests diving procedures, equipment, and small diving vehicles.

◆ **1 sonar test barge**

IX 310 (no name) Actually, two barges moored in Lake Seneca, New York; subordinated to the Naval Underwater Sound Laboratory, Newport, Rhode Island. In service in 1971. IX-309, *Monob I*, is now numbered YAG-61.

◆ **1 U.S. Army FS-381-class torpedo-trials ship**

	Bldr	In serv.
IX 308 NEW BEDFORD (ex-AKL-17, ex-FS-289)	Wheeler SB, Brooklyn	3-45

D: 500 tons (800 fl)   **S:** 12 kts   **Dim:** 53.8 × 9.75 × 3.05
A: 1/324-mm TT   **Fuel:** 67 tons   **Electric:** 225 kw
M: 2 GM 6-278A diesels; 2 props; 1,000 hp   **Range:** 4,100/10

REMARKS: Operated by the Coast Guard for the Army during World War II; transferred to the Navy as a cargo ship on 1-3-50. Converted as a torpedo-trials ship in 1963. Operated by the Naval Torpedo Station, Keyport, Washington.

◆ **1 explosives-testing instrumentation ship**

IX 307 BRIER (ex-WLI-299)

D: 178 tons (fl)   **S:** 8.5 kts   **Dim:** 30.5 × 7.3 × 1.6
M: 2 GM diesels, electric drive; 2 props; 600 hp

UNCLASSIFIED MISCELLANEOUS SHIPS (*continued*)

REMARKS: Former Coast Guard inland buoy tender, built in 1943. Acquired on 10-3-69; redesignated on 29-8-70. Employed at Naval Ordnance Center, Solomons Island, Maryland, explosives-testing facility.

◆ **1 U.S. Army FS-330DC-class torpedo-trials ship**

	Bldr	In serv.
IX 306 (ex-FS-221)	Higgins Ind., New Orleans	1-45

D: 460 tons (906 fl) **S:** 12 kts **Dim:** 54.81 × 9.75 × 4.32
A: 1/533-mm TT **Fuel:** 62 tons **Electric:** 225 kw
M: 2 Enterprise diesels; 2 props; 800 hp

REMARKS: Employed by the Army as a cargo ship until transferred to the Navy on 1-1-69 as a torpedo- and general-experimentation trials ship for the Naval Underwater Weapons Research and Engineering Center, Newport, R.I., at the Atlantic Underwater Test and Evaluation Center (AUTEC) in the Bahamas. Naval and civilian crew. Painted white with blue bow; torpedo-tube exits on starboard bow.

◆ **1 ocean construction platform** Bldr: Missouri Valley Br. & Iron, Ind.

	Laid down	L	In serv.
SEACON (ex-YFNB-33)	16-1-45	22-3-45	25-10-45

D: 2,780 tons (fl) **S:** 7 kts **Dim:** 79.25 × 14.63 × 2.9
Man: 50 men **Electric:** 575 kw
M: 1 GM 12-71 diesel, 2 GM 6-71 diesels; 3 Voith-Schneider 14E/87 vertical cycloidal props; 1,020 hp

REMARKS: A large covered barge belonging to the Navy and used by NASA for transporting rockets, the *Seacon* was converted 1974-76 to serve as a seagoing work ship for the Navy Ocean Engineering and Construction Project Office. Intended to be towed at up to 11 knots to work locations and then use own propulsion for precision maneuvering. Can be used to lay cable and has open work deck 40 × 14 aft. Unique in having no ship or yard-craft number.

EXPERIMENTAL CRAFT

◆ **1 surface-effect ship**

Rohr SES design

D: 2,200 tons (3,000 fl) **S:** 80-100 kts **Dim:** 81.5 × 32.9 × . . .
A: *See* remarks **Man:** 125 men
M: 4 LM-2500A gas turbines; 4 pump-jets; 80,000 hp (plus 2 LM-2500A gas turbines to drive lift fans)

REMARKS: Rohr Marine, San Diego, won a competition with Bell Aerospace to design and construct a prototype surface-effect ship of nearly 3,000 tons. Although it was originally to have been armed, the Secretary of Defense announced in 1977 that only limited military sensors and armament would be fitted—effectively making the ship into yet another systems prototype. The armament originally proposed included two SH-3 Sea King helicopters, two 20-mm Vulcan-Phalanx Gatling AA guns, six Mk-32 ASW TT (III × 2), and four twin Harpoon launchers. The design has rigid side walls with flexible skirts fore and aft to trap the air-cushion "bubble." Actual construction has been indefinitely deferred, although money continues to be spent on the program. No money was appropriated for the program under FY 80, thus probably terminating it.

◆ **1 Aerojet General prototype surface-effect ship**

	Bldr	In serv.
SES 100A	Tacoma Boatbuilding	7-72

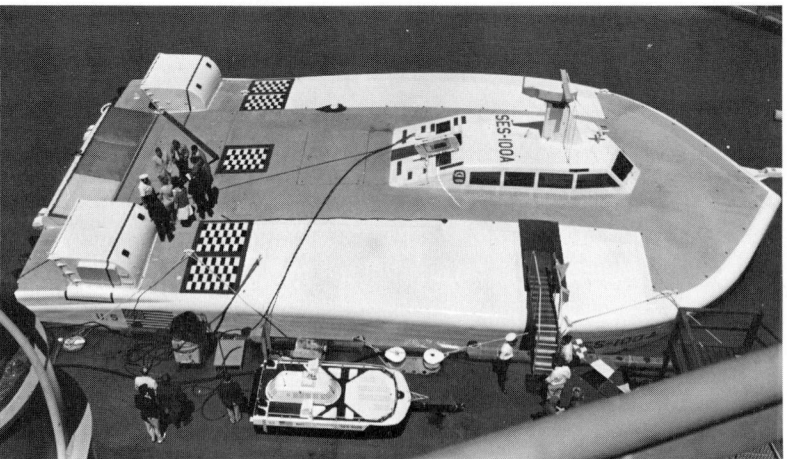

SES 100A – SES 100B model in foreground   A. Baker, 1976

D: 100 tons **S:** 76 kts **Dim:** 25.0 × 12.5 × . . .
Man: 1 officer, 3 men, plus 6 technicians
M: 4 Avco TF-35 gas turbines (12,000 hp) driving two water jets and 3 lift fans

REMARKS: A rigid-side-wall design developed in competition with Bell's SES-100B. Can carry 10 tons of test equipment.

◆ **1 Bell Aerospace prototype surface-effect ship**

	Bldr	In serv.
SES 100B	Bell, Michoud, Louisiana	2-72

D: 100 tons **S:** 82.3 kts **Dim:** 23.8 × 10.7 × . . .

UNCLASSIFIED MISCELLANEOUS SHIPS (*continued*)

SES 100B at 40 knots   1973

Man: 1 officer, 3 men, plus 6 technicians
M: 3 Pratt & Whitney FT-12 gas turbines; 2 props; 13,500 hp (with United Aircraft of Canada ST-6J-70 gas turbines (1,500 hp) driving 8 lift fans)

REMARKS: Employed in 1976 in trials with vertically launched Standard-ARM antiship missiles while under way at 80 kts.

◆ **1 SWATH (Small Waterplane Area, Twin Hull) prototype**

SSP 1 KAIMALINO   Bldr: U.S. Coast Guard, Curtis Bay, Md.

D: 190 tons (217 fl)   **S:** 25 kts   **Dim:** 27.1 × 13.7 × . . .
M: 2 T-64 gas turbines; 2 props; 5,000 hp

REMARKS: Launched on 7-3-73. Catamaran hull with cigar-shaped flotation pontoons. Helicopter deck. Operated by the Naval Ocean Systems Center, Hawaii Laboratory. The SWATH concept shows great promise as an economical, high-performance/high-endurance ASW ship, but has been hampered in its development by a lack of funding.

◆ **3 Asheville-class engineering-trials ships**   Bldr: Tacoma Boat building

	In serv.
ATHENA I (ex-*Chehalis*, PG-94)	11-8-69
ATHENA II (ex-*Grand Rapids*, PG-98)	9-5-70
ATHENA III (ex-*Douglas*, PG-100)	6-2-71

D: 225 tons (235 fl)   **S:** 40 kts   **Dim:** 50.14 × 7.28 × 2.9
Range: 325/37, 1,700/16   **Fuel:** 50 tons   **Electric:** 100 kw
M: CODOG: 1 GE 7LM-1500-PE 102 LM 1500 gas turbine (12,500 hp), 2 Cummins VT12-875M diesels (1,400 hp); 2 controllable-pitch props

REMARKS: These craft are regarded as equipment and therefore do not have USN hull numbers. Operate from Mayport, Florida, for the Naval Ships Research and Development Center, Carderock. Have civilian crews and are disarmed. *Athena-I* reclassified on 21-8-75, *Athena-II* on 1-10-77, and *Athena-III* in 1979. Have a 10-ton instrumentation payload.

◆ **1 gas-turbine engine-trials craft**   Bldr: Sewart, Berwick, La.

PTF 25

D: 72 tons (102 fl)   **S:** 40 kts   **Dim:** 28.86 × 7.06 × 2.1
A: Removed   **Man:** . . .
M: 2 Garrett GT PF 990 GT; 2 water jets; 6,000 hp

REMARKS: Built in 1968. New engines, installed in 9-79, replace two Napier Deltic T18-37K diesels. Former fast patrol craft now to be used for propulsion trials for possible future small combatants. Aluminum construction. One 40-mm AA, two 20-mm AA (I × 2), and one 81-mm mortar removed. Sisters PTF-23, PTF-24, and PTF-26 sold in 1979.

◆ **2 Cove-class former inshore minesweepers**   Bldr: Bethlehem SY, Bellingham, Wash.

	Laid down	L	In serv.
MSI 1 COVE	1-2-57	8-2-58	20-11-58
MSI 2 CAPE	1-5-57	5-4-58	27-2-59

Cape   1959

D: 200 tons (240 fl)   **S:** 12 kts   **Dim:** 34.1 × 7.1 × 3.0
M: 2 GM diesels; 2 props; 650 hp   **Man:** . . . (civilians)

REMARKS: Wooden construction; sweep gear removed. MSI-1 has been operated by the Applied Physics Laboratory of Johns Hopkins University since 31-7-70. MSI-2 serves the Naval Ocean Systems Center, San Diego. Sisters operate as minesweepers in the Iranian and Turkish navies.

DEEP-SUBMERGENCE RESEARCH CRAFT

◆ **1 nuclear research submarine for deep diving**

	Bldr	Laid down	L	In serv.
NR-1	Electric Boat Co.	10-6-67	25-1-69	27-10-69

Authorized: FY 66

D: 400 tons surfaced/700 submerged   **Dim:** 42.67 × 3.75 × 4.45
Man: 2 officers, 3 men, 2 scientists
M: 1 pressurized-water reactor, turboelectric drive; 2 props

DEEP-SUBMERGENCE RESEARCH CRAFT (*continued*)

NR-1   1969

REMARKS: Project approved 18-4-65. Fitted for all oceanographic missions, military and
civilian, and for bottom salvage. Thick cylindrical hull. Wheels for moving on ocean
bottom. A very successful vehicle, but cost three times the original estimate. No
periscope, uses television cameras. Four ducted maneuvering thrusters.

◆ **2 DSRV class**   Bldr: Lockheed Missile & Space Co., Sunnyvale, Calif.

	In serv.	Accepted
DSRV-1 MYSTIC	6-8-71	4-11-77
DSRV-2 AVALON	28-7-72	1-1-78

D: 30.5 tons   **S:** 5 kts   **Dim:** 15.0 × 2.5 × . . .   **Man:** 3 men
M: 1 electric motor; 1 shrouded-pivoting prop; 15 hp

REMARKS: The DSRVs are intended to: operate at a maximum depth of 3,500 feet
(1,070 m); stand pressure equal to 9,000 feet (2,750 m); dive and rise at 100 feet a
minute; make a maximum speed of 5 knots while submerged; remain submerged for
30 hours at 3 knots; maintain station in a 1-knot current; and operate all machinery
even while submerged at a 45° angle. DSRVs can bring to the surface as many as 24
men at one time. Motor powered by a silver-zinc battery turns a regular propulsion
propeller and two thrusters, one forward and one aft, which can be positioned to permit a close approach to a sunken object. Their size and weight were determined by the
possible need to airlift them in an Air Force Starlifter (Lockheed C-141A) cargo plane.
Additional equipment, especially a truck transport for the DSRV, would be carried in
a second Starlifter. In addition, SSNs have received the equipment necessary to fas-
ten a DSRV to their decks and carry it at 15 knots. The SSN will serve as a base for
the DSRV while it awaits the arrival of a *Pigeon*-class rescue ship (ASR). Hull consists of two HY-140 steel spheres surrounded by a fiberglass outer hull.
    A cost overrun of nearly 1,500 percent prevented the procurement of any more
DSRVs. Twelve were originally planned. Names were assigned in 1977.

◆ **2 Turtle class**   Bldr: General Dynamics, Groton, Conn.

DSV-3 TURTLE (ex-*Autec-I*)   DSV-4 SEA CLIFF (ex-*Autec-II*)

D: 21 tons   **S:** 2 kts   **Dim:** 7.9 × 2.4 (3.7 over thrusters)
Man: 2 men + 1 scientist   **M:** 1 electric motor; 1 prop; 2 thrusters

REMARKS: Launched on 11-12-68. Could originally descend to 1,980 m. Spherical pressure hull of HY-100 steel. The *Turtle* was modified in 1979 to descend to 3,000 meters,
and the *Sea Cliff* is scheduled to receive a titanium pressure sphere in 1981-82, permitting 6,100-m descents. Air transportable. Fitted with external manipulator arms.
Eight hours' endurance at 1 knot.

Sea Cliff and Turtle—at "launch"   1968

◆ **1 Alvin-class**   Bldr: General Mills, Minneapolis, Minn., 1965

DSV-2 ALVIN

D: 16 tons   **S:** 2 kts   **Dim:** 6.9 × 2.4 × . . .
M: Electric motors; 1 prop; 2 thrusters   **Man:** 1 man + 2 scientists

REMARKS: Operated by civilian Woods Hole Oceanographic Institute on contract to the
navy. Sank on 16-10-68 but raised, repaired, and returned to service in 11-72. Single
titanium pressure sphere permits descents to 3,600 m.

◆ **1 Trieste class**   Bldr: Castellammare, Italy, 1953

DSV-1 TRIESTE-II

D: 84 tons surfaced/220 submerged   **S:** 2 kts   **Dim:** 22.86 × 4.58
Man: 3 men   **Range:** 8 hours at 2 kts
M: Electric propulsion; 3 props; 1 ducted thruster; 19.5 hp

REMARKS: The U.S. Navy bought Professor Piccard's *Trieste* in 1958, modified it, and
renamed it *Trieste-II.* Subsequently so modified that it is an entirely new design. Rebuilt with new float, 1965-66. Can dive as deep as 6,100 m.

SERVICE CRAFT

NOTE: As of 1 January 1980, the U.S. Navy had 1,007 service craft, some 115 of which
were in reserve. Few such craft are being built, and the force consists mostly of
craft built during World War II. The units currently operational are listed below;
those marked with an asterisk are non-self-propelled.

◆ **6 AFDB large auxiliary floating dry docks***

REMARKS: AFDB-1 and AFDB-2 are ten-section docks, capable of lifting 90,000 tons.
Sections A, G, H, and I of AFDB-1 were stricken 1978. AFDB-3 is a nine-section dock,
capable of lifting 81,000 tons. AFDB-4 to AFDB-7 are seven-section docks capable
of lifting 55,000 tons. Built 1943-45. Only Sections A, B, E, and G of AFDB-7, *Los
Alamos,* are active. AFDB-1 named *Artisan,* 5-79.

◆ **6 AFDL small auxiliary floating docks***

AFDL-1 ENDEAVOR	AFDL-7 ABILITY	AFDL-47 RELIANCE
AFDL-6 DYNAMIC	AFDL-23 ADEPT	AFDL-48 DILIGENCE

SERVICE CRAFT (*continued*)

REMARKS: AFDL-1, AFDL-6, AFDL-7, and AFDL-23 are of 1,000-ton capacity; AFDL-47 (ex-ARD-33) is of 6,500-ton capacity, and the capacity of AFDL-48 is not available. All are active. Built 1943-44.

◆ 4 AFDM medium auxiliary floating dry docks*

AFDM-5 RESOURCEFUL	AFDM-7 SUSTAIN
AFDM-6 COMPETENT	AFDM-8 RICHLAND

REMARKS: AFDM-5 to AFDM-8 are all of 18,000-ton capacity. AFDM-8 named *Richland*. All active. 189.6 × 37.8 m. Built 1943-44.

◆ 16 APL barracks craft*

REMARKS: Built 1944-45. All active. 2,660 tons (fl), 79.6 × 15.0 × 2.6.

◆ 4 ARD auxiliary repair dry docks*

ARD-5 WATERFORD, ARD-7 WEST MILTON	**Dim:** 149.9 × 21.6
ARD-24, ARD-30 SAN ONOFRE	**Dim:** 149.9 × 24.7

REMARKS: All active, all 3,500-ton capacity. Built 1943-44.

◆ 4 ARDM medium auxiliary repair docks*

ARDM-1 OAKRIDGE, ARDM-2 ALAMAGORDO, ARDM-3 ENDURANCE, ARDM-4 SHIPPINGPORT

Capacity: 3,500-ton   **Dim:** 149.9 × 24.7

REMARKS: Built 1943-44, except ARDM-4: 1979. ARDM-4 *Shippingport* built by Bethlehem, Sparrows Point, delayed in delivery 1978-79 by design problems.

◆ 1 YAG miscellaneous auxiliary

YAG 61 MONOB I (ex-IX-309, ex-YW-87)

REMARKS: Former 53-m water tanker used as a tender to Naval Mine Defense Laboratory, Panama City, Fla., since 5-79. Built 1943.

◆ 231 YC open lighters*

REMARKS: Built 1915-77. Eight are in reserve. Five new construction requested under FY 80. YC-1517 to YC-1522 built 1976-77. Majority are 33.53 × 9.75, displacing 206 tons light (692 fl).

◆ 1 YCF car float*

YCF-16

REMARKS: Built 1941. 45.72 × 10.21; used to transport railroad cars. Active.

◆ 5 YCV aircraft transportation lighters*

YCV-8 to YCV-11   YCV-15   YCV-16

REMARKS: Built 1943. 28.96 × 9.14; 80-ton capacity. All active.

◆ 70 YD floating cranes*

REMARKS: Built 1913-70s. Sixty-four are active. YD-171, ex-German, has largest capacity: 350 tons. Most U.S. Navy YD are rectangular barges. Typical data: 1,630 tons (fl), 42.7 × 21.3, 90-100 tons capacity.

◆ 4 YDT diving tenders

YDT-3 (ex-YFNG-1): 90 tons, 24.7 × 8.2, 400 hp

YDT-14 PHOEBUS (ex-YC-294), YDT-15 SUITLAND (ex-YF 336): 600 tons, 40.4 × 9.1, 1 Union diesel: 600 hp

YDT-16* TOM O'MALLEY (ex-YFNB-43): 2,000 tons (fl), 79.6 × 14.6

REMARK: Built 1941-43.

◆ 3 YF covered lighters

YF-862, YF-866 KODIAK, YF-885 KEYPORT: 675 tons, 40.2 × 9.1, 1 160-hp diesel.

REMARKS: Built 1944. YF-885 active.

◆ 6 YFB ferryboats

YFB-83	**D:** 500 tons (fl)	**S:** 8.5 kts	**Dim:** 49.4 × 17.7
M: 2 diesels	**Cargo:** 500 passengers, 38 vehicles		
YFB-87	**D:** 773 tons (fl)	**Dim:** 54.9 × 18	**M:** 2 diesels

YFB-88 to YFB-91 (ex-LCU-1636, ex-LCU-1638 to LCU-1640)   **D:** 390 tons (fl)   **Dim:** 41.0 × 9.0

M: 4 GM diesels; 2 props; 1,200 hp

REMARKS: Built 1965-69. Modified 1969-70. All active.

◆ 1 YFD yard floating dry dock*

YFD-71   **Capacity:** 14,000-ton   **Dim:** 182.3 × 36.0

REMARKS: Built 1944. Active. Eight sisters on loan to commercial activities.

◆ 174 YFN covered lighter*

REMARKS: Built 1940-70s. 167 active. Majority are 685 tons (fl), 33.5 × 9.8. Large rectangular deckhouse.

◆ 15 YFNB large covered lighters*

REMARKS: Built 1945. Twelve active. All 831 tons light (2,780 fl), 79.2 × 14.6 × 2.9.

◆ 3 YFND dry-dock companion craft*

YFND 5   YFND-27   YFND-29

REMARKS: All 33.53 × 9.75, converted YFN. YFND-5 in reserve. Built 1943-44.

◆15 YFNX special-purpose lighters*

REMARKS: 14 active. Most converted YFN. Built 1943-45.

◆ 4 YFP floating power barges*

YFP-3   YFP-11   YFP-12

REMARKS: All converted YC, YFN.

YFP-14 INDUCTANCE (ex-Army BD-6235)

REMARKS: Built 1943-45. Transferred 1-10-77.

◆ 1 YFR refrigerated cargo lighter

YFR-888   **D:** 610 tons (fl)   **Dim:** 40.2 × 9.1   **M:** 1 Union diesel; 600 hp.

REMARKS: Built 1944. In reserve.

◆ 6 YFRN refrigerated cargo lighters

REMARKS: Built 1941-44. Two active. Most 45.7 × 10.4, 340-ton capacity.

SERVICE CRAFT (*continued*)

◆ 5 YFRT covered lighter range tenders

YFRT-287	YFRT-418	YFRT-451	YFRT-520	YFRT-523

   D: 650 tons (fl)   **S:** 10 kts   **Dim:** 40.4 × 9.1   **M:** 1 diesel; 600 hp

REMARKS: YF converted for duties on weapon-trials range. YFRT-520 has 3/324-mm MK-32 ASW TT (III × 1). YFRT-418 in reserve.

◆ 17 YFU harbor utility craft

YFU-50 (ex-LCU-1486): *See* LCU-1466 class data; in reserve

YFU-71, YFU-72, YFU-74 to YFU-77, YFU-79, YFU-81 (1967-68): Sisters to IX-506 (ex-YFU-82). All in reserve.

YFU-83, YFU-91, YFU-94, YFU-97, YFU-98, YFU-100 to YFU-102: All LCU-1610 class converted, except YFU-83, built for purpose. YFU-94 in reserve. Built 1955-68.

◆ 6 YGN garbage lighters*

REMARKS: Most approx. 110 tons light (500 fl), 36.6 × 10.7 rectangular barges. Have hopper-type bottoms to permit dumping at sea. Four active.

◆ 2 YHLC salvage lift craft, heavy*

YHLC-1 CRILLEY	YHLC-2 CRANDALL

REMARKS: Ex-*Hiev* and ex-*Griep* purchased from Germany for Vietnam War duties. Built in 1940s. Now in the Maritime Commission Reserve fleet, but remain Navy property.

◆ 6 YM dredge

YM-17	YM-32	YM-33	YM-35	YM-37	YM-38

REMARKS: Characteristics vary. YM-32 and YM-33 in reserve. Built 1930s-.

◆ 2 YNG gate craft*

YNG-11   YNG-17   **Dim:** 33.5 × 10.5.

REMARKS: Built 1941 to tend harbor-defense nets.

◆ 17 YO fuel-oil barges

YO-47 CASING HEAD   **D:** 2,660 tons (fl)   **Dim:** 71.6 × 11.3 × 4.6
   M: 2 Enterprise diesels; 820 hp. In reserve.

YO-106, YO-129, YO-171, YO-174, YO-200, YO-202, YO-203, YO-220, YO-223 to YO-225, YO-230, YO-241 (ex-YOG-5), YO-251 (ex-YOG-72), YO-264 (ex-YOG-105)

   D: 1,400 tons (fl)   **Dim:** 53.0 × 9.8 × 4.1
   M: 1-2 diesels; 560-640 hp. Five in reserve.

YO-153:   **D:** 1,076 tons (fl)   **Dim:** 47.6 × 9.3 × 3.6   **M:** 1 diesel, 525 hp.
REMARKS: In reserve. Built 1941-46.

◆ 8 YOG gasoline barges

YOG-58, YOG-68, YOG-78, YOG-79, YOG-87, YOG-88, YOG-93, YOG-196 (ex-YO-196)
   D: 1,390 tons (fl)   **Dim:** 53.0 × 9.8 × 4.1
   M: 1 or 2 diesels; 1 prop; 560-640 hp.

REMARKS: Four in reserve. Built 1945-46. Carry aviation fuel.

◆ 13 YOGN gasoline barges*

REMARKS: Built 1943-. . . All active. Carry aviation fuel.

◆ 49 YON fuel-oil barges

REMARKS: Built 1901-76. All active. Typical unit: 1,445 tons (fl); 50.3 × 12.0 × 2.7. Two new YON requested under FY 80. YON-255 and later (30 units) were built 1964-76. Five are ex-U.S. Army. YON-235 is ex-YW-73. Can carry a variety of fuels.

◆ 12 YOS oil-storage barges*

REMARKS: Built 1944-65. All active. Ten: 100 tons light; 24.4 × 10.4; others: 140 tons light; 33.5 × 10.4.

◆ 22 YP patrol craft

YP-654 to YP-675
   D: 60 tons (71 fl)   **S:** 13.3 kts   **Dim:** 24.51 × 5.72 × 1.6
   M: 2 GM 6-71 diesels; 2 props; 590 hp   **Man:** 2 officers, 8 men, 50 midshipmen

REMARKS: Built 1965-79. Used for navigation and maneuvering training at Naval Academy, Annapolis, and Naval Officer Candidate School, Newport. Not armed. YP-673 to YP-675 completed 1979 by Peterson Builders, Sturgeon Bay, Wisconsin.

◆ 6 YPD floating pile drivers*

REMARKS: Built 1943-65. In reserve. Most built on standard 24.4 × 10.4 barge hulls.

◆ 23 YR floating workshops*

REMARKS: Built 1941-45. Twenty-one active. Most 520 tons light (770 fl); 46.6 × 10.7 × 1.8. Differ in equipment.

◆ 4 YRB repair and berthing barges*

YRB-1	YRB-2	YRB-22	YRB-25

REMARKS: All 33.5 × 9.1. Built 1940-45. Support submarines.

◆ 22 (+ 9) YRBM repair, berthing, and messing barges*

REMARKS: Built 1955-81. All active; support submarines and ships in overhaul. Marinette SB constructing YRBM-31 to YRBM-36 during 1979-81: 688 tons; 44.5 × 14.0 × 1.3; accommodations for 26 officers, 231 men. Three more requested under FY 80.

◆ 4 YRDH floating dry-dock workshops, hull*

REMARKS: Built 1946. One active. All converted YR: 770 tons (fl), 46.6 × 10.7 × 1.8

◆ 4 YRDM floating dry-dock workshops, machinery*

REMARKS: Built 1945-49. One active. All converted YR: 770 tons (fl) 46.6 × 10.7 × 1.8.

◆ 14 YRR radiological repair barges*

REMARKS: Built 1942-46. All active. Most converted YR: 770 tons (fl) 46.6 × 10.7 × 1.8. Before conversion, some served as YRDH/YRDM.

◆ 5 YRST salvage-craft tender*

REMARKS: Built 1942-44. All active. YRST-1 to YRST-3 former YDT, YRST-6 former YFNX.

◆ 6 YSD seaplane wrecking derricks

YSD-15	YSD-39	YSD-53	YSD-63	YSD-74	YSD-77

SERVICE CRAFT (continued)

D: 270 tons (fl)   **Dim:** 31.7 × 9.5 × 1.2
M: 2 Superior diesels; 2 props; 320 hp

REMARKS: Built 1941-45. Employed as 10-ton capacity, self-propelled cranes.

◆ 23 YSR sludge-removal barges*

REMARKS: Built 1932-46. Eighteen active. Most either 24.4 × 9.8 or 33.5 × 10.4.

◆ 81 YTB large harbor tugs (SCB-147/147A type)

YTB 752 EDENSHAW	YTB-783 REDWING	YTB-810 ANOKA
YTB 753 MARIN	YTB-784 KALISPELL	YTB-811 HOUMA
YTB-756 PONTIAC	YTB-785 WINNEMUCCA	YTB-812 ACCOMAC
YTB-757 OSHKOSH	YTB-786 TONKAWA	YTB-813 POUGHKEEPSIE
YTB-758 PADUCAH	YTB-787 KITTANNING	YTB-814 WAXAHATCHIE
YTB-759 BOGALUSA	YTB-788 WAPATO	YTB-815 NEODESHA
YTB-760 NATICK	YTB-789 TOMAHAWK	YTB-816 CAMPTI
YTB-761 OTTUMWA	YTB-790 MENOMINEE	YTB-817 HYANNIS
YTB-762 TUSCUMBIA	YTB-791 MARINETTE	YTB-818 MECOSTA
YTB-763 MUSKEGON	YTB-792 ANTIGO	YTB-819 IUKA
YTB-764 MISHAWAKA	YTB-793 PIQUA	YTB-820 WANAMASSA
YTB-765 OKMULGEE	YTB-794 MANDAN	YTB-821 TONTOGANY
YTB-766 WAPAKONETA	YTB-795 KETCHIKAN	YTB-822 PAWHUSKA
YTB-767 APALACHICOLA	YTB-796 SACO	YTB-823 CANONCHET
YTB-768 ARCATA	YTB-797 TAMAQUA	YTB-824 SANTAQUIN
YTB-769 CHESANING	YTB-798 OPELIKA	YTB-825 WATHENA
YTB-770 DAHLONEGA	YTB-799 NATCHITOCHES	YTB-826 WASHTUENA
YTB-771 KEOKUK	YTB-800 EUFAULA	YTB-827 CHETEK
YTB-774 NASHUA	YTB-801 PALATKA	YTB-828 CATAHECASSA
YTB-775 WAUWATOSA	YTB-802 CHERAW	YTB-829 METACOM
YTB-776 WEEHAWKEN	YTB-803 NANTICOKE	YTB-830 PUSHMATAHA
YTB-777 NOGALES	YTB-804 AHOSKIE	YTB-831 DEKANAWIDA
YTB-778 APOPKA	YTB-805 OCALA	YTB-832 PETALESHARO
YTB-779 MANHATTAN	YTB-806 TUSKEGEE	YTB-833 SHABONEE
YTB-780 SAUGUS	YTB-807 MASSAPEQUA	YTB-834 NEGWAGON
YTB-781 NIANTIC	YTB-808 WENATCHEE	YTB-835 SKENANDOA
YTB-782 MANISTEE	YTB-809 AGAWAN	YTB-836 POKAGON

D: 286 tons (346 fl)   **S:** 12.5 kts   **Dim:** 33.05 × 9.3 × 4.14
M: 1 diesel; 1 prop; 2,000 hp   **Man:** 12 men   **Range:** 2,000/12

REMARKS: Built 1959-75. YTB-752 to YTB-759 have a less-streamlined superstructure and are considered a separate class (SCB 147 type). All active. Three also built for Saudi Arabia.

◆ 9 YTL small harbor tugs

YTL-422	YTL-431	YTL-434	YTL-438	YTL-439	YTL-558
YTL-583	YTL-588	YTL-602			

D: 70 tons (80 fl)   **S:** 8 kts   **Dim:** 20.1 × 5.5 × 2.4
M: 1 Hoover, Owens, Rentschler diesel; 375 hp   **Man:** 4 men

REMARKS: Built 1944-45. Four in reserve. All will probably soon be disposed of. Survivors of several hundred YTL-422 class; many still in foreign navies.

◆ 58 YTM medium harbor tugs

◆ 3 YTM-138 class

YTM-178 DEKAURY	YTM-180 MADOKAWANDO	YTM-189 NEPANET

D: 260 tons (310 fl)   **S:** 12 kts   **Dim:** 30.8 × 8.5 × 3.4
M: 1 Enterprise diesel; 1 prop; 820 hp   **Man:** 19 men

REMARKS: Built 1943. YTM-178 active; others in reserve.

◆ 6 YTM-174 class

YTM-252 DEKANISORA	YTM-359 PAWTUCKET	YTM-380 CHANAGI
YTM-381 CHEPANOC	YTM-382 COATOPA	YTM-383 COCHALI

D: 210 tons (320 fl)   **S:** 12 kts   **Dim:** 31.1 × 7.6 × 3.0
M: 2 GM diesels; 1 prop; 820 hp   **Man:** 15 men

REMARKS: Built 1942-44. Two active, four in reserve.

◆ 2 YTM-265 class

YTM-265 HIAWATHA	YTM-268 RED CLOUD

D: 230 tons (310 fl)   **S:** 12 kts   **Dim:** 30.5 × 8.5 × 3.0
M: 1 Enterprise diesel; 1 prop; 820 hp   **Man:** 14 men

REMARKS: Built 1942-43. Both in reserve.

◆ 19 YTM-364 class

YTM-364 SASSABA	YTM-395 WINGINA	YTM-404 COSHECTON
YTM-366 WAUBANSEE	YTM-397 YANEGUA	YTM-405 CUSSETA
YTM-390 GANADOGA	YTM-398 NATAHKI	YTM-406 KITTATON
YTM-391 ITARA	TYM-399 NUMA	YTM413 PORTOBAGO
YTM-392 MECOSTA	YTM-400 OTOKOMI	YTM-415 SECOTA
YTM-393 NAKARNA	YTM-403 PITAMAKAN	YTM-417 TACONNET
YTM-394 WINAMAC		

D: 260 tons (310 fl)   **S:** 10.5 kts   **Dim:** 30.8 × 8.5 × 3.4
M: 2 Fairbanks-Morse diesels; 1 prop; 820 hp   **Man:** 14 men

REMARKS: Built 1944-45. Eleven active, eight in reserve.

◆ 1 YTM-192 class

YTM-496 (no name)

D: 240 tons (340 fl)   **S:** 11 kts   **Dim:** 30.8 × 7.9 × 3.3
M: 2 Fairbanks-Morse diesels; 1 prop; 805 hp   **Man:** 11 men

REMARKS: Built 1942. In reserve.

◆ 19 YTM-518 class

YTM-521 NABIGWON	YTM-536 NAHOKE	YTM-547 YANABA
YTM-522 SAGAWAMICK	YTM-542 CHEGODEGA	YTM-548 MATUNAK
YTM-523 SENASQUA	YTM-543 ETAWINA	YTM-549 MIGADAN
YTM-524 TUTAHACO	YTM-544 YATANOCAS	YTM-701 ACOMA
YTM-526 WAHAKA	YTM-545 ACCOHANOC	YTM-702 ARAWAK
YTM-527 WAHPETON	YTM-546 TAKOS	YTM-704 MORATOC
YTM-534 NADLI		

D: 260 tons (310 fl)   **S:** 11 kts   **Dim:** 30.8 × 8.5 × 3.3
M: 2 GM diesels; 1 prop; 820 hp   **Man:** 8 men

REMARKS: Built 1945-46. Sixteen active, three in reserve.

SERVICE CRAFT (*continued*)

◆ **1 YTM-747 class**

YTM-748 YUMA (ex-Army LT-2078)

  D: 470 tons (fl)   **S:** 12 kts   **Dim:** 32.6 × 8.0 × 4.5
  M: 2 diesels; 1 prop; 1,200 hp

REMARK: In reserve.

◆ **1 ex-U.S. Army tug**

YTM-750 HACKENSACK (ex-Army LT-2089)

REMARK: Active.

◆ **2 YTM-760 class**

YTM-760 MASCOUTAH (ex-YTB-772)   YTM-761 MENASHA (ex-YTB-773)

  D: 200 tons (fl)   **S:** 12 kts   **Dim:** 25.9 × 7.3 × 3.4
  M: 2 GM 6-71 diesels; 2 Voith-Schneider vertical cycloidal props; 2,000 hp
  Man: 8 men

REMARKS: Built 1965-66. The U.S. Navy's only cycloidal-prop tugs. Both active.

◆ **4 YTM-764 class**

YTM-768 APOHOLA (ex-YTB-502)   YTM-770 MIMAC (ex-YTB-507)
YTM-776 HIAMONEE (ex-YTB-513)   YTM-779 POCASSET (ex-YTB-516)

  D: 260 tons (350 fl)   **S:** 11 kts   **Dim:** 30.8 × 8.5 × 3.7
  M: 2 Enterprise diesels; 1 prop; 1,270 hp   **Man:** 8 men

REMARKS: Built 1945-46. Two active, two in reserve.

◆ **11 YW water barges**

YW-83   YW-101   YW-113   YW-123   YW-127
YW-86   YW-108   YW-119   YW-126   YW-128
YW-98

  D: 1,235 tons (fl)   **S:** 8 kts   **Dim:** 53.0 × 9.7 × 4.6
  M: 2 diesels; 1 prop; 560 hp   **Man:** 22 men

REMARKS: Built 1944-45. YW-113, YW-119, YW-123, YW-128 active; others in reserve. Same basic design as YO and YOG classes.

◆ **7 YWN water barges***

REMARKS: Built 1944-45. Six active. Most 220 tons light; 50.3 × 10.7 × 2.4.

NOTE: In addition to the above yard and service craft, all of which have hull numbers and are carried on the Navy List, there are more than 1,000 small craft that are listed as property. Among the larger of these are a class of torpedo-retrievers:

  D: 110 tons light (165 fl)   **S:** 18 kts   **Dim:** 31.0 × 6.4 × 2.4
  Range: 1,920/10   **Fuel:** 7 tons
  M: 2 GM 12V-149 diesels; 2 props; 1,350 hp   **Man:** 15 men

REMARKS: Design based on PGM-59-class patrol boat. Ramp at stern. Stowage for 17 tons of recovered ordnance. There are also a number of 19.8-m torpedo-retrievers based on a patrol-craft design; the same design has also been built as an air/sea rescue boat.

San Onofre—YFND-27 alongside   1970

YFU-83   Defoe SB, 1971

YOG 89—YO and YW nearly identical

YP-660   A. Baker, 1978

SERVICE CRAFT (*continued*)

YFNB-24   1969

Dahlonega   C. Dragonette, 1978

Mascoutah   PH3 E. Pichette, 1964

Crandall   JO1 J. Todd, 1974

31.1-m torpedo-retriever   Peterson Builders, 1969

YR26   1969

MILITARY SEALIFT COMMAND

This quasi-military organization was founded in 1949 as the Military Sea Transportation Service, and given its current name on 1-8-70. It is headed by a flag officer of the U.S. Navy, whose deputy and three area commanders are also flag officers. Its ships, which are not armed, are considered to be noncommissioned, and are manned by civilians, are described below in the order of their hull type numbers. The prefix "T" is appended to the hull numbers of its ships, whose missions are fleet support, transportation of bulk military cargo, and scientific research and survey.

NOTE: MSC ships are painted gray (AGOR/AGS: white) and have blue and gold-yellow stack bands. They do *not* display hull numbers.

STORES SHIP

◆ **1 Rigel class**

	Bldr	L	In serv.
T-AF 58 RIGEL	Ingalls, Pascagoula	15-3-55	2-9-55

Rigel   C. Martinelli, 1977

D: 7,950 tons (15,540 fl)   **S:** 20 kts   **Dim:** 153.0 × 22.0 × 8.8
Electron Equipt: Radars: 1/SPS-40, 1/navigational   **Range:** 11,000/18
M: 1 set GE GT; 1 prop; 16,000 hp   **Boilers:** 2 Combustion Engineering

REMARKS: 10,781 grt/8,112 dwt. Twelve 10-ton booms. Cargo: 5,975 m³ dry, 5,400 m³ refrigerated. Provides fleet support.

HYDROGRAPHIC RESEARCH SHIP

◆ **1 Victory class**   Bldr: California SB Corp.

	Laid down	L	In serv.
T-AG 164 KINGSPORT (ex-*Kingsport Victory*, AK-239)	1-44	24-5-44	12-7-44

D: 7,190 tons light (10,680 fl)   **S:** 16.5 kts   **Dim:** 138.7 × 18.9 × 6.7
Man: 13 officers, 42 men, 15 technicians   **Range:** 20,000/16.5
Boilers: 2 Babcock & Wilcox, 37 kg/cm² pressure—superheat 399°C
M: 1 set Westinghouse GT; 1 prop; 8,500 hp   **Fuel:** 2,824 tons

REMARKS: 7,607 grt/6,123 dwt. Acquired by the Navy on 1-3-50 as a cargo ship. Modified 1961-62 as a satellite-communications relay ship; reassigned to hydrographic research in 1966. Operated for Naval Electronics Systems Command. Helicopter deck aft.

Kingsport   MSC, 1976

RANGE INSTRUMENTATION SHIPS

◆ **1 Mariner class**

	Bldr	L	In serv.
T-AGM 23 OBSERVATION ISLAND (ex-AG-154, ex-*Empire State Mariner*)	New York SB, Camden, N.J.	15-8-53	5-12-58

Observation Island — as AG-154   1972

RANGE INSTRUMENTATION SHIPS (continued)

D: 16,076 tons (fl)   **S:** 20 kts   **Dim:** 171.6 × 23.27 × 8.8
Man: . . .   **Range:** 17,000/13
Boilers: 2 Combustion Engineering, 42.3 kg/cm² pressure—superheat 467°C
M: 1 set GE GT; 1 prop; 22,000 hp

REMARKS: Former ballistic-missile trials ship. Acquired by the Navy on 10-9-56; used for Polaris and Poseidon missile trials until placed in reserve on 29-9-72. Under conversion between 7-79 and 7-81 to carry Cobra Judy missile-tracking, fixed-array radar aft, aimed to starboard. Will be operated for the U.S. Air Force in the Pacific.

◆ **1 converted Haskell-class attack transport**   Bldr: Permanente Metals, Richmond, Cal.

	L	In serv.
T-AGM 22 RANGE SENTINEL (ex-*Sherburne*, APA-205)	10-7-44	20-9-44

Range Sentinel—tracking radars now in geodesic domes   MSC, 1971

D: 11,860 tons (fl)   **S:** 15.5 kts   **Dim:** 138.7 × 18.9 × 8.8
Man: 14 officers, 54 men, 27 technicians   **Range:** 10,000/15.5
Boilers: 2 Combustion Engineering, 37 kg/cm² pressure—superheat 399°C
M: 1 set GT; 1 prop; 8,500 hp   **Fuel:** 1,197 tons

REMARKS: 8,306 grt/5,301 dwt. Converted between 10-69 and 14-10-71 as support ship for the Poseidon (and later, Trident) program. Victory-type hull and propulsion; forecastle deck now extends three-quarters of her length and she has four large tracking radars forward.

◆ **1 Vanguard class**   Bldr: Marine Ship, Sausalito, Cal.

	In serv.
T-AGM 20 REDSTONE (ex-*Johnstown*, ex-*Mission de Pala*, AO-114)	22-4-44

D: 21,626 tons (fl)   **S:** 16 kts   **Dim:** 181.4 × 22.9 × 7.6
Man: 20 officers, 71 men, 120 technicians   **Range:** 27,000/16
Boilers: 2 Babcock & Wilcox "D", 42.3 kg/cm² pressure—superheat 440°C
M: 1 set GE GT, electric drive; 1 prop; 10,000 hp   **Fuel:** 3,995 tons

REMARKS: 16,060 grt/16,255 dwt. Former T2-SE-A2-type tanker converted 1964-66 to serve as tracking and communications ship for NASA manned space flights; 22 meters added amidships. Sister *Mercury* (T-AGM-21) stricken in 1969 after very little use, and sister *Vanguard* (T-AGM-19) redesignated AG in 1978.

Redstone—tracking radars now in geodesic domes   USAF, 1970

◆ **2 General H. H. Arnold class**   Bldr: Kaiser, Richmond, Cal.

	In serv.	Conv.
T-AGM 9 GENERAL H. H. ARNOLD (ex-*General R. E. Callan*, T-AP-139)	8-8-44	1963
T-AGM 10 GENERAL HOYT S. VANDENBERG (ex-*General Harry Taylor*, T-AP-145)	8-5-44	1963

General Hoyt S. Vandenberg   MSC, 1976

D: 16,600 tons (fl)   **S:** 17 kts   **Dim:** 168.5 × 21.8 × 7.9
Man: 21 officers, 71 men, 113 technicians   **Range:** 18,000/17
Fuel: 2,685 tons
Boilers: 2 Babcock & Wilcox, 32.7 kg/cm² pressure—superheat 407°C
M: 1 set Westinghouse GT; 1 prop; 9,000 hp

RANGE INSTRUMENTATION SHIPS (*continued*)

REMARKS: 12,848 grt/3,950 dwt. Converted C4-S-A1-class troop transports, originally under the Air Force but assigned to MSC in 7-64.

◆ **1 converted "Victory"-class (VC2-S-AP3 type)**   Bldr: Oregon SB, Portland

	In serv.	Conv.
T-AGM 8 WHEELING (ex-*Seton Hall Victory*)	6-45	28-5-64

Wheeling

D: 10,680 tons (fl)	**S:** 16.5 kts	**Dim:** 138.7 × 18.9 × 8.8
Man: 13 officers, 46 men, 62 technicians		**Range:** 20,000/16.5

Fuel: 2,824 tons
Boilers: 2 Babcock & Wilcox, 37 kg/cm² pressure—superheat 399°C
M: 1 set GT; 1 prop; 8,500 hp

REMARKS: 8,319 grt/10,650 dwt. Now in ready reserve. Only survivor of six "Victory"-class cargo ships converted to AGM. Hangar and flight deck for two helicopters.

OCEANOGRAPHIC RESEARCH SHIPS

◆ **2 Gyre class (SCB 734 type)**   Bldr: Halter Marine, New Orleans

	Laid down	L	In serv.
AGOR 21 GYRE	9-10-72	7-6-73	14-11-73
AGOR 22 MOANA WAVE	9-10-72	23-6-73	16-1-74

D: 950 tons (1,190 fl)	**S:** 12.5 kts	**Dim:** 53.14 × 11.05 × 3.05

Man: 10 men plus 11 researchers
M: 2 Caterpillar diesels; 2 controllable-pitch props; 1,700 hp (plus 170 hp retractable maneuvering prop)

REMARKS: *Not under MSC control but listed here for simplicity.* On completion, assigned to Texas A&M University and University of Hawaii. Modified oil-field supply ships using modular equipment vans on long open fantail.

NOTE: The *Chain* (AGOR-17, ex-ARS-20) was stricken on 30-12-77.

◆ **1 Hayes class (SCB 726 type)**   Bldr: Todd SY, Seattle

	Laid down	L	In serv.
T-AGOR 16 HAYES	12-11-69	2-7-70	21-7-71

D: 3,080 tons (fl)	**S:** 15 kts	**Dim:** 75.1 (67.0 pp) × 22.9 × 6.6
Man: 11 officers, 33 men, 30 researchers		**Range:** 6,000/13.5

Fuel: 368 tons

Hayes   1977

Hayes   1977

Electron Equipt: Sonars: 1/3.5 kHz mapping, 1/16 kHz	**Electric:** 850 kw

M: 4 high-speed diesels; 2 controllable-pitch props; 5,400 hp (plus 2 165-hp diesels for low-speed operations, 2 to 4 kts)

REMARKS: 3,677 grt/393 dwt. Catamaran, each hull 7.3 m beam. Suffered at first from severe pitching problems. Numerous equipment-handling gallows up to 15-ton capacity. Extremely well equipped.

OCEANOGRAPHIC RESEARCH SHIPS (*continued*)

◆ **2 Melville class (SCB 710 type)**   Bldr: Defoe SB, Bay City, Mich.

	Laid down	L	In serv.
AGOR 14 MELVILLE	12-7-67	10-7-68	27-8-69
AGOR 15 KNORR	9-8-67	21-8-68	14-1-70

Melville   1970

D: 1,915 tons (2,080 fl)   **S:** 12.5 kts   **Dim:** 74.7 (67.0 pp) × 14.1 × 4.6
Man: 9 officers, 16 men, 25 researchers   **Range:** 10,000/12
M: 2 Enterprise diesels; Voith-Schneider cycloidal props; 2,500 hp

REMARKS: *Under Navy, not MSC, control, but listed here for simplicity.* Operated for the Office of Naval Research, AGOR-14 by Scripps Institute, AGOR-15 by Woods Hole Oceanographic Institution. One vertical cycloidal propeller forward, larger unit aft; intended for precise maneuvering but, because mechanical rather than electric drive was used, have proven troublesome. AGOR-19 and AGOR-20 of this class therefore canceled. AGOR-14 seldom operates and may be placed in reserve.

◆ **7 Robert D. Conrad class (SCB 185 and 710* types)**

	Bldr	L	In serv.
AGOR 3 ROBERT D. CONRAD	Gibbs, Jacksonville	26-5-62	29-11-62
T-AGOR 4 JAMES M. GILLIS	Christy Corp., Wisc.	19-5-62	5-11-62
T-AGOR 7 LYNCH	Marinette, Wisc.	17-3-65	27-3-65
AGOR 9 THOMAS G. THOMPSON	Marinette, Wisc.	18-7-64	24-8-65
AGOR 10 THOMAS WASHINGTON	Marinette, Wisc.	1-8-64	27-9-65
T-AGOR 12 DE STEIGUER*	N.W. Marine, Portland	3-6-66	28-2-69
T-AGOR 13 BARTLETT*	N.W. Marine, Portland	24-5-66	31-3-69

D: 1,200 tons (1,380 fl)   **S:** 13.5 kts   **Dim:** 63.7 × 11.4 × 4.7
Man: 9 officers, 17 men, 18 researchers   **Range:** 12,000/12
Electron Equipt: Radar: 1/R.C.A. CRM-N1A-75   **Electric:** 850 kw
M: 2 Caterpillar D-378 diesels, electric drive; 1 prop; 1,000 hp   **Fuel:** 211 tons

REMARKS: All civilian crews; 3 under Navy control, 4 under MSC. Assigned: AGOR-3: Lamont Geophysical Lab., Columbia U.; T-AGOR-4: U. of Miami for Navy research;

Thomas Washington   1965

De Steiguer   1969

T-AGOR-7: MSC for Oceanographer of the Navy; AGOR-9: U. of Washington for Navy; AGOR-10: Scripps Inst. of Oceanography; T-AGOR-12 and T-AGOR-13: MSC for Oceanographer of the Navy. Vary in details and paint (see photos). *Sands* (T-AGOR-6) on loan to Brazil, *Charles H. Davis* (T-AGOR-5) to New Zealand. Large stack contains 620-hp gas-turbine generator set used to drive main shaft at speeds up to 6.5 kts for experiments requiring "quiet" conditions. Also have retractable electric bow thruster/propulsor which provides up to 4.5 kts.

◆ **1 Eltanin class**   Bldr: Avondale Marine, New Orleans, La.

	L	In serv.	Conv.
T-AGOR 11 MIZAR (ex-T-AK-272)	7-10-57	22-11-57	1962

Mizar   J.-C. Bellonne, 1971

OCEANOGRAPHIC RESEARCH SHIPS (continued)

D: 2,040 tons light (4,942 fl) **S:** 13 kts **Dim:** 79.9 × 15.7 × 6.9
Man: 11 officers, 30 men, 15 technicians **Range:** 14,000/12
M: 4 Alco diesels, Westinghouse motors; 2 props; 3,200 hp **Fuel:** 675 tons

REMARKS: 2,486 grt/1,850 dwt. Former sister to *Mirfak* (T-AK-271). Reclassified on 15-4-64. Operates for the Naval Electronics Command. Icebreaker hull; covered well on centerline for lowering equipment. Sister *Eltanin* (T-AGOR-8) loaned to Argentina in 12-73 as *Islas Orcadas*, returned in 8-79 and stricken.

OCEAN SURVEILLANCE SHIPS

◆ **3 T-AGOS class**

	Bldr	Laid down	L	In serv.
T-AGOS-1 N . . .	. . .	. . .	. . .	. . .
T-AGOS-2 N . . .	. . .	. . .	. . .	. . .
T-AGOS-3 N . . .	. . .	. . .	. . .	. . .

Authorized: 2 in FY 79, 1 in FY 80

D: 2,400 tons (fl) **S:** 11 kts **Dim:** 67.5 (61.0 wl) × 12.8 × 4.6
Man: 17 men + 9 technicians **Range:** 2,000/11, 6,400/3
Electron Equipt: Radars: 2/navigational Sonar: SURTASS
M: 4 Caterpillar D-348 diesels, electric drive; 2 props; 2,200 hp

REMARKS: The original program called for the construction of twelve of these ships, but delays have been numerous and costs have risen. Three were requested for FY 80, but only one was appropriated for. The first T-AGOS had not been contracted for as of 12-31-79. SURTASS is a very long, linear, hydrophone array deployed over the ship's stern in a flexible, neutrally buoyant cable. Crew will be mainly civilian, but the Navy will supply men to monitor the SURTASS. Will have satellite communications and precision-navigation equipment. Main-engine motor/generator sets also supply ship's service power; there is a 250-kw emergency generator. Will have passive roll stabilization. Intended to conduct ninety-day patrols and to be at sea 300 days per year.

SURVEYING SHIPS

◆ **1 converted cargo ship (C4-SA type)** Bldr: National Steel, San Diego, Calif.

	L	In serv.
T-AGS 38 H. S. HESS (ex-*Canada Mail*)	3-65	16-1-78

D: 17,874 tons (fl) **S:** 21 kts **Dim:** 171.8 (160.93 pp) × 23.16 × 9.6
Man: 48 men **Range:** 14,000/20 **Fuel:** 3,178 tons
Boilers: 2 Foster-Wheeler, 43.3 kg/cm² pressure — superheat 457°C
M: 1 set GE GT; 1 prop; 19,250 hp **Electric:** 1,400 kw

REMARKS: Mariner-type passenger-cargo ship acquired from the Maritime Administration on 9-7-76 for conversion to replace the *Michelson* (T-AGS-23) in SSBN navigational support program. Retains original six cargo holds but most cargo booms removed.

◆ **2 Chauvenet class (SCB 723 type)** Bldr: Upper Clyde SB, Glasgow, G.B.

	Laid down	L	In serv.
T-AGS 29 CHAUVENET	24-5-67	13-5-68	13-11-70
T-AGS 32 HARKNESS	30-6-67	12-6-68	29-1-71

D: 3,000 tons (4,200 fl) **S:** 15 kts **Dim:** 119.8 (101.8 pp) × 16.5 × 4.9
Man: MSC: 13 officers, 56 men + Navy: 6 officers, 49 men + 12 civilian scientists

Harkness   Pradignac & Léo, 1972

Chauvenet   1971

Range: 15,000/12 **Fuel:** 824 tons **Electric:** 1,500 kw
Endurance: 90 days
M: 2 Alco diesels, Westinghouse motor; 1 controllable-pitch prop, 3,600 hp

REMARKS: 2,890 grt/1,030 dwt. Very complete navigation and communications systems. Can carry four small survey launches; hangar and flight deck for two helicopters. Operated for the Oceanographer of the Navy; some naval personnel aboard. T-AGS-32 to be placed in reserve in 1980.

◆ **4 Silas Bent class (SCB 226, 725*, and 728** types)**

	Bldr	L	In serv.
T-AGS 26 SILAS BENT	American SB, Lorain	16-5-64	23-7-65
T-AGS 27 KANE	Christy, Sturgeon Bay	20-11-65	19-5-67
T-AGS 33 WILKES*	Defoe, Bay City, Mich.	31-7-69	28-6-71
T-AGS 34 WYMAN**	Defoe, Bay City, Mich.	30-10-69	3-11-71

SURVEYING SHIPS (*continued*)

Kane

Pradignac & Léo, 1977

D: 1,935 tons (2,420 to 2,558 fl) **S:** 15 kts **Dim:** 86.9 × 14.6 × 4.6
Man: 12 officers, 35 men, 30 scientists **Range:** 14,000/15 **Fuel:** 461 tons
Electron Equipt: Radar: 1/CRM-N1A-75, 1/SPS-53
M: 2 Alco diesels, Westinghouse motor; controllable-pitch prop; 3,600 hp (plus 350-hp bow thruster)

REMARKS: Operated for Oceanographer of the Navy. T-AGS-33 has been in Ready Reserve since shortly after completion.

◆ **2 Bowditch class** Bldr: Oregon SB, Portland, South Coast Co.

	L	Conv.
T-AGS 21 BOWDITCH (ex-*South Bend Victory*)	30-6-45	8-10-58
T-AGS 22 DUTTON (ex-*Tuskegee Victory*)	8-5-45	30-9-58

D: 14,512 tons (fl) **S:** 16.5 kts **Dim:** 138.76 (133.05 pp) × 18.98 × 7.62
Man: 14 officers, 47 men, 40 technicians **Range:** 20,000/16.5
Fuel: 2,824 tons
Boilers: 2 Combustion Engineering, 37 kg/cm² pressure—superheat 399°C
M: 1 set GT; 1 prop; 8,500 hp

REMARKS: 7,783 grt/8,350 dwt. Victory-class cargo ships converted to support the SSBN program. Used for sea-floor charting and magnetic mapping. Sister *Michelson* (T-AGS-23) stricken in 1975.

Dutton

CARGO SHIPS

◆ **14 T-AKX class (proposed)**

REMARKS: At the end of 1979 the Carter administration indicated that the first increment of a total of fourteen logistic-support ships was to be requested in FY 81. The ships will support a "new" concept of a Rapid Deployment Force, which would also include a number of new, large, cargo aircraft to be operated by the Air Force. The fourteen T-AKX would be combat-loaded with sufficient gear for three Marine Corps brigades and positioned in forward "areas." It had not been determined whether the ships were to be new or conversions from existing ships. This concept was proposed by the Johnson administration in the late 1960s as the "Fast Logistics Support Ship" (FDL), a new-construction gas-turbine-propelled design with helicopter facilities and bow and stern cargo ramps; it was rejected then by Congress on the grounds that it would make it too easy to involve the United States in foreign conflicts. The New T-AKX is believed to be a considerably more austere concept.

◆ **1 ballistic-missile support ship**

	Bldr	L	In serv.
T-AK 284 N . . .	. . .	1943-45	1982

D: Approx. 16,000 tons (fl) **S:** 18 kts
Dim: 149.96 (141.73 pp) × 21.18 × 8.4
M: 1 set GT; 1 prop; 8,500 hp
Boilers: 2, 30.6 kg/cm² pressure—superheat 407°C

REMARKS: A converted C-3 cargo ship intended to act as transport for Trident missiles and support supplies for SSBNs. Will replace one *Norwalk*-class T-AK in service. Design funds requested in FY 80; conversion to be funded under FY 81. Presumably, the ship will be drawn from the Maritime Administration's reserve fleet.

◆ **1 Andromeda class** Bldr: Moore DD, Oakland, Calif.

	L	In serv.
T-AK 283 WYANDOT (ex-T-AKA-92)	28-6-44	30-9-44

D: 7,430 tons light (14,200 fl) **S:** 16.5 kts
Dim: 139.96 (132.59 wl) × 19.2 × 8.03
Range: 14,000/15.5 **Fuel:** 1,503 tons **Electric:** 900 kw
Boilers: 2 Combustion Engineering, 31.7 kg/cm² pressure—superheat 399°C
M: 1 set GE GT; 1 prop; 6,000 hp

REMARKS: 8,895 grt/6,450 dwt. Cargo: 10,734 m³ dry/453 m³ refrigerated. Built as an attack cargo ship. Winterized for Arctic service. Renumbered T-AK-283 on 1-1-69. In Maritime Administration's reserve fleet.

◆ **3 Norwalk class**
Bldr: Oregon SB, Portland (T-AK-281: Permanente, Richmond, Calif.)

	L	Conv.
T-AK 280 FURMAN (ex-*Furman Victory*)	18-5-45	7-10-64
T-AK 281 VICTORIA (ex-*Ethiopia Victory*)	28-4-44	15-10-65
T-AK 282 MARSHFIELD (ex-*Marshfield Victory*)	15-5-44	28-5-70

D: 6,700 tons light (11,150 fl) **S:** 16.5 kts
Dim: 138.76 (133.05 pp) × 18.90 × 7.32 **Man:** 80 to 90 men
Fuel: 2,824 tons **Range:** 20,000/16.5 **M:** 1 set GT; 1 prop; 8,500 hp
Boilers: 2, 37 kg/cm² pressure—superheat 399°C

REMARKS: 7,491 grt/9,649 dwt. Hold No. 3 accommodates 16 vertically stowed Poseidon

CARGO SHIPS (continued)

Marshfield—others retain original superstructure   1970

or Polaris SLBM. Ships support SSBN activities. Carry torpedoes, submarine spares etc.; also carry 18,000 barrels cargo fuel (7,566 bbl diesel/10,434 bbl fuel oil). 40-ton cargo booms. Small Navy security detachment aboard. *Norwalk* (T-AK-279) stricken 1-8-79; a second will strike in 1981, another in 1982, and the last in 1987.

NOTE: The *Schuyler Otis Bland* (T-AK-277) was stricken on 15-8-79 and *Mirfak* (T-AK-271) on 15-12-79.

◆ **5 Victory class (VC2-S-AP3 and AP2 types)**   Bldrs: T-AK-237: Calship, L.A.; T-AK-240, T-AK-274: Oregon SB, Portland; T-AK-242, T-AK-254: Permanente Metals, Richmond, Calif.

	Laid down	L	In serv.
T-AK 237 GREENVILLE VICTORY	21-3-44	28-5-44	8-7-44
T-AK 240 PVT. JOHN R. TOWLE (ex-*Appleton Victory*)	9-12-44	19-1-45	23-3-45
T-AK 242 SGT. ANDREW MILLER (ex-*Radcliffe Victory*)	22-2-45	4-4-45	28-4-45
T-AK 254 SGT. TRUMAN KIMBRO (ex-*Hastings Victory*)	30-9-44	30-11-44	22-12-44
T-AK 274 LT. JAMES E. ROBINSON (ex-T-AG-170, ex-T-AK-274 ex-AKV-3, ex-*Czechoslovakia Victory*)	25-11-43	20-1-44	11-3-44

D: 6,700 tons light (12,450 fl)   **S:**   17 kts (T-AK-254: 15)
Dim: 138.76 (133.05 pp) × 18.9 × 8.69   **Man:**   49 men   **Range:**   20,000/16.5
Fuel: 2,824 tons   **Boilers:**   2, 37 kg/cm² pressure—superheat 399°C
Electric: 600 kw   **M:**   1 set GT; 1 prop; 8,500 hp (T-AK-254: 6,000 hp)

REMARKS: 7,607 grt/10,681 dwt. Acquired from the Maritime Administration in 1950. T-AK-240 active; others in Maritime Administration's reserve fleet, remaining on Navy List. Approx. 12,600 m³ dry cargo (varies). T-AK-254 is a VC2-S-AP2 type. T-AK-274 was the second Victory ship to be completed. T-AK-237 can accommodate 83 passengers. T-AK-240 has new cranes.

Pvt. John R. Towle

◆ **2 Pvt. Leonard C. Brostrom class (C4-S-B1 type)**   Bldr: Sun SB & DD, Chester, Pa.

	Laid down	L	In serv.
T-AK 255 PVT. LEONARD C. BROSTROM (ex-*Marine Eagle*)	5-12-42	10-5-43	18-9-43
T-AK 267 MARINE FIDDLER	15-12-44	15-5-45	31-8-45

Pvt. Leonard C. Brostrom

D: 7,526 tons light (22,094 fl)   **S:**   15.8 kts
Dim: 158.5 (153.3 pp) × 21.8 × 10.1
Man: 14 officers, 43 men   **Range:**   10,000/15.8   **Fuel:**   2,052 tons
Boilers: 2 Babcock & Wilcox, 32.7 kg/cm² pressure—superheat 399°C
M: 1 set GE GT; 1 prop; 9,000 hp   **Electric:**   900 kw

CARGO SHIPS (*continued*)

REMARKS: 11,164 grt/13,504 dwt. Cargo: 19,512 m³ dry cargo + 38,000 bbl. fuel oil. T-AK-255, acquired on 9-8-50, is in service. T-AK-267, acquired on 7-2-52, is in the Maritime Administration's reserve fleet. Both converted 1954 to heavy-lift configuration, with two 150-ton-capacity booms.

VEHICLE CARGO SHIPS

◆ **1 Meteor class (C4-ST-67a type)**   Bldr: Puget Sound Bridge & DD

	Laid down	L	In serv.
T-AKR 9 METEOR (ex-*Sea Lift*)	19-5-64	18-4-64	25-5-67

Meteor   1968

D: 11,130 tons light (21,700 fl)   **S:** 20 kts   **Dim:** 164.7 × 25.5 × 8.8
Man: 62 men   **Fuel:** 2,511 tons   **Range:** 10,000/20
M: 1 set GT; 2 props; 19,400 hp   **Boilers:** 2

REMARKS: 16,467 grt/12,326 dwt. Cargo: 26,819 m³ vehicle parking volume. Stern and four side ramps for Ro-Ro loading/unloading. Can carry 12 passengers. Authorized as T-AK-278, completed as T-LSV-9, retyped T-AKR 14-8-69. Renamed 12-9-75.

◆ **1 Comet class (C3-ST-14A type)**   Bldr: Sun SB & DD, Chester, Pa.

	Laid down	L	In serv.
T-AKR 7 COMET	15-5-56	31-7-57	27-1-58

D: 7,605 tons light (18,150 fl)   **S:** 18 kts   **Dim:** 152.1 × 23.8 × 8.9
Man: 73 men   **Range:** 12,000/18   **Fuel:** 2,423 tons
M: 1 set GE GT; 2 props; 13,200 hp   **Boilers:** 2 Babcock & Wilcox

Comet   J. Jedrlinic, 1979

REMARKS: 13,792 grt/10,111 dwt. Cargo: more than 700 military vehicles in holds totaling 19,370 m³ volume. Side and stern ramps. Denny-Brown fin stabilizers. Authorized as T-AK-269, changed to T-LSV-7 on 1-6-63, then to T-AKR-7 on 1-1-69.

OILERS

◆ **6 Neosho class (SCB 82 type)**

Bldr: New York SB, Camden, N.J. (T-AT-143: Bethlehem, Quincy, Mass.)

	L	In serv.	To MSC
T-AO 143 NEOSHO	10-11-53	24-9-54	25-5-78
T-AO 144 MISSISSINEWA	12-6-54	18-1-55	15-11-76
T-AO 145 HASSAYAMPA	12-9-54	19-4-55	17-8-78
T-AO 146 KAWISHWI	11-12-54	6-7-55	1-10-79
T-AO 147 TRUCKEE	10-3-55	23-11-55	20-9-79
T-AO 148 PONCHATOULA	9-7-55	12-1-56	. . .

D: 11,600 tons light (38,000 fl)   **S:** 20 kts
Dim: 199.65 (195.07 wl) × 26.21 × 10.67
Man: 105 men   **Fuel:** 5,000 tons   **Electric:** 1,500 kw

Mississinewa   1978

OILERS (*continued*)

Electron Equipt: Radars: 1/SPS-10, 1/SPS-53
Boilers: 2 Babcock & Wilcox, 42.2 kg/cm² pressure – superheat 357°C
M: 2 sets GE GT; 2 props; 28,000 hp

REMARKS: 19,553 grt/36,840 dwt. Carry 180,000 bbl. liquid cargo (approx. 23,600 tons) Helicopter platform aft in all but T-AO-148. Operated by MSC as underway-replenishment ships for the Navy. Transferred to MSC as a cost-saving measure (Navy crew was 360 total).

◆ **5 Mispillion class (jumboized T3-S2-A3 type)** Bldr: Sun SB, Chester, Pa.

	L	In serv.	To MSC
T-AO 105 MISPILLION	10-8-45	29-12-45	26-7-73
T-AO 106 NAVASOTA	30-8-45	27-2-46	13-8-75
T-AO 107 PASSUMPSIC	31-10-45	1-4-46	24-7-73
T-AO 108 PAWCATUCK	19-2-46	10-5-46	15-7-75
T-AO 109 WACCAMAW	30-3-46	25-6-46	24-2-75

Waccamaw 1976

D: 11,000 tons light (33,750-34,179 fl) **S:** 16 kts
Dim: 196.9 × 22.9 × 10.8
Electron Equipt: Radars: 1/SPS-10, 1/SPS-53 **Man:** 110 men
Fuel: 2,250 tons
Boilers: 4 Babcock & Wilcox, 32.7 kg/cm² pressure – superheat 393°C
M: 2 sets Westinghouse GT; 2 props; 13,500 hp

REMARKS: 19,294 grt/23,250 dwt. Cargo: 107,000 bbl. fuel oil, diesel, etc. plus dry cargo. Fleet support units transferred from the Navy and intended for underway replenishment. Had four single 76.2-mm guns, but now disarmed. Helicopter deck forward. All lengthened 28.3 m during the mid-1960s.

◆ **2 Cimarron class (T3-S2 A1 type)** Bldr: Bethlehem, Sparrows Point, Md.

	L	In serv.	To MSC
T-AO 57 MARIAS	21-12-43	12-2-44	2-10-73
T-AO 62 TALUGA	10-7-44	25-8-44	4-5-72

D: 24,450 tons (fl) **S:** 18 kts **Dim:** 168.56 × 22.86 × 10.1
Man: 107 men **Fuel:** 2,205 tons **Electric:** 950 kw
Electron Equipt: Radars: 1/SPS-10, 1/SPS-53
Boilers: 4 Foster-Wheeler, 31.7 kg/cm² pressure – superheat 399°C
M: 2 sets GT; 2 props; 13,500 hp

Marias 1975

REMARKS: 12,000 grt/18,400 dwt. Cargo: 87,000 bbl. fuel oil, diesel, etc. Fleet support ships intended for underway replenishment. To be stricken before 30-9-80.

TRANSPORT OILERS

◆ **4 Falcon class** Bldr: Ingalls SB, Pascagoula, Miss.

	L	In serv.	Acquired
T-AOT 182 COLUMBIA (ex-*Falcon Lady*)	12-9-70	11-3-71	15-1-76
T-AOT 183 NECHES (ex-*Falcon Duchess*)	30-1-71	4-8-71	11-2-76
T-AOT 184 HUDSON (ex-*Falcon Princess*)	8-1-72	4-5-72	23-4-76
T-AOT 185 SUSQUEHANNA (ex-*Falcon Countess*)	2-10-71	13-1-72	11-5-76

D: 45,877 tons (fl) **S:** 16.5 kts **Dim:** 204.9 (194.46 pp) × 27.13 × 11.13
Man: ... **Range:** 16,000/16.5 **Fuel:** 2,620 tons
M: 2 Colt-Pielstick 16PC-2V400, 16 cyl. diesels; 1 prop; 15,000 hp

Hudson J. Jedrlinic, 1979

TRANSPORT OILERS (continued)

REMARKS: 20,571 grt/37,267 dwt. Cargo: 310,000 bbl. fuels. Originally on bareboat charter to MSC, later purchased. Operated by civilian contractor. Redesignated T-AOT on 30-9-78.

◆ **1 Potomac class**   Bldr: Ingalls SB, Pascagoula, Miss.

	Laid down	In serv.
T-AOT 181 POTOMAC (ex-*Shenandoah*, ex-*Potomac*, T-AO-150)	9-6-55	1-57/14-12-64

Potomac

D: 35,000 tons (fl)	**S:** 18 kts	**Dim:** 189.0 × 25.5 × 10.4	
Man: . . .	**Range:** 18,000/18	**Fuel:** 4,321 tons	
M: 1 set GT; 1 prop; 20,460 hp	**Boilers:** 2		

REMARKS: 15,739 grt/27,467 dwt. Carries 200,000 bbl. fuel plus 878 m³ dry cargo. Originally belonging to the *Maumee* class, she was heavily damaged in 1961; only her stern was salvaged. Rebuilt by Sun SB & DD, Chester, Pa., and operated on charter to MSC as the *Shenandoah* from 1964 until purchased on 12-1-76. Operated by a civilian contractor. Reclassified T-AOT on 30-9-78.

◆ **9 Sealift class**   Bldrs: First four: Todd, Los Angeles; others: Bath Iron Works

	L	In serv.
T-AOT 168 SEALIFT PACIFIC	13-10-73	14-8-74
T-AOT 169 SEALIFT ARABIAN SEA	26-1-74	6-5-75
T-AOT 170 SEALIFT CHINA SEA	20-4-74	9-5-75
T-AOT 171 SEALIFT INDIAN OCEAN	27-7-74	29-8-74
T-AOT 172 SEALIFT ATLANTIC	26-1-74	26-8-74
T-AOT 173 SEALIFT MEDITERRANEAN	9-3-74	6-11-74
T-AOT 174 SEALIFT CARIBBEAN	8-6-74	10-2-75
T-AOT 175 SEALIFT ARCTIC	31-8-74	22-5-75
T-AOT 176 SEALIFT ANTARCTIC	26-10-74	1-8-75

Sealift Pacific   1974

D: 33,000 tons (fl)	**S:** 16 kts	**Dim:** 178.9 (170.8 pp) × 25.6 × 10.5	
Man: 10 officers, 20 men, 2 cadets	**Range:** 12,000/16	**Fuel:** 3,444 tons	
Electric: 2,600 kw			
M: 2 Colt-Pielstick, 14PC-2V400 14-cyl., 520-rpm diesels; 1 controllable-pitch prop; 14,000 hp			

REMARKS: 17,157 grt/27,217 dwt (vary slightly). Cargo: 225,154 barrels fuel oil, diesel, etc. Equipped with bow-thruster. MSC chartered these ships for twenty years and has a commercial contractor operating them. Equipped with bow-thruster. All redesignated T-AOT on 30-9-78.

◆ **1 American Explorer class (T5-S-RM2A type)**   Bldr: Ingalls SB, Pascagoula, Miss.

	Laid down	L	In serv.
T-AOT 165 AMERICAN EXPLORER	9-7-57	11-5-58	27-10-59

D: 8,400 tons light (31,300 fl)	**S:** 20 kts	**Dim:** 187.5 × 24.4 × 9.8	
Man: 53 men	**Range:** 14,000/20	**Fuel:** 3,482 tons	
M: 1 set GT; 1 prop; 22,000 hp	**Boilers:** 2		

REMARKS: 14,984 grt/24,226 dwt. Cargo: 174,000 bbl. fuel oil, diesel, etc. plus 878 m³ dry cargo. Operated commercially. Retyped AOT on 30-9-78. Similar to *Maumee* class.

◆ **3 Maumee class (T5-S-12A type)**

	Bldr	Laid down	L	In serv.
T-AOT 149 MAUMEE	Ingalls SB	8-3-55	16-2-56	12-12-56
T-AOT 151 SHOSHONE	Sun SB, Chester	15-8-55	17-1-57	15-4-57
T-AOT 152 YUKON	Ingalls SB	16-5-55	16-3-56	17-5-57

D: 32,000 tons (fl)	**S:** 18 kts	**Dim:** 189.0 × 25.5 × 9.8	
Man: 62 men	**Range:** 18,000/18	**Fuel:** 4,321 tons	
M: 1 set GT; 1 prop; 20,460 hp	**Boilers:** 2		

TRANSPORT OILERS (*continued*)

Shoshone

REMARKS: 15,626 grt/26,943 dwt. Cargo: 187,000 bbl. fuel oil, diesel, etc. plus 878 m³ dry cargo. T-AOT-149 has ice-reinforced bow. Sister *Potomac* (T-AO-150, now T-AOT-181) rebuilt to different design. All retyped T-AOT on 30-9-78.

◆ 1 Mission class (T2-SE-A2 type)   Bldr: Marineship, Sausalito, Calif.

	Laid down	L	In serv.
T-AOT 134 MISSION SANTA YNEZ	9-9-43	19-12-43	13-3-44

D: 5,730 tons light (22,380 fl)   **S:** 16.5 kts
Dim: 159.7 (153.3 pp) × 20.7 × 9.4
Man: 52 men   **Range:** 13,000/14.5   **Fuel:** 1,375 tons
Electric: 1,120 kw
Boilers: 2 Babcock & Wilcox, 42.2 kg/cm² pressure—superheat 441°C
M: 1 set GE GT, electric drive; 1 prop; 10,000 hp

REMARKS: 10,461 grt/17,056 dwt. Acquired by the Navy on 22-10-47. Cargo: 16,500 tons liquid (approx. 134,000 bbl.) In reserve since 6-3-75. Retyped T-AOT on 30-9-78.

◆ 6 Suamico class (T2-SE-A1 type)   Bldr: Sun SB & DD, Chester, Pa.

	Laid down	L	In serv.
T-AOT 50 TALLULAH (ex-*Valley Forge*)	. . .	25-6-42	5-9-42
T-AOT 67 CACHE (ex-*Stillwater*)	. . .	7-9-42	3-11-42
T-AOT 73 MILLICOMA (ex-*Conastoga*, ex-*King's Mountain*)	4-8-42	21-1-43	5-3-43
T-AOT 75 SAUGATUCK (ex-*Newton*)	16-9-42	7-7-42	19-2-43
T-AOT 76 SCHUYLKILL (ex-*Louisburg*)	24-9-42	16-2-43	9-4-43
T-AOT 78 CHEPACHET	. . .	10-3-43	27-4-43

D: 5,782 tons light (21,880 fl)   **S:** 15 kts
Dim: 159.7 (153.3 pp) × 20.7 × 9.4
Man: 52 men   **Range:** 13,000/14.5   **Fuel:** 1,375 tons
Electric: 1,100-1,160 kw
Boilers: 2 Babcock & Wilcox, 42.2 kg/cm² pressure—superheat 441°C
M: 1 set GE GT, electric drive; 1 prop; 8,250 hp (T-AOT-67 and T-AOT-75: 1 set Westinghouse GT, electric drive; 1 prop; 6,600 hp)

REMARKS: 10,296 grt/16,500 dwt. Taken over by the Navy while under construction and completed as fleet oilers. Transferred to MSTS (later MSC) in 1949 and operated with civilian crews until placed in the Maritime Administration's reserve fleet between 1972 and 1975. Cargo: 141,000 bbl. All reclassified T-AOT on 30-9-78. T-AOT-78 loaned to U.S. Department of Energy on 9-11-78 for five years for experiments with the OTEC (Ocean Thermal Energy Conversion) concept for electric-power generation;

the ship will be extensively altered and will no longer be capable of acting as a transport oiler.

GASOLINE TANKERS

◆ 2 Alatna class (T1-MET-24a type)   Bldr: Bethlehem, Staten I., NY

	L	In serv.
T-AOG 81 ALATNA	1956	7-57
T-AOG 82 CHATTAHOOCHIE	4-12-56	22-10-57

Alatna

D: 7,300 tons (fl)   **S:** 12 kts   **Dim:** 92.0 × 18.6 × 7.0
Man: 51 men   **Range:** 5,760/10   **Fuel:** 535 tons
M: 4 Alco diesels, Westinghouse electric motors; 2 props; 4,000 hp

REMARKS: 3,459 grt/4,933 dwt. Icebreaker-type hulls; originally intended as Arctic/Antarctic support ships. Cargo: 30,000 bbls. light petroleum products. Both placed in the Maritime Administration's reserve fleet on 8-8-72; reactivated in 1979 to replace T-AOG-77 and T-AOG-79. Were to receive new diesel engines. Small helicopter deck aft.

◆ 1 Peconic class (T1-M-BT2 type)   Bldr: Todd SY, Houston, Texas

	Laid down	L	In ser.
T-AGO 78 NODAWAY (ex-*Tarcoola*)	19-2-45	15-5-45	11-9-50

D: 2,060 tons light (6,083 fl)   **S:** 10 kts   **Dim:** 99.1 × 14.7 × 5.9
Man: 41 men   **Range:** 6,000/10   **Fuel:** 154 tons   **Electric:** 515 kw
M: 2 Nordberg diesels; 1 prop; 1,400 hp

REMARKS: 3,160 grt/3,933 dwt. Cargo: 31,284 bbl. light fuels (diesel, JP-5, gasoline). The *Rincon* (T-AOG-77) and *Petaluma* (T-AOG-79) were stricken in 1979 and 1980 when replaced by the reactivated T-AOG-81 and T-AOG-82.

TRANSPORTS

NOTE: The transports listed below are maintained in the Maritime Administration's reserve fleet but remain the Navy's property, earmarked for the MSC, should the requirement arise. Most were placed in reserve in 1969 and 1970.

TRANSPORTS (continued)

◆ 2 Barrett class (P2-S1-DN3 type)   Bldr: New York SB, Camden, N.J.

	L	In serv.
T-AP 197 GEIGER (ex-*President Adams*)	9-10-50	13-9-52
T-AP 198 UPSHUR (ex-*President Hayes*)	19-1-51	20-12-52

D: 6,720 tons light (17,600 fl)   **S:** 19 kts
Dim: 162.69 (153.3 pp) × 22.33 × 8.26
Man: 219 men   **Range:** 17,000/19   **Fuel:** 3,393 tons
Electric: 2,400 kw
Boilers: 2 Babcock & Wilcox, 43.3 kg/cm² pressure−superheat 454°C
M: 2 sets GE GT; 2 props; 12,500 hp

REMARKS: 13,319 grt/6,934 dwt. Cargo: 1,943 passengers plus 2,719 m³ dry cargo. Sister *Barrett* (ex-T-AP-196) stricken in 7-73.

◆ 5 Admiral class (P2-S2-R1 type)   Bldr: Bethlehem, Alameda, Calif.

	L	In serv.
T-AP 122 GENERAL ALEXANDER M. PATCH (ex-*Admiral R. E. Coontz*)	22-4-44	21-11-44
T-AP 123 GENERAL SIMON B. BUCKNER (ex-*Admiral E. W. Eberle*)	14-6-44	24-1-45
T-AP 125 GENERAL NELSON M. WALKER (ex-*Admiral H. T. Mayo*)	26-11-44	24-4-45
T-AP 126 GENERAL MAURICE ROSE (ex-*Admiral Hugh Rodman*)	25-2-45	10-7-45
T-AP 127 ex-GENERAL WILLIAM O. DARBY (ex-*Admiral W. S. Sims*)	4-6-45	27-9-45

D: 12,657 tons light (22,574 fl)   **S:** 19 kts
Dim: 185.6 (174.65 wl) × 23.01 × 8.07
Man: 319 men   **Range:** 15,000/19   **Fuel:** 3,877 tons
Electric: 2,000 kw
Boilers: 4 Combustion Engineering "D," 42.2 kg/cm² pressure−superheat 449°C
M: 2 sets GE GT, electric drive; 2 props; 18,000 hp

REMARKS: 16,039 grt/9,944 dwt. All operated by the Army Transportation Service until 1-3-50, when transferred to MSTS (later MSC). Active into the late 1960s. Can carry 1,757 troops, 2,889 m³ dry cargo. Sister *Hugh J. Gaffey* (T-AP-121) redesignated IX-507 on 1-11-78 and used as a barracks ship. All could originally carry 5,100 troops. T-AP-127 officially lost her name in 1974 when it was proposed that she become a prison ship. Two others stricken.

◆ 3 General class (P2-S2-R2 type)   Bldr: Federal SB & DD, Kearny, N.J.

	L	In serv.
T-AP 110 GENERAL JOHN POPE	21-3-43	5-8-43
T-AP-117 GENERAL W. H. GORDON	7-5-44	29-6-44
T-AP 119 GENERAL WILLIAM WEIGEL (ex-*General C. H. Barth*)	3-9-44	6-1-45

D: 11,450 tons light (20,700 fl)   **S:** 21 kts   **Dim:** 189.77 × 23.01 × 7.77
Man: . . .   **Range:** 11,000/19   **Fuel:** 3,043 tons   **Electric:** 1,600 kw
Boilers: 4 Foster-Wheeler "D," 32.7 kg/cm² pressure−superheat 407°C
M: 2 sets de Laval GT; 2 props; 17,000 hp

REMARKS: T-AP-110: 17,927 grt/7,479 dwt; others vary. Can carry from 2,154 to 3,825 passengers or troops. One sister sold commercially, seven others stricken.

CABLE SHIPS

◆ 1 new construction   Bldr: National Steel, San Diego, Calif.

	Laid down	L	In serv.
T-ARC 7 N . . .	. . .	. . .	12-82

Authorized: FY 79

D: 8,370 tons light (14,157 fl)   **S:** 15 kts
Dim: 153.2 (138.4 pp) × 22.3 × 7.3
Man: 16 officers, 61 men, 25 technicians   **Range:** 10,000/15

General Alexander M. Patch   1965

T-ARC 7 − artist's rendering   1978

CABLE SHIPS (*continued*)

Electric: 3,500 kw
M: 3 diesels, electric drive; 2 props; 9,000 hp

REMARKS: Ordered in 8-79. Cost $107 million. Will replace T-ARC-3. Second unit no longer programmed. Two bow and two stern thrusters for precision maneuvering. Two 5-ton cranes.

◆ **2 Neptune class (S3-S2-BP1 type)** Bldr: Pusey & Jones, Wilmington, Del.

	L	In serv.
T-ARC 2 NEPTUNE (ex-*Wm. H. G. Bullard*)	1945	1-6-53
T-ARC 6 ALBERT J. MEYER	1945	13-5-63

Neptune   G. Arra, 1975

D: T-ARC-2: 4,960 tons light (7,810 fl); T-ARC-6: 5,030 tons light (7,815 fl)
S: 14 kts   **Dim:** 110.3 (98.1 pp) × 14.3 × 5.5
Man: 74-85 men   **Range:** 7,400/11.5   **Fuel:** 1,031 tons (T-ARC-2: 905 tons)
Boilers: 2 Combustion Engineering
M: 2 Skinner Uniflow, 5-cyl. reciprocating steam; 2 props; 4,340 hp

REMARKS: T-ARC-2: 3,929 grt/2,000 dwt; T-ARC-6: 4,013 grt/4,332 dwt. Differ in detail. Last reciprocating steam-propelled ships in USN/MSC service. T-ARC-2 to MSC from Navy 8-11-73. T-ARC-6 from U.S. Army in 1953. T-ARC-2 has a helicopter deck aft; T-ARC-6 does not. Both have been modernized. T-ARC-2: 112.8-m overall.

◆ **1 Aeolus class** Bldr: Walsh Kaiser, Providence, R.I.

	L	In serv.	Conv.
T-ARC 3 AEOLUS (ex-*Turandot*, AKA-47)	1945	18-6-45	14-5-55

D: 4,283 tons light (7,040 fl)   **S:** 15.5 kts
Dim: 133.5 (121.9 pp) × 17.7 × 4.88

Aeolus—foremast now stepped atop bridge   1970

Man: 86 men   **Range:** 9,700/14   **Fuel:** 1,247 tons
Boilers: 2 sets Westinghouse GT, electric drive; 2 props; 6,000 hp
M: 2 sets Westinghouse GT, electric drive; 2 props; 6,000 hp

REMARKS: 6,064 grt/2,757 dwt. S4-SE2-BE1 attack cargo ship converted by Bethlehem Steel to a cable-layer 1955-56. Sister *Thor* (T-ARC-4) stricken on 17-7-75. T-ARC-3 is in poor condition but must be retained until T-ARC-7 is completed.

FLEET TUGS

◆ **7 Powhatan class** Bldr: Marinette Marine, Wisc.

	Laid down	L	In serv.
T-ATF 166 POWHATAN	30-9-76	24-6-78	15-6-79
T-ATF 167 NARRAGANSETT	5-5-77	12-5-79	31-10-79
T-ATF 168 CATAWBA	14-12-77	22-9-79	5-80
T-ATF 169 NAVAJO	14-12-77	12-79	8-80
T-ATF 170 MOHAWK	22-3-79	1-80	9-80
T-ATF 171 SIOUX	22-3-79	6-80	11-80
T-ATF 172 APACHE	22-3-79	11-80	81

Authorized: 1 in FY 75, 3 in FY 76, 3 in FY 78

Powhatan   1979

FLEET TUGS (continued)

D: 2,000 tons (2,400 fl) **S:** 15 kts **Dim:** 73.2 (68.9 pp) × 12.8 × 4.6
Man: 4 officers, 12 men + 4 Navy communications team **Range:** 10,000/15
M: 2 GM diesels; 2 Kort-nozzle, controllable-pitch props; 4,500 hp
Fuel: 600 tons

REMARKS: Modified oilfield-supply-boat design built to merchant marine specifications. If required, could mount two 20-mm AA (I × 2) and two 12.7-mm machine guns (I × 2). Five were requested under FY 78, three approved. Have a 300-hp bow thruster and one 10-ton electrohydraulic crane. This class has been subjected to serious delays because of a strike at the shipyard. No additional units are planned despite dwindling number of U.S. Navy tugs. Consideration has been given to chartering commercial tugs.

◆ **4 Cherokee and Achomawi class** Bldrs: T-ATF-76 and T-ATF-85: United Eng., Alameda, Calif; others: Charleston SB, S.C.

	Laid down	L	In serv.
T-ATF 76 UTE	27-2-42	24-6-42	31-12-42
T-ATF 85 LIPAN	30-5-42	17-9-42	29-4-43
T-ATF 149 ATAKAPA	17-2-44	11-7-44	8-12-44
T-ATF 158 MOSOPELIA	2-1-45	7-3-45	28-7-45

Atakapa—in Navy service   PH1 R. Varney, 1971

D: 1,235 tons (1,675 fl) **S:** 16.5 kts **Dim:** 62.48 (59.44 wl) × 11.73 × 4.67
Man: 34 men + 6 Navy communications team **Range:** 7,000/15, 15,000/8
Fuel: 363 tons (T-ATF-76: 300)
Electron Equipt: Radar: 1/SPS-53 **Electric:** 400 kw
M: 4 GM 12-278A (T-ATF-76 and T-ATF-85: 12-278) diesels, electric drive; 1 prop; 3,000 hp

REMARKS: T-ATF-85 and T-ATF-158 to MSC in 7-73; the others in mid-1974. T-ATF-76 and T-ATF-85 are to be stricken before 30-9-80. All have large stacks. Six sisters remain in Navy service.

MSC COMMERCIAL FLEET

In addition to the government-owned ships listed in detail above, the Military Sealift Command must also charter a large number of merchant ships in order to meet its transportation and other obligations. In December 1978, this chartered fleet comprised no less than thirty-two ships, two of which were even under foreign (Panamanian) registry. Under charter were twenty-five cargo ships, five tankers, and two scientific-support ships—all manned by contractor personnel. In addition the MSC is responsible for six Strategic Petroleum Reserve special tanker charters.

NOTE: In addition to the ships listed above for the U.S. Navy and Military Sealift Command, there exist several hundred former naval ships, ranging from aircraft carriers and cruisers to auxiliaries and yard craft, which have been officially stricken but not yet scrapped or otherwise disposed of. Although many might be recalled to service in an emergency, listing them is beyond the scope of this book.

COAST GUARD

GENERAL

The Revenue Marine, which was created in 1790, became the Coast Guard on 28 January 1915 by act of Congress. Until 1 April 1967 the Coast Guard was part of the Department of the Treasury; at that time it was transferred to the Department of Transportation. The act that created the service calls for it to operate in time of crisis under the control of the Navy. The principal responsibilities of the Coast Guard are:
—preparation and training for combat in cooperation with the Navy;
—enforcement of the laws of the sea and the policing of navigation;
—control of territorial waters, suppression of smuggling, and policing and assisting the fishing industry;
—surveillance of the coasts and protection of access to ports and bases;
—search and rescue at sea, including transocean air routes;
—manning and maintaining aids to navigation: lighthouses, beacons, buoys, lightships, and Loran stations (46,000 in all);
—control of piloting and the investigation of accidents at sea;
—control of the safety and seaworthiness aspects of shipbuilding;
—international ice patrols (keeping track of drifting icebergs);
—protection of offshore oil installations;
—pollution control and protection of the environment;
—meteorologic, oceanographic, and hydrographic surveying.
The Coast Guard played an active part in the war in Vietnam (patrolling the coasts, inspecting junks, protecting convoys, port security, maritime salvage, and shore fire support).

ORGANIZATION

The Coast Guard is divided into two main components, one for the Pacific and one for the Atlantic. Each of these area commands is headed by a rear admiral. Just as the Navy is divided into Naval Districts, the Coast Guard is further divided into twelve Coast Guard Districts in order to fulfill its responsibilities along the U.S. coastline (more than 10,000 nautical miles, not including Hawaii).

A four-star admiral heads the Coast Guard. He is appointed for four years and is assisted by a general staff, whose headquarters are in the Department of Transportation building. The Commandant reports to the Secretary of Transportation and not the Joint Chiefs of Staff.

COMPOSITION OF THE FLEET

Coast Guard patrol ships have their names preceded by USCGC (United States Coast Guard Cutter). Cutters and patrol craft are white, icebreakers have red hulls, buoy tenders, black. All ships and craft carry a diagonal red stripe and the USCG shield on the hull.

As of 1-1-80 the in-service, seagoing USCG fleet was composed of the following:

◆ **9 high-endurance cutters (WHEC):**

12 *Hamilton* class, 3,050 tons (fl)
5 *Secretary* class, 2,656 tons (fl) (1 in reserve)
1 *Casco* class, 2,800 tons (fl)

◆ **23 medium-endurance cutters (WMEC)** from 860 to 1,745 tons (fl)

◆ **6 icebreakers (WAGB)**

◆ **23 patrol boats (WPB)**, 105-tons (fl)

◆ **53 Point-class patrol boats,** 67 to 69 tons (fl)

◆ **29 tugs (WYTM and WYTL)**

◆ **3 oceanographic research ships (WAGO)**

◆ **50 seagoing buoy tenders (WLB and WLM)**

◆ **1 officer training ship (WIX)**

◆ **1 reserve training ship (WTR)**

◆ **3 lightships (WLV)**

A program to rejuvenate the Coast Guard so that it will be able to meet its new commitments covers the period 1977-1986 and includes plans to build from eleven to twenty-five *Bear*-class medium-endurance cutters and ten *Katmai Bay*-class icebreaking tugs. Plans to build up to thirty 33-meter patrol boats have been postponed in favor of modernizing the Cape class.

AVIATION

As of 1-1-79, the Coast Guard operated 55 fixed-wing aircraft, which included:
25 HC-130 Hercules long-range search and rescue aircraft
17 HC-131 Convair twin-engined turboprop transports transferred in 1977 and 1978 from the U.S. Air Force's reserve stocks for use in patrolling the 200-nautical-mile economic zone
11 HU-16 Albatross amphibians for patrol and rescue duties
1 Grumman VC-4A Gulfstream-I as a personnel (VIP) transport
1 Grumman VC-11A Gulfstream-II as a personnel (VIP) transport
Helicopters in use included:
38 HH-3F Pelican for rescue duties
80 HH-52A Sea Guard for rescue duties
The dwindling number of HU-16 Albatross and the aged HC-131 are to be replaced by forty-one HU-25 Falcon-20G twin-jet patrol aircraft, ordered in 1-77; a version of the Dassault Mystère-20, the first of these new aircraft was scheduled for delivery in 1980. In 6-79, ninety Aerospatiale SA-366N SRR (Short-Range Recovery) helicopters were ordered from France; these will be powered by U.S.-built Lycoming LTS 101-700 turboshaft engines and will replace the HH-52A helicopters.

USCG HG-130 Hercules

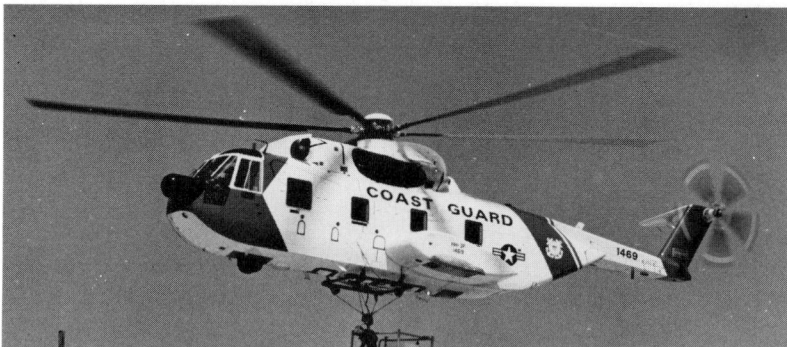

USCG HH-3F Pelican

USCG HH-52A Sea Guard

HIGH-ENDURANCE CUTTERS

◆ **12 Hamilton class (378-ft class)** Bldr: Avondale SY, Westwego, La.

	Laid down	L	In serv.
WHEC 715 HAMILTON	1-65	18-12-65	20-2-67
WHEC 716 DALLAS	7-2-66	1-10-66	1-10-67
WHEC 717 MELLON	25-7-66	11-2-67	22-12-67
WHEC 718 CHASE	15-10-66	20-5-67	1-3-68
WHEC 719 BOUTWELL	12-12-66	17-6-67	14-6-68
WHEC 720 SHERMAN	13-2-67	23-9-67	23-8-68
WHEC 721 GALLATIN	17-4-67	18-11-67	20-12-68
WHEC 722 MORGENTHAU	17-7-67	10-2-68	14-2-69
WHEC 723 RUSH	23-10-67	16-11-68	3-7-69
WHEC 724 MUNRO	18-2-70	5-12-70	10-9-71
WHEC 725 JARVIS	9-9-70	24-4-71	30-12-71
WHEC 726 MIDGETT	5-4-71	4-9-71	17-3-72

Morgenthau　　　　　　　　　　　　　A. Baker, 1976

Gallatin　　　　　　　　　　　　　J. Jedrlinic, 1979

D: 2,716 tons (3,050 fl)　　**S:** 29 kts

Dim: 115.37 (106.68 pp) × 13.06 × 4.27 (6.2 over sonar)

Man: 15 officers, 149 men　　**Range:** 2,400/29, 9,600/19 on gas turbines

A: 1/127-mm 38-cal. DP−2/40-mm Mk-64 grenade launchers (I × 2)−2/20-mm AA (I × 2)−6/324-mm Mk-32 ASW TT (III × 2)−1/HH-52A helicopter

Electron Equipt:　Radars:　1/SPS-53 navigational, 1/SPS-64 surface-search, 1/SPS-29 air-search, 1/Mk-35

　　　　　　　　　Sonar:　SQS-38

Electric: 1,500 kw　　**Fuel:** 800 tons

M: CODOG: 2 Fairbanks-Morse 38TD⅛, 12-cyl. diesels, 3,500 hp each; 2 Pratt & Whitney FT4-A6 gas turbines, 18,000 hp each; 2 controllable-pitch props, 36,000 hp

REMARKS: A single, 1.20-m-diameter, 360-degree trainable bow propeller linked to a 350-hp electric motor, used for close-quarters maneuvering at slow speeds, retracts into the hull. Bilge keels. Helicopter platform, 26.82 × 12.2; weather-balloon shelter at forward end of flight deck is used as a helicopter shop/storage area. Living spaces air-conditioned. Laboratories for weather and oceanographic research. Welded hull; aluminum superstructure. Named after secretaries of the treasury and Coast Guard

Boutwell　　　　　　　　　　　　　1972

heroes. Thirty-six planned, only twelve built. Mk-56 radar gunfire-control director and Mk-309 ASW fire-control system installed. There are plans to replace the 127-mm gun and Mk-56 gunfire-control system with a 76-mm Mk-75 (OTO Melara Compact) gun and Mk-92 radar gunfire-control system, and to add one 20-mm Vulcan-Phalanx Gatling AA gun and eight Harpoon SSM (IV × 2). The grenade launchers have replaced the 81-mm mortars formerly carried. The helicopter hangars have been blanked off in several.

HIGH-ENDURANCE CUTTERS (*continued*)

◆ **6 Secretary class (327-ft class)**

	Bldr	Laid down	L	In serv.
WHEC 31 BIBB	Charleston NSY	15-8-35	14-1-37	19-3-37
WHEC 32 CAMPBELL	Philadelphia NSY	1-5-35	3-6-36	22-10-36
WHEC 33 DUANE	Philadelphia NSY	1-5-35	3-6-36	16-10-36
WHEC 35 INGHAM	Philadelphia NSY	1-5-35	3-6-36	6-11-36
WHEC 36 SPENCER	New York NSY	11-9-35	6-1-37	13-5-37
WHEC 37 TANEY	Philadelphia NSY	1-5-35	3-6-36	24-10-36

Taney—with weather radar   1973

Duane   1979

D: 2,216 tons (2,656 fl)   **S:** 19.8 kts   **Dim:** 99.67 (93.88 wl) × 12.55 × 4.57
Man: 13 officers, 131 men   **Range:** 4,000/19.8, 8,000/10.5   **Fuel:** 572 tons
A: 1/127-mm 38-cal. DP—2/40-mm Mk-64 grenade launchers (I × 2)
Electron Equipt: Radars: 1/SPS-64, 1/SPS-29 (not in WHEC-35)
Boilers: 2 Babcock & Wilcox, 28.2 kg/cm² pressure
M: 2 sets Westinghouse GT; 2 props; 6,200 hp

REMARKS: WHEC-36 has been in reserve since 1-2-74; she is used as a stationary engineering training ship at the Coast Guard Yard, Curtis Bay, Md. WHEC-37 has a dome above her bridge for WSR-S1 weather radar, while WHEC-35 has an egg-shaped radome in place of the antenna for SPS-29 on the after mast. All gunfire-control and ASW equipment removed.

◆ **5 Owasco class (255-ft class)**   Bldr: Western Pipe & Steel, San Pedro, Calif. (WHEC-69 and WHEC-70: Coast Guard Yard, Curtis Bay, Md.)

	Laid down	L	In serv.
WHEC 41 CHAUTAUQUA	22-12-43	15-5-44	4-4-45
WHEC 65 WINONA	8-11-44	22-4-45	15-8-46
WHEC 67 MINNETONKA (ex-*Sunapee*)	22-12-44	21-11-45	20-9-46
WHEC 69 MENDOTA	1-6-43	29-2-44	2-6-46
WHEC 70 PONTCHARTRAIN (ex-*Okeechobee*)	1-7-43	29-4-44	28-7-45

D: 1,563 tons (1,913 fl)   **S:** 18.4 kts   **Dim:** 77.42 × 13.11 × 5.18 (max.)
Man: 12 officers, 127 men   **Range:** 6,000/18.4, 12,000/10
A: 1/127-mm 38-cal. DP   **Electron Equipt:** Radars: 1/SPS-53, 1/SPS-29
Boilers: 2 Foster-Wheeler, 44.7 kg/cm² pressure—superheat 399°C
M: 1 set Westinghouse GT, electric drive; 1 prop; 4,000 hp

REMARKS: In reserve: WHEC-41, WHEC-69, WHEC-70 at Baltimore, Md., and WHEC-65 and WHEC-67 at Alameda, Calif. Survivors of a class of thirteen. Not a very successful design and unlikely to see further service. All ASW equipment removed.

◆ **1 Casco class (311-ft class)**   Bldr: Associated SB, Seattle

	Laid down	L	In serv.
WHEC 379 UNIMAK (ex-WTR, ex-WHEC, ex-AVP-31)	12-2-42	27-5-43	31-12-43

D: 1,766 tons (2,800 fl)   **S:** 17 kts   **Dim:** 94.7 × 12.52 × 3.65
Man: 13 officers, 137 men   **Range:** 8,000/17, 20,000/10   **Fuel:** 400 tons
A: 1/127-mm 38-cal. DP—2/40-mm Mk-64 grenade launchers (I × 2)
Electron Equipt: Radar: 1/SPS-64   **Electric:** 600 kw
M: 4 Fairbanks-Morse 38D8⅛ diesels; 2 props; 6,080 hp

REMARKS: The last of a series of small seaplane tenders (AVP), eighteen of which were transferred to the Coast Guard, 1947-48; seven were given to South Vietnam beginning in 1970, and eight have been taken out of service since 1968. WHEC-379 was a training ship from 11-69 until placed in reserve on 30-5-75. She was recommissioned on 15-8-77 for patrol duties in the 200-nautical-mile economic zone. Gunfire-control and ASW systems have been removed.

MEDIUM-ENDURANCE CUTTERS

◆ **9 (+ 7) Bear class (270-ft class)**

	Bldr	Laid down	L	In serv.
WMEC 901 BEAR	Tacoma Boatbldg.	23-8-79	5-80	81
WMEC 902 TAMPA	Tacoma Boatbldg.	5-80	81	81
WMEC 903 HARRIET LANE	Tacoma Boatbldg.	9-80	81	82
WMEC 904 NORTHLAND	Tacoma Boatbldg.	81	81	82
WMEC 905 SENECA	...	...	...	...
WMEC 906 PICKERING	...	...	...	...
WMEC 907 ESCABANA	...	...	...	...
WMEC 908 LEGARE	...	...	...	...
WMEC 909 ARGUS	...	...	...	...
WMEC 910 TAHOMA	...	...	...	...
WMEC 911 ERIE	...	...	...	...
UMEC 912 McCULLOCH	...	...	...	...

MEDIUM-ENDURANCE CUTTERS (*continued*)

WMEC 913 EWING	...	...	...	...	...
WMEC 914 N ...	...	...	...	...	...
WMEC 915 N ...	...	...	...	...	...
WMEC 916 N ...	...	...	...	...	...

Authorized: 4 in FY 77, 2 in FY 79, 3 in FY 80
To be requested: 2 in FY 81, 2 in FY 83, 2 in FY 84

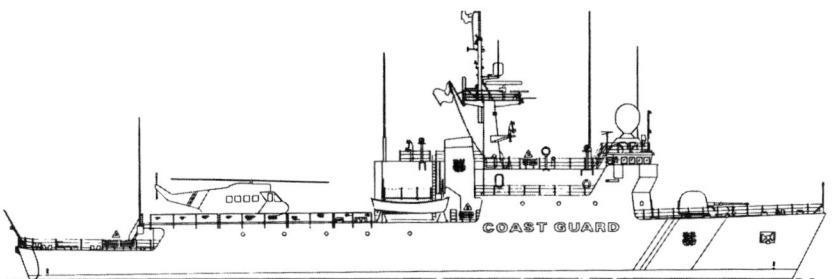

Bear class   J. J. Henry Co., 1978

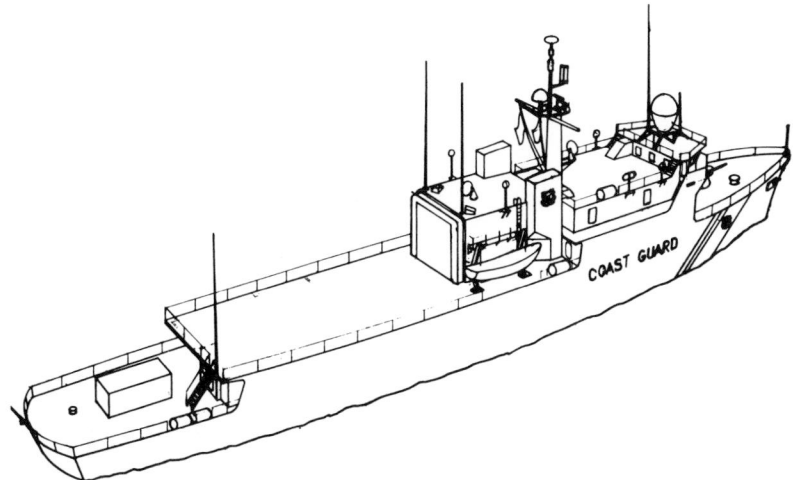

Bear class   1977

D: 1,728 tons (fl)   **S:** 19.7 kts   **Dim:** 82.3 × 11.58 × 4.11
Man: 15 officers, 94 men   **Range:** 6,800/13.5
A: 1/76-mm Mk-75 DP – 1/HH-52A or LAMPS-III helicopter
Electron Equipt: Radars: 1/navigational, 1/Mk-92 fire-control
               Sonar: Provision for SQR-19A TASS
               ECM: SLQ-32(v)1, 4/Mk-36 Super RBOC chaff
M: 2 Fairbanks-Morse diesels; 2 controllable-pitch props; 7,000 hp

REMARKS: Names listed will be used as ships are authorized. Intended to be able to act as ASW escorts in wartime, using LAMPS-III ASW helicopter. No hull-mounted sonar or on-board ASW weapons. Space and weight reserved for Vulcan-Phalanx 20-mm Gatling AA gun and two quadruple Harpoon missile-launch canisters. Satellite-communications system will be carried. Can carry van-mounted towed passive sonar array on fantail. Telescoping hangar, fin stabilization. This entire program is much behind schedule, the first unit originally having been planned to complete on 28-11-80. As many as nine additional units are planned.

◆ **16 Reliance class (210-ft A* and 210-ft B class)**

	Bldr	L	In serv.
WTR 615 RELIANCE*	1	25-5-63	20-6-64
WMEC 616 DILIGENCE*	1	20-7-63	26-8-64
WMEC 617 VIGILANT*	1	24-12-63	3-10-64
WMEC 618 ACTIVE*	2	31-7-65	17-9-66
WMEC 619 CONFIDENCE*	3	8-5-65	19-2-66
WMEC 620 RESOLUTE	3	30-4-66	8-12-66
WMEC 621 VALIANT	4	14-1-67	28-10-67
WMEC 622 COURAGEOUS	4	18-5-67	10-4-68
WMEC 623 STEADFAST	4	24-6-67	25-9-68
WMEC 624 DAUNTLESS	4	21-10-67	10-6-68
WMEC 625 VENTUROUS	4	11-11-67	16-8-68
WMEC 626 DEPENDABLE	4	16-3-68	27-11-68
WMEC 627 VIGOROUS	4	4-5-68	2-5-69
WMEC 628 DURABLE	3	29-4-67	8-12-67
WMEC 629 DECISIVE	3	14-12-67	23-8-68
WMEC 630 ALERT	3	19-10-68	4-8-69

Bldrs: 1. Todd Shipyards – 2. Christy Corp., Sturgeon Bay, Wis. – 3. Coast Guard SY, Curtis Bay, Md. – 4. American SB, Lorain, Ohio.

D: 759 tons (993* or 1,007 fl)   **S:** 18 kts
Dim: 64.16 (60.96 pp) × 10.36 × 3.2

Dauntless – with HH-52A helicopter   1972

MEDIUM-ENDURANCE CUTTERS (*continued*)

Man: 7 officers, 54 men   **Range:** 2,700/18, 6,100/14 (*: 2,100/18, 6,100/13)

A: 1/76.2-mm Mk-22 DP—2/40-mm Mk-64 grenade launchers (I × 2)—1/HH-52A helicopter

Electron Equipt: Radars: 2/navigational   **Endurance:** 15 days

Electric: 500 kw

M: 2 Alco 251B 16-cyl. diesels, 2,500 hp each; 2 controllable-pitch props; (WTR-615 to WMEC-619: CODAG: 2 Solar-Saturn T-1000S gas turbines, 1,000 hp each, and 2 Cooper-Bessemer FVBM12-T diesels, 1,500 hp each; 2 controllable-pitch props; 5,000 hp)

REMARKS: WTR-615 replaced WHEC-379 as reserve training cutter in 1974; she retains full WMEC capabilities. CODAG propulsion in WTR-615 to WMEC-619; not installed in the others because it provided no speed advantage, despite the extra horsepower, and it cut the endurance; the engines exhaust through the stern. No hangar. Designed to operate up to 500 miles off the coast. High superstructure permits 360-degree visibility. Can tow a 10,000-ton ship. Air-conditioned. The 76.2-mm single-fire gun is to be replaced by two 20-mm AA (I × 2).

◆ **2 Diver class (213-ft class)**   Bldr: Basalt Rock Co., Napa, Calif.

	Laid down	L	In serv.
WMEC 167 ACUSHNET (ex-WAGO-167, ex-WAT-167, ex-*Shackle*, ARS-9)	26-10-42	1-4-43	6-2-44
WMEC 168 YOCONA (ex-WAT-168, ex-*Seize*, ARS-26)	28-9-43	8-4-44	3-11-44

Acushnet   1975

D: 1,557 tons (1,745 fl)   **S:** 15.5 kts   **Dim:** 65.08 (63.09 wl) × 12.5 × 4.57

Man: 7 officers, 65 men   **Range:** 9,000/15.5, 20,000/7   **Fuel:** 300 tons

A: None   **Electron Equipt:** Radars: 2/SPS-53   **Electric:** 460 kw

M: 4 Cooper-Bessemer GSB-8 diesels, electric drive; 2 props; 3,000 hp

REMARKS: Former salvage ships, taken over from the Navy in 1946. WMEC-167 served as WAGO-167 from 1968 to 1978, then retyped WMEC. WMEC-168 has a small tripod mast atop the pilothouse and a tall mainmast just forward of the stack.

◆ **2 Sotoyomo class (143-ft class)**   Bldrs: WMEC-194: Levingston SB, Orange, Texas; WMEC-202: Gulfport Boiler, Port Arthur, Texas

	Laid down	L	In serv.
WMEC 194 MODOC (ex-*Bagaduce*, ATA-194)	7-11-44	4-12-44	14-2-45
WMEC 202 COMANCHE (ex-*Wampanoag*, ATA-202)	24-8-44	10-10-44	8-12-44

Comanche   1969

D: 534 tons (860 fl)   **S:** 13.5 kts   **Dim:** 43.59 × 10.31 × 4.27

Man: 5 officers, 42 men   **Range:** 7,300/13.5, 12,000/8.5   **Fuel:** 178 tons

A: 2/40-mm Mk-64 grenade launchers (I × 2)   **Electric:** 120 kw

Electron Equipt: Radar: 1/SPS-53

M: 2 GM 12-278A diesels, electric drive; 1 prop; 1,500 hp

REMARKS: Former auxiliary ocean tugs. WMEC-194 to the Coast Guard from the Maritime Commission on 15-4-59; WMEC-202 from the Navy on loan on 25-2-59, and permanently on 1-6-69.

◆ **1 Storis class (230-ft class)**   Bldr: Toledo SB, Toledo, Ohio

	Laid down	L	In serv.
WMEC 38 STORIS (ex-*Eskimo*)	14-7-41	4-4-42	30-9-42

Storis   1971

MEDIUM-ENDURANCE CUTTERS (*continued*)

D: 1,715 tons (1,925 fl) **S:** 14 kts **Dim:** 70.1 × 13.1 × 4.6
A: 1/76.2-mm Mk-22 DP **Man:** 10 officers, 96 men
Range: 12,000/14, 22,000/8
M: 2 diesels, electric drive; 1 prop; 1,800 hp

REMARKS: Rated as WAG until 1966, and WAGB until 1-7-72, when she was retyped WMEC. Resembles a *Balsam*-class buoy tender, but is larger. Has an icebreaker hull but is no longer considered capable of acting as such. The 76.2-mm gun aft is to be removed.

◆ 3 Cherokee and Achomawi class (205-ft class)

	Bldr	Laid down	L	In serv.
WMEC 153 CHILULA (ex-ATF-153)	Charleston SB	13-7-44	1-12-44	5-4-45
WMEC 165 CHEROKEE (ex-ATF-66)	Bethlehem, Staten I.	23-12-38	10-11-39	26-4-40
WMEC 166 TAMAROA (ex-*Zuni*, ATF-95)	Commercial Iron Works, Portland, Oregon	8-3-43	13-7-43	9-10-43

Tamaroa   R. Scheina, 1979

D: 1,235 tons (1,731 fl) **S:** 16.2 kts
Dim: 62.48 (59.44 pp) × 11.73 × 5.18
Man: 7 officers, 65 men **Range:** 6,500/16.2, 15,000/8 **Fuel:** 315 tons
A: 1/76.2-mm Mk-22 DP **Electron Equipt:** Radars: 2/navigational
M: 4 GM 12-278 diesels, electric drive; 1 prop; 3,000 hp **Electric:** 260 kw

REMARKS: WMEC-165 and WMEC-166 were the first and last of their numerous class to be built; WMEC-153 is one of a later version that has similar appearance but her diesels are GM 12-278A. The 76.2-mm gun is to be removed. Former U.S. Navy fleet tugs loaned to the Coast Guard in 1946 and transferred outright on 1-6-69.

ICEBREAKERS

◆ 2 Polar Star class (399-ft class) Bldr: Lockheed SB, Seattle

	Laid down	L	In serv.
WAGB 10 POLAR STAR	15-5-72	17-11-73	19-1-76
WAGB 11 POLAR SEA	27-11-73	24-6-75	23-2-78

Polar Star   1978

Polar Sea and Polar Star   1978

D: 10,863 tons (12,087 fl) **S:** 18 kts
Dim: 121.91 (102.78 pp) × 25.45 × 1.14
Man: 13 officers, 125 men, 10 scientists **Range:** 16,000/18, 28,275/13
Fuel: 3,555 tons
M: CODAG; 6 Alco 16V-251 diesels, 3,000 hp each; 3 Pratt & Whitney FT-4A12 gas turbines, 25,000 hp each, down-rated; electric drive; 3 controllable-pitch props; 66,000 hp

REMARKS: No additional units planned. Carry two HH-52A helicopters, painted red. Can break 2-meter ice at 3 knots, 6.4-meter ice maximum. Propulsion plant completely

ICEBREAKERS (continued)

cross-connected and automatic. Two 15-ton cranes. Four 20-mm AA (I × 4) and two 40-mm Mk-64 grenade launchers (I × 2) can be installed. Both homeported at Seattle.

◆ **1 Glacier class (310-ft class)**   Bldr: Ingalls SB, Pascagoula, Miss.

	Laid down	L	In serv.
WAGB 4 GLACIER	3-8-53	27-8-54	27-5-55

Glacier   1972

D: 5,100 tons (8,449 fl)   **S:** 17.6 kts   **Dim:** 94.5 (88.4 pp) × 22.6 × 8.8
Man: 14 officers, 215 men   **Range:** 12,000/17.6, 29,000/12
A: 2/40-mm Mk-64 grenade launchers (I × 2)−2/HH-52A helicopters
Electron Equipt: Radar: SPS-53
M: Diesel-electric propulsion; 10 Fairbanks-Morse 38-D8⅛ diesels and 2 Westinghouse electric motor-generators; 21,000 hp

REMARKS: Built for the U.S. Navy and transferred to the Coast Guard on 1-7-66. SPS-6 air-search radar, carried atop mast, believed removed. Guns removed. Two 12.5-ton cranes.

◆ **2 Wind class (269-ft class)**   Bldr: Western Pipe & Steel, San Pedro, Calif.

	Laid down	L	In serv.
WAGB 281 WESTWIND (ex-AGB-6, ex-*Severniy Polyus*)	24-8-42	31-3-43	18-9-44
WAGB 282 NORTHWIND	10-7-44	22-2-45	28-7-45

D: 3,500 tons (6,515 fl)   **S:** 16 kts   **Dim:** 81.99 (76.2 pp) × 19.36 × 8.84
Man: 135 men   **Range:** 16,000/16, 38,000/10.5   **Electric:** 400 kw
M: 4 Enterprise diesels, electric drive; 2 props; 10,000 hp

REMARKS: Can make way in 2.7-m ice. Double hull entirely welded. Telescoping hangar of alloy metal; one HH-52A helicopter can be carried. Both reengined 1973-75. SPS-6 radar atop bridge probably removed. Two 12.5-ton cranes. WAGB-281, which was in the Soviet Navy from 31-3-45 to 6-12-51, is on the Great Lakes. Five sisters stricken, including the *Burton Island* (WAGB-283) on 9-5-78.

Westwind   1974

◆ **1 Mackinaw class (290-ft class)**   Bldr: Toledo SB, Toledo, Ohio

	Laid down	L	In serv.
WAGB 83 MACKINAW (ex-*Manitowoc*)	20-3-43	4-3-44	20-12-44

Mackinaw−now has red hull   1971

D: 5,252 tons (fl)   **S:** 18.7 kts   **Dim:** 88.39 × 22.66 × 5.79
Man: 10 officers, 117 men   **Range:** 10,000/18.7, 41,000/9
M: 4 Fairbanks-Morse 38D8⅛ diesels, electric drive; 3 props (2 aft, 1 fwd); 10,000 hp

REMARKS: Built for use on the Great Lakes. Helicopter platform. Fitted with two 12-ton cranes. Can break 1.2-m solid ice and 11-m broken ice.

PATRIL CRAFT

PATROL CRAFT

◆ **25 95-ft Cape class** Bldr: Coast Guard Yard, Curtis Bay, Md., 1953-59

WPB 95300 CAPE SMALL	WPB 95314 CAPE FAIRWEATHER
WPB 95301 CAPE CORAL	WPB 95316 CAPE FOX
WPB 95302 CAPE HIGGON	WPB 95317 CAPE JELLISON
WPB 95304 CAPE GULL	WPB 95318 CAPE NEWAGEN
WPB 95305 CAPE HATTERAS	WPB 95319 CAPE ROMAIN
WPB 95306 CAPE GEORGE	WPB 95320 CAPE STARR
WPB 95307 CAPE CURRENT	WPB 95321 CAPE CROSS
WPB 95308 CAPE STRAIT	WPB 95322 CAPE HORN
WPB 95309 CAPE CARTER	WPB 95324 CAPE SHOALWATER
WPB 95310 CAPE WASH	WPB 95326 CAPE CORWIN
WPB 95311 CAPE HEDGE	WPB 95328 CAPE HENLOPEN
WPB 95312 CAPE KNOX	WPB 95332 CAPE YORK
WPB 95313 CAPE MORGAN	

Cape Strait   J. Jedrlinic, 1979

D: 105 tons (fl)   **S:** 18 kts (cruising, fl)   **Dim:** 28.95 × 6.1 × 1.55
A: 2/40-mm Mk-64 grenade launchers (I × 2)   **Man:** 1 officer, 13 men
Range: WPB-95300 to WPB-95311: 460/20, 2,600/9; WPB-95312 to WPB-95320: 460/20, 3,000/9; WPB-95321 to WPB-95332: 500/20, 2,800/9
M: 4 Cummins VT-12-M diesels; 2 props; 2,324 hp   **Electric:** 40 kw

REMARKS: Two transferred to Haiti (1956), two to Ethiopia (1958), four to Thailand, and one to Saudi Arabia. Nine were given to South Korea (1969-70). Several others have been scrapped. Twenty-three of those remaining are being reengined and rehabilitated, 1977-81, in lieu of building thirty new WPBs. WPB-95302 and WPB-95305 are out of service, being held for modernization.

NOTE: The hydrofoil *Flagstaff* (WPGH-1), transferred by the Navy to the Coast Guard on 29-9-76, was stricken on 18-9-78.

◆ **53 83-ft Point class** Bldr: Coast Guard Yard, Curtis Bay, Md. (except WPB-82345 to WPB-82349: J. Martinac SB, Takoma, Wash.)

In serv: WPB-82302 to WPB-82314: 1960-61; WPB-82318 to WPH-82370: 1961-67; WPB-82371 to WPB-82379: 1970

WPB 82302 POINT HOPE	WPB 82354 POINT EVANS
WPB 82311 POINT VERDE	WPB 82355 POINT HANNON
WPB 82312 POINT SWIFT	WPB 82356 POINT FRANCIS
WPB 82314 POINT THATCHER	WPB 82357 POINT HURON
WPB 82318 POINT HERRON	WPB 82358 POINT STUART
WPB 82332 POINT ROBERTS	WPB 82359 POINT STEELE
WPB 82333 POINT HIGHLAND	WPB 82360 POINT WINSLOW
WPB 82334 POINT LEDGE	WPB 82361 POINT CHARLES
WPB 82335 POINT COUNTESS	WPB 82362 POINT BROWN
WPB 82336 POINT GLASS	WPB 82363 POINT NOWELL
WPB 82337 POINT DIVIDE	WPB 82364 POINT WHITEHORN
WPB 82338 POINT BRIDGE	WPB 82365 POINT TURNER
WPB 82339 POINT CHICO	WPB 82366 POINT LOBOS
WPB 82340 POINT BATAN	WPB 82367 POINT KNOLL
WPB 82341 POINT LOOKOUT	WPB 82368 POINT WARDE
WPB 82342 POINT BAKER	WPB 82369 POINT HEYER
WPB 82343 POINT WELLS	WPB 82370 POINT RICHMOND
WPB 82344 POINT ESTERO	WPB 82371 POINT BARNES
WPB 82345 POINT JUDITH	WPB 82372 POINT BROWER
WPB 82346 POINT ARENA	WPB 82373 POINT CAMDEN
WPB 82347 POINT BONITA	WPB 82374 POINT CARREW
WPB 82348 POINT BARROW	WPB 82375 POINT DORAN
WPB 82349 POINT SPENCER	WPB 82376 POINT HARRIS
WPB 82350 POINT FRANKLIN	WPB 82377 POINT HOBART
WPB 82351 POINT BENNETT	WPB 82378 POINT JACKSON
WPB 82352 POINT SAL	WPB 82379 POINT MARTIN
WPB 82353 POINT MONROE	

Point Huron   G. Arra, 1976

D: 64 tons (67-69 fl)   **S:** 23.7 kts (*see* Remarks)   **Dim:** 25.3 × 5.23 × 1.95
Man: 1 officer, 7 men   **Range:** 460/23.7, 1,400-1,500/8-9
A: 2/40-mm Mk-64 grenade launchers (I × 2) or none
M: 2 Cummins VT-12-M diesels; 2 props; 1,600 hp

REMARKS: Hull in mild steel. High-speed diesels controlled from the bridge. The heavier WPB-82371 and later make 22.6 knots, and have a range of 320/22.6, 1,200/8. WPB-82314 had two gas turbines with 1,000 hp (27-knot potential) and controllable-pitch propellers, but was again equipped with diesels. Well equipped for salvage and towing. Beginning in 6-65, twenty-six were sent to Vietnam.

OCEANOGRAPHIC CUTTERS

◆ **1 Balsam class (180-ft class)**

WAGO 295 EVERGREEN (ex-WLB-295)

Evergreen   1973

REMARKS: Data as for *Balsam*-class buoy tenders. Built in 1944. Reconstruction for
service as an oceanographic research ship completed in 2-73. Equipped with COGLAD
(Coast Guard Loran Assist Device), which gives a continuous real-time plot of ship's
position. Bow-thruster fitted, also enlarged superstructure. Operates on International Ice Patrol when not doing research. Has two 40-mm Mk-64 grenade launchers
(I × 2).

TRAINING CUTTER

◆ **1 Horst Wessel class** Bldr: Blohm & Voss, Hamburg, Germany

	L	In serv.
WIX 327 EAGLE (ex-*Horst Wessel*)	13-6-36	1-46

Eagle   1977

D: 1,816 tons (fl)   **S:** 18 kts   **Dim:** 89.9 (70.4 wl) × 11.9 × 5.2
Man: 19 officers, 46 men, 195 cadets   **Electric:** 450 kw
Electron Equipt: Radar: 1/Raytheon 1500
M: 2 M.A.N. diesels; 1 prop; 750 hp (10.5 kts); 2,355 m² sail area

REMARKS: Training ship at the Coast Guard Academy, New London. Sisters operate in
the Brazilian Navy and Soviet merchant marine.

NOTE: The training cutter *Cuyahoga* (WIX-157) was rammed and sunk on 20-10-78.
She has been replaced as enlisted training craft at Yorktown, Va., by the *Ojibwa*
(WYTM-97).

BUOY TENDERS, SEAGOING

◆ **32 Balsam class** Bldrs: WLB-297: Coast Guard Yard; others: Marine Iron SB,
Duluth, or Zenith Dredge Co., Duluth, Minn., 1942-44

WLB 290 GENTIAN	WLB 308 PAPAW	WLB 397 MARIPOSA
WLB 291 LAUREL	WLB 309 SWEETGUM	WLB 399 SAGEBRUSH
WLB 292 CLOVER	WLB 388 BASSWOOD	WLB 400 SALVIA
WLB 296 SORREL	WLB 389 BITTERSWEET	WLB 401 SASSAFRAS
WLB 297 IRONWOOD	WLB 390 BLACKHAW	WLB 402 SEDGE
WLB 300 CITRUS	WLB 391 BLACKTHORN	WLB 403 SPAR
WLB 301 CONIFER	WLB 392 BRAMBLE	WLB 404 SUNDEW
WLB 302 MADRONA	WLB 393 FIREBUSH	WLB 405 SWEETBRIER
WLB 305 MESQUITE	WLB 394 HORNBEAM	WLB 406 ACACIA
WLB 306 BUTTONWOOD	WLB 395 IRIS	WLB 407 WOODRUSH
WLB 307 PLANETREE	WLB 396 MALLOW	

Madrona   R. Scheina, 1979

D: 935 tons (1,025 fl)   **S:** 12.8-13 kts   **Dim:** 54.9 × 11.3 × 4.0
Man: 6 officers, 47 men   **Fuel:** Varies
Range: Most: 4,600/12-18, 14,000/7.4; WLB-297, WLB-306 to WLB-308, WLB-388,
WLB-390, WLB-396, WLB-401: 8,000/13, 23,500/7.5; WLB-305, WLB-392,
WLB-406, WLB-407: 10,500/13, 31,000/7.5
M: 2 diesels, electric drive; 1 prop; WLB-295 to WLB-302: 1,000 hp; WLB-297, WLB-
305 to WLB-407: 1,200 hp; WLB-404: 1,800 hp.

REMARKS: The *Evergreen* (WAGO-295) converted to oceanographic research ship.
WLB-296, WLB-300, WLB-390, WLB-392, WLB-402, WLB-403, and WLB-404 have

BUOY TENDERS, SEAGOING (*continued*)

strengthened hulls for icebreaking, but all have icebreaker hull form. All have 20-ton derrick. These ships have been or are being modernized, and rebuilt engines and propulsion motors, improved habitability, hydraulic cargo-handling gear, and bow thrusters. WLB-290 and WLB-296 were in special reserve in 1979, awaiting modernization. WLB-404 has a maximum speed of 15 knots. Modernized ships have greater endurance.

BUOY TENDERS, COASTAL

◆ **5 Red class (157-ft class)** Bldr: Coast Guard Yard, Curtis Bay, Md.

WLM 685 RED WOOD	WLM 687 RED BIRCH	WLM 689 RED OAK
WLM 686 RED BEECH	WLM 688 RED CEDAR	

White Sage   1976

◆ **3 Hollyhock class (175-ft class)**

WLM 212 FIR	WLM 220 HOLLYHOCK	WLM 252 WALNUT

Red Cedar   G. Arra, 1976

> **D:** 471 tons (512 fl)   **S:** 12 kts   **Dim:** 47.9 × 10.1 × 1.9
> **Man:** 4 officers, 27 men   **Range:** 2,248/12.8, 3,055/11.6
> **M:** 2 diesels; 2 controllable-pitch props; 1,800 hp

REMARKS: WLM-685 and WLM-686 built in 1964, WLM-687 in 1965, WLM-688 in 1970, and WLM-689 in 1971. Can break light ice. Have 10-ton derrick, and a bow thruster.

◆ **7 White class (133-ft class)**

WLM 540 WHITE SUMAC	WLM 545 WHITE HEATH
WLM 542 WHITE BUSH	WLM 546 WHITE LUPINE
WLM 543 WHITE HOLLY	WLM 547 WHITE PINE
WLM 544 WHITE SAGE	

> **D:** 435 tons (600 fl)   **S:** 9.8 kts   **Dim:** 40.5 × 9.4 × 2.7
> **Man:** 1 officer, 20 men   **Range:** 2,100/9.8, 4,500/5.1
> **M:** 2 Union diesels; 2 props; 600 hp

REMARKS: WLM-540 built in 1943, WLM-542 and WLM-543 in 1944, others in 1942. Former U.S. Navy YF (covered lighter, self-propelled). One 10-ton boom.

Fir   1974

> **D:** 989 tons (fl)   **S:** 12 kts   **Dim:** 53.4 × 10.4 × 3.7
> **Man:** 5 officers, 35 men
> **Range:** 6,500/12, 10,000/7.5; WLM-212: 5,650/12, 8,675/7.5
> **M:** 2 diesels; 2 props; 1,350 hp

REMARKS: WLM-220 built in 1937, others in 1939. WLM-220 and WLM-252, reengined 1958-59, have shorter stacks. All have a 20-ton boom. Redesignated from WLB to WLM on 1-1-65.

NOTE: The *Juniper* (WLM-224) was stricken on 31-10-78.

BUOY TENDERS, INLAND

◆ 1 Buckthorn class (100-ft class)

WLI 642 BUCKTHORN

    D: 200 tons (fl)   **S:** 11.9 kts   **Dim:** 30.5 × 7.3 × 1.2
    Man: 1 officer, 13 men   **Range:** 1,300/11.9, 2,000/7.3
    M: 2 diesels; 2 props; 600 hp

REMARKS: Built in 1963. Bow rectangular at main deck. Has one 5-ton boom. Based on the Great Lakes.

◆ 2 Bayberry class (65400 class)

WLI 65400 BAYBERRY   WLI 65401 ELDERBERRY

    D: 68 tons (fl)   **S:** 11.3 kts   **Dim:** 19.8 × 5.2 × 1.2
    Man: 5 men   **Range:** 800/11.3, 1,700/6   **M:** 2 diesels; 2 props; 400 hp

REMARKS: Built in 1954.

◆ 2 Blackberry class (65300 class)

WLI 65303 BLACKBERRY   WLI 65304 CHOKEBERRY

    D: 68 tons (fl)   **S:** 9 kts   **Dim:** 19.8 × 5.2 × 1.2
    Man: 5 men   **Range:** 700/9, 1,500/5   **M:** 1 diesel; 1 prop; 220 hp

REMARK: Built in 1946.

NOTE: The surviving five WLI of the *Cosmos* class were reclassified WLIC in 1979. The *Loganberry* (WLI-65305) was stricken on 30-9-76. The *Tern* (WLI-80801) was stricken on 1-7-77, and the *Azalea* (WLI-641) was stricken on 31-10-78.

BUOY TENDERS, RIVER

◆ 9 Gasconade class (75-ft class)

WLR 75401 GASCONADE	WLR 75406 KICKAPOO
WLR 75402 MUSKINGUM	WLR 75407 KANAWHA
WLR 75403 WYACONDA	WLR 75408 PATOKA
WLR 75404 CHIPPEWA	WLR 75409 CHENA
WLR 75405 CHEYENNE	

    D: 141 tons (fl)   **S:** 7.6-8.7 kts   **Dim:** 22.9 × 6.7 × 1.2
    Man: 12 men   **Range:** 1,600/7.6, 3,100/6.5   **M:** 2 diesels; 2 props; 600 hp

REMARKS: WLR-75401 built in 1964; WLR-75402, WLR-75403, and WLR-75404 in 1965; WLR-75405 in 1966; WLR-75406 and WLR-75407 in 1969; and WLR-75408 and WLR-75409 in 1970. Flat-ended, bargelike hulls. WLR-75401 and WLR-75405 have associated buoy barges which they push; they also have slightly larger crews. One 1-ton crane. All operate on the Mississippi River and its tributaries.

◆ 6 Ouachita class (65-ft class)

WLR 65501 OUACHITA	WLR 65503 OBION	WLR 65505 OSAGE
WLR 65502 CIMARRON	WLR 65504 SCIOTO	WLR 65506 SANGAMON

    D: 139-143 tons (fl)   **S:** 10 kts   **Dim:** 20.1 × 6.4 × 1.5
    Man: 10 men   **Range:** 1,700/10.5, 3,500/6   **M:** 2 diesels; 2 props; 600 hp

REMARKS: WLR-65501 and WLR-65502 built in 1960, others in 1962. WLR-65504 has an associated push-type buoy barge with a 3-ton crane, and a larger crew. All have a 3-ton crane aboard. Operate on the Mississippi River and its tributaries.

◆ 1 Sumac class (115-ft class)

WLR 311 SUMAC

    D: 404 tons (478 fl)   **S:** 10.6 kts   **Dim:** 35.1 × 9.1 × 1.8
    Man: 1 officer, 22 men   **Range:** 5,000/10.6, 11,600/5
    M: 3 diesels; 3 props; 2,250 hp

REMARKS: Built in 1943. Has a 1-ton crane. Based at St. Louis.

◆ 1 Lantana class (80-ft class)

WLR 80310 LANTANA

    D: 235 tons (fl)   **S:** 10 kts   **Dim:** 24.3 × 9.1 × 1.8
    Man: 1 officer, 19 men   **Range:** 5,000/10   **M:** 3 diesels; 3 props; 945 hp

REMARK: Built in 1943.

◆ 1 Dogwood class (114-ft class)

WLR 259 DOGWOOD

    D: 230 tons (310 fl)   **S:** 11 kts   **Dim:** 34.8 × 7.9 × 1.2
    Man: 1 officer, 20 men   **Range:** 1,300/11, 2,800/5.5
    M: 2 diesels; 2 props; 800 hp

REMARKS: Built in 1940. Sisters *Forsythia* (WLR-263) and *Sycamore* (WLR-268) discarded in 1977. Other recently discarded river buoy tenders: *Foxglove* (WLR-285) and *Oleander* (WLR-7364), both in 1977.

CONSTRUCTION TENDERS, INLAND

◆ 4 Pamlico class (160-ft class)   Bldr: Coast Guard Yard, Curtis Bay, Md.

WLIC 800 PAMLICO	WLIC 803 KENNEBEC
WLIC 801 HUDSON	WLIC 804 SAGINAW

Pamlico   1976

    D: 413 tons (459 fl)   **S:** 11.5 kts   **Dim:** 49.1 × 9.1 × 1.2
    Man: 1 officer, 13 men   **Range:** 1,300/11
    Electron Equipt: Radar: 1/LN-66
    M: 2 Cummins D379, 8-cyl. diesels; 2 props; 1,000 hp

CONSTRUCTION TENDERS, INLAND (*continued*)

REMARKS: WLIC-800 and WLIC-801 built in 1976; others in 1977. Design combines capabilities of the *Anvil* class and their associated equipment barges. One 9-ton crane.

◆ **10 Anvil class (75-ft class)**

WLIC 75301 ANVIL	WLIC 75305 VISE	WLIC 75308 SPIKE
WLIC 75302 HAMMER	WLIC 75306 CLAMP	WLIC 75309 HATCHET
WLIC 75303 SLEDGE	WLIC 75307 WEDGE	WLIC 75310 AXE
WLIC 75304 MALLET		

D: 145 tons (fl) **S:** 9.1 kts **Dim:** 22.9 × 6.7 × 1.2
M: 2 diesels; 2 props; 600 hp **Man:** 0 or 1 officer, 9 men **Range:** 2,200/5

REMARKS: Built between 1962 and 1965. Most have an associated push-type work barge with a 9-ton crane. WLIC-75306 to WLIC-75310 are 23.2 m overall and can make 9.4 knots.

◆ **5 Cosmos class (100-ft class)**

WLIC 293 COSMOS	WLIC 315 SMILAX
WLIC 298 RAMBLER	WLIC 316 PRIMROSE
WLIC 313 BLUEBELL	

D: 178 tons (fl) **S:** 10.5 kts **Dim:** 30.5 × 7.3 × 1.5
Electron Equipt: Radar: 1/LN-66 **Man:** 1 officer, 14 men
M: 2 diesels; 2 props; 600 hp **Range:** 1,400/10.5, 2,700/7

REMARKS: WLIC-293 built in 1942, WLIC-313 in 1945, the others in 1944. Reclassified from WLI on 1-10-79. WLIC-293 and WLIC-298 have associated construction barges, while WLIC-316 has a piledriver on her bow. All have a 5-ton crane.

ICEBREAKING TUGS

◆ **10 Katmai Bay class (140-ft class)** Bldr: Tacoma BB, Tacoma, Wash.

	Laid down	L	In serv.
WTGB 101 KATMAI BAY	7-11-77	8-4-78	8-1-79
WTGB 102 BRISTOL BAY	13-2-78	22-7-78	5-4-79
WTGB 103 MOBILE BAY	13-2-78	11-11-78	6-5-79
WTGB 104 BISCAYNE BAY	29-8-78	3-2-79	6-8-79
WTGB 105 NEAH BAY	. . .	. . .	. . .
WTGB 106 MORRO BAY	. . .	. . .	. . .
WTGB 107 PENOBSCOT BAY	. . .	. . .	. . .
WTGB 108 THUNDER BAY	. . .	. . .	. . .
WTGB 109 STURGEON BAY	. . .	. . .	. . .
WTGB 110 N . . .			

Authorized: 1 in FY 76, 3 in FY 77, 2 in FY 78, 1 in FY 79
Proposed: 1 in FY 81, 1 in FY 82, 1 in FY 83

D: 662 tons (fl) **S:** 14.7 kts **Dim:** 42.67 (39.62 pp) × 11.43 × 3.66
Man: 3 officers, 14 men **Range:** 1,800/14.7, 4,000/12 **Electric:** 250 kw
M: 2 Fairbanks-Morse 38D8⅛ diesels, Westinghouse electric drive; 1 prop; 2,500 hp

REMARKS: Reclassified from WYTM on 5-2-79; beginning with WGTB-103 have white hulls (the first two will be repainted). Initial units to operate on the Great Lakes. Can break 45–50-mm ice. Have portable bubble-generator system housed in a removeable deckhouse on the fantail. Two fire-fighting monitors atop the pilothouse, which provides near 360-degree viewing. One 2-ton crane handles a 4.9-m plastic workboat. Initially intended to replace the older WYTMs in service.

Katmai Bay 1979

HARBOR TUGS, MEDIUM

◆ **13 110-ft class**

Bldr: Ira S. Bushey, Brooklyn, N.Y. (WYTM-60 and WYTM-61: Coast Guard Yard, Curtis Bay, Md.)

WYTM 60 MANITOU	WYTM 92 NAUGATUCK
WYTM 61 KAW	WYTM 93 RARITAN
WYTM 71 APALACHEE	WYTM 96 CHINOOK
WYTM 72 YANKTON	WYTM 97 OJIBWA
WYTM 73 MOHICAN	WYTM 98 SNOHOMISH
WYTM 90 ARUNDEL	WYTM 99 SAUK
WYTM 91 MAHONING	

Chinook 1977

U.S.A. (*continued*)

HARBOR TUGS, MEDIUM (*continued*)

D: 370 tons (384 fl)   **S:** 11.2 kts   **Dim:** 33.54 × 8.29 × 3.51
Electron Equipt: Radar: 1/LN-66   **Man:** 1 officers, 19 men
Range: 1,845/11.2, 4,000/8
M: 2 GM or Ingersoll-Rand 8-cyl. diesels, electric drive; 1 prop; 1,000 hp

REMARKS: WYTM-90 to WYTM-93 were built in 1939, the others in 1943. WYTM-61 scheduled to strike in 1979, others to follow as *Katmai Bay*-class WTGB complete. WYTM-97 is enlisted training ship at Yorktown, Va., replacing the *Cuyahoga* (WIX-157).

◆ **1 85-ft class**

WYTM 85009 MESSENGER

D: 230 tons (fl)   **S:** 9.5 kts   **Dim:** 25.9 × 7.0 × 2.7
Man: 10 men   **Range:** 2,000/9.5, 3,000/5   **M:** 1 diesel; 1 prop; 700 hp

REMARK: Built in 1944.

HARBOR TUGS, SMALL

◆ **15 65-ft class**

WYTL 65601 CAPSTAN	WYTL 65606 CATENARY	WYTL 65611 LINE
WYTL 65602 CHOCK	WYTL 65607 BRIDLE	WYTL 65612 WIRE
WYTL 65603 SWIVEL	WYTL 65608 PENDANT	WYTL 65613 BITT
WYTL 65604 TACKLE	WYTL 65609 SHACKLE	WYTL 65614 BOLLARD
WYTL 65605 TOWLINE	WYTL 65610 HAWSER	WYTL 65615 CLEAT

Capstan   R. Scheina, 1979

D: 72 tons (fl)   **S:** 9.8 (first 6: 10.5)   **Dim:** 19.8 × 5.8 × 2.1
Man: 10 men
Range: 850/9.8, 2,700/5.8 (WYTL-65601 to WYTL-65606: 3,600/6.8, 8,900/10.5
Electron Equipt: Radar: 1/LN-66   **M:** 1 diesel; 1 prop; 400 hp

REMARK: Built between 1961 and 1967.

LIGHTSHIPS

◆ **2 28-ft class**

WLV 604 LIGHTSHIP COLUMBIA   WLV 612 LIGHTSHIP NANTUCKET

D: 607 tons (fl) (WLV-604: 617 tons)   **S:** 11 kts   **Dim:** 39.0 × 9.1 × 3.4
Range: 14,000/11, 28,000/4.8   **M:** 1 diesel; 1 prop; 550 hp

REMARKS: Built in 1950. Most lightships have now been replaced by fixed installations. WLV-604 is assigned to Astoria, Oregon; WLV-612 to Boston, Mass., for the Nantucket Shoals station. WLV-604 range: 14,000/10.7, 25,000/6.1. The relief lightship WLV-605 has been sold.

FERRIES

NOTE: The following three ships are not commissioned cutters of the U.S. Coast Guard but are under Coast Guard control. Their status is "in service" and they are civilian-manned. Former U.S. Army units, they operate from Governors Island in New York Harbor.

LT. SAMUEL S. COURS   PVT. NICHOLAS MINUE

D: 869 tons   **S:** 12 kts   **Dim:** 54.9 × 18.9 × 3.0
M: Diesel-electric drive; . . . props; 1,000 hp

REMARK: The *Lt. Samuel S. Cours* was built in 1956.

THE TIDES

D: 744 tons (fl)   **S:** 12 kts   **Dim:** 56.4 × 16.8 × 2.7
M: Diesel-electric drive; . . . props; 1,350 hp

REMARK: Built in 1946.

URUGUAY

PERSONNEL: 5,200, including 500 officers, 3,700 enlisted, and 1,000 Marines

MERCHANT MARINE (1978): 48 ships – 174,357 grt
(tankers: 6 ships – 111,981 grt)

NAVAL AVIATION: Fixed-wing aircraft include 3 Grumman S-2A Tracker ASW patrol, 3 Beech SNB-5 (C-45) utility transports, 1 Embraer EMB-110B Bandeirante, 3 North American SNJ (T-6 Texan) trainers, and 1 Beech T-34B Mentor trainer. Helicopters include 2 Bell 47G and 2 Sikorsky SH-34C.

SUBMARINES

◆ **2 German Type-209 class** Bldr: Howaldtswerke, Kiel

		Laid down	L	In serv.
S . . .	N . . .	. . .	. . .	. . .
S . . .	N . . .	. . .	. . .	. . .

D: 980 tons surfaced, 1,390 submerged **S:** 21 kts submerged, 12 snorkeling
Dim: 55.0 × 6.6 × 5.9 **Man:** 5 officers, 26 men **Fuel:** 50 tons
A: 8/533-mm TT fwd — 6 reload torpedoes
M: 4 MTU 12V 493 TY60 diesels, 1 Siemans electric motor; 1 prop; 3,600 hp

REMARK: Ordered on 18-9-78.

FRIGATES

◆ **1 ex-U.S. Dealey class** Bldr: Bath Iron Works, Me.

	Laid down	L	In serv.
DE 3 18 DE JULIO (ex-*Dealey*, DE-1006)	15-10-52	8-11-53	3-6-54

D: 1,450 tons (1,914 fl) **S:** 25 kts
Dim: 95.86 × 11.2 × 4.04 (5.27 over sonar)
Man: 11 officers, 150 men **Range:** 4,400/11 **Fuel:** 360 tons
A: 4/76.2-mm DP (II × 2) — 6/324-mm Mk 32 ASW TT — 1/depth-charge rack
Electron Equipt: Radars: 1/SPS 5D, 1/SPS 6E, 2/SPG 34
Sonar: 1/SQS-29 series
Boilers: 2 Foster-Wheeler "D", 42 kg/cm² pressure — superheat 510°C
M: 1 set de Laval GT; 1 prop; 20,000 hp

REMARKS: First and least-modified of her class. One sister survives in the Colombian Navy. Two Mk-63 gunfire-control radars. New superstructure added abreast the stack. Purchased on 28-7-72.

◆ **2 ex-U.S. Cannon class** Bldr: Federal SB & DD, Newark, N.J.

	Laid down	L	In serv.
DE 1 URUGUAY (ex-*Baron*, DE-166)	30-11-42	9-5-43	5-7-43
DE 2 ARTIGAS (ex-*Bronstein*, DE-189)	26-8-43	14-11-43	13-12-43

Artigas

D: 1,240 tons light (1,900 fl) **S:** 19 kts **Dim:** 93.27 × 11.15 × 3.56 (hull)
Man: 160 men **Range:** 8,300/14 **Fuel:** 315 tons **Electric:** 680 kw
A: 3/76.2-mm DP (I × 3) — 2/40-mm AA (II × 1) — 1/Mk 11 Hedgehog — 8/Mk 6 depth-charge projectors — 1/Mk 9 depth-charge rack
Electron Equipt: Radars: 1/SPS 5, 1/SPS 6C, 1/navigational
Sonars: SQS-4 series
M: 4 GM 16-278A diesels, electric drive; 2 props; 6,000 hp

REMARKS: DE-1 was transferred in 5-52 and DE-2 in 3-52. Modernized in late 1960s with new radars. No radar fire control but do have Mk-51 range-finder for 76.2-mm guns and Mk-51, mod. 2, lead-computing director for 40-mm AA. DE-1 does not have stub mainmast.

CORVETTES

◆ **1 ex-U.S. Agile-class former minesweeper** Bldr: Bellingham SY, Bellingham, Wash.

	L	In serv.
MS 33 MALDONADO (ex-*Bir Hakeim*, ex-MSO-451)	1-10-53	24-2-54

D: 700 tons (795 fl) **S:** 13.5 kts **Dim:** 52.27 × 10.71 × 4.2
A: 1/40-mm AA **Man:** 54 men **Range:** 3,000/10 **Fuel:** 47 tons
M: 2 GM 8-278A diesels; 2 controllable-pitch props; 1,600 hp

REMARKS: On completion, transferred to France as the *Bir Hakeim* (M-614). Returned to U.S. Navy's control and retransferred to Uruguay in 9-70. All portable minesweeping gear offloaded. Wooden construction.

◆ **1 ex-U.S. Auk-class former minesweeper**

Bldr: Defoe Boiler & Machine Works, Bay City, Mich.

	Laid down	L	In serv.
MS 31 COMANDANTE PEDRO CAMPBELL (ex-*Chickadee*, MSF-59)	21-8-41	20-7-42	9-11-42

Comandante Pedro Campbell

CORVETTES (*continued*)

D: 890 tons (1,250 fl)   **S:** . . .   **Dim:** 67.41 (65.53 wl) × 9.78 × 3.28
A: 1/76.2-mm DP−4/40-mm AA (II × 2)−4/20-mm AA (II × 2)
Electron Equipt: Radars: 1/navigational, 1/SO 8   **Man:** 105 men
M: 4 Alco 539 diesels, electric drive; 2 props; 3,118 hp   **Electric:** 300 kw

REMARKS: Transferred on 18-8-66 and purchased on 18-8-76. Retains some minesweeping equipment, but has no ASW capability.

PATROL BOATS

◆ **3 French Vigilante class**   Bldr: CMN, Cherbourg

	L	In serv.		L	In serv.		L	In serv.
N . . .	. . .	10-80	N . . .	. . .	11-80	N . . .	. . .	12-80

D: 166 tons (190 fl)   **S:** 25 kts   **Dim:** 41.5 (38.0 pp) × 6.8 × 2.1
A: 1/40-mm AA−1/20-mm AA   **Man:** 3 officers, 22 men
Electron Equipt: Radar: 1/Decca TM 1226   **Range:** 2,400/15
M: 2 MTU diesels; 2 props; 5,400 hp

REMARKS: Ordered in 1978. Diminutive version of La Combattante-II design.

◆ **1 ex-U.S. Adjutant-class former minesweeper**

    Bldr: National Steel SB, San Diego, Cal.

	In serv.
MS 32 RIO NEGRO (ex-*Marguerite*, ex-*MSC-94*)	3-54

Rio Negro−most minesweeping gear now removed

D: 300 tons (372 fl)   **S:** 13 kts   **Dim:** 43.0 (41.5 pp) × 7.95 × 2.95
A: 2/20-mm AA (II × 1)   **Man:** 38 men   **Range:** 2,500/10
Electron Equipt: Radar: 1/DRBN 31   Sonar: UQS 1D
M: 2 GM 8-268A diesels; 2 props; 1,200 hp

REMARKS: On completion, transferred to France, then to Uruguay on 10-11-69. Wooden construction. Most minesweeping equipment, including sweep winch and cable drum, now removed.

PATROL CRAFT

◆ **1 U.S. 85-foot commercial cruiser**   Bldr: Sewart Seacraft, Morgan City, La.

PR 12 PAYSANDU

D: 43.5 tons (54 fl)   **S:** 22 kts   **Dim:** 25.91 × 5.69 × 2.1
A: 3/12.7-mm machine guns (I × 3)   **Man:** 8 men   **Range:** 800/21
Electron Equipt: Radar: 1/Raytheon 1500B   **Electric:** 40 kw
M: 2 GM 16V71N diesels; 2 props; 1,400 hp

REMARKS: Built under U.S. Military Assistance Program. Launched in 11-68. Aluminum construction.

◆ **1 ex-German FL-9 class**   Bldr: Krögerwerft, Rendsburg, 1955

PR 11 CARMELO

D: 67 tons (73 fl)   **S:** 30 kts   **Dim:** 28.8 (27.9 pp) × 5.0 × 1.6
A: 1/20-mm AA   **Man:** 8 men   **Range:** 600/25
Electron Equipt: Radar: 1/Decca 12
M: 2 Maybach 12-cyl. diesels; 2 props; 3,000 hp

REMARKS: One of five sisters built as air-sea rescue craft for the British Royal Air Force. Transferred to Uruguay in about 1961. Wooden construction.

◆ **1 ex-U.S. 63-foot AVR class**

PRIO COLONIA

D: 25 tons (34 fl)   **S:** 28 kts   **Dim:** 19.3 × 4.67 × 1.22
A: 4/12.7-mm machine guns (II × 2)   **Man:** 8 men   **Range:** 450/25, 600/15
M: 2 Hall-Scott Defender V-12 gasoline engines; 2 props; 1,260 hp
Fuel: 4.3 tons

REMARKS: Former air-sea rescue boat, launched on 4-7-44. Transferred in about 1945. Wooden construction. No radar.

NOTE: There are a number of small patrol launches with pendant numbers in the PM series.

AMPHIBIOUS WARFARE CRAFT

◆ **3 U.S. LCM (6)-class landing craft**

LD 41   LD 42   LD 43

D: 24 tons (57 fl)   **S:** 10 kts   **Dim:** 17.07 × 4.37 × 1.17
M: 2 Gray Marine 64HN9 diesels; 2 props; 450 hp   **Range:** 130/9

REMARKS: LD-41 and LD-42 were transferred in 10-72. LD-43 was built in Uruguay in 1978. **Cargo:** 30 tons.

HYDROGRAPHIC SHIPS

◆ **1 Paysandu-class former patrol boat**   Bldr: CNR, Ancona

GS 24 SALTO

D: 150 tons (180 fl)   **S:** 17 kts   **Dim:** 42.1 × 5.8 × 1.58
M: 2 Krupp-Germania diesels; 2 props; 1,000 hp   **Man:** 26 men
Range: 4,000/10

REMARKS: Launched on 11-8-35. Survivor of a class of three, placed on present duties as a survey craft and navigational-buoy tender in 1972.

URUGUAY (*continued*)

HYDROGRAPHIC SHIPS (*continued*)

◆ **1 former yacht and training ship**

Bldr: Soc. Española de Const. Naval, Cadiz, Spain, 1930

GS 20 CAPITÁN MIRANDA

   D: 516 tons (550 fl)   **S:** 10 kts   **Dim:** 54.6 (45.0 pp) × 8.4 × 3.0
   M: 1 M.A.N. diesel; 1 prop; 500 hp   **Man:** 49 men   **Fuel:** 45 tons

◆ **3 inshore-survey craft**

PS 1   PS 2   PS 3

REMARK: No data available.

AUXILIARY SHIPS

◆ **1 supertanker** Bldr: Kawasaki, Kobe, Japan, 1975

AO 27 JUAN A. LAVALLEJA (ex-*Solfonn*)

   D: 145,000 tons (fl)   **S:** 15.5 kts   **Dim:** 273.0 × 44.1 × 15.7
   M: 2 sets GT; 1 prop; 24,500 hp   **Boilers:** 2   **Man:** . . .

REMARKS: Literally, the world's largest naval ship, by a wide margin. Laid up by Norwegian owner on 13-10-75, when she was completed. Purchased by Uruguay on 13-1-77 for use by ANCAP, the state petroleum monopoly, in commercial service with a naval crew. 131,663 dwt, 68,931 grt. No underway replenishment capability.

◆ **1 tanker** Bldr: Bazán, Spain, 1971

AO 28 PRESIDENTE RIVERA

   D: 36,000 tons (fl)   **S:** 16.5 kts   **Dim:** 194.0 (191.0 pp) × 25.4 × 9.8
   M: 1 diesel; 1 prop; 15,300 hp   **Man:** 58 men

REMARKS: Used in commercial service, with a naval crew, by ANCAP, the state petroleum monopoly. 31,885 dwt, 19,656 grt.

NOTE: The third tanker in commercial service, the *Presidente Oribe* (AO-9) was stricken in 1978.

◆ **1 ex-U.S. Cohoes-class salvage ship** Bldr: Commercial Ironworks, Portland, Ore.

	Laid down	L	In serv.
AM 25 HURACAN (ex-*Nahant*, AN-83, ex-*YN-102*)	31-3-45	30-6-45	24-8-45

   D: 650 tons (855 fl)   **S:** 12.3 kts   **Dim:** 51.36 (44.5 pp) × 10.31 × 3.3
   A: 3/20-mm AA (I × 3)   **Electron Equipt:** Radar: 1/SPS 5   **Man:** 48 men
   M: 2 Busch-Sulzer B.S.539 diesels, electric drive; 1 prop; 1,200 hp

REMARKS: Former netlayer. Transferred in 12-68. A decompression chamber for divers was added in 1974.

◆ **1 ex-U.S. harbor tug** Bldr: Bellingham Iron Works, Bellingham, Wash., 1944

AM 26 VANGUARDIA (ex-*YTL-589*)

   D: 100 tons   **S:** 12 kts   **Dim:** 20.17 × 5.18 × . . .
   M: 1 Hoover-Owens-Rentschler diesel; 1 prop; 300 hp

REMARK: Transferred in 9-65.

VENEZUELA

PERSONNEL: 7,500 men, including 4,000 marines

MERCHANT MARINE (1978): 201 ships—823,543 grt
(tankers: 23 ships—368,077 grt)

NAVAL AVIATION: The small naval aviation component operates six Grumman S-2E Tracker ASW patrol aircraft, four Grumman HU-16A Albatross air-sea rescue amphibians, two Douglas C-47 transports, one Hawker-Siddeley (BAe) HS-748 transport and two Cessna 337 liaison aircraft, as well as two Bell mod. 47J helicopters. Twelve Agusta-Bell AB-212 helicopters are on order for the *Lupo*-class frigates.

SUBMARINES

◆ **4 209 type** Bldr: Howaldtswerke, Kiel

	L	In serv.		L	In serv.
S 31 SABALO	21-8-75	6-8-76	S-33 N . . .	. . .	. . .
S 32 CONGRIO	16-12-75	11-3-77	S-34 N . . .	. . .	. . .

   D: 980 tons surfaced, 1,230 submerged   **S:** 10/22 kts
   Dim: 55.0 × 6.6 × 5.9   **Man:** 5 officers, 26 men
   A: 8/533-mm TT—torpedoes
   M: Diesel-electric propulsion: 4 MTU Type 12V-492-Tb-90 diesels; Siemens electric motor, 3,600 hp

REMARK: S-31, S-32 ordered 1971; S-33, S-34 ordered 10-3-77.

◆ **2 ex-U.S. Guppy II**

	Bldr	Laid down	L	In serv.
S 21 TIBURON (ex-*Cubera*, SS-347)	Electric Boat Co.	11-5-44	17-6-45	19-12-45
S 22 PICUDA (ex-*Grenadier*, SS-525)	Boston NSY	8-2-44	15-12-44	10-2-51

   D: 2,040 surfaced, 2,420 submerged   **S:** 18/16 kts
   Dim: 93.57 × 8.33 × 5.18   **Man:** 82 men
   A: 10/533-mm TT (6 fwd, 4 aft)   **Electron Equipt:** Radar: 1/SS-2
                                                    Sonar: BQR-2
   M: 4 GM 16-278A (S-22: Fairbanks-Morse 38D8⅛) diesels, electric drive; 2 props; 4,160 hp

REMARKS: S-21 sold to Venezuela 5-1-72; S-22 purchased 15-5-73. S-22 was completed as a Guppy II, S-21 converted 1948. Four 126-cell batteries. Both have high sails.

NOTE: Ex-U.S. Balao-class submarine *Carite* (S-11), ex-*Tilefish* (SS-307), stricken 28-1-77.

DESTROYERS

◆ **1 ex U.S. Allen M. Sumner FRAM-II class** Bldr: Todd-Pacific SY, Seattle, Wash.

	Laid down	L	In serv.
D 22 FALCON (ex-*Robert K. Huntington*, DD-781)	29-2-44	5-12-44	3-3-45

   D: 2,200 tons (3,320 fl)   **S:** 30 kts   **Dim:** 114.75 × 10.45 × 5.8 (max.)
   A: 6/127-mm DP (II × 3)—6/324-mm Mk-32 ASW TT (III × 2)—2/Mk-11 Hedgehogs

DESTROYERS (continued)

Electron Equipt: Radars: 1/SPS-10, 1/SPS-29, 1/Mk 25
Sonar: SQS-29 series   ECM: BLR-3
Range: 1,260/30, 4,800/15   **Man:** 14 officers, 260 men
Boilers: 2 Babcock & Wilcox and 2 Foster-Wheeler; 43.3 kg/cm² pressure—super-heat 454°C
Electric: 1,200 kw   **Fuel:** 650 tons
M: 2 sets Allis-Chalmers GT; 2 props; 60,000 hp

REMARKS: Purchased 31-10-73. Did not have VDS. Retains DASH (Drone Antisubmarine Helicopter) hangar and deck and can operate Venezuela's Bell-475 helicopters. One Mk-37 gunfire-control director.

◆ **1 ex-U.S. Allen M. Sumner class** Bldr: Bethlehem Steel, Staten I.

	Laid down	L	In serv.
D 21 CARABOBO (ex-Beatty, DD-756)	30-11-44	1-5-45	31-3-45

D: 2,375 tons (3,310 fl)   **S:** 33 kts   **Dim:** 114.75 × 10.45 × 4.37 (6.25 sonar)
A: 6/127-mm DP (II × 3)—1/40-mm AA—2/Hedgehogs—6/324-mm Mk-32 ASW TT (III × 2)—1/depth-charge rack
Electron Equipt: Radar: 1/SPS-10, 1/SPS-6C, 1/Mk 25
Sonar: SQS-29 series   ECM: BLR-1
Boilers: 2 Babcock & Wilcox and 2 Foster Wheeler; 43.3 kg/cm² pressure—super-heat 454°C
Range: 850/33, 3,300/12   **Fuel:** 500 tons   **Man:** 14 officers, 260 men
M: 2 sets GE GT; 2 props; 60,000 hp   **Electric:** 1,100 kw

REMARKS: Purchased 14-7-72. Forty-millimeter antiaircraft mount added aft in 1978. Has Mk-37 gunfire-control system forward, and Mk-51, Mod. 2, (no radar) aft.

NOTE: The *Nueva Esparta* (D-11) was stricken in 1-79 for use as a target. The *Zulia* (D-12) was stricken on 1-9-79.

◆ **6 Italian Lupo class** Bldr: CNR, Riva Trigoso, Italy

	Laid down	L	In serv.
F 21 MARISCAL SUCRE	19-11-76	28-9-78	11-19-79
F 22 ALMIRANTE BRION	6-77	22-2-79	4-80
F 23 GENERAL URDANETA	1978	1979	1980
F 24 GENERAL SOUBLETTE	. . .	. . .	1981
F 25 GENERAL SALOM	. . .	. . .	1981
F 26 JOSÉ FELIX RIBAS	. . .	. . .	1982

Mariscal Sucre   C. Martinelli, 1978

D: 2,208 tons (2,525 fl)   **S:** 35 kts
Dim: 112.8 (106.0 pp) × 11.98 × 3.6 (hull)
A: 8/Otomat SSM (I × 8)—1/Albatros SAM system (VIII × 1, no reloads)—1/127-mm DP OTO Melara—4/40-mm Breda Dardo AA (II × 2)—6/324-mm Mk-32 ASW TT (III × 2, for A244 torpedoes)—2/AB-212 ASW helicopters
Electron Equipt: Radar: 1/3 RM 20 navigational, 1/SMA SPQ-2F surface search, 1/MM-SPS-74 air search, 2/NA-10, 2/Dardo
Sonar: Edo 610E   ECM: Lambda, 2/SCLAR chaff launchers
Range: 1,050/31.7, 5,500/16   **Electric:** 3,120 kw   **Man:** 185 men
M: CODOG: 2 Fiat GE LM-2500 gas turbines, 25,000 hp each; 2 GMT A230-2M diesels, 3,900 hp each; 2 controllable-pitch props

REMARKS: Ordered 24-10-75. Maximum speed on diesels is 21 knots. Fin stabilizers fitted. Gun (127-mm) and missile fire control by two Elsag Mk-10, Mod. 0, systems with NA-10 radar directors. The Albatros system uses Aspide missiles, a re-engineered version of NATO Sea Sparrow. Each twin 40-mm antiaircraft mount has an associated radar director. All weapons controlled by a Selenia IPN-10 computerized data system. Fixed, non-telescopic hangar. Near-sisters in the Italian and Peruvian navies.

◆ **2 Almirante Clemente class** Bldr: Ansaldo, Livorno

	Laid down	L	In serv.
F 10 GENERAL JOSÉ TRINIDAD MORAN	5-5-54	12-12-54	1956
F 11 ALMIRANTE CLEMENTE	5-5-54	12-12-54	1956

D: 1,300 tons (1,500 fl)   **S:** 29 kts   **Dim:** 97.6 × 10.84 × 2.6
A: 2/76-mm OTO Melara DP (I × 2)—2/40-mm AA (II × 2)—6/324-mm ASW TT (III × 2)
Electron Equipt: Radar: 1/Decca 1226, 1/Plessey AWS-2, 1/RTN-10X
Sonar: Plessey MS-26
Boilers: 2 Foster-Wheeler; 43.3 kg/cm² pressure—superheat 454°C
Range: 2,500/18, 4,000/15   **Fuel:** 350 tons
M: GT; 2 props; 24,000 hp

REMARKS: Survivors of a class of six: *General José de Austria* stricken 1976, *General José Garcia* stricken 1977, and *General Juan José Flores* and *Almirante Brion* stricken 1978. Both were extensively refitted by Cammell Laird, Birkenhead, from 1968 to 1975-76 (much delay caused by financial and labor problems). New radars, sonar, and armament fitted, with OTO Melara Compact mounts replacing the original four 102-mm dual-purpose (II × 2). When new, could make 32 knots. Very lightly built, with much use of aluminum alloy. Denny-Brown fin stabilizers.

PATROL BOATS AND CRAFT

◆ **6 Constitución class** Bldr: Vosper Thornycroft, Portsmouth, G.B.

	Laid down	L	In serv.
P 11 CONSTITUCIÓN	1-73	1-6-73	16-8-74
P 12 FEDERACIÓN	8-73	26-2-74	25-3-75
P 13 INDEPENDENCIA	2-73	24-7-73	20-9-74
P 14 LIBERTAD	9-73	5-3-74	12-6-75
P 15 PATRIA	3-73	27-9-73	9-1-75
P 16 VICTORIA	3-73	3-9-74	22-9-75

D: 150 tons (170 fl)   **S:** 31 kts   **Dim:** 36.88 (33.53 wl) × 7.16 × 1.73
A: P-11, P-13, P-15: 1/76-mm OTO Melara Compact
P-12, P-14, P-16: 2/Otomat SSM (I × 2)—1/40-mm AA
Electron Equipt: 1/SPQ-2D; P-11, P-13, P-15: RTN-10X also

PATROL BOATS AND CRAFT (*continued*)

Constitución   Vosper, 1975

Range: 1,350/16   **Electric:** 250 kw   **Man:** 3 officers, 14 men
M: 2 MTU MD 16V 538 TB90 diesels; 1 props; 7,080 max. hp/5,900 sust. hp

REMARKS: Ordered 4-72. All equipped with Vosper fin stabilizers. New hull numbers assigned 1978. Maximum sustained speed is 27 knots.

◆ **21 Rio Orinoco-class patrol craft**

Bldrs: First 10: INMA, La Spezia; Others: Dianca, Puerto Cabello; 1974-. . .

C 87 RIO ORINOCO	C 94 RIO SAN JUAN	C 132 N . . .
C 88 RIO VENTUARI	C 95 RIO TUCUYO	C 133 N . . .
C 89 RIO CAPARO	C 96 RIO TURBIO	C 134 N . . .
C 90 RIO VENAMO	C 128 RIO GUAICAIPURO	C 135 N . . .
C 91 RIO TORRES	C 129 RIO TAMANACO	C 136 N . . .
C 92 RIO ESCALANTE	C 130 RIO MANAURE	C 137 N . . .
C 93 RIO LIMON	C 131 RIO ARA	C 138 N . . .

D: 65 tons (fl)   **S:** 25 kts   **Dim:** 28.3 × 4.8 × 1.5
A: 1/12.7-mm machine gun
M: 2 MTU diesels; 2 props; 2,200 hp

REMARKS: Wooden construction. Most operational by 1977.

AMPHIBIOUS WARFARE SHIP

◆ **1 ex-U.S. Terrebone Parrish-class landing ship**

Bldr: Ingalls, Pascagoula

	Laid down	L	In serv.
T 51 AMAZONAS (ex-*Vernon County*, LST-1161)	14-4-52	1952	1954

Amazonas   1977

D: 2,590 tons (5,786 fl)   **S:** 13 kts   **Dim:** 117.35 × 16.76 × 5.18
A: 6/76.2-mm DP (II × 3)   **Electric:** 600 kw   **Man:** 116 men
Electron Equipt: 1/Decca navigational, 1/SPS-21, 2/SPG-34
M: 4 GM 16-278A diesels; 2 controllable-pitch props; 6,000 hp

REMARKS: Loaned 29-6-73, purchased outright 30-12-77. Cargo: 2,200 tons vehicles and stores, 395 troops. Two Mk-63 gunfire-control systems. Normally carries 2 LCVPs.

◆ **1 ex-U.S. Achelons-class former repair ship**

Bldr: Chicago Bridge & Iron Co., Seneca, Ill.

	Laid down	L	In serv.
T 31 GUYANA (ex-*Quirinus*, ARL-39, ex-LST-1151)	3-3-45	4-6-45	15-6-45

D: 4,100 tons (fl)   **S:** 11.6 kts   **Dim:** 99.98 × 15.24 × 3.4
A: 8/40-mm AA (IV × 2)   **Electric:** 420 kw   **Man:** 11 officers, 70 men
M: 2 GM 12-567A diesels; 2 props; 1,800 hp

REMARKS: Loaned 6-62, purchased outright 30-12-77. Repair equipment removed and ship used as a transport. Retains operable bow door.

◆ **4 ex-U.S. LSM 1-class medium landing ships**   Bldr: Brown SB Co., Houston, Tex.

	Laid down	L	In serv.
T 21 LOS MONJES (ex-LSM-548)	14-7-45	25-8-45	1-2-46
T 22 LOS ROQUES (ex-LSM-543)	7-7-45	18-8-45	27-12-45
T 23 LOS FRAILES (ex-LSM-544)	7-7-45	18-8-45	4-1-46
T 24 LOS TESTIGOS (ex-LSM-545)	7-7-45	25-8-45	8-1-46

Los Monjes—wearing old number   1969

AMPHIBIOUS WARFARE SHIPS (*continued*)

D: 1,095 tons (fl) **S:** 12.5 kts **Dim:** 62.03 (59.9 wl) × 10.52 × 2.54
A: 2/40-mm AA (II × 1) — 8/20-mm AA (II × 4) **Electric:** 240 kw
Electron Equipt: Radar: 1/Raytheon 1404 **Cargo:** 400 tons
Fuel: 165 tons **Range:** 9,000/11 **Man:** 59 men
M: 2 Fairbanks-Morse 38D8⅛ diesels; 2 props; 2,800 hp

REMARKS: Transferred 1959-60 under Military Aid Program. Beaching displacement at 1.6-meters draft: 743 tons.

◆ **12 U.S. LCVP-class landing craft** Bldr: Dianca, Puerto Cabello, 1976-77

D: 12 tons (fl) **S:** 9 kts **Dim:** 10.9 × 3.2 × 1.0
M: 1 diesel; 1 prop; 225 hp **Range:** 110/9

REMARKS: Follow design of U.S.-built LCVP. Several other LCVP and LCPL transferred with U.S. Navy ships probably survive.

AUXILIARY SHIPS

◆ **1 projected oceanographic research ship**

H . . . N . . .

D: Approx. 1,600 (fl) **S:** 14 kts **Dim:** 68.4 × 11.8 × 4.2
M: 2 diesels; 1 prop; 2,180 hp — bow thruster

REMARKS: Ordered 10-78 from a French shipyard. Bulbous bow, ramp at stern, two survey launches.

◆ **1 ex-U.S. Cohoes-class survey ship** Bldr: Commercial Iron Works, Portland, Ore.

	Laid down	L	In serv.
H 11 PUERTO SANTO (ex-*Marietta*, AN-82, ex-YN-101)	17-2-45	27-4-45	25-6-45

D: 650 tons (855 fl) **S:** 12 kts **Dim:** 48.2 (44.5 wl) × 10.3 × 3.6
A: 3/20-mm AA (I × 3) **Electric:** 240 kw **Fuel:** 110 tons
Man: 46 men
M: 2 Busch-Sulzer BS 539 diesels, electric drive; 1 prop; 1,500 hp

REMARKS: Ex-net tender. Transferred 1-61 under Military Aid Program; purchased outright 30-12-77. Converted for use as a hydrographic survey ship in 1962 by U.S. Coast Guard Yard, Curtis Bay, Md. Original bow horns removed, reducing overall length from 51.4 meters. Retains 12-ton boom forward. Bridge superstructure raised one deck. Sisters *Puerto Miranda* (ex-*Waxsaw*, AN-91) and *Puerto de Nutrius* (ex-*Tunxis*, AN-90) stricken 1977.

◆ **2 Gabriela-class survey craft**

Bldr: Abeking & Rasmussen, Lemwerder, West Germany

	Laid down	L	In serv.
P 119 GABRIELA	10-3-73	29-11-73	5-2-74
P 121 LELY	28-5-73	12-12-73	7-2-74

D: 90 tons (fl) **S:** 20 kts **Dim:** 27.0 × 5.6 × 1.5
M: 2 MTU diesels; 2 props; 2,300 hp **Man:** 16 men

REMARK: Civilian-manned.

◆ **2 Maracaibo-class cargo ships** Bldr: Canadian Vickers, Montreal

T 41 MARACAIBO (ex-*Ciudad de Maracaibo*)
T 42 VALENCIA (ex-*Ciudad de Valencia*)

D: Approx. 8,100 tons (fl) **S:** 15 kts **Dim:** 128.15 × 16.76 × 6.78
M: 1 Nordberg diesel; 1 prop; 4,275 hp

REMARKS: Built 1949 (T-41) and 1953 (T-42). Transferred from State Shipping Co. in 1973 and 1977. Five cargo holds; 4,297 grt/5,885 dwt. Additional superstructure added on stern to increase accommodations.

◆ **1 Punta Cabana-class transport** Bldr: Uraga DY, Japan

T . . . PUNTA CABANA

D: 3,200 tons (fl) **S:** 17 kts **Dim:** 114.0 × 16.0 × 7.0
M: 1 diesel; 1 prop; 17 kts **Range:** 6,000/15

T . . . LAS AVES (ex-*Dos de Diciembre*) Bldr: Dubigeon

Las Aves

D: 944 tons (fl) **S:** 15 kts **Dim:** 71.4 (64.5 pp) × 10.2 × 3.0
A: 4/20-mm AA (II × 2) **Range:** 2,520/14
M: 2 diesels; 2 props; 1,600 hp **Cargo:** 215 tons + troops

REMARK: Launched 29-12-54. Also fitted as the presidential yacht.

◆ **3 ex-U.S. Achomawi-class fleet tugs** Bldr: Charleston SB & DD, S.C.

	Laid down	L	In serv.
R 21 FELIPE LARRAZABEL (ex-*Utina*, ATF-163)	6-6-45	31-8-45	30-1-46
R 22 ANTONIO PICARDI (ex-*Nipmuc*, ATF-157)	2-12-44	12-4-45	7-7-45
R 23 MIGUEL RODRIGUEZ (ex-*Salinin*, ATF-161)	13-4-45	20-7-45	11-9-45

D: 1,235 tons (1,675 fl) **S:** 16.5 kts **Dim:** 62.48 (59.44 wl) × 11.74 × 4.67
A: R-21 only: 1/76.2-mm DP
Electron Equipt: Radar: 1/SPS-53 (R-21: SPS-5)
Electric: 400 kw **Fuel:** 300 tons **Range:** 7,000/15 **Man:** 85 men
M: 4 GM 16-278A diesels, electric drive; 1 prop; 3,000 hp

REMARKS: R-21 loaned 3-9-71; purchased outright 30-12-77. R-22, R-23 purchased 1-9-78.

◆ **1 sail training ship** Bldr: Ast. Celeya, Bilbao, Spain

SIMON BOLIVAR

D: 934 grt **S:** 10.5 kts **Dim:** 76.2 (56.1 pp) × 10.6 × 4.2
M: 1 GM 12V149 diesel; 1 prop; 700 hp **Man:** 10 officers, 66 men

REMARKS: Sister Ecuadorian *Guayas*. Three-masted bark. Ordered 7-78.

SERVICE CRAFT

◆ **1 large harbor tug** Bldr: Dianca, Puerto Cabello, 1978

C 142

VENEZUELA (*continued*)

SERVICE CRAFT (*continued*)

    D: . . .   **S:** . . .   **Dim:** . . . × . . . × . . .
    M: 2 Werkspoor diesels; 2 props; 1,600 hp

REMARKS: Ordered 1973. Used for navy by Dianca SY. Three sisters operated by Ministry of Communications: C-139, C-140, C-141.

◆ **2 ex-U.S. large harbor tugs** Bldr: Ira S. Bushey, Brooklyn, NY

	Laid down	L	In serv.
R 14 FABIO GALLIPOLI (ex-*Wannalancey*, YTB-385)	28-9-43	12-1-44	19-5-44
R 15 DIANA-III (ex-*Sassacus*, YBT-193)	26-1-42	4-5-42	8-9-42

    D: 260 tons (340 fl)   **S:** 12 kts   **Dim:** 30.73 × 7.62 × 3.35
    Electric: 40 kw   **Man:** 11 men   **Fuel:** 70 tons
    M: 1 Fairbanks-Morse diesel; 1 prop; 805 hp

REMARK: Loaned 8-65 and 1-1-63; purchased outright 30-12-77.

◆ **1 ex-U.S. medium harbor tug** Bldr: Ramsey & sons, New Orleans, La.

R 11 FERNANDO GOMEZ (ex-*Dudley*, YTM-744)

    D: 161 tons   **S:** 15 kts   **Dim:** 24.5 × 5.8 × 2.4
    M: 1 Clark 6-cyl. diesel; 1 prop; 380 hp   **Man:** 10 men

REMARKS: Built 1938. Acquired by U.S. Navy 1-42; sold to Venezuela 1-47.

NOTE: *José Felix Ribas* (R-13, ex-*Oswegatehie*, YTM-778, ex-YTB-515) has been discarded, as have been five ex-U.S. small harbor tugs (YTL).

◆ **1 ex-U.S. floating repair barge** Bldr: Mare Isl. NSY, Cal.

. . . (ex-YR-48)

    D: 520 tons (770 fl)   **Dim:** 46.6 × 13.1 × 2.1
    Electric: 220 kw   **Fuel:** 75 tons   **Man:** 46 men

REMARKS: Launched 30-5-43. Leased 7-61; purchased outright 30-12-77.

◆ **1 ex-U.S. ARD-12-class floating dry dock** Bldr: Pacific Bridge, Alameda, Cal.

DF 11 GOLFO DE CARIACO (ex-ARD-13)

    Dim: 149.9 × 24.7 × 1.7 (light)   **Capacity:** 3,500 tons

REMARKS: In service 11-43. Leased 2-62, purchased 30-12-77. Pointed, ship-type bow

◆ **1 floating crane**   **Capacity:** 40 tons

NATIONAL GUARD

PATROL CRAFT

◆ **12 Rio Meta class** Bldr: N. de l'Estérel, Cannes, France

RIO META	RIO URIBANTE	. . .	. . .	. . .	. . .
RIO PORTUGUESA	. . .	. . .	. . .	. . .	. . .

    D: 45 tons   **S:** 30 kts   **Dim:** 27.0 × 4.9 × 1.5
    A: 1/20-mm AA – 1/12.7-mm machine gun   **Range:** 1,500/15
    M: 2 MTU diesels; 2 props; 3,300 hp   **Man:** 12 men

REMARK: Six built 1970-71, other six built 1976-77.

◆ **8 Rio Apure class** Bldr: C. N. de l'Estérel, Cannes, Frances, 1955

RIO APURE	RIO CABRALES	RIO GUARICO	RIO NEVERI
RIO ARAUCA	RIO CARONI	RIO NEGRO	RIO TUY

    D: 38.5 tons   **S:** 27 tons   **Dim:** 28.0 (25.0 pp) × 4.65 × 1.25
    A: 1/12.7-mm machine gun   **Man:** 12 men   **Range:** 750/24
    M: 2 Mercedes-Benz MB820 diesels; 2 props; 1,350 hp

REMARK: Wooden construction.

◆ **1 patrol craft**

GOLFO DE CARIACO

    D: 37 tons   **S:** 19 kts   **Dim:** 20.0 × 5.5 × 2.8
    M: 2 diesels; 2 props; . . . hp   **Man:** 10 men

◆ **1 patrol craft**

RIO SANTO DOMINGO

    D: 40 tons   **S:** 24 kts   **Dim:** 22.0 × 4.6 × 1.9
    M: 2 GM diesels; 2 props; 1,250 hp   **Man:** 10 men

VIETNAM

MERCHANT MARINE (1978): 80 ships – 162,585 grt
(tankers: 10 ships – 33,906 grt)

NOTE: The following listings include ships known to have been in North Vietnamese service in 1975, those units left behind in South Vietnam that did not escape the communist victory, and a number of ships known to have been turned over to Vietnam by the Soviet Union since 1975. The operability of much of the former U.S. equipment is questionable, but several of the larger units have been seen at sea. New ship names are not known.

FRIGATES

◆ **2 ex-Soviet Petya-II class**

    D: 950 tons (1,150 fl)   **S:** 30 kts   **Dim:** 82.3 × 9.1 × 3.2
    A: 4/76.2-mm DP (II × 2) – 3/533-mm TT (III × 2) – 4/RBU-2500 ASW rocket launchers (XVI × 4) – 2/depth-charge racks – mines
    Electron Equipt: Radars: 1/Don-2, 1/Strut Curve, 1/Hawk Screech
                        Sonar: 1/high frequency – ECM: 2/Watch Dog
    Range: 4,000/10 (diesel), 500/30 (CODAG)   **Man:** 80-90 men
    M: CODAG: 2 gas turbines, 15,000 hp each; 1 diesel, 6,000 hp; 3 props

REMARKS: Of the same export version as has been transferred to India and Syria. Transferred 1978.

FRIGATES (*continued*)

◆ 1 ex-U.S. Savage-class former radar picket

Bldr: Consolidated Steel Corp., Orange, Texas

	Laid down	L	In serv.
ex-TRAN KHANH DU (ex-*Forster*, DER-334)	31-8-43	13-11-43	25-1-44

D: 1,590 (1,850 fl)   **S:** 20 kts   **Dim:** 93.3 (91.4 wl) × 11.2 × 4.3 (hull)
A: 2/76.2-mm DP (I × 2)−6/324-mm Mk-32 ASW TT (III × 2)−1/81-mm mortar−
2/12.7-mm machine guns
Electron Equipt: Radars: 1/SPS-10, 1/SPS-29, 1/SPG-34
                    Sonar: SQS-29 series
Fuel: 310 tons   **Man:** Approx. 170 men   **Range:** 10,000/15
M: 4 Fairbanks-Morse 38D8⅛ diesels; 2 props; 6,000 hp   **Electric:** 580 kw

REMARKS: Transferred to South Vietnam 25-9-71. Was in overhaul at Saigon in 1975 and may not have been re-activated by the new government. Mk-63 radar GFCS forward, Mk-51, Mod. 2, optical GFCS aft.

◆ 1 ex-U.S. Barnegat class   Bldr: Lake Washington SY, Houghton, Wash.

	Laid down	L	In serv.
ex-THAM NGU LAO (ex-U.S.C.G. *Absecon*, WHEC-374, ex-AVP-23)	23-7-41	8-3-42	28-1-43

D: 1,766 tons (2,800 fl)   **S:** 18 kts   **Dim:** 94.7 (91.4 wl) × 12.5 × 4.1
A: 1/127-mm 38-cal. DP−2/81-mm mortars (I × 2)
Electron Equipt: Radars: 1/SPS-21, 1/SPS-29, 1/Mk-26
Fuel: 26 tons   **Range:** 20,000/10   **Man:** Approx. 200 men
M: 4 Fairbanks-Morse 38D8⅛ diesels; 2 props; 6,080 hp   **Electric:** 600 hp

REMARKS: Transferred to South Vietnam in 1971, having served in the U.S. Coast Guard since 1948. Believed to have been made operational by Vietnam. Has probably had 37-mm antiaircraft added to armament.

CORVETTES

◆ 2 ex-U.S. Admirable-class former fleet minesweepers

	Bldr	Laid down	L	In serv.
ex-KY HOA (ex-*Sentry*, MSF-299)	Winslow Marine Railway, Winslow, Wash.	16-5-43	15-8-43	30-5-44
ex-HA HOI (ex-*Prowess*, IX-305, ex-MSF-280)	Gulf SB, Chickasaw, La.	15-9-43	17-2-44	27-9-44

D: 650 tons (945 fl)   **S:** 14.8 kts   **Dim:** 56.2 (54.9 wl) × 10.1 × 3.0
A: 2/57-mm AA (II × 1)−2/37-mm AA (I × 2)−6/23-mm AA (II × 3)
Electron Equipt: Radar 1/SPS-53   **Man:** Approx. 80 men
Electric: 280 kw
M: 2 Cooper-Bessemer GSB-8 diesels; 1,710 hp

REMARKS: Transferred to South Vietnam 8-62 and 6-70, respectively. All minesweeping gear removed before transfer, and antisubmarine warfare gear removed during overhauls in early 1970s. At least one, now numbered HQ-07, is operational, rearmed with Soviet or Chinese weapons.

GUIDED-MISSILE PATROL BOATS

◆ 2 ex-Soviet Komar class

D: 71 tons (82 fl)   **S:** 40 kts   **Dim:** 25.3 × 7.0 × 1.8

A: 2/SS-N-2 Styx SSM (I × 2)−1/25-mm AA (I × 2)
Electron Equipt: Radar: 1/Square Tie   **Man:** 19 men   **Range:** 400/30
M: 4 MSO-F diesels; 4 props; 4,800 hp

REMARKS: Transferred 1972. One sister sunk 19-12-72. Wooden construction. Design based on P-6 torpedo boat. Missile tubes mounted on hull sponsons. Probably in poor condition.

TORPEDO BOATS

◆ 2 Soviet Shershen class

D: 180 tons (fl)   **S:** 45 kts   **Dim:** 34.0 × 7.2 × 1.5
A: 4/30-mm AA (II × 2)−4/533-mm TT−2/depth-charge racks
Electron Equipt: Radar: 1/Pot Drum, 1 Drum Tilt   **Man:** 19 men
M: 3 M-503A diesels; 2 props; 12,000 hp   **Range:** 450/34, 700/20

REMARKS: Transferred 1979, possibly without torpedo tubes.

◆ 6 ex-Chinese P-6 class

D: 66.5 tons (fl)   **S:** 43 kts   **Dim:** 25.3 × 6.1 × 1.6
A: 4/25-mm (II × 2)−2/533-mm TT−depth charges
Electron Equipt: Radar: 1/Skin Head   **Man:** 12 men
M: 4 M50-F diesels; 4 props; 4,800 hp   **Range:** 400/32, 700/15

REMARKS: Transferred during the late 1960s. Wooden construction; copy of Soviet version. Probably in poor condition.

◆ 4 ex-Chinese P-4 class

D: 22.5 tons (fl)   **S:** 55 kts   **Dim:** 19.0 × 3.3 × 1.0
A: 2/14.5-mm machine guns (II × 1)−2/450-mm TT
Electron Equipt: Radar: 1/Skin Head
M: 2 M50 diesels; 2 props; 2,400 hp

REMARKS: Transferred 1961-64; several lost in action. Aluminum construction. Probably in poor condition.

PATROL BOATS

◆ 3 Soviet Zhuk class

D: 60 tons (fl)   **S:** 34 kts   **Dim:** 24.6 × 5.2 × 1.9
A: 4/14.5-mm AA (II × 2)   **Man:** 18 men
M: 2 MSO-F diesels; 2 props; 2,400 hp

REMARKS: Transferred 1978.

◆ up to 18 PGM-59 and PGM-71 class

Bldrs: ex-PGM-59 to ex-PGM-63: J. M. Martinac SB, Seattle, Wash.; ex-PGM-64 to ex-PGM-69: Marinette Marine, Marinette, Wisc.; others: Peterson Bldrs, Sturgeon Bay, Wisc., 1963-67

ex-HQ 600 ex-PHU DU (ex-PGM-64)	ex-HQ 610 ex-DINH HAI (ex-PGM-69)
ex-HQ 601 ex-TIEN MOI (ex-PGM 65)	ex-HQ 611 ex-TRUONG SA (ex-PGM-70)
ex-HQ 602 ex-MINH HOA (ex-PGM-66)	ex-HQ 612 ex-THAI BINH (ex-PGM-72)
ex-HQ 603 ex-KIEN VANG (ex-PGM-67)	ex-HQ 613 ex-THI TU (ex-PGM-73)
ex-HQ 605 ex-KIM QUI (ex-PGM-60)	ex-HQ 614 ex-SONG TU (ex-PGM-74)
ex-HQ 606 ex-MAY RUT (ex-PGM-59)	ex-HQ 615 ex-TAT SA (ex-PGM-80)
ex-HQ 607 ex-NAM DU (ex-PGM-61)	ex-HQ 616 ex-HOANG SA (ex-PGM-82)
ex-HQ 608 ex-HOA LU (ex-PGM-62)	ex-HQ 617 ex-PHU QUI (ex-PGM-81)
ex-HQ 609 ex-TO YEN (ex-PGM-63)	ex-HQ 619 ex-THO CHAU (ex-PGM-91)

PATROL BOATS (continued)

ex-Dinh Hai   1967

D: 102 tons light (142 fl)   **S:** 17 kts   **Dim:** 30.81 × 6.45 × 2.3
A: 1/40-mm AA − 4/20-mm AA (II × 2) − 4/12.7-mm machine guns (II × 2)
Range: 1,000/17   **Fuel:** 16 tons   **Man:** 30 men   **Electric:** 30 kw
M: ex-PGM-59 to ex-PGM-70: 2 Mercedes-Benz MB 820 Db diesels; 2 props; 1,900 hp
     ex-PGM-71 to ex-PGM-91: 8 GM 6-71 diesels; 2 props; 2,040 hp

◆ 3 ex-Soviet S.O.-1 class

D: 215 tons (fl)   **S:** 28 kts   **Dim:** 42.0 × 6.1 × 1.9
A: 4/25-mm AA (II × 2) − 4/RBU-1200 ASW rocket launchers − 2/depth-charge racks − mines
Electron Equipt: Radar: 1/Pot Head   Sonar: 1/high frequency
Range: 1,100/13   **Man:** 30 men
M: 3 diesels; 3 props; 7,500 hp

REMARKS: Transferred 1960-66; one other sunk 2-66. Probably in poor condition.

◆ 8 ex-Chinese Shanghai-II class

D: 155 tons (fl)   **S:** 28 kts   **Dim:** 38.8 × 5.4 × 1.6
A: 4/37-mm AA (II × 2) − 4/25-mm AA (II × 2)   **Man:** 25 men
Electron Equipt: Radar: Skin Head
M: 4 M50 diesels; 4 props; 4,800 hp

REMARKS: Transferred four in 1966 and four in 1968. Probably in very poor condition. Very unsophisticated craft.

◆ up to 14 ex-Chinese Swatow class

D: 80 tons (fl)   **S:** 28 kts   **Dim:** 25.1 × 6.0 × 1.8
A: 4/37-mm AA (II × 2) − 2/12.7-mm machine guns (I × 2)
M: 4 diesels; 4 props; 3,000 hp   **Man:** 25 men

REMARKS: Transferred beginning in 1958; many lost in action. Those remaining are probably in very poor condition. Steel hulls; some had single 37-mm antiaircraft vice twin. A few had Skin Head radar.

◆ 26 ex-U.S. Coast Guard Point Class   Bldr: Coast Guard Yard, Curtis Bay, Md., 1950s

ex-HQ 700 ex-LE PHUOC DUI (ex-*Pt. Garnet*, WPB 82310)
ex-HQ 701 ex-LE VAN NGA (ex-*Pt. League*, WPB 82304)
ex-HQ 702 ex-HUYNH VAN CU (ex-*Pt. Clear*, WPB 82315)
ex-HQ 703 ex-NGUYEN DAO (ex-*Pt. Gammon*, WPB 82328)
ex-HQ 704 ex-DAO THUC (ex-*Pt. Comfort*, WPB 82317)
ex-HQ 705 ex-LE NGOC THAN (ex-*Pt. Ellis*, WPB 82330)
ex-HQ 706 ex-NGUYEN NGOC THACH (ex-*Pt. Slocum*, WPB 82313)
ex-HQ 707 ex-DANG VAN HOANH (ex-*Pt. Hudson*, WPB 82322)
ex-HQ 708 ex-LE DINH HUNG (ex-*Pt. White*, WPB 82308)
ex-HQ 709 ex-THUONG TIEN (ex-*Pt. Dume*, WPB 82325)
ex-HQ 710 ex-PHAM NGOC CHAU (ex-*Pt. Arden*, WPB 82309)
ex-HQ 711 ex-DAO VAN DANG (ex-*Pt. Glover*, WPB 82307)
ex-HQ 712 ex-LE DGOC AN (ex-*Pt. Jefferson*, WPB 82306)
ex-HQ 713 ex-HUYNH VAN NGAN (ex-*Pt. Kennedy*, WPB 82320)
ex-HQ 714 ex-TRAN LO (ex-*Pt. Young*, WPB 82303)
ex-HQ 715 ex-BUI VIET THANH (ex-*Pt. Partridge*, WPB 82305)
ex-HQ 716 ex-NGUYEN AN (ex-*Pt. Caution*, WPB 82301)
ex-HQ 717 ex-NGUYEN HAN (ex-*Pt. Welcome*, WPB 82329)
ex-HQ 718 ex-NGO VAN QUYEN (ex-*Pt. Banks*, WPB 82327)
ex-HQ 719 ex-VAN DIEN (ex-*Pt. Lomas*, WPB 82321)
ex-HQ 720 ex-HO DANG LA (ex-*Pt. Grace*, WPB 82323)
ex-HQ 721 ex-DAM THOAJ (ex-*Pt. Mast*, WPB 82316)
ex-HQ 722 ex-HUYNH BO (ex-*Pt. Grey*, WPB 82324)
ex-HQ 723 ex-NGUYEN KIM HUNG (ex-*Pt. Orient*, WPB 82319)
ex-HQ 724 ex-HO DUY (ex-*Pt. Cypress*, WPB 82326)
ex-HQ 725 ex-TROUNG BA (ex-*Pt. Maromec*, WPB 82331)

ex-Ngo Van Quyen   1969

D: 64 tons (67 fl)   **S:** 23.7 kts   **Dim:** 25.3 × 5.23 × 1.95
A: 1/81-mm mortar combined with 12.7-mm machine gun − 4/12.7-mm machine guns (I × 4)
Range: 460/23.7, 1,400/8   **Man:** 12 men
M: 2 Cummins VT-12-M diesels; 2 props; 1,600 hp

REMARKS: Had been operating in Vietnamese waters with U.S. Coast Guard crews when transferred to South Vietnam in 1969-70. Probably rearmed, if operational.

PATROL BOATS (*continued*)

♦ **1 or more ex-U.S. LSSL-1-class fire-support gunboats**

Bldr: Commercial Iron Works, Portland, Ore.

	Laid down	L	In serv.
ex-HQ 230 ex-NGUYEN NGOC LONG (ex-LSSL-96)	18-12-44	6-1-45	24-1-45

ex-Nguyen Ngoc Long   1969

D: 227 tons light (387 fl)   **S:** 14.4 kts   **Dim:** 48.16 × 7.21 × 1.73
A: 1/76.2-mm DP – 4/40-mm AA (II × 2) – 4/20-mm AA (II × 2) – 4/12.7-mm machine guns (I × 4) – 2/81-mm mortars (I × 2)
Electron Equipt: Radar: 1/Raytheon 1500B   **Electric:** 120 kw
Fuel: 76 tons   **Range:** 5,500/12   **Man:** Approx. 70 men
M: 8 GM 6-71 diesels; 2 controllable-pitch props; 1,320 hp

REMARKS: Transferred to South Vietnam 12-65 after serving in the Japanese Navy 1953-64. Had been refitted and modernized with additional armor at Guam in the early 1970s.

PATROL CRAFT

♦ **up to 107 ex-U.S. Swift Mk-1 and Mk-2 class**

D: 19 tons (fl – Mk 2: 19.2)   **S:** 25 kts   **Man:** 6 men
Dim: Mk 1: 15.28 × 3.99 × 1.07; Mk 2: 15.64 × 4.14 × 1.07
A: 1/81-mm mortar combined with 12.7-mm machine gun – 2/12.7-mm machine guns (II × 1)
Range: 400/24
M: 2 GM 12V71N diesels; 2 props; 860 hp

REMARKS: Built 1968-70. Transferred on completion. Most believed still serviceable.

RIVERINE WARFARE CRAFT

♦ **up to 9 ex-U.S. CCB (command and control boat) class**

CCB class   1967

D: 160 tons light (75.5 fl)   **S:** 8.5 kts   **Dim:** 18.29 × 5.33 × 1.0
A: 1/20-mm AA – 1/12.7-mm machine gun – 2/7.62-mm machine guns (I × 2) – 1/60-mm mortar
Man: 11 men   **Range:** 160/8
M: 2 Gray Marine 64HN9 diesels; 2 props; 450 hp

REMARKS: Built 1969-70. Equipped with communications facility in well occupied by 105-mm mortar in otherwise similar LCM monitor class. Can tow disabled craft. Some had three 20-mm antiaircraft (I × 3) with an ASPB-type turret forward.

♦ **up to 84 ex-U.S. ASPB (assault support patrol boat) class**

D: 30 tons light (38 fl)   **S:** 14 kts   **Dim:** 15.3 × 5.32 × 1.22
A: 2/20-mm AA (I × 2) – 2/76.2-mm machine guns (I × 2) – 2/40-mm grenade launchers
Range: 200/10   **Man:** 5 men
M: 2 GM 12V71N diesels; 2 props; 1,050 hp

REMARKS: Built 1969-70. Two armored turrets with interchangeable armaments of one 20-mm antiaircraft, two 12.7-mm machine guns, or two 40-mm grenade launchers (or a combination thereof). A few had an 81-mm mortar aft in an open well.

♦ **up to 42 ex-U.S. monitor Mk-V class**

Art

D: 60.3 tons light (75.5 fl)   **S:** 8.5 kts   **Dim:** 18.29 × 5.33 × 1.0
A: 2/20-mm AA (I × 2) – 2/12.7-mm machine guns (I × 2) – 4/7.62-mm machine guns – 1/81-mm mortar
Range: 160/8   **Man:** 11 men
M: 2 Gray Marine 64HN9 diesels; 2 props; 450 hp

REMARKS: Built 1969-70. Originally built as monitors, rather than converted as the class below. A few had a turret-mounted 105-mm howitzer in place of the bow 20-mm turret and 81-mm mortar in well. All had screen and "venetian-blind-like" bar armor to break up projectiles. Towing rig on stern of most.

RIVERINE WARFARE CRAFT (*continued*)

Monitor Mk-V class   1967

◆ **up to 22 ex-U.S. converted LCM(6) monitors**

D: 75 tons (fl)   **S:** 8 kts   **Dim:** 18.29 × 5.2 × 1.0
A: 1/40-mm AA (in some) − 1/20-mm AA − 2/12.7-mm machine guns − 1/81-mm mortar (or 2 M10-8 flame throwers)
M: 2 Gray Marine 64HN9 diesels; 2 props; 450 hp   **Man:** 10 men

REMARKS: Converted from LCM(6)-class landing craft. Transferred 1964-67.

◆ **up to 100 ex-U.S. ATC (armored troop carrier) class**

ATC class − note bar armor   1967

D: 55.8 tons light (70 fl)   **S:** 8.5 kts   **Dim:** 17.09 × 5.33 × 3.0
A: 1/20-mm AA − 2/12.7-mm machine guns (I × 2) − 2-6/7.62-mm machine guns (I × 2-6) − 2/40-mm grenade launchers (I × 2)
M: 2 Gray Marine 64HN9 diesels; 2 props; 450 hp   **Man:** 7 men

REMARKS: Transferred 1969. Converted LCM(6)-class landing craft. Can carry up to 40 troops. Bow ramp. Bar armor on hull and superstructure, bullet-proof awning over troop space. A few had a small helicopter platform in place of the awning. Others were configured for refuelling with 4,500-liter tank in the cargo well. Four CSB (combat salvage boat) versions of the LCM(6) design were also left in Vietnam, having been transferred 1969-70.

◆ **up to 293 ex-U.S. PBR (patrol boat, riverine) Mk-II class**

PBR Mk II   1974

D: 6.7 tons light (8 fl)   **S:** 24 kts   **Dim:** 9.73 × 3.53 × 0.6
A: 3/12.7-mm machine guns (II × 1, I × 1) − 1/60-mm mortar
Man: 4 men   **Range:** 150/23
M: 2 GM 6V53N diesels; 2 Jacuzzi water jets; 430 hp

REMARK: Built 1968-70.

◆ **up to 27 ex-U.S. RCP (riverine craft patrol) class**

D: 14 tons (fl)   **S:** 14 kts   **Dim:** 10.9 × 3.15 × 1.1
A: 4/12.7-mm machine guns (II × 2) − 2/7.62-mm machine guns (I × 2)
M: 2 Gray Marine 64HN9 diesels; 2 props; 450 hp   **Man:** 6 men

REMARKS: Unsuccessful predecessor to the PBR type, transferred 1965-69. Others serve in the Thai Navy. Probably few operational.

MINE WARFARE CRAFT

◆ **up to 8 ex-U.S. MSB-5-class minesweeping boats**

MINE WARFARE CRAFT (*continued*)

D: 30 tons (42 fl)   **S:** 12 kts   **Dim:** 17.45 × 4.83 × 1.32
A: Several 12.7-mm machine guns   **Man:** 6 men   **Fuel:** 15.8 tons
M: 2 Packard 2D850 diesels; 2 props; 600 hp

REMARKS: Transferred 1970. Built 1952-56; Wooden construction. Two sweep-current generators; capable of sweeping magnetic, contact, and acoustic mines.

◆ up to 8 ex-U.S. MSR (minesweeper, riverine) class

D: 30 tons light (38 fl)   **S:** 14 kts   **Dim:** 15.3 × 5.32 × 1.22
A: 2/12.7-mm machine guns (II × 1) − 1/7.62-mm machine gun − 1/60-mm mortar
Range: 200/10   **Man:** 5 men
M: 2 GM 12V71N diesels; 2 props; 1,050 hp

REMARKS: Built 1970. A minesweeping version of the ASPB class. Some were equipped with a pipe frame projecting ahead of the craft to explode contact mines. Others had four 88.9-mm rocket launch tubes mounted on the twin machine gun turret on the bow. One or two 40-mm grenade launchers could also be carried.

◆ up to 8 ex-U.S. MSM (minesweeping monitor) river minesweepers

D: 70 tons (fl)   **S:** 8.5 kts   **Dim:** 17.09 × 5.33 × 3.1
A: 2/20-mm AA (I × 2) − 1/12.7-mm machine gun − 2/40-mm grenade launchers
M: 2 GM 64HN9 diesels; 2 props; 450 hp   **Man:** 5 men

REMARKS: Converted LCM(6)-class landing craft, transferred in 1970. Not all had the 20-mm antiaircraft. Bar armor fitted to sides. Retained bow ramp. Could sweep mechanical and acoustic mines.

◆ up to 10 ex-U.S. MLMS (motor launch minesweeper) class

D: 25 tons (fl)   **S:** 8 kts   **Dim:** 15.29 × 4.01 × 1.31
M: 1 Navy DB diesel; 1 prop; 60 hp   **Man:** 4 men

REMARKS: Standard 50-foot wooden motor launches converted for minesweeping in the late 1950s. Transferred in 1963. May no longer be serviceable.

AMPHIBIOUS WARFARE SHIPS

◆ 3 ex-U.S. LST-1- and LST-542-class tank landing ships

	Bldr	Laid down	L	In serv.
ex-HQ 501 ex-DA NANG	Bethlehem,	12-7-44	15-8-44	9-9-44
(ex-*Maricopa County*, LST-938)	Hingham, Mass.			
ex-HQ 503 ex-VUNG TAU	Chicago B & I,	10-12-43	15-4-44	15-5-44
(ex-*Coconino County*, LST-603)	Seneca, Ill.			
ex-HQ 504 ex-QUI NHON	Jeffersonville	7-10-43	23-11-43	8-1-44
(ex-*Bullock County*, LST-509)	B & M, Ind.			

D: 1623 tons light (4,080 fl)   **S:** 11.6 kts
Dim: 99.98 × 15.24 × 4.29   **A:** 8/40-mm AA (II × 2, I × 4)
Electron Equipt: Radar: 1/SPS-53   **Man:** Approx. 100 men
Electric: 300 kw   **Fuel:** 590 tons   **Range:** 6,000/9 (loaded)
M: 2 GM 12-567A (ex-HQ 501: GM 12-278A) diesels; 2 props; 1,700 hp

REMARKS: Transferred to South Vietnam 7-62, 7-69, and 4-70, respectively. All believed to be operational. Several other ex-U.S. LSTs may have been transferred to Vietnam by China, at least one configured as a fuel tanker.

◆ 4 ex-U.S. LSM-1-class medium landing ships

	Bldr	Laid down	L	In serv.
ex-HQ 401 ex-HAN GIANG	Brown SB,	7-10-44	28-10-44	25-11-44
(ex-Fr. LSM-9012, ex-LSM-110)	Houston			
ex-HQ 403 ex-NINH GIANG	Brown SB,	22-8-44	15-9-44	12-10-44
(ex-LSM-85)	Houston			
ex-HQ 405 ex-TIEN GIANG	Pullman Car,	16-3-44	24-5-44	25-6-44
(ex-LSM-313)	Chicago			
ex-HQ 406 ex-HAU GIANG	Federal SB,	11-8-44	20-9-44	16-10-44
(ex-LSM-276)	Newark, N.J.			

e -Ninh Giang   1960s

D: 520 tons light (1,095 fl)   **S:** 12.5 kts   **Dim:** 62.03 × 10.52 × 2.54
A: 2/40-mm AA (II × 1) − 4 or 5/20-mm AA (I × 4 or 5) − 4/12.7-mm machine guns
   (I × 4)
Range: 4,900/12   **Fuel:** 160 tons   **Man:** Approx. 70 men
M: 2 Fairbanks-Morse 38D8⅛ diesels (ex-HQ 406: GM-278A); 2 props; 2,880 hp

REMARK: Transferred to South Vietnam 10-55 (after service in French Navy), 10-56, 6-62, and 3-63, respectively.

◆ 14 ex-U.S. LCU 1466-class utility landing craft

ex-LCU 1475	ex-LCU 1485	ex-LCU 1502
ex-LCU 1479	ex-LCU 1493	ex-LCU 1594
ex-LCU 1480	ex-LCU 1494	ex-LCU 1595
ex-LCU 1481	ex-LCU 1498	ex-YFU 90 (ex-LCU-1582)
ex-LCU 1484	ex-LCU 1501	

D: 367 tons (fl)   **S:** 8 kts   **Dim:** 35.14 × 10.36 × 1.5
A: 4/20-mm AA (II × 2)   **Electron Equipt:** Radar: 1/Raytheon 1500B
Fuel: 11 tons   **Range:** 1,200/6   **Man:** 14 men   **Cargo:** 167 tons.

REMARK: Transferred 1954-70 (ex-YFU-90 in 7-71).

◆ 1 ex-U.S. LCU 501 (LCT(6)) class utility landing craft

ex-LCU 1221   Bldr: Bison SB, Buffalo, N.Y.

D: 143 tons light (309 fl)   **S:** 8 kts   **Dim:** 36.42 × 9.75 × 1.3
A: 4/20-mm AA (II × 2)   **Man:** 13 men   **Range:** 1,200/7
M: 3 Gray Marine 64HN9 diesels; 3 props; 675 hp   **Fuel:** 11 tons
Cargo: 150 tons.

REMARKS: Launched 27-8-44. Transferred to South Vietnam 11-55. Three half-sisters

VIETNAM (*continued*)

AMPHIBIOUS WARFARE SHIPS (*continued*)

converted as salvage lift craft were also left behind in 1975: ex-YLLC-1 (ex-LCU-1348), ex-YLLC-3 (ex-YFU-33, ex-LCU-1195), and ex-YLLC-5 (ex-YFU-2, ex-LCU-529).

NOTE: A number of U.S. LCU(6), LCM(8), LCVP, and LCP-type landing craft were also abandoned; many have probably been returned to service.

SERVICE CRAFT

◆ **3 ex-U.S. 174-foot-class gasoline tankers**

Bldr: George Lawley & Sons, Neponset, Mass. (ex-YOG-56: R.T.C. SB, Camden, N.J.)

	Laid down	L	In serv.
ex-HQ 472 (ex-YOG-67)	26-1-45	17-3-45	4-5-45
ex-HQ 473 (ex-YOG-71)	11-6-45	24-7-45	27-8-45
ex-HQ 475 (ex-YOG-56)	17-5-44	30-9-44	19-2-45

D: 440 tons light (1,390 fl) **S:** 11 kts **Dim:** 53.04 (51.2 pp) × 9.75 × 3.94
A: 2/20-mm AA (I × 2) **Electric:** 80 kw **Fuel:** 25 tons
Man: 23 men **Cargo:** 860 tons
M: 1 GM diesel (ex-YOG-56: Union diesel); 1 prop; 640 hp (ex-YOG-56: 540 hp)

REMARKS: Transferred to South Vietnam in 7-67, 3-70, and 6-72. Employed in transporting diesel fuel.

◆ **1 ex-U.S. 174-foot-class water tanker**

Bldr: Nav. Mec. Castellamare, Italy, 1956

ex-HQ 9118 (ex-YW 152)

D: 1,250 tons (fl) **S:** 9 kts **Dim:** 54.4 × 9.8 × 4.3
A: 2/20-mm AA (I × 2) **Man:** 23 men
M: 1 Ansaldo diesel; 1 prop; 600 hp

REMARKS: Built with U.S. funds for South Vietnam under the Offshore Procurement Program. Also possibly remaining in service is ex-HQ 9113 (ex-YWN-153), a non-self-propelled water barge built in 1955.

◆ **up to 9 ex-U.S. YTL-type small harbor tugs**

ex-YTL 152	ex-YTL 245	ex-YTL 457
ex-YTL 200	ex-YTL 452	ex-YTL 586
ex-YTL 206	ex-YTL 456	. . .

D: 70 tons (80 fl) **S:** 10 kts **Dim:** 20.16 × 5.18 × 2.44
Electric: 40 kw **Fuel:** 7 tons **Man:** 4 men
M: 1 Hoover-Owens-Rentschler diesel; 1 prop; 300 hp

REMARKS: Built 1941-45. Four transferred to South Vietnam in 1955-56, two in 1969, and two in 1971; the original identity of the ninth unit, left behind by the French, is not known.

NOTE: In addition to the ships and craft listed above, the Vietnamese Navy undoubtedly employs many smaller craft ("junks") in patrol and logistics duties. Cargo ships of up to several hundred deadweight tons capacity were built in North Vietnamese shipyards during the Vietnamese War for infiltration purposes; many of these armed craft may still be in military service.

VIRGIN ISLANDS
British

ROYAL VIRGIN ISLANDS POLICE FORCE

◆ **1 patrol craft** Bldr: Brooke Marine, Lowestoft, G.B., 1975

VIRGIN CLIPPER

D: 15 tons **S:** 22 kts **Dim:** 12.2 × 3.7 × 0.6
A: 1/7.62-mm machine gun **Man:** 4 men
Electron Equipt: Radar: 1/Decca 101
M: 2 Caterpillar diesels; 2 props; 370 hp

YEMEN
People's Democratic Republic of (South Yemen)

PERSONNEL: Over 450 officers and men

MERCHANT MARINE (1978): 24 ships—10,061 grt

CORVETTE

◆ **1 ex-Soviet T-58 class**

D: 900 tons (fl) **S:** 18 kts **Dim:** 70.0 × 9.1 × 2.5
A: 4/57-mm AA (II × 2) — 2/RBU-1200 ASW rocket launchers—mines
Electron Equipt: Radar: 1/Don-2, 1/Muff Cob
Sonar: 1/high frequency
M: 2 diesels; 2 props; 4,000 hp **Man:** Approx. 60 men

REMARKS: Former minesweeper. Built in the late 1950s, transferred 1978. Minesweeping equipment deleted.

GUIDED-MISSILE PATROL BOATS

◆ **2 ex-Soviet OSA-II class**

D: 205 tons (245 fl) **S:** 39 kts **Dim:** 39.0 × 7.7 × 1.8
A: 4/SS-N-2B Styx SSM (I × 4) — 4/30-mm AA (II × 2)
Electron Equipt: Radar: 1/Square Tie, 1/Drum Tilt
Man: 30 men **Range:** 450/34, 700/20
M: 3 M-504 diesels; 3 props; 15,000 hp

REMARKS: Transferred 1974. Additional units can be expected.

YEMEN (*continued*)

TORPEDO BOATS

◆ **2 Soviet MOL class**

D: 170 tons (210 fl)   **S:** 40 kts   **Dim:** 39.0 × 7.6 × 1.8
A: 4/30-mm AA (II × 2) – 4/533-mm TT
Electron Equipt: Radar: 1/Pot Drum, 1/Drum Tilt
Range: 450/34, 700/20   **Man:** 30 men
M: 3 M503 diesels; 3 props; 12,000 hp

REMARKS: Transferred 1978. New construction design, based on Osa-class guided-missile patrol boat. Sisters in Somali and Sri Lankan navies.

◆ **2 ex-Soviet P-6 class**

D: 66.5 tons (fl)   **S:** 43 kts   **Dim:** 25.3 × 6.1 × 1.6
A: 4/25-mm AA – 2/533-mm TT – depth charges
Electron Equipt: Radar: 1/Skin Head or Pot Head   **Man:** 12 men
Range: 400/32, 700/15
M: 4 M50-F diesels; 4 props; 4,800 hp

REMARKS: Transferred 1971. Wooden construction. Probably in poor condition, and possibly replaced by the craft above.

PATROL BOATS

◆ **2 ex-Soviet Zhuk class**

D: 50 tons (60 fl)   **S:** 30 kts   **Dim:** 26.0 × 4.9 × 1.5
A: 2/14.5-mm machine guns (II × 1)   **Man:** 12-14 men
M: 2 M50 diesels; 2 props; 2,400 hp

REMARK: Transferred in 2-75.

◆ **2 ex-Soviet S.O.-1 class**

D: 190 tons (215 fl)   **S:** 28 kts   **Dim:** 42.0 × 6.1 × 1.9
A: 4/25-mm AA (II × 2) – 2/RBU-1200 ASW rocket launchers – 2/depth-charge racks – mines
Electron Equipt: Radar: 1/Pot Head   Sonar: 1/high frequency
Range: 1,100/13   **Man:** 30 men
M: 3 diesels; 3 props; 7,500 hp

REMARK: Transferred in 4-72 in bad condition.

◆ **1 ex-Soviet Poluchat-I class**

D: 80 tons (90 fl)   **S:** 18 kts   **Dim:** 29.6 × 5.8 × 1.5
A: 2/14.5-mm AA (II × 1)   **Man:** 12 men
M: 2 M50 diesels; 2 props; 2,400 hp

REMARKS: May be a torpedo-retriever vice patrol-boat version. Transferred in the early 1970s.

AMPHIBIOUS WARFARE SHIPS

◆ **4 ex-Soviet Polnocny-B-class medium landing ships**

Bldr: Polnocny SY, Gdansk, Poland

D: 950 tons (fl)   **S:** 18 kts   **Dim:** 74.0 × 8.5 × 2.0
A: 2/14.5-mm machine guns or 2/30-mm AA (II × 1) – 2/140-mm barrage rocket launchers (XVIII × 2)

Electron Equipt: Radar: 1/Spin Trough, possibly 1/Drum Tilt
M: 2 diesels; 2 props; 4,000 hp   **Man:** 40 men

REMARKS: Two delivered 8-73, one in 7-77 and one in 1979.

◆ **3 ex-Soviet T-4 class landing craft**

D: 35 tons light (93 fl)   **S:** 10 kts   **Dim:** 19.9 × 5.6 × 1.4
M: 2 3D6 diesels; 2 props; 600 hp   **Range:** 1,500/10

REMARKS: Transferred 11-70. Resemble U.S. LCM(6) class.

MINISTRY OF THE INTERIOR

◆ **5 Tracker-2 class**   Bldr: Fairey Marine, G.B.

D: 31 tons (fl)   **S:** 29 kts   **Dim:** 19.25 × 4.98 × 1.45
A: 1/20-mm AA   **Man:** 11 men   **Range:** 650/25
M: 2 MTU 8V331 TC diesels; 2 props; 2,200 hp

REMARKS: Ordered 8-77; delivered 1977-78. Used in customs duties.

◆ **4 Spear class**   Bldr: Fairey Marine, G.B.

D: 4.5 tons (fl)   **S:** 26 kts   **Dim:** 9.1 × 2.8 × 0.8
A: 3/7.62-mm machine guns   **M:** 2 diesels; 2 props; 290 hp

REMARKS: Three delivered 20-9-75; fourth during 1978. Used in customs duties. Fiberglass construction.

◆ **1 Interceptor class**   Bldr: Fairey Marine, G.B.

REMARKS: Catamaran with two 135-hp outboard motors, can carry eight 25-man life rafts, and intended for rescue duties. Overall: 7.6 meters.

YEMEN ARAB REPUBLIC
(North Yemen)

PERSONNEL: Approximately 200 men

MERCHANT MARINE (1978): 4 ships – 1,436 grt

TORPEDO BOATS

◆ **3 ex-Soviet P-4 class**

D: 22.5 tons (fl)   **S:** 55 kts   **Dim:** 19.0 × 3.3 × 1.0
A: 2/14.5-mm machine guns (II × 1) – 2/450-mm TT
Electron Equipt: Radar: 1/Skin Head   **Man:** 12 men
M: 2 M50 diesels; 1 props; 2,400 hp

REMARKS: Built in mid-1950s; transferred in late 1960s. Aluminum construction. One other unit discarded.

YEMEN ARAB REPUBLIC (NORTH YEMEN) *(continued)*

PATROL BOATS

◆ **3 Broadsword class** Bldr: Halter Marine, New Orleans, La., 1978

200 SANA'A   300 13TH JUNE   400 25TH SEPTEMBER

13th June   1978

D: 90 tons (fl)   **S:** 28 kts   **Dim:** 32.0 × 6.3 × 1.9
A: 2/23-mm AA (II × 1) − 2/14.5-mm AA (II × 1) − 2/12.7-mm machine guns (I × 2)
Electron Equipt: Radar: 1/Decca 914   **Man:** 14 men   **Fuel:** 16.3 tons
M: 3 GM 16V71 T1 diesels; 3 props; . . . hp   **Electric:** 120 kw

REMARKS: Ordered 1977. Armament, added after delivery, is of Soviet origin.

◆ **2 Soviet Zhuk class**

D: 60 tons (fl)   **S:** 34 kts   **Dim:** 24.6 × 5.2 × 1.9
A: 4/14.5-mm AA (II × 2)   **Man:** 18 men
M: 2/ M50-F diesels; 2 props; 2,400 hp

REMARKS: Built 1978; transferred 1978. Unlike other units of this class, the North Yemeni units have their twin antiaircraft in enclosed gun houses with hemispherical covers.

SERVICE CRAFT

◆ **2 Soviet T-4-class landing craft**

D: 35 tons light (95 fl)   **S:** 10 kts   **Dim:** 19.9 × 5.6 × 1.4
M: 2 3D6 diesels; 2 props; 600 hp   **Range:** 1,500/10

REMARKS: Transferred around 1970. Resemble U.S. LCM(6) class.

◆ **1 Soviet Poluchat-1-class torpedo-retriever**

D: 80 tons (90 fl)   **S:** 18 kts   **Dim:** 29.6 × 5.8 × 1.5
A: 2/14.5-mm AA (II × 1)   **Man:** 12 men
M: 2 M50-F diesels; 2 props; 2,400 hp

REMARKS: Transferred late 1960s to support the P-4-class torpedo boats. Has stern ramp for recovering torpedoes. Also used as a patrol craft.

YUGOSLAVIA

PERSONNEL: 14,000 men

MERCHANT MARINE (1978): 468 ships − 2,365,630 grt
(tankers: 29 ships − 214,779 grt)

NAVAL AVIATION: One squadron of Soviet Ka-25 Hormone ASW helicopters, several Soviet Mi-8 and U.S. Sikorskiy S-55 liaison helicopters, and two Canadian DHC-2 Beaver STOL light transports.

SUBMARINES

◆ **2 Sava class submarine** Bldr: Split SY

	Laid down	L	In serv.
831 SAVA	1975	1977	1978
832 N . . .	1977	. . .	. . .

D: 964 tons, submerged   **S:** 16 kts, submerged
Dim: 55.8 × 5.05 × . . .   **Man:** 35 men   **Endurance:** 28 days
A: 6/533-mm TT − 10 torpedoes or 20 mines
M: Diesel-electric: 1 prop; 2,400 hp

REMARKS: Maximum diving depth: 300 meters. Completion of second unit delayed. Very strongly resemble the Heroj class.

◆ **3 Heroj class** Bldr: Uljanik, Pula

	Laid down	L	In serv.
821 HEROJ	1965	1966	1968
822 JUNAK	1966	1967	1969
823 USKOK	. . .	. . .	1970

Heroj   1968

SUBMARINES (*continued*)

D: 1,068 tons standard, 1,170 surfaced, 1,350 submerged   **S:** 16/10 kts
Dim: 64.0 × 6.6 × 5.0   **Man:** 55 men   **Range:** 9,700/8
A: 6/533-mm TT   **M:** 2 diesels, electric motors; 1 prop; 2,400 hp

◆ **2 Sutjeska class**   Bldr: Uljanik, Pula

		Laid down	L	In serv.
811	SUTJESKA	1957	28-9-58	9-60
812	NERETVA	1957	1959	1962

Neretva—now has bulbous bow   G. Arra, 1969

D: 700 tons standard, 820 surfaced, 945 submerged   **Dim:** 55.0 × 6.6 × 4.8
S: 14/9 kts   **Man:** 38 men   **Range:** 4,400/8.6
A: 6/533-mm TT   **M:** 2 Sulzer diesels, electric motors; 1,800 hp

REMARK: First submarines built in Yugoslavia. New bow sonar arrays added during the early 1970s.

◆ **2 or more Mala-class midget submarines**

D: . . .   **S:** . . . kts   **Dim:** 8.2 × 1.9 (diameter)
M: 1 electric motor   **Man:** 2 men

DESTROYER

◆ **1 Split class**   Bldr: "3 Maj" Brodogradiliste, Rijeka

		Laid down	L	In serv.
11	SPLIT (ex-*Spalado*, ex-*Split*)	7-39	1940	4-7-58

D: 2,400 tons (3,000 fl)   **S:** 24 kts   **Dim:** 120.0 (114.7 pp) × 12.0 × 3.7
A: 4/127-mm DP (I × 4) – 12/40-mm AA (IV × 1, II × 2, I × 4) – 5/533-mm TT (V × 1) – 2/Mk-11 Hedgehogs – 6/Mk-6 depth-charge projectors – 2/Mk-9 depth-charge racks   **Man:** 240 men
Electron Equipt: Radars: 1/974, 1/SG-1, 1/SC, 1/Mk 12, 1/Mk 22, 1/Mk 34
           Sonar: QCU series
M: 2 sets GT; 2 props; 50,000 hp   **Boilers:** 2   **Fuel:** 590 tons

REMARKS: Original plans from Chantiers Loire, France. Equipped to lay 40 mines. U.S. electronics and weapons dating from World War II. Mk-37 gunfire-control system with Mk-12 and Mk-22 radars forward, one Mk-63 gunfire-control radar with Mk-34 radar on the 40-mm quadruple mount aft, two Mk-51, Mod. 2, GFCS for the twin 40-mm mounts. Probably now immobile; one boiler known to be inoperable.

NOTE: Although Yugoslavia is building training frigates of considerable sophistication (combined diesel/gas turbine propulsion, modern ordnance) for Iraq and Indonesia, there are no indications of construction of such a ship for the Yugoslav Navy itself. One might be expected during the 1980s, however, as a replacement for the aged flagship *Split*.

CORVETTES

◆ **2 Mornar class**   Bldr: Tito SY, Kraljevica

		Laid down	L	In serv.
PBR 551	MORNAR	1957	1958	10-9-59
PBR 552	BORAC	1964	1965	1965

Borac   1973

D: 330 tons (430 fl)   **S:** 19 kts   **Dim:** 51.8 × 6.97 × 2.0
A: 2/40-mm AA (I × 2) – 2/20-mm AA (I × 2) – 4/RBU-1200 ASW rocket launchers – 2/Mk-6 depth-charge projectors – 2/Mk-9 depth-charge racks
Electron Equipt: Radar: 1/Decca navigational   Sonar: 1/high frequency
Range: 2,000/15, 3,000/12   **Man:** 60 men
M: 4 SEMT-Pielstick 14-cyl. diesels; 2 props; 3,240 hp

REMARKS: Modernized 1970-73 at Sava Kovacevic Naval Yard, Tivat. Original two 76.2-mm dual purpose, two 40-mm antiaircraft older model, Mousetrap ASW rocket launchers replaced by new Bofors guns and Soviet ASW rocket launchers.

◆ **1 French Le Fougueux class**   Bldr: F. C. Méditerranée, Le Havre

		Laid down	L	In serv.
PBR 581	UDARNIK (ex-P-6, ex-PC-1615)	1954	21-12-54	1-56

D: 325 tons (402 fl)   **S:** 18.7 kts   **Dim:** 53.10 (50.9 wl) × 6.4 × 2.1
A: 2/40-mm AA (I × 2) – 2/20-mm AA (I × 2) – 1/Mk-11 Hedgehog – 4/Mk-6 depth-charge projectors – 2/Mk-9-depth-charge racks
Electron Equipt: Radar: 1/navigational   Sonar: 1/high frequency
Range: 3,300/15, 6,350/12   **Man:** 62 men   **Fuel:** 53 tons
M: 4 SEMT-Pielstick 14-cyl. diesels; 2 props; 3,240 hp   **Electric:** 60 kw

REMARKS: Built with U.S. Offshore Procurement Funds as U.S. PC-1615; transferred on completion. One sister in the Tunisian Navy. Engines can produce 3,840 hp for brief periods.

CORVETTES (*continued*)

Udarnik

GUIDED-MISSILE PATROL BOATS

◆ **5 Rade Končar class** Bldr: Tito SY, Kraljevica

	L	In serv.
RT 401 RADE KONČAR	15-10-76	4-77
RT 402 VLADO ČETKOVIĆ	28-8-77	1977
RT 403 RAMIZ SADIKU	1978	10-9-78
RT 404 HASAN ZAHIROVIČ LASA	1979	11-79
RT 405 JORDAN NIKOLOV-ORCE	1979	1980

Rade Končar   1971

D: 250 tons (fl)   **S:** 40 kts   **Dim:** 45.0 × 8.4 × 1.8
A: 2/SS-N-2B Styx SSM – 2/57-mm Bofors AA
Electron Equipt: 1/Decca navigational – 1/9LV200 system

Rade Končar   1977

Range: 500/35   **Man:** 30 men
M: CODAG: 2 Rolls-Royce Proteus gas turbines, 5800 hp each; 2 MTU diesels, 2,600 hp each; 4 controllable-pitch props; 18,800 hp

REMARKS: Of Yugoslav design, using Swedish (Svensk Philips) fire control and guns and Soviet missiles. Have on Soviet Square Head IFF interrogator. Styx missiles chosen over the Exocet originally planned.

◆ **10 ex-Soviet Osa-I class**

RC 301 M. ACEV	RC 306 N. MARTINOVIC
RC 302 V. BAGAT	RC 307 J. MAZAR
RC 303 P. DRAPSIN	RC 308 K. ROJC
RC 304 S. FILIPOVIC	RC 309 F. ROZMAN-STANE
RC 305 V. SKORPIK	RC 310 Z. JOVANOVIC-SPANAC

M. Acev

GUIDED-MISSILE PATROL BOATS (*continued*)

D: 175 tons (210 fl)   **S:** 36 kts   **Dim:** 39.0 × 7.7 × 1.8
A: 4/SS-N-2 Styx SSM—4/30-mm AA (II × 2)   **Man:** 25 men
Electron Equipt: Radars: 1/Square Tie, 1/Drum Tilt
                          IFF: 1/High Pole B, 2/Square Head
M: 3 M 503A diesels; 3 props; 12,000 hp   **Range:** 450/34, 700/20

REMARK: Transferred 1965-69.

TORPEDO AND GUN BOATS

◆ **14 Soviet Shershen class**   Bldr: 4 in USSR; others: Tito SY, Kraljevica, 1966-71

TC 211 to TC 224

Known names: BIKOVAC, CRVENA ZVIJEZDA, IVAN, JADRAN, KOMAT, PARTIZAN,
PARTIZAN II, PIONIR, PROLETER, STRJELKO, TOPCIDER

D: 150 tons (180 fl)   **S:** 45 kts   **Dim:** 34.0 × 7.2 × 1.5
A: 4/30-mm AA (II × 2)—4/533-mm TT—mines   **Man:** 22 men
Electron Equipt: Radars: 1/Pot Drum, 1/Drum Tilt
                          IFF: 1/High Pole B, 1/Square Head
M: 3 M503A diesels; 3 props; 12,000 hp   **Range:** 450/34, 700/20

REMARK: Ten built in Yugoslavia under license, after four were transferred in 1965.
No depth-charge racks, as on Soviet units.

◆ **8 158-type former torpedo boats**   Bldr: Yugoslavia, 1950s

D: 55-60 tons   **S:** 26 kts   **Dim:** 21.0 × 6.5 × 1.5
A: 1/40-mm AA—2/12.7-mm machine guns (II × 2)—2-4 mines
Electron Equipt: Radar: 1/Decca 45   **Man:** 14 men
M: 3 Junkers motors; 3 props; 3,300 hp

REMARKS: Copied after U.S. Higgins 78-foot torpedo boat, but used aircraft engines
captured from Germany. Formerly had two torpedo tubes. Possibly deleted. Wooden
construction. Some had two 40-mm guns (I × 2).

PATROL BOATS

◆ **12 131-type coastal patrol craft**   Bldr: Trogir SY, 1965-68

PC 131 to PC 140:

BRESICE	GRANICA	KOZUF	RUDNIK
CER	KALNIK	LOVCEN	TRIVAL
DURMITOR	KOTOR	ROMANIJA	VELIBIT

Kotor

D: 85 tons (120 fl)   **S:** 17 kts   **Dim:** 32.0 × 5.5 × 2.5
A: 6/20-mm Hispano Suiza HS831 AA (III × 2)
Electron Equipt: Radar: 1/Kelvin-Hughes 14/9
M: 2 diesels; 2 props; 900 hp

REMARK: May serve in the Maritime Border Brigade, an organization similar to a coast
guard.

◆ **up to 6 Kraljevica class**   Bldr: Tito SY, Kraljevica

PBR 510	PBR 511	PBR 512	PBR 519	PBR 521	PBR 524

PBR 512—before rearmament

PATROL BOATS (*continued*)

D: 190 tons (202 fl)   **S:** 18 kts   **Dim:** 41.0 × 6.3 × 2.2
A: 2/40-mm AA (II × 2) − 4/20-mm AA − 2/RBU-1200 ASW rocket launchers − 2/Mk-6 depth-charge projectors − 2/depth-charge racks
Electron Equipt: Radar: 1/Decca 45
                          Sonar: QCU-2 or Soviet high frequency
Range: 1,000/12   **Man:** 44 men
M: 2 M.A.N. W8V 30/38 diesels; 2 props; 3,300 hp

REMARKS: Units of this class have been transferred to Sudan, Ethiopia, and Bangladesh. A number have been scrapped. Were produced in two series, some having a U.S. 76.2-mm dual purpose forward and others a U.S. Hedgehog. Survivors all believed to be armed as above.

MINE WARFARE SHIPS

◆ 4 French Sirius-class coastal minesweepers

Bldrs: M 161: Mali Losinj SY, Yugoslavia; others: A. Normand, Le Havre, France

M 151 VUKOV KLANAC (ex-*Hrabi*, ex-MSC-229)
M 152 PODGORA (ex-*Smeli*, ex-MSC-230)
M 153 BLITVENICA (ex-*Slobodni*, ex-MSC-231)
M 161 GRADAC (ex-*Snazhi*)

Blitvenica, Podgora, and Vukov Klanac—with old numbers   1956

D: 400 tons (440 fl)   **S:** 15 kts (sweeping: 11.5)
Dim: 46.4 (42.7 pp) × 8.55 × 2.5   **Man:** 40 men
A: 1/40-mm AA − 1/20-mm AA   **Range:** 3,000/10   **Fuel:** 48 tons
M: 2 SEMT-Pielstick 16-cyl. diesels; 2 props; 2,000 hp

REMARKS: First three built with U.S. Offshore Procurement funds. M 161 in service 1960. Wooden-planked hulls on metal framing.

◆ 4 British "-ham"-class minesweepers   Bldr: Yugoslavia, 1964-66

M 141 N . . . (ex-MSI-98)   M 143 IZ (ex-MSI-100)
M 142 BRSEC (ex-MSI-99)   M 144 OLIB (ex-MSI-101)

D: 123 tons (164 fl)   **S:** 14 kts   **Dim:** 32.43 × 6.45 × 1.7
A: 1/40-mm   **Man:** 22 men   **Range:** 1,500/12, 2,000/9
M: 2 Paxman YHAXM diesels; 2 props; 1,100 hp   **Fuel:** 15 tons

REMARKS: Built under U.S. Offshore Procurement Program. Composite construction: wooden planking over a metal-framed hull.

◆ 6 117-class inshore minesweepers   Bldr: Yugoslavia, 1966-68

ML 117   ML 118   ML 119   ML 120   ML 121   ML 122

D: 120 tons (131 fl)   **S:** 12 kts   **Dim:** 30.0 × 5.5 × 1.5
A: 1/20-mm AA − 2/12.7-mm machine guns (I × 2)
M: 2 GM diesels; 1,000 hp   **Man:** 25 men

REMARK: Also used for coastal patrol.

◆ 3 Nestin-class river minesweepers   Bldr: Brodotehnika, Belgrade

M 331 NESTIN   M 332 MOTAJICA   M 333 BELEGIS

D: 65 tons   **S:** 15 kts   **Dim:** 27.0 × 6.3 × 1.6
A: 2/20-mm AA (I × 2) − mines   **M:** 2 diesels; 2 props; 520 hp

REMARKS: M 331 launched 20-12-75, M 332 launched 18-12-76, and M 333 launched 1-77. Hull of light metal alloy. Additional units may have been completed. Has been offered for export. Very low freeboard. Used on the Danube.

◆ 14 small river minesweepers

RML 301 to RML 314

D: 38 tons   **S:** 12 kts   **A:** 1/20-mm AA

REMARKS: Built 1951-53. Used on the Danube. Being phased out.

AMPHIBIOUS WARFARE SHIPS

NOTE: An LST design of some 2,980 tons, 102.0 × 14.2 × 3.1, has been offered for export, but there are no indications that any are being built for the Yugoslav Navy itself. The ships would have two diesels totaling 6,800 hp, two 40-mm antiaircraft (I × 2) and would be able to transport 1,500 tons of cargo.

◆ 24 DTM-211 class landing craft   Bldr: Yugoslavia, 1950s

DTM 211 to DTM 234

D: 240 tons (410 fl)   **S:** 10.3 kts   **Dim:** 49.8 × 6.6 × 1.35
A: *See* Remarks   **Man:** 27 men   **Range:** 500/9.3
M: 3 Gray Marine 64HN9 diesels; 3 props; 625 hp

REMARKS: Near duplicates of the World War II German MFP-D class. Nearly all have been equipped with hull sponsons extending beam to 8.6 meters and providing space for two mine rails with a total capacity of up to 100 small mines. Armament has included one 40-mm antiaircraft or four 20-mm antiaircraft (IV × 1) and two 12.7-mm machine guns. Bow ramp. Can carry 140 tons of vehicles or 200 men.

◆ 15 601-class landing craft   Bldr: Yugoslavia, 1976-. . .

DSC 601 to DSC 615

D: 35 tons   **S:** 22 kts   **Dim:** 21.4 × 4.6 × 0.6
A: 1/20-mm AA   **M:** 2 diesels; 2 props; 1,125 hp

REMARKS: Fiberglass construction. Bow ramp. Offered for export also.

AUXILIARY SHIPS

◆ **1 Soviet Moma-class hydrographic ship**   Bldr: Gdansk, Poland, 1971

PH 33 ANDRIJA MOHOROVIČIĆ

Andrija Mohorovičić   1971

D: 1,260 tons (1,540 fl)   **S:** 17 kts   **Dim:** 73.3 × 10.8 × 3.8
Range: 8,700/11   **Man:** 56 men
M: 2 Sgoda 6TD48 diesels; 2 controllable-pitch props; 3,600 hp

REMARKS: Transferred in 1972. Carries one survey launch. Five-ton crane for navigational buoy handling. Four laboratories totalling 35 m² deck space. Used for oceanographic research, hydrographic surveys, and buoy tending.

◆ **1 salvage vessel**   Bldr: Tito SY, Belgrade

PS 12 SPASILAC

D: 750 tons   **S:** 16 kts   **Dim:** 53.0 × 8.0 × 3.9
M: 2 diesels; 2 props; 3,000 hp

REMARKS: In service 10-9-76. Replacement for a salvage ship of the same name that was built in 1929 and has now been scrapped.

◆ **1 presidential yacht**   Bldr: C.R.D.A., San Marco, Trieste

Jadranka

	Laid down	L	In serv.
JADRANKA (ex-*Biokovo*, ex-*Beli Orao*, ex-*Zagaria*, ex-*Alba*)	23-12-38	3-6-39	10-39

D: 567 tons (660 fl)   **S:** 17 kts (trials: 18.5)
Dim: 60.45 × 7.93 × 2.7
M: 2 Sulzer diesels; 2 props; 1,900 hp

REMARKS: Served in Italian Navy during World War II. Can carry two 40-mm antiaircraft (I × 2), two 20-mm antiaircraft (I × 2).

◆ **1 cadet training ship**   Bldr: Ansaldo, Genoa, 1938

GALEB (ex-*Kuchuk*, ex-*Ramb III*)

Galeb

D: 5,182 tons   **S:** 16 kts   **Dim:** 117.3 × 15.6 × 5.6
A: None   **M:** 2 Ansaldo diesels; 2 props; 7,200 hp

REMARKS: Begun as a commercial banana carrier; used as an auxiliary cruiser and minelayer by the Italian Navy during World War II. Ceded to Yugoslavia after the war. Can be fitted with four 40-mm antiaircraft (I × 4). Has been used as the presidential yacht but is mostly used as a cadet training ship.

◆ **1 topsail training schooner**   Bldr: Blohm & Voss, Hamburg, 1932

JADRAN

D: 720 tons   **S:** 8 kts   **Dim:** 58.0 × 8.8 × 4.2
M: 1 Linke-Hoffman diesel; 375 hp   **Sail area:** 800 m²

REMARK: Accommodations for 150 cadets.

◆ **2 command ships**

VIS

REMARKS: Built in Yugoslavia in 1956. Serves as flagship for missile boats.

KOZARA

REMARKS: Former presidential yacht, now reportedly flagship of the Danube River Flotilla.

YUGOSLAVIA (*continued*)

SERVICE CRAFT

◆ **4 PN-13-class fuel tankers** Bldr: Yugoslavia, 1955-56

PN 13   PN 14   PN 15   PN 16

   D: 420 tons (650 fl)   **S:** 7 kts   **Dim:** 43.2 × 7.0 × 4.2
   M: 1 Burmeister & Wain diesel; 1 prop; 300 hp   **Range:** 1,500/7
   Cargo: 300 tons

REMARK: Sister PN 17 transferred to Sudan in 1969.

◆ **2 PN-24-class fuel tankers** Bldr: Split SY, 1950s

PN 24   PN 25

   D: 300 tons (430 fl)   **S:** 7 kts   **Dim:** 46.4 × 7.2 × 3.2
   M: 1 Burmeister & Wain diesel; 1 prop; 300 hp

◆ **4 PT-71-class cargo lighters** Bldr: Split SY, 1950s

PT 71   PT 72   PT 73   PT 74

   D: 310 tons (428 fl)   **S:** 7 kts   **Dim:** 43.1 × 7.2 × 4.85
   M: 1 Burmeister & Wain diesel; 1 prop; 300 hp

◆ **6 PT-61-class cargo lighters** Bldr: Pula and Sibenik SYs, 1951-59

PT 61   PT 62   PT 63   PT 64   PT 65   PT 66

   D: 695 tons fl   **S:** 7 kts   **Dim:** 46.4 × 7.2 × 3.2
   M: 1 Burmeister & Wain diesel; 1 prop; 300 hp

◆ **4 PO-52-class ammunition lighters** Bldr: Split SY, 1950s

   D: 695 tons (fl)   **S:** 7 kts   **Dim:** 46.4 × 7.2 × 3.2
   M: 1 Burmeister & Wain diesel; 1 prop; 300 hp

◆ **3 water tankers**

PV 11   PV 12   PV 13

   D: 250 tons   **S:** . . .   **Dim:** 32.2 × . . . × . . .
   M: 1 diesel; 1 prop; . . . hp   **Cargo:** 125 tons

◆ **4 PR-37-class coastal tugs**

PR 37   PR 38   PR 39   PR 40

◆ **8 LR-67-class harbor tugs**

LR 67   LR 68   LR 69   LR 70   LR 71   LR 72   LR 73   LR 74

ZAIRE

PERSONNEL: 300 men

MERCHANT MARINE (1978): 34 ships — 109,785 grt

TORPEDO BOATS

◆ **4 Chinese Hu Chwan-class semi-hydrofoils**

   D: 39 tons (fl)   **S:** 54 kts   **Dim:** 21.8 × 4.9 (7.5 over foils) × 1.0
   A: 4/14.5-mm AA (II × 2) — 2/533-mm TT
   M: 3 M50 F diesels; 3 props; 3,600 hp   **Range:** 500/20

REMARKS: Date of transfer not known; may actually be the similar P-4/North Korean design listed directly below.

◆ **3 ex-North Korean-built Soviet P-4 class**

   D: 22.5 tons (fl)   **S:** 55 kts   **Dim:** 19.0 × 3.3 × 1.0
   A: 2/14.5-mm AA (II × 1) — 2/450-mm TT   **Man:** 12 men
   M: 2 M50 F diesels; 2 props; 2,400 hp

REMARKS: Transferred in 1974. May in fact be of a similar, indigenous North Korean design with 533-mm torpedo tubes.

PATROL BOATS

◆ **4 Chinese Shanghai-II class**

101   102   103   104

   D: 155 tons (fl)   **S:** 28 kts   **Dim:** 38.8 × 5.4 × 1.6
   A: 4/37-mm AA (II × 2) — 4/25-mm AA (II × 2)   **Man:** 25 men
   Electron Equipt: Radar: 1/Pot Head
   M: 4 M50 F diesels; 4 props; 4,800 hp

REMARK: Transferred two in 1976, two in 1978.

PATROL CRAFT

◆ **12 Arcoa class** Bldr: Arcoa, France

REMARKS: Ordered in 7-74; no other data available. For use on lakes and rivers. All delivered by 1976.

◆ **6 ex-U.S. Swift Mk-II class** Bldr: Swiftships, Morgan City, La., 1971

   D: 19.2 tons (fl)   **S:** 25 kts   **Dim:** 15.64 × 4.14 × 1.07
   A: 6/12.7-mm machine guns (II × 1, I × 4)   **Man:** 12 men
   M: 2 GM 12 V 71N diesels; 2 props; 860 hp   **Range:** 400/24

REMARKS: Used on inland lakes. Aluminum construction. One earlier unit of similar design, purchased in 1968, may still exist.

NOTE: There are a number of additional small riverine patrol and logistics support craft.

ZANZIBAR

Although part of the United Republic of Tanzania, Zanzibar has internal autonomy and its own armed forces.

◆ **4 patrol craft**   Bldr: Vosper Thornycroft, G.B.

   D: 70 tons   **S:** 24.5 kts   **Dim:** 22.9 × 6.0 × 1.5
   A: 2/20-mm AA (I × 2)   **Range:** 800/20   **M:** 2 diesels; 2 props; 1,840 hp

REMARKS: The first two units were delivered in 7-73, the last two in 1974. Fiberglass construction.

INDEX OF SHIPS

All ships are indexed by their full names, e.g., Almirante Domecq Garcia.

ADDENDA

ARGENTINA

◆ *1 new construction antarctic supply ship*
Bldr: Principe & Menghe SY, Maciel Isl.

	Laid down	L	In serv.
N . . .	6–79	. . .	9–80

D: 9,200 tons (fl)   **S:** 18 kts   **Dim:** 130.7 (120.0 pp) × 19.5 × 7.0

A . . .   **Man:** 180 men   **Fuel:** 300 tons

M: 2 diesels; 2 controllable-pitch props; . . . hp

REMARKS: Will be able to transport 450 passengers, plus 3,500 m³ dry and 250 m³ refrigerated stores. Two helicopters.

FRIGATES

Now only four MEKO-360-class frigates are to be built, all in Germany. They will be supplemented by a new Blohm & Voss-design frigate class displacing 1,400 tons (fl), the MEKO 140, six of which are to be built at AFNE, Rio Santiago.

An oceanographic ship of 390 dwt, 55.0 × 11.0 × 1.7, is to be delivered by Hitachi Zosen, Japan, in 6–80; it will be capable of 13.9 knots on diesel engines.

AUSTRALIA

The destroyer *Vampire* (D–11) is scheduled to become a training ship in 4–80, assisting *Jervis Bay*. Her sister *Vendetta* (D–08) was stricken in 1979.

The new replenishment oiler to replace the *Supply* will be laid down in Australia in 1981 for delivery in 7–83. The design will generally follow that of the French *Durance*, and will displace 18,100 tons (fl).

CANADA

COAST GUARD

◆ *2 new construction icebreakers*

N . . .	N . . .		

D: 42,000 tons (fl)   **S:** 20 kts   **Dim:** 119.0 × 32.2 × 12.5

Man: 124 men

M: Nuclear reactor and gas turbines; . . . props; 150,000 hp

REMARKS: Still in the programming stage. To cost 10 million Canadian dollars. Would be, by far, the world's most powerful icebreakers. At best, will not be laid down before 1984.

A third *Franklin*-class icebreaker will be laid down in 1980, as will two 21-meter search and rescue boats, four motor lifeboats, and an ocean rescue tug.

The buoy tender *Dumit* (no data available) was completed in 7–79 by Allied Ship-building, Vancouver.

The old icebreaker/navigational buoy tenders *N. B. McLean* and *Ernest Lapointe* were stricken in 1979.

CUBA

A second Soviet Foxtrot attack submarine was delivered to Cuba in 1–80.

DENMARK

The submarine *Narhvalen* capsized in dry dock in 9–79. It is considered a total loss.

Nils Juel   1980

DJIBOUTI REPUBLIC

A U.S. Navy LCU-1610-class landing craft was to be transferred during 1980.

EGYPT

Transfer of the U.S. Gearing FRAM-1-class destroyers has been cancelled because of the poor material condition of the ships, which were even older than the Soviet *Skory*-class destroyers they were to have replaced.

FRANCE

A new personnel transport of the *Ariel* class, *Naiade* (Y . . .), is to enter service early in 1980.

Three new 2,600-hp seagoing tugs are to enter service during 1980: *Belier* (A . . .), *Buffle* (A . . .), and N . . . (A . . .).

FEDERAL REPUBLIC OF GERMANY

SUBMARINES

Wilhelm Bauer 1979

GREAT BRITAIN

♦ . . . type 2400 attack submarine

D: 2,160 tons surfaced/2,400 tons submerged   **S:** 12/20 kts

Dim: 70.0 × 7.6 × . . .

A: 6/533-mm tubes fwd for MK–24 and U.S. Mk–48 torpedoes and/or Sub-Harpoon SSM (18 total weapons)

Man: 30 to 50 men   **Range:** 8,000/8 (snorkel)   **Endurance:** over 28 days

M: 2 Paxman Valenta 16 RPA 200S 16-cyl. diesels, 2,000 hp each, electric drive; 1 6-bladed prop; 3,000 hp

REMARKS: A design prepared by Vickers as successor to the *Oberon* class. Primarily intended for ASW. First unit would not be operational before the late 1980s. Diving depth would be over 200 meters. Two 240-cell lead-acid batteries.

The *Tiger*-class cruiser *Blake* was put in Reserve in 3–80, and will be moth-balled. The *Tiger*, placed in Reserve on 4–5–79, is to be placed on the disposal list.

The following Tribal-class frigates are to be placed in Reserve, in the "Standby Squadron": *Eskimo, Gurkha, Mohawk, Nubian,* and *Zulu*. A plan has been made by Vosper-Thornycroft to modernize these ships for foreign sale. A helicopter hangar would be added at the expense of the after gun, and the two stacks would be combined into one.

D: 2,700 tons   **S;** 27 kts   **Dim:** 109.7 × 12.9 × 5.5

A 1/114–mm Mk–5 DP—2/Sea Cat GWS 21 SAM systems (IV × 2)—2/20–mm AA (1 × 2)—2/Lynx helicopters

Electron Equipt: Radars: 1/Decca TM 1226, 1/Marconi S820, 1/Marconi ST802 1/Sapphire
Sonar: Graseby GI 777K—2/Knebworth-Corvus chaff

Range: 5,300/12   **Man:** 13 officers, 240 men

M: COSAG: 1 set GT/1 gas turbine: 20,000 hp

♦ *1 Type-24-class general purpose frigate*
Bldr: Yarrow, Scotstoun

	Laid down	L	In serv.
F . . . N . . .	. . .	. . .	1983

D: 2,785 tons (3,100 trials)   **S:** 31.0 kts   **Dim:** 122.0 (116.0 pp) × 14.8 × . . .

A: 4/Sea Wolf SAM launchers (II × 4)—8/MM 40 Exocet SSM (IV × 2)—1/114–mm Vickers Mk–8 DP—4/30–mm Oerlikon GCM AA—6/324–mm ASW TT (III × 2)—2/WG 13 Lynx helicopters (16 Sea Skua ASM)

Electron Equipt: Radars: 1/Decca 1229C, 1/HSA ZWO–8, 1/Plessey AWS–5, 2/HSA VM40
Sonars: 1/Graseby 850, 1/162M—CAAIS–450 data system
ECM: Decca Cutlass, Decca RCM, 2/Sea Fan chaff launchers

Electric: 3,200 kw   **Range:** 7,800/16, 9,650/13   **Man:** 14 officers, 146 men

M: CODOG: 2 Rolls-Royce Olympus TM 3B gas turbines; 28,000 hp each; 2 Paxman Valenta 18CM diesels, 6,080 hp each; 2 controllable-pitch props

REMARKS: The first unit of this class *may* be built on speculation of foreign sale; original plans called for completion by 1983. Alternative armament suits are also offered. The Sea Wolf system will use light weight automatic reloading twin launchers. Maximum speed on diesels: 17.5 knots. Will have SCOT satellite communication system. If built, and if foreign interest does not develop, ship may be incorporated into the Royal Navy.

NOTE: A Type–23 frigate, of admiralty (vice commercial) design, is also in the planning stages as a successor to the Type 22.

The *Rothesay*-class frigate *Londonderry* (F–108) as trials ship has no armament and has been equipped with two additional tall pylon masts. A small helicopter deck has been added at the after end of the forecastle, which has been extended toward the stern.

♦ *4 new construction offshore patrol vessel Mk-2 class*

D: 1,450 tons   **S:** 22 kts   **Dim:** 81.0 (75.0 pp) × 7.3 × 3.4

A: . . .   **Range:** 10,000/12   **Man:** . . .   **Fuel:** 180 tons

Electron Equipt: Radars: 1/1006, 1/HSA M20 series—CANES navigational system
Sonar: Thomson-CSF DUEM-21A

M: 2 diesel engines; 2 controllable-pitch props; 5,640 hp

REMARKS: Intended to follow the Island class in production for the Royal Navy and also to be offered for foreign sale. Main armament may include the Rarden 105–mm low-angle gun or 76–mm OTO Melara Compact, while several different close-defense guns are under consideration. The flight deck will be able to accommodate a Sea King-sized helicopter, while the hangar would be able to house a Sea Lynx. ASW sensors and ordnance could be carried, and four Exocet launch canisters could be mounted on the forecastle.

The salvage ship *Reclaim* (A–231) was stricken in 12–79; the *Seaforth Clansman* is to be retained for several more years on charter.

The accommodations hulk *Berry Head* (A–191, ex-repair ship) was stricken in 12–79, as were net tender *Laymoor* (P–190), replenishment ship *Resurgent* (A–280), and minehunter *Shoulton* (M–1182).

The Hunt-class minehunter *Brecon* (M–29) in service 6–12–79; the *Ledbury* was launched 5–12–79. The sixth unit of this class will be named the *Brocklesby*.

INDIA

The Leopard-class frigate *Brahmaputra* (F–31) has had her after twin 114–mm mount replaced by a large deckhouse to accommodate naval cadets.

♦ *British Leander-class frigate*

Taragiri 1979

The oiler *Lok Adhar* has been stricken.

INDONESIA

FRIGATES

Fatahilah 1979

Fatahilah 1979

AUXILIARY SHIPS

Submarine tender Ratulangi 1979

Replenishment oiler Sorong 1979

IRAN

AUXILIARY SHIPS

Water tanker Kangan   1979

IRAQ

The new training frigate under construction in Yugoslavia is to be named the *Ibn Khaldum*.

Construction of several frigates in Italy (*Lupo* class?) may be under consideration, because an export license for General Electric LM–2500 gas turbines to be used in their propulsion plants was turned down by the U.S. government in 2–80.

IRELAND

Two additional patrol ships are to be built by Verolme, Cork. Larger than the *Emer* class, they will have a helicopter hangar and flight deck and will be armed with a 76–mm OTO Melara Compact gun. First is to be laid down in 1980 and delivered in 1982; the second unit is to be laid down in 1981.

A 10.6–meter sailboat has been acquired for cadet training and for participation in European sailing races.

ITALY

The first *Nazario Sauro*-class submarine, *Nazario Sauro*, has had its entry into service delayed by the necessity of replacing the original batteries with ones of Swedish manufacture. The second ship, *Carlo Fecia di Cossato*, became the first fully active unit of the class, at the end of 12–79. *Nazario Sauro* made 20.2 knots for 30 minutes submerged on trials, 18–10–79, with the new batteries.

JAPAN

MARITIME SELF-DEFENSE FORCE

The Japanese cabinet has approved the following new ships under the FY 80 program: two 2,900-ton destroyers, one *Ishikari*-class (1,400-ton) frigate, one *Yushio*-class (2,200-ton) submarine, two *Hatsushima*-class (440-ton) minesweepers, one 490-ton yard oiler, one 30-ton yard tug, and one 11-ton personnel launch. Construction of a new 3,600-ton submarine rescue ship/tender to replace the *Chihaya* was deferred, as were several yardcraft. Aircraft acquisitions approved included ten P–3C Orion, two HSS–2B helicopters, one US–1 seaplane, and two TC–90 training aircraft. Active personnel strength for 1980 is to be 43,897 total.

The destroyer *Akizuki* (DD–161) has had her Hedgehogs replaced by a deckhouse, atop which is a 375-mm Bofors ASW rocket launcher (IV x 1); her sister *Teruzuki* was similarly refitted in 1976–77. Both have six 324-mm ASW torpedo tubes (III x 2).

All three *Minegumo* (DD–116)-class destroyers are equipped with an ASROC launcher aft in place of the drone helicopter installation, but only *Minegumo* has the OTO Melara 76-mm gun in place of the after twin 76.2-mm gunmount.

MARITIME SAFETY AGENCY

The Fiscal Year 1980 budget request by the Maritime Safety Agency included the following ships and aircraft: two modified PL–01 class, three 1,000-ton PL–101 class, three 500-ton PM, six 30-meter PC (to replace three older craft), one 23-meter PC, nine 15-meter PC (to replace eight older craft), two FM–01-class fireboats, one 2,500-ton HL surveying ship (to replace an older ship), five Beech 200T utility aircraft, and 16 Bell 212 helicopters (thirteen land-based and three ship-landing-configured to replace seven older helicopters).

PL–04, PL–118, PL–122, and PL–124 are to receive one 35-mm Oerlikon antiaircraft gun vice their 40-mm antiaircraft gun. Other units of the *Soya* (PL 01) and *Shiretoko* (PL 101) class may be backfitted later.

♦ *Yamayuri-class patrol craft construction data*

	Bldr	L	In serv.
CL 205 YAGURUMA	Sumidagawa		31-7-79
CL 207 SUZURAN	Sumidagawa		31-7-79
CL 208 ISOGIKU	Sumidagawa	20-8-79	
CL 209 ISEGIKO	Sumidagawa	6-8-79	
CL 210 AYAME	Yokohama Yacht		29-10-79
CL 212 HIMAWARI	Yokohama Yacht		29-10-79
CL 213 HAZAKURA	Yokohama Yacht	9-8-79	
CL 215 HAMAGIKU	Yokohama Yacht	22-8-79	
CL 216 FUYUME	Ishihara		30-7-79
CL 217 TSUBAKI	Ishihara		10-8-79
CL 218 SAZANKA	Ishihara	31-7-79	
CL 219 AOI	Sumidagawa		31-10-79
CL 220 SUISEN	Yokohama Yacht		29-10-79
CL 222 AKEBI	Yokohama Yacht		29-10-79
CL 223 SHIRAHAGI	Sumidagawa	25-12-79	
CL 224 BENIBANA	Sumidagawa	25-12-79	
CL 225 MURATSUBAKI	Ishihara		20-12-79
CL 227 ASHIBI	Ishihara		20-12-79
CL 229 YUKITSUBAKI	Ishihara	21-12-79	

◆ *Shiretoko (PL–101) class construction data*

	Bldr	L	In serv.
PL 111 REBUN	Narazaki		21-11-79
PL 112 CHOKAI	Nihonkai		30-11-79
PL 114 OKI	Tsuneishi		16-11-79
PL 115 NOTO	Miho Zosen		30-11-79
PL 121 GENKAI	Miho Zosen		31-1-80
PL 124 HATERUMA	Osaka DY	1-11-79	

Other new construction data: The three *Takatori* (PM–79)-class patrol boats for the 1980 program (PM–95–PM–97) have already been laid down, one by Usukine DY on 3-12-79, one by Shikoku DY on 6-12-79, and one by Utsumi on 6-12-79. The "130-ton" patrol craft *Akaqi* (PS–101) was launched by Sumidagawa on 30-11-79. The large buoy tender *Ginga* (LL–13) was launched on 16-12-79 by Kawasaki; she is a sister to the *Ginga* (LL–12), described in the text. Small buoy tenders *Kamihikari* (LS–209) and *Shimahikari* (LS–210) were completed by Yokohama Yacht on 17-12-79.

Recent Maritime Safety Agency strikings: patrol ships: *Rebun* (PM–04) 16-10-79; *Oki* (PM–06) 15-10-79; *Hachijo* (PM–08) 26-9-79; *Noto* (PM–13) 29-10-79; *Mikura* (PM–15) 29-10-79; *Koshiki* (PM–16) 24-12-79; *Kozu* (PM–20) 25-9-79. Large patrol craft: *Shimakaze* (CL–22) 15-10-79; *Hatsuyuke* (CL–307) 17-10-79; *Akishimo* (CL–312) 6-12-79; *Shiratae* (CL–313) 6-12-79. Small patrol craft: *Kisaragi* (CS–107) 15-10-79; *Yamabuki* (CS–123) 15-10-79; *Akebi* (CS–126) 12-10-79. Small buoy tenders: *Himihikari* (LS–212) and Kotohikari (LS–213) 3-12-79.

LIBERIA

◆ *3 patrol boats*
Bldr: Karlskrona, Sweden

D: 50 tons (fl)   **S:** 25 kts   **Dim:** 26.7 × 5.2 × 1.1
A: . . . .   **Man:** . . .   **Range:** 1,000/18
M: 2 MTU 8V331 C82 diesels; 2 props; 1,866hp
REMARK: Ordered late in 1979.

NETHERLANDS

The destroyer *Friesland* (D–812) was striken on 29-6-79.

The *Van Speijk*-class frigate *Van Galen* (F–803) was modernized 15-7-77 to 1-12-79; *Van Nes* (F–805) 31-3-78 to 1-8-80; and *Tjerk Hiddes* (F–804) 15-12-79 to 1-6-81.

The *Kortenaer*-class frigate *Pieter Florisz* (F–812) was launched on 15-12-79. The *Philips van Almonde* (F–823) was launched on 11-8-79.

Construction of the 2,300-ton "M"-class frigates may be deferred due to lack of funds.

SENEGAL

CORVETTE

◆ *1 French PR 72 MS class*
Bldr: Soc. Française de Construction Navale, Villeneuve-la-Garonne

	Laid down	L	In serv.
N . . .	. . .	. . .	6–81

D: 381 tons (451 fl)   **S:** 30 kts   **Dim:** 58.7 × 8.22 × 2.18
A: 2/76-mm DP OTO Melara (I × 2)—2/20-mm AA (I × 2)
Range: 2,50υ/16   **Man:** 46 men
M: 4 SACM AGO 195V16 CZSHR diesels; 4 props; 12,800 hp
REMARKS: Ordered 11-79. Similar to units in the Moroccan Navy.

TURKEY

The U.S. *Gearing* FRAM-I-class destroyer *Meredith* (DD–890), stricken from the U.S. Navy on 29-6-79, is to be transferred to Turkey in early 1980.

The U.S. *Tang*-class submarine *Tang* (SS–563) has been leased to Turkey for five years; transferred 29-2-80, she has been renamed *Piri Reis* (SS–343).

U.S.S.R.

Cruiser Programs: According to an authoritative article in the U.S. press, the U.S.S.R. now has no less than *four* cruiser construction programs under way. Two are described in the text, but a summary of all is given here:

1. The first 27,000-ton *Kirov*-class nuclear-powered cruiser is expected to go to sea for the first time early in 1980, with the second following in 1982. The armament includes vertically-launched missiles.

2. At least four 7,800-ton cruisers are being built, presumably those at Zhdanov Shipyard, Leningrad. The first will be completed in 1980, with the others following at the rate of one per year. Armament includes cruise missiles, long-range guns, *mines*, and "modern defensive weapon systems."

3. The gas-turbine-powered follow-on class to the Kara-construction program at Nikolayev displaces 12,500 tons and includes at least three ships, with the first to be completed in 1981. Armament will include cruise missiles and guns.

4. Three ASW cruisers of 8,400 tons are reported to be under construction at an unidentified facility, with the first to be completed in 1981 and two others a year later.

These programs total twelve new cruiser-sized combatants, all to be delivered in the early 1980s, and it can be expected that additional units of some or all of the four new classes will appear as the decade progresses.

U.S.A.

The new ARS class, the first of which is to be constructed under the FY 81 budget, is to be a repeat of the forty-year-old *Bolster* class.

Beginning with the *John Hancock* (DD–981), *Spruance*-class destroyers are being equipped with the SLQ–32 ECM system; earlier units have WLR–1.

Spruance-class destroyer *Harry W. Hill* (DD–986) entered service on 17-11-79; her sister *O'Bannon* (DD–987) entered service on 15-12-79 and *Thorn* (DD–988) on 16-2-80. *Deyo* (DD–989), *Ingersoll* (DD–990), *Fife* (DD–991), and *Fletcher* (DD–992) were scheduled to enter service on 22-3-80, 12-4-80, 3-5-80, and 7-6-80, respectively.

Under the FY 81 Defense Budget, the administration has requested the following Navy/Marine Corps aircraft: 48 F/A–18 Hornet, 24 F–14 Tomcat, 3 EA–6B Prowler,

Thorn—on trials

Litton Industries, 1980

14 CH–53 Sea Stallion, 6 E–2C Tracer, 8 p–3C Orion, and long-lead items in preparation for production of the SH–60B LAMPS III.

Oliver Hazard Perry-class frigate *McInerney* (FFG–8) entered service on 19-11-79, while others scheduled to enter service were: *Wadsworth* (FFG–9) on 8-3-80, *Duncan* (FFG–10) on 26-4-80, *Clark* (FFG–11) on 17-5-80, *Samuel Eliot Morison* (FFG–13) on 26-7-80, and *George Philip* (FFG–12) on 12-8-80.

Submarines scheduled to enter service: *Bremerton* (SSN–698) on 31-3-80, *Jacksonville* (SSN–699) on 30-4-80, and *Dallas* (SSN–700) on 21-6-80. *Indianapolis* (SSN–697) in service on 5-1-80. *Nautilus* (SSN–571) is to be decommissioned on 3-3-80; *Wahoo* (SS–565) is scheduled to be stricken on 31-3-80

Belknap (CG–26) is scheduled for recommissioning on 3-5-80. *Albany* (CG–10) is scheduled to be decommissioned on 29-8-80; *Chicago* (CG–11) was decommissioned on 1-3-80.

The Maritime Commission C–333-type cargo ship *Bay* (ex-*Mormacbay*) has been selected for conversion under FY 81 as a Trident missile support ship. The following data supersede the listing in the text:

T-AK-284 N . . . (ex-*Bay*, ex-*Mormacbay*)
  D: . . .   **S:** 18 kts   **Dim:** 147.2 × 20.7 × 9.4   **Man:** . . .
  Range: 14,000/18   **Fuel:** 2,318 tons
  M: 1 set GT; 1 prop; . . . hp

REMARKS: Launched 1960. Before conversion: 9,252 grt/12,460 dwt, 12,040 cubic meters dry cargo. Cargo booms can lift up to 75 tons. The ship has been in the Maritime Commission Reserve in the James River, Virginia.

Kawishiwi (AO–1456) and *Truckee* (AO–147) were transferred to the Military Sealift Command as T-AO on 10-10-79 and 30-1-80, respectively; sister *Ponchatoula* (AO–148) is scheduled for transfer on 1-9-80. *Marias* (T-AO–57) and *Taluga* (T-AO–62) are scheduled for transfer to the Military Sealift Command ready reserve on 30-9-80.

Ammunition ship *Mauna Kea* (AE–22) was transferred to Naval Reserve Force control on 1-10-79; sister *Pyro* (AE–24) was scheduled for transfer on 1-9-80. *Preserver* (ARS–8) was transferred to the Naval Reserve Force on 1-11-79; *Durham* (LKA–114) and Charleston (LKA–113) were transferred on 1-10-79 and 21-11-79, respectively; sister *Mobile* is scheduled for transfer on 1-9-80. *Tulare* (LKA–112) was decommissioned on 15-2-80 and placed in reserve.

Peleliu (LHA–5) is scheduled to enter service on 10-5-80.

Paul Revere (LPA–248) was decommissioned on 1-10-79 and transferred to Spain on 17-1-80.

Narragansett (T-ATF–167) in service on 9-11-79; sisters *Catawba* (T-ATF–168), *Navaho* (T-ATF–169), and *Mohawk* (T-ATF–170) are scheduled to enter service 20-5-80, 3-7-80, and 30-9-80, respectively. *Shakori* (ATF–162) was decommissioned on 29-

2-80; half-sisters *Ute* (T-ATF–76) and *Lipan* (T-ATF–85) are scheduled for decommissioning on 30-9-80.

Frank Cable (AS–40) entered service on 20-10-79; *Howard W. Gilmore* (AS–16) is scheduled to be decommissioned on 30-9-80.

Kingsport (T-AG–164) is to be stricken during 1980, after several years of inactivity

Compass Island (AG–153) is scheduled for decommissioning to the reserve on 1-5-80.

Cimarron (AO–177) is scheduled to enter service on 18-7-80.

Shenandoah (AD–26) is scheduled for decommissioning on 1-4-80; *Yellowstone* (AD–41) is to enter service on 19-5-80.

Yellowstone

1979